Explore Your World!

Focus on Primary Sources to Understand History.

Bring world history to life by exploring history through primary sources. Features and activities, both within your textbook and online, allow you to relive history.

Interact with Exciting Online Activities.

Journey to different parts of the world by using dynamic online activities. At PHSchool.com you're only one web code away from exciting interactivities on geography, history and culture. Use the web codes listed in the Go Online boxes throughout each chapter to travel through history.

Explore the Hagia Sophia
The Church of the Holy Wisdom, commonly known as Hagia Sophia, is a former Greek Orthodox church converted to a mosque, now a museum, in Istanbul. It is universally acknowledged as one of the great buildings of the world, architecturally. The Hagia Sophia has many features of ancient Roman art and architecture, such as mosaics, arches, and domes. It adapts these features for use

PEARSON
Prentice Hall

Hagia Sophia
The Hagia Sophia is a magnificent church built in Constantinople in the sixth century by the Byzantine emperor Justinian. Hagia Sophia means "Holy Wisdom." After Constantinople fell to the Turks in 1453, the Hagia Sophia was converted to a mosque. Constantinople is now the city of Istanbul, located in Turkey.

Hagia Sophia | Cutaway | Mosaic of Jesus and St. John | Mosaic of Mary and Jesus

Move the slider to each label to learn about the Hagia Sophia.

Go Online
PHSchool.com

For: An activity on the Trojan War
Visit: PHSchool.com
Web Code: lbd-2601

Get Hands-on with the Historian's Apprentice Activity Pack.

Hands-on activities allow you to think like a historian! Use authentic primary sources to answer intriguing historical questions. Each activity pack includes authentic documents such as maps, data, and primary sources to make learning history fun!

PRENTICE HALL

HISTORY OF OUR WORLD

PEARSON

Prentice Hall

Boston, Massachusetts
Upper Saddle River, New Jersey

Program Consultants

Heidi Hayes Jacobs, Ed.D.

Heidi Hayes Jacobs has served as an education consultant to more than 1,000 schools across the nation and abroad. Dr. Jacobs serves as an adjunct professor in the Department of Curriculum on Teaching at Teachers College, Columbia University. She has written two best-selling books and numerous articles on curriculum reform. She received an M.A. from the University of Massachusetts, Amherst, and completed her doctoral work at Columbia University's Teachers College in 1981. The core of Dr. Jacobs's experience comes from her years teaching high school, middle school, and elementary school students. As an educational consultant, she works with K–12 schools and districts on curriculum reform and strategic planning.

Michal L. LeVasseu

Michal LeVasseur is the Eve Director of the National Council for Geocy Education. She is an instructor in the Colleg Education at Jacksonville State Universid works with the Alabama Geographic AlliaHer undergraduate and graduate work were i fields of anthropology (B.A.), geogr (M.A.), and science education (Ph.D.). Dr. LeVar's specialization has moved increasingly intc area of geography education. Since 1996 she hrved as the Director of the National Geographicety's Summer Geography Workshops. As ducational consultant, she has worked with tlational Geographic Society as well as with schcand organizations to develop programs and ciula for geography.

Senior Reading Consultants

Kate Kinsella

Kate Kinsella, Ed.D., is a faculty member in the Department of Secondary Education at San Francisco State University. A specialist in second-language acquisition and adolescent literacy, she teaches coursework addressing language and literacy development across the secondary curricula. Dr. Kinsella earned her M.A. in TESOL from San Francisco State University and her Ed.D. in Second Language Acquisition from the University of San Francisco.

Kevin Feldman

Kevin Feldman, Ed.D., is the ector of Reading and Early Intervention with 1Sonoma County Office of Education (SCOE) aan independent educational consultant. At thCOE, he develops, organizes, and monitors procms related to K–12 literacy. Dr. Feldman han M.A. from the University of California, Rivere, in Special Education, Learning Disabilitiand Instructional Design. He earned his Ed.D. iurriculum and Instruction from the Universibf San Francisco.

Acknowledgments appear on pages 780–784, which constitute an extension of this copyright page.

ISBN 0-13-203771-8
5678910   10 09 08

Cartography Cosultant

DK **Andrew Heritage**

Andrew Heritage has been puishing atlases and maps for more than 25 years. 1991, he joined the leading illustrated nonficth publisher Dorling Kindersley (DK) with the task (building an international atlas list from scrch. The DK atlas list now includes some 10 titlewhich are constantly updated and appea n new editions either annually or every other ar.

Academic Reviewers

Africa
Barbara B. Brown, Ph.D.
African Studies Center
Boston University
Boston, Massachusetts

Ancient World
Evelyn DeLong Mangie, Ph.D.
Department of History
University of South Florida
Tampa, Florida

Central Asia and the Middle East
Pamela G. Sayre
History Department,
    Social Sciences Division
Henry Ford Community College
Dearborn, Michigan

East Asia
Huping Ling, Ph.D.
History Department
Truman State University
Kirksville, Missouri

Eastern Europe
Robert M. Jenkins
Center for Slavic, Eurasian and
    East European Studies
University of North Carolina
Chapel Hill, North Carolina

Latin America
Dan La Botz
Professor, History Department
Miami University
Oxford, Ohio

Medieval Times
James M. Murray
History Department
University of Cincinnati
Cincinnati, Ohio

North Africa
Barbara E. Petzen
Center for Middle Eastern Studies
Harvard University
Cambridge, Massachusetts

Religion
Charles H. Lippy, Ph.D.
Department of Philosophy
    and Religion
University of Tennessee
    at Chattanooga
Chattanooga, Tennessee

Russia
Janet Vaillant
Davis Center for Russian
    and Eurasian Studies
Harvard University
Cambridge, Massachusetts

South Asia
Robert J. Young
Professor Emeritus
History Department
West Chester University
West Chester, Pennsylvania

United States and Canada
Victoria Randlett
Geography Department
University of Nevada, Reno
Reno, Nevada

Western Europe
Ruth Mitchell-Pitts
Center for European Studies
University of North Carolina
    at Chapel Hill
Chapel Hill, North Carolina

Reviewers

Sean Brennan
Brecksville-Broadview Heights
    City School District
Broadview Heights, Ohio

Stephen Bullick
Mt. Lebanon School District
Pittsburgh, Pennsylvania

William R. Cranshaw, Ed.D.
Waycross Middle School
Waycross, Georgia

Dr. Louis P. De Angelo
Archdiocese of Philadelphia
Philadelphia, Pennsylvania

Paul Francis Durietz
Social Studies
    Curriculum Coordinator
Woodland District #50
Gurnee, Illinois

Gail Dwyer
Dickerson Middle School,
    Cobb County
Marietta, Georgia

Michal Howden
Social Studies Consultant
Zionsville, Indiana

Rosemary Kalloch
Springfield Public Schools
Springfield, Massachusetts

Deborah J. Miller
Office of Social Studies,
    Detroit Public Schools
Detroit, Michigan

Steven P. Missal
Newark Public Schools
Newark, New Jersey

Catherine Fish Petersen (Retired)
East Islip School District
Islip Terrace, New York

Joe Wieczorek
Social Studies Consultant
Baltimore, Maryland

HISTORY OF OUR WORLD

Develop Skills

Use these pages to develop your reading, writing, and geography skills.

Focus on History

Learn about the geography, history, and cultures of the world from the beginnings of history to our world today.

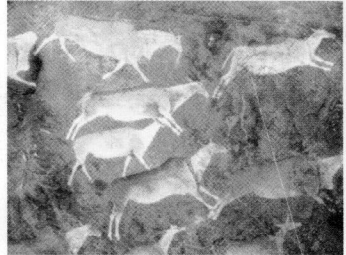

Unit 2 Ancient Egypt, India, and China 64

Unit 5   Age of Encounter................390

- Learn map skills with the MapMaster Skills Handbook.
- Practice your skills with every map in this book.
- Interact with every map online and on CD-ROM.

Maps and illustrations created by DK help build your understanding of the world. The DK World Desk Reference Online keeps you up to date.

The History of Our World Video Program takes you on field trips to study countries around the world.

The History of Our World Interactive Textbook online and on CD-ROM uses inter-active maps and other activities to help you learn.

Special Features

Literature

Focus On

Skills for Life

Links

Links Across Time

Links Across the World

Links to Art

Links to Economics

Links to Government

Links to Language Arts

Links to Math

Citizen Heroes

Discovery CHANNEL SCHOOL

Target Reading Skills

Maps and Charts

MAP★MASTER™

MAP★MASTER™ Interactive

Go online to find an interactive version of every MapMaster™ map in this book. Use the Web Code provided to gain direct access to these maps.

How to Use Web Codes:

1. Go to **www.PHSchool.com**.

2. Enter the Web Code.

3. Click Go!

Charts, Graphs, and Tables

Building Geographic Literacy

Learning about a country often starts with finding it on a map. The MapMaster™ system in *History of Our World* helps you develop map skills you will use throughout your life. These three steps can help you become a MapMaster!

The MAP★MASTER™ System

1 Learn

You need to learn geography tools and concepts before you explore the world. Get started by using the MapMaster™ Skills Handbook to learn the skills you need for success.

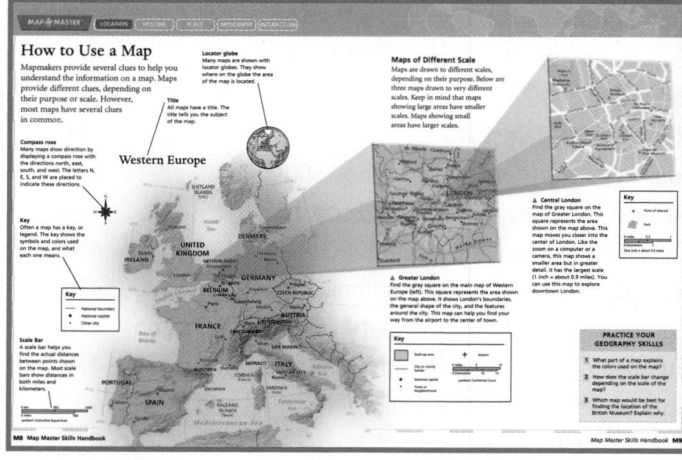

MAP★MASTER™ Skills Activity

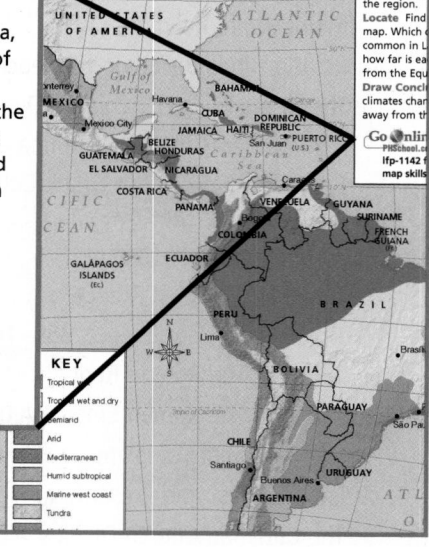

Location The Equator runs through parts of Latin America, but it is far from other parts of the region.

Locate Find the Equator on the map. Which climates are most common in Latin America, and how far is each climate region from the Equator?

Draw Conclusions How do climates change as you move away from the Equator?

Go Online
PHSchool.com Use Web Code **lfp-1142** for step-by-step **map skills practice.**

2 Practice

You need to practice and apply your geography skills frequently to be a MapMaster. The maps in *History of Our World* give you the practice you need to develop geographic literacy.

3 Interact

Using maps is more than just finding places. Maps can teach you many things about a region, such as its climate, its vegetation, and the languages that the people who live there speak. Every MapMaster™ map is online at **PHSchool.com,** with interactive activities to help you learn the most from every map.

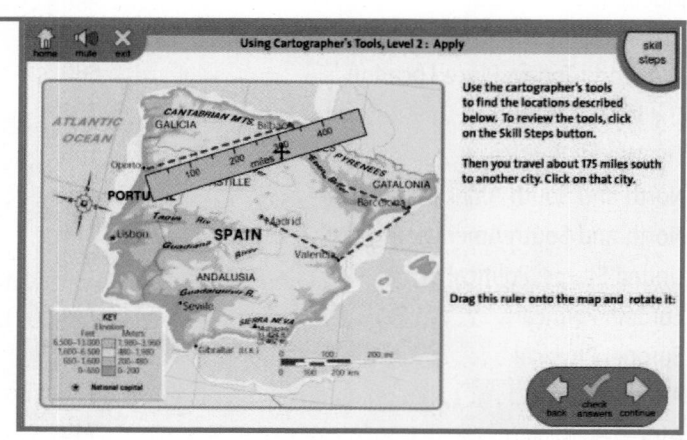

Learning With Technology

You will be making many exciting journeys across time and place in *History of Our World*. Technology will help make what you learn come alive in your classroom.

Explore the first great migration.

World Studies Video Program

You are going to learn about many new people, places, and thousands of years of history. The History of Our World Video Program created by our partner, Discovery Channel School, will bring this new information to life. Look for the video reference in every chapter!

For a complete list of features for this book, use Web Code muk-1000.

For: An activity on the Trojan War
Visit: PHSchool.com
Web Code: lbd-2601

Go Online at PHSchool.com

Use the Web Code in each Go Online box to access exciting information or activities at **PHSchool.com**.

How to Use the Web Code:
1. Go to **www.PHSchool.com**.
2. Enter the Web Code.
3. Click Go!

Interactive Textbook

The *World Studies* Interactive Textbook brings your textbook to life. Learn about the world, using interactive maps and other activities. Define and understand vocabulary words at the click of a mouse.

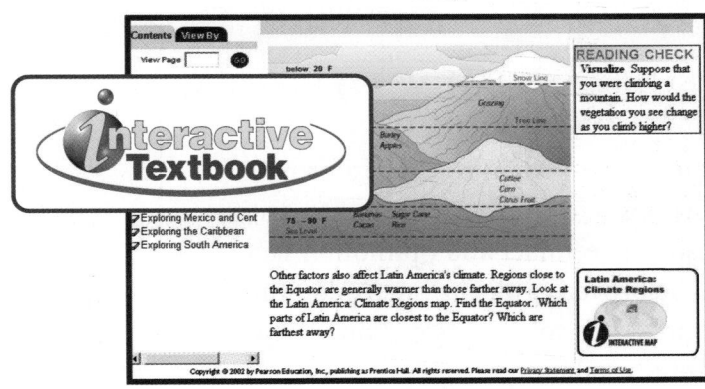

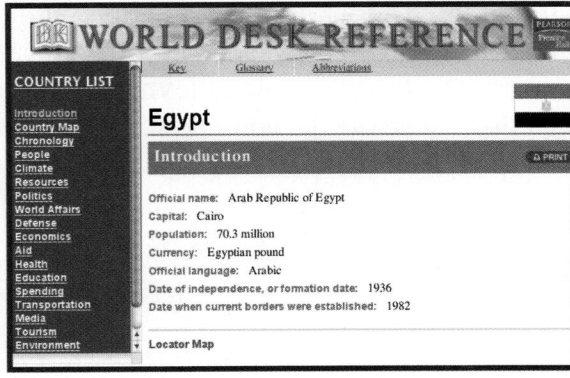

 **World Desk Reference Online**

There are more than 190 countries in the world. To learn about them, you need the most up-to-date information and statistics. The **DK World Desk Reference Online** gives you instant access to the information you need to explore each country.

Reading Informational Texts

Reading a magazine, an Internet page, or a textbook is not the same as reading a novel. The purpose of reading nonfiction texts is to acquire new information. On page M18 you'll read about some 🎯 **Target Reading Skills** that you'll have a chance to practice as you read this textbook. Here we'll focus on a few skills that will help you read nonfiction with a more critical eye.

Analyze the Author's Purpose

Different types of materials are written with different purposes in mind. For example, a textbook is written to teach students information about a subject. The purpose of a technical manual is to teach someone how to use something, such as a computer. A newspaper editorial might be written to persuade the reader to accept a particular point of view. A writer's purpose influences how the material is presented. Sometimes an author states his or her purpose directly. More often, the purpose is only suggested, and you must use clues to identify the author's purpose.

Distinguish Between Facts and Opinions

It's important when reading informational texts to read actively and to distinguish between fact and opinion. A fact can be proven or disproven. An opinion cannot—it is someone's personal viewpoint or evaluation.

For example, the editorial pages in a newspaper offer opinions on topics that are currently in the news. You need to read newspaper editorials with an eye for bias and faulty logic. For example, the newspaper editorial at the right shows factual statements in blue and opinion statements in red. The underlined words are examples of highly charged words. They reveal bias on the part of the writer.

> More than 5,000 people voted last week in favor of building a new shopping center, but the opposition won out. The margin of victory is irrelevant. Those radical voters who opposed the center are obviously self-serving elitists who do not care about anyone but themselves.
>
> This month's unemployment figure for our area i 10 percent, which rep resents an increase o about 5 percent over th figure for this time las year. These figures mea unemployment is gettin worse. But the people wh voted against the mal probably do not care abou creating new jobs.

Identify Evidence

Before you accept an author's conclusion, you need to make sure that the author has based the conclusion on enough evidence and on the right kind of evidence. An author may present a series of facts to support a claim, but the facts may not tell the whole story. For example, what evidence does the author of the newspaper editorial on the previous page provide to support his claim that the new shopping center would create more jobs? Is it possible that the shopping center might have put many small local businesses out of business, thus increasing unemployment rather than decreasing it?

Evaluate Credibility

Whenever you read informational texts, you need to assess the credibility of the author. This is especially true of sites you may visit on the Internet. All Internet sources are not equally reliable. Here are some questions to ask yourself when evaluating the credibility of a Web site.

- ❏ Is the Web site created by a respected organization, a discussion group, or an individual?
- ❏ Does the Web site creator include his or her name as well as credentials and the sources he or she used to write the material?
- ❏ Is the information on the site balanced or biased?
- ❏ Can you verify the information using two other sources?
- ❏ Is there a date telling when the Web site was created or last updated?

Writing for Social Studies

Writing is one of the most powerful communication tools you will ever use. You will use it to share your thoughts and ideas with others. Research shows that writing about what you read actually helps you learn new information and ideas. A systematic approach to writing— including prewriting, drafting, revising, and proofing—can help you write better, whether you're writing an essay or a research report.

Narrative Essays

Writing that tells a story about a personal experience

1 Select and Narrow Your Topic

A narrative is a story. In social studies, it might be a narrative essay about how an event affected you or your family.

2 Gather Details

Brainstorm a list of details you'd like to include in your narrative.

3 Write a First Draft

Start by writing a simple opening sentence that conveys the main idea of your essay. Continue by writing a colorful story that has interesting details. Write a conclusion that sums up the significance of the event or situation described in your essay.

4 Revise and Proofread

Check to make sure you have not begun too many sentences with the word *I*. Replace general words with more colorful ones.

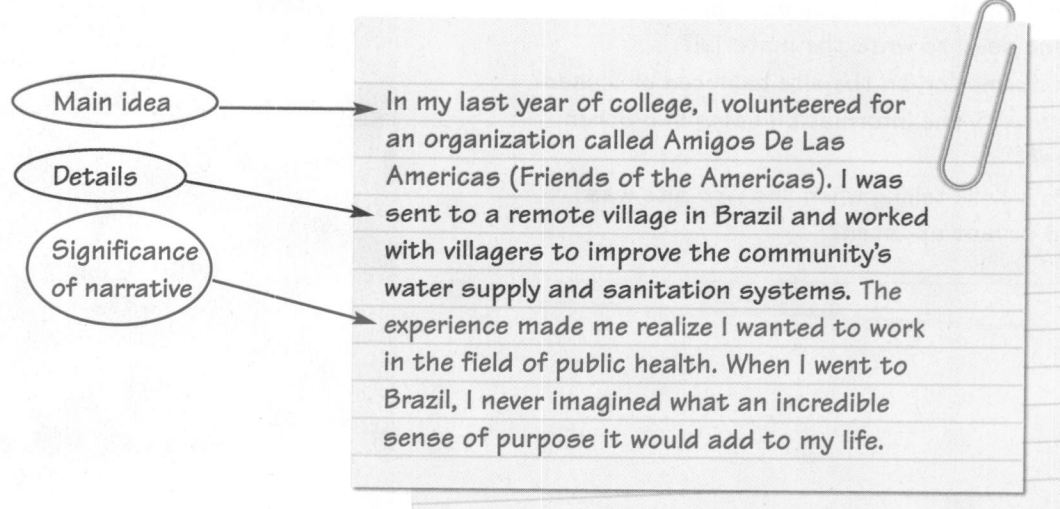

Main idea

Details

Significance of narrative

In my last year of college, I volunteered for an organization called Amigos De Las Americas (Friends of the Americas). I was sent to a remote village in Brazil and worked with villagers to improve the community's water supply and sanitation systems. The experience made me realize I wanted to work in the field of public health. When I went to Brazil, I never imagined what an incredible sense of purpose it would add to my life.

Persuasive Essays

Writing that supports an opinion or position

1 Select and Narrow Your Topic

Choose a topic that provokes an argument and has at least two sides. Choose a side. Decide which argument will appeal most to your audience and persuade them to understand your point of view.

2 Gather Evidence

Create a chart that states your position at the top and then lists the pros and cons for your position below, in two columns. Predict and address the strongest arguments against your stand.

3 Write a First Draft

Write a strong thesis statement that clearly states your position. Continue by presenting the strongest arguments in favor of your position and acknowledging and refuting opposing arguments.

4 Revise and Proofread

Check to make sure you have made a logical argument and that you have not oversimplified the argument.

Main Idea → It is vital to vote in elections. When people vote, they tell public officials how to run the government. Not every proposal is carried

Supporting (pro) argument → out; however, politicians do their best to lis-

Opposing (con) argument → ten to what the majority of people want.

Transition words → Therefore, every vote is important.

Expository Essays

Writing that explains a process, compares and contrasts, explains causes and effects, or explores solutions to a problem

1 Identify and Narrow Your Topic

Expository writing is writing that explains something in detail. It might explain the similarities and differences between two or more subjects (compare and contrast). It might explain how one event causes another (cause and effect). Or it might explain a problem and describe a solution.

2 Gather Evidence

Create a graphic organizer that identifies details to include in your essay.

Cause 1	Cause 2	Cause 3
Most people in the Mexican countryside work on farms.	The population in Mexico is growing at one of the highest rates in the world.	There is not enough farm work for so many people.

Effect
As a result, many rural families are moving from the countryside to live in Mexico City.

3 Write Your First Draft

Write a topic sentence and then organize the essay around your similarities and differences, causes and effects, or problem and solutions. Be sure to include convincing details, facts, and examples.

4 Revise and Proofread

Research Papers

Writing that presents research about a topic

1 Narrow Your Topic

Choose a topic you're interested in and make sure that it is not too broad. For example, instead of writing a report on Panama, write about the construction of the Panama Canal.

2 Acquire Information

Locate several sources of information about the topic from the library or the Internet. For each resource, create a source index card like the one at the right. Then take notes using an index card for each detail or subtopic. On the card, note which source the information was taken from. Use quotation marks when you copy the exact words from a source.

Source #1
McCullough, David. *The Path Between the Seas: The Creation of the Panama Canal, 1870-1914.* N.Y., Simon and Schuster, 1977.

3 Make an Outline

Use an outline to decide how to organize your report. Sort your index cards into the same order.

Outline
I. Introduction
II. Why the canal was built
III. How the canal was built
   A. Physical challenges
   B. Medical challenges
IV. Conclusion

Introduction

Building the Panama Canal

Ever since Christopher Columbus first explored the Isthmus of Panama, the Spanish had been looking for a water route through it. They wanted to be able to sail west from Spain to Asia without sailing around South America. However, it was not until 1914 that the dream became a reality.

Conclusion

It took eight years and more than 70,000 workers to build the Panama Canal. It remains one of the greatest engineering feats of modern times.

4 Write a First Draft

Write an introduction, a body, and a conclusion. Leave plenty of space between lines so you can go back and add details that you may have left out.

5 Revise and Proofread

Be sure to include transition words between sentences and paragraphs. Here are some examples:

To show a contrast—*however, although, despite.*

To point out a reason—*since, because, if.*

To signal a conclusion—*therefore, consequently, so, then.*

Evaluating Your Writing

Use this table to help you evaluate your writing.

	Excellent	Good	Acceptable	Unacceptable
Purpose	Achieves purpose—to inform, persuade, or provide historical interpretation—very well	Informs, persuades, or provides historical interpretation reasonably well	Reader cannot easily tell if the purpose is to inform, persuade, or provide historical interpretation	Purpose is not clear
Organization	Develops ideas in a very clear and logical way	Presents ideas in a reasonably well-organized way	Reader has difficulty following the organization	Lacks organization
Elaboration	Explains all ideas with facts and details	Explains most ideas with facts and details	Includes some supporting facts and details	Lacks supporting details
Use of Language	Uses excellent vocabulary and sentence structure with no errors in spelling, grammar, or punctuation	Uses good vocabulary and sentence structure with very few errors in spelling, grammar, or punctuation	Includes some errors in grammar, punctuation, and spelling	Includes many errors in grammar, punctuation, and spelling

CONTENTS

Go Online
PHSchool.com Use Web Code **lap-0000** for all of the maps in this handbook.

Five Themes of Geography

Studying the geography of the entire world is a huge task. You can make that task easier by using the five themes of geography: location, regions, place, movement, and human-environment interaction. The themes are tools you can use to organize information and to answer the where, why, and how of geography.

LOCATION

1 Location answers the question, "Where is it?" You can think of the location of a continent or a country as its address. You might give an absolute location such as 22 South Lake Street or 40° N and 80° W. You might also use a relative address, telling where one place is by referring to another place. *Between school and the mall* and *eight miles east of Pleasant City* are examples of relative locations.

▲ **Location**
This museum in England has a line running through it. The line marks its location at 0° longitude.

REGIONS

2 Regions are areas that share at least one common feature. Geographers divide the world into many types of regions. For example, countries, states, and cities are political regions. The people in any one of these places live under the same government. Other features, such as climate and culture, can be used to define regions. Therefore the same place can be found in more than one region. For example, the state of Hawaii is in the political region of the United States. Because it has a tropical climate, Hawaii is also part of a tropical climate region.

MOVEMENT

4 Movement answers the question, "How do people, goods, and ideas move from place to place?" Remember that what happens in one place often affects what happens in another. Use the theme of movement to help you trace the spread of goods, people, and ideas from one location to another.

PLACE

3 Place identifies the natural and human features that make one place different from every other place. You can identify a specific place by its landforms, climate, plants, animals, people, language, or culture. You might even think of place as a geographic signature. Use the signature to help you understand the natural and human features that make one place different from every other place.

INTERACTION

5 Human-environment interaction focuses on the relationship between people and the environment. As people live in an area, they often begin to make changes to it, usually to make their lives easier. For example, they might build a dam to control flooding during rainy seasons. Also, the environment can affect how people live, work, dress, travel, and communicate.

◄ **Interaction**
These Congolese women interact with their environment by gathering wood for cooking.

PRACTICE YOUR GEOGRAPHY SKILLS

1 Describe your town or city, using each of the five themes of geography.

2 Name at least one thing that comes into your town or city and one that goes out. How is each moved? Where does it come from? Where does it go?

Understanding Movements of Earth

The planet Earth is part of our solar system. Earth revolves around the sun in a nearly circular path called an orbit. A revolution, or one complete orbit around the sun, takes 365 ¼ days, or one year. As Earth orbits the sun, it also spins on its axis, an invisible line through the center of Earth from the North Pole to the South Pole. This movement is called a rotation.

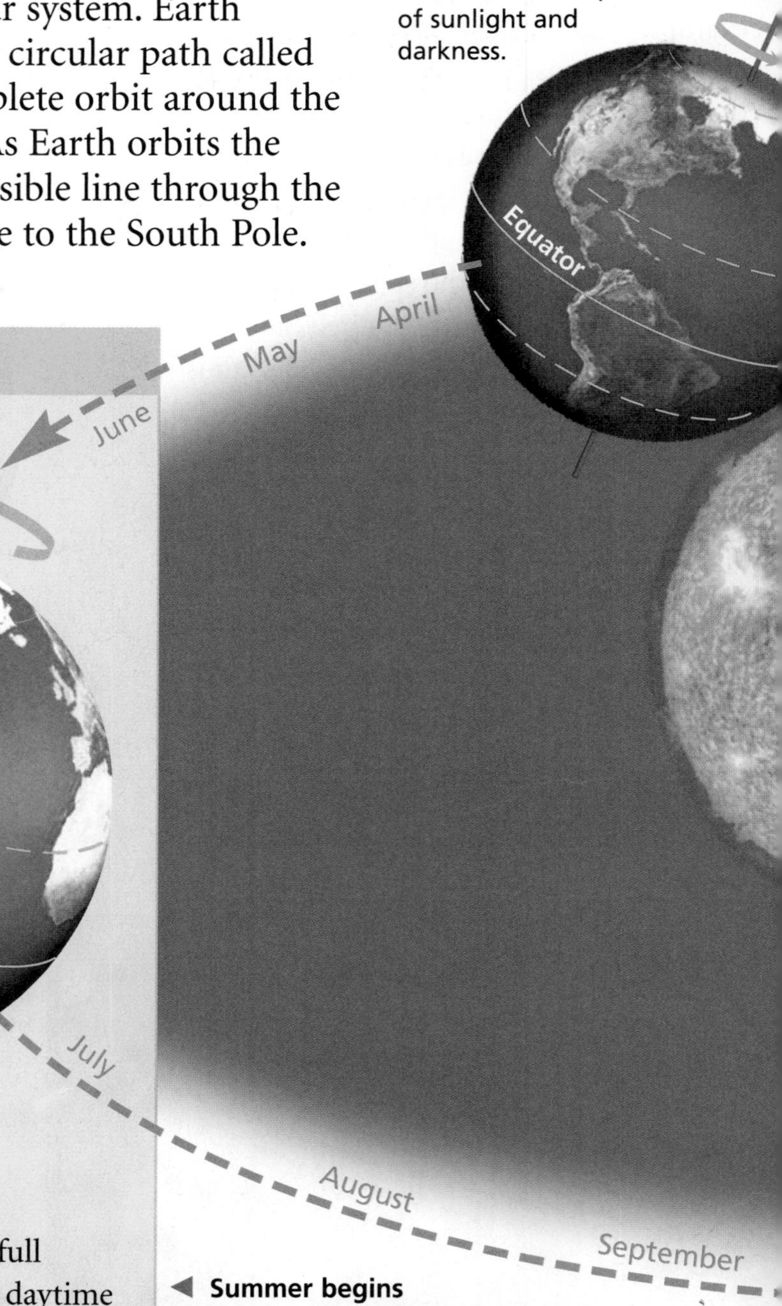

▼ **Spring begins**
On March 20 or 21, the sun is directly overhead at the Equator. The Northern and Southern Hemispheres receive almost equal hours of sunlight and darkness.

How Night Changes Into Day

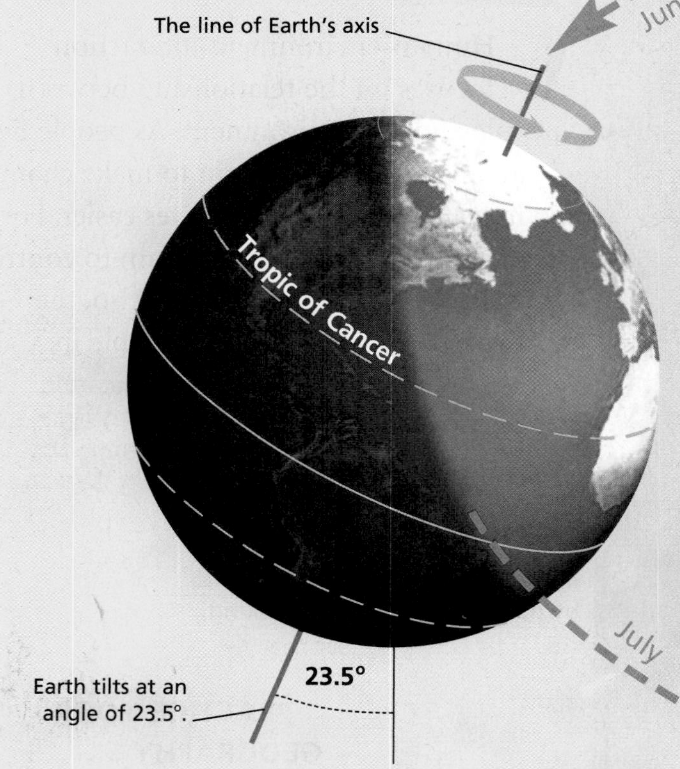

The line of Earth's axis

Tropic of Cancer

June

May

April

Equator

July

Earth tilts at an angle of 23.5°.

23.5°

August

September

Earth takes about 24 hours to make one full rotation on its axis. As Earth rotates, it is daytime on the side facing the sun. It is night on the side away from the sun.

◄ **Summer begins**
On June 21 or 22, the sun is directly overhead at the Tropic of Cancer. The Northern Hemisphere receives the greatest number of sunlight hours.

The Seasons

Earth's axis is tilted at an angle. Because of this tilt, sunlight strikes different parts of Earth at different times in the year, creating seasons. The illustration below shows how the seasons are created in the Northern Hemisphere. In the Southern Hemisphere, the seasons are reversed.

PRACTICE YOUR GEOGRAPHY SKILLS

1 What causes the seasons in the Northern Hemisphere to be the opposite of those in the Southern Hemisphere?

2 During which two days of the year do the Northern Hemisphere and Southern Hemisphere have equal hours of daylight and darkness?

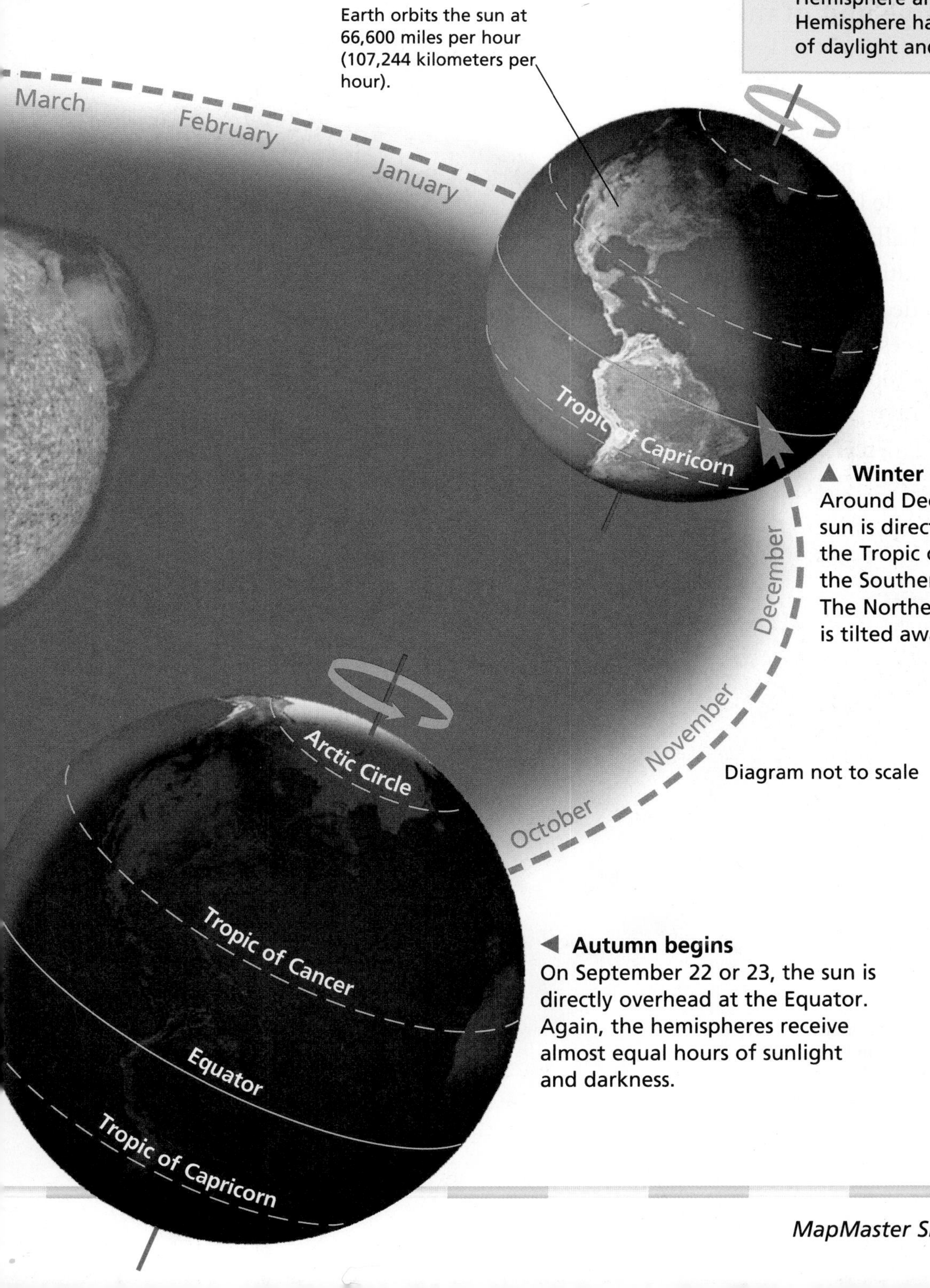

Earth orbits the sun at 66,600 miles per hour (107,244 kilometers per hour).

March
February
January

Tropic of Capricorn

December
November
October

Diagram not to scale

Arctic Circle

▲ **Winter begins**
Around December 21, the sun is directly overhead at the Tropic of Capricorn in the Southern Hemisphere. The Northern Hemisphere is tilted away from the sun.

Tropic of Cancer

Equator

Tropic of Capricorn

◄ **Autumn begins**
On September 22 or 23, the sun is directly overhead at the Equator. Again, the hemispheres receive almost equal hours of sunlight and darkness.

Understanding Globes

A globe is a scale model of Earth. It shows the actual shapes, sizes, and locations of all Earth's landmasses and bodies of water. Features on the surface of Earth are drawn to scale on a globe. This means that a small unit of measure on the globe stands for a large unit of measure on Earth.

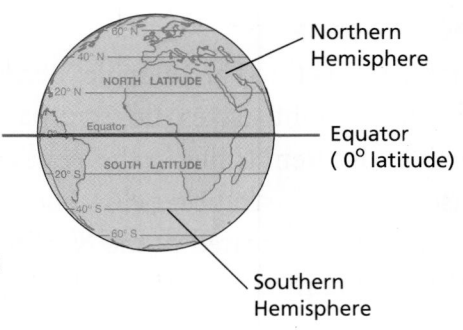

Northern Hemisphere

Equator (0° latitude)

Southern Hemisphere

Parallels of Latitude

Geographers divide the globe along imaginary horizontal lines called parallels of latitude. One of these latitude lines is the Equator, located halfway between the North and South Poles. Parallels of latitude are measured in degrees (°). One degree of latitude represents a distance of about 69 miles (111 kilometers).

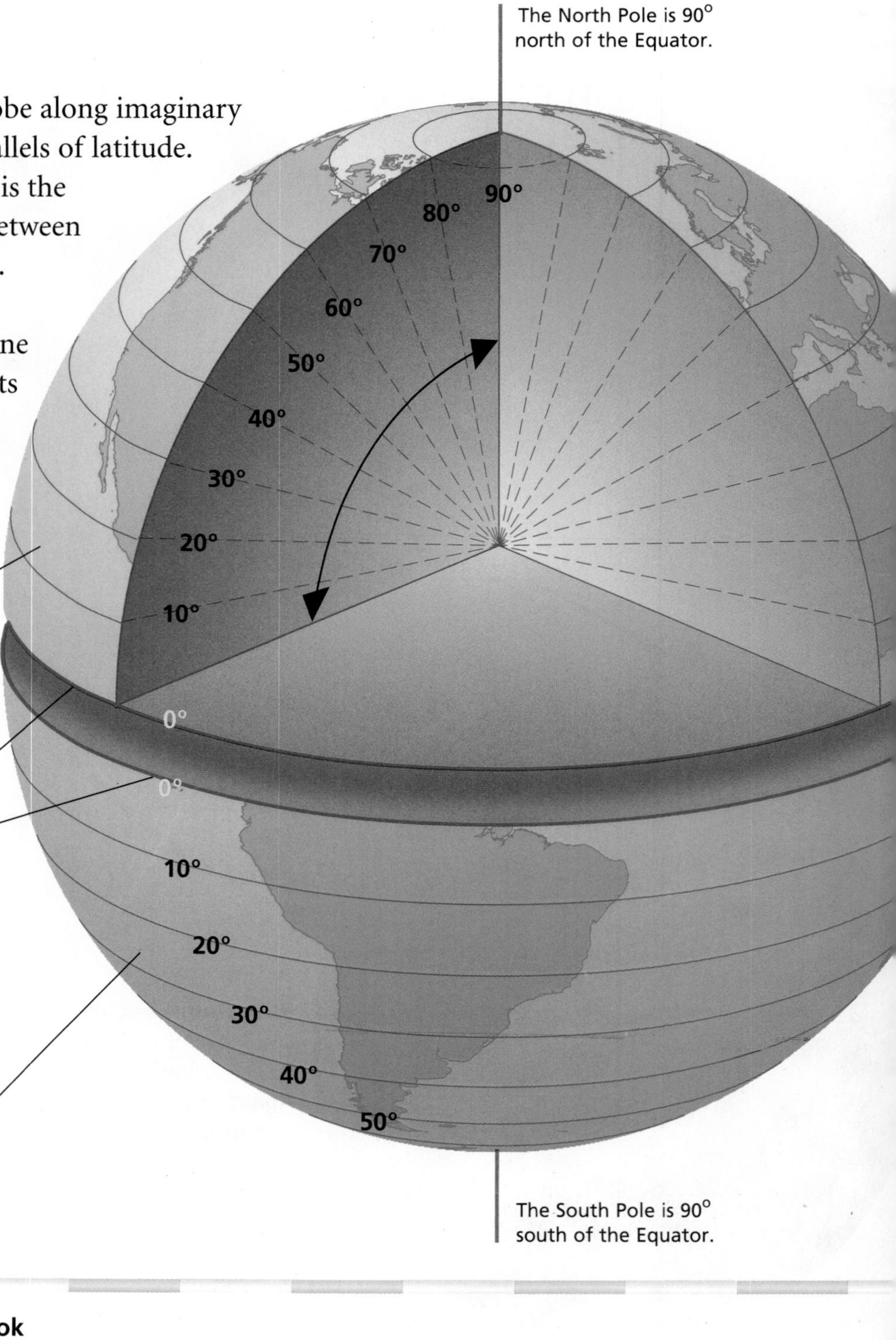

The North Pole is 90° north of the Equator.

90° 80° 70° 60° 50° 40° 30° 20° 10° 0°

All the latitudes, land, and water north of the Equator are in the Northern Hemisphere.

The Equator marks 0° latitude and divides Earth into the Southern and Northern Hemispheres.

0° 10° 20° 30° 40° 50°

All the latitudes, land, and water south of the Equator are in the Southern Hemisphere.

The South Pole is 90° south of the Equator.

Meridians of Longitude

Geographers also divide the globe along imaginary vertical lines called meridians of longitude, which are measured in degrees (°). The longitude line called the Prime Meridian runs from pole to pole through Greenwich, England. All meridians of longitude come together at the North and South Poles.

PRACTICE YOUR GEOGRAPHY SKILLS

1 Which continents lie completely in the Northern Hemisphere? In the Western Hemisphere?

2 Is there land or water at 20° S latitude and the Prime Meridian? At the Equator and 60° W longitude?

All the longitudes, land, and water west of the Prime Meridian are in the Western Hemisphere.

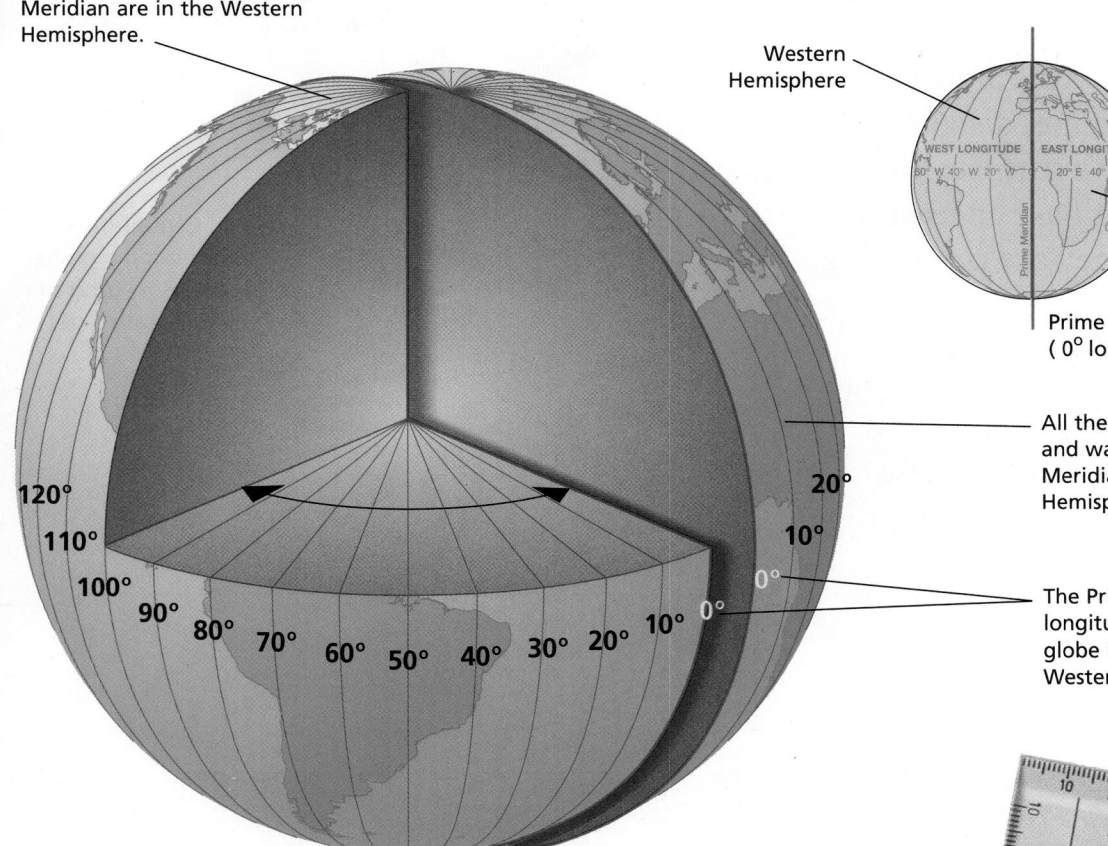

Western Hemisphere

WEST LONGITUDE   EAST LONGITUDE
60° W 40° W 20° W   20° E 40° E 60° E

Eastern Hemisphere

Prime Meridian (0° longitude)

All the longitudes, land, and water east of the Prime Meridian are in the Eastern Hemisphere.

The Prime Meridian marks 0° longitude and divides the globe into the Eastern and Western Hemispheres.

120° 110° 100° 90° 80° 70° 60° 50° 40° 30° 20° 10° 0°

20° 10° 0°

The Global Grid

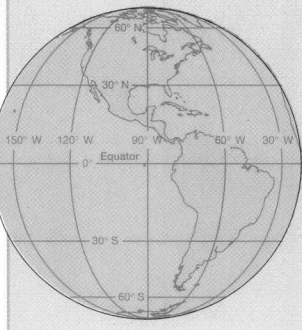

60° N

30° N

150° W 120° W   90° W   60° W   30° W

0°   Equator

30° S

60° S

Together, the pattern of parallels of latitude and meridians of longitude is called the global grid. Using the lines of latitude and longitude, you can locate any place on Earth. For example, the location of 30° north latitude and 90° west longitude is usually written as 30° N, 90° W. Only one place on Earth has these coordinates—the city of New Orleans, in the state of Louisiana.

▲ **Compass**
Wherever you are on Earth, a compass can be used to show direction.

Map Projections

Maps are drawings that show regions on flat surfaces. Maps are easier to use and carry than globes, but they cannot show the correct size and shape of every feature on Earth's curved surface. They must shrink some places and stretch others. To make up for this distortion, mapmakers use different map projections. No one projection can accurately show the correct area, shape, distance, and direction for all of Earth's surface. Mapmakers use the projection that has the least distortion for the information they are presenting.

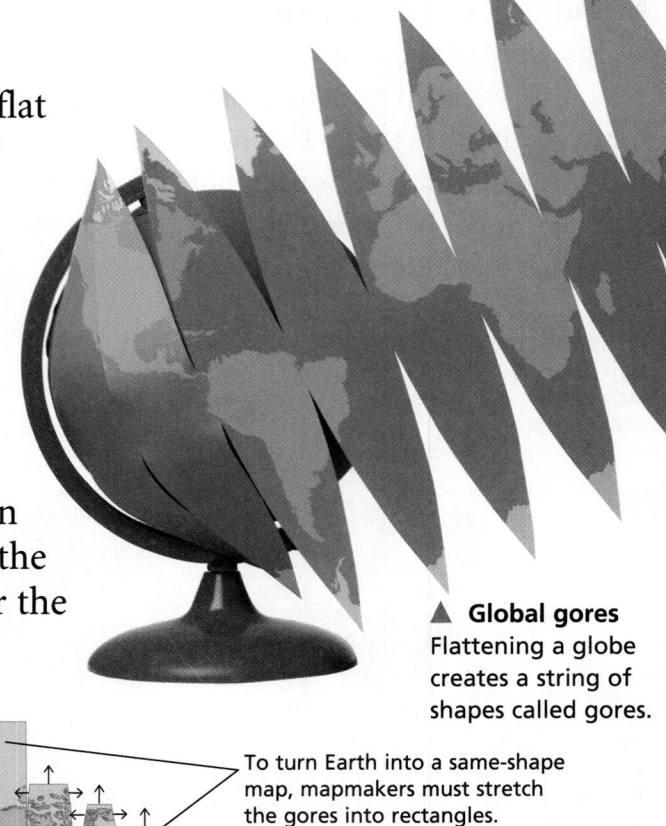

▲ **Global gores**
Flattening a globe creates a string of shapes called gores.

Same-Shape Maps

Map projections that accurately show the shapes of landmasses are called same-shape maps. However, these projections often greatly distort, or make less accurate, the size of landmasses as well as the distance between them. In the projection below, the northern and southern areas of the globe appear more stretched than the areas near the Equator.

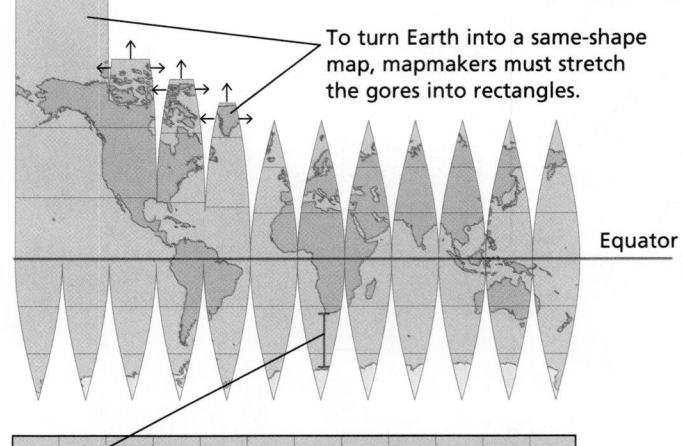

To turn Earth into a same-shape map, mapmakers must stretch the gores into rectangles.

Equator

Stretching the gores makes parts of Earth larger. This enlargement becomes greater toward the North and South Poles.

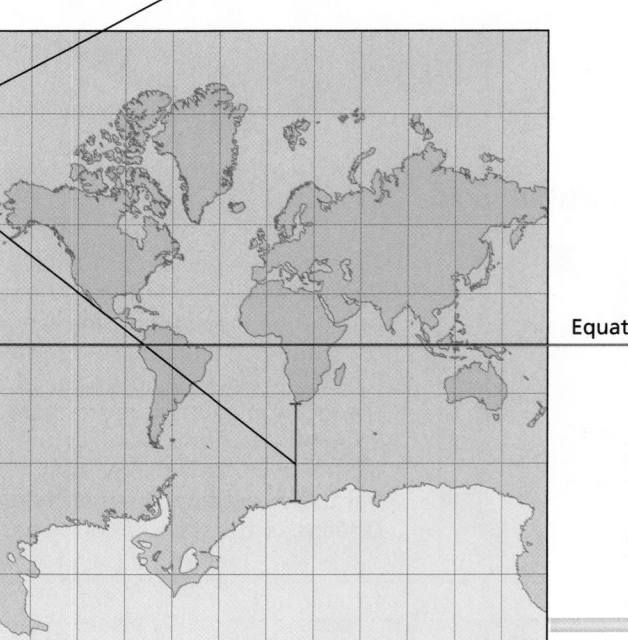

Mercator projection ▶
One of the most common same-shape maps is the Mercator projection, named for the mapmaker who invented it. The Mercator projection accurately shows shape and direction, but it distorts distance and size. Because the projection shows true directions, ships' navigators use it to chart a straight-line course between two ports.

Equator

Equal-Area Maps

Map projections that show the correct size of landmasses are called equal-area maps. In order to show the correct size of landmasses, these maps usually distort shapes. The distortion is usually greater at the edges of the map and less at the center.

PRACTICE YOUR GEOGRAPHY SKILLS

1 What feature is distorted on an equal-area map?

2 Would you use a Mercator projection to find the exact distance between two locations? Tell why or why not.

To turn Earth's surface into an equal-area map, mapmakers have to squeeze each gore into an oval.

The tips of all the gores are then joined together. The points at which they join form the North and South Poles. The line of the Equator stays the same.

Equator

North Pole

Equator

South Pole

Robinson Maps

Many of the maps in this book use the Robinson projection, which is a compromise between the Mercator and equal-area projections. The Robinson projection gives a useful overall picture of the world. It keeps the size and shape relationships of most continents and oceans, but distorts the size of the polar regions.

The entire top edge of the map is the North Pole.

The map is least distorted at the Equator.

Equator

The entire bottom edge of the map is the South Pole.

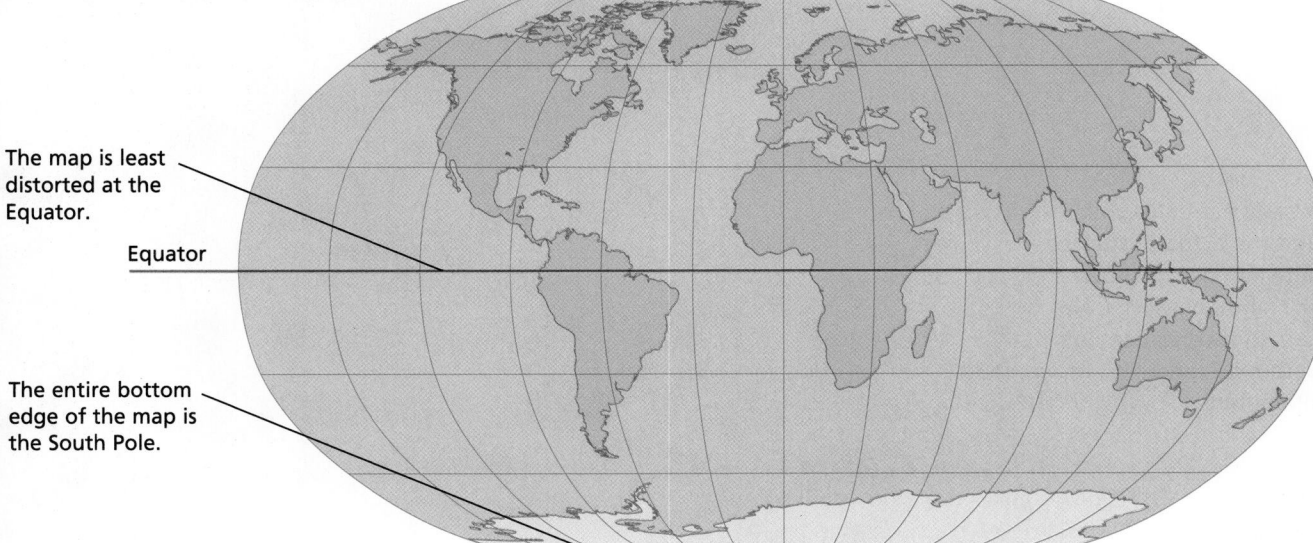

How to Use a Map

Mapmakers provide several clues to help you understand the information on a map. Maps provide different clues, depending on their purpose or scale. However, most maps have several clues in common.

Locator globe
Many maps are shown with locator globes. They show where on the globe the area of the map is located.

Title
All maps have a title. The title tells you the subject of the map.

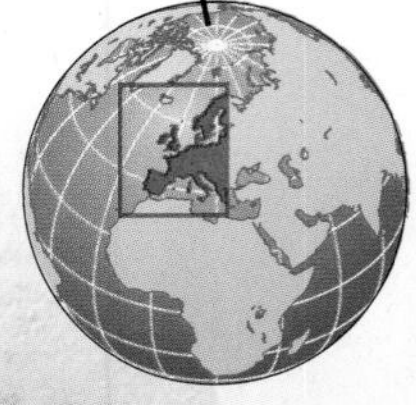

Compass rose
Many maps show direction by displaying a compass rose with the directions north, east, south, and west. The letters N, E, S, and W are placed to indicate these directions.

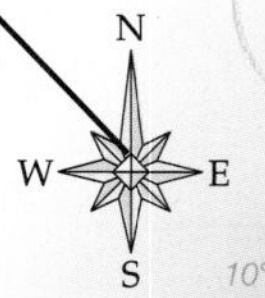

Key
Often a map has a key, or legend. The key shows the symbols and colors used on the map, and what each one means.

Western Europe

Key

——	National border
⊛	National capital
•	Other city

Scale bar
A scale bar helps you find the actual distances between points shown on the map. Most scale bars show distances in both miles and kilometers.

0 miles   300
0 kilometers   300
Lambert Azimuthal Equal Area

SHETLAND ISLANDS (U.K.)

North Sea

Glasgow

Copenhagen

DENMARK

UNITED KINGDOM

Dublin

IRELAND

Hamburg
Berlin

NETHERLANDS
Amsterdam

London

The Hague

GERMANY

Brussels

Prague

BELGIUM

Frankfurt

CZECH REPUBLIC

LUXEMBOURG

Paris

Luxembourg

Munich

Vienna

AUSTRIA

English Channel

FRANCE

Bern LIECHTENSTEIN

SWITZERLAND

Bay of Biscay

Lyon

Milan

SAN MARINO

Toulouse

MONACO

ITALY

Marseille

Adria
Se

ANDORRA

CORSICA
(France)

VATICAN CITY
Rome

PORTUGAL

Madrid

Barcelona

SARDINIA
(Italy)

Tyrrhenian
Sea

Lisbon

SPAIN

BALEARIC
ISLANDS
(Spain)

Seville

Mediterranean Sea

SICILY
(Italy)

Maps of Different Scales

Maps are drawn to different scales, depending on their purpose. Here are three maps drawn to very different scales. Keep in mind that maps showing large areas have smaller scales. Maps showing small areas have larger scales.

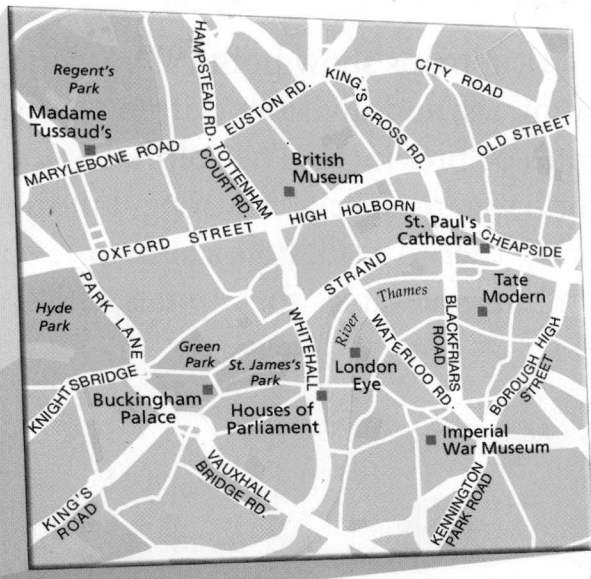

▲ **Greater London**

Find the gray square on the main map of Western Europe (left). This square represents the area shown on the map above. It shows London's boundaries, the general shape of the city, and the features around the city. This map can help you find your way from the airport to the center of town.

▲ **Central London**

Find the gray square on the map of Greater London. This square represents the area shown on the map above. This map moves you closer into the center of London. Like the zoom on a computer or a camera, this map shows a smaller area but in greater detail. It has the largest scale (1 inch represents about 0.9 mile). You can use this map to explore downtown London.

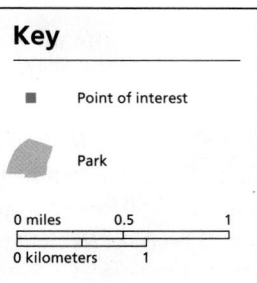

Key

■ Point of interest

Park

0 miles   0.5   1
0 kilometers   1

Key

Built-up area   ✈ Airport

City or county border

0 miles   10   20
0 kilometers   20
Lambert Conformal Conic

⊛ National capital

• Town or neighborhood

PRACTICE YOUR GEOGRAPHY SKILLS

1. What part of a map explains the colors used on the map?

2. How does the scale bar change depending on the scale of the map?

3. Which map would be best for finding the location of the British Museum? Explain why.

Political Maps

Political maps show political borders: continents, countries, and divisions within countries, such as states or provinces. The colors on political maps do not have any special meaning, but they make the map easier to read. Political maps also include symbols and labels for capitals, cities, and towns.

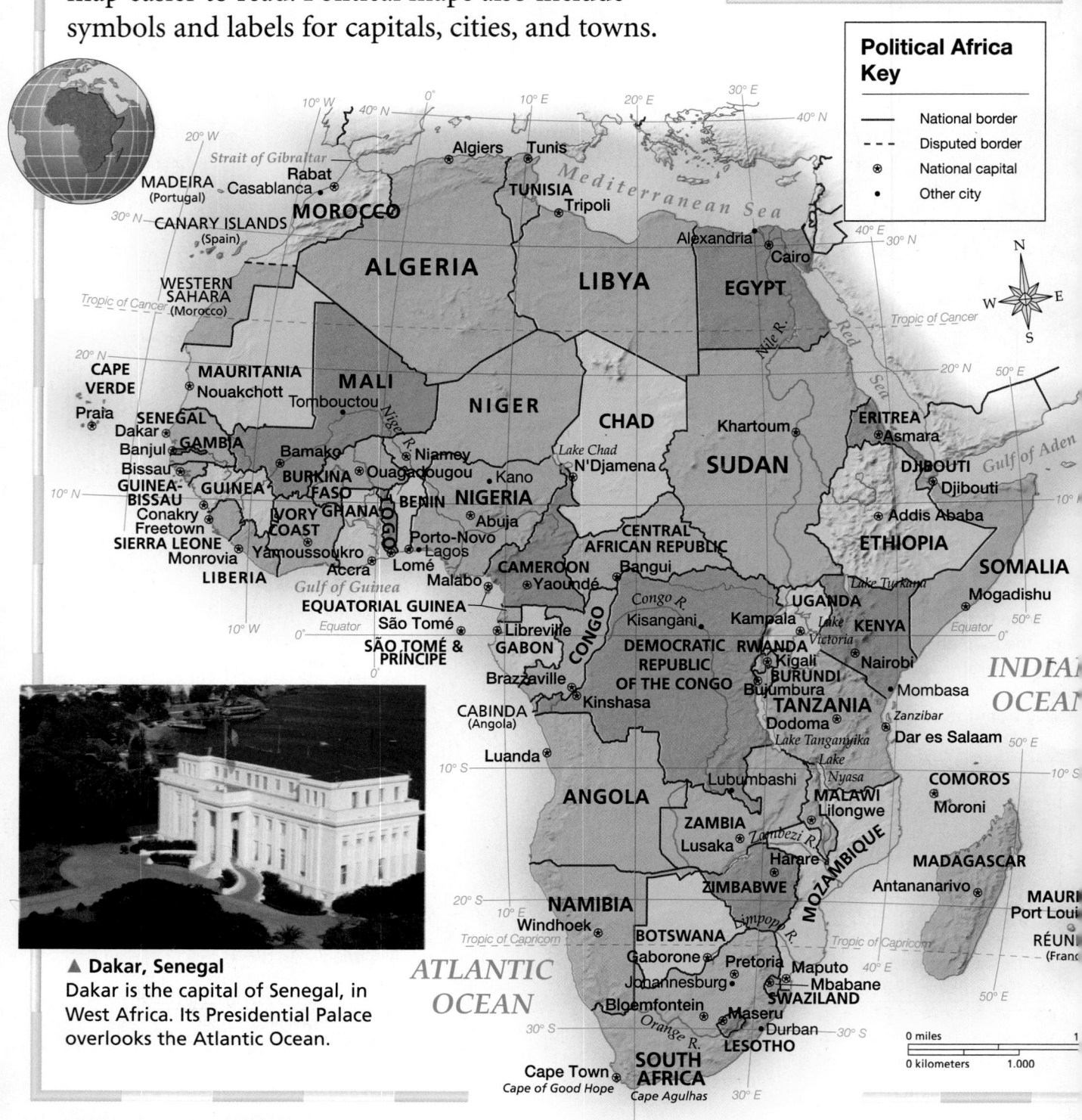

Political Africa Key

——	National border
- - -	Disputed border
⊛	National capital
•	Other city

▲ **Dakar, Senegal**
Dakar is the capital of Senegal, in West Africa. Its Presidential Palace overlooks the Atlantic Ocean.

Physical Maps

Physical maps represent what a region looks like by showing its major physical features, such as hills and plains. Physical maps also often show elevation and relief. Elevation, indicated by colors, is the height of the land above sea level. Relief, indicated by shading, shows how sharply the land rises or falls.

PRACTICE YOUR GEOGRAPHY SKILLS

1 Which areas of Africa have the highest elevation?

2 How can you use relief to plan a hiking trip?

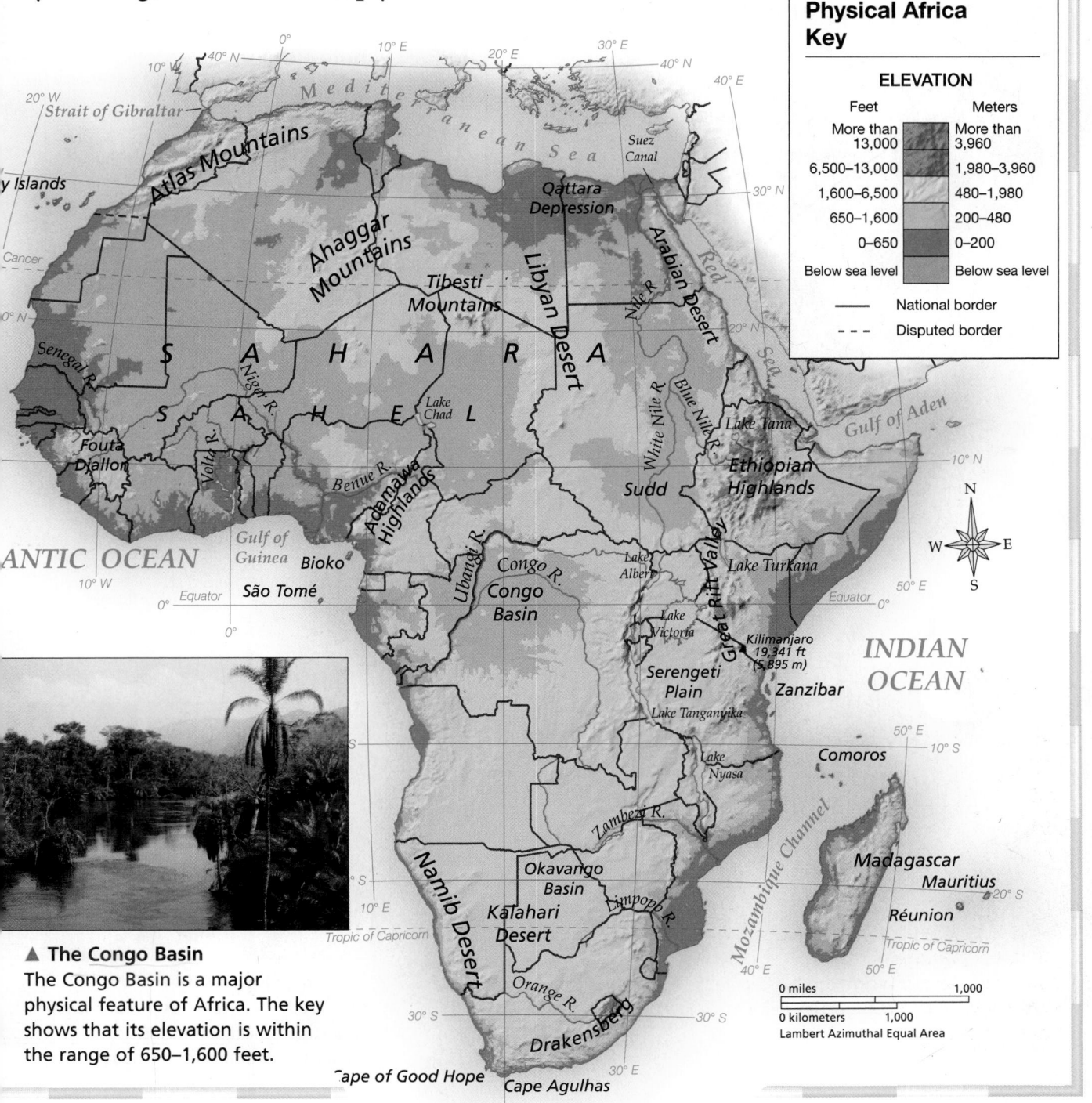

Physical Africa Key

ELEVATION

Feet		Meters
More than 13,000		More than 3,960
6,500–13,000		1,980–3,960
1,600–6,500		480–1,980
650–1,600		200–480
0–650		0–200
Below sea level		Below sea level

——— National border

- - - Disputed border

▲ **The Congo Basin**
The Congo Basin is a major physical feature of Africa. The key shows that its elevation is within the range of 650–1,600 feet.

Special-Purpose Maps: Climate

Unlike the boundary lines on a political map, the boundary lines on climate maps do not separate the land into exact divisions. For example, in this climate map of India, a tropical wet climate gradually changes to a tropical wet and dry climate.

PRACTICE YOUR GEOGRAPHY SKILLS

1 What part of a special-purpose map tells you what the colors on the map mean?

2 Where are arid regions located in India? Are there major cities in those regions?

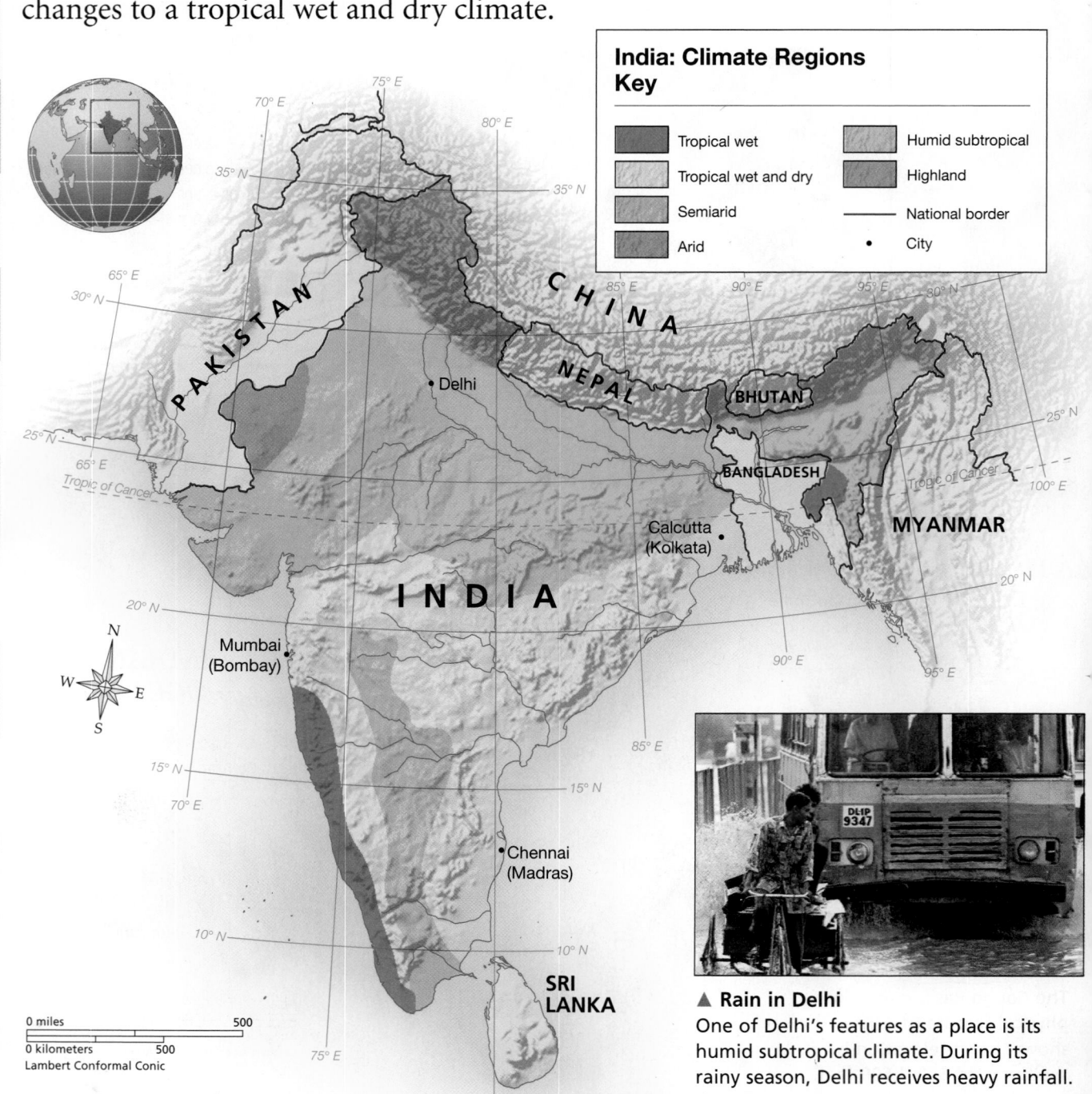

India: Climate Regions Key

- Tropical wet
- Tropical wet and dry
- Semiarid
- Arid
- Humid subtropical
- Highland
- National border
- • City

▲ **Rain in Delhi**
One of Delhi's features as a place is its humid subtropical climate. During its rainy season, Delhi receives heavy rainfall.

Special-Purpose Maps: Language

This map shows the official languages of India. An official language is the language used by the government. Even though a region has an official language, the people there may speak other languages as well. As in other special-purpose maps, the key explains how the different languages appear on the map.

PRACTICE YOUR GEOGRAPHY SKILLS

1 What color represents the Malayalam language on this map?

2 Where in India is Tamil the official language?

The Hindi language ▶
Hindi is the most widely spoken language in India. It is also the most popular language in Delhi.

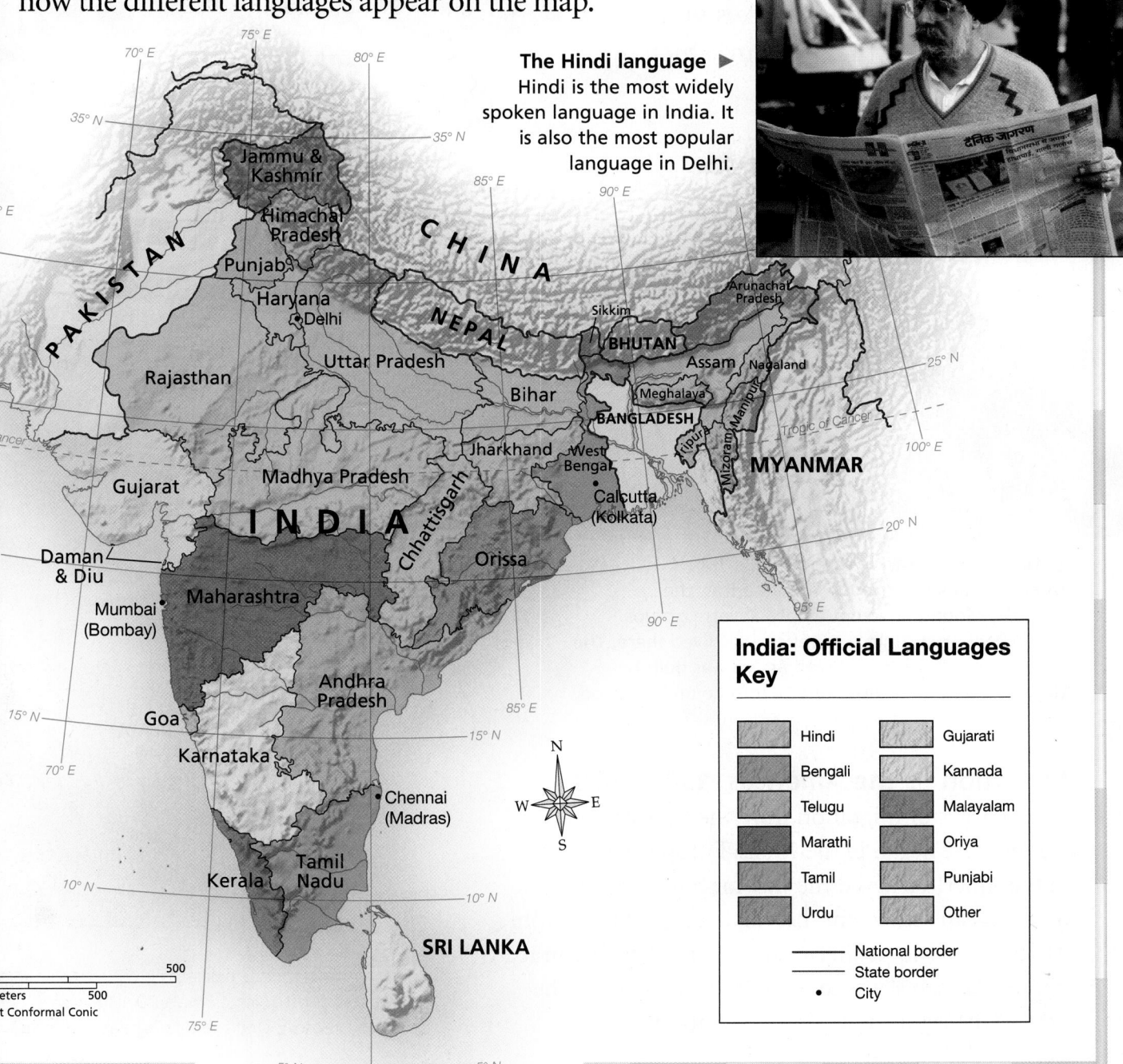

India: Official Languages Key

Hindi	Gujarati
Bengali	Kannada
Telugu	Malayalam
Marathi	Oriya
Tamil	Punjabi
Urdu	Other

—— National border
—— State border
• City

Human Migration

Migration is an important part of the study of geography. Since the beginning of history, people have been on the move. As people move, they both shape and are shaped by their environments. Wherever people go, the culture they bring with them mixes with the cultures of the place in which they have settled.

Explorers arrive ▼
In 1492, Christopher Columbus set sail from Spain for the Americas with three ships. The ships shown here are replicas of those ships.

▲ **Native American pyramid**
When Europeans arrived in the Americas, the lands they found were not empty. Diverse groups of people with distinct cultures already lived there. The temple-topped pyramid shown above was built by Mayan Indians in Mexico, long before Columbus sailed.

Migration to the Americas, 1500–1800

A huge wave of migration from the Eastern Hemisphere began in the 1500s. European explorers in the Americas paved the way for hundreds of years of European settlement there. Forced migration from Africa started soon afterward, as Europeans began to import African slaves to work in the Americas. The map to the right shows these migrations.

ATLANTIC OCEAN

NEW SPAIN
(Spain)
Mexico City

Caribbean Sea

Panama City

DUTCH GUIANA
(Netherlands)

FRENCH GUIANA
(France)

NEW GRENADA
(Spain)

Amazon R.

PERU
(Spain)
Lima
Cuzco

BRAZIL
(Portugal)

Potosí

RIO DE LA PLATA
(Spain)

Concepción

Buenos Aires

0 miles   1,000
0 kilometers   1,000
Wagner VII

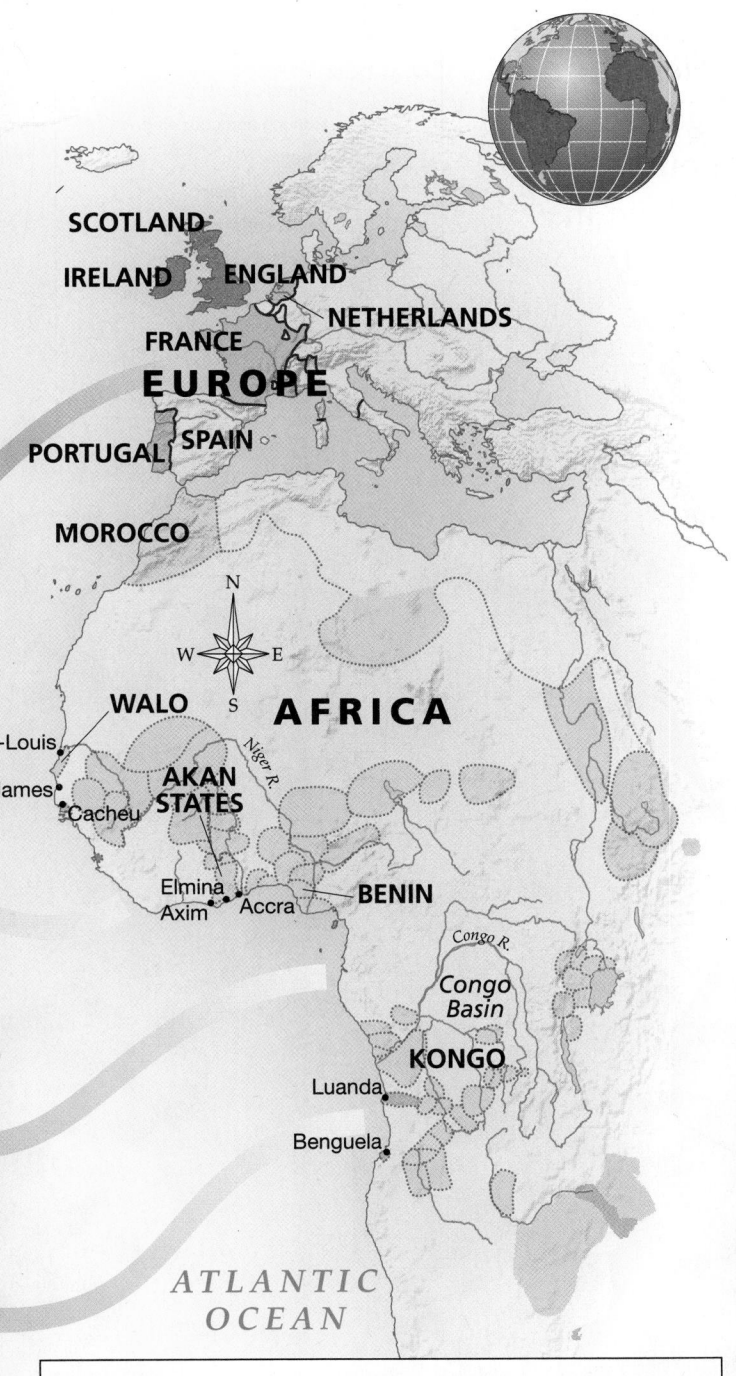

SCOTLAND
IRELAND ENGLAND
FRANCE NETHERLANDS
EUROPE
PORTUGAL SPAIN
MOROCCO

N
W E
S

AFRICA

t-Louis
James
Cacheu
WALO
AKAN
STATES
Niger R.
Elmina
Axim Accra
BENIN
Congo R.
Congo
Basin
KONGO
Luanda
Benguela

ATLANTIC OCEAN

Migration to Latin America, 1500–1800 Key

←	European migration	▨ Spain and possessions
←	African migration	▨ Portugal and possessions
——	National or colonial border	▨ Netherlands and possessions
·····	Traditional African border	▨ France and possessions
▨	African State	▨ England and possessions

PRACTICE YOUR GEOGRAPHY SKILLS

1 Where did the Portuguese settle in the Americas?

2 Would you describe African migration at this time as a result of both push factors and pull factors? Explain why or why not.

"Push" and "Pull" Factors

Geographers describe a people's choice to migrate in terms of "push" factors and "pull" factors. Push factors are things in people's lives that push them to leave, such as poverty and political unrest. Pull factors are things in another country that pull people to move there, including better living conditions and hopes of better jobs.

▲ **Elmina, Ghana**
Elmina, in Ghana, is one of the many ports from which slaves were transported from Africa. Because slaves and gold were traded here, stretches of the western African coast were known as the Slave Coast and the Gold Coast.

World Land Use

People around the world have many different economic structures, or ways of making a living. Land-use maps are one way to learn about these structures. The ways that people use the land in each region tell us about the main ways that people in that region make a living.

World Land Use Key

	Nomadic herding
	Hunting and gathering
	Forestry
	Livestock raising
	Commercial farming
	Subsistence farming
	Manufacturing and trade
	Little or no activity
——	National border
- - - -	Disputed border

▲ **Wheat farming in the United States**
Developed countries practice commercial farming rather than subsistence farming. Commercial farming is the production of food mainly for sale, either within the country or for export to other countries. Commercial farmers like these in Oregon often use heavy equipment to farm.

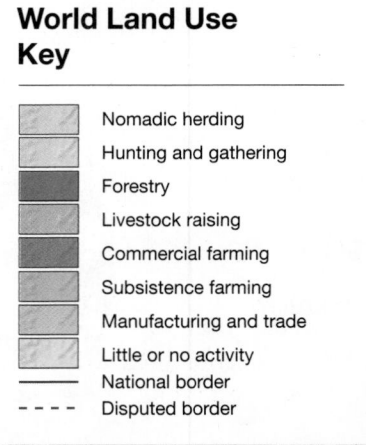

NORTH AMERICA

SOUTH AMER

Levels of Development

Notice on the map key the term *subsistence farming*. This term means the production of food mainly for use by the farmer's own family. In less-developed countries, subsistence farming is often one of the main economic activities. In contrast, in developed countries there is little subsistence farming.

▲ **Growing barley in Ecuador**
Subsistence farmers like this one in Ecuador use hand tools to harvest barley. They use most of their crop to feed themselves or their farm animals.

0 miles

0 kilometers   2,000

Robinson

M16   MapMaster Skills Handbook

▲ Growing rice in Vietnam
Women in Vietnam plant rice in wet rice paddies, using the same planting methods their ancestors did.

PRACTICE YOUR GEOGRAPHY SKILLS

1 In what parts of the world is subsistence farming the main land use?

2 Locate where manufacturing and trade are the main land use. Are they found more often near areas of subsistence farming or areas of commercial farming? Why might this be so?

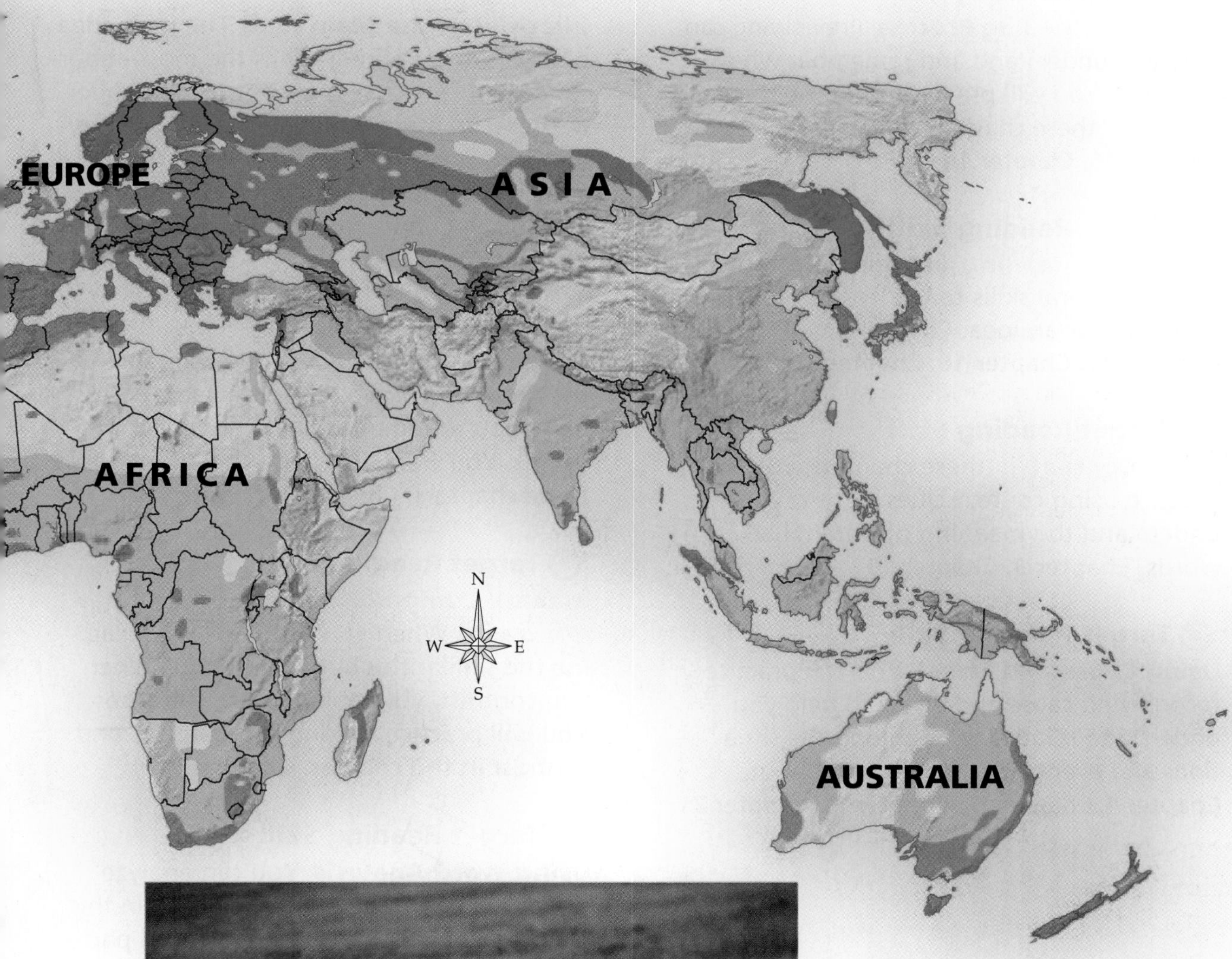

EUROPE

ASIA

AFRICA

N
W E
S

AUSTRALIA

◄ Herding cattle in Kenya
Besides subsistence farming, nomadic herding is another economic activity in Africa. This man drives his cattle across the Kenyan grasslands.

 # Target Reading Skills

The Target Reading Skills introduced on this page will help you understand the words and ideas in this book and in other social studies reading you do. Each chapter focuses on one of these reading skills. Good readers develop a bank of reading strategies, or skills. Then they draw on the particular strategies that will help them understand the text they are reading.

Target Reading Skill

Using the Reading Process Previewing can help you understand and remember what you read. You will practice using the reading process in these chapters: **Chapter 1, Chapter 10, Chapter 18**

Target Reading Skill

Clarifying Meaning In these chapters, you will use several skills to clarify the meaning of a word or an idea. **Chapter 2, Chapter 11, Chapter 16, Chapter 22**

Target Reading Skill

Using Context In these chapters, you will practice using context clues to help you understand the meaning of unfamiliar words. **Chapter 3, Chapter 19**

Target Reading Skill

Using Cause and Effect You will practice recognizing cause and effect to help you understand relationships among the situations and events you are reading about. **Chapter 4, Chapter 13, Chapter 15, Chapter 21**

Target Reading Skill

Identifying the Main Idea The main idea of a section or paragraph is the most important point, the one you want to remember. In these chapters, you will practice identifying both stated and implied main ideas and identifying supporting details. **Chapter 5, Chapter 9, Chapter 12, Chapter 17, Chapter 20**

Target Reading Skill

Using Sequence Understand sequence—the order in which a series of events occurs—helps you to remember and understand events. You will practicing using sequence in these chapters. **Chapter 6, Chapter 14**

Target Reading Skill

Making Comparisons and Contrasts When you compare, you examine the similarities between things. When you contrast, you look at the differences. You will practice making comparisons and contrast in this chapter. **Chapter 7**

Target Reading Skill

Using Word Analysis You can analyze words to determine their meanings. In this chapter, you will practice using word parts (such as roots, prefixes, and suffixes) and recognizing word origins. **Chapter 8**

HISTORY OF OUR WORLD

To understand today's world, we must learn about its past. Ancient civilizations laid strong foundations for modern cultures. The early ages of world history have added greatly to those cultures. In this book, you will learn how the ideas, events, and people of the past have shaped our lives.

Guiding Questions

The text, photographs, maps, and charts in this book will help you discover answers to these Guiding Questions.

1. **Geography** How did physical geography affect the development and growth of societies around the world?

2. **History** How did each society's belief system affect its historical accomplishments?

3. **Culture** What were the beliefs and values of people in these societies?

4. **Government** What types of governments were formed in these societies and how did they develop?

5. **Economics** How did each society develop and organize its economic activities?

Project Preview

You can also discover answers to the Guiding Questions by working on projects. Several project possibilities are listed on page 662 of this book.

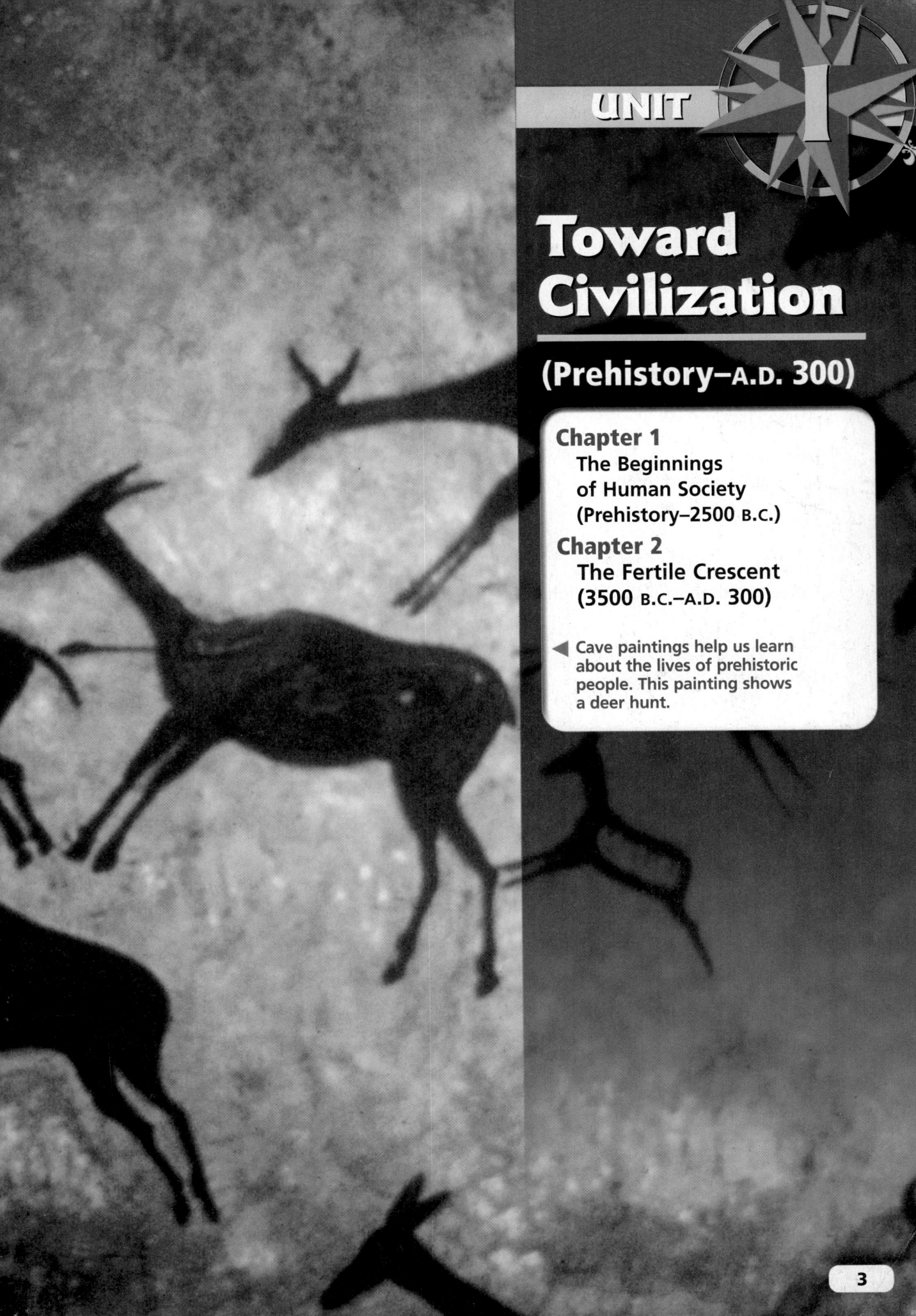

Toward Civilization

(Prehistory–A.D. 300)

Chapter 1
The Beginnings
of Human Society
(Prehistory–2500 B.C.)

Chapter 2
The Fertile Crescent
(3500 B.C.–A.D. 300)

◀ Cave paintings help us learn
about the lives of prehistoric
people. This painting shows
a deer hunt.

Chapter

1

The Beginnings of Human Society

Chapter Preview

In this chapter you will find out how archaeologists learn about the past. You will also learn about the connections between geography and history.

Section 1
Geography and History

Section 2
Prehistory

Section 3
The Beginnings of Civilization

Target Reading Skill

Reading Process In this chapter you will focus on previewing to help you understand and remember what you read.

▶ Cave painting from about 5000 B.C., Argentina

Early Migration of Modern Humans

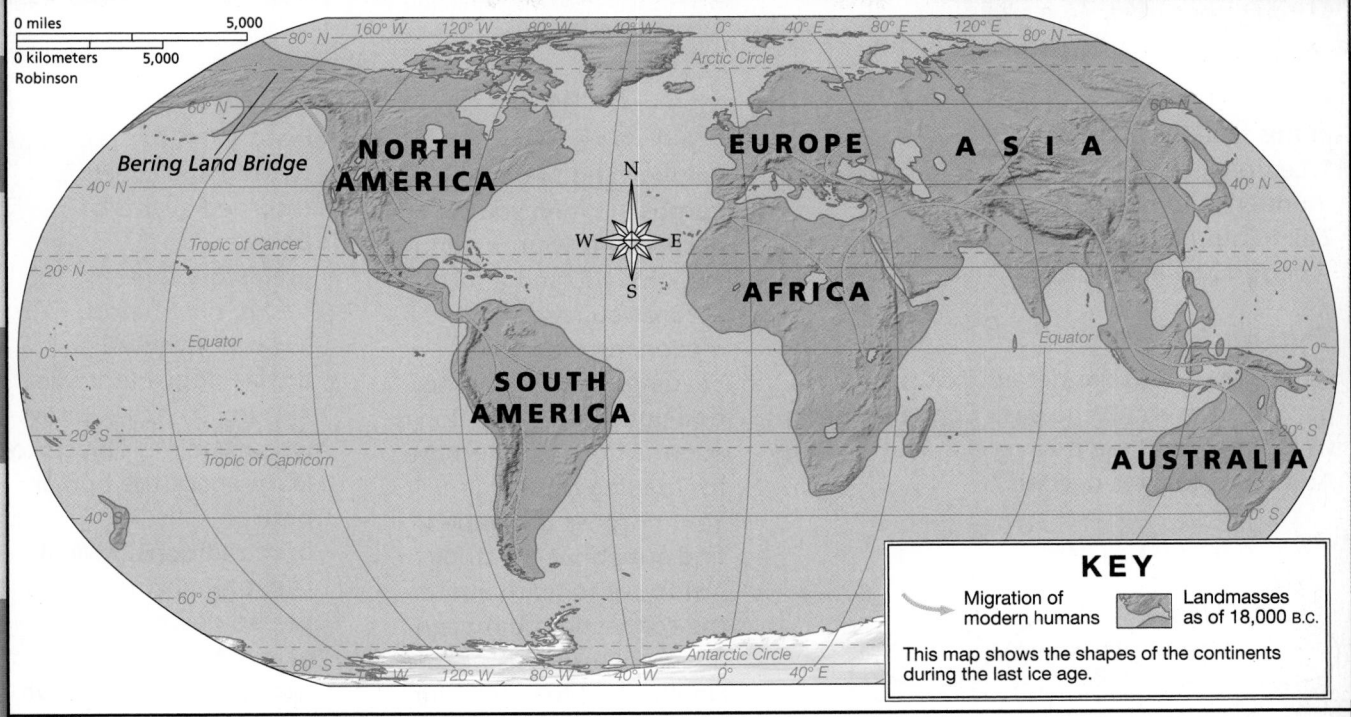

0 miles   5,000
0 kilometers   5,000
Robinson

Bering Land Bridge

NORTH AMERICA

EUROPE   **A S I A**

AFRICA

SOUTH AMERICA

AUSTRALIA

Arctic Circle
Tropic of Cancer
Equator
Tropic of Capricorn
Antarctic Circle

KEY

 Migration of modern humans

Landmasses as of 18,000 B.C.

This map shows the shapes of the continents during the last ice age.

Movement Modern humans may have originated more than 100,000 years ago in Africa before spreading to other parts of the world. This migration most likely took place over many thousands of years. **Identify** What landmass did modern humans cross to travel from Asia into North America? **Infer** Why did the migration of humans from Africa to the rest of the world take place so slowly? Explain your answer.

Go Online
PHSchool.com Use Web Code **lbp-2111** for step-by-step **map skills practice.**

Prepare to Read

Objectives

In this section you will

1. Learn what tools are used to understand history.
2. Find out about the connections between geography and history.

Taking Notes

As you read, look for details that tell how people learn about the past. Copy the concept web below, and use it to record your findings. Add more ovals as needed.

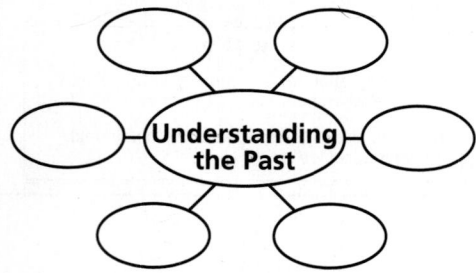

Understanding the Past

Target Reading Skill

Preview and Set a Purpose When you set a purpose for your reading, you give yourself a focus. Before you read this section, preview the headings and pictures to find out what the section is about. Then set a purpose for reading this section. Your purpose might be to find out about the study of history, or to learn about the connections between geography and history. Finally, read to meet your purpose.

Key Terms

- **history** (HIS tuh ree) *n.* written and other recorded events of people
- **prehistory** (pree HIS tuh ree) *n.* time before writing was invented
- **archaeologist** (ahr kee AHL uh jist) *n.* a scientist who examines objects to learn about the human past
- **oral traditions** (AWR ul truh DISH unz) *n.* stories passed down by word of mouth
- **geography** (jee AHG ruh fee) *n.* the study of Earth's surface and the processes that shape it

A scientist recovers the body of the ancient Iceman from a glacier in the Alps.

He is called the Iceman. His frozen body was found in a mountain pass in the Alps, on the Italian-Austrian border in Europe.

Two hikers discovered the Iceman by chance in 1991. His body and possessions were taken to a laboratory, where scientists learned more about him. His clothing, tools, and his body were well preserved. They provided clues about the Iceman's life and death. Scientists used these clues to build a story of his life. To learn how the Iceman died, see the Links to Science on the next page.

Scientists determined that the Iceman lived about 5,000 years ago, in about 3000 B.C. The Iceman's finely stitched animal skins showed that he probably came from a community that included people who were skilled in sewing.

The most important clue about the Iceman's life was his copper ax. Copper was the first metal used by Europeans, beginning about 4000 B.C. The ax left no doubt that the Iceman lived after people had learned to use copper. In many ways, the story of the Iceman helps us to understand the story of our past.

Understanding History

The scientists' curiosity about the Iceman's life was natural. As human beings, we are curious about our earliest origins. What was life like many thousands of years ago?

Before and After Writing About 5,000 years ago, peoples in Southwest Asia and in Africa developed systems of writing. They began to keep written records of their experiences. These developments marked the beginning of **history,** the written and other recorded events of people. By adding the prefix *pre-,* which means "before," you form the word *prehistory.* **Prehistory** is the time before history. Prehistory is the period of time before writing was invented.

Prehistory: Digging Up the Past To learn about life in prehistoric times, scientists must rely on clues other than written records. **Archaeologists** (ahr kee AHL uh jists) are scientists who examine objects to learn about past peoples and cultures. They sift through the dirt of prehistoric camps to find bones, tools, and other objects. These objects may tell them something about the people who lived there. For example, the size of stone spear points shows what kinds of game the people hunted. To kill big game, such as bears, hunters had to use large, heavy spear points. Such points, however, would not work very well with birds and small animals.

Links to
Science

Cause of Death At first, scientists believed that the Iceman had frozen to death. But ten years after the discovery of the Iceman, scientists found an arrowhead lodged in his shoulder. Later, they found a knife wound on his hand. Now scientists believe the Iceman may have died from injuries he received during an armed struggle.

The stone amulet, above, is similar to the one found with the Iceman. The knife and its grass case, left, were among his belongings.

A museum model of the Iceman, right, shows how he may have dressed.

Prehistoric rock painting in South Africa

History: A Record in Writing Historians do not rely only on the objects discovered by archaeologists to learn about the past. They also study the written records of human life and accomplishments to understand a society—its wars, its religion, and its rulers, among other things. Historians also look at what other groups living at the same time wrote about that society.

A Record of the Spoken Word The written records studied by historians often began as **oral traditions,** stories passed down by word of mouth. Oral traditions can include a family's history, such as stories of parents, grandparents, and great-grandparents. They can also tell stories about heroes or events in the past.

Oral traditions are still an important part of many societies today. Not all oral stories are historically accurate. Stories often change as they are told and retold. Like myths and legends, they often contain facts mixed with personal beliefs and exaggerations about heroes. Still, oral traditions tell how a society lived and what the people considered important.

Set a Purpose
If your purpose is to learn about the study of history, how does reading about oral traditions help you to achieve your purpose?

✓ **Reading Check** **Why are historians interested in oral traditions?**

Carrying on a Tradition
In West Africa, a professional storyteller called a griot (GREE oh) keeps oral traditions alive.
Draw Conclusions
How does a community benefit from knowing about its recent and ancient past?

Linking Geography and History

Knowing when something happened is important. Understanding why historic events took place is also important. To do this, historians often turn to **geography,** the study of Earth's surface and the processes that shape it. Geography also refers to the features of a place, including its climate, landscape, and location. Knowing the connections between geography and history is often the key to understanding why events happened. Weather patterns, the water supply, and the landscape of a place all affect the lives of the people who live there. For example, to explain why the ancient Egyptians developed a successful civilization, you must look at the geography of Egypt.

Egyptian civilization was built on the banks of the Nile River in Africa. Each year the Nile flooded, depositing soil on its banks. Because the soil was rich, Egyptian farmers could grow enough crops to feed the large numbers of people in the cities. That meant everyone did not have to farm, so some people could perform other jobs that helped develop the civilization. Without the Nile and its regular flooding, Egyptian civilization would not have become so successful.

A farm in Egypt's Nile delta

✓ **Reading Check** **Give one example of geography's effect on history.**

Section 1 Assessment

Key Terms
Review the key terms at the beginning of this section. Use each term in a sentence that explains its meaning.

Target Reading Skill
How did having a reading purpose help you understand this section?

Comprehension and Critical Thinking
1. (a) Recall What do scientists study to learn about prehistory?
(b) Generalize What do we know about societies that leave behind written records?

(c) Draw Inferences Analyze the clothes you wear and the things you carry to school. What do they say about your life? How does your story compare to the Iceman's story?
2. (a) Identify Name some examples of familiar geographic features.
(b) Explain How can geography help us to understand history?
(c) Identify Cause and Effect What effect has geography had on the way people in your community live?

Writing Activity
Ask a classmate to share a story with you. The story should be about an important event in the person's life. Write the story from your classmate's point of view.

For: An activity on archaeology
Visit: PHSchool.com
Web Code: lbd-2101

A wall painting from the ancient city of Knossos, Greece, founded in 2500 B.C.

The post above was used to secure the reins on an animal's harness. It is from the ancient city of Ur, founded in 3500 B.C. in Mesopotamia.

When you study history, you must learn about many different events and the dates on which they occurred. However, a whole page filled with dates can be hard to follow. For that reason, writers often use a simple diagram called a timeline. A timeline shows the order in which events happened. At a glance, a timeline can give you a picture of a certain time period.

Learn the Skill

Refer to page 11 as you follow the steps below.

1 **Read the title of the timeline.** The title tells you what the timeline will show.

2 **Determine the time span.** Look at the beginning and the endpoint of the timeline to determine the time span. If the timeline shows ancient history, it is sometimes divided into two parts. The dates on the left side are marked with the letters B.C. The dates on the right side are marked with the letters A.D. The letters B.C. are an abbreviation of "before Christ" and refer to the years before Jesus' birth. The letters A.D. mean "anno Domini," which is Latin for "in the year of our Lord." The letters A.D. refer to the time after Jesus' birth.

Notice that with B.C., you count backward. The numbers get larger as you go backward in time. Also note the letter *c.* before some dates. An abbreviation for the Latin word *circa*, *c.* means "about." Historians often use *circa* or *c.* before dates.

3 **Determine the intervals of time.** A timeline is divided into intervals of time that are marked by vertical lines. Determine how many years occur between the vertical lines. Timelines that show a long span of time have longer intervals, such as 100 or 1,000 years. Timelines that show a short span of time have shorter intervals, such as 10 or 20 years.

4 **Study the events on the timeline.** Each event has a date and is connected to the timeline by a dot and a line. Notice when each event happened. Be sure to notice whether a date has more than one event.

Practice the Skill

Use the timeline below to practice the skill.

1 Find the title of the timeline. Based on the title, do you think this timeline will show a long or a short time span?

2 Determine the time span. Find the beginning of the timeline at the left. Notice that the first date is followed by B.C. Next, find the endpoint of the timeline. Notice that the last date is preceded by A.D. What is the span of time between these two dates?

3 Determine the intervals. Look at the dates marked by vertical lines on the timeline. How far is one date from another?

4 Study the events on the timeline. Notice the kinds of events that are shown and whether they are connected. How can you tell whether some events occurred closer together than others? Look at the abbreviations used with the dates on this timeline. Why is the event "Jesus is born" an important event to show on this particular timeline?

Apply the Skill

Turn to the table titled Early Cities on page 22. Create a timeline based on the information in the table. Follow the steps you used to practice this skill to help you create your timeline.

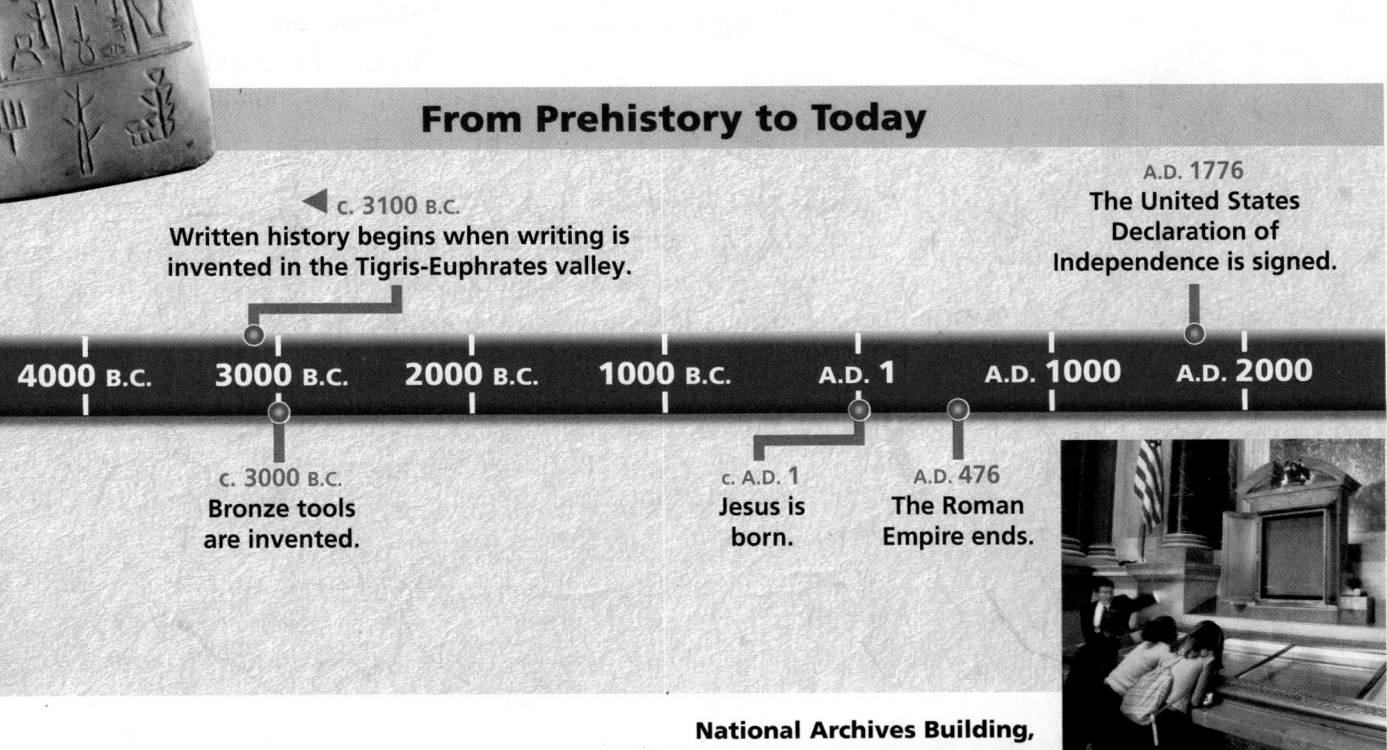

From Prehistory to Today

◀ c. 3100 B.C.
Written history begins when writing is invented in the Tigris-Euphrates valley.

A.D. 1776
The United States Declaration of Independence is signed.

4000 B.C.   3000 B.C.   2000 B.C.   1000 B.C.   A.D. 1   A.D. 1000   A.D. 2000

c. 3000 B.C.
Bronze tools are invented.

c. A.D. 1
Jesus is born.

A.D. 476
The Roman Empire ends.

National Archives Building, Washington, D.C., which houses the Declaration of Independence

Prepare to Read

Objectives

In this section you will

1. Discover how hunter-gatherers lived during the Stone Age.
2. Learn about the beginning of farming.

Taking Notes

As you read, look for details about survival during the Stone Age. Copy the table below, and use it to record your findings.

Topic	Details
Tools	
Hunting	
Gathering	
Fire	
Settlement	
Farming	
Animals	

Target Reading Skill

Preview and Predict
Making predictions about your text helps you to remember what you read. Before you read this section, preview it by looking at the headings and pictures. Then predict what the text might discuss about prehistory. For example, you might predict that the text will explain important events that happened in prehistory. As you read, connect what you read to your prediction. If what you learn doesn't support your prediction, revise your prediction.

Key Terms

- **hominid** (HAHM uh nid) *n.* a modern human or a member of an earlier group that may have included ancestors or relatives of modern humans
- **Stone Age** (stohn ayj) *n.* a period of time during which hominids made lasting tools and weapons mainly from stone; the earliest known period of prehistoric culture
- **nomad** (NOH mad) *n.* a person who has no settled home
- **domesticate** (duh MES tih kayt) *v.* to adapt wild plants or tame wild animals and to breed them for human use

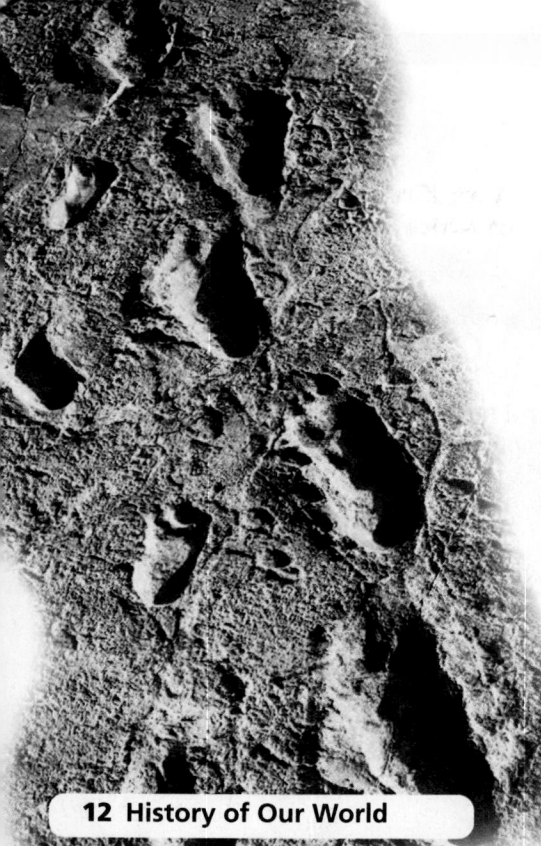

About three and a half million years ago, a huge explosion shook a part of East Africa. A volcano spit out clouds of fine ash that fell on the surrounding land. Then rain came. It turned the blanket of ash into thick mud. Before the mud dried, two individuals walked across the landscape. As they walked, they left their footprints in the mud.

In 1976, a group of scientists discovered the footprints, preserved in stone. They were amazed at their find. The footprints are almost identical to those made by modern humans walking in wet sand. Such evidence may help scientists understand early **hominids,** a term that refers both to modern humans and to earlier groups that may have included ancestors or relatives of modern humans.

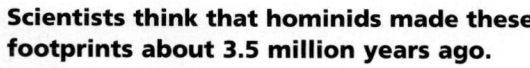

Scientists think that hominids made these footprints about 3.5 million years ago.

Stone Age Hunting and Gathering

A million years after the footprints were made, early hominids began making stone tools. By studying these tools, we learn about the development of prehistoric culture.

Stone Age Culture The first use of stone to create tools began the earliest period of human culture: the Stone Age. The **Stone Age** was a period during which hominids, including modern humans, made lasting tools mainly from stone. They also made tools from wood and animal bones. Scientists think that the Stone Age continued for hundreds of thousands of years, until people learned to use metal for tools.

Archaeologists divide the Stone Age into three periods: the Old Stone Age, the Middle Stone Age, and the New Stone Age. During the Old Stone Age, modern humans and other hominids did not yet know how to farm. They were hunter-gatherers who survived by hunting animals and gathering wild plants. Almost all of human prehistory took place during the Old Stone Age.

Fire! Between about 1,400,000 and 500,000 years ago, early hominids learned how to use fire. No one knows for sure how they learned. Perhaps one day a small band of hunters saw a grass fire caused by lightning on the open plain. Although terrified by the fire, they learned how to keep it going. With fire, they could ward off dangerous animals, who were also afraid of the flames.

Finally, early hominids discovered how to create fire. They probably did this by rubbing two sticks together or by striking stones together to produce a spark. The ability to create fire was an important step for our ancestors. With this great advance, they could move to areas with colder climates.

Links to Science

How Old Is It? After archaeologists find bones, tools, or other objects, they ask themselves that question. Scientists use different tests for dating different objects. One very useful test is called radiocarbon dating. All plants and animals have tiny amounts of a substance called radiocarbon in their bodies. After they die, the radiocarbon changes into another substance. Scientists know how long this change takes. They have tests that measure how much radiocarbon remains. Scientists can then calculate the age of the material. Because the ancient comb, below, is made from the antler of a deer or an elk, radiocarbon dating could be used to determine its age.

A wildfire on the grasslands of Africa

Target Skill

Predict Based on what you have read so far, is your prediction on target? If not, change your prediction now.

Discovery CHANNEL SCHOOL Video

Explore the first great migration.

Nomadic Herding
A young shepherd guides her flock to graze in the Taza Province of Morocco in North Africa. **Predict** *What factors might influence this nomad's decision to move her sheep from one area to another?*

Settling New Areas As early hominids developed the use of tools, they left their original homes in Africa. Their move may have begun as early as one million years ago. Many early hominids were nomads. **Nomads** are people who have no settled home. They moved around to places where they thought they would find food and stayed there for several days. When they had gathered all the food around them, they moved on.

Early hominids eventually spread out over much of Earth. There is evidence that early hominids were living in Asia and Europe at least 500,000 years ago. Many scientists believe that modern humans originated more than 100,000 years ago in Africa and then spread to other parts of the world. Perhaps 30,000 years ago humans crossed from Asia into North America. By 10,000 B.C., humans had reached Chile in South America. Compared with today, humans then were few in number. But as we can today, they survived in all sorts of geographical conditions. They lived in the steamy rain forests of Africa and Asia, the cold lands near the Arctic Circle, and the high altitudes of the Andes in South America.

✓ **Reading Check** **What was life like during the Stone Age?**

The Beginning of Farming

For tens of thousands of years, our ancestors continued to live as hunter-gatherers. However, some societies entered the Middle Stone Age, which was characterized by the use of more refined, or advanced, tools. Those who began the practice of farming would enter the New Stone Age.

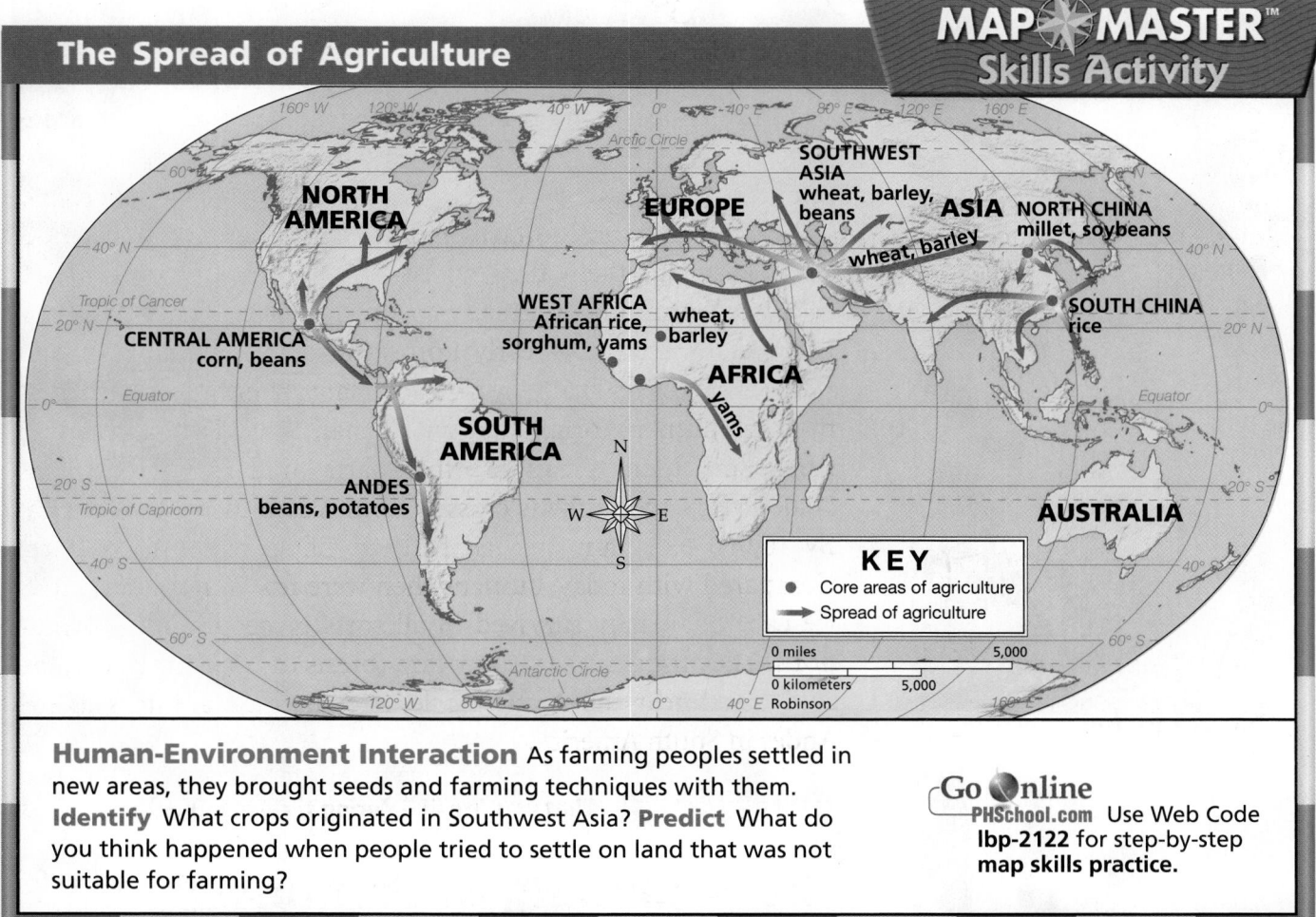

The Spread of Agriculture

MAP★MASTER™
Skills Activity

NORTH AMERICA

CENTRAL AMERICA
corn, beans

SOUTH AMERICA

ANDES
beans, potatoes

WEST AFRICA
African rice,
sorghum, yams

wheat,
barley

EUROPE

SOUTHWEST ASIA
wheat, barley,
beans

wheat, barley

ASIA

NORTH CHINA
millet, soybeans

SOUTH CHINA
rice

AFRICA

yams

AUSTRALIA

Arctic Circle
Tropic of Cancer
Equator
Tropic of Capricorn
Antarctic Circle

KEY
● Core areas of agriculture
→ Spread of agriculture

0 miles   5,000
0 kilometers   5,000
Robinson

Human-Environment Interaction As farming peoples settled in new areas, they brought seeds and farming techniques with them. **Identify** What crops originated in Southwest Asia? **Predict** What do you think happened when people tried to settle on land that was not suitable for farming?

Go **Online**
PHSchool.com Use Web Code
lbp-2122 for step-by-step
map skills practice.

Early Farmers About 11,000 years ago, people in Southwest Asia made an amazing discovery. They learned that if they planted the seeds of wild grasses, new crops of grasses would come up. Thus began the New Stone Age in Southwest Asia. It was called the New Stone Age because people began to grow their own food. They did not have to be nomads, although they still depended on stone tools. However, in many other parts of the world, the Old and Middle Stone Ages continued for many thousands of years. In some areas, Old Stone Age societies even existed into the 1900s.

At the same time that people began to grow their own food, some people became pastoral nomads. That is, they raised livestock and traveled from place to place in search of grazing areas for their animals. Many people, such as the desert-roaming Bedouins of present-day Iraq, Syria, and other areas, are still pastoral nomads.

In most societies, women were responsible for gathering plants and seeds. Therefore they may have been the first to plant seeds. Men usually were the hunters. Women began planting and harvesting their crops in the same place year after year.

Farming Techniques
Over time, people have made important advances in farming. In Bali, Indonesia, top, farmers build terraces, or platforms, into the hillsides for growing rice. In 5000 B.C., people grew ears of corn, above left, about 1 inch (2.5 cm) long. By A.D. 1500, years of careful breeding produced much larger corn, above right, about 5 1/3 inches (13.6 cm) long.
Analyze Images *What advantages do farmers gain from such techniques as terrace farming and plant breeding?*

Farming Around the World Some places were better for farming than others. Soil in some areas was very fertile, or rich in the substances that plants need to grow. Because plants also need light and warmth, areas that had long springs and summers were good places to farm. Gentle rains are important sources of water for plants. People gradually discovered that the soil, the water, and the length of the growing seasons in several places around the world were good for plants. These people took up the farming way of life.

About 9,000 years ago, Chinese farmers began planting rice and other crops. A little later in Central America, people began to grow corn, beans, and squash. The map on page 15 shows where certain crops were first planted and how their use spread.

Plant Selection While the kinds of plants grown by those first farmers are still important today, the plants looked very different then. When people first began to plant crops, they carefully chose seeds from the biggest, best-tasting plants. In doing so, they began to **domesticate** plants, or adapt wild plants for human use. Very gradually, this careful selection of seeds and roots from each crop led to the kinds of food that we eat today. The photograph of ears of corn on this page shows the domestication of corn over time.

Raising Animals Just as humans learned to domesticate plants, they also learned to domesticate animals. During the New Stone Age, humans learned to tame wild animals and breed them for human use. The first domesticated animals may have been dogs, because they were valuable in hunting. By taming larger animals such as sheep, goats, and pigs, people developed ready sources of meat, milk, wool, and skins. Through gradual and careful breeding, herders developed animals that were gentler than their wild ancestors and provided more milk or wool. By about 2500 B.C., cattle, camels, horses, and donkeys were trained to carry heavy loads.

The Challenge of Domestication Over the course of history, humans have tried and failed to domesticate many species. Since ancient times, many animals have been captured in the wild and tamed. The people of ancient India tamed wild elephants for use in battle. Ancient Assyrians and Egyptians trained wild cheetahs for hunting. But these animals and many other species are not easy to breed in captivity. In fact, only a few species of large animals have been suitable for use in agriculture or transportation.

A caravan of camels used by nomads in Iran

 **Reading Check** What skills did people develop during the New Stone Age?

Section 2 Assessment

Key Terms
Review the key terms at the beginning of this section. Use each term in a sentence that explains its meaning.

Target Reading Skill
What did you predict about this section? How did your prediction guide your reading?

Comprehension and Critical Thinking
1. (a) Recall Describe how hominids of the Old Stone Age survived.

(b) Infer What important skills did hominids of the Old Stone Age use to find food?
(c) Synthesize How did survival skills change as people began to settle?
2. (a) Identify What marked the beginning of the New Stone Age?
(b) Contrast How was life in the New Stone Age different from life in the Old Stone Age?
(c) Apply Information What are the effects of geography and climate on farming?

Writing Activity
Suppose you are a hunter-gatherer. You think of an idea for growing your own food. Write a journal entry describing what gave you the idea, and how your idea might affect your people.

For: An activity on the Stone Age
Visit: PHSchool.com
Web Code: lbd-2102

Focus On
Hunter-Gatherers

Spears ready, they hide behind rocks and trees. Their hand axes have been sharpened to a fine edge. They are hungry, and the wait seems endless. Then one of them spies the prey and gives a signal to the group. The hunt is on!

Hunter-gatherers lived in the wild. They built their own shelter and made their own clothes. They ate fruits, roots, leaves, and nuts. When they wanted meat, hunting in groups worked best.

Hunting in Groups Big game, such as the mammoth shown here, was valuable for its meat, hide, and bones. Mammoths—now extinct—thrived during the last ice age, which ended about 10,000 years ago.

Hunting big game was dangerous and required team-work. A hunter could easily be crushed by a mammoth, or speared by its sharp tusks.

Scientists have different ideas about how such game was hunted. The animals may have been wounded by spears and then lured into hidden pits and killed. Or, hunters may have attacked the animals near watering holes. Some evidence suggests that hunters would herd animals until they were forced over bluffs, falling to their deaths.

The illustration above shows the mammoth being butchered after a hunt. Once the hide was removed, it was stretched and scraped clean. Damaged weapons were then repaired and made ready for the next hunt.

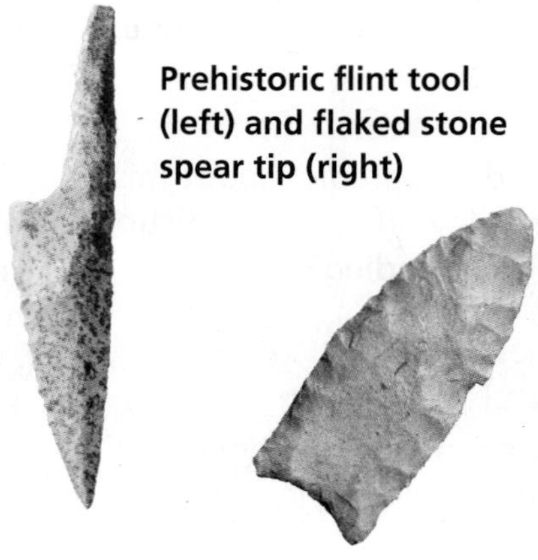

Prehistoric flint tool (left) and flaked stone spear tip (right)

Ancient Art

During the last Ice Age, a time when glaciers covered much of Earth, hunter-gatherers painted animal forms and symbols on cave walls. Charcoal and other materials were used for pigments. Paintings have been found in Africa, Europe, and Australia. The painting above is from a cave in Alsace, France.

Creating Shelter

Hunter-gatherers lived in caves or human-made shelters. Long ago, hunter-gatherers in parts of Europe made huts of mammoth bones and tusks, like the model shown above. The shelters were probably covered by large animal hides. Firepits, dug into the hut floor, provided heat.

Go Online
PHSchool.com Use Web Code **mup-0815** for an interactivity on life in the Ice Age.

Tools

Hunter-gatherers made their own tools and weapons using stone, wood, bone, and animal sinew.

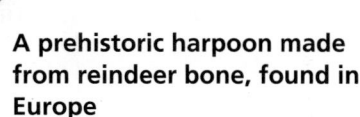

A prehistoric harpoon made from reindeer bone, found in Europe

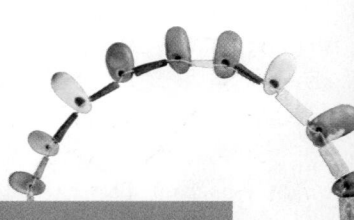

A shell and bone necklace found in Israel

Assessment

Describe What methods did hunter-gatherers use to hunt large animals?

Infer Describe the importance of animals to the survival of hunter-gatherers long ago.

Prepare to Read

Objectives

In this section you will

1. Find out about the advantages people gained from settling down in one place.
2. Learn about the growth of early cities.
3. Understand how the first civilizations formed and spread.

Taking Notes

As you read, summarize changes that lead to the growth of civilization. Copy the chart below, and use it to record your findings.

The Growth of Civilization

People begin to farm and raise animals.

↓ ↓ ↓

Farming creates food surpluses.

↓ ↓ ↓

Target Reading Skill

Preview and Ask Questions Before you read this section, preview the headings and pictures to find out what the section is about. As you read, write two questions that will help you remember something important about the beginnings of civilization. For example, you might ask yourself, What is a city? Or, How did early civilizations form? Find the answers to your questions as you read.

Key Terms

- **irrigation** (ihr uh GAY shun) *n.* supplying land with water through a network of canals
- **surplus** (SUR plus) *n.* more than is needed
- **artisan** (AHR tuh zun) *n.* a worker who is especially skilled at crafting items by hand
- **civilization** (sih vuh luh ZAY shun) *n.* a society with cities, a central government, job specialization, and social classes
- **social class** (SOH shul klas) *n.* a group of people with similar backgrounds, incomes, and ways of living

Caring for irrigation trenches in Libya, North Africa

Under a fierce desert sun, long lines of people are digging a trench that will soon become a deep canal. Other people lift heavy baskets of dirt dug from the canal onto their shoulders. They dump the dirt near the river where another crew is building a huge earthen dam.

These are some of the world's first construction workers. They are building a system of **irrigation,** supplying land with water from another place using a network of canals. One person directs the work at each site. Like the big construction projects of today, this job takes teamwork.

Soon, the dam will hold back the spring floodwaters of the river. A group of people are building wooden gates in the dam. Officials will open the gates in the dry season, allowing water to flow through the canals and irrigate the growing crops. Farming techniques like this irrigation system were important in creating early communities.

Advantages of a Settled Life

Farming was much harder work than hunting and gathering. However, it had far greater rewards. People who produced their own food could have a steady supply of food year-round. This meant they no longer had to travel from place to place. People often even had a food **surplus**—more than what is needed. Surplus food could be stored for use at another time.

The Population Grows Having surplus food also affected the size of families. The hunting-gathering life did not allow parents to have many children. How could they feed them all? Now, food surpluses would feed many more people.

Larger families brought rapid population growth. Scientists estimate that about 10,000 years ago, the population of the world was about 5 million people, which is about the number of people living in Minnesota today. By 7,000 years ago, many people had settled into the farming life. The world's population then was as much as 20 million.

Early Villages and Towns People lived in New Stone Age farming settlements for many centuries. Gradually, as the population increased, the settlements grew into towns.

With food surpluses, people did not have to spend all their days producing food. Some people were able to switch from farming to other kinds of work. For example, some people became artisans. An **artisan** is a worker who is especially skilled in crafting items by hand. Artisans make items such as baskets, leather goods, tools, pottery, or cloth.

✓ **Reading Check** What effect did food surpluses have on people living in settlements?

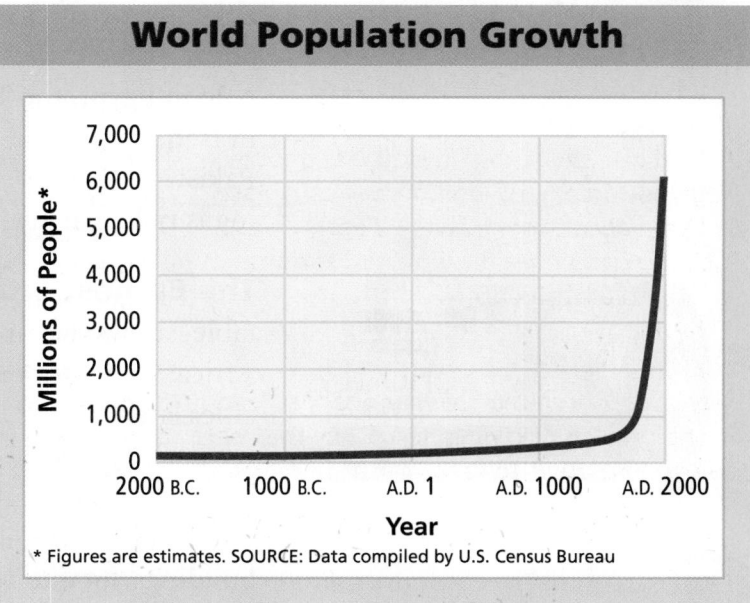

World Population Growth

* Figures are estimates. SOURCE: Data compiled by U.S. Census Bureau

Graph Skills

By A.D. 1000, the world's population had reached about 275 million.
Identify By what date had the population reached more than 6 billion?
Generalize How would you describe the rate of population growth before the year A.D. 1?

The ruins of Çatal Hüyük in Turkey, a settlement from around 7000 B.C.

The Growth of Cities

Although some farming settlements grew into cities, many others did not. Cities were more likely to develop in areas where rich soil created large surpluses of food. People also needed a dependable source of drinking water and materials to build shelters. Some of the earliest cities grew up along large rivers, such as the Nile in Egypt, the Tigris (TY gris) and Euphrates (yoo FRAY teez) in Iraq, the Huang (hwahng) in China, and the Indus (IN dus) in Pakistan. Cities grew up in these areas because the soil for farming is rich near riverbeds.

The Earliest Cities Look at the table titled Early Cities. The table shows when some of the first cities developed in Asia, Africa, and Europe. You will learn more about some of these cities later.

Early cities were different from farming villages in some important ways. Cities were larger, of course. Cities also had large public buildings. There were buildings to store surplus grain, buildings for the worship of gods, and buildings where people could buy and sell goods. In villages, most people were farmers. In cities, workers had a wide variety of occupations. Most worked at a craft. As new skills developed, so did new occupations.

Ask Questions
Ask (and answer) a question about how settlements grew into cities.

Discovery CHANNEL SCHOOL Video
Explore the birthplaces of civilizations.

Chart Skills

Cities arose at different times in different places. Ruins from Knossos, right, are part of a palace built circa, or around, 1550 B.C. In the table, c. stands for *circa*.
Identify Where were the cities of Ur and Anyang located, and when were these cities founded?
Compare In the text, you learned about the geographic conditions in the areas where the earliest cities developed. What geographic factor do you think the cities of Ur and Anyang had in common?

Early Cities

City	Present-Day Location	Date Founded
Ur	Iraq	c. 3500 B.C.
Memphis	Egypt	c. 3100 B.C.
Mohenjo-Daro	Pakistan	c. 2700 B.C.
Knossos	Greece	c. 2500 B.C.
Anyang	China	c. 1700 B.C.

Governments Form As the population of cities grew, governments formed. Governments kept order in society and provided services. They also settled disputes and managed public building and irrigation projects.

✓ Reading Check **Along which rivers did early cities grow?**

The First Civilizations

Over time, some New Stone Age societies grew into civilizations. A **civilization** is a society that has cities, a central government run by official leaders, and workers who specialize in various jobs. Writing, art, and architecture also characterize a civilization.

The Bronze Age By 6600 B.C., artisans in Europe and Asia had learned a key skill. They discovered that melting a certain rock at high temperatures would separate the metal copper from the rock. By 3000 B.C., artisans had learned to mix copper with another metal, tin, to make a mixture called bronze. Ancient peoples may have discovered bronze-making by accident. In nature, small amounts of tin are sometimes found with copper deposits. This discovery marked the beginning of the Bronze Age.

The first people to refine copper with tin had discovered a valuable new metal. Because bronze is much harder than copper, it could be used to make items more durable, or long-lasting. For example, bronze was used to make weapons, tools, helmets, and shields more durable.

Bronze Tools
Shown are half of a stone mold for pins and a bronze pin, top, from Switzerland, around 1000 B.C., and a bronze razor from Denmark, bottom. **Infer** *How are these tools signs of early civilizations?*

Trade and the Spread of Ideas Traders took valuable items such as pottery, tools and weapons, baskets, cloth, and spices to faraway cities. They traded these items for food and goods that people at home wanted.

By around 3500 B.C., some civilizations had developed a simple but amazing invention: the wheel and axle. An axle is a rod on which a wheel turns.

With the wheel and axle, trade goods could be loaded into carts and pushed through the city to market. More goods could be transported farther and more easily.

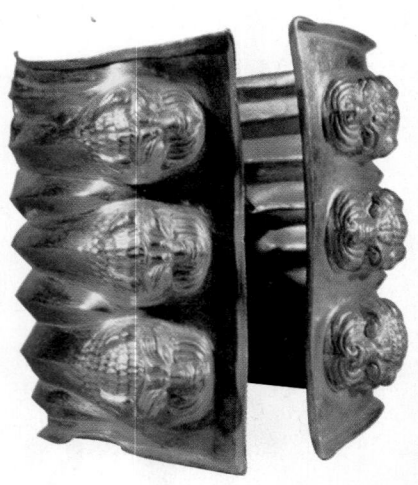

Social Status
Ancient jewelry can provide clues to the social status of its owner or to the type of artisans in a society. The decorative bracelet above comes from the area of present-day Iran. *Infer What does the bracelet tell us about the ancient society it came from?*

Trade over water also developed. Merchant ships now carried goods across seas and rivers. With all this travel, people of many different cultures came into contact with one another. New tools and ideas from one society soon spread to other societies as people traded information along with goods.

Social Classes Develop Growing trade links brought new prosperity to the cities. Prosperity led to another major change in society—the development of social classes. A **social class** is a group of people having similar backgrounds, incomes, and ways of living.

In the large cities, the king was the most powerful person. Next in importance were two classes of people. One class was made up of the priests of the city's religion. The other class was made up of nobles, who were government officials and military officers. Below them were the artisans, small traders, and merchants. Common workers and farmers were the lowest ranked free members of society.

Slaves, human beings owned as property by other people, formed a separate social class. Most slaves worked in cities, often as household servants and as laborers. Their status, or rank, was beneath that of free people.

✓ **Reading Check** **What skills and practices were important in the growth and spread of early civilizations?**

Section 3 Assessment

Key Terms
Review the key terms at the beginning of this section. Use each term in a sentence that explains its meaning.

Target Reading Skill
What questions did you ask to help you learn or remember something about this section?

Comprehension and Critical Thinking
1. (a) Describe How did people's lives change when they began to produce their own food?

(b) Identify Effects What effects did food surpluses have on people and populations?

2. (a) Recall What resources were necessary for villages to grow into cities?

(b) Compare and Contrast What were the similarities and differences between villages and cities?

3. (a) Name What developments occurred as societies grew into civilizations?

(b) Draw Conclusions How did prosperity lead to the development of social classes?

Writing Activity
Suppose you are an early trader bringing tools and weapons made of bronze to people who have never seen bronze before. Write a speech in which you try to persuade these people to trade for your bronze goods.

Writing Tip Write an opener for your speech that will grab the listener's attention. Write a list of reasons why bronze tools are better than tools made of copper. Refer to this list when writing your speech.

Review and Assessment

◆ Chapter Summary

Section 1: Geography and History

- The study of tools, bones, and other objects can help to explain prehistoric life.
- The development of writing marks a turning point in the story of our past.
- The geography of a place can explain why historic events happened there.

Section 2: Prehistory

- During the Old Stone Age, our ancestors survived by hunting animals and gathering plant foods.
- Gradually, our ancestors moved from Africa and spread out over much of Earth.
- During the New Stone Age, some people began to farm and to domesticate animals.

Section 3: The Beginnings of Civilization

Knossos

- The advantage of a steady food supply helped early farming settlements to prosper.
- Farming settlements grew into cities because of their geographical locations.
- The first civilizations developed in cities and spread with the help of trade.

Camel caravan

◆ Reviewing Key Terms

Fill in the blanks in Column I using the key terms from Column II.

Column I

1. Stories passed down by word of mouth are _____.

2. The _____ was the earliest known period of human culture.

3. Human ancestors learned how to _____, or tame, animals.

4. Making items such as baskets, jewelry, and pottery is the job of a(n) _____.

5. A society that has cities, a central government, and specialized workers is a(n) _____.

6. _____ is the period of time before writing was developed.

Column II
civilization
archaeologist
oral traditions
artisan
Stone Age
prehistory
domesticate
irrigation

◆ Comprehension and Critical Thinking

7. (a) Identify What is the difference between history and prehistory?
(b) Explain How can we learn about people who lived before written history?
(c) Draw Inferences Suppose that large, heavy spear points are found at a prehistoric site. What might they tell us about the people who once lived there?

8. (a) Describe How did early hominids find food during the Old Stone Age?
(b) Make Generalizations What characterized the Old Stone Age, the Middle Stone Age, and the New Stone Age?
(c) Sequence What is the connection between farming and the growth of early cities?

9. (a) Recall What survival skills did our human ancestors learn throughout the Stone Age?
(b) Identify Effects How did the discovery of the use of fire affect early hominids?
(c) Identify Causes What developments allowed early nomads to move from Africa to many parts of the world?

10. (a) Recall Describe aspects of the earliest cities.
(b) Explain How did cities benefit from a central government?
(c) Draw Conclusions What was the relationship between government and the social classes of early civilizations?

◆ Skills Practice

Using Timelines In the Skills for Life activity in this chapter, you learned how to use a timeline to gain a better understanding of a certain time period. You then created your own timeline. Review the steps you follow for this skill and study the timeline on page 11. Then reread Chapter 1 looking for events that fit within the timeline span. Redraw the timeline with the additional events.

◆ Writing Activity: Science

Form conclusions the way archaeologists do. Choose a place you know well, such as your classroom. Then, pick two or three objects found there and make detailed notes on them. What do your notes tell you about the people who use the objects?

MAP MASTER™ Skills Activity

The World

Place Location For each place listed below, write the letter from the map that shows its location.
1. Central America
2. Southwest Asia
3. North China
4. South America
5. West Africa
6. South China

Go Online
PHSchool.com Use Web Code **lbp-2133** for an **interactive map**.

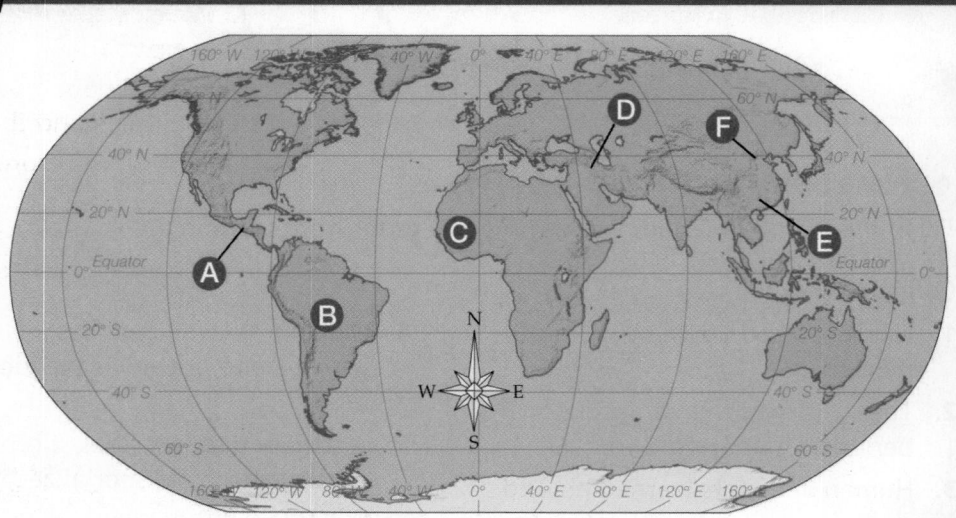

Standardized Test Prep

Test-Taking Tips

Some questions on standardized tests ask you to analyze a reading passage for causes and effects. Read the paragraph below. Then follow the tips to answer the sample question.

> The Sumer civilization arose in the region between the Tigris and Euphrates rivers. Similarly, early Egyptian civilization developed along the Nile River. Ancient China had its origins along the Huang River. A fresh water supply and rich soil made these river valleys "cradles of civilization."

TIP Identify the main idea, or most important point, as you read a paragraph or passage.

Pick the letter that best completes the statement.

The author wrote this passage to give information about the effect of

A geography on early civilizations.

B agriculture on early civilizations.

C geography on the economies of early civilizations.

D migration on the environment.

TIP Restate this as a question: Which effect was the author writing about?

Think It Through Start with the main idea: Early civilizations developed near rivers in many places. Keep the main idea in mind as you try to answer the question. Rivers are a part of geography, so you can eliminate B and D. Rivers do have an effect on economies, but the paragraph does not discuss that topic. The correct answer is A.

Practice Questions

Use the tips above and other tips in this book to help you answer the following questions.

1. Prehistory describes the time period before
   A people existed.
   B people used tools.
   C clothes were made from animal skins.
   D writing was invented.

2. During which time period did farming develop?
   A the Bronze Age
   B the Old Stone Age
   C the Middle Stone Age
   D the New Stone Age

3. As food surpluses developed,
   A population growth increased.
   B towns grew into farming settlements.
   C people left the cities.
   D more artisans became farmers.

Read the passage below, and then answer the question that follows.

Oral history, while important, does not give an accurate history of a society. Stories may exaggerate or only focus on certain things. Archaeology is also incomplete. Bones and objects tell us only part of the story of the past. Any accurate history must take into account the written records of human life.

4. Which statement best reflects the main idea of the passage?
   A Historians must have written records to fully understand the past.
   B Written records are not very important.
   C Written records are almost as important as stories and archaeology.
   D Historians value oral stories the most.

Use Web Code lba-2103
for **Chapter 1 self-test.**

Chapter 2

The Fertile Crescent

Chapter Preview

This chapter will introduce you to the civilizations of an ancient region of the Middle East known as the Fertile Crescent.

Section 1
Land Between Two Rivers

Section 2
Fertile Crescent Empires

Section 3
The Legacy of Mesopotamia

Section 4
Mediterranean Civilizations

Section 5
Judaism

Target Reading Skill

Clarifying Meaning In this chapter you will focus on clarifying, or better understanding, the meaning of what you read.

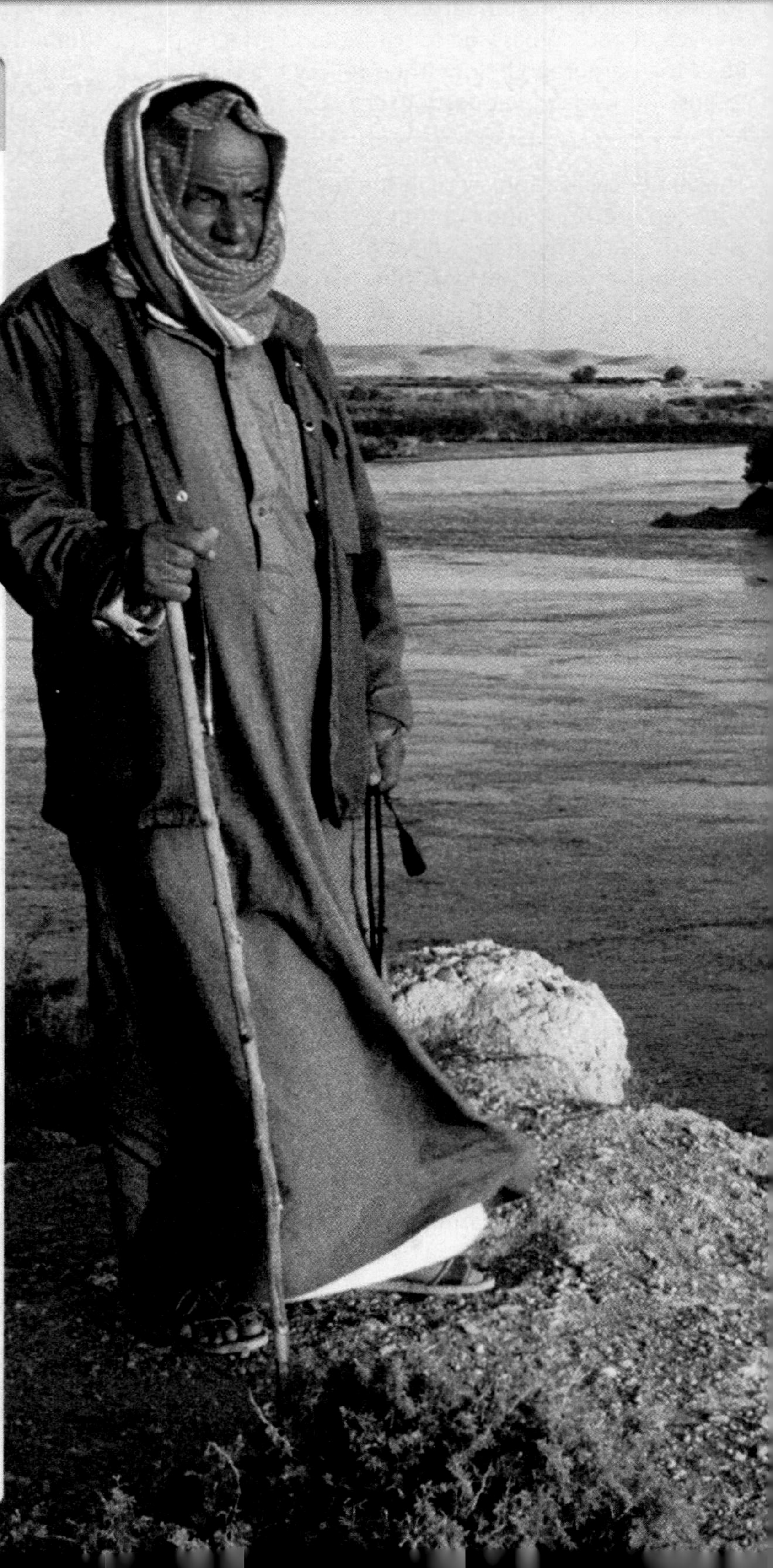

▶ A shepherd grazes his sheep along the banks of the Euphrates River in Syria.

The Fertile Crescent

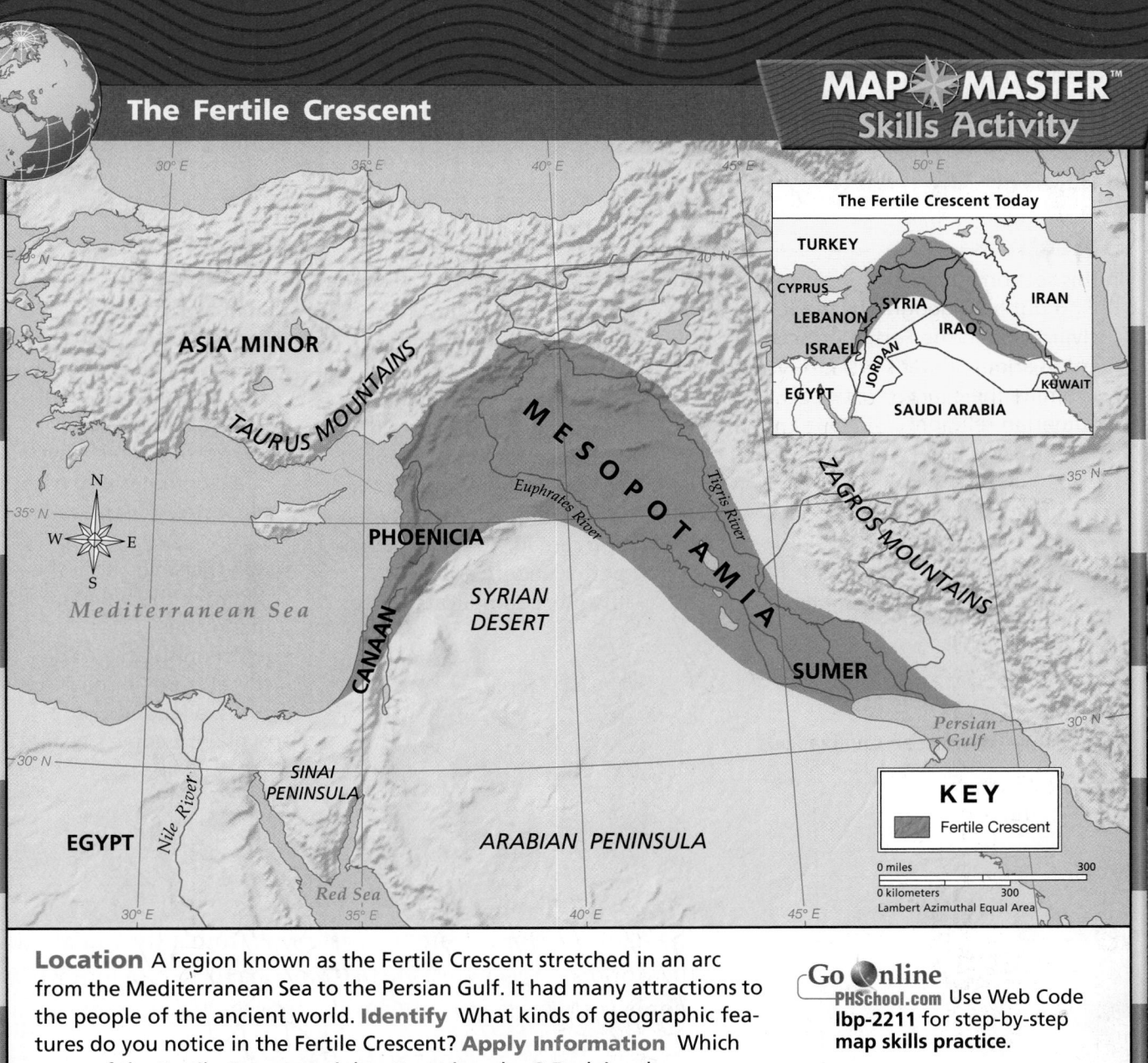

The Fertile Crescent Today

TURKEY
CYPRUS
LEBANON SYRIA
ISRAEL IRAQ IRAN
EGYPT JORDAN KUWAIT
SAUDI ARABIA

ASIA MINOR

TAURUS MOUNTAINS

M E S O P O T A M I A

Euphrates River

Tigris River

ZAGROS MOUNTAINS

PHOENICIA

Mediterranean Sea

CANAAN

SYRIAN DESERT

SUMER

Persian Gulf

N
W   E
S

SINAI PENINSULA

Nile River

EGYPT

Red Sea

ARABIAN PENINSULA

KEY

Fertile Crescent

0 miles   300
0 kilometers   300
Lambert Azimuthal Equal Area

Location A region known as the Fertile Crescent stretched in an arc from the Mediterranean Sea to the Persian Gulf. It had many attractions to the people of the ancient world. **Identify** What kinds of geographic features do you notice in the Fertile Crescent? **Apply Information** Which areas of the Fertile Crescent might attract invaders? Explain why.

Go Online
PHSchool.com Use Web Code
lbp-2211 for step-by-step
map skills practice.

Land Between Two Rivers

Prepare to Read

Objectives

In this section you will
1. Find out how geography made the rise of civilization in the Fertile Crescent possible.
2. Learn about Sumer's first cities.
3. Examine the characteristics of Sumerian religion.

Taking Notes

As you read, look for details about Mesopotamia and Sumer. Copy the outline below, and use it to record your findings.

> **I. The geographic setting**
>   **A. Mesopotamia**
>   1.
>   2.
>   **B. The Tigris and Euphrates rivers**
> **II.**

Target Reading Skill

Reread Rereading is a strategy that can help you to understand words and ideas in the text. If you do not understand a certain passage, reread it to look for connections among the words and sentences. When you reread, you may gain a better understanding of the more complicated ideas.

Key Terms

- **scribe** (skryb) *n.* a professional writer
- **Fertile Crescent** (FUR tul KRES unt) *n.* a region in Southwest Asia; site of the first civilizations
- **city-state** (SIH tee stayt) *n.* a city that is also a separate, independent state
- **polytheism** (PAHL ih thee iz um) *n.* the belief in many gods
- **myth** (mith) *n.* a traditional story; in some cultures, a legend that explains people's beliefs

The Work of Scribes
The language on this tablet—Sumerian—is the oldest known written language. **Analyze Information** *Why were scribes important in Sumer?*

The following words from the past come from a student at one of the world's first schools. He tells what happened to him when his homework was sloppy or when he spoke without permission.

> **❝My headmaster read my tablet and said, 'There is something missing,' and hit me with a cane. . . . The fellow in charge of silence said, 'Why did you talk without permission?' and caned me. ❞**
>
> —*A Sumerian student*

The first known schools were set up in the land of Sumer (SOO mur) over 4,000 years ago. Sumerian schools taught boys—and possibly a few girls—the new invention of writing. Graduates of the schools became **scribes,** or professional writers. Scribes were important because they kept records for the kings and priests. Learning to be a scribe was hard work. Students normally began school at about the age of eight and finished about ten years later. The writings Sumerian scribes left behind help to tell the story of this early civilization.

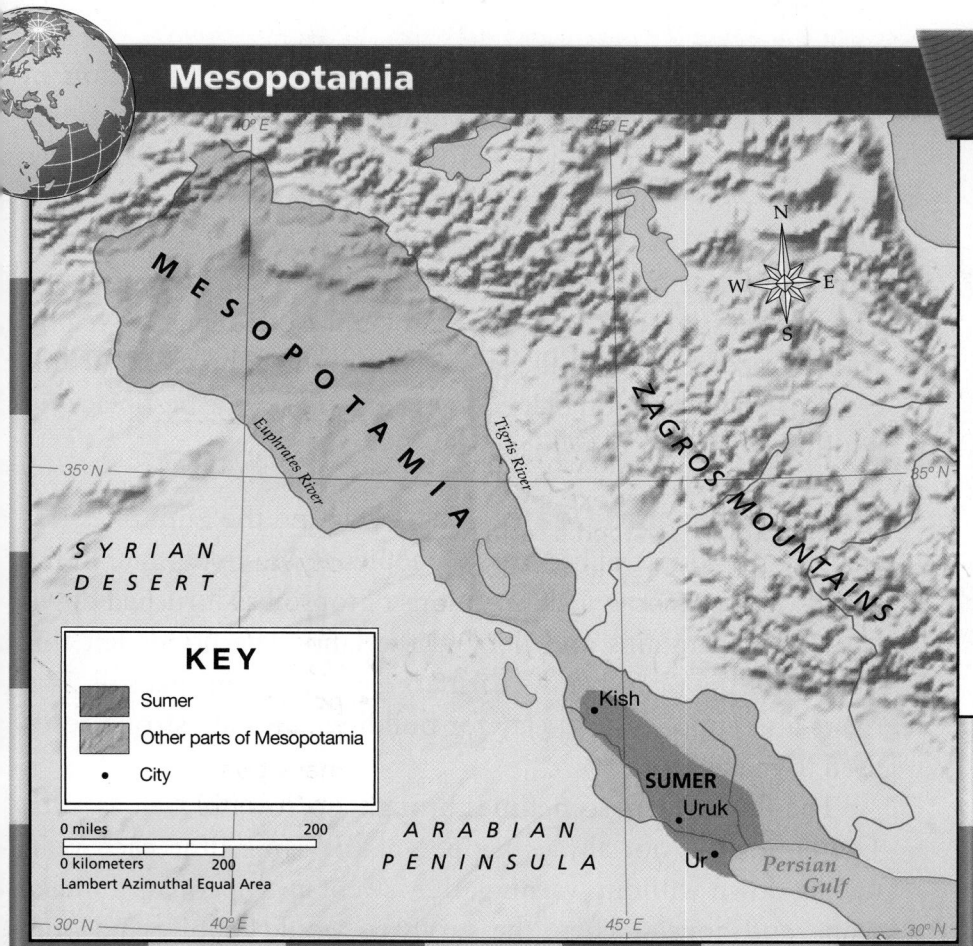

M E S O P O T A M I A

Euphrates River

Tigris River

ZAGROS MOUNTAINS

S Y R I A N
D E S E R T

N
W   E
S

40° E

45° E

35° N   35° N

30° N   30° N

40° E   45° E

KEY

Sumer

Other parts of Mesopotamia

• City

0 miles   200
0 kilometers   200
Lambert Azimuthal Equal Area

• Kish

SUMER
• Uruk

Ur •   *Persian Gulf*

A R A B I A N
P E N I N S U L A

MAP MASTER™
Skills Activity

Place The Tigris and the Euphrates rivers provided excellent conditions for human settlement.
Identify Name the physical features shown on the map.
Draw Conclusions Which of the physical features shown on the map would discourage human settlement? Explain why.

Go Online
PHSchool.com Use Web Code **lbp-2221** for step-by-step **map skills practice**.

The Geographic Setting

Sumer was located in a region called Mesopotamia (mes uh puh TAY mee uh). Look at the map titled Mesopotamia. Like the place where you live, ancient Mesopotamia had special attractions that drew people to settle there. Most important, it had rich soil and life-giving rivers. These attractions drew people who became farmers and city builders. Sumer's central location within the ancient world drew many traders from other regions. Sumer became one of the most prosperous areas of the ancient world.

The Location of Mesopotamia

Mesopotamia's name describes its location. The word *Mesopotamia* comes from Greek words that mean "between the rivers." The map above shows that Mesopotamia lies between two rivers, the Tigris and the Euphrates.

The ruins of Uruk, an ancient Sumerian city on the Euphrates River, northwest of Ur

Mesopotamia is part of the **Fertile Crescent,** a region in Southwest Asia that was the site of the world's first civilizations. Turn to the map titled The Fertile Crescent on page 29. To see how this region got its name, place your finger at the eastern edge of the Mediterranean Sea (med uh tuh RAY nee un) on the map. Move eastward from the Mediterranean coast to Mesopotamia. Then move southeast to the Persian Gulf. Notice that the region you've traced is shaped like a crescent moon. The rivers of this crescent-shaped region helped to make it one of the best places in Southwest Asia for growing crops.

Rivers of Life and Death   The Tigris and the Euphrates rivers were the source of life for the peoples of Mesopotamia. In the spring, melting snow picked up tons of topsoil as it rushed down from the mountains and flooded the land. The floods left this topsoil on the plain below. Farmers grew crops in this soil. The rivers also supplied fish, clay for building, and tall, strong reeds used to make boats.

The floodwaters sometimes brought sorrows as well as gifts. The floods did not always happen at the same time each year. Racing down without warning, they swept away people, animals, crops, and houses. Then, the survivors would rebuild and pray that the next flood would not be so destructive.

✔ Reading Check   **How did flooding rivers affect people who settled in Mesopotamia?**

Peacetime in Sumer
Around 2500 B.C., artists from the Sumerian city-state of Ur created this mosaic recording of peacetime activities. Shown are two out of the three rows of figures.
❶ The king sits facing members of the royal family at a banquet.
❷ Servants stand ready to wait upon the royal family.
❸ A musician playing a harp and a singer provide entertainment.
❹ Servants deliver animals, fish, and other items for the feast.
Infer *How do the activities shown provide clues about jobs and social classes in Ur?*

The First Cities

As farming succeeded in Mesopotamia, communities began to build up surpluses of food. In time, food surpluses encouraged the growth of cities. By 3500 B.C., some of the earliest known cities arose in the southern region of Sumer, along the Tigris and Euphrates rivers.

Independent Cities Form Although cities in Sumer shared a common culture and language, they did not unite under a single ruler. Instead, they remained politically independent city-states. A **city-state** is a city that is also a separate, independent state. Each Sumerian city acted as an independent state, with its own special god or goddess, its own government, its own army, and, eventually, its own king.

A Brief Tour of a Sumerian City Public squares bustled with activity. In the marketplaces, merchants displayed goods in outdoor stalls. Musicians, acrobats, beggars, and water sellers filled the streets. For a fee, scribes wrote letters for those who could not read or write. Sumerian houses faced away from the crowded streets, onto inner courtyards where families ate and children played. On hot nights, people slept outdoors on their homes' flat roofs. Oil lamps supplied light for Sumerian homes.

✓ **Reading Check** **How were the cities of Sumer governed?**

Discovery SCHOOL Video Find out about the ancient city of Petra.

Target Skill

Rereading Reread the paragraph at left. In what ways did Sumerian cities act as states?

Sumerian Religion

A stranger coming to a Sumerian city could easily notice a giant brick building at the heart of the city. It was the ziggurat (ZIG oo rat), the site of the temple to the main god or goddess of the city.

Sumerian Temples Religious, social, and economic activities all took place at the temple sites. Ziggurats were pyramids made of terraces, one on top of another, linked by ramps and stairs. Some were more than seven stories high. At the top of each ziggurat was a shrine. The Sumerians believed that gods descended to Earth using the ziggurat as a stairway.

Ancient Religious Beliefs The people of Sumer worshiped many gods and goddesses. This practice is known as **polytheism,** a belief in many gods. To understand this word, break it up into its parts. *Poly-*, a Greek prefix, means "many." *Theism* means "belief in a god or gods."

Sumerian **myths,** or stories about gods that explain people's beliefs, warned that the gods would punish people who angered them. The myths also promised rewards to people who served the gods well.

Sumerians placed prayer figures on altars. The eyes of the worshiping figures were made wide, as though they were fixed on the gods.

Stairway to the Heavens
This partially restored brick ziggurat was part of the ancient city of Ur. **Analyze Images** *Why do you think the Sumerians believed the gods could use the ziggurat to descend to Earth?*

Honoring the Gods The Sumerians honored their gods in religious ceremonies. Temple priests washed the statues of gods before and after each meal was offered. Music sounded and incense burned as huge plates of food were laid before them. In most ancient religions, the food was often eaten after it was presented to the gods. Perhaps the worshipers thought that by eating the offering, they would be taking in the qualities they admired in the gods. The religious beliefs of the Sumerians give us an idea of what was important to them. Poetry was also used to express what was important to them:

> **Behold the bond of Heaven and Earth, the city. . . .**
> **Behold . . . its well of good water.**
> **Behold . . . its pure canal.**

—*A Sumerian poem*

A reconstructed musical instrument called a lyre (lyr), about 2500 B.C., from Ur

The Fall of Sumer   Unfortunately for Sumer, its wealth became its downfall. Sumerian city-states fought each other over land and the use of river water. Rulers from various city-states won and lost control of all of Sumer. Around 2300 B.C., Sumer was conquered by the armies of neighboring Akkad (AK ad). Its ruler, King Sargon, united the Sumerian city-states and improved Sumer's government and its military. Sumer remained united for about 100 years until it dissolved once more into independent city-states. Sumer was no longer a major power after 2000 B.C. It fell to a northern rival, Babylonia, in the 1700s B.C.

✔ Reading Check **What weakened the cities of Sumer?**

 **Section 1 Assessment**

Key Terms
Review the key terms at the beginning of this section. Use each term in a sentence that explains its meaning.

Target Reading Skill
What word or idea were you able to clarify by rereading certain passages?

Comprehension and Critical Thinking
1. (a) Recall Describe the geography of Mesopotamia.

(b) Find the Main Ideas How did Mesopotamia's geography help civilizations to develop in the area?

2. (a) Compare In what ways were Sumerian cities alike?

(b) Contrast In what ways were the cities of Sumer different?

3. (a) Explain How did Sumerians practice religion?

(b) Infer What do the religious practices of the Sumerians tell us about their values?

Writing Activity
Write a journal entry from the viewpoint of a student scribe in Sumer. Describe what you see on your walk to school.

For: An activity on Sumer
Visit: PHSchool.com
Web Code: lbd-2201

Farming in Mesopotamia

Farming the land "between the rivers" required skill and determination. The life-giving rivers could be generous one year and stingy the next. Frosts, droughts, floods, weeds, or insects could bring starvation. For survival, families worked together in farming communities. As cities rose above the Mesopotamian plain, governments created huge farms. From the river-fed land, farmers cultivated the crops—wheat, barley, cucumbers, and figs—that nourished kingdoms for many years to come.

Working the Fields Farmers in Mesopotamia were allowed a certain amount of water each year to prepare their soil for planting and to water their crops. Local officials often decided when to open the floodgates in canals, allowing water into the fields.

Farmers would let their animals graze in the wet soil, to trample and eat the weeds. The earliest farmers then broke up the soil using hand tools. This work became easier with the invention of the ox-drawn plow. After plowing, the seeds could be planted.

At first, farmers spread seeds by hand. In the 2000s B.C., they attached a funnel to the plow, as shown in the illustration, to spread the seeds easily and more evenly. After the grain was harvested, it was threshed, or pounded to separate the grain from the straw.

Farming Tools

Early farmers in Mesopotamia first used simple tools—sticks for plowing and stone-bladed sickles, like the one shown here, for harvesting grain. In time, more efficient tools were invented.

Assessment

Analyze Information Describe how farmers in Mesopotamia prepared the soil and planted their crops.

Draw Conclusions How did Mesopotamians improve their farming methods over time?

Pottery

The pottery made by Mesopotamians had many uses. The spouted vessel above, from about 3000 B.C., was found in Iraq. It may have been used to carry water. The cup, dated to 2200–1900 B.C., was found in Israel. It was probably used to measure grain.

Prepare to Read

Objectives

In this section you will

1. Learn about the three most important empires of the Fertile Crescent.
2. Find out what characterized the Babylonian and Assyrian empires.
3. Investigate the achievements of the Persian Empire.

Taking Notes

As you read, note the similarities and the differences between Babylonia and Assyria. Copy the Venn diagram below, and record your findings in it.

Mesopotamian Empires

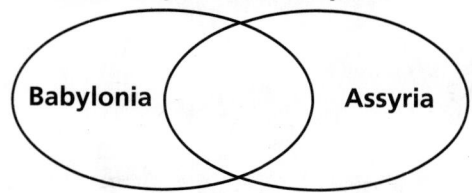

Babylonia   Assyria

Target Reading Skill

Paraphrase When you paraphrase, you restate what you have read in your own words. You could paraphrase the first paragraph of this section this way: "King Sargon II of Assyria learned that two kingdoms were joining together to resist him. In 714 B.C., he attacked the weaker forces of Urartu and Zikirtu."

As you read, paraphrase or "say back" the information following each red or blue heading.

Key Terms

- **empire** (EM pyr) *n.* many territories and peoples controlled by one government
- **Babylon** (BAB uh lahn) *n.* the capital of Babylonia; a city of great wealth and luxury
- **caravan** (KA ruh van) *n.* a group of travelers journeying together
- **bazaar** (buh ZAHR) *n.* a market selling different kinds of goods
- **Zoroastrianism** (zoh roh AS tree un iz um) *n.* a religion that developed in ancient Persia

King Sargon II of Assyria (center) and two officials

King Sargon II of Assyria (uh SEER ee uh) heard the news: Assyria had attacked the nearby kingdoms of Urartu and Zikirtu as planned. But the two kingdoms had then joined forces against him. How dare they resist the most powerful monarch in the world? In the summer of 714 B.C., King Sargon II set out to confront his enemies.

The two kingdoms were no match for the powerful Assyrian ruler. His armies quickly overcame the forces of Urartu and killed all who resisted. The Assyrians howled with laughter when they saw the king of Urartu fleeing on an old horse. Sargon II let him go. He knew that the defeated king would serve as a warning to others who might later be tempted to challenge the mighty Assyrians. Sargon II was one of many kings who ruled the Fertile Crescent after the fall of Sumer.

The Babylonian Empire

A ruler who conquered all of Mesopotamia created an **empire**, or an area of many territories and peoples that is controlled by one government. Rulers of empires gained great wealth from trade and agriculture. Hammurabi (hah muh RAH bee) created the Babylonian Empire in 1787 B.C. by conquering cities in Sumer. Then he conquered lands far to the north. The beautiful city of **Babylon** was the capital of the Babylonian empire. Find the boundaries of the empire on the map titled Fertile Crescent Empires, on page 39.

The Babylonians built roads throughout the empire. The roads made travel easier, which encouraged trade. Babylon's location made it a crossroads of trade. **Caravans**, or groups of travelers, stopped in Babylon on their way between Sumer to the south and Assyria to the north. In the city's **bazaars**, or markets, shoppers could buy cotton cloth from India and spices from Egypt.

Trade made Babylon rich. But all the wealth that Babylon had gathered could not save it from conquest. The empire that Hammurabi had conquered shrank and was finally destroyed by invaders in the early 1500s B.C.

✓ **Reading Check** **Who was Hammurabi, and what did he accomplish?**

Links to
Math

Babylonian Mathematics
The Babylonians developed a useful system of mathematics for solving everyday problems. For example, they learned to calculate areas of geometric shapes. Such calculations were important for making building plans. Their number system was based on numbers from 1 to 60. We still divide minutes and hours into 60 parts.

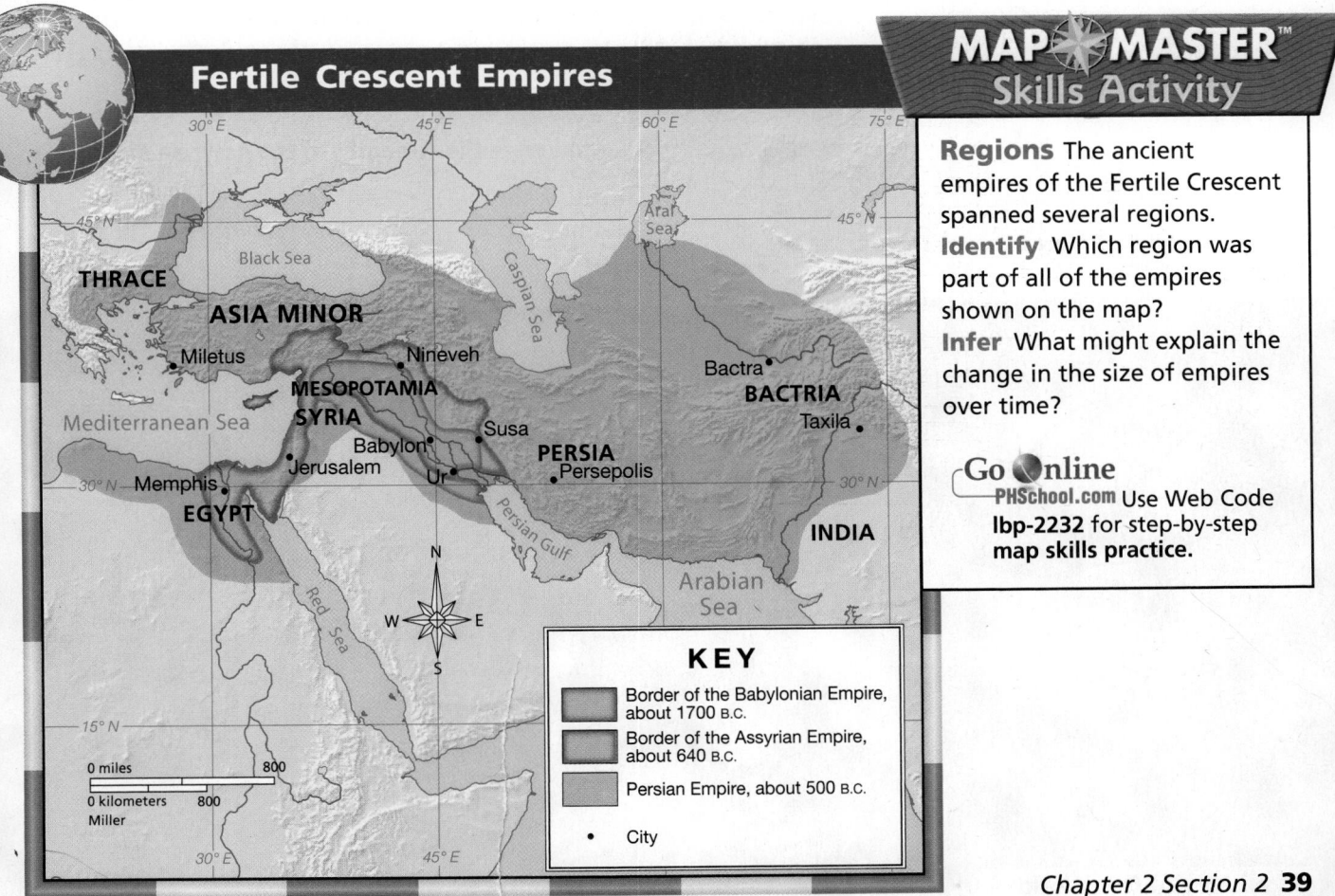

Fertile Crescent Empires

THRACE
Black Sea
ASIA MINOR
Miletus
Nineveh
MESOPOTAMIA
SYRIA
Mediterranean Sea
Babylon
Jerusalem
Memphis
Ur
EGYPT
Susa
PERSIA
Persepolis
Bactra
BACTRIA
Taxila
INDIA
Arabian Sea
Caspian Sea
Aral Sea
Persian Gulf
Red Sea

KEY
Border of the Babylonian Empire, about 1700 B.C.
Border of the Assyrian Empire, about 640 B.C.
Persian Empire, about 500 B.C.
• City

0 miles 800
0 kilometers 800
Miller

MAP MASTER™
Skills Activity

Regions The ancient empires of the Fertile Crescent spanned several regions.
Identify Which region was part of all of the empires shown on the map?
Infer What might explain the change in the size of empires over time?

Go Online
PHSchool.com Use Web Code **lbp-2232** for step-by-step map skills practice.

The Empire of the Assyrians

The kingdom of Assyria lay in open land, making it easy for other peoples to invade. Since they were constantly defending themselves, the Assyrians became skilled warriors. About 1365 B.C., they decided the best method of defense was to attack. By 650 B.C., Assyria had conquered a large empire. It stretched across the Fertile Crescent, from the Nile River to the Persian Gulf.

Assyria's Contributions   The Assyrians were clever when it came to waging war. They invented the battering ram, a powerful weapon having a wooden beam mounted on wheels. Battering rams pounded city walls to rubble. Warriors used slings to hurl stones at the enemy. Expert archers were protected with helmets and armor. But most feared were the armed charioteers who slashed their way through the enemy troops.

As the empire grew, Assyria's capital of Nineveh (NIN uh vuh) became a city of great learning. It had a remarkable library that held thousands of clay tablets with writings from Sumer and Babylon. Because the Assyrians kept these records, we now know a great deal about life in early Mesopotamia.

Assyria Overthrown   The Assyrians had few friends in the lands that they ruled. Conquered peoples attempted a number of revolts against Assyrian rule. Two groups, the Medes (meedz) and Chaldeans (kal DEE unz), joined together to defeat the Assyrian Empire in 612 B.C.

✓ **Reading Check**   What were the strengths of the Assyrian Empire?

Assyrian warriors carry off goods from a defeated enemy.

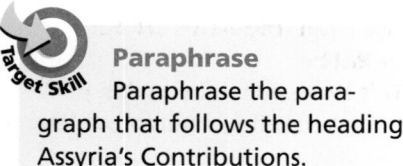

Target Skill

Paraphrase
Paraphrase the paragraph that follows the heading Assyria's Contributions.

Babylonia Rises Again

Under the Chaldeans, Babylon rose again to even greater splendor. It became the center of the New Babylonian Empire. The New Babylonian Empire controlled the entire Fertile Crescent.

Nebuchadnezzar, King of Babylon King Nebuchadnezzar II (neb you kud NEZ ur) rebuilt the city of Babylon, which the Assyrians had destroyed. He put up massive walls around the city for protection. He also built a gigantic palace, decorated with colored tiles. Nebuchadnezzar's royal palace was built on several terraces that rose to the height of some 350 feet (110 meters). It had a dazzling landscape of trees and gardens. According to legends, he built the towering palace and gardens for his wife, who hated the dry plains of Mesopotamia.

Advances in Learning Under the rule of the Chaldeans, Babylon again became a center of learning and science. Building on earlier Babylonian knowledge of mathematics, Chaldean astronomers charted the paths of the stars and measured the length of a year. Their measurement was only a few minutes different from the length modern scientists have found. And Chaldean farmers raised "the flies that collect honey"—honey bees.

Like other Mesopotamian empires, the Chaldeans were open to attack by powerful neighbors. In 539 B.C., the New Babylonian Empire fell to the Persians, led by Cyrus the Great. But the city of Babylon was spared.

✓ Reading Check **Who was Nebuchadnezzar II?**

Assyrian and Arab Troops in Battle
This stone panel shows Assyrian soldiers fighting Arabs mounted on camels.
❶ Sturdy shields protected the Assyrian soldiers.
❷ The Arab archers fought from swift camels.
❸ The Assyrians fought from horseback and from chariots.
❹ The Assyrian army was well armed and highly trained.
Predict *Judging by what you have read about the Assyrian army, who is likely to have won the battle shown on this carving?*

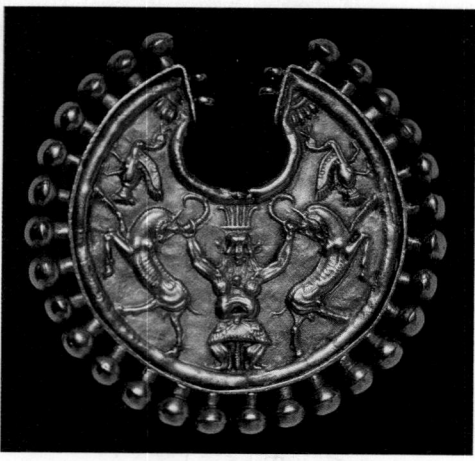

An Ancient Persian Earring
This golden earring shows the Zoroastrian god, Ahura Mazda.
Synthesize *What does this object show about Persian culture?*

The Persian Empire

Just to the east of the plains of Mesopotamia is a region of mountains, valleys, and deserts that is today the nation of Iran. This region was the homeland of the Persians who conquered Babylon in 539 B.C. The Persians built the largest empire that the Fertile Crescent had ever known. By 490 B.C., their empire stretched from Greece in the west to India in the east.

A Rich and Tolerant Culture Persian culture included **Zoroastrianism**, an ancient Persian religion. Zoroastrians originally worshiped one god, unlike their neighbors, who worshiped many. To rule their giant empire, the Persians developed a bureaucracy, or a complex structure of government offices. The Persians also built a road network across their vast empire, which enabled trade with neighboring civilizations.

The Persians tolerated peoples with different cultures. For example, they freed Jews who had been held captive in Babylon. They also supported Babylonian science and mathematics.

Lasting Influence Through conquest and trade, the Persians spread their religion, their system of bureaucracy, and Babylonian science to neighboring peoples, including the Greeks of Europe. These Persian cultural achievements survived to help shape our modern civilization.

Go Online
PHSchool.com Use Web Code
mup-0816 for an interactivity on Persia's capital, Persepolis.

√ **Reading Check** **How did the Persians promote trade?**

Section 2 Assessment

Key Terms
Review the key terms at the beginning of this section. Use each term in a sentence that explains its meaning.

Target Reading Skill
Paraphrase the last paragraph in this section.

Comprehension and Critical Thinking
1. (a) Identify Where was the city of Babylon located, and why was it important?

(b) Analyze How did the New Babylonian Empire build on the achievements of earlier empires?
2. (a) Recall How did the Assyrians build an empire?
(b) Compare How was the Assyrian empire similar to or different from other Fertile Crescent empires?
3. (a) Identify Where was the homeland of the Persians?
(b) Synthesize What were the main achievements of the Persians and what has been their lasting influence?

Writing Activity
Epitaphs are messages carved into tombstones. They praise and honor the deceased. Write an epitaph in remembrance of Nebuchadnezzar II.

Writing Tip Keep your message short and to the point. To get started, summarize what you know about Nebuchadnezzar II.

The Legacy of Mesopotamia

Prepare to Read

Objectives

In this section you will
1. Learn about the importance of Hammurabi's Code.
2. Find out how the art of writing developed in Mesopotamia.

Taking Notes

As you read, look for details summarizing the achievements of Mesopotamian civilizations. Copy the table below, and record your findings in it.

The Legacy of Mesopotamia	
Hammurabi's Code	**The Art of Writing**

Target Reading Skill

Summarize You can better understand a text if you pause to restate the key points briefly in your own words. A good summary includes important events and details, notes the order in which the events occurred, and makes connections between the events or details.

Use the table at the left to help you summarize what you have read.

Key Terms

- **code** (kohd) *n.* an organized list of laws and rules
- **Hammurabi** (hah muh RAH bee) *n.* the king of Babylon from about 1792 to 1750 B.C.; creator of the Babylonian Empire
- **cuneiform** (kyoo NEE uh fawrm) *n.* groups of wedges and lines used to write several languages of the Fertile Crescent

Sometimes the customs and laws of other countries may seem strange to us. Imagine what it would be like to have to obey the laws set down by early civilizations.

> **If a man has destroyed the eye of a man of the class of gentlemen, they shall destroy his eye. If he has broken a gentleman's bone, they shall break his bone. If he has destroyed the eye of a commoner or broken a bone of a commoner, he shall pay one mina [measure of weight] of silver. If he has destroyed the eye of a gentleman's slave, or broken a bone of a gentleman's slave, he shall pay half [the slave's] price. If a gentleman's slave strikes the cheek of a gentleman, they shall cut off [the slave's] ear.**
>
> —*from Hammurabi's Code*

King Hammurabi standing before Shamash, the sun god and the god of justice

Hammurabi's Code

What kind of justice system do you think we would have if our laws were not written down? What would happen if a judge were free to make any law he or she wanted, or if the judge could give any punishment? Would people think that the laws were fair? A written **code,** or organized list of laws, helps people know what is expected of them and what punishment they will receive if they disobey a law.

We live by the idea that all laws should be written down and applied fairly. The Babylonians held similar beliefs about law. **Hammurabi** ruled Babylonia from about 1792 to 1750 B.C. He set down rules for everyone in his empire to follow. These rules are known as Hammurabi's Code. The code told the people of Babylonia how to settle conflicts in all areas of life.

Hammurabi's Code, which was based partly on earlier Sumerian codes, contained 282 laws organized in different categories. These included trade, labor, property, and family. The code had laws for adopting children, practicing medicine, hiring wagons or boats, and controlling dangerous animals.

An Eye for an Eye Reread the first law from the quotation on page 43. Hammurabi's Code was based on the idea of "an eye for an eye." In other words, punishment should be similar to the crime committed. However, the code did not apply equally to all people. The harshness of the punishment depended on how important the victim and the lawbreaker were. The higher the class of the victim, the greater the penalty was. For example, an ox owner would pay half a mina of silver if the ox gored a noble. If the victim was a slave, however, the owner would pay only one third of a mina.

A person who accidentally broke a law was just as guilty as someone who meant to break the law. People who could not always control the outcome of their work, such as doctors, had to be very careful, as the following law shows:

> **If a surgeon performed a major operation on a citizen with a bronze lancet [knife] and has caused the death of this citizen . . . his hand shall be cut off.**

—from Hammurabi's Code

Summarize
Summarize the paragraph at the right. Give the main point and two details.

This clay lion once stood guard at a Babylonian temple.

Laws for Everyone You probably know many rules. There are rules for taking tests, playing ball, and living in your home. People have followed—or broken—rules for thousands of years. What, then, was the importance of Hammurabi's Code?

The laws are important to us because they were written down. With written laws, everyone could know the rules—and the punishments. Hammurabi's punishments may seem harsh to us, but they improved upon previous laws. Hammurabi's laws were not the first attempt by a society to set up a code of laws. But his laws are the first organized, recorded set that we have found.

✔ **Reading Check** What was Hammurabi's Code?

- If any one steal the minor son of another, he shall be put to death.
- If any one is committing a robbery and is caught, then he shall be put to death.
- If any one open his ditches to water his crop, but is careless, and the water flood the field of his neighbor, then he shall pay his neighbor corn for his loss.
- If a man adopt a child [as his] son, and rear him, this grown son cannot be demanded back again.
- If a son strike his father, his hands shall be hewn (cut) off.

■ **Chart Skills**

The table above shows five of the nearly 300 laws that make up Hammurabi's Code. At the left is a detail of the stone pillar on which the laws were carved. **Identify** Which of the laws in the table deals with the crime of kidnapping? **Generalize** What do the laws shown above tell us about the Babylonians' ideas of justice?

The Art of Writing

Think how much more difficult life would be if no one knew how to read and write. But writing did not suddenly appear. It took a long time for the art of writing to be developed.

Ancient Scribes Writing first developed in Mesopotamia around 3100 B.C. Long before Hammurabi issued his code, the people of Sumer had developed a system of writing. Writing met the need Sumerians had to keep records. Record keepers were very important—and busy—people in Sumer. The Sumerians' earliest written documents are records of farm animals. Since only a few people could write, it was one of the most valuable skills in the ancient world. Scribes held positions of great respect in Mesopotamia.

The scribes of Sumer recorded sales and trades, tax payments, gifts for the gods, and marriages and deaths. Some scribes had special tasks. Military scribes calculated the amount of food and supplies that an army would need. Government scribes figured out the number of diggers needed to build a canal. Written orders then went out to local officials who had to provide these supplies or workers. None of these records were written on paper, however. Paper had not yet been invented. Instead, the scribes of Mesopotamia kept their notes and records on clay.

Links Across Time

New Discoveries In 2000, archaeologists uncovered a small stone with an unfamiliar type of ancient writing inscribed upon it. Scientists estimate that the stone, found in the present-day country of Turkmenistan, dates back to about 2300 B.C. The stone and other findings in the area indicate the existence of an ancient culture that had been entirely unknown.

A Record in Clay The Tigris and the Euphrates rivers provided scribes with the clay they used to write on. Each spring, the rivers washed down clay from the mountains. Scribes shaped the soft, wet clay into smooth, flat surfaces called tablets. They marked their letters in the clay with sharp tools. When the clay dried, it was a permanent record.

The shape and size of a tablet depended on its purpose. Larger tablets were used for reference purposes. Like the heavy atlases and dictionaries in today's libraries, they stayed in one place. Smaller tablets, the size of letters or postcards, were used for personal messages. Even today, these personal tablets can be fun to read. They show that Mesopotamians used writing to express the ups and downs of everyday life:

> **❝This is really a fine way of behaving! The gardeners keep breaking into the date storehouse and taking dates. You yourselves cover it up and do not report it to me! Bring these men to me—after they have paid for the dates. ❞**
>
> —from a Mesopotamian tablet

Scribes sometimes enclosed a message (above) in an envelope (top) made from wet clay. As the envelope dried, it formed a seal around the tablet. A sharpened reed (below) is used to write cuneiform script on soft clay.

How Writing Was Invented Like most inventions, writing developed over time. Long before the Sumerians invented writing, they used shaped pieces of clay as tokens, or symbols. They used the clay tokens to keep records. Tokens could keep track of how many animals were bought and sold, or how much food had been grown. By around 3100 B.C., this form of record keeping had developed into writing.

At first, written words were symbols that represented specific objects. Grain, oxen, water, or stars—each important object had its own symbol. As people learned to record ideas as well as facts, the symbols changed. Eventually, scribes combined symbols to make groups of wedges and lines known as **cuneiform** (kyoo NEE uh fawrm). Cuneiform script could be used to represent different languages. This flexibility was highly useful in a land of many peoples.

The Development of Cuneiform

Word	Outline Character, About 3000 B.C.	Sumerian, About 2000 B.C.	Assyrian, About 700 B.C.	Chaldean, About 500 B.C.
Sun				
God or heaven				
Mountain				

Chart Skills

The table at the left shows how cuneiform changed over time. **Identify** The simplest symbols came from which time period? **Generalize** How did the symbols for each word change over time?

Refer to the table above titled The Development of Cuneiform. Notice how the symbols developed over time. Scholars believe that the Sumerians developed their system of writing independently. That means that they did not borrow ideas from the writing systems of other civilizations. Working independently meant that they had many decisions to make. They decided that the symbols should be set in rows, that each row should be read from left to right, and that a page should be read from top to bottom. What other languages are written this way?

✔ **Reading Check** **When, where, and how did writing first develop?**

Go Online
PHSchool.com Use Web Code **mup-0817** for an interactivity on ancient writing.

Section 3 Assessment

Key Terms

Review the key terms at the beginning of this section. Use each term in a sentence that explains its meaning.

Target Reading Skill

Summarize the information in the last paragraph of this section.

Comprehension and Critical Thinking

1. (a) Recall What was Hammurabi's Code, and what was its purpose in ancient Babylonia?

(b) Analyze What does the expression "an eye for an eye" mean in relation to the laws in Hammurabi's Code?

(c) Apply Information Hammurabi's Code was fair in some ways and unfair in other ways. Explain.

2. (a) Describe What were some uses of writing in Sumer?

(b) Contrast How do the early forms and methods of writing differ from the way we write today?

(c) Draw Inferences Why was the development of writing an important step in human history?

Writing Activity

Reread the quote on page 46 in which the writer complains about the gardeners. Write a law that applies to the gardeners who stole the dates. What do you think should happen to the people who didn't tell about the theft?

For: An activity on cuneiform writing
Visit: PHSchool.com
Web Code: lbd-2203

Mediterranean Civilizations

Prepare to Read

Objectives

In this section you will

1. Understand how the sea power of the Phoenicians helped spread civilization throughout the Mediterranean area.
2. Learn about the major events in the history of the Israelites.

Taking Notes

As you read, create an outline of the history of the Phoenicians and the Israelites. Copy the outline below, and record your findings in it.

> I. The Phoenicians
>   A. Sea-trading power
>   1.
>   2.
>   B. Phoenician alphabet
>   1.
>   2.
> II. The Israelites

Target Reading Skill

Read Ahead Reading ahead is a strategy that can help you to understand words and ideas in the text. If you do not understand a certain passage, read ahead, because a word or idea may be clarified later on. Use this strategy as you read this section.

Key Terms

- **alphabet** (AL fuh bet) *n.* a set of symbols that represent the sounds of a language
- **monotheism** (MAHN oh thee iz um) *n.* the belief in one god
- **famine** (FAM in) *n.* a time when there is so little food that many people starve
- **exile** (EK syl) *v.* to force someone to live in another country

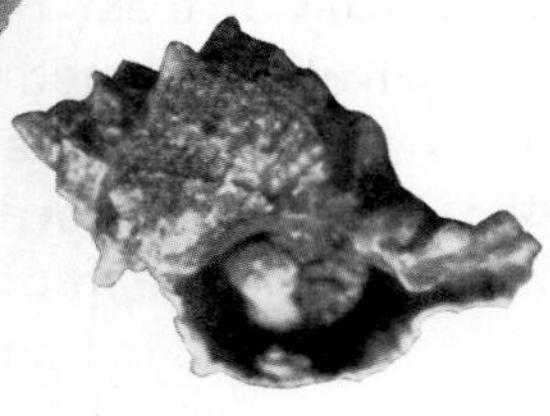

Above, ancient vats from a site in Tel Dor, Israel, once contained purple dye of the type used by the Phoenicians. The stained pottery piece in the middle probably came from a vessel that held the dye. The purple dye comes from the glands of the murex snail, shown at the right.

While the great empire of Hammurabi was rising and falling, the people of a city on the shores of the Mediterranean Sea were becoming rich by gathering snails.

The snails collected near the coastal city of Tyre (tyr) were not ordinary snails. These snails produced a rich purple dye. Cloth made purple with the dye was highly valued by wealthy people throughout the Mediterranean region. Ships from Tyre sold the purple cloth at extremely high prices. The profits helped make Tyre a wealthy city.

Phoenician Sea Power

Tyre was the major city in a region called Phoenicia (fuh NISH uh). Locate Phoenicia and its colonies on the map below. The Phoenicians' outlook was westward, toward the Mediterranean Sea and the cities that were growing around it.

Masters of Trade The Phoenicians had settled in a land that had limited, but very important, resources. Besides the snails used to dye cloth, Phoenicia had a great amount of dense cedar forests. The Phoenicians sold their dyed cloth and the wood from their forests to neighboring peoples.

As trade grew, the Phoenicians looked to the sea to increase their profits. In time, they controlled trade throughout much of the Mediterranean. From about 1100 to 800 B.C., Phoenicia was a great sea power. Phoenician ships sailed all over the Mediterranean Sea and into the stormy Atlantic Ocean. They came back from these trips with stories of horrible monsters that lived in the ocean depths. These stories helped keep other peoples from trying to compete for trade in the Atlantic.

A silver coin from Sidon showing a Phoenician galley, a ship powered by oars

MAP MASTER™ Skills Activity

Phoenician Colonies and Trade Routes

KEY
- Phoenicia
- Phoenician colonies
- → Phoenician trade routes
- • Phoenician trading centers

EUROPE

ATLANTIC OCEAN

Black Sea

ASIA MINOR

Euphrates River

GREECE

PHOENICIA

Sidon
Tyre•
Jerusalem

Cadiz•

Carthage

Mediterranean Sea

0 miles 500
0 kilometers 500
Lambert Azimuthal Equal Area

AFRICA

EGYPT

Location The Phoenicians usually sailed close to the coast.
Identify Name a city in Phoenicia and the trading center that is the farthest west of the city. Use your finger to trace a route between the two points.
Conclude How did the Phoenicians control the sea trade far from Phoenicia?

Go Online
PHSchool.com Use Web Code lbp-2244 for step-by-step map skills practice.

Exotic Marketplaces Trade brought valuable goods from lands around the Mediterranean Sea to the Phoenician cities of Tyre and Sidon (SY dun). Bazaars swelled with foods brought from faraway places. These foods included figs, olives, honey, and spices. In the bazaars, merchants sold strange animals, such as giraffes and warthogs from Africa and bears from Europe.

The overflowing markets of Tyre awed visitors. Here is one description of Tyre's bazaars:

> **"When your wares came from the seas, you satisfied many peoples. With your great wealth and merchandise, you enriched the kings of the earth. "**
>
> —the Bible, Ezekiel 27:33

✓ **Reading Check** What resources did the Phoenicians first use to build their wealth?

The Phoenician Alphabet

The Phoenicians relied on writing to help them conduct trade. They developed a writing system that used just 22 symbols. This system was the Phoenician **alphabet,** a set of symbols that represents the sounds of the language. It forms the basis of the alphabet used in many languages today, including English. In the Phoenician alphabet, however, each letter stood for one consonant sound.

The simple Phoenician alphabet was far easier to learn than cuneiform. Before the alphabet, only highly educated scribes were skilled in writing. Now many more people could write using the new alphabet. The alphabet simplified trade between people who spoke different languages. The Phoenician sea trade, in turn, helped the alphabet to spread.

✓ **Reading Check** How did the Phoenician alphabet differ from cuneiform script?

The Phoenician Alphabet

Letter	Symbol	Letter	Symbol
A		N	
B		O	
C		P	
D		Q	
E		R	
F		S	
G		T	
H		U	
I		V	
J		W	
K		X	
L		Y	
M		Z	

■ Chart Skills

The chart at the left shows the Phoenician letters that correspond to our alphabet. The symbols for A, E, I, O, and U originally represented consonant sounds. The Greeks later used the symbols to represent vowel sounds. The Phoenician stone inscription above dates to about 391 B.C. **Identify** Which letters in the Phoenician alphabet seem similar to the letters in our alphabet? **Identify Effects** How did the Phoenician alphabet affect other civilizations?

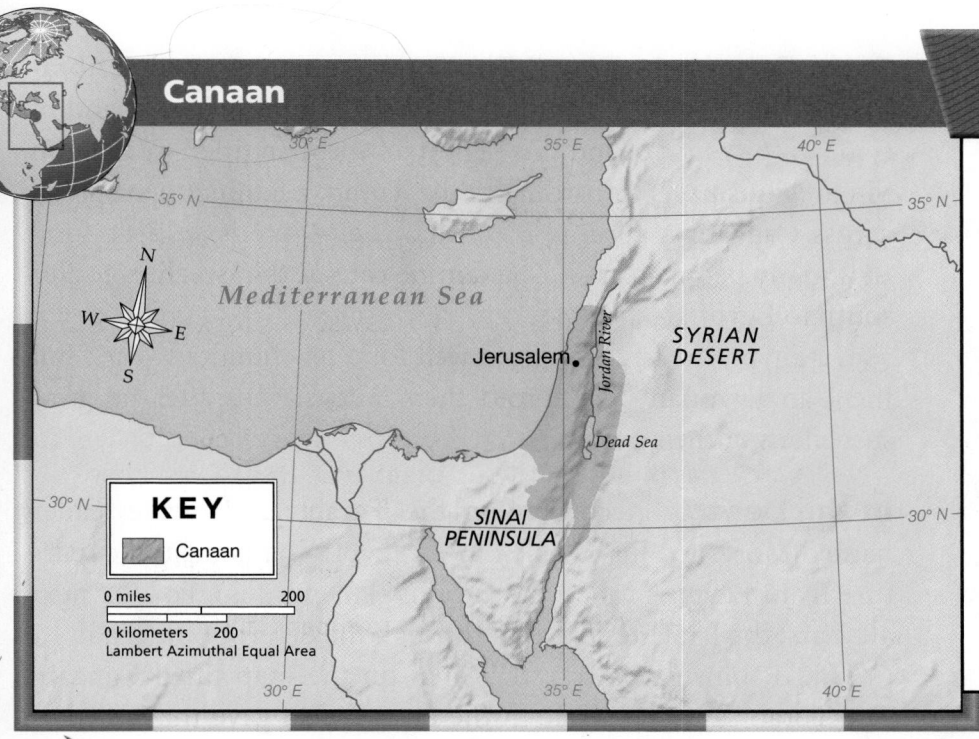

Canaan

MAP★MASTER™
Skills Activity

Movement The Israelites are said to have spent 40 years in the desert of the Sinai Peninsula trying to reach the land of Canaan. **Locate** In what direction did the Israelites travel to return to Canaan from the Sinai Peninsula? **Infer** What physical features of Canaan made it suitable for settlement?

Go Online
PHSchool.com Use Web Code **lbp-2254** for step-by-step map skills practice.

The Rise of the Israelites

South of Phoenicia, a small band of people settled in the hills around the Jordan River valley. Called Hebrews at first, they later became known as Israelites. Although the Israelites never built a large empire, they had a great influence on our civilization.

Much of what is known about the early history of the Israelites comes from stories told in the Torah (TOH ruh), the Israelites' most sacred text. Historians compare biblical and other religious stories with archaeological evidence to piece together events from the past. In this way they have determined that Abraham, whose story follows, may have lived around 2000 B.C.

Abraham the Leader The Israelites traced their beginnings to Mesopotamia. For hundreds of years, they lived as shepherds and merchants who grazed their flocks outside Sumerian cities.

According to the Torah, a leader named Abraham taught his people to practice monotheism, a belief in one god. *Mono-* is the Greek prefix for "one." The Torah says that God told Abraham to leave Mesopotamia and settle elsewhere:

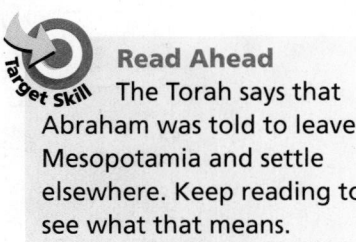

Read Ahead The Torah says that Abraham was told to leave Mesopotamia and settle elsewhere. Keep reading to see what that means.

> **"Get you out of your country, and from your kindred [relatives], and from your father's house, to the land that I will show you. And I will make of you a great nation."**
>
> —*Genesis 12:1–2*

From Canaan to Egypt The Torah goes on to say that Abraham led the Israelites from Mesopotamia to settle in the land of Canaan (KAY nun). Find this region on the map titled Canaan on the previous page. According to the Torah, a famine then spread across Canaan. A **famine** is a time when there is so little food that many people starve. The famine caused the Israelites to flee south to Egypt.

In Egypt, the Israelites lived well for a few hundred years. But then, an Egyptian king forced them into slavery after he grew suspicious of their power.

In the Desert According to the Torah, an Israelite leader named Moses led his people out of Egypt. The Israelites' departure from Egypt is called the Exodus (EKS uh dus). For the next 40 years, the Israelites traveled through the desert of the Sinai (SY ny) Peninsula. Locate the Sinai on the map titled Canaan. The Torah says that while in the desert, God gave the Israelites the Ten Commandments, a code of laws. Eventually, the Israelites returned to Canaan. There, over time, the Israelites moved from herding to farming and built their own cities.

This photograph shows the Western Wall, a Jewish Holy place located in Jerusalem.

Settlement in Canaan As they moved farther north, the Israelites were able to settle in many parts of Canaan. They united under their first king, Saul, who defended them against their enemies. The next king, David, established his capital in the city of Jerusalem.

A Divided Kingdom After David died, his son, Solomon, inherited the kingdom and built a temple in Jerusalem. After Solomon's death, the country split into two kingdoms. The northern kingdom was called Israel. The southern kingdom took the name Judah. The divided kingdom was ripe for invasion. Its neighbor, Assyria, conquered the Israelites and gained control of Judah.

Sent Into Exile In 722 B.C., the Israelites resisted Assyrian rule. In response, the Assyrians exiled thousands of people to distant parts of their empire. To **exile** means to force people to live in another place or country. The Assyrians controlled Judah until 612 B.C., when Assyria was conquered by the Chaldeans. Judah then fell under control of the Chaldean Babylonians. Later, in 587 B.C., the King of Judah rebelled against the Chaldeans. King Nebuchadnezzar responded by destroying the capital city of Jerusalem, including the holy temple. He exiled the people of Judah to Babylonia.

King Solomon

✓ Reading Check **Who were the Israelites?**

Section 4 Assessment

Key Terms
Review the key terms at the beginning of this section. Use each term in a sentence that explains its meaning.

Target Reading Skill
What word or idea were you able to clarify by reading ahead?

Comprehension and Critical Thinking
1. (a) Identify Who were the Phoenicians?
(b) Recall How did the Phoenicians gain their wealth and power?

2. (a) Explain What are some features of the Phoenician alphabet?
(b) Identify Effects Describe the importance of the Phoenician alphabet. How did it affect the Mediterranean world and later civilizations?
3. (a) Identify Sequence Briefly trace the history of the Israelites from the leadership of Abraham to King Solomon.
(b) Identify Central Issues What important events in the history of the Israelites were shaped by movement and by war?

Writing Activity
Reread the description of Tyre. Using what you have read, write a poetic verse about Tyre's markets. Or work with a partner to write song lyrics on the same subject.

Writing Tip Poetic verses and song lyrics don't have to rhyme, but they usually have rhythm. To supply rhythm to your verse or lyrics, it sometimes helps to think of a familiar song as you write. Match words and phrases in your verse to the beats and phrases of the music.

"That movie was really confusing," Brandon said to his friend Juan as they left the theater.

"The action was great, though," said Juan. "Can you believe how much that explorer had to go through to find the treasure?"

Juan's comment gave Brandon an idea. "I guess that was the whole point of the movie—to show all the adventures they had while they tried to find the lost treasure."

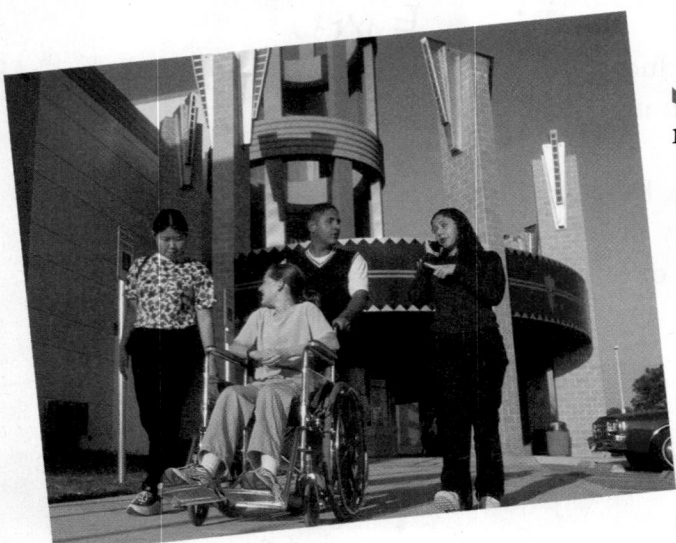

Juan and Brandon were right. To understand anything you read or see, you need to identify the main idea.

Learn the Skill

These steps will explain how to find the main idea in a written paragraph or in any kind of information that carries a message or a theme.

1. **Look for an idea that all the sentences in the paragraph have in common.** In a well-written paragraph, most of the sentences provide details that support or explain a particular idea.

2. **Identify the subject of the paragraph.** You may find the subject stated in several sentences. Or, you may find the subject in a topic sentence, one sentence that tells what the paragraph is about. The subject may also be stated in a title.

3. **State the main idea in your own words.** Write one or two versions of the main idea or topic. Then reread the passage to make sure that what you wrote accurately identifies the main idea.

Practice the Skill

Read the text in the box below, and then use the steps on page 54 to identify the main idea of the text.

1 What idea do the sentences in the paragraph have in common?

2 This paragraph does not have a title, so you will need to find the sentence or sentences that state the main idea. Is there a topic sentence?

3 First, try to come up with a title for the paragraph. Then turn the title into a complete sentence that identifies the main idea.

> In 1901, an archaeologist discovered a stone pillar with an ancient set of laws— Hammurabi's Code. The black stone is almost eight feet tall and more than seven feet around. At its top is a carving of Hammurabi receiving the code of laws from the Babylonian god of justice. About 3,500 lines of cuneiform characters are carved into the stone. These inscriptions are Hammurabi's Code.

Apply the Skill

Turn to page 44, and read the paragraph titled An Eye for an Eye. Follow the steps on page 54 to identify the main idea of the paragraph.

The stele, or stone pillar, on which Hammurabi's Code was written

Prepare to Read

Objectives

In this section you will
1. Learn about the basic beliefs of Judaism.
2. Find out about the effect that Judaism has had on other religions.

Taking Notes

As you read, list details that characterize Judaism. Copy the concept web below, and use it to help you summarize this section.

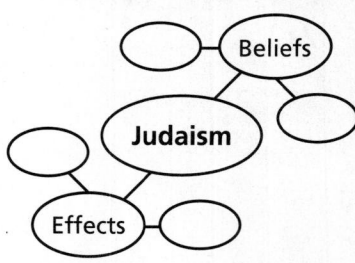

Target Reading Skill

Summarize When you summarize, you review and state, in the correct order, the main points you have read. Summarizing what you read is a good technique to help you comprehend and study. As you read, pause to summarize the main ideas about Judaism. The diagram you are using to take notes may help you to summarize.

Key Terms

- **covenant** (KUV uh nunt) *n.* a binding agreement
- **Moses** (MOH zuz) *n.* an Israelite leader whom the Torah credits with leading the Israelites from Egypt to Canaan
- **prophet** (PRAHF it) *n.* a religious teacher who is regarded as someone who speaks for God or for a god
- **diaspora** (dy AS pur uh) *n.* the scattering of people who have a common background or beliefs

Reading from the Torah

The Torah, the most sacred text of Judaism, says God made a promise to the Israelite leader Abraham:

> **"I will make you exceedingly fruitful; and I will make nations of you, and kings shall come forth from you. And I will . . . be God to you and to your descendants . . . "**

—*Genesis 17: 6–7*

The ancient Israelites viewed this promise as the beginning of a long relationship between themselves and God.

The early Israelites came to believe that God was taking part in their history. The Torah records events and laws important to the Israelites. It makes up the first five books of the Jewish Bible. They are called Genesis (JEN uh sis), Exodus, Leviticus (luh VIT ih kus), Numbers, and Deuteronomy (doo tur AHN uh mee). Later, Christians adopted the Jewish Bible as the Old Testament of the Christian Bible. The promise that you just read is from the Book of Genesis. In Genesis, we learn of the very beginnings of Judaism, the world's first religion that was monotheistic. *Monotheistic* means "having only one god."

The Beliefs of Judaism

To the Israelites, history and religion were closely connected. Each event showed God's plan for the Israelite people. Over time, Israelite beliefs developed into the religion we know today as Judaism. You already know that Judaism was monotheistic from its beginning. It differed from the beliefs of nearby peoples in other ways as well.

A Promise to the Israelites Most ancient people thought of their gods as being connected to certain places or people. The Israelites, however, believed that God is present everywhere. They believed that God knows everything and has complete power.

According to the Torah, God promised Abraham that his people would become kings and build nations. God said to Abraham, "I will keep my promise to you and your descendants in future generations as an everlasting covenant." Because of this **covenant,** or binding agreement, the Israelites believed they were expected to follow God's laws and be just and kind to others. This covenant was later renewed by **Moses,** an Israelite leader who lived sometime around 1200 B.C. He told the Israelites that God would lead them to Canaan, "the promised land." In return, the Israelites had to obey God faithfully.

The Dead Sea Scrolls
The Dead Sea Scrolls (above) were discovered in 1947 in jars like the one shown at the left. The scrolls helped historians reconstruct the early history of the Israelites.
Generalize *What is the importance of archaeological finds like the Dead Sea Scrolls?*

Target Skill

Summarize
Summarize the paragraph at the left. Be sure to include the key points and important details about God's promise to the Israelites.

Links Across
Time

Kosher In Judaism, laws require that certain foods be kosher (KOH shur), meaning "fit for use." These laws are based on passages from the Hebrew Bible. For seafood to be kosher, for example, it must have scales and fins. So, codfish is kosher, but clams are not. Other laws tell how animals meant for consumption should be slaughtered and how food must be prepared and eaten. Not all Jews follow these strict dietary laws today.

The Ten Commandments At the heart of Judaism are the Ten Commandments. The Israelites believed that God delivered the Commandments to them through Moses. Some Commandments set out religious duties toward God. Others are rules for correct behavior. Here are some of the Commandments.

> **I the Lord am your God who brought you out of the land of Egypt. . . . You shall have no other gods beside Me. . . . Honor your father and your mother, as the Lord your God has commanded. . . . You shall not murder. You shall not steal.**
>
> —the Ten Commandments

In addition to the Ten Commandments, the Torah set out many other laws. Some had to do with everyday matters, such as how food should be prepared. Others had to do with crimes. Like Hammurabi's Code, many of the Israelites' laws tried to match punishments to crimes. At the same time, religious teachers called on leaders to carry out the laws with justice and mercy.

Judaism and Women Some laws protected women. One of the Commandments, for example, requires that mothers be treated with respect. As in many other ancient cultures, women had different duties than men. A man who was head of a family was responsible for his wife and children. A father could choose husbands for his daughters with the daughters' consent. Only a husband could seek a divorce.

Early in Israelite history a few women, such as the judge Deborah, won honor and respect as religious leaders. Later on, women were not given many religious leadership roles.

Before sunset on Friday evenings, Jewish women light white Shabbat candles and say a blessing.

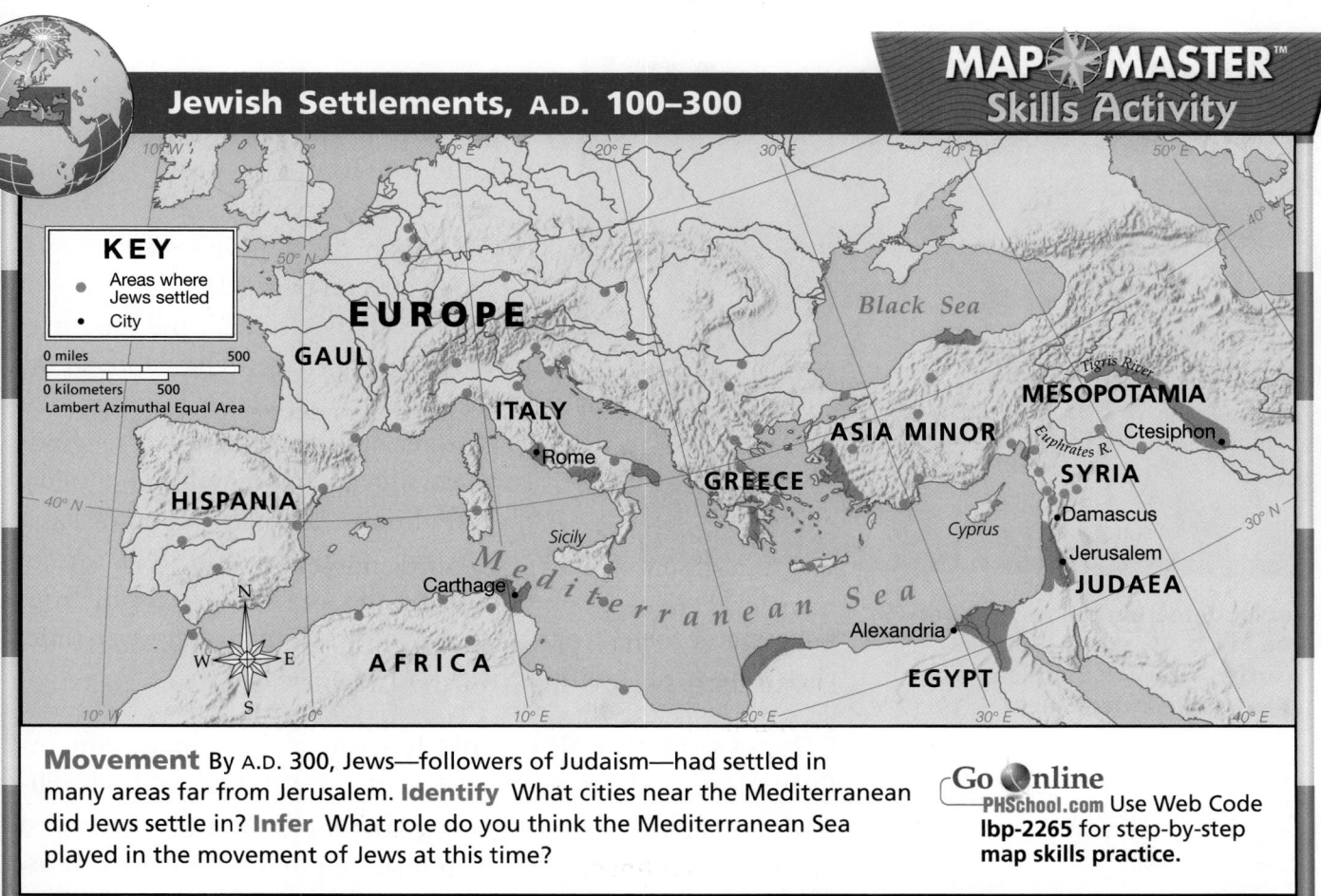

KEY
● Areas where Jews settled
• City

0 miles 500
0 kilometers 500
Lambert Azimuthal Equal Area

EUROPE
GAUL
ITALY
•Rome
HISPANIA
Sicily
Carthage•
AFRICA

Black Sea

MESOPOTAMIA
Tigris River
ASIA MINOR
Ctesiphon•
Euphrates R.
GREECE
SYRIA
•Damascus
Cyprus
•Jerusalem
Mediterranean Sea
JUDAEA
Alexandria•
EGYPT

Movement By A.D. 300, Jews—followers of Judaism—had settled in many areas far from Jerusalem. **Identify** What cities near the Mediterranean did Jews settle in? **Infer** What role do you think the Mediterranean Sea played in the movement of Jews at this time?

Go Online
PHSchool.com Use Web Code
lbp-2265 for step-by-step
map skills practice.

Justice and Morality The history of the Israelites tells of **prophets,** or religious teachers who are regarded as speaking for God. The prophets told the Israelites how God wanted them to live. They warned the people not to disobey God's law.

Prophets preached a code of ethics, or moral behavior. They urged the Israelites to live good and decent lives. They also called on the rich and powerful to protect the poor and weak. All people, the prophets said, were equal before God. In many ancient societies, a ruler was seen as a god. To the Israelites, however, their leaders were human. Kings had to obey God's law just as shepherds and merchants did.

✓ Reading Check **What did the prophets tell the Israelites?**

The Effects of Judaism

After their exile from Judah in 586 B.C., the Jews, or people who follow Judaism, saw their homeland controlled by various foreign powers, including the Romans. The Romans drove the Jews out of Jerusalem in A.D. 135. While many Jews remained in the region, others moved to different parts of the world.

After defeating the Jews in battle in A.D. 70, Roman soldiers carried off precious objects from the temple in Jerusalem.

New Settlements The Romans carried on the Jewish **diaspora** (dy AS pur uh), the scattering of a group of people, begun by the Assyrians and Chaldeans. See the map titled Jewish Settlements, A.D. 100–300, on page 59.

Wherever they settled, the Jews preserved their heritage. They did so by living together in close communities. They took care to obey their religious laws, worship at their temples, and follow their traditions. The celebration of Passover is one such tradition. It is a celebration of the Israelites' freedom from slavery and their departure, or Exodus, from Egypt. Over time, such long-held traditions helped to unite Jews.

Effects on Later Religions Judaism had an important influence on two later religions, Christianity and Islam. Both religions have their beginnings in Judaism. Both faiths originated from the same geographical area. Both were monotheistic. Jews, Christians, and followers of Islam all honor Abraham, Moses, and the prophets. They also share the same moral point of view that the Israelites first developed.

✓ Reading Check **How did the Jews preserve their heritage?**

 **Section 5 Assessment**

Key Terms
Review the key terms at the beginning of this section. Use each term in a sentence that explains its meaning.

 Target Reading Skill
Write a summary of the last paragraph in this section.

Comprehension and Critical Thinking
1. (a) **Identify** What promise did the Israelites believe God made to Abraham?

(b) **Explain** What did God's covenant with Abraham require of the Israelites?
(c) **Analyze Information** Why did the Israelites believe that they were God's chosen people?
2. (a) **Recall** What religious laws did the Israelites follow?
(b) **Compare and Contrast** How does Judaism compare and contrast with the beliefs of other peoples in the ancient world?
(c) **Draw Inferences** What do the laws of Judaism say about the moral values of the Israelites?

Writing Activity
Suppose you have a friend who wants to learn more about Judaism. Write him or her a letter explaining the basic beliefs and history of Judaism.

Writing Tip When writing a letter, remember to include the date, a salutation, or greeting, and a closing. It might help to have a specific friend in mind when you write your letter.

Review and Assessment

◆ Chapter Summary

Cuneiform tablet

Section 1: Land Between Two Rivers

- Mesopotamia's attractive location between two rivers drew people to settle there.
- Some of the earliest cities grew up in Sumer, in the region of Mesopotamia.
- Sumerians worshiped and honored many gods.

Section 2: Fertile Crescent Empires

- The Babylonian Empire included the conquered cities of Sumer and lands reaching into Asia Minor.
- The Assyrians overthrew the Babylonians and created an even larger empire.
- The Assyrian Empire fell to the Chaldeans, who created the New Babylonian Empire under Nebuchadnezzar II.
- The Persians created the largest empire the Fertile Crescent had ever known and tolerated the cultures of conquered peoples.

Section 3: The Legacy of Mesopotamia

- The earliest existing set of written laws, known as Hammurabi's Code, established rules and punishments for Babylonians.
- Writing developed in Mesopotamia in about 3500 B.C., and was first used to keep records.

Section 4: Mediterranean Civilizations

- Phoenicia was a major sea power from 1100 to 800 B.C. Its wealth came from trade.
- The Phoenician alphabet forms the basis of alphabets used in English and other languages.
- The Israelites practiced monotheism and established a capital in the city of Jerusalem.

Section 5: Judaism

- The religion practiced by the Israelites was very different from other religions practiced in the ancient world.
- The Ten Commandments are the core beliefs of Judaism.
- Judaism has influenced other major religions of the world.

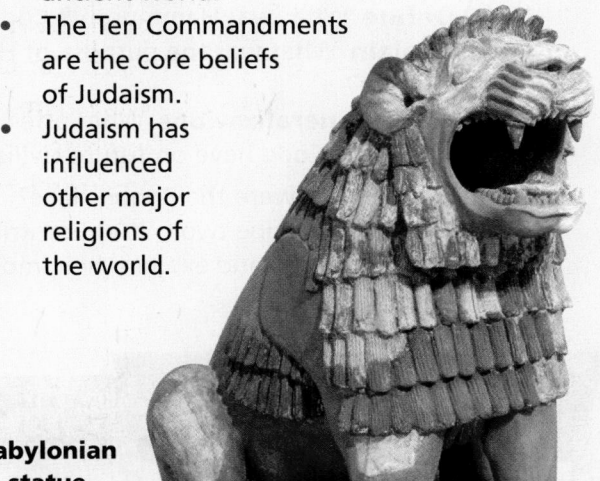

Babylonian statue

◆ Key Terms

Use each key term below in a sentence that shows the meaning of the term.

1. city-state
2. polytheism
3. myth
4. empire
5. caravan
6. bazaar
7. code

8. cuneiform
9. monotheism
10. famine
11. exile
12. covenant
13. prophet
14. diaspora

Review and Assessment (conti

◆ Comprehension and Critical Thinking

15. (a) Identify What is the Fertile Crescent?
(b) Apply Information Explain the importance of the Tigris and the Euphrates rivers in the Fertile Crescent.
(c) Draw Conclusions How did the geography of the Fertile Crescent help the Sumerians to prosper?

16. (a) Recall Describe the Babylonian, Assyrian, New Babylonian, and Persian empires.
(b) Identify Cause and Effect Explain how the Fertile Crescent's location shaped the development of its civilizations.
(c) Find the Main Ideas What patterns do you see in the rise and fall of the many civilizations in the Fertile Crescent?

17. (a) Define What was Hammurabi's Code?
(b) Explain What was the purpose of Hammurabi's Code?
(c) Make Generalizations What effect did Hammurabi's Code have on future civilizations?

18. (a) Name Who were the Phoenicians?
(b) Explain Describe two cultural contributions of the Phoenicians and explain their importance.

(c) Compare and Contrast Compare and trast cuneiform and the Phoenician alphabe

19. (a) Recall Who were the Israelites and wh they believe?
(b) Explain Describe two major events in history of the Israelites.
(c) Analyze Information Choose an ever from the history of the Israelites and descr its importance.

◆ Skills Practice

Identifying Main Ideas In the Skills for Life ity, you learned how to identify main ideas. You learned how to summarize main ideas in a bri statement. Review the steps you followed to l this skill. Then turn to page 45 and read the t paragraphs on that page under the heading Th of Writing. Identify the main ideas and then su rize them in a few sentences.

◆ Writing Activity: Math

Turn to page 3 at the beginning of this unit. Ac ing to the dates for Chapter 2, how long did t ancient civilizations of the Fertile Crescent last Write a sentence explaining your answer.

MAP MASTER
Skills Activity

The Fertile Crescent

Place Location For each place listed below, write the letter from the map that shows its location.
1. Tigris River
2. Euphrates River
3. Mesopotamia
4. Fertile Crescent
5. Canaan
6. Mediterranean Sea

Go Online
PHSchool.com Use Web Code
lbp-2275 for an **interactive map.**

Standardized Test Prep

Test-Taking Tips

Some questions on standardized tests ask you to draw conclusions by analyzing a reading passage. Read the paragraph below. Then follow the tips to answer the sample question.

> Sumerian priests washed the statues of gods before and after each meal was offered. Music sounded and incense burned as huge plates of food were laid before them. In most ancient religions, the food was often eaten after it was presented to the gods. Perhaps the worshipers thought that by eating the offering, they would be taking in the qualities they admired in the gods.

TIP Reread if necessary before answering.

Pick the letter that best completes the statement.

TIP Use logic—or good reasoning—to choose your answer.

Which conclusion can you reach, based on the passage?

- A The Sumerians were not as intelligent as modern people.
- B Only priests were allowed into temples.
- C The Sumerians did not like to waste food.
- D Religious ceremonies were important to the Sumerians.

Think It Through You can rule out B. The passage does not say that only priests were allowed in the temples. The practices of the Sumerians may seem odd to us, but odd does not mean unintelligent. So A is not correct. The passage states that people possibly ate offerings to honor their gods. So C is not the best answer. The correct answer is D.

Practice Questions

Use the tips above and other tips in this book to help you answer the following questions.

1. Where was Mesopotamia located?
   - A along the Nile River
   - B between the Tigris and the Euphrates rivers
   - C in the Arabian Desert
   - D in present-day Egypt

2. Which civilization mastered seafaring?
   - A Phoenicia
   - B Sumer
   - C Assyria
   - D Babylonia

Read the passage below, and then answer the questions that follow.

The Assyrians invented the battering ram to tear down city walls. They trained people to hurl stones with slings, and they created special armor to protect their archers. They also perfected the skill of fighting while on horse-drawn chariots.

3. What can you conclude about the Assyrians from this passage?
   - A They were inexperienced warriors.
   - B They liked inventing new things.
   - C They disliked fighting.
   - D They had fought many wars.

4. Judaism differed from other early religions in that it
   - A was polytheistic.
   - B treated men and women equally.
   - C was monotheistic.
   - D developed in the Fertile Crescent.

Go Online
PHSchool.com
Use Web Code lba-2205 for
Chapter 2 self-test.

Ancient Egypt, India, and China

(3100 B.C.–A.D. 500)

◀ The Pyramids at Giza, Egypt, are one of the Seven Wonders of the Ancient World.

Ancient Egypt and Nubia

Chapter Preview

This chapter will introduce you to the civilizations of Ancient Egypt and Nubia.

Section 1
The Geography of the Nile

Section 2
The Rulers of Egypt

Section 3
Egyptian Religion

Section 4
Ancient Egyptian Culture

Section 5
The Cultures of Nubia

Target Reading Skill

Context In this chapter you will focus on using context to help you understand unfamiliar words. The context of a word includes the words, phrases, and sentences surrounding the word.

▶ **A tomb painting of Egyptian fishermen, dating from about 1292 to 1225** B.C.

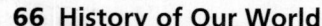

MAP MASTER™ Skills Activity

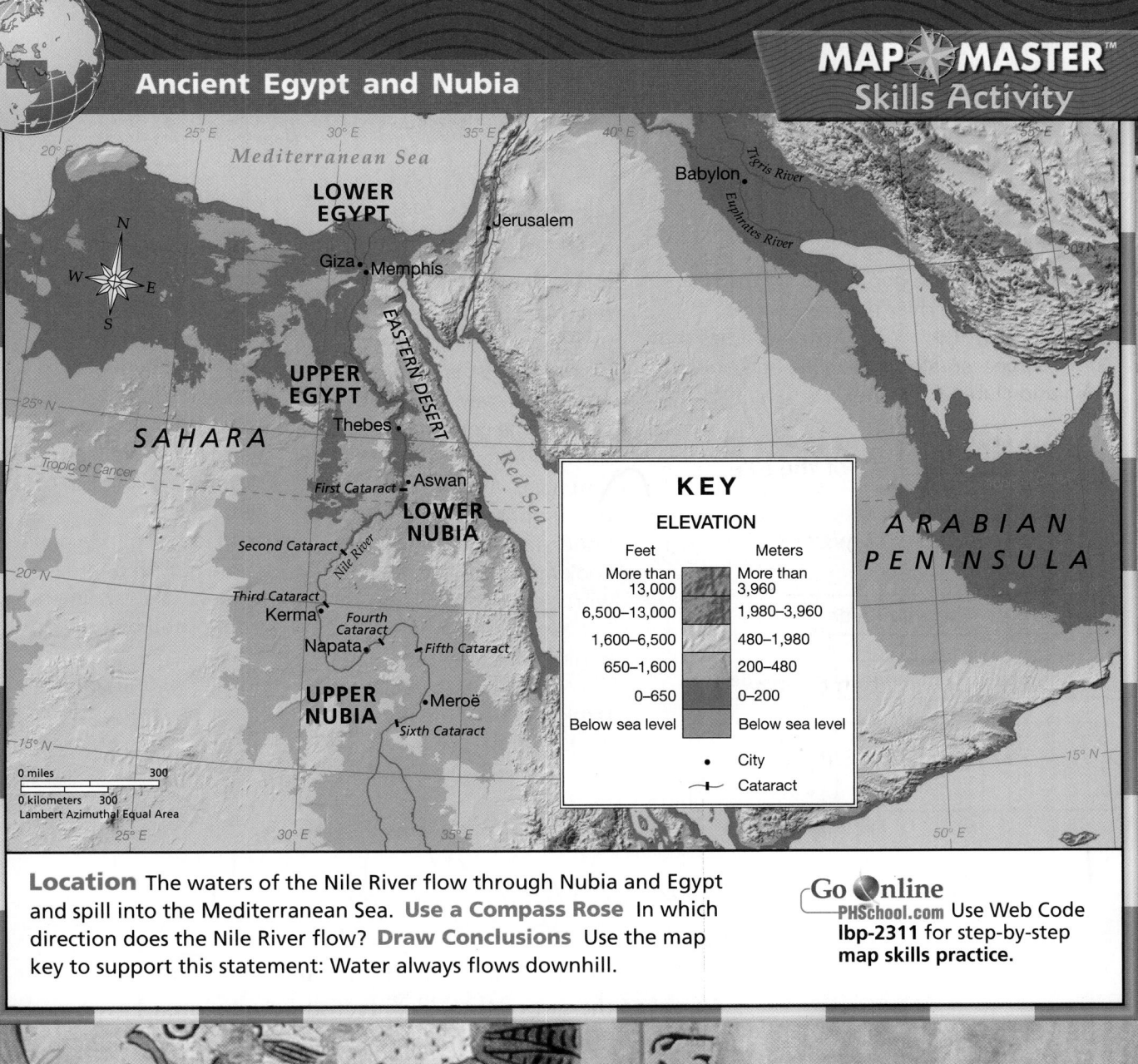

Ancient Egypt and Nubia

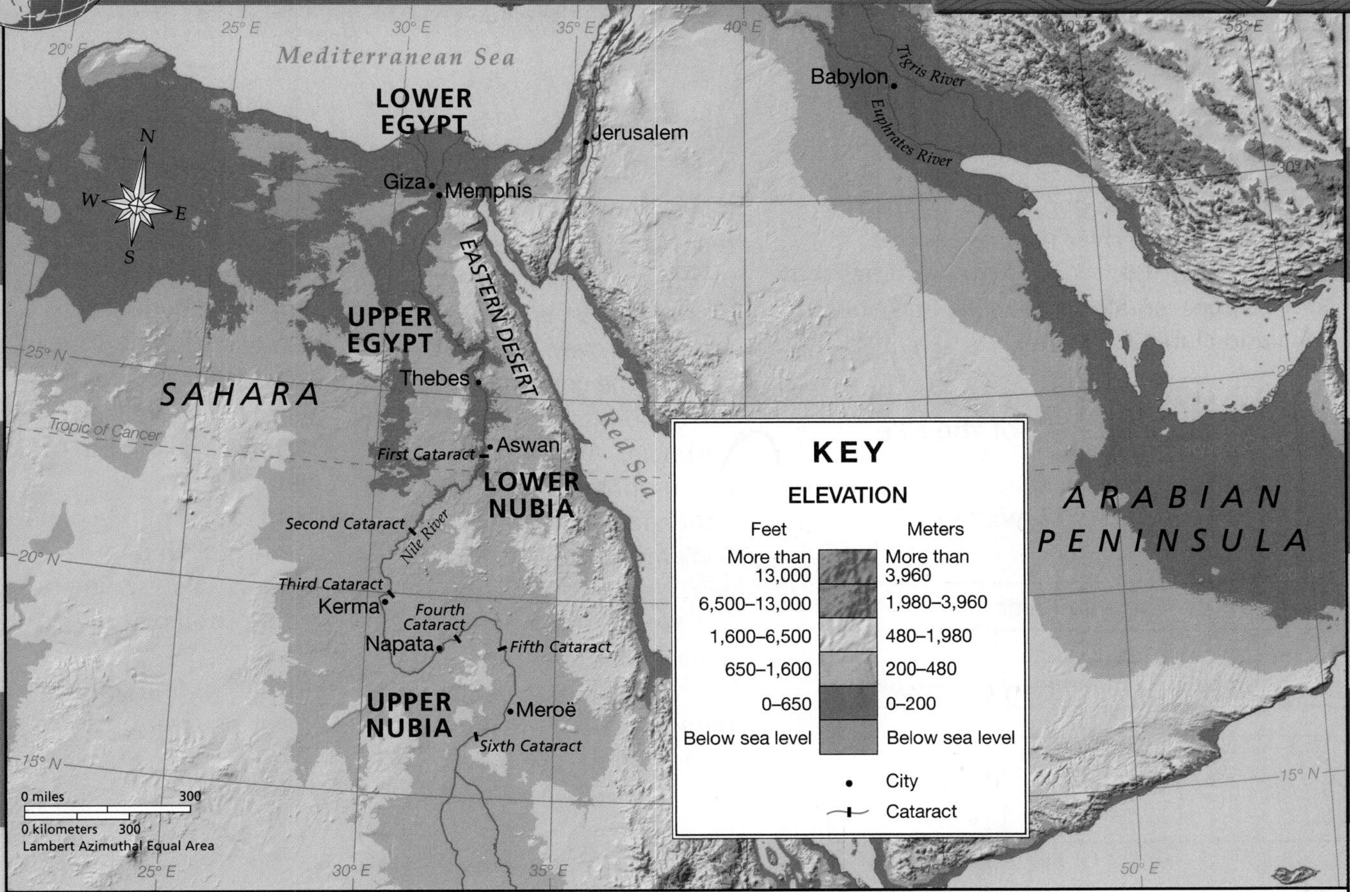

Mediterranean Sea
LOWER EGYPT
Giza
Memphis
Jerusalem
Babylon
Tigris River
Euphrates River
EASTERN DESERT
UPPER EGYPT
Thebes
SAHARA
Tropic of Cancer
First Cataract
Aswan
Red Sea
LOWER NUBIA
Second Cataract
Nile River
Third Cataract
Kerma
Fourth Cataract
Napata
Fifth Cataract
UPPER NUBIA
Meroë
Sixth Cataract
ARABIAN PENINSULA
N
S
E
W
20° E
25° E
30° E
35° E
40° E
50° E
55° E
30° N
25° N
20° N
15° N
0 miles 300
0 kilometers 300
Lambert Azimuthal Equal Area
KEY
ELEVATION
Feet
Meters
More than 13,000
More than 3,960
6,500–13,000
1,980–3,960
1,600–6,500
480–1,980
650–1,600
200–480
0–650
0–200
Below sea level
Below sea level
City
Cataract

Location The waters of the Nile River flow through Nubia and Egypt and spill into the Mediterranean Sea. **Use a Compass Rose** In which direction does the Nile River flow? **Draw Conclusions** Use the map key to support this statement: Water always flows downhill.

Go Online PHSchool.com Use Web Code **lbp-2311** for step-by-step **map skills practice.**

Section 1

The Geography of the Nile

Prepare to Read

Objectives

In this section you will

1. Find out how the geography of the Nile changes as the river runs its course.
2. Learn about the types of communities that first appeared along the Nile, and how the Nile was used for trade.

Taking Notes

As you read, note the effects the Nile had on the growth of communities and trade. Copy the chart below, and use it to record your findings.

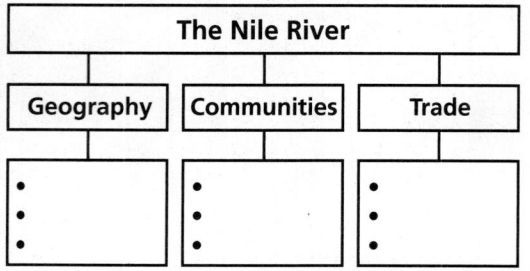

The Nile River

Geography	Communities	Trade
•	•	•
•	•	•
•	•	•

Target Reading Skill

Use Context Clues When reading, you may come across an unfamiliar word, or a word that is used in an unfamiliar way. Look for clues in the context—the surrounding words, sentences, and paragraphs—to help you understand the meaning. Look at the context for the word *sediment* on page 70 in the paragraph that begins with The Gifts of the Nile. What do you think *sediment* means?

Key Terms

- **Nubia** (NOO bee uh) *n.* an ancient region in the Nile River Valley, on the site of present-day southern Egypt and nothern Sudan
- **cataract** (KAT uh rakt) *n.* a large waterfall; any strong flood or rush of water
- **delta** (DEL tuh) *n.* a plain at the mouth of a river, formed when sediment is deposited by flowing water
- **silt** (silt) *n.* fine soil found on river bottoms

The Greek historian Herodotus (huh RAHD uh tus) wrote, "Egypt is the gift of the Nile." Herodotus explored Egypt in the 400s B.C. On his journey, he saw the life-giving waters of its great river. He traveled upriver until he was stopped by churning rapids of white water. Forced to turn back, he never found the source of the river.

Herodotus wrote down his observations of Egypt and other lands. His writings still make interesting reading today. Despite his failure to locate the source of the Nile, Herodotus had learned a basic truth: There would be no Egypt without the Nile.

River of Life
An Egyptian uses a throwstick, a sort of boomerang, to hunt for birds from his boat. **Analyze Images** *What gifts of the Nile are shown in this painting?*

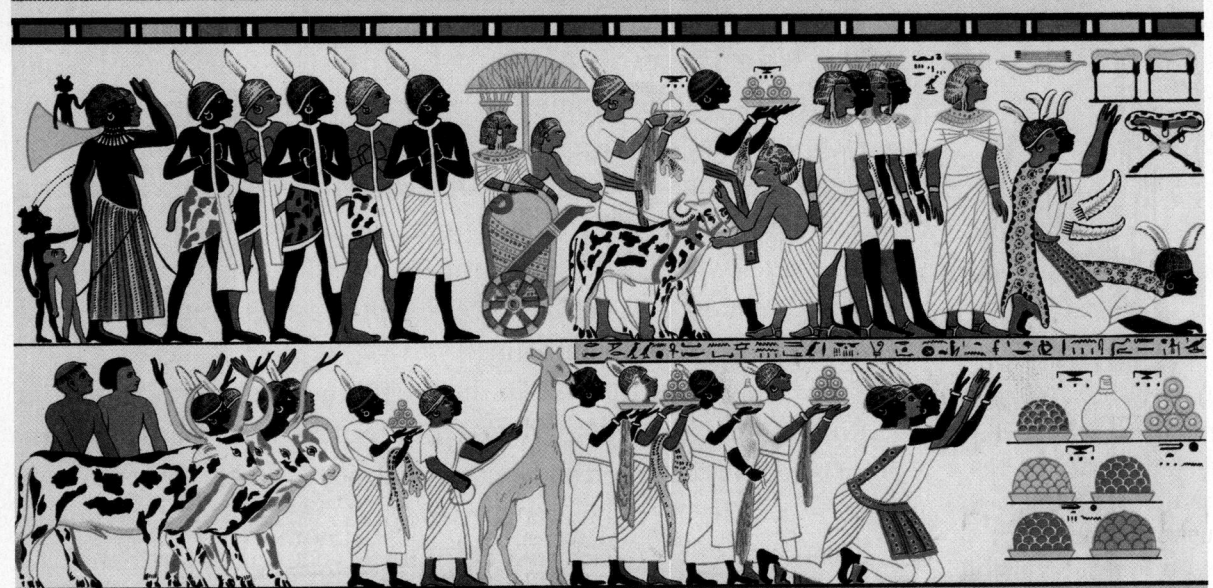

The Course of the Nile River

The Nile River is the world's longest river. It flows north from its sources in East Africa to the Mediterranean Sea for more than 4,000 miles (6,400 kilometers). That is about the distance from New York to Alaska. The Nile has two main sources. The Blue Nile rises in the highlands of the present-day country of Ethiopia and races down to the desert in thundering torrents. The White Nile is calmer. It begins deep in East Africa and flows northward through swamps. The two rivers meet in the present-day country of Sudan. There, the Nile begins its journey through desert lands to the Mediterranean Sea.

The Nile Through Ancient Nubia Just north of the point where the Blue Nile and White Nile meet, the Nile makes two huge bends. It forms an S shape 1,000 miles (1,600 kilometers) in length. The northern tip of the S is at the city of Aswan in Egypt. Along this stretch of the Nile was **Nubia,** an ancient region in the Nile River valley.

The Nubian section of the Nile contained six **cataracts,** or rock-filled rapids. Between the first and second cataracts was Lower Nubia. In that region, the desert and granite mountains lined the riverbanks, leaving very little land for farming. Because it rarely rained in Lower Nubia, people had to live close to the Nile for their water supply.

Farther south, between the second and sixth cataracts, lies the area that was known as Upper Nubia. In that region, rain does fall, so people could plant in the fall and then harvest in the spring. But the farmland was in a very narrow strip, no more than 2 miles (3 kilometers) wide on each side of the river.

Learn about life on the Nile.

The Nile Through Ancient Egypt The Nile ran for about 700 miles (1,100 kilometers) through ancient Egypt, from the First Cataract at Aswan to the Mediterranean Sea. On its way, it passed through a narrow region called Upper Egypt. This fertile strip had an average width of around 6 miles (10 kilometers) on each side of the river. In the north, the Nile spread out to form a fertile, marshy area called Lower Egypt. Deserts stretched on each side of the river's green banks.

At the end of the Nile in the north, the river split into several streams that flowed to the Mediterranean Sea. These streams formed an area called the delta. A **delta** is a plain at the mouth of a river. The flowing water deposited mineral-rich sediment. Because of this, the Nile delta contained very fertile farmland.

The Gifts of the Nile Every spring, far away in the highlands of Africa, waters began to rush downstream. As they flowed, they brought a rich, fertile sediment called silt. **Silt** is fine soil found on river bottoms. By late summer, the Nile spilled over its banks all the way to the delta. The floodwaters deposited a thick layer of silt, making the land ideal for farming. In gratitude, the Egyptians praised Hapi (HAH pea), the god of the Nile:

> **"Hail to you, O Nile, who flows from the Earth and comes to keep Egypt alive."**
>
> —ancient Egyptian prayer

Target Skill **Using Context Clues** In the paragraph at the right, sediment is described as being mineral rich and carried by water. If you read ahead, you will learn that silt is a kind of sediment What is the meaning of *sediment*?

Black Land and Red Land The ancient Egyptians called their land Kemet (KEH met), "the black land," because of the dark soil left by the Nile's floods. The timing of the floods and the height of the floodwaters might vary from year to year. But unlike the Mesopotamians, the Egyptians usually did not have to worry about flash floods. Dry years were rare in Egypt, but they could cause famine.

Beyond the fertile river banks lay the "red land," the vast desert. It spread out on either side of the river. Most of the Sahara lay to the west, and the part of the Sahara called the Eastern Desert lay to the east. These lands were not friendly to human life. They were useless for farming. Only those who knew the deserts well dared travel over this blistering-hot land.

Desert Protection The hot sands shielded Egypt and Nubia from foreign attacks. That was a protection Mesopotamia did not have. The land between the Tigris and Euphrates rivers was wide open to outsiders. The people of Mesopotamia often faced invasions. Over a period of 2,000 years, the people of ancient Egypt and Nubia faced few invasions. Yet they were not isolated. The Nile valley provided a path for trade with Central Africa. The Mediterranean Sea and the Red Sea provided access to Southwest Asia.

✓ **Reading Check** How did the people of Nubia and Egypt benefit from the geography of the region?

Geography and Civilization
In the large photo below, you can see the date palms and fields that line the Nile River near the city of Luxor. The small photo shows the desert landscape that surrounds the Nile. **Analyze Images** *Compare the two photos. What are the challenges of living in the desert? What are the advantages of living along the Nile?*

The Growth of Communities and Trade Along the Nile

Settled hunting and fishing communities may have appeared in Nubia around 6000 B.C. Unlike the communities of the Fertile Crescent that settled after taking up agriculture, the Nubians formed settlements before they began to farm. Settled farming communities began to appear in both Egypt and Nubia sometime around 5000 B.C. As these communities grew, trade also expanded.

Living Along the Nile Egypt's early farming communities settled in the delta and valley regions of the Nile. The people of the delta built villages around the fertile river beds. Their homes were built of straw or of bricks made from a mix of mud and straw. To the south, in Upper Egypt, people built scattered farming villages along the banks of the Nile.

Nubia had less farmland along the Nile than Egypt. Because of the shortage of farmland, Nubians added to their diet by fishing in the Nile and hunting ducks and other birds along its banks.

Links Across Time

Saving Monuments To control flooding, the Egyptians built the Aswan High Dam on the Nile River in the 1960s. The water held back by the dam created Lake Nasser. During its creation, Lake Nasser threatened to flood ancient monuments that had been carved in the cliffs above the Nubian Nile. Egypt, with the help of about 50 nations, saved some of the monuments. At a site called Abu Simbel, the temple of Ramses II (below) was saved. Workers cut the temple into blocks. They moved the blocks to higher ground and then rebuilt the temple.

A Highway for Trade In Egypt, the Nile was used to transport goods. Ships could travel north on the Nile because it was moving downriver. But they could also sail upriver with the help of the winds that blew toward the south. Other trade links ran east across the desert to the Red Sea ports or to Mesopotamia. Caravans loaded with gold, silver, copper, and fine pottery traveled the overland trade routes. Valuable goods such as cedar from the eastern coast of the Mediterranean Sea and gold from Nubia were sold in the bazaars of Egypt's towns.

Routes Through Nubia Because of the cataracts, people could not travel through Nubia by river. Instead, the Nubians developed trade routes over land. The Nubians became famous traders of the ancient world. They carried goods from central Africa and Nubia into Egypt and southwestern Asia and brought other goods back.

One Nubian caravan that traveled into Egypt had 300 donkeys. The donkeys carried ebony wood, ivory from elephant tusks, ostrich feathers and eggs, and panther skins. Another popular object was a throwstick, a type of boomerang that Africans used for hunting.

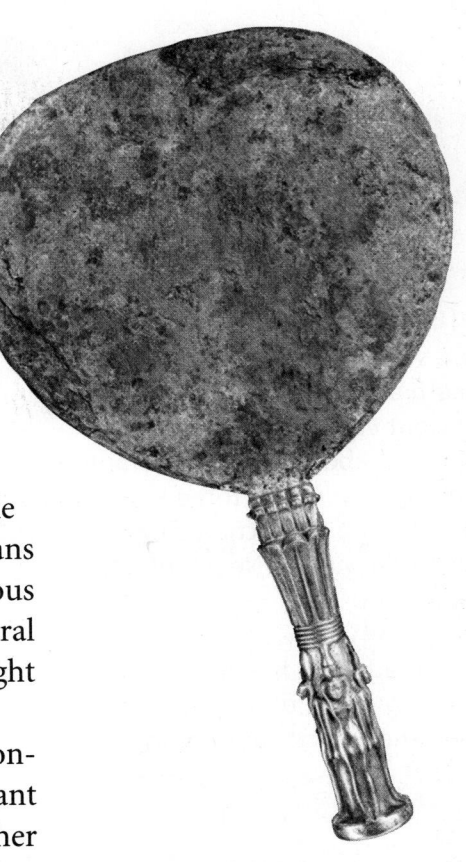

Nubians traded many valuable goods. This Nubian bronze mirror with a gilt silver handle, from about 700 B.C., was found in present-day Sudan.

✔ **Reading Check** How did the Nile operate as a "highway for trade"?

Section 1 Assessment

Key Terms
Review the key terms at the beginning of this section. Use each term in a sentence that explains its meaning.

Target Reading Skill
Find the word *torrents* on page 69. Use context clues to find the meaning of *torrents*.

Comprehension and Critical Thinking
1. (a) Recall Describe the course of the Nile River from its source all the way to the delta.

(b) Identify Cause and Effect How did the Nile River affect the lives of the early Egyptians and Nubians?

(c) Predict If the Nile did not flood regularly, how might life along the river have been different in ancient times?

2. (a) List What kinds of trade goods passed through Nubia on their way to Egypt?

(b) Identify Effects How did the cataracts of the Nile River affect Nubian trade?

(c) Draw Conclusions How did the Nubians become famous as traders?

Writing Activity
Suppose that you are traveling along the Nile from its source to the Nile delta. Write a journal entry about the changes you notice in the river as you travel.

For: An activity on the Nile River
Visit: PHSchool.com
Web Code: lbd-2301

The Rulers of Egypt

Prepare to Read

Objectives

In this section you will

1. Learn about the history of kingship in ancient Egypt.
2. Find out about Egypt's accomplishments during each of the three kingdom periods.
3. Understand what characterized the rule of Egypt during the New Kingdom period.

Taking Notes

As you read, look for the main ideas about ancient Egyptian rulers. Copy the diagram below, and record your findings in it.

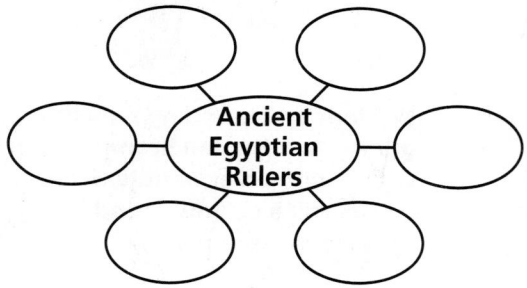

Ancient Egyptian Rulers

Target Reading Skill

Use Context Clues When you read an unfamiliar word, you can sometimes figure out its meaning from clues in the context. Sometimes the context will restate the word. The following phrase, for example, restates the meaning of *sphinx*: "a legendary creature with a lion's body and a human head." As you read, look at the context for the word *timber* on page 76. What do you think *timber* means?

Key Terms

- **pharaoh** (FEHR oh) *n.* the title of the kings of ancient Egypt
- **dynasty** (DY nus tee) *n.* a series of rulers from the same family or ethnic group
- **absolute power** (AB suh loot POW ur) *n.* complete control over someone or something
- **regent** (REE junt) *n.* someone who rules for a child until the child is old enough to rule

A sculpture of Queen Hatshepsut as a sphinx, a legendary creature with a lion's body and a human head

She seized control of Egypt's throne and made herself **pharaoh** (FEHR oh), the title used by the kings of Egypt. Hatshepsut (haht SHEP soot) was not the only woman to rule Egypt. But the title of pharaoh was traditionally held by men. Hatshepsut took on all the responsibilities of a pharaoh. Sometimes she even wore the false beard traditionally worn by pharaohs. Like all Egyptian pharaohs, Hatshepsut controlled the wealth and power of a great civilization.

Egyptian Kingship

Hatshepsut was one of many famous Egyptian pharaohs who ruled Egypt. Some, like her, were wise. Others were careless or cruel. Egypt's fortunes rested on the strength of its pharaohs.

From Dynasty to Dynasty The history of ancient Egypt is the history of each of its dynasties. A dynasty is a series of rulers from the same family or ethnic group. Egypt had 31 dynasties, from about 3100 B.C. until it was conquered in 332 B.C. Historians group Egypt's dynasties into three major time periods, called kingdoms. The earliest major time period is called the Old Kingdom. Next comes the Middle Kingdom. The latest time period is called the New Kingdom. The timeline titled Major Time Periods in Ancient Egypt on page 76 shows the approximate dates of each kingdom. Remember, these kingdoms are not places. They are time periods.

The gaps between the kingdoms were times of troubles—wars, invasions, or weak rulers. These in-between periods were rare, however. For most of ancient Egyptian history, rule was stable.

Egypt Is Unified According to legend, Egypt's first dynasty began when a king named Menes (MEE neez) united Upper and Lower Egypt. Menes built a city named Memphis near the present-day city of Cairo (KY roh). From there, he ruled over the Two Lands, the name the ancient Egyptians gave to Upper and Lower Egypt. Carvings from Menes' time show a pharaoh named Narmer wearing two crowns—the white crown of Upper Egypt and the red crown of Lower Egypt. Some historians believe that Menes and Narmer may have been the same man. The unification of Egypt was the beginning of one of the most stable civilizations in history.

All-Powerful Pharaohs The pharaohs had **absolute power,** or complete control over their people. For help in making decisions, they could turn to their advisors or appeal to Ma'at, the goddess of truth. In the end, whatever the pharaoh decided became law. For example, he decided when the fields would be planted. At harvest time, he demanded crops from the workers in the fields.

The Narmer Palette
This two-sided tablet honors the unification of Upper and Lower Egypt by a king named Narmer.
❶ Narmer wears symbols of Egyptian kingship: the cone-shaped crown of Upper Egypt and a false beard and tail. He prepares to strike the enemy.
❷ The falcon represents Horus, the god of kingship.
❸ Reed plants, which grow in the Nile delta, represent Lower Egypt.
❹ A royal sandal bearer carries Narmer's shoes. **Predict** *Narmer wears a different crown on the opposite side of the tablet. What crown do you think he wears?*

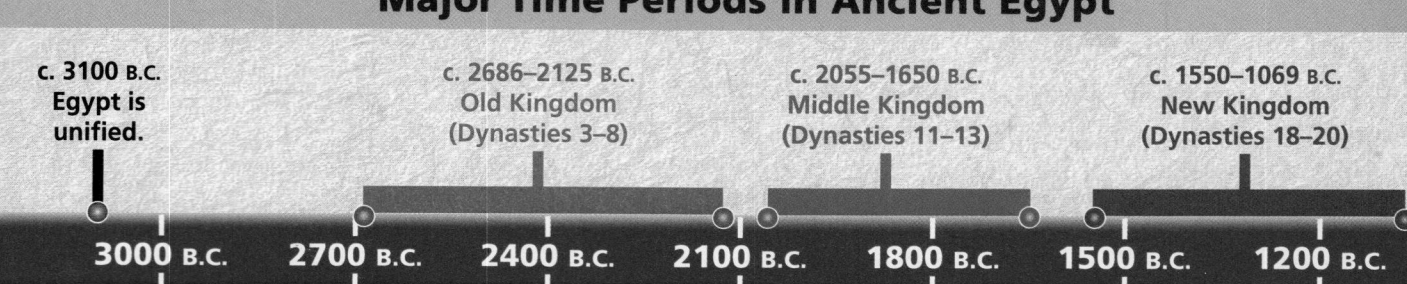

Major Time Periods in Ancient Egypt

c. 3100 B.C.
Egypt is unified.

c. 2686–2125 B.C.
Old Kingdom (Dynasties 3–8)

c. 2055–1650 B.C.
Middle Kingdom (Dynasties 11–13)

c. 1550–1069 B.C.
New Kingdom (Dynasties 18–20)

3000 B.C. 2700 B.C. 2400 B.C. 2100 B.C. 1800 B.C. 1500 B.C. 1200 B.C.

Old Kingdom
- c. 2589 B.C.
Builders begin Great Pyramid.
- c. 2533 B.C.
Great Sphinx statue is completed.

Middle Kingdom
- c. 1991–1786 B.C.
Egypt expands into Lower Nubia. Literature and art flourish.

New Kingdom
- c. 1503–1482 B.C.
Queen Hatshepsut rules.
- c. 1504–1450 B.C.
Reign of Thutmose III; empire expands into Syria.

■ Timeline Skills

Notice the three time periods called kingdoms, as well as the number of years between the kingdoms. **Identify** How many dynasties ruled from 2686 to 2125 B.C.? How many ruled from 2125 to 2055 B.C.? **Infer** During which of those two time periods was Egypt most stable? Explain your answer.

Use Context Clues If you do not know what timber is, look for context clues. Find a restatement of the word *timber*. Then reread what the Egyptians used timber for. What is timber?

Ancient Egyptians believed that their pharaohs were the earthly form of Horus, the falcon god. Over time, pharaohs came to be connected with other gods, including the sun god Re (ray). In this way, the pharaohs were god-kings. It was the pharaoh, Egyptians believed, who provided his people with the Nile's yearly floods and the harvests that followed.

> **He is the god Re whose beams enable us to see.**
> **He gives more light to the Two Lands than the sun's disc.**
> **He makes Earth more green than the Nile in flood.**
> **He has filled the Two Lands with strength and life.**
>
> —*an official of ancient Egypt*

✓ **Reading Check** **Who was Menes and what did he accomplish?**

The Three Kingdoms

Important events and achievements marked each of Egypt's three kingdoms. The Old Kingdom was noted for its well-run system of government.

The Old Kingdom The Old Kingdom pharaohs kept the peace and traded with Nubia, with only occasional conflicts. They sent merchants to the eastern coast of the Mediterranean to find timber, or trees used for building. The timber was used to make houses, boats, and furniture. Merchants may have traveled north across the Mediterranean in search of trade items.

Toward the end of the Old Kingdom, governors in the provinces began to challenge the power of the pharaohs' government. Egypt's unity crumbled, and the dynasties grew weak.

Egyptian Empire, About 1450 B.C.

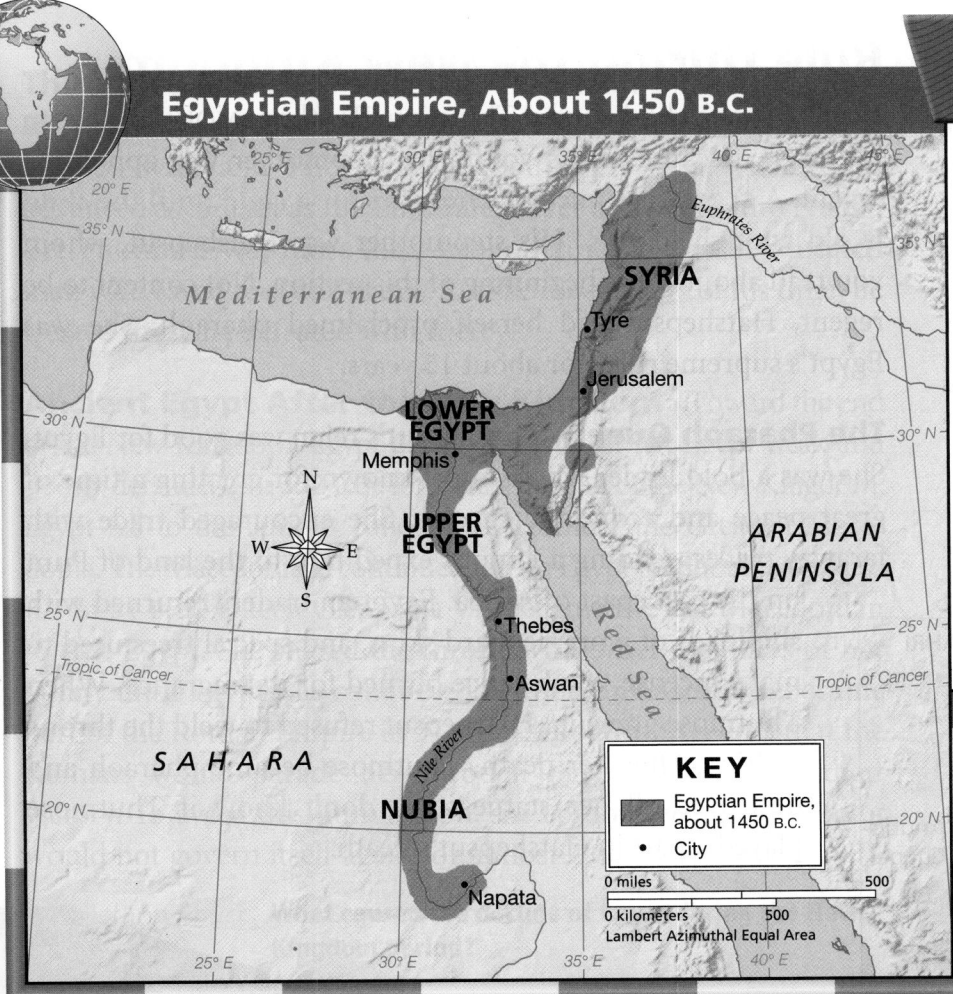

KEY

Egyptian Empire, about 1450 B.C.

• City

0 miles 500
0 kilometers 500
Lambert Azimuthal Equal Area

Movement Egypt expanded its rule during the New Kingdom. As the empire grew, Egyptian goods and ideas reached new places. **Identify** Which waterways could the Egyptians use to transport goods? **Infer** How did the empire's access to waterways help it to control the empire?

Go Online
PHSchool.com Use Web Code **lbp-2322** for step-by-step map skills practice.

The Middle Kingdom The early rulers of the Middle Kingdom restored order and reunited the country. Pharaohs spent the nation's wealth on public works instead of on wars. For example, they constructed buildings and irrigation projects. Egypt grew even richer. However, weaker and less able rulers followed. In time, they lost control of the country to foreign invaders.

The New Kingdom Egyptian princes became strong enough to drive out the foreign invaders. This event marks the start of the New Kingdom, which began in 1567 B.C. The first pharaohs of the New Kingdom wanted to build an empire. They created huge armies of foot soldiers, mounted warriors, and charioteers. Bronze swords and body armor made the Egyptians nearly unbeatable. One New Kingdom pharaoh is of special interest to scholars. King Tutankhamen became ruler of Egypt while he was still a child. At about age 18 he died and was buried with many precious objects. An archaeologist discovered his tomb in 1922. Since then, studies of Tutankhamen's funeral treasures have taught us a great deal about the ancient Egyptians.

A gold portrait mask was one of the many treasures found in King Tutankhamen's tomb.

✓ **Reading Check** **What characterized each of the three kingdoms?**

Egyptian Religion

Prepare to Read

Objectives

In this section you will

1. Learn about Egyptian gods and goddesses.
2. Find out about the Egyptians' belief in the afterlife.
3. Discover how and why the pharaohs' tombs were built.

Taking Notes

As you read, take notes to summarize the religious beliefs and practices of the ancient Egyptians. Copy the chart below, and use it to record your notes.

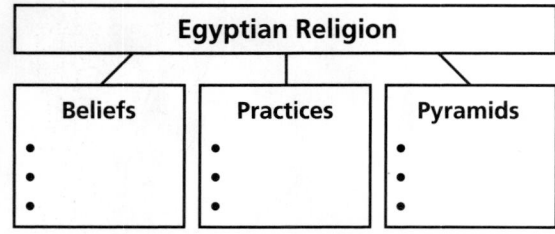

Egyptian Religion		
Beliefs	Practices	Pyramids
•	•	•
•	•	•
•	•	•

Target Reading Skill

Use Context Clues When reading, you may find a word that is unfamiliar or even a word you know that is used in an unfamiliar way. Look for clues in the surrounding words and sentences, to help you understand the meaning of the word. For example, look at the context for the word *linen* in the second paragraph on this page. Find the explanation of how linen was used in mummification. What do you think *linen* means?

Key Terms

- **afterlife** (AF tur lyf) *n.* a life after death
- **mummy** (MUM ee) *n.* a dead body preserved in lifelike condition
- **pyramid** (PIH ruh mid) *n.* a huge building with four sloping triangle-shaped sides; built as royal tombs in Egypt
- **Giza** (GEE zuh) *n.* an ancient Egyptian city; the site of the Great Pyramid

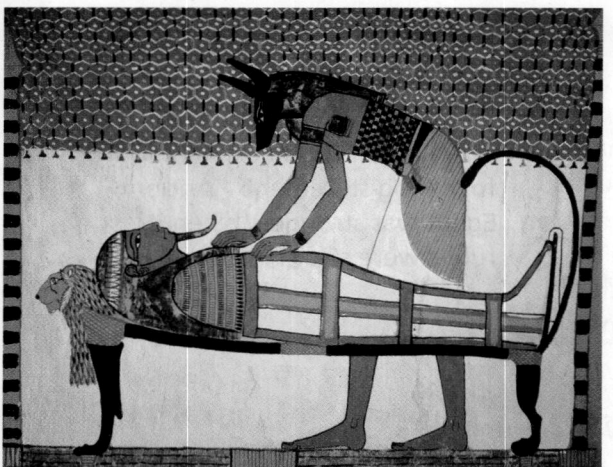

Anubis, god of the dead, tends a dead pharaoh. According to Egyptian myth, Anubis invented mummification.

As the royal family wept over the pharaoh's body, the priest chanted:

> **"You will live again. You will live forever. Behold, you will be young forever."**
>
> —*ancient Egyptian prayer*

One hundred days had passed since the pharaoh had died. During that time, the royal officials had been carefully preparing his body. Now, they wrapped the body in many strips of fine linen and placed it in a gold-covered coffin decorated to resemble the king in all of his royal glory.

The Egyptians believed in an **afterlife,** a life after death. They said prayers during the funeral, hoping to help the pharaoh's soul on its way to the afterlife. Then the nobles and royal family followed the body as it was carried to the royal tomb. Workers closed the tomb and the mourners went home. The pharaoh's journey to the afterlife had begun.

Egyptian Gods and Goddesses

Religion was an important part of daily life in ancient Egypt. The Egyptians believed that their gods and goddesses controlled the workings of nature. They built temples to honor their gods, and offered them food, gifts, and prayers.

Regional Differences   Early on, Egyptian towns had their own gods and goddesses with their own temples. These included gods who were often shown as humans with animal heads. All Egyptians also worshiped certain principal gods, such as the sun god, Re and the falcon god, Horus. Over time, however, all ancient Egyptians came to believe in several groups of gods.

Important Gods   The chief god of the ancient Egyptians was Amon-Re (ah mun RAY). He protected the rich and the poor alike. The Egyptians believed that Amon-Re was born each morning in the east with the sunrise. Each evening he died in the west with the setting sun. That is why the desert area to the west was believed to be the home of the dead.

Other powerful gods included Osiris (oh SY ris), the god of the living and the dead. The goddess Isis (EYE sis) was his wife. She was worshiped as the great mother who protected her children. The sky god, Horus, was their son.

✓ Reading Check   **Who was Osiris?**

Egyptian Gods and Goddesses
The ancient Egyptians believed that their gods controlled life, death, and all of nature.
❶ Horus, the sky god and the god of kingship
❷ Osiris, the god of the afterlife
❸ Isis, the goddess of women
❹ Thoth, the god of wisdom and of writing
❺ Amon-Re, the sun god and god of creation

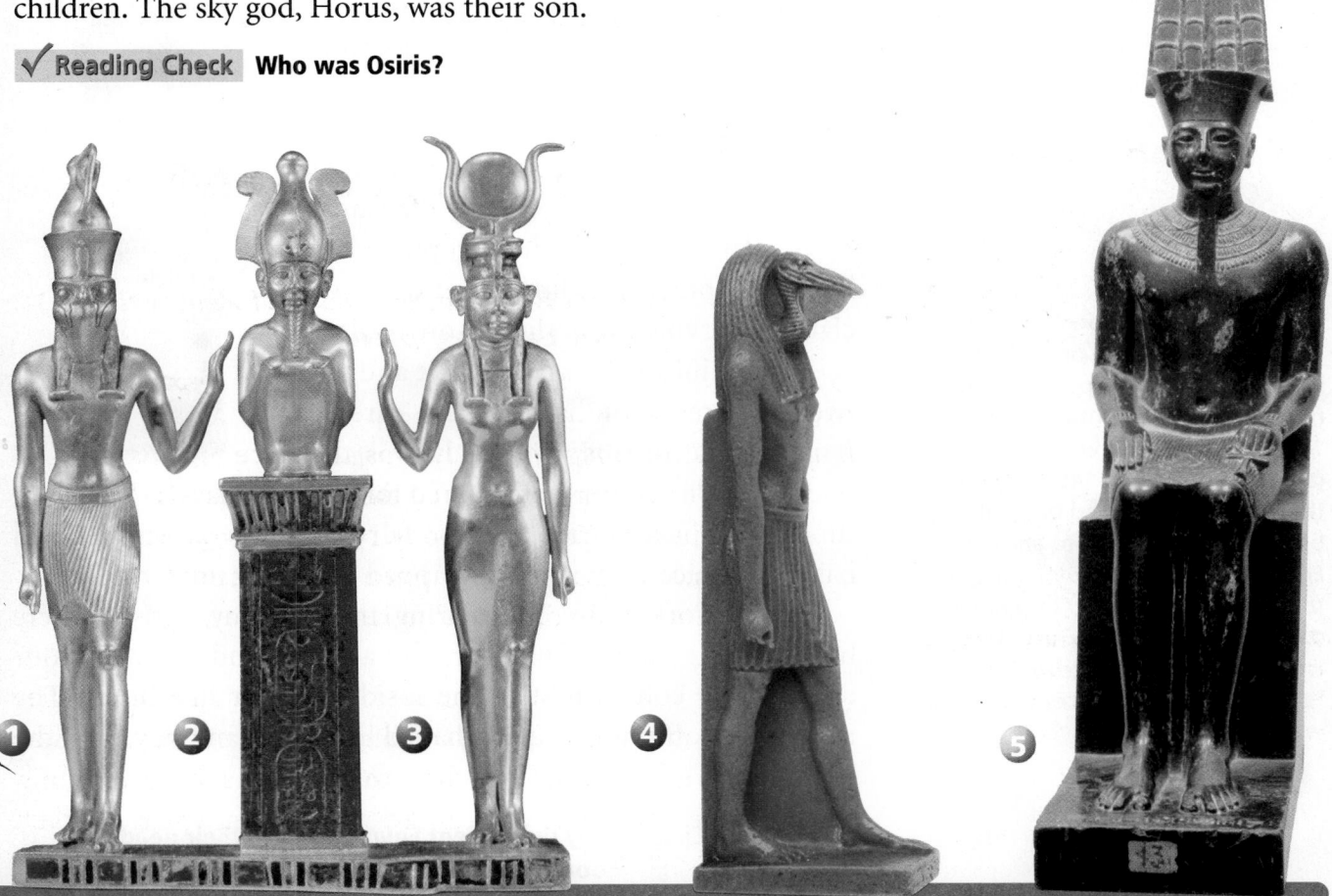

Links Across
The World

A King With One God
Amenhotep IV (ah mun HOH tep) became pharaoh in 1352 B.C. Five years later, he changed his name to Akhenaton (ah keh NAH tun) to show his devotion to the god, Aton, the life-giving disk of the sun. Like the Israelites, Akhenaton worshiped only one god. He ordered workers to remove the names of other Egyptian gods from temples. Most Egyptians rejected the practice of monotheism. After the king's death, they went back to worshiping many gods.

Belief in an Afterlife

Like the people of many civilizations, the ancient Egyptians believed in life after death. Evidence of this belief is often found in the art and artifacts they left behind.

Journey to the Afterlife The ancient Egyptians believed the spirits of the dead made their way to the afterlife in heavenly boats. If they had pleased the gods in this world, they joined Osiris and lived a life of ease and pleasure. They spent their days eating, drinking, and visiting with friends and family members who had died. Because the souls of the dead could not survive without food, clothing, and other items from this life, their possessions were buried with them.

During the Old Kingdom, the afterlife was thought to be only for kings and their associates. But beginning in the Middle Kingdom, people of all classes looked forward to an afterlife.

Preparing the Dead Before the building of pyramids, most Egyptians were buried in the desert in shallow pits. Egypt's climate dried out a person's remains, creating a **mummy,** the preserved body of a dead person. According to religious beliefs, the soul would leave the mummy, but return to it to receive food offerings. The preserved appearance of the body allowed it to be recognized by the person's spirit. By the time of the Fourth Dynasty, the Egyptians had begun to practice mummification, artificially preserving the bodies before burial.

Mummification was expensive and took two or three months. Workers carefully removed the organs. The body was then filled with a natural salt and stored for about 40 days. During that time, it completely dried out. Once dry, the body was cleaned and bathed in spices. It was then wrapped with long linen bandages.

While workers were preparing the mummy, artisans were busy carving the coffin. Pharaohs actually had three or four coffins. The coffins nested one inside another like boxes. The innermost coffin was usually shaped like a human body, with the dead person's face painted on the cover.

Burials, rich and poor
The decorative coffin on the right held the expensively preserved internal organs of King Tutankhamen. The reed coffin tied with rope (above), from about 1450 B.C., holds the naturally preserved body of a baby. **Infer** *According to ancient Egyptian religious beliefs, which of the two souls would enjoy a more comfortable afterlife? Explain.*

✓ Reading Check **Why did ancient Egyptians bury their dead with food and other possessions?**

The Great Pyramid

For more than 4,000 years, the Great Pyramid at Giza stood taller than any other human-made structure in the world. About 480 feet (147 meters) high, it still stands today. It has four triangle-shaped sides and a square base.

These stones spread the weight of the pyramid above, preventing the whole structure from collapsing.

Graffiti carved into these slabs records the names of the workers who built the chamber.

The pharaoh's outer coffin is larger than the entrance to the chamber, meaning that the pyramid was built around it.

Inside the Grand Gallery
In the 1800s, Napoleon Bonaparte of France ordered a study of the pyramids. His scientists made drawings as they passed through the Grand Gallery to the King's Chamber.

The King's Chamber lay at the center of the pyramid.

A temple held the pharaoh's body before burial.

Building the King's Chamber
The King's Chamber was hidden away at the heart of the Great Pyramid. The pharaoh's mummy was sealed into the chamber and lay undisturbed until grave robbers stole it.

The pharaoh's body was carried to the burial chamber through secret tunnels. Some tunnels were false, leading to dead ends.

Granite blocks sealed off the Grand Gallery route to the King's Chamber.

ANALYZING IMAGES
What did the builders of the Great Pyramid at Giza do to keep out grave robbers?

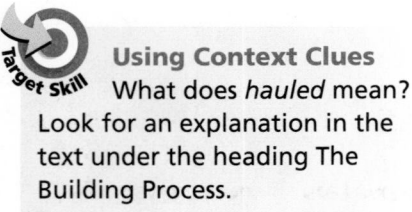

Go Online
PHSchool.com **Use Web Code mup-0819** for an interactivity on Egyptian pyramids.

Using Context Clues
What does *hauled* mean? Look for an explanation in the text under the heading The Building Process.

The Pharaohs' Tombs

The planning for a pharaoh's tomb began soon after he was crowned. The earliest royal tombs were made of mud brick. As time went on, however, tomb building became a complex art.

The Pyramids   The pharaohs of the Fourth Dynasty built the largest and most famous tombs. These were the **pyramids,** huge buildings with four sloping triangle-shaped sides. Most of the pyramids were built during the Old Kingdom. The largest is called the Great Pyramid, built for Khufu (KOO foo), the second king of the Fourth Dynasty. The Great Pyramid was built in the ancient city of **Giza.** Find Giza on the map at the beginning of this chapter.

The Building Process   Building the pyramids required a great deal of organization. The Great Pyramid is made up of more than 2 million stones. The average weight of each stone is 5,000 pounds (2,270 kilograms). Each stone had to be hauled up the side of the pyramid and put into its proper place.

The Great Sphinx is a portrait of King Kafre with the body of a lion. Kafre's pyramid is behind and to the right of the Sphinx.

A pyramid could take more than 20 years to build. The project began with the selection of a site on the west bank of the Nile. Remember that the west was thought to be the land of the dead. Once the site was chosen, workers cleared the ground. Engineers set the pyramid square so that the sides faced the main points of the compass—north, south, east, and west.

Workers then cut the building blocks. Stone for the inside of the pyramid came from nearby quarries. But fine stone for the outside came from farther away. Some stone came all the way from Nubia. It had to be loaded onto barges and carried to the building site either along the Nile or along canals near the Nile.

Teamwork To get the blocks of stone into place, workers used sleds, wooden rollers, and levers. They dragged and pushed the huge blocks up ramps of packed rubble to the level they were working on.

Building pyramids was dangerous work. Each year, men lost their lives, crushed by falling blocks. Some modern archaeologists believe that the pyramid workers were not slaves but rather peasants from throughout Egypt. The peasants were forced to work for a few months at a time under the supervision of skilled craftsmen.

Carpenters at work, from a painting in an official's tomb

 **Reading Check** **Why did the Egyptians build pyramids?**

Section 3 Assessment

Key Terms
Review the key terms at the beginning of this section. Use each term in a sentence that explains its meaning.

Target Reading Skill
Find the word *quarries* in the second paragraph of this page. What do you think it means?

Comprehension and Critical Thinking
1. (a) Identify What were the religious beliefs of the ancient Egyptians?

(b) Describe In what ways did the ancient Egyptians use religion to understand nature?

2. (a) Explain Why did the Egyptians mummify their dead?

(b) Analyze How do we know that the afterlife was important to the ancient Egyptians?

3. (a) Recall Why were the pharaohs concerned about the condition of their tombs?

(b) Sequence Describe how the ancient Egyptians organized the building of the pyramids.

Writing Activity
Suppose the pharaoh invites you to go with him to inspect his pyramid as it is being built. Write a journal entry describing what you see on your visit.

Go Online PHSchool.com

For: An activity on the religion of the ancient Egyptians
Visit: PHSchool.com
Web Code: lbd-2303

The Pyramid Builders

In the shadow of the three pyramids at Giza, archaeologists are uncovering a lost city. It is the workers' city, a sprawling site on which as many as 20,000 men and women lived and worked about 4,500 years ago. The workers came from all over Egypt. They included pyramid builders and their bosses, administrators, priests, cooks, doctors, metalworkers, masons, weavers, and gravediggers. Laborers could be forced to work, but some probably volunteered to build the sacred tombs.

Preheating
Pot tops warm up over an open fire.

Baking
Pots filled with dough are set in hot ashes and topped with the preheated pots.

Copper Smelting
This carving shows workers blowing on flames to smelt copper, a process in which heat was used to remove impurities from the metal. Copper tools like the one shown at the top of this page were pounded into wedges to split rock.

An Ancient Bakery Without bread to feed the workers, the pyramids could not have been built. In the workers' city, bakers ground barley and wheat into flour for the bread dough. Wild airborne yeast helped the dough to rise. (The Egyptians, however, believed it rose by the power of the gods.) Workers set covered pots of dough onto a bed of hot ashes for baking. The finished loaves were heavy and filling—enough to feed a hungry pyramid builder.

The workers' site also included buildings for preparing meat and fish, to complete the workers' diet. There was one drawback to the bread-making process. Tiny pieces of the grain-grinding stones often wound up in the loaves, creating life-threatening dental diseases for the Egyptians.

Cooling Bread
After the bread bakes, it cools.

Making Bread Dough
Flour and water are mixed in a large terra-cotta vat.

Egyptian Medicine
In the workers' city, doctors set bones and treated a variety of ailments. Egyptians believed the household god Bes, whose statue is shown at the left, could protect them from danger.

Assessment

Identify Who were the people who lived in the lost city near the pyramids at Giza?

Infer Why was a city of workers needed to build the pyramids?

Section 4

Ancient Egyptian Culture

Prepare to Read

Objectives

In this section you will

1. Find out about the everyday life of the ancient Egyptians.
2. Learn about writing in ancient Egypt.
3. Discover advances made by the Egyptians in science and medicine.

Taking Notes

As you read, look for details about ancient Egyptian culture. Copy the flowchart below and record your findings in it.

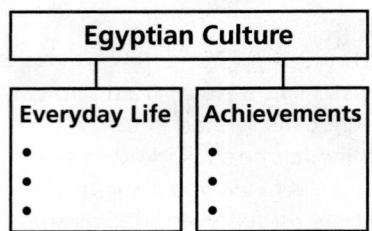

Target Reading Skill

Use Context Clues Cause-and-effect clues can help you understand the meaning of an unfamiliar word. In the following sentence, a cause-and-effect clue points to the meaning of *scattered:* When the farmer scattered the seeds, he caused them to fly and land in many directions. What do you think *scattered* means?

Key Terms

- **hieroglyphs** (HY ur oh glifs) *n.* pictures and other written symbols that stand for ideas, things, or sounds
- **papyrus** (puh PY rus) *n.* an early form of paper made from a reed plant found in the marshy areas of the Nile delta; the plant used to make this paper
- **astronomer** (uh STRAHN uh mur) *n.* a scientist who studies the stars and other objects in the sky

A high official of ancient Egypt and his wife

Uni was a high-ranking Egyptian of the Old Kingdom. His life story—a success story—is recorded in his tomb.

Uni began his career in a simple way—running a storehouse. Later, he was promoted to groundskeeper of the royal pyramid. In his job, he oversaw the delivery of stone from the quarry, the site where stone was cut, to the pyramid. Uni must have worked hard, because later he was made a general. Then, he became Governor of Upper Egypt, in charge of goods and taxes for half the kingdom. By the time of his death, Uni had become royal tutor at the palace and an honored companion of the pharaoh. Uni and many other people like him were part of everyday life in ancient Egypt.

The Lives of the Egyptians

Most of what we know about the everyday life of the Egyptians is based on paintings that cover the walls of tombs and temples. Written records also tell us much about their lives.

Social Classes Historians often turn to Egyptian art to learn about the social classes of ancient Egypt. Egyptian paintings and carvings show royalty and ordinary people involved in all aspects of life. Like Uni, most Egyptians were busy and hard-working people. They also had a sense of fun and a love of beauty.

Egyptian society itself resembled a pyramid. At the very top stood the pharaoh. Beneath him was a small upper class. This group included priests, members of the pharaoh's court, and nobles who held the largest estates. The next level was the middle class, made up of merchants and skilled workers. At the base of the pyramid was by far the largest class, the peasants. Mostly, the peasants did farm labor. But they also did other kinds of labor, such as building roads and temples. A person could rise to a higher class. Generally, the way to rise was through service to the pharaoh, as Uni did.

Slavery Prisoners captured in wars were made slaves. Slaves formed a separate class, which was never very large. Egyptian society was flexible, however. Even slaves had rights. They could own personal items and inherit land from their masters. They could also be set free.

Citizen Heroes

Nekhebu, Royal Architect
A man named Nekhebu worked his way up from the bottom of society to become an architect during the Old Kingdom. At first, he carried other builders' tools for them. Eventually, his hard work paid off. The pharaoh made him Royal Architect. Nekhebu believed in always doing the best possible work, and in "never going to bed angry against anybody."

Working in Egypt
Models showing scenes from everyday life were often placed in tombs. This wood model shows workers in a bakery. **Infer** *Why do you think such scenes are useful to archaeologists?*

Lives of the Peasants Although peasants could own land, most worked the land of wealthier people. During the flood season, the peasants worked on roads, temples, and other buildings. As soon as the waters left the land, they had to plant the fields. The work had to be done quickly while the soil was still moist. One farmer plowed the black earth with a team of oxen while another followed behind, scattering the seeds.

The harvest was the busiest season for Egypt's peasants. All men, women, and older children went into the fields to gather the crops of wheat or barley. Work went on from sunrise to sunset. Once the crops were gathered, the villagers feasted. They offered food and drink to the gods in thanks for their help.

Women of Egypt Egyptian women were looked upon as living models of Isis, the wife of the god Osiris. They had most of the rights that men had. They could own property, run businesses, and enter into legal contracts. For the most part, women traveled about freely. Egyptian paintings often show them supervising farm work or hunting. And women performed many roles—from priestess to dancer.

Noble women held a special position in Egyptian society. Sometimes they were in charge of temples and religious rites. They could also use their position to influence the pharaoh. Some women acted as regents until the pharaoh was old enough to rule on his own.

 **Reading Check** How was Egyptian society organized?

Women's Lives
The women shown above are wearing scented wax cones on their heads. The wax melted in the heat, surrounding the women with perfume. At the right, a woman works in a field with her husband. **Conclude** *Which social classes do you think the women in the paintings belonged to? Explain your answer.*

A		P	
AH		F	
AY		M	or
EE		N	
U		L	
B		H	
H		Q	
S		K	
SH		T	

Writing in Ancient Egypt

The records and writings left by the ancient Egyptians allow us to learn more about their culture. From these records, we know that they possessed an amazing amount of knowledge.

A New System of Writing In ancient Egypt, as in Mesopotamia, ideas were written down in picturelike symbols called **hieroglyphs** (HY ur oh glifs). In this script, some pictures stand for ideas or things. For example, a picture of two legs means "go." Other pictures stand for sounds. For example, a drawing of an owl stands for the "m" sound.

The Egyptians began to use hieroglyphs because they needed a way to keep track of the kingdom's growing wealth. As the Egyptian empire grew, it became necessary to create more pictures for more complicated ideas.

Writing Materials At first, the Egyptians wrote on clay and stone, as the Sumerians did. But they needed a more convenient writing surface. They found it in **papyrus** (puh py ruhs), an early form of paper made from a reed found in the marshy areas of the Nile delta. The plant used to make this paper is also called papyrus. To make the paper, the inner stalks of the plant were cut into narrow strips. The strips were cut to the same length and placed side by side by side in one layer. Another layer of strips was placed crosswise on top to form a sheet. Papyrus makers wet the sheet, pressed it flat, and dried it in the sun. Sap from the plant glued the strips together. Pasted side by side, the sheets formed a long strip that could be rolled up.

■ Chart Skills

The text of the *Book of the Dead* (top left) was meant to guide the dead on their journey to the afterlife. The book's hieroglyphs are written on papyrus. The table (above) shows some hieroglyphs and the sounds they stood for. **Identify** What is the hieroglyph for the "p" sound? **Analyze Images** What are some English words you could spell using the hieroglyphs in the chart?

Use Context Clues
What does *sap* mean? Look for cause-and-effect clues in the text. Sap from the plant glues the strips of papyrus together. What does that tell you about sap?

Unlocking a Mystery The meaning of ancient Egypt's hieroglyphic writing was lost after the A.D. 400s. Scholars could not read the mysterious pictures. It wasn't until about 200 years ago, in 1799, that an important find took place. A soldier digging a fort near the Nile found a large black stone with three different types of writing on it. The upper part showed hieroglyphs, the middle part showed a later Egyptian script called demotic, and the lower part showed Greek letters. The stone was named the Rosetta Stone because it was found near Rosetta, a city in the Nile delta near the Mediterranean Sea.

The three texts on the stone held the same meaning. Therefore, many scholars tried to use the Greek letters on the Rosetta Stone to figure out the meaning of the hieroglyphs. But it was not an easy task. Then, in the 1820s, a young French scholar named Jean François Champollion (zhahn frahn SWAH shahm poh LYOHN) finally figured it out. When Champollion published his results, a new window onto the world of ancient Egypt opened.

✓ **Reading Check** What was the significance of the Rosetta Stone?

Clues to the Past
The circled hieroglyphs on the Rosetta Stone (above left) spell the name of King Ptolemy V. Jean François Champollion (above right) realized that hieroglyphs stood for sounds in the Egyptian language and was able to decipher the hieroglyphs used to spell Ptolemy's name.
Generalize *Why was the translation of hieroglyphs an important discovery in the study of Egyptian history?*

Science and Medicine

In addition to their developments in writing, the ancient Egyptians made important advances in such fields as astronomy and medicine. Among the people of the ancient world, Egypt was known as a land of great learning.

Keeping Track of Time Because they were an agricultural people, the Egyptians needed to be able to predict when the Nile would flood. Astronomers noticed that the Nile appeared to rise rapidly about the same time that they could see Sirius (SIHR ee us), the Dog Star, in the sky shortly before sunrise. **Astronomers are** scientists who study the stars and other objects in the sky. They worked out the average time between the appearances of the star. They found that it came to about 365 days. This became the length of their year.

Mathematics The Egyptians used basic mathematics in finding solutions to problems they faced every day. We know they could add, subtract, multiply, and divide. We also know they used simple fractions. Mathematics helped Egyptians measure stone so that it could be cut to the proper size to build pyramids. They used geometry to measure area so that they could figure out the amount of taxes for a plot of land.

Medicine Religion and medicine were closely related in ancient Egypt. Doctors were specially trained priests who used religious practices and their knowledge of illnesses to try to heal the sick. Probably because of their work on mummies, the ancient Egyptians knew a great deal about the body. By studying the body, they learned to perform surgery. They could set broken bones and treat many minor injuries.

The Egyptians also understood herbalism, the practice of creating medicines from plants. They used these natural remedies to help ease everyday illnesses such as stomachaches and headaches. Mothers prepared their own home remedies, or cures, to reduce children's fevers. The Egyptians wrote much of their medical knowledge down on papyrus. Centuries later, the ancient Greeks and Romans used these records.

✔ **Reading Check** **Why was it important for the Egyptians to figure out the length of their year?**

Section 4 Assessment

Key Terms
Review the key terms at the beginning of this section. Use each term in a sentence that explains its meaning.

Target Reading Skill
Find the word *remedies* in the last paragraph in this section. Use cause-and-effect clues to figure out its meaning.

Comprehension and Critical Thinking
1. (a) Describe How were the lives of Egypt's peasants ruled by the seasons?

(b) Draw Conclusions How did the seasons affect all of Egyptian society?

2. (a) Recall Describe how the Egyptians used hieroglyphs to communicate.

(b) Analyze Information What was the importance of writing in Egyptian society?

3. (a) List What areas of science and medicine did the ancient Egyptians study?

(b) Link Past and Present How did the learning achievements of the Egyptians affect later civilizations?

Writing Activity
Suppose you are an Egyptian scribe. Write a description that shows how you use your skill in the service of the pharaoh. Then, use the table of hieroglyphs in this section to create a word.

Writing Tip Scribes kept records and accounts for the pharaohs. They also wrote prayers on the wall paintings of tombs. Think about some other work a scribe might perform for a pharaoh. Then write your description from the scribe's point of view.

Skills for Life

Using Route Maps

The leader of the caravan turned and saw the storm approaching in the distance. Then he looked ahead, straining to see some glimpse of Assur. The caravan had been traveling for many days, carrying goods from Giza. Although his men were tired, the leader signaled for them to move faster. He wanted to reach the city before the storm came.

For years, the caravan leader had brought goods from Lower Egypt to Syria and Sumer. This particular road, however, was new to him. He hoped that they would reach Assur soon.

A silver jug from ancient Egypt

The leader of the caravan might have found a route map useful. Although maps did exist in ancient times, most people's knowledge of roads was passed along by word of mouth. Today, most road travel is fairly easy. You just need to know how to read a route map.

Learn the Skill

Use the following steps to read a route map.

1 **Read the title of the map, and become familiar with the map's features.** What is the purpose of the map? What type of map is it—physical or political, modern or historical, or a standard road map?

A camel caravan in the Sahara

2 **Study the key to understand its symbols.** Colors are generally used on route maps to show different routes or different types of roads.

3 **Trace routes on the map.** Using the scale of miles, you can calculate distances. A physical map will show the geographic features of a route.

4 **Interpret the map.** Draw conclusions about which routes would be fastest, safest, most scenic, or the easiest to follow.

Practice the Skill

Use the steps on page 94 and the map at the right to gather and interpret information about ancient trade routes.

1 Write down the purpose of the map. What does the map show?

2 Look at the key to see information about Egyptian trade routes. Identify the purple region on the map. Find routes that travel over land and water. Identify the landmarks indicated in the map key.

3 Using the compass rose, note the general direction of the trade routes. Identify the geographic features of the routes. Look for geographic features that the routes seem to avoid.

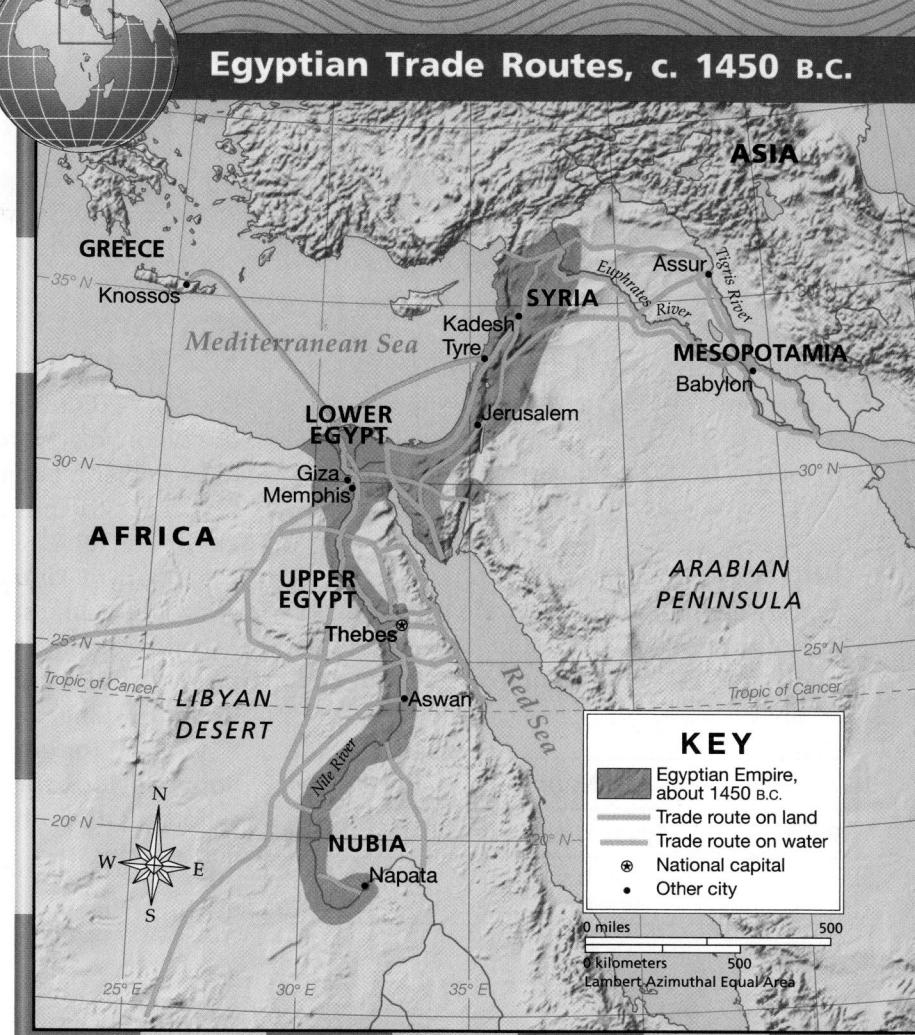

Egyptian Trade Routes, c. 1450 B.C.

KEY

Egyptian Empire, about 1450 B.C.
Trade route on land
Trade route on water
⊗ National capital
• Other city

4 Write a paragraph that draws conclusions about Egyptian trade routes. Answering these questions might help you: Why did most of the trade routes run through the purple area? How did geography influence the paths that traders took? Why does the map show no direct road connecting the major Egyptian cities of Thebes and Giza?

Apply the Skill

Draw a map showing the route you take from your home to your school. Add a scale and a compass rose. Mark the location of your school and your home with symbols. Explain the symbols in a map key.

When you are finished, exchange maps with a classmate. Identify the symbols used in the map key. Determine the distance from your classmate's home to school.

Prepare to Read

Objectives

In this section you will
1. Examine the relationship between Nubia and Egypt.
2. Learn about the Nubian kingdoms centered in Kerma, Napata, and Meroë.

Taking Notes

As you read, find details on the resources and culture of ancient Nubia. Copy the table below, and fill in the columns to record your findings.

Nubia			
Relations With Egypt	Kerma	Napata	Meroë
• •	• •	• •	• •

Target Reading Skill

Use Context Clues You can use synonyms, words that have similar meanings, to figure out the meaning of an unfamiliar word. Find the synonym for *ultimate* in the following sentence: Taharka received the *ultimate* prize, the greatest honor possible. *Greatest* is a synonym for *ultimate*. As you read, look for synonyms and other context clues.

Key Terms

- **ore** (awr) *n.* a mineral or a combination of minerals mined for the production of metals
- **Lower Nubia** (LOH ur NOO bee uh) *n.* the region of ancient Nubia between the first and second Nile cataracts
- **Upper Nubia** (UP ur NOO bee uh) *n.* the region of ancient Nubia between the second and sixth Nile cataracts
- **artisan** (AHR tuh zun) *n.* a worker who is skilled in crafting goods by hand

This Egyptian bronze statue shows Pharaoh Taharka making an offering to the falcon god.

Prince Taharka of Nubia loved a good contest. He once held a 5-hour, 30-mile race across the desert. The athletes, Taharka's soldiers, ran at night to avoid the blazing heat. In the end, he gave prizes to the winners and losers alike.

In 690 B.C., Taharka himself would receive the ultimate prize: He was to be crowned king of both Nubia and Egypt. He would become the greatest ruler of his dynasty. Taharka's mother traveled 1,200 miles from Nubia north to Memphis to see her son made king. Their homeland of Nubia gave birth to some of the world's oldest cultures.

Nubia and Egypt

Archaeologists have found pottery, weapons, and jewelry at Nubian burial sites. Some of these items date to about 6000 B.C. Findings also show that trade existed among these early peoples. From about 3100 B.C., many Nubian kingdoms arose, only to die out as their rulers lost power.

Land of the Bow Recall that the region of Nubia was located south of ancient Egypt, beyond the first cataract of the Nile River. For most of their long history, Nubia and Egypt were peaceful, friendly neighbors. The Egyptians called Nubia Ta Sety (tah SEHT ee), the "land of the bow." They were probably referring to the Nubians' skill as archers. The Nubian archers were so skilled that Egypt hired many of them for its armies.

Valuable Resources Egypt valued Nubia for its rich mineral resources, such as gold, copper, and iron ore. An **ore** is a mineral or a combination of minerals mined for the production of metals. Because of its location, Nubia became a bridge for goods traveling between central Africa and Egypt. Early in its history, Egypt benefited from goods that came from **Lower Nubia,** the region between the first and second Nile cataracts. Later, powerful kingdoms began to rise to the south, in **Upper Nubia,** the region between the second and sixth Nile cataracts. These kingdoms rivaled Egypt for control of land. The most powerful of these kingdoms were in the cities of Kerma (KUR muh), Napata (nuh PAY tuh), and Meroë (MEHR oh ee). Find these cities on the map on page 98. These kingdoms were ruled by Kushites, people who lived in southern Nubia.

✓ **Reading Check** Why did Nubia and Egypt become rivals?

Links to
Science

Nubia and Egypt A recent discovery of a Nubian incense burner has some scientists thinking about Nubia's early relationship with Egypt. Some scientists think the object was made around 3100 B.C., or even earlier. Carved on its side are a seated king and other figures that later became the symbols of Egyptian pharaohs. Scholars are debating whether Nubia or Egypt had the first kings.

Nubian Archers
A model shows an army of Nubian archers. The Egyptians admired the Nubians' skill in archery. **Conclude** *Why was Nubia called the "land of the bow"?*

Human-Environment Interaction The natural resources of Nubia formed the basis of its wealth.

Locate Which metal was found between the second and third cataracts of the Nile River?

Identify Effects How did Nubia's metal resources affect its relationship with Egypt?

Go Online
PHSchool.com Use Web Code **lbp-2335** for step-by-step map skills practice.

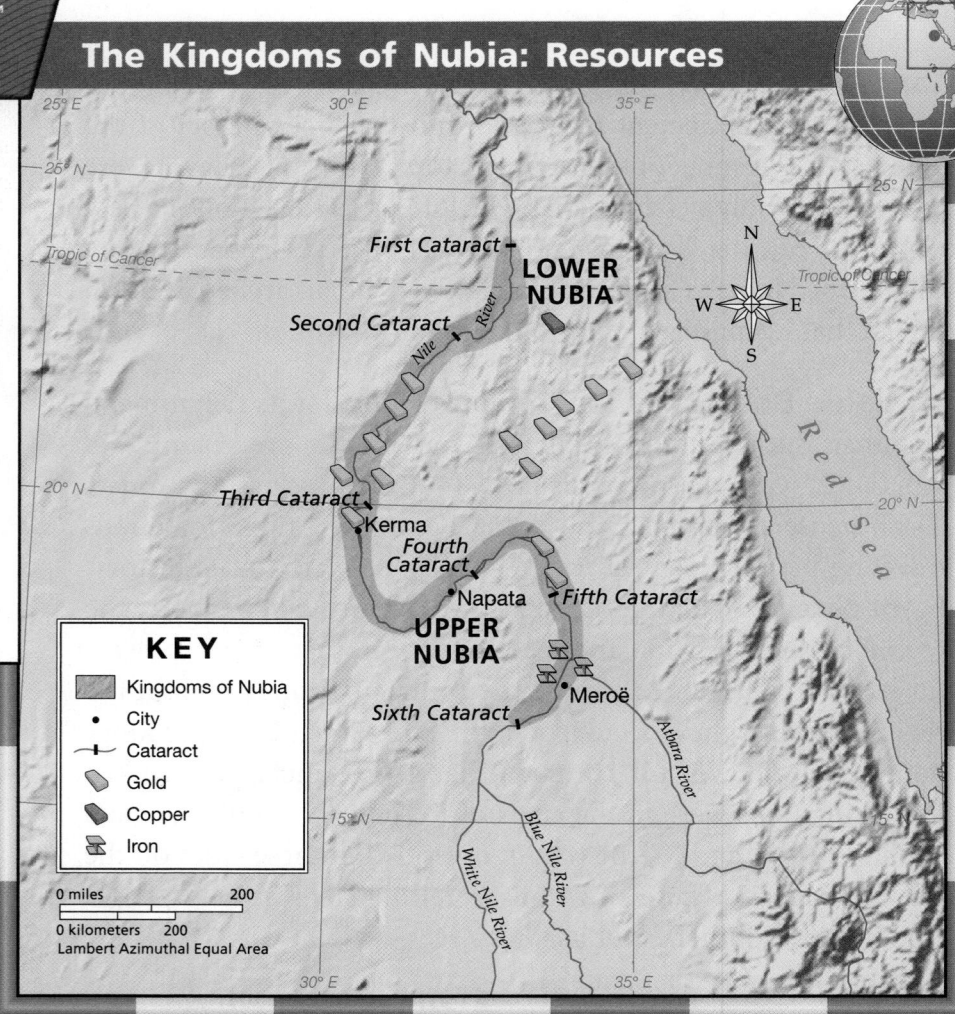

KEY

▨	Kingdoms of Nubia
•	City
┼	Cataract
▨	Gold
▨	Copper
▨	Iron

0 miles 200
0 kilometers 200
Lambert Azimuthal Equal Area

The Kerma Culture

The Kushites came to power at a time when Egypt was weakening. By about 1600 B.C., the Kushite kingdom had expanded from the city of Kerma into parts of southern Egypt. These Nubians are known as the Kerma culture. Their kingdom lasted from about 2000 to 1500 B.C.

Kerma's Wealth Kerma had gained not only power but wealth, mainly from controlling the trade between Central Africa and Egypt. It was noted for its **artisans,** or workers skilled at crafting items by hand. They made highly prized, delicate pottery. Items made by Kerma artisans have been found in the tombs of pharaohs.

Like the Egyptians, the people of Kerma devoted a great deal of energy and resources to royal burials. They buried their kings in mounds of earth as large as football fields. Inside their tombs, the kings' bodies rested on top of gold-covered beds surrounded by jewelry, gold, and ivory.

A Kerma pottery bowl

Conflict With Egypt Around the 1500s B.C., Egypt began to recover its strength and to reclaim control of the area. Pharaoh Thutmose I sent his armies into Nubia. After a war that lasted about 50 years, the Egyptians took control of Nubia as far south as the fourth cataract. Egypt ruled Nubia for about the next 700 years.

During this period, the Nubians adopted many Egyptian ways. They even began to worship Egyptian gods along with their own. Throughout these times of conflict and peace, people and goods continued to pass between Nubia and Egypt. The two cultures became mixed.

Use Context Clues Do you know what *recover* means? Find a synonym for *recover* later in the same sentence. What does it mean?

✓ **Reading Check** **What were some characteristics of Kerma?**

Napata and Meroë

South of Kerma lay the Nubian cities of Napata and Meroë, in the ancient land called Kush. After centuries of Egyptian rule, the Kushites rose again to power. Their kingdom was centered in the Nubian city of Napata and then later in Meroë.

The Capital of Napata In the late 700s B.C., Egypt was once again weak and divided. From their capital in Napata, the Kushites expanded their power into Egypt.

The Napatan kings gradually took control of more of Egypt. They moved their capital city first to Thebes and then to Memphis. By the time of Taharka, whose coronation you read about earlier, the Nubians controlled all of Egypt. The pharaohs of Egypt's Twenty-fifth Dynasty were Nubians.

The Napatan kings admired Egyptian culture. They brought back many old Egyptian ways and preserved them. They even began building pyramids in which to bury their kings. The ruins of these small Nubian pyramids can still be seen today.

The rule of the Napatan kings did not last very long. About 660 B.C., they were forced back into Nubia. They retreated to Napata and then gradually moved their capital south to Meroë. The Nubians never again controlled Egyptian land.

Monuments of Napata
The pyramids of Napata (top) and a ram statue (bottom) from the entrance to the Great Amum Temple at Napata reflect the ties between Nubian culture and Egyptian culture. **Contrast** *How do the Nubian pyramids differ from the Egyptian pyramids shown in the photo on page 84?*

Links to
Government

The Women of Nubia
Women held very high status in Nubian society. Most often, the children of the ruler's sister would be next in line for the throne. Compared to Egypt, Nubia had many more women as rulers. In ancient artwork, the queens of Meroë have large and powerful figures. The queens were considered ideal beauties, and their weight reflected their wealth and rank.

The Capital of Meroë After moving south of Egypt's reach, the Nubians founded a royal court in the ancient city of Meroë. This city was located on the Nile between the fifth and sixth cataracts. It became the center of an empire that included much of Nubia. It also stretched south into central Africa.

The rocky desert east of Meroë held large deposits of iron ore. The Nubians used the ore to make iron weapons and tools. Iron plows allowed them to produce generous supplies of food. Iron weapons allowed them to control trade routes that ran all the way to the Red Sea. There they traded goods from central Africa for articles from India, the Arabian Peninsula, and Rome. Meroë grew rich from this trade.

Today, Meroë remains largely a mystery. The Nubians of Meroë created their own system of hieroglyphic writing. Scholars have so far been unable to fully understand these hieroglyphics, which are found on the temples and tombs of the kingdom.

Meroë began to weaken in the A.D. 200s, and it fell to the African kingdom of Axum in the next century. Features of Nubian culture, however, have lasted for 3,500 years. To this day, Nubian styles of pottery, furniture, jewelry, braided hairstyles, and clothing survive among people of the modern-day African country of Sudan.

✓ **Reading Check** **How did the people of Meroë use iron ore?**

Section 5 Assessment

Key Terms
Review the key terms at the beginning of this section. Use each term in a sentence that explains its meaning.

Target Reading Skill
Find *articles* in the second paragraph on this page. If it is used in an unfamiliar way, find a synonym to understand its meaning.

Comprehension and Critical Thinking
1. (a) Explain What was the relationship between Egypt and Nubia?

(b) Apply Information How did the Nubians and the Egyptians borrow from each other's cultures?
2. (a) Recall What were the resources of Kerma?
(b) Identify the Main Idea What part did Kerma's wealth play in its conflict with Egypt?
3. (a) Explain How are the histories of Napata and Meroë tied to Egypt?
(b) Link Past and Present What signs of Nubian culture exist in Africa today? Do you think present-day Africans are likely to be interested in Nubian culture? Explain why or why not.

Writing Activity
List the names of the three major Nubian cities you learned about in this section. Write a brief description of each of the cities, and include its importance in the history of Nubia.

Writing Tip Before you begin, reread Section 5. As you read, look for important details about each city of Nubia. Your list should include the most important and most interesting details. Refer to the list when you write your description.

Review and Assessment

Hunting in ancient Egypt

◆ Chapter Summary

Section 1: The Geography of the Nile

- Beginning from two sources, the Nile flows northward in a varied course until it reaches the Mediterranean Sea.
- The Nile provided the ancient Egyptian and Nubian peoples with water, food, and fertile soil.
- The Nile River and its valley were central trade routes for the ancient Egyptians and Nubians.

Section 2: The Rulers of Egypt

- Egyptian kings had absolute power and were thought to be gods.
- Ancient Egypt prospered during three major time periods, the Old Kingdom, the Middle Kingdom, and the New Kingdom.
- After Hatshepsut died, Thutmose III rose to power and became one of the greatest pharaohs of the New Kingdom.

Section 3: Egyptian Religion

- Egyptians were deeply religious and believed in several gods and goddesses.
- Egyptians believed in life after death and carefully prepared their dead for the afterlife.
- Pharaohs began the long, difficult process of building their tombs as soon as they came into power.

Section 4: Ancient Egyptian Culture

- The Egyptian social order resembled a pyramid, with the pharaoh at the top, and the largest class, the peasants, at the base.
- The ancient Egyptians used a pictorial writing system similar to that used in Mesopotamian civilization.
- Egyptians also studied the stars and practiced medicine.

Section 5: The Cultures of Nubia

- Throughout its history, Nubia was both a friend and a rival of Egypt.
- The Nubian kingdom of Kerma was known for its skilled artisans.
- The people of Meroë were the first Africans to work with iron.

Nubian Pharaoh and falcon god

◆ Key Terms

Match the definitions in Column I with the key terms in Column II.

Column I

1. a strong rush of water
2. a skilled worker
3. a series of rulers from the same family
4. a picturelike symbol
5. a building with four triangle-shaped sides
6. minerals mined for the production of metal
7. fertile soil deposited by flooding rivers

Column II

A ore

B dynasty

C pyramid

D artisan

E hieroglyph

F cataract

G silt

◆ Comprehension and Critical Thinking

8. **Recall** Describe the geography of the Nile River and the lands that surround it.
   (a) Explain Why did the people of Egypt and Nubia consider their deserts to be a blessing?
   (b) Identify Effects In what ways did the Nile river affect ancient civilizations?

9. **List** Name and describe the three major periods in ancient Egyptian history.
   (a) Describe What was the role of the pharaoh in Egyptian government and society?
   (b) Compare and Contrast Compare the pharaohs' rule of Egypt with Hammurabi's rule of Babylonia. How are the rulers similar or different?

10. **(a) Identify** What was the purpose of the pyramids in ancient Egypt?
    (b) Generalize Why was religion so important to the people of ancient Egypt?
    (c) Analyze Why did the idea of the afterlife appeal to the ancient Egyptians?

11. **(a) Recall** List the accomplishments of the ancient Egyptians.
    (b) Conclude Choose one accomplishment of the ancient Egyptian civilization and describe its importance.

12. **(a) Explain** Why was it in the interests of Egypt and Nubia to maintain friendly relations?
    (b) Compare and Contrast Compare the length of time Egypt's and Nubia's civilizations lasted with that of the Assyrians and the Babylonians. How do you account for the differences?

◆ Skills Practice

Using Route Maps In the Skills for Life lesson in this chapter, you learned how to analyze and interpret route maps. You also learned how to create your own route map.

Review the steps for this skill. Using your route map, complete the following: (a) Add another route between your home and your school. It could be a shortcut, or a longer route. (b) Explain the advantages and disadvantages of your alternate route.

◆ Writing Activity: Language Arts

Think about the Nile River and how important it was to the ancient Egyptians and Nubians. Then write a poem about the Nile, from the point of view of an ancient Egyptian or Nubian.

The poem can be in any form, rhyming or unrhyming. Be sure to include details that show the importance of the river. Reread Section 1 to refresh your memory on the geography of the Nile.

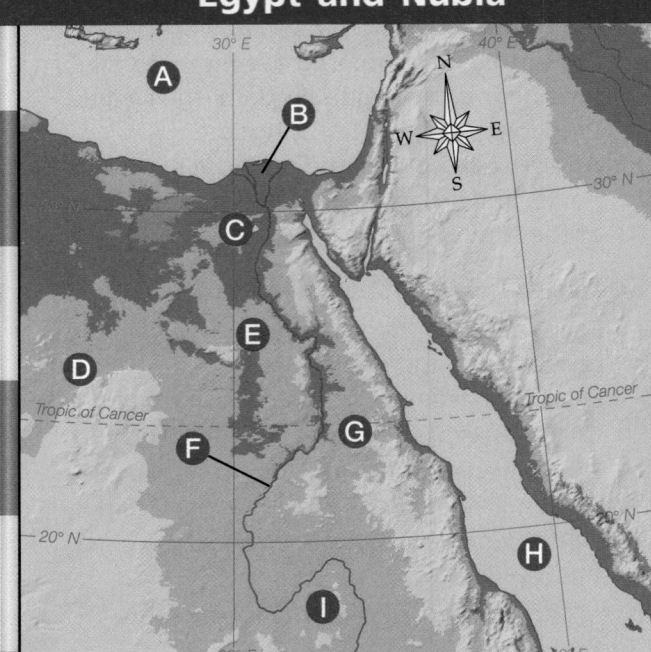

MAP✶MASTER™ Skills Activity

Egypt and Nubia

Place Location For each place listed below, write the letter from the map that shows its location.

1. Nile River
2. Mediterranean Sea
3. Red Sea
4. Upper Nubia
5. Lower Nubia
6. Sahara
7. Upper Egypt
8. Lower Egypt

Go Online
PHSchool.com Use Web Code **lbp-2345** for an **interactive map.**

Standardized Test Prep

Test-Taking Tips

Some questions on standardized tests ask you to draw conclusions by analyzing a table. Study the table below. Then follow the tips to answer the sample question.

BUILDING THE GREAT PYRAMID

Number of blocks	2 million
Weight of each block	5,000 pounds
Height of pyramid	450 feet
Time to build	about 20 years

Pick the letter that best completes the statement.

The information in the table could be used to show the

   A importance of the Nile River in Egypt.

   B division of Egyptian society into classes.

   C cruelty of the Egyptian pharaohs.

   D organization and skills of the Egyptians.

Think It Through All of the information in the table has to do with the construction of the pyramids. You can rule out answer A, because it has to do with the river. You can eliminate C, because it has to do with the characteristics of the pharaohs. Of B and D, which answer has the most to do with the construction of the pyramids? The answer is D. It states correctly that the pyramids show the organization and skill of the Egyptians.

TIP Preview the question first and think about it as you study the table.

TIP Eliminate answer choices that don't make sense. Then decide which remaining choice is BEST.

Practice Questions

Use the tips above and other tips in this book to help you answer the following questions.

1. Why did the Nubians develop trade routes over land?

   A Cataracts on the Nile River limited travel.

   B The Egyptians tended to attack by boat.

   C Nubians had no ship-building skills.

   D Travel in the desert was easy.

Study the table below, and then answer the question that follows.

Ancient Civilizations

Location	Time Span
Ancient Mesopotamia	About 3500 – 539 B.C.
Ancient Egypt	About 3100 – 31 B.C.
Ancient Nubia	About 3100 B.C. – A.D. 350

2. Which sentence accurately describes the information in the table?

   A All ancient civilizations ended before A.D. 1.

   B The civilizations of Mesopotamia began after those of Egypt and Nubia.

   C The civilizations of ancient Egypt and Nubia both lasted about 1,000 years.

   D Several ancient civilizations lasted thousands of years.

3. Egyptian society was pyramid-shaped, with

   A the pharaoh at the top and peasants at the bottom.

   B the pharaoh at the top and priests at the bottom.

   C priests at the top and no peasants.

   D priests and peasants at the top.

Use Web Code lba-2305 for **Chapter 3** self-test.

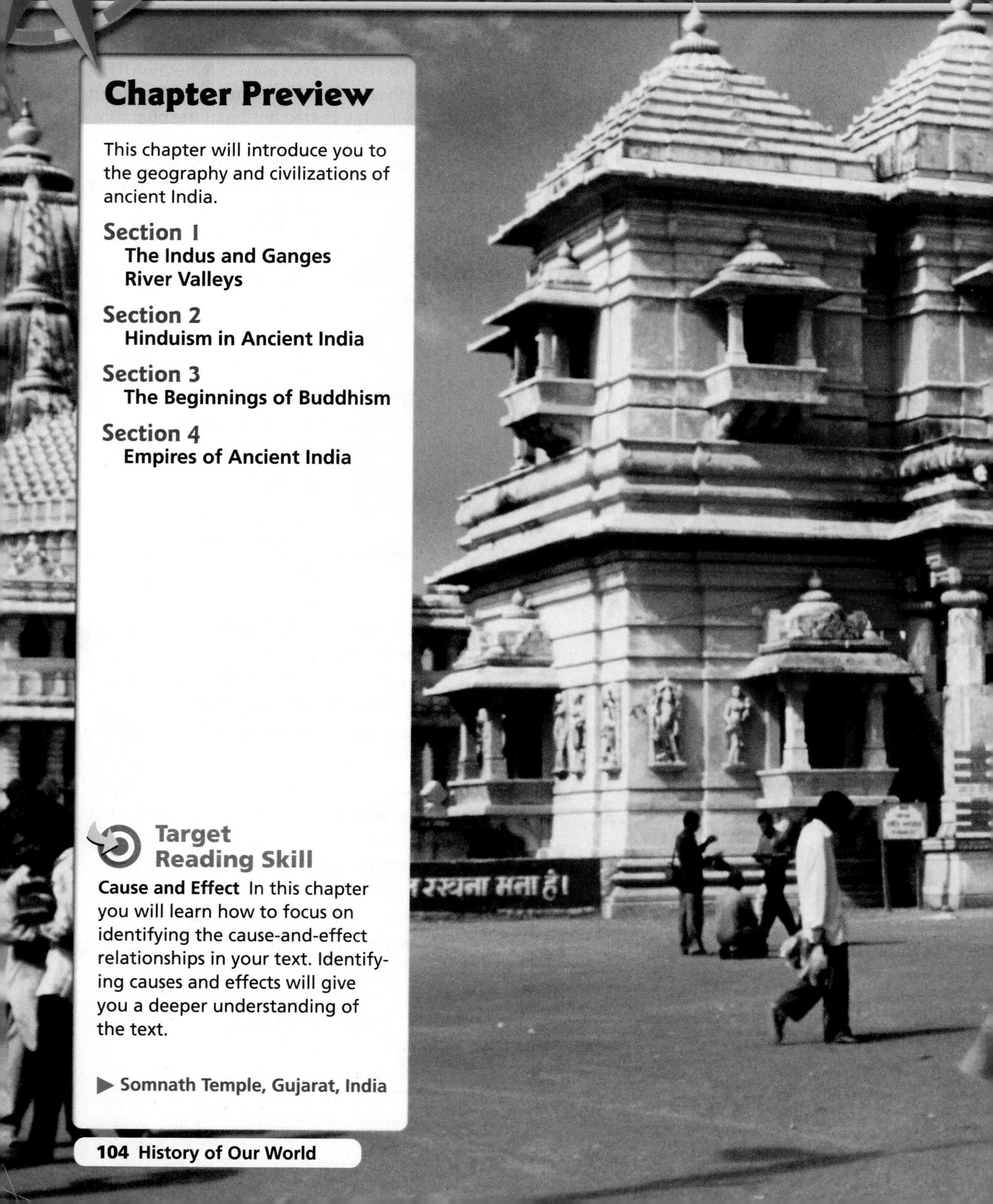

Chapter Preview

This chapter will introduce you to the geography and civilizations of ancient India.

Target Reading Skill

Cause and Effect In this chapter you will learn how to focus on identifying the cause-and-effect relationships in your text. Identifying causes and effects will give you a deeper understanding of the text.

▶ Somnath Temple, Gujarat, India

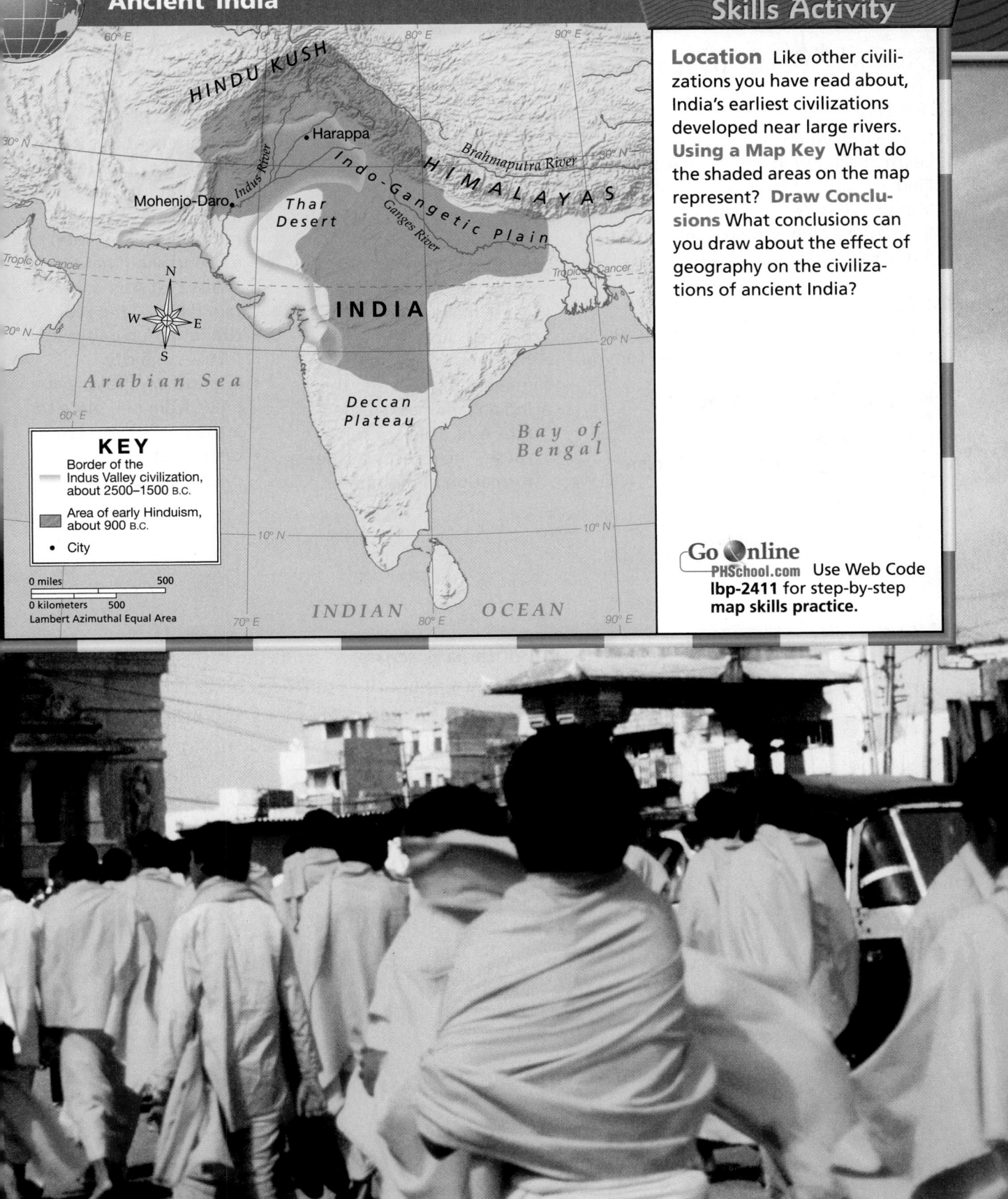

Location Like other civilizations you have read about, India's earliest civilizations developed near large rivers. **Using a Map Key** What do the shaded areas on the map represent? **Draw Conclusions** What conclusions can you draw about the effect of geography on the civilizations of ancient India?

HINDU KUSH

• Harappa

Indo-Gangetic Plain

Brahmaputra River

HIMALAYAS

Mohenjo-Daro•

Indus River

Thar Desert

Ganges River

Tropic of Cancer

INDIA

Tropic of Cancer

Arabian Sea

Deccan Plateau

Bay of Bengal

KEY

Border of the Indus Valley civilization, about 2500–1500 B.C.

Area of early Hinduism, about 900 B.C.

• City

0 miles 500
0 kilometers 500
Lambert Azimuthal Equal Area

INDIAN OCEAN

Go Online
PHSchool.com Use Web Code **lbp-2411** for step-by-step **map skills practice.**

The Indus and Ganges River Valleys

Prepare to Read

Objectives

In this section you will

1. Learn about India's geographic setting.
2. Find out about life in an ancient city of the Indus River valley.
3. Examine the rise of a new culture in the Indus and Ganges river valleys.

Taking Notes

As you read, create an outline of this section. The outline below has been started for you.

I. India's geographic setting
   A. Monsoon climate
      1.
      2.
   B.
      1.
      2.
II. Life in the Indus River valley

Target Reading Skill

Identify Causes and Effects Determining causes and effects can help you understand the relationships among situations or events. A cause makes something happen. An effect is what happens. For example, millions of years ago the Indian landmass crashed into Asia. Think of this as a cause. The effect was the formation of mountains.

Key Terms

- **subcontinent** (SUB kahn tih nunt) *n.* a large landmass that juts out from a continent
- **monsoon** (mahn SOON) *n.* a strong wind that blows across East Asia at certain times of the year
- **citadel** (SIT uh del) *n.* a fortress in a city
- **migrate** (MY grayt) *v.* to move from one place to settle in another area
- **caste** (kast) *n.* a social class of people

The land of India is separated from the rest of the world by a great wall. Rising along India's northern border, the wall is more than 1,500 miles (2,400 kilometers) long and nearly 5 miles (8 kilometers) high. The wall is not made of stone or bricks. It is a wall of snow-capped peaks and icy glaciers. This great barrier is the Himalayas, the highest mountain range in the world.

The Himalayas

India's Geographic Setting

Stretching south from the Himalayas, the kite-shaped land of India juts out from Asia into the Indian Ocean. Geographers call this land a **subcontinent,** or a large landmass that juts out from a continent. Historians refer to the entire subcontinent as India, although today it is divided into several countries, including India, Pakistan, and Bangladesh.

For centuries, geography limited the contact the people of the Indian subcontinent had with the rest of the world. Turn to the map titled Ancient India on page 105. Notice how the Himalaya and the Hindu Kush mountain ranges separate India from the rest of Asia. Like these mountains, the bodies of water around India separated it from surrounding regions.

A Climate of Monsoons India's climate is dominated by the **monsoons,** strong winds that blow across the region at certain times of the year. Look at the map below titled India: Monsoons. From October to May, the winter monsoon blows from the northeast, spreading dry air across the country. Then, in the middle of June, the wind blows in from the Indian Ocean. This summer monsoon picks up moisture from the ocean. It carries rains that drench the plains and river valleys daily.

Links to
Science

The Creation of the Himalayas Millions of years ago, all of today's continents were part of a single continent called Pangaea (pan JEE uh). Then Pangaea slowly broke apart. Eventually, India broke loose from Africa and began moving northeast. About 55 million years ago, India began crashing into Asia. The force of the collision pushed up layers and layers of rock to form the Himalayas.

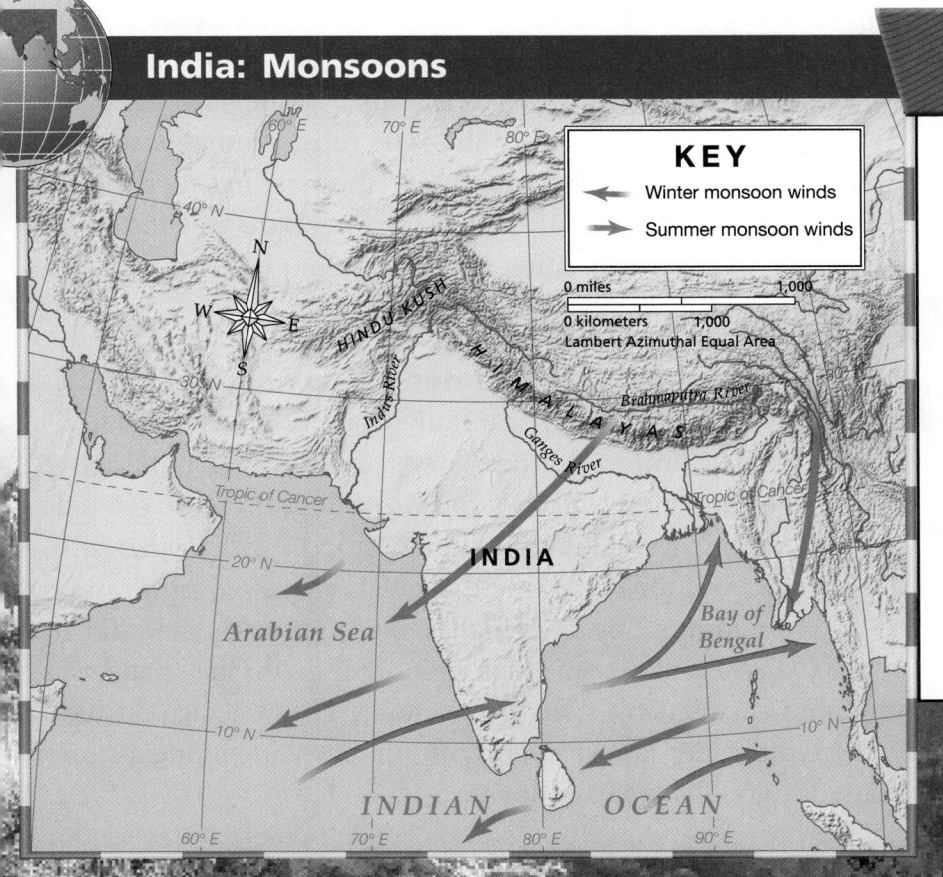

India: Monsoons

KEY
← Winter monsoon winds
→ Summer monsoon winds

0 miles 1,000
0 kilometers 1,000
Lambert Azimuthal Equal Area

MAP MASTER™
Skills Activity

Place India's distinct geographic features have influenced its history and culture. **Identify** What geographic features do you notice on this map?
Analyze Which winds bring rain to India, winter or summer? Which winds bring dry, cool air? Explain why.

Go Online
PHSchool.com Use Web Code **lbp-2421** for step-by-step **map skills practice.**

Identify Causes and Effects

What cause-and-effect relationships are described in the paragraph at the right?

The people of India depend on summer monsoons to provide life-giving rain. If the monsoon is late or weak, crops die, causing famine. If it brings too much rain, overflowing rivers may cause deadly floods.

Barriers and Pathways   Although the mountains separate India from other lands, they do have openings. For thousands of years, passes through the Hindu Kush mountain range have served as highways for migration and invasion. The earliest people of northern India probably entered the Indus River valley through these pathways.

Great rivers begin in the mountains. The Indus (IN dus) River crosses the Himalayas and empties into the Arabian Sea. The Ganges (GAN jeez) River flows from the Himalayas into the Bay of Bengal. Fed by melting snow and rain, the Indus and Ganges rivers cut through the mountains. They flow across northern India and make farming possible in the river valleys.

✓ **Reading Check**   **How do winter monsoons differ from summer monsoons?**

Life in the Indus River Valley

From the rich soil of the Indus valley, early farmers harvested a surplus of wheat and other grains. With a surplus of food, the population grew. Some villages grew to become cities. From around 2500 to 1500 B.C., well-planned cities flourished in the valley. Two such cities were Harappa (huh RAP uh) and Mohenjo-Daro (moh HEN joh DAH roh), both located in present-day Pakistan. To find these cities, return to the map titled Ancient India on page 105. Mohenjo-Daro was the larger of the two cities, and it lay along the banks of the Indus River.

Stone Seals
Merchants of Mohenjo-Daro may have used seals like these to identify their goods.
Compare *How do these seals compare to the ways that present-day merchants identify their goods?*

Ancient City Planners   The ruins of Mohenjo-Daro show how carefully the city was planned. To help protect it from floods, the city was built above ground level. Homes and workshops made up one side of the city. Public buildings stood on the other side. Streets separated these regular blocks of homes and buildings. The city's highest point served as a **citadel,** or **fortress.** Built on a high mound of earth, the citadel was probably enclosed by a high brick wall. This wall would have protected the city's most important buildings, including a storehouse for grain and a bath house.

Unlike most other cities of the time, Mohenjo-Daro had a drainage system. Clay pipes ran under the brick streets. They carried waste from homes and public buildings away from the city. Outside the city, canals ran along the Indus River, which often flooded. The canals helped to control flooding by catching overflow from the river. The water was then directed where it was most needed.

A mythical animal on a stone seal

Life in Mohenjo-Daro In Mohenjo-Daro, merchants and artisans sold their wares from shops that lined the streets. Carts loaded with grain rolled through the city. Traders came from as far away as Mesopotamia to buy and sell precious goods. The citizens of Mohenjo-Daro lived in homes that opened onto courtyards. Children played with toys and pets. Adults enjoyed games and music. Artisans fashioned jewelry and bright cotton clothing for the people to wear.

The language of the people is still a mystery. Their writings appear on square seals, but experts have not yet been able to figure out what the symbols mean. The form of government and the religion of Mohenjo-Daro are also unknown. No royal tombs or great temples have been found. But evidence found in the city's ruins suggests that the people had a number of gods.

Ancient City
The baked-brick ruins of Mohenjo-Daro are in the present-day country of Pakistan. **Analyze Images** *How does the photograph below suggest that Mohenjo-Daro was probably a crowded city?*

Farming the Indus Valley
In Ladakh, India, farming is part of an ancient tradition. **Generalize** *How did farmers help make civilization possible in the Indus valley?*

A Mysterious Decline   Around 2000 B.C., Indus valley farmers began to abandon their land. The climate may have changed, turning the fertile soil into desert. Or great earthquakes may have caused floods that destroyed the canals. Without enough food, people began to leave the cities of the Indus valley. Between 2000 and 1500 B.C., newcomers from the north entered the valley. These newcomers eventually gained power throughout the region.

✓ **Reading Check** **When did the Indus valley civilization begin to decline?**

A New Culture Arises

The newcomers called themselves Aryans (AYR ee unz), which in their language meant "noble" or "highborn." They **migrated, or moved,** from their homelands in central Asia. For several centuries, waves of these nomadic herders swept into India.

The Aryans drove horse-drawn chariots that helped them gain power. The chariots overwhelmed the enemy's slow-moving foot soldiers and settled populations. In time, local people adopted the language and some of the beliefs of the Aryans. Gradually, a new Aryan culture developed. This culture combined the traditions of the original inhabitants with ideas and beliefs brought by the newcomers. Marriages between members of the two groups created a mixed population.

Aryan Culture Spreads   This new culture first developed in the northern Indus valley. Gradually, it spread into the Ganges valley to the east, where people also adopted the Aryan language. By about 800 B.C., the people of northern India had learned to make tools and weapons out of iron. With iron axes, these people cleared areas of the thick rain forests of the northeast. There they built farms, villages, and even cities.

Aryan Life Most of what we know of early Aryan life comes from religious books called Vedas, which means "knowledge." The Vedas tell us that the earliest Aryans were herders and warriors who lived in temporary villages. Often on the move, these people did not at first build cities or spacious homes.

The Aryans organized their society around three classes. Aryan priests, called Brahmans, performed religious services and composed hymns and prayers. Ranked below them was a class of warriors and nobles. Next came the artisans and merchants. Gradually, a low-ranking fourth class was formed. It was made up of farm workers, laborers, and servants.

The Social Order By 500 B.C., there was a strict division of classes. Europeans later called it the caste system. At first, each **caste,** or class, performed special duties. Under the caste system, people always had to stay in the caste of their parents. Over time, the caste system became more complicated. The main castes divided into hundreds of different groups, in which each person had the same occupation. Since people could not leave their caste, they did the same work that their parents and other group members did.

The caste system still exists in present-day India, but it is much less rigid. For example, people of different castes interact more freely. Also, many modern professions have no caste ranking.

✓ **Reading Check** **How was Aryan society organized?**

Indian Society
In the caste system, a weaver's son would be a weaver. A barber's daughter would marry a barber. The manuscript page above shows workmen building a royal city.
Summarize *How did the caste system develop in India?*

Section 1 Assessment

Key Terms
Review the key terms at the beginning of this section. Use each term in a sentence that explains its meaning.

Target Reading Skill
What may have caused the decline of Indus valley civilizations around 2000 B.C.? What was the effect of this decline?

Comprehension and Critical Thinking
1. (a) Recall Describe the geography of the Indus and Ganges river valleys.

(b) Identify Effects How do the monsoons affect India and its climate?
2. (a) Explain How did geography influence the building of Mohenjo-Daro?
(b) Draw Conclusions How was Mohenjo-Daro similar to modern cities?
3. (a) Identify Who were the Aryans?
(b) Analyze Information How was it possible for the Aryans to spread their influence over the Indus and Ganges river valleys so successfully?

Writing Activity
List some words that describe the city and the people of Mohenjo-Daro. Use these words to write a paragraph about life in that city.

Writing Tip Use vivid language when writing a description. Reread the text on Mohenjo-Daro to see what life was like in the ancient city. When you write your description, carefully choose adjectives that will bring Mohenjo-Daro to life.

The advertisement shown below is fiction, of course, but the details are quite true. While villagers in ancient Mesopotamia and Egypt were living in mud huts, Indus valley dwellers lived in relatively high style—especially in the two large cities of Harappa and Mohenjo-Daro. Discovered by archaeologists in 1922, Mohenjo-Daro was a feat of engineering, architecture, design, mathematics, and social organization.

Homes available in fashionable Mohenjo-Daro! Houses feature from 1 to 24 rooms in cool, brick buildings, some with courtyards. Good security. Indoor baths and well water in most units. Close to the Indus River and to downtown area. Dogs, cats, chickens, pigs, goats, mules, and sheep welcome.

Corridor
A channel of the Indus River or a canal may have flowed between the lower city and the citadel.

A street scene from the lower city

A lamp found in the ruins of Mohenjo-Daro

City Life From its beginnings in around 2500 B.C., Mohenjo-Daro was a booming city where more than 35,000 people lived and worked. Planners divided the city into two sections: a western side for public facilities, known as the citadel, and a residential east side, known as the lower city. Built on mud-brick platforms to protect it from floods, Mohenjo-Daro was laid out with mathematical precision on one square mile.

Artisans of Mohenjo-Daro created jewelry, crafted copper and bronze objects, and found a way to mass-produce pottery. Cotton fabric found in the city's ruins is the earliest evidence of a textile industry for which India would later become famous. Yet despite these signs of success, we find no great tombs of kings or priests. Few clues remain as to who built this city and extended its influence for thousands of miles.

Lower City
Homes and shops

Citadel
Public buildings

Great Bath
The pool was 8 feet (2.5 meters) deep. It may have been used for religious ceremonies.

Granary
Vents in the building kept the grain from spoiling.

Assessment

Identify Describe the citadel and the lower-city sections of Mohenjo-Daro.

Draw Conclusions What do the features of Mohenjo-Daro tell us about the people who lived there?

Prepare to Read

Objectives

In this section you will
1. Find out about the beginning of Hinduism.
2. Learn about the teachings of Hinduism.
3. Examine the practice of Hinduism.

Taking Notes

As you read, find details about the basic beliefs of Hinduism. Copy the concept web below, and record your findings in it.

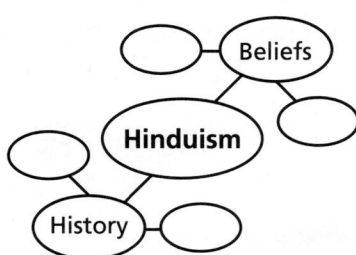

Target Reading Skill

Recognize Cause-and-Effect Signal Words Sometimes certain words, such as *affect, from,* and *as a result,* signal a cause or an effect. In the following sentence, *from* signals both a cause and an effect: "*From* this blending of ideas and beliefs came one of the world's oldest living religions, Hinduism." The cause is a blend of ideas and beliefs, and the effect is Hinduism. As you read, look for signals announcing other causes and effects.

Key Terms

- **brahman** (BRAH mun) *n.* a single spiritual power that Hindus believe lives in everything
- **avatar** (av uh TAHR) *n.* a representation of a Hindu god or goddess in human or animal form
- **reincarnation** (ree in kahr NAY shun) *n.* the rebirth of the soul in the body of another living being
- **dharma** (DAHR muh) *n.* the religious and moral duties of Hindus
- **ahimsa** (uh HIM sah) *n.* the Hindu idea of non-violence

Shiva, one of the most important Hindu gods

The following prayer was part of one of the early Aryan Vedas:

❝O Lord of the storm gods, . . . [d]o not hide the sun from our sight. O Rudra, protect our horseman from injury. . . . Your glory is unbounded, your strength unmatched among all living creatures, O Rudra, wielder [handler] of the thunderbolt. Guide us safely to the far shore of existence where there is no sorrow.❞

—*Aryan Vedas*

The prayer praises Rudra and other gods of nature. What parts of the prayer ask the gods for their protection?

The Beginnings of Hinduism

Aryan prayers were passed down through generations. As Aryan culture mixed with India's existing cultures, new ideas and beliefs became part of the Vedas. From this blending of ideas and beliefs came one of the world's oldest living religions, Hinduism.

A Blend of Religions

As Hinduism developed over 3,500 years, it absorbed many beliefs from other religions. Hinduism became very complex over time, with many different practices existing side by side. Hindus believe that since people are different, they need many different ways of approaching god.

Hinduism is one of the world's major religions, and a way of life for more than 850 million people in India today. Its beliefs have influenced people of many other religions. Yet Hinduism is unlike other major world religions.

Hinduism has no one single founder, but Hindus have many great religious thinkers. Hindus worship many gods and goddesses. However, they believe in one single spiritual power called **brahman**, which lives in everything. Hindus believe that there is more than one path to the truth.

Hindu Gods and Goddesses

The gods and goddesses of Hinduism stand for different parts of brahman. An ancient Hindu saying expresses this idea: "God is one, but wise people know it by many names." The most important Hindu gods are Brahma, the Creator; Vishnu, the Preserver; and Shiva, the Destroyer.

Hindu gods take many different forms, called avatars. An **avatar** is the representation of a Hindu god or goddess in human or animal form.

Hindu teachings say that the god Brahma was born from a golden egg. He created Earth and everything on it. However, he is not as widely worshiped as Vishnu and Shiva.

Bathing in the Ganges
People practice the ancient ritual of cleansing in the Ganges River. Hindus believe the waters of the Ganges to be sacred. **Infer** *Why do you think Hindus believe the Ganges to be sacred?*

Hindu Temple
The Hindu temple of Kandarya Mahadeva was built in central India around A.D. 1000. The temple is covered with carvings of Hindu gods. **Synthesize** *In what ways are the gods of Hinduism complex, or many-sided?*

Hindus believe that Vishnu is a kindly god who is concerned with the welfare of human beings. Vishnu visits Earth from time to time in different forms. He does this to guide humans or to protect them from disaster.

Unlike Vishnu, Shiva is not concerned with human matters. He is very powerful. Shiva is responsible for both the creative and the destructive forces of the universe. Shiva developed from the god Rudra, the "wielder of the thunderbolt" in the prayer at the beginning of this section.

Hindu gods have their own families. Many Hindus, for example, worship Shiva's wife, the goddess Shakti. Hindus believe Shakti plays a role in human life. Like her husband, she is both a destroyer and a creator. She is both kind and cruel.

✓ **Reading Check** **What are the three main Hindu gods?**

The Teachings of Hinduism

All Hindus share certain central beliefs that are contained in religious writings or sacred texts.

The Upanishads   One of the Hindu religious texts is the Upanishads (oo PAN uh shadz). *Upanishad* means "sitting near a teacher." Much of the Upanishads is in the form of questions by pupils and responses by teachers. For example, a pupil asks, "Who created the world?" The teacher replies, "Brahman is the creator, the universal soul." When asked to describe brahman, the teacher explains that it is too complicated for humans to understand. Brahman has no physical form.

Reincarnation   One important idea in the Upanishads is **reincarnation,** or rebirth of the soul. Hindus believe that when a person dies, the soul is reborn in the body of another living thing. Hindus believe that every living thing has a soul. This idea is an important part of other Asian beliefs as well.

According to Hindu belief, the actions of a person in this life affect his or her fate in the next. Good behavior is always rewarded. Bad behavior is always punished. Faithful followers of Hinduism will be reborn into a higher position. Those whose acts have been bad may be born into a lower caste, or may even return as animals. If a person leads a perfect life, he or she may be freed from this cycle of death and rebirth. As a result, the person's soul becomes one with brahman.

A Hindu's Duties   To become united with the one spirit and escape the cycle of death and rebirth, a person must obey his or her dharma (DAHR muh). **Dharma** is the religious and moral duties of each person. These duties depend on such factors as a person's class, age, and occupation. In Hinduism, it is a man's duty to protect the women in his family, and it is a ruler's duty to protect his subjects. Another important idea of Hinduism is **ahimsa** (uh HIM sah), or nonviolence. To Hindus, people and living things are part of brahman and therefore must be treated with respect. For that reason, many Hindus do not eat meat and try to avoid harming living things.

✔ **Reading Check**   **According to Hindu belief, what happens to a person's soul after death?**

Links to
Language Arts

Common Roots The Hindu sacred books were written in a language called Sanskrit. It is one of the oldest known languages. Sanskrit is related to many other languages in the world, such as Greek and Latin. Modern languages, including Spanish, German, and English, also have roots in common with ancient Sanskrit. The page shown below is from an ancient Indian book written in Sanskrit.

Recognize Cause-and-Effect Signal Words
What does *as a result* signal?

The Practice of Hinduism

As you have read, Hinduism teaches that there is more than one path to the truth. Because of this view, Hinduism allows its followers to worship in various ways.

The Yogas   Many non-Hindus know yoga (YOH guh) as a physical activity, a system of special exercises and breathing. Hindus believe yoga exercises help free the soul from the cares of the world. In this way, the soul may unite with brahman. In fact, the word *yoga* means "union." For Hindus, there are many yogas that may be used as paths to brahman. Physical activity is one yoga. Another is the yoga of selfless deeds, such as giving to the poor. By learning the sacred writings, a Hindu practices the yoga of knowledge. And by honoring a personal god, a Hindu follows the yoga of devotion.

Private Devotion   Hindus worship in public by praying and performing rituals in temples. They also show devotion privately at home. It is common for Hindus to choose a personal god, and to honor that god by offering food, gifts, and prayers at a home altar. A Hindu's devotion to the god brings the soul closer to brahman.

Home Altar
Many Hindus, like the woman shown above, worship before altars in their homes. **Contrast** *What are some differences between public and private worship for Hindus?*

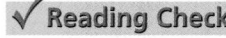 Reading Check   **How is yoga practiced by Hindus?**

Section 2 Assessment

Key Terms
Review the key terms at the beginning of this section. Use each term in a sentence that explains its meaning.

 **Target Reading Skill**
Return to the fourth paragraph on page 117 and find the signal word *affect*. What cause-and-effect relationships are described in the two sentences that follow?

Comprehension and Critical Thinking
1. (a) Explain How did the early Aryan religion grow into Hinduism?

(b) Compare and Contrast
How is Hinduism different from other religions you have learned about? How is it similar?
2. (a) Analyze Information
What is the relationship between good and bad behavior and the Hindu idea of reincarnation?
(b) Find the Main Idea What does "escaping the cycle of birth and death" mean to Hindus?
3. (a) Describe In what ways do Hindus practice their faith?
(b) Draw Conclusions How do you think the yogas bring Hindus closer to brahman?

Writing Activity
Hindu teachers often instruct their students through questions and answers. Write a dialogue in which a student asks questions about Hindu beliefs and the teacher responds.

> **Writing Tip** A dialogue is similar to a script for a play. When you write your dialogue, make it clear that either the student or the teacher is speaking. Try to make the dialogue sound like a conversation.

The Beginnings of Buddhism

Prepare to Read

Objectives

In this section you will

1. Learn about the Buddha and his teachings.
2. Find out how Buddhism was received inside and outside India.

Taking Notes

As you read, find details on the beginnings of Buddhism. Copy the flowchart below, and record your findings in it.

Beginnings of Buddhism

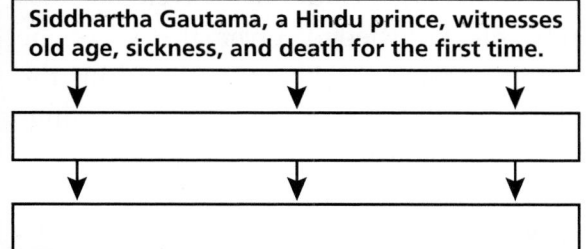

Target Reading Skill

Recognize Multiple Causes A cause is what makes something happen. An effect is what happens. Sometimes an effect can have more than one cause. For example, in the story that begins this section, Siddhartha Gautama witnesses three events that cause him to change the direction of his life. Can you identify the three causes? As you read, look for effects that have multiple causes.

Key Terms

- **meditate** (MED uh tayt) *v.* to focus the mind inward in order to find spiritual awareness or relaxation
- **nirvana** (nur VAH nuh) *n.* the lasting peace that Buddhists seek by giving up selfish desires
- **missionary** (MISH un ehr ee) *n.* a person who spreads his or her religious beliefs to others

Indian statue of the young Buddha

According to Buddhist tradition, a young Hindu prince once lived a life of luxury in his palace in northern India. The prince was surrounded by beauty and youth. He had never witnessed old age, sickness, or death.

Then, around the age of 30, the prince traveled outside the palace walls. What he saw changed his life. He met a bent and tired old man. Then he saw a man who was very sick. Finally, he saw a corpse, or dead body, as it was carried to a funeral.

This suffering and death troubled the young man greatly. He wondered why there was so much misery and pain in the world. He decided he must change his life to find the answer. He gave up his wealth, his family, and his life of ease in order to find the causes of human suffering. The young man was named Siddhartha Gautama (sih DAHR tuh GOW tuh muh). What he discovered after seven years of wandering led to the beginnings of a major world religion: Buddhism.

The Buddha and His Teachings

As Gautama traveled in the 500s B.C., he sought answers to his questions about the meaning of life. At first, Gautama studied with Hindu philosophers, but their ideas did not satisfy him. He could not accept the Hindu belief that only priests could pass on knowledge.

The Search for Understanding Gautama decided to stop looking outwardly for the cause of suffering. Instead, he tried to find understanding within his own mind. To do this, he decided to **meditate,** to focus the mind inward in order to find spiritual awareness. Meditation was an ancient Hindu practice used by Indus valley civilizations. Buddhist tradition says that Gautama fasted and meditated under a fig tree. After 49 days, he found the answers he sought. He believed he finally understood the roots of suffering.

For the next 45 years, Gautama traveled across India and shared his knowledge. Over the years, he attracted many followers. His followers called him the Buddha (BOO duh), or "Enlightened One." His teachings became known as Buddhism.

The Middle Way Buddhism teaches people to follow the Eightfold Path, also called the Middle Way. By following this path, a person avoids a life of extreme pleasure or extreme unhappiness.

The Buddha believed that selfish desires for power, wealth, and pleasure cause humans to suffer. By giving up selfish pleasures, a person can become free from suffering. He taught that the way to end human suffering is by following the Eightfold Path. To overcome selfish desires, Buddhists must learn to be wise, to behave correctly, and to develop their minds.

The Practice of Buddhism: The Eightfold Path

1. Right Understanding
Having faith in the Buddhist view of the universe

2. Right Intention
Making a commitment to practice Buddhism

3. Right Speech
Avoiding lies and mean or abusive speech

4. Right Action
Not taking life, not stealing, and not hurting others

5. Right Livelihood
Rejecting jobs and occupations that conflict with Buddhist ideals

6. Right Effort
Avoiding bad attitudes and developing good ones

7. Right Mindfulness
Being aware of one's own body, feelings, and thoughts

8. Right Concentration
Thinking deeply to find answers to problems

SOURCE: *Encyclopaedia Britannica*

The Eightfold Path
The Eightfold Path outlines the steps a person should take to lead a balanced life.
Analyze *Which steps direct followers to lead a moral life?*

Release From Reincarnation To find this Middle Way, the Buddha taught, people must act unselfishly toward others and treat people fairly. They must tell the truth at all times. People should also avoid violence and the killing of any living thing. If people follow the Buddha's path, their suffering will end. They will eventually find **nirvana,** or lasting peace. By reaching nirvana, people will be released from the cycle of reincarnation.

Followers of Buddhism Buddhism also taught that all people are equal. Anyone, the Buddha declared, could follow the path to nirvana, regardless of his or her social class. This idea appealed to many people living under the caste system.

Like other religions, Buddhism has priests. Although monastery life is difficult, people of any social class can work to become a Buddhist priest or monk. The Buddha encouraged his followers to establish monasteries. There they would learn, meditate, and teach. He also urged monks to become **missionaries,** or people who spread their religious beliefs to others.

✓ **Reading Check** Why do Buddhists try to follow the Middle Way?

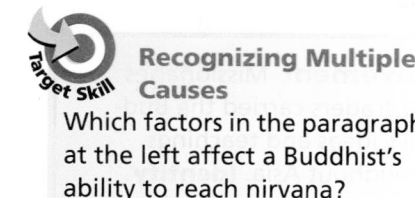

Recognizing Multiple Causes
Which factors in the paragraph at the left affect a Buddhist's ability to reach nirvana?

Reclining Buddha
Like many statues of the Buddha, this sculpture in Vientiane, Laos, located in Southeast Asia, shows the Buddha lying down. The pose may be linked to one of the great events of the Buddha's life, his reaching nirvana. **Analyze** *Describe the importance of nirvana.*

Indian Temple Painting
This painting comes from a temple carved into the Ajanta Caves during the Gupta period. **Infer** *What details suggest that this is a religious painting?*

The Gupta Empire

After Asoka died, the Maurya Empire weakened and eventually split into smaller states. For centuries, India faced internal conflicts and foreign invasions.

However, in A.D. 320, the Gupta dynasty rose to power. By 400, the Guptas had built an empire across northern India. Invasions from Central Asia weakened the Gupta Empire. After 540, India again split into small states.

Under the Guptas, India enjoyed a rich culture. Indians invented the technique of printing cloth in this period. Hindu scholars and students gathered in colleges where they developed advanced schools of philosophy. Kalidasa (kah lee DAH suh), one of the greatest Indian writers of all time, wrote poems and plays. Indian mathematicians invented the decimal point and the system of numbers that we use today.

✓ **Reading Check** **How did learning advance under the Guptas?**

Section 4 Assessment

Key Terms
Review the key terms at the beginning of this section. Use each term in a sentence that explains its meaning.

Target Reading Skill
Reread Chandragupta's Legacy on page 127. What were the effects of wealth on the Maurya Empire?

Comprehension and Critical Thinking
1. (a) Recall How was India governed before the Maurya Empire?
(b) Evaluate What were some of the costs and benefits of Chandragupta's rule for Indians?
2. (a) Describe What were some of Asoka's accomplishments?
(b) Identify Cause and Effect How did Buddhism influence Asoka's rule of the empire?
3. (a) Identify What part of India did the Guptas control?
(b) Explain Why have some historians called the Gupta period a golden age?
(c) Draw Conclusions What Indian inventions under the Gupta have had a lasting impact?

Writing Activity
Asoka wrote many rules of conduct for himself and for others to follow. Write a list of rules of conduct that you would like to see today's leaders follow.

Go Online
PHSchool.com

For: An activity on Asoka
Visit: PHSchool.com
Web Code: lbd-2404

Practice the Skill

In this text, you are learning about some of the world's major religions. Read the table at the right to find out more about those religions.

1 Study the kinds of information shown in the table.

2 Suppose you want to locate information on where Judaism was founded. Under which column heading would you look? Which row has the information you want?

3 Use the table to answer these questions: Which religion was founded most recently? Which religions were founded in India? How might this information be useful to you when reading about ancient history?

Major World Religions

Religion	Date Founded	Place of Origin
Buddhism	c. 525 B.C.	India
Christianity	c. A.D. 30	Southwest Asia
Hinduism	c. 1500 B.C.	India
Islam	c. A.D. 622	Southwest Asia
Judaism	c. 1800 B.C.	Southwest Asia

Candle Orders for Fundraiser

Seller	Green	Red	Blue
Katelyn			
Troy	2		5
Rashid			
Madelyn		3	
Indira	6		
Michael			
Elizabeth			

Apply the Skill

Now try making a table yourself. Interview at least four of your classmates to find out each person's favorite food, movie, and sport. Create a table to show the results.

Exchange tables with a classmate. Analyze the information in your classmate's table.

Empires of Ancient Ind

Prepare to Read

Objectives

In this section you will
1. Learn about the rise of the Maurya Empire.
2. Study Asoka's leadership.
3. Investigate the Gupta Empire.

Taking Notes

As you read, compare and contrast the rulers of the Maurya Empire. Copy the Venn diagram below. Write similarities in the overlapping space and differences in the outside ovals.

Rulers of Maurya

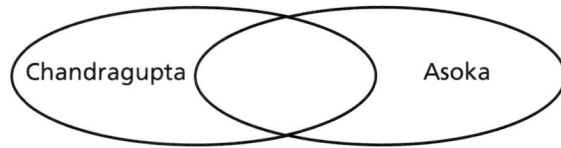

Chandragupta   Asoka

Target Reading Skill

Understand Effects Sometimes one cause may produce several effects. Turn to page 127 and read the paragraph after the heading Chandragupta's Legacy. What were the effects of wealth on the Maurya Empire?

Key Terms

- **Maurya Empire** (MOWR yuh EM pyr) *n.* Indian empire founded by Chandragupta, beginning with his kingdom in northeastern India and spreading to most of northern and central India
- **convert** (kun VURT) *v.* to change one's beliefs; in particular, to change from one religion to another
- **tolerance** (TAHL ur uns) *n.* freedom from prejudice

Terra-cotta figure of a mother goddess worshiped in India, 200s B.C.

Around 321 B.C., a new ruler came to the throne of a kingdom in northeastern India. Within 35 years, the tiny kingdom had grown into the giant Maurya (MOWR yuh) Empire. Chandragupta (chun druh GUP tuh) Maurya founded India's **Maurya Empire**.

Chandragupta had been born to a poor family and sold into slavery at a young age. But later, when he became king, Chandragupta enjoyed luxuries from all parts of Asia. When he appeared before his subjects, he was often seated in a golden chair carried on his servants' shoulders. Sometimes he rode on an elephant covered with jewels.

The Rise of the Maurya Empire

India was made up of a number of warring states before Chandragupta came to power. Strong and ruthless, Chandragupta's armies overthrew kingdoms along the Ganges River. Turning west, the armies advanced into the Indus River valley. In only a few years, Chandragupta's power extended over most of northern and central India.

Absolute Rule Chandragupta was guided by the basic belief that a ruler must have absolute power. According to legend, one of Chandragupta's advisors gave him a book of advice called *Arthasastra*. The book urged kings to maintain control of their subjects and to establish an army of spies to inform on them.

Chandragupta commanded a huge army. Thousands of foot soldiers and mounted troops were ready to enforce the law and to crush any revolts. The army also had a herd of 9,000 war elephants, which struck fear into the hearts of opponents.

Under Chandragupta, the empire enjoyed great economic success. Most of its wealth came from farming. The Maurya Empire also built up trade with such faraway places as Greece, Rome, and China.

However, as his rule continued, Chandragupta became fearful for his life. Afraid of being poisoned, he made servants taste his food. He slept in a different room every night to ward off assassins, or people who murder rulers or political figures. One story says that near the end of his life, Chandragupta left the throne to his son and became a monk in southern India. Fasting and praying, he starved himself to death.

Chandragupta's Legacy Chandragupta did not gain wealth for himself only. Although his rule was harsh, he used his wealth to improve his empire. New irrigation systems brought water to farmers. Forests were cleared, and more food was produced. Government officials promoted crafts and mining. A vast network of roads made it easier for Maurya traders to exchange goods with foreign lands. Chandragupta's leadership brought order and peace to his people.

✓ **Reading Check** **What kind of ruler was Chandragupta?**

Links to
Economics

The Emperor's Guidebook
Both Chandragupta and his grandson Asoka benefited from a book titled *Arthasastra*. *Artha* means "property and economics." Chandragupta used the book's advice on government as his guide to building an empire. Kautilya, the book's author, also served as an advisor to Chandragupta. Although Kautilya wrote about ways to achieve material success, he did not live in great luxury himself.

Go Online
PHSchool.com Use Web Code **mup-0821** for an interactivity on Indian classic dance.

Fighting for Empire
Chandragupta's army rode elephants into war, causing fear and panic. This painting from the 1600s shows an elephant charging toward the enemy.
Evaluate *How did Chandragupta use his army to create an empire?*

Place Under Asoka's rule, the Maurya Empire covered a vast amount of territory.
Identify What physical feature formed the northeast boundary of Asoka's empire?
Conclude What challenges came with governing such a great amount of territory?

Go ●nline
PHSchool.com Use Web Code **lbp-2444** for step-by-step **map skills practice.**

KEY

Maurya Empire, about 250 B.C.

0 miles 1,000
0 kilometers 1,000
Lambert Azimuthal Equal Area

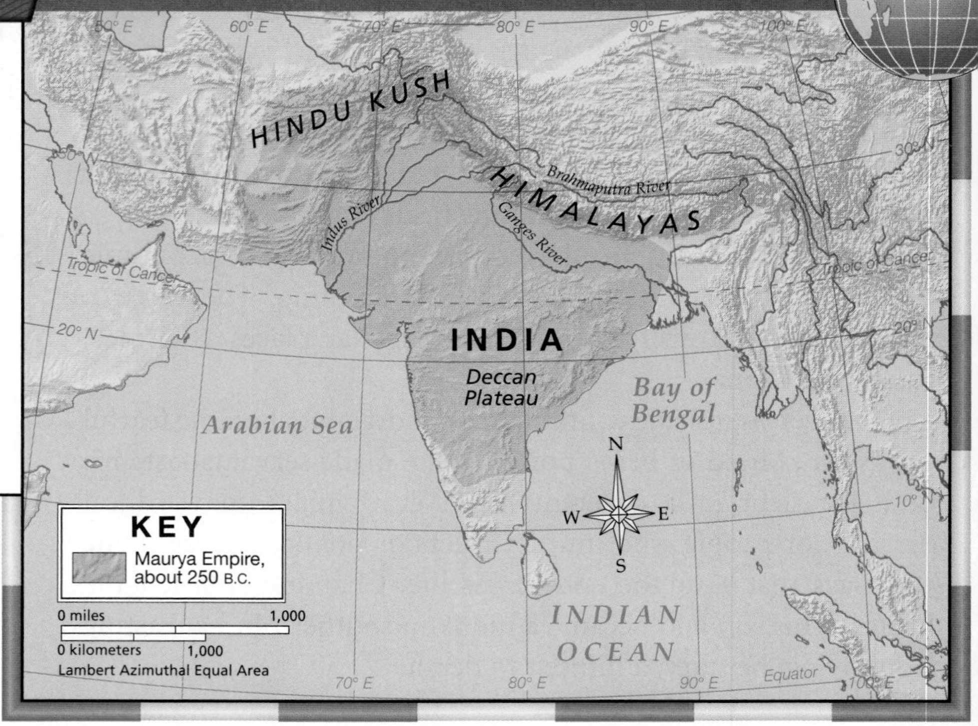

Asoka's Leadership

Chandragupta passed the leadership of the Maurya Empire on to his son. After the son died in 273 B.C., Chandragupta's grandson, Asoka, gained power. Asoka, whose name means "without sorrow," further expanded Chandragupta's empire. By the end of his lengthy rule in 232 B.C., Asoka had built the greatest empire India had ever seen.

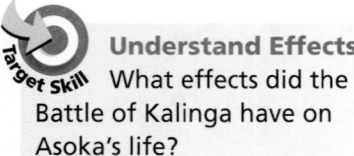

Understand Effects
Target Skill What effects did the Battle of Kalinga have on Asoka's life?

The Battle of Kalinga For more than 35 years, Asoka ruled an empire that included much of the Indian subcontinent. During the first years of his rule, Asoka was as warlike as his grandfather had been. He conquered new territories which were not yet part of the empire.

Early in his rule, Asoka led his army south into the state of Kalinga. In about 261 B.C., he won a bloody battle in which thousands and thousands of people were injured or died. The great slaughter at Kalinga was a turning point in Asoka's life. He was filled with sorrow over the bloodshed. He gave up war and violence. He freed his prisoners and restored their land. Later, he chose to **convert,** or change his beliefs, to Buddhism. Asoka also spread the message of Buddhism to the people of his empire.

The Buddhist Ruler   Asoka practiced and preached the teachings of the Buddha. He did not allow the use of animals for sacrifices. He gave up hunting, the traditional sport of Indian kings.

Asoka thought of his people as his children and was concerned about their well-being. He had hospitals built throughout his kingdom. He even had wells dug every mile beside the roads so that travelers and animals would not go thirsty.

Asoka was also concerned with his people's moral and spiritual life. To carry the Buddha's message throughout his vast empire, Asoka issued writings of moral advice. Some writings urged people to honor their parents. Others asked people not to kill animals. Still others encouraged people to behave with truthfulness and **tolerance,** or freedom from prejudice. Asoka practiced religious tolerance toward the Hindus.

Still, Buddhism grew under Asoka. He sent missionaries far and wide to spread its message. Buddhist missionaries spread the religion to Sri Lanka, China, Southeast Asia, and eventually to Korea and Japan.

✔ **Reading Check**   **How did Asoka spread Buddhism?**

Find out about the
Mauryas' elephant army.

Honoring the Buddha
This stupa, or Buddhist monument, was built sometime between 100 B.C. and A.D. 100, in Sanchi, India. The umbrella at the very top represents protection. **Transferring Information** *How did Asoka's rulings reflect the teachings of the Buddha?*

Indian Temple Painting
This painting comes from a temple carved into the Ajanta Caves during the Gupta period. **Infer** *What details suggest that this is a religious painting?*

The Gupta Empire

After Asoka died, the Maurya Empire weakened and eventually split into smaller states. For centuries, India faced internal conflicts and foreign invasions.

However, in A.D. 320, the Gupta dynasty rose to power. By 400, the Guptas had built an empire across northern India. Invasions from Central Asia weakened the Gupta Empire. After 540, India again split into small states.

Under the Guptas, India enjoyed a rich culture. Indians invented the technique of printing cloth in this period. Hindu scholars and students gathered in colleges where they developed advanced schools of philosophy. Kalidasa (kah lee DAH suh), one of the greatest Indian writers of all time, wrote poems and plays. Indian mathematicians invented the decimal point and the system of numbers that we use today.

✓ **Reading Check** **How did learning advance under the Guptas?**

 **Section 4 Assessment**

Key Terms
Review the key terms at the beginning of this section. Use each term in a sentence that explains its meaning.

Target Reading Skill
 Reread Chandragupta's Legacy on page 127. What were the effects of wealth on the Maurya Empire?

Comprehension and Critical Thinking
1. (a) Recall How was India governed before the Maurya Empire?

(b) Evaluate What were some of the costs and benefits of Chandragupta's rule for Indians?
2. (a) Describe What were some of Asoka's accomplishments?
(b) Identify Cause and Effect How did Buddhism influence Asoka's rule of the empire?
3. (a) Identify What part of India did the Guptas control?
(b) Explain Why have some historians called the Gupta period a golden age?
(c) Draw Conclusions What Indian inventions under the Gupta have had a lasting impact?

Writing Activity
Asoka wrote many rules of conduct for himself and for others to follow. Write a list of rules of conduct that you would like to see today's leaders follow.

For: An activity on Asoka
Visit: PHSchool.com
Web Code: lbd-2404

Review and Assessment

◆ Chapter Summary

Section 1: The Indus and Ganges River Valleys

Mohenjo-Daro seal

- India's geographic setting limited the contact the ancient peoples of the Indian subcontinent had with the rest of the world.
- Well-planned cities, such as Mohenjo-Daro, flourished along the banks of the Indus River.
- Aryans migrated in great waves from central Asia into India, influencing Indian life and culture.

Section 2: Hinduism in Ancient India

- Hinduism is a complex religion that developed over a span of about 3,500 years.
- Hindus believe in nonviolence, and that good behavior will be rewarded and bad behavior will be punished.
- Hindus take many paths in their search for truth.

nskrit text

Sections 3: The Beginnings of Buddhism

- Buddhism was founded by a Hindu prince who preached nonviolence and unselfish behavior.
- Buddhism flourished in India, along with Hinduism, but it eventually declined there. Missionaries carried the Buddha's message to cultures throughout Asia.

Section 4: Empires of Ancient India

- Chandragupta's Maurya Empire extended over northern and central India.
- Chandragupta's grandson, Asoka, greatly expanded the Maurya Empire and embraced Buddhism.
- Under the Guptas, India made progress in textiles, philosophy, literature, and mathematics.

Indian warriors

◆ Reviewing Key Terms

Circle the underlined key term that best completes the sentence.

1. A <u>citadel, subcontinent</u> is a large landmass that juts out from a continent.

2. <u>Dharma, Nirvana</u> is the religious and moral duties of a Hindu.

3. To <u>meditate, migrate</u> is to move from one place to settle in another area.

4. Hindus and Buddhists believe in <u>ahimsa, reincarnation</u>, which is the rebirth of the soul.

5. Under the <u>caste, avatar</u> system, a weaver's son always became a weaver and a barber's daughter always married a barber.

6. Buddhism spread to other countries with the help of <u>monsoons, missionaries</u>.

7. Asoka encouraged his people to behave with <u>tolerance, dharma</u>, or freedom from prejudice.

Review and Assessment (continued)

◆ Comprehension and Critical Thinking

8. (a) Describe What were the geography and climate of ancient India?
(b) Identify Effects How did India's geography and climate affect the people of Mohenjo-Daro?
(c) Infer How do we know that the people of Mohenjo-Daro created a highly organized civilization?

9. (a) Identify Who were the Aryans?
(b) Explain What were some characteristics of Aryan culture?
(c) Summarize What influence did the Aryans have on the people of the Indus valley?

10. (a) Recall Describe the beginnings of ancient Hinduism.
(b) Summarize What are some of the basic beliefs of Hinduism?
(c) Evaluate Information Why is Hinduism considered to be a complex religion?

11. (a) Identify Who was the Buddha?
(b) Explain What is the central idea of Buddhism, and why did the religion appeal to so many people?
(c) Draw Inferences Buddhism and Hinduism were able to coexist in India for some time. Why do you think this was possible?

12. (a) Recall List Asoka's achievements as ruler of the Maurya Empire.
(b) Explain How did Asoka's actions show that he was a Buddhist?
(c) Compare How did Siddhartha Gautama's life-changing experience with suffering compare to Asoka's?

◆ Skills Practice

Reading Tables In the Skills for Life activity, you learned how to read tables and how to create your own table.

Review the steps you follow to do this skill. Return to the concept web you created to take notes on Section 2 of this chapter. Organize that same information into a table. Then, write a brief explanation of how a table makes comparing information from the section easy.

◆ Writing Activity: Language Arts

Asoka helped spread the Buddha's message by having his teachings carved into stone pillars. Turn to pages 120 and 121 and reread the text and the chart titled The Practice of Buddhism: The Eightfold Path. Write at least five full sentences that could be carved into a pillar to teach people about Buddhism.

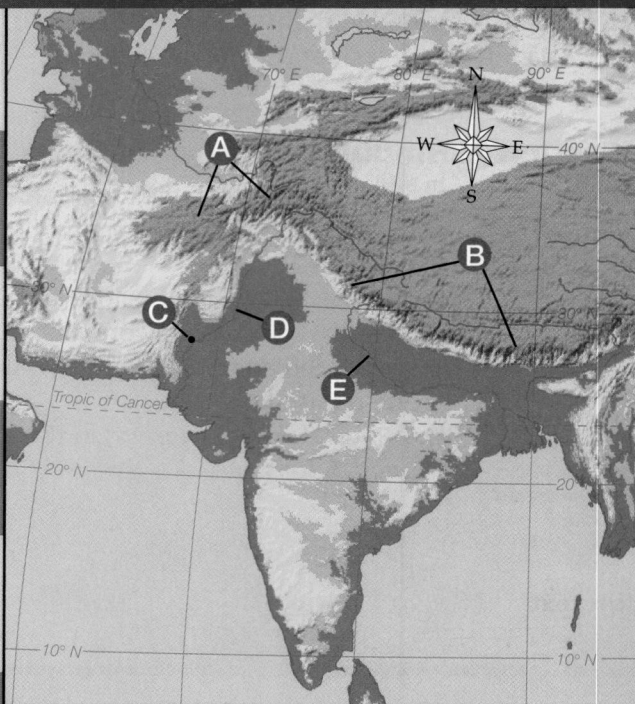

MAP✹MASTER™
Skills Activity

Ancient India

Place Location For each place listed below, write the letter from the map that shows its location.
1. Himalayas
2. Hindu Kush
3. Indus River
4. Ganges River
5. Mohenjo-Daro

Go Online
PHSchool.com Use Web Code **lbp-2454** for an **interactive map**.

Standardized Test Prep

Test-Taking Tips

Some questions on standardized tests ask you to analyze a reading selection for the main ideas. Read the passage below. Then follow the tips to answer the sample question.

> Buddhist missionaries spread their religion throughout Asia. Buddhism took root in China and grew there. Millions of Chinese became Buddhists. Gradually, Buddhist ideas mixed with earlier Chinese teaching. Buddhism then spread from China to Korea and Japan.

Pick the letter that best answers the question.

Which topic sentence is missing from this paragraph?

- **A** Buddhism died out in Turkey but took root in many parts of Asia.
- **B** Buddhist monasteries became centers of thought in China.
- **C** Buddhism died out in India but took root in many parts of Asia.
- **D** Today, Buddhism is a part of many Asian cultures.

Think It Through Start with the main idea of the paragraph. Each sentence tells about the spread of Buddhism. You can rule out answer B because the paragraph is not about monasteries. Nor is the paragraph about Buddhism today, so you can rule out D. That leaves A and C. Did Buddhism spread from Turkey or from India? The answer is India. Even if you were not sure, you might guess that India is much closer to China and the eastern part of Asia. Therefore, the best answer is C.

TIP Some paragraphs have a topic sentence that states the main idea. All sentences in the paragraph support this idea.

TIP Read all of the answer choices before making a final pick. You can't be sure you have the best answer until you have read every one.

Practice Questions

Use the tips above and other tips in this book to help you answer the following questions.

1. The Vedas are
   - **A** a mountain range in northern India.
   - **B** Aryan religious books.
   - **C** nomadic herders who moved into the Indus River valley.
   - **D** early inhabitants of the Indus River valley.

Read the passage below, and then answer the questions that follow.

Under Chandragupta, the Maurya Empire prospered. Asoka expanded and strengthened the empire. He encouraged the spread of Buddhism and united the various Indian states.

2. Which of the following would serve as the best topic sentence for this passage?
   - **A** Asoka was the "Father of Buddhism."
   - **B** The Maurya Empire grew and prospered under two leaders, Chandragupta and Asoka.
   - **C** Chandragupta believed in absolute power.
   - **D** Asoka converted to Buddhism.

3. Unlike other major world religions, Hinduism
   - **A** had no single founder.
   - **B** has had no influence on other religions.
   - **C** has no sacred texts.
   - **D** has no great thinkers.

Go Online
PHSchool.com

Use Web Code **lba-2404** for a
Chapter 4 self-test.

Chapter Preview

This chapter will introduce you to the history of ancient China.

**Target
Reading Skill**

Main Idea In this chapter you will focus on skills you can use to identify the main ideas as you read.

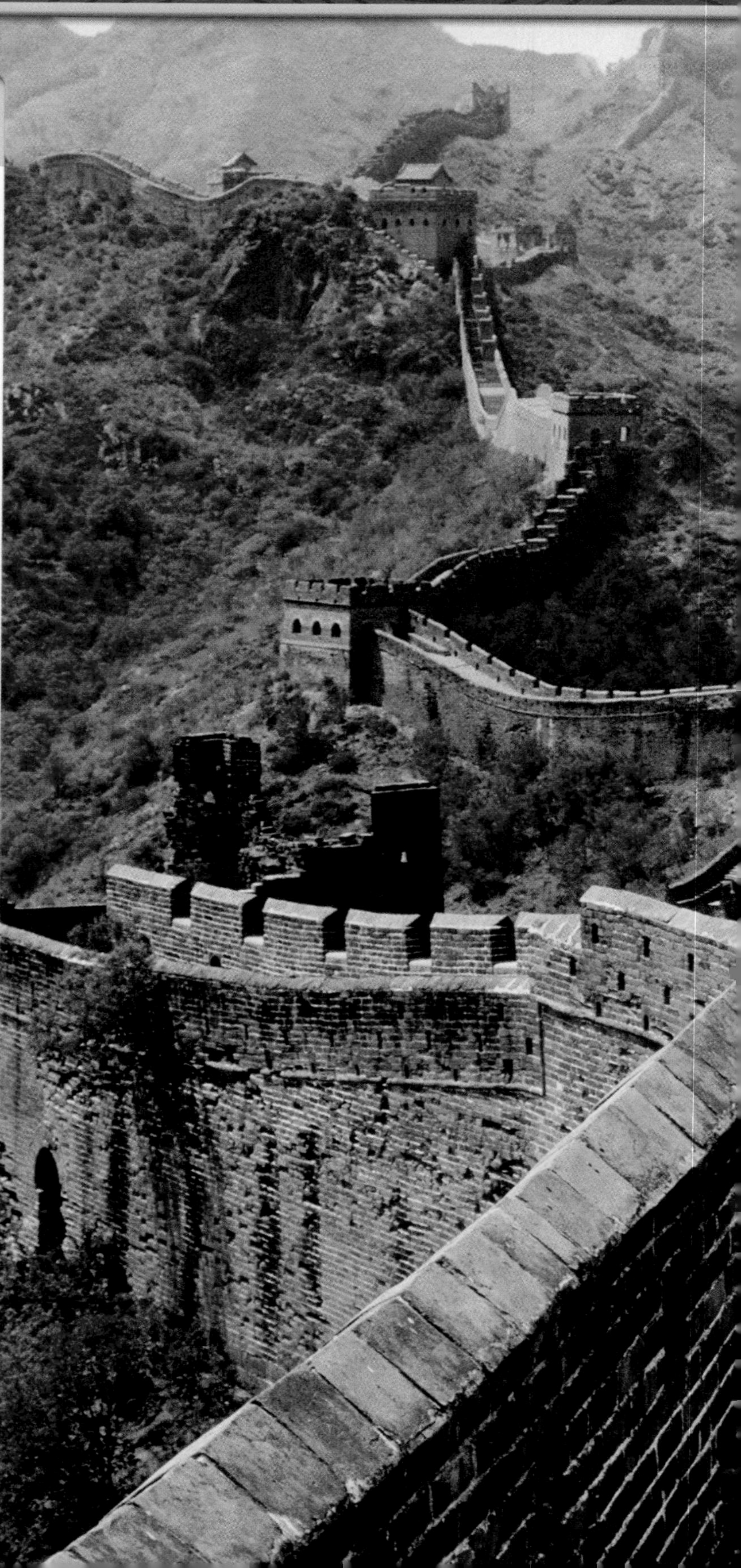

▶ The Great Wall of China

Ancient China

MAP MASTER™ Skills Activity

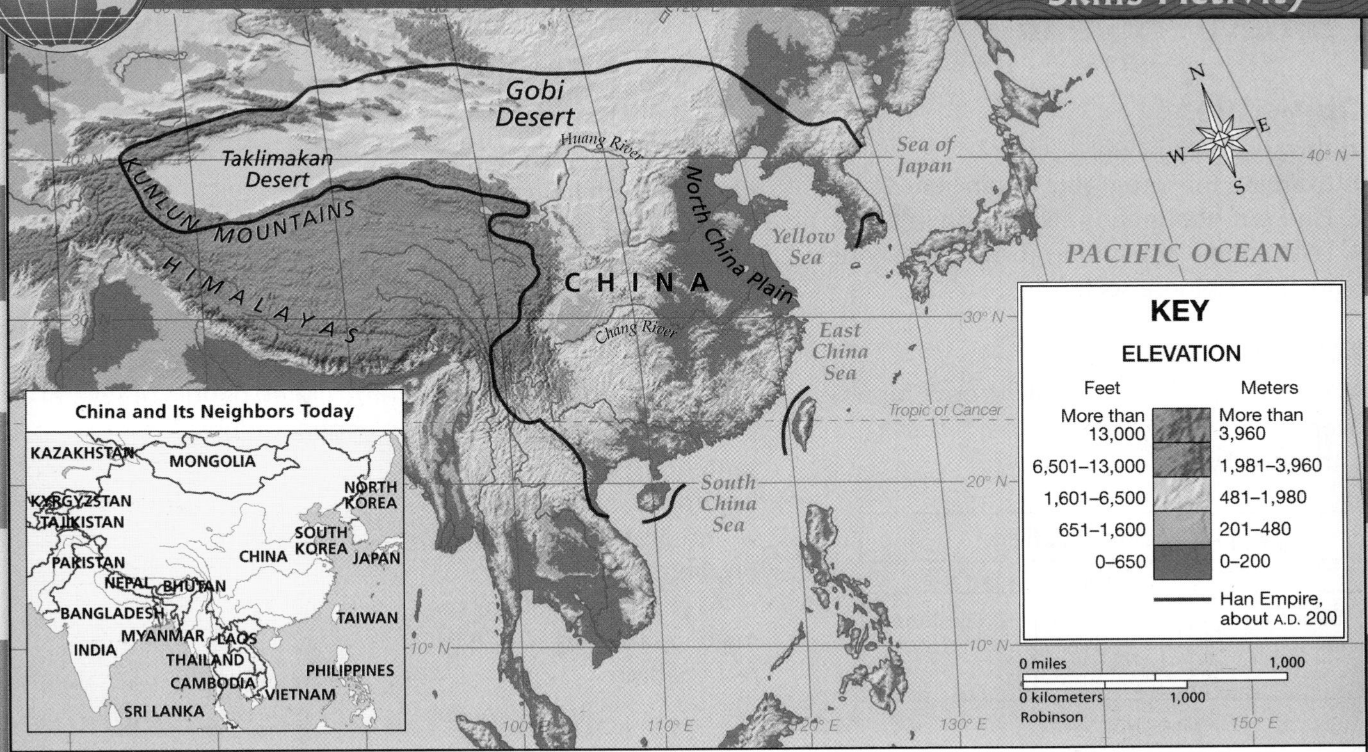

Gobi Desert
Taklimakan Desert
KUNLUN MOUNTAINS
HIMALAYAS
Huang River
North China Plain
CHINA
Chang River
Sea of Japan
Yellow Sea
East China Sea
South China Sea
PACIFIC OCEAN
Tropic of Cancer
40° N
30° N
20° N
10° N
100° E
110° E
120° E
130° E
150° E
N
E
S
W
KEY
ELEVATION
Feet
Meters
More than 13,000
More than 3,960
6,501–13,000
1,981–3,960
1,601–6,500
481–1,980
651–1,600
201–480
0–650
0–200
Han Empire, about A.D. 200
0 miles
1,000
0 kilometers
1,000
Robinson
China and Its Neighbors Today
KAZAKHSTAN
MONGOLIA
NORTH KOREA
KYRGYZSTAN
TAJIKISTAN
SOUTH KOREA
CHINA
JAPAN
PAKISTAN
NEPAL
BHUTAN
BANGLADESH
TAIWAN
MYANMAR
LAOS
INDIA
THAILAND
PHILIPPINES
CAMBODIA
VIETNAM
SRI LANKA

Location Notice that the boundaries of ancient China are marked by seas and mountains. **Identify** What other geographical features do you notice about ancient China? **Draw Conclusions** Choose a place on the map where you think Chinese civilization might have begun, and explain your choice.

Go Online
PHSchool.com Use Web Code **lbp-2511** for step-by-step **map skills practice.**

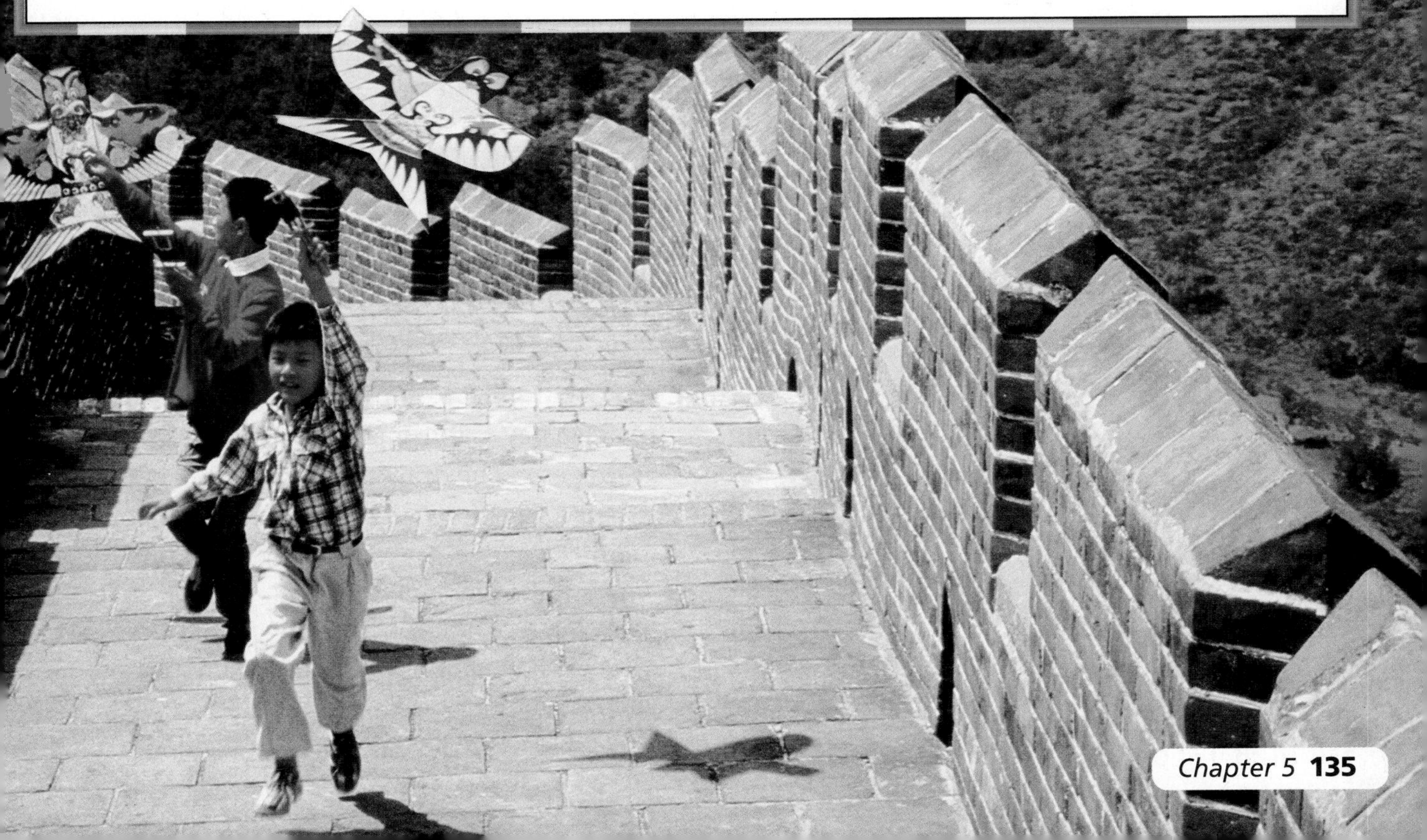

The Geography of China's River Valleys

Prepare to Read

Objectives

In this section you will
1. Examine the geography of ancient China.
2. Find out about early civilization in China.
3. Learn about the importance of family ties in early Chinese society.

Taking Notes

As you read, look for details about China's river valleys. Copy the chart below, and use it to record your findings.

China's River Valleys		
Geography • •	**Civilization** • •	**Families** • •

🎯 Target Reading Skill

Identify Main Ideas
The main idea is the most important point in a section of text. On page 137, the main idea for the section titled The Geography of Ancient China is stated in this sentence: "The climate, soil, landforms, and waterways varied greatly, depending on the region."

As you read, look for the main idea stated after each red heading.

Key Terms

- **loess** (LOH es) *n.* yellow-brown soil
- **dike** (dyk) *n.* a protective wall that controls or holds back water
- **extended family** (ek STEN did FAM uh lee) *n.* closely related people of several generations

What words would you use to describe dragons? You might think of these imaginary beasts as being fierce and scary. People of some cultures would agree with you. But to the ancient Chinese people, the dragon was a respected spirit, not a terrible monster. In ancient China, dragons were friendly beasts that brought good luck. Dragon gods were believed to be responsible for the rains that made the fields fertile. In China, dragon rain ceremonies date as far back as the 500s B.C.

The Chinese also used the image of this respected spirit to show the importance of their rivers. They traditionally described their rivers as dragons. The dragon's limbs were the smaller streams. They flowed into the dragon's body, or main river. The dragon's mouth was the delta, where the river flowed into the sea. Rivers were important to the development of civilization in China. Other landforms and climate played an important role as well.

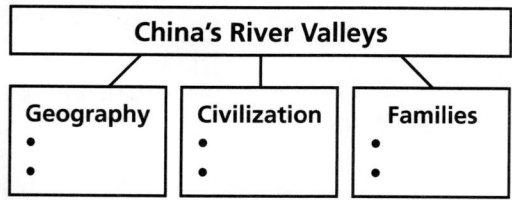

A sculpture of a Chinese dragon

The Geography of Ancient China

Ancient China covered a large area. The climate, soil, landforms, and waterways varied greatly, depending on the region. Turn to the map on page 135 to study the geography of ancient China.

Contrasting Climate and Landforms The North China Plain is located in East Asia. It is built up of soil deposits from the Huang (hwahng) River.

The North China Plain and its surrounding highlands, as well as far northern China, have only a brief, but intense, summer rainy season caused by monsoon winds. However, the region doesn't get much rain the rest of the year. As a result, the climate is very dry.

The climate in the south, in contrast, is warm and wet. Monsoons from the South China Sea bring heavy rains to southern China from March to September. Light rain falls the rest of the year.

A painting of a river voyage in China

Effects on Civilization Geographic barriers such as mountains and seas separated China from other lands. As a result, the Chinese had little knowledge of the civilizations of Egypt, India, Greece, and Rome. They were so sure that they lived at the center of the world that they called themselves the Middle Kingdom.

China's rivers overflowed their banks each spring, bringing fresh, fertile topsoil to the land. For that reason, China's first farming villages developed along its rivers. Civilization began along the Huang River and later spread south to wetter land along the Chang, China's longest river.

Terrace Farming
A man grows a crop of millet in northern China. **Apply Information** *Why does it make sense to grow crops on terraces in this part of China?*

A woman collects water from the Huang River. ▶

Yellow River The Huang is the second-longest river in China. The word *huang* means "yellow" in Chinese. It is called the "yellow river" because of the **loess** (LOH es), or yellow-brown soil, that its waters carry along. When the Huang floods, it deposits loess on the surrounding plain. Over many years, the Huang has carpeted the North China Plain with a thick layer of fertile soil. There, the Chinese grow a grain called millet. Millet has been an important part of the Chinese diet for thousands of years.

China's Sorrow The Chinese people also called the Huang China's Sorrow. It brought life to the land, but it also took life away. Destructive floods could come without warning, sometimes as often as every two years. Some floods drowned thousands of people. At times, the floodwaters ran with such force that they cut an entirely new path over the land. As a result, the course of the river could change by hundreds of miles.

Flood Control To help control the flooding, early Chinese people built dikes along the banks of the Huang. A **dike** is a protective wall that holds back the waters. As more loess settled to the bottom of the river, the level of the river rose. Eventually, the river rose high enough to overflow the dikes, causing even more deadly floods. Despite such dangers, the early Chinese people continued to settle along the banks of the Huang.

✓ **Reading Check** **What did the Chinese do to control flooding?**

The Yellow River
You can see from this photograph why the Huang's Chinese name means "yellow river." **Analyze Images** *How is the land near the river used?*

Early Civilization in China

Early farmers of the North China Plain probably were once nomads who moved from place to place to hunt and gather food. Historians do not know exactly when the first farming settlements developed in the Huang Valley. Some think it was as early as 5000 B.C. These early farming societies grew into civilizations that controlled parts of the Huang Valley.

The Shang Dynasty The Shang dynasty was the first civilization in China. It probably arose sometime around 1760 B.C. The Shang people built China's first cities. Among their many accomplishments was the production of some of the finest bronze work of ancient China.

The Shang people also produced the first Chinese writing system. Like Mesopotamia's cuneiform and our own alphabet, the Chinese writing system could be used for different languages. This was helpful for communication, because China had many regional languages.

About 600 years after the founding of the Shang dynasty, a new group emerged. This group, known as the Zhou (joh) people, lived in the Wei Valley to the west of the Shang people.

The Zhou Dynasty The territory of the Zhou people partly bordered the Shang territory. Sometimes these two neighbors lived peacefully side by side. At other times, they fought over territory. Finally, the Zhou conquered the Shang in about 1122 B.C. The Zhou dynasty ruled over ancient China for almost 1,000 years. This long period is divided into two parts—the earlier Western Zhou dynasty and the later Eastern Zhou dynasty. It was near the end of the Eastern Zhou dynasty that a period known as the Warring States began. During that time, small kingdoms fought for control over one another until a new dynasty—the Qin (chin)— finally emerged.

Mandate of Heaven Sometimes Chinese rulers inherited the throne. At other times, they fought for the right to rule. In either instance, the Chinese believed that rulers came to power because it was their destiny, or fate. This idea was called the Mandate of Heaven. A mandate is a law, or an order. The Mandate of Heaven supported a leader's right to rule his people. It also gave a father authority over his family.

✓ **Reading Check** What was the Mandate of Heaven?

Target Skill Identify Main Ideas Which sentence states the main idea under the heading Early Civilization in China?

A Shang dynasty turtle shell shows one of the earliest examples of Chinese writing.

A Chinese Family
Wealthy Chinese families could afford to have their portraits painted, like this one dating from the late 1700s. **Analyze Images** *How do we know that the family members in this portrait are probably part of an extended family?*

Bronze statue of a Chinese girl with a lamp, around 100 B.C. ▶

Importance of the Family

The family was the center of early Chinese society. It was considered to be of far more importance than the individual or the nation. A person's first responsibility was always to the family. The family, in turn, was each person's chief source of well-being.

Traditional Families A household in ancient China might contain as many as five generations living together. This meant that small children lived with their great-great-grandparents as well as their parents, uncles and aunts, cousins, brothers and sisters, and so on. These closely related people are called an **extended family.** In rich families, the members might live together in one big home. But most of China's people were poor. In farming villages, members of the extended family might live in separate one-room cottages. The cottages were within easy walking distance from one another.

Family Authority The status of each person in a Chinese extended family depended on his or her age and sex. The center of authority was usually the oldest man. He had the most privileges and the most power in the family. He decided who his children and grandchildren would marry. When children were disrespectful, he punished them severely. After the oldest male died, by tradition all his lands were divided among his sons. Each son then started his own household.

Women's Roles Women were considered to be of lower status than men. According to tradition, women were bound by what were called the three obediences: to obey their fathers in youth, their husbands after their marriage, and their sons in widowhood. Four virtues also guided women's behavior in ancient China: morality, modesty, proper speech, and domestic skills. When a woman married, she left her household and became part of her husband's family. In her new household, she was expected to obey her husband and respect the wishes of her mother-in-law.

Family Names In the 300s B.C., Chinese established the practice of using inherited family names along with a personal name. The inherited name was passed down from father to child. The other was for the individual. Examples of present-day family names include Mao, Chan, and Lu. Of course, people in the United States also use two names. In Chinese society, however, the family name comes first. If this system were used in American society, you would know the first President of the United States as Washington George, not George Washington. Think of other famous people in American history. What would their names be in the Chinese naming style?

The tradition of using family names first dates back to China's earliest times. It showed how important the family was in China. Centuries later, a great philosopher, or thinker, called Confucius (kun FYOO shus) had ideas about the role of the family in Chinese society. These ideas would have a great effect on the Chinese people.

Royal Seals
Emperors used seals, like the decorated cube above, to mark their names in ink. The characters shown at the top left representing the emperor's name are carved into the bottom face of the cube. **Infer** *Why do you think the ancient Chinese began using family names in addition to personal names?*

✔ **Reading Check** **What factors determined a person's status within early Chinese families?**

Section 1 Assessment

Key Terms
Review the key terms at the beginning of this section. Use each term in a sentence that explains its meaning.

Target Reading Skill
State the main ideas of each of the red headings in Section 1.

Comprehension and Critical Thinking
1. (a) Identify Effects How did the Huang River affect ancient Chinese civilization?
(b) Compare What do you think ancient China had in common with the ancient civilizations of Mesopotamia, Egypt, and India?

2. (a) Recall What was the first known civilization in China?
(b) Draw Conclusions Describe the importance of China's first civilization. What effect do you think it had on later civilizations in ancient China?
3. (a) Recall Describe the importance of family in early China.
(b) Apply Information In ancient China, members of an extended family often lived together in one home. How do you think the ancient Chinese benefited from their family structure?

Writing Activity
Suppose you were a member of an ancient Chinese family. Write a description of what your life would have been like.

Writing Tip Specific details will bring your description to life. First focus on one important aspect of life in ancient China that you want to describe. Then choose two or three interesting details to make your description more colorful.

Making Valid Generalizations

Sometimes people make broad generalizations that are not really true.

"People who like to read a lot are not interested in sports."

"Dog owners do not like cats."

A broad statement about a group of people is called a stereotype. A stereotype is not based on factual knowledge, and it is often untrue and unfair.

To avoid using stereotypes, be careful when you make a generalization. Some generalizations are valid—that is, they have value or worth. They are probably true, because they are based on specific facts. Other generalizations are not valid. They might be based on rumors or impressions instead of on facts. A stereotype is a generalization that may not be valid.

Learn the Skill

To make a valid generalization, follow these steps:

1 **Identify the specific facts that are contained within a source.** Become familiar with the facts in a piece of text, a table, or some other source.

2 **State what the facts have in common, and look for patterns.** Do any of the facts fit together in a way that makes a point about a broad subject? Do the data in a table or a graph point toward some kind of general statement?

3 **Make a generalization, or broad conclusion, about the facts.** Write your generalization as a sentence or paragraph.

4 **Test the generalization, and revise it if necessary.** You can test the validity of a generalization by using the guidelines in the box at left.

Testing a Generalization

- Are there enough facts in your source to support the generalization?
- Do any other facts support the generalization?
- Which are stronger, the examples of the generalization or the exceptions to it?
- Does the statement generalize too broadly or stereotype a group of people? Look for words such as *all, always,* or *every,* which can make a generalization invalid.
- Words such as *some, many, most,* and *often* help prevent a statement from being too general.

Flno

Practice the Skill

Turn to page 137, and reread the second paragraph that follows the title Effects on Civilization.

1 The title of the text will help you understand the topic. Find and write down at least three facts that relate to that topic.

2 From reading these facts, what major ideas can you learn about the topic? Do the facts suggest any ideas about China's rivers that are not specifically stated in the text?

3 Make a generalization about China's rivers and how they affected the growth of Chinese civilization. Make sure the facts support your statement.

4 If your statement does not meet the test for a valid generalization, try making it valid by rewriting it so that it is more limited.

The Huang River, China

Apply the Skill

We generalize in everyday speech: "Everybody loves the summer." "Most kids I know are into sports." "Nobody rents videos anymore. They rent DVDs." Find and write down three valid generalizations, and explain why they are valid. You can use generalizations that you find in your textbook, or you can write your own based on facts you know. Write down the facts that support each generalization.

Section 2

Confucius and His Teachings

Prepare to Read

Objectives

In this section you will
1. Learn about the life of Confucius.
2. Find out about the teachings of Confucius.
3. Understand the influence Confucianism had on Chinese society.

Taking Notes

As you read, summarize the teachings of Confucius and the influence they had on China. Copy the chart below, and use it to record your findings.

Confucius

Life	Teachings	Effects
• • • •	• • • •	• • • •

Target Reading Skill

Identify Supporting Details The main idea of a section of text is supported by details. These details may explain the main idea or give examples. On the next page, the main idea for the text under the heading The Life of Confucius is stated in this sentence: "Confucius was the most famous—and important—of the early Chinese thinkers."

As you read, note the details following each of the blue headings that tell more about the life of Confucius.

Key Terms

- **Confucius** (kun FYOO shus) *n.* (551– 479 B.C.) a Chinese philosopher and teacher whose beliefs had a great influence on Chinese life
- **philosophy** (fih LAHS uh fee) *n.* a system of beliefs and values
- **civil service** (SIV ul SUR vis) *n.* the group of people whose job it is to carry out the work of the government

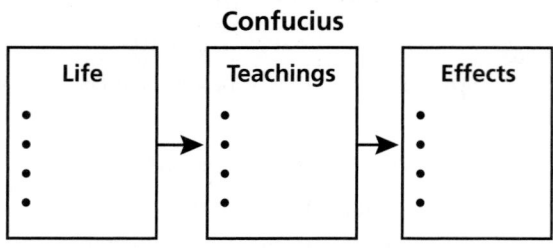

One day, the Chinese teacher and philosopher **Confucius** and his students were walking through the countryside. In the distance, they heard a woman crying. As they came around a bend in the road, they saw the woman kneeling at a grave. "Why are you crying?" they asked her. "Because," she answered, "a tiger killed my husband's father. Later, the tiger also killed my husband. Now, the tiger has killed my son as well."

They then asked the woman, "Why do you stay in this place after these terrible things have happened?" The woman answered, "Because there are no cruel rulers here." Confucius turned to his students and said, "Remember this. A cruel ruler is fiercer and more feared than a tiger."

After the death of Confucius, people told many stories about him. Like the story of the woman and the tiger, most stories contained an important lesson.

Confucius, c. 551– 479 B.C.

The Life of Confucius

Confucius was the most famous—and important—of the early Chinese thinkers. The Chinese called him Kong Fu Zi (kong foo dzih), or "Master Kong." *Confucius* is the Latinized version of this name.

The Early Years Confucius was born in 551 B.C. to a noble but poor family of the North China Plain. He loved learning and was mostly self-taught. He hoped to advance to an important government office, but he never succeeded in that way. Instead, he decided to try teaching.

A Pioneer Teacher Many historians think that Confucius was China's first professional teacher. Confucius charged students a fee to take classes. He taught the students his views of life and government. He was a dedicated teacher:

> **"From the very poorest upward . . . none has ever come to me without receiving instruction. I instruct only a student who bursts with eagerness."**
>
> —*Confucius*

Later in his life, Confucius searched for a ruler who would follow his teachings, but he could find no such ruler. He died in 479 B.C. at age 73. By the time of his death, he believed his life had been a failure. He had no way of knowing that his teachings would be followed for many centuries.

Identify Supporting Details
What detail in the paragraph at the left supports the idea that Confucius was an important Chinese thinker?

 **Reading Check** **What kind of students did Confucius like to teach?**

Relationships Based on the Teachings of Confucius

▼ **Ruler and ruled**

Husband and wife ►

▲ **Father and son**

Older brother and younger brother ►

Five Human Relationships
Confucius believed that Chinese society was built upon the five relationships shown above. **Conclude** *According to Confucius, how does a fair and just ruler benefit society?*

Confucius' ideas were studied in books like this one.

The Teachings of Confucius

Confucius did not claim to be an original thinker. He felt that his role was to pass on the forgotten teachings of wise people from an earlier age. In many of his teachings he tried to persuade rulers to reform. He also hoped to bring peace, stability, and prosperity to China's kingdoms.

Confucianism Confucius himself never wrote down his teachings. Instead, his students gathered a collection of his sayings after his death. Together, these writings made up a system of beliefs and values, or a **philosophy**. That philosophy became known as Confucianism. Confucianism was one of several important philosophies of ancient China. Over time, it began to govern many aspects of life there.

Bringing Order to Society Confucius lived during a time of frequent warfare in China. Powerful rulers of several Chinese states, or kingdoms, fought one another for the control of land. They seemed more interested in gaining power than in ruling wisely. Confucius hoped to persuade these rulers to change their ways and bring peace and order to China.

The goal of Confucius was to bring order to society. He believed that if people could be taught to behave properly toward one another, order and peace would result. Society would prosper.

▼ **Friend and friend**

Respecting Others Confucius said that people should know their place in the family and in society. They ought to respect the people above and below them and treat others justly. He described five human relationships: ruler and ruled; father and son; husband and wife; older brother and younger brother; and friend and friend. Then he explained how people should behave in each of these relationships. Confucius said that people in authority—princes or parents—must set good examples. For example, if a ruler was fair, his people would follow his example and treat one another fairly, too. Confucius summarized his ideas about relationships in a simple way. It is similar to what Christians and Jews call the Golden Rule: "Do not do to others what you would not want done to yourself."

Religious Traditions Although Confucianism is a philosophy, it has also functioned as a religion for many people. Like Hindus or Buddhists, those who practice Confucianism are part of a moral community. The teachings of Confucius helped guide many of the ancient Chinese in how to behave. But many ancient Chinese also practiced Confucianism alongside their existing religious traditions.

Ancient China was home to many kinds of religious beliefs and practices: the worship of ancestors, the honoring of gods, and the belief in spirits. Most Chinese believed that life should be lived in harmony with nature. Happiness came from living a balanced life. A religious philosophy known as Taoism (DOW iz um) supported these ideas. Taoism was based on the writings of Laozi (LOW dzuh), a Chinese thinker who lived in the 500s B.C. The Taoists loved nature, and they believed in leading simple and selfless lives.

At times, Taoism would rival Confucianism for popularity in China. But overall, the teachings of Confucius would remain the most widely studied of Chinese philosophies.

Go **Online**
PHSchool.com Use Web Code **mup-0822** for an interactive tour of the temple of Confucius.

A painting of Laozi riding a buffalo, attended by a servant

✓ Reading Check **Describe the religious traditions of ancient China.**

A Chinese emperor oversees students at a civil service exam.

The Influence of Confucius

The teachings of Confucius came to have a major effect on Chinese government. They became part of the basic training for members of the civil service. The **civil service** is the group of people who carry out the work of government.

A Merit System   Before the ideas of Confucius took hold, government posts were generally given to the sons of powerful people. Afterward, any man could hold a government post based on merit—that is, on how qualified he was or how well he did his job. Candidates for government jobs had to pass official examinations. These exams were based on the teachings of Confucius.

Rising to High Positions   The examination system did not open government jobs to everyone. Candidates still had to know how to read. This rule made it difficult for a poor man to enter the government. But it was not impossible. Many talented but poor young men learned to read and rose to high government positions.

Confucius would have been surprised at the influence he had on China. He did not consider himself particularly wise or good. But he left a lasting mark on Chinese life.

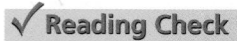 **Reading Check**   **Why was it difficult for poor men to work in the civil service?**

 ## Section 2 Assessment

Key Terms
Review the key terms at the beginning of this section. Use each term in a sentence that explains its meaning.

 **Target Reading Skill**
State the details that support the main idea on page 145.

Comprehension and Critical Thinking
1. (a) Recall How did Confucius become a teacher?
(b) Transfer Information
Confucius would teach only those students who wanted to learn. How does his rule apply to your experience as a student?

2. (a) List What were the basic teachings of Confucius?
(b) Explain Why did Confucius think it was important to teach rulers how to behave?
3. (a) Describe How did the ideas of Confucius change the way civil servants were chosen in ancient China?
(b) Predict Confucius hoped to become a government worker, but he became a teacher instead. Do you think his influence on Chinese society would have been different if he had gotten his wish? Explain your answer.

Writing Activity
Suppose that you are a government official in a small state in northern China. One day, a wandering teacher named Confucius arrives. Write a journal entry that describes what Confucius says and how your ruler reacts to him.

For: An activity on Confucius
Visit: PHSchool.com
Web Code: lbd-2502

Prepare to Read

Objectives

In this section, you will
1. Learn about the rise of the Qin dynasty.
2. Find out how Emperor Shi Huangdi attempted to unify the economy and culture of China.
3. Examine the actions of the Han dynasty's leaders.

Taking Notes

As you read, find details about Chinese rulers and life in China during the Qin and the Han dynasties. Copy the table below, and use it to record your findings.

Qin Dynasty	Han Dynasty
•	•
•	•
•	•

Target Reading Skill

Identify Implied Main Ideas Sometimes main ideas are not stated directly. However, all the details in a section of text add up to a main idea. For example, after reading and adding up all the details on page 150 following the heading The Qin Dynasty, you could state the main idea this way: "China was unified and strengthened by its first emperor, Shi Huangdi."

Carefully read the details in the paragraphs below. Then state the main idea.

Key Terms

- **Shi Huangdi** (shur hwahng DEE) *n.* founder of the Qin dynasty and China's first emperor
- **currency** (KUR un see) *n.* the type of money used by a group or a nation
- **Liu Bang** (LYOH bahng) *n.* the founder of the Han dynasty
- **Wudi** (woo dee) *n.* Chinese emperor who brought the Han dynasty to its greatest strength
- **warlord** (WAWR lawrd) *n.* a local leader of an armed group

In 1974, several farmers were digging a well in a grove of trees in northern China. Six feet down, they found some terra cotta, a reddish type of pottery. Another five feet down, they unearthed the terra-cotta head of a man. Archaeologists took over and began digging. They discovered more than 6,000 life-sized statues of soldiers and horses, along with wood and bronze chariots and metal weapons. It was a terra-cotta army. For more than 2,000 years, these buried soldiers had kept watch at the tomb of China's first emperor, **Shi Huangdi** (shur hwahng DEE).

With his underground army, Shi Huangdi had planned to rule a second empire in the afterlife. He had also made grand plans for the real-life empire he created in China. His dynasty, he boasted, would last for 10,000 generations.

These terra-cotta warriors guarded Shi Huangdi's tomb in the ancient city of Chang'an, China.

The Great Wall of China
The Great Wall winds its way across the mountains and plains of northern China. **Infer** *What does the size of the wall tell you about Shi Huangdi's enemies?*

Discovery CHANNEL SCHOOL Video
Explore the Great Wall of China.

The Qin Dynasty

Shi Huangdi's dynasty lasted only two generations, but that was still a huge accomplishment. Before that time, China was divided into seven warring kingdoms. Shi Huangdi conquered these kingdoms to unify China.

China's First Emperor Shi Huangdi's original name was Zhao Zheng (jow jeng). He ruled the Qin (chin) people, who lived along China's western border. By 221 B.C., Zheng had extended his rule over most of the land that makes up modern-day China. When Zheng established the Qin dynasty, he took the name Shi Huangdi, meaning "First Emperor." Because Qin is sometimes spelled *Ch'in*, the name China comes from the Qin dynasty.

Strengthening the Empire Shi Huangdi sought to strengthen China through strong and harsh rule. One of his first tasks was to protect the new empire from its enemies.

Throughout history, nomads had attacked China along its vast northern border. Shi Huangdi had a plan to end these border wars. He ordered what became the largest construction project in Chinese history. It is now called the Great Wall of China. Turn to page 152 and locate the wall on the map titled Qin and Han Empires.

Previous rulers had built walls along the border. Shi Huangdi decided to connect them. He ordered farmers from their fields and merchants from their stores to form an army of hundreds of thousands of workers. Shi Huangdi's wall took about ten years to construct. After Shi Huangdi died, the wall fell into disrepair. Over time, other emperors repaired the wall and added new sections to it. Because some sections overlap, the Great Wall is really a system of walls. In all, the Great Wall stretches about 4,500 miles (7,200 kilometers) in length.

Organizing the Government To help put down rebellions within the empire, Shi Huangdi put thousands of farmers to work building roads. The new roads enabled his armies to rush to the scene of any uprisings. The emperor killed or imprisoned any local rulers who opposed him. Shi Huangdi divided all of China into areas called districts. Each district had a government run by the emperor's trusted officials.

✓ Reading Check **How was China's Great Wall built?**

Unifying Economy and Culture

Shi Huangdi was not content to unify the government of China. He also wanted the many peoples of his united kingdom to have one economy and one culture.

Economic and Cultural Improvements Shi Huangdi declared that one **currency,** or type of money, be used throughout China. The new currency was a round coin with a square hole in the middle. A common currency made it easier for one region of China to trade goods with another. Shi Huangdi also ordered the creation of common weights and measures, an improved system of writing, and a law code.

Restricting Freedoms Shi Huangdi also tried to control the thoughts of his people. In 213 B.C., he outlawed the ideas of Confucius and other important thinkers. Instead, he required that people learn the philosophies of Qin scholars.

The Qin believed in legalism, the idea that people should be punished for bad behavior and rewarded for good behavior. Legalists thought that the people of China should work to serve the government and the emperor. The Qin dynasty practiced a strict and sometimes brutal form of legalism. Shi Huangdi commanded that all the books in China be burned except those about medicine, technology, and farming. Hundreds of scholars protested the order. Shi Huangdi had them all killed.

The End of a Dynasty Shi Huangdi's death in 210 B.C. was followed by four years of chaos and civil war that ended in the murder of his son. Power then passed to Shi Huangdi's grandson, but he could not hold China together. Rebellions broke out. The dynasty that was supposed to last for 10,000 generations lasted for only 15 years.

✓ Reading Check **How did Shi Huangdi try to limit his people's freedoms?**

Bronze cooking pot, Shang dynasty

The Rise and Fall of Chinese Dynasties

A new dynasty rises.
• A strong ruler defeats other local rulers.
• The new dynasty expands China's borders.

The new dynasty rules.
• It restores peace.
• It chooses loyal officials.
• It makes reforms.

The dynasty grows weak.
• The large empire becomes difficult to govern.
• Leaders lose control of the provinces.

A period of violence follows. Local rulers fight for power.

Lady of the Emperor's court, statue, A.D. 600s

The dynasty falls. Rebellions destroy the weakened dynasty.

■ **Diagram Skills**

Although many different dynasties ruled China throughout its long history, each rose and fell in a similar pattern. **Describe** Why do dynasties fall? **Analyze Information** Why might a dynasty become weaker as it grows larger?

Human-Environment Interaction Both natural and human-made features shaped the borders of the Qin and Han empires. **Identify** What feature formed the northern border of the Qin Empire? **Infer** What geographical feature may have limited the expansion of the Han Empire to the southwest?

Go Online
PHSchool.com Use Web Code **lbp-2523** for step-by-step map skills practice.

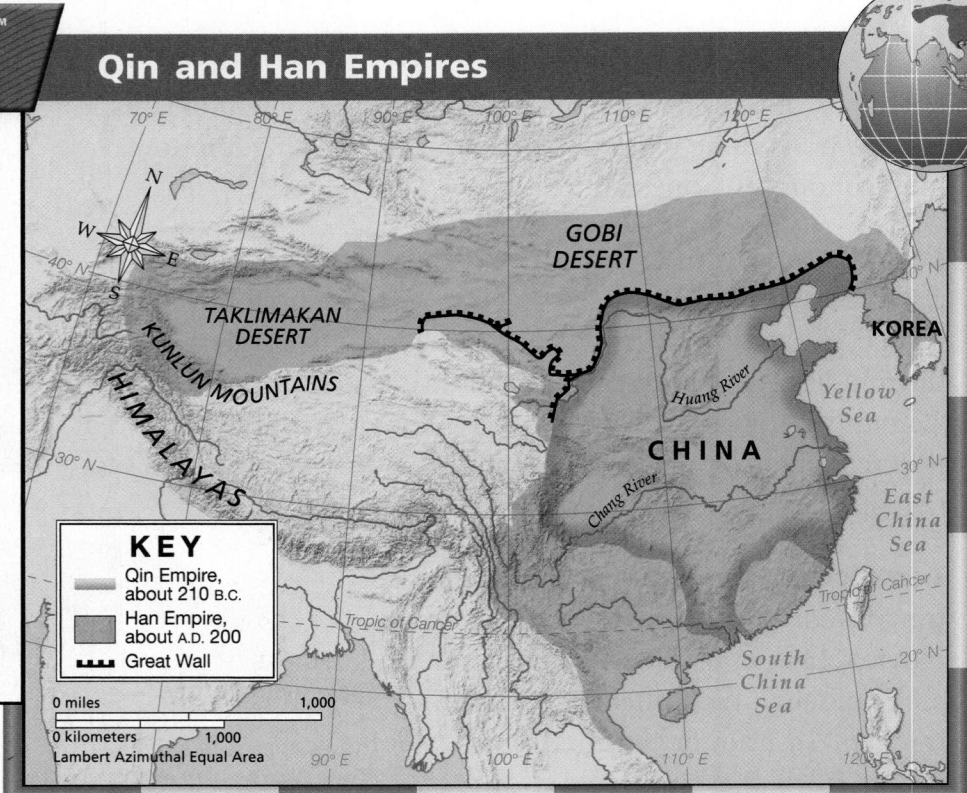

KEY
- Qin Empire, about 210 B.C.
- Han Empire, about A.D. 200
- Great Wall

0 miles 1,000
0 kilometers 1,000
Lambert Azimuthal Equal Area

Go Online
PHSchool.com Use Web Code **mup-0823** for an interactivity on military technology in China.

The Han Dynasty

One of the rebels who helped overthrow the Qin dynasty was a talented ruler named Liu Bang (LYOH bahng). By 202 B.C., **Liu Bang** won out over his rivals and became emperor of China. Born a peasant, Liu Bang became the first emperor of a new dynasty: the Han (hahn). Liu Bang created a stable government, but one that was was less harsh than Shi Huangdi's.

Stable governments were a feature of the Han dynasty, which lasted for about 400 years. Han rulers realized that they needed educated people to work in the government. They set up the civil service system based on Confucianism to meet that need.

Wudi: The Warrior Emperor In 140 B.C., Liu Bang's great-grandson, Wudi, came to power. Under **Wudi** (woo dee), the Han dynasty reached its greatest power. About 15 years old when he took the throne, Wudi ruled for more than 50 years.

Wudi's main interests were war and military matters. In fact, his name means "Warrior Emperor." He made improvements to Shi Huangdi's Great Wall. He also strengthened the army. By the end of Wudi's reign, Chinese rule stretched west into Central Asia, east into present-day northern and central Korea, and south into present-day Vietnam. Locate the Han Empire on the map titled Qin and Han Empires.

Links to Art

Han Dynasty Bronze Work Han dynasty artisans created beautiful objects of bronze, including finely made mirrors. On one side of the mirror, the metal was polished enough to show a reflection. The back was decorated with gems, animal symbols, and writing. Mirrors were important in China because they symbolized self-knowledge. At the right is the decorated side of a bronze mirror.

The End of the Han Empire   The great emperor Wudi died in 87 B.C. China's stability and prosperity continued under later Han emperors. Many new ideas and technologies developed. But over time, the empire began to weaken. A series of very young emperors—one was only 100 days old—ruled the empire. People within the government struggled for power over these young emperors. While they struggled, no one paid attention to running the empire. Roads and canals fell into disrepair.

As the rule of the emperors weakened, **warlords,** local leaders of armed groups, gained power. The last Han emperor was kept in power by one such warlord, named Cao Pei. At first Cao Pei tried to control the empire through the emperor. In A.D. 220, he declared an end to the Han dynasty. In its place, he set up his own Wei dynasty. However, the Wei dynasty had control only over parts of northern China. It ended after about 50 years, and China broke up into a number of smaller kingdoms.

✓ Reading Check   **What happened in A.D. 220?**

Identify Implied Main Ideas
In one sentence, state what all the details in the paragraph at the left imply.

This bronze statue of a man on horseback dates from the Han dynasty.

Section 3 Assessment

Key Terms
Review the key terms at the beginning of this section. Use each term in a sentence that explains its meaning.

Target Reading Skill
State the three main ideas in Section 3.

Comprehension and Critical Thinking

1. (a) Describe What measures did Shi Huangdi take to strengthen the empire and organize the government?
(b) Summarize Why is Shi Huangdi a major figure in Chinese history?

2. (a) Identify What measures did Shi Huangdi take to unite the economy and culture of China?
(b) Analyze Information How did all of Shi Huangdi's efforts strengthen the empire? How did his leadership hurt the empire?
3. (a) Recall What characterized the government of China during the Han dynasty?
(b) Compare and Contrast Compare the ways the emperors of the Qin dynasty and the emperors of the Han dynasty viewed the ideas of Confucius. How were their viewpoints similar or different?

Writing Activity
The farmers who discovered Shi Huangdi's terra-cotta army made one of the most important archaeological finds in history. Write a list of questions that you would like to ask them about their discovery.

Writing Tip   Write your questions in a logical order. For instance, you could begin with a few general questions. Later, narrow your focus with more specific questions.

Swooping down from the Mongolian plain, the legendary Xiongnu (shong noo) warriors came not to conquer, but to steal. They came on horseback, wild, dust-covered, and fierce. In attacks that terrorized Chinese border towns, the Xiongnu stole Chinese silks and other luxuries, galloping off with all they could carry. The great Han warrior emperor, Wudi, devoted his long half-century reign (140–87 B.C.) to taming China's frontier and exploring civilizations beyond the known world of his time.

The Expeditions Emperor Wudi chose Zhang Qian (jahng chyen) to lead a dangerous expedition to the western frontier. Zhang, an officer in Wudi's imperial guard, led the caravan (shown at the right) from the Han capital of Chang'an in 138 B.C. His mission was to befriend the Yuezhi (yooeh jur), enemies of the Xiongnu, and to rally them to war. Thirteen years later, Zhang returned—to tell Wudi not of war, but of unimagined wealth to be gained in trade with western societies. So Wudi sent him west again, in 119 B.C., to open government and economic ties with other lands.

During his travels, Zhang learned of swift horses owned by the people of the Fergana Valley. Wudi's forces later captured some of the Fergana horses (depicted in the bronze statue at the top of this page). Wudi's warriors ultimately drove the Xiongnu far from China's borders and opened a gateway to the west.

Han Bowl and Spoon
Everyday goods, such as this Han dynasty pottery, would have been useful on the expedition.

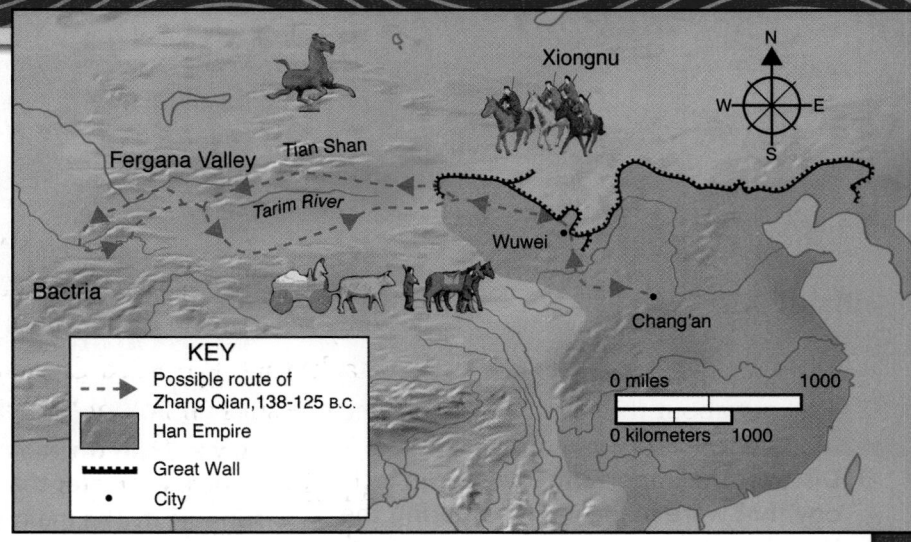

KEY
- - → Possible route of Zhang Qian, 138-125 B.C.
▬ Han Empire
▬▬ Great Wall
• City

The First Expedition On their journey, Zhang and his men were captured by the Xiongnu. After ten years, they escaped. By the time Zhang met the Yuezhi, they were settled peacefully and had no appetite for war. Zhang continued west to gold-rich Bactria before heading home.

Assessment

Explain Why did Emperor Wudi send expeditions to China's western frontier?

Identify Effects How did these expeditions benefit China?

Connecting Roads   The Silk Road was a series of routes covering more than 4,000 miles (6,400 kilometers), a little less than the distance from present-day Chicago to Hawaii. Follow the routes on the map above titled The Silk Road.

The Silk Road followed a challenging route through mountainous country and desert land. The road passed through Persia and Mesopotamia. Finally, it turned north to the city of Antioch (AN tee ahk), in present-day Turkey. From there, traders shipped goods across the Mediterranean to Rome, Greece, Egypt, and other lands that bordered the Mediterranean.

A terra-cotta statue of a traveler on a camel, about A.D. 700

Prepare to Read

Objectives
In this section you will
1. Learn about the Silk Road.
2. Find out about the Han dynasty's respect for tradition and learning.

Target Reading Skill
Identify Supporting Details Details in a section of text may explain the main idea

Key Terms
- **Silk Road** (silk rohd) *n.* an ancient trade route between China and Europe

Making Silk
A scroll from the 1100s shows Chinese women beating silk fibers in a trough. Silk was used to make musical instruments, fishing line, and even paper. **Infer** *Why was the Silk Road named after this material?*

A Route for Goods   Few travelers ever journeyed the entire length of the Silk Road. Generally, goods were passed from trader to trader as they crossed Asia. With each trade along the route, the price of the goods went up. By the time the goods arrived at the end of their journey, they were very expensive.

The Silk Road got its name from **silk,** a valuable cloth originally made only in China. Han farmers had developed new methods for raising silkworms, the caterpillars that made the silk. Han workers found new ways to weave and dye the silk. These methods were closely guarded secrets. The penalty for revealing them was death.

The arrival of silk in Europe created great excitement. Wealthy Romans prized Chinese silk and were willing to pay high prices for it. And wealthy people in China would pay well for glass, horses, ivory, woolens, and linen cloth from Rome.

A Route for Ideas   More than goods traveled the road. New ideas did, too. For example, missionaries from India traveled to China along a section of the road and brought the religion of Buddhism with them. By the time the Han dynasty ended, Buddhism was becoming a major religion in China.

✓ **Reading Check** **What are silkworms?**

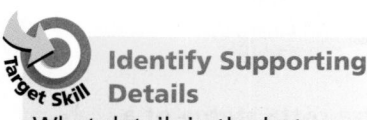

Tradition and Learning

Traditional Chinese ideas flourished during the Han dynasty. People returned to the teachings of Confucius. A renewed interest in learning led one Han scholar to record the early history of China. His efforts helped the people of China understand their past.

Identify Supporting Details
What details in the last paragraph on this page tell about tradition and learning during the Han dynasty?

Respect for Learning   Han rulers found that during troubled times in the past, many people had lost respect for their traditions. As a way of bringing back this respect, rulers encouraged people to return to the teachings of Confucius. Rulers of the Han and later dynasties also required members of the civil service to be educated in Confucian teachings.

The arts and scholarship flourished under the Han dynasty. Expressive poetry reflected Chinese culture. Chinese scholars put together the first dictionary of the Chinese language. But the greatest advances happened in the field of history.

The Silk Road

KEY

	Han Empire
—	Silk Road
▪▪▪▪	Great Wall
•	City

0 miles 1,000
0 kilometers 1,000
Robinson

Map labels: ASIA MINOR, Antioch, Mediterranean Sea, MESOPOTAMIA, Ctesiphon, Tigris R., Euphrates R., Caspian Sea, PERSIA, Marakanda, Kuldja, TIAN SHAN, Kashgar, PAMIR MTS., Aksu, Khotan, Taklimakan Desert, Turfan, GOBI DESERT, Anxi, NAN SHAN, ASIA, HIMALAYAS, Indus River, Ganges River, INDIA, INDIAN OCEAN, Huang River, Chang'an, Chang River, CHINA, Mekong River, South China Sea, Tropic of Cancer

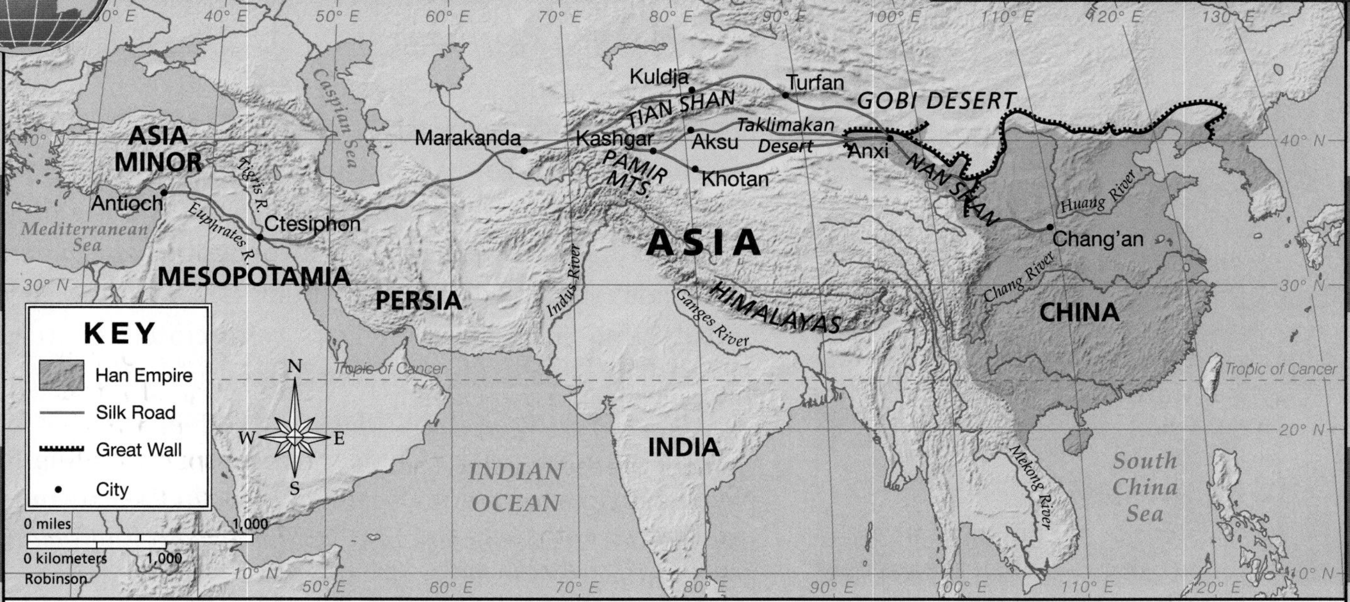

Movement Travel along the Silk Road was very dangerous. Travelers faced geographical and human-made barriers, attacks by robbers, and extreme weather conditions. **Note** Why did the Silk Road split into two routes in Central Asia? **Analyze Information** Judging from the map, what might have been the most difficult part of the route?

Go Online
PHSchool.com Use Web Code
lbp-2534 for step-by-step
map skills practice.

The Silk Road

The Emperor Wudi's conquests in the west brought the Chinese into contact with the people of Central Asia. Trade with these people introduced the Chinese to such new foods as grapes, walnuts, and garlic. In turn, Chinese goods and ideas passed to the peoples living to the West. This exchange of goods gave rise to a major trade route—the Silk Road. This ran all the way from China to the Mediterranean Sea.

Connecting Roads The Silk Road was a series of routes covering more than 4,000 miles (6,400 kilometers), a little less than the distance from present-day Chicago to Hawaii. Follow the routes on the map above titled The Silk Road.

The Silk Road followed a challenging route through mountainous country and desert land. The road passed through Persia and Mesopotamia. Finally, it turned north to the city of Antioch (AN tee ahk), in present-day Turkey. From there, traders shipped goods across the Mediterranean to Rome, Greece, Egypt, and other lands that bordered the Mediterranean.

A terra-cotta statue of a traveler on a camel, about A.D. 700

Making Silk
A scroll from the 1100s shows Chinese women beating silk fibers in a trough. Silk was used to make musical instruments, fishing line, and even paper. **Infer** *Why was the Silk Road named after this material?*

Identify Supporting Details
What details in the last paragraph on this page tell about tradition and learning during the Han dynasty?

A Route for Goods Few travelers ever journeyed the entire length of the Silk Road. Generally, goods were passed from trader to trader as they crossed Asia. With each trade along the route, the price of the goods went up. By the time the goods arrived at the end of their journey, they were very expensive.

The Silk Road got its name from **silk,** a valuable cloth originally made only in China. Han farmers had developed new methods for raising silkworms, the caterpillars that made the silk. Han workers found new ways to weave and dye the silk. These methods were closely guarded secrets. The penalty for revealing them was death.

The arrival of silk in Europe created great excitement. Wealthy Romans prized Chinese silk and were willing to pay high prices for it. And wealthy people in China would pay well for glass, horses, ivory, woolens, and linen cloth from Rome.

A Route for Ideas More than goods traveled the road. New ideas did, too. For example, missionaries from India traveled to China along a section of the road and brought the religion of Buddhism with them. By the time the Han dynasty ended, Buddhism was becoming a major religion in China.

✓ Reading Check **What are silkworms?**

Tradition and Learning

Traditional Chinese ideas flourished during the Han dynasty. People returned to the teachings of Confucius. A renewed interest in learning led one Han scholar to record the early history of China. His efforts helped the people of China understand their past.

Respect for Learning Han rulers found that during troubled times in the past, many people had lost respect for their traditions. As a way of bringing back this respect, rulers encouraged people to return to the teachings of Confucius. Rulers of the Han and later dynasties also required members of the civil service to be educated in Confucian teachings.

The arts and scholarship flourished under the Han dynasty. Expressive poetry reflected Chinese culture. Chinese scholars put together the first dictionary of the Chinese language. But the greatest advances happened in the field of history.

A History of China   Until the time of the Han dynasty, the Chinese people had little knowledge of their own history. They knew only myths that had been passed down from generation to generation. Often, these stories were in conflict with one another. No one was sure exactly when the various Chinese rulers had lived or what each had accomplished.

The scholar Sima Qian (sih MAH chen) decided to solve the problem. **Sima Qian** spent his life writing a history of China from mythical times to the reign of Wudi. Sima described his work:

> **❝**I wish to examine all that encircles heaven and man. I want to probe the changes of the past and present.**❞**
>
> —Sima Qian

Sima Qian's work, called *Historical Records,* is a major source of information about ancient China.

✓ **Reading Check**   **What problem did Sima Qian solve?**

Han Technology

Because the Han government was stable, the Chinese could turn their attention to improving their society. During the Han dynasty, China became the most advanced civilization in the world.

Advances in Technology   The Chinese made significant advances in farming tools and other technologies. Some of these advances are shown in the chart at the right, titled Achievements in Ancient China. During the Han dynasty, the Chinese invented many practical devices that did not reach Europe until centuries later. Among these was paper—something the world still depends on every day.

Achievements in Ancient China

The Arts
- Silk weaving
- Bronze working
- Architecture (temples and palaces)
- Poetry and history
▶ Jade carving

Medicine
◀ Acupuncture—the treatment of disease using needles
- Herbal remedies—the use of plants in the practice of medicine
- Circulatory system—the discovery that blood travels through the body

Technology
- Paper made from wood pulp
- Iron plow for breaking up soil
- Rudder—a device used to steer ships
- Seismoscope—a device that registers the occurrence of earthquakes
- Compass
▼ Wheelbarrow

Arts, Medicine, and Technology
The Chinese made great advances during the Han dynasty. **Analyze** *Which two inventions were especially useful to farmers? Explain your answer.*

The Invention of Paper The Chinese first used wooden scrolls and bones to keep records. Later, they wrote messages and even whole books on silk. Then, around A.D. 105, the Chinese recorded one of their greatest achievements: the invention of paper. Archaeological evidence shows that paper may have already been in use before that time. Early paper was made from materials such as tree bark, hemp, and old rags. The materials were soaked in water, beaten into pulp, and dried flat on a screen mold.

The availability of paper greatly influenced learning and the arts in China. After several centuries, the use of paper spread across Asia and into Europe. Eventually, paper replaced papyrus from Egypt as the material for scrolls and books.

The Han dynasty came to an end in the A.D. 200s. But its accomplishments were not forgotten. Today, people in China still call themselves "the children of Han."

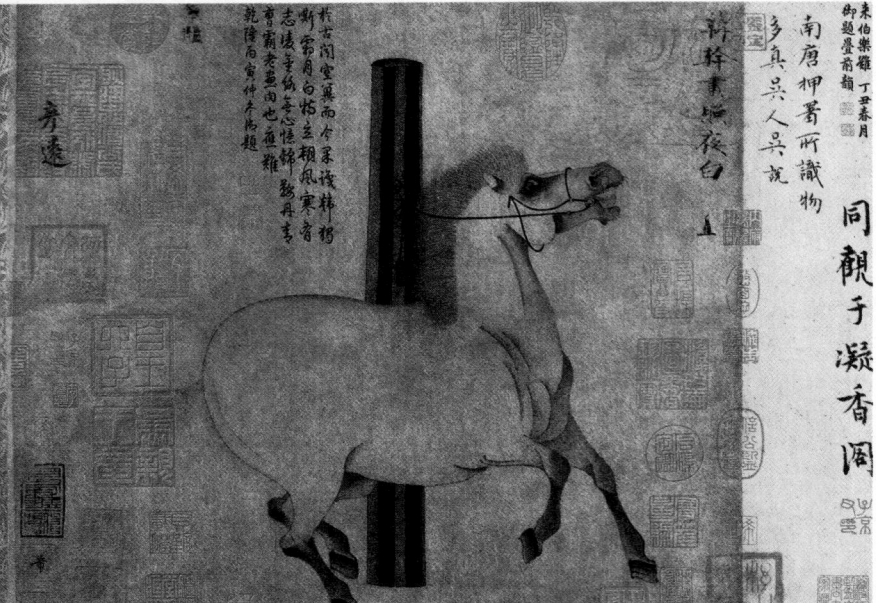

A Chinese emperor's favorite horse, named Night-Shining White, is shown in this painting from the A.D. 700s.

 **Reading Check** What did the Chinese write on before they invented paper?

Section 4 Assessment

Key Terms

Review the key terms at the beginning of this section. Use each term in a sentence that explains its meaning.

Target Reading Skill

State the details that support the main idea on page 156.

Comprehension and Critical Thinking

1. (a) Locate Describe the route of the Silk Road.
(b) Infer Why were the secrets of silk-making so closely guarded?

2. (a) List In what ways did the Han dynasty show a respect for Chinese traditions?
(b) Draw Conclusions Describe the importance of Sima Qian's role in preserving Chinese traditions.
3. (a) Recall Name three important inventions or achievements during the Han dynasty.
(b) Predict How did the achievements of the Han dynasty affect later generations of Chinese people, as well as other peoples?

Writing Activity

Suppose that you are a poet living in ancient Chang'an, at one end of the Silk Road. Write a poem about what you have seen or heard about the Silk Road from living in Chang'an.

For: An activity on ancient Chinese technology
Visit: PHSchool.com
Web Code: lbd-2504

Review and Assessment

Terra-cotta warriors

◆ Chapter Summary

Section 1: The Geography of China's River Valleys

- Flooding rivers, monsoon rains, and mountain and ocean barriers greatly affected China's early peoples.
- China's first known civilization, the Shang dynasty, arose in the Huang Valley.
- The family, headed by the eldest man, was at the heart of early Chinese society.

Section 2: Confucius and His Teachings

- Confucius was a poor noble from the North China Plain who became a professional teacher.
- Confucius believed that a peaceful, orderly society was possible only when rulers treated others justly.
- Confucianism reformed Chinese government by requiring that civil service workers be hired based on merit.

Confucius

Section 3: Warring Kingdoms Unite

- Several warring states became one China under Shi Huangdi of the Qin dynasty.
- China's first emperor built the Great Wall to protect the empire. He also organized local governments by dividing China into districts.
- Under the Qin dynasty, some attempts to unify China's economy and culture benefited the people, while others caused unrest.
- China's second ruling dynasty, the Han, remained in power for about 400 years. China then broke into smaller kingdoms.

Section 4: Achievements of Ancient China

- The Silk Road opened China to trade with lands to the west.
- The Han dynasty embraced the ideas of Confucius.
- The Chinese made many advances in learning and technology under the Han dynasty.

◆ Key Terms

Match each definition in Column I with the correct key term in Column II.

Column I

1. a kind of money
2. a fine yellow soil
3. a protective wall built along a river to hold back the waters
4. several generations of closely related people
5. a system of beliefs and values
6. a valuable cloth first made in China
7. a group of people who carry out the government's work
8. a local leader of armed groups

Column II

A extended family

B dike

C civil service

D loess

E currency

F philosophy

G warlord

H silk

Review and Assessment (continued)

◆ Comprehension and Critical Thinking

9. **(a) Recall** Describe the geographic setting of China's first known civilization.
   (b) Infer Why did the early Chinese have so little contact with other ancient civilizations?
   (c) Compare and Contrast Think about the other ancient civilizations you have read about. How were the earliest Chinese civilizations similar? How were they different?

10. **(a) Describe** According to Confucius, how should rulers and other people in authority behave?
    (b) Explain Why did Confucius think his ideas were necessary and important?
    (c) Analyze Information Some Chinese people thought the ideas of Confucius were dangerous. Who felt most threatened by his ideas? Explain why. How do we know that others found his ideas useful?

11. **(a) Name** Identify three actions the emperor Shi Huangdi took to unite China.
    (b) Draw Conclusions Why is the rule of Shi Huangdi judged as harsh?
    (c) Identify Causes How did the harsh rule of Shi Huangdi help bring about Liu Bang's rise to power?

12. **(a) Describe** What characterized the rule of the Han dynasty?

(b) Make Generalizations Why is the Han dynasty considered to be an important part of Chinese history?
(c) Make Inferences Why do people in China today call themselves "the children of Han"?

13. **(a) Identify** What was the route of the Silk Road?
    (b) Explain How was the Silk Road used?
    (c) Apply Information What was the importance of the Silk Road to other civilizations?

◆ Writing Activity: Language Arts

Reread the story about Confucius and the grieving woman on page 144. Many legends about Confucius were written by scholars long after his death. Use what you know about Confucius and China to write a similar brief story. Use his ideas about family or government to write the moral, or lesson, of the story.

◆ Skills Practice

Making Valid Generalizations Review the steps you followed to learn this skill. Then reread Traditional Families on page 140. Using the skills you learned, make a generalization about traditional families in ancient China. Use the steps you have learned to make sure your generalization is valid.

Ancient China

MAP ✶ MASTER™
Skills Activity

Place Location For each place listed below, write the letter from the map that shows its location.

1. Huang River
2. Chang River
3. North China Plain
4. Great Wall of China
5. Silk Road

Go **O**nline
PHSchool.com Use Web Code **lbp-2544** for an **interactive map.**

Standardized Test Prep

Test-Taking Tips

Some questions on standardized tests ask you to analyze a graphic organizer. Study the concept web below. Then follow the tips to answer the sample question.

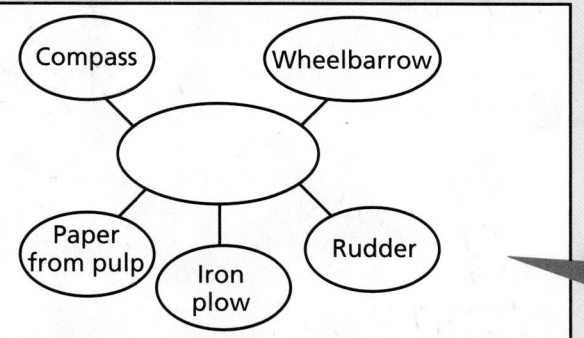

Choose the letter that best answers the question.

Which title should go in the center of the web?

A Gunpowder

B Inventions of Ancient Japan

C Inventions of Ancient China

D Technology

Think It Through The question asks for a title that describes all of the information in the smaller ovals. You can rule out A, because it does not describe all of the outer ovals. D could be a title, but it is not the *best* answer. To evaluate answers B and C, use your knowledge of history. Do you know where any of the items were first invented? If you recognize the origin of even one item shown in the web, then you know that the correct answer is C.

TIP When you study a chart or concept web, pay attention to the kind of information that goes in each part of it.

TIP Use what you already know about history, geography, government, and culture to help you answer the question.

Practice Questions

Use the tips above and other tips in this book to help you answer the following questions.

1. The Chinese called the Huang River China's Sorrow because

    A it was hard to navigate.

    B it flooded and destroyed property.

    C foreigners used it to invade China.

    D it carried no loess to use in farming.

2. What was the main goal of Confucianism?

    A to create original ideas

    B to produce written texts of philosophy

    C to bring order to society

    D to reward important people in society

3. Paper, the wheelbarrow, and iron farming tools were all invented during which dynasty?

    A the Qin   C the Shang

    B the Zheng   D the Han

Study the chart below and then answer the question that follows.

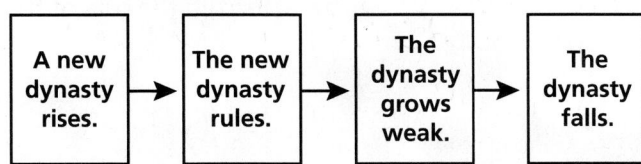

4. "Rulers lose control of the provinces" belongs under which of the headings above?

    A A new dynasty rises.

    B The new dynasty rules.

    C The dynasty grows weak.

    D The dynasty falls.

Use Web Code lba-2504 for **Chapter 5 self-test.**

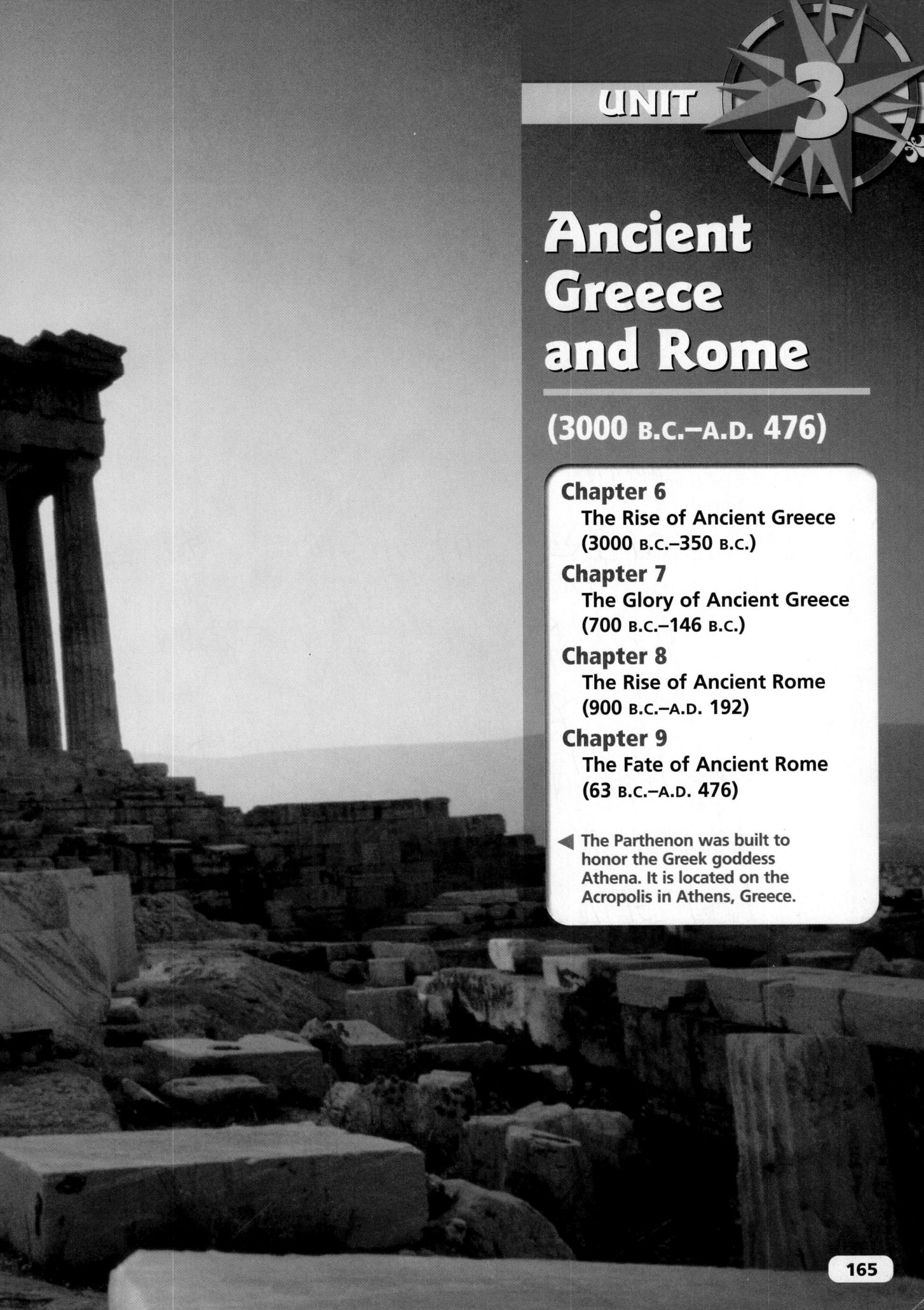

Ancient Greece and Rome

(3000 B.C.–A.D. 476)

◀ The Parthenon was built to honor the Greek goddess Athena. It is located on the Acropolis in Athens, Greece.

Chapter

6

The Rise of Ancient Greece

Chapter Preview

This chapter will examine the rise of Ancient Greece and the development of democracy, philosophy, and the arts during the Golden Age of Athens.

Section 1
The Rise of Greek Civilization

Section 2
Religion, Philosophy, and the Arts

Target Reading Skill

Sequence In this chapter, you will focus on using sequencing to help you understand how events are related to one another. Sequencing helps you see the order in which events happened and can help you understand and remember them.

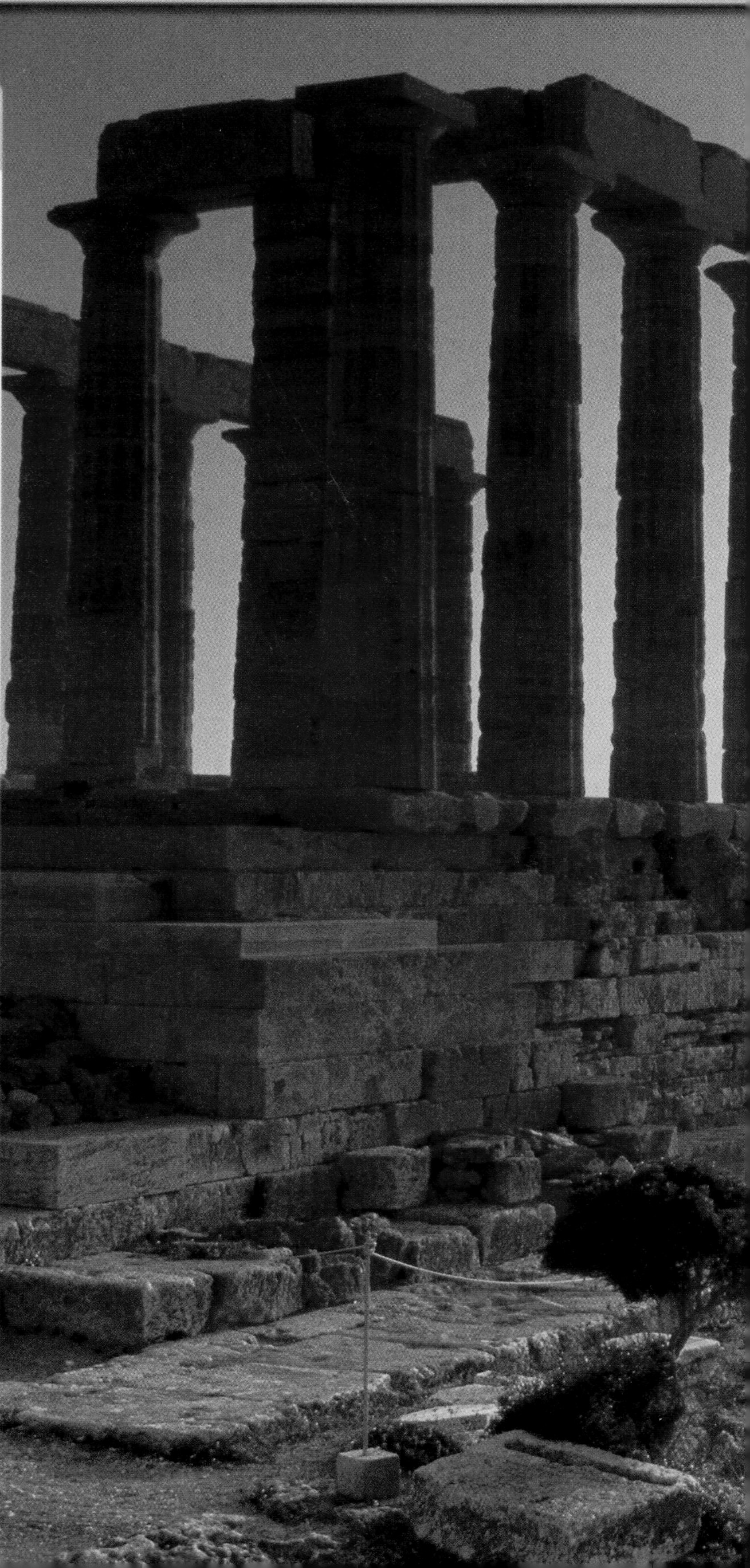

▶ **The ruins of the Temple of Poseidon in Greece**

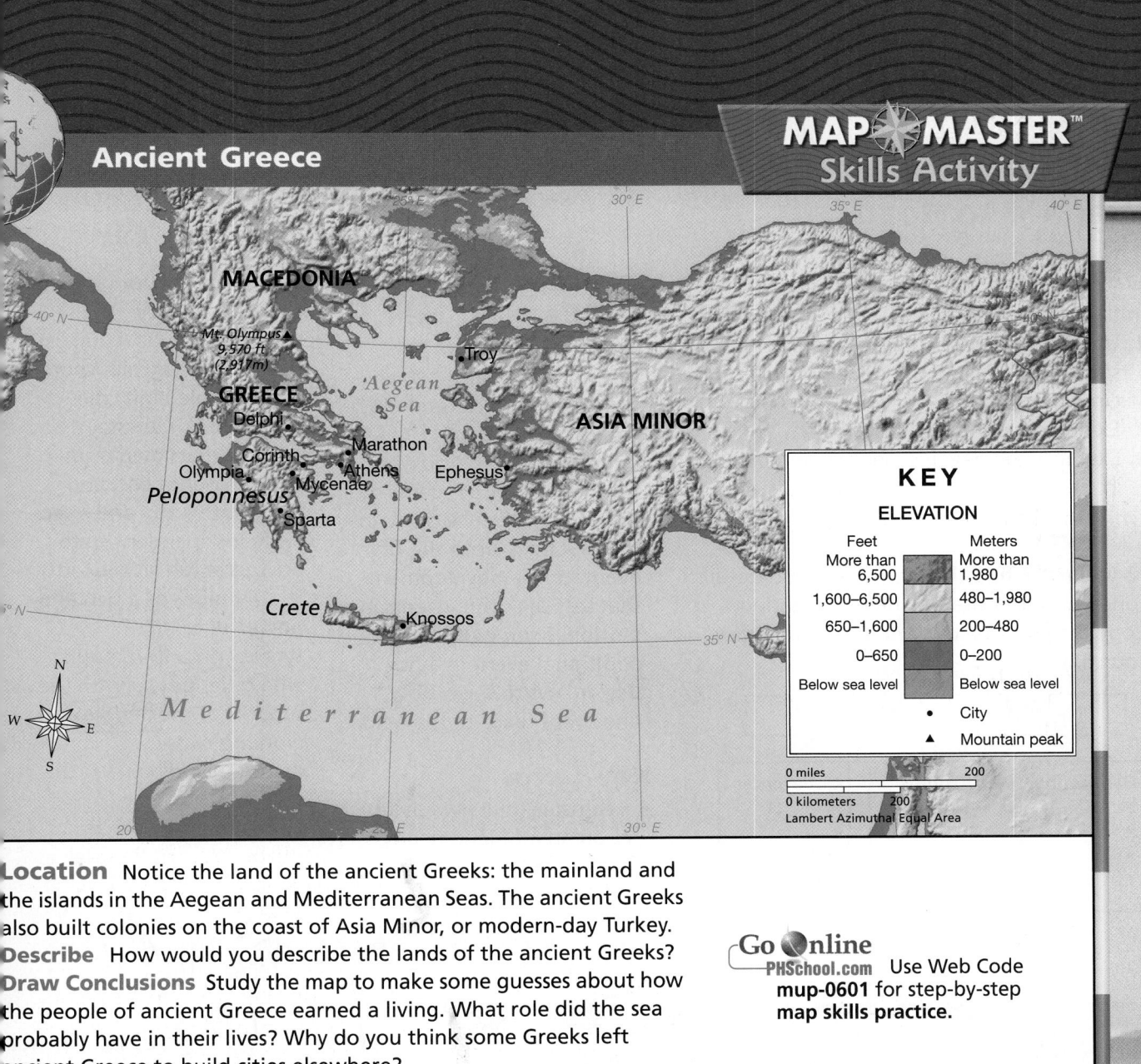

MAP MASTER™
Skills Activity

MACEDONIA

Mt. Olympus ▲
9,570 ft
(2,917m)

GREECE

Delphi

Corinth
Olympia
Mycenae
Athens
Marathon

Peloponnesus

Sparta

*Aegean
Sea*

Troy

ASIA MINOR

Ephesus

Crete

Knossos

M e d i t e r r a n e a n   S e a

N
W E
S

KEY
ELEVATION

Feet		Meters
More than 6,500		More than 1,980
1,600–6,500		480–1,980
650–1,600		200–480
0–650		0–200
Below sea level		Below sea level
•	City	
▲	Mountain peak	

0 miles   200
0 kilometers   200
Lambert Azimuthal Equal Area

Location   Notice the land of the ancient Greeks: the mainland and the islands in the Aegean and Mediterranean Seas. The ancient Greeks also built colonies on the coast of Asia Minor, or modern-day Turkey.
Describe   How would you describe the lands of the ancient Greeks?
Draw Conclusions   Study the map to make some guesses about how the people of ancient Greece earned a living. What role did the sea probably have in their lives? Why do you think some Greeks left ancient Greece to build cities elsewhere?

Go Online
PHSchool.com   Use Web Code
mup-0601 for step-by-step
map skills practice.

The Rise of Greek Civilization

Prepare to Read

Objectives

In this section you will

1. Understand how Greece's geographic setting influenced the development of Greek civilization.
2. Examine early Greek history.
3. Examine the development of democracy in Greece.

Taking Notes

As you read, find the main ideas and details concerning the rise of Greek civilization. Copy the chart below, and use it to record your findings.

```
        The Rise of Greek Civilization
    ┌──────────┬──────────┬──────────────┐
 Geography     Origins      Government
   •             •              •
   •             •              •
   •             •              •
   •             •              •
```

Target Reading Skill

Identify Sequence
Noting the order in which events take place can help you understand and remember them. You can track the order of events by making a sequence chart. In the first box, write the first event, or the development that sets the other events in motion. Then write each additional event in a box. Use arrows to show how one event leads to the next.

Key Terms

- **peninsula** (puh NIN suh luh) *n.* an area of land nearly surrounded by water
- **epic** (EP ik) *n.* a long poem that tells a story
- **acropolis** (uh KRAH puh lis) *n.* a high, rocky hill where early people built cities
- **city-state** (SIH tee stayt) *n.* a city with its own traditions, government, and laws; both a city and a separate independent state
- **aristocrat** (uh RIS tuh krat) *n.* a member of a rich and powerful family
- **tyrant** (TY runt) *n.* a ruler who takes power with the support of the middle and working classes
- **democracy** (dih MAHK ruh-see) *n.* a form of government in which citizens govern themselves

Following their defeat of the Titans, Zeus and his brothers and sisters battled the giants. The gods Apollo and Artemis, above left, confront a group of helmeted giants.

First there was nothing. Then came Mother Earth. The gods of Night and Day appeared next, and then the starry Sky. Earth and Sky created the Twelve Titans (TYT unz). These great gods rebelled against their father Sky and took away his power. The youngest of the Titans, Cronos (KROH nus), ruled in his father's place. In time, Cronos had six children. The youngest, mighty Zeus (zoos), toppled Cronos from his throne.

With such stories, the people of ancient Greece described the struggles of their gods. Like their gods, the people of Greece had to struggle for power and independence. Their struggles began with the land itself.

Greece's Geographic Setting

The land of Greece looks as if the sea had smashed it to pieces. Some pieces have drifted away to form small, rocky islands. Others barely cling to the mainland. Greece is a country made up of peninsulas. A **peninsula** is an area of land surrounded by water on three sides. Look at the map titled *Ancient Greece*. As you can see, no part of Greece is very far from the sea.

Mountains are the major landform of Greece. Greece's islands are mostly mountain peaks. Mountains wrinkle the mainland, so there are only small patches of farmland. Only about one fifth of Greece is good for growing crops. No wonder the Greeks became traders and sailors. At times, they left Greece to found colonies far away.

What was life like for people living in Greece 3,000 years ago? In a way, the ancient Greeks were all islanders. Some lived on real islands completely surrounded by water or on small peninsulas. Others lived on what could be thought of as land islands. Instead of water, mountains separated these small communities from one another. The geography of Greece made it hard for people from different communities to get together.

For this reason, it is no surprise that ancient Greek communities thought of themselves as separate countries. Each one developed its own customs and beliefs. Each believed its own land, traditions, and way of life were the best. And each was more than ready to go to war to protect itself. In fact, for most of their history, the Greeks were so busy fighting among themselves that it is easy to forget that they shared a common heritage, spoke the same language, and worshiped the same gods.

✓ **Reading Check** **What do we mean when we say the ancient Greeks were all islanders?**

Greece's Coastline
Several typical geographic features appear in this picture of the northwestern coast of Greece. These features include a rocky coastline and rugged mountains.
Critical Thinking *How did the geographic features shown affect the way ancient people lived in this area?*

Greek Beginnings

Early Greek civilization arose on and off the Greek mainland. Two ancient peoples, the Minoans (mih NOH unz) and the Mycenaeans (my suh NEE unz), made an important impact on Greek history.

Early Greek Cultures
The fresco from the 1500s B.C., shown below, illustrates Minoan naval combat. A Mycenaean princess appears in the above photo. **Conclude** *How do we know that both the Minoans and the Mycenaeans developed advanced cultures?*

Minoan Civilization From about 3000 to about 1100 B.C., Bronze Age people called the Minoans lived on the island of Crete (kreet). Washed by the waters of the Aegean (ee JEE un) and Mediterranean Seas, Crete was an ideal place for the Minoans to develop a broad sea trade network. Mainland Greece and other Greek islands, as well as Egypt and Sicily, traded with the Minoans, who at one time dominated the Aegean. Archaeological finds show that the Minoans had developed a vibrant culture. Samples of Minoan writing have been found on thousands of clay tablets. A grand palace once stood in the ancient Crete city of Knossos (NAHS us). Palace ruins hint at rooms once covered with fanciful wall paintings. Various statues found within suggest that the Minoans worshiped goddesses. In the middle of the 1400s B.C., Knossos was destroyed, and Minoan civilization declined. People from mainland Greece, the Mycenaeans, were the likely invaders.

The Mycenaeans After the Mycenaeans came into power, mainland and island cultures blended. However, the focus of these cultures moved to the mainland, where the city of Mycenae was located. At the height of their power, around 1400 B.C., the Mycenaeans controlled the Aegean Sea and parts of the Mediterranean. Like the Minoans, the Mycenaeans also used writing. Studies of the Mycenaeans' script show that they spoke an early form of modern Greek.

The Minoans had gained much of their power through trade. Although the Mycenaeans traded widely, they relied upon conquest to spread their power.

The Trojan War Greek myth tells the story of the Trojan War, a long struggle between Greece and the city of Troy on the west coast of Asia Minor, in present-day Turkey. It's possible that Mycenaean warriors inspired this legend.

According to the myths, the Greeks conquered Troy by using a trick—the Trojan Horse. Greek warriors hid inside a huge wooden horse. The horse was rolled to the city gates. Thinking it was a gift, the Trojans brought the horse into their city. During the night the Greek soldiers climbed out of the horse and let the rest of their army into Troy. The Greeks burned and looted Troy and then returned home.

Two **epics**, or long story-telling poems, about the Trojan War survive today. They are the *Iliad* (IL ee ud) and the *Odyssey* (AHD ih see). These epics may have been composed by many people, but they are credited to a poet called Homer. The poems were important to the Greeks. They taught them what their gods were like and how the noblest of their heroes behaved. Today, people think these poems came from stories memorized by several poets and passed down by word of mouth through many generations. Homer may have been the last and greatest in this line of poets who told about the Trojan War.

Most historians agree that the Trojan War did not happen exactly as Homer described it. Some believe that Homer's epics were inspired by a long battle between the Greeks and Trojans, but others argue that the epics were inspired by a series of minor battles. Troy was destroyed by a large fire in the mid-1200s B.C., an act that some historians believe may have been committed by invaders from Greece.

✓ **Reading Check** Contrast how Minoans and Mycenaeans spread their power.

Learn about two classic Greek epics.

Links to Science

Troy Discovered Over the years, people came to believe that Troy and the Trojan War were fiction. An amateur archaeologist, Heinrich Schliemann (HYNrik SHLEE mahn), disagreed. In the late 1800s he used clues in the *Iliad* to pinpoint the location of Troy. When he and later archaeologists dug there, they found nine layers of ruins from ancient cities. One was possibly the Troy of the *Iliad* and the *Odyssey*.

about 1450 B.C.
Fire destroys many towns and palaces on Crete.

Mid-1200s B.C.
Troy is destroyed by fire.

| 3000 B.C. | 2500 B.C. | 2000 B.C. | 1500 B.C. | 1000 B.C. | 500 B. |

about 3000 B.C.
Minoan culture begins to flourish on the island of Crete.

about 1600 B.C.
Mycenaean culture begins to flourish in Mycenae on mainland Greece.

about 1200 B.C.
Mycenaean civilization collapses, possibly because of invasion.

1100s–750 B.C.
Dark Ages in Greece.

Timeline Skills

Two ancient peoples, the Minoans and the Mycenaeans, made an important impact on Greek history.
Identify Where and when did Minoan culture begin to flourish? **Analyze** How did the location of Mycenaean culture differ from the location of the Minoan culture?

Pottery painting of a Greek cobbler

The Dark Ages of Greece

Not long after the end of the Trojan War, civilization in Greece collapsed. No one knows exactly why. Life went on, but poverty was everywhere. People no longer traded for food and other goods beyond Greece. They had to depend on what they could raise themselves. Some were forced to move to islands and to the western part of Asia Minor. They were so concerned with survival that they forgot the art of writing.

These years, from the early 1100s B.C. to about 750 B.C., have been called Greece's Dark Ages. Without writing, people had to depend on word of mouth to keep their traditions and history alive. Old traditions were remembered only in the myths that were told and retold.

Greece's Dark Ages were not completely bleak. During this time, families gradually began to resettle in places where they could grow crops and raise animals. Some of these family farms may have developed into villages. When they chose where to build their farms, people favored places near rocky, protected hills. Here they built structures to protect them from attack. The name for such a fortified hill was **acropolis,** meaning "high city."

After 800 B.C., people in Greece began writing again. It was during this period that Homer is believed to have composed his epic about the Trojan War.

✓ Reading Check What happened during Greece's Dark Ages?

Temple of Artemis

The Temple of Artemis at Ephesus was the largest of all ancient Greek buildings. The temple was considered one of the seven wonders of the ancient world. In 1869 British archaeologist John Turtle Wood uncovered the remains of the temple. His discovery marked the first time an ancient Greek site had been excavated, or uncovered. Ancient Greeks worshipped Artemis as the goddess of wild animals and the hunt.

Ruins of the Temple
Fragments of marble are all that remain of the Temple of Artemis, located in present-day Turkey.

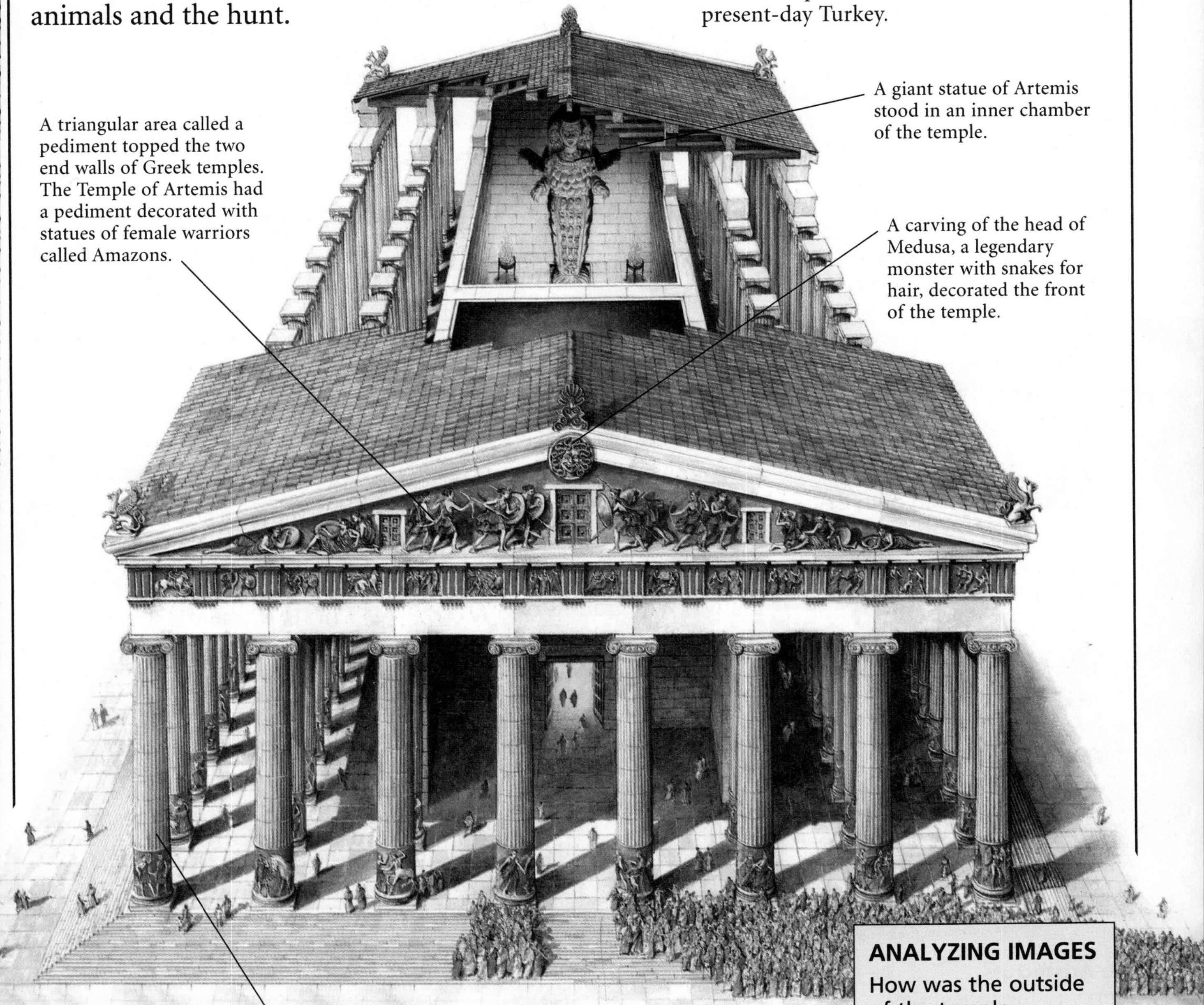

A giant statue of Artemis stood in an inner chamber of the temple.

A triangular area called a pediment topped the two end walls of Greek temples. The Temple of Artemis had a pediment decorated with statues of female warriors called Amazons.

A carving of the head of Medusa, a legendary monster with snakes for hair, decorated the front of the temple.

The columns stood more than 60 feet (18 meters) high. They numbered 127 in all.

ANALYZING IMAGES
How was the outside of the temple decorated?

City-States Develop

Historians believe that sometime around 750 B.C., villages in a small area probably joined to form a city in the shadow of an acropolis. At that time, each city began to develop its own traditions and its own form of government and laws. Today, we call these tiny nations city-states. A **city-state** is not only a city, but also a separate independent state. Each city-state included a city and the villages and fields surrounding it. Hundreds of Greek city-states grew up, each more or less independent.

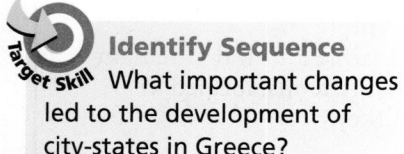

Identify Sequence What important changes led to the development of city-states in Greece?

Aristocracy: Nobles Rule The earliest rulers of city-states were probably chieftains or kings who were military leaders. By the end of Greece's Dark Ages, most city-states were ruled by **aristocrats,** members of the rich and powerful families. Aristocrats controlled most of the good land. They could afford horses, chariots, and the best weapons to make themselves stronger than others.

A New Type of Ruler As the Greeks sailed to foreign ports trading olive oil, marble, and other products, the city-states became richer. A middle class of merchants and artisans developed. They wanted some say in the government of their cities. These people could not afford to equip themselves with horses and chariots for war. However, they could afford armor, swords, and spears. With these weapons, large groups of soldiers could fight effectively on foot. Gradually, military strength in the cities shifted from aristocrats to merchants and artisans.

As a result of these changes, aristocratic governments were often overthrown and replaced by rulers called tyrants. A **tyrant** was a ruler who seized power by force. Tyrants were usually supported by the middle and working classes. Today, we think of tyrants as being cruel and violent. That was true of some Greek tyrants, but others ruled wisely and well.

✓ Reading Check **What kind of ruler often replaced aristocratic governments?**

The Aristocrats
Some wealthy ancient Greeks owned chariots. **Analyze** *How did the aristocrats use their wealth to gain power?*

Democracy in Greece

Eventually, the people of many city-states overthrew tyrants. Some of the cities adopted a form of government called democracy. In a **democracy,** citizens govern themselves. The city-state in which democracy was most fully expressed was Athens.

About 594 B.C., a wise Athenian leader called Solon (SOH lun) won the power to reform the laws. Solon was well known for his fairness. His laws reformed both the economy and the government of Athens. One of his first laws canceled all debts and freed citizens who had been enslaved for having debts. Another law allowed any male citizen of Athens aged 18 or older to have a say in debating important laws. These laws and others allowed Athens to become the leading democracy of the ancient world.

Not everyone living in ancient Athens benefited from democracy. Only about one in five Athenians was a citizen. To be a citizen, a man had to have an Athenian father and mother. Some of the people living in Athens were enslaved. These people did not take part in democracy, nor did women or men with non-citizen parents. Men who were citizens of Athens were free and self-governing.

Tools of Democracy
Athenians used a machine to help select juries. A colored ball, top, dropped into an allotment machine, bottom, would fall at random next to the slots containing names of potential jurors. In the middle is a voting tablet used in Athens. **Infer** *How do you think voting helped to strengthen Athenian democracy?*

 **Reading Check** **Why did some Athenians benefit more from democracy than others?**

Section 1 Assessment

Key Terms
Review the key terms listed at the beginning of this section. Use each term in a sentence that explains its meaning.

Target Reading Skill
Place these events in the correct order: rise of the city-state, height of Minoan civilization, Greek Dark Ages.

Comprehension and Critical Thinking
1. (a) Recall Describe the geographic setting of ancient Greece.

(b) Predict What effect do you think the geography of Greece had on the kind of communities that developed there?

2. (a) Recall Describe early Greek civilization.

(b) Make Generalizations How were the Minoan and Mycenaean civilizations similar?

3. (a) Identify What two kinds of government first developed in the Greek city-states after the Greek Dark Ages?

(b) Cause and Effect How did the rise of the middle class help shape government in ancient Greece?

Writing Activity
Write a description of the conditions in Greece during the period between the 1100s B.C. and the 700s B.C. Why are these years referred to as Greece's Dark Ages?

For: An activity on the Trojan War
Visit: PHSchool.com
Web Code: mud-0610

Drama was an important part of Greek culture. Many Greek plays were tragedies. These were often based on myth and were solemn and poetic. The main character was usually a good but imperfect person faced with a difficult choice. His or her struggles usually ended in death. Comedies dealt with well-known people and problems of the day. Greek plays were performed by only a few actors who played several roles. Instead of makeup, actors wore masks to indicate the kind of characters they played. A chorus danced, chanted, and commented on the action.

The Theater Early Greek theaters were probably just open areas in cities or next to hillsides. The audience would watch and listen to a chorus singing about the adventures of a god or hero. Later, theaters became much more complex but remained outdoors and open to the sky, much like a stadium today. The *theatron,* or "viewing place," was where the spectators sat. The theater illustrated to the right could seat 17,000 spectators! Rows of seats curved halfway around a large semicircular area called an *orchestra*. Behind the *orchestra* was a building called the *skene*. The *skene* was usually decorated as a palace or temple, depending on what background was needed for a particular play. Actors could enter and exit through the doors of the *skene*.

Scene from Ancient Greek Play
These present-day actors are performing an ancient Greek play. They wear masks, just as their ancient counterparts did.

Assessment

Describe Suppose that you have attended a play at an ancient Greek theater. Write a letter to a friend describing your experience.

Compare How did the experience of attending a Greek theater differ from that of attending a play today?

A Great Greek Playwright
Sophocles was one of three great writers of Greek tragedies. Only seven of his plays have survived.

The teacher looked at Lisa and asked, "How did the people of Athens feel about drama?"

Lisa had read the assignment, but there wasn't anything in the book about how Athenians felt about drama. She did remember a few facts, though. "They had a lot of theaters and put on a lot of plays. They had play-writing contests. So I guess if they had so many plays, drama must have been pretty important to them."

Greek actor's mask

Like Lisa, when you draw a conclusion, you figure out something based on the information you have read or seen. Drawing conclusions is a skill that will help you benefit from your schoolwork and anything you read.

Learn the Skill

Use these steps to learn how to draw a conclusion:

1. **Gather factual information about the topic.** Find out as many factual details as you can by reading about your topic and then talking with people who know about the subject.

2. **Combine the facts with other information you already know.** Add the information you find in your research to what you already know.

3. **Write a conclusion that follows logically.** A conclusion is usually an educated guess.

Practice the Skill

Turn to page 171, and reread the first four paragraphs of text in the main column. Use this information to draw conclusions about the Trojan War.

1. The text tells you about the people who may have inspired the legend of the war. It tells where the war was fought, and it describes the heroes, how they fought, and how the story was handed down to us. Choose one of these topics. Write down facts about that topic.

2. Combine whatever facts you already know with the facts you have just read. You might know something about stories of other wars or about how people react to war stories.

3. Try to form an educated guess about your topic—something that is not specifically stated in the text. Your conclusion might answer a question starting with *why*. For instance: Why has the history of the Trojan War fascinated so many people through the centuries? Check your conclusion to make sure it is supported by the facts.

Apply the Skill
Turn to page 175, and reread the paragraphs titled Democracy in Greece. Use facts from that text plus facts you already know to draw conclusions about American democracy.

The Trojan horse inside the ancient city of Troy

Religion, Philosophy, and the Arts

Prepare to Read

Objectives

In this section you will
1. Identify the religious beliefs of the ancient Greeks.
2. Explore how the Greeks searched for knowledge about the world.
3. Describe the relationship between the rise of democracy and the spread of new ideas in Greek city-states.

Taking Notes

As you read, look for details about the religion, philosophy, and the arts of the ancient Greeks. Use a copy of the outline below to record your findings.

> I. The Golden Age of Athens
>   A. Period from 479 to 431 B.C.
>   B. Sources of wealth
>   1.
>   2.
>   3.
> II. Ancient Greek religious beliefs

Target Reading Skill

Recognize Sequence Signal Words Signals point out relationships among ideas or events. This section discusses life in the Golden Age of Athens. To help keep the relationship between leaders, thinkers, and writers clear, look for words like *first, at that time,* and *in [date]* that signal the order in which these people were active.

Key Terms

- **tribute** (TRIB yoot) *n.* a payment made by a less powerful state or nation to a more powerful one
- **immortal** (ih MAWR tul) *n.* someone or something that lives forever
- **oracle** (AWH uh kul) *n.* in ancient Greece, a sacred site used to consult a god or goddess; any priest or priestess who spoke for the gods
- **philosopher** (fih LAHS uh fur) *n.* someone who used reason to understand the world; in Greece the earliest philosophers used reason to explain natural events
- **tragedy** (TRAJ uh dee) *n.* a type of serious drama that ends in disaster for the main character

Pericles led the Athenians in peace and war. The helmet he wears reminds us that he was a skilled general.

The Athenian leader Pericles (PEHR uh kleez) reminded the citizens that Athens was unique.

> **"Our constitution does not copy the laws of neighbouring states; we are rather a pattern to others than imitators ourselves. Its administration favours the many instead of the few; this is why it is called a democracy. If we look to the laws, they afford equal justice to all . . . [P]overty [does not] bar the way, if a man is able to serve the state. In short, I say that as a city we are the school of [Greece] . . ."**
>
> — The History of the Peloponnesian War
> *Thucydides*

Pericles' words had special meaning: They were spoken during the first year of a war with Sparta, another Greek city-state. Eventually, it was conflict with Sparta that ended Athens' golden age of accomplishment.

The Golden Age of Athens

The years from 479 B.C. to 431 B.C. are called the Golden Age of Athens. During the Golden Age, Athens grew rich from trade and from silver mined by slaves in regions around the city. **Tribute,** or payments made to Athens by its allies, added to its wealth.

Athenians also made important achievements in the arts, philosophy, and literature, and democracy reached its high point. For about 30 years during the Golden Age, Pericles was the most powerful man in Athenian politics. This well-educated, intelligent man had the best interests of his city at heart. When he made speeches to the Athenians, he could move and persuade them.

Pericles was a member of an aristocratic family, but he supported democracy. Around 460 B.C., he became leader of a democratic group. He introduced reforms that strengthened democracy. The most important change was to have the city pay a salary to its officials. This meant that poor citizens could afford to hold public office.

One of the greatest accomplishments under the rule of Pericles was the construction of the Parthenon (PAHR thuh nahn) between 447 and 432 B.C. The construction of the Parthenon was part of the general reconstruction of the Acropolis at Athens. Many of the buildings there had been destroyed by invaders from Persia about three decades earlier. The Parthenon was a temple built to honor the patron, or protector, of Athens, the goddess Athena.

An ancient Athenian silver coin bearing an owl, a symbol of the city

A vase depicting citizenship in Athens

✓ Reading Check   **How did Pericles strengthen democracy?**

Ancient Greek Religious Beliefs

Greeks worshiped a family of gods and goddesses called the Twelve Olympians (oh LIM pea unz). Each ruled different areas of human life and the natural world. The chart titled "A Family of Gods" gives you more information about some of the Olympians.

The Greeks took great care when honoring their gods. They wished to give thanks and to receive blessings. They also tried to avoid angering the gods.

Gods and Goddesses Wherever the Greeks lived, they built temples to the gods. Because the gods had human forms, they also had many human characteristics. The main difference between gods and humans was that the gods were **immortal, which meant they lived forever.** They also had awesome power.

Mythology tells us that the Greeks worshiped gods led by Zeus, the king of the gods. From Mt. Olympus, Greece's highest mountain, Zeus ruled the gods and humanity. In addition to worshiping gods, the Greeks also honored mythical heroes like Achilles (uh KIL eez), whose great deeds are told in the *Iliad*.

Although the Greeks worshiped all their gods, each city-state honored one of the twelve gods, in part by building a temple to that god. Athena (uh THEE nuh), for example, was the patron goddess of Athens. The Greeks also honored their gods by holding festivals and by sacrificing animals and offering food to the gods. To honor Zeus, the city-states came together every four years for an Olympian festival and games. Modern Olympic Games are based on this tradition.

Poseidon, Athena, Apollo, and Artemis are shown in this relief.

Delphi
The Tholos Temple at the Sanctuary of Athena Pronaia was once the gateway to Delphi. In the vase painting, Aegeus, a legendary Athenian king, consults a priestess at Apollo's oracle in Delphi. **Conclude** *Why did the ancient Greeks visit oracles?*

The Oracles In ancient cultures, people often looked to their gods for signs or advice. They wanted the gods to show them how to live or how to behave. The Greeks visited **oracles,** sacred sites where it was believed the gods spoke. At these shrines, the people would ask the gods to give them advice or to reveal the future. Sometimes the advice came through dreams. Often a response would come in the form of a riddle, delivered by priests or priestesses thought to be capable of hearing the voice of the gods. Oracles of various gods were located throughout Greece. Heads of state often sought advice on governing and wars from the oracle of the god Apollo at Delphi (DEL fy), an ancient town in central Greece. Because such advice was taken very seriously, the oracles had a great impact on Greek history.

✓ **Reading Check** How did the Greeks honor their gods?

Chart Skills

The Greeks believed the world was ruled by gods and goddesses. Ten of them are listed in the table below. **Identify** Who was considered to be the leader of all gods and goddesses? **Analyze** Why do you think this chart is titled "A Family of Gods?"

A Family of Gods

Zeus (zoos)	Ruler of all gods and humanity
Hera (HIHR uh)	Goddess of marriage and childbirth
Apollo (uh PAHL oh)	God of music, poetry
Artemis (AHR tuh mis)	Goddess of hunting
Athena (uh THEE nuh)	Goddess of wisdom and war
Ares (EHR eez)	God of war
Aphrodite (af ruh DY tee)	Goddess of love
Hermes (HUR meez)	Messenger of the gods
Poseidon (poh SY dun)	God of earthquakes and the ocean
Demeter (dih MEE tur)	Goddess of fertility

The Search for Knowledge

Most Greeks believed that their gods were responsible for all natural events. But a few thinkers disagreed. About 150 years before the Golden Age of Athens, some people thought about new ways to understand the world.

Greek Science and Philosophy You learned earlier about philosophy, which is a system of beliefs or values. **Philosophers believed that people could use the powers of the mind and reason to understand natural events.** One of the first philosophers, Thales (THAY leez), believed that water was the basic material of the world. Everything was made from it. Over the years, various philosophers had other ideas about the universe. They did not do experiments. But they were careful observers and good thinkers. Democritus (dih MAHK ruh tus), who lived in the 400s B.C., thought that everything was made of tiny particles he called atoms. More than 2,000 years later, modern science showed that he had been correct.

Socrates During the Golden Age and later, several important philosophers taught in Athens. One was a man called Socrates (SAHK ruh teez). People in the marketplace of Athens could not help but notice this sturdy, round-faced man. He was there at all hours of the day, eagerly discussing wisdom and goodness.

Socrates wanted people to consider the true meaning of qualities such as justice and courage. To do this, he asked questions that made others think about their beliefs. Sometimes they became angry because Socrates often showed them that they didn't know what they were talking about. "Know thyself" was his most important lesson.

Target Skill

Recognize Sequence and Signal Words
What words signal that Democritus lived in the same century as Pericles?

Go Online
PHSchool.com Use Web Code **mup-0824** for an interactivity on Greek philosophers.

Death of Socrates
Socrates urged his students to question and critically examine all around them. For "corrupting the youth" in this way, an Athenian jury sentenced him to death.
Conclude *Why do you think some people believed Socrates corrupted the youth of Athens?*

In 399 B.C., Socrates was brought to trial. The authorities accused him of dishonoring the gods and misleading young people. He was sentenced to death by forced suicide, a common sentence in Athens at the time. Socrates drank a cup of hemlock, a poison, and died.

Plato and Aristotle Much of what is known about Socrates comes from the writings of Plato (PLAY toh), one of his students. Socrates' death caused Plato to mistrust democracy. In *The Republic,* Plato wrote that society should be made up of three groups: workers, soldiers, and philosopher-rulers. Plato founded a school in Athens called the Academy, where he taught a student named Aristotle (AR uh staht ul). Aristotle believed that reason should guide the pursuit of knowledge. He later founded his own school, the Lyceum.

✓ Reading Check **How did Socrates challenge the values of the people of Athens?**

The Acropolis
Once the religious center of Athens, the Acropolis now serves as a monument to Greek architecture.
1 The Propylaia, the entrance to the Acropolis, was completed in 432 B.C.
2 The Odeion (theater) of Herodes Atticus was built in A.D. 161.
3 The Erechtheion, named after a legendary king of Athens, was completed in 406 B.C.
4 Completed in 438 B.C., the Parthenon served as a temple to Athena, the patron goddess of Athens.
Predict *Why do you think the Athenians built the Acropolis?*

Visual and Dramatic Arts

The ancient Greeks devoted great attention to their arts. The Greeks used visual arts, such as architecture and sculpture, to glorify and honor their gods. The ancient Greeks are also known as the first playwrights, or people who write plays.

The Parthenon Today, the Athenian leader Pericles is probably best known for making Athens a beautiful city. The Acropolis, the religious center of Athens, had been destroyed in 480 B.C., during one of the city's many wars. Pericles decided to rebuild the Acropolis and create new buildings to glorify the city.

The builders of the new Acropolis brought Greek architecture to its highest point. Their most magnificent work was the Parthenon, a temple to the goddess Athena. The temple was made of fine marble. Rows of columns surrounded it on all four sides. Within the columns was a room that held the statue of Athena, made of wood, ivory, and gold. The statue rose 40 feet (12 m), as high as a four-story building.

The great statue of Athena disappeared long ago. However, much of the sculpture on the inside and outside of the temple still exists. Many of the scenes that decorate the Parthenon have three important characteristics. First, they are full of action. Second, the artist carefully arranged the figures to show balance and order. Third, the sculptures are lifelike and accurate. However, they are ideal, or perfect, views of humans and animals. These characteristics reflect the goal of Greek art. This goal was to present images of perfection in a balanced and orderly way.

Dramas In addition to their achievements in architecture and sculpture, Athenians were the first people known to write dramas. Among the city's greatest achievements were the plays written and produced in the 400s B.C., during the Golden Age.

Some of the most famous Greek plays were tragedies. A **tragedy** is a serious story that usually ends in disaster for the main character. Often, tragedies told of fictional humans who were destroyed when forced to make impossible choices. A Greek tragedy consisted of several scenes that featured the characters of the story. Between the scenes, a chorus chanted or sang poems. In most plays, the author used the chorus to give background information, comment on the events, or praise the gods.

Comedies During the 400s B.C. in Athens, poets wrote comedies that made fun of well-known citizens and politicians and also made jokes about the customs of the day. Because of the freedom in Athens, people accepted the humor and jokes.

✓ Reading Check **What was the role of the chorus in Greek drama?**

Greek actors performed in outdoor theaters, such as the one shown above at Epidauros. By using different masks, such as the one at top, actors could play a variety of roles.

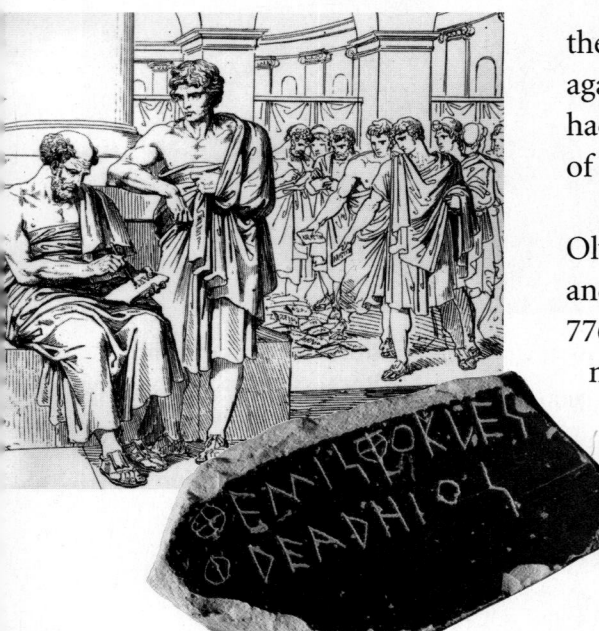

Aristides, a general at the Battle of Marathon, writes his name for someone who wants him banished from Athens. Inset photo is of a voting tablet used in Aristides' trial.

Many City-States, One People

The citizens of Greek city-states such as Athens had strong patriotic feelings and valued their freedoms. For these reasons, they took a very active role in their government. They were able to develop new ideas in philosophy, religion, government, and the arts in part because of the value they placed on free thinking. The spread of education and growing wealth through trade with Egypt, Sicily, and other places gave the Greeks the freedom to explore new ideas.

Though Athens was the most important city-state, it was not the only one in Greece at this time. City-states in Greece competed against one another, but their citizens spoke the same language and had many of the same customs. They thought of themselves as part of the same people, calling themselves Hellenes.

One example of the common culture of the city-states was the Olympic Games, which were held every four years throughout ancient Greece. The first recorded Olympic Games were held in 776 B.C. Other Olympic Games were held fairly regularly over the next thousand years. Athletes from city-states around Greece competed for prizes in competitions in running, horse racing, boxing, and many other events.

✓ Reading Check **What role did education and growing wealth play in the development of philosophy and the arts in ancient Greece?**

Section 2 Assessment

Key Terms
Review the key terms listed at the beginning of this section. Use each term in a sentence that explains its meaning.

Target Reading Skill

Review the section "The Search for Knowledge" on pages 184–185. Find the words that signal time related to the lives of the philosophers.

Comprehension and Critical Thinking
1. (a) Define What was the Golden Age of Athens?

(b) Draw Conclusions Why do you think Pericles called Athens "the school of all Greece"?
2. (a) Explain How did the Greeks attempt to understand the world?
(b) Explore Details What did Socrates mean when he said, "Know thyself"?
3. (a) Explain What characteristics did people in city-states throughout Greece share?
(b) Infer How did the growth of wealth through trade contribute to the spread of new ideas in Greece?

Writing Activity
Write a brief essay describing the achievements of Athenians during the Golden Age.

For: An activity on Greek architecture
Visit: PHSchool.com
Web Code: mud-0620

Review and Assessment

◆ Chapter Summary

Section 1: Early Greek Civilization

- The geography of Greece encouraged the growth of independent communities that shared a common culture.
- The dominance of the Minoans and then of the Mycenaeans was followed by a collapse of these Greek civilizations.
- Greeks lost the art of writing and other advancements during Greece's Dark Ages, and people began living in villages.
- Greece's traditionally independent cities provided the foundation for government rule by the people.

Minoan naval battle

Section 2: Religion, Philosophy and the Arts

- During the 400s B.C., Athens enjoyed a golden age of achievement in philosophy and the arts.
- Greeks worshiped many different gods and goddesses and sought their advice at oracles.
- Greek philosophers introduced new ways to think about the world.
- Visual arts, such as architecture and sculpture, and literary arts, such as drama, flourished during the Golden Age of Athens.
- Although city-states in Greece competed against one another, their citizens shared a common culture.

The Golden Age of Athens

◆ Key Terms

Write a definition for each of the key terms listed below.

1. peninsula
2. epic
3. acropolis
4. city-state
5. aristocrat
6. tyrant
7. democracy
8. tribute
9. philosopher
10. tragedy

Review and Assessment (continued)

◆ Comprehension and Critical Thinking

11. (a) **Identify** Who were the Minoans and the Mycenaeans?
(b) **Generalize** Describe the period in Greek history that followed the dominance of the Minoans and the Mycenaeans.
(c) **Infer** How did the story of the Trojan War help the ancient Greeks understand their history?

12. (a) **Recall** How did city-states arise in ancient Greece?
(b) **Explain** Why did tyrants replace aristocrats as rulers of the city-states?
(c) **Identify Effects** How did rule by tyrants affect the city-states?

13. (a) **List** Identify two characteristics that describe Greek religion.
(b) **Describe** What was the importance of the oracles to the Greeks?
(c) **Apply Information** According to Greek philosophers, how could people understand natural events?

14. (a) **Generalize** What arts were important in ancient Greece?
(b) **Compare** Describe the two types of dramas developed by ancient Greeks.
(c) **Draw Conclusions** How did the comedies affect the free exchange of ideas in ancient Greece?

◆ Skills Practice

Drawing Conclusions In the Skills for Life Activity, you learned how to draw conclusions from information that is not specifically stated in the text.

Review the steps you follow to apply this skill. Reread the passage in Section 2 titled Socrates. Use what you have read and your own observations of human nature to draw conclusions about Socrates and the impact of his ideas on future civilizations.

◆ Writing Activity Language Arts

Choose at least five terms from the Key Terms list on the previous page. Write a brief poem, essay, or dialogue about ancient Greece that uses the terms you have chosen.

MAP✷MASTER™ Skills Activity

The Rise of Ancient Greece

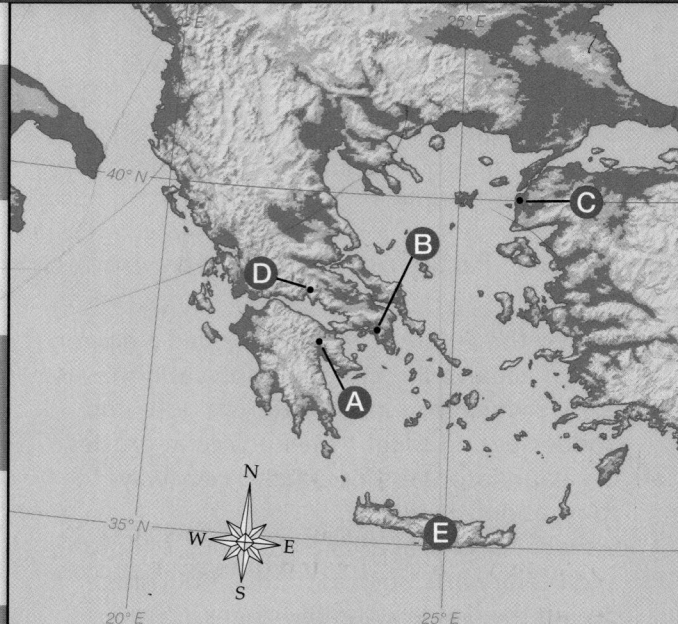

Place Location For each place listed below, write the letter from the map that shows its location.
1. Athens
2. Mycenae
3. Crete
4. Delphi
5. Troy

Go Online
PHSchool.com Use Web Code **mup-0602** for step-by-step **map skills practice.**

Standardized Test Prep

Test-Taking Tips

Some questions on standardized tests ask you to analyze an outline. Study the outline below. Then follow the tips to answer the sample question.

TIP Use key words in the text to help you.

I Solon's Reforms
   A Outlawed slavery based on debt
   B Opened high offices to more citizens
   C _____
   D Gave the assembly more power
II Limited Rights
   A Allowed only male citizens to participate
   B Restricted citizenship
   C Left many slaves without rights

TIP Think about how the text is organized. Use that information to help you answer the question.

Pick the letter that best answers the question.
Which of the following belongs in I-C?
  A Later reforms under another ruler
  B Allowed male citizens to debate important laws
  C Life in Athens
  D Did not allow women to share in public life

Think It Through This outline is organized by major topics and subtopics. The question asks you to find a subtopic under Solon's Reforms. Answer C is too general; it could be the subject of an entire outline. Answer A is also general; it could be the subject of another topic in this outline. Answer D does not fit under Solon's Reforms. The key word reforms means "changes" or "improvements." Therefore, answer B is correct.

Practice Questions

Use the tips above and other tips in this book to help you answer the following questions.

1. Why did the ancient Greeks think of their communities as separate countries?
  A A different language was spoken in each community.
  B Each community's people came from a different country.
  C Each community practiced a different religion.
  D Geographical features cut communities off from one another.

2. Philosophers believed that they could understand the world around them by
  A using the powers of reason.
  B building shrines to the gods.
  C seeking answers at the oracle at Delphi.
  D paying tribute to their allies.

Study the outline below, and then answer the following question.

I Greek Beginnings
   A Minoan Civilization
      1. Lived on the island of Crete
      2.
   B Mycenaean Civilization

3. Which answer belongs in the space numbered 2 in the outline above?
  A Spoke an early form of modern Greek
  B Spread their power through conquest
  C Fought in the Trojan War
  D Dominated the Aegean Sea through trade

Use Web Code **mua-0603** for **Chapter 6 self-test.**

The Sirens
A Greek Myth From *The Adventures of Ulysses*
Retold by Bernard Evslin

Prepare to Read

Background Information

Have you ever been persuaded to go somewhere, do something, or buy something because someone made it sound fun or exciting? Messages like these can sometimes lead people in the wrong direction.

The Sirens (SY runz) in this myth are creatures who use their songs to lead sailors to destruction. The hero, Ulysses (yoo LIS eez), is warned about the Sirens as he tries to sail home to Greece after the Trojan War.

Ulysses is the name the Roman people gave to the Greek hero Odysseus (oh DIS ee us). The tale of Ulysses and the Sirens comes from a series of tales told in Homer's *Odyssey*. The clever Ulysses had expected an easy journey home. Instead, he was delayed by adventures that tested his body and spirit.

Like Homer himself and other storytellers, Bernard Evslin has retold the ancient story of the Sirens in his own words. The events are the same as those in the Odyssey myth. But the author has added many details to make the story his own.

Objectives
In this selection you will
1. Learn about the Greek ideas of leadership and heroism.
2. Think about the roles temptation and danger play in this story and in people's lives.

Sculpture of a Siren

In the first light of morning Ulysses awoke and called his crew about him.

"Men," he said. "Listen well, for your lives today hang upon what I am about to tell you. That large island to the west is Thrinacia, where we must make a landfall, for our provisions run low. But to get to the island we must pass through a narrow strait. And at the head of this strait is a rocky islet where dwell two sisters called Sirens, whose voices you must not hear. Now I shall guard you against their singing, which would lure you to shipwreck, but first you must bind me to the mast. Tie me tightly, as though I were a dangerous captive. And no matter how I struggle, no matter what signals I make to you, do not release me, lest I follow their voices to destruction, taking you with me."

Thereupon Ulysses took a large lump of the beeswax that was used by the sail mender to slick his heavy thread and kneaded it in his powerful hands until it became soft. Then he went to each man of the crew and plugged his ears with soft wax; he caulked their ears so tightly that they could hear nothing but the thin pulsing of their own blood.

Thrinacia (thrih NAY shee uh) *n.* mythological island that might have been Sicily

strait (strayt) *n.* narrow water passage between two pieces of land

islet (EYE lit) *n.* small island

caulk (kawk) *v.* to stop up and make tight

Then he stood himself against the mast, and the men bound him about with rawhide, winding it tightly around his body, lashing him to the thick mast.

They had lowered the sail because ships cannot sail through a narrow strait unless there is a following wind, and now each man of the crew took his place at the great oars. The polished blades whipped the sea into a froth of white water and the ship nosed toward the strait.

Ulysses had left his own ears unplugged because he had to remain in command of the ship and had need of his hearing. Every sound means something upon the sea. But when they drew near the rocky islet and he heard the first faint <u>strains</u> of the Sirens' singing, then he wished he, too, had stopped his own ears with wax. All his strength suddenly <u>surged</u> toward the sound of those magical voices. The very hair of his head seemed to be tugging at his scalp, trying to fly away. His eyeballs started out of his head.

For in those voices were the sounds that men love:

Happy sounds like birds <u>railing</u>, sleet hailing, milk pailing....

Sad sounds like rain leaking, trees creaking, wind seeking....

Autumn sounds like leaves tapping, fire snapping, river <u>lapping</u>....

Quiet sounds like snow flaking, spider waking, heart breaking....

strain (strayn) *n.* tune

surge (surj) *v.* to rise or swell suddenly

rail (rayl) *v.* to cry, complain

lap (lap) *v.* to splash in little waves

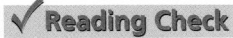
Reading Check

What does Ulysses do to keep his men from hearing the voices of the Sirens?

A Greek jar showing Ulysses and his men as they encounter the Sirens

purl (purl) *v.* to make a soft murmuring sound like a flowing stream

spume (spyoom) *n.* foam

hawser (HAW zur) *n.* a large rope

It seemed to him then that the sun was burning him to a cinder as he stood. And the voices of the Sirens purled in a cool crystal pool upon their rock past the blue-hot flatness of the sea and its lacings of white-hot spume. It seemed to him he could actually see their voices deepening into a silvery, cool pool and must plunge into that pool or die a flaming death.

He was filled with such a fury of desire that he swelled his mighty muscles, burst the rawhide bonds like thread, and dashed for the rail.

But he had warned two of his strongest men—Perimedes (pehr ih MEE deez) and Eurylochus (yoo RIHL uh kus)—to guard him close. They seized him before he could plunge into the water. He swept them aside as if they had been children. But they had held him long enough to give the crew time to swarm about him. He was overpowered—crushed by their numbers—and dragged back to the mast. This time he was bound with the mighty hawser that held the anchor.

The men returned to their rowing seats, unable to hear the voices because of the wax corking their ears. The ship swung about and headed for the strait again.

Louder now, and clearer, the tormenting voices came to Ulysses. Again he was aflame with a fury of desire. But try as he might he could not break the thick anchor line. He strained against it until he bled, but the line held.

The men bent to their oars and rowed more swiftly, for they saw the mast bending like a tall tree in a heavy wind, and they feared that Ulysses, in his fury, might snap it off short and dive, mast and all, into the water to get at the Sirens.

Now they were passing the rock, and Ulysses could see the singers. There were two of them. They sat on a heap of white bones—the bones of shipwrecked sailors—and sang more beautifully than senses could bear. But their appearance did not match their voices, for they were shaped like birds, huge birds, larger than eagles.

A Siren

About the Selection

Homer's tale of Ulysses and the Sirens is only a few dozen verses long. This version of the tale, "The Sirens," as well as many other tales from Homer's *Odyssey,* can be found in *The Adventures of Ulysses,* by Bernard Evslin. The book was published in 1969.

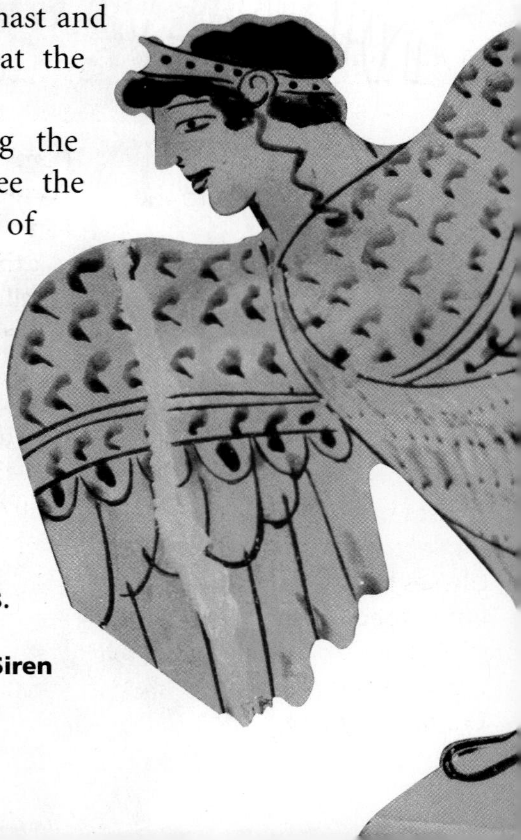

They had feathers instead of hair, and their hands and feet were claws. But their faces were the faces of young girls.

◀ **The eastern coast of Sicily, Italy**

When Ulysses saw them he was able to forget the sweetness of their voices because their look was so fearsome. He closed his eyes against the terrible sight of these bird-women perched on their heap of bones. But when he closed his eyes he could not see their ugliness, then their voices maddened him once again, and he felt himself straining against the bloody ropes. He forced himself to open his eyes and look upon the monsters, so that the terror of their bodies would blot the beauty of their voices.

But the men, who could only see, not hear the Sirens, were so <u>appalled</u> by their <u>aspect</u> that they swept their oars faster and faster, and the black ship scuttled past the rock. The Sirens' voices sounded fainter and fainter and finally died away.

When Perimedes and Eurylochus saw their captain's face lose its madness, they unbound him, and he signaled to the men to unstop their ears. For now he heard the whistling gurgle of a whirlpool, and he knew that they were approaching the narrowest part of the strait, and must pass between <u>Scylla</u> and <u>Charybdis</u>.

appall (uh PAWL) *v.* horrify
aspect (AS pekt) *n.* the way something looks
Scylla (SIL uh) *n.* a monster who ate sailors passing through the Straits of Messina, between Italy and Sicily
Charybdis (kuh RIB dis) *n.* a monster in the form of a deadly whirlpool near Scylla

✓ **Reading Check**

What are the Sirens doing on their rocky islet?

Review and Assessment

Thinking About the Selection

1. (a) **Identify** What are the Sirens?
(b) **Explain** How do the Sirens bring ships to destruction?
(c) **Apply Information** Why do you think temptation is sometimes described as a "siren song"?
2. (a) **Recall** What fears does Ulysses have about the voyage?
(b) **Infer** Give two reasons Ulysses leaves his own ears unplugged during the voyage.
(c) **Draw Conclusions** Do you think Ulysses is a good leader? Explain why or why not.

Writing Activity

Retell the Story in a Different Form "The Sirens" is in the form of a short story. Use another form of writing to retell it. You might choose to make it into a poem. You could retell it as a movie script with dialog and scene descriptions. Or, you might write an instruction manual for sailors to follow when they have to travel near the Sirens.

About the Author

Homer Although "The Sirens" is retold here by Bernard Evslin, the tale was made famous by Homer. Homer was a Greek poet who lived around 750 B.C. Scholars believe that he drew on legends passed down by word of mouth to compose the epic poems the *Iliad* and *Odyssey*.

Chapter

7 The Glory of Ancient Greece

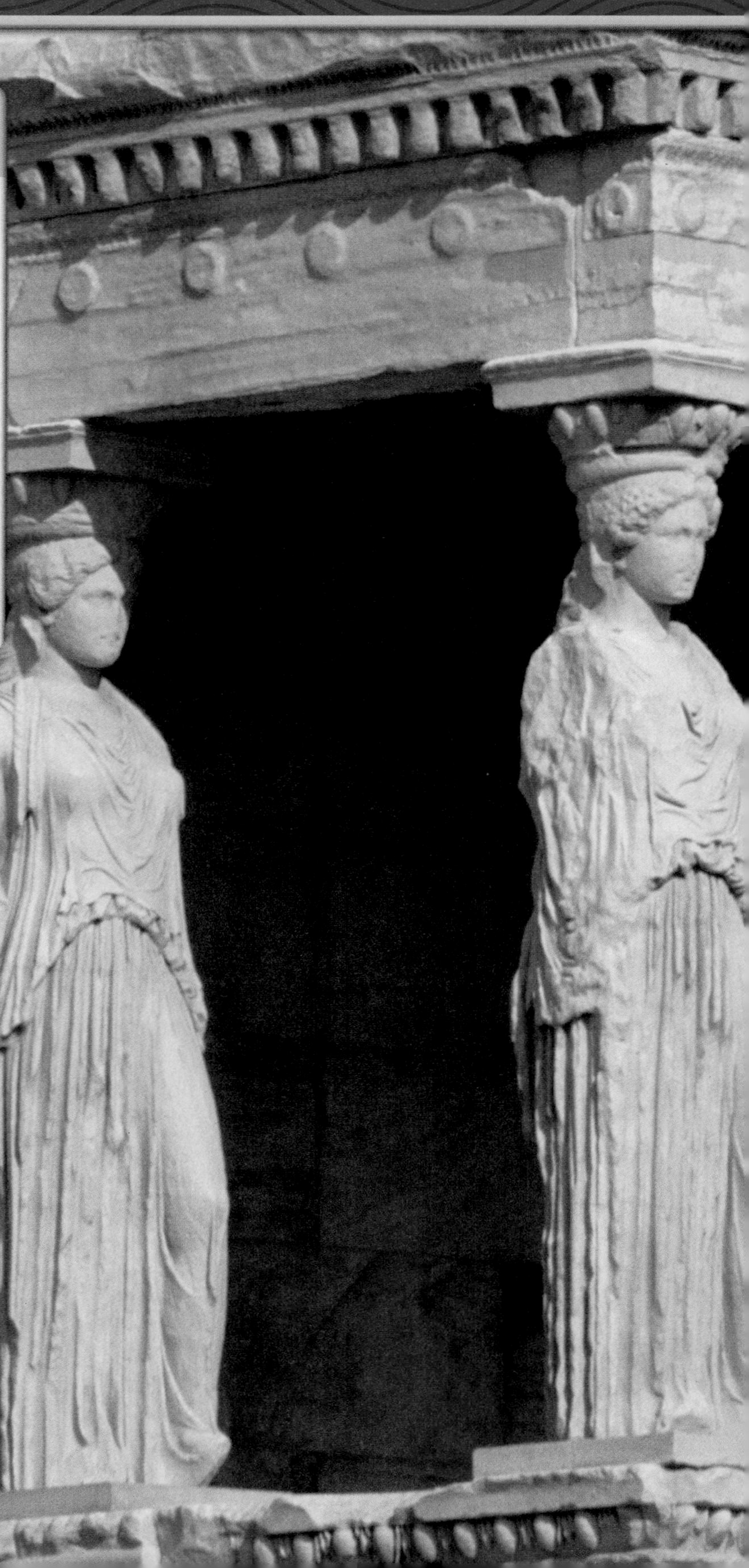

Chapter Preview

This chapter will introduce you to

Section 1
Daily Life in Athens

Section 2
Athens and Sparta

Section 3
The Spread of Greek Culture

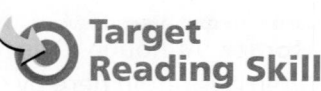

Target Reading Skill

Make Comparisons and Contrasts In this chapter you will learn to compare and contrast to help you sort out and analyze information.

▶ At the Acropolis in Athens, these statues on the porch of the Erectheion are called *Caryatids,* possibly because women called the *Karyai* were the models.

MAP MASTER™ Skills Activity

The Glory of Ancient Greece

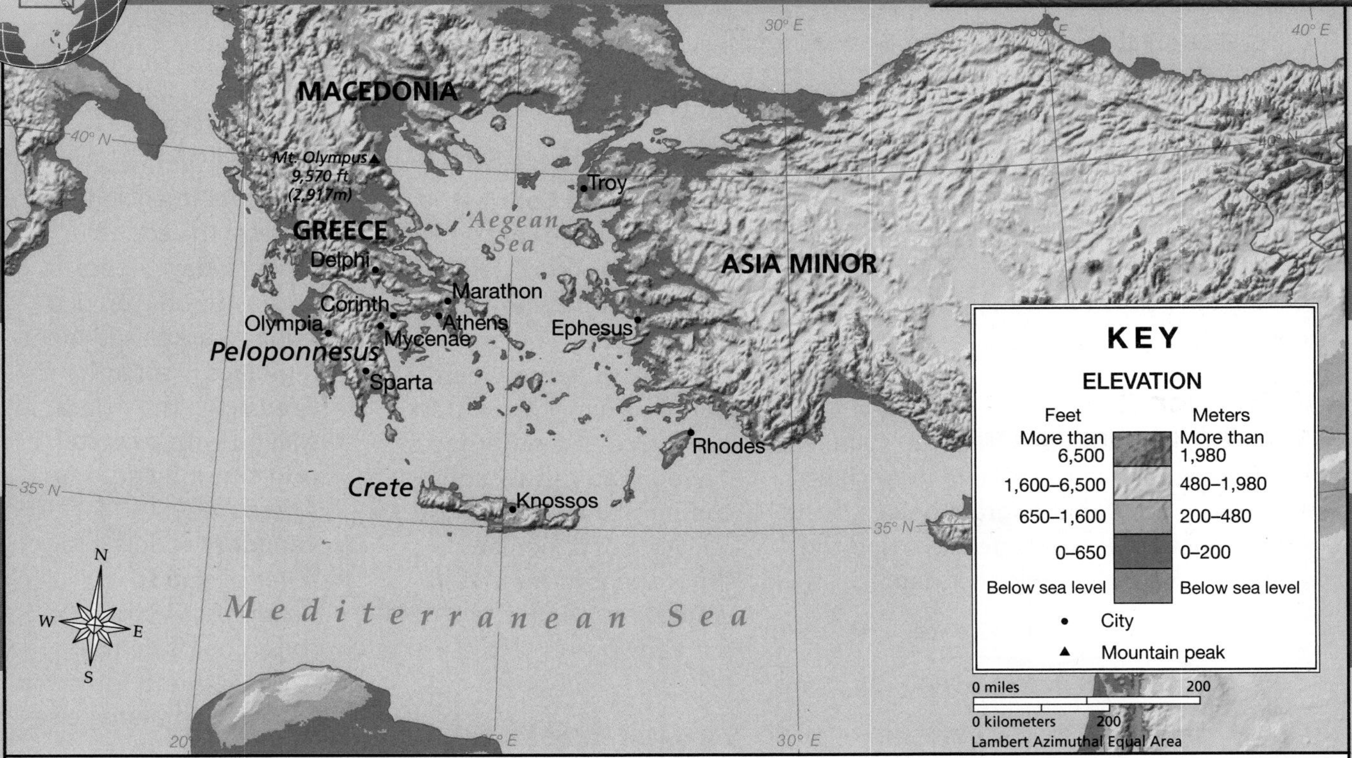

MACEDONIA
Mt. Olympus
9,570 ft
(2,917m)
GREECE
Aegean Sea
Troy
Delphi
Marathon
Corinth
Athens
Olympia
Mycenae
Peloponnesus
Sparta
Ephesus
ASIA MINOR
Rhodes
Crete
Knossos
Mediterranean Sea
40° N
35° N
30° E
40° E
20°
N
S
E
W
KEY
ELEVATION
Feet
Meters
More than 6,500
More than 1,980
1,600–6,500
480–1,980
650–1,600
200–480
0–650
0–200
Below sea level
Below sea level
City
Mountain peak
0 miles 200
0 kilometers 200
Lambert Azimuthal Equal Area

Location In the Mediterranean civilization of the fifth century B.C. travel over land was difficult and dangerous. **Identify** Examine the map to discover how many cities are close to the sea. **Draw Conclusions** Use the topographical features of the map to determine what other reason might cause cities to be located where they are. Use the same features to explain why overland travel was difficult.

Go Online
PHSchool.com Use Web Code **mup-0701** for step-by-step **map skills practice.**

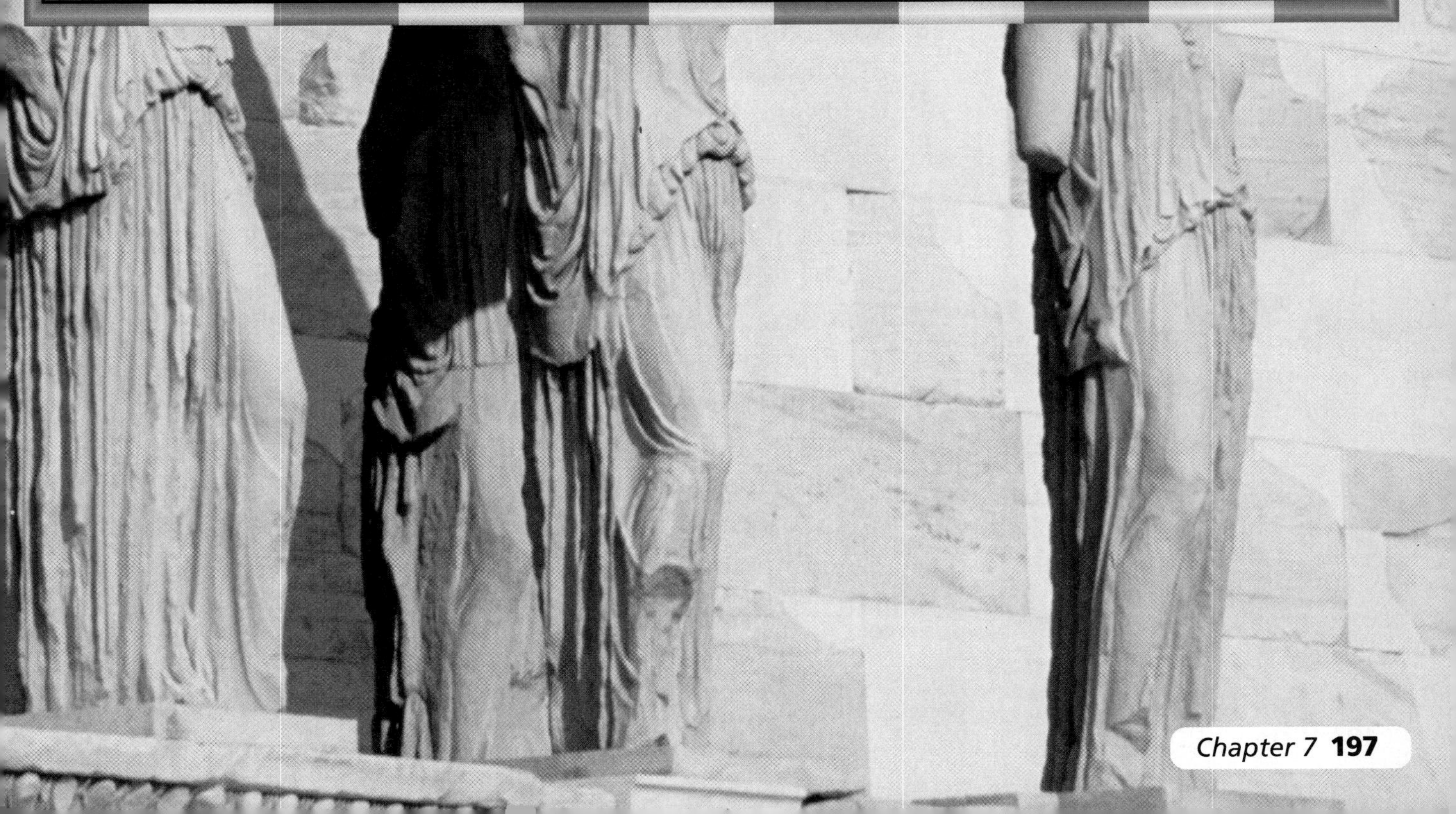

Daily Life in Athens

Prepare to Read

Objectives

In this section you will

1. Learn about public life in Athens.
2. Find out how Athenians spent their time when they were at home.
3. Understand how slavery operated in ancient Greece.

Taking Notes

As you read, look for ways that life is similar and different for various people in Ancient Greece. Copy the Venn diagram below. Write the differences in the outside areas and the similarities where the circles overlap.

Life in Ancient Greece

Target Reading Skill

Compare and Contrast Comparing and contrasting can help you sort out and analyze information. When you compare, you examine the similarities between things. When you contrast, you look at the differences. As you read this section, compare and contrast the daily life of Athenians. Write the information in your Taking Notes diagram.

Key Terms

- **Athens** (ATH unz) *n.* a city-state in ancient Greece; the capital of modern-day Greece
- **agora** (AG uh ruh) *n.* a public market and meeting place in an ancient Greek city; the Agora, spelled with a capital a, refers to the agora of Athens
- **vendor** (VEN dur) *n.* a seller of goods
- **slavery** (SLAY vur ee) *n.* condition of being owned by, and forced to work for, someone else

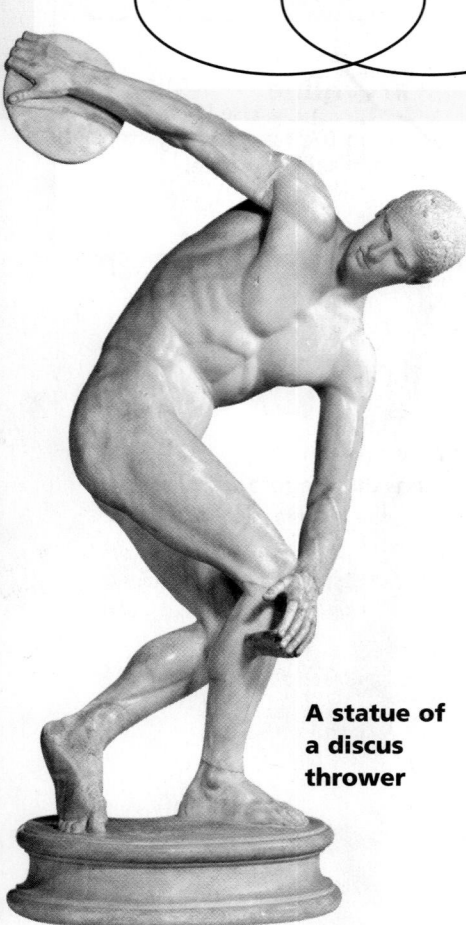

A statue of a discus thrower

The light from the courtyard was still gray when the young boy awoke. He sat up on his hard bed and felt the morning air on his face. It was time to get up for school. The boy swallowed his breakfast, pulled his cloak around him, and left the house.

On the way to school, the boy met other students. All were carrying wooden tablets covered with wax. They would write their lessons on the tablets. They talked about their lesson, a long passage of history that they had to memorize.

The best part of the day came after school. Then, the boy spent the afternoon at the training ground. All the boys exercised and practiced wrestling and throwing a flat plate called a discus. Sometimes they watched older athletes training to compete in the Olympic Games, held in honor of Zeus.

This story shows how a boy might have spent his day in **Athens, a city-state in ancient Greece.** A look at daily life in ancient Athens will help you understand how many people lived in the early days of Greece.

Public Life

Boys growing up in Athens needed only to look around to understand that it was the men who were active in politics, in society, and in other aspects of Athenian public life. The boys knew that they could look forward to assuming an important role in Athenian public life as they became adults.

The Marketplace On their way to school, the boys passed through the Agora of Athens. The Acropolis was the center of Athens' religious life, and the Agora was the center of its public life. The Agora was near the Acropolis, which rose in splendor above it. All Greek cities had **agoras,** or public markets and meeting places. The Agora in Athens was probably the busiest and most interesting of them all. The mild climate of Athens made it possible to carry on business in the open.

The Business of Men In the morning, many Athenian men made their way to the Agora. In the Agora, the men talked of politics, philosophy, or events in their community.

As they talked, they heard the cries of **vendors,** or sellers of goods. Buyers and vendors commonly haggled, or bargained, for the best prices. The streets were lined with shops. Farmers and artisans also sold their wares from stands set up under shady trees. Just about any food an Athenian would want could be found in the Agora. Other goods were also for sale—sheep's wool, pottery, hardware, cloth, and books.

Public Buildings Temples and government buildings lined the Agora. The buildings were often beautiful structures, for Athenians greatly admired beauty in architecture. The Greek classical style of architecture, or the style developed during the Golden Age, continues to influence how buildings are built in our time. Many government buildings in Europe and the United States were patterned after Greek architecture.

✔ **Reading Check** What business did Athenian men conduct in the Agora?

Go Online
PHSchool.com Use Web Code **mup-0825** for an interactivity on education in ancient Greece.

Community Life
The ruins of an agora are shown above. Greeks used agoras as public markets and meeting places. A vase from the 400s shows two Greeks discussing philosophy. **Analyze** *Why do you think the Agora was the center of public life in Athens?*

At Home in Athens

The splendor of public buildings in Athens contrasted with the simplicity of people's houses, even in the Golden Age.

Ancient Greek wine vessel

Private Life Throughout Greece, private homes were plain. Made of mud bricks, Greek houses consisted of rooms set around an open courtyard that was hidden from the street. The courtyard was the center of the household. Other rooms might include a kitchen, storerooms, a dining room, and bedrooms. Some homes even had bathrooms. Water had to be carried from a public fountain.

The ancient Greeks ate simple foods. Breakfast might be just bread. For midday meals, Athenians might add cheese or olives to the bread. Dinner would be a hot meal that was more filling. It might consist of fish and vegetables followed by cheese, fruit, and even cakes sweetened with honey. Most Athenians ate little meat. Even wealthy families ate meat only during religious festivals.

Women of Athens If you had walked through the Agora, you would have noticed that most of the people there were men. If you had asked where the women were, an Athenian man might have replied, "At home."

Home was where most Athenian women spent their days. Women led secluded lives. Athenian men thought that women needed to be protected. Keeping them out of the public eye, men thought, gave women the most protection.

Target Skill
Compare and Contrast
Where did Athenian men spend most of their time? Where did Athenian women spend most of their time? What was similar about their daily lives?

Greek Women
The women of ancient Greece making bread, as shown in the figure at right.
Predict *Use what you know about the lives of ancient Greeks to predict where girls might gather to play games.*

Most Greeks thought that women needed to be guided by men. Women had almost none of the freedom their husbands, sons, and fathers took for granted. They could not take any part in politics. Nor could they vote. They could not own property. About the only official activity allowed them was to be priestesses in religious groups.

Running the home and family was the job of women. In some wealthy families, men and women had completely separate quarters. Women organized the spinning and weaving, looked after supplies of food and wine, and cared for young children. They also kept track of the family finances. If a family was wealthy enough to have slaves, they were the woman's responsibility as well. She directed them, trained them, and cared for them when they were sick.

If a woman lived in a poor household, she often worked outside of the home. Women who had little money found jobs making pottery, tending sheep, or manufacturing cloth from wool.

Although women throughout Greece did important work, they were expected to be almost invisible. As Pericles once said: "The greatest glory belong to the woman who is least talked about by men, either they praise her or find fault with her."

✓ **Reading Check** **What kinds of foods did Athenians eat?**

Links to **Art**

Painting Their Lives
Athenians were known for their beautiful pottery. They decorated vases, jars, and cups with black or reddish-tan figures. Many scenes were mythological, but others showed Athenian daily life. Some of the pottery was used in religious ceremonies. However, much of it was used in Athenian households to carry water, serve food, and hold flowers.

Slavery in Ancient Greece

Slaves did a great deal of work throughout the city-states of Greece. It was the labor of the slaves that gave Athenian men the leisure time to go to the Agora, participate in government, and develop a love of the arts.

Slavery, the condition of being owned by someone else, was common in Athens. Historians estimate that as many as 100,000 slaves may have lived in Athens. This would mean that almost one third of the city's population were slaves. Today, we consider slavery a crime. However, in ancient times free people rarely questioned slavery, even in democratic Athens.

Who Were the Slaves? Many free people became enslaved when they were captured by armies during war or by pirates while traveling on ships. Children born into slave families automatically became slaves.

Some Greeks were uncomfortable owning other Greeks. Greeks with such scruples, or ethical objections to a situation, solved this problem by owning foreign slaves. A large number of slaves in Greece were foreigners.

The Slaves of Athens
In this detail from a vase, a servant attends to a seated woman. **Draw Conclusions** *Based on what you have read, draw a conclusion about the ancient Greek's attitudes toward slavery.*

The Lives of Slaves Slaves did not have any of the privileges taken for granted by the rest of Greek society. Citizenship in Greece was very restricted, so it follows that slaves, on the lowest rung of Greek society, were not citizens. They had no political rights or personal freedom and they received no formal education. Slaves could only become free if they bought their own freedom or if their master freed them.

Remember that without the labor of the slaves, Greek citizens—that is, Greek men—would not have had the leisure to participate in government and the arts. Slaves did many kinds of work. Some provided labor on farms. Others dug silver and other metals in mines. Still others assisted artisans by making pottery and other decorative items. Some slaves helped construct buildings. Others helped forge weapons and armor. Most Greek households could not have operated without slaves. They cooked and served food, tended children, cleaned, and wove cloth.

A painting from a cup shows a male slave balancing two vessels.

✔ **Reading Check** What kinds of labor did slaves perform?

Section 1 Assessment

Key Terms
Review the key terms at the beginning of this section. Use each term in a sentence that explains its meaning.

Target Reading Skill
Name two ways in which the lives of Athenian men and women were similar. Name two ways in which they differed.

Comprehension and Critical Thinking
1. (a) Describe What activities took place in the Agora of Athens?
(b) Explore Main Ideas and Details What does the Agora tell us about the culture of Athens?

2. (a) Recall Describe the home life of the Athenians.
(b) Compare What were the responsibilities of men compared to those of women in ancient Athens?
(c) Draw Conclusions Considering your answer to the previous question, what conclusions can you make about society in ancient Athens?
3. (a) Recall Describe the various roles of slaves in Athens and of those in the rest of ancient Greece.
(b) Draw Inferences Free people rarely questioned slavery in ancient Greece. Why do you think this was so?

Writing Activity
Write a description of your school-day routine. How does your day compare with that of the Greek boy you read about at the beginning of this section?

For: An activity on the women of ancient Greece
Visit: PHSchool.com
Web Code: mud-0710

Focus On
The Agora of Athens

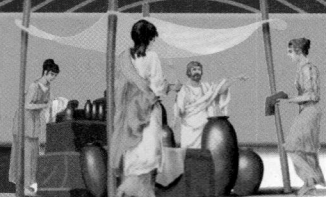

In the center of town stands the town hall, a grocery store, a church, a library, and a firehouse. These buildings enclose a public square. The square looks like countless town squares throughout America and Europe, yet its roots lie in ancient Greece. The busy heart of a Greek city was called the *agora,* or "marketplace." Some agoras were laid out as squares or rectangles. The Athenian agora shown here followed a more rambling style.

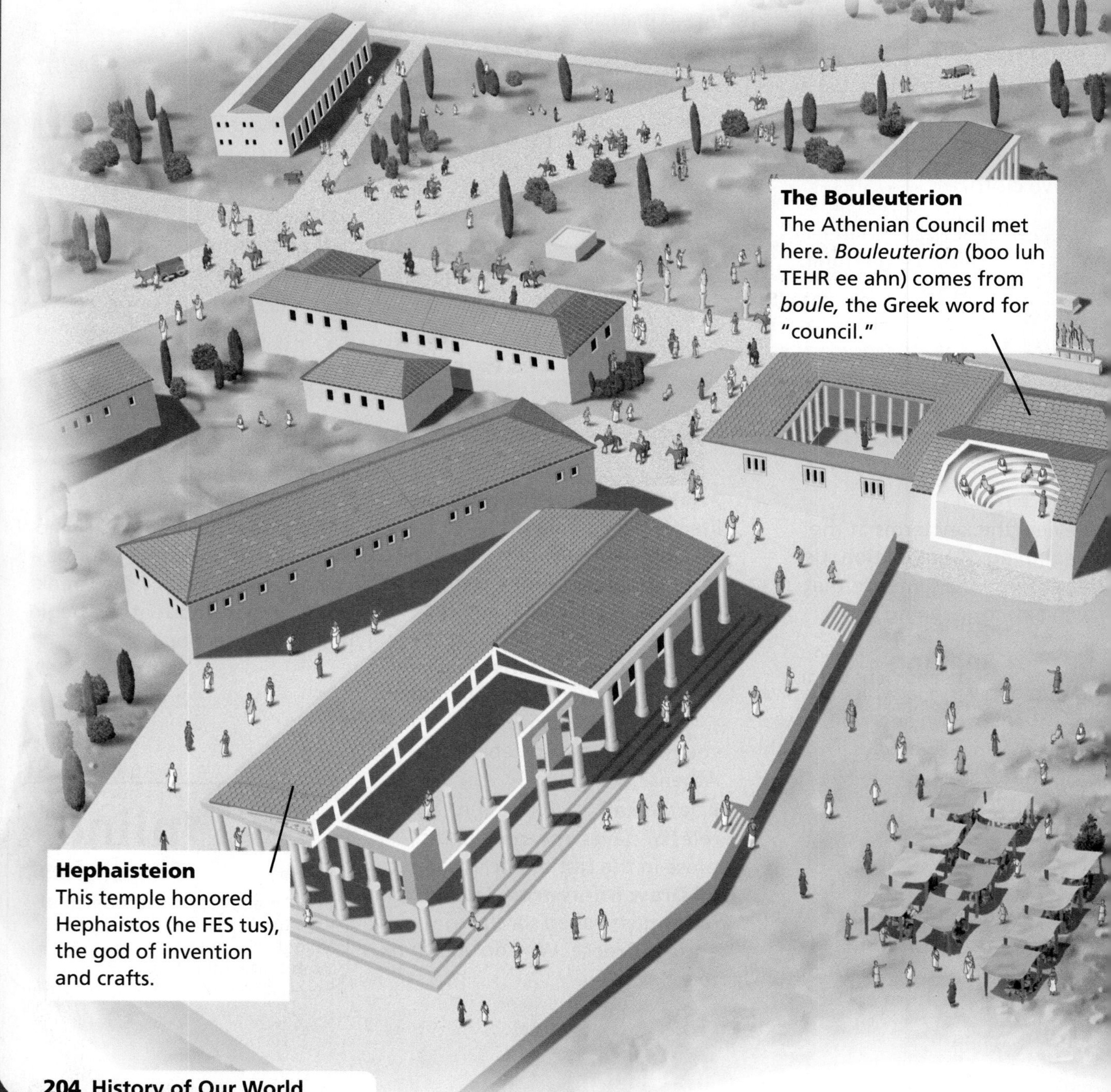

The Bouleuterion
The Athenian Council met here. *Bouleuterion* (boo luh TEHR ee ahn) comes from *boule,* the Greek word for "council."
Hephaisteion
This temple honored Hephaistos (he FES tus), the god of invention and crafts.

Hephaisteion Ruins
This temple was built in the 400s B.C. Among all the Agora ruins, it is the best preserved.

The Odeion of Agrippa
This concert hall could seat 1,000 people.

Stoa of Attalos
Merchants housed their *stoae* (STOH ee), or "shops," here.

The Tholos
Council members ate and slept in this round building.

The Athenian Marketplace The Agora symbolized the Greeks' love of public participation—political, religious, economic, judicial, and scholarly. Public buildings surrounded open spaces for the exchange of news, ideas, and goods. In the shadow of the Acropolis, Athens built a magnificent agora. There, the orator Pericles spoke, and the philosopher Socrates taught and was sentenced to death. Generals rallied the city to war, and priests paid respect to the gods. There, democracy was born as Athenian citizens voted for their leaders and sat on juries. Although the Agora was once adorned with fountains, gardens, and sculpture, little is left of it today.

Assessment

Describe What kinds of activities took place in the Agora?

Compare In what ways is the Agora similar to the citadel section of Mohenjo-Daro (shown on pages 112–113)?

Prepare to Read

Objectives

In this section you will

1. Learn how people lived in ancient Sparta.
2. Discover some results of the Persian invasion of Greece.
3. Understand the conflicts that the Athenian empire faced.

Taking Notes

As you read, look for ways in which Spartans differed from Athenians. Copy the chart below, and use it to record those differences.

Differences Between Spartans and Athenians	
Spartans	**Athenians**
• Boys trained in military arts • •	• Boys educated in arts, history, and physical training • • •

Target Reading Skill

Identify Contrasts When you contrast two peoples or cultures, you examine how they differ. In this section, you will read about the Spartan people. Although they had many of the same elements of Greek culture that the Athenians did, they differed in other ways. As you read, list the differences between Athens and Sparta. Record your findings in your Taking Notes chart.

Key Terms

- **Sparta** (SPAHR tuh) *n.* a city-state in ancient Greece
- **helots** (HEL uts) *n.* In ancient Sparta, the term for slaves who were owned by the state
- **Peloponnesian War** (pel uh puh NEE shun wawr) *n.* (431–404 B.C.), a war fought between Athens and Sparta in ancient Greece; almost every other Greek city-state was involved in the war
- **plague** (playg) *n.* a widespread disease
- **blockade** (blah KAYD) *n.* an action taken to isolate the enemy and cut off its supplies

A Spartan warrior

The boy stood still and straight beside his companions as their trainer approached. "You," the trainer barked, "Are you sick? Don't think you'll get out of sword practice—and why are you holding your belly? Hiding something?"

The trainer gave the boy's cloak a sharp tug. It fell to the ground, freeing a fox that streaked off into the underbrush. The boy fell to the ground. His cloak was blood red. His side was shredded with deep cuts and bites. The boy had stolen the fox for his dinner. Hidden beneath the cloak, the fox had clawed and bit him.

Later, the boy died from his wounds. He had endured terrible pain without giving any sign of his distress. To the Spartans, this was the sign of true character.

This Spartan story of the boy and the fox may be true, or it might be just a legend. However, it tells us much about the people of **Sparta**, a city-state in southern Greece.

Living in Sparta

Life in Athens was free and open, but life for the citizens of Sparta was just the opposite. Life in Sparta was harsh and even cruel. The Spartans themselves were tough, silent, and grim. Sparta's army easily equaled that of Athens' in the 400s B.C. However, Sparta never came close to equaling Athens' other achievements.

In its early days, Sparta was similar to other Greek cities. Then, in the 600s B.C., wars inside and outside the city led to changes in the government and the way people lived. The changes turned Sparta into a powerful war machine. The city-state established one basic rule: Always put the city's needs above your own.

Early in its history, the Spartans conquered the land around their city. They turned the conquered people into **helots**, or slaves owned by the city-state of Sparta. Helots did all the farm work on the land owned by Spartan citizens. This system left the Spartans free to wage war. However, the helots far outnumbered the Spartans. Living in fear of a helot revolt, the Spartans turned their city into an armed camp. They treated the helots very harshly.

✓ **Reading Check** **What type of people were the Spartans?**

Sparta lies in a fertile valley with mountains on three sides. Sparta spent its money and energy on its army instead of fine buildings. Today, few ruins remain to tell us about this important city-state.

Growing Up in Sparta

The life of every Spartan was in the hands of the government from birth. Only the healthiest children were raised because the Spartans wanted only the healthiest people in their city.

Growing Up Male Training began early. At seven, a Spartan boy left his home to live in barracks with other boys. His training continued for the next 13 years.

By the age of 12, a boy had spent long hours practicing with swords and spears. He had only one cloak and a thin mat to sleep on. He could hardly live on the small amount of food he was given, so he was urged to steal. The Spartans thought that a boy who learned to steal would know how to live off the land during a war. However, if the boy were caught stealing, he was severely punished. Boys were expected to bear pain, hardship, and punishment in silence. Through this rigid discipline, Spartan youths became excellent soldiers.

When he became 20, a young man officially became a soldier. Men remained soldiers until their sixtieth birthdays. At the age of 30, a man was able to take his place in the assembly, a council consisting of all the male citizens born in Sparta. As in Athens, only non-slave males were considered citizens in Sparta. The council approved the decisions made by the council of elders who, in turn, acted as advisors to the king.

Helmet worn by Greek soldiers

Spartan soldiers were trained to be excellent warriors. Many armies suffered defeat at the hands of Spartan fighting forces.

Growing Up Female Like the boys, girls also trained and competed in wrestling and spear throwing. No one expected girls to become soldiers. However, Spartans did believe that girls who grew up strong and healthy would have strong, healthy children. Therefore, unlike other Greek women, Spartan women were trained to exercise and build up their bodies.

Spartan women had a somewhat better life than women in other Greek city-states. They were allowed to own land and even take some part in business. However, like their Athenian sisters, they had to obey the males—the fathers, husbands, or brothers—in their lives. Because the men were so involved in military matters, some Spartan women took on larger responsibilities, such as the running of their farms or estates.

Spartan Attitudes The Spartans did not mingle with other Greeks. They were not allowed to travel. They looked down on the desire for wealth and on those engaged in trade. They lacked the interest in the arts that the Athenians and some other Greeks cultivated. However, Spartan warriors were known for their skill and bravery. The Spartan fighting force played a key role in the Greek wars against the Persians, a people who lived across the Aegean Sea, east of Greece.

✓ **Reading Check** **What was the Spartan attitude about trade?**

Identify Contrasts Contrast the life of Spartan women to that of Athenian women. Enter your findings on your Taking Notes chart.

■ Timeline Skills

The timeline below covers events that occured during Classical Greece, an era that lasted from about 500 B.C. to 323 B.C. **Identify** What event occured near the end of the Persian Wars? **Analyze** After which war did Athens surrender to Sparta?

The Persians Invade

Much of Greek history tells of wars the Greeks fought among themselves. Near the beginning of the 400s B.C., a new threat loomed—the growing might of Persia. The Greeks put aside their differences and joined forces to defend their peninsula.

The Expanding Persian Empire Cyrus the Great had founded the Persian Empire in the mid-500s B.C. Cyrus and the rulers who followed him extended the original empire. By 520 B.C., the Persians had gained control of the Greek colonies on the west coast of Asia Minor.

Battle at Marathon In the fall of 490 B.C., a force including thousands of Persians landed in Greece. The Persian soldiers gathered at Marathon (MAR uh thahn), about 25 miles (40 km) north of Athens. The Athenians hastily put together a small army. However, the Persians outnumbered them by at least two to one. For several days, the armies stared tensely at each other across the plain of Marathon.

Then, without warning, the Athenians rushed the Persians, who were overwhelmed by the furious attack. By one account, at the end of the battle the Athenians had killed 6,400 Persians but had lost only 192 soldiers themselves. The Persian losses may have been exaggerated. However, it is true that in a short time this tiny state had defeated the giant that had come to destroy it.

✓ **Reading Check** **What happened during the battle at Marathon?**

Classical Greece

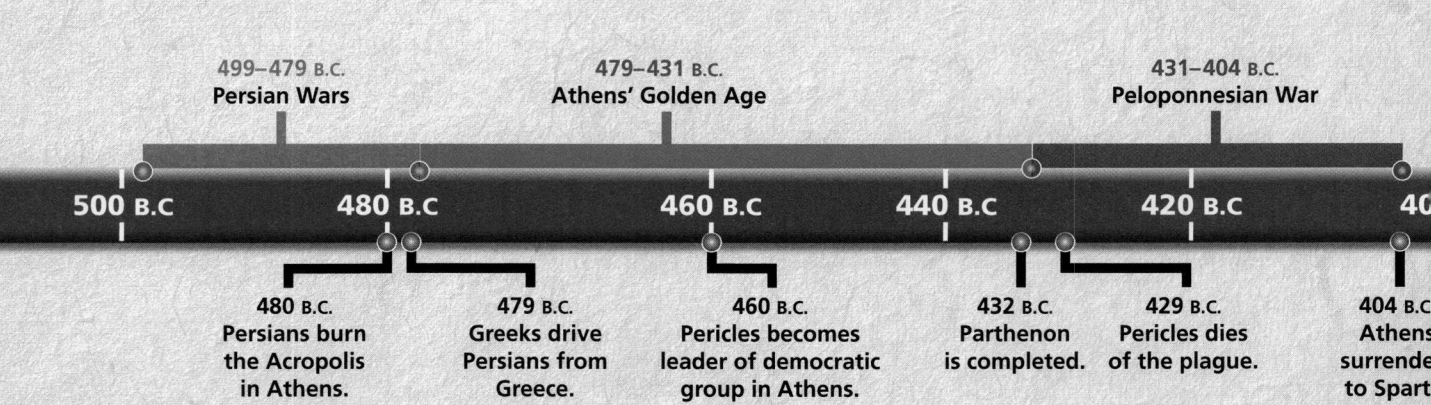

499–479 B.C. **Persian Wars**

479–431 B.C. **Athens' Golden Age**

431–404 B.C. **Peloponnesian War**

500 B.C   480 B.C   460 B.C   440 B.C   420 B.C   40

480 B.C. Persians burn the Acropolis in Athens.

479 B.C. Greeks drive Persians from Greece.

460 B.C. Pericles becomes leader of democratic group in Athens.

432 B.C. Parthenon is completed.

429 B.C. Pericles dies of the plague.

404 B.C. Athens surrende to Spart

These warriors decorate a vase from the 500s B.C. The background is the natural color of the baked clay. The black figures were made by using a glossy black pigment.

Conflict and the Athenian Empire

More battles with Persia followed. As a common enemy, Persia distracted the Greek city-states from fighting one another. Briefly united, Greece drove away the Persians.

Their victory over the Persians increased the Greeks' sense of their own importance. They believed that the gods had favored them and had therefore influenced the outcome of the wars.

Athens emerged from the war as the most powerful city-state in Greece. Its influence spread over much of eastern Greece. Athens joined other city-states in the Delian League (DEE lee un leeg), named after the island of Delos (DEE lahs), where the league's treasury was kept. In time, however, these cities were treated more like subjects of Athens and less like allies. Athens came to dominate the league and used it to create its own empire.

Ironically, while Athens was expanding its empire and forcing other city-states to bow to its will, Athens came to champion political freedom at home. Athens did support democratic groups within the other city-states, but its focus was on freedom for its own people. The years following the Persian Wars were the Golden Age of Athens that you read about in Chapter 6.

✓ **Reading Check** Why did Greeks believe they had won their wars with Persia?

Citizen Heroes

Working Together

In one of the wars against the Persians, some 6,000 Greeks had to defend a mountain pass leading into southern Greece. They faced nearly 200,000 Persians. Most of the Greeks retreated, but 300 Spartan soldiers stood their ground. All of them died in the battle. They didn't hold back the Persians, but they earned undying praise for their brave sacrifice.

Movement By the early 400s B.C., the Persian Empire had spread from India to just north of the Greek mainland. **Identify** What cities were Persian capitals? **Infer** What advantage would the Persians gain from winning control over Greece?

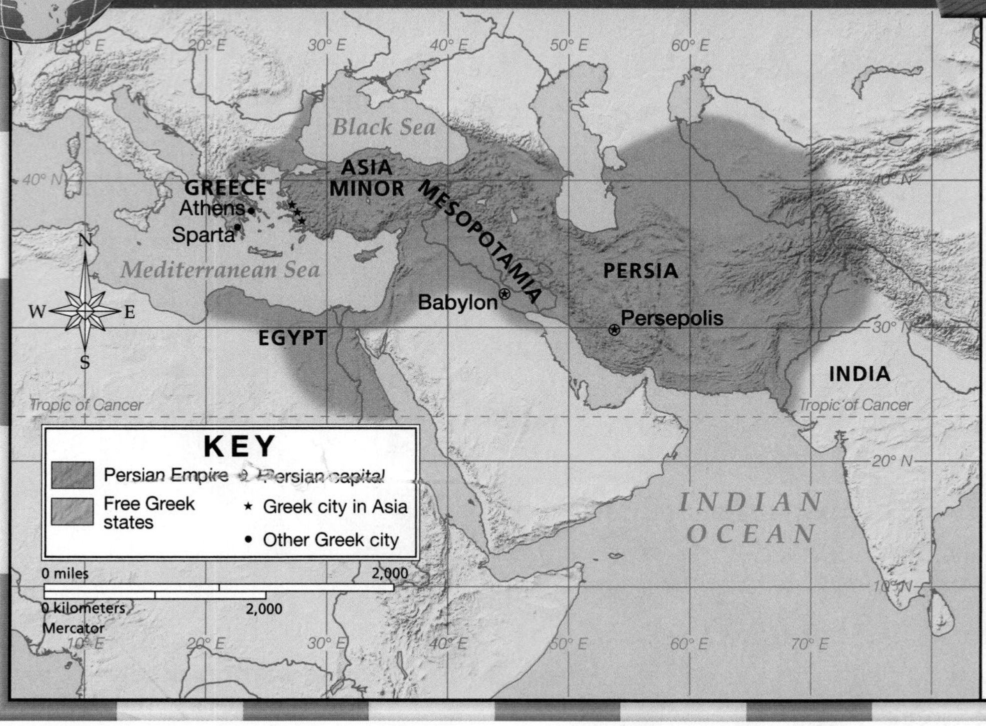

KEY

▨ Persian Empire	⊛ Persian capital
☐ Free Greek states	★ Greek city in Asia
	• Other Greek city

0 miles 2,000
0 kilometers 2,000
Mercator

Go Online
PHSchool.com Use Web Code **lbp-2624** for step-by-step **map skills practice.**

Greek warrior figurine

Learn about Sparta's warriors.

Sparta and Athens at War

Athens may have been a democracy at home, but it began to act unfairly toward other city-states. At first, allies of Athens had paid tribute to the city-state for protection, in case the Persians caused more trouble. Later, Athens moved the treasury from Delos to Athens and used the money that was supposed to help defend its allies to build the Parthenon and to finance other projects.

The Peloponnesian War The people of these city-states began to fear and resent Athens' power. They looked to Sparta, which had not joined the alliance, to protect them. To counter the Delian League, Sparta formed the Peloponnesian League, named after Peloponnesus, the southern Greek peninsula where Sparta was located. In 431 B.C., Sparta and its allies fought against Athens and its allies. Thus began the **Peloponnesian War**, a conflict between Athens and Sparta that lasted for 27 years.

Even though Athens had a fine navy and more wealth than the other city-states, its geography was a great disadvantage in the war. Sparta, located inland, could not be attacked from the sea. However, Sparta had only to march north to attack Athens by land.

When Sparta invaded Athens, the statesman Pericles, whom you read about in Chapter 6, let the people from the surrounding countryside move inside the city walls. The overcrowded conditions led to a **plague**, or widespread disease. By the time the plague ended five years later, about one third of the people of Athens had died from it. Among the dead was Pericles. The power struggles of those who sought to take Pericles' place also undermined the city's government.

The Fall of Athens Athens never recovered from its losses during the plague. To make matters worse, Sparta allied itself to its former common enemy to have the advantage of the Persian navy. In 405 B.C., with their new allies, the Spartans staged a **blockade,** an action taken to isolate the enemy and cut off its supplies. The Spartans surrounded and closed the harbor where Athens received food shipments. Starving and beaten, the Athenians surrendered in 404 B.C.

The victorious Spartans knocked down the walls of Athens. They destroyed its navy and decimated its empire. Athens never again dominated the Greek world.

Athens Defeated
Shields and spears, such as those carried by the warriors below, could not spare the Athenians from the plague. **Analyze** *What factors contributed to the fall of Athens?*

 **Reading Check** **What did Greek city-states do to overcome oppression by Athens?**

Section 2 Assessment

Key Terms
Review the key terms listed at the beginning of this section. Use each term in a sentence that explains its meaning.

Target Reading Skill
Look at the chart you made of the differences between the Spartans and the Athenians. Name one of the differences that led to the outcome of the Peloponnesian War.

Comprehension and Critical Thinking
1. (a) Recall Describe what life was like for boys living in Sparta.
(b) Explain What was the Spartan attitude toward wealth?

(c) Draw Inferences How did the Spartans' attitude toward wealth affect their trade and travel?
2. (a) Describe How did the Greeks overcome the Persian invasion?
(b) Evaluate Information What was at stake for the people of Athens at the Battle of Marathon?
(c) Predict How might the history of Greece have changed if the Persians had succeeded at Marathon?
3. (a) Recall What happened to the Greeks' attitude about themselves after defeating the Persians?
(b) Summarize How did the Athenian empire develop after its victory over Persia?

(c) Synthesize Information How did Athens play a part in its own downfall?

Writing Activity
Reread the story that begins this section. From a trainer's point of view, write a report that explains the event to other Spartan officers.

For: An activity on politics in Sparta
Visit: PHSchool.com
Web Code: mud-0720

Section 3 — The Spread of Greek Culture

Prepare to Read

Objectives

In this section you will

1. Learn how King Philip of Macedonia came to power and how Alexander the Great built his empire.
2. Understand what role the conquests of Alexander the Great played in spreading Greek culture.

Taking Notes

As you read, look for details about the spread of Greek culture. Copy the chart below, and use it to record your findings.

The Spread of Greek Culture	
Alexander's Empire	The Hellenistic Age
•	•
•	•
•	•

Target Reading Skill

Make Comparisons Comparing two or more situations, people, or items enables you to see how they are alike. As you read this section, compare the ideas of Alexander the Great to those of his predecessors.

Key Terms

- **barbarian** (bahr BEHR eeun) *n.* a person who belongs to a group that others consider wild, or uncivilized
- **assassinate** (uh SAS uh nayt) *v.* to murder for political reasons
- **Alexander the Great** (alig ZAN dur thuh grayt) *n.* (356–323 B.C.) king of Macedonia; conquered Persia and Egypt and invaded India
- **Hellenistic** (hel uh NIS tik) *adj.* describing Greek history or culture after the death of Alexander the Great, including the three main kingdoms formed by the breakup of Alexander's empire

A sculpture of King Philip of Macedonia

King Philip of Macedonia (mas uh DOH nee uh) had not wasted the money he spent on Greek tutors for his son. Young Alexander was a fine and eager student. The boy wanted to learn as much as he could, especially about the ideas and deeds of the Greeks.

The kingdom of Macedonia lay just north of Greece. Alexander thought of himself as Greek and spoke the Greek language. However, people who lived to the south did not accept the Macedonians as Greeks. They thought the Macedonians were **barbarians**, or wild, uncivilized people.

Alexander's tutor was the Greek philosopher Aristotle (AIR uh STAHT ul). Aristotle taught the boy Greek literature, philosophy, and science. Aristotle also passed on his strong feelings that the Greeks were a superior people and, therefore, deserved to rule.

Alexander loved his tutor, but his role model was Achilles, the warrior hero of the *Iliad*. Alexander vowed to visit the site of ancient Troy and lay a wreath at the tomb of his hero.

"... I will say that, from the day on which I mounted the throne, I have not ceased to consider by what means I may rival those who have preceded me in this post of honour, and increase the power of Persia as much as any of them. ... [A]t last I have found out a way whereby we may at once win glory, and likewise get possession of a land which is as large and as rich as our own.... My intent is to ... march an army through Europe against Greece, that thereby I may obtain vengeance from the Athenians for the wrongs committed by them against the Persians and against my father."

—Herodotus, a Greek historian, quoting the Persian King Xerxes in his *History*. Herodotus was a small child in a Greek city at the time Xerxes supposedly made this speech.

"... [E]vil-minded men taught headstrong Xerxes what to think: they told him that the vast wealth [his father] handed on was won at spearpoint while he, not half the man, secretly played toy spears at home and added nothing to inherited prosperity. Hearing such taunts over and again from evil-minded men, he planned his expedition and the invasion of Greece."

—Aeschylus, a Greek playwright, quoting Xerxes' mother Atossa in his play *Persians*. Aeschylus was a Greek soldier at the time of Xerxes' invasion.

Practice the Skill

If you were to come across the three quotations above while doing research, how would you evaluate them as historical sources? Ask yourself the following questions:

1. Who was Herodotus? Who was Aeschylus? How did their reasons for writing differ?

2. When were the two quotes written? Did the authors hear the people quoted first-hand? How accurate are these quotes likely to be?

3. Is either author likely to be a neutral source on the Persian invasion of Greece? Does either show any bias? Explain why one account might be more accurate than the other.

4. What purpose might each author have had for writing? Did each author write to inform or for some other reason?

Apply the Skill

Research a recent event, using reliable online or library primary sources. Find and read through two sources on the same subject, and determine whether the sources are biased or reliable.

The Spread of Greek Culture

Prepare to Read

Objectives

In this section you will

1. Learn how King Philip of Macedonia came to power and how Alexander the Great built his empire.
2. Understand what role the conquests of Alexander the Great played in spreading Greek culture.

Taking Notes

As you read, look for details about the spread of Greek culture. Copy the chart below, and use it to record your findings.

The Spread of Greek Culture	
Alexander's Empire	The Hellenistic Age
•	•
•	•
•	•

Target Reading Skill

Make Comparisons
Comparing two or more situations, people, or items enables you to see how they are alike. As you read this section, compare the ideas of Alexander the Great to those of his predecessors.

Key Terms

- **barbarian** (bahr BEHR eeun) *n.* a person who belongs to a group that others consider wild, or uncivilized
- **assassinate** (uh SAS uh nayt) *v.* to murder for political reasons
- **Alexander the Great** (alig ZAN dur thuh grayt) *n.* (356–323 B.C.) king of Macedonia; conquered Persia and Egypt and invaded India
- **Hellenistic** (hel uh NIS tik) *adj.* describing Greek history or culture after the death of Alexander the Great, including the three main kingdoms formed by the breakup of Alexander's empire

A sculpture of King Philip of Macedonia

King Philip of Macedonia (mas uh DOH nee uh) had not wasted the money he spent on Greek tutors for his son. Young Alexander was a fine and eager student. The boy wanted to learn as much as he could, especially about the ideas and deeds of the Greeks.

The kingdom of Macedonia lay just north of Greece. Alexander thought of himself as Greek and spoke the Greek language. However, people who lived to the south did not accept the Macedonians as Greeks. They thought the Macedonians were **barbarians**, or wild, uncivilized people.

Alexander's tutor was the Greek philosopher Aristotle (AIR uh STAHT ul). Aristotle taught the boy Greek literature, philosophy, and science. Aristotle also passed on his strong feelings that the Greeks were a superior people and, therefore, deserved to rule.

Alexander loved his tutor, but his role model was Achilles, the warrior hero of the *Iliad*. Alexander vowed to visit the site of ancient Troy and lay a wreath at the tomb of his hero.

Philip Comes to Power

Like his predecessors, the other Macedonian rulers before him, Philip had Greek ancestors and thought of himself as Greek. Also like his predecessors, Philip had maintained ties to his Greek neighbors. When he was young, Philip had studied in Greece. His experience of studying there led to his hiring of Aristotle to tutor Alexander.

When Philip came to power, he dreamed of conquering the rich city-states of Greece. He would accomplish this by using diplomacy as well as military force.

Before King Philip seized power in 359 B.C., Macedonia was poor and divided. Philip united Macedonia and then formed alliances with many of the Greek city-states by threatening or bribing them. He built an army even stronger than Sparta's. With this army and his talent for waging war, Philip captured one Greek city-state after another.

Demosthenes (dih MAHS thuh neez), who was a master of elocution (eluh KYOO shun), or the art of public speaking, tried to warn his fellow Athenians of the danger to the north:

> **"He is always taking in more, everywhere casting his net round us, while we sit idle and do nothing. When, Athenians, will you take the necessary action? What are you waiting for?"**

In 338 B.C., Athens and another city-state, Thebes (theebz), at last joined to try to stop Philip. However, they were unsuccessful. Philip gained control of all of Greece.

✓ **Reading Check** Why did King Philip think Greece would be easy to conquer?

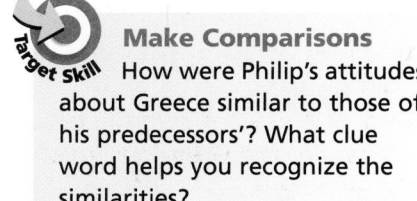

Make Comparisons
How were Philip's attitudes about Greece similar to those of his predecessors'? What clue word helps you recognize the similarities?

In an effort to unite the people of his country and preserve Greek freedom, Demosthenes issued powerful speeches against King Philip of Macedonia. These speeches came to be known as Philippics. This term is still used today to describe strong appeals against someone or something.

Alexander Builds an Empire

After he had conquered all of Greece, Philip then planned to attack Persia. But in 336 B.C., before he could carry out his plan, Philip was **assassinated,** or murdered for political reasons, by a rival. At just 20 years old, Alexander became king. He now had a chance to be as great as his hero Achilles.

Alexander's Conquests Although he was young, Alexander was already an experienced soldier. One of his first actions was to invade the Persian Empire. The empire was much weaker than it had been in the days when Persia had attempted to conquer Greece. However, it was still huge, stretching from Egypt to India. In 334 B.C., Alexander won his first battle in the vast empire. He then led his army through Asia Minor, where together they won battle after battle. He then led them on to Judaea (earlier known as Canaan), Egypt, and Babylon, the Persian capital. Alexander's forces crossed the Indus River into India, taking extensive territory wherever they fought.

Within 11 short years, the Macedonian king had conquered Persia, Egypt, and lands extending beyond the Indus River in the east. He had earned the right to be called **Alexander the Great**.

Wherever Alexander went, he established cities. Many of them he named after himself. Even today, there are numerous cities named Alexandria or Alexandroupolis (ah lek sahn DROO puh lis) throughout western Asia.

Fighting the Persian Empire
The mosaic, at right, shows the Battle of Issus, in which Alexander the Great, above, defeated an army of Persians in 333 B.C. **Infer** *Why do you think Alexander is called "Alexander the Great"?*

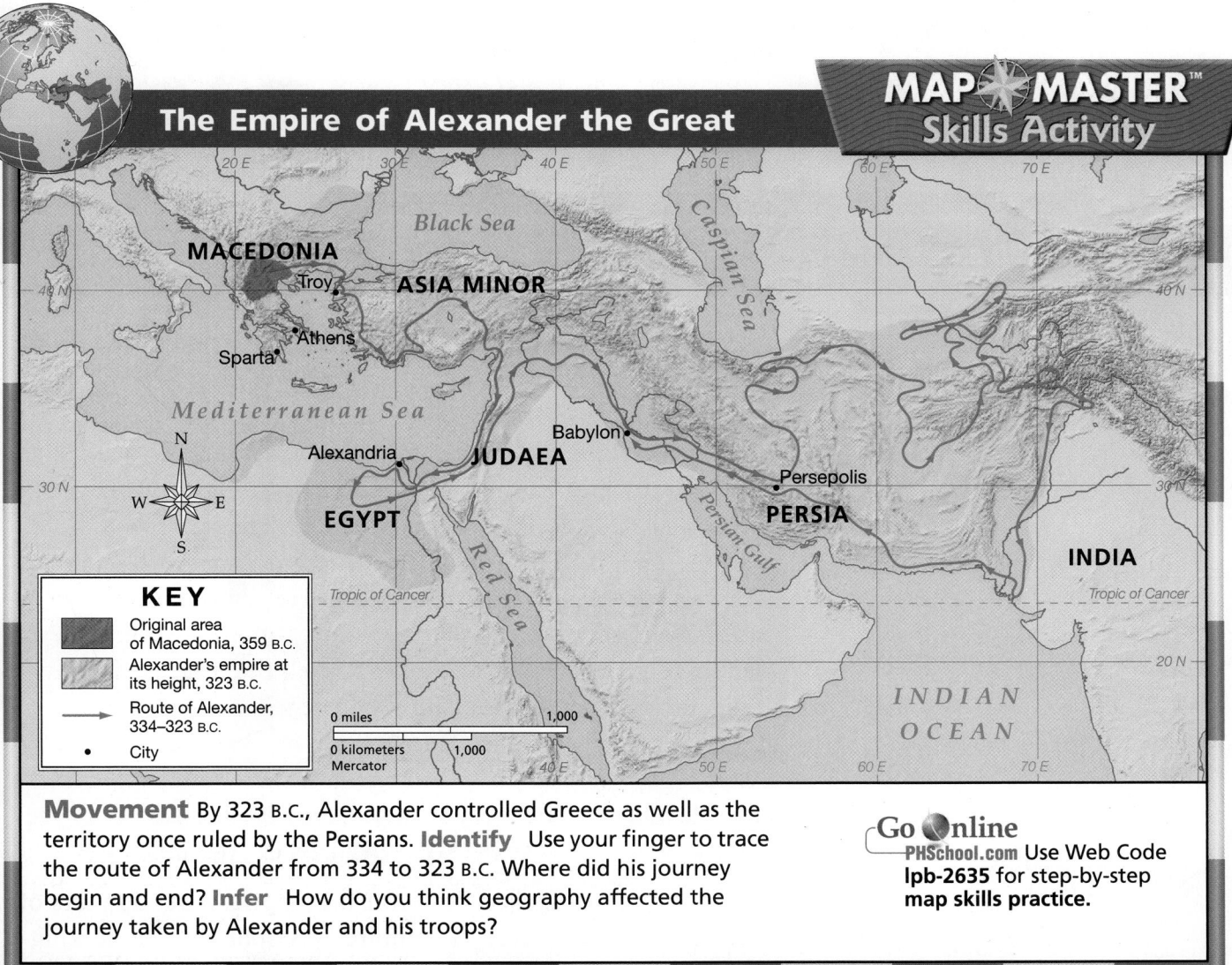

The Empire of Alexander the Great

MAP★MASTER™
Skills Activity

KEY

Original area of Macedonia, 359 B.C.

Alexander's empire at its height, 323 B.C.

Route of Alexander, 334–323 B.C.

• City

0 miles 1,000
0 kilometers 1,000
Mercator

Movement By 323 B.C., Alexander controlled Greece as well as the territory once ruled by the Persians. **Identify** Use your finger to trace the route of Alexander from 334 to 323 B.C. Where did his journey begin and end? **Infer** How do you think geography affected the journey taken by Alexander and his troops?

Go Online
PHSchool.com Use Web Code **lpb-2635** for step-by-step map skills practice.

Alexander's Last Battle Alexander's energy and military genius helped him succeed. This leader drove himself and his army hard, advancing across vast lands at lightning speed. His soldiers grumbled, but they obeyed him. He traveled far into the east, never losing a battle.

At last, not far beyond the Indus River, his weary troops refused to go another step east. Alexander was angry, but he turned back. Alexander got as far as Babylon (BAB uh lahn), where he came down with a fever. In 323 B.C., only 13 years after he had come to the throne, Alexander died. Like the legendary warrior Achilles, Alexander had died young. However, he had gone far beyond the deeds of his hero. His conquests spread Greek culture throughout a vast area.

✓ **Reading Check** Why was Alexander so successful as a military leader?

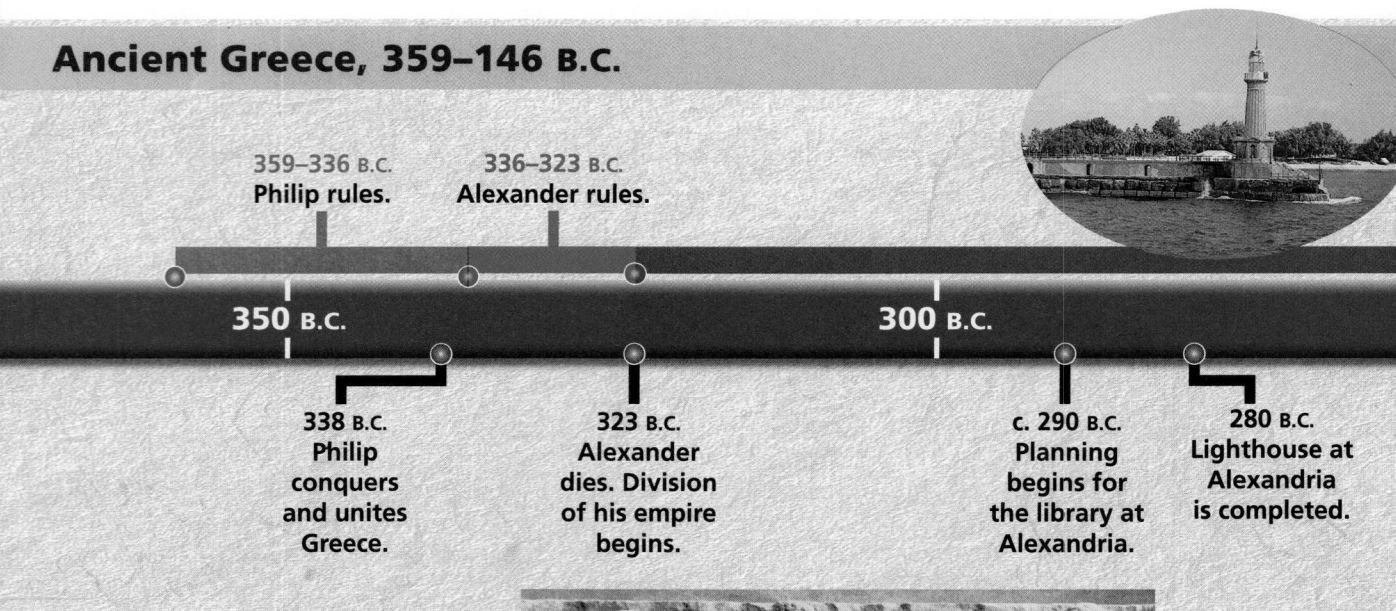

359–336 B.C.
Philip rules.

336–323 B.C.
Alexander rules.

350 B.C.

300 B.C.

338 B.C.
Philip conquers and unites Greece.

323 B.C.
Alexander dies. Division of his empire begins.

c. 290 B.C.
Planning begins for the library at Alexandria.

280 B.C.
Lighthouse at Alexandria is completed.

Greek Culture Spreads

Alexander's death spelled death for his empire. After 50 years of confusion and disorder, the empire was split into three kingdoms, with each kingdom ruled by one of Alexander's former commanders. One commander ruled Greece and Macedonia, which were combined into one kingdom. The other two commanders ruled the kingdoms of Egypt and Persia. For the next three hundred years, the descendants of these commanders fought over the lands that Alexander had conquered.

As Alexander had done before them, his successors created new cities throughout the new kingdoms. Many Greek soldiers remained in the new kingdoms after Alexander's death and settled in those cities. Soon thousands of Greek traders and artisans followed. These emigrants, or people who leave their country to settle in another, ensured that Greek culture would remain alive and well in these Hellenistic kingdoms, as they came to be called. The word **Hellenistic** describes Greek history and culture after the death of Alexander the Great. *Hellenistic* comes from the word *Hellas*—the name Greeks gave their land.

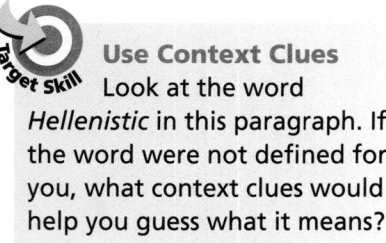

Use Context Clues Look at the word *Hellenistic* in this paragraph. If the word were not defined for you, what context clues would help you guess what it means?

200 B.C.

150 B.C.

212 B.C.
Archimedes
dies.

146 B.C.
Greece is
conquered
by Romans.

Timeline Skills

The Hellenistic Age began
with the death of Alexander.
Identify How long did the
Hellenistic Age last?
Predict Why do you think
historians mark the end of
the Hellenistic Age as
146 B.C.?

The Hellenistic Kingdoms When Alexander took control of lands, he tried not to destroy the cultures of the defeated people. Instead, he hoped that the local cultures would mix with Greek culture in his new cities. Unfortunately, this mixing did not happen in the three Hellenistic kingdoms.

The cities of the Hellenistic world were modeled after Greek cities. Greek kings ruled, and Greeks held the most important jobs. The cities were designed with Greek temples and agoras. Citizens gathered at large theaters for performances of Greek tragedies. The Greek language was spoken in the cities for hundreds of years, even though people in the countryside continued to speak their local languages.

Greek Culture in Egypt The greatest of all Hellenistic cities was Alexandria in Egypt. Alexander had founded this city in 332 B.C. at the edge of the Nile delta. Alexandria became the capital of Egypt. Over the years, it grew famous as a center for business and trade. Its double harbor was dominated by a huge lighthouse that rose about 350 feet (106 m) in the air. The tower was topped by a flame that guided ships safely into port.

The important Hellenistic cities were centers of learning, but Alexandria outdid them all. It boasted the largest library in the world, with half a million scrolls. It was the learning capital of the Greek world. Scholars and writers from all over came to use the huge library.

✓ Reading Check   Why was Alexandria in Egypt such an important city?

Math and Science

Mathematics and science also flourished in Alexandria. Around 300 B.C., a mathematician named Euclid (YOO klid) developed the branch of mathematics called geometry. He started with accepted mathematical laws. Then, he wrote step-by-step proofs of mathematical principles. The proofs helped explain the qualities of such figures as squares, cubes, angles, triangles, and cones. Mathematicians today still use Euclid's system.

Unlike the people who lived at the time of Columbus, many scientists in Hellenistic times knew that the Earth was round. A scientist named Eratosthenes (ehr uh TAHS thuh neez) even calculated the distance around the Earth. Eratosthenes used mathematics that were advanced for his time. His result was very close to the correct distance as it is known today.

Probably the greatest scientist of the times was Archimedes (ar kuh MEE deez). Archimedes studied in Alexandria. He discovered that people can use pulleys and levers to lift very heavy objects. One story says that he hoisted up a loaded ship with these devices. Once he boasted: "Give me a lever long enough and a place to stand on, and I will move the Earth."

✓ **Reading Check** **How did scientists of Hellenistic times differ from scientists of Columbus's time in their thinking about the Earth?**

Section 3 Assessment

Key Terms
Review the key terms listed at the beginning of this section. Use each term in a sentence that explains its meaning.

 ## Target Reading Skill
What goals did Alexander and his father King Philip have in common?

Comprehension and Critical Thinking
1. (a) Recall Who was Alexander's tutor when he was young?
(b) Identify Cause and Effect How did Alexander's upbringing affect his attitudes about Greek culture?

(c) Draw Conclusions Alexander the Great wanted the cultures of his defeated cities to survive and mix with Greek culture. What happened instead? Why?
2. (a) Describe What features of Greek culture were carried over to the Hellenistic kingdoms?
(b) Make Inferences Name one way that the domination of Greek culture in the Hellenistic countries might have been an advantage. Name one way that it might have been a disadvantage.
(c) Evaluate Describe the importance of the contributions made by Euclid, Eratosthenes, and Archimedes.

Writing Activity
What do you think of Alexander's education? Write a short paragraph that supports your opinion.

For: An activity on Greek culture
Visit: PHSchool.com
Web Code: mud-0730

Review and Assessment

◆ Chapter Summary

Women kneading dough

Section 1: Daily Life in Athens

- Greek men conducted business and social activities in the marketplace.
- Greek women stayed at home, tending to the running of the household.
- Slavery, especially of foreigners, was common in ancient Greece.

Section 2: Athens and Sparta

- Life in ancient Sparta was strictly ruled by the state in order to create a powerful army.
- Although outnumbered, the army of Athens fought back a force of invading Persians that threatened to take over all of Greece.
- Athens grew into an empire, but eventually it was destroyed by the forces of Sparta.

Spartans in battle

Section 3: The Spread of Greek Culture

- King Philip of Macedonia conquered all of Greece before he was killed in 336 B.C.
- Philip's son, Alexander the Great, conquered Persia, Judaea, Egypt, and lands extending beyond the Indus River in the East.
- After Alexander's death, Greek culture spread to the areas he had conquered.

Alexander the Great

◆ Key Terms

Each of the statements below contains a key term from the chapter. If the statement is true, write true. If it is false, rewrite the statement to make it true.

1. Athenian women lived in agoras, where they supervised spinning and other household activities.

2. The term Hellenistic refers to the period of Greek history after the death of Alexander the Great.

3. Helots were marketplaces where Greek men conducted business.

4. A plague is a disease that kills many people.

5. A barbarian is a person thought to be wild and savage by a group that considers itself to be more civilized.

6. Slavery is the owning of human beings.

7. If you were to assassinate someone, you would be worshiping that person as a god.

8. A vendor is someone who trains boys in the skill of military arts.

◆ Comprehension and Critical Thinking

9. **(a) Compare** Describe the roles of free men, free women, and slaves in Athenian life.
(b) Predict How would the daily lives of Athenians have been affected if slavery had not been common in Athens?

10. **(a) Describe** How did the Spartans become skilled warriors?
(b) Compare How did the Spartan emphasis on military training differ from Athenian ideas on how to train young men?
(c) Evaluate Information Do you think the basic differences in the way that Sparta and Athens trained their young men accounted for what eventually happened to the two city-states? Explain your answer.

11. **(a) Recall** What event caused the Greek city-states to put aside their differences?
(b) Analyze Information Why was the Athenian victory in the Battle at Marathon significant?
(c) Link Past and Present How has the Battle of Marathon been immortalized in the present time?

12. **(a) Identify Sequence** What events led to the Peloponnesian War?
(b) Draw Conclusions How did Athens lose its dominance over the rest of Greece?

13. **(a) Recall** Describe the empire of Alexander the Great before and after his death.
(b) Explain Why did the empire begin to fall apart after Alexander's death?
(c) Predict What might Alexander have done to make sure that his empire would hold together?

◆ Skills Practice

Analyzing Primary Source In the Skills for Life Activity, you learned how to analyze primary sources to determine whether they are reliable. Explain how you would decide whether an article about the Egyptian city of Alexandria under Hellenistic rule did or did not show bias.

◆ Writing Activity: Science

Choose one achievement in science or math that was made by the Greeks. Write at least two paragraphs about the difference that achievement has made in the modern world.

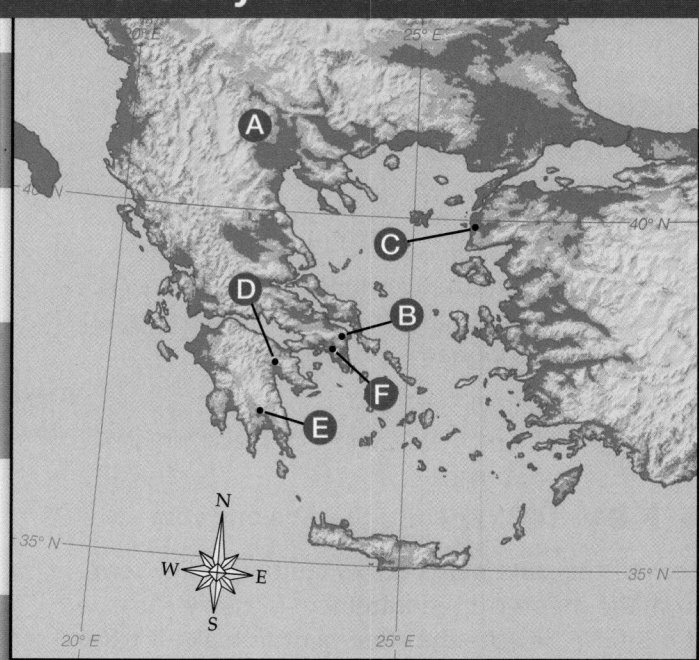

MAP MASTER™
Skills Activity
The Glory of Ancient Greece

Place Location For each place listed below, write the letter from the map that shows its location.
1. Athens
2. Sparta
3. Macedonia
4. Troy
5. Marathon
6. Mycenae

Go Online
PHSchool.com Use Web Code **mud-0702** for step-by-step **map skills practice.**

Standardized Test Prep

Test-Taking Tips

Some questions on standardized tests ask you to analyze an outline. Study the outline below. Then follow the tips to answer the sample question.

I Alexander's Conquests
  A Invaded Persia
  B Marched through Asia Minor
  C Invaded Egypt
  D Took territory across Indus River
II Alexander's Legacy
  A Invaded Persia
  B Created centers of learning
  C _____

TIP Use key words in the text to help you.

TIP Think about how the text is organized. Use that information to help you answer the question.

Choose the letter of the response that best answers the question.
Which of the following belongs in II-C?
  A Taught by Aristotle
  B Spread Greek culture throughout empire
  C Died in Babylon from a fever
  D Wanted to mix Greek culture and local cultures

Think It Through This outline is organized by major topics and subtopics. The question asks you to find a subtopic under Alexander's Legacy. Answers A and C introduce subtopics not covered in the outline. Answer D is something that Alexander wanted, but it did not happen. The correct answer is B.

Practice Questions

Use the tips above and other tips in this book to help you answer the following questions.

1. What was the role of women in ancient Greece?
   A Greek women sat on the councils that made all the decisions in Greece.
   B Greek women worked like slaves.
   C Greek women were protected and isolated in their homes.
   D Greek women went to war along with the men.

2. Most of the work in ancient Greece was performed by
   A slaves.
   B philosophers.
   C women.
   D boys.

3. For which of the following were Spartans well known?
   A art and architecture
   B war skills
   C philosophy
   D an open society

Study the partial outline below, and then answer the following question.

II The Aftermath of the Persian Wars
  A The Athenians feel favored by the gods.
  B _____
  C Athens' allies become more like subjects.

4. Which answer belongs in the space following letter B?
   A Sparta and its allies fight against Athens.
   B A plague kills one-third of the Athenians.
   C Athens becomes the most powerful city-state in Greece.
   D Sparta puts a blockade around the city.

Use Web Code **mua-0704** for **Chapter 7 self-test.**

Chapter 8

The Rise of Ancient Rome

Chapter Preview

This chapter will examine the rise of the Roman Republic and the Roman Empire.

Section 1
The Roman Republic

Section 2
The Roman Empire

Target Reading Skill

Word Analysis In this section you will learn how to recognize and pronounce unfamiliar words by recognizing word origins and by breaking down words into prefixes, suffixes, and roots.

▶ The ruins of Ephesus (EF ih sus), a Roman city in Asia Minor

The Roman Empire

MAP MASTER™ Skills Activity

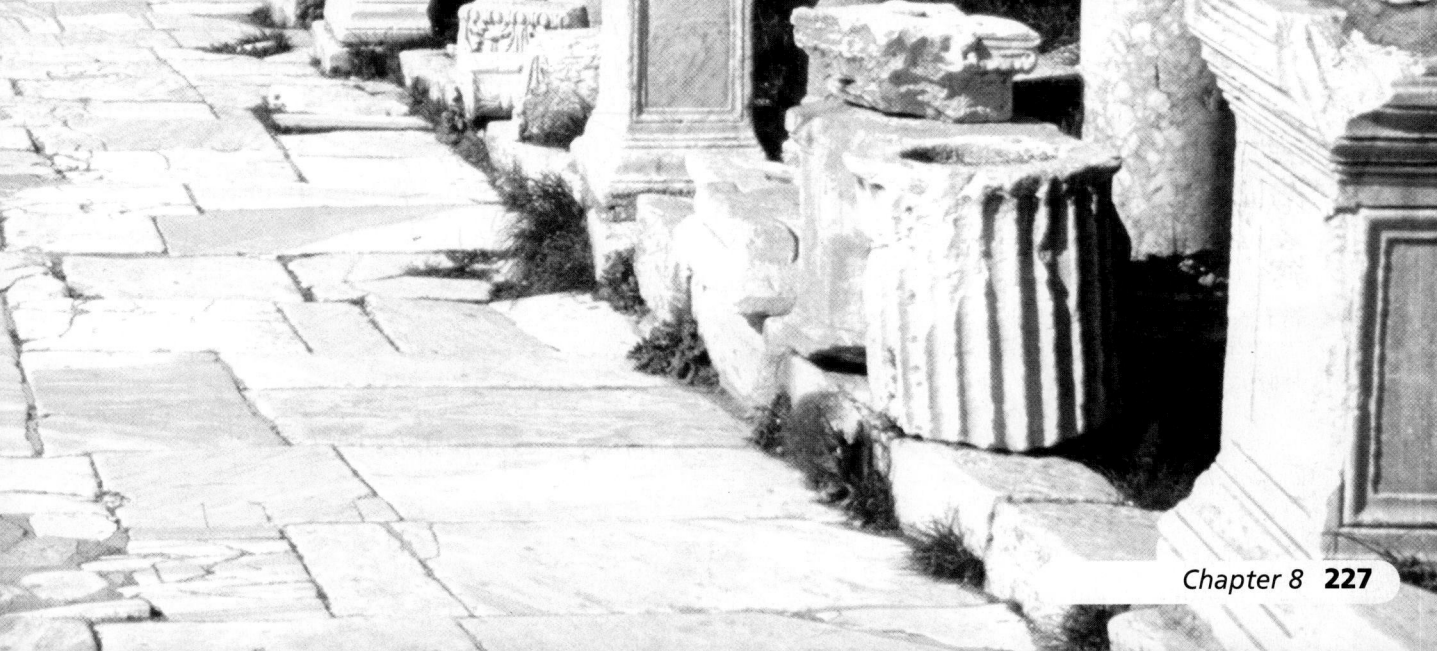

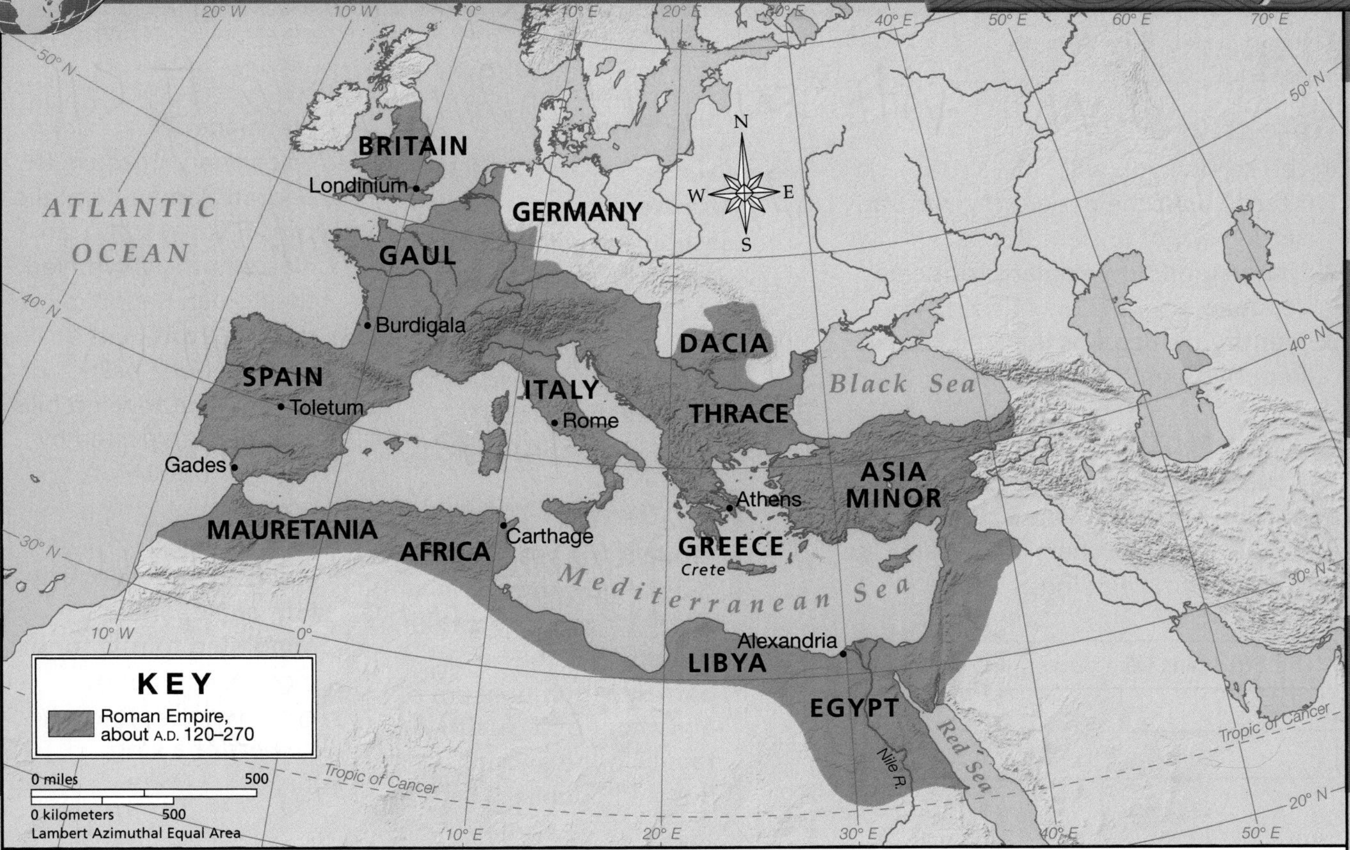
ATLANTIC OCEAN
BRITAIN
Londinium
GERMANY
GAUL
Burdigala
SPAIN
Toletum
Gades
MAURETANIA
AFRICA
Carthage
ITALY
Rome
DACIA
THRACE
Black Sea
ASIA MINOR
Athens
GREECE
Crete
Mediterranean Sea
Alexandria
LIBYA
EGYPT
Nile R.
Red Sea
N
S
E
W
KEY
Roman Empire, about A.D. 120–270
0 miles 500
0 kilometers 500
Lambert Azimuthal Equal Area
Tropic of Cancer
50° N
40° N
30° N
20° N
20° W
10° W
0°
10° E
20° E
30° E
40° E
50° E
60° E
70° E

Location Over a period of about 500 years Rome grew from a village fighting to protect its borders to a great city in control of the world around it. **Identify** How are the positions of Rome and Athens similar? How does the size of Italy compare to the other areas identified on the map? **Draw Conclusions** Athens dominated the world for a short time, but Roman rule lasted for centuries. What means of travel and transport did the Romans need in order to keep control of their empire?

Go Online PHSchool.com Use Web Code **mup-0801** for step-by-step **map skills practice.**

Prepare to Read

Objectives

In this section you will

1. Learn about the geography and early settlement of ancient Rome.
2. Understand how Romans formed a republic.
3. Identify the reasons that the Roman Republic went into decline.

Taking Notes

As you read the section, look for details about the rise and collapse of the Roman Republic. Copy the chart below, and use it to record your findings.

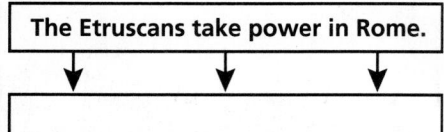

The Etruscans take power in Rome.

↓   ↓   ↓

Target Reading Skill

Use Word Parts In this section you will read the word *reorganized*. Break it into a prefix and root to try to learn its meaning. The prefix *re-* means "again." The root "organized" means "to put in order."

Key Terms

- **republic** (rih PUB lik) *n.* a type of government in which citizens select their leaders
- **patrician** (puh TRISH un) *n.* a member of a wealthy family in the ancient Roman Republic

- **plebeian** (plih BEE un) *n.* an ordinary citizen in the ancient Roman Republic
- **consul** (KAHN sul) *n.* an elected official who led the Roman Republic
- **veto** (VEE toh) *n.* the power of one branch of government to reject bills or proposals passed by another branch of government
- **dictator** (DIK tay tur) *n.* a person in the ancient Roman Republic appointed to rule for six months in times of emergency, with all the powers of a king

In ancient times, young Romans learned about the founding of their state. But it was a story that mixed a little fact with a great deal of legend. The main characters in the story were twin brothers, Romulus (RAHM yuh lus) and Remus (REE mus). They were the children of a princess and Mars, the Roman god of war. A jealous king feared that the twins would someday seize power from him. He ordered them to be drowned. But the gods protected the infants. A female wolf rescued them. Then a shepherd found the twins and raised them as his own. The twins grew up, killed the unjust king, and went off to build their own city. At a place where seven hills rise above the Tiber River, the twins founded the city of Rome.

The Tiber River in Rome

Rome's Geography and Early Settlement

We can learn much from the story of Rome's founding—even if the tale is mostly legend. We learn that the Romans valued loyalty and justice. People who broke the law were severely punished, just as Romulus and Remus punished the king. We also learn that the Romans highly valued the favor of the gods.

Geographical Advantages   The first settlers on Rome's seven hills were not thinking about building a great empire. They chose that site because it seemed to be a good place to live. The hills made the area easy to defend. The soil was fertile, and the site had a river. From the mountains of central Italy, the Tiber River flowed through Rome before emptying into the Tyrrhenian (tih REE nee un) Sea. As centuries passed, Romans discovered that the location of their city gave them other advantages. Rome was at the center of a long, narrow peninsula we now call Italy. Italy juts out into the Mediterranean Sea, and the Mediterranean Sea was at the center of the known Western world.

The Dolomite Mountains are part of the Italian Alps. This mountain range stood as a great divide between Italy and the rest of Europe.

The Etruscans We know very little about the people who actually founded Rome. We do know, however, that their first settlements date from about 900 B.C. Rome grew slowly as the Romans fought their neighbors for land.

About 600 B.C., a people called the Etruscans (ih TRUS kunz) held power in Rome. From the many examples of their writing that have been found, we know that the Etruscans spoke a language unlike most other ancient Italian languages. For example, it was unrelated to Latin, the language of the Romans.

For a time, Etruscans ruled as kings of Rome, but many Romans did not like being ruled by an all-powerful king and having no say in how they were governed. Some ancient Roman historians claimed that in 509 B.C. the Romans revolted against the harsh reign of Tarquinius Superbus (tahr KWIN ee us soo PUR bus) and drove the Etruscans from power. Many modern historians doubt the truth of this story and are not sure exactly how and when the rule of the Etruscan kings ended and the Roman Republic began.

Although the Romans defeated the Etruscans, the victors adopted Etruscan ideas. For example, many of the Roman gods were originally Etruscan gods. The Romans also borrowed the Greek alphabet that the Etruscans used. The Roman garment called the toga came from the Etruscans as well.

✓ **Reading Check** **What is known about the Etruscans?**

Etruscan Art
This Etruscan sarcophagus dates from about 510 B.C. Like many ancient peoples, the Etruscans used sarcophagi as coffins. This one was made for a married couple.
Analyze Images *How can you tell that this sarcophagus was found in pieces and then reassembled?*

KEY

- Greeks
- Etruscans
- Carthaginians
- City

0 miles 200
0 kilometers 200
Lambert Conformal Conic

ALPS

Italy

Tiber River

APENNINES

Adriatic Sea

Corsica

Rome

Sardinia

Tyrrhenian Sea

Sicily

Africa

Carthage

N
W E
S

Movement In its origins Rome was only one of many cities and villages inhabited by a tribe called the Latins. Other more powerful peoples controlled much of the Italian peninsula.

Identify Use the key to locate the three civilizations that were established nearby as Rome began to expand.

Infer Study the locations of Greeks and Carthaginians in Italy. Why do you think these settlers from other places chose these locations?

Go Online
PHSchool.com Use Web Code **mup-0812** for step-by-step map skills practice.

Romans Form a Republic

After removing the last Etruscan king, the Romans vowed never again to put so much trust in kings. They wanted a government that did not rely on one ruler. Over the next several centuries, Rome expanded its territory and found ways to govern that better represented the will of its citizens.

By 264 B.C., the Romans had gained control of the entire Italian peninsula (the area that makes up present-day Italy) and had firmly established a new form of government—a republic. In a **republic,** citizens who have the right to vote select their leaders. The leaders rule in the name of the people.

The Roman Senate In the Roman Republic, the most powerful part of the government was the senate. The Roman senate was the basis for our own legislative branch of government—the branch that proposes and votes on new laws. At first, the senate was made up only of 300 upper-class men called patricians. A **patrician** was a member of a wealthy family in the Roman Republic. Ordinary citizens were known as **plebeians.** In the early republic, plebeians could not hold office or be senators.

Daily life activities were often the subjects of Roman art.

The Roman Consuls Two chief officials called **consuls** led the government. The consuls, like our U.S. President, were the chief executives of the government. They were responsible for enforcing the Republic's laws and policies. The consuls were elected by the assembly of citizens. Before 367 B.C., plebeians could not be consuls. The senate advised the consuls on foreign affairs, laws, and finances, among other things.

Consuls ruled for one year only. They almost always did what the senate wanted them to do. Power was divided equally between the consuls. Both had to agree before the government could take any action. If only one consul said, "Veto" ("I forbid"), the matter was dropped. A **veto** is the rejection of any planned action by a person in power. Today, we use "veto" to mean the rejection of a proposed law by the President of the United States.

Other Important Officials The Romans knew that their government might not work if the two consuls disagreed. For this reason, Roman law held that a dictator could be appointed to handle an emergency. In the Roman Republic, a **dictator** was a Roman official who had all the powers of a king but could hold office for only six months.

Praetors (PREE turz) were other important officials. At first they functioned as junior consuls, but later, they served as judges in civil-law trials—trials that settled disputes about money, business matters, contracts, and so on. Thus, the *praetors* helped to develop some of the first rules for Roman courts of law.

■ **Timeline Skills**

The Roman Republic lasted for almost 500 years. **Identify** By what year did Rome control the Italian peninsula? **Analyze** About how long did the republic's main period of conquests around the Mediterranean Sea last? What event occured near the end of that period?

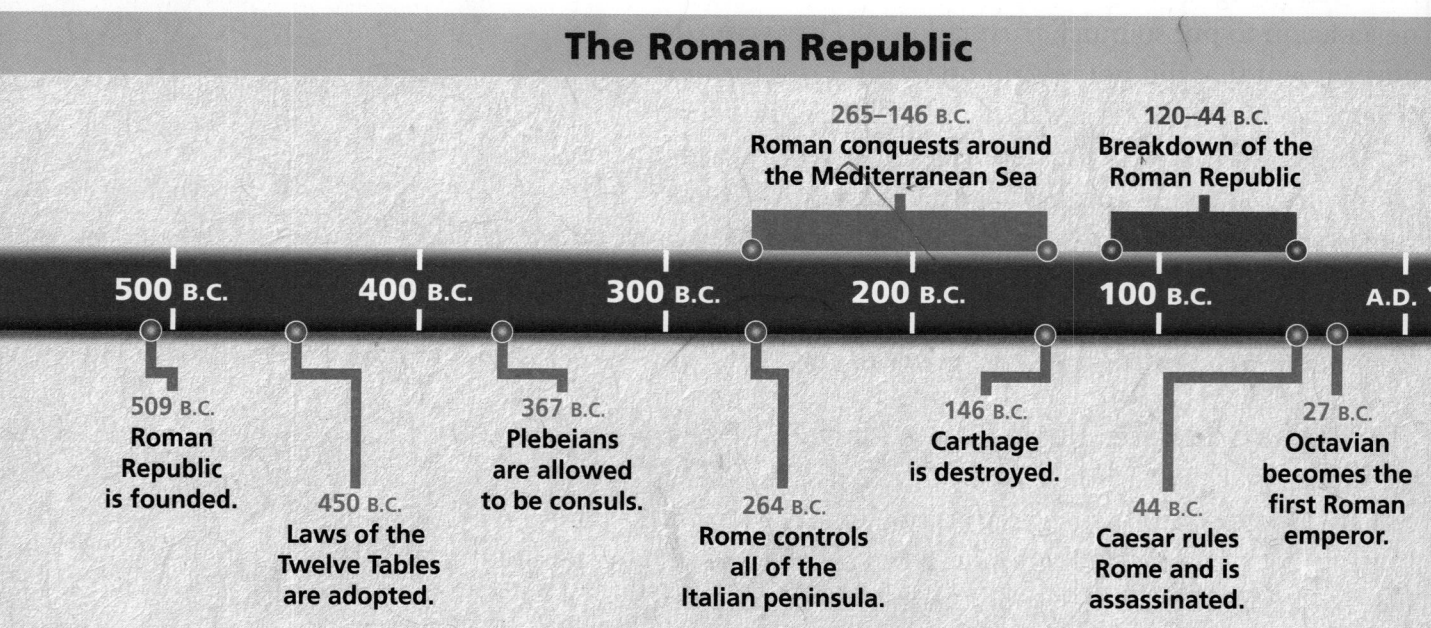

The Roman Republic

265–146 B.C.
Roman conquests around the Mediterranean Sea

120–44 B.C.
Breakdown of the Roman Republic

500 B.C.   **400** B.C.   **300** B.C.   **200** B.C.   **100** B.C.   A.D.

509 B.C.
Roman Republic is founded.

450 B.C.
Laws of the Twelve Tables are adopted.

367 B.C.
Plebeians are allowed to be consuls.

264 B.C.
Rome controls all of the Italian peninsula.

146 B.C.
Carthage is destroyed.

44 B.C.
Caesar rules Rome and is assassinated.

27 B.C.
Octavian becomes the first Roman emperor.

Patricians Versus Plebeians The expansion of Rome's influence throughout Italy caused growing troubles between patricians and plebeians. Patricians and plebeians had different attitudes and interests. Patricians thought of themselves as leaders. They fought hard to keep control of the government. Plebeians believed that they had a right to be respected and treated fairly. Plebeians did not trust the actions of the patrician senate. They believed that the senate was often unfair to the plebeians. Therefore, plebeians formed their own groups to protect their interests.

Many patricians grew wealthy because of Rome's conquests. They took riches from those they had defeated in war. Then they bought land from small farmers and created huge farms for themselves. Plebeians did not work on these farms. Rather, the work was done by slaves brought back from conquests. Many plebeian farmers found themselves without work. The cities, especially Rome, were filled with jobless plebeians.

Eventually, angry plebeians refused to fight in the Roman army. It was then that the patricians gave in to one of the main demands of the plebeians. This demand was for a written code of laws which was called the Laws of the Twelve Tables. The Twelve Tables applied equally to all citizens. They were hung in marketplaces so that everyone could know what the laws were. Despite this victory, the plebeians never managed to gain power equal to that of the patricians.

Master of the Mediterranean While patricians and plebeians fought for power in Rome, Roman armies were conquering new territories. Roman armies invaded territories controlled by Carthage, a North African city in what is now the country of Tunisia. The Romans drove the Carthaginians from the coast of Spain. By 146 B.C., after a series of bloody wars, the Romans had completely destroyed Carthage. Other Roman armies conquered Greece in that same year. Then the Romans gradually took control of the rest of Spain and the land of Gaul, most of which is present-day France.

The Sack of Carthage
The artist Tiepolo portrayed the final destruction of Carthage by the Romans in his painting. At the final surrender, the city that once had a population of more than a quarter million people was left with only 50,000 survivors.
Analyze Images *What other titles might be appropriate for Tiepolo's depiction of the war with Carthage?*

✓ Reading Check **What complaints did the plebeians have against the patricians?**

Julius Caesar was a powerful dictator of the Roman Republic. Later Roman leaders adopted his name as a title. In time, *Caesar* came to mean "emperor."

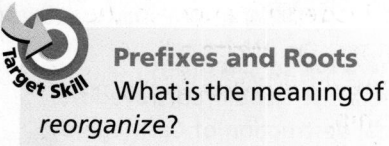

Target Skill

Prefixes and Roots
What is the meaning of *reorganize*?

The Decline of the Republic

Even though it ruled a large area, Rome was in trouble by 120 B.C. Some leaders tried to break up estates and give land to the plebeians. The patricians fought back, and plebeian leaders were murdered.

Over the next seventy-five years, a number of the most successful Roman generals gathered private armies around them and fought for power. Consuls no longer respected each other's veto power. Rome dissolved into civil war, with private armies roaming the streets and murdering enemies. As Rome seemed about to break up, Julius Caesar (JOOL yus SEE zur) arose as a strong leader.

The Rise of Julius Caesar Caesar was a smart leader, eager for power. From 58 to 51 B.C., he led the army that conquered Gaul. Caesar's conquest brought millions of people and a vast new territory under Roman control. His strong leadership won him the loyalty of his troops. They would follow him anywhere—even back to Rome to seize power.

In 49 B.C., Caesar violated the terms of his military assignment when he crossed the Rubicon River into Italy. War broke out between Caesar and Pompey, backed by the senate and the nobility. Caesar became dictator of the Roman world in 48 B.C. Recall that under Roman law, a dictator could rule for only six months. Caesar's rule, however, lasted far longer than that. Although some elements of the republic remained, Caesar ruled with great power, taking much of the power that had once belonged to the senate.

The Death of a Dictator For four years, the civil war continued, and Caesar fought a series of battles against his opponents in different parts of the Roman world. Meanwhile, Caesar took over important public offices. In 45 B.C., he became the only consul. In 44 B.C., he became dictator for life. Caesar took many useful steps to reorganize the government. But it seemed to many senators that Rome once again had a king. They hated this idea.

On March 15, 44 B.C., Caesar had plans to attend a meeting of the senate. His wife sensed danger and urged him not to go, but Caesar insisted. At the meeting, a group of senators gathered around Caesar. Suddenly, they pulled out knives and stabbed him. He fell to the ground, dead. Caesar had been a strong leader. However, many Romans felt that he had gone too far and too fast in gathering power.

From Republic to Empire Civil war followed Caesar's death. When the war ended after thirteen years, Caesar's adopted son, Octavian (ahk TAY vee un), held power. In 27 B.C., the senate awarded Octavian the title of Augustus (aw GUS tus), which means "highly respected." He was the first emperor of Rome. The rule of Augustus marked the beginning of the Roman Empire and the end of the Roman Republic.

The Roman Republic had lasted nearly 500 years. The government worked well for much of that time. As a republic, Rome grew from a city-state to a holder of vast territories. It developed the largest elected government the world had seen up to that time. But civil war and the ambition of powerful political figures ate away at Rome's republican forms of rule. For the next 500 years, the great Roman civilization would be ruled, not by the people, but by an all-powerful emperor.

In the next section, you will read about how the Roman emperors ruled their vast empires and about some of the innovations in technology and law that developed during the Roman Empire.

In addition to receiving the title **Augustus**, Octavian was later honored as *Pater Patriae*, or father of his country.

✔ **Reading Check** **What did Julius Caesar do to become dictator of Rome?**

Section 1 Assessment

Key Terms
Review the key terms listed at the beginning of this section. Use each term in a sentence that explains the term's meaning.

Target Reading Skill
Apply your knowledge of the prefix *re-*. What does re-create mean?

Comprehension and Critical Thinking
1. (a) Recall Describe the geography and early settlement of Rome.

(b) Explain Why did the Romans overthrow the Etruscans?
2. (a) List What were the important features of the Roman Republic?
(b) Analyze Why did the Romans want the republic to have two consuls rather than one?
3. (a) Identify Describe the features of the rule of Julius Caesar.
(b) Draw Conclusions Why would the Roman senate be likely to lead the opposition to Caesar's growing power?

Writing Activity
Julius Caesar was a strong leader, but his leadership angered the Roman senate. Write a list of pros and cons about Julius Caesar's leadership.

For: An activity on the geography of Rome
Visit: PHSchool.com
Web Code: mud-0810

Focus On
The Roman Senate

The Roman Senate was the most powerful governing body in the Roman Republic. It began as a group of advisors to the king. When the king was exiled in 510 B.C., the Senate took control of the government. At that time, it was decided that there would be two consuls who would rule with advice from the Senate. Consuls had power for one year and then became senators. Senators usually served for life. The Senate advised on home and foreign policy, laws, and questions of money and religion. It dealt with foreign powers and settled disputes among the Roman provinces.

A Senate Debate During most of the Roman Republic, the Senate had 300 members. Not all senators had to be present in order for a debate to take place. Only a quorum—a percentage of the whole group—had to be in attendance.

A senator had to be a good orator, or highly skilled at public speaking. Orators were known for their precise choice of words, their expert use of description, and their powers of persuasion. Famous orators like Cicero (106–43 B.C.) were sometimes able to sway the opinion of the entire city of Rome with their arguments.

In the illustration, Cicero is addressing the Senate. He and his fellow senators wore togas, which were the most dignified type of Roman dress. Senators' togas had a broad purple stripe. Like other Roman men, senators were typically clean-shaven and wore their hair short.

Cicero
In the scene below, Cicero is shown making a speech shortly after becoming consul. His forceful speaking skills helped him win office.

A Senator's Toga
Roman senators wore togas edged with a broad purple stripe, as shown in the present-day photo.

Assessment

Explain What was the role of the Roman Senate?

Infer The United States also has a Senate. Why might the Founding Fathers have chosen this name for the American governing body?

Skills for Life
Synthesizing Information

During his trip to Rome with his family, William was most impressed by the ancient ruins in the center of the city. It was here that government business of the Roman Republic had been conducted. The tour guide pointed out that many of America's present-day methods of government are borrowed from the ancient Roman Republic: an elected chief executive, a senate, and a court system based on laws designed to protect all citizens.

William told his parents, "When we return from vacation, I would like to make a report to my class on the government of the Roman Republic. What should my first step be?"

William's mother replied, "You will have to synthesize all the information you learned while in Rome."

William gulped, "Synthesize information? How do I do that?"

When you are asked to synthesize information, you should find the main ideas and weave them into a conclusion. Synthesizing information is a skill that can help you in all of your subjects in school.

Learn the Skill

When you synthesize information, you summarize. Use the following steps to synthesize:

1. **Identify the main idea of each piece of information.** Main ideas are broad, major ideas that are supported by details.

2. **Identify details that support your main ideas.** You may want to make notes or create a chart. The details will give information about your main ideas.

3. **Look for connections between pieces of information.** These connections may be similarities, differences, causes, effects, or examples.

4. **Draw conclusions based on the connections you found.** Do not think about details at this point, but of the main ideas and the general, overall statements you can make to tie these together.

Government of the Roman Republic	
Main Ideas	**Supporting Details**
1. Executive official	• Consul
	• dictator
2. Senate	

Practice the Skill

Use the steps above to synthesize information about the government of the Roman Republic. Rely mainly on Section 1 of this chapter, especially the material under the heading Romans Form a Republic.

1 Study the information about the government of the Roman Republic, and add one or two main ideas in the first column of the chart. Two are already supplied.

2 Now write details that support each main idea. Do this for other main ideas that you have identified.

3 Do the main ideas show contrasts or similarities among the branches of the government of the Roman Republic? Jot down any connections.

4 Your main ideas should help you write a one- or two-sentence conclusion that answers questions such as "What kind of government did ancient Rome have before the first emperor took over?"

Apply the Skill

Use the steps on this page to synthesize information about the government of the Roman Empire in a brief, well-organized paragraph. Refer to the main text of Section 2 of this chapter, but you may also use maps, photographs, captions, and other sources. Do not summarize everything you read about the Roman Empire. Concentrate on the form of government.

The Roman Empire

Prepare to Read

Objectives

In this section you will
1. Learn how Rome ruled an empire.
2. Understand the Greek influence on Rome.
3. Identify key aspects of Roman architecture and technology.
4. Learn about key aspects of Roman law.

Taking Notes

As you read, find main ideas and details about the Roman Empire. Copy the outline below, and use it to record your findings. Expand the outline as needed.

> I. Governing the empire
>   A. Boundaries and territory
>   1.
>   2.
>   B. Augustus

Target Reading Skill

Recognize Word Origins You can decode an unfamiliar word by knowing the word's origin. For instance, you might not know the key term aqueduct, but you can uncover the meaning if you know that it comes from the Latin words *aqua* (water) + *ductus* (act of leading).

Key Terms

- **province** (PRAH vins) *n.* a unit of an empire
- **Colosseum** (kahl uh SEE um) a large amphitheater built in Rome around A.D. 70; site of contests and combats
- **aqueduct** (AK wuh dukt) *n.* a structure that carries water over long distances
- **polytheism** (PAHL ih thee iz um) *n.* a belief in more than one god
- **arch** (ahrch) *n.* a curved structure used as a support over an open space, as in a doorway

Located on the grounds of the Colosseum, the arches were built in honor of Constantine's victory over Maxentius. The arches are inscribed with the saying, "Constantine overcame his enemies by divine inspiration."

In his epic poem the *Aeneid* (ee NEE id), Virgil challenges Romans to play to their strengths. The following passage expresses his beliefs and hopes for Rome:

> **❝Others . . . will do better**
> **At making breathing figures out of metal**
> **Or giving lumps of marble living faces;**
> **They will be better orators, better astronomers;**
> **But you, Roman, remember, you are to rule**
> **The nations of the world: your arts will be**
> **To bring the ways of peace, be merciful**
> **To the defeated and smash the proud completely.❞**
>
> —from the *Aeneid*

Virgil says that other cultures may produce beautiful art or fine philosophers and astronomers. But Romans are most fit to govern, he says, and will do so wisely and fairly. Virgil was not alone in his hopes for just rule under Augustus, the first Roman emperor.

Ruling an Empire

When Augustus came to power, Roman control had already spread far beyond Italy. Under Augustus and the emperors who followed him, Rome gained even more territory. Look at the map titled The Roman Empire at the beginning of this chapter. The Roman Empire stretched from Britain to Egypt. Rome controlled all the lands around the Mediterranean. With pride, Romans called the Mediterranean *mare nostrum* (MAH ray NAWS trum), or "our sea."

The Power of Augustus Augustus was an intelligent ruler. When he was struggling for power, he often ignored the senate and its laws. But after he won control, he changed his manner. He showed great respect for the senate and was careful to avoid acting like a king. He did not want to suffer the same fate as Julius Caesar. Augustus often said that he wanted to share power with the senate. He even said that he wanted to restore the republic.

What really happened was quite different. Romans were so grateful for Rome's peace and prosperity that they gave Augustus as much power as he wanted.

Governing Conquered Peoples The Romans took some slaves after a conquest, but most of the conquered people remained free. To govern, the Romans divided their empire into provinces. Each **province,** or area of the empire, had a Roman governor supported by an army. Often, the Romans built a city in a new province to serve as its capital.

Wisely, the Romans did not usually force their way of life on conquered peoples. They allowed these people to follow their own religions. Local rulers ran the daily affairs of government. As long as there was peace, Roman governors did not interfere in conquered peoples' lives. Rather, they kept watch over them. Rome wanted peaceful provinces that would supply the empire with the raw materials it needed. Rome also wanted the conquered people to buy Roman goods and to pay taxes. Many of the conquered people adopted Roman ways. Many learned to speak Latin, the language of the Romans, and worshiped Roman gods.

Augustus, First Emperor of Rome
With the rule of Augustus, a period of stability and prosperity known as the Pax Romana, or "Roman peace," began. **Generalize** *Use what you have read in the text to describe the kind of ruler Augustus was.*

Marcus Aurelius was the last of the five "good emperors." In this stone sculpture, he pardons the barbarians whose attacks weakened the Roman Empire.

The Five "Good Emperors" Augustus died in A.D. 14. For eighty-two years after his death, Roman history was a story of good, bad, and terrible emperors. Two of the worst were Caligula (kuh LIG yuh luh) and Nero. Both may have been insane. Caligula proclaimed himself a god and was a cruel, unfair ruler. Nero murdered his half-brother, his mother, and his wife. In fact, Caligula and Nero were so despised that Romans later tried to forget them by removing mention of their reigns from official records.

In A.D. 96, Rome entered what is called the age of the five "good emperors." Only the last of these emperors had a son. Each of the others adopted the best young man he could find to be the next emperor.

Perhaps the greatest of the five "good emperors" was Hadrian (HAY dree un). He worked hard to build a good government. His laws protected women, children, and slaves. He issued a code of laws so that all laws were the same throughout the empire. Hadrian reorganized the army so that soldiers were allowed to defend their home provinces. This gave them a greater sense of responsibility. Hadrian traveled throughout his empire, commissioning many buildings and other structures. He even traveled to the British Isles, where he commissioned a great wall to be built, parts of which still stand today. Hadrian also encouraged learning.

The last of the "good emperors," Marcus Aurelius (MAHR kus aw REE lee uhs), chose his son Commodus (KAHM uh dus) to follow him. Commodus was a terrible leader who ruled with great brutality. His reign ended the age of peace and prosperity that Rome had enjoyed under its five previous emperors.

The Empire in Decline During the reign of Commodus, things started going badly for the Roman Empire. In Chapter 9, you will learn how bad government, economic problems, and foreign invaders all helped contribute to the fall of the Roman Empire.

✓ Reading Check **Why was Hadrian considered one of the five "good emperors"?**

The Greek Influence on Rome

The Romans had long admired Greek achievements. People said that Hadrian spoke Greek better than he spoke Latin. Marcus Aurelius wrote a famous book of philosophy in Greek. Many Romans visited Greece to study Greek art, architecture, and ideas about government.

Religion Greek religion influenced Roman religion. Like the Greeks, Romans practiced **polytheism**—the belief in more than one god—and offered prayers and sacrifices to their gods. Many Roman gods and goddesses had Greek counterparts. For example, the Roman god of the sky, Jupiter, shared characteristics with the Greek god Zeus. The Roman goddess of arts and trades, Minerva, is similar to the Greeks' Athena. The Romans also adopted heroes from Greek mythology, such as Heracles—known as Hercules to the Romans. As their empire spread, Romans appealed to and adopted other foreign gods as well.

Building on Ideas Both the Greeks and the Romans valued learning, but in different ways. The Greeks were interested in ideas. They sought to learn truths about the world through reason. They developed studies such as mathematics, philosophy, and astronomy, or the study of the stars and planets. The Romans benefited from the study of these subjects, but they were more interested in using these studies to build and organize their world. Under the Romans, architecture and engineering blossomed. With these skills, the Romans built their empire.

✓ **Reading Check** In what ways did the Greeks and Romans value learning?

Word Origins The word *polytheism* comes from the Greek words *poly* and *theos*. If theos means "god," what does *poly* mean?

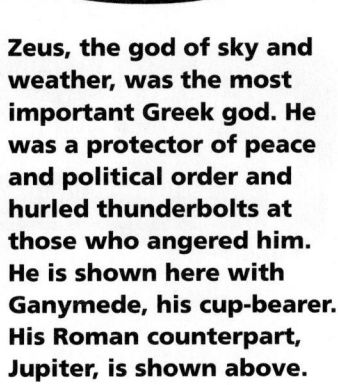

GIOVE SERAPIDE

Zeus, the god of sky and weather, was the most important Greek god. He was a protector of peace and political order and hurled thunderbolts at those who angered him. He is shown here with Ganymede, his cup-bearer. His Roman counterpart, Jupiter, is shown above.

Architecture and Technology

Early Roman art and architecture copied the Etruscan style. Then, the Romans studied and copied Greek sculpture and architecture. Later, they developed their own art and architecture styles.

The Roman Style Roman statues and buildings were heavier and stronger in style than those of the Greeks. The Romans made advances in the use of the **arch**—a curved structure used as a support over an open space, as in a doorway. Romans used arches to build larger structures. They used wide arched ceilings to create large open spaces inside buildings.

In earlier times, most large buildings had been built of bricks and then covered with thin slabs of marble. However, Romans developed an important new building material—concrete. Concrete was a mix of stone, sand, cement, and water that dried as hard as rock. Concrete helped the Romans construct buildings that were taller than any previously built.

The Colosseum Possibly the greatest Roman building was the **Colosseum,** the site of contests and combats between people and between people and animals. This giant arena held 50,000 spectators. Its walls were so well built that the floor of the arena could be flooded for mock naval battles in real boats. Stairways and ramps ran through the building. There were even elevators to carry wild animals from dens below up to the arena.

Roads and Aqueducts Roman engineers built roads from Rome to every part of the empire. Do you know the saying "All roads lead to Rome"? In Roman times all of the major roads did lead to Rome, so no matter what road travelers started out on, they could get to Rome. These roads allowed the Roman military to maintain firm control by traveling quickly to all parts of the empire. These roads also helped trade to spread throughout the empire and made the empire more prosperous.

Romans were famous for their **aqueducts,** structures that carried water over long distances. The aqueducts were huge lines of arches, often many miles long. A channel along the top carried water from the countryside to the cities. Roman aqueducts tunneled through mountains and spanned valleys. Some are still being used today. To learn more, see the Eyewitness Technology feature titled The Roman Aqueduct.

✓ **Reading Check** What are some characteristics of Roman buildings?

The Roman Aqueduct

The Romans built aqueducts to bring fresh water to the city. Sources of water had to be at elevations higher than the city, as pumping was not a practical way of moving water. Engineers tunneled through mountains and bridged valleys to create a gradual, even slope. Follow the numbers to see how the water flowed from the mountains to the city.

Roman Arches
Water traveled through hollow passages in the stonework, which was supported by arches.

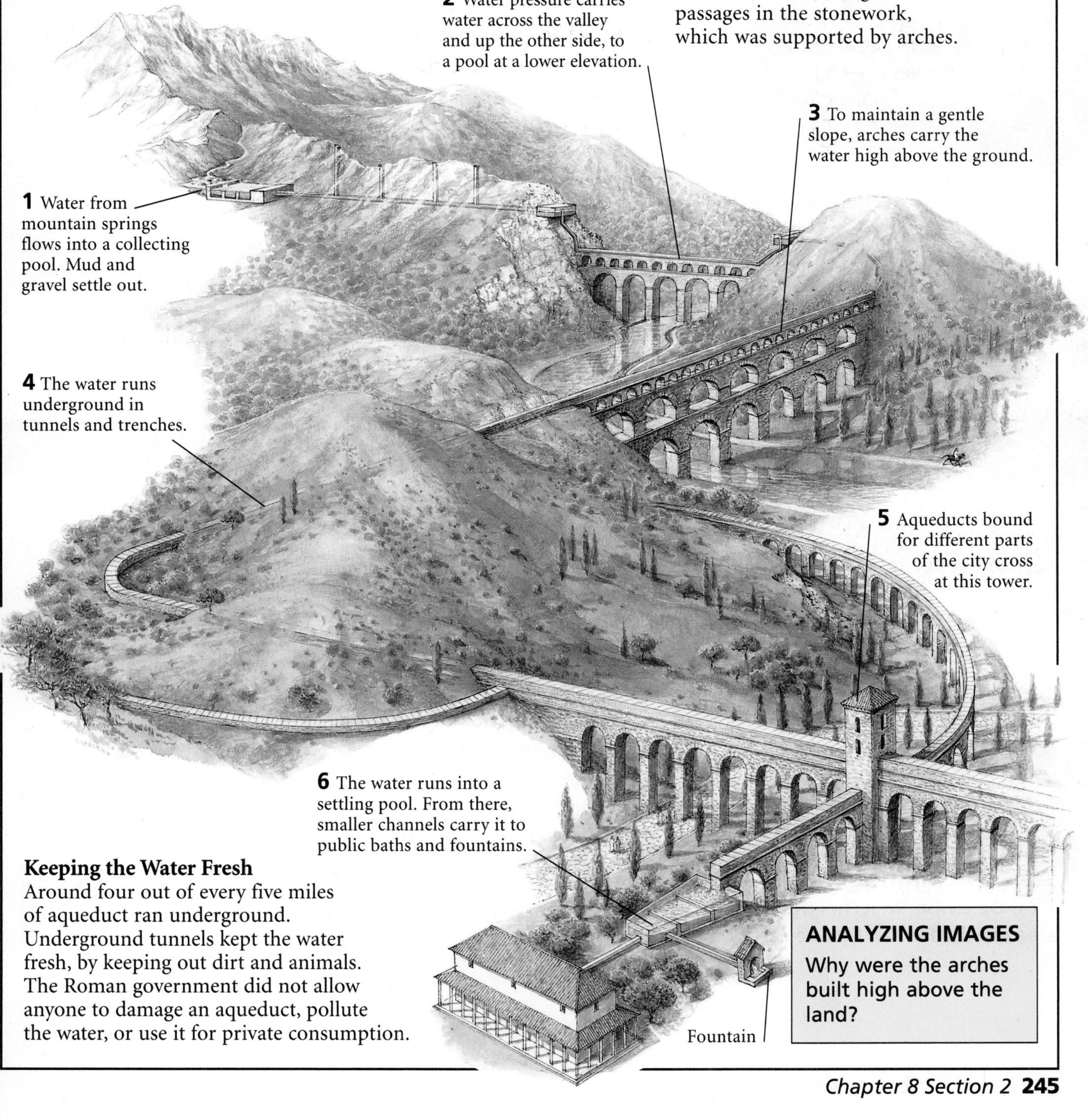

2 Water pressure carries water across the valley and up the other side, to a pool at a lower elevation.

3 To maintain a gentle slope, arches carry the water high above the ground.

1 Water from mountain springs flows into a collecting pool. Mud and gravel settle out.

4 The water runs underground in tunnels and trenches.

5 Aqueducts bound for different parts of the city cross at this tower.

6 The water runs into a settling pool. From there, smaller channels carry it to public baths and fountains.

Keeping the Water Fresh
Around four out of every five miles of aqueduct ran underground. Underground tunnels kept the water fresh, by keeping out dirt and animals. The Roman government did not allow anyone to damage an aqueduct, pollute the water, or use it for private consumption.

Fountain

ANALYZING IMAGES
Why were the arches built high above the land?

Roman Law

Like Roman roads, Roman law spread throughout the empire. The great Roman senator Cicero (SIS uh roh) expressed Roman feeling about law when he said, "What sort of thing is the law? It is the kind that cannot be bent by influence, or broken by power, or spoiled by money."

A later ruler named Justinian (juh STIN ee un) created a code of justice from Roman law. That code includes these laws:

Knowledge of the laws and legal procedures of Rome was helpful in pursuing a government career. Many Roman officials, such as the Senators depicted in this sculpture, argued cases in court and served as judges.

> **No one suffers a penalty for what he thinks. No one may be forcibly removed from his own house. The burden of proof is upon the person who accuses. In inflicting penalties, the age and inexperience of the guilty party must be taken into account.**
>
> —*Code of Justinian*

Roman law was passed on to other cultures, including our own. In fact, Roman ideas of justice are basic to our system of laws. For example, under Roman law, persons accused of crimes had the right to face their accusers. If reasonable doubt existed about a person's guilt, that person would be considered innocent.

✓ **Reading Check** Recall two features of Justinian's code, and explain their meaning.

Section 2 Assessment

Key Terms
Review the key terms listed at the beginning of this section. Use each term in a sentence that explains the terms meaning.

Target Reading Skill

If the Latin word *colosseus* means "colossal" or "very large," what might you guess about the Colosseum?

Comprehension and Critical Thinking
1. (a) Describe At its height, what area did the Roman Empire cover?

(b) Explain How did Rome handle the difficulties of governing its large empire?

2. (a) List What did the Romans learn from the Greeks?

(b) Explore the Main Idea How did the Roman's technological achievements help them strengthen their empire?

3. (a) Name What was the Justinian code of law?

(b) Draw Conclusions What did Cicero mean when he said that the law "cannot be bent by influence, or broken by power, or spoiled by money"?

Writing Activity
Write down a few ideas for guidelines that you would give to every new governor of a Roman province. For example, how should the governor treat the people of the province?

For: An activity on the Roman Empire
Visit: PHSchool.com
Web Code: mud-0820

Review and Assessment

◆ Chapter Summary

Section 1: The Roman Republic
- Rome's geographic setting helped the city grow into an important civilization.
- Rome's early ruling people, the Etruscans, were overthrown by the Romans who established a Republic.
- Julius Caesar took over the weakened republic and became Rome's dictator.
- After Caesar's murder and a long civil war, Augustus emerged as the first emperor of Rome.

Section 2: The Roman Empire
- The expanding Roman Empire was a challenge for Augustus and other emperors who ruled it.
- The Greeks influenced Roman learning and religion.
- The Romans were masters at creating large public buildings and road networks.
- Roman law spread throughout the empire and continues to influence civilizations today.

Sarcophagus of the Spouses

The Arch of Constantine

◆ Key Terms

Choose the correct word(s) for each of the definitions below.

1. an ordinary citizen in the ancient Roman Republic
   - **A** patrician
   - **B** dictator
   - **C** plebeian
   - **D** consul

2. an arena in ancient Rome
   - **A** villa
   - **B** Colosseum
   - **C** aqueduct
   - **D** province

3. an elected official who led the ancient Roman Republic
   - **A** consul
   - **B** dictator
   - **C** plebeian
   - **D** patrician

4. a unit of an empire
   - **A** emperor
   - **B** province
   - **C** plebeian
   - **D** citizen

5. a structure that carries water over a long distances
   - **A** arch
   - **B** dictator
   - **C** patrician
   - **D** aqueduct

Review and Assessment (continued)

◆ Comprehension and Critical Thinking

6. **(a) Recall** How were the Etruscans governed?
   (b) Explain How was the Roman republican form of government different from Etruscan rule?

7. **(a) Identify** What power allowed the consul to reject any proposed government policy?
   (b) Draw Inferences During the Republic, what problem in the two-consul setup was addressed by appointing a dictator?

8. **(a) Contrast** What were the main differences between the patricians and the plebeians?
   (b) Identify Effects What measure was taken to address the complaints of the plebeians?

9. **(a) Identify Causes** What led to the decline of the Roman Republic?
   (b) Identify Effects How did the decline of the Roman Republic affect the governing of Rome?

10. **(a) Recall** How did Augustus come to power?
    (b) Compare and Contrast Why did the Roman Senate strike down Caesar, but hand more power to Augustus?

11. **(a) Identify** What was the Colosseum?
    (b) Explain What does the saying "all roads lead to Rome" mean?

12. **(a) Identify** What contributions did Romans make to law? To technology?
    (b) Generalize What was the importance of these contributions?

◆ Skills Practice

Synthesizing Information In the Skills Activity in this chapter, you learned about the importance of synthesizing information. When synthesizing information, find the main ideas and use them to formulate a conclusion.

Reread the section on Architecture and Technology from Section 2 of this chapter. Create an outline in which you synthesize the most important information from this section.

◆ Writing Activity: Government

Suppose that you are a speechwriter for a Roman senator around the time that Augustus becomes the first emperor of Rome. Write a speech addressed to the senate that argues either for or against giving Augustus more power.

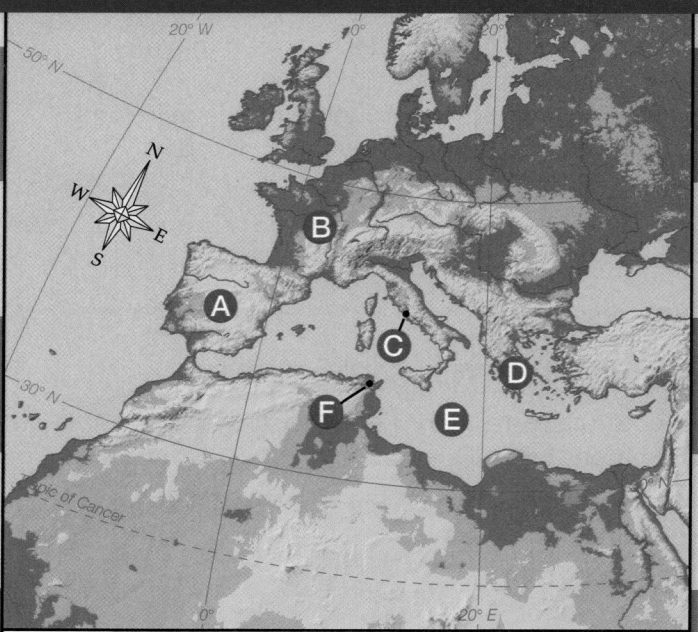

MAP MASTER™
Skills Activity

The Rise of the Roman Empire

Place Location For each place listed below, write the letter from the map that shows its location.

1. Rome
2. Mediterranean Sea
3. Gaul
4. Spain
5. Greece
6. Carthage

Go Online
PHSchool.com Use Web Code **mup-0803** for step-by-step **map skills practice.**

Standardized Test Prep

Test-Taking Tips

Some questions on standardized tests ask you to analyze a timeline. Study the timeline below. Then follow the tips to answer the sample question.

A	B	C	D
509 B.C.	146 B.C.	48 B.C.	27 B.C.

TIP When you read a timeline, line up each date with the significant event that occurred on that date. Place as many events as you know above the proper dates to help you eliminate wrong answers.

Choose the letter that best answers the question.

Where would "the first Roman emperor" go on the timeline?

A point A

B point B

C point C

D point D

TIP Carelessness costs points on multiple-choice tests. Think carefully about each date and event on the timeline.

Think It Through As you look over the timeline, ask yourself, When did the first emperor take office? It must have happened after all the trouble and turmoil surrounding the rule of the dictator Julius Caesar and his murder by a group of senators. If you know that, then you know that the first emperor took office after Caesar was murdered in 44 B.C. The only possible answer, then, is D.

Practice Questions

Use the tips above and other tips in this book to help you answer the following questions.

1. In the Roman Republic, what happened if the republic faced an emergency?

   A A dictator was appointed.

   B A third consul was appointed.

   C The senate made the final decision.

   D All citizens voted.

2. The Romans were heavily influenced by

   A the Greeks.

   B the Chinese.

   C the Persians.

   D the plebeians.

3. Which of the following is a key feature of a republican government?

   A rule by a king

   B dictatorship

   C polytheism

   D elected officials

Use the timeline below to answer Question 4.

A	B	C	D
509 B.C.	146 B.C.	48 B.C.	27 B.C.

4. At which point on the timeline did the Romans overthrow the last Etruscan king?

   A point A

   B point B

   C point C

   D point D

Use Web Code **mua-0800** for **Chapter 8 self-test.**

Chapter 9

The Fate of Ancient Rome

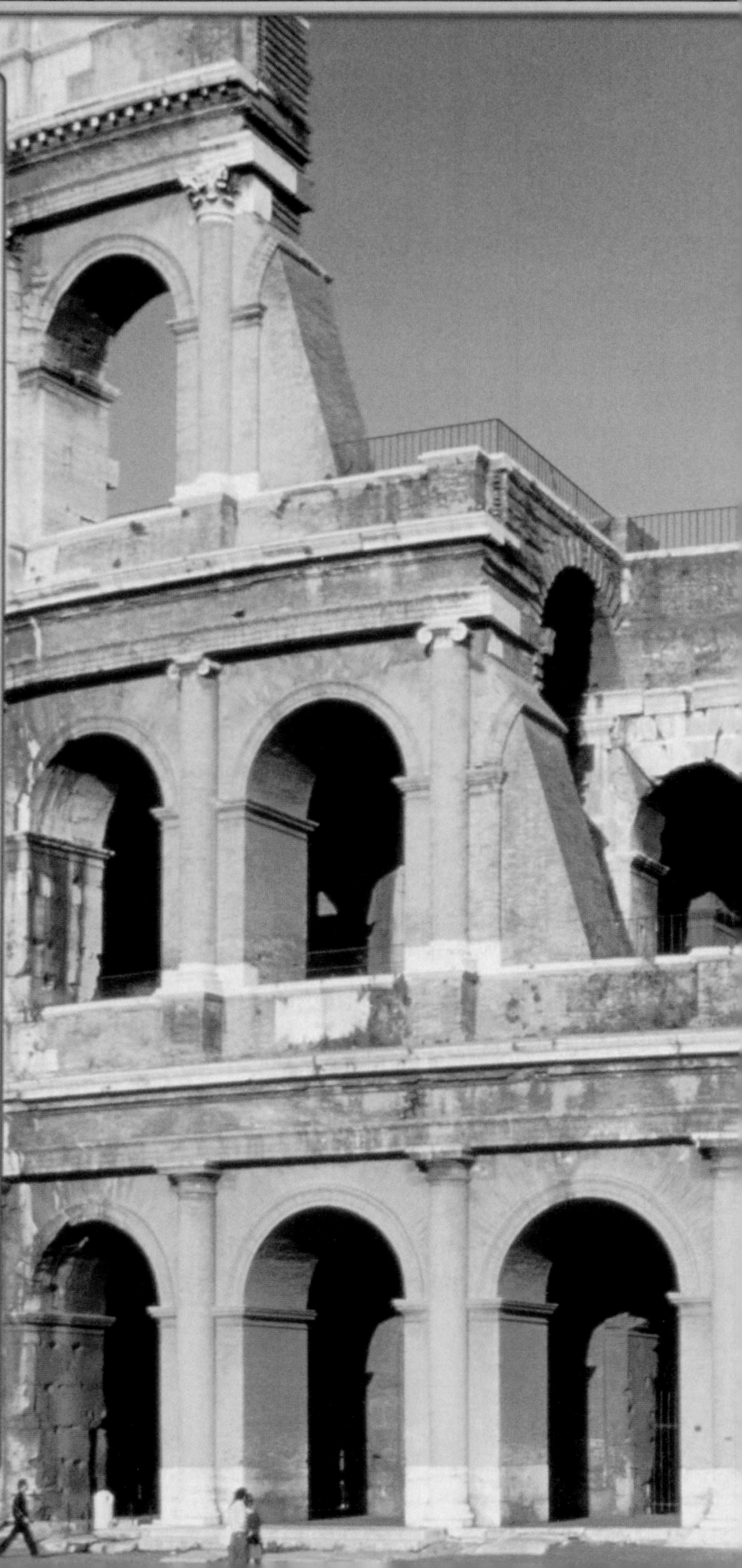

Chapter Preview

In this chapter you will discover how people lived in ancient Rome. You will also learn about the birth of Christianity, its effect on Rome, and the collapse of the Roman Empire.

Section 1
Roman Daily Life

Section 2
Christianity and the Roman Empire

Section 3
The Fall of Rome

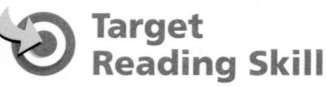

Target Reading Skill

Main Idea In this chapter you will identify the main idea of a paragraph or section. Identifying main ideas will help you better understand what you read. This skill also includes identifying supporting details and implied main ideas, or ideas that are not stated directly.

▶ **Romans knew the Colosseum as the Flavian Amphitheatre. In use for almost 500 years, it held audiences of more than 45,000 for its bloody spectacles.**

MAP MASTER™
Skills Activity

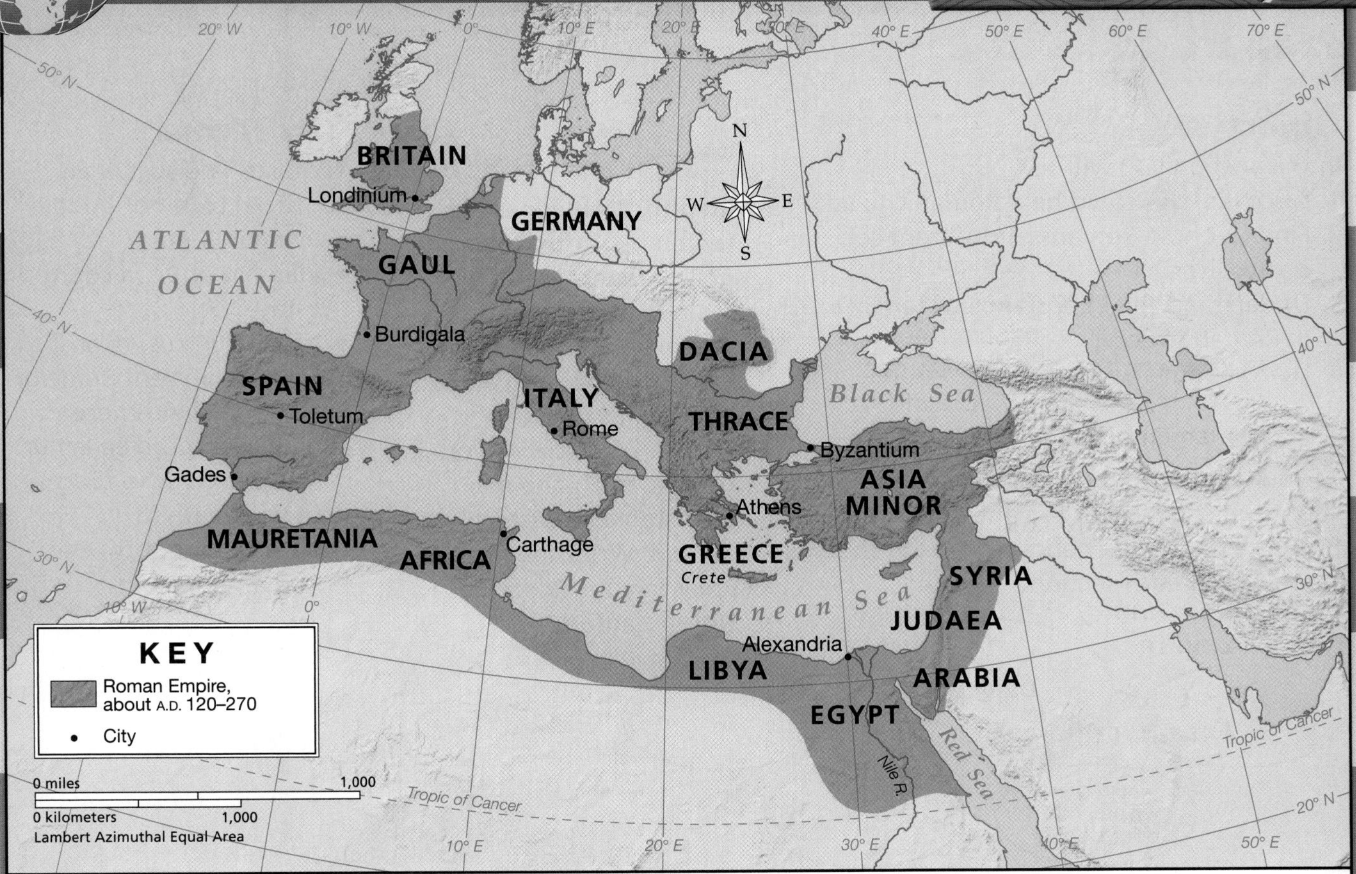

The Roman Empire

BRITAIN
• Londinium

ATLANTIC
OCEAN

GERMANY

GAUL

• Burdigala

SPAIN
• Toletum

Gades •

MAURETANIA

ITALY
• Rome

AFRICA

• Carthage

DACIA

THRACE

Black Sea

GREECE
Crete

Byzantium •

ASIA
MINOR

• Athens

Mediterranean Sea

SYRIA

JUDAEA

• Alexandria

LIBYA

ARABIA

EGYPT

Nile R.

Red Sea

Tropic of Cancer

N
W   E
S

KEY
Roman Empire,
about A.D. 120–270
• City

0 miles   1,000
0 kilometers   1,000
Lambert Azimuthal Equal Area

Tropic of Cancer

Location The Romans extended their empire to include all those
areas that would serve their political and economic interests.
Use the Legend What was the northernmost province of the empire?
Southernmost? What was the widest extent of the empire in miles east
and west? How far was Judaea from Rome? **Apply Information** Which
city on the map would be most difficult for the Roman Army
to reach? Why?

Go Online
PHSchool.com Use Web Code
mup-0901 for step-by-step
map skills practice.

Roman Daily Life

Prepare to Read

Objectives

In this section you will

1. Discover who could be a Roman citizen.
2. Find out how Romans of different social classes lived.
3. Understand the importance of family life in Roman society.
4. Learn about slavery in ancient Rome.

Taking Notes

As you read, note the most important points about the daily life of the ancient Romans. Copy the diagram. Then fill it in with the main idea of each section.

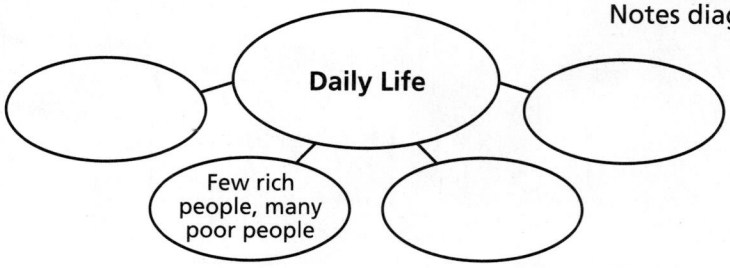

Daily Life

Few rich people, many poor people

Target Reading Skill

Identify Main Ideas To remember information, good readers identify main ideas as they read. The main idea is the most important point in a text. Sometimes the main idea is stated directly. As you read, identify the main idea stated in each section. Write the main ideas in your Taking Notes diagram.

Key Terms

- **census** (SEN sus) *n.* an official count of people living in a place
- **villa** (VIL uh) *n.* a country estate
- **circus** (SUR kus) *n.* an arena in ancient Rome or the show held there
- **gladiator** (GLAD ee ayt ur) *n.* a person who fought to the death as entertainment for the Roman public

At the height of its glory, Rome had perhaps the most beautiful monuments and public buildings in the world. Wealth and goods flowed into Rome from all parts of the empire. Its marketplaces and shops had more goods than any other city. Not everyone was thrilled with the excitement. The poet Martial (MAHR shul), grumbled about the noise:

> **There is no place in town . . . where a poor man can either think or rest. One cannot live for the school-masters in the morning, corn grinders at night, and braziers' hammers all day and night. . . . Who can enumerate the various interruptions to sleep at Rome?**

An ancient wall painting from Pompeii, Italy

Roman Citizens

Rome was a huge city, teeming with people. As the capital of an immense empire, it was first among the cities of its time. The poet Martial also used poetry to celebrate Rome's size and importance:

Take a look at life in ancient Rome.

> "**Rome, goddess of the earth and its people, to whom there is nothing equal, nothing second . . .**"

In its day, ancient Rome had no equal. In terms of its population, however, it was actually the size of some cities today. Rome actually had too many people. A million or more people lived within its limits by the time of Augustus. The citizens of Rome had to put up with noise and crowding every day.

Being Counted as a Citizen

Despite the problems caused by overpopulation, being a Roman citizen was a matter of great pride. In the republic and during the early years of the empire, only residents of the city of Rome itself enjoyed citizenship. Every five years Roman men registered for the census, or official count of people living in Rome. Registering for the census was the only way to claim citizenship. Roman men declared their families, slaves, and wealth to authorities at census time. If a man did not register, he ran the risk of losing his property. Worse yet, he could be sold into slavery. Women, girls, slaves, and those who had been freed from slavery were not counted as citizens. Their place in Roman society was determined only by their relationship to citizens.

This bronze tablet is an official Roman document granting citizenship to a group of people in a Roman province.

Citizens and City As the Roman Empire expanded, people beyond Rome gained Roman citizenship. But this expanded citizenship did not change the special love that residents of Rome felt for their city. Rome was everything to them. Its buildings and monuments were a constant reminder that their city was the center of religion, politics, and culture. Lively banquets and other gatherings made Rome the scene of all social life.

Go Online
PHSchool.com Use Web Code **mup-0828** for an interactivity on the Roman city of Pompeii.

✓ Reading Check **How did a person claim Roman citizenship?**

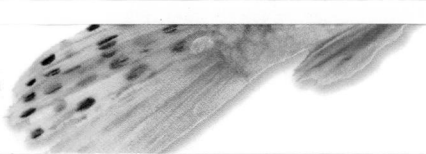

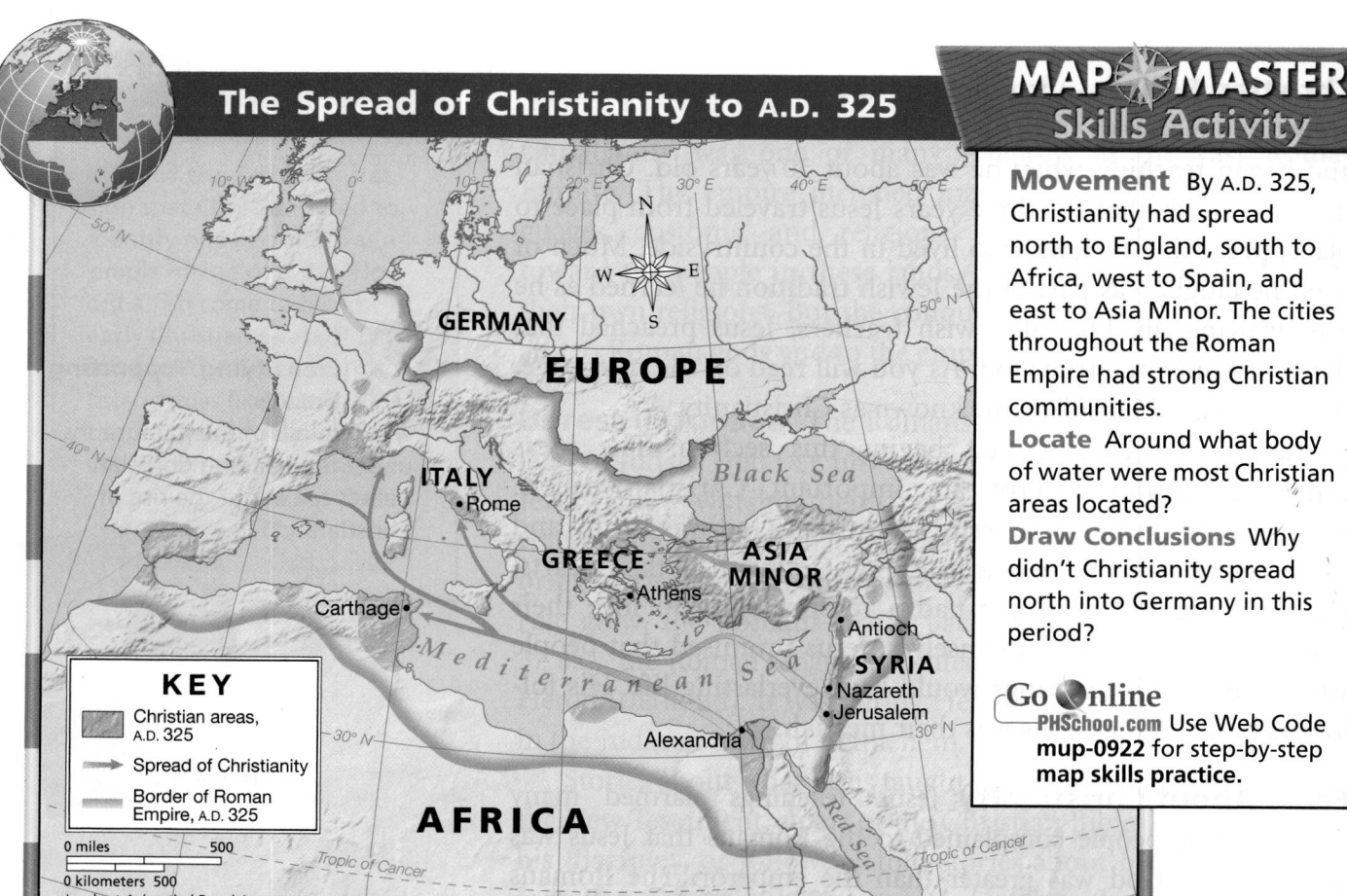

GERMANY

EUROPE

ITALY
•Rome

Black Sea

GREECE
•Athens

ASIA MINOR

Carthage•

Mediterranean Sea

•Antioch

SYRIA
•Nazareth
•Jerusalem

Alexandria•

AFRICA

Red Sea

KEY

- Christian areas, A.D. 325
- → Spread of Christianity
- — Border of Roman Empire, A.D. 325

0 miles 500
0 kilometers 500
Lambert Azimuthal Equal Area

Movement By A.D. 325, Christianity had spread north to England, south to Africa, west to Spain, and east to Asia Minor. The cities throughout the Roman Empire had strong Christian communities.

Locate Around what body of water were most Christian areas located?

Draw Conclusions Why didn't Christianity spread north into Germany in this period?

Go Online
PHSchool.com Use Web Code **mup-0922** for step-by-step map skills practice.

Christianity Spreads

The Greek equivalent of the word *messiah* was *christos* (KRIS tohs). Many educated people of Jesus' time spoke Greek. As these people accepted the teachings of Jesus, they began calling him Christ. After his death, Jesus' followers, called Christians, spread the new religion from Jerusalem across the empire, and finally to Rome itself.

The Letters of Paul One of the most devoted followers of Jesus' teachings was a Jew whose original name was Saul. Saul was well educated and spoke Greek, the common language of the eastern Roman Empire. According to the New Testament, Saul at first rejected the Christian message. One day, however, he believed he had a vision in which Jesus spoke to him. After this experience, Saul changed his name to Paul and carried Christianity to the cities around the Mediterranean, spreading Jesus' teachings as he traveled.

Paul's writings also helped turn the Christian faith into an organized religion. Paul wrote many **epistles,** or letters, to Christian groups in distant cities. Some of these epistles became a part of the Christian Bible.

The Apostle St. Paul
by Marco Pino

Christianity Moves to the Cities Others also helped spread Christian beliefs throughout the Roman world. By A.D. 100, groups of Christians were gathering for worship in Alexandria, Antioch (AN tee ahk), Corinth (KAWR inth), Ephesus (EF ih sus), Thessalonica (thes uh LAHN ih kuh), and even Rome. The new religion gained many followers in cities. Many poor city dwellers welcomed the message of Christianity as good news. These early Christians used the word *paganus* (pah GAH nus) for anyone who did not share their beliefs. *Paganus* means "country dweller" in Latin. It is the root of the English word *pagan*. Today, *pagan* is used to describe someone who is not a Christian, a Jew, or a Muslim.

Go Online PHSchool.com Use Web Code mup-0829 for an interactivity on the travels of Paul.

Ways of Worship Early Christians shared a common faith in the teachings of Jesus and a common way of worship. Over time, their scattered communities organized under a structured Church. Christians borrowed some practices from Jewish worship. They prayed and sang. They also read from the scripture or from one of Paul's letters. Often someone interpreted these readings for those gathered. Christians set aside Sunday, the day they believed Jesus had risen from the dead, as their day of worship.

As Jesus had instructed, Christians also practiced two rites, or holy acts. In the rite of baptism, a believer was dipped in water to wash away his or her sin. Baptism made the person a member of the church. In the rite of the Lord's Supper, Christians shared bread and wine in a sacred meal called the Eucharist. They did this in memory of Jesus, whose last supper was described in the Gospels. Christians believed that through the Eucharist they were receiving the body and blood of Jesus.

The Baptism of Constantine is a painting by Raphael and is displayed at the Vatican palace in Rome.

✓ **Reading Check** **Why did Christianity find many followers in the cities of the Roman Empire?**

Rome Reacts

The fast-growing new religion alarmed the Roman government. Christians refused to worship the Roman gods and did not show the emperor the respect that was required. Some Christians turned away from their responsibilities as Roman citizens, such as serving in the army. Many Roman officials began to view Christians as enemies of the empire.

The Burning of Rome
After the fire, rumors placed the blame on Nero for the fire that destroyed the city. Legend suggests that in his glee for the ruin of Rome, Nero played his lyre while standing atop the Palatine. The legend is depicted above. **Infer** *Why was Nero so quick to blame Christians?*

Rome Burns Under the emperor Nero, the first official campaign against the Christians began in A.D. 64. One night, a fire started in some shops in Rome. The fire spread and burned for nine days, and it left much of the city in ruins.

According to some accounts, Nero blamed the Christians. He ordered the arrest of Christians, who were sent to their deaths. Some were forced to fight wild animals in the Colosseum. Others were soaked with oil and burned alive; others were crucified. Paul was imprisoned for two years and then killed.

Treatment of Christians The Romans persecuted Christians at various times for another 250 years. To *persecute* means to treat repeatedly in a cruel or an unjust way. During these years, the Roman Empire began to lose its power. To explain the decline, Romans looked for people to blame. They found them among the followers of the new religion. As one Roman wrote:

> **If the Tiber River reaches the walls, if the Nile fails to rise to the fields, if the sky doesn't move or the Earth does, if there is famine or plague, the cry is at once: 'The Christians to the Lions.'**

In the Roman world it had become a crime just to be a Christian. As you have read, the punishment for following the new religion was death.

The Appeal of Christianity Despite the persecution of its followers, Christianity continued to spread throughout the empire. The help that Christian communities gave to widows, orphans, and the poor drew people to the new religion. Its messages of love, forgiveness, and a better life after death appealed to many. The figure of Jesus also attracted followers. Jesus was not a hero from myth. He had actually lived among people of the empire. The writings known as the Gospels helped spread Jesus' teachings. The simple style of the Gospels also made Jesus' teachings easy to grasp. They were written in the language that ordinary people used.

As the Christian religion gained more followers, emperor after emperor tried to halt its spread. Actions against Christians were especially severe under Domitian (duh MISH un), Marcus Aurelius, Decius (DEE shus), and Valerian (vuh LIHR ee un). The emperor Diocletian (dy uh KLEE shuhn) was determined to stamp out the new religion, but not even he could stop the growth of Christianity. He outlawed Christian services, imprisoned Christian priests, and put many believers to death. Diocletian's actions accomplished the opposite of what he wanted, however. Many Romans admired the Christians. They saw them as martyrs and heroes. A **martyr** is someone who dies for a cause. By the A.D. 300s, about one in every ten Romans had accepted the Christian faith.

According to tradition, Saint Agnes, shown above, died for her beliefs under the persecution of Christians by Diocletian.

 **Reading Check** How did the Romans persecute Christians?

Section 2 Assessment

Key Terms
Review the key terms listed at the beginning of this section. Use each term in a sentence that explains the term's meaning.

Target Reading Skill
List three details that support the main idea of the section under the heading Rome Reacts.

Comprehension and Critical Thinking
1. (a) Describe What ideas did Jesus teach?

(b) Draw Conclusions Why do you think the Roman governor had Jesus put to death?

2. (a) Recall To what new groups did Paul want to spread the teachings of Jesus?

(b) Draw Inferences Why might Christians have borrowed ways of worship from the Jewish religion?

3. (a) Explain Why did Roman officials consider Christians enemies of the empire?

(b) Identify Cause and Effect What effect did Diocletian's actions have on the growth of Christianity? Explain.

Writing Activity
You are a Roman citizen who has just learned about Christianity. Write a paragraph describing what you now know about it.

For: An activity on the spread of Christianity
Visit: PHSchool.com
Web Code: mud-0920

The Roman soldier was a citizen and a professional, committed to serving on the battlefield for at least 25 years. Away from his homeland for years at a time and forbidden to marry during his service, he formed strong bonds of loyalty to his commander and his comrades. If he survived to complete his dangerous service, he could expect to be well rewarded with land or money.

Pocket Sundial
This travel-sized Roman sundial was used to keep time.

Ruins of a Roman military camp built near the Dead Sea in Israel

Making Camp Foot soldiers, called legionaries (LEE juh nehr eez), sometimes marched 20 miles a day, weighed down by about 70 pounds (32 kilograms) of armor and gear. At the end of their march, the legion, or army, would make a temporary camp. Scouts traveled ahead of the legion to choose a level piece of land near a water source, such as a river or a stream.

When the legionaries arrived, some stood guard while others set to work building ramparts—banks of earth to protect them from attack. First they cut strips of turf from the ground. Then they dug trenches about 10 feet (3 meters) deep. The earth piled up from the trenches formed the ramparts, which were then covered with turf. Finally, stakes driven into the ramparts created a fence. Inside the camp, tents were pitched in orderly rows. The entire job probably took about two hours.

Armor
Various styles of armor were introduced throughout the army's history.

Tools
The men used pickaxes and turf cutters to build the camp's defenses.

Centurions
These officers led the legionaries into battle and directed them in their duties.

Iron Tools
Roman soldiers used many different kinds of tools. The axe (left) and a hook (right) used to lift cauldrons from a fire date from the A.D. 100s.

Assessment

Describe What types of challenges did legionaries face during their service in the Roman army?

Generalize Why do you think Roman soldiers developed a strong sense of loyalty to the army during their service?

Suppose your teacher gave you this extra-credit project: Write a paper comparing and contrasting the ancient empire of Rome with China during the Qin dynasty.

To compare means to find similarities. (Sometimes people use *to compare* to mean to find similarities *and* differences. Be sure to ask your teachers what they mean when they ask you to compare.) You also know that *to contrast* means to find differences. For this project, you need to find out how Rome and China were alike and how they were different.

Learn the Skill

Whenever you are asked to compare and contrast, follow these steps:

1 **Identify a topic and purpose.** What do you want to compare, and for what purpose? For example, you may want to:
- make a choice
- understand a topic
- discover patterns
- show that items are more alike or more different

2 **Identify categories of comparison, and fill in details for each category.** You will need to take notes. You may want to organize your notes in a chart. Make a column for each item you want to compare, and make a row for each category of comparison. Then fill in specific information under each of your categories.

3 **Identify similarities and differences.** If you make a chart, you can mark an *S* for similar or a *D* for different items.

4 **Draw conclusions.** Write a sentence telling whether the items you're comparing have more similarities or more differences.

Practice the Skill

Use the chart below to practice comparing and contrasting.

1. Examine the headings in the chart below to identify the chart's topic and its purpose.

2. What are the main categories of comparison in the chart? How do the details shown support each category?

3. Fill in *S* or *D* in the last column of the chart to identify the similarities and the differences between the two empires.

4. As you write your conclusion, keep in mind the topic and the purpose of the chart.

The remains of an ancient Roman road in Sicily

The Roman Empire and the Qin Dynasty

Characteristic	Roman Empire	Qin Dynasty	Similar or Different
Length of empire	About 520 years (44 B.C.–A.D. 476)	About 15 years (221–206 B.C.)	
Major characteristics	• Built a network of roads • Created local governments • Established code of laws • Created a money system (currency) • Supported literature and the arts	• Built a network of roads • Created local governments • Established code of laws • Created a money system (currency) • Restricted the freedoms of scholars	
Religion or philosophy	Roman religion; later Christianity	Philosophy of legalism	

An ancient Chinese road

Apply the Skill

Use the steps on this page to compare and contrast features of Roman life with life in the United States today. Take notes or put your comparisons in a chart. Write a sentence that draws a conclusion about your findings.

The Fall of Rome

Prepare to Read

Objectives

In this section you will
1. Explore how bad government contributed to the decline of the Roman Empire.
2. Understand the fall of the Roman Empire.
3. Discuss Constantine's role in support for Christianity.
4. Learn how northern invaders contributed to the collapse of the Roman Empire.

Taking Notes

As you read, identify each section's main idea and details. For each section, copy the diagram below. Fill in each main idea and details.

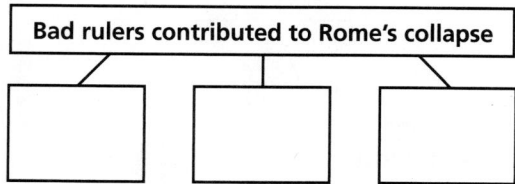

Bad rulers contributed to Rome's collapse

Target Reading Skill

Identify Implied Main Ideas Sometimes main ideas are not stated directly. The details in a section or paragraph hint at a main idea, but you must state it yourself. As you read, study the details in each section. Then write the section's main idea and supporting details in your Taking Notes diagram.

Key Terms

- **Constantine** (KAHN stun teen) (C. A.D. 286–337) emperor of Rome from A.D. 312 to 337; encouraged the spread of Christianity
- **mercenary** (MUR suh neh ree) *n.* a soldier who serves for pay in a foreign army
- **inflation** (in FLAY shun) *n.* an economic situation in which the government issues more money with lower value

This statue of Emperor Constantine originally towered over 30 feet (9m). Today, only the head remains.

Emperor Constantine (KAHN stun teen) stood with his troops near a bridge spanning the Tiber River. On that day in A.D. 312, the sky was full of clouds and Constantine was filled with doubts. His enemies were waiting on the other side of the river.

As Constantine stood, hoping for victory, the sun broke through the clouds. According to one story, Constantine saw a cross in the sky. Above the cross was written in Latin: "Under this sign you will conquer!"

A different story claims that Constantine had a dream. Because of this dream, Constantine had his soldiers' shields marked with a Christian symbol. In the battle, Constantine's army won an overwhelming victory. Constantine believed that the victory had come from the Christian God. Constantine vowed to become a Christian.

Historians today debate whether Constantine had these religious experiences—or whether they are just legend. But **Constantine**, Rome's emperor from A.D. 312 to 337, strongly encouraged the spread of Christianity.

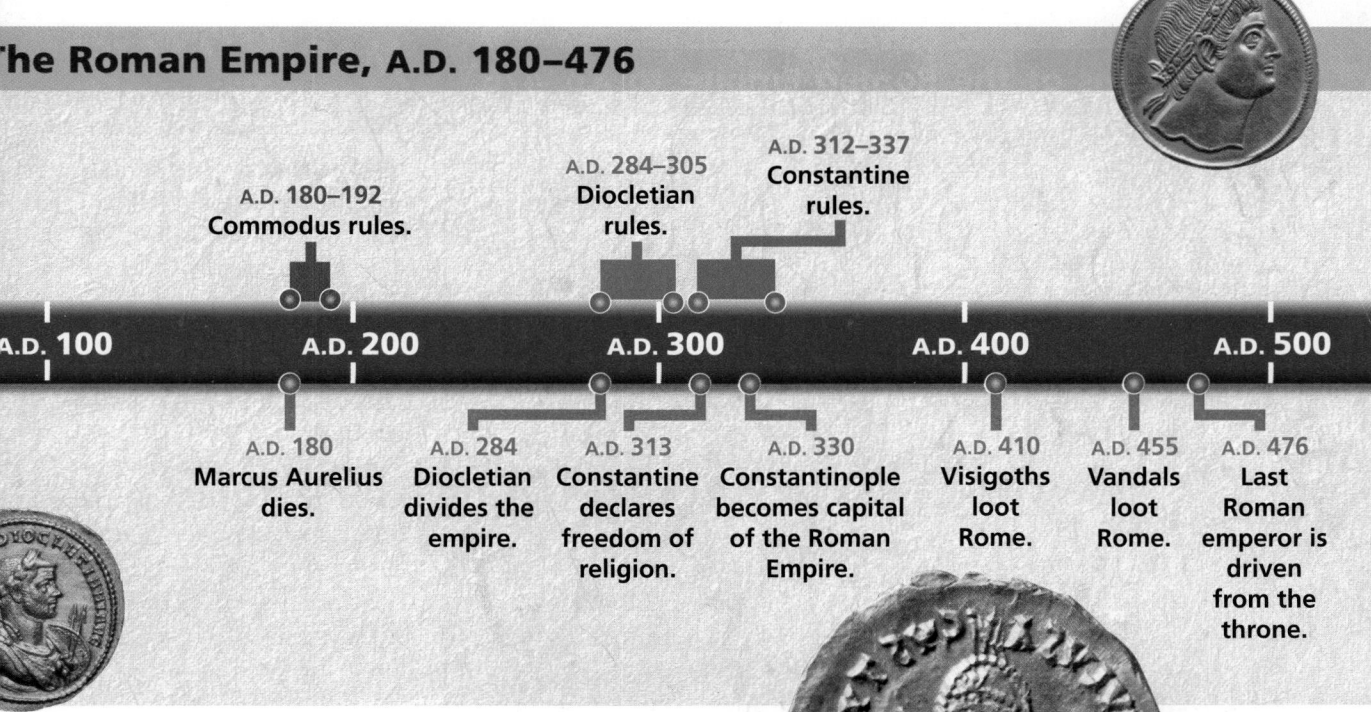

A.D. 180–192
Commodus rules.

A.D. 284–305
Diocletian rules.

A.D. 312–337
Constantine rules.

A.D. 100 | A.D. 200 | A.D. 300 | A.D. 400 | A.D. 500

A.D. 180
Marcus Aurelius dies.

A.D. 284
Diocletian divides the empire.

A.D. 313
Constantine declares freedom of religion.

A.D. 330
Constantinople becomes capital of the Roman Empire.

A.D. 410
Visigoths loot Rome.

A.D. 455
Vandals loot Rome.

A.D. 476
Last Roman emperor is driven from the throne.

From Good Rule to Bad

The Christian Church provided comfort and authority at a time when the mighty Roman Empire was close to collapse. By the time Constantine took power, he could do little to stop the empire's fall. The trouble had started 125 years earlier, when Marcus Aurelius died. The emperor left his son Commodus in power in A.D. 180.

Commodus was only eighteen when he became emperor. Marcus Aurelius was aware that his son was not qualified to rule the empire. But Commodus was in line to inherit power. Marcus Aurelius may have believed that Commodus would grow to be a good emperor as time went by.

Commodus allowed others to help him run the empire, but he made poor choices. He stood by as others worked to destroy the power and prestige of the senate. Commodus himself showed little use for the senate by not seeking its approval before he acted. He kept a grip on power by bribing the army to support him.

His bold, extravagant, and savage ways were his downfall. He loved the bloodshed of the gladiators. He took part in the games himself, dressed as the hero Hercules as well as in other costumes. Commodus had planned to appear as a gladiator on the first day of 193, but he was assassinated on New Year's Eve in 192.

✔ **Reading Check** **What happened to the Roman senate under the emperor Commodus?**

■ Timeline Skills

These timeline entries show the decline and collapse of the Roman Empire. **Identify** When did Diocletian divide the Roman Empire? **Summarize** Summarize the important events from the timeline.

Identify Implied Main Ideas

In one sentence, state the main idea that all the details in this section support.

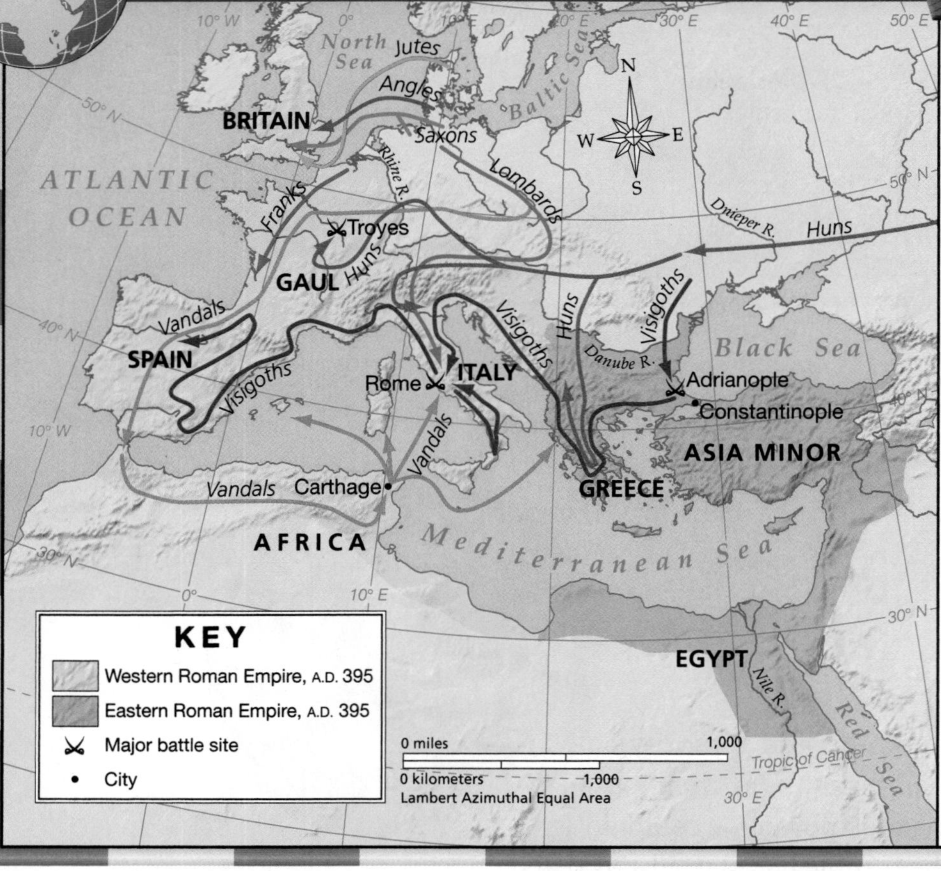

MAP MASTER™
Skills Activity

Invasions of the Roman Empire to A.D. 476

BRITAIN

Jutes

Angles

Saxons

ATLANTIC OCEAN

Franks

Lombards

Rhine R.

North Sea

Baltic Sea

Troyes

GAUL

Huns

Huns

Dnieper R.

Huns

Vandals

SPAIN

Visigoths

Rome

ITALY

Visigoths

Danube R.

Visigoths

Black Sea

Adrianople

Constantinople

ASIA MINOR

Vandals

Carthage

Vandals

GREECE

AFRICA

Mediterranean Sea

EGYPT

Nile R.

Red Sea

Tropic of Cancer

KEY

Western Roman Empire, A.D. 395

Eastern Roman Empire, A.D. 395

✗ Major battle site

• City

0 miles 1,000

0 kilometers 1,000

Lambert Azimuthal Equal Area

Movement The Roman Empire in the west fell to German invaders in A.D. 476. The eastern part of the empire survived as the Byzantine Empire.
Identify What groups of invaders entered the Roman Empire?
Compare and Contrast In which part of the empire did most invasions take place?

Go Online
PHSchool.com Use Web Code **mup-0933** for step-by-step map skills practice.

The Empire Crumbles

The decline of the Roman Empire began under Commodus. Historians do not agree on any one cause for this decline. They believe that several problems led to the fall of Rome.

Weak, Corrupt Rulers After Commodus, emperors were almost always successful generals, not politicians. They often stole money from the treasury. They used the money to enrich themselves and pay for the loyalty of their soldiers. The government and the economy became weak and the senate lost power. Would-be rulers gained the throne by violence. Between A.D. 180 and A.D. 284, Rome had 29 emperors. Most were assassinated.

A Mercenary Army In earlier times, the Roman army had been made up of citizen soldiers ready to defend their land. Now the army was filled with **mercenaries,** foreign soldiers who serve for pay. Mercenaries were motivated by money, not by loyalty to any cause. They often switched sides if doing so could work to their personal advantage. Rome's strength had depended on a strong army that was loyal to the empire. This was now a memory.

Relief showing a barbarian fighting a Roman soldier

The Size of the Empire The Roman Empire had grown too large. Enemies launched attacks all over the empire. Many conquered territories regained their independence. The Roman army spent its time defending the empire instead of extending its authority. Consequently, the empire shrank.

Serious Economic Problems When Rome stopped conquering new lands, new sources of wealth were no longer available. The empire struggled to pay its army. To raise money, the government raised taxes. Meanwhile, the people of the empire suffered severe unemployment.

Food was scarce, so its price went up. To pay for food, the government produced more coins. The value of those coins was dependent upon the amount of silver in them. But because the government did not have much silver, less of this metal was put in each coin. This change resulted in **inflation,** an economic situation in which more money circulates, but the money has less value. When inflation is not controlled, money buys less and less. Roman coins soon became worthless.

Efforts to Stop the Decline Some emperors tried to stop the empire's decline. Diocletian worked to strengthen Rome. He enlarged the army, built new forts at the borders, and improved the tax system. Diocletian also divided the empire into two parts to make it easier to rule. He ruled the wealthier eastern part of the empire, and appointed a co-emperor to rule the western part.

✓ **Reading Check** **What problems did having a mercenary army cause for the empire?**

Roman warship

Christianity in the Roman Empire

Above is the church of St. John the Theologian in Ephesus, an ancient city whose ruins are located in present-day Turkey. Ephesus was an early base of Christianity within the Roman Empire. **Summarize** *How did Constantine encourage the spread of Christianity?*

Constantine and Christianity

Diocletian and his co-emperor stepped down in A.D. 305. A struggle for power followed. For seven years, generals fought one another for power until one—Constantine—became the winner. As you read earlier, Constantine reported that the Christian God had helped his army win the battle for control of Rome. The victory at the bridge over the Tiber made Constantine sole ruler of the Roman Empire in the West. In the East, rule of the Roman Empire was shared by Licinius (ly SIN ee us) and Maximinus (mak suh MEE nus). In 313 Licinius took complete control of the eastern parts of the empire.

Freedom of Religion Also in 313, Constantine and Licinius proclaimed freedom of worship for people across the empire. Under Diocletian and others, Christians had been tortured and punished for their beliefs. Now Rome would no longer persecute the Christians. They were free to practice their religion openly. They could organize churches. Property that had been taken from them was returned. Christianity would soon became the official religion of the Roman Empire.

Another Christian Victory In 324 Constantine won several battles against Licinius for control of the eastern half of the Roman Empire. Now Constantine was emperor of both East and West. Although Licinius and Constantine had agreed to tolerate all religions when they began sharing power in 313, Licinius had continued to allow the persecution of Christians in the East. Constantine saw his victory over Licinius as further proof that the Christian God was working through him.

Building a Faith During his 25 years as emperor, Constantine worked to strengthen the Christian church. In 325 he stepped in to help solve a religious crisis. The church almost split apart when eastern and western church leaders disagreed on certain issues of faith. Constantine led a meeting in Nicaea (ny SEE uh) that brought the two sides together and kept the church whole.

Constantine was a leading force behind the construction of important Christian places of worship. He helped plan and pay for the construction of a church in Jerusalem on the spot where Jesus was crucified, buried, and is said to have risen from the dead. The church of St. Peter in Rome was also built with his help. Constantine also supported the building of churches in the city that would become the empire's new capital.

A New Capital In 330, Constantine moved the capital of the Roman Empire east to the city of Byzantium (bih ZAN tee um), in what is now Turkey. It was a natural move for the emperor. He had grown up in the East and had lived in the eastern Roman city of Nicomedia (ni kuh MEED ee uh) at the court of the emperor Diocletian. The move east also made sense for the empire. Rome had not been its political center for some time.

Constantine spared no expense in enlarging Byzantium and filling it with riches. When he dedicated the city as the new capital of the empire, he called it New Rome. Soon, however, the capital was known by a different name, Constantinople (kahn stan tuh NOH pul), "the city of Constantine." With the emperor and the empire's capital in Constantinople, the power of the Roman Empire was now firmly in the East.

✓ Reading Check **What city became the new capital of the Roman Empire?**

This shows the Hagia Sophia in Sultan Ahmet Square in Constantinople, the capital of the eastern Roman Empire. Today, Constantinople is known as Istanbul, Turkey.

Links Across Time

Vandals Today, we call someone who destroys property and valuable things a vandal. The Vandals were one of the Germanic tribes that invaded the Roman Empire. They looted Rome in A.D. 455, stealing artwork and other highly prized items. Their name came to be connected with this kind of destructive behavior.

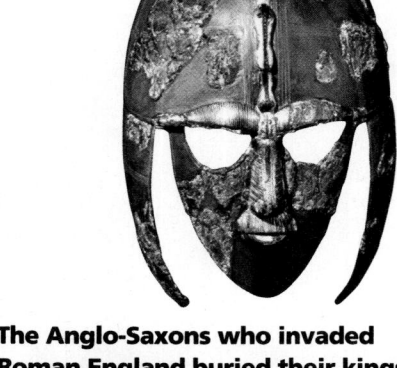

The Anglo-Saxons who invaded Roman England buried their kings in ships. At a site discovered in England in 1939, the ancient ship had rotted. Yet many items, including this helmet remained.

Invasions and Collapse

Constantine struggled to keep the empire together, but the forces pulling it apart were too great. After his death, invaders swept across Rome's borders and overwhelmed the empire. The invaders belonged to northern tribes. Today, we call them Germanic tribes. The Romans called them barbarians. In the past, the Roman army had been able to defeat these tribes. Now, however, they could not stop the intruders. In the 400s, the Germanic tribes overran the empire. One tribe, the Visigoths (VIZ ee gahths), captured and looted Rome in 410. The Vandals (VAN dulz), another Germanic tribe, took Rome in 455. The Roman emperor was almost powerless.

The last Roman emperor was 14-year-old Romulus Augustulus (RAHM yuh lus oh GUS chuh lus). His name recalled more than 1,000 years of Roman glory. But the boy emperor did not win glory for himself. In 476, a German general took power and sent the emperor to work on a farm. After Romulus Augustulus, no emperor ruled over Rome and the western part of the empire.

However, even after Rome fell, the eastern part of the empire remained strong. Its capital, Constantinople, remained the center of another empire, the Byzantine Empire, for a thousand years.

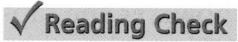

✓ **Reading Check** Who was Romulus Augustulus, and what was his fate?

Section 3 Assessment

Key Terms
Review the key terms listed at the beginning of this section. Use each term in a sentence that explains the term's meaning.

Target Reading Skill
State the main idea of the section Constantine and Christianity.

Comprehension and Critical Thinking
1. (a) Recall How is Marcus Aurelius remembered?
(b) Analyze Was Commodus a good choice for emperor?

2. (a) Identify What factors contributed to the Roman Empire's decline?
(b) Identify Cause and Effect How did each cause you listed affect the empire's stability?
3. (a) Describe What did Constantine do to show that he accepted Christianity?
(b) Draw Conclusions Why did Constantine take steps to strengthen the Christian church?
4. (a) Recall What events led to the fall of Rome?
(b) Analyze Information Why was the Roman army unable to resist the invading armies?

Writing Activity
The fall of the western Roman Empire was a turning point in history, but many people in those days may not have noticed any change. Why might this be true?

For: An activity on the fall of the Roman Empire
Visit: PHSchool.com
Web Code: mud-0930

9 Review and Assessment

◆ Chapter Summary

Section 1: Roman Daily Life

- As the Roman Empire expanded, people beyond Rome gained Roman citizenship.
- A small number of people in ancient Rome were wealthy, but many people were poor.
- Men held a great deal of power compared with that of women and children in the Roman family.
- Slavery was common in ancient Rome.

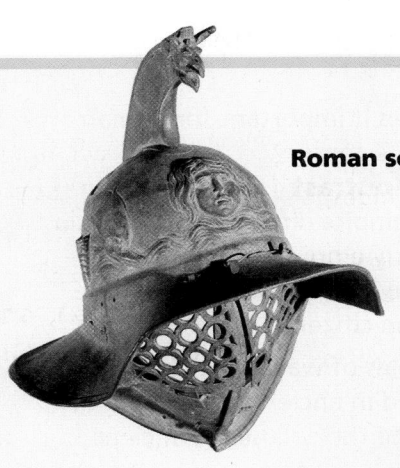

Roman soldier's helmet

Section 2: Christianity and the Roman Empire

- According to the Christian Bible, Jesus' followers thought he was their savior.
- After Jesus' death, Christianity spread throughout the Roman Empire.
- Roman officials viewed Christians as enemies of the empire and persecuted them.

Symbols of Christianity

Section 3: The Fall of Rome

- Political and economic problems brought about the decline of the Roman Empire.
- The emperor Constantine strengthened the Christian church and made Constantinople the empire's capital.
- Germanic tribes invaded the empire, and Rome's last emperor stepped down in 476.

Present-day Constantinople

◆ Key Terms

Match each definition with the correct term.

1. an official count of people living in a place
   - A circus
   - B census
   - C inflation
   - D martyr

2. an arena in ancient Rome
   - A villa
   - B circus
   - C gladiator
   - D census

3. a follower of a person or belief
   - A epistle
   - B disciple
   - C gladiator
   - D martyr

4. an economic situation in which there is more money with lower value
   - A circus
   - B inflation
   - C census
   - D epistle

Review and Assessment (continued)

◆ Comprehension and Critical Thinking

5. **(a) Explain** Why was it important for Roman men to register in the census?
   (b) Compare and Contrast How did Roman citizens in the later empire differ from citizens in the republic and early empire?
   (c) Draw Inferences Why might someone be proud to be a Roman citizen?

6. **(a) List** Give examples of ways the rich, the poor, and slaves lived in ancient Rome.
   (b) Identify Describe the circuses of ancient Rome.
   (c) Summarize In what ways did the Roman circuses bring the rich, poor, and slaves together?

7. **(a) Recall** What were some of the teachings of Jesus?
   (b) Draw Conclusions Why did poor Romans and slaves find Christianity appealing?

8. **(a) Explain** Why did the Roman government view Christians as enemies of the empire?
   (b) Identify Causes Why did Nero start a campaign against Christians?
   (c) Identify Effects How did the decline of the Roman Empire affect Christians?

9. **(a) Identify** Name a weak and corrupt Roman ruler.
   (b) Explore the Main Idea Explain how this ruler contributed to the decline of the empire.

10. **(a) Recall** What happened to the western part of the empire after Romulus Augustulus was removed from power?
    (b) Predict How do you think life in the West changed after the fall of Rome?

◆ Skills Practice

Comparing and Contrasting In the Skills Activity in this chapter, you learned how to compare and contrast. You learned to identify how different ideas, objects, historical figures, or situations are alike or different.

Review the steps you followed to learn this skill. Reread the part of Section 1 in Chapter 8 describing the decline of the Roman Republic. Then reread the part of Section 3 in this chapter describing the fall of the Roman Empire. Create a chart to help identify the similarities and differences between the two events. Finally, use your findings to draw conclusions about the events.

◆ Writing Activity History

Suppose you were a resident of Rome in A.D. 476, when northern invaders entered the city. Write a letter about the experience to a relative who lives in Constantinople. Also discuss your hopes and fears for the future.

MAP MASTER™ Skills Activity

The Roman Empire

Place Location For each place listed below, write the letter from the map that shows its location.
1. Rome
2. Mediterranean Sea
3. Nazareth
4. Jerusalem
5. Constantinople

Go Online
PHSchool.com Use Web Code **mud-0902** for step-by-step map skills practice.

Standardized Test Prep

Test-Taking Tips

Some questions on standardized tests ask you to analyze a timeline. Study the timeline below. Then follow the tips to answer the sample question.

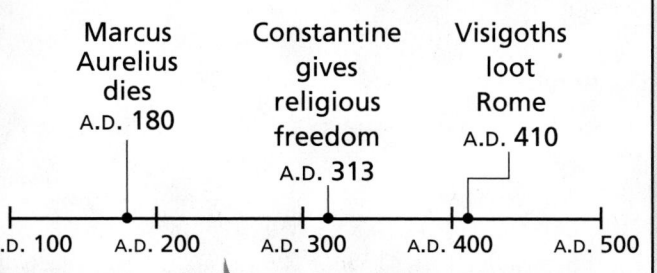

TIP When you read a timeline, align each event with the nearest date. Make sure you can read a date for each point on the timeline.

Pick the letter that best answers the question.

Where would the event "Last Roman emperor driven from power" go on the timeline?

- **A** between A.D. 100 and A.D. 200
- **B** between A.D. 200 and A.D. 300
- **C** between A.D. 300 and A.D. 400
- **D** between A.D. 400 and A.D. 500

TIP Carelessness costs points on multiple-choice tests. Think carefully about each date and event on the timeline.

Think It Through Review the timeline. Ask yourself, "When did the last emperor rule Rome?" It must have happened near the end of the Roman Empire; that means you can rule out A and B. Even if you don't know the exact date, make a thoughtful guess. The last emperor ruled after the Visigoths looted Rome. The correct answer is D.

Practice Questions

Use the tips above and other tips in this book to help you answer the following questions.

1. The Roman government gave family support to the upper classes to
   - **A** reduce their power over their households.
   - **B** encourage them to increase their families.
   - **C** allow wealthy women more independence.
   - **D** gain political power for the emperor.

2. Followers of Jesus believe that he was the
   - **A** messiah.
   - **B** emperor.
   - **C** disciple.
   - **D** ruler.

3. Paul's epistles became part of
   - **A** the Torah.
   - **B** the Gospels.
   - **C** the Greek language.
   - **D** the Christian Bible.

Use the timeline below to answer Question 4.

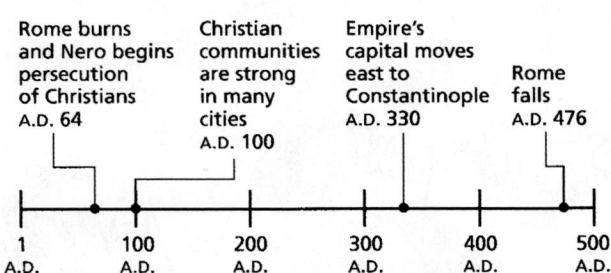

4. How many years passed between the capital's move to Constantinople and the fall of Rome?
   - **A** 142
   - **B** 100
   - **C** 146
   - **D** 64

Go Online
PHSchool.com

Use Web Code **mua-0904** for **Chapter 9 self-test.**

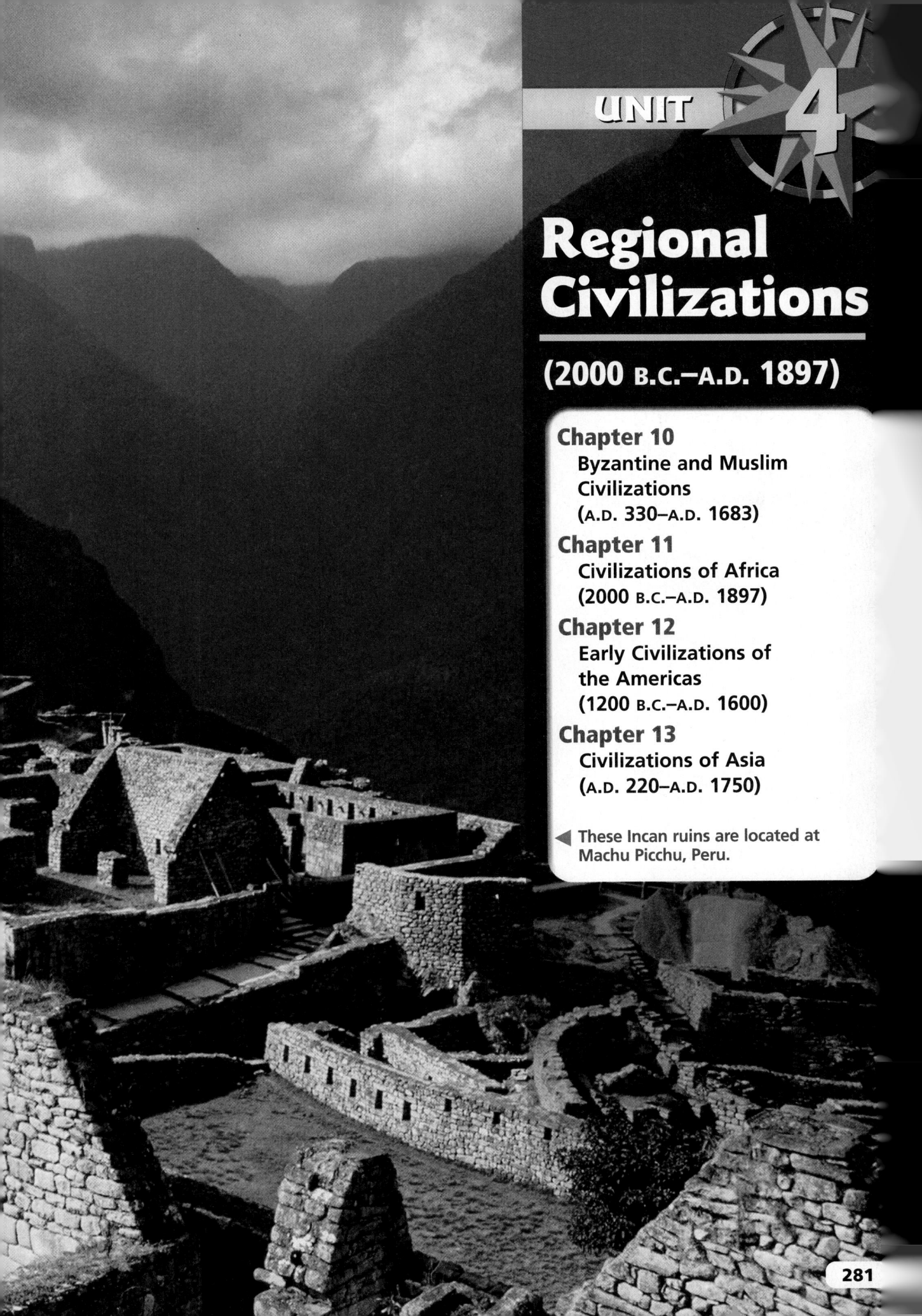

Regional Civilizations

(2000 B.C.–A.D. 1897)

◀ These Incan ruins are located at
Machu Picchu, Peru.

Chapter

10 Byzantine and Muslim Civilizations

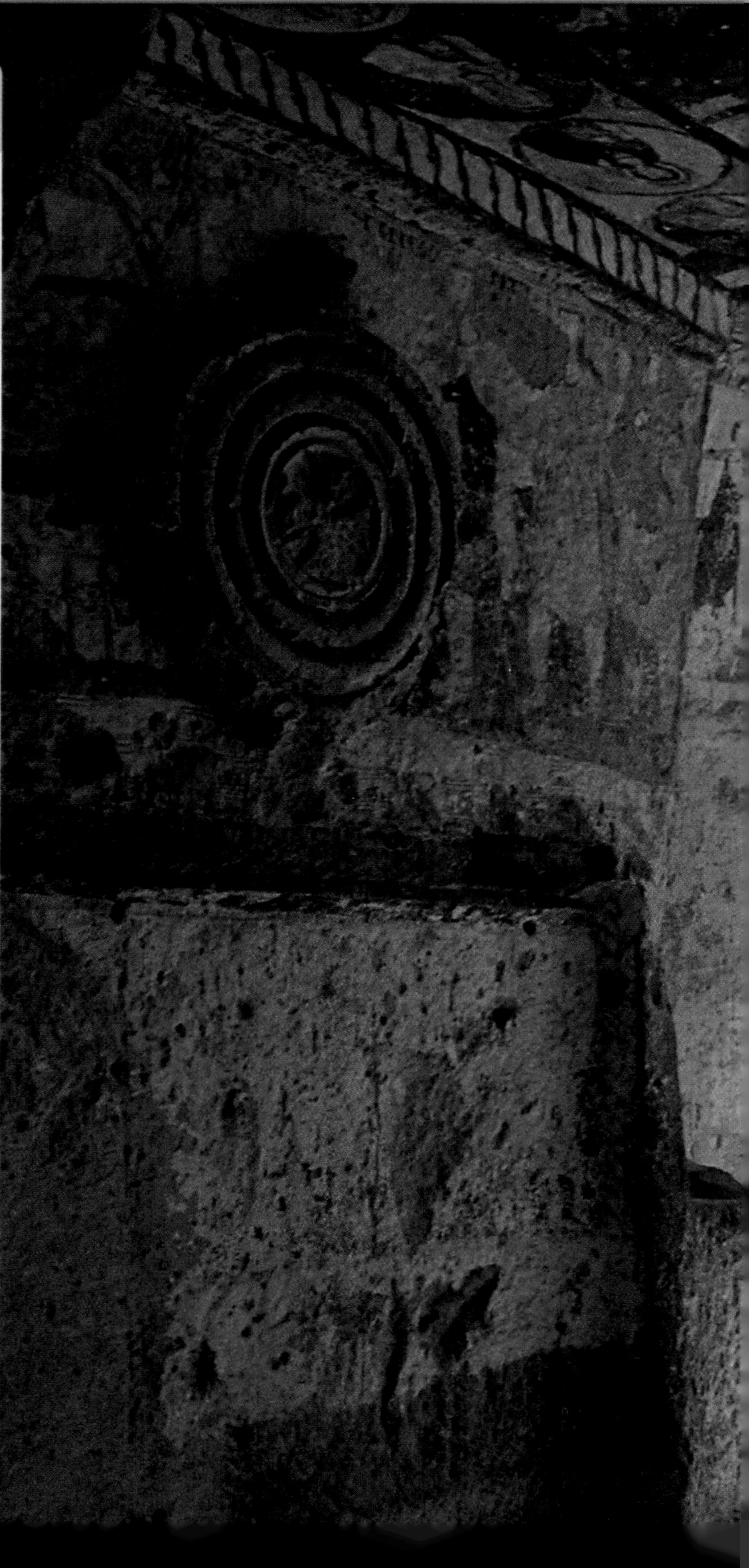

Chapter Preview

This chapter will introduce you to the Byzantine Empire, the religion of Islam, and the golden age of Muslim civilization.

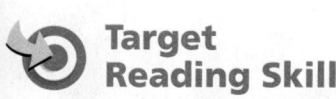

Target Reading Skill

Reading Process In this chapter you will focus on the reading process by using previewing to help you understand and remember what you read.

▶ **Interior of a Byzantine church in present-day Turkey**

ATLANTIC
OCEAN

Kiev

Volga R.

Dnieper R.

Venice

Danube R.

Black Sea
Bosporus

Caspian Sea

Córdoba

Rome

Constantinople

Asia
Minor

Aegean Sea

Antioch

Tigris R.

Indus R.

Crete

Cyprus

Euphrates R.

Baghdad

Mediterranean Sea

Jerusalem

Persian Gulf

Tropic of Cancer

Alexandria

Tropic of Cancer

Arabian
Sea

Red Sea

Medina

Nile R.

Mecca

INDIAN
OCEAN

Arabian
Peninsula

KEY

Byzantine Empire,
about A.D. 1000

Islamic rule,
about A.D. 1000

Roman Empire,
about A.D. 120

• City

0 miles   1,000

0 kilometers   1,000
Lambert Azimuthal Equal Area

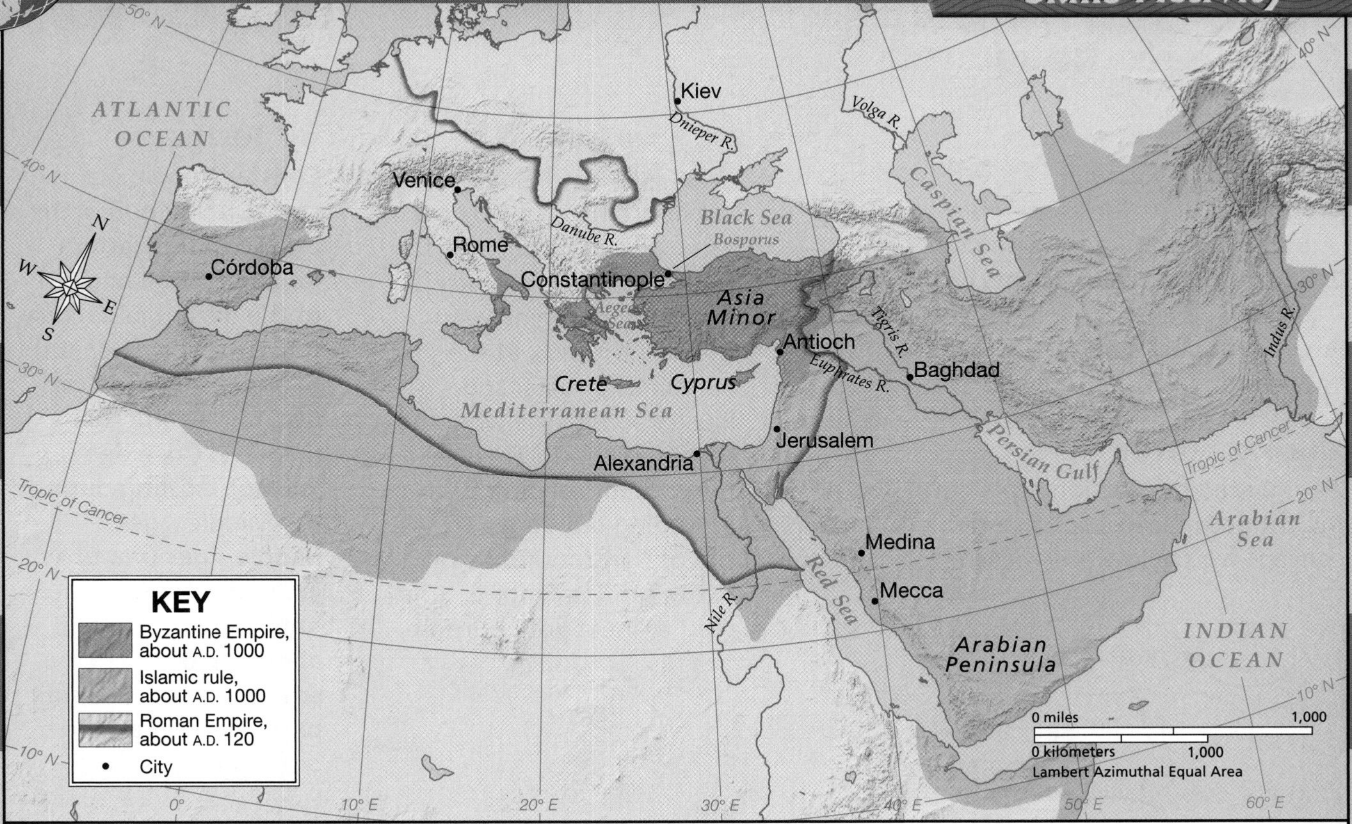

Regions Notice the three political regions on this map.
Identify Which empire was the earliest? The largest? **Conclude** Find
Constantinople. How do you think its location contributed to its
growth and importance?

Go Online
PHSchool.com Use Web Code
lgp-8111 for step-by-step
map skills practice.

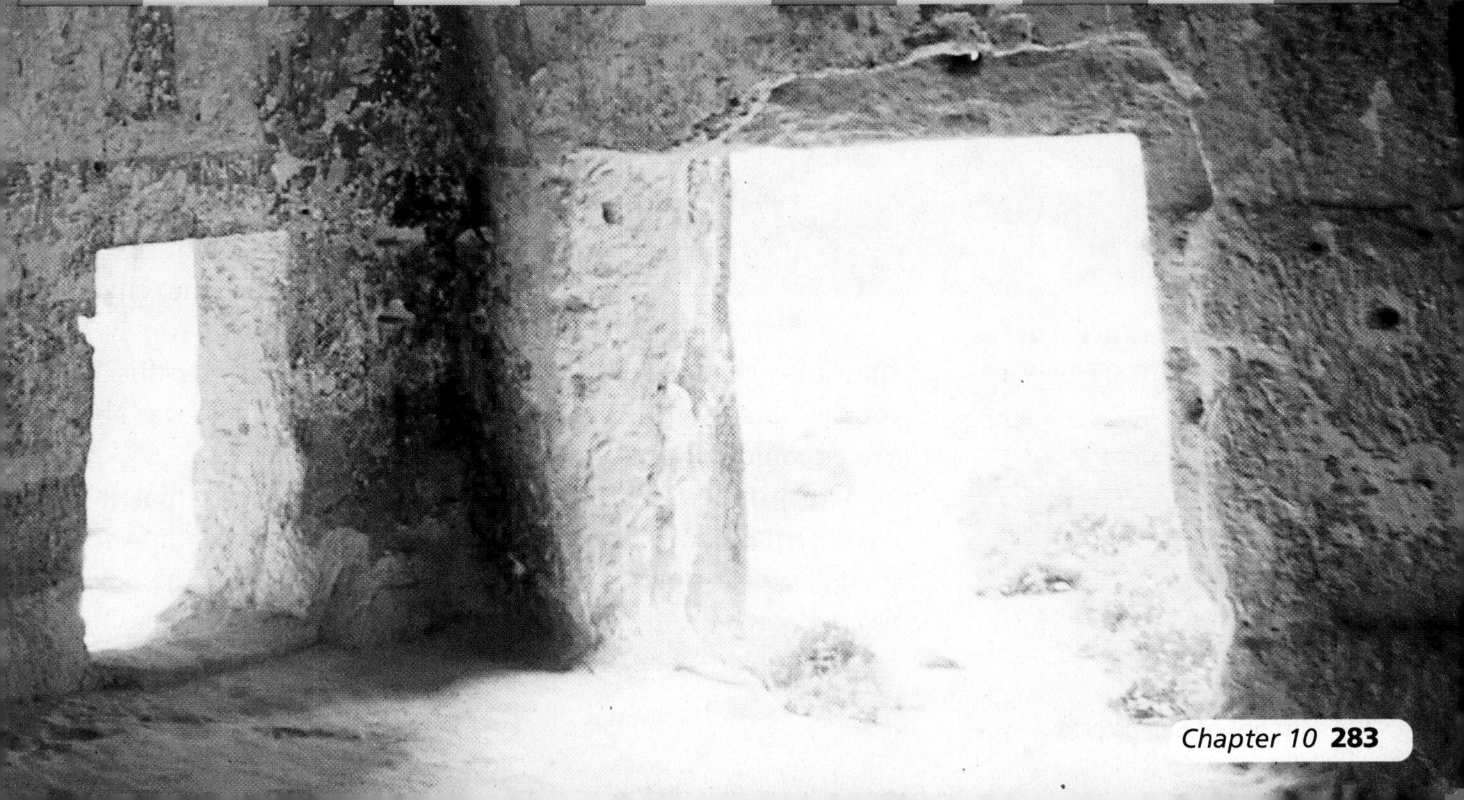

1
The Byzantine Empire

Prepare to Read

Objectives

In this section you will
1. Find out how Constantinople and the Byzantine Empire became powerful.
2. Discover the achievements of the Age of Justinian.
3. Learn about the later years of the Byzantine Empire.

Taking Notes

As you read this section, take notes about the Byzantine Empire's capital and rulers. Copy the concept web below and record your data in it.

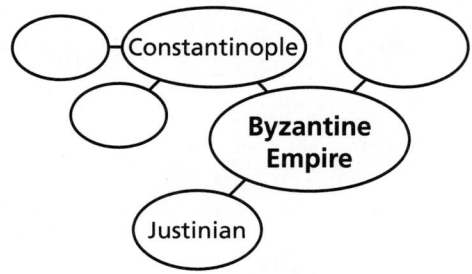

Target Reading Skill

Preview and Set a Purpose
When you set a purpose for reading, you give yourself a focus. Before you read this section, look at the headings, photos, and illustrations to see what the section is about. Then set a purpose for reading, such as finding out about the city of Constantinople or the Byzantine Empire. Now read to meet your purpose.

Key Terms

- **Constantinople** (kahn stan tuh NOH pul) *n.* the capital of the eastern Roman Empire and later of the Byzantine Empire
- **Justinian** (jus TIN ee un) *n.* one of the greatest Byzantine emperors
- **medieval** (mee dee EE vul) *adj.* existing during the Middle Ages
- **Middle Ages** (MID ul AY jiz) *n.* the period between A.D. 476 and about 1500
- **schism** (SIZ um) *n.* a split, particularly in a church or religion

Greek fire being used in battle, as shown in a Byzantine manuscript

Prince Igor (EE gawr) of Kiev, which was then an important city in Russia, watched as a large force of his warships sailed across the Black Sea in A.D. 941. The prince was sure that **Constantinople,** capital of the Byzantine (BIZ un teen) Empire, would soon be his.

As his fleet drew close to the city, the prince's excitement turned to horror. Byzantine ships shot "Greek fire" at the invaders. Anything this "fire" touched burst into flames. Soon, most of Igor's fleet was ablaze. Water could not put out the flames.

Greek fire was made from a formula so secret that it was never written down. Even today, no one knows exactly how it was made, except that it contained petroleum. But this deadly weapon gave the Byzantines tremendous power throughout the Mediterranean area.

Constantinople at a Crossroads

At its height, the ancient Roman Empire controlled the lands surrounding the Mediterranean Sea. It also ruled parts of northern Europe and the region we now call the Middle East. In the centuries after Rome's power faded, these lands went through a tug of war. Two groups—the Christian Byzantines and the Muslim Arabs and Turks—developed powerful civilizations at this time. These two groups sometimes shared control and sometimes fought over the region.

Constantine and His Capital The emperor Constantine began his rule of the enormous Roman Empire in A.D. 306. As you have read, his reign was marked by two important changes. First, Constantine became a Christian and stopped the persecution of Christians. Second, after 20 years of ruling from the city of Rome, Constantine decided to build a new imperial capital.

Constantine chose Byzantium, an ancient city founded by the Greeks, at the eastern end of the empire. He spared no expense building and fortifying his capital, which was renamed Constantinople (kahn stan tuh NOH pul), the "city of Constantine." By the early 500s, Constantinople had large markets, forums or public squares, paved roads, a cathedral, a palace, public baths, and a hippodrome, or circus. An estimated half a million people lived there. Although the name of their city had changed, the people who lived there were still called Byzantines.

Fortress City
Notice the walls that protect Constantinople in the painting (bottom) and in the diagram of the city (middle). The photograph (top) shows ruins of a city wall. **Infer** *Why would the aqueduct, which carried water, and the cisterns, which stored water, also be important if the city were attacked?*

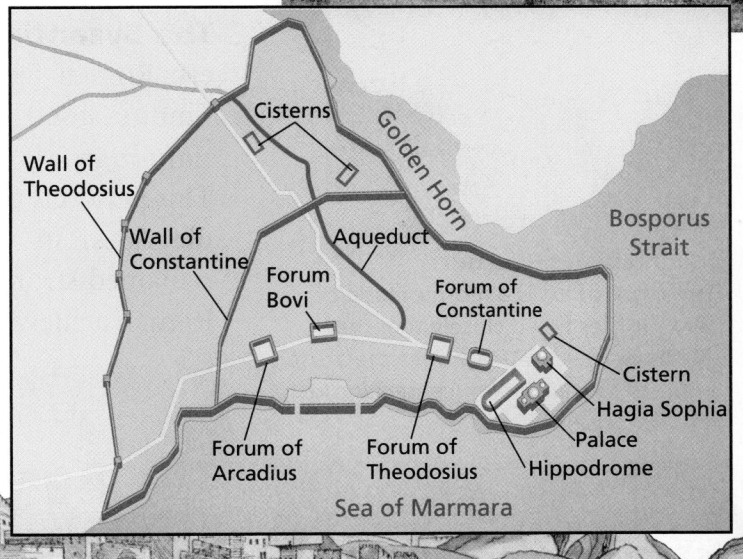

Gold coin from Constantinople ▶

Go Online
PHSchool.com Use Web Code
mup-0830 for an interactivity
on the Hagia Sophia.

Justinian and His Court
This work of art is a mosaic made of
ceramic tiles fitted closely together.
Analyze Images *How does the artist
indicate that Justinian (center) is the
most important person?*

The emperors who followed Constantine continued to rule from Constantinople, in the eastern part of the empire. When the Roman Empire split into two parts, the eastern half proved to be by far the stronger. One reason for its strength was military. The Byzantines had the strongest army in the region. Another reason for the Byzantines' strength was trade.

Trade Constantinople was built at a major crossroads of land and sea trade routes. Find it on the map on page 283. Notice that it is located on the Bosporus. The Bosporus is a strait, or narrow channel that links two bodies of water. It connects the Black Sea and the Sea of Marmara, which flows into the Mediterranean Sea. Two continents, Europe and Asia, meet at the Bosporus.

Goods came to Constantinople from Kiev in the north, from Egypt in the south, and from as far away as China in the east. The Byzantines charged taxes on all goods that went through the city. Over time, the Byzantine Empire grew rich.

The Byzantines Stand Alone As you have read, the western Roman Empire fell. After it fell, the eastern or Byzantine Empire stood alone. The period from the fall of the Roman Empire in A.D. 476 to about 1500 is known as the **Middle Ages.** This period is also labeled **medieval,** or existing during the Middle Ages. In the early Middle Ages, the Byzantine Empire remained strong. This allowed the Byzantines to preserve many Roman achievements and traditions.

✓ **Reading Check** **Why did Constantinople become rich and powerful?**

The Age of Justinian

As Rome was falling to invaders, strong fortifications and an excellent army protected Constantinople. But these were not the city's only strengths. The early Byzantine Empire had many excellent rulers who were wise as well as popular. They encouraged education and made reforms to laws and government. This kind of leadership also contributed to the strength of their empire.

The Emperor Justinian One of the greatest Byzantine emperors was **Justinian** (jus TIN ee un), whose rule began in 527. Justinian was an energetic ruler who rarely gave up on a task until it was completed. He had been born into a poor family, and he listened to the ideas of all his subjects—whether they were wealthy nobles or poor peasants.

Justinian's Code One of Justinian's most lasting contributions was a system of laws. When he became emperor, the empire was using a disorganized system of old Roman laws. Some laws even contradicted others. It was difficult to make sense of them—or to enforce them. Justinian appointed a team to collect and summarize centuries of Roman laws. The result was **Justinian's Code,** an organized collection and explanation of Roman laws for use by the Byzantine Empire. Eventually, this code became the basis for the legal systems of most modern European countries.

Byzantine Culture In addition to preserving the principles of Roman law, Byzantine scholars also kept and copied the works of the ancient Greeks. At its peak, Byzantine civilization blended Greek, Roman, and Christian influences. Later, when the empire was in decline, scholars took the ancient manuscripts and their knowledge of the rich Byzantine culture to the newly powerful city-states of Italy. In Chapter 15, you will read how, hundreds of years later, these influences helped spark a cultural movement called the Renaissance.

✓ Reading Check **What cultures influenced Byzantine civilization?**

Hagia Sophia
It took 10,000 workers five years to build the Hagia Sophia cathedral in Constantinople. Since the fall of the empire, it has been used as a mosque. **Infer** *Why do you think Justinian built such a majestic church?*

The Importance of Icons
This icon shows the Virgin Mary and the baby Jesus. The ban on icons was finally lifted in A.D. 843, and they are important in Eastern Orthodox Christianity to this day. **Identify Frame of Reference** *Why might medieval Christians have valued icons?*

The Empire's Later Years

After Justinian's death in 565, the Byzantine Empire began to decline. Later emperors had to fight wars against many neighboring enemies—including Persians and Turks to the east, Arabs to the south, and Germanic peoples to the north and west. The Byzantine Empire was shrinking in both size and power. As the Byzantines struggled to keep nearby enemies from invading Constantinople, religious and political arguments were weakening the empire from within.

A Religious Dispute Although most Byzantines were Christians, they did not practice Christianity the same way as the people in Western Europe did. Byzantine Christians rejected the authority of the pope, the leader of the church in Rome. The Byzantine emperor had to approve the choice of the patriarch, or highest church official in Constantinople. Greek was the language of the Byzantine church, while Latin was the language of the Roman church. The two branches of Christianity began to grow apart.

At that time, many Christians prayed to saints or holy people, represented by icons, or paintings of these people. In the 700s, a Byzantine emperor outlawed the use of icons, saying that they violated God's commandments. The pope disagreed, and banished the emperor from the church.

Byzantines felt that the pope did not have the authority to banish the emperor from the church. These disputes led to a schism, or split, in the Christian church in 1054. Now there were two distinct forms of Christianity: the Roman Catholic Church in the west and the Eastern (Greek) Orthodox Church in the east.

A Second Golden Age From about 900 until the mid-1000s, the Byzantine Empire experienced a final period of greatness. Trade increased and merchants came to Constantinople from as far away as Venice and Russia. Once again the population of the city grew in size and diversity.

As the economy grew in strength, so did the government. The long reign of Basil II—from 976 until 1025—was the most exceptional period of Byzantine history since the rule of Justinian. The empire regained some of the land it had lost. There was a burst of creativity in the arts.

The Fall of Constantinople During the 1000s, however, Muslim peoples to the east were also gaining power. By the late 1100s, Turks had taken the inland areas of Asia Minor away from the weakening Byzantine Empire.

The Byzantines were also threatened by Europeans. In 1171, disagreements over trade led to a war with Venice. And in the early 1200s, Constantinople was attacked by Christian crusaders. Western Christians ruled the city for 50 years. In 1261, the Byzantines regained their capital, but little was left of their empire.

In 1453, a force of about 70,000 Turks surrounded Constantinople. They came both by sea and by land, and they brought cannons to attack the city's walls. The defending force, which numbered about 7,000, held out for two months. Then the Byzantine capital—which had been a defensive fortress for more than 1,000 years—finally fell.

However, like Constantine before them, the new rulers would rebuild the city and make it an imperial capital. Renamed Istanbul, the city at the crossroads became a great center of Muslim culture and the capital of the Ottoman Empire.

 **Reading Check** **Why did Constantinople finally fall?**

The Turks Take Constantinople
The Turks dragged some of their ships overland and launched them into Constantinople's harbor. **Synthesize** *From what you know about the city's fortifications, why was this a good strategy?*

Section 1 Assessment

Key Terms
Review the key terms at the beginning of this section. Use each term in a sentence that explains its meaning.

Target Reading Skill
What was your purpose for reading this section? Did you accomplish it? If not, what might have been a better purpose?

Comprehension and Critical Thinking
1. (a) Locate Where was Constantinople located?

(b) Identify Effects How did its location contribute to its growth and to the strength of the Byzantine Empire?
2. (a) Recall What qualities made Justinian a good and successful ruler?
(b) Draw Conclusions Why was Justinian's Code so important?
3. (a) Explain What was the dispute that split the medieval Christian church?
(b) Draw Conclusions Why might that split have weakened the empire?

Writing Activity
Write a letter to a friend or family member from the point of view of a foreign merchant traveling to Constantinople during the reign of Justinian. Describe the city and its location as well as what you have heard about the emperor.

For: An activity on the Byzantines
Visit: PHSchool.com
Web Code: lgd-8101

Using a Table to Write a Paragraph

Mr. Perez's students have just finished studying the Byzantine Empire. Now they are studying modern Turkey, which occupies some of the same land. They have learned that Istanbul is the modern name of Constantinople. Mr. Perez has asked the students to use a table of information about Istanbul and Constantinople to write a paragraph that compares the two cities.

Byzantine cup

Information—words or numbers—presented in graphs, charts, or tables is called data. When you use this type of data to write a paragraph, you are transferring information from one medium to another.

Learn the Skill

Follow these steps to write a paragraph based on data from a table.

1. **Identify the topic of the table.** First read the title. Then look at the table to get a general idea of its purpose.

2. **Identify the key pieces of information.** Headings tell the main topics. Read both across and down to understand how the data relate to the headings.

Modern Istanbul

3. **Look for similarities and differences in data.** The columns of a table often compare and contrast information.

4. **Analyze the meaning of the information.** What information seems most important? List several conclusions you can draw from the data.

5. **Write a paragraph that states and supports your conclusions.** Your main conclusion can be your topic sentence. Support it with examples from the data.

Istanbul Past and Present

Characteristic	Constantinople in A.D. 540	Istanbul Today
Importance	Capital of Byzantine Empire, largest city in Byzantine Empire	Turkey's largest city
Population	About 500,000	About 10 million
Major Religion	Christianity	Islam
Sources of Wealth	Trade	Textiles, manufacturing, tourism
Language	Greek	Turkish
Challenges	Overpopulation, disease, earthquakes, attacks by foreigners	Overpopulation, earthquakes, pollution

Practice the Skill

Use the steps in Learn the Skill to transfer the information in the table above into a paragraph.

1. What is the title of the table? In your own words, state what the table is about.

2. What are the important headings? How do you find key information, such as the major religion of present-day Istanbul?

3. Note how Istanbul is similar to Constantinople and how it is different.

4. Which headings or topics represent the most important information? Are the similarities or the differences more important?

5. What is the most important thing you've learned about the two cities? Use your conclusion as the topic sentence, and support it with data from the table.

Apply the Skill

Study the table at the right, and draw a conclusion about the information in it. Write a paragraph that uses data from the table to support your conclusion.

The Christian Church Divides, A.D. 1054

Characteristic	Eastern Orthodox	Roman Catholic
Head of Church	Patriarch	Pope
Had Most Power Over Church	Emperor	Pope
Main Location	Eastern Europe	Western Europe
Language	Greek	Latin
Practices	• Priests could marry • Pope's authority was not recognized	• Priests could not marry • Pope had supreme authority

Prepare to Read

Objectives

In this section you will
1. Learn about the Arabian Peninsula, its nomadic people, and its centers of trade.
2. Find out about the life and mission of the Muslim prophet Muhammad.
3. Learn about Muslim beliefs.

Taking Notes

As you read this section, keep track of the most important ideas about the beginnings of Islam. Copy the outline started below, and add to it as you read.

> **I. The Arabian Peninsula**
>   **A. Nomadic Bedouins**
>   1.
>   2.
>   **B. Mecca: A center of trade**

Target Reading Skill

Preview and Predict
Making predictions about your text helps you set a purpose for reading and remember what you read. Before you begin, look at the headings, photos, and anything else that stands out. Then predict what the text might be about. For example, you might predict that this section will tell about the origins of Muslim beliefs. As you read, if what you learn doesn't support your prediction, revise your prediction.

Key Terms

- **Muhammad** (muh HAM ud) *n.* the prophet and founder of Islam
- **nomads** (NOH madz) *n.* people with no permanent home, who move from place to place in search of food, water, or pasture
- **caravan** (KA ruh van) *n.* a group of traders traveling together for safety
- **Mecca** (MEK uh) *n.* an Arabian trading center and Muhammad's birthplace
- **Muslim** (MUZ lum) *n.* a follower of Islam
- **mosque** (mahsk) *n.* a Muslim house of worship
- **Quran** (koo RAHN) *n.* the holy book of Islam

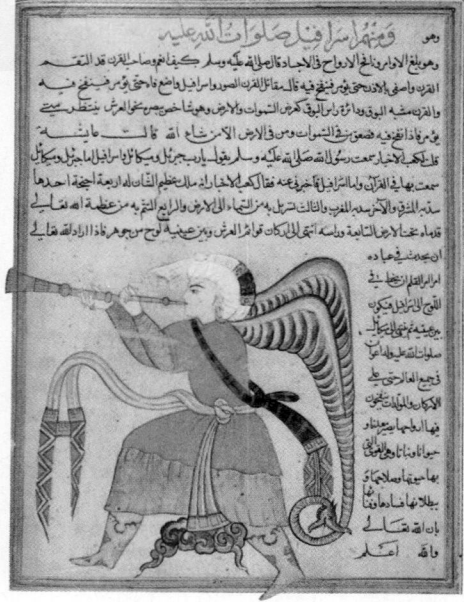

In this illustration, an angel's announcement is symbolized by the blowing of a horn.

The religion of Islam (IS lahm) teaches that in about 610, the prophet **Muhammad** (muh HAM ud) went into a cave in the Arabian mountains to pray. (A prophet is a person who is regarded as speaking for God.) It is said that while Muhammad was inside the cave, he heard the voice of an angel. God told Muhammad through the angel that there was only one God, that God had created people, and that God would teach His people. The angel told Muhammad that Muhammad was to be God's messenger.

According to Islamic teaching, Muhammad was frightened and unsure that he was worthy of such an important mission. But he obeyed. God continued to send Muhammad messages, which Muhammad shared with the people of the Arabian Peninsula. These teachings formed Islam, a religion that brought great changes to the region. In the centuries after Muhammad's death, the new religion spread to many parts of the world.

The Arabian Peninsula

In Muhammad's time, as today, much of the Arabian Peninsula was covered by desert. Although surrounded by water, the peninsula has no major rivers and receives little rainfall. Trade with neighboring peoples supported the growth of towns along trade routes. And many groups of Bedouins (BED oo inz) made their homes among the shifting sand dunes of the desert.

Nomadic Bedouins The Bedouins were **nomads,** or people who have no permanent home but move from place to place in search of food, water, and pasture. The Arabian desert yielded little food for the Bedouins or for their herds of sheep, camels, and goats. Water was also scarce—for people as well as for animals.

To make their way across the desert, the Bedouins followed traditional routes from one oasis to another. An oasis is a green area within a desert, fed by underground water. These all-important oases provided plenty of water for the nomads and their animals.

Because of their knowledge of the desert and its oases, the Bedouins also worked as guides for traders. They helped traders travel across the desert in large groups called **caravans.** These desert caravans depended on camels, which carried both people and their goods. Camels are sturdy animals with a special ability to store water for long periods.

Bedouins Today
These Bedouins in the Sinai desert of Egypt are still nomads like their ancestors. **Predict** *What kinds of events and conditions might prevent the Bedouins from continuing their traditional way of life?*

Mecca: A Center of Trade The oases on the Arabian Peninsula became busy trading centers. One of the most important was **Mecca** (MEK uh). From Mecca, great caravans traveled northwest to markets in what is now Syria. From Syria, goods could be shipped across the Mediterranean Sea to Europe. Other caravans traveled northeast from Mecca. They made a dangerous journey across the desert to markets in the area now known as Iraq. Trade was also conducted with Yemen to the south. Precious goods traded along these routes included perfume and spices, incense, expensive cloth, elephant tusks, and gold.

✓ **Reading Check** **Why did Bedouins make good guides for traders?**

Muhammad

Muhammad was born and grew up in the trading center of Mecca. His great-grandfather had been a wealthy merchant. However, by the time Muhammad was born in about 570, his family was poor. As a young man, Muhammad worked on caravans. His job took him to distant places, including Syria, which was then part of the Byzantine Empire.

Muhammad's Mission Muhammad liked to walk in the mountains outside Mecca. Troubled by problems he saw in society, he liked to be alone to pray and think. According to Islam, when Muhammad was 40 years old, he first heard God speak to him through the angel in the cave. God told him that people would submit to, or agree to obey, the one true God. In time, a person who accepted the teachings of Muhammad came to be known as a **Muslim** (MUZ lum), "a person who submits." The religion of Muslims is called Islam.

Many Arabs traveled to Mecca in order to pray at an ancient shrine called the Kaaba (KAH buh). Many people in Mecca thought Muhammad's teachings threatened their old gods. They feared that abandoning their old gods would end Mecca's importance as a religious center. People in Mecca also feared that Muhammad might gain political power. Although Islam taught that all people were brothers and sisters in a community established by God, few people in Mecca accepted his message.

Muhammad in Medina In 622, Muhammad and his followers were invited to Yathrib (yah THREEB), a city north of Mecca. The people there regarded Muhammad as a prophet. This movement of early Muslims is known as the hijra (hih JY ruh), or "the migration." The year of the hijra—622 in the calendar used in the United States—became year 1 on the Muslim calendar.

After the hijra, the name of Yathrib was changed to Medina. This name means "city" and is short for "city of the prophet." Medina quickly became an important Islamic center. But Islam did not remain limited to Medina. In 630, Muhammad returned to Mecca—this time in triumph. By the time Muhammad died two years later, the new religion of Islam had spread all across the Arabian Peninsula.

✔ **Reading Check** **Why did Muhammad go to Yathrib?**

Go Online
PHSchool.com Use Web Code
mup-0831 for an interactivity on the five pillars of Islam.

Muslim Belief

A muezzin (myoo EZ in), a man who calls Muslims to worship, looks out over the city and begins his loud call. The muezzin's voice echoes in all directions: "There is no god but God, and Muhammad is the messenger of God." In Arabic, the word for God is *Allah*. Five times each day, Muslims are called to worship in this way. And five times a day, every faithful Muslim stops whatever he or she is doing to pray.

Some Muslims gather in a house of worship called a **mosque** (mahsk). Others kneel outside. Wherever Muslims are in the world—in the Arabian Peninsula, in North Africa, or in the United States—they kneel in a direction that faces toward Mecca. "There is no god but God," the faithful respond, "and Muhammad is the messenger of God."

The Five Pillars of Islam Basic Muslim beliefs are expressed in the five pillars of Islam. These practices, shown in the table above, are the foundations of Islam. Muslims regard these pillars as sacred duties. The fifth pillar—the hajj (haj), or pilgrimage to the Kaaba—is required only of those who are able to travel to Mecca.

The Five Pillars of Islam

Pillar	Description
Declaration of Faith	Muslims must regularly declare the belief that there is only one God and Muhammad is God's messenger.
Prayer	Muslims must pray five times each day, facing in the direction of the holy city of Mecca.
Almsgiving	Muslims must give alms, or money that goes to the needy.
Fasting	Muslims must fast during daylight hours in the month of Ramadan.
Pilgrimage	Muslims must make a pilgrimage to Mecca at least one time in their lives if they are able.

Chart Skills

The photo above shows Muslim men and boys worshiping at a mosque in Brunei, in Southeast Asia. **Identify** Which pillar of Islam are they fulfilling? **Analyze Information** Which one of the five pillars would it be most difficult to fulfill? Explain why.

The Hajj
Muslims making a hajj to the Kaaba wear special white, seamless garments. The large photo shows a modern hajj. The small painting is from a 1410 manuscript. **Compare** *What can you conclude about this tradition by comparing the two pictures?*

Preview and Predict
Based on what you have read so far, is your prediction on target? If not, revise or change your prediction now.

The Quran The holy book of Islam is called the **Quran** (koo RAHN). According to Muslim belief it contains the messages God revealed to Muhammad, including the rules of Islam. Many Muslims have memorized the Quran. Muslims believe that the meaning and beauty of the Quran are best appreciated in its original language. Therefore, many converts to Islam learn Arabic. This shared language has helped unite Muslims from many regions.

Like the Jewish Bible and the Christian Bible, the Quran contains many kinds of writing, including stories, promises, warnings, and instructions. There is a reason for the similarity of the Quran to Jewish and Christian holy books. Muslims, like Jews and Christians, believe in one God. They regard Adam, Noah, Abraham, Moses, and Jesus as important people in their religious history. Muhammad saw himself as the last prophet in a long line of prophets that included all these men. Muhammad felt respect for Jews and Christians, whom he called "people of the Book."

The Role of Women Before Islam, in most of Arab society, women were not regarded as equal to men, and female children were not valued. The Quran, however, taught that men and women were spiritually equal. It also gave women more rights under the law, such as the right to inherit property and to get an education. Muslim women could not be forced to marry against their will, and they had the right to divorce.

A Split Among Muslims You have already read about a schism that split the Christian church at the time of the Byzantine Empire. A schism, or split, also occurred among followers of Islam.

In 656, Uthman (OOTH mahn), the leader of the Muslim community, was assassinated. His death split the Muslim world in two. Muslims disagreed over who should be their rightful leader. Over the next several decades, two main groups gradually emerged on opposite sides of this disagreement.

The smaller group, called Shiites (SHEE yts), argued that the ruler should be a man who was a direct descendant of Muhammad. They believed that Muhammad's descendants would be inspired by God, just as Muhammad had been. They felt that their leader should explain the meanings of the messages Muhammad received from God, which are found in the Quran.

The larger group, called Sunnis (SOO neez), argued that any truly religious Muslim man of Muhammad's tribe could lead the community. They believed that no one man, not even the leader of Islam, should tell Muslims what God's messages meant. The Sunnis argued that a group of Muslim scholars could best explain the Quran. Today, about 85 percent of all Muslims are Sunnis.

Illustrated manuscript pages from a 1500s Quran

✓ **Reading Check** **What issues split the Shiites and Sunnis?**

Section 2 Assessment

Key Terms
Review the key terms at the beginning of this section. Use each term in a sentence that explains its meaning.

Target Reading Skill
What did you predict about this section? How did your prediction guide your reading?

Comprehension and Critical Thinking
1. (a) Note What geographic feature covers most of the Arabian Peninsula?

(b) Identify Effects How did geography affect trade and settlement there?
(c) Conclude Why do you think the Bedouins became nomads?
2. (a) Recall What were the main events of Muhammad's life?
(b) Synthesize What are the main beliefs of Islam?
(c) Compare and Contrast What beliefs do Sunnis and Shiites share? Which beliefs separate them?

Writing Activity
Write a poem or a paragraph describing what it might have been like to travel in a caravan. How would it feel to ride a camel? To cross the desert? To stop for a rest at an oasis?

Writing Tip Review the illustrations in this section. Then think about the sights, sounds, and smells you would expect to experience as part of caravan life. Use vivid descriptive words and phrases to describe what you see and feel.

Focus On
Bedouin Life

The air is hot and dry. A blinding, bright sun scorches the sand. At times, a screaming wind sweeps across the land, blowing clouds of sand that block the sun. These are the desert lands of the Arabian Peninsula. By the time of the prophet Muhammad in the A.D. 600s, the Bedouins of Arabia had been thriving in the desert for hundreds of years. These nomadic peoples lived in tents and moved camp frequently in their search for water. Some of their descendants still live in the desert today.

Surviving in the Desert The ancient Bedouins depended upon the desert, the camel, their fellow tribe members, and the family tent. Plants gathered from the desert were used for food and medicine. Camels provided transportation, as well as milk, meat, and hides. Family members worked together to search for water and to herd their camels, goats, and sheep. The family tent sheltered the Bedouins in the harsh desert climate.

Women were responsible for the tents. They spun goats' hair into yarn to make the tent panels. When it was time to move their camp, the women took down the tents and then pitched them at the new campsite.

It was the men's job to herd camels and other livestock. Sometimes Bedouin men would raid villages or other tribes for goats, sheep, camels, and other goods.

The illustration at the right shows a Bedouin family in their tent. Bedouin women created jewelry, like the necklace shown at the top of this page.

Hospitality
Bedouin men served their guests thick, bitter coffee.

Goatskin Bag
Bags made from goatskin carried precious water.

Bedouin Coffee Pot
The Bedouins served coffee from copper or brass pots.

Water
Carried in goatskin bags, water came from oases and wells.

Cooking
Fires were fueled by camel dung, twigs, and dry plants.

Assessment

Identify Name the four things the Bedouins depended upon most.

Analyze How did the Bedouins survive in the desert?

Prepare to Read

Objectives

In this section you will
1. Find out how the religion of Islam spread.
2. Learn about the golden age of Islam under the rule of the caliphs.
3. Investigate the Ottoman Empire.

Taking Notes

As you read this section, jot down key events of early Muslim history and when they occurred. Copy the timeline below and use your data to complete it.

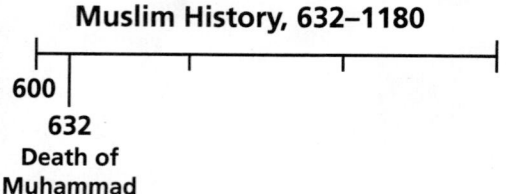

Muslim History, 632–1180

600
632
Death of
Muhammad

Target Reading Skill

Preview and Ask Questions Before you read this section, preview the headings and illustrations to see what the section is about. Then write two questions that will help you understand or remember something important in the section. For example, you might ask, "How did Islam spread beyond the Arabian Peninsula?" Then read to answer your question.

Key Terms

- **Omar Khayyam** (OH mahr ky AHM) *n.* a Muslim poet, mathematician, and astronomer
- **caliph** (KAY lif) *n.* a Muslim ruler
- **Sufis** (SOO feez) *n.* a Muslim group that believed they could draw closer to God through prayer, fasting, and a simple life
- **sultan** (SULTun) *n.* a Muslim ruler, particularly the ruler of the Ottoman Empire

The cover of a book of verses by Omar Khayyam

Almost one thousand years ago, Persia boasted great scientists, mathematicians, and poets. One man was all three. **Omar Khayyam** (OH mahr ky AHM) was a skilled Muslim astronomer, one of the most famous mathematicians in the world, and a great poet. The poems he wrote in the Persian language are still read today. This is one of his poems:

> **When I was a child, I sometimes went to a teacher. And sometimes I taught myself, but eventually I learned The limits to all knowledge: we come into this world upon the waters, we leave it on the wind.**
>
> —*Omar Khayyam*

Although Khayyam writes of limits to knowledge, his was a time when mathematics, science, and poetry were all making new breakthroughs and expanding the boundaries of knowledge. It was considered a golden age of Muslim civilization, and it took place across a wide geographic area.

The Spread of Islam

Within 150 years after Muhammad's death in 632, Islam spread west to North Africa, and into present-day Spain. It also spread north into Persia and east to the borders of northern India and China.

Many New Converts Arab merchants traveled to many parts of Asia and North Africa and along the Mediterranean coast. Many of these traders were Muslims, and they helped to spread their new religious beliefs. Arab armies also conquered neighboring regions. This was another way that Islam spread.

In 717, the Arabs attacked Constantinople, but they were unable to take the great fortress. Even so, most Christians who lived along the eastern and southern Mediterranean eventually converted to Islam. By the 700s, Muslims had also crossed from North Africa into Spain. In 732, Arab forces were defeated by European soldiers at the Battle of Tours, in present-day France. This battle halted the Muslim advance into Christian Europe.

The Battle of Tours

The Spread of Islam

MAP MASTER™ Skills Activity

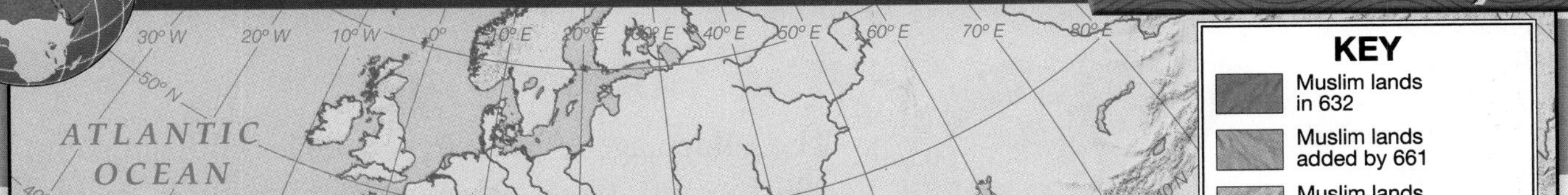

KEY

- Muslim lands in 632
- Muslim lands added by 661
- Muslim lands added by 800
- Muslim lands added by 1180
- Muslim lands added by 800 but lost by 1180
- Armenian and Crusader states, 1180
- • City

ATLANTIC OCEAN

Tours
FRANCE
SPAIN
Córdoba
Granada
Rome
Black Sea
Constantinople
Caspian Sea
NORTH AFRICA
Mediterranean Sea
Damascus
Euphrates R.
Tigris R.
Baghdad
PERSIA
Alexandria
Jerusalem
Cairo
SAHARA
EGYPT
Medina (Yathrib)
ARABIAN PENINSULA
Mecca
Muscat
Persian Gulf
Arabian Sea
INDIA
Bay of Bengal
Nile R.
Red Sea
Gulf of Aden
INDIAN OCEAN

0 miles 1,000
0 kilometers 1,000
Lambert Azimuthal Equal Area

Movement Islam began to spread even during Muhammad's lifetime. **Identify** When did Islam spread to North Africa? Where did the Muslims lose lands after 800? **Conclude** What role do you think the Mediterranean Sea played in the spread of Islam?

Go Online PHSchool.com Use Web Code **lgp-8123** for step-by-step map skills practice.

Preview and Ask Questions

Ask a question that will help you learn something important from the paragraph at the right. Now read the paragraph, and answer your question.

Reasons for Success In the centuries before Muhammad, Arab peoples had not been able to conquer neighboring regions. The strong Roman Empire made invasions of these lands nearly impossible. And the later Byzantine and Persian empires successfully blocked Arabs from advancing north. So why were the Muslims successful after Muhammad's death?

By that time, the three empires that might have stopped the Arab expansion north and east were either defeated or weakened. Also, a shared religion now united the Arab peoples into one community. And once they began to work together, the Muslims quickly grew powerful.

Under Muslim Rule Unlike Byzantine leaders of the time—who did not accept different religions—Muslims tolerated other faiths. Muslim rulers allowed Christians and Jews to practice their own religions and pursue their own business affairs. Non-Muslim citizens did have fewer rights than Muslims, however. For example, they were forbidden to carry weapons and could not serve in the military. They also paid a special tax, which helped support the government.

✔ **Reading Check** **Compare Muslim rulers and Byzantine rulers.**

A Royal Gift
The caliph Harun ar-Rashid presented this water jug to Charlemagne, the ruler of a Christian empire in Europe. He hoped to form an alliance with Charlemagne. *Infer What can you infer about Harun from this gift?*

The Golden Age

The golden age of Muslim culture lasted from about 800 to 1100. Great advances were made in mathematics and science, and lasting works of literature and architecture were created. Why did so much happen at that time?

The Age of the Caliphs One reason was the great wealth of the Arab world. Under Muslim rulers called caliphs (KAY lifs), an empire developed and grew rich. Its wealth came both from the many lands it controlled and from trade. Baghdad was the capital of the Muslim empire during the golden age. Find it on the map titled The Spread of Islam on page 301. You can see that Baghdad, like Constantinople, was a natural center for trade. With your finger, trace a route from India to Baghdad. Now trace a route from the Mediterranean Sea to Baghdad. Traders from all over the world brought their goods to the caliph's court. The caliph was considered to be Muhammad's successor, or the next person who had the right to rule.

Achievements of the Golden Age

Arab scholars not only created new works but also built on the earlier achievements of other cultures. This approach led Muslim scholars to make great advances in mathematics, science, and literature.

Mathematics and Science Arab scholars studied both Greek and Indian mathematics. They learned about the idea of zero from Indian scholars. And they borrowed the so-called Arabic numerals that we use today from India, too. The Muslim mathematician al-Khwarizmi (al KWAHR iz mee) wrote a book explaining Indian arithmetic. He also helped invent algebra. These advances later formed the basis for great discoveries in astronomy, physics, and chemistry.

The famous Muslim scientist and philosopher Ibn Sina (IB un SEE nah) lived from 980 to 1037. Also known as Avicenna (ahv ih SEN uh), he organized the medical knowledge of the Greeks and Arabs into the *Canon of Medicine.*

Literature Muslim writers created many lasting works of literature. Poetry was particularly important in the Islamic world. One group of Muslims used poetry to teach their ideas and beliefs.

This group, called the **Sufis** (SOO feez), were Muslims who believed that they could draw close to God through prayer, fasting, and a simple life. They taught that careful attention could unlock the world's mysteries. Sufi missionaries also helped spread Islam to Central Asia, India, and Africa.

The most famous Sufi poet, Rumi (ROO mee), wrote:

> **The morning wind spreads its fresh smell.**
> **We must get up and take that in,**
> **that wind that lets us live.**
> **Breathe before it's gone.**

—*Rumi*

✔ Reading Check **What did Muslim mathematicians invent?**

Arab Contributions to Mathematics and Science

Medicine
Arabs trained the first professional pharmacists, who sold spices, herbs, and other medicines to the public.

Mathematics
Arab mathematicians made important contributions to algebra. They studied formulas like this one. It explains how to find the length of one side of a right triangle when you know the length of the other sides.

Machines
Water-driven machines fascinated Arab scientists. In this diagram, water falling into the cups causes the globe at the top to turn.

The Ottoman sultan, Selim II, in the blue jacket, with his troops

The Ottoman Empire

After about 900, the power of the caliphs declined. In 1258, invading Mongols killed the last caliph in Baghdad. Much of the Muslim world was now controlled by Mongols and Turks, peoples originally from Central Asia.

A group of Muslim Turks, the Ottomans, began to expand their territory around 1300. With their strong armies, they conquered the last bits of the Byzantine Empire in present-day Turkey and Greece. The Byzantine capital, Constantinople, fell in 1453. The Ottoman ruler, or **sultan,** now held much of southeastern Europe and Turkey. Over the next 200 years, the Ottomans conquered most of southeastern Europe, North Africa, and the Middle East. Once again, much of the Muslim world was united under one ruler.

The Ottoman lands were also home to many Christians and Jews. The Ottomans treated these groups with tolerance. This tolerance helped to strengthen the Ottoman Empire.

Over time, however, the empire weakened. Corrupt officials used their jobs for private gain. Meanwhile, European nations grew stronger. After Europeans defeated the Ottomans in 1683, the Ottoman Empire began a long decline.

✓ **Reading Check** **How did the Ottomans gain power?**

Section 3 Assessment

Key Terms
Review the key terms at the beginning of this section. Use each term in a sentence that explains its meaning.

Target Reading Skill
What questions helped you learn something important from this section? What are the answers to your questions?

Comprehension and Critical Thinking
1. (a) Recall Describe the two main ways that Islam spread beyond the Arabian Peninsula.

(b) Synthesize Information Why might the Arabs have chosen Baghdad as their capital?
(c) Generalize How do geography and trade contribute to a city's prosperity and power?
2. (a) Identify Name three Arab contributions to mathematics and science.
(b) Analyze How do these contributions combine borrowed knowledge and new ideas?
3. (a) Recall What earlier empire did the Ottomans conquer?
(b) Infer How might control of this earlier empire, including its capital city, have increased the power of the Ottomans?

Writing Activity
Write an essay explaining why the Ottoman sultans might have adopted a policy of religious tolerance. Begin with a statement of your basic argument and then support it with reasons and facts about the Ottomans or about other civilizations you have studied.

For: An activity on Islam's golden age
Visit: PHSchool.com
Web Code: lgd-8103

Review and Assessment

◆ Chapter Summary

Justinian

Section 1: The Byzantine Empire

- After Constantine established his capital at Constantinople, the city became the capital of the powerful Byzantine Empire. It grew rich from its location at the intersection of several trade routes.
- Justinian, one of the greatest Byzantine emperors, organized a system of laws called Justinian's Code.
- After Justinian's death, the Byzantine Empire shrank in size and power. It later enjoyed a second golden age. A schism split the Christian church into eastern and western branches.

Section 2: The Beginnings of Islam

- Although much of the Arabian Peninsula is covered by desert, important cities, such as Mecca, grew up on trade routes.
- The Muslim prophet Muhammad preached in Mecca and Medina. His teachings became the religion of Islam.
- The Five Pillars of Islam and the Quran are the basis of Muslim beliefs. A dispute among Muslims led to the split between Shiites and Sunnis.

Section 3: Muslim Civilization

- After the death of Muhammad, the religion of Islam spread to many neighboring regions by both trade and conquest.
- During the golden age of Islam, caliphs ruled the Muslim world, which made great achievements in mathematics, science, and literature.
- The sultans of the Ottoman Empire later ruled over much of the Muslim world.

A caliph's water jug

◆ Key Terms

Match each key term with its definition from the list at the right.

1. mosque
2. sultan
3. nomads
4. caliph
5. Justinian
6. caravan
7. schism
8. Omar Khayyam

A   a Muslim ruler

B   a group of traders traveling together for safety

C   emperor of the Byzantine Empire

D   ruler of the Ottoman Empire

E   Muslim house of worship

F   a Muslim astronomer, mathematician, and poet

G   people with no permanent home, who move from place to place

H   a split, particularly in a church or religion

◆ Comprehension and Critical Thinking

9. (a) **Recall** In what part of the old Roman Empire was Constantinople located?
   (b) **Identify Cause and Effect** How did Constantinople's location affect the culture that developed there?
   (c) **Compare and Contrast** What enabled the eastern part of the Roman Empire to survive after the western Roman Empire "fell"?

10. (a) **Define** What was Justinian's Code?
    (b) **Infer** How did Justinian's Code help make the Byzantine Empire strong and successful?

11. (a) **Describe** How did Muhammad first receive God's message?
    (b) **Infer** Why do you think Muhammad did not give up preaching when few people listened?

12. (a) **Recall** What do Muslims, Jews, and Christians have in common?
    (b) **Contrast** How do the beliefs of Sunni and Shiite Muslims differ?

13. (a) **Recall** When and where did the golden age of Muslim civilization occur?
    (b) **Synthesize** Explain in your own words why these years are called a golden age.

◆ Skills Practice

Using a Table to Write a Paragraph In the Skills for Life activity in this chapter, you learned how to use the data in a table to write a paragraph. Review the steps you followed to learn the skill.

Now review the table The Five Pillars of Islam on page 295. Use the data in the table to draw a conclusion about the topic. Write a paragraph that states your conclusion and that uses data from the table as supporting details.

◆ Writing Activity: Language Arts

A monologue is a speech by one person. In drama, a monologue is spoken directly to the audience. Choose one of the rulers you have read about in this chapter. Write a monologue that this ruler might speak in a theatrical performance. It can be about the person's whole life or about one important event. Do further research on the ruler if you wish. You may want to perform your monologue for your class.

MAP MASTER™ Skills Activity

Place Location For each place or feature listed below, write the letter from the map that shows its location.

1. Rome
2. Mecca
3. Constantinople
4. Mediterranean Sea
5. Bosporus
6. Baghdad
7. Arabian Peninsula

Go Online
PHSchool.com Use Web Code **lgp-8133** for an **interactive map.**

The Byzantine Empire and the Spread of Islam

Standardized Test Prep

Test-Taking Tips

Some questions on standardized tests ask you to evaluate a source for a research assignment. Read the passage below. Then use the tip to help you answer the sample question.

Vera is writing a research paper about Justinian's Code. At the school library, she found four books that she might use.

Think It Through Even if you don't know about Justinian's Code, you can eliminate A because it is fiction—an invented story. You can also rule out C because it is about a merchant's travels, not about Justinian's Code. That leaves B and D. Justinian's Code refers to laws, not to copying Roman and Greek books. The correct answer is B.

Pick the letter that best answers the question.

Which one of the following books would be best for Vera's topic?

A *Justinian's Bride*—a novel about the Empress Theodora

B *The Birth of Law*—a nonfiction book about the Byzantine legal system

C *The Journal of Ignatius*—a firsthand account of a merchant's travels during the time of Justinian

D *The Rescue of Knowledge*—the story of how Byzantine scholars copied and cared for books of ancient Rome and Greece

TIP Rule out choices that don't make sense. Then choose the best answer from the remaining choices.

Practice Questions

Use the tip above and other tips in this book to help you answer the following questions.

1. Miguel's history class has been studying the Byzantine Empire. Miguel has decided to write a research paper about the empire's capital, Constantinople. He would like to find out the population of Constantinople at the time of Justinian's rule.

   Which one of the following would be the best choice for this information?

   A *An Atlas of Modern Turkey*—a nonfiction book that includes maps and factual data

   B *Our Trip to Istanbul*—a new Web site that tells about a family's vacation to the city formerly called Constantinople

   C *An Atlas of the Ancient World*—a nonfiction book that includes historical maps and other historical data

   D *Population Growth of Major U.S. Cities*—a nonfiction book that includes charts and maps

Pick the letter of the word or phrase that best completes each sentence.

2. Muslims are called to worship _____.

   A once a day
   B four times a month
   C five times a day
   D once a year

3. Constantine was the first _____ to rule the Roman Empire.

   A Muslim
   B Jew
   C Sufi
   D Christian

4. The _____ links the Black Sea and the Sea of Marmara, which flows into the Mediterranean Sea.

   A Bosporus
   B Arabian Peninsula
   C Mecca
   D hijra

Use Web Code **lga-8103**
for a **Chapter 10 self-test.**

Chapter 11

Civilizations of Africa

Chapter Preview

This chapter will introduce you to the early history of Africa and to some of its great civilizations.

Section 1
Africa and the Bantu

Section 2
Kingdoms of West Africa

Section 3
East Africa's Great Trading Centers

Target Reading Skill

Clarifying Meaning In this chapter, you will focus on clarifying meaning by learning how to reread, how to paraphrase, and how to summarize.

▶ Ruins of the Great Mosque of Kilwa, in present-day Tanzania, East Africa

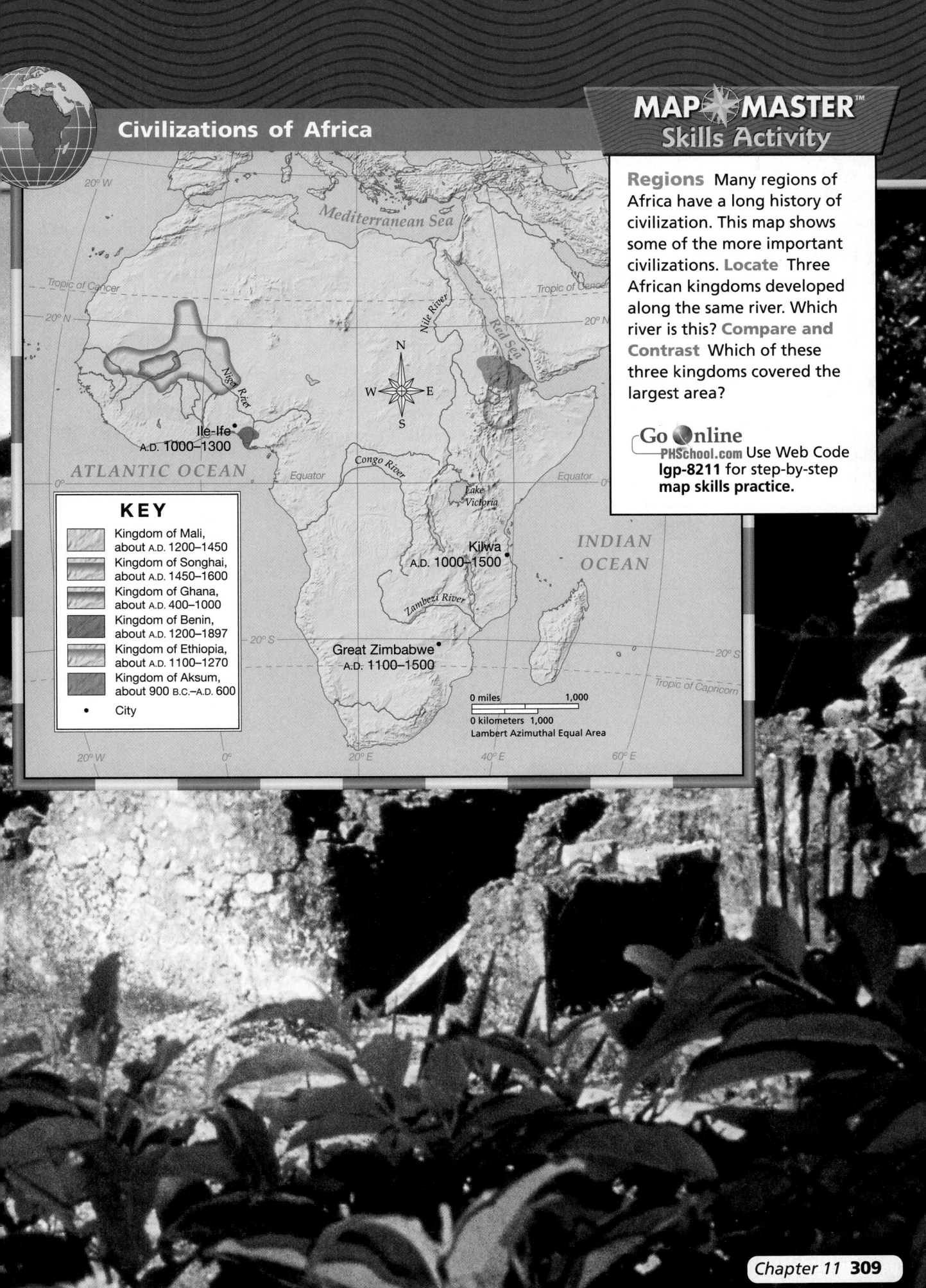

Civilizations of Africa

Mediterranean Sea

20° W

Tropic of Cancer

Tropic of Cancer

20° N

20° N

Nile River

Red Sea

N
W   E
S

Ile-Ife
A.D. 1000–1300

Niger River

ATLANTIC OCEAN

Congo River

Equator

Equator

Lake Victoria

Kilwa
A.D. 1000–1500

INDIAN OCEAN

Zambezi River

20° S

Great Zimbabwe
A.D. 1100–1500

20° S

Tropic of Capricorn

20° W   0°   20° E   40° E   60° E

Regions Many regions of Africa have a long history of civilization. This map shows some of the more important civilizations. **Locate** Three African kingdoms developed along the same river. Which river is this? **Compare and Contrast** Which of these three kingdoms covered the largest area?

Go Online
PHSchool.com Use Web Code **lgp-8211** for step-by-step **map skills practice.**

KEY

	Kingdom of Mali, about A.D. 1200–1450
	Kingdom of Songhai, about A.D. 1450–1600
	Kingdom of Ghana, about A.D. 400–1000
	Kingdom of Benin, about A.D. 1200–1897
	Kingdom of Ethiopia, about A.D. 1100–1270
	Kingdom of Aksum, about 900 B.C.–A.D. 600
•	City

0 miles   1,000
0 kilometers 1,000
Lambert Azimuthal Equal Area

Section 1

Africa and the Bantu

Prepare to Read

Objectives

In this section, you will
1. Learn about the physical geography of Africa.
2. Find out about the Bantu and their movement across the continent.

Taking Notes

As you read this section, look for information about the major physical features of Africa. Copy the table below, and record your findings in it.

Physical Features of Africa	
Deserts	• •
Savannas	• •
Rain Forests	• •

Target Reading Skill

Reread or Read Ahead If you do not understand a passage, reread it to look for connections among the words and sentences. Reading ahead can also help. Words and ideas may be clarified further on.

Key Terms

- **migration** (my GRAY shun) *n.* the movement from one country or region to settle in another
- **Bantu** (BAN too) *n.* a large group of central and southern Africans who speak related languages
- **savanna** (suh VAN uh) *n.* an area of grassland with scattered trees and bushes
- **Sahara** (suh HA ruh) *n.* a huge desert stretching across most of North Africa
- **oral history** (AWR ul HIS tuh ree) *n.* accounts of the past that people pass down by word of mouth
- **clan** (klan) *n.* a group of families who trace their roots to the same ancestor

Zulu women in traditional dress in South Africa

About 4,000 years ago, many families left the places where they lived in West Africa. They would never return to their homeland. Some families had to climb over rocky hills. Others journeyed through forests or across lands baked by the sun. Mothers, fathers, and children carried everything they owned with them. After traveling for many miles, these people settled somewhere new.

No one knows exactly why they first moved. The population may have grown very quickly. If so, there may not have been enough land and resources to support all of the people. Over many years, later generations moved farther away from their original homes. They kept searching for better land for farming. Over time, their **migration** (my GRAY shun), or movement from one region to settle in another, took them across most of Africa south of the Equator. Today, their descendants number more than 200 million. The name **Bantu** (BAN too) describes both this large group of Africans and the related languages they speak.

Africa's Physical Geography

Look at the map titled Africa: Natural Vegetation. Notice the tropical rain forests that are located on either side of the Equator. They have hot, moist climates.

Surrounding these forests are bands of **savanna,** areas of grassland with scattered trees and bushes. Much of Africa is savanna. Africa's lions, zebras, and elephants live mainly on the savannas. Deserts stretch north and south of the savannas. The **Sahara** (suh HA ruh) is a desert stretching across most of North Africa. It is the world's largest desert. The Sahara is a hot, dry place of sand dunes and rocky mountains. A band of lakes, deep valleys, and rugged mountains runs north to south through East Africa.

Africa's physical geography has affected its people's ways of life. For example, there is little farming in Africa's deserts, because there is too little water. People herd cattle on the savannas, but cattle cannot survive in the rain forests. Flies and other pests in the rain forests carry diseases that are deadly for cattle.

An Oasis in the Sahara
An oasis (oh AY sis) is an area of vegetation within a desert, fed by springs and underground water.
Infer How might oases help travelers crossing a desert?

Africa: Natural Vegetation

Tropic of Cancer

SAHARA

Tropic of Cancer

20° N

Nile

20° N

Niger R.

0°

Equator

0°

Congo

N

W   E

S

Zambezi R.

20° S

20° S

Tropic of Capricorn

KEY

- Tropical rain forest
- Coniferous forest
- Mediterranean forest
- Tropical savanna
- Temperate grassland
- Desert scrub
- Desert (no vegetation)

20° W   0°   20° E   40° E   60° E

0 miles   1,500
0 kilometers   1,500
Lambert Azimuthal Equal Area

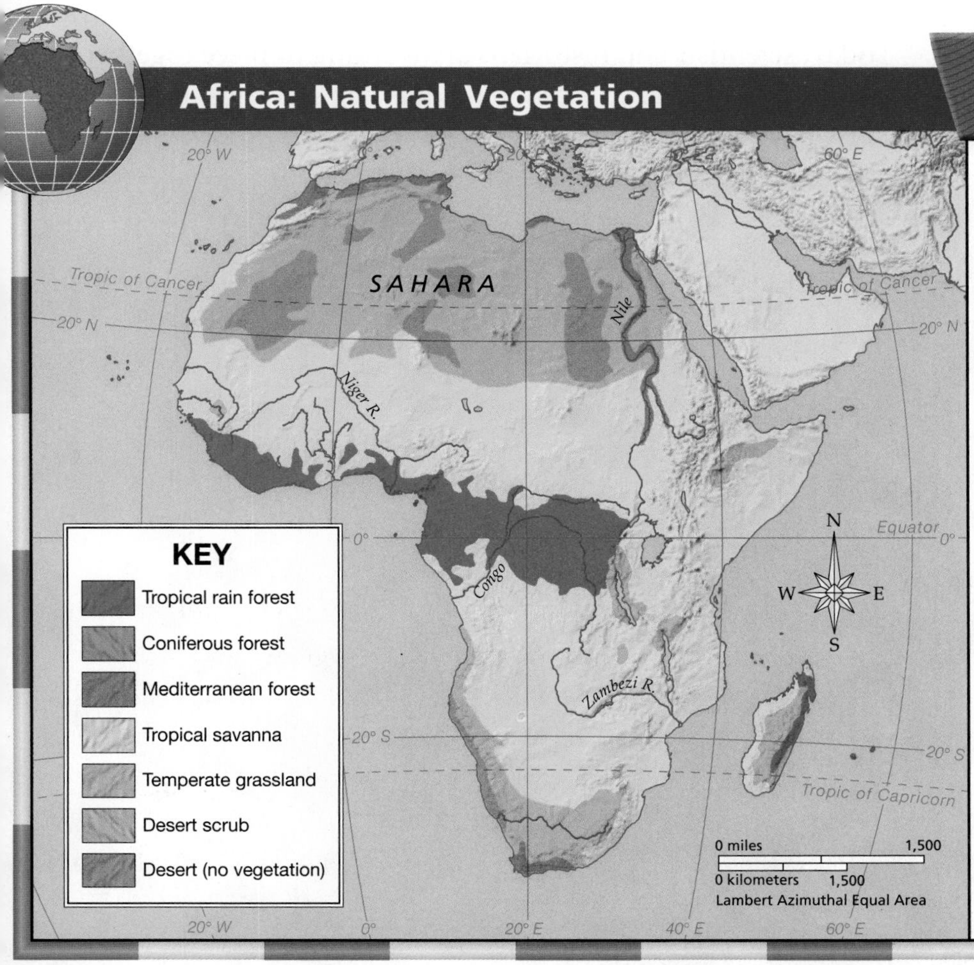

MAP MASTER™
Skills Activity

Human-Environment Interaction Deserts and rain forests are barriers to travel. Each area of natural vegetation supports different kinds of crops and livestock, but few crops or animals can survive in deserts.
Describe Which type of natural vegetation covers the largest area in Africa? Which occurs only at the northern and southern edges of the continent? **Infer** If people need crops and livestock for food, which parts of Africa do you think would have the fewest people?

Go Online
PHSchool.com Use Web Code lgp-8221 for step-by-step map skills practice.

Groups that share the same environment may live differently. For example, Mbuti (em BOO tee) people of Africa's rain forest live mainly by hunting animals and gathering plants, but neighboring peoples live mainly by farming.

✓ **Reading Check** **How do Africa's physical features affect people's ways of life?**

The Bantu Migrations

The physical barriers formed by lakes, forests, mountains, and rivers did not stop the movement of people across Africa. The map titled Bantu Migrations, on page 313, traces the major routes of the Bantu people. These migrations continued for more than 1,000 years. They are among the largest population movements in all of human history.

The History of Sub-Saharan Africa Historians know a great deal about North Africa's history. But they have only a sketchy knowledge of the history of Africa south of the Sahara. That area is called sub-Saharan Africa. Until modern times, the Sahara cut off this larger part of Africa from Europe. European historians have found it difficult to study sub-Saharan Africa. Today, scientists and historians are working to piece together the history of this area. In many ways, it is like solving a puzzle.

Target Skill

Reread
Reread the last four paragraphs, under the heading Africa's Physical Geography, to understand how Africa's physical features might have been a barrier to movement.

The Zambezi River plunges over Victoria Falls, on the Zambia-Zimbabwe border.

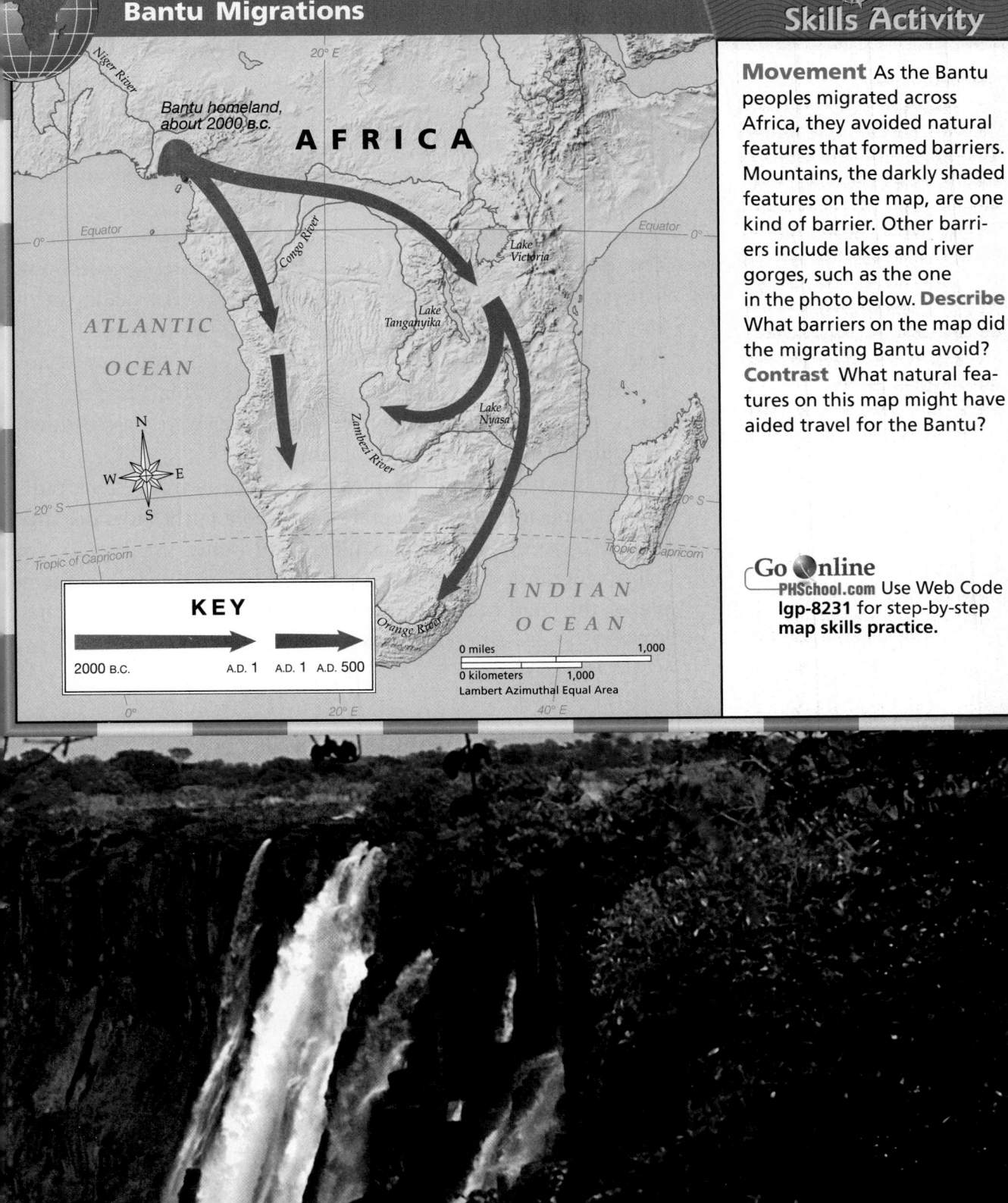

Bantu Migrations

AFRICA

Bantu homeland, about 2000 B.C.

Niger River

20° E

Equator

Congo River

ATLANTIC OCEAN

Lake Victoria

Lake Tanganyika

Lake Nyasa

Zambezi River

N
W E
S

20° S

Tropic of Capricorn

Orange River

INDIAN OCEAN

40° E

KEY

2000 B.C. → A.D. 1   A.D. 1 → A.D. 500

0 miles 1,000
0 kilometers 1,000
Lambert Azimuthal Equal Area

Movement As the Bantu peoples migrated across Africa, they avoided natural features that formed barriers. Mountains, the darkly shaded features on the map, are one kind of barrier. Other barriers include lakes and river gorges, such as the one in the photo below. **Describe** What barriers on the map did the migrating Bantu avoid? **Contrast** What natural features on this map might have aided travel for the Bantu?

Go Online
PHSchool.com Use Web Code **lgp-8231** for step-by-step map skills practice.

Links Across
Time

Bantu Languages As the Bantu speakers moved through Africa, they also spread their languages. Today, more than 200 million Africans speak Bantu languages. In fact, about 500 of the languages spoken in Africa south of the Sahara belong to the Bantu language family.

One reason this puzzle is difficult is that the wood and clay that many African peoples used for building have disintegrated. Even iron tools and weapons have not lasted, because iron rusts fairly quickly. However, modern techniques and inventions have helped scientists uncover new information. Stories told by traditional African storytellers have led to new areas of exploration. That is because these stories are often **oral history,** accounts of the past that people pass down by word of mouth.

The Bantu In early times, most Bantu-speaking peoples were fishers, farmers, and herders. Their villages were made up of families from the same **clan** (klan), or group of families who traced their roots to the same ancestor. Many of these clans traced their ancestry through mothers rather than fathers. For this reason, property and positions of power were passed down through the mother's side of the family.

The Bantu-speaking peoples moved slowly from their traditional homelands. Each generation moved a fairly short distance in their search for better farmland and better grazing. As the Bantu migrated, they entered different environments. In many places, they had to change the way they lived. For example, they learned to raise different crops or different kinds of animals.

These women in Windhoek, Namibia, belong to a present-day Bantu group, the Herero.

The Spread of Bantu Culture Often, Bantu people moved into areas where other people already lived. When this happened, they sometimes joined the groups living there. The older cultures then usually adapted to Bantu culture. For example, the Bantu introduced crops such as yams to other parts of Africa. At other times, however, the Bantu forced the people already living there to leave their homes.

As the Bantu migrated, they also carried a knowledge of metalworking with them. Iron tools gave the Bantu more control over their environment than older cultures had. With hard axes, they could cut down trees and clear the land. Their sharp, iron-headed spears and arrows were powerful weapons for hunting and for warfare.

These migrations continued over many generations, with groups moving whenever an area became crowded. In time, the Bantu had settled throughout Central and Southern Africa.

✓ **Reading Check** What kinds of skills did the Bantu carry with them?

Making Iron Tools
Bantu peoples heated rocks containing iron in furnaces to produce a lump of iron, shown above at the far left. They then gradually hammered it to shape a useful tool, such as the hoe above at the right. **Draw Conclusions** *How might iron tools have given the Bantu an advantage over people who lacked metal tools?*

Section 1 Assessment

Key Terms
Review the key terms at the beginning of this section. Use each term in a sentence that explains its meaning.

Target Reading Skill
What were you able to clarify about Africa's physical features by rereading?

Comprehension and Critical Thinking
1. (a) Identify Describe the main physical features of Africa.

(b) Synthesize Information How do Africa's physical features affect people's ways of life?
2. (a) Recall Over how many years did the Bantu migrations occur?
(b) Summarize Tell what happened when the Bantu met other African peoples.
(c) Conclude Why are the Bantu migrations an important part of African history?

Writing Activity
Consider the Bantu people's long history of migration and adaptation to new environments. Write a paragraph to answer the following question: What does this history suggest about the kind of people the Bantu were?

For: An activity on the Bantu migration
Visit: PHSchool.com
Web Code: lgd-8201

Grace was writing a paper about the Nok culture, the earliest known Iron Age culture in West Africa. She found this passage in a book called *Great Civilizations of Ancient Africa,* published in 1971. It was written by the historian Lester Brooks. Was this passage a good source for Grace's paper?

"The Nok peoples are known to have had a sophisticated agricultural society and . . . the ability to produce weapons of iron at this early time. They undoubtedly must have had relations—peaceful or otherwise—with other peoples over a wide expanse of the African interior. . . .

"But the truth . . . is that we just do not know who the Nok peoples were or how they lived. We have no written records, we have no legends or myths that explain them."

Nok statue

All books are not equally reliable. Use the skill below to help you determine how reliable a piece of writing is.

Learn the Skill

To decide whether a piece of writing is reliable, use the following steps:

1 **Look at the date of the source.** A source might have been written near the time of an event or many years later. Eyewitness accounts can tell you how an event was understood at the time it happened. Later writing may be based on respected research. New discoveries might have been made since the passage above was written.

2 **Identify the author's qualifications and purpose.** A "historian" should be a reliable source. But think about the sentence beginning, "The Nok peoples are known to have had a . . ." Who is it who *knows?* Where might this author have gotten his information?

3 **Decide whether the author has a bias.** Look for opinions, beliefs that cannot be proved. "They undoubtedly must have had relations . . ." is an opinion, not a fact. Also look for loaded words and phrases. The word *sophisticated* gives a positive impression that may or may not be accurate. Sometimes biased writers leave out information that does not support their bias.

4 **Decide how reliable the source is and why.** Consider your purpose: Are you writing about how an event seemed to the people who experienced it? Or, do you need the latest research to support your conclusions about the event?

The following passage is from *Travels in Asia and Africa 1325–1354*, written by a North African merchant named Ibn Battutah. He describes a journey through the Sahara.

"[W]e passed ten days of discomfort because the water there is bitter and the place is plagued with flies. . . . We passed a caravan on the way and they told us that some of their party had become separated from them. We found one of them dead under a shrub of the sort that grows in the sand. . . ."

Practice the Skill

Read the passage above. Then follow the steps in Learn the Skill to decide if it is a reliable source.

1 When was the passage written? Would this information be more reliable if it had been written more recently? Explain why or why not.

2 What qualifies the author to describe the Sahara? Do you think he was an accurate observer?

3 Identify an example of loaded language in the passage. Could this statement be proved true or false? Is it possible that the writer has left important information out of his account?

4 Do you consider this passage a reliable source? How might your purpose in using the passage affect your decision?

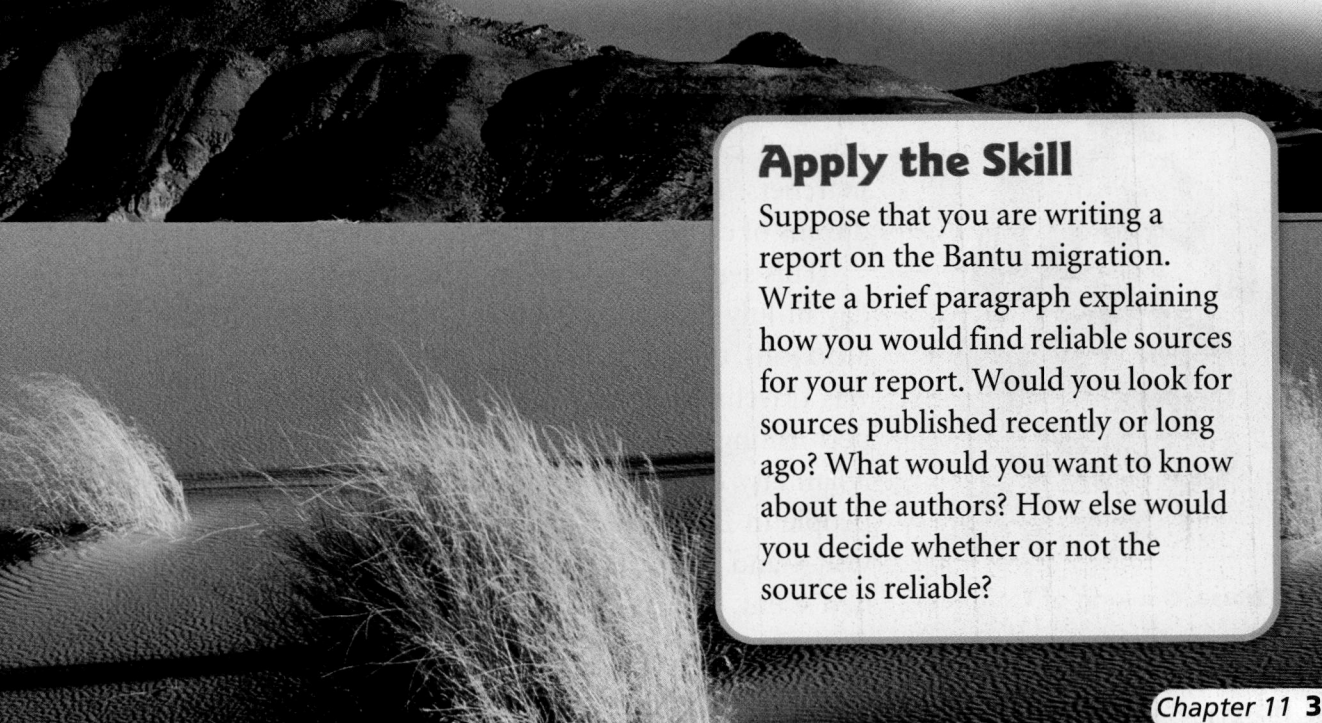

Sand dunes in the Sahara

Apply the Skill

Suppose that you are writing a report on the Bantu migration. Write a brief paragraph explaining how you would find reliable sources for your report. Would you look for sources published recently or long ago? What would you want to know about the authors? How else would you decide whether or not the source is reliable?

Kingdoms of West Africa

Prepare to Read

Objectives

In this section, you will
1. Learn about the trading kingdoms of the West African savanna.
2. Investigate the kingdoms of the West African rain forests.

Taking Notes

As you read this section, look for the main ideas and details about different African cultures. Create an outline of the section using the example below as a model.

```
I. Kingdoms of the savanna
   A. Ghana
      1.
      2.
   B.
II.
```

🎯 Target Reading Skill

Paraphrase When you paraphrase, you restate what you have read in your own words. For example, you could paraphrase the first paragraph below this way: "Thousands of people and dozens of camels carrying gold marched in a group."

As you read this section, paraphrase the information after each red or blue heading.

Key Terms

- **Mansa Musa** (MAHN sah MOO sah) *n.* a king of Mali in the 1300s
- **Mali** (MAH lee) *n.* a rich kingdom of the West African savanna
- **Ghana** (GAH nuh) *n.* the first West African kingdom based on the gold and salt trade
- **Songhai** (SAWNG hy) *n.* a powerful kingdom of the West African savanna
- **Ile-Ife** (EE lay EE fay) *n.* the capital of a kingdom of the West African rain forest
- **Benin** (beh NEEN) *n.* a kingdom of the West African rain forest

Mansa Musa, the king of Mali

Soldiers whose swords hung from gold chains rode horses decorated with gold. Hundreds of government officials marched along with the soldiers. Thousands of slaves, each one dressed in silk and carrying a staff made of gold, also accompanied the marchers. The procession included more than 60,000 people and dozens of camels, each camel loaded with many pounds of gold.

This sight greeted the astonished people of Cairo, Egypt, one day in July 1324. It was the caravan of **Mansa Musa** (MAHN sah MOO sah), the powerful king of Mali, in West Africa. The caravan was traveling from Mali across North Africa. Mansa Musa was performing his duty as a Muslim by traveling to the Southwest Asian city of Mecca, the holiest city of Islam. Many years later, people in Egypt were still talking about Mansa Musa's amazing visit—and about the amount of gold that he and his officials had spent.

Kingdoms of the Savanna

Mansa Musa ruled **Mali** (MAH lee), a rich kingdom of the West African savanna. The kingdoms of the savanna controlled important trade routes across the Sahara. The Niger River, which flows through the region, was another important trade route. Traders traveling through these lands had to pay taxes on all their goods. This made the kingdoms rich. In return, the rulers kept peace and order throughout the land. Thus, merchants—and their caravans of valuable goods—could travel safely from one place to another.

Ghana, a Kingdom Built on Trade Salt and gold were the basis of West African trade. Most of the salt came from mines in the central Sahara. Salt was very valuable. People needed it to flavor food, to preserve meat, and to maintain good health. Salt was scarce in the rain forest region. So people from the forest region of West Africa sold gold in exchange for salt. Some gold was sold to traders on their way to North Africa. These traders returned with glass and other precious North African goods. Traders could travel hundreds of miles across the dry Sahara because their camels could travel for days without water.

The first West African kingdom to be based on the wealth of the salt and gold trade was **Ghana** (GAH nuh). By about A.D. 400, the people of Ghana took control of the trade routes across the Sahara. Ghana's location was ideal. Find Ghana on the map titled Civilizations of Africa, on page 309. Ghana was just north of the rich gold fields. Land routes south from the Sahara went through Ghana. By about A.D 800, Ghana was a major trading kingdom.

Go **Online**
PHSchool.com Use Web Code
mup-0832 for an interactivity on Mansa Musa.

The Salt Trade in Africa
Camel caravans like the one shown at the bottom of the page carried slabs of salt from salt mines in the Sahara. Slabs of salt were traded in markets like the one below, in Mopti, Mali.
Apply Information *When traders from the forest region bought salt, what might they have offered in exchange?*

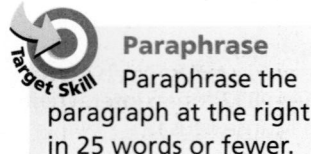
Ghana's capital, Kumbi Saleh, was divided into two cities. One was the center of trade. The other was the royal city, where the king had his court and handed down his decisions. Around A.D. 1000, the power of Ghana began to weaken. Invaders from the north overran the capital and other cities. By the 1200s, Ghana had broken into small, independent states. Soon, most of the trade in the area was controlled by a powerful new kingdom, the kingdom of Mali.

The Powerful Kingdom of Mali Mali was centered in the Upper Niger Valley. Under the leadership of Sundiata (sun JAH tah), who united the kingdom about 1230, Mali took control of the salt and gold trade. Sundiata conquered surrounding areas and increased the size of the kingdom. By 1255, when Sundiata died, Mali had grown rich from trade. It had become the most powerful kingdom in West Africa. Mali continued to grow in the years after Sundiata's death.

In 1312, Mansa Musa became ruler of Mali. By this time, traders from North Africa had brought a new religion, Islam, to West Africa. Muslims, or people who practice Islam, worship one god. Mansa Musa greatly expanded his kingdom and made Islam the official religion. Mansa Musa's trip to the holy city of Mecca created new ties between Mali and the Muslim peoples of North Africa and Southwest Asia.

The Great Mosque at Djenné
The mosque below is in the city of Djenné, an important trading center in the kingdoms of Mali and Songhai. A mosque is a Muslim place of worship. **Analyze Images** *What does the scale of this mosque suggest about the importance of Islam to people in this region?*

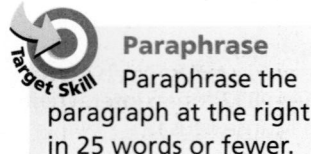

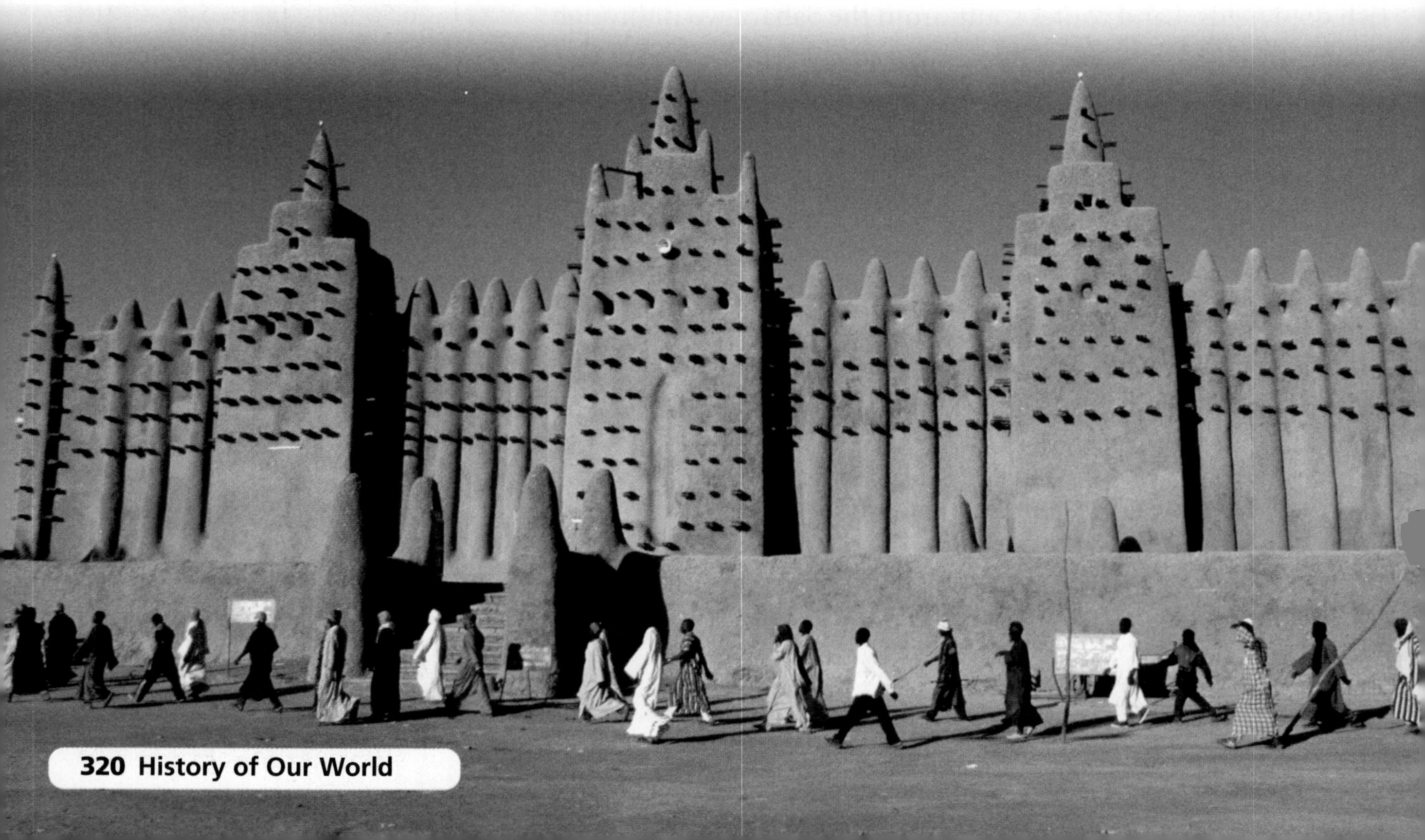

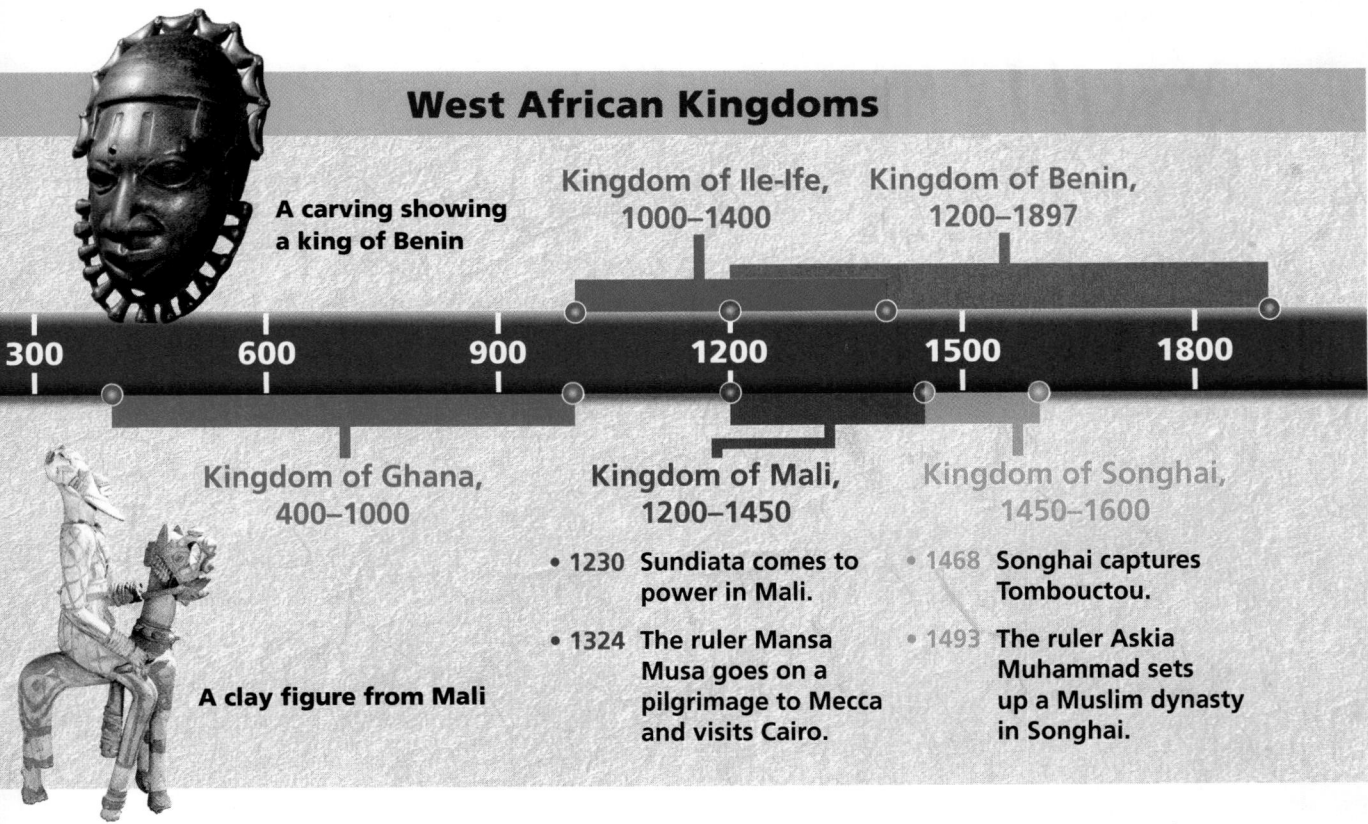

West African Kingdoms

A carving showing a king of Benin

Kingdom of Ile-Ife, 1000–1400

Kingdom of Benin, 1200–1897

300   600   900   1200   1500   1800

Kingdom of Ghana, 400–1000

A clay figure from Mali

Kingdom of Mali, 1200–1450

- 1230 Sundiata comes to power in Mali.
- 1324 The ruler Mansa Musa goes on a pilgrimage to Mecca and visits Cairo.

Kingdom of Songhai, 1450–1600

- 1468 Songhai captures Tombouctou.
- 1493 The ruler Askia Muhammad sets up a Muslim dynasty in Songhai.

During his 25-year rule, Mansa Musa used his new ties to these Muslim peoples to make Mali a center of learning. Scholars came to teach religion, mathematics, medicine, and law. In the late 1300s, however—about 50 years after Mansa Musa died—Mali's power began to fade. Raiders attacked from the north, and fighting broke out within the kingdom. Several provinces broke away and became independent. One of these former provinces became an empire in its own right. It was called Songhai (SAWNG hy).

The Rise and Fall of Songhai Songhai became the leading kingdom of the West African savanna during the 1400s. Like the rulers of Ghana and Mali, Songhai's leaders controlled trade routes and the sources of salt and gold. Songhai's wealth and power grew when it conquered the rich trading city of Tombouctou in 1468. Find Songhai on the map titled Civilizations of Africa on page 309.

In less than 100 years, however, the kingdom of Songhai began to lose power. In the late 1500s, the people of Songhai began fighting among themselves. The kingdom became weaker. And it easily fell to the guns and cannons of an army from Morocco, in North Africa. The era of the rich and powerful trading empires of West Africa was at an end.

✓ **Reading Check** Name the two most important trade items in West Africa.

■ Timeline Skills

This timeline shows five West African kingdoms. Vertical lines mark specific dates. Horizontal bars show periods of time. The kingdoms of the savanna are at the bottom of the timeline. The forest kingdoms are at the top. **Identify** Which kingdom lasted the longest? Which lasted the shortest time? **Analyze** Which forest kingdoms overlapped in time with the kingdom of Mali?

Kingdoms of the Forest

Ghana, Mali, and Songhai developed on West Africa's savanna. At the same time, other kingdoms arose in the rain forests to the south of these grasslands. The peoples of the rain forests were not Muslim. They practiced religions with hundreds of different gods.

Two of the most important kingdoms of the West African forests were centered around the cities of **Ile-Ife** (EE lay EE fay) and **Benin** (beh NEEN). Both of these cities were located in the present-day nation of Nigeria. As with the kingdoms of the savanna, trade made these forest kingdoms powerful and wealthy. With their wealth and stability, these kingdoms supported larger populations than other African rain forest regions could support.

Ile-Ife: A Center of Culture and Trade

About A.D. 1000, Ile-Ife became a major cultural and trading center. The powerful leaders of this kingdom were called onis (OH neez). Traditional stories told by these people described Ile-Ife as "the place where the world was created," but historians know little about the early city or the people who lived there.

One of the reasons that we know little about Ile-Ife is that the modern town of Ife is located on top of the earlier city. Also, the region is thickly forested and damp. Trees have covered old sites outside the town, and rains have washed away old mud buildings. Dampness has also rusted iron and long since rotted wood and fabrics.

Among the most important artifacts that have survived are sculptures. Many were discovered only in the last 100 years. Scientists have dated these works of art to the years between the 1100s and the 1300s. Many of these sculptures are lifelike and may be portraits of the powerful onis of Ile-Ife.

The rain forests of West Africa have a damp climate and lush vegetation.

Benin Rules an Empire The city of Benin dates to the 1200s. At that time, workers in the region mined copper, iron, and gold. Benin's leaders, called obas (OH buz), also sold slaves to African traders. Many of these slaves were forced to work as servants for rich families on the savanna. Others joined slaves from Europe and Asia to work in North Africa.

By the 1500s, Benin reached its greatest strength and size. The oba controlled a large army, priests, government workers, and less important local chiefs. The city of Benin ruled the trade routes along the rivers to the north and south. It became immensely rich. It ruled much of present-day southern Nigeria. Benin remained strong until the late 1600s, when the kingdom began to lose its power over the region.

Like Ile-Ife, the city of Benin also became a center of art. The obas hired skilled artists to make many beautiful objects from bronze, brass, ivory, and copper. These artists may have borrowed some cultural traditions from Ile-Ife, but the exact relationship between the two kingdoms is unclear. The artists of Benin and other West African kingdoms have in turn influenced modern artists in Europe and the Americas.

✓ **Reading Check** What were the leaders of Ile-Ife and Benin called?

Links to Art

Bronze Plaques Benin artists made bronze plaques and sculptures for the royal palaces of the obas. For example, one sculpture shows a man playing a flute and wearing an animal-skin skirt. After 1897, the British ruled this region and removed many objects. Today, hundreds of Benin plaques can be seen in museums in Europe and the United States. This plaque is about 300 years old.

Section 2 Assessment

Key Terms
Review the key terms at the beginning of this section. Use each term in a sentence that explains its meaning.

Target Reading Skill
Find the second paragraph under the heading Kingdoms of the Forest, on page 322. Paraphrase this paragraph by rewriting it in your own words.

Comprehension and Critical Thinking
1. (a) List What were the names of the three major kingdoms of the West African savanna?

(b) Identify Causes What made each of the three kingdoms rich?
(c) Apply Information What do the powerful countries of today have in common with these kingdoms?
2. (a) Recall Describe some of the art objects that the people of Ile-Ife and Benin left behind.
(b) Identify Cause and Effect Why are these objects among the few things that have survived from these cultures?

Writing Activity
Suppose that you are a foreign visitor who has traveled to the kingdom of Benin in the late 1500s. You will be allowed to meet briefly with the current oba. Write a list of five or six questions that you would like to ask him about his daily life, his kingdom, and the people he rules.

> **Writing Tip** Be sure that your questions are worded in a way that shows respect for the powerful ruler and his kingdom. Also be sure to include a brief introduction identifying yourself and the purpose of your visit.

From the salt mines of the Sahara, caravan leaders drove their camels through the hot desert sand. Heavily weighted with slabs of salt, the camel train headed south. Meantime, trade caravans from West Africa's gold mines traveled north. They met in the West African city of Tombouctou (tohm book TOO). In the 1500s, salt was as valuable as gold in the city's markets.

A Marketplace of Goods and Ideas Business was brisk in Tombouctou's markets. Buyers and sellers traded for metal wares and wood; grains and nuts; fish, camel meat, milk, water, and dates; rugs and linen; precious ivory, gold, salt, and even slaves.

By the mid-1500s, about 60,000 people lived in Tombouctou. Artisans such as weavers, dyers, and metalsmiths had shops in the busy city.

More than just a marketplace, this city drew scholars from all over the Islamic world to study and exchange ideas. Many people within the city spoke Arabic. Muslims could pray at three impressive dried-mud mosques.

The illustration at the right shows a market scene in Tombouctou with a mosque in the background. The illustration at the top of the page is of an ancient manuscript that was found in the city.

The Salt and Gold Trade

Salt from mines in the Sahara was traded in the markets of Tombouctou. At one time, about 25,000 camels traveled from Taoudenni in the Sahara to Tombouctou yearly. Gold came from the southern areas of West Africa.

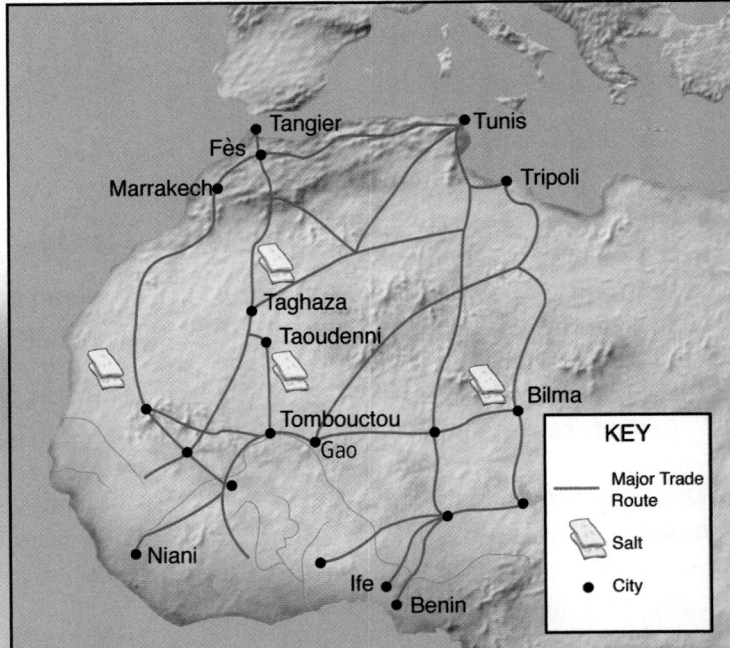

KEY

— Major Trade Route

▨ Salt

● City

Map cities: Tangier, Tunis, Fès, Tripoli, Marrakech, Taghaza, Taoudenni, Bilma, Tombouctou, Gao, Niani, Ife, Benin

Assessment

Describe What was Tombouctou like in the 1500s?

Conclude What was the importance of salt and gold in Tombouctou?

Weights for Gold Dust
Merchants and traders in medieval Africa used the metal pieces at the right to measure the weight of gold dust.

Prepare to Read

Objectives

In this section, you will

1. Learn about powerful East African civilizations whose cities included Aksum and Lalibela.
2. Find out why the coastal cities of East Africa were important.

Taking Notes

As you read this section, look for the major events in this period of East Africa's history. Copy the timeline below, and add events and dates in the proper places on it.

A.D. **100** ⊢——————————————⊣ A.D. **1600**

Target Reading Skill

Summarize When you summarize, you review and state, in the correct order, the main points you have read. Summarizing can help you understand and study. As you read, pause occasionally to summarize what you have read.

Key Terms

- **Kilwa** (KEEL wah) *n.* one of many trading cities on the East African coast
- **Aksum** (AHK soom) *n.* an important East African center of trade

- **city-state** (SIH tee stayt) *n.* a city that is also a separate, independent state
- **Swahili** (swah HEE lee) *n.* a Bantu language with Arabic words, spoken along the East African coast
- **Great Zimbabwe** (grayt zim BAHB way) *n.* a powerful southeast African city

The ruins of the Great Mosque of Kilwa in Tanzania

The port was full of hurrying people, bobbing ships, and bundles of goods. The bright sun reflected off the water. Some traders were unloading glass beads, rice, spices, and expensive jewels carried from India. Others were bringing honey and wheat from Southwest Asia. Rich silks and fragile porcelains were also arriving after the long voyage from faraway China.

This was the bustling scene at **Kilwa** (KEEL wah), one of many trading cities along the coast of East Africa. Find Kilwa on the map titled Civilizations of Africa on page 309. Located in present-day Tanzania, Kilwa was an Islamic city with a royal palace and lush orchards and gardens. Kilwa's rulers charged taxes on all goods that entered their port. These taxes made Kilwa rich. Ibn Battutah (IB un bat TOO tah)—a famous Muslim traveler from North Africa—visited in the 1330s. He wrote that Kilwa was "one of the most beautiful and best-constructed towns in the world."

Ancient Ethiopia

Thousands of years ago, rich civilizations began to develop in southern Arabia and northeastern Africa along the Red Sea. By A.D. 1, the city of **Aksum** (AHK soom), located in present-day Ethiopia, was an important East African center of trade.

Aksum, a Center of Trade and Christianity Although the city of Aksum was located in the mountains about 100 miles (160 kilometers) inland, it controlled a trading port at Adulis (AD oo lis) on the Red Sea. Over time, Aksum conquered much of modern Ethiopia and southwestern Arabia. It grew steadily in strength and wealth.

The merchants of Aksum traded goods at ports as far away as India. One of the main trade goods they controlled was ivory. Ivory, the white material from elephant tusks, was highly valued for carving. As they traded goods with foreign merchants, the people of Aksum also exchanged ideas and beliefs with them.

During the A.D. 300s, King Ezana (ay ZAH nuh) of Aksum learned about a new religion—Christianity. Soon, the king became a Christian himself and made Christianity the official religion of his kingdom. Over time, most people under Aksum's rule converted to Christianity.

For several hundred years, Aksum kept its control of the major trade routes linking Africa with Europe and Asia. Then in the A.D. 600s, Muslims fought with the rulers of Aksum for control of the Red Sea trade routes. Eventually, the Muslims conquered the coastal ports. The Muslim conquest of the coast ended the trade that had given Aksum its power and wealth.

Christianity in Ethiopia
The city of Aksum, at top, remains an important religious center today. The St. Mary of Zion Church is at the right. The young priest above is holding a Coptic cross, a symbol of Ethiopian Christianity. **Compare and Contrast** *How do these images of Christianity compare to Christian imagery in the United States?*

St. George's Church, Lalibela
At top, worshipers surround St. George's Church, one of the churches that King Lalibela had carved into the rock about A.D. 1200. Above, a priest at the church's entrance.
Apply Information *How long has this church been in use?*

Lalibela and the Spread of Christianity

After Aksum had lost power, the Christian kings of the region built churches and monasteries. But these kings did not build a new capital. Instead, they moved from place to place around the kingdom. They lived in royal tents and were accompanied by thousands of citizens and servants.

Many neighboring lands converted to Islam, but present-day Ethiopia remained Christian. Cut off in their mountainous home, the Ethiopians had little direct contact with other Christian peoples. In time, their churches developed unique customs and traditions. In one such tradition, churchgoers rest their foreheads against the outside wall of a church and kiss it to show respect.

Another unique feature of the region's Christianity is a group of churches built about A.D. 1200 under King Lalibela (lah lee BAY lah). The king had his people build new churches—but not from the ground up. Instead, the people were to carve the churches down into the solid red rock. The flat rooftops of the buildings are level with the surrounding land. The churches are in a town named Lalibela in honor of the king. These fascinating churches are still used today by the Christians of Ethiopia.

✓ **Reading Check** **Describe the churches of Lalibela.**

Rich Centers of Trade

After Muslims gained control of Indian Ocean trade, trade centers developed along the east coast of Africa. Each of these ports was a **city-state** (SIH tee stayt), a city with its own government that controls much of the surrounding land. By 1400, there were about 30 such city-states along Africa's Indian Ocean coast.

Trade thrived in East Africa because the region supplied goods such as gold and ivory that were very scarce outside Africa. In return, Muslim traders brought luxury goods that could not be found in Africa. Muslim traders from Arabia also brought their religion and language to these African city-states.

The City-State of Kilwa The merchants of Kilwa traded goods from inland regions of Africa for the foreign goods that traders brought to the port by sea. Contact between Africans and Arabs in Kilwa and other coastal city-states led to a new culture and language. Called **Swahili** (swah HEE lee), this Bantu language has words borrowed from Arabic. Swahili was spoken all along the East African coast. Most people on this coast converted to Islam.

In the 1500s, Portuguese troops sailing from Europe captured and looted Kilwa and the other coastal city-states. Portugal took over the prosperous trade routes. But the influence of Swahili culture remained. Today, Swahili is an official language in Kenya and Tanzania, and most East Africans use Swahili for business. Islam is still an important religion in the region.

Great Zimbabwe Much of the gold traded at Kilwa was mined in an inland area to the south, between the Zambezi and Limpopo rivers. This was the region controlled by the powerful southeastern African city of **Great Zimbabwe** (grayt zim BAHB way). Like other medieval African centers that you have read about, Great Zimbabwe grew rich and powerful through trade.

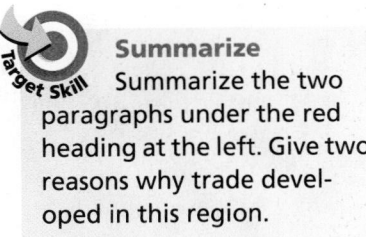
Summarize
Summarize the two paragraphs under the red heading at the left. Give two reasons why trade developed in this region.

Discovery CHANNEL SCHOOL Video
Learn about Great Zimbabwe and explore its ruins.

Mombasa Harbor, Kenya
Like Kilwa, the port of Mombasa on the Indian Ocean has a long history of trade. Wooden sailing ships like the ones below carried the trade of these city-states. **Infer** *Why were the East African city-states located along the coast?*

Stone-walled ruins at Great Zimbabwe, in the present-day nation of Zimbabwe

Historians believe that the city of Great Zimbabwe had been founded by about 1100. Its Bantu-speaking people were the ancestors of today's Shona (SHOHN uh) people. Most people in this area were poor farmers. For those who were better off, large herds of cattle were an important form of wealth. Richest of all were the leaders who controlled the gold trade. These powerful leaders and their families lived among impressive stone-walled structures.

Great Zimbabwe thrived for hundreds of years. Historians believe that the city reached its peak before the early 1400s. By 1500, the city had fallen. Trade routes may have moved to favor other centers. Farmers also may have worn out the soil. In either case, the glory of Great Zimbabwe was not entirely lost. Its stone ruins still stand, and its history is a source of pride for the present-day nation of Zimbabwe.

 **Reading Check** What were two possible causes for the collapse of Great Zimbabwe?

 **Section 3 Assessment**

Key Terms
Review the key terms at the beginning of this section. Use each term in a sentence that explains its meaning.

Target Reading Skill
Write a summary of the two paragraphs at the top of this page.

Comprehension and Critical Thinking
1. (a) Recall What change did King Ezana of Aksum make in the A.D. 300s?

(b) Identify What are some of the most famous sites in Ethiopia today?
(c) Synthesize Information How are these famous sites related to the changes made by King Ezana?
2. (a) Explain What connection was there between Great Zimbabwe and Kilwa?
(b) Analyze Information How did the locations of Kilwa and Great Zimbabwe make them powerful and rich?

Writing Activity
Study the photo of the rock-cut church of Lalibela on page 328. Write a description of this unusual church to a friend or relative. Where is it located? What does the building look like? How was it built? In what ways is it similar to or different from other buildings?

For: An activity on historic Ethiopia
Visit: PHSchool.com
Web Code: lgd-8203

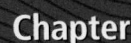 
Review and Assessment

◆ Chapter Summary

Section 1: Africa and the Bantu

- The physical geography and natural vegetation of Africa are diverse, from tropical rain forests along the Equator to the world's largest desert.
- More than 2,000 years ago, the Bantu-speaking people of West Africa began migrating across central and southern Africa, carrying their culture wherever they went.

Section 2: Kingdoms of West Africa

- Powerful trading kingdoms, including Ghana, Mali, and Songhai, controlled the savannas of West Africa for hundreds of years.
- The cities of Ile-Ife and Benin were important centers of trade and art in the West African rain forests.

Section 3: East Africa's Great Trading Centers

- Strong kings built lasting monuments and brought changes to the lands they ruled in present-day Ethiopia.
- City-states along the East African coast and the inland city of Great Zimbabwe grew rich from trade.

A bronze plaque from Benin

◆ Key Terms

Each statement below includes a key term from this chapter. If the statement is true, write *true*. If it is false, rewrite the statement to make it true.

1. Swahili is a language based on Portuguese, with Bantu words, that is spoken in West Africa.

2. Movement from one country or region to settle in another is called migration.

3. Mansa Musa ruled the kingdom of Mali.

4. A city-state is a city with its own government that controls much of the surrounding land.

5. The Sahara is the world's longest river.

6. Oral history is an account of the past that is passed down from generation to generation by word of mouth.

◆ Comprehension and Critical Thinking

7. **(a) Locate** Where are Africa's tropical rain forests located?
   (b) Describe What are some important features of Africa's savannas?
   (c) Compare and Contrast In what ways are Africa's rain forests and savannas alike? In what ways are they different?

8. **(a) List** Name two things that have helped modern historians study the history of Africa south of the Sahara.
   (b) Explain Why is studying this history "like solving a puzzle"?

9. **(a) Summarize** When and why did African Muslims fight the rulers of Aksum?
   (b) Analyze Why was this fight important?

10. **(a) Recall** In which two rain forest kingdoms did artists make bronze sculptures?
    (b) Generalize Why might an artist depict a powerful king in his or her work?

11. **(a) Identify** Where did Mansa Musa and his caravan stop in July 1324?
    (b) Infer Why might a large caravan need to stop in the middle of a very long journey?

◆ Skills Practice

Using Reliable Information In the Skills for Life activity in this chapter, you learned how to judge whether information is reliable. Review the steps for this skill. Suppose you found the text below in a recent travel guide to Africa. Use the steps for this skill to decide whether the information is reliable. Write a sentence that explains why or why not.

"The mosque at Djenné is the most magnificent building in all of Africa. It must have been built by a powerful ruler with a strong religious faith. Every traveler to Africa should visit this mosque."

◆ Writing Activity: Science

You have read about the importance of iron tools and weapons to early peoples. Do research, using reliable sources, to find out how Africans made these early iron tools. What were the different steps in the process? What equipment did they use? What kind of tools did they make? Write a short report on your findings.

MAP◆MASTER™ Skills Activity

Place Location For each place or feature listed below, write the letter from the map that shows its location.

1. Great Zimbabwe
2. Sahara
3. Kilwa
4. Kingdom of Ghana
5. Equator
6. Kingdom of Benin
7. Kingdom of Mali

Go Online
PHSchool.com Use Web Code **lgp-8214** for an **interactive map.**

Sub-Saharan Africa

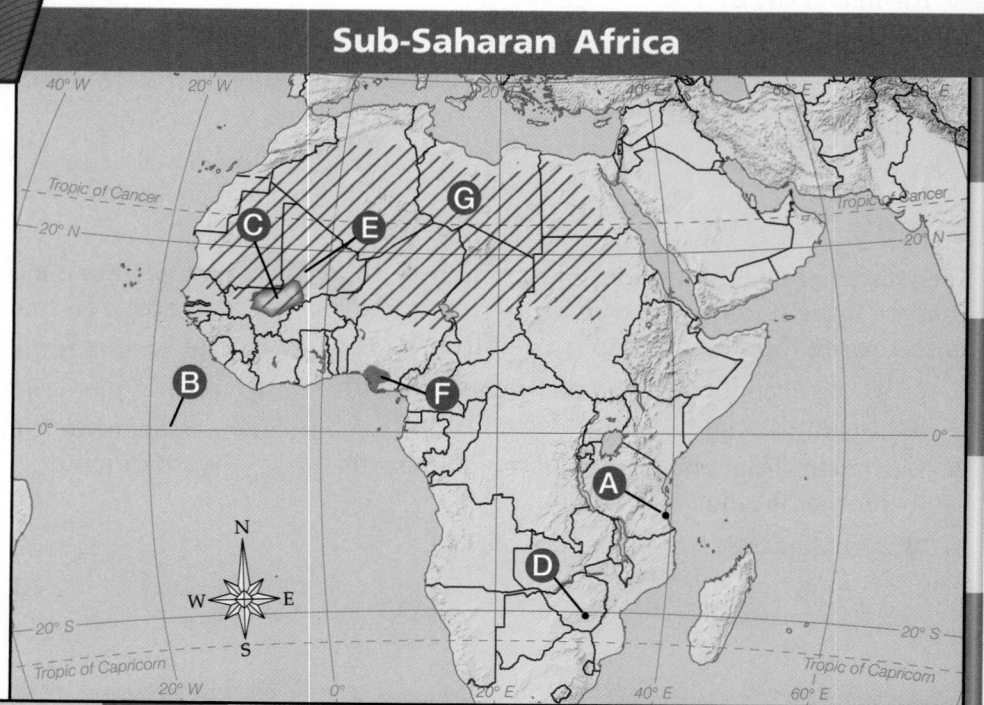

Standardized Test Prep

Test-Taking Tips

Some questions on standardized tests ask you to find main ideas. Read the paragraph below. Then follow the tips to answer the sample question.

Imagine trading a pound of salt for a pound of gold. At today's prices, a pound of salt costs only about 50 cents, but a pound of gold is worth thousands of dollars. That has not always been true everywhere. In parts of Africa, salt was as scarce as gold in medieval times. People needed salt to preserve their food. They needed it to stay healthy, too. So they traded their gold for nearly the same weight of salt.

TIP As you read the paragraph, try to identify its main idea, or most important point. In some cases, the main idea may be stated. In other cases, such as this one, you have to add up the details to find the main idea.

Pick the letter that best answers the question.

The main idea of this paragraph is that

A today, a pound of salt costs only about 50 cents.

B in medieval Africa, salt was nearly as valuable as gold because it was needed and scarce.

C people need salt to stay healthy.

D in medieval Africa, gold was easier for traders to carry than salt.

TIP Look for key words in the answer choices or question that connect to the paragraph. In this case, two key words are *salt* and *gold*.

Think It Through The paragraph's main idea is that Africans traded gold for salt long ago, when salt was hard to get. Look at all four choices. A and C both just give details about salt. They do not compare the values of salt and gold. That leaves B and D. D gives information that is not in the paragraph. So, the correct answer is B, which is the main idea of the paragraph.

Practice Questions

Use the tips above and other tips in this book to help you answer the following questions.

1. In Africa, tropical rain forests lie along
   A Madagascar.
   B the Equator.
   C an oasis.
   D the Nile.

2. The kingdom of Mali rose to power after this West African kingdom weakened.
   A Songhai
   B Benin
   C Ghana
   D Nigeria

3. Which Christian king of East Africa had his people carve underground churches?
   A Sundiata
   B Ezana
   C Mansa Musa
   D Lalibela

Read the paragraph below, and answer the question that follows.

Medieval traders sold East African ivory in India. Ivory comes from elephant tusks. India has its own elephants, so why did Indians buy East African ivory? East African elephants have softer tusks. East African ivory is better for carving.

4. The main idea of this paragraph is that
   A ivory comes from elephant tusks.
   B Indians bought East African ivory because it was good for carving.
   C trading elephant tusks is illegal today.
   D East African elephants have softer tusks than Indian elephants.

Use Web Code **lga-8201** for a **Chapter 11 self-test**.

Chapter 12

Early Civilizations of the Americas

Chapter Preview

This chapter will introduce you to the civilizations that existed in the Americas before the arrival of Europeans.

Section 1
South America and the Incas

Section 2
Cultures of Middle America

Section 3
Cultures of North America

Target Reading Skill

Main Idea In this chapter you will focus on finding and remembering the main idea, or the most important point, of sections and paragraphs.

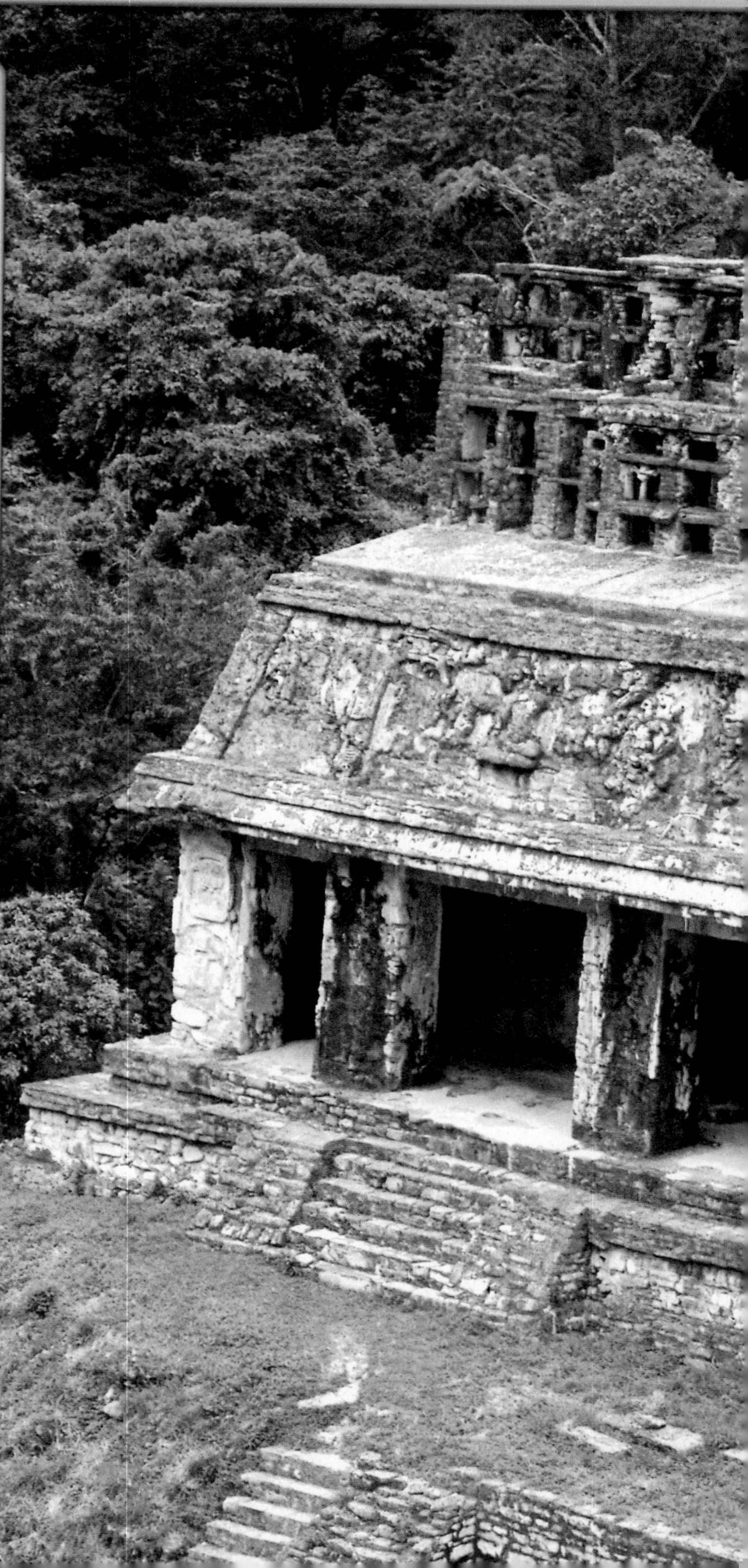

▶ Temple of the Cross, Palenque, Mexico

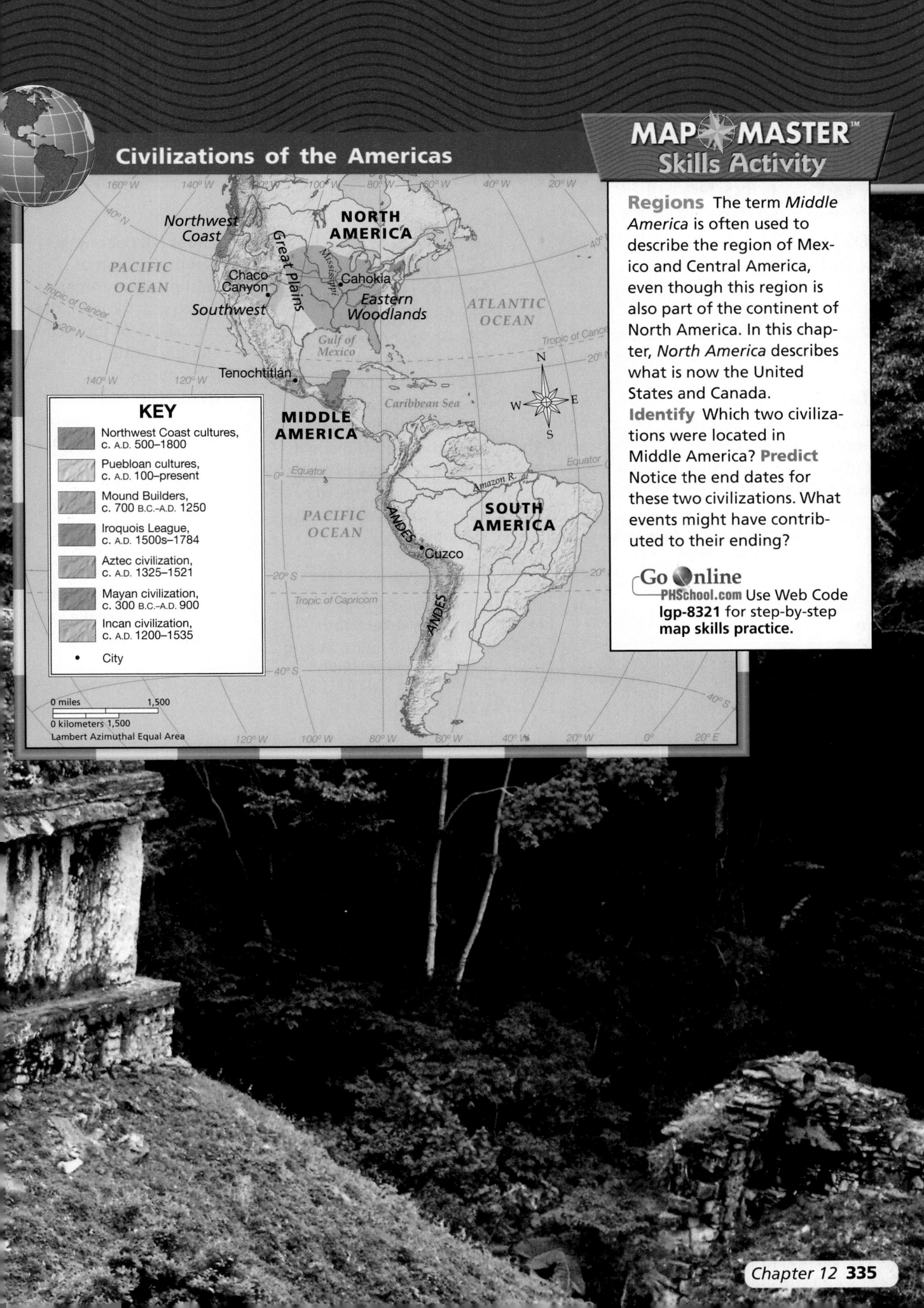

Civilizations of the Americas

NORTH AMERICA

Northwest Coast

Great Plains

Chaco Canyon

Southwest

Mississippi

Cahokia

Eastern Woodlands

PACIFIC OCEAN

Gulf of Mexico

Tenochtitlán

Caribbean Sea

ATLANTIC OCEAN

MIDDLE AMERICA

Amazon R.

PACIFIC OCEAN

SOUTH AMERICA

ANDES

Cuzco

ANDES

160° W, 140° W, 100° W, 80° W, 60° W, 40° W, 20° W

Tropic of Cancer

40° N

20° N

140° W, 120° W

Tropic of Cancer

Equator

Equator

20° S

Tropic of Capricorn

40° S

120° W, 100° W, 80° W, 60° W, 40° W, 20° W, 0°, 20° E

KEY

- Northwest Coast cultures, c. A.D. 500–1800
- Puebloan cultures, c. A.D. 100–present
- Mound Builders, c. 700 B.C.–A.D. 1250
- Iroquois League, c. A.D. 1500s–1784
- Aztec civilization, c. A.D. 1325–1521
- Mayan civilization, c. 300 B.C.–A.D. 900
- Incan civilization, c. A.D. 1200–1535
- • City

0 miles 1,500
0 kilometers 1,500
Lambert Azimuthal Equal Area

Regions The term *Middle America* is often used to describe the region of Mexico and Central America, even though this region is also part of the continent of North America. In this chapter, *North America* describes what is now the United States and Canada.
Identify Which two civilizations were located in Middle America? **Predict** Notice the end dates for these two civilizations. What events might have contributed to their ending?

Prepare to Read

Objectives

In this section, you will
1. Find out about the geography of the Americas.
2. Learn about the empire established by the Incas of South America.

Taking Notes

As you read this section, record key points about the Incan Empire. Copy the start of the outline below, and then add more information to complete it.

> I. The mountain empire of the Incas
>   A. Growth of an empire
>   1.
>   2.
>   B.
> II.

Target Reading Skill

Identify Main Ideas Good readers identify the main idea in every written passage. The main idea is the most important, or the biggest, point of the section. It includes all of the other points made in the section. As you read, note the main idea of each paragraph or written passage.

Key Terms

- **Incas** (ING kuhz) *n.* people of a powerful South American empire during the 1400s and 1500s
- **Andes** (AN deez) *n.* a mountain chain of western South America
- **Cuzco** (KOOS koh) *n.* the capital city of the Incan Empire, located in present-day Peru
- **census** (SEN sus) *n.* an official count of people in a certain place at a certain time
- **quipu** (KEE poo) *n.* a group of knotted strings used by the Incas to record information
- **terraces** (TEHR us iz) *n.* steplike ledges cut into mountains to make land suitable for farming

Machu Picchu, Peru

Clouds cluster around the peaks of the towering mountains. As the sun breaks through, its rays fall upon stone walls and roofless buildings. These structures cling to the steep mountain slopes. Surrounding the quiet ruins are green grasses and shrubs. This is Machu Picchu (MAH chooh PEEK chooh). The thousands of people who once lived here have been gone for centuries.

This spectacular site was built by the **Incas** (ING kuhz), people of a powerful empire that ruled part of South America in the 1400s and 1500s. Their huge empire was located in the **Andes** (AN deez), a mountain chain that snakes along the western coast of the continent. Look at the map on page 335 to locate the Incan Empire. This empire stretched through what are now the countries of Ecuador (EK wuh dawr), Peru, Bolivia, Chile (CHIL ee), and Argentina.

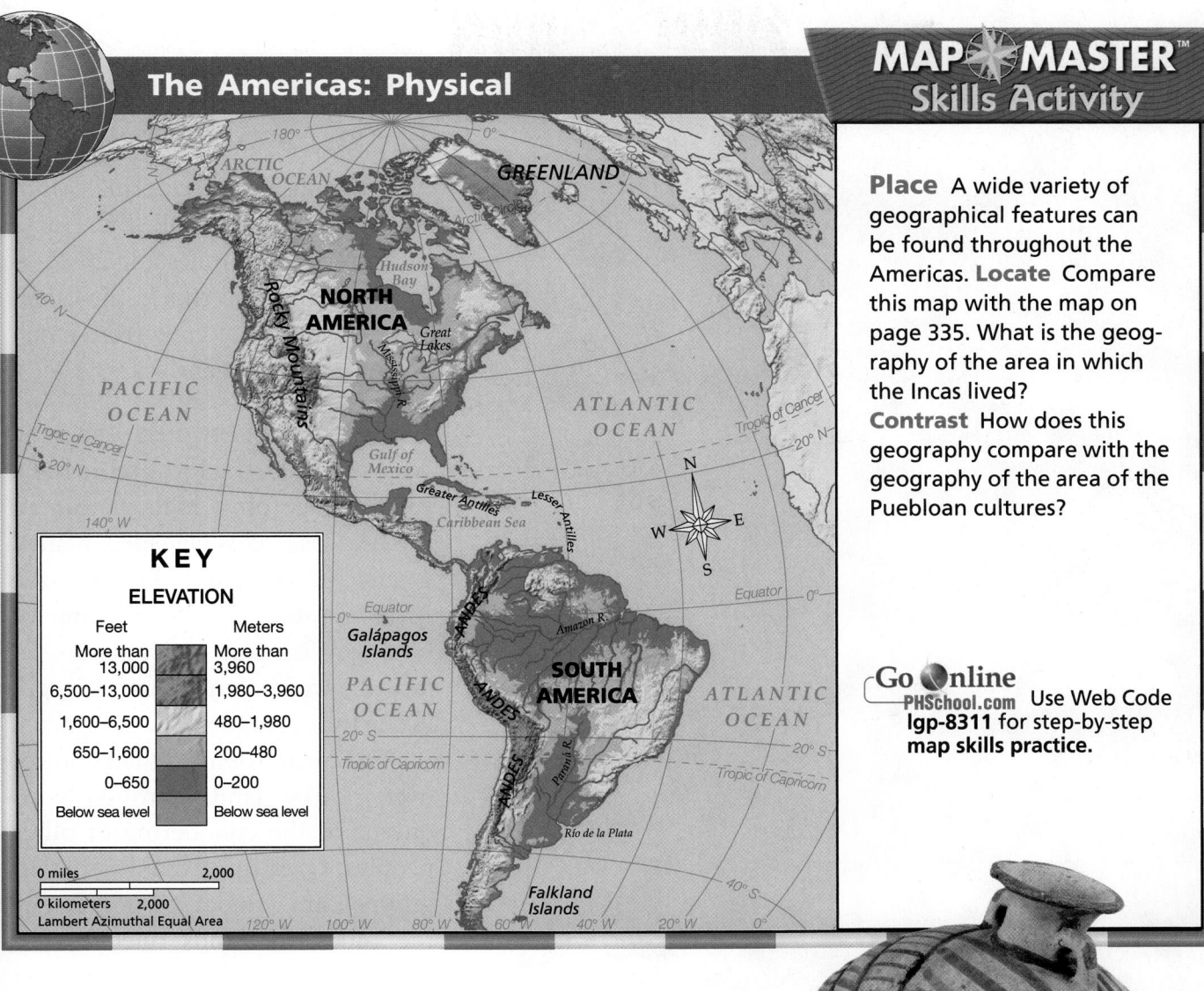

MAP MASTER™
Skills Activity

KEY
ELEVATION

Feet		Meters
More than 13,000		More than 3,960
6,500–13,000		1,980–3,960
1,600–6,500		480–1,980
650–1,600		200–480
0–650		0–200
Below sea level		Below sea level

0 miles   2,000
0 kilometers   2,000
Lambert Azimuthal Equal Area

Place A wide variety of geographical features can be found throughout the Americas. **Locate** Compare this map with the map on page 335. What is the geography of the area in which the Incas lived? **Contrast** How does this geography compare with the geography of the area of the Puebloan cultures?

Go Online
PHSchool.com Use Web Code **lgp-8311** for step-by-step map skills practice.

Geography of the Americas

The Incas were not the first culture to develop in the Americas. Many groups had lived in the region for thousands of years. Individual cultures developed different ways of life to fit their geographic settings. Some peoples made their homes in dense forests or fertile river valleys. Other peoples lived among rocky cliffs in areas that were dry for much of the year.

Locate the mountain ranges on the map above. Find the Mississippi and Amazon rivers, which drain two of the largest river systems in the world. Now, compare this map to the map on page 335, at the beginning of this chapter. Notice that the Incas lived in the mountainous Andes and along the Pacific coast. Compare the homeland of the Incas with that of the Mound Builders. Consider how people might have developed different cultures to help them live in different geographic settings.

This earthenware vessel was designed to be carried on the back of a llama.

✓ **Reading Check** In what geographic setting did the Incas live?

The Mountain Empire of the Incas

At its peak, the powerful South American empire of the Incas measured 2,500 miles (4,020 kilometers) from one end to the other. This great empire grew from small beginnings over many years.

Growth of an Empire About the year A.D. 1200, the Incas settled in a small village on a high plateau in the Andes. This village, named **Cuzco** (KOOS koh), became the Incas' capital city and a center of both government and religion. In fact, the word *cuzco* means "center" in the Incan language.

The Incas extended their control over nearby lands through conquests, or the conquering of other peoples. Over time, many different groups came under their rule. By the 1400s, the lands ruled by the Incas had grown into an empire. At its height, the Incan Empire included as many as 12 million people.

Even when the empire included millions of people, it was run in an orderly way. Incan rulers had a complex system of gathering knowledge about events that happened hundreds of miles away from their capital city.

Festival of the Sun
Thousands of people gather at the ruins of an Incan fortress in Cuzco for the yearly Festival of the Sun, which celebrates the winter solstice.
Infer *How can you tell which people are part of the festival and which are just watching?*

Quipus in Incan Life
In the drawing below, dating from the 1500s, an official gives a noble a quipu like the one at left. The quipu may have been created hundreds of miles away. **Analyze Images** *What details in the drawing tell which person is the noble?*

Incan Government The Incan ruler was called Sapa Inca, or "the emperor." The people believed that their emperor was related to the sun-god. The emperor, and only he, owned all the land and divided it among those under his rule. Under the Sapa Inca was the noble class. Nobles oversaw government officials, who made sure the empire ran smoothly.

Officials used a **census,** or an official count of the people, to keep track of everyone's responsibilities. The census helped to make sure that everyone paid taxes. It recorded which men worked as soldiers or on public projects such as gold mining and road building. Farmers had to give the government part of their crops, while women had to weave cloth. In return, the empire took care of the poor, the sick, and the elderly.

The official spoken language of the empire was Quechua (KECH wuh), but the Incas did not have a written language. Instead, they invented a complex system for keeping detailed records. Information such as births, deaths, and harvests was recorded on a group of knotted strings called a **quipu** (KEE poo). Each quipu had a main cord with several colored strings attached. The colors represented different items, and knots of varying sizes recorded numbers.

Incan relay runners carried quipus across vast networks of roads and bridges to keep the government informed about distant parts of the empire. These roads also carried the Incan armies and trade caravans, both of which helped to unify the vast empire.

Go Online
PHSchool.com Use Web Code **mup-0833** for an interactive tour of Incan roads.

Links Across Time

Rope Bridges This rope bridge, strung across a gorge in the Andes, is similar to those used by the Incas. A gorge is a narrow pass between steep cliffs or walls. Incan bridges were made with strong cords of braided vines and reeds. Some peoples in the Andes still make bridges from vines and reeds today. Modern steel suspension bridges in other parts of the world use the engineering principles developed by the Incas hundreds of years ago when they built their rope-and-vine bridges.

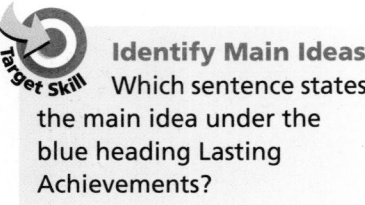

Identify Main Ideas Which sentence states the main idea under the blue heading Lasting Achievements?

Lasting Achievements The achievements of the Incas still amaze people today. They constructed thousands of miles of paved roads, massive walls, and mountaintop buildings. And they did all this with only stone hammers and bronze chisels. Remarkably, much of what the Incas built hundreds of years ago with only primitive tools still stands today.

The Incas took advantage of their environment. They used stone—plentiful in the Andes—for many purposes. Sometimes they used enormous stones whole. At other times, they carefully broke stones into smaller blocks. First they cut a long groove into a rock's surface. Then they drove stone or wooden wedges into the groove until the rock split.

When Incan stonemasons made a wall, they made sure its large, many-sided stones fit together perfectly. After a wall was complete, the fit was so tight that not even a very thin knife blade could be slipped between two blocks. Construction without mortar, or cement, also allowed the massive stones to move and resettle during earthquakes without damaging the wall.

Among their many ingenious uses of stone was a method to increase farm production. The Andes are steep, dry, and rocky. There is little natural farmland. By building **terraces,** or steplike ledges cut into the mountains, the Incas could farm on slopes that would otherwise have been too steep. Stone terraces held the soil in place so it would not be washed away by rain. A complex system of aqueducts, or stone-lined channels, carried water to these farms. One of these aqueducts was 360 miles (579 kilometers) long.

The Decline of the Incan Empire The power of the Incan Empire peaked in the 1400s. After that, it lasted for less than 100 years. A number of factors contributed to the fall of the empire. Members of the ruling family began to fight among themselves for control. Also, many workers started to rebel against the strict government.

Then, in the 1530s, a Spanish conquistador (kahn KEES tuh dawr), or conqueror, named Francisco Pizarro arrived in South America. Pizarro had heard of the wealthy Incan Empire. He wanted to explore the region and conquer its peoples. The Incan emperor welcomed Pizarro. But when he and his unarmed men met the conquistador, they walked into a trap. Pizarro captured the emperor and killed his men.

The Spanish had superior weapons. They also carried diseases, such as smallpox and measles, to which the Incas had never been exposed. These diseases killed much of the Incan population. The Spanish quickly gained control of the vast Incan Empire. For decades, the Incas tried to regain rule of their land, but they never succeeded.

A wooden cup made for Pizarro shows Spanish and Incan figures.

✓ Reading Check **Which Spanish conquistador conquered the Incas?**

Section 1 Assessment

Key Terms
Review the key terms at the beginning of this section. Use each term in a sentence that explains its meaning.

Target Reading Skill
State the main idea of the first paragraph on this page.

Comprehension and Critical Thinking
1. (a) Identify Name two geographic settings in which peoples of the Americas lived.
(b) Synthesize Information What are the climates of those two regions?

(c) Infer How might the people who lived in these regions have adapted to their geography and climate?
2. (a) Recall How much land did the Incan Empire cover at its greatest extent?
(b) Explain How did the government in Cuzco keep track of distant parts of the empire?
(c) Draw Conclusions What do you think were the major problems of keeping such a large empire running smoothly? Explain your answer.

Writing Activity
If you could interview a stonemason from the Incan Empire, what would you ask? Make a list of questions you would ask in order to learn how these skilled workers accomplished so much so long ago. Then write a paragraph explaining why you want to ask the questions.

Go Online
PHSchool.com

For: An activity on the Incas
Visit: PHSchool.com
Web Code: lgd-8301

Wondering why things happen is something every human being does. Why does the sun rise in the east? Why does the United States have a president and not a king? Why did the Incas build Machu Picchu? This curiosity has driven people to ask how history has shaped our world. When we ask "why" about something, we are really trying to figure out causes and effects.

A cause is something that makes an event or a situation happen. An effect is a result of a cause. When you identify cause and effect, you understand how an action or several actions led to a particular result. Causes and effects can be short term or long term.

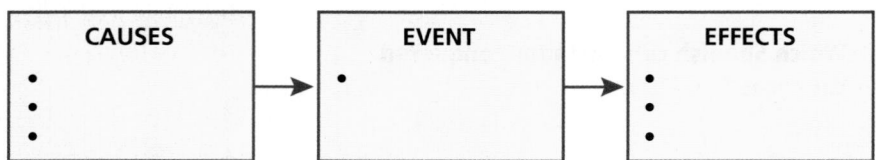

Learn the Skill

Use these steps to understand cause-and-effect relationships.

1. **Choose one event or condition as a starting point.** Determine whether in this case it is a cause or an effect.

2. **Look at earlier events or conditions for possible causes.** Also look for clue words that signal cause, such as *because*, *so*, and *since*. Words such as *therefore*, *then*, *reason*, and *as a result* signal effects.

3. **Make a cause-and-effect diagram.** A diagram like the one above can help you understand cause-and-effect relationships. Remember that sometimes an effect becomes a cause for another effect.

4. **Summarize the cause-and-effect relationships.** Be sure to include all of the causes and effects.

An Incan woman weaving

Incan Taxes

The Incas did not use money. Even so, villages had to pay taxes on their harvest and herds. To do so, they gave one third of their crops and animals to the empire. Villages could also pay their taxes by having their people do special work.

For this reason, every village sent a few young men and women to work for the empire. Some made jewelry, textiles, or pottery for nobles. Many men worked as soldiers or miners. Others built buildings or inspected roads or bridges.

In return, the government gave something back to the villages. The poor, the old, and the sick received government help.

Practice the Skill

Follow the steps in Learn the Skill to look for causes and effects in the passage above.

1 Read the passage. Find one event or condition that can serve as your starting point. Decide if it is a cause or an effect. How might the title help you?

2 What facts or conditions led to the way Incas paid taxes? What clue words in the second paragraph signal cause and effect?

3 Make a cause-and-effect diagram. Check for effects that in turn become causes for other effects. Expand your diagram if you need to.

4 Summarize the cause-and-effect relationships you have discovered.

Incan men building a fortress

Apply the Skill

Reread the two paragraphs under the heading The Decline of the Incan Empire on page 341. Use the steps in this skill to identify the causes and effects described in the passage. Make a cause-and-effect diagram or write a paragraph explaining the cause-and-effect relationships you find.

Prepare to Read

Objectives

In this section, you will
1. Learn about the Mayan culture of Middle America.
2. Find out about the powerful Aztec Empire.

Taking Notes

As you read this section, look for the characteristics of the Mayan and Aztec civilizations. Copy the web diagram below and record your findings for the Mayas. Then make a similar diagram for the Aztecs.

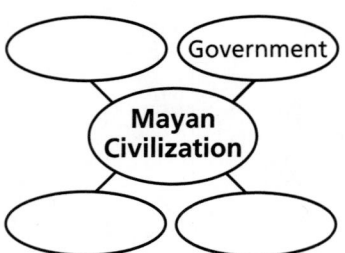

Target Reading Skill

Identify Supporting Details Sentences in a paragraph may give further details that support the main idea. These details may give examples, explanations, or reasons. In the first paragraph on page 345, this sentence states the main idea: "Thousands of years before the Aztecs built Tenochtitlán, other cultures thrived in Middle America." Note three details that support this main idea.

Key Terms

- **Aztecs** (AZ teks) *n.* a people who lived in the Valley of Mexico
- **Tenochtitlán** (teh nawch tee TLAHN) *n.* capital city of the Aztecs
- **Mayas** (MAH yuhz) *n.* a people who established a great civilization in Middle America
- **slash-and-burn agriculture** (slash and burn AG rih kul chur) *n.* a farming technique in which trees are cut down and burned to clear and fertilize the land
- **maize** (mayz) *n.* corn
- **hieroglyphics** (hy ur oh GLIF iks) *n.* the signs and symbols that made up the Mayan writing system

This page dating from the 1500s illustrates the Aztec legend. A version of it forms part of the Mexican flag today.

In about 1325, the **Aztecs** (AZ teks), a people who lived in the Valley of Mexico, began looking for a place to build a new capital. According to legend, the Aztecs asked their god of war where they should build this capital. He replied, "Build at the place where you see an eagle perched on a cactus and holding a snake in its beak."

When the Aztecs found the sign their god had described, they were surprised. The cactus on which the eagle perched was growing on a swampy island in the center of Lake Texcoco. It was an unlikely setting for an important city. But they believed their god had given them this sign, and so this was the place where the Aztecs built **Tenochtitlán** (teh nawch tee TLAHN), their capital. It would become one of the largest and finest cities of its time.

The Culture of the Mayas

Thousands of years before the Aztecs built Tenochtitlán, other cultures thrived in Middle America. One of these ancient peoples, called the Olmec (AHL mek), lived along the Gulf Coast from about 1200 B.C. until about 600 B.C. The Olmec are known for their pyramid-shaped temples and huge carved stone heads.

Somewhat later, an important culture developed in parts of Central America and the Yucatán Peninsula to the north. The Yucatán Peninsula is located at Mexico's southeastern tip. These people, called the **Mayas** (MAH yuhz), established a great civilization and built many cities in this region of Middle America. The Mayas may have been influenced by Olmec culture. The Mayan way of life lasted for many centuries. Its greatest period was from about A.D. 250 until 900.

Olmec statues like this one were usually several feet tall.

A Farming Culture Mayan life was based on farming. To grow crops, Mayan farmers used a technique called **slash-and-burn agriculture.** They first cleared the land by cutting down trees. They then burned the tree stumps, saving the ash to use as fertilizer. Finally, they planted seeds. After a few years, however, the soil would be worn out. The farmers would then have to clear and plant a new area.

Mayan farmers grew a variety of crops, including beans, squash, peppers, papayas (puh PY uz), and avocados. But their most common crop was **maize** (mayz), or corn. In fact, maize was so important to the Mayas that one of the gods they worshiped was a god of corn. And since the corn needed the sun and rain to grow, it is not surprising that the Mayas also worshipped a rain god and a sun god.

Tikal—Ruins of a Great City
Tikal, located in Guatemala, was once a thriving Mayan city. The city and its surrounding areas had a population of nearly 100,000. **Infer** *Judging from the photo, what challenge probably faced Mayan farmers who lived in this region?*

Mayan Counting The Mayas created a number system to count and record information. Dots stood for single numbers. For example, three dots in a row represented the number three. Bars stood for groups of five. Unlike our number system, which is based on 10, the Mayas' number system was based on 20. So, to record a number larger than 19, they used one large dot standing alone to represent the number 20, and more large dots for larger numbers divisible by 20. Dots and bars were used to make up the rest of the number. In the Mayan book at left, the number 29 is circled in white.

Go Online
PHSchool.com Use Web Code **mup-0834** for an interactive tour of a Mayan city.

Centers of Religion and Government The Mayan region was divided into several city-states. Each city-state had its own ruler and a city that served as a religious and governmental center. Priests and nobles were also important leaders. These leaders lived in large palaces within the city. Ordinary people lived on the edges of the city. Each city held great festivals to honor the many Mayan gods. The large temple-pyramids were the site of major religious ceremonies, which included human sacrifice.

Skilled mathematicians, Mayan priests developed calendars to follow the seasons and to plan religious celebrations. The Mayas also created a system of writing using signs and symbols called hieroglyphics. They used these hieroglyphics to record information in books made from the bark of fig trees.

A Mayan Game Cities also had outdoor courts where a special ball game called pok-ta-tok was played. A court was about the size of a football field, and the game was a bit like soccer and basketball combined. The ball was made of hard rubber. Players tried to knock it through a stone hoop set on a wall. They could hit the ball with their elbows, knees, or hips—but not with their hands or feet. The ball could not touch the ground.

The Mayas Abandon Their Cities Around A.D. 900, Mayan civilization began to decline. The people stopped building cities. They moved back into villages. The reasons probably included drought, crop failures, war, disease, overuse of natural resources, or a people's rebellion against their leaders. Today, however, millions of Mayas live in Middle America. Many continue some of the cultural traditions of their Mayan ancestors.

Identify Supporting Details
What details in the paragraph at right support the main idea that Mayan civilization declined?

✓ Reading Check **What did Mayan priests do?**

The Aztec Empire

You have already read that the Aztecs built their new capital, Tenochtitlán, in the middle of a lake in about 1325. They had first settled in the Valley of Mexico in the 1100s. By the 1470s, the Aztecs had conquered the surrounding lands. Their large empire stretched from the Gulf of Mexico in the east to the Pacific Ocean in the west. A single powerful leader, the Aztec emperor, ruled these lands. All the people he conquered were forced to pay him tribute, or heavy taxes, in the form of food, gold, or slaves.

Waterways and Gardens In spite of its swampy origins, Tenochtitlán became a magnificent capital city. At its center were an open plaza and one or more towering pyramid-temples. There were schools for the sons of the nobles and large stone palaces. Raised streets of hard earth, called causeways, connected the city to the surrounding land. To supply the city with enough fresh water, the Aztecs also built aqueducts. These special channels carried spring water from distant sources to storage areas in the city.

As the population of Tenochtitlán grew, the Aztecs realized they needed more farmland. Their solution was to build many island gardens in the shallow lakes around the capital. These raised fields, called chinampas (chih NAM puz), were made from rich soil dredged up from the lake bottom. Trees planted along the edges prevented soil from washing away. Between the fields were canals. Farmers used the canals to transport produce by boats to a huge marketplace near the capital.

Find out how Cortés defeated the Aztecs.

Floating Gardens Today
A man poles a boat among the chinampas on the outskirts of Mexico City. **Draw Conclusions** *List some advantages and disadvantages of growing crops on chinampas.*

Aztec Gods and Goddesses

The Aztec God Quetzalcoatl (top) was the god of priests, and was believed to have invented the Aztec calendar. Above is the Aztec maize goddess. Both figures appear often in Aztec art.

Make Generalizations *What does the worship of gods and goddesses such as these tell you about Aztec society?*

Religion and Learning To bring about good harvests, Aztec priests held ceremonies that would win the favor of their gods. Their most important god was the sun god. Aztec religion taught that the sun would not have the strength to rise and cross the sky every day without human blood. Of course, if the sun did not rise, crops could not grow, and the people would starve. Therefore, Aztec religious ceremonies included human sacrifice. The Aztecs also prayed to their gods for victory in war. Prisoners captured in war often served as human sacrifices.

To schedule their religious festivals and farming cycles, Aztec priests created a calendar based on the Mayan calendar and their own knowledge of astronomy. The calendar had 13 periods, like months, of 20 days each. The Aztecs also kept records using hieroglyphs similar to those used by the Mayas.

Tenochtitlán had schools and a university. Boys from noble families attended these schools. They studied to be government officials, teachers, or scribes.

Aztec Society Aztec society had a strict class structure. The emperor, of course, was most important. Next were members of the royal family, nobles, priests, and military leaders. Soldiers were next in importance. Below soldiers came artisans—skilled creators of jewelry, pottery, sculpture, and other goods—and merchants. Then came the farmers. They made up the largest class of people. The lowest position in Aztec society was held by slaves, most of whom were prisoners captured in battle.

War was a part of life in the Aztec Empire, as new territory was conquered. Most young men over the age of 15 served as soldiers for a period of time. They were well trained and well equipped. Soldiers had swords and bows and arrows. For protection, they had special armor made from heavy quilted cotton. Priests and government officials did not serve in the military.

Aztec women were not allowed to work as soldiers or military leaders, though they could train to be priestesses. Most women— even women from noble families—had to be skilled at weaving. Some of the cloth they wove was used for trade. Some was used to decorate temples. The finest cloth was used to make clothing for the Aztec royal family and nobles. Before teenage girls learned to weave, they were expected to grind flour, make tortillas, and cook meals.

The End of an Empire In 1519, Spanish conquistadors invaded the Aztec Empire. Some of the peoples whose lands the Aztecs had conquered joined forces with the Spanish. Together, they fought the Aztecs and tried to overthrow the Aztec emperor, Moctezuma. The two sides waged fierce battles. Diseases carried by the Spanish spread to the Aztecs and killed many of them. In 1521, the Aztecs surrendered to the Spanish. The once-powerful Aztec Empire was at an end.

✔ Reading Check **Describe the levels of Aztec society.**

Aztec Feather Headdress
Moctezuma's head covering was decorated with feathers—an important symbol in the Aztec religion.

Section 2 Assessment

Key Terms
Review the key terms at the beginning of this section. Use each term in a sentence that explains its meaning.

Target Reading Skill
State three details that support the main idea of the first paragraph under the heading Aztec Society.

Comprehension and Critical Thinking
1. (a) Recall What activity was the basis of Mayan life?

(b) Explain How did Mayan religion reflect the importance of this activity?
(c) Infer What do you think is the most likely reason the Mayas abandoned their cities? Explain your choice.
2. (a) Describe How did the Aztec Empire expand?
(b) Synthesize How did the Aztecs treat the peoples they conquered in war?
(c) Draw Conclusions Why might some of the peoples conquered by the Aztecs have wanted to overthrow the emperor?

Writing Activity
The Mayas and the Aztecs created great civilizations. How were their cultures alike? How were they different? Write a paragraph comparing and contrasting the two civilizations.

Writing Tip First take notes on the similarities and differences. You may want to use a chart to help you organize. Be sure to write a topic sentence for your paragraph, and then support it with details from your notes.

Focus On
The Great Temple

In 1521, the Spanish conquered the Aztecs and began to destroy the Aztec capital of Tenochtitlán. On the site of the ruined Aztec city, they built a new capital: Mexico City. For many years, an important piece of Mexico's past—the Great Temple of the Aztecs—remained buried under this new city. Scholars were not sure where the site of the Great Temple lay. Then in 1978, electrical workers dug up an old stone carving. Experts who studied the carving knew that it had been made by the Aztecs. The site of the Great Temple had been found.

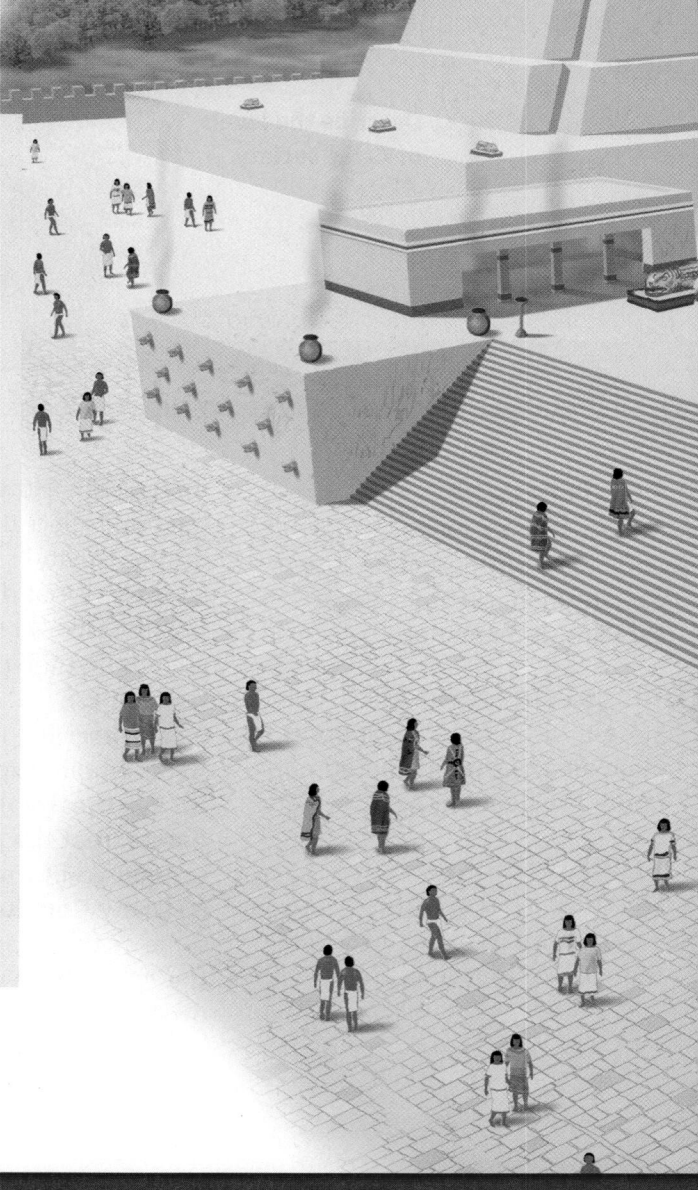

Building the Temple The Great Temple honored two Aztec gods: Tlaloc (tlah LOHK), the god of earth and rain, and Huitzilopochtli (weets eel oh POHCH tlee), the god of sun and sky. The Aztecs first built the temple about 1325. A solid, earth-filled pyramid, the heavy temple soon began to sink into the soft soil of Tenochtitlán. To save their sinking monument, the Aztecs rebuilt it six times within the next 200 years.

The Aztecs rebuilt each new temple over the previous temple. After rebuilding, they honored their gods with human sacrifices in the temple's shrines. A figure called a chacmool, at the top left, was used to hold offerings to the gods.

The illustration at the right shows some of the temple layers. By the time the Spanish began to destroy Tenochtitlán in 1521, the Great Temple had been built seven times.

Sacred Ornament

The double-headed serpent was a symbol of Tlaloc, the god of earth and rain. A high priest probably wore this ornament on his chest.

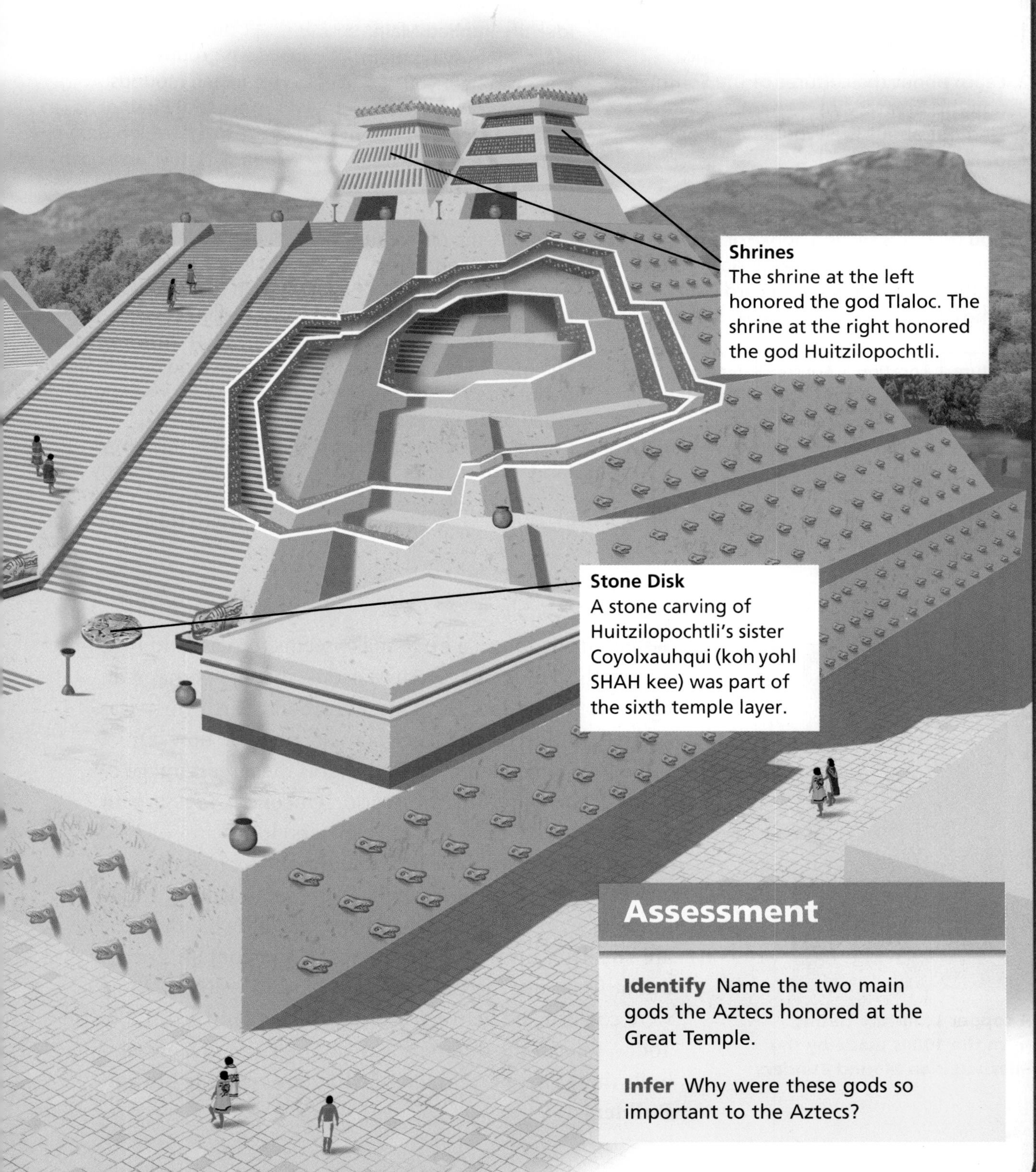

Shrines

The shrine at the left honored the god Tlaloc. The shrine at the right honored the god Huitzilopochtli.

Stone Disk

A stone carving of Huitzilopochtli's sister Coyolxauhqui (koh yohl SHAH kee) was part of the sixth temple layer.

Assessment

Identify Name the two main gods the Aztecs honored at the Great Temple.

Infer Why were these gods so important to the Aztecs?

Cultures of North America

Prepare to Read

Objectives

In this section, you will
1. Find out about the Mound Builders who lived in eastern North America.
2. Learn about the cultures of the Southwest and the Great Plains.
3. Find out about the Woodland peoples of North America.

Taking Notes

As you read this section, look for information about three major Native American cultures. Copy the table below and record your findings in it. Add categories as needed.

Culture	Location	Source of Food	Type of Dwelling

Target Reading Skill

Identify Implied Main Ideas Identifying main ideas can help you remember what you read. Even if a main idea is not stated directly, the details in a paragraph add up to the main idea. For example, the details in the paragraph under the heading The Eastern Mound Builders add up to this main idea: The Mound Builders, hunters and gatherers who relied on the land's resources, became settled farmers over time.

Key Terms

- **Mound Builders** (mownd BIL durz) *n.* Native American groups who built earthen mounds
- **Ancestral Puebloans** (an SES trul PWEB loh unz) *n.* early Native American peoples of the Southwest
- **pueblo** (PWEB loh) *n.* a cluster of Native American stone or adobe dwellings
- **kiva** (KEE vuh) *n.* a round room used by the Pueblo peoples for religious ceremonies
- **Great Plains** (grayt playnz) *n.* a mostly flat and grassy region of western North America

A copper sculpture dating from the 1000s made by the Mississippian Mound Builders

Seen from above, a huge snake seems to twist and turn across the landscape. A mysterious shape—perhaps an egg?—is at its mouth. This enormous earthwork was created hundreds of years ago in what is now Ohio. Called the Great Serpent Mound, it is the largest image of a snake anywhere in the world. Uncoiled, the serpent would be about 1,349 feet (411 meters) long.

Archaeologists have found thousands of earthworks across eastern North America. They were made by thousands of workers moving baskets of earth by hand. There are small mounds and large ones. Some contain graves, but others—like the Great Serpent Mound—do not. Most were constructed between around 700 B.C. and A.D. 1250. Today, we call the different Native American groups who built these curious and long-lasting mounds the **Mound Builders**.

The Eastern Mound Builders

The Mound Builders lived in eastern North America. They occupied the region roughly between Minnesota and Louisiana, and between the Mississippi River and the Atlantic Ocean. The Mound Builders lived along the area's many rivers, which provided them with plenty of fish and fresh water. They hunted wild animals for food, including deer, turkeys, bears, and even squirrels. They also gathered nuts such as acorns, pecans, and walnuts to supplement their diet. Over time, these communities began to grow their own food. This meant they did not have to move as much in search of food and could form settlements.

Early Mound Builders: The Adena Archaeologists have discovered evidence of early Mound Builders who lived about 600 B.C. in the Ohio Valley. Called the Adena (uh DEE nuh), these people constructed mounds that are usually less than 20 feet high. Certain mounds were tombs that contained weapons, tools, and decorative objects in addition to bodies. Some items were made from materials not found locally, such as copper and seashells. Thus, historians believe that the Adena must have taken part in long-distance trade. Little is known about the daily life of the Adena, but they seem to have declined about 100 B.C.

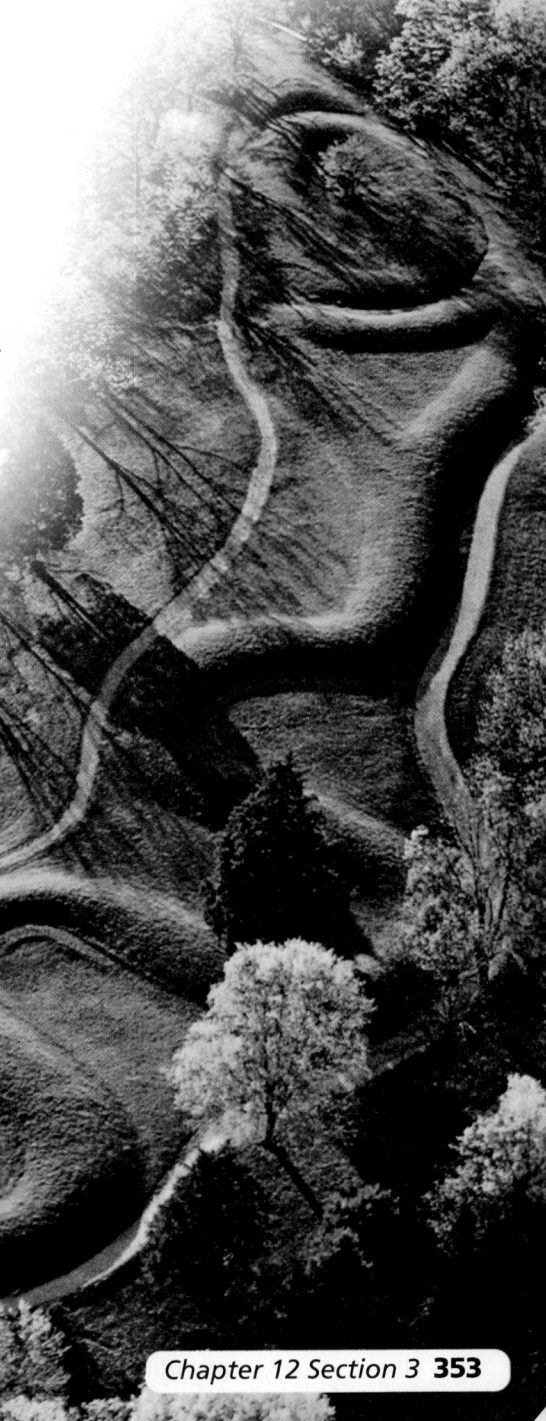

Great Serpent Mound
The Great Serpent Mound snakes across Ohio's countryside.
Infer *What about the mound suggests that it may have had religious importance?*

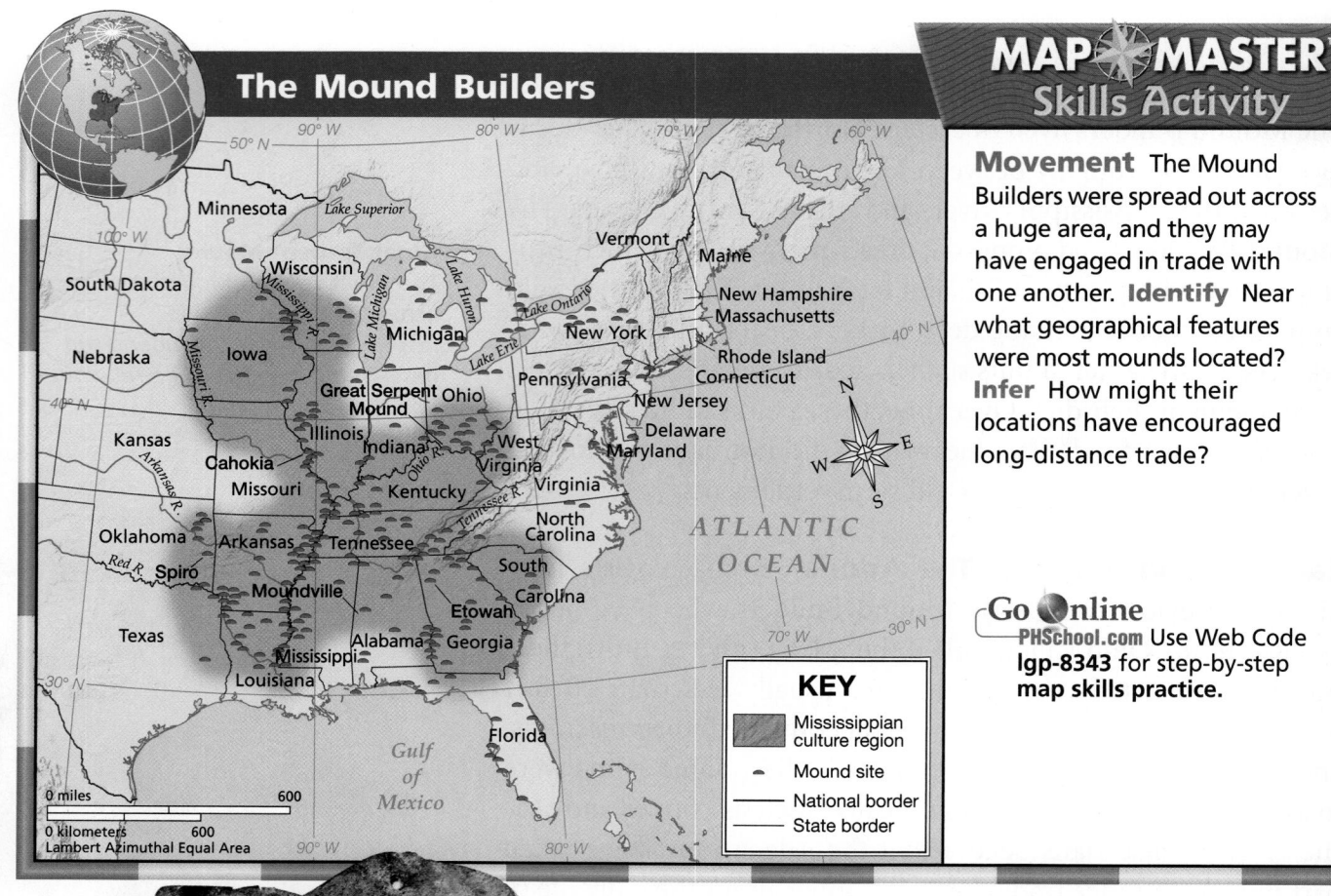

MAP MASTER™
Skills Activity

Movement The Mound Builders were spread out across a huge area, and they may have engaged in trade with one another. **Identify** Near what geographical features were most mounds located? **Infer** How might their locations have encouraged long-distance trade?

Go Online
PHSchool.com Use Web Code **lgp-8343** for step-by-step map skills practice.

KEY
- Mississippian culture region
- Mound site
- National border
- State border

0 miles   600
0 kilometers   600
Lambert Azimuthal Equal Area

The Hopewell made figures like the copper raven (above) and the hand (bottom right), which is made of mica, a soft mineral.

The Hopewell Culture About 100 years before the Adena disappeared, another culture appeared along the Ohio and upper Mississippi rivers. Called the Hopewell, these peoples built larger mounds. The Hopewell did not have a highly organized society with a single ruler. Instead, they lived in many small communities with local leaders.

The Hopewell peoples grew a greater variety of crops than did the Adena. They also seem to have traded over a wider area. There is evidence that goods were traded from the Gulf of Mexico to present-day Canada and from the Rocky Mountains to the Atlantic Ocean. Hopewell sites have silver from the Great Lakes region and alligator teeth from present-day Florida.

About A.D. 400, the long-distance trade across eastern North America seems to have faded out. Also, the Hopewell stopped building new mounds. Historians are not sure why. The climate may have turned colder and hurt agriculture. The Hopewell may have suffered a severe drought or been invaded. Overpopulation is also a possible reason for their decline.

The Mississippians By about A.D. 700, a new and important culture called Mississippian (mis uh SIP ee un) began to flower in eastern North America. These peoples inhabited both small and large communities. Like the earlier Mound Builders, the Mississippians lived along rivers and built mounds. They, too, grew new kinds of crops. Maize and beans became important parts of their diet. Both foods are easily dried and stored in large amounts. This helped the Mississippians protect themselves against years of drought and bad harvests.

The Mississippian culture spread over a wide area in the present-day South and Midwest. During this period, long-distance trade revived. Populations increased over time, and major centers of government and religion developed. These include Moundville in present-day Alabama, and Etowah (ET uh wah) in present-day Georgia. The largest center was Cahokia (kuh HOH kee uh), located in what is now Illinois. One of Cahokia's mounds, around 100 feet tall, was the largest mound in North America.

Cahokia was a large city for its day. Historians estimate that it reached its peak about 1100. At that time, as many as 20,000 to 30,000 people may have lived there. But by 1250, the population dropped. The disappearance of the last of the Mound Builders is as mystifying as the many earthworks they left behind.

✓ **Reading Check** **How did the Mississippians live?**

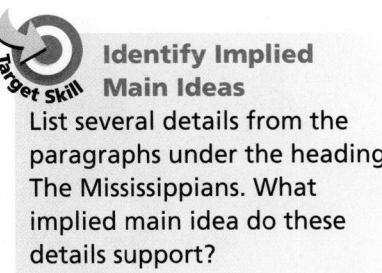

Identify Implied Main Ideas
List several details from the paragraphs under the heading The Mississippians. What implied main idea do these details support?

An archaeologist digs at Chaco Canyon, New Mexico.

Peoples of the Southwest and the Great Plains

The mounds of the Mound Builders are not the only impressive structures built by early Native American cultures. Other peoples in North America adapted to different landscapes and climates to create distinctive structures. One of these groups created tall multistory homes from the available materials of the Southwest.

Ancestral Puebloans The **Ancestral Puebloans**, also known as Anasazi, were early Native American peoples of the Southwest. Ancestral Puebloan culture began about A.D. 100. Historians think that Chaco Canyon, in present-day New Mexico, was a trading center for the region. A network of roads connected distant Ancestral Puebloan villages to Chaco Canyon. Archaeologists have found tens of thousands of turquoise pieces as well as baskets, pottery, shells, and feathers in Chaco Canyon.

Cliff Village
Entire villages of Ancestral Puebloans lived under the shelter of rock cliffs like this one in Colorado. Ancestral Puebloan craftspeople decorated pottery like the jar above with black and white patterns.
Analyze Images *What might be some advantages to living under cliffs like these?*

The American Southwest has cold, dry winters and hot, dry summers. The soil is mostly poor, and there is little water. To capture rainwater for their fields, the Ancestral Puebloans created a system of canals and dams. This system allowed them to grow maize, beans, and squash for food. They also grew cotton for cloth.

For their homes, the Ancestral Puebloans constructed **pueblos** (PWEB lohz). These clusters of stone and adobe dwellings helped to keep people warm in the winter and cool in the summer. Pueblos had thick walls. Round rooms called **kivas** (KEE vuz) were used for special religious ceremonies. As the population grew, so did the pueblos. Some pueblos were five stories tall and had hundreds of rooms. Between 1275 and 1300, however, severe droughts hit the region. The Ancestral Puebloans abandoned all their major pueblos, never to return.

Later Pueblo Peoples Ancestral Puebloan customs survived among later groups who lived in the same region. They are called Pueblo peoples, or simply Pueblos. These groups also built apartment-style stone and adobe dwellings with kivas. Like the Ancestral Puebloans, their crafts included weaving, basket-making, and pottery. They were also skilled farmers.

The region of New Mexico and Arizona where the Pueblos lived receives only 8 to 13 inches of rain a year, but it does have rivers. The Pueblos planted corn, squash, beans, and other crops in the river bottoms near their dwellings. They relied on intensive irrigation to raise these crops. Hunting and gathering provided the Pueblos with the food they could not grow.

The Pueblos believed in many spirits, called kachinas (kuh CHEE nuz). They wanted to please these spirits, who they believed controlled the rain, wild animals, and harvests. Many times a year, the Pueblos gathered for ceremonies that involved prayer, dancing, and singing. They also appealed to their ancestors, another type of kachina. Today the modern Pueblo peoples, including the Hopi and the Zuni, keep many of these traditions alive.

The Plains Indians West of the Mississippi River and east of the Rocky Mountains is a mostly flat and grassy region called the **Great Plains.** For centuries, this land was home to diverse groups of Native Americans called Plains Indians. Individual groups had their own languages and traditions. They used a form of sign language to trade with one another.

Some groups, such as the Mandan, were farmers. They lived in fenced villages along the Missouri River, in lodges made of earth and wood. Others, such as the Sioux (soo), followed herds of bison that roamed the plains. Dwellings such as tipis (TEE peaz)—easy to take apart, carry, and set up again—were ideal for such a lifestyle.

After the arrival of Europeans, the lives of Plains Indians changed rapidly. They had to share their land with eastern Native Americans, such as the Omaha, who had been forced west by white settlers. Newly introduced horses, guns, and railroads altered their traditions. Most groups suffered from diseases brought by Europeans and lost their land to European settlement. Many Native American cultures began to break down. Today, there is a strong effort to revive these traditional cultures.

✓ Reading Check How did the Sioux live?

Links Across The World

The Arrival of the Horse
The arrival of the horse in the Americas brought major changes to the lives of many Plains Indians. Native Americans on horseback became expert buffalo hunters. They came to depend more and more on the buffalo for their existence, using the animal for food, clothing, and shelter. Many previously settled Indian groups became nomadic. They rode their horses across the plains, following the great herds of buffalo.

Peoples of the Woodlands

Native American groups lived in woodlands in different parts of present-day Canada and the United States. The peoples of the Northwest Coast hunted in the forests and fished in rivers full of salmon as well as in the Pacific Ocean. They lived in settlements of wooden homes. Like the Mound Builders and the Pueblos, early Native Americans of the Northwest Coast created remarkable structures. They were called totem poles.

Totem poles were carved and painted logs stood on end. They typically had images of real or mythical animals. Often the animals were identified with the owner's family line, much as a family crest is used in European cultures. Totem poles were a symbol of the owner's wealth, as were ceremonies called potlatches. At a potlatch, a person of high rank invited many guests and gave them generous gifts.

In the eastern woodlands, Native American groups such as the Iroquois (IHR uh kwoy) not only hunted in the forests but also cleared land for farms. Because the men were often at war, the women were the farmers. In the 1500s, five Iroquois nations—Mohawk, Onondaga, Cayuga, Seneca, and Oneida—formed a peace alliance. Nations of the Iroquois League governed their own villages, but they met to decide issues that affected the group as a whole. This was the best-organized political system in the Americas when Europeans arrived.

Totem pole in Vancouver, Canada

✓ **Reading Check** What was the Iroquois League?

Section 3 Assessment

Key Terms

Review the key terms at the beginning of this section. Use each term in a sentence that explains its meaning.

Target Reading Skill

State the main ideas in Section 3.

Comprehension and Critical Thinking

1. (a) Sequence List the three groups of Mound Builders, from earliest to latest.

(b) Compare In what ways were the three groups alike?

2. (a) Identify What is the climate of southwestern North America?

(b) Identify Cause and Effect Why did peoples of this region build pueblos rather than other types of structures?

3. (a) Define What are totem poles and potlatches?

(b) Infer How were totem poles and potlatches symbols of a family's wealth?

Writing Activity

Study the photograph of the Ancestral Puebloan cliff dwellings on pages 356–357. Write a paragraph describing the site. What are the buildings like? Where are they located? What might it be like there at night or during a storm?

> **Writing Tip** Use descriptive adjectives for colors, textures, and shapes. Also include any sounds and smells you might experience there at different times of the day or year.

Standardized Test Prep

Test-Taking Tips

Some questions on standardized tests ask you to analyze a timeline. Study the timeline below. Then follow the tips to answer the sample question.

A.D. 250–900
The Mayas are at their strongest.

A.D. 1200–1535
The Incas rule from Cuzco.

200 400 600 800 1000 1200 1400 1600

A.D. 700–1250
Mississippian culture thrives.

A.D. 1325–1521
The Aztecs rule from Tenochtitlán.

Choose the letter of the best answer.

Based on the timeline, which statement is true?

A Mississippian culture ended at A.D. 1100.

B The Incas ruled from Cuzco for more than 400 years.

C The Aztecs and the Incas did not live at the same time.

D Mississippian culture began to thrive about A.D. 700.

TIP Use the lines at the beginning and end of each civilization bracket to calculate how long each civilization lasted.

Think It Through You can see that the line marking the end of Mississippian culture falls after 1200. Therefore A is incorrect. "The Incas rule from Cuzco" starts at 1200 and ends before 1600, so you can rule out B, too. The brackets on the timeline show that the Incas and the Aztecs did live at the same time. And the dates for the Aztecs, 1325–1521, overlap with the dates for the Incas, 1200–1535. So C is incorrect. That leaves only D. You can see that the line marking the start of Mississippian culture does indeed fall halfway between 600 and 800. D is the correct answer.

TIP Preview the question and skim over the answer choices before you look at the timeline. Keep the questions and possible answers in mind as you study the timeline.

Practice Questions

Use the timeline above to help you choose the letter of the best answer.

1. Based on the timeline, which statement is true?

   A The Incas began to rule from Cuzco about A.D. 1000.

   B The Aztecs and the Incas did not live at the same time.

   C The Mayas were at their strongest for more than 600 years.

   D Mississippian culture lasted for only 200 years.

Choose the letter of the best answer to complete each sentence.

2. The _____ built stone and adobe dwellings close together.

   A Incas

   B Hopewell peoples

   C Ancestral Puebloans

   D Adena

3. The spectacular site of Machu Picchu is located in

   A the Great Plains.

   B South America.

   C North America.

   D Lake Texcoco.

4. The _____ lived along rivers in eastern North America.

   A Mound Builders

   B Aztecs

   C Mayas

   D Pueblo peoples

Use Web Code lga-8303 for a **Chapter 3 self-test.**

13 Civilizations of Asia

Chapter Preview

This chapter will introduce you to the civilizations that thrived in China, Japan, and India during the medieval period.

Section 1
Golden Ages of China

Section 2
Medieval Japan

Section 3
The Great Mughal Empire in India

Target Reading Skill

Cause and Effect In this chapter you will focus on determining cause and effect in order to help you understand relationships among situations and events.

▶ A large stone statue of the Buddha in the Qian Qi Temple Cave, China, carved during the Tang dynasty

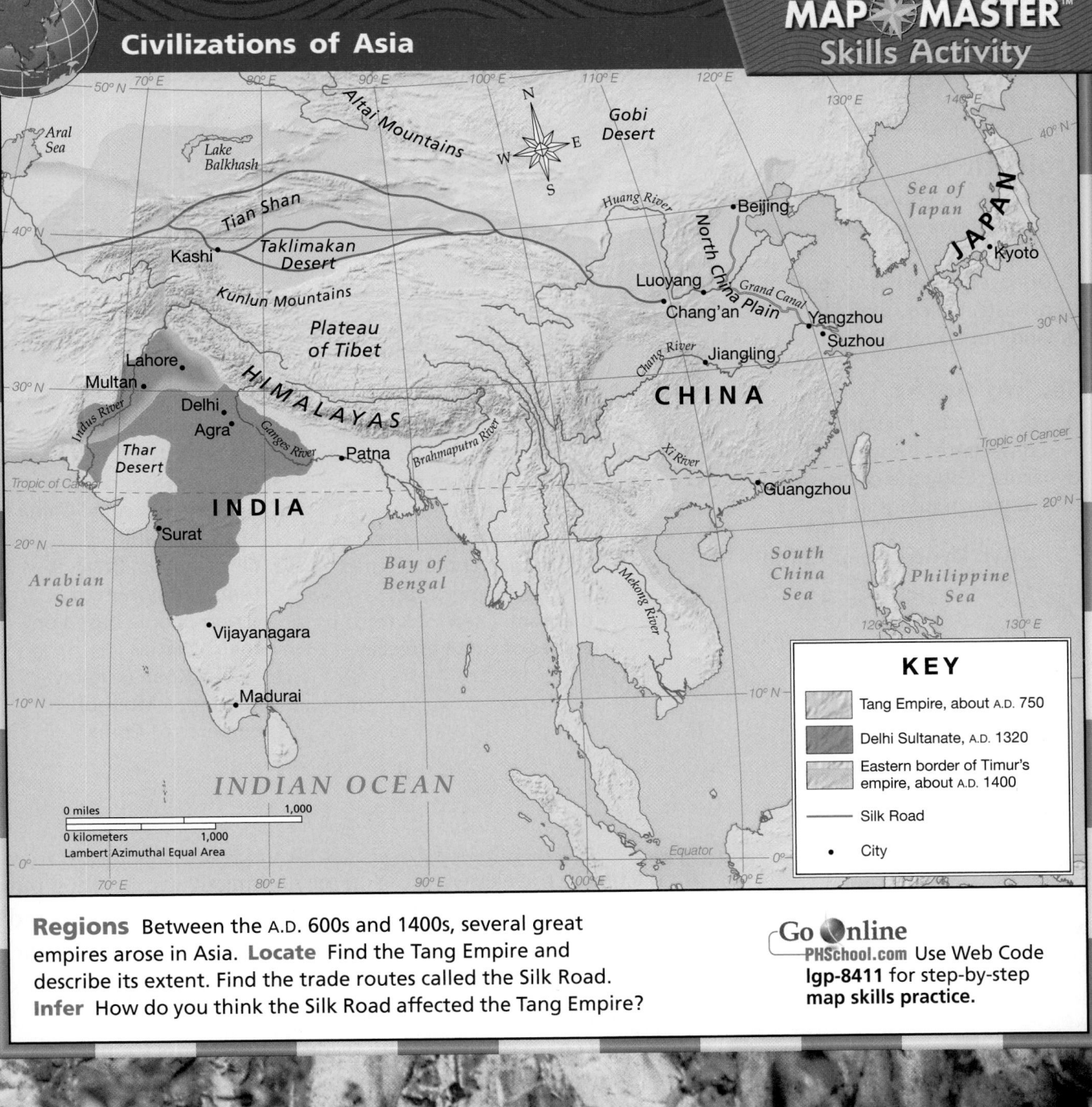

KEY

- Tang Empire, about A.D. 750
- Delhi Sultanate, A.D. 1320
- Eastern border of Timur's empire, about A.D. 1400
- —— Silk Road
- • City

Regions Between the A.D. 600s and 1400s, several great empires arose in Asia. **Locate** Find the Tang Empire and describe its extent. Find the trade routes called the Silk Road. **Infer** How do you think the Silk Road affected the Tang Empire?

Go Online
PHSchool.com Use Web Code
lgp-8411 for step-by-step
map skills practice.

Prepare to Read

Objectives

In this section you will

1. Learn about the Golden Age of the Tang dynasty.
2. Discover the achievements of the Song dynasty, which ruled China after the Tang.
3. Find out about Mongol rule of China.

Taking Notes

As you read this section, look for similarities and differences between the Tang and Song dynasties. Copy the diagram below and record your findings in it.

Two Dynasties of China

Tang   Song

Target Reading Skill

Identify Causes and Effects A cause makes something happen. An effect is what happens. Determining causes and effects helps you understand relationships among situations and events. As you read this section, think of the cultures of the Tang and Song dynasties as effects. Write their characteristics in your Taking Notes diagram. Then look for the causes of these effects.

Key Terms

- **Silk Road** (silk rohd) *n.* a chain of trade routes stretching from China to the Mediterranean Sea
- **dynasty** (DY nus tee) *n.* a series of rulers from the same family
- **Tang** (tahng) *n.* a dynasty that ruled China for almost 300 years
- **Song** (sawng) *n.* a dynasty that ruled China after the Tang
- **merit system** (MEHR it SIS tum) *n.* a system of hiring people based on their abilities
- **Kublai Khan** (KOO bly kahn) *n.* a Mongol emperor of China

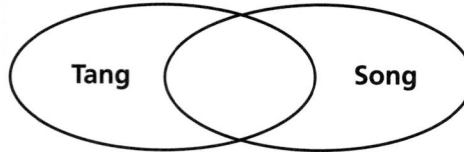

Silk from the Tang dynasty

A Chinese traveler wrote, "You see nothing in any direction but the sky and the sands, without the slightest trace of a road; and travelers find nothing to guide them but the bones of men and beasts." He was describing crossing the Gobi Desert along the Silk Road. In spite of its name, the **Silk Road** was not a single road. It was a long chain of connecting trade routes across Central Asia. These routes stretched about 4,000 miles (6,400 kilometers), all the way from China to the eastern Mediterranean Sea.

For centuries, camels, horses, and donkeys carried traders and their precious goods along the Silk Road. Travelers braved blowing desert sands, cold and rocky mountain passes, and even robbers. Most of the goods they carried were small and very valuable. One—a beautiful, lightweight fabric called silk—was so important that it gave the route its name.

The Tang Dynasty

China covers much of East Asia. It is an immense land with a varied landscape. In the east are lowland and coastal regions. Fertile valleys lie along the Chang and the Huang (hwahng) rivers. To the north and west of these farmlands are great deserts and mountainous regions, including the Gobi Desert in the north and the Plateau of Tibet in the west.

Look at the map titled Tang and Song Empires on page 366. Notice that under the Tang, the land under Chinese control stretched westward into Central Asia. Peoples from these distant areas and traders traveling along the Silk Road introduced new ideas—as well as new goods—to China. In return, the Chinese traded their tea, jade, ivory, ceramics, and silk. Chinese ideas and inventions also spread to other nations. Such exchanges helped China become an important center of trade and culture.

Guarding the Silk Road
This beacon tower along the Silk Road is in western China. **Infer** *Why do you think towers like this were built along the Silk Road?*

Dynasties Rule China Throughout its long history, China has been ruled by many different dynasties. A **dynasty** is a series of rulers from the same family. For example, the Han dynasty ruled China from 206 B.C to A.D. 220. After the collapse of the Han dynasty, China broke up into several kingdoms, but Chinese culture survived. Buddhism spread throughout China, and the arts and learning continued to develop. In 581, the Sui (swee) dynasty came to power. The Sui ruled only until 618, but they united the north and south of China for the first time in centuries.

A Golden Age Begins In 618, the Sui dynasty was overthrown. The **Tang** came to power and ruled China for almost 300 years. The Tang dynasty was a golden age of political and cultural achievement. Under Tang rule, China grew in both area and population. Its capital, Chang'an (chahng ahn), was the world's largest city at that time. Historians estimate that it was home to about one million people. Chang'an was shaped like a rectangle and surrounded by tall walls for protection. A variety of foods, entertainment, and fine goods were available to those who lived there.

Tang Taizong

The Grand Canal China enjoyed great prosperity under the Tang dynasty. One source of China's economic strength was the Grand Canal, which had been greatly extended under the earlier Sui dynasty.

The Grand Canal was a waterway that linked the Huang River and the Chang River. At more than 1,000 miles (1,600 kilometers) long, it is still the longest canal ever built. The Grand Canal helped join northern and southern China and made it possible to supply the capital with large amounts of grain grown in the south.

A Great Ruler The greatest ruler of the Tang dynasty was Tang Taizong (tahng ty ZAWNG). He began his military career at the age of 16, and helped his father establish the Tang dynasty. During his rule, from 626 to 649, he was not only a successful general, but also a scholar and historian. In addition, Tang Taizong was a master of calligraphy, the art of beautiful handwriting.

MAP MASTER™
Skills Activity

Regions Notice the difference in the areas controlled by the Tang and the Song dynasties. **Identify** Under which dynasty did China lose control of much of the Silk Road? **Infer** How might that have affected China's trade with lands to the west?

Go Online
PHSchool.com Use Web Code **lgp-8421** for step-by-step map skills practice.

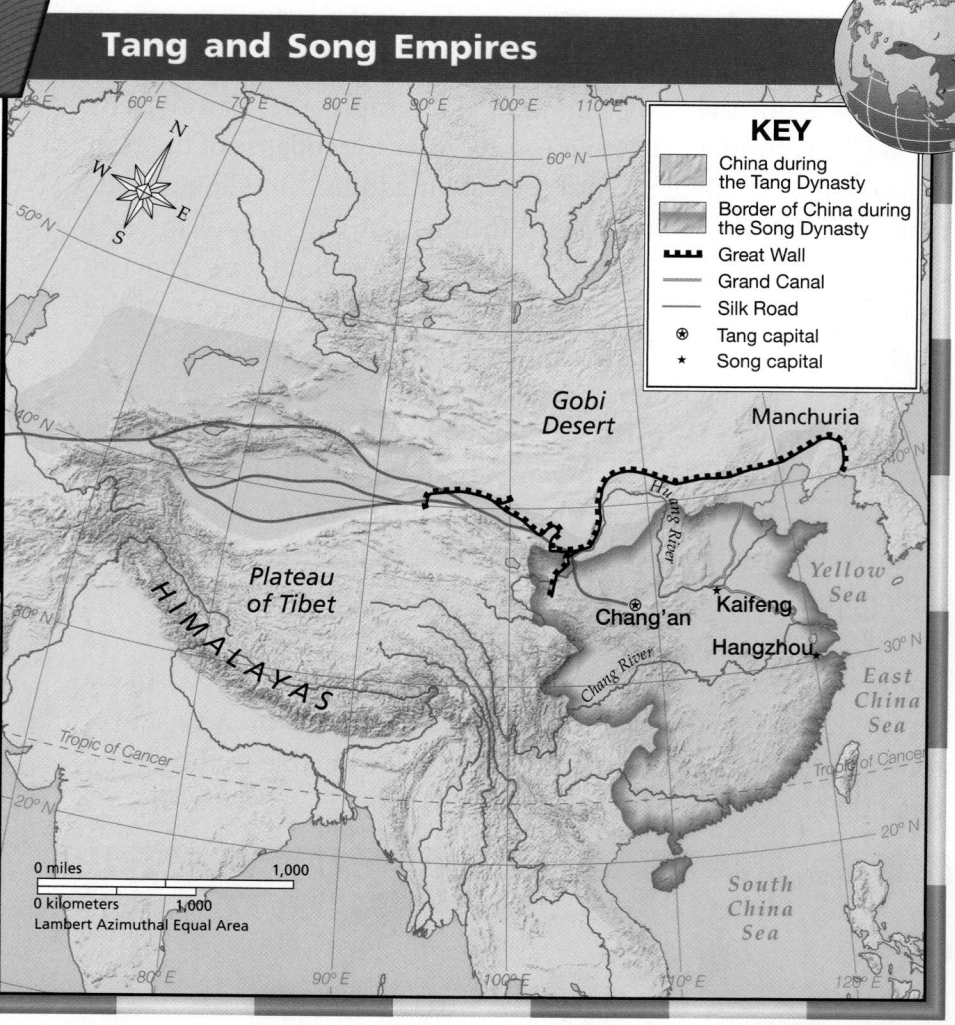

Tang and Song Empires

KEY
- China during the Tang Dynasty
- Border of China during the Song Dynasty
- Great Wall
- Grand Canal
- Silk Road
- ⊛ Tang capital
- ★ Song capital

Gobi Desert

Manchuria

Plateau of Tibet

HIMALAYAS

Chang'an

Kaifeng

Hangzhou

Yellow Sea

East China Sea

South China Sea

Tropic of Cancer

0 miles 1,000
0 kilometers 1,000
Lambert Azimuthal Equal Area

Tang Taizong worked to strengthen law and order and his own power by promoting the teachings of Confucius (kun FYOO shus). Confucius was an ancient Chinese teacher who had taught that all people had duties and responsibilities. Confucius had wanted to bring peace and stability to China. To create this kind of society, Confucius said, all people must treat one another with respect.

Tang Taizong began to reform the government according to Confucius's ideas. The Tang government hired officials trained in Confucian philosophy. It also began land reform, giving more land to the peasants who farmed it.

✓ **Reading Check** What are some achievements of Tang Taizong?

The Song Dynasty

After 850, China's control of its westernmost lands weakened. Then fighting among different groups within China ended the Tang dynasty. Order was restored about 50 years later by the **Song** (sawng), the dynasty that ruled China from 960 to 1279.

Changes in Government At the beginning of the Song dynasty, the Chinese capital was located at Kaifeng (KY fung), along the Grand Canal. After the Song lost control of regions to the north, they moved the capital to Hangzhou (hahn JOH), near the coast.

The Song rulers made many advances in government. They expanded the **merit system** of hiring government officials. Under this system, officials had to pass tests and prove their ability to do the work. Before the Song, officials came from rich and powerful families. They were allowed to keep their positions for life even if they did not do a good job. Hiring people based on their abilities, rather than on their wealth or social position, greatly improved the Chinese government.

Improvements in Agriculture During the Song dynasty, new strains of rice and better irrigation methods helped peasants grow more rice. These two improvements allowed farmers to produce two crops a year instead of one. Food surpluses meant that more people could follow other trades or pursue the arts.

Links to
Language Arts

Poems and Legends Poetry was popular and respected during the Tang dynasty. Li Bo and Du Fu were two of the greatest poets of the era. Li Bo was also famous for his adventurous life—once he was even accused of treason. His poems, however, dealt with quieter subjects, such as nature and friendship. After Li Bo died, this legend spread about his death: Li Bo was in a boat at night. The moon's reflection was so beautiful that he reached out to seize it, fell overboard, and drowned. This painting shows Li Bo at a waterfall.

The Arts and Trade Chinese rulers supported many different forms of art, including music and poetry. During the Song dynasty, artists created the earliest known Chinese landscape paintings. They were painted on silk and featured peaceful scenes of water, rocks, and plants. The Chinese believed that such scenes helped both the painter and the viewer think about important forces in the natural world.

Song rulers also prized graceful art objects, such as those made from porcelain (PAWR suh lin), a white and very hard type of ceramic. Because it was first made in China, porcelain is often called *china*. For hundreds of years, Chinese craftspeople produced the finest ceramics. Because the Chinese produced the best porcelain in the world, it became an important item for trade.

Another item of great beauty and value was silk. It was so beautiful that it was called the queen of fibers. Silk comes from the cocoons of caterpillars called silkworms. For a long time, only the Chinese knew how to make silk. Even after others learned the method, Chinese silk was still the highest quality in the world. People in southwest Asia and Europe were willing to pay high prices for Chinese silk.

Links to
Economics

From China to Boston Tea drinking has been a part of Chinese culture since at least A.D. 350. The custom of drinking tea spread from China to Japan and other Asian countries, and tea became a major Chinese export crop. European countries began importing tea around 1600. The English sent tea from England to their colonies in North America. Late in the 1700s, the colonists' desire for tea—and the British government's desire to tax tea—contributed to the colonies' movement toward independence.

Chinese Ceramics
Europeans paid dearly for Song dynasty wares, such as these beautiful ceramics.
Analyze Images *If you were a European trader, which of these objects would you buy? Explain your answer.*

◀ Gunpowder
The Chinese invented gunpowder in the 800s. At first, they used it to make fireworks. By about 1300, however, it was being used in weapons.

◀ Compass
In the 1000s, Chinese sailors were using the magnetic compass for navigaon long voyages. At the left is a replica of a compass from the Song dynasty.

▼ Movable Type
About 1045, Chinese printers began using individual characters carved on small blocks to create a page of text. The blocks could be reused in a different order to produce various pieces of writing.

Smallpox Vaccine
As early as the 900s, the Chinese fought smallpox with a vaccine. They gave tiny doses of smallpox to healthy people so that they would develop an immunity to, or ability to avoid infection by, the deadly disease.

Printing, Books, and Learning One of the historic Song inventions was a new way to print books. For centuries, the Chinese had carved the characters of each page onto a wood block. They brushed ink over the carving and laid a piece of paper on it to print the page. Printers could make many copies of a book using these blocks, but carving the block for each page took a long time. Around 1045, Bi Sheng (bee sheng) developed a printing method that used movable type. He made many separate characters out of clay and rearranged them to make each page.

During the Song dynasty, books became less expensive. In earlier times, only the rich could buy them. With more people able to afford books, the number and kinds of books increased. More people, including women, also learned to read and write. By the 1200s, books about farming, medicine, religion, and poetry were in print. They helped to spread knowledge throughout China. This Song saying reflects the new importance of books:

> **To enrich your family, no need to buy good land: Books hold a thousand measures of grain. For an easy life, no need to build a mansion: In books are found houses of gold. "**
>
> — *A Song emperor*

✔ Reading Check **What does the Song emperor's saying mean?**

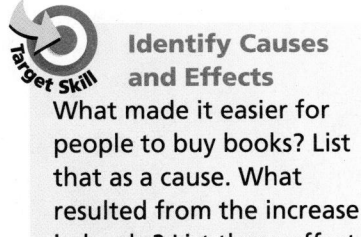

Identify Causes and Effects
What made it easier for people to buy books? List that as a cause. What resulted from the increase in books? List those effects.

Go **O**nline
PHSchool.com Use Web Code **mup-0835** for an interactivity on a Chinese ship.

The Mongols Conquer China

The Mongols were nomads from the plains of Central Asia, north of China. They were fierce warriors, said to "live in the saddle" because they spent so much time on horseback. By the 1200s, they were a tough military force. Under the leadership of Genghis Khan, they began forging an empire that eventually included China and Korea in the east, stretched into Russia and Eastern Europe in the west, and extended to the southwest as far as the Persian Gulf.

The Mongols Attack China
This illustration from the 1400s shows Kublai Khan's armies crossing a bridge to attack a Chinese fortress. **Conclude** *Use details in the illustration to draw conclusions about the dress, equipment, and methods of Kublai Khan's armies.*

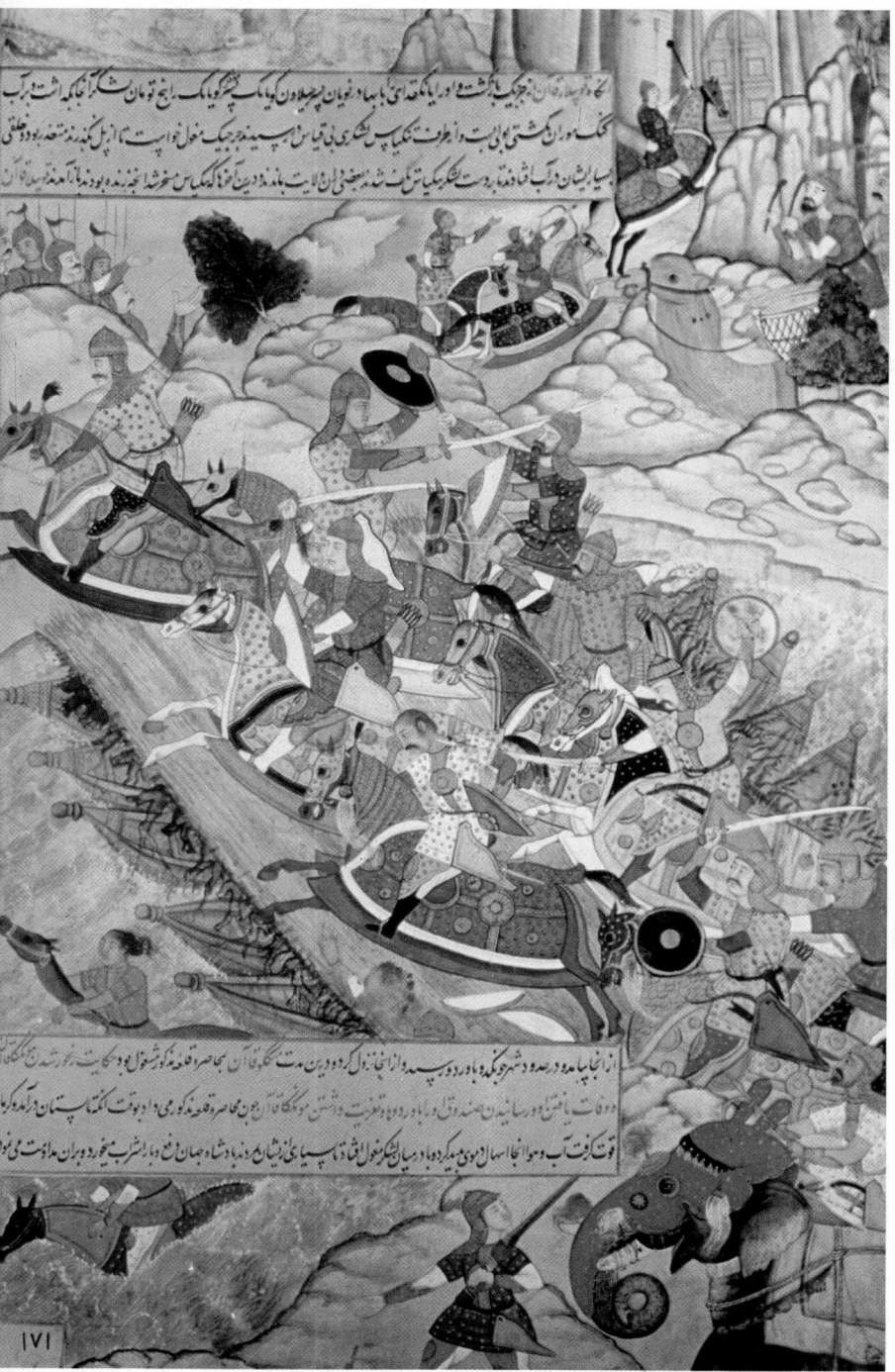

Kublai Khan, Mongol Ruler of China Genghis Khan had conquered all of northern China by 1215. But the southern Song empire continued to resist. It was left to Genghis Khan's grandson **Kublai Khan** to complete the conquest of China and to rule it.

Kublai Khan came to power in 1259. Within 20 years, he had toppled the last Song emperor. From his capital at the present-day city of Beijing, Kublai Khan declared himself emperor of China. He named his new dynasty *Yuan,* which means "beginning," because he intended that Mongol rule of China would last for centuries.

China Under Mongol Rule The Mongols centralized government in China. They did not allow the old Chinese ruling class to govern. High government positions were reserved for Mongols and were even given to foreigners rather than to Chinese. The Mongols also kept their own language and customs rather than adopting Chinese culture. They did, however, allow the practice of many religions.

Marco Polo at Kublai Khan's Court
The Italian Marco Polo, shown kneeling before Kublai Khan, worked for the khan for 17 years. **Analyze Images** *What detail in the painting indicates that Polo is reporting to Kublai Khan?*

Visitors from all lands were welcome at Kublai Khan's court. One of these was Ibn Battutah, an African Muslim. Another was a Christian from Europe, Marco Polo. He came from Venice in present-day Italy in 1271. After returning to Europe, Polo wrote about his travels. He described the riches of Kublai Khan's palace, China's efficient mail system, and its well-maintained roads.

Marco Polo's writings sparked increased trade between Europe and China. China prospered under Kublai Khan, but not under the khans, or emperors, who followed him. In 1368, a Chinese peasant led an uprising that overthrew the foreign rulers and ended Mongol rule of China.

Explore the history of kung fu.

✓ **Reading Check** **Describe Mongol rule of China.**

Section 1 Assessment

Key Terms
Review the key terms at the beginning of this section. Use each term in a sentence that explains its meaning.

Target Reading Skill
What were two effects of the Mongol rule of China?

Comprehension and Critical Thinking
1. (a) Recall What is the Grand Canal?

(b) Synthesize Why was it important?
2. (a) Identify Describe one important change in government made by the Song.
(b) Identify Effects How did this change affect China?
3. (a) Summarize How did the Mongols conquer China?
(b) Identify Frame of Reference Why do you think the Mongols did not adopt Chinese customs?

Writing Activity
During the Song dynasty, printed materials became available to many more people. What would life be like today without books and other printed materials? Write a journal entry to express your thoughts.

For: An activity on Chinese inventions
Visit: PHSchool.com
Web Code: lgd-8401

Skills for Life

Making an Outline

An outline is a way to organize information. It identifies the main ideas and supporting details. You can use an outline to take notes on what you read or to plan a report that you will write.

Learn the Skill

1 **Identify the most important points or main ideas, and list them with Roman numerals.** If you are outlining a text, look for headings stating these ideas.

2 **Decide on important subtopics for each main idea, and list them with capital letters.** Indent these entries under the main ideas, as shown in the sample outline below.

3 **Use Arabic numerals to list supporting ideas or details under each subtopic.** Indent these entries. Because an outline is a type of summary, you don't have to be as detailed or complete as your source. See the sample outline below.

4 **Check your outline for balance.** Make sure that the entries with Roman numerals are the most important ideas. Check that the ideas and information listed under the main ideas support those ideas. Make sure that main topics have at least two supporting subtopics or details.

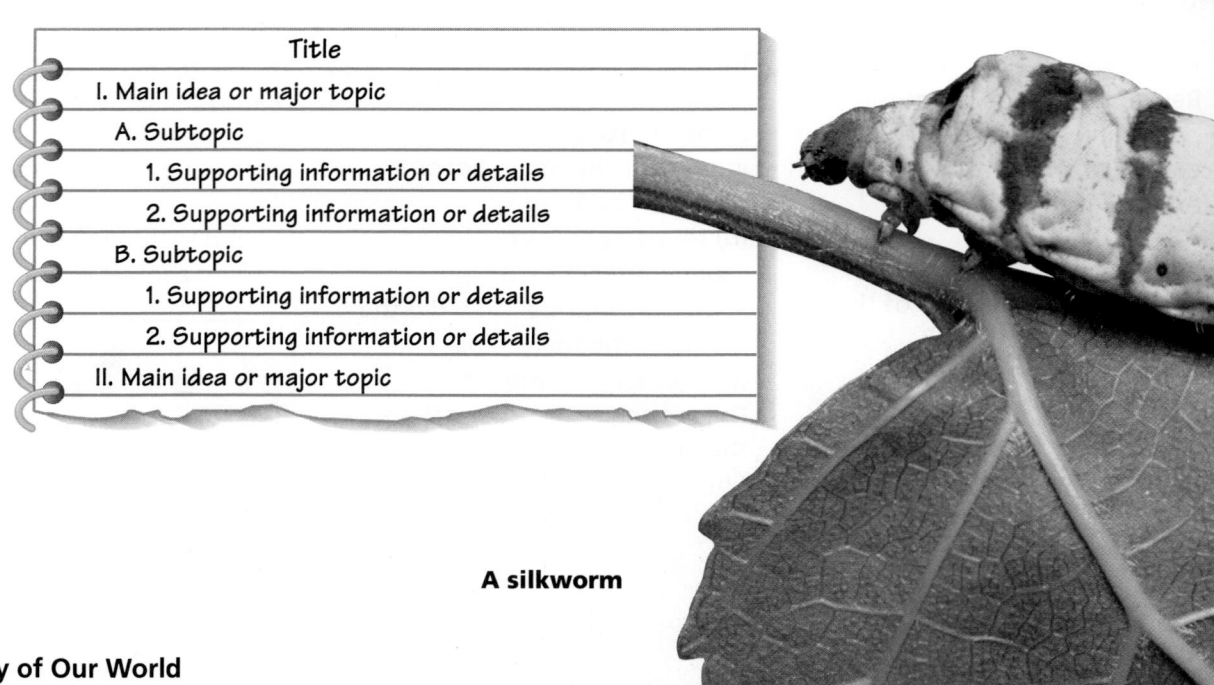

Title
I. Main idea or major topic
  A. Subtopic
    1. Supporting information or details
    2. Supporting information or details
  B. Subtopic
    1. Supporting information or details
    2. Supporting information or details
II. Main idea or major topic

A silkworm

Women preparing newly woven silk

Practice the Skill

Suppose you are outlining an article on silk making. You want to cover two main ideas: The Chinese were the first to make silk, and silk became an important trade product for China. Use the passage at the right as the source for the beginning of your outline. Then follow the steps below to outline it.

1. What is the main idea of the passage? Make it Roman numeral I of your outline.

2. Identify at least two important subtopics, and list them with capital letters.

3. Which details support the important topics or ideas? List those with Arabic numerals under the appropriate subtopics.

4. Reread your outline to be sure you have included all the important ideas and details. Make sure your outline correctly indicates which ideas are the most important and how other ideas and details support the main ideas.

Chinese Silk Making The fabric known as silk is made from the cocoons of caterpillars called silkworms. The cocoons are unwound very carefully, to avoid breaking the fibers. This process is long and difficult if done by hand—as it was in ancient China. The silk strands are then twisted together to form yarn, which is woven into fabric on a loom.

Silk making in China dates back more than 3,000 years. It is said that the empress Hsi Ling Shi, called the Goddess of Silk, invented the loom to weave this valuable fabric. She was a patron of the silk industry, which involved tending silkworms and cultivating the mulberry trees on which the caterpillars fed. This laborious work was done by women.

Silk was so beautiful and expensive that only royalty and nobles could afford to wear it. Because the fabric was so valuable and desirable, the Chinese kept the silk-making process a secret.

Apply the Skill

Reread the portion of text titled The Song Dynasty on pages 367–369. Make an outline of that text.

Prepare to Read

Objectives

In this section you will
1. Learn about the geography of Japan.
2. Discover the changes that occurred during the Heian period of Japanese history.
3. Find out about feudalism and the rule of the shoguns in Japan.

Taking Notes

As you read this section, look for details about the major periods of Japan's history. Copy the table below and record your findings in it.

Japan, 794–1867	
Period	**Characteristics**
Heian period	
Rise of the samurai	
Kamakura shogunate	
Tokugawa shogunate	

Target Reading Skill

Understand Effects An effect is what happens as the result of a specific cause or factor. For example, you can see in the paragraphs on the next page that the geography of Japan has had several effects on that nation. This section also discusses how contact with the outside world affected Japan. As you read, note the effects on Japan of the contact with the Mongols and with Europeans.

Key Terms

- **archipelago** (ahr kuh PEL uh goh) *n.* a group or chain of many islands
- **Kyoto** (kee OH toh) *n.* the capital city of medieval Japan
- **feudalism** (FYOOD ul iz um) *n.* a system in which poor people are legally bound to work for wealthy landowners
- **samurai** (SAM uh ry) *n.* Japanese warriors
- **shogun** (SHOH gun) *n.* the supreme military commander of Japan

Japanese woodcut of Mount Fuji

In A.D. 882, a group of more than 100 officials sailed across the sea to Japan. They were from a kingdom in Manchuria, north of China. They carried greetings for the Japanese emperor, as well as gifts of tiger skins and honey. When the emperor heard the news, he was pleased. This visit would give the Japanese a chance to display their achievements. The emperor's name was Yozei (yoh zay ee). At the time, he was only 14 years old.

Yozei sent expensive gifts of food and clothing to the visitors. He also sent people to escort them to his capital. The officials from Manchuria had landed in the north, and the capital was far to the south. The journey over land would take five months. The Japanese quickly fixed roads and bridges along the way. When the visitors arrived, there was a celebration. Japan's nobles, government leaders, and best poets were invited. Horse races, archery, and a poetry contest took place. A great feast was held, too, with much music and dancing.

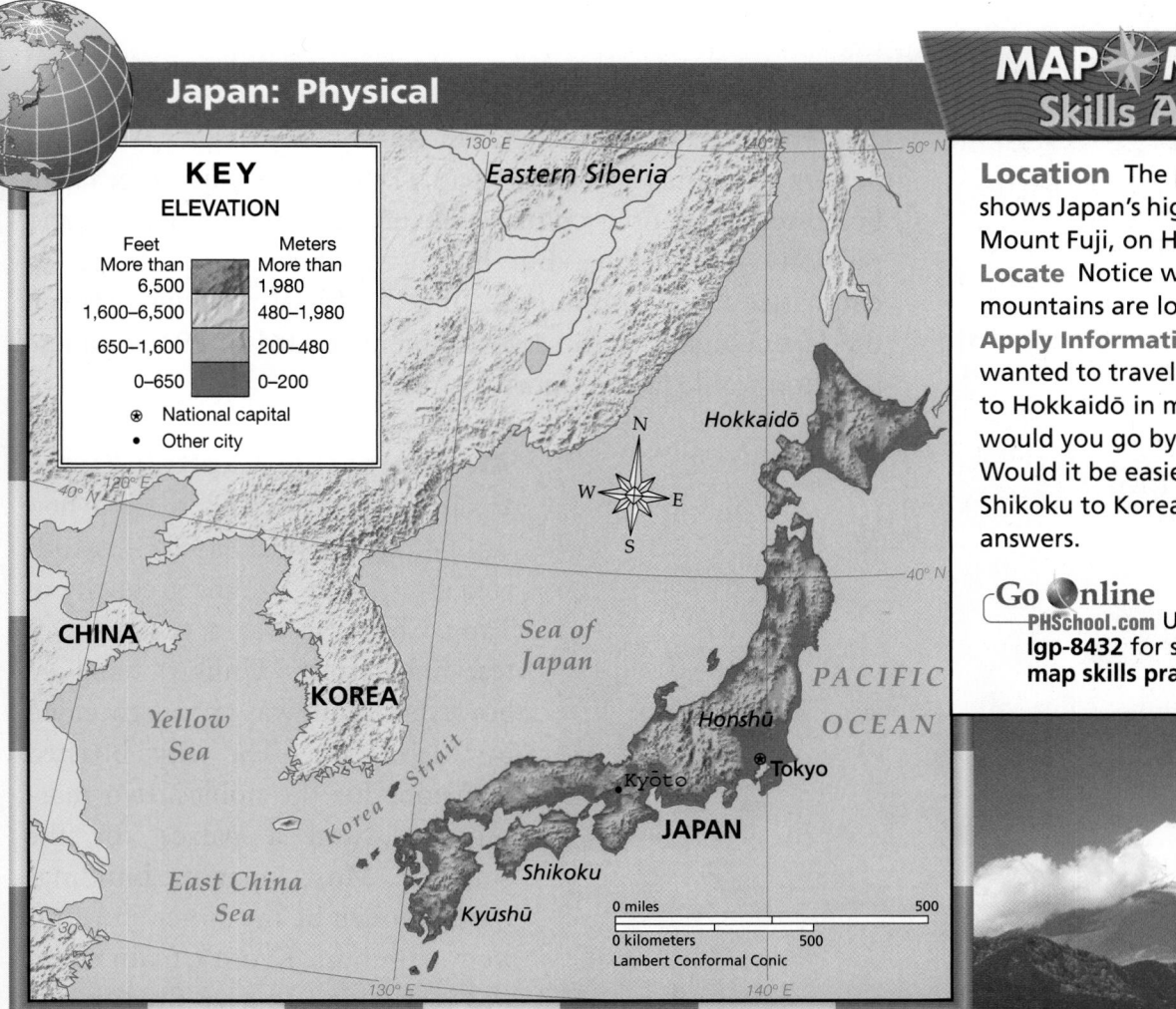

MAP★MASTER™
Skills Activity

KEY
ELEVATION

Feet		Meters
More than 6,500		More than 1,980
1,600–6,500		480–1,980
650–1,600		200–480
0–650		0–200

⊛ National capital
• Other city

Eastern Siberia

Hokkaidō

N
W — E
S

CHINA

Sea of Japan

40° N

Yellow Sea

KOREA

PACIFIC OCEAN

Honshū

Korea Strait

Kyōto

⊛ Tokyo

East China Sea

Shikoku

JAPAN

Kyūshū

0 miles 500
0 kilometers 500
Lambert Conformal Conic

130° E   140° E

Location The photo below shows Japan's highest mountain, Mount Fuji, on Honshū island.
Locate Notice where Japan's mountains are located.
Apply Information If you wanted to travel from Shikoku to Hokkaidō in medieval Japan, would you go by land or by sea? Would it be easier to go from Shikoku to Korea? Explain your answers.

Go Online
PHSchool.com Use Web Code **lgp-8432** for step-by-step **map skills practice.**

A Country of Islands

The visitors from Manchuria had a long trip over both land and sea to Japan. Japan is an **archipelago** (ahr kuh PEL uh goh), or chain of many islands, in the Pacific Ocean off the coast of the Asian mainland. It is about 500 miles (800 kilometers) from the coast of China but it is only 100 miles (160 kilometers) from Korea. The islands of Japan were formed by volcanoes, and earthquakes are common in the region.

Look at the map above. Notice that the islands of Japan are mountainous. The mountains make traveling by land difficult. As a result, the sea became an important highway for the Japanese— even for those traveling from place to place on the same island. On the other hand, for centuries, the sea helped to protect Japan from invaders. Over time, this isolation also led the Japanese to develop a distinctive way of life.

✓ **Reading Check** Describe Japan's geography.

The Heian Empire

The emperor Yozei ruled Japan during the Heian (HAY ahn) period, which lasted from 794 to 1185. Before this time, Japan borrowed much of its culture—including its literature, laws, and religion—from China. But during the 800s, Japan began to emphasize its own traditions. In fact, official relations between the Japanese and Chinese governments ended in 894. Japanese isolation would last for more than 500 years.

Modern Kyoto
The traditional Japanese pagoda, or shrine, in the foreground is still an important part of the modern, bustling city. **Infer** *What does this blend of architecture suggest about modern Japanese culture?*

An Impressive Capital: Kyoto

Heian emperors ruled from a new capital, **Kyoto** (kee OH toh). Modeled after Chang'an, the great city of Tang China, it was a rectangle of tree-lined streets. Unlike Chang'an, however, Kyoto was not surrounded by high walls. The city boasted mansions for the nobles, two marketplaces, and a palace for the emperor. Most Japanese buildings were wooden at the time, and fires were common. Kyoto's main street was very wide—to keep fires on one side from spreading to the other. Canals running through the capital also provided water to help put out any fires.

The Japanese Nobility The Heian period was a mostly peaceful time, during which Japanese culture thrived. Fine architecture, literature, and beautiful gardens all became a part of life for the nobility. Life for most of the population, however, was very different. Farmers, fishers, traders, and builders were usually poor and spent their time doing hard work.

The nobles believed that the importance of their families and their positions within the government set them apart from others. But even among the nobles, people belonged to different ranks, or classes. In fact, noblemen wore specially colored robes related to their position in society. Noblewomen were not affected by such rules because they could not hold official positions in the government.

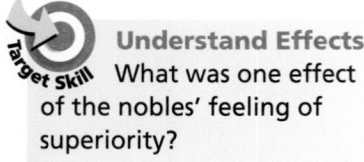

Target Skill
Understand Effects
What was one effect of the nobles' feeling of superiority?

✓ Reading Check **How did nobles live during the Heian period?**

Feudalism in Japan

During the 1000s, the Japanese emperor began to lose power. He continued to rule the capital, but he had less control over the rest of Japan. At the same time, the nobles gained greater power and wealth. They owned estates, or large tracts of land, outside the capital. The work on these estates was done by peasants. This kind of economic system, in which poor people are legally bound to work for wealthy landowners, is called **feudalism.**

Samurai Warriors Rich estate owners became so independent that they often disobeyed the emperor. They even hired private armies. The nobles paid these armies to defend them, their estates, and the peasants who worked for them. The armies were made up of warriors called **samurai** (SAM uh ry).

Samurai warriors followed a strict set of rules for behavior, called *bushido* (BOO shee doh). They swore an oath to follow these rules without question. According to bushido, honor meant more than wealth or even life itself. This code said that a samurai must never show weakness or surrender to an enemy. The true samurai had no fear of death, and would rather die than shame himself. He was expected to commit ritual suicide rather than betray the code of bushido.

Go Online
PHSchool.com Use Web Code **mup-0836** for an interactive tour of a Japanese castle.

Prepared for War
Samurai armor was made of small metal and leather scales tied with silk and leather. The painting below shows the charge of a samurai on horseback. **Analyze Images** *What do these two images suggest about samurai warriors?*

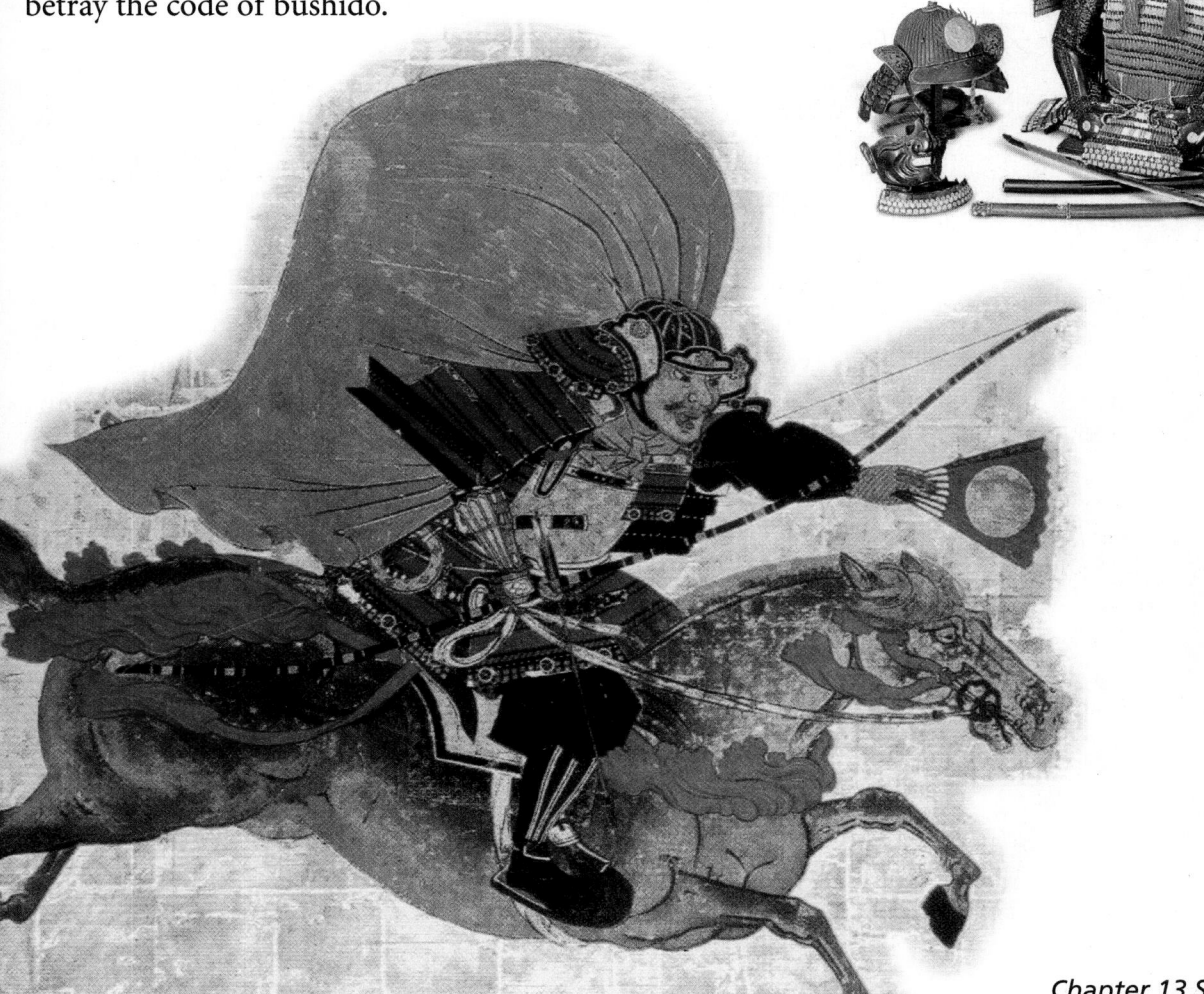

A New Class Gains Power Over time, the samurai warriors grew in number and formed their own clans. Each clan promised loyalty to a powerful warlord, or daimyo (DY myoh). The daimyo expected his samurai warriors to be willing to give their lives for him. As the different warlords grew in power, small wars broke out among them. Eventually the Minamoto clan became the most powerful.

In 1192, the emperor gave the title of **shogun** (SHOH gun), **or supreme military commander,** to the leader of the Minamoto clan. Minamoto Yoritomo (mee nah MOH toh yoh ree TOH moh) became the supreme ruler of all Japan. He set up the Kamakura (kah mah KUR ah) shogunate, a series of military dynasties.

✓ Reading Check **How did the samurai become powerful?**

Japan and the Outside World

Within a century after shogun rule began, Japan was threatened by outsiders. One group came from Mongolia, north of China. Under their fierce and brilliant leader Kublai Khan, the Mongols had already conquered China and Korea. Kublai Khan tried to invade Japan twice, and failed both times. For nearly 300 years after the Mongols were defeated in the 1200s, few foreigners came to Japan.

The Arrival of Europeans In 1543, several Portuguese ships were blown off course and landed on Japan's coast. The Japanese showed great interest in these foreigners—especially in their guns. In the years that followed, a lively trade developed between East and West. Many European traders and missionaries made the long voyage to these islands in the Pacific. And thousands of Japanese converted to Christianity. The European influence in Japan did not last long, however.

The Tokugawas Unify Japan In 1603, Tokugawa Ieyasu (toh koo GAH wah ee yay AH soo) became shogun. Ieyasu was determined to bring order to the country. To end the fighting among warring samurai bands, Ieyasu divided Japan into about 250 regions. The daimyo of each region promised to serve the shogun and swore loyalty to him. To control these local leaders, the Tokugawas required each daimyo to live in the shogun's capital Edo (now called Tokyo) for several months every other year.

Citizen Heroes

A Peasant Warrior

Toyotomi Hideyoshi (toh yoh TOH mee hee duh YOH shee) started life as a peasant. Through hard work, he became a respected warrior. Because of his great military skills, he became a chief lieutenant in the army of a powerful daimyo. When the daimyo died in 1582, Hideyoshi took his place. A skillful leader, he went on to unite Japan. He then tried, but failed, to conquer Korea and China. Nevertheless, Hideyoshi, shown below, became one of the most admired heroes in Japan.

The Tokugawa shogunate ruled Japan until 1867. It was a period of peace. The economy thrived. Food was plentiful, the population increased, trade flourished inside Japan, and a merchant class developed. Cities grew, and the arts flourished. A type of Buddhism called Zen became popular in Japan. It emphasized meditation, the practice of good deeds, and reverence for nature.

Theater and poetry also thrived under the Tokugawas. Haiku—three-line poems that express a feeling or picture in only 17 syllables—were greatly admired. Plays featuring life-size puppets were popular. So was the Kabuki theater. Kabuki combines drama, dance, and music.

Kabuki Theater
Even today, men play women's roles in Kabuki theater, and many of the plays recount tales of feudal Japan. **Analyze Images** *What do the elaborate makeup, costumes, and gestures suggest about Kabuki performances?*

Japan Becomes Isolated Again At the same time, the Tokugawa shogunate was isolating Japan from foreign influences. Even Tokugawa Ieyasu had worried that Europeans might try to conquer Japan. He and the shoguns who ruled after him decided that Japan should remain isolated from Westerners. They outlawed Christianity and forced Europeans to leave. By 1638, they had closed Japan's ports, banning most foreign travel and trade. The shoguns also stopped the building of large ships that could travel long distances. For more than 200 years, the Japanese would remain cut off from the outside world.

 **Reading Check** **How did the Tokugawas change Japan?**

Section 2 Assessment

Key Terms
Review the key terms at the beginning of this section. Use each term in a sentence that explains its meaning.

Target Reading Skill
What were two effects of the growing power of the daimyo?

Comprehension and Critical Thinking
1. (a) Describe What are the geographical features of Japan?

(b) Identify When did Japan start to develop its own traditions?
(c) Identify Causes What led to Japan's isolation?
2. (a) Recall What happened to the emperor and the nobles during the 1000s?
(b) Identify Causes What led to the establishment of shoguns?
3. (a) Recall How did trade develop between Japan and Europe in the 1500s?
(b) Synthesize How and why did the Tokugawas isolate Japan?

Writing Activity
Suppose you could interview a samurai. Write five questions that you would ask him. Then write a paragraph to introduce your interview.

For: An activity about the samurai
Visit: PHSchool.com
Web Code: lgd-8402

Focus On
A Japanese Home

In 1649, authorities of the Tokugawa government sent a decree to Japanese villages: "[Peasants] must not buy tea . . . to drink, nor must their wives. . . . The husband must work in the fields, [and] the wife must work at the loom. Both must do night work. However good-looking a wife may be, if she neglects her household duties, she must be divorced. Peasants must wear only cotton or hemp—no silk." This decree shows how the Tokugawa government tried to maintain a firm grip on Japanese society. Both outside and inside the home, the lives of the Japanese were guided by tradition and by law.

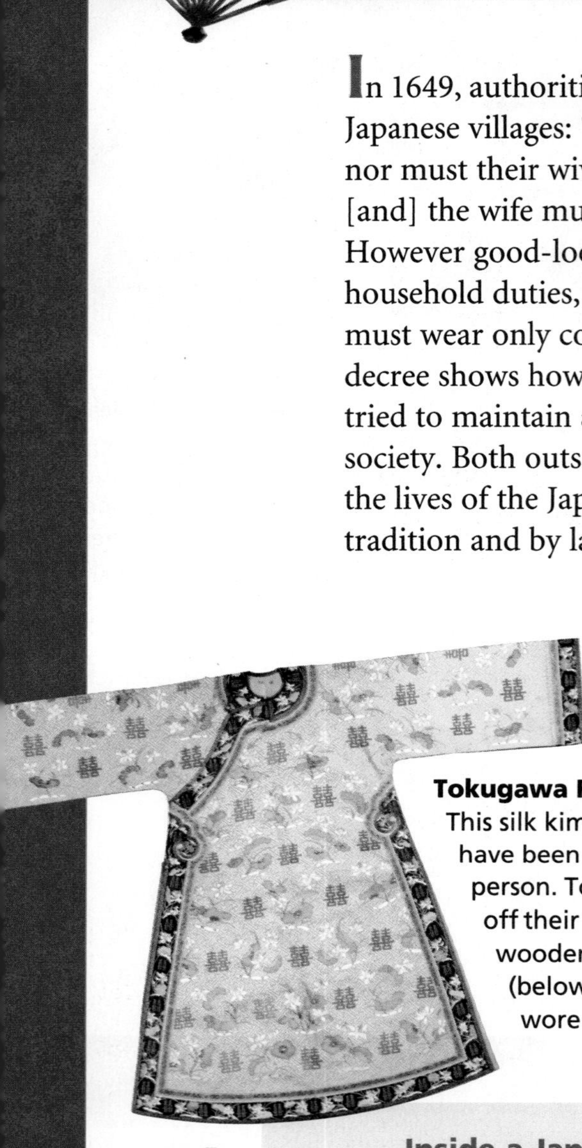

Tokugawa Fashions
This silk kimono, or robe, would have been worn by a wealthy person. Townspeople kept mud off their feet by wearing raised wooden clogs called geta (below). Peasants usually wore straw sandals.

Inside a Japanese Farmhouse The illustration at the right shows a typical farmhouse during the Tokugawa shogunate. In Tokugawa Japan, most houses had a main room with a sunken fire pit. The family gathered around the fire pit, and sat according to rank. At night, they slept on the floor on thin mattresses, which had been stored away in cupboards during the day.

Not shown are the two back rooms. One of these was the zashiki, a formal room used for receiving guests. Inside it was a butsudan, a Buddhist altar, and a tokonoma, a recessed space decorated with a flower vase, candlestick, and incense burner. The other back room was the nando, used for sleeping and for storage. In some farmhouses, women raised silkworms on a second floor.

The illustration shows raised wood floors covered with straw mats called tatami. It was customary to remove one's shoes before stepping onto the tatami. This custom is still practiced in Japan today.

Hiroma
This was the family's living and dining room.

Doma
This earthen-floored area was used for cooking and working, and sometimes, for sheltering farm animals.

Assessment

Describe Identify the features of a Japanese farmhouse during the Tokugawa shogunate.

Compare and Contrast Compare the Japanese farmhouse with the Bedouin tent on pages 298–299. How are they similar? How are they different?

Prepare to Read

Objectives

In this section you will

1. Find out about the geography of the Indian subcontinent.
2. Learn about the Delhi Sultanate, a period of Muslim rule.
3. Learn about the founding and achievements of the Mughal Empire.

Taking Notes

As you read this section, look for important events in India's history, and note when they occurred. Copy the timeline below and record your findings on it.

India's History, 600–1707

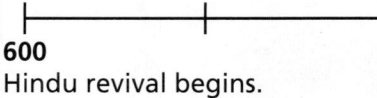

600
Hindu revival begins.

Target Reading Skill

Recognize Cause-and-Effect Signal Words Sometimes certain words, such as *because, affect,* or *as a result,* signal a cause or an effect. In this section, you will learn about invasions of India and the rise and fall of two Indian empires. Look for signal words to help you understand the causes and effects of these events.

Key Terms

- **sultan** (SUL tun) *n.* a Muslim ruler
- **caste system** (kast SIS tum) *n.* a Hindu social class system that controlled every aspect of daily life
- **Mughal Empire** (MOO gul EM pyr) *n.* a period of Muslim rule of India from the 1500s to the 1700s
- **Akbar** (AK bahr) *n.* the greatest Mughal leader of India
- **Taj Mahal** (tahzh muh HAHL) *n.* a tomb built by Shah Jahan for his wife

Timur, from an Indian manuscript

Even before Timur (tee MOOR) invaded India, people there had heard of this Mongol conqueror. He had destroyed entire cities and their populations in other parts of Asia. In 1398, he and his troops marched into northern India, in search of fabled riches. They ruined fields of crops and quickly captured Delhi (DEL ee), the capital city. Timur and his troops killed many people and took hundreds of slaves. They also carried away great treasures—pearls, golden dishes, rubies, and diamonds.

For a brief time, Delhi became part of the huge empire that Timur controlled from his capital, Samarkand (sam ur KAND). But Timur was more interested in conquering new lands than in governing those he had defeated. Not long after the Mongols invaded Delhi, they departed. Once again, a **sultan,** or Muslim ruler, took control of the city. But Delhi did not regain its command over the region, as you will see.

India's Geography

The triangular Indian subcontinent forms the southernmost part of Central Asia. A mountain range called the Himalayas stretches across the north of India. Although these mountains have helped to isolate India from lands to the north, the passes through the Himalayas have allowed some conquerors from the north to enter the subcontinent. To the west of India is the Arabian Sea, and to the east is the Bay of Bengal.

A large plain lies to the south of the Himalayas. It is dominated by major river systems, including the Indus and Ganges rivers. These rivers are fed by melting mountain snows, and much of the land here is well suited to farming. Farther to the south are highlands and plains.

✓ **Reading Check** **Describe India's geography.**

The Delhi Sultanate

The Mongols led by Timur were not the first people to invade India. Long before they came, India's riches had tempted others. Muslim invaders began raiding the Indian subcontinent around A.D. 1000. From 1206 to 1526, a series of sultans controlled northern India as well as parts of present-day Bangladesh and Pakistan. This period of India's history is called the Delhi Sultanate—after the capital city, Delhi.

A Himalayan Mountain Pass
Even today, it is difficult to cross the Himalayas. **Infer** *Why do you think modern travelers are still using pack animals rather than trucks or automobiles to cross these mountains?*

A Hindu Revival At the time of the Muslim invasion, the region was experiencing a revival of the ancient Hindu religion. This revival had begun about A.D. 600. Hindus accept many gods, but they believe that all of these gods are just different aspects of one supreme being. Hindus also believe that social classes are part of the natural order of the universe.

In India at this time, the Hindu **caste system**—a strict system of social classes—controlled everyday life. Caste determined a person's job and status. At the top of the caste system were priests, teachers, and judges. Warriors were second. Then came farmers and merchants. The fourth class included craftspeople and laborers. Finally, there was a group of poor and powerless people who were called untouchables.

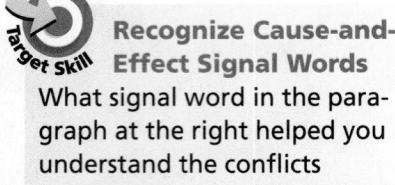

Recognize Cause-and-Effect Signal Words

What signal word in the paragraph at the right helped you understand the conflicts between Hindus and Muslims?

The Muslims who controlled the Delhi Sultanate did not become part of Hindu society. As you read in Chapter 10, Muslim culture is based on beliefs that are very different from those of Hindu culture. These differences caused conflicts between the two groups. In fact, religious disagreements still divide the Hindus and Muslims who live in India today.

The Fall of the Delhi Sultanate In 1526, a Mongol prince named Babur (BAH bur) took advantage of the weakened Delhi Sultanate. Babur was a Muslim descendant of the Mongol conqueror Timur. Even though Babur and his troops were outnumbered almost ten to one, they attacked the sultan's army.

The sultan's forces had 100 elephants to help them fight. Babur's troops had none. But the Mongols had cannons—and they were better fighters. The prince defeated the sultan and went on to control the capital city, Delhi. A new period of India's history would now begin.

√ **Reading Check** How was the Delhi Sultanate defeated?

Akbar Holds Court

Akbar supported many kinds of artists, including those who made beautiful miniature paintings like this one. **Conclude** *What can you conclude about Akbar's court from this painting?*

The Mughal Empire

Babur founded the celebrated **Mughal Empire,** whose Muslim rulers controlled India until the 1700s. (*Mughal* is another word for "Mongol.") About 25 years after Babur's death, the empire came under the control of Babur's grandson. His name was **Akbar** (AK bahr), and he would become the greatest Mughal leader of India.

Akbar the Great When Akbar came to power, he was only 13 years old. He grew up to become a talented soldier. Through conquest, treaties, and marriage, he greatly expanded the Mughal Empire.

Akbar also encouraged the arts. He set up studios for painters at his court. He supported poets, although he himself never learned to read or write. Akbar also brought together scholars from different religions for discussions. He consulted with Muslims, Hindus, Buddhists, and Christians.

Although he was a Muslim, Akbar gained the support of his Hindu subjects through his policy of toleration. He allowed Hindus to practice their religion freely, and he ended unfair taxes that had been required of non-Muslims.

The Delhi Sultanate and Mughal Empire

MAP MASTER™ Skills Activity

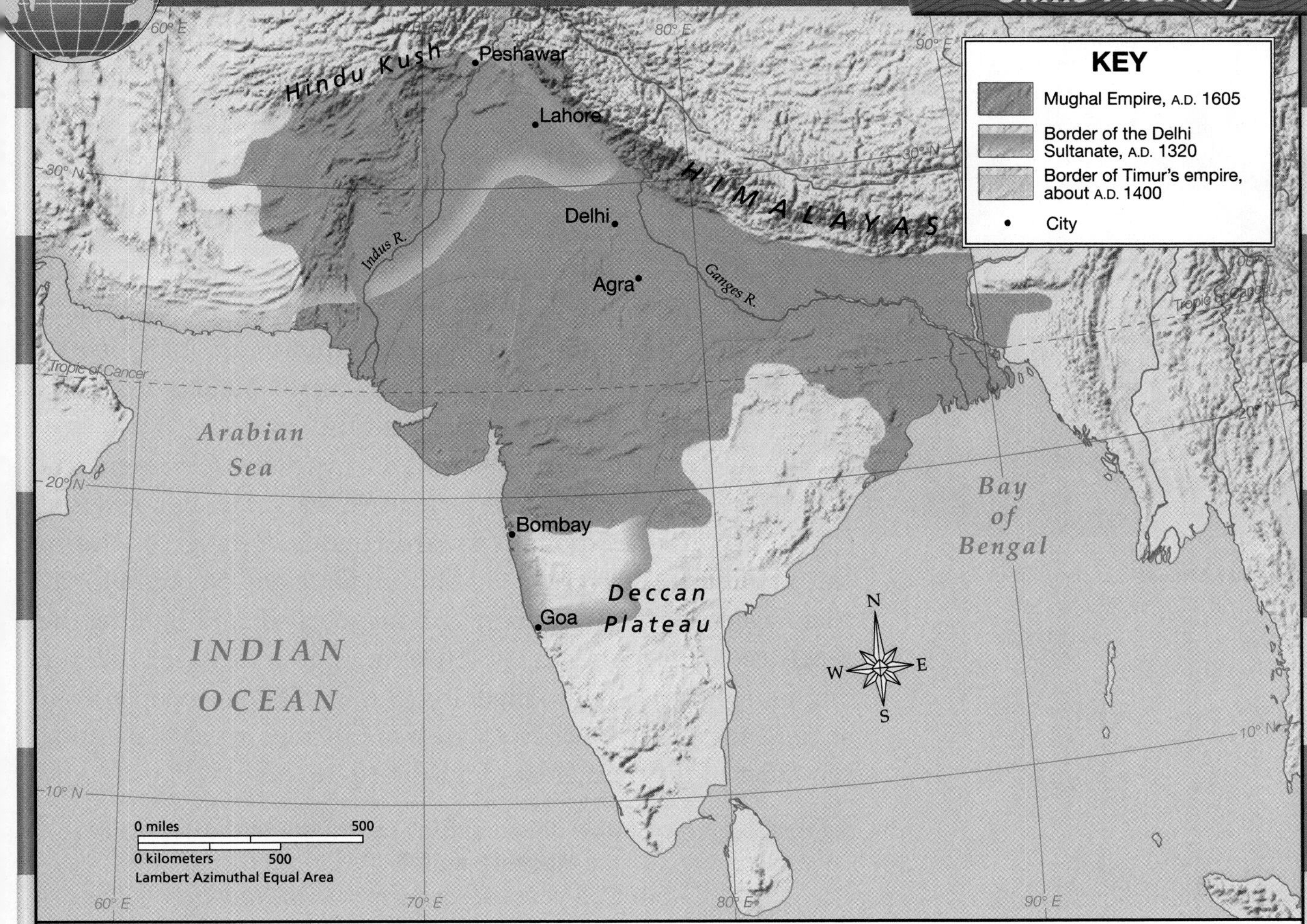
KEY
Mughal Empire, A.D. 1605
Border of the Delhi Sultanate, A.D. 1320
Border of Timur's empire, about A.D. 1400
City
Hindu Kush
Peshawar
Lahore
HIMALAYAS
Delhi
Agra
Indus R.
Ganges R.
Tropic of Cancer
Arabian Sea
Bay of Bengal
Bombay
Goa
Deccan Plateau
INDIAN OCEAN
N
S
E
W
60° E
70° E
80° E
90° E
30° N
20° N
10° N
0 miles 500
0 kilometers 500
Lambert Azimuthal Equal Area

Regions Notice the physical features as well as the borders of the empires on the map. **Locate** Which empire was the oldest? Which one gained control of the mouths of India's two most important rivers? **Infer** Why do you think neither the sultans nor the Mughals extended their empires farther north?

Go Online PHSchool.com Use Web Code **lgp-8443** for step-by-step **map skills practice.**

Akbar created a strong central government, and he gave government jobs to qualified people, whatever their religion or caste. Hindus served as generals, governors, administrators, and clerks. These policies helped Hindus and Muslims live together more peacefully. They also strengthened Mughal power in India.

In 1605, when Akbar died, most of northern India was under his control. Akbar had ruled the Mughal Empire for 49 years, earning himself the nickname "the Great." During this long reign, his system of government had become firmly established in India. This system allowed the empire to continue developing and expanding for the next 100 years—even under rulers who were less capable than Akbar the Great.

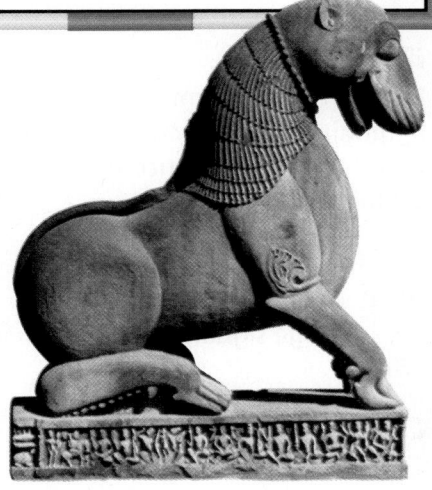

Royal emblem from the Gujari Palace, India

The Taj Mahal

The Reign of Shah Jahan More than 100 years after Akbar's death, the Mughal Empire began to fall apart. Akbar's grandson, Shah Jahan (shah juh HAHN), became emperor in 1628. Jahan spent a fortune on extravagant buildings. The most famous of these is the **Taj Mahal** (tahzh muh HAHL), a tomb for the emperor's wife, Mumtaz Mahal (mum TAHZ muh HAHL).

When his wife died, Jahan was overcome with grief. The two had been constant companions, and Jahan had asked his wife's opinion on many issues. After she died, Jahan set out to build a tomb "as beautiful as she was beautiful."

Jahan's son, Aurangzeb (AWR ung zeb), spent still more money on expensive wars. He also reversed Akbar's policies toward Hindus. Aurangzeb tried to force Hindus to convert to the Muslim faith, and he began to tax them again. As a result, many Hindus rebelled, and fighting the rebels cost still more money. After Aurangzeb died in 1707, the empire split into small kingdoms. But to this day, people from around the globe journey to see his mother's tomb—a lasting reminder of the once great Mughal Empire.

✓ Reading Check **How did Aurangzeb contribute to the decline of the Mughal Empire?**

Section 3 Assessment

Key Terms
Review the key terms at the beginning of this section. Use each term in a sentence that explains its meaning.

Target Reading Skill
What words in the last paragraph on this page signal cause and effect?

Comprehension and Critical Thinking
1. (a) Identify What are the major geographic features of the Indian subcontinent?

(b) Predict How might India's history have been different if there had been no mountain passes in the north?
2. (a) Define What was the Delhi Sultanate?
(b) Synthesize How did Hindus and Muslims live together in India during this time?
3. (a) Explain Why was Akbar called "the Great"?
(b) Identify Causes What caused the decline of the Mughal Empire?

Writing Activity
Suppose that Akbar is a leader under a system of government like the United States government. He is running for reelection, and you are his campaign manager. Write a short speech stating why voters should reelect him.

Writing Tip Remember to support your position with specific examples.

◆ Chapter Summary

Section 1: Golden Ages of China

Kublai Khan's court

- The Tang dynasty ruled China for almost 300 years. That period was the beginning of a golden age, during which China's territory increased, and Chinese culture and trade flourished.
- The Song dynasty, which ruled China after the Tang, expanded the merit system and promoted the spread of knowledge.
- The Mongols conquered China, and their leader, Kublai Khan, centralized China's government.

Section 2: Medieval Japan

- Japan is a mountainous island country of East Asia. The sea has provided both transportation and protection for the people of Japan.
- During the Heian period, the Japanese built a new capital and began to develop a distinctive culture.
- Warriors, called samurai, and powerful military leaders, called shoguns, took control away from the emperor. The shoguns eventually closed Japan to outsiders.

Section 3: The Great Mughal Empire in India

- The Indian subcontinent is shaped like a triangle, with mountains to the north and seas to the east and west.
- During the Delhi Sultanate, Muslim rulers called sultans ruled India.
- Mongols conquered India and established the Mughal Empire. Akbar the Great was the greatest Mughal leader.

Kabuki performer

◆ Key Terms

Define each of the following terms.

1. Silk Road
2. Tang
3. shogun
4. sultan
5. caste system

6. Kublai Khan
7. archipelago
8. samurai
9. Taj Mahal
10. dynasty

Review and Assessment (continued)

◆ Comprehension and Critical Thinking

11. (a) Identify Name two Chinese products that were important for trade.
(b) Explain Why were these products valued by other countries?
(c) Identify Effects How did trade in these products affect China?

12. (a) Recall How did the Song, and then the Mongols, change Chinese government?
(b) Evaluate Which changes benefited China? Which were harmful? Explain.

13. (a) Identify What are the major geographic features of Japan? Of India?
(b) Compare and Contrast How did the geography of these two places affect their history and culture?

14. (a) Define What is a shogunate?
(b) Summarize How did shoguns gain power in Japan?
(c) Identify Causes Why did shoguns ban most foreign travel and trade?

15. (a) Identify Whose rule led to the breakup of India's Mughal Empire?
(b) Contrast How was his rule different from that of his great-grandfather, Akbar?
(c) Analyze What factors contributed to the downfall of the Mughal Empire?

◆ Skills Practice

Making an Outline In the Skills for Life activity in this chapter, you learned how to make an outline. Review the steps you followed to learn the skill. Then reread the text under the heading The Mughal Empire on pages 384–386. Make an outline of that text.

◆ Writing Activity: Science

Use encyclopedias, other reliable books, or reliable Internet sources to research one Chinese invention of the Tang or Song dynasty. Describe the invention, how it works, when and how it was invented, and why it was important. Write your findings as an essay or as an illustrated report that you can display in your classroom.

MAP★MASTER™ Skills Activity

Civilizations of Asia

Place Location For each feature or place listed, write the letter from the map that shows its location.

1. Himalayas
2. Delhi
3. Silk Road
4. Japan
5. Delhi Sultanate
6. Ganges River
7. China during the Tang dynasty

Go Online
PHSchool.com Use Web Code **lpg-8453** for an **interactive map.**

Standardized Test Prep

Test-Taking Tips

Some questions on standardized tests may ask you to identify the main topic or the topic sentence of a passage. Read the paragraph below. Then use the tip to help you answer the sample question.

> Beginning in the 1600s, the powerful shoguns of Japan outlawed Christianity. The shoguns forced Europeans to leave the country. They also closed Japanese ports to foreigners and banned foreign trade. Through their efforts to isolate Japan, the shoguns hoped to protect it from foreign invasion.

Think It Through Read all four choices. Answers A and D tell about specific actions, not broad ideas or main topics. Even though C is the first sentence of the passage, it also describes one particular action. Therefore, it is not more important than A or D. Because B summarizes the information of the other sentences, it is the correct answer.

Pick the letter that best answers the question.

Which of these sentences states the <u>main topic</u> of the passage?

A They also closed Japanese ports to foreigners and banned foreign trade.

B Through their efforts to isolate Japan, the shoguns hoped to protect it from foreign invasion.

C Beginning in the 1600s, the powerful shoguns of Japan outlawed Christianity.

D The shoguns forced Europeans to leave the country.

TIP Many paragraphs have one sentence that states the main topic. The other sentences in the paragraph all support this topic sentence. The first and last sentences are the most likely to be the topic sentence.

Practice Questions

Pick the letter that best answers the question.

1. Read the passage below. Which of the sentences that follow states the main topic of the passage?

> Hideyoshi was born a poor peasant in Japan in the 1500s. Through hard work, he became a samurai warrior. Because of his military skills, Hideyoshi was promoted to an important position working for a powerful warlord. In 1582, the warlord was killed, and Hideyoshi took his place. A skillful leader from poor beginnings, Hideyoshi became ruler of Japan.

A Through hard work, he became a samurai warrior.

B Hideyoshi was born a poor peasant in Japan in the 1500s.

C A skillful leader from poor beginnings, Hideyoshi became ruler of Japan.

D In 1582, the warlord was killed, and Hideyoshi took his place.

Read each of the following statements. If the statement is true, write *true*. If it is false, write *false*.

2. The samurai warriors of Japan followed a set of strict rules for behavior.

3. Song rulers used the merit system in Chinese government.

4. The Indian subcontinent could not be invaded from the north.

5. Akbar was a great Mughal ruler of India.

6. Japan's islands are mostly flat, and traveling by land is easy.

Go Online
PHSchool.com

Use Web Code **lga-8403** for a **Chapter 13 self-test.**

Age of Encounter

(500–1800)

◀ The ship is a replica of *The Golden Hind*, the ship used by explorer Sir Francis Drake during the late 1500s.

Chapter

14

Europe in the Middle Ages

Chapter Preview

This chapter will introduce you to life in Europe during the Middle Ages.

**Target
Reading Skill**

Sequence In this chapter you will focus on using sequence to note the order in which events take place. This skill will help you understand and remember those events.

▶ The medieval castle at Carcassonne, France

MAP MASTER™ Skills Activity

Europe in 1300

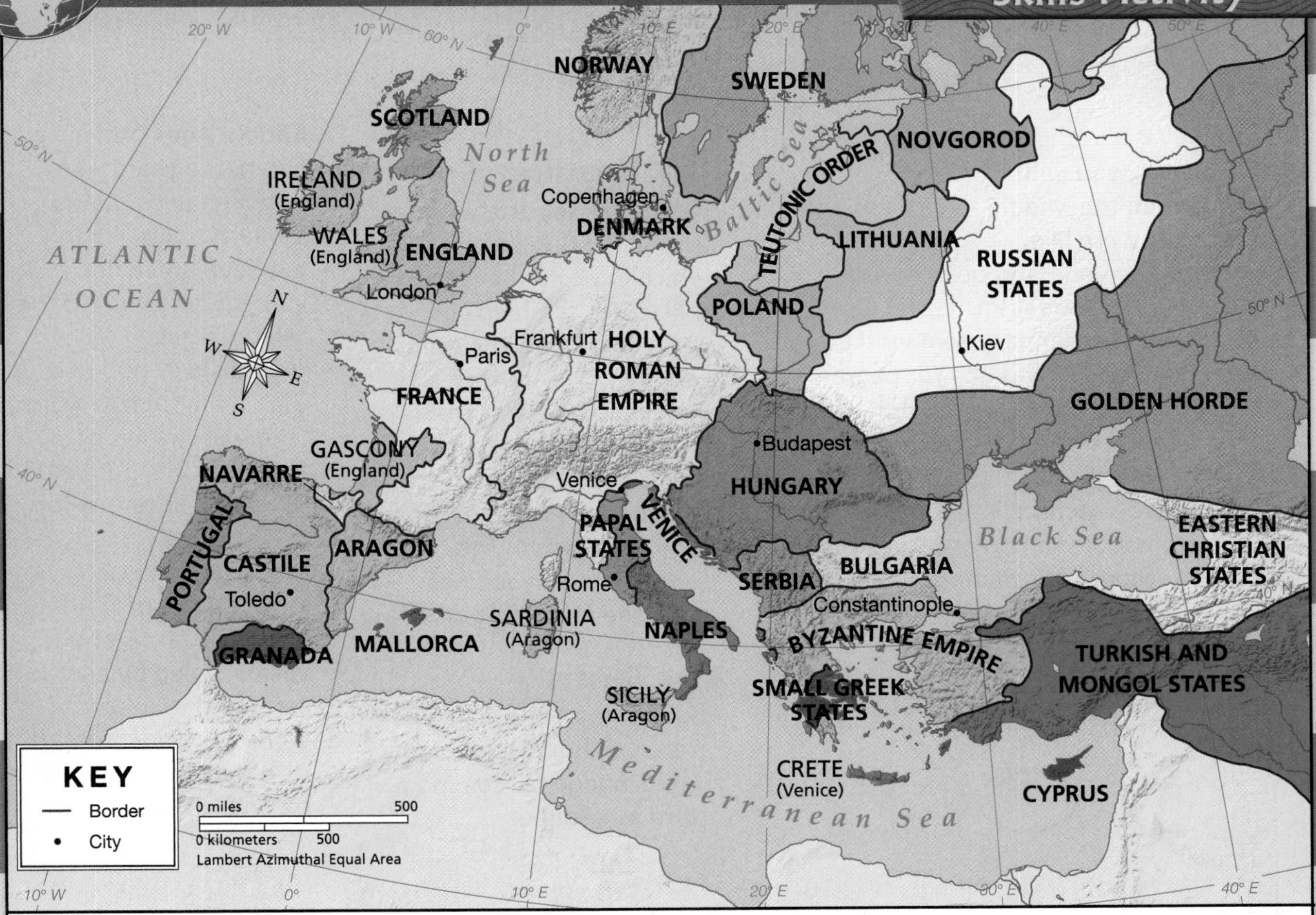

NORWAY
SWEDEN
SCOTLAND
North Sea
NOVGOROD
TEUTONIC ORDER
IRELAND (England)
Copenhagen
Baltic Sea
WALES (England)
ENGLAND
DENMARK
LITHUANIA
ATLANTIC OCEAN
London
RUSSIAN STATES
POLAND
Frankfurt
HOLY ROMAN EMPIRE
Paris
Kiev
FRANCE
GOLDEN HORDE
GASCONY (England)
Budapest
NAVARRE
Venice
HUNGARY
PORTUGAL
CASTILE
ARAGON
PAPAL STATES
VENICE
Black Sea
EASTERN CHRISTIAN STATES
SERBIA
BULGARIA
Toledo
Rome
Constantinople
SARDINIA (Aragon)
NAPLES
BYZANTINE EMPIRE
GRANADA
MALLORCA
TURKISH AND MONGOL STATES
SICILY (Aragon)
SMALL GREEK STATES
CRETE (Venice)
CYPRUS
Mediterranean Sea
KEY
Border
City
0 miles 500
0 kilometers 500
Lambert Azimuthal Equal Area
N
S
E
W
20° W
10° W
0°
10° E
20° E
30° E
40° E
50° E
60° N
50° N
40° N

Regions In 1300, Europe was made up of many separate kingdoms and states. **Identify** Which names on the map are familiar to you? Which are not? **Apply Information** What route might merchants traveling from Constantinople to Venice take? Which states and bodies of water would they cross?

Go Online PHSchool.com Use Web Code **lgp-8511** for step-by-step **map skills practice.**

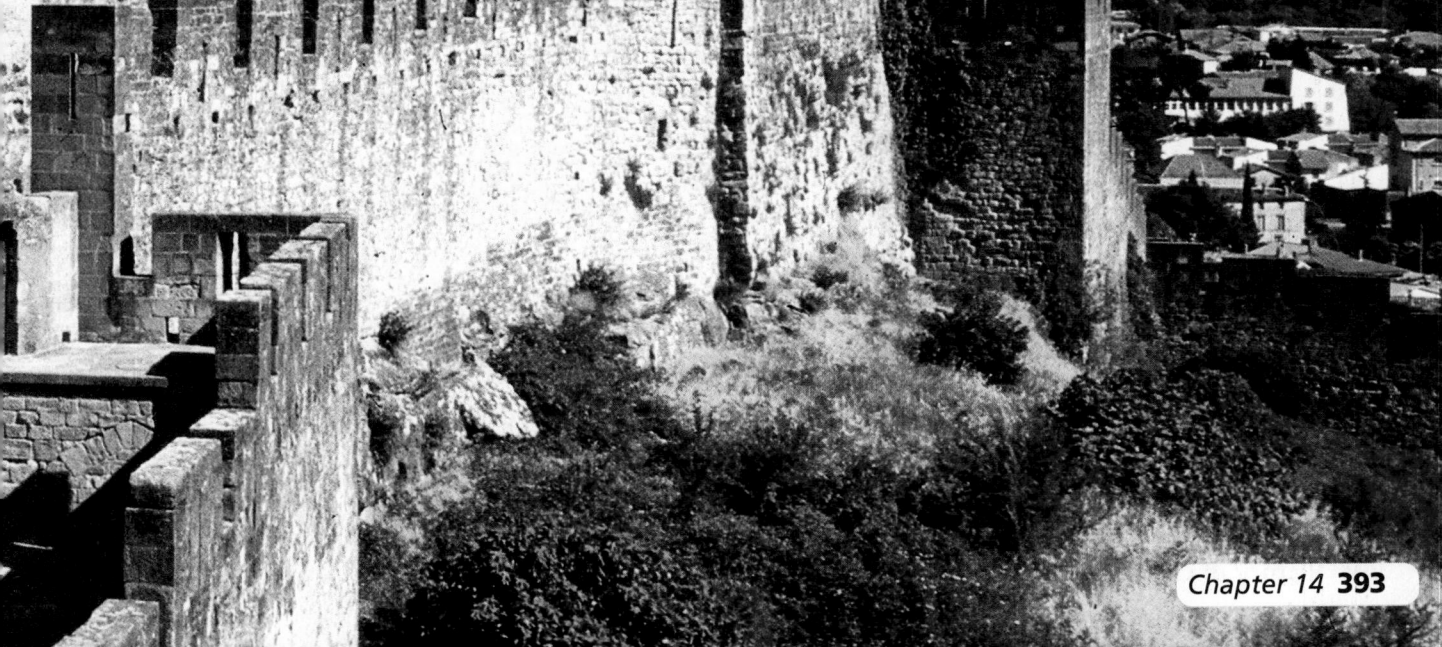

Feudalism and the Manor System

Prepare to Read

Objectives

In this section, you will

1. Learn when the Middle Ages were and what they were like.
2. Find out how land and power were divided under feudalism.
3. Learn how the manor system worked.
4. Discover what life was like for peasants and serfs.

Taking Notes

As you read this section, look for the major features of feudalism. Copy the web diagram below and record your findings in it.

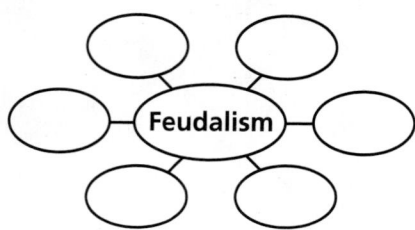

Target Reading Skill

Recognize Sequence Signal Words Noting the order in which important events take place can help you understand how the events relate to one another. Sequence signal words, such as *first, then, began,* and *in [date],* point out relationships in time. Look for such words in this section to help you understand the Middle Ages.

Key Terms

- **knight** (nyt) *n.* a man who received honor and land in exchange for serving a lord as a soldier
- **Middle Ages** (MID ul Ay juz) *n.* the years between ancient and modern times
- **medieval** (mee dee EE vul) *adj.* referring to the Middle Ages
- **feudalism** (FYOOD ul iz um) *n.* a system in which land was owned by kings or lords but held by vassals in return for their loyalty
- **manor** (MAN ur) *n.* a large estate, often including farms and a village, ruled by a lord
- **serf** (surf) *n.* a farm worker considered part of the manor on which he or she worked

A knighting ceremony

As darkness fell, a young man put on a white tunic and red and black cloaks. Then he walked to the church, where he spent the long night alone, praying. Soon he would no longer be a mere squire, or knight-in-training. He would become a real **knight,** who would receive honor and land in exchange for serving his lord as a soldier.

The next morning, the squire entered the castle courtyard, where knights and ladies had gathered. His lord presented him with his sword, spurs, and shield. The squire knelt. Then he felt the lord's sword lightly tap him on each shoulder. "In the name of God, Saint Michael, and Saint George, I call you a knight," declared the lord. "Be loyal, brave, and true."

A knight was expected to be loyal to the lord who knighted him. His lord was loyal to a more powerful lord or king. Knights and lords protected the less powerful people loyal to them. This system held society together.

The Middle Ages

A thousand years ago, scenes like the one you just read about took place throughout Western Europe. These were the times of knights in shining armor, lords and ladies, and castles and cathedrals. These were the **Middle Ages**, the years between ancient times and modern times.

Historians usually say that ancient times lasted until about A.D. 500 and that modern times started about 1500. The period in the middle, the Middle Ages, is also called the **medieval** period. *Medieval* comes from Latin words that mean "middle ages."

The Collapse of the Roman Empire The Middle Ages began with the collapse of the Roman Empire in Western Europe. For centuries, the Roman Empire had provided order and stability in the region. It had spread its culture, the Latin language, and Christianity across the continent. Over time, however, the Roman Empire grew weak. It suffered economic and social troubles. Worse, the Roman Empire also suffered from invasions by peoples from the north.

Go Online PHSchool.com Use Web Code **mup-0837** for an interactivity on two feudal societies.

Bronze plaque of a Lombard warrior

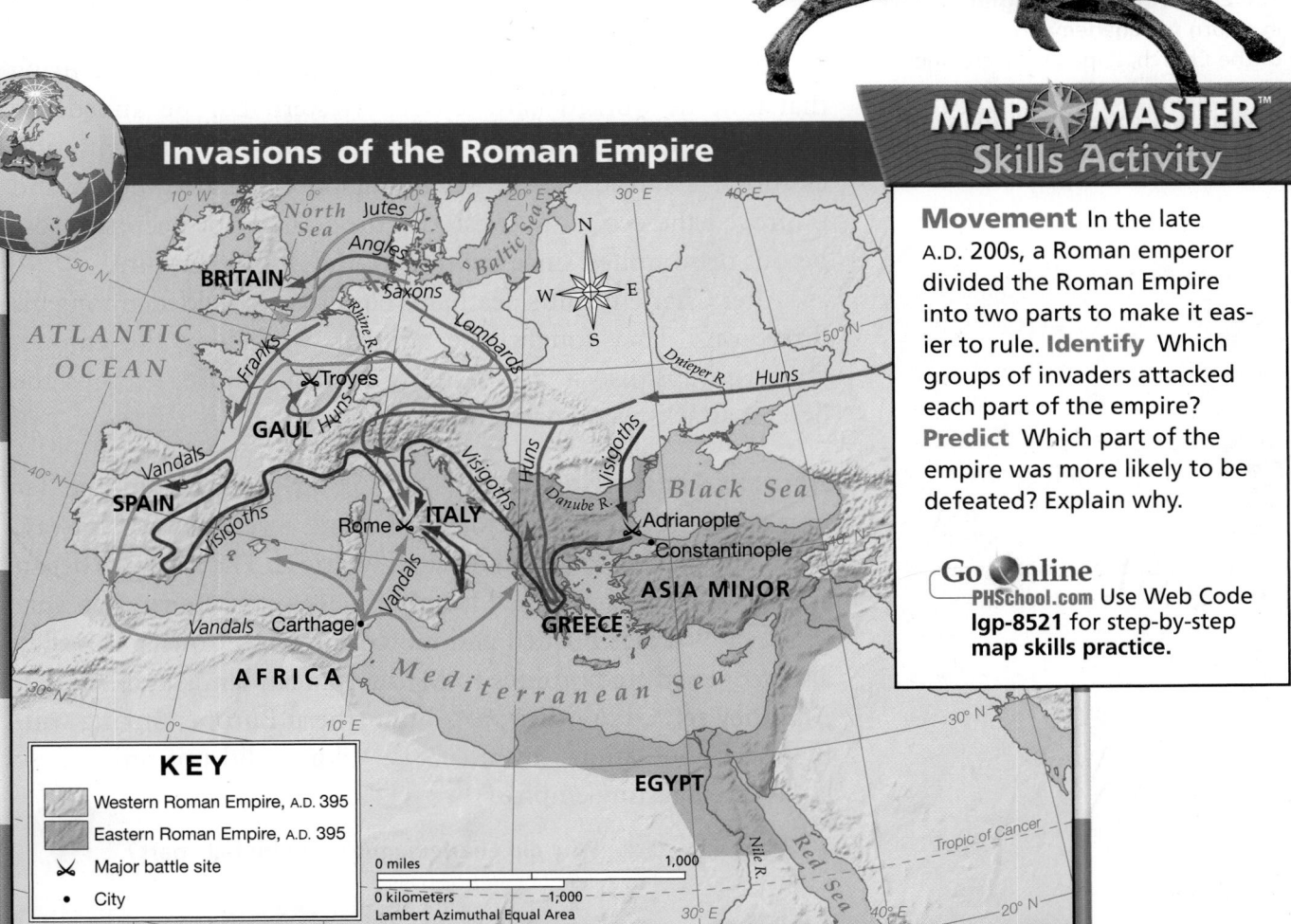

Invasions of the Roman Empire

MAP MASTER™ Skills Activity

Movement In the late A.D. 200s, a Roman emperor divided the Roman Empire into two parts to make it easier to rule. **Identify** Which groups of invaders attacked each part of the empire? **Predict** Which part of the empire was more likely to be defeated? Explain why.

Go Online PHSchool.com Use Web Code **lgp-8521** for step-by-step **map skills practice**.

KEY

- Western Roman Empire, A.D. 395
- Eastern Roman Empire, A.D. 395
- ✗ Major battle site
- • City

0 miles 1,000
0 kilometers 1,000
Lambert Azimuthal Equal Area

The Emperor Charlemagne
In return for Charlemagne's support of the Church, Pope Leo III crowned him emperor in 800. **Analyze Images** *How does this statue show Charlemagne's greatness and power?*

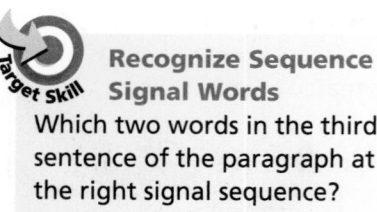

Recognize Sequence Signal Words
Which two words in the third sentence of the paragraph at the right signal sequence?

In wave after wave, the invaders destroyed Roman towns and cut off trade routes. They claimed parts of the empire for themselves. Because these peoples kept their own languages and laws, they broke the bonds that had held the Roman Empire together.

By about A.D. 500, the Roman Empire in Western Europe had completely collapsed. It was replaced by a patchwork of small kingdoms. Reading and writing were in danger of disappearing from Europe because many of the invading groups could not do either.

Charlemagne Reunites Western Europe One of the invading groups was the Franks. They claimed the area called Gaul, which is now France. In fact, the name *France* comes from the word "Franks." In 768, a skilled military leader named Charlemagne (SHAHR luh mayn) became king of the Franks.

At the time, the many small kingdoms of Western Europe were often at war with one another. Charlemagne expanded his kingdom by conquering these weaker kingdoms. Soon, he ruled an empire that stretched across most of Western Europe.

Charlemagne ruled his empire for nearly 50 years. During that time he worked hard to keep Western Europe united. He established schools throughout the land to promote learning and culture. He spread the Christian religion. He issued money and improved the economy. Western Europe had not been so prosperous or so united since the time of the Roman Empire.

After Charlemagne's death, his empire was divided among his three sons. They fought one another, weakening the empire. Other groups also attacked the weakened empire. Perhaps the fiercest attacks were made by the Vikings.

Attacks From the North The Vikings came from the far north of Europe—present-day Denmark, Sweden, and Norway. They were skilled sailors and tough warriors. Their attacks began around 800 and continued for about 300 years. Relying on surprise, the Vikings burned and looted European towns. But they also reopened trade routes to Mediterranean lands and beyond. And they settled in other parts of northern Europe, mixing with the local populations. Even so, the Vikings did not unite these lands into a lasting empire.

✓ **Reading Check** **Why did Charlemagne's empire fall apart?**

Feudalism

Charlemagne's empire was gone. Western Europe was again divided into many small kingdoms. Viking attacks were a constant threat. Life was dangerous. Slowly, the people of Europe worked out a new system for meeting their military, political, and economic needs.

The Feudal System The system that developed was called feudalism. Under **feudalism**, land was owned by kings or lords but held by vassals in return for their loyalty. By about 1000, feudalism was the way of life throughout Western Europe. It would last for hundreds of years.

In medieval Europe, power belonged to those who controlled the land. These landowners were nobles, such as barons and princes. They gave a share of land, called a fief (feef), to each of their vassals, or people who promised to follow the landowner's laws and to fight for him. A vassal could also be a lord.

Feudal Duties Lords promised to treat their vassals with honor. In addition, the chief duty of lords was to protect their vassals and their lands. If a vassal with young children died, for example, the lord became the children's protector. The lord also asked his vassals' advice before making laws or going to war.

Vassals were expected to raise and lead armies that would fight for their lord. Many of these vassals were knights —professional horse soldiers who led other men into battle. Vassals also appeared at the lord's court when commanded to do so. And they paid taxes, often in the form of crops, to their lords.

✓ **Reading Check** What did lords give vassals in exchange for the vassals' loyalty?

The Manor System

In medieval Europe, feudalism was a system of power and economic relations across regions. Manorialism was a system of economic and political life at the local level. This system was based on the **manor**, a large estate that included farm fields, pastures, and often an entire village. It also included a large house, called the manor house, where the lord, or ruler, of the manor lived.

Links Across
The World

Vikings in America The Vikings did not limit their conquests to Europe. They went as far south as North Africa. Viking ships, such as the one shown below, also traveled westward to Greenland and beyond. An Icelandic saga, or story, gives clues about the location of Vinland, a Viking settlement in lands west of Greenland. Historians who have studied these clues and examined ruins in North America think that Vinland was probably in what is now Newfoundland, Canada.

A medieval knight in armor

Noblewomen at Home
The larger illustration shows a lady in charge of a dinner where her guests are seated according to rank. A noblewoman sits at her desk in the smaller illustration. **Generalize** *What can you infer about the lives of noblewomen from these illustrations?*

Lords and Manors The lord of the manor was typically a vassal of a king or of a more powerful lord. The manor was part of his fief. Most manors were far from towns, villages, and other manors. Therefore, they had to be self-sufficient, or able to supply their own needs. Food, clothing, and other things needed by the people who lived on the manor were made there.

A lord depended on the wealth his manor provided. He ruled over his manor—and the poor people who lived there. He made the rules and acted as judge. He decided who would oversee the farming and other daily work. And he collected taxes from the peasants who lived on the manor.

The Role of Noblewomen Women of the noble classes also played an important part in feudal society. Like the men in her family, a noblewoman went to other noble families for training. Then, she took her place as lady of the household. She managed the household, performed necessary medical tasks, and supervised servants. When her husband or father was away fighting, she often served as "lord of the manor," making important decisions.

✓ **Reading Check** **Why did manors have to be self-sufficient?**

Peasants and Serfs

The majority of the people of medieval Europe were not lords, ladies, or knights. They were peasants, a group of people who made their living as farmers and laborers. Their lives were very different from the lives of the nobles.

Peasants were often very poor. They did all of the work on the manors of the Middle Ages. They farmed the lord's fields to raise food for his household. They were only allowed to farm a small strip of land for themselves. Even so, they had to give part of their own harvest to their lord.

Learn about the knights and castles of the Middle Ages.

Tied to the Manor Most peasants were also serfs. **Serfs were peasants who were considered to be part of the manor.** When a noble was given a manor as part of his fief, its serfs became his. They could not leave the manor, or even get married, without his permission.

Although serfs were tied to manors, they were not quite slaves. Successful serfs could save money to buy freedom and a plot of land of their own. A serf who escaped to a city and lived there for a year and a day without being caught also became free. Most serfs, however, remained serfs their whole lives.

A Hard Life Medieval peasants worked hard for most of their lives. They farmed their own fields and those of their lord. Men, women, and children were all required to work.

Peasants lived in one-room huts that often had only a single opening for a window. For heating and cooking, they built a fire on the dirt floor. Smoke filled the dark, cramped interior before drifting out of a hole in the roof. Peasants ate mostly simple foods such as black bread, cabbage, and turnips. They rarely ate meat, since the animals of the manor and surrounding land were reserved for their lord. Peasants even suffered when they slept: their mattresses were cloth sacks stuffed with straw.

Peasant Life
Peasant women worked in the fields along with the men. **Contrast** *Use this illustration and those on page 398 to contrast the lives of peasant women and noblewomen.*

✔ **Reading Check** **What was life like for medieval peasants?**

Section 1 Assessment

Key Terms
Review the key terms at the beginning of this section. Use each term in a sentence that explains its meaning.

Target Reading Skill
Review the text under the heading The Collapse of the Roman Empire. List the words that signal the order of events.

Comprehension and Critical Thinking
1. (a) Recall When were the Middle Ages?

(b) Identify Cause and Effect Why did the collapse of the Roman Empire lead to a new age in Western Europe?

2. (a) Define What was feudalism?

(b) Explain How did the system of feudalism work?

3. (a) Describe How was a manor organized?

(b) Conclude Why did a manor produce a wide variety of goods?

4. (a) Explain What was the relationship of a serf to his or her manor?

(b) Infer How and why might a serf become free?

Writing Activity
During the Middle Ages, most poor peasants remained poor their entire lives. Why do you think this was so? Write a paragraph explaining what you think the reason or reasons were.

For: An activity on feudalism
Visit: PHSchool.com
Web Code: lgd-8501

Although peasants and nobles led very different lives, their reliance on the lands of the manor estate bound them together. Peasants worked the land to pay what they owed to their lords. Nobles depended on what the peasants produced so that they could pay taxes to higher nobles and to the king. In addition to cash, taxes were paid in grain, bread, fence posts, shingles and planks, linen cloth, shirts, honey, chickens, eggs, cheese, and butter. All of these goods were produced on the manor estate.

A peasant's house

The Manor Estate Medieval manors included the lord's home, the homes of the peasants and serfs, a mill for grinding grain, and often a chapel or a church. Attached to the manor house, or in a separate building, was a bakery that peasants and serfs would use for baking bread.

Most people in medieval Europe were agricultural workers. The lands and forests surrounding the manor and peasant houses provided grain, fruits, and vegetables. Peasants grazed cattle, sheep, and goats in the manor fields. Their pigs roamed the manor's woodlands in search of food. Woodlands also provided timber for building and fuel. Hunting in the forests was reserved for the nobles.

The illustration on the facing page shows a manor estate of the Middle Ages. At the top of this page is a shield painted with a noble's coat of arms.

A Manor Feast ▶
This illustration from the 1400s shows a duke feasting with his family and friends. In medieval times, guests brought their own knives to feasts, and many foods were eaten with the fingers. Diners often shared cups and dishes. Musicians, acrobats, and jugglers provided entertainment.

Manor House
A lord's house could be built of wood, stone, or clay bricks.

Village
These houses were usually made of wood and roofed with thatch—tightly bundled straw or reeds.

Mill
Peasants paid a fee to grind their grain.

Fields
Crops were planted in strips in two fields. A third field lay fallow, or unplanted.

Assessment

Describe What are the characteristics of a medieval manor?

Draw Conclusions Describe the relationship between the nobles and peasants. How did they depend upon one another and on the manor's lands?

The Church and the Rise of Cities

Prepare to Read

Objectives

In this section you will

1. Learn why the Roman Catholic Church was so important and powerful during the Middle Ages.
2. Discover the connection between an increase in trade and the growth of towns.
3. Find out what life was like in a medieval town.
4. Understand the role of culture and learning in the Middle Ages.

Taking Notes

As you read this section, think about what caused towns to grow in the Middle Ages and the effects of this growth. Copy the diagram below and record your findings in it.

Target Reading Skill

Identify Sequence
Noting the order in which significant events occur can help you understand and remember them. You can track the order of events by making a list. Then use signal words and dates in the text to make sure your events are listed in the correct order.

Key Terms

- **clergy** (KLUR jee) *n.* persons with authority to perform religious services
- **excommunication** (eks kuh myoo nih KAY shun) *n.* expelling someone from the Church
- **guild** (gild) *n.* a medieval organization of crafts workers or tradespeople
- **apprentice** (uh PREN tis) *n.* an unpaid person training in a craft or trade
- **chivalry** (SHIV ul ree) *n.* the code of honorable conduct for knights
- **troubadour** (TROO buh dawr) *n.* a traveling poet and musician of the Middle Ages

The cathedral at Chartres, France, still dominates the city.

Tall spires reach toward the heavens. Gorgeous stained-glass windows feature rich colors. Sculptures and carvings of people, plants, and animals seem to be everywhere. Amazing flying buttresses—masses of stonework or brickwork attached to the walls—help hold the building up. What is this building? It is a Gothic cathedral.

Even today, these huge medieval churches dominate towns in many parts of Europe. During the Middle Ages, cathedrals were built not only to glorify God but also to be a credit to their city. Entire communities worked for decades to build the biggest, tallest, most beautiful cathedral.

Once completed, a cathedral served as a house of worship, a gathering place, and even as a religious school. Its beautiful glass windows and sculptures told Bible stories and presented the lives of the saints to a population that could not read or write.

The Church in the Middle Ages

Most Gothic cathedrals were built in Western Europe between 1100 and 1400. *Gothic* refers to the style of architecture, as you can see in the Eyewitness Technology feature on page 404. A cathedral was the church of a bishop, an important leader of the Roman Catholic Church. During the Middle Ages, nearly all people in Western Europe were Roman Catholic. The Roman Catholic Church had so much influence that it was known simply as "the Church." Why was the Church so powerful? There were many reasons.

Religious and Economic Power During the Middle Ages, life was short and hard for most people. They were comforted by the Christian belief that they would enjoy the rewards of heaven after death if they lived according to Church teachings. The Church also held that if people *didn't* obey those rules, they would be punished after death. The promise of reward combined with the threat of punishment made most people follow the teachings of the Church.

The Church also had great economic power. It gained great wealth by collecting taxes. It also took fiefs from lords in exchange for services performed by **clergy,** or persons with authority to perform religious services. In fact, the Church was the single largest owner of land in Europe during the Middle Ages.

Political Power of the Church The combination of religious and economic power enabled the Church to take on many of the roles that government performs today. It even made laws and set up courts to enforce them. People who did not obey the Church were threatened with being excommunicated. **Excommunication** means being expelled from membership in the Church and participation in Church life. This was a very serious threat. Few people would associate with someone who had been excommunicated.

High Church officials were advisors to kings and lords. The ever-present threat of excommunication gave Church officials great influence in political matters. The Church used its authority to limit feudal warfare. It declared periods of truce, or temporary peace. That was one reason warfare began to decline during the 1100s.

Teaching Tool
This stained glass window in Canterbury Cathedral, England, shows the three kings following a star to the birth of Jesus. **Infer** *How might this window have helped medieval people understand Church teachings?*

Gothic Cathedral

In the mid 1100s, Northern Europeans began to build large stone churches in a new style, called Gothic. This style allowed walls to be thinner and higher. The Gothic cathedral was an expression of medieval religion, and became a symbol of European medieval society.

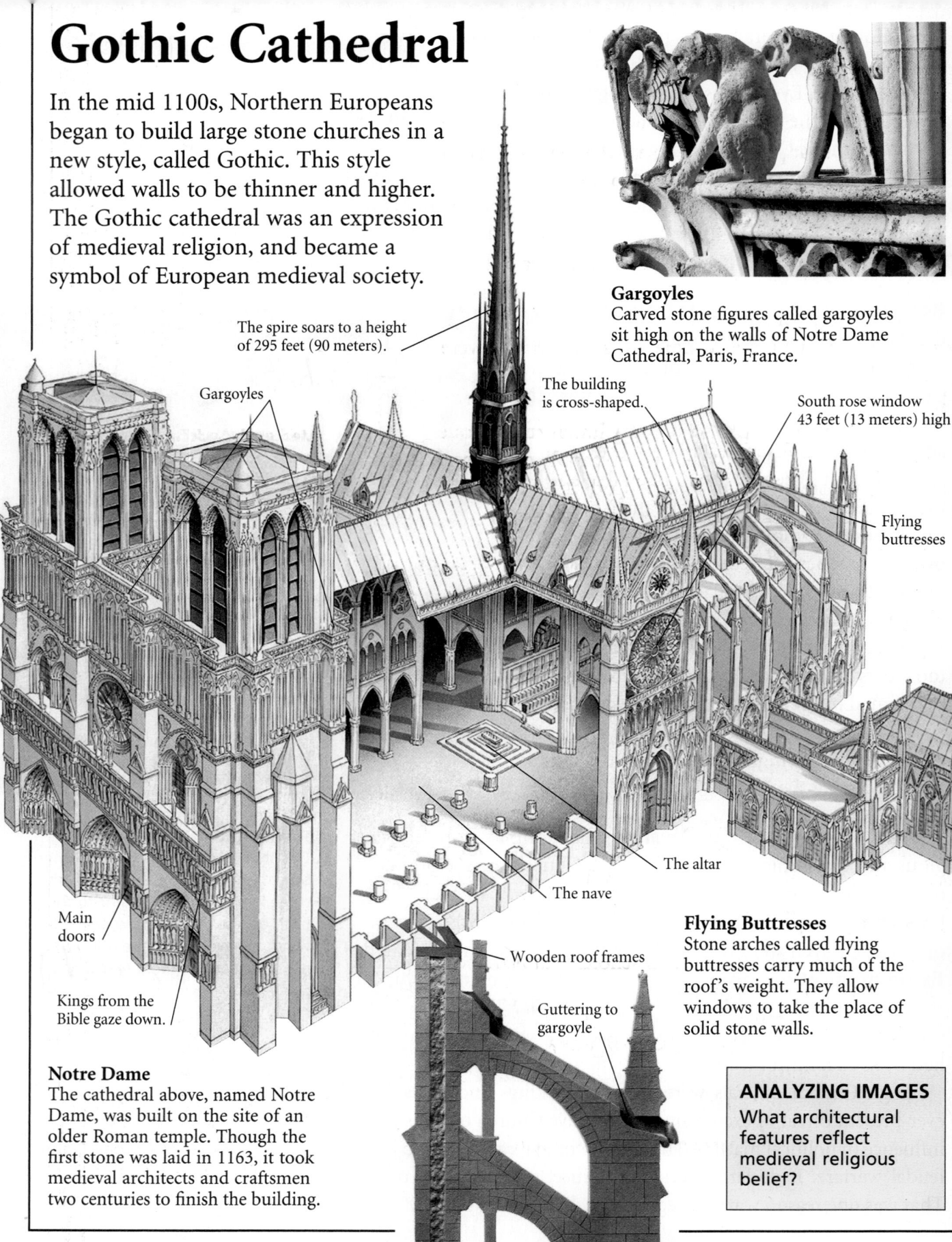

Gargoyles
Carved stone figures called gargoyles sit high on the walls of Notre Dame Cathedral, Paris, France.

The spire soars to a height of 295 feet (90 meters).

Gargoyles

The building is cross-shaped.

South rose window 43 feet (13 meters) high

Flying buttresses

The altar

The nave

Main doors

Kings from the Bible gaze down.

Wooden roof frames

Guttering to gargoyle

Flying Buttresses
Stone arches called flying buttresses carry much of the roof's weight. They allow windows to take the place of solid stone walls.

Notre Dame
The cathedral above, named Notre Dame, was built on the site of an older Roman temple. Though the first stone was laid in 1163, it took medieval architects and craftsmen two centuries to finish the building.

ANALYZING IMAGES
What architectural features reflect medieval religious belief?

Church Organization The Church was highly organized. Almost every village had a priest. A bishop supervised several priests and an archbishop supervised several bishops. Finally, the archbishops were under the authority of the pope. The papacy, or government of the Church, was based in Rome. These areas of Church authority overlapped and crossed the boundaries of kingdoms. Thus, the Church had power in every kingdom, every fief, and every village.

The Church in Everyday Life The medieval Church touched nearly all aspects of life. Think of any major event—the birth of a child, a serious illness, a marriage, or a death. During the Middle Ages, the clergy were almost always in attendance to offer a blessing or to perform a service.

The clergy helped people follow Church rules about how to live. They also listened when people came to church to confess their sins. In the name of God, the clergy then forgave them for the wrongs to which they had confessed.

Medieval Wedding
In the Middle Ages, ceremonies such as weddings had to be performed by a priest. **Conclude** *How did this requirement increase Church power?*

Monasteries and Convents Some religious men felt that they should dedicate their lives to God by living together in religious communities called monasteries. Religious women, called nuns, lived in similar communities called convents. This form of religious life is called monasticism.

These religious communities developed better ways of growing crops and tending livestock. In this way, the Church helped improve the economy of the Middle Ages, which was based mostly on farming. Monks and nuns also looked after the sick and set up schools. Monks were more educated than most people. Because they copied books from ancient times, they preserved knowledge that otherwise would have been lost. Convents gave women a rare opportunity to become educated.

Scholasticism Some Christian scholars studied ancient Greek texts that said people should use reason to discover truth. However, the Church taught that many ideas must be accepted on faith. These medieval scholars worked out a system that tried to resolve the two philosophies. Called scholasticism, it used reason to support Christian beliefs.

✓ Reading Check   **What were monasteries and convents?**

This detail from a medieval manuscript shows a monk copying a manuscript.

This beautiful bottle from Syria, made in the 1300s, would have been a valued trade item.

Trade Revives and Towns Grow

By about A.D. 1000—the middle of the Middle Ages—feudalism was well established in Europe and the Church was a stabilizing force. Europe was becoming a safer place, and the population was growing.

The Revival of Trade As people felt safer, they began to travel more and learn more about distant places. As you will read in Section 3, the crusaders brought many desirable goods back from Asia. Europeans began to demand such things as spices and cloth that they could get only from Africa and Asia. Ancient trade routes came into use again. European merchants traveled abroad to buy and sell valued goods.

The Growth of Towns At first, local goods were traded in the markets of small villages. As trade grew, so did these markets. Some developed into major trade fairs. You can find these market towns on the map below.

MAP MASTER™ Skills Activity

Movement As trade increased, towns along major trade routes held trade fairs and became important business centers. **Identify** Name the major trade centers of Castile. Name French towns with trade fairs. **Infer** Why do you think places such as Valencia, Naples, and Rome became important trade centers?

Go Online
PHSchool.com Use Web Code
lpg-8532 for step-by-step map skills practice.

Trade Centers in Europe

SCOTLAND

North Sea

Baltic Sea

Danzig

IRELAND (England)

WALES (England)

ENGLAND

Hamburg

Lübeck

London
Winchester

FLANDERS
Bruges
Ghent
Lille

HOLY ROMAN EMPIRE

ATLANTIC OCEAN

Paris
Provins
Var-sur-Aube
Troyes

FRANCE
Lyon
Milan
Turin
Venice
Verona
Genoa
Florence
Siena

VENICE

PAPAL STATES

NAVARRE
León
Bayonne
BÉARN

Rome
Naples

KINGDOM OF NAPLES

PORTUGAL
CASTILE
Toledo
Barcelona

ARAGON
SARDINIA (Aragon)

Valencia

Córdoba
Cádiz
GRANADA

Mediterranean Sea

SICILY (Aragon)

0 miles 500
0 kilometers 500
Lambert Azimuthal Equal Area

KEY
• Major trade center
○ Towns with major fairs
— Border as of 1400

Traders also gathered at convenient places for travelers, such as river crossings and along highways. They chose important monasteries and fortified places built by nobles. Before long, towns developed in these locations, too.

As trade grew, so did Europe's medieval towns and cities. The possibility of a better life and freedom from serfdom drew many people to the new, growing towns. The growth of these towns' population further increased their prosperity and trade.

✓ **Reading Check** Why did towns begin to grow?

Life in Towns and Cities

By about 1300, many towns in Western Europe were growing into cities. Paris, with a population approaching 100,000, was one of the largest cities in the world.

The Rise of a Middle Class Town life was not at all like farm or manor life. Towns and cities were not self-sufficient. Instead, their economies were based on the exchange of money for goods and services. A new class of people developed, made up of merchants, traders, and crafts workers. In status, it was between nobles and peasants, and so it was called the middle class.

The Role of Guilds In many towns and cities, the merchants, traders, and crafts workers began to form associations called guilds. A **guild** included all the people who practiced a certain trade or craft. Thus there was a guild of weavers, a guild of grocers, a guild of shoemakers, and so on.

Guilds set prices and prevented outsiders from selling goods in town. They set standards for the quality of their goods. Guild members paid dues. This money was used to help needy members or to support the families of members who had died.

It took a long time to become a member of a guild. Between the ages of about 8 and 14, a boy who wanted to learn a certain trade became an **apprentice,** or unpaid worker being trained in a craft. He lived and worked in the home of a master of that trade for as long as seven years. Then he could become a journeyman, or salaried worker. In time, if guild officials judged that the journeyman's work met their standards, he could join the guild.

Shops in a Paris Street
Notice the many kinds of shops in Paris in the early 1500s. Merchants were becoming an important part of society at this time. **Generalize** *What types of goods were available in European cities in the 1500s?*

◀ **A shield representing the Guild of Notaries, who prepared and verified documents**

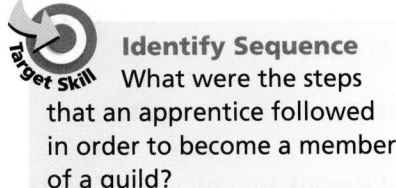

Identify Sequence
What were the steps that an apprentice followed in order to become a member of a guild?

Overcrowding and Disease Medieval towns and cities were extremely crowded. Their lack of sanitation, or procedures for keeping the town clean, bred disease, and the overcrowded conditions meant that disease spread quickly. One disease, the bubonic plague, wiped out one third of Europe's population between 1347 and 1351. Called the Black Death, it was spread by fleas living on the rats that thrived in the unsanitary towns.

✓ **Reading Check** **What was the Black Death?**

Troubadours provided entertainment and preserved traditional tales.

Medieval Culture

Despite its hardships, medieval life was not all a struggle for survival. The growing cities attracted traveling scholars, and young men flocked to cathedral schools. Many of these schools became great centers of learning. Much of the beautiful artwork of the Middle Ages was displayed in churches where many could enjoy it.

Stories, poems, and songs about chivalry were also very popular. **Chivalry** is the code of honorable conduct by which knights were supposed to live. Throughout Western Europe, traveling poets and musicians called **troubadours** or minstrels went from place to place singing about the brave deeds performed by knights to win the love of a beautiful and worthy woman.

✓ **Reading Check** **Describe some advantages of living in a medieval city.**

Section 2 Assessment

Key Terms
Review the key terms at the beginning of this section. Use each term in a sentence that explains its meaning.

Target Reading Skill
Identify and list in sequence three events or conditions that led to the growth of towns.

Comprehension and Critical Thinking
1. (a) Recall How was the Church important in everyday life?

(b) Identify Effects How did this importance contribute to the Church's power?
2. (a) List What factors led to the increase in trade in Western Europe?
(b) Infer How might the growth of trade have affected the life of an ordinary person?
3. (a) Define What were guilds?
(b) Draw Conclusions Why would someone join a guild?
4. (a) Explain What was chivalry?
(b) Infer Why was chivalry a popular topic for troubadours?

Writing Activity
During the Middle Ages, children began apprenticeships as early as the age of eight. Do you think that it is good to begin working at that age? Write a paragraph that answers this question.

Writing Tip Begin your paragraph with a topic sentence that tells whether or not you think eight years old is too young. Use supporting sentences to give reasons for your position.

Prepare to Read

Objectives

In this section you will
1. Learn about the causes of the Crusades.
2. Find out about the different Crusades and what they accomplished.
3. Discover the effects the Crusades had on life in Europe.

Taking Notes

As you read this section, look for the ways various people or groups contributed to the Crusades. Copy the table below and record your findings in it.

Person or Group	Contribution

Target Reading Skill

Recognize Sequence Signal Words Signal words point out relationships between ideas or events. This section discusses the Crusades, which took place over many years. To help keep the order of events clear, look for words such as *first, then, finally,* and *in [date]* that signal the order in which the events took place.

Key Terms

- **Holy Land** (HOH lee land) *n.* Jerusalem and parts of the surrounding area where Jesus lived and taught
- **Crusades** (kroo SAYDZ) *n.* a series of military expeditions launched by Christian Europeans to win the Holy Land back from Muslim control
- **Jerusalem** (juh ROOZ uh lum) *n.* a city in the Holy Land, regarded as sacred by Christians, Muslims, and Jews
- **pilgrim** (PIL grum) *n.* a person who journeys to a sacred place

On November 27, 1095, a crowd gathered in the town of Clermont, located in present-day France. They came to hear an urgent message from the pope:

> **“You common people who have been miserable sinners, become soldiers of Christ! You nobles, do not [quarrel] with one another. Use your arms in a just war! Labor for everlasting reward.”**
>
> —*Pope Urban II*

The crowd roared its approval. They shouted, "God wills it!"

Pope Urban II was calling the people of Europe to war. The purpose of this war was to capture the **Holy Land,** a region sacred to Christians because Jesus had lived and taught there. It was a small region on the eastern shore of the Mediterranean Sea known in ancient times as Judaea, today part of Israel and the West Bank. Now, said the pope, the Holy Land has fallen to the Muslims. Christians must win it back.

Pope Urban II calling for a war to win back the Holy Land

Embarking on a Crusade
Huge armies of crusader knights sailed to the Holy Land.
Conclude *What was involved in transporting these large armies?*

Causes of the Crusades

Over the next 200 years, the Church launched eight military expeditions, called the **Crusades**, to capture the Holy Land. The word comes from *crux,* the Latin word for "cross." People who carried the Christian cross into battle against the non-Christian enemy were called crusaders.

Pilgrims to the Holy Land Since about A.D. 200, European Christians had been traveling to **Jerusalem,** a city in the Holy Land regarded as sacred by Christians, Muslims, and Jews. These people were **pilgrims**—people who journey to a sacred place. Nobles and peasants alike made the long and difficult journey. They wanted to visit the places written about in the Bible.

The Rise of the Turks For centuries, Jerusalem had been controlled by Arab Muslims who generally welcomed Christian pilgrims. Then, in the 1000s, the Seljuk Turks (SEL jook turks) took control of the Holy Land. This Muslim group sometimes attacked the Christian pilgrims from Europe. Then they closed the pilgrimage routes to Jerusalem.

At the same time, the Turks were also conquering much of the Byzantine Empire. The Byzantine emperor in Constantinople asked Pope Urban II to send knights to defend his Christian empire. The pope agreed and called on the people of Europe to fight the Muslim Turks.

Many medieval Christians believed that Jerusalem was the center of the world, as this map from the 1200s shows.

Why Go to War? Why did Pope Urban II agree to organize a war against the Muslim Turks? Mainly, he wanted the Holy Land to be under the control of Christians. He wanted Christian pilgrims to be able to visit Jerusalem and other religious sites.

But he also had other reasons. The pope thought a crusade would unite Europeans against a common enemy—the Muslim Turks—and they would stop fighting among themselves. He also hoped to gain power and prestige for himself and the Church.

Some Europeans had other reasons for encouraging the Crusades. They wanted to control not only the Holy Land but also key trade routes between Africa, Asia, and Europe.

✓ **Reading Check** **Why did the pope want to conquer the Holy Land?**

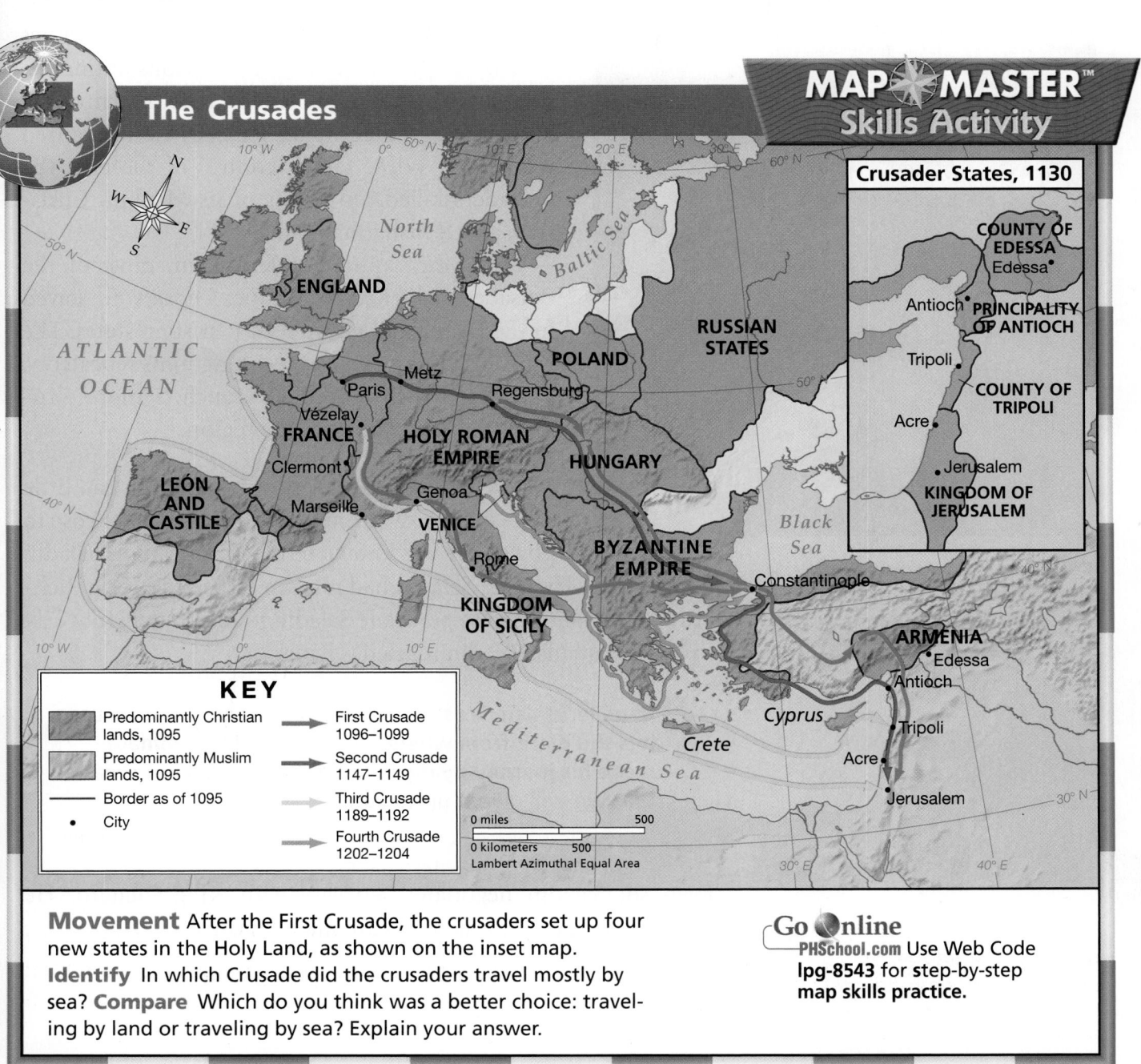

The Crusades

MAP★MASTER™
Skills Activity

Crusader States, 1130

COUNTY OF EDESSA
Edessa•
Antioch• PRINCIPALITY OF ANTIOCH
Tripoli•
COUNTY OF TRIPOLI
Acre•
•Jerusalem
KINGDOM OF JERUSALEM

KEY

▨ Predominantly Christian lands, 1095	➡ First Crusade 1096–1099
▨ Predominantly Muslim lands, 1095	➡ Second Crusade 1147–1149
— Border as of 1095	➡ Third Crusade 1189–1192
• City	➡ Fourth Crusade 1202–1204

0 miles 500
0 kilometers 500
Lambert Azimuthal Equal Area

Movement After the First Crusade, the crusaders set up four new states in the Holy Land, as shown on the inset map.
Identify In which Crusade did the crusaders travel mostly by sea? **Compare** Which do you think was a better choice: traveling by land or traveling by sea? Explain your answer.

Go Online
PHSchool.com Use Web Code lpg-8543 for step-by-step map skills practice.

Recognize Sequence Signal Words

What word in the paragraph at the right signals sequence? How does this clue help you understand the next few paragraphs?

A Series of Crusades

The pope's best hope for capturing the Holy Land rested with European lords and their knights. But before these armies could assemble, a band of common people set out for Jerusalem.

Peter the Hermit and the People's Crusade Peter, a small man who wore monk's robes, gathered an "army" of common people. They set out in 1096. When they got to Constantinople, the Byzantine emperor advised them to wait for help from an army of knights from Europe. Peter agreed, but his followers rebelled. His soldiers attacked the Turks, who easily defeated them. Only a small part of his army survived.

Crusaders led by Louis IX of France take the city of Damietta, near the Holy Land.

The First Crusade At last, the European armies sent by Pope Urban II reached Constantinople. Joined by what remained of Peter's army, the knights fought their way to Jerusalem and captured it in 1099. While taking control of the city, the crusaders killed thousands of its Muslim, Christian, and Jewish inhabitants.

After the capture of Jerusalem, most of the crusaders returned to Europe. Those who stayed in the Holy Land set up four Christian states. The Muslim Turks attacked these kingdoms repeatedly. European Christians then launched more Crusades to keep control of the region.

Later Crusades The Second Crusade had little success. Then a strong Arab Muslim leader rose to power. He was known to the Europeans as Saladin (SAL uh din). By 1187, Saladin had retaken Jerusalem. King Richard I of England tried to persuade Saladin to return the Holy City to the Christians. Saladin refused, saying,

> **To us Jerusalem is as precious . . . as it is to you, because it is the place from where our Prophet [Muhammad] made his journey by night to heaven. . . . Do not dream that we will give it up to you.**
>
> *—Saladin*

Even so, Saladin negotiated a treaty with King Richard. He agreed to reopen Jerusalem to Christian pilgrims.

✓ **Reading Check** Why did Saladin refuse to give up Jerusalem?

The Results of the Crusades

Although crusaders did capture the Holy Land for a while, they were never able to gain firm control of it. Still, the Crusades brought important and lasting changes to Europe.

Increased Trade The European ships that carried crusaders and their supplies to the Holy Land returned with rugs, jewelry, glass, and spices. Soon, these goods were in great demand in Europe. Thus, the Crusades helped revive trade, which in turn led to the growth of towns and cities.

The Crusades also encouraged the use of money in Europe. For much of the Middle Ages, most people bartered, or traded goods for other goods or for land or protection. But the crusaders went far from home, where they needed to *buy* supplies. In that case, it was easier to use money than it was to barter.

New Ideas Returning crusaders also brought new ideas and technology back to Europe. You have read about the advances made by Arabs in medicine, mathematics, and technology. The crusaders helped increase European knowledge of these techniques. Europeans learned how to make better ships and maps—skills that would help them become worldwide explorers.

Medieval Banking
A man deposits gold in a bank.
Synthesize *Why did banking increase after the Crusades?*

✓ **Reading Check** **Describe two effects of the Crusades.**

 # Section 3 Assessment

Key Terms
Review the key terms at the beginning of this section. Use each term in a sentence that explains its meaning.

Target Reading Skill
Reread the text on page 410 under the heading The Rise of the Turks. What signal words helped you understand the sequence of these events?

Comprehension and Critical Thinking
1. (a) Find Main Ideas What was the chief goal of the crusaders?

(b) Infer Why do you think Pope Urban II called the First Crusade a "just," or honorable, war?

2. (a) Sequence List the events of the First Crusade in order.
(b) Identify Frame of Reference How do you think European Christians viewed the Muslim Turks? How do you think Muslims living in the Holy Land viewed the crusaders?

3. (a) Identify Effects What were the main effects of the Crusades on life in Europe?
(b) Predict What might have happened in Europe if the Crusades had never taken place?

Writing Activity
Suppose that there were European newspapers that published editorials at the time of the Crusades. Write an editorial either in support of or against the First Crusade.

Writing Tip Remember that editorials are persuasive writing. State your position. Then use reasons and facts to convince readers that your opinion is the right one.

Distinguishing Fact and Opinion

Richard I was born on September 8, 1157. He became king of England in 1189 but spent most of his reign fighting in the Crusades. He led his armies to free the Holy Land. Richard loved to be in the midst of battle and always fought bravely. He spent only six months of his reign in England, but his people loved him anyway. They admired his great courage and called him Richard the Lion-Hearted.

Richard won many battles, but he failed to free the Holy Land. He did make peace with the Muslim leader Saladin, who allowed Christians to visit the holy city of Jerusalem. That was a great accomplishment. Richard died in 1199. He was a good and kind king.

King Richard I of England

Facts are statements that can be proved true. Opinions are personal beliefs or value judgments. You will often need to make your own judgments or decisions based on facts, so you must be able to recognize them.

Learn the Skill

To distinguish fact from opinion, use the following steps:

1. **Look for facts by asking what can be proved true or false.** A fact usually tells who, what, when, where, or how much. A fact can be proved true.

2. **Ask how you could check whether each fact is true.** Could you do your own test by measuring or counting? Could you find information in an encyclopedia or in another reliable reference book?

3. **Look for opinions by identifying personal beliefs or value judgments.** Look for words that signal personal feelings, such as *I think* or *I believe*. Look for words that judge, such as *great* or *brave*, or *should* or *ought to*. An opinion cannot be proved true or false.

4. **Decide whether facts or good reasons support each opinion.** A well-supported opinion can help you make up your own mind—as long as you recognize it as an opinion and not a fact.

Practice the Skill

Read the passage about Richard the Lion-Hearted until you are sure that you understand it. Then reread it for facts and opinions.

1️⃣ Identify facts in the paragraph that tell who, what, when, where, and how much.

2️⃣ Explain how each fact could be proved true or false.

3️⃣ **(a)** Identify two examples of words that show personal feelings. Can these statements be proved true or false? **(b)** Now identify one word that signals judgment. Can the statement containing this word be proved true or false?

4️⃣ The last sentence in the passage expresses an opinion. Is the opinion well supported with facts and reasons? Explain your answer.

Richard I riding into battle

Burying victims of the Black Death, 1349

Apply the Skill

Read the passage at the right. List two facts and two opinions from the passage. If you found this passage in a book, how useful would it be as a source for a research paper? Explain your answer.

The Black Death was the worst thing that happened in medieval Europe. The disease struck quickly. It caused horrible spots and almost certain death. The Black Death eventually killed so many people—more than 25 million—that normal life broke down. There was a labor shortage, and those workers who survived the disease unfairly demanded higher wages. Farmers turned from growing crops to grazing sheep, which required fewer workers. Fear of the disease and economic disruption caused riots all over Europe. That kind of reaction would never happen today.

The Power of Kings

Prepare to Read

Objectives

In this section you will
1. Learn about the forces that led to nation building in Europe.
2. Find out about nation building in England.
3. Discover how the Hundred Years' War affected England and France.

Taking Notes

As you read this section, think about what factors led to nation building in England and France. Copy the table below and record your findings in it.

Nation Building	
England	**France**
•	•
•	•

Target Reading Skill

Identify Sequence Noting the order of events can help you understand and remember them. Make a sequence chart of events that led to nation building in England. Write the first event in the first box. Then write each additional event in a box. Use arrows to show how one event led to the next.

Key Terms

- **nation** (NAY shun) *n.* a community of people that shares territory and a government

- **Magna Carta** (MAG nuh KAHR tuh) *n.* the "Great Charter," in which the king's power over his nobles was limited, agreed to by King John of England in 1215
- **Model Parliament** (MAHD ul PAHR luh munt) *n.* a council of lords, clergy, and common people that advised the English king on government matters
- **Hundred Years' War** (HUN drud yeerz wawr) *n.* a series of conflicts between England and France, 1337–1453

Pope Gregory VII forgiving King Henry IV

For three days, the king waited outside the castle where Pope Gregory VII was staying. Barefoot in the winter cold, the king begged forgiveness. Would the pope forgive King Henry IV?

During the Middle Ages, kings and popes quarreled over who should select bishops. Because bishops were Church officials, popes claimed the right to choose them. Kings wanted this right because bishops often controlled large areas of their kingdoms. They also wanted to play a role in the Church.

In 1077, Henry IV of Germany ruled much of Europe. He had been choosing bishops even though Pope Gregory had ordered him not to. In response, the pope had excommunicated the king and declared that his people no longer had to obey him. However, after putting Henry off for three long, cold days, the pope gave in. He allowed Henry to rejoin the Church.

Pope Gregory had made a serious mistake. In 1081, King Henry invaded Italy, where the pope lived. By 1084, Henry had replaced Pope Gregory with a new pope, who crowned Henry emperor of the Holy Roman Empire. Gregory was sent into exile.

Nation Building

Henry's success in overthrowing the pope was a hint of things to come. As later kings gained power, they often dared to put their own wishes before those of the Church. They would soon increase their power in other ways as well.

Castle Stronghold
This English castle is protected by walls and water. **Infer** *What would be involved in defending this castle from attack?*

The Power of Nobles When the 1200s began, Europe was still a feudal society. While kings reigned over kingdoms, the wealthiest lords also had great power. Many saw themselves as nearly the king's equal. In fact, it was not unusual for a noble to have more land, vassals, and knights than his king. But the nobles' power was based on the feudal system. If the feudal system began to decline, so would the nobles' power.

The Decline of Feudalism One reason for the decline of the feudal system was the growth of trade and towns. Kings began to support the new towns in exchange for money. They agreed to protect towns and made laws to help towns grow rich. Then, with the money paid by townspeople, kings hired armies and used them to attack troublesome nobles.

The Crusades also weakened the nobles. Many gave up land to raise money so they could join the Crusades. Other nobles were killed in the Crusades, and kings claimed their land.

The Birth of Nations Over time, kings became more and more powerful. Instead of a patchwork of fiefs ruled by many nobles, large areas of Europe became united under a single king. The kings became strong enough to challenge the Church.

Gradually, these larger kingdoms began to turn into nations. A **nation** is a community of people that shares territory and a government. A common language and culture also often unite the people of a nation. The process of combining smaller communities into a single nation with a national identity and a national government is called nation building.

In the late Middle Ages, the idea of nationhood was taking hold in Europe. A royal marriage united the two largest kingdoms in Spain. In Russia, rulers called tsars were expanding their territory and their power over other nobles. In France, a long line of kings slowly but surely increased royal power. Louis IX, who ruled from 1226 to 1270, was a deeply religious king. He strengthened both Christianity and the central government in his kingdom.

✓ **Reading Check** **What is nation building?**

Target Skill

Identify Sequence
What events described in the paragraph at the right led to increased power of the king? Write these events in a sequence chart.

Go Online
PHSchool.com Use Web Code **mup-0882** for an interactivity on the Magna Carta.

Changes in England

By the 1200s, England was already well on its way to becoming a unified nation. In 1066, William of Normandy, a duke from France, had conquered England in what is called the Norman Conquest. As king of England, William the Conqueror was a strong ruler who dominated his nobles. The kings who followed William—especially Henry I and Henry II—further increased the power of the king. Of course, the nobles began to resent this power. King John, a son of Henry II, would soon face their anger.

King John Angers the Nobles When John became king of England in 1199, he quickly moved to increase his wealth and power. He taxed people heavily. He jailed his enemies unjustly and without trial. Even the most powerful nobles were hurt by John's unfair actions.

John also angered Church leaders and clergymen. He seized Church property and tried to block the pope's choice for the chief bishop of England. When the pope's choice for bishop did take office, he backed the nobles who opposed the king's actions.

King John at Runnymede
The Magna Carta marked the beginning of limitations on the power of the king. This engraving shows King John surrounded by English nobles and clergymen. **Synthesize** *How did these groups benefit from the Magna Carta?*

The Magna Carta John was not strong enough to defy the nobles and clergy whom he had angered. With the backing of the bishops, English nobles demanded a meeting with the king. On June 15, 1215, about 2,000 English nobles gathered at Runnymede, a meadow along the Thames River. They presented John with a list of their demands.

John was forced to place the royal seal on the document, and it became law. Called the **Magna Carta** (MAG nuh KAHR tuh), or the "Great Charter," it limited the king's power. The king could no longer jail any freeman without just cause, and he could not raise taxes without consulting his Great Council of lords and clergy.

This council later became the **Model Parliament,** which included common people as well as lords and clergy. Eventually, Parliament evolved into a powerful legislature, or law-making assembly. As it gained power, Parliament also helped unify England. However, the Magna Carta also strengthened the power of the king. Because nobles now had a say in government, they were more likely to support what the king did.

✓ **Reading Check** How did the Magna Carta help unite England?

The Hundred Years' War

Despite the growth of nations, Western Europe was not at peace. Now, instead of nobles fighting each other, the emerging nations went to war. One long series of clashes between England and France was called the **Hundred Years' War.** It lasted from 1337 to 1453.

Causes of the War In the 1300s, the borders of England and France were not the ones we know today. As a result of marriage and inheritance, the English king had come to be the lord of many counties in present-day France.

You have read that William the Conqueror, who became king of England in 1066, was also Duke of Normandy in France. The 1152 marriage of King Henry II of England and the French noblewoman Eleanor of Aquitaine brought more French land under English control.

Then, in 1328, the French king died. King Edward III of England, whose mother had been a French princess, claimed to be king of France under feudal law. The French nobles did not agree. Determined to get his way, Edward III invaded France—and began the Hundred Years' War.

There were other causes of the war. Both England and France wanted to control the English Channel, the waterway that separates their countries. Each nation also wanted to control trade in the region and the wealth it brought.

Joan of Arc's Victory The Hundred Years' War dragged on, fought by one king after another. England won most of the battles, but the French continued to fight. However, the tide turned in 1429 when a peasant girl called Joan of Arc took charge of the French forces at the battle of Orléans (awr lay AHN). French troops at Orléans greeted her with hope and curiosity.

Under Joan's command, the French defeated the English at Orléans. She then led her forces to victory in other battles. In 1430, Joan was taken prisoner by allies of the English. England tried Joan for witchcraft. She was convicted and burned at the stake.

The French saw Joan of Arc as a martyr, and her death inspired them to many victories. By 1453, the English had been driven from most of France. With the English troops in retreat, France was on its way to becoming a strong and united nation.

Citizen Heroes

Joan of Arc

The young girl who would become one of France's greatest heroes was the daughter of a tenant farmer. Joan was very religious and believed that she saw heavenly visions. In 1429, when she was only 17, she journeyed to the court of Charles, the heir to the French throne. She convinced him that God had called her to lead the French forces at the battle of Orléans. Charles finally agreed. He gave Joan armor, attendants, horses, and a special banner to carry into battle. You can see that banner in this statue of Joan, which stands in Paris.

King Charles VII
The victory of Charles VII of France over the English in the Hundred Years' War increased his power in France. **Infer** *How might war with a foreign nation increase a ruler's power?*

The Growing Power of Kings The Hundred Years' War affected the balance of power in England and France. On the battlefield, new weapons such as the longbow and cannon increased the importance of footsoldiers. Armored knights, on the other hand, became less valuable in battle. Feudal castles could not stand up to the firepower of the new cannons. Kings now needed large armies, not small bands of knights, to fight for them.

The Hundred Years' War also led to national feeling. People began to think of themselves as citizens of England or of France, not simply as loyal to their local lords. Kings who had led their nations in battle became more powerful as the influence of nobles declined. On the other hand, the English king had been forced to ask Parliament for more and more money to fund the war. This helped Parliament win "the power of the purse" and increased its power in relation to the king. These two developments helped unify England.

The Hundred Years' War helped set the modern boundaries of England and France. Forced to give up their dream of an empire in Europe, the English later looked to more distant lands for trade and conquest. Leaving feudalism behind, Europe was becoming a continent of nations. And some of these nations, as you will read in Chapter 15, would soon rule much of the world.

 **Reading Check** **Explain two effects of the Hundred Years' War.**

Section 4 Assessment

Key Terms
Review the key terms at the beginning of this section. Use each term in a sentence that explains its meaning.

Target Reading Skill
Reread page 419. Write the events of Joan of Arc's life in a sequence chart.

Comprehension and Critical Thinking
1. (a) Recall How much power did kings have under feudalism?

(b) Identify Cause and Effect Why did feudalism decline, and how did this affect the power of kings?
2. (a) Identify What are two limits on the king's power established by the Magna Carta?
(b) Identify Effects How did the Magna Carta help unify England as a nation?
3. (a) Name Who fought the Hundred Years' War?
(b) Identify Effects How did this war help unify each of the two nations involved?

Writing Activity
Suppose that you are a French soldier preparing for the battle of Orléans. Describe your reaction to the news that a young peasant girl is your new commander.

For: An activity on the Hundred Years' War
Visit: PHSchool.com
Web Code: lgd-8504

Review and Assessment

◆ Chapter Summary

Lombard warrior

Section 1: Feudalism and the Manor System

- The Middle Ages was the period from about A.D. 500 to 1500.
- Medieval Europe's economic and political system was feudalism, in which nobles granted vassals land in return for loyalty.
- Local economic and political life was based on the manor system, in which people lived and worked on large estates owned by lords.
- Most people of the Middle Ages were peasants. Serfs were peasants who were considered part of the manors on which they worked.

Section 2: The Church and the Rise of Cities

- During the Middle Ages, the Roman Catholic Church was a powerful force that touched nearly every aspect of people's lives.
- An increase in trade led to the growth of towns and cities.
- The new middle class organized craft and trade guilds. Medieval towns and cities were crowded and unsanitary.
- Culture and learning were limited to only small groups of people. Troubadours brought stories of chivalry from place to place.

Section 3: The Crusades

- The Crusades were a series of wars launched by European Christians to capture the Holy Land from Muslim Turks.
- The First Crusade succeeded in capturing the holy city of Jerusalem.
- Later Crusades were launched to defend the Christian kingdoms in the Holy Land from Muslim Turk attacks.
- The Crusades changed life in Europe: trade increased, towns grew, the use of money increased, and the learning of the Arab world came to Europe.

Section 4: The Power of Kings

- Nation building in Europe began as feudalism declined and kings increased their power.
- The Magna Carta limited the power of the English king but also helped unify England into a nation.
- The Hundred Years' War helped unify both England and France into nations.

◆ Key Terms

Write one or two paragraphs about life in the Middle Ages. Use all of the following terms correctly in your paragraphs.

1. Middle Ages
2. feudalism
3. pilgrim
4. guild
5. manor

6. serf
7. clergy
8. apprentice
9. troubadour
10. Crusades

◆ Comprehension and Critical Thinking

11. (a) Recall In the feudal system, what was the role of a lord? Of a vassal?
(b) Synthesize How could one person be both a lord and a vassal at the same time?

12. (a) Describe What was a manor, and how did it meet people's needs?
(b) Explain What was the relationship of serfs to the manor?
(c) Draw Conclusions How did manorialism help support feudalism?

13. (a) Identify What was "the Church" in the Middle Ages?
(b) Draw Conclusions Why was the Church so powerful in the Middle Ages?

14. (a) Recall Where did towns spring up during the Middle Ages?
(b) Synthesize Information How was the growth of medieval towns related to the growth of guilds?

15. (a) Define What were the Crusades?
(b) Draw Conclusions Do you think the Crusades helped or hurt Europe? Explain.

16. (a) Define What is nation building?
(b) Identify Causes What factors led to nation building in Europe in the later Middle Ages?

17. (a) Recall Who was Joan of Arc?
(b) Identify Effects How did she influence the outcome of the Hundred Years' War?

◆ Skills Practice

Distinguishing Fact and Opinion In the Skills for Life activity in this chapter, you learned how to distinguish fact from opinion. Review the steps you followed to learn the skill. Then reread the opening paragraphs of Section 2 of this chapter on page 402. List the facts and opinions in this text. For each opinion, note whether or not you think the opinion is well supported and reliable.

◆ Writing Activity: Science

The bubonic plague—the Black Death that killed so many Europeans during the Middle Ages—still exists today. However, it is not nearly so common or deadly as it once was. Use an encyclopedia and other reliable sources to learn how modern medicine and sanitation prevent and control the disease. Write a brief report titled "The Bubonic Plague in Modern Times."

MAP ✦ MASTER™
Skills Activity

Europe and the Holy Land

Place Location For each place listed below, write the letter from the map that shows its location.
1. England
2. France
3. Jerusalem
4. Mediterranean Sea
5. Rome
6. Constantinople

Go Online
PHSchool.com Use Web Code **lgd-8554** for an **interactive map.**

Standardized Test Prep

Test-Taking Tips

Some questions on standardized tests ask you to identify cause and effect. Study the graphic organizer below. Then use the tip to help you answer the sample question.

```
┌─────────────────────────────────────┐
│              CAUSES                  │
│ • King John taxed people heavily.    │
│ • King John jailed enemies unfairly. │
│ • King John seized church property.  │
└─────────────────────────────────────┘
                  ↓
┌─────────────────────────────────────┐
│        EVENT: MAGNA CARTA            │
└─────────────────────────────────────┘
                  ↓
┌─────────────────────────────────────┐
│              EFFECTS                 │
│ • King couldn't jail nobles.         │
│ • King couldn't tax without consent. │
│ •                                    │
└─────────────────────────────────────┘
```

TIP Remember that a *cause* is what makes something happen. An *effect* is what happens as a result of something else. Is the question asking for a cause or an effect?

Pick the letter that best answers the question.

What information belongs with the last bullet (•) in the graphic organizer?

A King John clashed with the pope.

B It became law with King John's seal.

C It helped unite England.

D King John seized Church property.

Think It Through The question is asking for an effect: What else happened as a result of the Magna Carta? You can eliminate A and D because both were causes, or events leading up to the Magna Carta. That leaves B and C. The Magna Carta did become law with King John's seal, but that was not an *effect* of the law. The answer is C: the Magna Carta had the effect of helping to unite England.

Practice Questions

Choose the letter of the best answer.

1. Which of the following was a major cause of the growth of towns during the Middle Ages?

   A a decrease in the power of the Church

   B an increase in trade

   C a decrease in Europe's population

   D an increase in the number of manors

2. Which of the following was NOT an effect of the Crusades?

   A The demand for foreign goods increased.

   B Europeans learned new shipbuilding techniques.

   C The use of money became more common.

   D The Holy Land came under permanent European control.

3. The decline of _____ helped the growth of _____.

   A trade, towns

   B feudalism, manorialism

   C Charlemagne's empire, feudalism

   D the Roman Empire, trade

Study the diagram. Then use it to answer the question that follows.

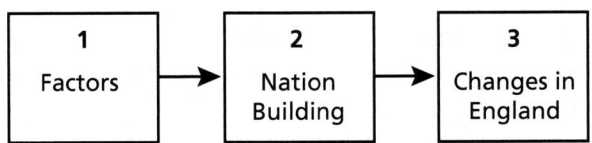

```
┌──────────┐     ┌──────────┐     ┌──────────┐
│    1     │ ──→ │    2     │ ──→ │    3     │
│ Factors  │     │  Nation  │     │Changes in│
│          │     │ Building │     │ England  │
└──────────┘     └──────────┘     └──────────┘
```

4. In the diagram,

   A **1** represents a single effect of nation building, and **2** and **3** represent several causes.

   B **1** represents a single cause of **2**, and **2** is a cause of **3**.

   C **2** is a cause of both **1** and **3**.

   D **1** represents several causes of **2**, and **3** represents how nation building affected England.

Go Online
PHSchool.com

Use Web Code lga-8504
for a **Chapter 14 self-test.**

Of Swords and Sorcerers:
The Adventures of King Arthur and His Knights
By Margaret Hodges and Margery Evernden

Prepare to Read

Background Information

How should a good and just ruler behave? What traits should a king or queen have? What do you admire in people who lead others?

People have read and enjoyed the stories of King Arthur for hundreds of years. To many, he symbolizes the virtue and justice of a good ruler. According to legend, he was loved and respected by all of his people.

Legends about King Arthur exist in many forms, and stories about him have been written and rewritten in several languages. The following selection is one tale of how Arthur met his friend Pellinore and found his sword, which was named Excalibur.

Objectives

As you read this selection, you will

1. Understand why King Arthur's subjects loved him.
2. Learn about some of the rules of honor in battle that were part of the code of chivalry.

petty (PET ee) *adj.* unimportant; of low rank

fealty (FEE ul tee) *n.* loyalty to a feudal lord

No king before Arthur had been able to unite the realm and rule it. This Arthur did. Lightnings and thunders surrounded him as he fought. In twelve great battles he defeated <u>petty</u> kings who had been constantly at war, laying waste all the land. The last to surrender was Arthur's own brother-in-law, King Lot of Orkney. When Lot laid down his arms and swore <u>fealty</u> to Arthur, he sent his sons to become knights at Camelot.

King Arthur standing with the crowns of 30 kingdoms, in an illustration from 1325

One son was Gawain, handsome and strong, whom Arthur called Gawain the Courteous. Another was Mordred, whose foxy smile and <u>gimlet eyes</u> concealed <u>malice</u> and a thirst for power. Gawain took the vows of knighthood in good faith, but Mordred's vows were insincere, and he soon began listening at the castle doors in hope of ferreting out secrets that might damage the court and someday play into his own hands. He saw that the time to strike had not yet come. The powers of heaven and earth all seemed to be on Arthur's side. The people loved him, and Camelot was in its glory.

Now there came a day when Arthur rode with Merlin seeking adventure, and in a forest they found a knight named Pellinore, seated in a chair, blocking their path.

"Sir, will you let us pass?" said Arthur.

"Not without a fight," replied Pellinore. "Such is my custom."

"I will change your custom," said Arthur.

"I will defend it," said Pellinore. He mounted his horse and took his shield on his arm. Then the two knights rode against each other, and each splintered his spear on the other's shield.

"I have no more spears," said Arthur. "Let us fight with swords."

"Not so," said Pellinore. "I have enough spears. I will lend you one."

Then a squire brought two good spears, and the two knights rode against each other again until those spears were broken.

"You are as good a fighter as ever I met," said Pellinore. "Let us try again."

Two great spears were brought, and this time Pellinore struck Arthur's shield so hard that the king and his horse fell to the earth.

Then Arthur pulled out his sword and said, "I have lost the battle on horseback. Let me try you on foot."

Pellinore thought it unfair to attack from his horse, so he dismounted and came toward Arthur with his sword drawn. Then began such a battle that both were covered with blood. After a while they sat down to rest and fought again until both fell to the ground. Again they fought, and the fight was even. But at last Pellinore struck such a blow that Arthur's sword broke into two pieces. Thereupon the king leaped at Pellinore. He threw him down and pulled off his helmet. But Pellinore was a very big man and strong enough to wrestle Arthur under him and pull off the

gimlet eyes (GIM lit eyez) *n.* eyes having a piercing quality
malice (MAL is) *n.* spite; a desire to damage or hurt someone

Knights in battle, in an illustration by N. C. Wyeth

✓ Reading Check

Why did Arthur and Pellinore fight?

king's helmet. All this time Merlin had watched, silent, but when he saw that Pellinore was about to cut off Arthur's head, he interfered.

"Do not kill this man," he said to Pellinore. "You do not know who he is."

"Why, who is he?" said the knight.

"It is King Arthur," said Merlin.

When he heard this, Pellinore trembled with fear of the royal <u>wrath</u>, for he would not knowingly have fought against the king. Then Merlin cast a spell of sleep on Pellinore so that he fell to the earth as if dead.

"Alas," said Arthur, "you have killed the best knight I ever fought."

"Have no fear," said Merlin. "He will awake in three hours as well as ever he was."

Then he mounted Pellinore's horse and led Arthur to a <u>hermit</u>, who bound up the king's wounds and healed them with good <u>salves</u>, so that he might ride again and go on his way.

But Arthur said, "I have no sword."

"Never fear," said Merlin. "Not far away is a sword that can be yours." So they rode on until they came to a broad lake of clear water. Far out in the middle of the lake Arthur saw an arm clothed in shining white and holding a noble sword, its golden hilt richly set with jewels.

"Lo," said Merlin, "yonder is the sword Excalibur."

wrath (rath) *n.* great anger or rage

hermit (HUR mit) *n.* a person who lives alone and away from others
salve (sahv) *n.* an oily substance used as medicine on the skin

King Arthur claiming Excalibur, in an illustration by N. C. Wyeth

Then they saw a lady floating toward them as if she walked on the water. Her garments were like a mist around her.

"That is the Lady of the Lake," said Merlin. "Within the lake is a rock, and within the rock is a palace, and within the palace lives this lady with many other ladies who serve her. She is called Vivien. Speak to her as a friend, and she will give you that sword."

So, when she had come close, Arthur said to her, "Lady, I wish that sword were mine, for I have no sword."

"It shall be yours," said the lady, and she showed Arthur a little boat lying at the edge of the lake. "Row out to the sword," she said. "Take it with its scabbard." Then she disappeared. Arthur and Merlin rowed out into the lake, and Arthur took the sword from the hand that held it. And the arm and the hand vanished under the water.

Arthur and Merlin rowed to shore and went on their way, and whenever Arthur looked on the sword, he liked it well.

"Which do you like better? asked Merlin. "The sword or the scabbard?"

"I like the sword better," said Arthur.

"The scabbard is worth ten such swords," said Merlin, "for while you wear the scabbard, you will never lose blood, no matter how sorely you are wounded."

So they rode back to Arthur's court, and all his knights marveled when they heard that the king risked his life in single combat as his poor knights did. They said it was merry to be under such a chieftain.

About the Selection

Of Swords and Sorcerers: The Adventures of King Arthur and His Knights was published in 1993. It includes nine episodes in the life of King Arthur.

scabbard (SKAB urd) *n.* a case or cover for a sword or dagger
chieftain (CHEEF tun) *n.* the head of a clan; leader of many people

✓ **Reading Check**

Which did Arthur like better, the sword or the scabbard?

Review and Assessment

Thinking About the Selection

1. **(a) Describe** How did Arthur and Pellinore fight?
(b) Predict How do you think the fight would have ended if Merlin had not interfered? Why do you think so?
2. **(a) Note** What did Arthur's knights think when they heard about his fight with Pellinore?
(b) Draw Conclusions What qualities does Arthur demonstrate in this episode that would make him a good ruler?

(c) Predict What kind of a ruler do you think Arthur would be in today's world? Explain your answer.

Writing Activity

Write a Poem or a Story Many characters in myths and legends have objects that protect them or give them special powers, as Arthur's sword and scabbard did for him. Write a poem or a story about a character who receives one such tool. What are its powers? How does it help the character?

About the Authors

Margaret Hodges, above, was a children's librarian and a storyteller for a children's radio program. She believed in the lasting value of myths. **Margery Evernden** has written children's books, biographies, and plays.

Chapter

15

The Renaissance and Reformation

Chapter Preview

This chapter will explore the sweeping cultural changes in Europe known as the Renaissance and the Reformation.

Target Reading Skill

Cause and Effect Determining causes and effects helps you understand the relationship between events. A cause makes something happen. An effect is something that results from another event or change. In this chapter you will focus on identifying and understanding historical causes and events.

▶ St. Peter's Basilica, shown here, is the spiritual center of the Roman Catholic Church. The church's arches and columns reflect the style of the Renaissance.

MAP MASTER™ Skills Activity

Europe in 1500

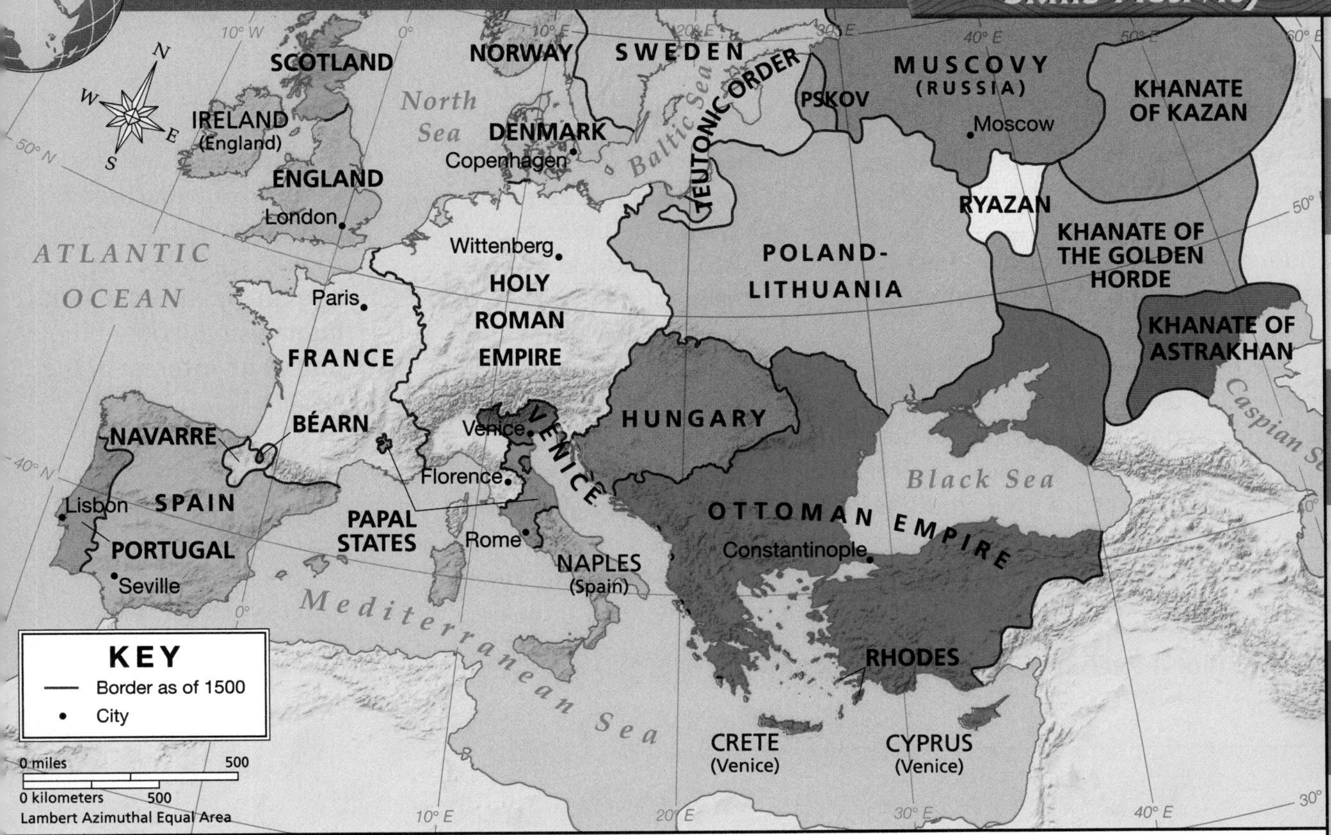

SCOTLAND
NORWAY
SWEDEN
TEUTONIC ORDER
PSKOV
MUSCOVY (RUSSIA)
Moscow
KHANATE OF KAZAN
IRELAND (England)
North Sea
DENMARK
Copenhagen
Baltic Sea
ENGLAND
London
RYAZAN
KHANATE OF THE GOLDEN HORDE
ATLANTIC OCEAN
Wittenberg
HOLY ROMAN EMPIRE
POLAND-LITHUANIA
Paris
FRANCE
KHANATE OF ASTRAKHAN
Caspian Sea
NAVARRE
BÉARN
Venice
VENICE
HUNGARY
Florence
Black Sea
Lisbon
SPAIN
PAPAL STATES
OTTOMAN EMPIRE
Rome
Constantinople
PORTUGAL
NAPLES (Spain)
Seville
Mediterranean Sea
RHODES
CRETE (Venice)
CYPRUS (Venice)
KEY
Border as of 1500
City
0 miles 500
0 kilometers 500
Lambert Azimuthal Equal Area
10° W
0°
10° E
20° E
30° E
40° E
50° E
60° E
50° N
40° N
30°
N
S
E
W

Movement Traders from Venice and other Italian cities used the Mediterranean Sea as a route to the East. **Explain** Why did Italy have an advantage over Western Europe in trade with eastern lands? **Predict** How might Western Europe overcome Italy's advantage?

Go Online PHSchool.com Use Web Code **mup-1512** for step-by-step **map skills practice.**

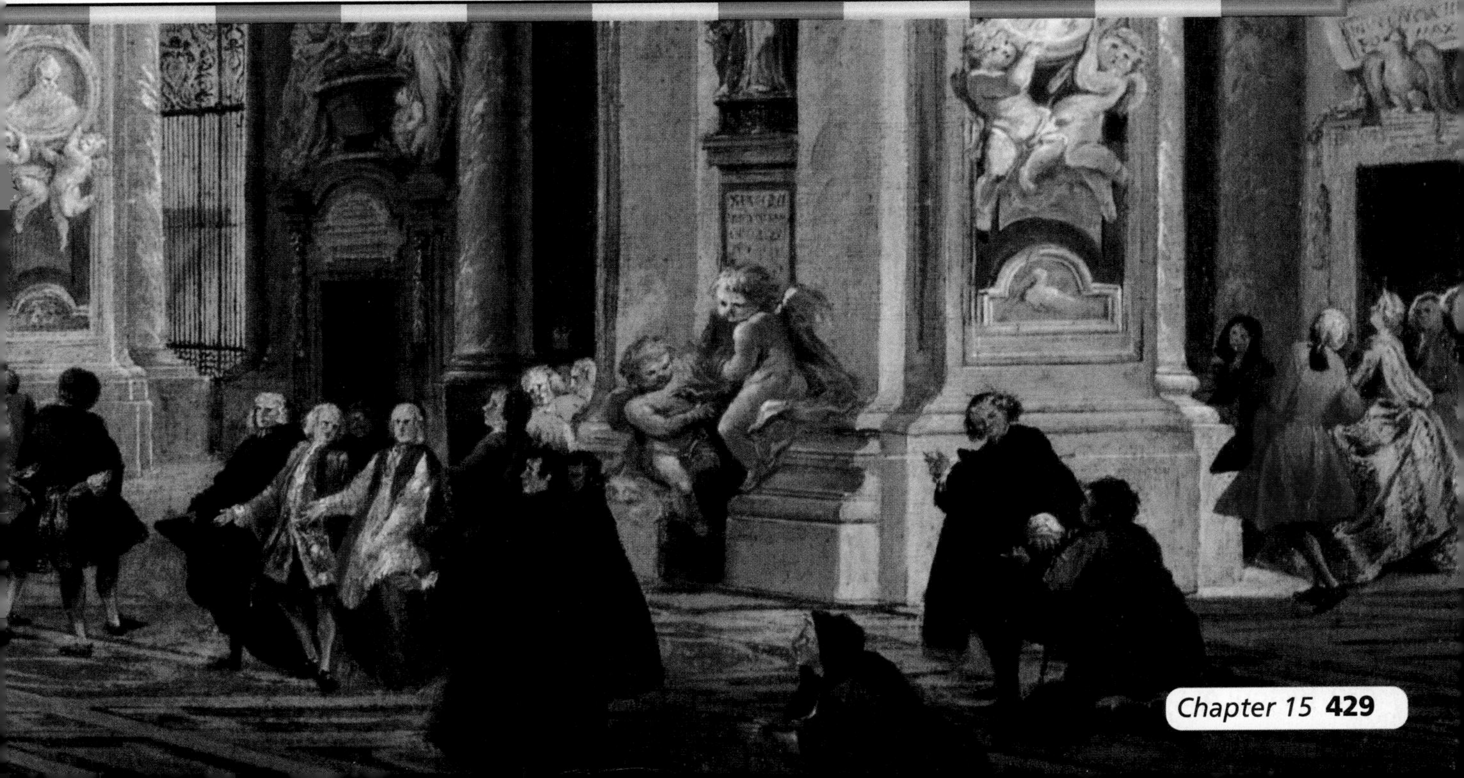

The Renaissance Begins

Prepare to Read

Objectives

In this section you will

1. Find out why Italy was the birthplace of the Renaissance.
2. Understand how literature and art were transformed during the Renaissance.

Taking Notes

As you read, look for reasons why the Renaissance began in Italy and how literature and art changed during this period. Copy the outline below, and record your findings in it.

> I. Why the Renaissance started in Italy
> A.
> B.
> II. The effects of the Renaissance
> A.
> B.

Target Reading Skill

Identify Causes and Effects To understand a historical period or event, it is helpful to know what caused it to happen and what effects it had. As you read this section, identify the causes of the Renaissance in Italy, as well as the effects. Write the causes and effects in your Taking Notes diagram.

Key Terms

- **Renaissance** (REN uh sahns) *n.* a widespread change in culture that took place in Europe, beginning with the 1300s
- **humanism** (HYOO muh niz um) *n.* an interest in the classics

La Gioconda (lah joh KAHN duh) is another name for the *Mona Lisa*.

The *Mona Lisa* is perhaps the most famous piece of art in the world. It is one of the masterpieces created by the great Italian artist, Leonardo da Vinci (lee uh NAHR doh duh VIN chee). Like many of da Vinci's works, however, the *Mona Lisa* may have never been finished. It is possible that da Vinci was drawn to another project without finishing the painting, as he had done on other projects. Da Vinci was not only a painter. He was also one of the world's greatest inventors and scientists.

The story of da Vinci and the *Mona Lisa* reveals much about the Renaissance. This is the term historians use for the period between 1300 and 1650 in Europe. During that time, the culture of Europe changed dramatically. Artists used new skills and techniques to create works of great beauty and charm. Scholars began looking at the world and its people in new ways. The spirit of the Renaissance is clearly seen in the life of Leonardo da Vinci. His great skills and wide interests reflect much of the spirit and character of the era.

The Renaissance Begins in Italy

The **Renaissance** was a widespread change in culture that took place in Europe beginning with the 1300s. The movement began in Italy.

Look at the map on this page, and notice Italy's place on the Mediterranean Sea. Because of this location, Italy became a center of European trade with the rich lands of the East during the late Middle Ages. While feudalism still dominated the rest of Europe, Italy's merchants were building great fortunes.

Italy's trade was based in its cities. Over time, these cities became centers of power and wealth. Successful merchants bought up feudal lands, and many nobles moved to the cities to seek their fortunes. The most powerful Italian cities became independent city-states. They were not under the control of a king or a noble. Even the Roman Catholic Church held little power in these cities.

✓ **Reading Check** **Why did the Renaissance begin in Italy?**

Identify Causes and Effects
What causes led to the birth of the Renaissance in Italy?

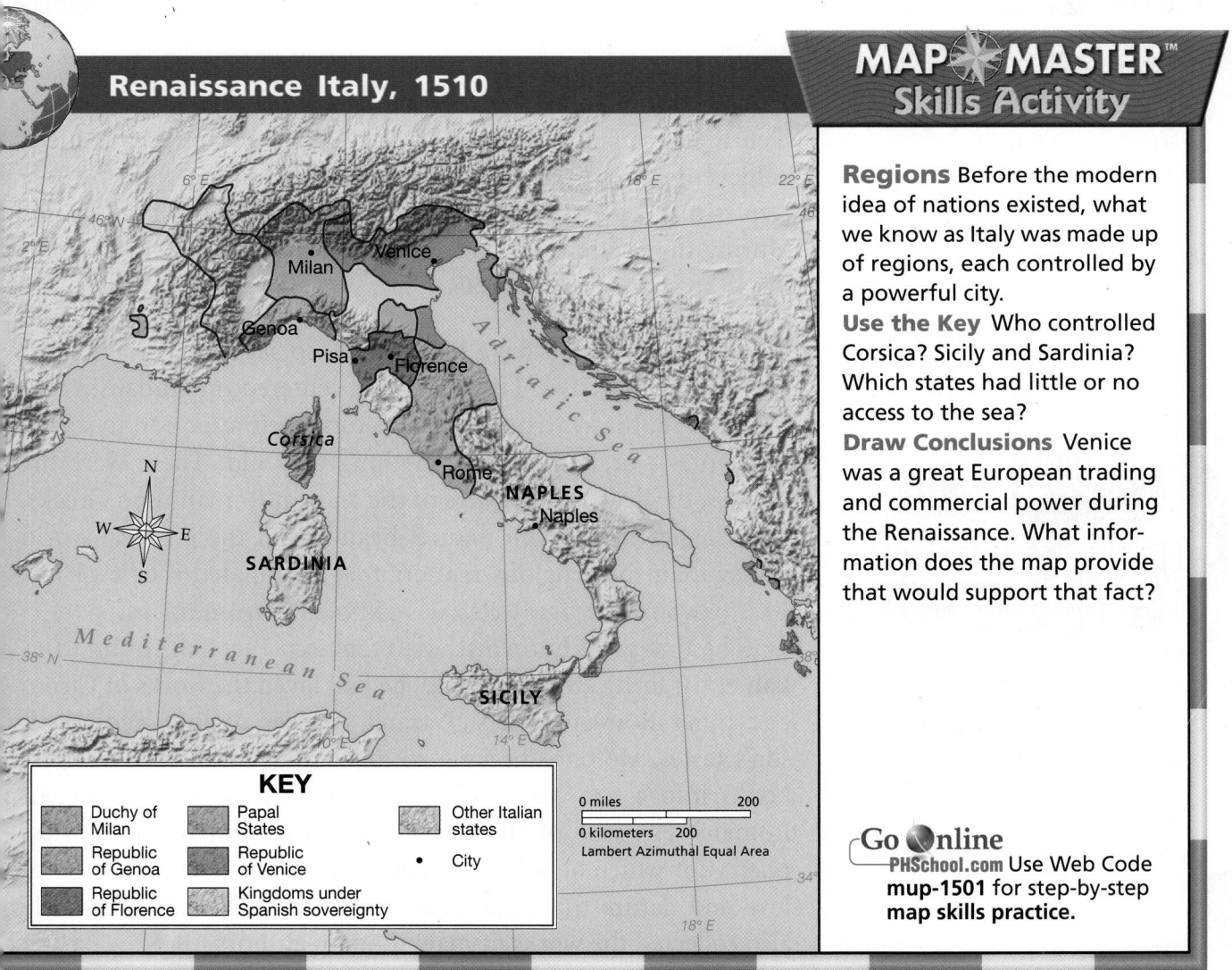

Renaissance Italy, 1510

MAP★MASTER™
Skills Activity

Regions Before the modern idea of nations existed, what we know as Italy was made up of regions, each controlled by a powerful city.

Use the Key Who controlled Corsica? Sicily and Sardinia? Which states had little or no access to the sea?

Draw Conclusions Venice was a great European trading and commercial power during the Renaissance. What information does the map provide that would support that fact?

KEY

Duchy of Milan	Papal States
Republic of Genoa	Republic of Venice
Republic of Florence	Kingdoms under Spanish sovereignty
Other Italian states	
•	City

0 miles 200
0 kilometers 200
Lambert Azimuthal Equal Area

Go Online
PHSchool.com Use Web Code **mup-1501** for step-by-step map skills practice.

![School of Athens painting by Raphael]

Renaissance Art

In this painting, *School of Athens*, Raphael, a Renaissance painter, depicted many of the great thinkers of Ancient Greece.
Analyze *Why do you think Raphael included the Greek philosophers in this painting?*

Discovery
CHANNEL
SCHOOL Video
Explore the art and science of Leonardo da Vinci.

Renaissance Art and Literature

The Renaissance is celebrated today as a time of great artistic achievement. Artists in all fields created stunning works. These efforts marked a sharp change from the art of the Middle Ages. During that period, art had focused on the Church. That focus began to change in the 1300s.

Literature As you have read, a new social system was taking shape in Italy's cities. Life no longer centered on feudalism and the Church. Many writers began to turn their attention to something new—or, rather, to something very old. These were the classics, or ideas and writings of the ancient Romans and Greeks. The classics focused on nature, beauty, and the physical world rather than the religious matters that dominated medieval life. This new interest in the classics is known as **humanism.**

The first great humanist was Francesco Petrarch (frahn CHES koh PEA trahrk). Even as a child, he had loved the works of Cicero and other Roman writers. Petrarch's father disapproved of his son's tastes. He once became so angry that he threw Petrarch's books into a fire. Yet Petrarch continued to study the ancient Romans. His love of the classics is clearly seen in the flawless poetry for which he is known. Petrarch's sonnets reveal a view of love and nature that is far different from medieval sonnets. He also collected the works of many Roman authors.

Visual Art Medieval art had dealt mostly with religious topics. Like Renaissance writers, however, artists of the Renaissance began to focus on nature and the human form. Painters and sculptors still created religious scenes. These works, however, showed the human body with great accuracy and detail.

You have read about Leonardo da Vinci and his great works. Da Vinci also became famous for the more than 4,000 notebook pages that he filled with sketches and notes about the world around him. The Italian Renaissance also produced such masters as Michelangelo (my kul AN juh loh). His greatest work may be the famous ceiling of the Sistene Chapel. Like da Vinci's *Mona Lisa*, this work is among the most beloved and recognized paintings in history.

In the early to mid-1400s, the sculptor Donatello (doh nuh TEL oh) worked in the city of Florence, creating life-like sculptures of the human body. He was inspired by the Greeks and Romans of antiquity. Some of Donatello's most famous works are a series of sculptures of the Biblical figure David. Donatello was a master of many techniques, using a variety of materials, including marble and bronze, for his sculptures.

✓ **Reading Check** **What was the main focus of Renaissance visual artists?**

Cosimo de Medici

Section 1 Assessment

Key Terms
Review the key terms at the beginning of this section. Use each term in a sentence that explains its meaning.

Target Reading Skill
Explain the causes that brought about the Renaissance in Italy.

Comprehension and Critical Thinking
1. (a) Recall What activity helped transform life in Italy in the late Middle Ages?

(b) Identify Cause and Effect What affect did the rise of cities have on feudal life in Italy?

2. (a) Identify What was the major influence on writers of the Renaissance?

(b) Summarize How did the interest in Greek and Roman classical literature affect Renaissance authors?

3. (a) Explain How did the focus of Italian artists change during the Renaissance?

(b) Analyze Images What details from Raphael's painting on page 432 illustrate the key features of Renaissance art?

Writing Activity
From the perspective of a person living in an Italian city-state at the start of the Renaissance, write a letter to a relative living somewhere in feudal Europe. Describe some of the changes you see taking place in the world around you.

For: An activity on the Renaissance in Northern Italy
Visit: PHSchool.com
Web Code: mud-1510

Prepare to Read

Objectives

In this section you will

1. Understand how the Renaissance spread from Italy to the north.
2. Identify key literary figures and ideas of the Northern Renaissance.
3. Identify key artists and artistic ideas of the Northern Renaissance.

Taking Notes

As you read, look for material that explains how Renaissance ideas spread and developed throughout Europe. Copy the graphic organizer below. Record your findings in it.

Renaissance North of Italy		
Renaissance Spreads North	**Literature of the Northern Renaissance**	**Art of the Northern Renaissance**
• •	• •	• •

Target Reading Skill

Recognize Multiple Causes Historical events can be complicated; sometimes several factors cause an event to happen. As you read this section, identify the multiple reasons why the Renaissance spread to the North.

Key Terms

- **movable type** (MOO vuh bul typ) *n.* individual letters and marks that can be arranged and rearranged quickly

The artisan's work was painstaking. At his bench was a block of wood. With great care, he carved away the surface. His task was to create a raised surface that could then be smeared with ink and pressed onto a flat material. What was the result of all this effort? It was a single page of a book.

In the mid-1400s, a German printer named Johannes Gutenberg (yoh HAHN us GOOT un burg) began work on a project that would create a new way of printing books. He would develop a system of **movable type**—individual letters and marks that could be arranged and rearranged quickly.

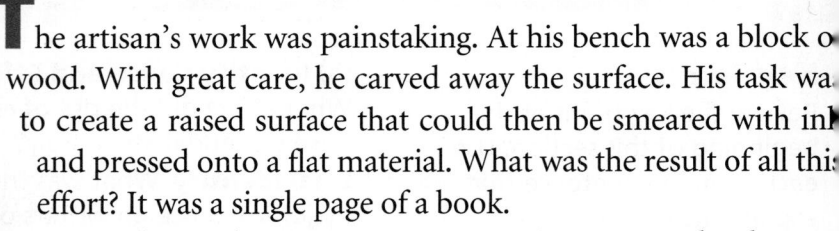

Gutenberg also developed a printing press, a machine that used movable type to print pages. The availability of books would change the way information and ideas traveled in Europe and the world.

Movable type allowed printers to use the same letters for different pages.

Renaissance Thought and Literature Spread

Over time, the changes that supported the birth of the Renaissance in Italy moved northward into western and northern Europe. Northern industry and trade expanded. The feudal and religious base of medieval society weakened. These changes were followed by changes in literature, art, and culture. Renaissance ideas, along with developments such as Gutenberg's printing methods, helped bring great change to the entire European continent.

As had happened in Italy, many scholars in northern and western Europe became interested in humanism. Renaissance thinkers throughout Europe applied the ideas of humanism to religious thinking, a movement called Christian humanism. These thinkers were concerned with the study of Christianity, rather than with the study of Greek and Roman texts. The leading figure of Christian humanism was Dutch-born Desiderius Erasmus (des uh DIHR ee us ih RAZ mus) (1466–1536).

Erasmus was a Roman Catholic priest. However, in one of his most famous works, *In Praise of Folly*, he mocked certain Church practices. These practices, he believed, had little to do with true faith. In fact, Erasmus thought that such practices often covered up corruption. Erasmus was also a leading scholar of Greek and Latin. His efforts had a powerful impact on education in Europe.

One of Erasmus's close friends was England's Sir Thomas More (sur TAHM us mawr). More was a lawyer. He may have been influenced by Greek thinkers such as Plato and Aristotle. His famous work *Utopia* (yoo TOH pea uh) describes an ideal world that is based on Greek philosophy. By writing about this perfect place, More was actually pointing out problems he saw in his own world, such as divisions between people who were politically weak and others who were politically powerful.

Recognize Multiple Causes

What are some of the causes that allowed Renaissance ideas to spread northward?

✓ **Reading Check** What did *In Praise of Folly* reveal about Erasmus's beliefs concerning many Church practices?

Gutenberg built this printing press to produce the Bible.

Literature of the Northern Renaissance

Many writers in northern and western Europe were influenced by new literary ideas developed during the Italian Renaissance. Like Petrarch and other Italian writers, these authors experimented with new ideas and unfamiliar literary forms.

François Rabelais (frahn SWAH rab uh LAY) of France was a devoted follower of Erasmus. Rabelais's best-known work is *Gargantua and Pantagruel* (gahr GAN choo uh and pan tuh groo EL), a tale that uses comedy to express the ideas of humanism.

A group of seven French poets known as the Pleiade (play YAD) applied ancient Greek and Roman forms to create new poetry in French. These poems focused on common themes, such as love and patriotism.

The spread of Renaissance ideas also brought new energy to poets in England. Sir Thomas Wyatt and the Earl of Surrey helped introduce a popular Italian form of poetry, the sonnet, to English audiences in the early 1500s.

England's best-known poet, William Shakespeare (WIL yum SHAYK spihr) (1564–1616), wrote at least 37 verse plays, many of them based on plots borrowed from ancient works. Shakespeare changed details of these ancient stories to appeal to the audiences of his day, and he created many memorable characters, including Romeo and Juliet. Shakespeare's interest in the human character was a key feature of the Renaissance.

✓ **Reading Check** What common theme was shared by many Renaissance writers in France and England?

The Globe Theater
The Globe, one of the public theaters in London during the Renaissance, saw the production of many of Shakespeare's plays. A modern staging of *A Midsummer Night's Dream* is pictured at right. **Name** *What other Shakespeare plays do you know?*

Art of the Northern Renaissance

Several artists in northern and western Europe distinguished themselves during the Renaissance. Flemish painter Jan van Eyck (yahn van yk), who lived in the early 1400s, was a master of realistic portraits. Van Eyck used multiple layers of oil paints to create rich visual effects. His bright colors and eye for realism show the details of everyday life in the region that is now part of Belgium and the Netherlands. He was only one of several well-known Renaissance painters from the Netherlands.

Germany's Albrecht Dürer (AHL brekt DYOOR ur) (1471–1528) was a painter as well as a master of woodcuts and engravings. In the late 1400s, Dürer visited Italy to see firsthand the work of Italian Renaissance masters. This visit had a deep impact on the young artist, whose work began to reflect the Italian style.

Dürer was a person of wide interests. In the early 1500s, his work began to reflect events that were just then shaking the religious foundation of Europe. In the next lesson you will read about these events, which are known collectively as the Reformation.

✓ **Reading Check** From which country did Jan Van Eyck come?

©The Portrait of Giovanni Arnolfini and his Wife Giovanna Cenami (The Arnolfini Marriage) 1434 (oil on panel), Eyck, Jan van (c.1390-1441)National Gallery, London, UK

One of Van Eyck's most famous paintings, *The Marriage of Giovanni Arnolfini and Giovanna Cenami*

Section 2 Assessment

Key Terms
Review the key terms listed at the beginning of this section. Use each term in a sentence that explains its meaning.

Target Reading Skill
What caused the Renaissance to spread beyond Italy?

Comprehension and Critical Thinking
1. (a) Explain What developments in Europe help explain why the Renaissance spread north from Italy?

(b) Synthesize Information Why did Renaissance developments in northern and eastern Europe lag behind those of Italy?

2. (a) List Identify two literary figures of the Renaissance in western and northern Europe.

(b) Summarize How would you summarize the spread of Renaissance literary ideas in western and northern Europe?

3. (a) List Identify two artists who were part of the Northern Renaissance.

(b) Make Generalizations What features did the art of Dürer and Van Eyck share with Italian Renaissance art?

Writing Activity
With a classmate, write a debate about whether the Renaissance in Italy was more spectacular than the Renaissance in northern and western Europe. Have one student argue in favor of Italy and the other argue in favor of northern and western Europe.

For: An activity on the Renaissance in the North
Visit: PHSchool.com
Web Code: mud-1520

Focus On
Renaissance Printing

Suppose that in order to create a new book, you had to copy every word by hand. Or you had to brush ink on individual letters and stamp each one on paper. Either process would be enormously time-consuming. There would be very few books in existence and limited ways for people to share knowledge and discoveries. The invention of the printing press around 1450 solved this problem. The printing press helped satisfy the great desire for learning and books fueled by the Renaissance.

The Printing Press Johannes Gutenberg, a German inventor, is credited with inventing the printing press. His press was adapted from machines used to press grapes. It used movable type—separate pieces of raised metal type that could be used again and again.

As he prepared to print, the printer took pieces of type, letter-by-letter, from a box, or type case. He then arranged the letters and screwed or tied them in place. He inked the type. Then he placed paper on the type. By turning a huge screw on the press, he brought down a wooden block against the paper to create a printed page.

If you entered a Renaissance print shop like the one shown in this illustration, you might see a highly skilled master printer and an apprentice, or student printer. A journeyman who had completed his apprenticeship and was qualified to work as a printer might also be there. The first books were literary and scientific works, as well as religious texts. Therefore, a scholar might also be present. His job was to advise on the accuracy of the texts.

An Early Bible
Artists decorated printed pages with bright colors and elaborate paintings and designs.

Assessment

Explain Why was the printing press an important tool for spreading new ideas during the Renaissance?

Apply You may have used the stamping technique described on the opposite page in art class, perhaps carving letters or a design into a potato to use as a stamp. Compare this method of printing with using a printing press.

Prepare to Read

Objectives

In this section you will
1. Understand the developments that led to the Reformation.
2. Learn about Luther's criticism of the Church.
3. Understand the immediate effects of Luther's ideas in Europe.

Taking Notes

As you read, look for the effects of the Church's behavior. Copy the diagram below, and record your findings in it.

```
┌─────────────────────────────┐
│          CAUSES             │
│                             │
└─────────────────────────────┘
              ↓
┌─────────────────────────────┐
│ EVENT: Luther posts his     │
│ "95 Theses"                 │
└─────────────────────────────┘
              ↓
┌─────────────────────────────┐
│          EFFECTS            │
│                             │
└─────────────────────────────┘
```

Target Reading Skill

Understand Effects
A cause makes an effect happen. Sometimes a cause creates several effects. As you read this section, think of the behavior of the Church as a cause. What was the effect of this cause? Write the effects in your Taking Notes diagram.

Key Terms

- **indulgence** (in DUL juns) *n.* an official pardon for a sin given by the pope in return for money
- **salvation** (sal VAY shun) *n.* to go to heaven, in religious terms
- **Reformation** (ref ur MAY shun) *n.* the term used to describe Luther's break with the Church and the movement it inspired

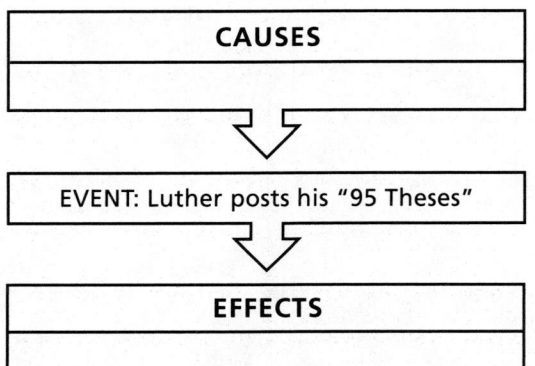

Reformers tried to stop Church abuses by distributing leaflets such as the one above.

The preacher was Johann Tetzel (YOH hahn Tet sul), and in return for a contribution to the Church, Tetzel said, a person could receive an indulgence. An **indulgence** allowed the buyer to escape punishment for sins. Moreover, Tetzel said, an indulgence could be used to help a loved one who had died. In vivid language, Tetzel told of the torment of the dead as they suffered for their sins. This suffering could be avoided, Tetzel suggested, for a small sum.

The granting of indulgences was not new in the Church. It had been taking place for centuries. In the early 1500s, the Church was trying to raise money for a glorious new church to be built in Rome. Tetzel was selling indulgences as part of this effort. However, attitudes towards this and other Church practices were changing. For a German monk named Martin Luther (MAHRT un LOO thur), Johann Tetzel's actions went too far.

This German woodcut from the Reformation visually expresses religious conflicts. **Critical Thinking** *Note the details in the two halves of the woodcut. Which half represents Protestants and which represents Catholics?*

The Church at the Time of Luther

As you have read, the Church had been at the very heart of medieval European life. In fact, during the medieval period, the Church had become one of the most powerful political institutions in Europe. It carried out wars and made alliances with other states. Its leader, the Pope, was a major public figure. His power was very like that of a king. Often, it seemed that the Church was involved as much in the affairs of the world as in questions of faith.

You have read about Erasmus and other humanist writers of the Renaissance. Many of these thinkers called attention to the changes in the Church. They observed that Church leaders had, in some cases, lost sight of the Church's main purpose—to guide people's religious life.

In the early 1500s, one of those who was dissatisfied with the Church was a monk named Martin Luther. For several years, Luther had struggled with his belief in Church teachings. For example, he was troubled by the Church's belief in the importance of doing good works as a way to get to heaven.

It was while Luther was struggling with these questions that Johann Tetzel began his campaign to sell indulgences. When Luther heard of Tetzel's efforts, he became angry. He decided to issue an official criticism to the Church.

✓ Reading Check   **How did the Church's great power lead to criticism of the Church during the Renaissance?**

Understand Effects In this section, you have read about Luther's criticisms of the Church. What effects did Luther's criticisms have on the Church? How did Church leaders respond to his actions and statements?

Go Online
PHSchool.com Use Web Code **mup-0839** for an interactivity on Luther's legacy.

Luther Starts the Reformation

In October 1517, Luther wrote a document in which he challenged the Church on the issue of indulgences. This document featured 95 *theses,* or arguments. Luther posted his Ninety-five Theses on the Church door at Wittenberg, Germany.

Church officials tried to silence Luther. Luther responded by widening his criticism of the Church. For example, he argued that people could achieve salvation through faith alone. **Salvation,** in religious terms, means to go to heaven. This differed from Church teachings on the importance of doing good works. Luther also challenged the role of priests. In Church teachings, only a priest could perform certain Church rituals. Wrote Luther, "A priest . . . is nothing else than an officeholder."

Luther also challenged the authority of the pope to rule on religious matters. He said that the Bible was the only true authority. If the pope's teachings did not follow the Bible, Luther said, people could disobey the pope.

Luther's ideas outraged Church officials. They tried to force German officials to have Luther punished. Luther refused to take back what he had said and written. "Here I stand, may God help me. Amen," he said.

In 1521 the Church succeeded in having Luther labeled an outlaw in Germany. However, Luther's popularity was growing, and his ideas were spreading quickly. The judgment against him was never enforced.

✔ **Reading Check** What did Luther say was the final authority in religious matters?

The portrait above shows Martin Luther. In the illustration to the right, members of the upper class look on as Luther posts his Ninety-five Theses.

The Reformation Succeeds

The **Reformation** is the term used to describe Luther's break with the Church and the movement it inspired. This movement continued in the 1520s.

©The delivery of the Augsburg Confession, 25th June 1530, 1617 (oil on panel) German School (17th Century) Georgenkirche, Eisenach, Germany/Bridgeman Art Library

There are many reasons for the Reformation's success. Many Germans were attracted to Luther's teachings. Some nobles resented the pope and the power of Rome. They welcomed a break with the Church. The poor were encouraged by what they saw as Luther's message of equality. In the 1520s, German peasants rose in revolt. They were disappointed when Luther spoke out against them. He believed that people should respect authority in nonreligious matters.

Still, Lutheranism (LOO thur un iz um), as the movement was called, took hold in many parts of Germany. It also spread to other parts of Europe, including Sweden and Norway. In 1555 the Church of Rome finally gave in. With the Peace of Augsburg (peas uv AWGS burg), Lutherans won the right to practice their religion.

The Peace of Augsburg did not end the Reformation. In the next section, you will read about how Reformation ideas affected other parts of Europe.

✓ Reading Check Why were peasants drawn to Luther's teachings?

In the painting above, German princes in 1530 present Emperor Charles V with the Augsburg Confession, in which Philip Melanchthon tried to present Lutheran theology in a form that Roman Catholics could accept. His attempt failed.

Section 3 Assessment

Key Terms
Review the key terms at the beginning of this section. Use each term in a sentence that explains its meaning.

Target Reading Skill
What effect did Martin Luther's teachings have on religion in Europe?

Comprehension and Critical Thinking
1. (a) Explain What was the role of the Church in European life in the Renaissance?

(b) Draw Inferences Why do you think the political power of the pope and Church officials troubled many people in Europe?

2. (a) Identify What action by Johann Tetzel upset Luther and led to the Ninety-Five Theses?

(b) Synthesize Information Which of Luther's key complaints against the Church did the selling of indulgences represent?

3. (a) Recall What happened to Luther after he was declared an outlaw in Germany?

(b) Analyze Information Why do you think the movement started by Martin Luther is known as the Reformation?

Writing Activity
The year is 1520. Write a memo to the pope, summarizing the events taking place in Germany. Briefly trace the story behind Martin Luther and his ideas. Explain how these ideas differ from Church teachings.

For: An activity on the Reformation
Visit: PHSchool.com
Web Code: mud-1530

Identifying Point of View

Karen, the leader of the student chorus, got right to the point during the planning meeting. "A lot of people would come out to see a spring musical," she said. "We have a number of strong singers, and we had very good attendance at our holiday musical."

"I don't know," replied Jason. "Some of the students who want to be in a spring play aren't involved in chorus, and some of us who are in chorus would rather act than sing."

Sandra, chairperson of the school theater committee, had to decide whether their class should put on a musical or a play in the spring.

After thinking all afternoon about what Karen and Jason had said, Sandra realized that Karen really wanted to do a spring musical, but that Jason preferred to put on a play. She would have to decide between their points of view.

I dentifying point of view helps you understand different viewpoints and make judgments about them.

Learn the skill

Use the steps below to identify point of view.

1 **Consider what you know about the background of each speaker and how that background might affect the speaker's viewpoint.** Sandra knew that Karen wanted to do another musical in the spring, but she also knew that Jason and other students would rather act than sing.

2 **Consider facts and other evidence that the speakers give to support their points of view.** Karen used the attendance at the holiday musical as a reason for a spring musical. Jason gave the example of students who would rather act than sing.

3 **Identify and explain each speaker's point of view, basing your conclusions on what you know about the speaker and the evidence that the speaker gives.** Sandra knew that Karen supported a spring musical because Karen enjoyed singing and that Jason preferred a spring play because he wanted to include students who weren't involved in chorus.

In this painting, Martin Luther is shown defending himself to Charles V at the Diet of Worms.

Practice the Skill

Reread The Church at the Time of Luther and Luther Starts the Reformation in Section 3 of this chapter. Then use the steps above to identify different points of view.

1. Answer these questions to help you identify the backgrounds of speakers: Who was Martin Luther? How did Catholic Church leaders live at this time?

2. Consider the facts and other evidence given about the points of view expressed. State your ideas in this form: "X said he believed Y because . . . " For example, "Church officials believed that Martin Luther should be declared an outlaw because he challenged their power."

3. From the questions you have answered and the statements you have written, what is each side's point of view?

Apply the Skill

Turn to Section 4 of this chapter and read the passage titled The Reformation After Luther. Use the steps in this skill to identify the points of view of various Protestant groups, such as the Calvinists, Zwinglians, and Anabaptists.

Prepare to Read

Objectives

In this section you will

1. Learn that Luther was the first of several religious reformers.
2. Identify other religious movements of the 1500s in Europe.
3. Understand how the Catholic Church responded to the Reformation.

Taking Notes

As you read, look for ways that the Reformation inspired new religious groups and changed the Catholic Church. Copy the diagram below, and record your findings in it.

Spread of Reformation Ideas	
Other Religious Movements	Changes in the Catholic Church
•	•
•	•
•	•

Target Reading Skill

Recognize Cause-and-Effect Signal Words

Causes and effects follow one another in a certain sequence. This section contains information about the spread of Reformation ideas. To help keep the order of events clear, look for words and phrases like *so, suddenly, finally, for this reason,* and *as a result.* These terms signal the relationship between a cause and its effects.

Key Terms

• **Protestant** (PRAHT us tunt) *adj.* refers to Christian groups that separated from the Catholic Church

A portrait of Henry VIII by Dutch painter Hans Holbein the Younger

© Hans the Younger Holbein (1497/8–1543), Dutch, *"Portrait of Henry VIII"*, 16th Century / Bridgeman Art Library

Henry VIII, King of England, was unhappy. He wanted very much to have a male child to inherit his throne. He and his wife, Catherine, had only one surviving child, a girl. So Henry decided that it was time to marry another woman. First, however, he needed the Church of Rome to officially end his marriage to Catherine. The pope refused Henry's request.

Henry had always been a strong supporter of the Church. In 1521 he had written an attack on Martin Luther's ideas. In response, the pope had given Henry the title of Defender of the Faith. Now, however, Henry attacked the Church and its practices. Still, the Church would not end his marriage. Finally, in 1534, Henry officially broke from the Catholic Church and became the head of a new church—the Church of England, or Anglican Church. Suddenly, the people of England were part of the Reformation.

The Reformation After Luther

Many people in Europe adopted Martin Luther's ideas in the mid-1500s and several other Protestant groups appeared. **Protestant** refers to Christians who separated from the Catholic Church.

John Calvin began his preaching in the 1530s in Switzerland. He believed that faith alone could win salvation and that God had determined long ago who would be saved, a belief known as predestination.

Also from Switzerland came Ulrich Zwingli (ool rik ZWING lee). His church was formed in the 1520s. Zwinglians (ZWING lee unz) believed that the Bible contained all religious truth.

The Anabaptists (an uh BAP tists) also formed at this time. They did not believe in the baptism of infants. Only older people, they argued, could have the faith that this religious practice required.

✔ **Reading Check** **Where did the Zwinglians first appear?**

John Calvin

MAP✦MASTER™ Skills Activity

Major Religions in Europe in the 1500s

KEY

- Mainly Roman Catholic
- Mainly Anglican
- Mainly Lutheran
- Mainly Calvinist
- Mainly Eastern Orthodox
- Mainly Muslim
- — Border
- • City

NORWAY · SWEDEN · RUSSIA · SCOTLAND · IRELAND (England) · ENGLAND · DENMARK · North Sea · Baltic Sea · POLAND-LITHUANIA · Woodstock · London · Münster · Wittenberg · Wartburg · HOLY ROMAN EMPIRE · Paris · Worms · Augsburg · HUNGARY · FRANCE · ATLANTIC OCEAN · Geneva · Trent · Venice · VENICE · PAPAL STATES · Adriatic Sea · Black Sea · PORTUGAL · SPAIN · Corsica · Rome · NAPLES (Spain) · Sardinia · OTTOMAN EMPIRE · Mediterranean Sea · Sicily

0 miles 500
0 kilometers 500
Lambert Azimuthal Equal Area

Movement This map shows how Reformation ideas and groups spread across Europe in the 1500s. **List** The map identifies the major Protestant groups that existed in Europe around 1600. List these groups. **Making Generalizations** In what part of Europe did the Reformation fail to weaken the hold of the Catholic Church?

Go Online
PHSchool.com Use Web Code **mup-1543** for step-by-step map skills practice.

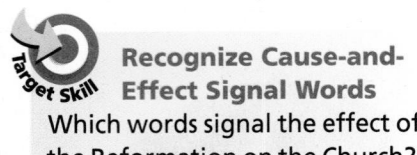

Recognize Cause-and-Effect Signal Words
Which words signal the effect of the Reformation on the Church?

The Council of Trent addressed the abuses that prompted the Reformation, but it did not reunite the Church.

The Catholic Church Reforms

The Reformation was a significant challenge to the Church of Rome. As you have read, much of Europe was swept up in the Reformation. As a result, the Church carried out its own reforms in the mid-1500s. These helped the Church survive and regain strength in much of Europe. The initial reforms of Luther and others became known as the Protestant Reformation. The Catholic Church's reforms were called the Catholic Reformation.

One key development of the Catholic Reformation was the establishment of the Society of Jesus in 1540. This was a religious order, or group, led by Ignatius Loyola (ig NAY shus loy OH luh). The Jesuits (JEZH oo its), as they came to be called, worked tirelessly to educate people and spread the Catholic faith. Their efforts helped build Church strength in southern Europe.

The Catholic Church was also strengthened by Paul III, who became pope in 1534. Paul III helped focus the Church on many of the abuses that had led to the Reformation. These included corrupt practices among the clergy. In 1542 Paul III called for a meeting now known as the Council of Trent. This meeting helped return the Church's focus to matters of religion and spirituality.

✓ **Reading Check** **What was the function of the Jesuits?**

 **Section 4 Assessment**

Key Terms
Review the key terms at the beginning of this section. Use each term in a sentence that explains its meaning.

 **Target Reading Skill**
Reread the description of Henry VIII's break with the Church of Rome. Which words signal the cause-and-effect relationship that led to the founding of the Church of England?

Comprehension and Critical Thinking
1. (a) Explain How did the Reformation develop following Luther's break with the Church?
(b) Draw Conclusions Why did other reformers follow Luther?
2. (a) List Name three religious reformers who established a Protestant faith in Europe.
(b) Compare What basic idea did the Protestant reformers share?
3. (a) Explain How did the Catholic Church respond to the Reformation?
(b) Summarize How did the Jesuits help the Catholic Church?

Writing Activity
Summarize the Reformation in Europe in the mid-1500s. Explain key features of the groups, and identify the places in which the new movements were strongest.

Go Online
PHSchool.com

For: An activity on the spread of the Reformation
Visit: PHSchool.com
Web Code: mud-1540

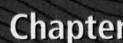

Review and Assessment

◆ Chapter Summary

Luther

Section 1: The Renaissance Begins

- The Renaissance began in Italy because Italy's geography encouraged trade and the development of large trade cities.
- Ancient ideas inspired humanism and helped transform the literature of Italy.
- Renaissance art flourished as new techniques helped artists produce works of great beauty.

Section 2: The Renaissance Moves North

- Renaissance ideas spread northward from Italy into the rest of Europe.
- Key literary figures of the Renaissance in northern and western Europe included François Rabelais and William Shakespeare.
- Renaissance art in northern Europe was led by masters such as Jan van Eyck and Albrecht Dürer.

A Shakespeare Play

Section 3: Martin Luther and the Reformation

- Martin Luther opposed such Roman Catholic Church practices as the selling of indulgences.
- Luther's challenge to Church authority and teaching touched off the Reformation.
- In spite of Church opposition, Lutheran ideas spread to many parts of Europe.

Section 4: Reformation Ideas Spread

- Other Protestant reformers followed Martin Luther in breaking with the Roman Catholic Church.
- The Catholic Church responded to the Reformation with reforms of its own.

John Calvin

◆ Key Terms

Each of the statements below contains a key term from the chapter. If the statement is true, write "true." If it is false, rewrite the statement to make it true.

1. The **Reformation** began in Italy, which was a center of commerce

2. All **Protestants** were alike in that they opposed certain beliefs and practices of the Catholic Church

3. **Humanists** believed that the ideas and values of the ancient world were corrupt.

4. Martin Luther believed that a person could achieve **salvation** through faith alone.

5. Erasmus was best known for his development of **movable type,** which helped make possible the large-scale printing of books.

6. Luther was a firm believer in the practice of selling **indulgences.**

7. **Renaissance** art featured an interest in realistic depiction of the human form.

Review and Assessment (continued)

◆ Comprehension and Critical Thinking

8. **(a) List** List some of the accomplishments of Leonardo da Vinci.
   (b) Synthesize Information Why is da Vinci considered a true example of a Renaissance artist and thinker?

9. **(a) Recall** What was the Renaissance?
   (b) Identify Cause and Effect How did Italy's location help shape its economic life at the start of the Renaissance?

10. **(a) List** Name two Renaissance writers from northern or western Europe.
    (b) Identify Frame of Reference How did William Shakespeare's work reflect Renaissance ideas?

11. **(a) Recall** When did Luther first begin to question Catholic teachings and practices?
    (b) Draw Inferences Why was Luther's idea that scriptures were the final authority in religious matters so radical?

12. **(a) Recall** How did the Church respond to Luther's challenges?
    (b) Identify Cause and Effect How did Luther's popularity in Germany change after his challenge of the Roman Catholic Church?

13. **(a) Explain** What was Henry VIII's reason for breaking with the Church?
    (b) Draw Inferences What can you infer about Henry VIII's views of Church teachings?

◆ Skills Practice

Identifying Point of View In the Skills for Life activity, you learned how to identify point of view. Review the steps you follow to use this skill. Reread the Citizen Heroes passage in Section 1 about Cosimo de Medici. Use what you read and your own thinking to identify de Medici's view of the changes that Renaissance ideas brought to Italy.

◆ Writing Activity: Art

You are an art critic in Italy during the Renaissance. Artists of the day are painting pictures that are amazingly realistic; for example, round objects look round. The technique these artists use is called *perspective*. Research and write a brief report on this technique. Explain how an artist can make a flat surface look "deep."

MAP✦MASTER™
Skills Activity
Renaissance Italy, 1510

Place Location For each place listed below, write the letter that indicates its location on the map.
1. Republic of Florence   4. Pisa
2. Republic of Venice   5. Florence
3. Rome

Go Online
PHSchool.com Use Web Code **mup-1502** for an **interactive map.**

Standardized Test Prep

Test-Taking Tips

Some questions on standardized tests ask you to find main ideas. Read the paragraph below. Then follow the tips to answer the sample question.

> The Renaissance supported a spirit of adventure and a wide-ranging curiosity that led people to explore new worlds. The Italian navigator Christopher Columbus represented that spirit. So did Nicolaus Copernicus, a Polish scientist who revolutionized the way people viewed the universe. Renaissance writers and artists, eager to experiment with new forms, also demonstrated that adventurous spirit.

TIP As you read the passage, identify its main ideas, or most important points.

Choose the statement that best reflects the main idea.

This passage shows that—
- **A** art influenced science
- **B** curiosity led to new ways of thinking and exploration.
- **C** exploration inspired curiosity.
- **D** exploration led to adventure.

TIP Look for a key word in the question or answer choices that connects to the paragraph. In this case, the word is *curiosity*.

Think It Through Start with the main idea—the curious nature of Renaissance thinkers encouraged changes in science, art, and exploration. You can link this idea to the key word, *curiosity*. You can rule out A and D, which do not discuss curiosity. C is a statement linking exploration to curiosity, but the statement does not reflect main point of the passage. The correct answer is B.

Practice Questions

Use the tips above and other tips in this book to help you answer the following questions.

1. How did the growth of Italian cities at the dawn of the Renaissance affect the feudal system?
   - **A** The growth of cities strengthened feudal power.
   - **B** The growth of cities weakened feudal power.
   - **C** The growth of cities forced nobles to fight one another.
   - **D** The growth of cities expanded the feudal system into a city environment.

2. Which of the following was one of Luther's central Reformation ideas?
   - **A** The Jesuits should spread religious faith.
   - **B** Infants should not be baptized.
   - **C** Women should be allowed into the priesthood.
   - **D** Faith, not good works, was the key to salvation.

Use the passage below to answer question 3.

> "Dare we believe, my brothers, that St. Benedict had such expensive horses and mules as we now see many a [Church official] possess? Certainly not!"

3. Which of the following best summarizes the main idea of this passage?
   - **A** St. Benedict should have had better horses.
   - **B** The Church is much better off today than it was during the Renaissance.
   - **C** Church officials live too well and should follow the example of St. Benedict.
   - **D** Expensive horses are better than expensive mules

Use Web Code **mua-1505** for **Chapter 15 self-test.**

Chapter Preview

This chapter will examine European exploration in Africa and Asia between the 1400s and 1700s.

Section 1
European Exploration Begins

Section 2
Europeans in India and Southeast Asia

Section 3
Europe Explores East Asia

Target Reading Skill

Clarifying Meaning In this chapter you will focus on clarifying, or better understanding, the meaning of what you read.

▶ In Lisbon, Portugal, the Monument to the Discoveries honors Prince Henry, the first in Europe to run a school for navigators. It includes statues of Magellan and Vasco da Gama.

MAP MASTER™ Skills Activity

Ocean Trade Beyond Europe, 1700

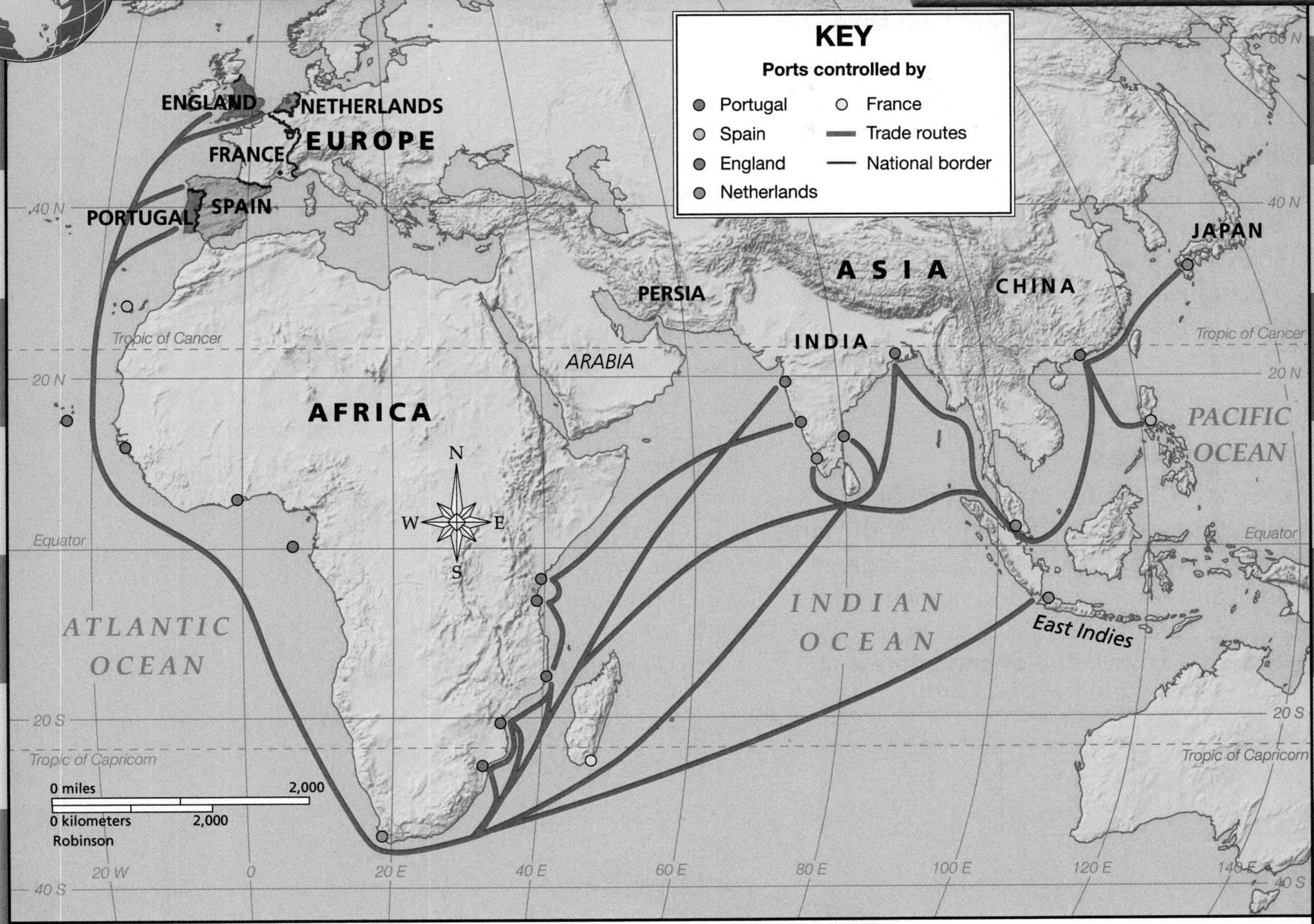
KEY
Ports controlled by
Portugal
Spain
England
Netherlands
France
Trade routes
National border
ENGLAND
NETHERLANDS
EUROPE
FRANCE
PORTUGAL
SPAIN
ASIA
PERSIA
ARABIA
INDIA
CHINA
JAPAN
AFRICA
PACIFIC OCEAN
ATLANTIC OCEAN
INDIAN OCEAN
East Indies
Tropic of Cancer
Tropic of Capricorn
Equator
N
S
E
W
0 miles 2,000
0 kilometers 2,000
Robinson
60 N
40 N
20 N
20 S
40 S
20 W
0
20 E
40 E
60 E
80 E
100 E
120 E
140 E

Movement The lure of profit led Europeans to risk their lives on the sea in search of cargo that they could sell at home. **Use the Key** Which country controlled ports on the east coast of Africa? In which ocean did all four countries have to follow the same route? **Apply Information** Which destination in the Pacific Ocean required the longest voyage? Approximately how many miles did a ship from the Netherlands have to sail in order to reach the East Indies?

Go Online PHSchool.com Use Web Code **mup-1601** for step-by-step **map skills practice.**

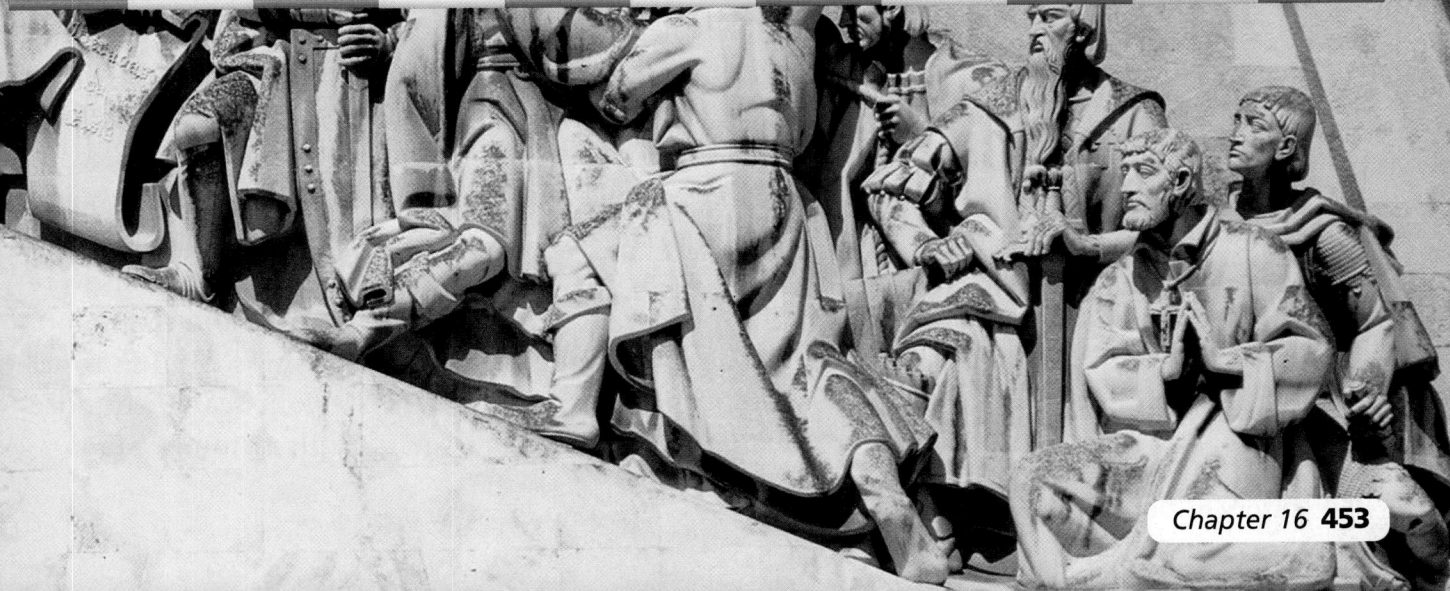

Section 1

European Exploration Begins

Prepare to Read

Objectives

In this section you will

1. Learn why Europeans began exploring the world in the 1400s.
2. Identify the early achievements of Portuguese exploration under Prince Henry the Navigator.
3. Understand how Portugal's efforts inspired early Spanish exploration.

Taking Notes

As you read, look for information about the earliest oceangoing explorations of the land beyond Europe. Copy the graphic organizer below, and record your findings in it.

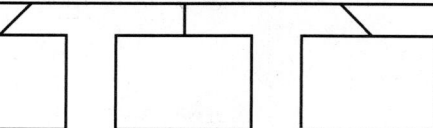

Growing knowledge of and interest in the world beyond Europe

Target Reading Skill

Paraphrase Paraphrasing can help you understand what you read. When you paraphrase, you restate what you have read in your own words. You could paraphrase the first paragraph of this section this way: "European sailors in the 1300s did not know what to expect, so they were afraid to sail their ships very far into the ocean."
As you read, paraphrase or "say back" the information following each red or blue heading.

Key Terms

- **circumnavigation** (sur kum nav ih GAY shun) *n.* going completely around the Earth, especially by water
- **isthmus** (IS mis) *n.* a narrow strip of land connecting two larger areas of land

The use of the sun and moon to determine latitude and longitude led to the creation of navigational tools. Early tools gave way to the sextant, as shown above.

What was out there in the ocean, beyond the horizon? In the 1300s, no European knew for sure. Were there monsters that could gobble ships whole? Did the waters of the sea reach the boiling point if you sailed too far to the south? Some European sailors actually held such fears. In fact, there was little firsthand knowledge of the open ocean. European vessels did not sail there.

That was about to change, however. As you learned in Chapter 15, Europe was emerging from the Middle Ages. Europeans were growing more interested in faraway lands and were learning more about them. Merchants were looking for ways to expand their trade and wealth. Kings and queens were looking for power and glory—for themselves and their God.

These were some of the reasons that ships from Europe first sailed out into the deep and mysterious sea. With those first ocean journeys, Europe's age of exploration began.

Why Europe Looked to the East

You have already read about the journey of Marco Polo and about the Crusades. These events helped increase European awareness of the wonders of the East. In the last chapter you also read about the successful merchants of the Italian city-states. These merchants made fortunes bringing spices and other goods from Asia and northern Africa. In fact, Italians controlled this trade when the Renaissance began. But other Europeans also were interested in expanded trade.

The Crusades also drove Europe's explorations. The spirit of the Crusades lived on in some parts of Europe. The desire to defeat the Muslims and spread Christianity remained strong, especially on the Iberian Peninsula. This is the peninsula on which Portugal and Spain are located. Here Christians had been fighting to remove the Moors, Muslims who had arrived on the Iberian Peninsula in the 700s.

√ Reading Check **What two factors caused Europeans to look to the East during the Renaissance?**

The Spice Trade
Europeans traded with merchants in the East for spices. **Explain** *Why were spices considered prize trade items?*

Prince Henry the Navigator at the conquest of Ceuta in 1415

Portuguese Exploration

Prince Henry the Navigator was born in 1394. The third son of Portugal's King João I (king zhoo OW), Henry became a driving force behind Portuguese exploration. Under Henry's guidance, Portuguese navigation and trade advanced significantly.

As a young man, Henry took part in the conquest of Ceuta (say OO tah), in North Africa. Ceuta was a rich Muslim trading city. For several years after Ceuta's capture, Henry served as its governor. The capture of this city gave the prince and his country a taste for the wealth that was available in trade. First, however, Portugal would have to break through—or sail around—Muslim domination of the region.

Exploring the African Coast The conquest of Ceuta also helped the Portuguese learn more about the continent of Africa. Before taking Ceuta, they knew little about this land and the riches it held. The conquest of Ceuta allowed the Portuguese to have access to excellent maps of North Africa.

In 1419, Prince Henry decided to press Portugal's exploration of the African coast. He hired many of Europe's best navigators, scientists, mapmakers, and shipbuilders. He also provided money for these journeys of discovery.

Soon Prince Henry's ships were sailing into the unknown. Over several decades, these voyages pushed farther and farther down Africa's western coast, establishing trade with the newly discovered areas. Many historians believe that Henry's ships sailed as far south as modern-day Sierra Leone. Unfortunately, these journeys also began the terrible practice of the European trade in slaves. In the mid-1400s, Portuguese ships were returning to port with African captives. It was a practice that grew rapidly in the centuries ahead.

Prince Henry died in 1460. He left behind a strong tradition of Portuguese exploration.

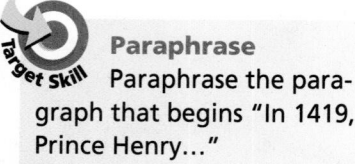

Paraphrase
Paraphrase the paragraph that begins "In 1419, Prince Henry..."

Bartolomeu Dias The Portuguese continued their quest of exploration. Bartolomeu Dias (bahr too loo MEE oo DEE us) had taken part in explorations of Africa's western coast. In 1487, he left Portugal to find the southern tip of Africa. In spite of a terrible storm, he succeeded in traveling around Africa's southern tip in 1488. He named the tip the Cape of Storms. The name was later changed to the Cape of Good Hope.

Vasco da Gama Dias's journey led the way for another Portuguese explorer. In November 1497, Vasco da Gama (VAHS koh duh GAM uh) sailed around the Cape of Good Hope and into the Indian Ocean. In 1498, da Gama sailed into the port of Calicut (KAL uh kut) in India. Da Gama was celebrated as a hero at home. A Portuguese poet wrote of da Gama's rank at the top of history's brave explorers:

> "Cease All, whose Actions ancient Bards [poets] exprest:
> 'A brighter Valour rises in the West'"
>
> —The Lusiad, *Luis de Camões*

As you will read in the next section, the European presence in Asia continued to expand in the coming years.

✔ **Reading Check** What two Portuguese voyages took place after Prince Henry's death?

Links to Science

Navigation The astrolabe (AS troh layb) was one of the devices that helped make possible the exploits of European ocean explorers. The mariner's astrolabe made it possible for sailors to figure out their latitude. Sailors did this by taking measurements of the sun or stars.

Astrolabes were developed by the ancient Greeks. Muslim scholars helped perfect astrolabe technology. They also introduced the astrolabe to Europe.

A King's Blessing
Below, King Manuel I of Portugal blesses da Gama and his expedition to Asia. Da Gama was later hailed a hero for successfully sailing around the Cape of Good Hope, as visible in the map on the left. Compare and Contrast *Compare this map with the one on page 453. How are the maps similar? How are they different?*

European Voyages of Exploration

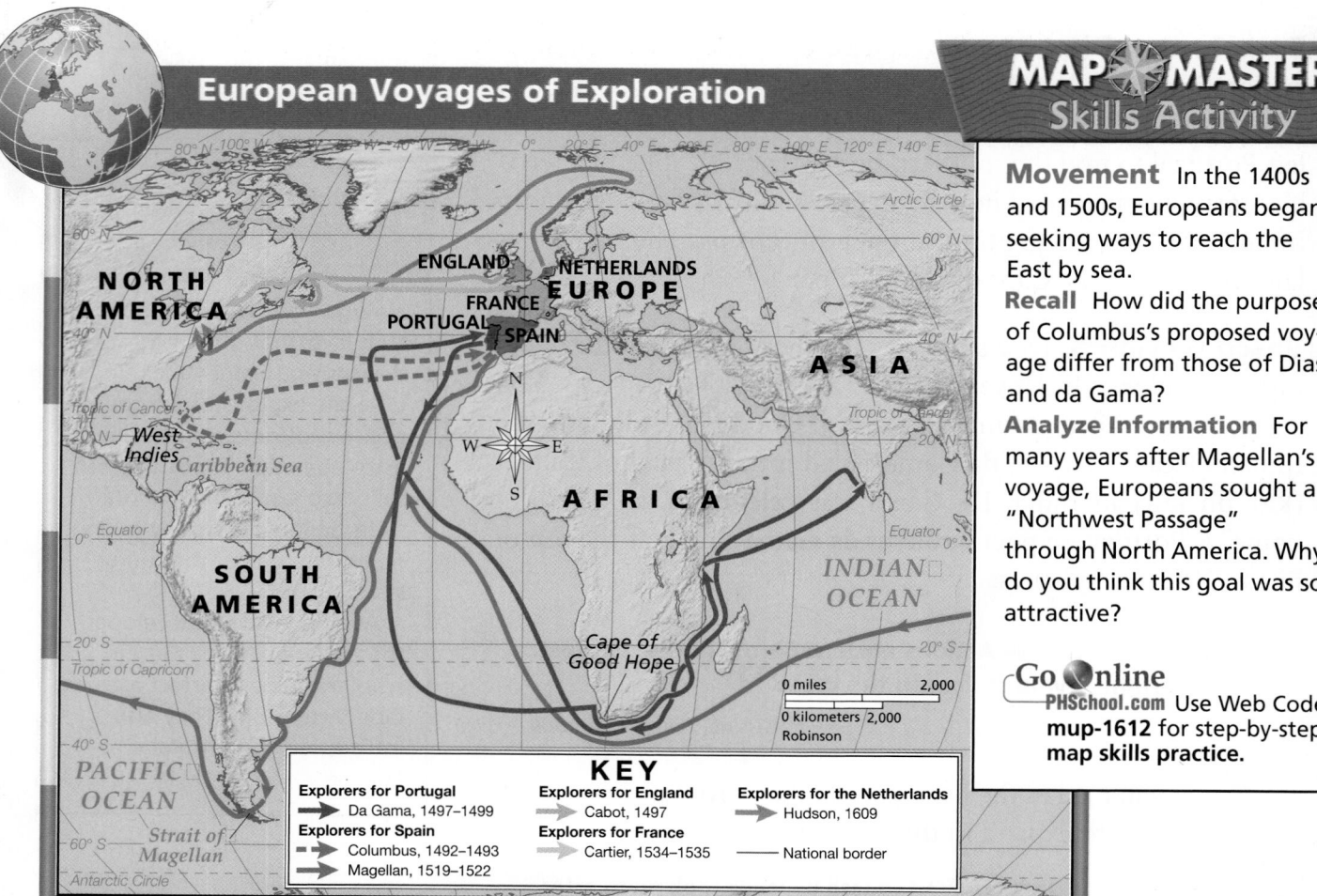

Movement In the 1400s and 1500s, Europeans began seeking ways to reach the East by sea.

Recall How did the purpose of Columbus's proposed voyage differ from those of Dias and da Gama?

Analyze Information For many years after Magellan's voyage, Europeans sought a "Northwest Passage" through North America. Why do you think this goal was so attractive?

Go Online
PHSchool.com Use Web Code **mup-1612** for step-by-step map skills practice.

KEY

Explorers for Portugal
→ Da Gama, 1497–1499

Explorers for Spain
- - - Columbus, 1492–1493
→ Magellan, 1519–1522

Explorers for England
→ Cabot, 1497

Explorers for France
→ Cartier, 1534–1535

Explorers for the Netherlands
→ Hudson, 1609

—— National border

Citizen Heroes

Queen Isabella

In 1492, Spain had just completed its centuries-old struggle to push the Moors from the land. With this battle won, Isabella was willing to take on a challenge that had seemed hopeless to other European leaders: supporting Columbus's idea for a voyage to the West. Thanks to Isabella's backing, Columbus was able to set sail on his fateful journey.

Columbus Sails Under Spanish Flag

Christopher Columbus was born in or around Genoa, Italy, in 1451. Like many Genoese, he became a skilled sailor. He traveled to Portugal and, later, Spain. He also developed a plan to reach the rich lands of India and the East by sailing to the West.

Little was known about the globe at this time. Even though most people thought the Earth was flat, many scholars knew that it was round. Columbus believed that by sailing far enough to the west, a sailor would eventually arrive at the lands of the East.

Columbus tried unsuccessfully for several years to win support for his plan. But in 1492, Queen Isabella of Spain finally agreed to pay for the voyage. That year, Columbus led three ships, the *Niña*, the *Pinta*, and the *Santa Maria*. After ten weeks, Columbus and his weary crew reached an island in the area now known as the Caribbean. The date was October 12, 1492.

Columbus's journey changed history. Instead of reaching Asia, he had reached the Americas. In Chapter 17, you will read more about the results of Columbus's voyage.

✓ **Reading Check** How did Columbus believe one could reach Asia?

The *Santa Maria*

After years of preparation, Christopher Columbus sailed from Spain on August 3, 1492, on what would be his first voyage to the Americas. The *Santa Maria* was the flagship, or lead ship of Columbus's fleet of three ships. The *Santa Maria* was the biggest of the three. It was also the slowest and the hardest to handle. Thirty-three days of clear sailing brought the fleet across the Atlantic Ocean to a small island in the Bahamas, where Columbus landed on October 12, 1492.

Christopher Columbus
After successfully completing his voyage in 1492, Columbus was honored with the title Admiral of the Ocean Sea.

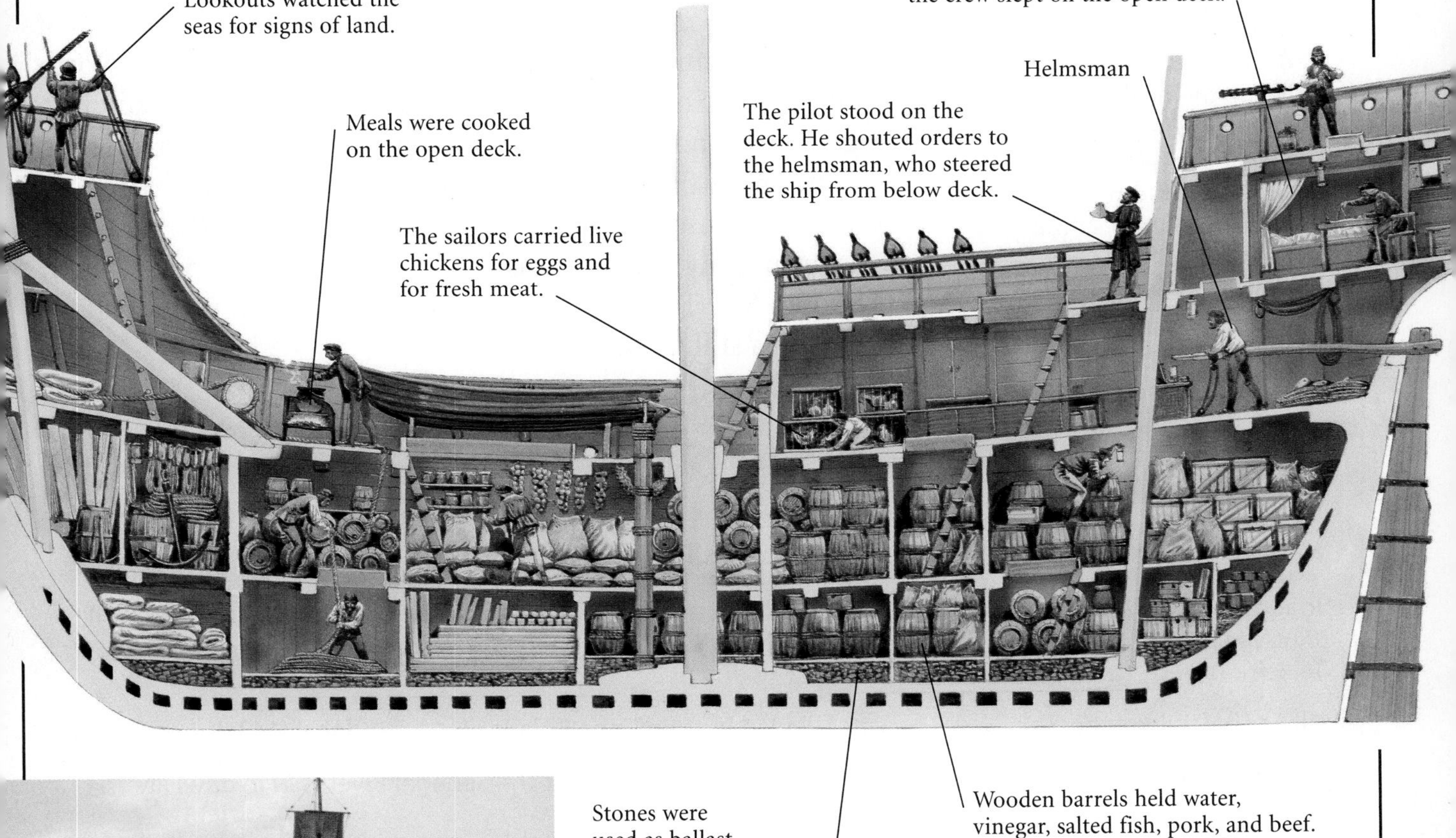

Columbus had his own cabin on board the *Santa Maria*. The rest of the crew slept on the open deck.

Lookouts watched the seas for signs of land.

Meals were cooked on the open deck.

Helmsman

The pilot stood on the deck. He shouted orders to the helmsman, who steered the ship from below deck.

The sailors carried live chickens for eggs and for fresh meat.

Stones were used as ballast, making the ship stable.

Wooden barrels held water, vinegar, salted fish, pork, and beef. Sacks held flour, rice, and beans.

Life-Sized Replicas
In this photo of life-sized replicas of Columbus's first fleet, the *Santa Maria* is in the lead. The *Pinta* and the *Niña* follow behind.

ANALYZING IMAGES
Why did the crew, except for Columbus, sleep on the open deck of the *Santa Maria*?

Other Explorers Look West

Europeans came to know the western lands Columbus had reached as America. The name can be traced to an Italian trader known as Amerigo Vespucci (ah meh REE goh ves POOT chee). In a letter to a government official in Florence, Italy, Vespucci claimed to have taken part in four voyages across the Atlantic Ocean. He wrote that in 1497 he explored the coast of what is now South America. The name America soon appeared on a map and came into common use.

For his part, Columbus never gave up the idea that the lands he had reached were part of Asia. By the early 1500s, however, Europeans knew that the Americas were not lands of the East.

Balboa Sees the Pacific In 1511, a Spanish explorer named Vasco Núñez de Balboa (VAHS koh NOO nyeth theh bal BOH uh) arrived on the Isthmus of Panama (IS mis uv PAN uh mah). An **isthmus** is a narrow strip of land connecting two larger areas of land. The Isthmus of Panama connects the continents of North America and South America. Balboa had heard stories about a huge ocean and gold treasure to the south. He organized an expedition to find both. After nearly a month, his expedition reached the shores of a sea that stretched far into the distance. This great body of water was the Pacific Ocean. Balboa called it the South Sea. Then he claimed it and all the lands it touched for Spain. Asia still lay beyond.

■ **Chart Skills**

Even before Magellan's historic voyages, Portuguese explorers and navigators of the 1400s made many important discoveries. **Identify** Name the navigator who rounded Cape Blanco in 1443.
Infer What can you infer from the fact that the Gambia River was spotted in 1446 but was not sailed upon until 1456?

Other Portuguese Navigators and Explorers

Names	Accomplishments
João Gonçalves Zarco (zhoo OW gohn SAHL veezh ZAHR koo) and Tristão Vaz Teixeira (treesh TOW vahsh tay SHAY ruh)	Rediscovered the islands of Porto Santo (PAWR toh SAHN toh) and Madeira (muh DIHR uh) (1418)
Gil Eanes (zhil YAH neesh)	Sailed around Cape Bojador (BOH juh dohr) (1434)
Dinís Dias (dee NEESH DEE us)	Reached the mouth of the Senegal River (SEN ih gawl RIV ur) (1445)
Nuño Tristão (NOO nyoo treesh TOW)	Rounded Cape Blanco (kayp BLANG koh) (1443), spotted the Gambia River (GAM bee uh RIV ur) (1446)
Diogo Gomes (DYOH goo GOH mish)	Explored the West African coast and sailed up the Gambia River (1456), landed on the Cape Verde Islands (kayp vurd EYE lundz) (1460)
Diogo Cão (DYOH goo kow)	Found the Congo River (1482), reached Cape Cross in present-day Namibia (nuh MIB ee uh) (1485–86)

Magellan's Voyage In 1519, the Portuguese navigator Ferdinand Magellan (FUR duh nand muh JEL un) set out to achieve Columbus's unfulfilled goal of reaching Asia by sailing west. With great difficulty, Magellan and three of his ships managed to reach the Pacific in 1520. In 1521 Magellan landed in the Philippines, where he was killed by native people. The crew pressed on, and the one remaining ship reached Spain in 1522. The voyage of nearly three years was the first circumnavigation of the globe. **Circumnavigation** means going completely around the earth, especially by water.

Quest for the Northwest Passage Magellan's voyage showed just how hard it was to circle the globe. For this reason, many Europeans sought a shortcut through North America. This hoped-for shortcut was referred to as the Northwest Passage. European explorers, including England's Henry Hudson, looked for such a shortcut for hundreds of years. It was not until the 1900s that a ship successfully traveled from the Atlantic Ocean to the Pacific Ocean by sailing north of Canada.

Ferdinand Magellan

✓ **Reading Check** What did Magellan's voyage have to do with the search for the Northwest Passage?

 **Section 1 Assessment**

Key Terms
Review the key term at the beginning of this section. Use each term in a sentence that explains its meaning.

Target Reading Skill
Paraphrase the achievements of early Portuguese explorers.

Comprehension and Critical Thinking
1. (a) Recall Which part of Europe dominated Asian trade at the start of the Renaissance?

(b) Synthesize Information What did the quests to expand trade and to spread Christianity have in common?
2. (a) Identify Why was the crusading spirit strong in Portugal?
(b) Summarize How did the conquest of Ceuta affect the Portuguese?
3. (a) Identify Where did Christopher Columbus first learn to be a sailor?
(b) Draw Inferences What can you infer from the fact that Columbus did not know about the existence of North and South America?

Writing Activity
Sailors in the 1400s and 1500s often did not know what they would find when they started their journeys. Write a diary entry from the point of view of a sailor leaving for his or her first voyage. Be sure to talk about both your hopes and your fears about what will happen to you.

For: An activity on the explorers of Portugal and Spain
Visit: PHSchool.com
Web Code: mud-1610

In the 1500s, a life at sea was a hard life. During lengthy voyages of exploration, sailors performed tiring physical labor, suffered from poor nutrition, and endured long stretches of boredom. They were often lonely, surrounded by vast and sometimes violent seas, far from home and family. They ate dried and salted food that was often infested with insects or gnawed by rats. They suffered injuries from their work or from fights with other sailors. Sailors' registries often identified men by their injuries, including crushed fingers and splinters embedded in the flesh.

Onboard a Ship Sailing was often the best job available for poor, uneducated men and orphaned boys who lived near busy ports. Boys as young as seven or eight served as ship's pages until they were about fifteen. A page's duties included scrubbing the ship and turning the sand clocks every half hour to mark the time. Unless they were assigned to specific officers, pages took orders from everyone on board. When they were old enough, pages became sailor's apprentices.

Apprentices were young men training to become sailors. They climbed the rigging in their bare feet to furl, or gather, the sails. They served as lookouts at the top of the masts, rowed smaller boats, and carried heavy cargo.

Sailors might work their way up to other positions, including that of ship's pilot, whose job it was to navigate. A very few men became the master of a ship. The master commanded the ship and was usually part owner of the vessel. The illustration at the right shows a vessel from the 1500s that sailed with about 45 crew members.

Sunken Treasures
This decorated plate and the pottery jug above were recovered from a Venetian shipwreck in the Adriatic Sea. The shipwreck probably occurred in the late 1500s.

Master's or Captain's Cabin
Common sailors slept on deck on straw-filled sacks.

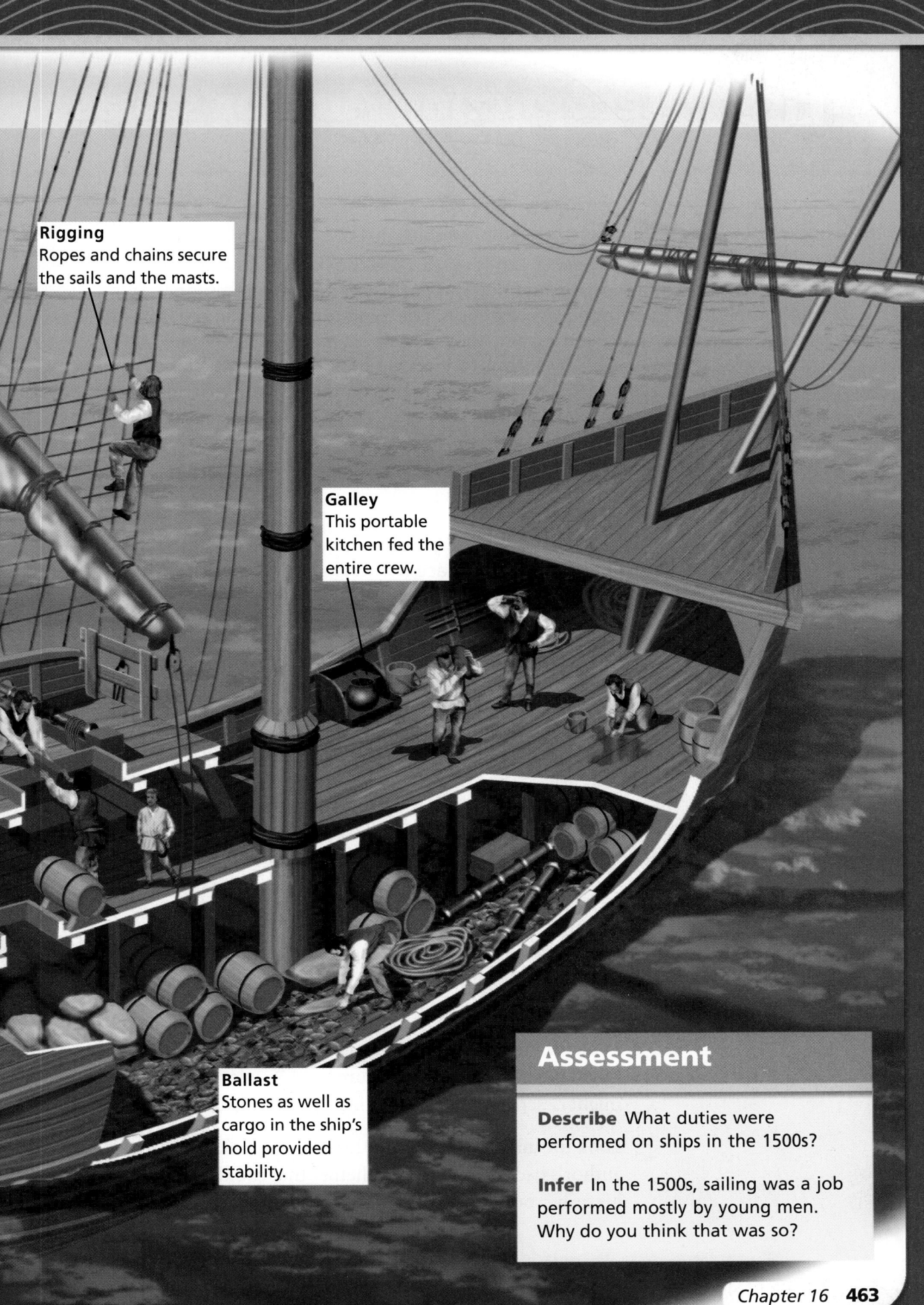

Rigging
Ropes and chains secure the sails and the masts.

Galley
This portable kitchen fed the entire crew.

Ballast
Stones as well as cargo in the ship's hold provided stability.

Assessment

Describe What duties were performed on ships in the 1500s?

Infer In the 1500s, sailing was a job performed mostly by young men. Why do you think that was so?

"Christopher Columbus discovered America in 1492."

This is a common statement. But it reveals the speaker's bias—a partial or narrow view of a fact or situation. This particular bias was common during the time of European exploration. The explorers arrived in areas that were new to them, so they felt they were *discovering* something. And in a sense they were—by encountering the unknown. But these lands were not new to everyone. Native people had lived there for thousands of years, so some would say that Columbus didn't really *discover* anything.

By studying what you read, you may find open or hidden bias in the author's statements. Recognizing an author's bias can help you to judge what you read and to place it in context.

This painting is an artist's representation of Captain Christopher Newport and his followers landing in Jamestown.

Learn the Skill

Use the following guidelines for becoming more alert to an author's possible bias.

1 **Look for one-sided language and evidence.** Look for words or information that seems to favor only one side of a situation or an argument.

2 **Ask what kind of sources the writer relies on.** Is the writing based on a balanced variety of sources, or does the writer rely only on sources that favor one side or viewpoint?

3 **Look for bias in descriptions.** For example, one author might describe a historical figure as an "explorer"; another might describe the same person as a "conqueror."

4 **Look for information about the author.** Look at the author's background to see whether that could influence his or her outlook.

Practice the Skill

Read the numbered sentences in the boxed advertisement at the right. Then answer the following questions.

1 Analyze the choice of words and use of language in sentence 1. Which words or phrases show bias?

2 Does sentence 2 use a balanced variety of sources? Explain.

3 How might the use of the word "Captain" influence the readers of this advertisement?

4 What does the author's background say about the possible bias of the ad? Would the preferred means of travel be the same if a flight attendant had written the advertisement?

1. Many people planning a trip around the world prefer ocean liners to airplanes.
2. A recent survey of ocean-liner travelers found that they place a high value on a leisurely pace of travel.
3. Captain Oswald Harris, a long-time skipper of big ocean liners, points out that the food and service are much better on cruise ships than on airplanes.
4. For more reasons to travel around the world by boat, come see me, Abe Fenster, represenative for Worldwide Ocean Cruises.

Apply the Skill

Reread the story of the encounter between Sir George Macartney and Qianlong in Section 3 of this chapter. Then write a biased version of the story, relating the events from the viewpoint of either Sir George Macartney or Qianlong. Use your imagination to invent new details or dialogue that will make your version persuasive and lively.

Europeans in India and Southeast Asia

Prepare to Read

Objectives

In this section you will
1. Learn how Portugal traded in India.
2. Understand how Portuguese trade expanded into India and the Spice Islands.
3. Identify the English and the Dutch as challengers to Portugal's power in Asia.

Taking Notes

As you read, look for information about European trading in Asia. Copy the graphic organizer below. Record your findings in it.

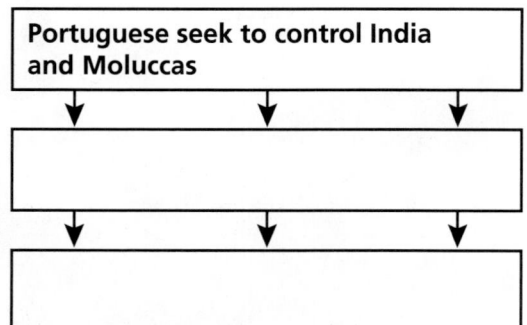

Portuguese seek to control India and Moluccas

Target Reading Skill

Summarize You can better understand a text if you pause to restate the key points briefly in your own words. A good summary includes important events and details, notes the order in which the events occurred, and makes connections. Use the graphic organizer at the left to summarize what you have read.

Key Terms

- **monopoly** (muh NAHP uh lee) *n.* the exclusive control of goods or services in a market
- **colony** (KAHL uh nee) *n.* a territory ruled over by a distant state

Ducats were gold coins used as currency in various European countries.

It was horrifying to think about: In 1519, Ferdinand Magellan had set out from Spain with a crew of more than 250 men on five ships. Nearly three years later—on September 6, 1522—the single remaining vessel from that voyage sailed into port under a different commander and with a ragged crew of eighteen.

The journey, however, was far from a total loss. The ship carried a valuable cargo: tons of cloves. The ship had picked up the cloves in the Moluccas (moh LUK uz)—islands in the East Indies also known as the Spice Islands. The value of these spices was 41,000 ducats (DUK utz). The entire voyage had cost a mere 20,000 ducats.

The people of Europe greatly prized spices. The spices you can now buy at your supermarket for just a few dollars were worth a small fortune hundreds of years ago.

At the beginning of the 1500s, even before Magellan's voyage, the Portuguese were the first Europeans to take advantage of these riches. They were followed, however, by other nations.

At the palace of the Zamorin, da Gama negotiated for trade rights and spices.

Portugal Gains a Foothold in India

As you have read, Portugal was the first European country to reach the rich ports of Asia. Vasco da Gama's voyage had reached the trading center of Calicut, India, in 1498 but da Gama left India empty-handed. Calicut traders had rejected the humble cloth, honey, and other trade goods he brought from Europe. The Portuguese soon returned, however. The next time, they were not disappointed in their quest for riches.

In 1500, Pedro Alvarez Cabral (PAY droh AL vuh rez kuh BRAHL) set out for India. This long journey included the first Portuguese landing in an area that is now southeastern Brazil. Cabral claimed this land for Portugal. The journey also included a shipwreck that took the life of Bartolomeu Dias, who was part of Cabral's crew.

Cabral eventually did reach Calicut. There, his efforts to trade for spices went slowly. A frustrated Cabral got into an armed conflict with Arab traders that left many people dead. In spite of the bloodshed, Cabral was able to establish a trading post in India. In 1501, he returned to Portugal with a load of spices. But this Portuguese show of force abroad was not to be the last.

Links to Math

Profits Magellan's voyage cost 20,000 ducats. It brought back a cargo worth 41,000 ducats. This means the profit on the voyage was 21,000 ducats.

✓ **Reading Check** Why did da Gama come home empty-handed on his first voyage to Calicut?

The Portuguese Empire Expands

Cabral's voyage was considered a great success. Soon Portugal was sending more ships to trade in Asia. They were also sending armed forces. With these forces, Portugal was able to gain control of many trading centers between the east coast of Africa and the west coast of India. These conquests were sometimes accomplished with bloodshed. Despite the cost in lives, Portugal succeeded in controlling the trade in the region.

Next Portugal looked further to the East. There lay the Moluccas—the Spice Islands, which lie in the northeastern part of present-day Indonesia. As you have read, these lands were the major source of cloves, a highly prized spice. In 1511, Afonso de Albuquerque (ah FAHN soh duh AL buh kur kee) led a mission to Malacca, located near these islands, which helped establish the Portuguese spice trade.

Portugal's hold on the East was vast. However, its control was limited mainly to trade. Portugal held very little territory. This Portuguese empire did not last very long, as you will read.

 **Reading Check** **What was Portugal's response to the success of Cabral's voyage?**

Troubles at Sea
Expeditions to the Spice Islands faced many challenges—storms at sea, tropical heat, sickness, and mutiny. **Link Past and Present** *What types of challenges do modern-day crews and their ships encounter?*

Challengers to Portugal

The Portuguese empire brought wealth to Portugal in the 1500s. Soon other powerful European nations became interested in the region.

The Rise of the Dutch The Dutch, the people from Holland (what we now call the Netherlands), soon challenged Portugal's leading role in the East. During the 1500s, the Dutch were growing into an economic and military power in Europe. As the century ended, they sought to control Portugal's empire of Asian trading posts. Portugal was unable to defend these posts against the more powerful Dutch.

In 1602, the Dutch East India Company was founded in Holland. The Dutch government gave this company a trade monopoly in Asia. A **monopoly** is complete control of the trade in a market or product.

The Dutch East India Company became a powerful force in Southeast Asia. From its base in modern-day Indonesia, it established many new trading posts and relationships. The company developed close ties with other Asian nations. It even had its own armies, which it used to seize land and people to serve its enterprise.

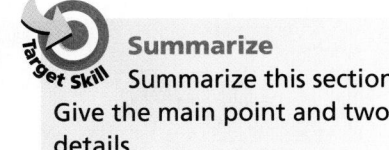

Summarize
Summarize this section. Give the main point and two details.

The English in Asia England was also interested in Asian trade. The East India Company, established in England in 1600, led this effort.

For a time, the British East India Company competed with the Dutch East India Company in the East Indies. The English soon moved their focus to India. First the English drove out the Portuguese. Then they expanded their own trading operations. Throughout the 1600s, they enjoyed great success, replacing the Portuguese as the area's leading trading power.

As the English made headway, the main power in India, the Mughal Empire, began to lose control of the country. Groups in India began to fight for power. The French East India Company, which was also trying to establish itself there, was among the groups battling for control. In the mid-1700s, the British emerged from these struggles as the leading power in India. Over the next hundred years, Britain tightened its hold. Eventually, in the mid-1800s, India became a colony of Great Britain. A **colony** is a territory ruled over by a faraway country.

European interest in Asia did not stop with India and the East Indies. In the next section, you will read about European involvement elsewhere in the region.

Trading port established by the British East India Company in Surat, India

✓ **Reading Check** **In what parts of Asia did the English and Dutch focus their efforts?**

Section 2 Assessment

Key Terms
Review the key terms at the beginning of this section. Use each term in a sentence that explains its meaning.

Target Reading Skill
Summarize the information in the last page of this section.

Comprehension and Critical Thinking
1. (a) Recall Why were the Portuguese interested in Asian trade?

(b) Draw Inferences What can you infer from the fact that the Portuguese sometimes used force in order to set up trading posts?

2. (a) Explain What was the Dutch East India company?

(b) Compare and Contrast How was the Dutch expansion into Asia similar to and different from the Portuguese expansion into Asia?

3. (a) Identify Which countries were England's main rivals for control of India?

(b) Cause and Effect Why were the English eventually able to gain total control over India?

Writing Activity
You are a Dutch businessperson in the late 1500s. Write a letter to colleagues in your business about possible business opportunities in Asia. Be sure to discuss the role of the Portuguese and other European rivals, such as the British.

Go Online
PHSchool.com

For: An activity on the explorers of Portugal and Spain
Visit: PHSchool.com
Web Code: mud-1620

Europe Explores East Asia

Prepare to Read

Objectives
In this section you will
1. Learn about European efforts to expand trade in East Asia.
2. Understand European encounters with China and Japan, 1600–1700.

Taking Notes
As you read, look for information about European efforts to expand trade in East Asia. Copy the graphic organizer below and record your findings in it.

> **I. Europeans seek trade in East Asia: 1500s and 1600s**
> A. Portuguese
> B.
> C.
> **II. China and the Europeans**
> A.
> B.
> **III. Japan and the Europeans**
> A.
> B.

Target Reading Skill
Reread or Read Ahead Rereading and reading ahead are strategies that can help you understand words and ideas in the text. If you do not understand a certain passage, reread it to look for connections among the words and sentences. It might also help to read ahead, because a word or idea may become clearer later on in the text.

Key Terms
- **missionary** (MISH un ehr ee) *n.* a person who is sent to do religious or charitable work in a foreign country
- **persecution** (pur sih KYOO shun) *n.* the causing of injury or distress to others because of their religion, race, or political beliefs

In 1793, the British government sent Sir George Macartney (sur jawrg muh KAHRT nee) to ask for greater British trading rights in China. He presented Qianlong (CHYAHN lawng), the Chinese emperor, with samples of fine British manufactured goods. The Chinese, however, were not moved. "We possess all things," wrote the emperor in his official response to George III. "I set no value on things strange or ingenious, and have no use for your country's manufactures." With that, the Chinese rejected the British requests.

Great Britain was not alone in seeking greater trade in East Asia from the 1500s through the 1700s. Nor was it the only country to come away disappointed. As you will read, the Portuguese, the Dutch, and the Spanish also tried to tap the riches of the region during this era. Few of them returned home with much to show for their efforts.

A Chinese export teapot from the 1700s decorated with a river landscape.

Go Online
PHSchool.com Use Web Code
mup-0840 for an interactivity
on world trade in 1700.

Expanding European Trade

European powers established trade and acquired some territory in India and Southeast Asia in the 1500s. Yet they were aware that another valuable prize existed nearby: the great riches of China. This land was famed for its porcelain, jade, and silk.

Even as Portugal seized control of Southeast Asia in the early 1500s, the country was beginning to explore trade in China. At first, the Chinese saw little reason to deal with the Portuguese, whom they viewed as little more than pirates. The Portuguese would not be denied, however; by 1557 they had secured a trading post at Macao (muh KOU). Yet China strictly limited and controlled this trade and did not formally recognize Portuguese control of Macao.

The Spanish also traded with China during this time. They operated from their colony of the Philippines. Recall that Magellan had landed—and died—in the Philippines during his ill-fated voyage. Spain later gained control of the entire chain of islands. Spain's trade with China was active. Spain used silver mined in Mexico to pay for fine silks and other goods from China.

It was also in the mid-1500s that Europeans first learned about Japan. In the 1540s, a Portuguese vessel landed there after being blown off course. More Europeans later returned to trade and to spread Christianity.

✓ **Reading Check** Who were the first Europeans to make contact with China in the early 1500s?

Links Across Time

The Philippines The Spanish colony of the Philippines was a center for Chinese trade. However, the Spanish also came to Asia to spread religion. In fact, they did convert many Filipinos to Christianity. Today, the Philippines remains largely Christian.

Jade and silk were two of the riches that attracted European powers to East Asia.

European Contacts with China and Japan

As you have read, the Dutch and the British replaced the Portuguese as the main trading powers in Asia in the 1600s. Like the Portuguese, they hoped to tap China's riches.

The China Trade Trade with China was difficult for Europeans in this era. The Chinese viewed themselves as the greatest empire in the world. They held little regard for "foreign devils," as they called the Europeans. The Europeans also tended to think of themselves as superior. This attitude sometimes caused conflict with the Chinese. When the Chinese did trade, they usually accepted silver for their goods. Some Europeans, such as the British, would have preferred trading their own manufactured goods.

Still, Europeans pressed for trade. The Dutch seized the southern part of the island of Taiwan in 1624. Their goal was to use Taiwan as a base for trade with China and Japan. However, the Chinese drove the Dutch from this base in 1661.

The British were also frustrated in their efforts. Chinese rulers allowed only tightly controlled trade. Sir George Macartney's unsuccessful mission of 1793 aimed at opening up this trade. For now, China was able to resist the British.

Learn about a trading mission to China.

Target Skill

Reread or Read Ahead
Reread to see why Europeans were not able to carry on wide trade with China in the 1600s and 1700s.

These workers are dyeing silk fabric.

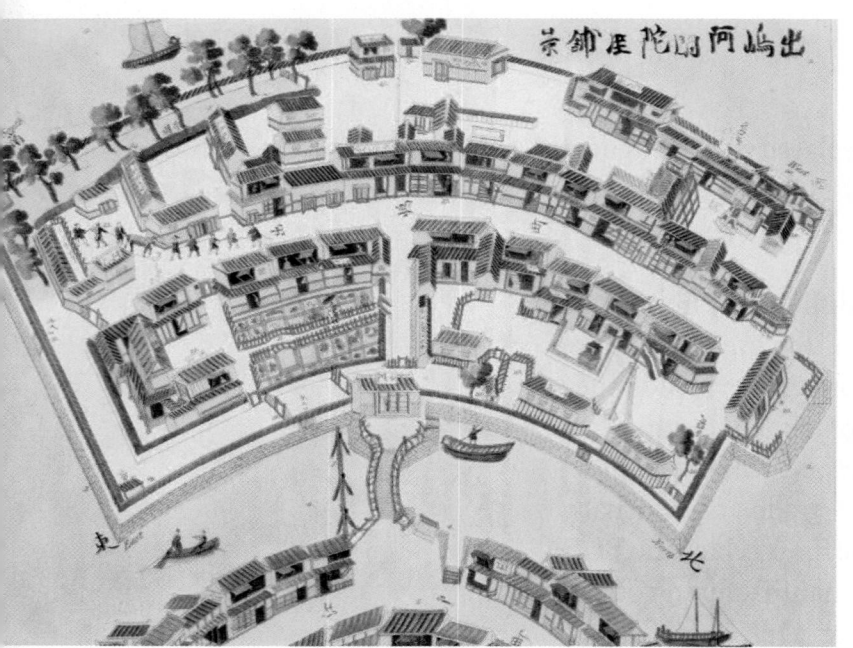

This plan shows the Dutch trading post on the island of Deshima at Nagasaki.

Europeans in Japan Earlier you read about the first Portuguese to reach Japan in the 1540s. Soon Portuguese traders and missionaries returned to Japan. A **missionary** is someone who travels to a foreign country to spread a religion or do charitable work. By the late 1500s, however, Japanese rulers had come to distrust the Portuguese. Religion was a major cause of this distrust. The missionaries and Japanese Christians were persecuted. **Persecution** is threatening or hurting someone because of his or her religion, race, or political beliefs. The Portuguese soon left Japan altogether.

In the early 1600s, the Dutch came to Japan seeking trade. They were allowed to build a trading post. This post was eventually moved to a human-made island called Deshima (DAY shee mah), near the city of Nagasaki (nah guh SAH kee). The Japanese closely controlled this trade. The Dutch remained the only Europeans to trade with Japan until the 1800s.

✓ Reading Check **Which country dominated trade with Japan starting in the 1600s?**

Section 3 Assessment

Key Terms
Review the key terms at the beginning of this section. Use each term in a sentence that explains its meaning.

Target Reading Skill
What idea from this section were you able to clarify by reading ahead?

Comprehension and Critical Thinking
1. (a) Recall What were Chinese attitudes toward trade in the 1500s?

(b) Compare and Contrast Compare and contrast Portugal's experience in China with its experience in Southeast Asia and India.

2. (a) Explain How did the Chinese regard the Europeans who arrived to trade with them?

(b) Draw Inferences What can you infer about China based on its leader's beliefs that it was superior to European countries?

3. (a) Identify Which countries succeeded in trading with Japan?

(b) Cause and Effect What was the effect of Portuguese efforts to spread Christianity in Japan?

Writing Activity
The year is 1550. You are a merchant for a major European firm. Write a letter to your company's directors describing your travels in Asia and the possibilities for trade in at least two Asian countries.

For: An activity on the explorers of Portugal and Spain
Visit: PHSchool.com
Web Code: mud-1630

Review and Assessment

◆ Chapter Summary

Section 1: European Exploration Begins

- At the start of the Renaissance, several European countries began to expand their interest and involvement in the wider world.
- Portugal led the way in ocean exploration.
- Spain was also a leader in seeking new ocean routes to Asia.

Section 2: Europeans in India and Southeast Asia

- The Portuguese became the first European country to establish trade in Asia.
- The Dutch followed the Portuguese and built an extensive trading network in Southeast Asia.
- The British dominated trade with India and eventually took direct control of the entire area.

Section 3: Europe Explores East Asia

- European nations sought trade in East Asia.
- China permitted trade, but only under strict Chinese controls.
- Japan also strictly limited trade with European powers.

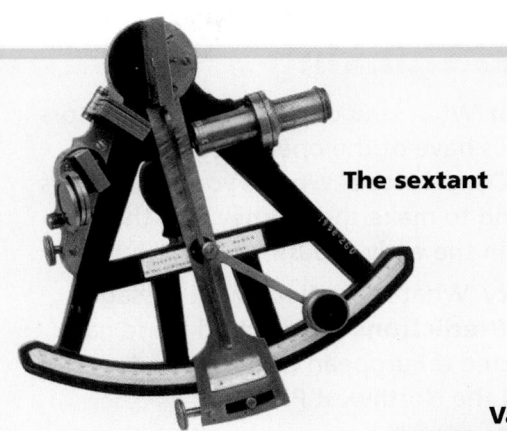
The sextant

Vasco da Gama negotiates trade rights

Chinese teapot from the 1700s

◆ Key Terms

Match each of the following terms with its definition.

1. missionary
2. circumnavigation
3. persecution
4. monopoly
5. colony

A Causing injury or distress to others because of religion, race, or political beliefs

B One who is sent to do religious or charitable work in a foreign country

C Traveling completely around the Earth, especially by water

D A territory ruled by a distant state

E Exclusive control of goods or services in a market

◆ Comprehension and Critical Thinking

6. (a) Explain What kind of knowledge did sailors in the 1300s have of the open ocean?
(b) Draw Conclusions Why do you think sailors were willing to make the journey into the unknown in the early 1400s?

7. (a) Identify What is the Northwest Passage?
(b) Make Predictions How would trade have been affected if European explorers had discovered the Northwest Passage?

8. (a) Identify Which nation replaced Portugal as a trading power in Asia?
(b) Draw Conclusions Basing your conclusion on Portugal's experience with this country, what can you infer about Portuguese military strength?

9. (a) Identify Over which country did Great Britain gain control in Asia?
(b) Sequence Describe the sequence of events that led to Britain's control of India.

10. (a) Recall Which European country colonized the Philippines?
(b) Evaluate Information In what area besides trade did the Spanish affect Philippine life?

11. (a) Explain What did Sir George Macartney hope to accomplish in China?
(b) Summarize Briefly summarize Qianlong's response to Macartney's presentation.

◆ Skills Practice

Recognizing Author's Bias In the Skills Activity in this chapter, you learned that authors sometimes show bias in their writing. You also learned that you can become a more informed and careful reader by learning to recognize an author's bias. Review the steps you followed to learn this skill. Then read an article on world trade or international affairs from an encyclopedia or from your local newspaper. Does the article show signs of bias? Explain your conclusions in a brief essay.

◆ Writing Activity: History

Using the library or the Internet, research the history of Korea in the era of the 1500s through the 1700s. Learn about Korea's relationships with China and Japan. Then write a brief report about what European traders of the era might find if they were to seek trading relationships with Korea.

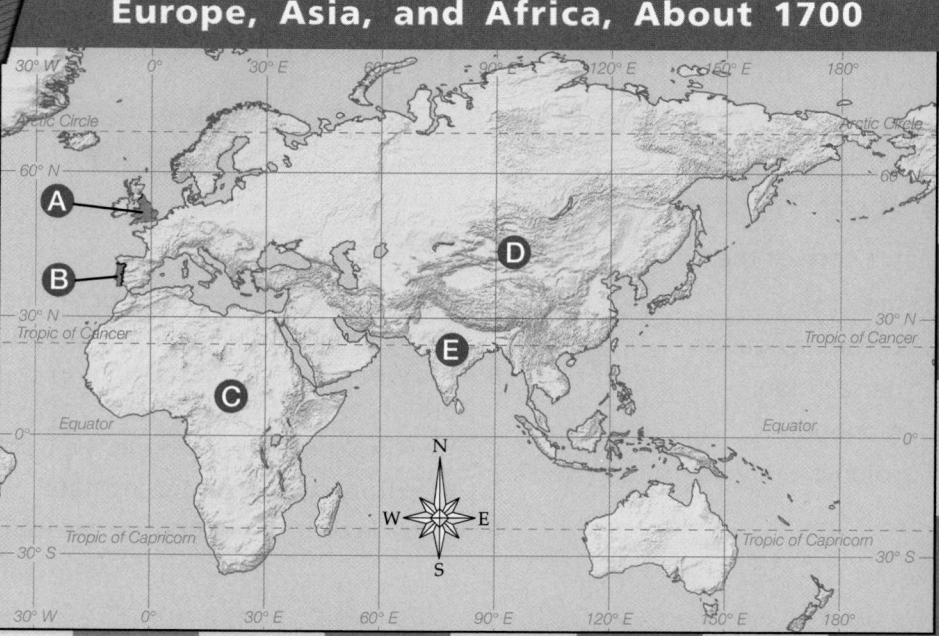

MAP MASTER™
Skills Activity

Europe, Asia, and Africa, About 1700

Place Location For each place listed below, write the letter from the map that shows its location.

1. Africa
2. Asia
3. India
4. Portugal
5. England

Go Online
PHSchool.com Use Web Code
mup-1602 for an **interactive map.**

Standardized Test Prep

Test-Taking Tips

Some questions on standardized tests ask you to analyze a reading selection. Read the paragraph and follow the tips to answer the sample question.

In 1519, Ferdinand Magellan sailed for South America with five ships. From the beginning, the voyage had serious problems. A mutiny occurred during the Atlantic crossing, but Magellan was able to overcome it and continue the expedition. After reaching the coast of South America, the crews of these ships refused to sail on. Once again, Magellan stopped the mutiny, and the ships continued searching for a passage to the other side of the continent.

> **TIP** When reading a paragraph, pay attention to the structure. Did the author order the paragraph by cause-and-effect, by topic, or by chronological order?

> **TIP** Use what you already know to help you answer multiple-choice questions.

Choose the letter that best answers the question.

What information would you expect to find in the next paragraph of an article about Ferdinand Magellan?

   A what Magellan's childhood was like

   B what happened after Magellan reached the Pacific Ocean

   C how Magellan's crew got through the Strait of Magellan

   D how Magellan died in the Philippines

Think It Through Start with the structure of the paragraph. It is in chronological order. You can rule out A, something that happened long before the voyage. You might also rule out D, which happened near the end of the voyage. You can use what you already know to determine that the passage through the Strait of Magellan would logically come before the crew reached the Pacific Ocean. The correct answer is C.

Practice Questions

Use the tips above and other tips in this book to help you answer the following questions.

1. Which of the following is linked to Prince Henry of Portugal?

   A the Crusades

   B the conquest of Ceuta

   C the East India Company

   D the discovery of the Americas

2. Which of the following took place at Deshima?

   A Sir George Macartney met Emperor Qianlong.

   B The Spanish tried to convert the people of the Philippines to Christianity.

   C The British established the headquarters of the East India Company.

   D The Dutch based their trade with Japan.

Read the diary entry below, and then answer the question that follows.

> "Wednesday, 10 October . . . Here the men lost all patience, and complained about the length of the voyage, but the Admiral encouraged them in the best manner he could, representing the profits they were about to acquire."

3. What might you find in the next diary entry?

   A how many men were part of the crew

   B how many fish the crew caught

   C a request from the crew to extend the voyage

   D the crew's reaction to the Admiral's reassurance

Use Web Code **mua-1604**
for **Chapter 16 self-test.**

Chapter Preview

This chapter will examine European expansion in the Americas and Africa.

Target Reading Skill

Main Idea   In this chapter you will focus on identifying the main idea of a paragraph or section. The main idea is the most important point—the one that includes all the other points in a paragraph or section. Identifying main ideas will help you better understand what you read.

▶ No other pyramid built before Columbus landed in the New World was as large as this, the Pyramid of the Sun in Teotihuacan, Mexico

European Land Claims in Africa and the Americas

MAP MASTER™
Skills Activity

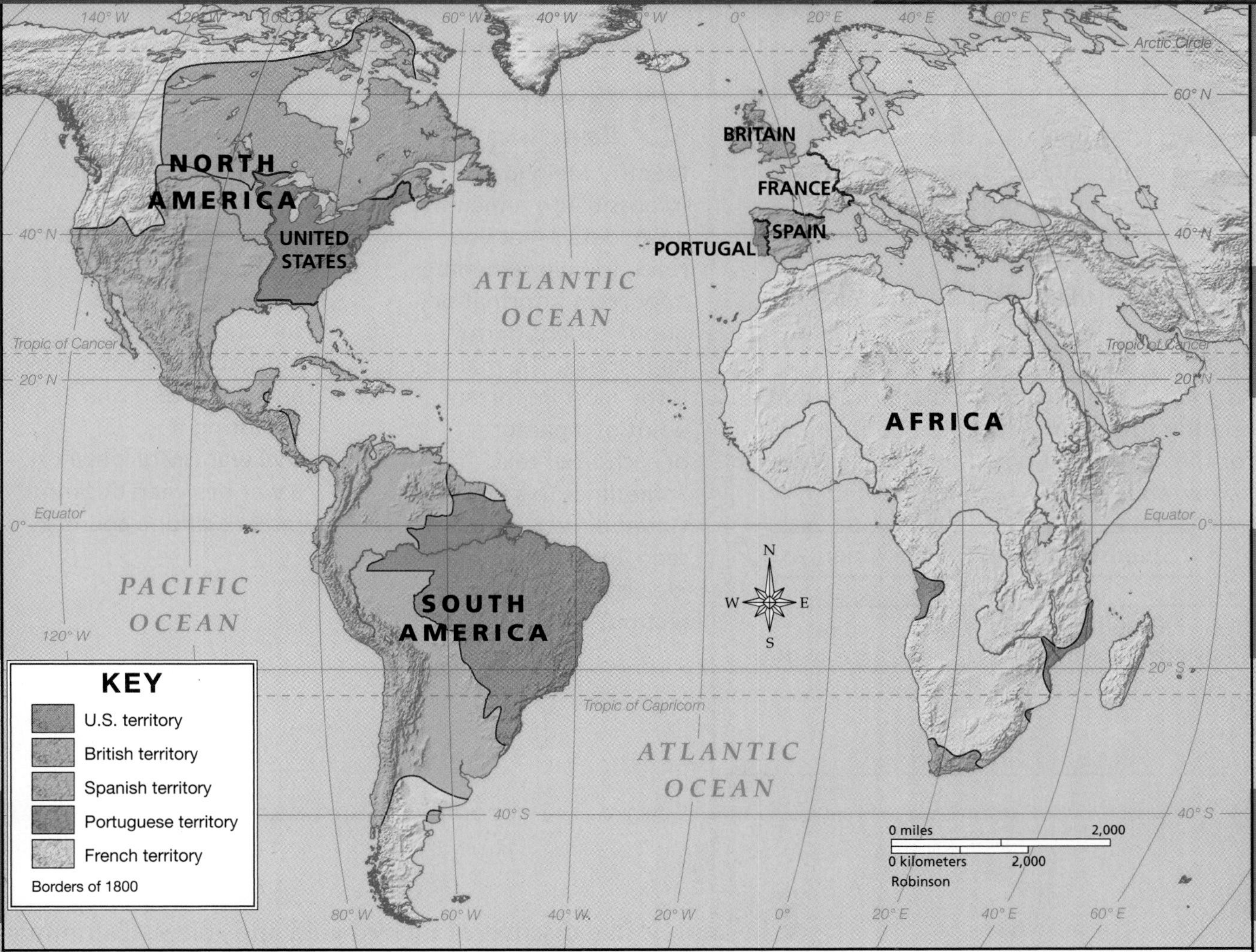

140° W 120° W 100° W 80° W 60° W 40° W 20° W 0° 20° E 40° E 60° E

Arctic Circle

60° N

NORTH AMERICA

BRITAIN
FRANCE
SPAIN
PORTUGAL

40° N   40° N

UNITED STATES

ATLANTIC OCEAN

Tropic of Cancer   Tropic of Cancer

20° N   20° N

AFRICA

Equator   Equator 0°

PACIFIC OCEAN

SOUTH AMERICA

N
W   E
S

120° W

20° S

KEY

	U.S. territory
	British territory
	Spanish territory
	Portuguese territory
	French territory

Borders of 1800

Tropic of Capricorn

ATLANTIC OCEAN

40° S   40° S

80° W   60° W   40° W   20° W   0°   20° E   40° E   60° E

0 miles   2,000
0 kilometers   2,000
Robinson

Location As European countries discovered new lands, they were eager to claim land for themselves in order to enrich their societies. **Identify** Find the areas claimed by Britain, Spain, and Portugal. Contrast the size of the European countries with their possessions. **Apply Information** Notice how small the claims in Africa are compared with those in North and South America. What reasons can you think of to account for the difference?

Go Online
PHSchool.com Use Web Code
mup-1701 for step-by-step map skills practice.

Prepare to Read

Objectives

In this section you will
1. Learn what attitudes and events led to the Spanish exploration of the Americas.
2. Find out how the Spanish conquered Mexico.
3. Learn how the Spanish conquered Peru.

Taking Notes

As you read this section, look for information relating to Spanish attitudes about and aims for the Americas. Copy the graphic organizer below, and record your findings in it.

> **Spanish Conquest in the Americas**
>
> | **Attitudes Towards the Americas** | **Aims for the Americas** |
> |---|---|
> | • | • |
> | • | • |
> | • | • |

Target Reading Skill

Identify Main Ideas It is impossible to remember every detail that you read. To help remember important information, good readers identify main ideas. The main idea is the most important point of a paragraph or section of text. Sometimes this idea is stated directly. As you read, identify the main idea stated in each section.

Key Terms

- **conquistador** (kahn KEES tuh dawr), *n.* a Spanish conqueror of the Americas in the sixteenth century
- **siege** (seej), *n.* the surrounding and blockading of a town by an army intent on capturing it
- **civil war** (SIV ul wawr), *n.* a war between different regions of one country

Columbus mistook the beautiful islands of the Caribbean for the Indies.

The land he had discovered offered gold and spices, Columbus wrote. "To these," Columbus added, "may be added slaves, as numerous as may be wished for."

Columbus was describing the Caribbean islands, which lie off the southeastern coast of North America. Columbus stumbled across these lands while searching for the Indies, a group of Southeast Asian islands. Native peoples, mainly a group called the Taínos (TY nohz), lived on the Carribean islands. Columbus thought that he was in the Indies, so he called these people Indians.

Columbus was mistaken about where he landed, but there was no mistaking the opportunities the Carribean presented. He claimed the islands and all their riches for Spain. As for the native people, Columbus believed that they posed no threat.

In this instance, Columbus was correct. Spain soon conquered the land of the Taíno. This was the first of many Spanish conquests in the Americas.

Aztec warriors attack Spanish conquistadors in the image on the left. A member of Moctezuma's army is shown below.

Duran, Diego (16th century), Codex Duran: Pedro de Alverado (c.1485-1541).

Spain's Exploration of the Americas

The Spanish completed their centuries-long quest to drive the Moors from the Iberian Peninsula in 1492, and now they were eager to explore and claim new territories. Late in that year, Queen Isabella and King Ferdinand sent Columbus on a voyage to the Indies. He returned to Spain with the exciting news of a new land.

The centuries of war with the Moors shaped Spanish culture. Spaniards admired the warriors who fought for glory and for their faith. The lands that Columbus discovered represented a new opportunity. The Americas were a place where the Spanish **conquistadors**, or conquerors, could seek glory for themselves, for Spain, and for their God, while winning great fortunes.

The Spanish set out to conquer the Americas. In the decades after Columbus's first voyage, conquistadors gained control of many islands in the Caribbean. They also conquered present-day Mexico, Central America, and parts of South America.

As you will discover in the next section, the Spanish also conquered two great civilizations. Some native groups put up resistance for a while. In general, however, the native people of the Americas were overwhelmed by the conquistadors' superior weapons. In addition, thousands of Native Americans died from diseases carried by the Spanish. Some peoples, such as the Taíno, disappeared entirely.

✓ **Reading Check** **What effect did the long struggle with the Moors have on the Spanish people?**

The Spanish Conquest of Mexico

In the sixteenth century, central Mexico was home to the great Aztec (AZ tek) empire. Its capital was Tenochtitlán (teh nawch tee TLAN), where the powerful Moctezuma (mahk tih ZOO muh) ruled. Moctezuma's empire was vast, and it included many conquered peoples.

In 1519, the conquistador Hernán Cortés (hur NAHN kohr TEZ) arrived in Mexico. Drawn by rumors of a wealthy Aztec empire, he journeyed to Tenochtitlán. With him traveled a force of several hundred soldiers. According to one legend, Moctezuma welcomed the Spanish because he feared that Cortés was a god named Quetzalcóatl (ket sahl koh AHT el). Aztec religious beliefs held that Quetzalcóatl, a pale-skinned god, would one day return to Mexico. Soon, however, the Aztec grew tired and suspicious of their visitors. Aztec soldiers surrounded Cortés and his men. The Spaniards fought their way out of the city.

Then Cortés gathered a large army, including reinforcements from Spain and thousands of Native Americans who resented Aztec rule. Cortés's army surrounded the city in a long siege. A **siege** is the surrounding and blockading of a town by an army. The battle ended in 1521 with Tenochtitlán in ruins. The Aztec empire that had controlled much of Mexico was utterly defeated.

✓ **Reading Check** Why did Moctezuma first welcome Cortés and his soldiers?

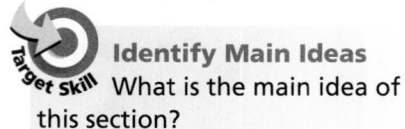

Identify Main Ideas
What is the main idea of this section?

Island City
In the sixteenth century, the city of Tenochtitlán was the capital of the great Aztec empire. Notice that passageways cross the water to connect the city to the mainland. Conclude *When Cortés attacked, how did the city's location help the Aztecs? What advantage did the water provide for Cortés and his men?*

The Spanish Conquest of Peru

The story of Cortés's success inspired many conquistadors. Among them was Francisco Pizarro (frahn SEES koh pea SAHR oh). Pizarro's goal was the conquest of the great Incan empire of present-day Peru. Like the Aztec, the Inca (ING kuh) were a great civilization with vast treasures of gold.

Pizarro arrived in Peru in 1532. The Incan empire at this time had been weakened by a **civil war**, a war between people of the same country. Pizarro managed to lead a small force of under 200 soldiers into the heart of Peru. The Inca king Atahualpa (ah tuh WAHL puh) watched the Spaniards closely. However, he made the mistake of visiting the Spaniards' camp, where Pizarro captured him. Although the Spanish force was small, its guns and horses overwhelmed Atahualpa's much larger army. The Incan soldiers had only spears and small weapons.

Pizarro forced the Inca to pay a ransom, a large sum of money, for the release of their king. Pizarro demanded that the Inca fill a room with gold if they wanted their king back alive. The Inca paid the ransom, but Pizarro had Atahualpa killed anyway. Now leaderless, the Inca were unable to mount an effective resistance against the conquest of their once-great empire. Spain added Peru to its list of conquests in the Americas.

✓ **Reading Check** What inspired Francisco Pizarro's interest in Peru?

The Incan civilization had vast treasures of gold. Some of the gold was sculpted, such as this gold figurine.

 ## Section 1 Assessment

Key Terms
Review the key terms at the beginning of this section.
Use each term in a sentence that explains its meaning.

Target Reading Skill
What are the three main ideas of Section 1?

Comprehension and Critical Thinking
1. (a) Explain Why was the year 1492 so important in Spanish history?

(b) Synthesize Information How did the struggle against the Moors prepare the Spanish for conquest in the Americas?

2. (a) Recall Who joined Cortés in his siege of Tenochtitlán?

(b) Draw Inferences Why do you think these people supported Cortés's attack of Tenochtitlán?

3. (a) Identify What conditions in the Inca empire favored Pizarro's conquest?

(b) Summarize How was Pizarro able to overcome the larger Incan force?

Writing Activity
Suppose that you are a Native American living in Central or South America in the 1500s. Write a brief summary of the history of your region from the point of view of Native American people.

For: An activity on Spanish conquests in the Americas
Visit: PHSchool.com
Web Code: mud-1710

Colonies in Middle and South America

Prepare to Read

Objectives

In this section you will
1. Learn how Spain and Portugal colonized the Americas and ruled their colonies.
2. Understand the economic systems of the Spanish colonies.

Taking Notes

As you read this section, look for information about European colonization of the Americas. Copy the graphic organizer below, and record your findings in it.

Spanish Colonization in the Americas		
Type of Government	Type of Economic System	Culture
• • •	• • •	• • •

Target Reading Skill

Identify Supporting Details The main idea of a paragraph or section is supported by details that give further information about it. These details may give examples or reasons to explain the main idea. As you read, look for details that support the main idea of each section.

Key Terms

- **viceroy** (VYS roy) *n.* a governor of a country or colony who rules as the representative of a king or queen
- **plantation** (plan TAY shun) *n.* a large estate or farm
- **encomienda** (en koh mee EN dah) *n.* a grant of Native American laborers to a Spanish colonist by the king
- **Columbian Exchange** (kuh LUM bee un eks CHAYNJ) *n.* the movement of plants and animals between the Western and Eastern hemispheres after the voyages of Columbus.

Native American gods, such as Quetzalcóatl, sometimes merged with Christian saints in religious art.

Following the conquest of the Americas, Catholic monks and priests spread out across Spain's new empire. They sought to convert the Native Americans to the Christian faith. They undertook this conversion process with great enthusiasm and enjoyed great success. One man named Toribio de Benevente (toh ree BEE oh duh bay nay VEN teh) claimed to have brought 300,000 Native Americans into the faith.

Although Europeans taught the Native Americans Christianity, the faith practiced by these new converts had its own special character. It blended Christian ideas with the people's traditions. For example, in religious art, Native American gods such as Quetzalcóatl merged with Christian saints. Stones from old Native American temples were placed in new Christian churches. Old native ceremonial sites became Christian holy places. This blend of Spanish Christianity and Native American religion formed part of the new culture of the Spanish colonies of the Americas.

Spain and Portugal's American Colonies

As you have read, the Spanish succeeded in conquering a large portion of the Americas in the 1500s. They eventually controlled territory that stretched from southern South America northward into the present-day United States. In some places, Native Americans, such as the Maya in Mexico and Central America, resisted the invasion. Spain, however, eventually won control of the Mayan region.

The Portuguese Colonies In South America, Brazil escaped Spanish control. Recall from Chapter 16 that Portugal's Pedro Alvarez Cabral had landed in 1500. Portugal based its claim to Brazil on this event. Eventually, Portugal established a colony in Brazil. However, the area lacked the gold and other rich treasures of Mexico and Peru, and it had no major cities. Fortunately, the land was rich in valuable brazilwood, a dense and colorful wood. Colonists sent many shiploads of this wood to Portugal. Over time, Portuguese settlements spread along the coast of Brazil.

Links to Math

Brazilwood In 1506, Portugal's king charged a group of Portuguese citizens 4,000 ducats for the right to go to Brazil and harvest its brazilwood. The land produced 20,000 units of wood. Each unit brought a profit of 2.5 ducats.

Go Online
PHSchool.com Use Web Code **mup-0841** for an interactivity on the Columbian Exchange.

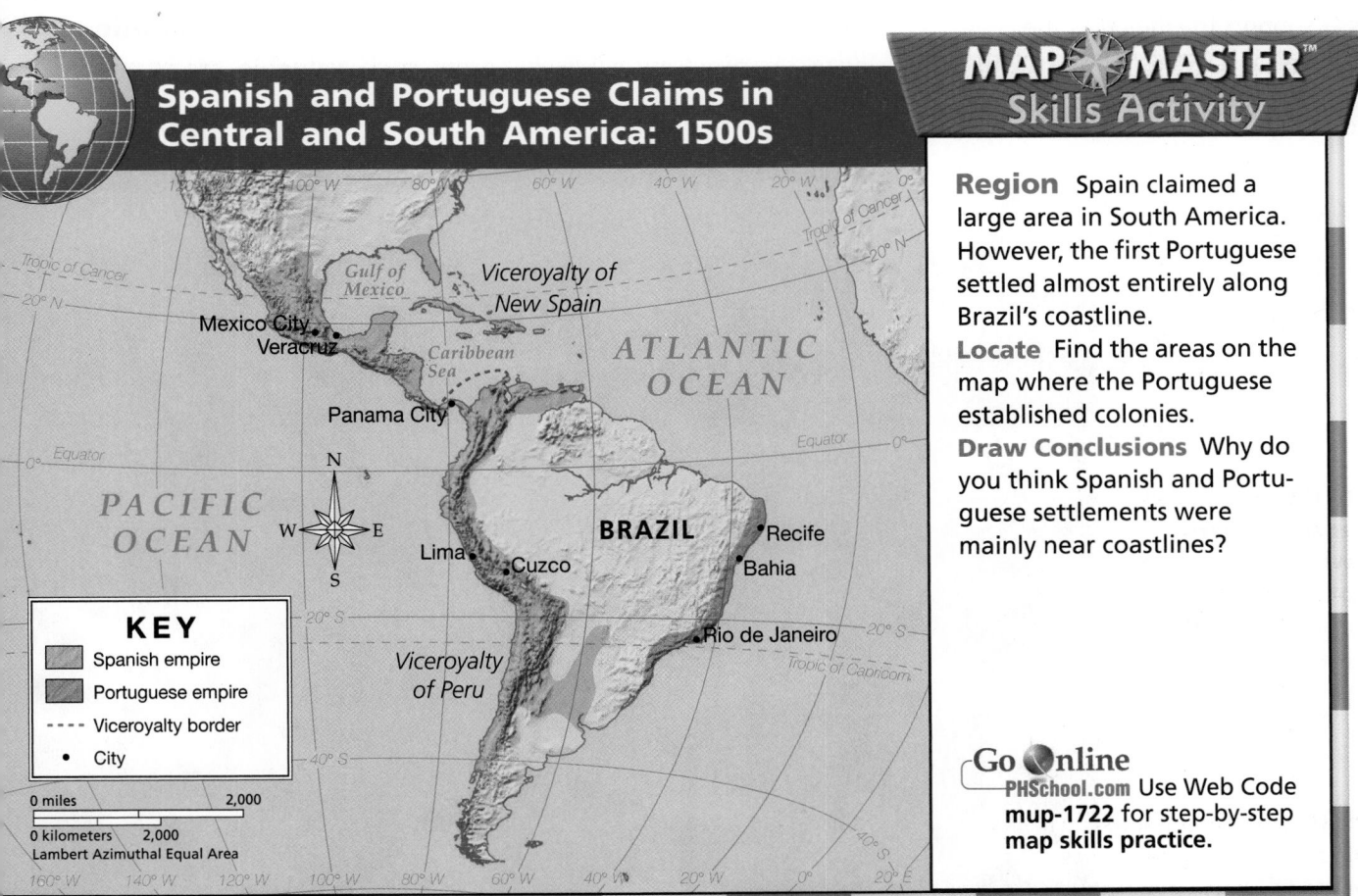

Spanish and Portuguese Claims in Central and South America: 1500s

- Viceroyalty of New Spain
- Mexico City
- Veracruz
- Gulf of Mexico
- Caribbean Sea
- Panama City
- ATLANTIC OCEAN
- PACIFIC OCEAN
- BRAZIL
- Lima
- Cuzco
- Recife
- Bahia
- Rio de Janeiro
- Viceroyalty of Peru
- Equator
- Tropic of Cancer
- Tropic of Capricorn

KEY
- Spanish empire
- Portuguese empire
- Viceroyalty border
- City

0 miles 2,000
0 kilometers 2,000
Lambert Azimuthal Equal Area

MAP MASTER Skills Activity

Region Spain claimed a large area in South America. However, the first Portuguese settled almost entirely along Brazil's coastline.

Locate Find the areas on the map where the Portuguese established colonies.

Draw Conclusions Why do you think Spanish and Portuguese settlements were mainly near coastlines?

Go Online
PHSchool.com Use Web Code **mup-1722** for step-by-step map skills practice.

Bartolomé de las Casas

Bartolomé de las Casas (bahr toh loh MAY day lahs KAS us) was a priest in the Spanish colonies in the Americas. He spoke out sharply against the Spanish treatment of the Native Americans. In particular, he believed that it was wrong to force Native Americans to work for the Spanish. At first he suggested that Native Americans be replaced by African slaves. Later, however, he spoke out against all slavery.

Identify Supporting Details

What details in this section support the idea that the Catholic Church played a large role in governing the Spanish colonies?

The Spanish Colonies To govern the Americas, Spain divided its lands into different units, called viceroyalties. Each viceroyalty was ruled by an official called a viceroy. A **viceroy** is a person who rules a colony in the name of the king or queen. Officials in Spain watched over the viceroys.

The Catholic Church also played a large role in governing the Spanish colonies. Although its main purpose for being in the Americas was to convert Native Americans to Christianity, the Church soon assumed a larger role. The clergy led the way in building Spanish-style settlements in the colonies. In many cases, the clergy acted as a sort of local government. Members of the clergy also intervened when they thought that the Spanish were abusing Native Americans.

Although the clergy forced Native Americans to adopt Spanish ways as well as beliefs, the priests also made it possible for some blending of the Native American and Spanish cultures.

✓ **Reading Check** How did the Spanish govern the people in the Americas?

The Economy of the Colonies

The new colonies produced great wealth for Spain. Shiploads of gold, silver, and other treasure crossed the ocean. **Plantations**—large farming enterprises—grew such valuable crops as sugar cane.

In this painting, enslaved Africans work as the owners of the sugar cane plantation ride away from the main house.

The Spanish needed workers to mine the gold and work the land. For their work, the Spanish used enslaved Africans. The Spanish brought these slaves to the Americas by the thousands. The Spanish encomienda system provided another source of labor. An **encomienda** was a document that gave a Spaniard the right to control a group of Native Americans. A Spaniard was supposed to care for the Native Americans under his control. In reality, conditions were often terrible for the Native Americans. The encomienda system faded as Native American populations were reduced by disease.

The economies of the American colonies and the Old World continents all benefited from the **Columbian Exchange,** or the movement of plants and animals between the Western and Eastern Hemispheres after the voyages of Columbus. Europeans brought crops and livestock such as wheat and cows to the Americas. Meanwhile, American crops took root in Europe, Africa, and Asia.

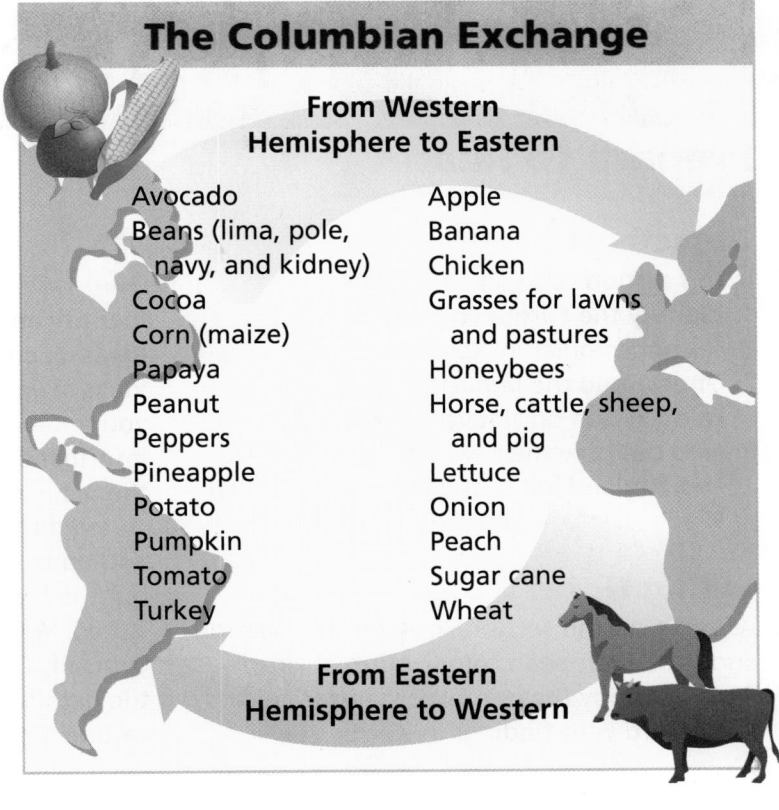

The Columbian Exchange

From Western Hemisphere to Eastern

Avocado	Apple
Beans (lima, pole, navy, and kidney)	Banana
	Chicken
Cocoa	Grasses for lawns and pastures
Corn (maize)	
Papaya	Honeybees
Peanut	Horse, cattle, sheep, and pig
Peppers	
Pineapple	Lettuce
Potato	Onion
Pumpkin	Peach
Tomato	Sugar cane
Turkey	Wheat

From Eastern Hemisphere to Western

 **Reading Check** **Why did the encomienda system end?**

Section 2 Assessment

Key Terms
Review the key terms at the beginning of this section. Use each term in a sentence that explains its meaning.

Target Reading Skill
List three details that support the main idea of the text following the heading The Spanish Colonies.

Comprehension and Critical Thinking
1. (a) Recall What European country claimed the territory of Brazil?
(b) Compare and Contrast How was the Portuguese colony in the Americas similar to and different from Spanish colonies?
2. (a) Explain What role did the Catholic Church play in the Spanish colonies?
(b) Synthesize Information How did the clergy affect the culture of the Native Americans?
3. (a) Define What was the encomienda system?
(b) Draw Inferences From your knowledge of the encomienda system, what can you infer about Spanish attitudes toward Native Americans?

Writing Activity
You are a newspaper reporter in the Spanish colonies. Write a report about the activities of Bartolomé de las Casas. Explain his complaints and relate proposed solutions.

For: An activity on Spanish conquests in the Americas
Visit: PHSchool.com
Web Code: mud-1720

Prepare to Read

Objectives

In this section you will

1. Identify the European countries that sought colonies in North America.
2. Understand the impact of European colonization on Native Americans.
3. Find out how the rivalry between France and England led to the French and Indian War.

Taking Notes

As you read this section, look for information about the European colonization of North America. Copy the graphic organizer below, and record your findings in it.

> I. Europeans in North America
>   A. Dutch Colonies
>   B.
>   C.
> II. European colonies affect Native Americans
>   A. Many Native Americans die from exposure to disease carried by the Europeans
>   B.

Target Reading Skill

Identify Implied Main Ideas Identifying main ideas as you read can help you remember important information. Sometimes the main ideas are not stated directly. The details add up to a main idea, but the idea itself is not stated. You must state it yourself. Carefully read the details of each section. Then state the main idea of each section.

Key Terms

- **emigrate** (EM ih grayt), *v.* to leave one country or region to settle in another
- **ally** (AL eye), *n.* a country or group that is united with another for a common purpose

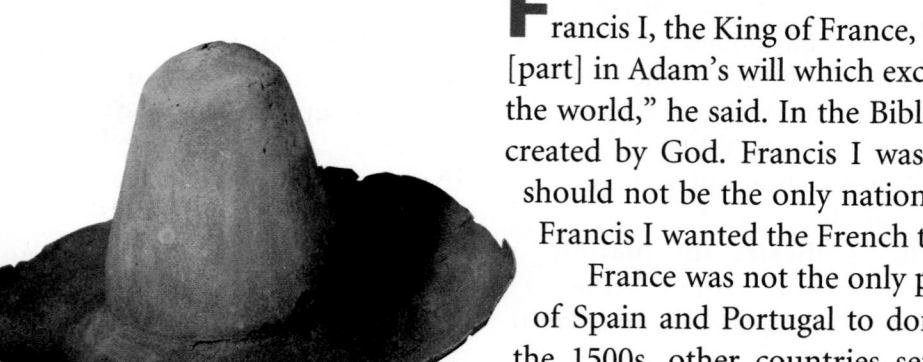

A pilgrim's hat from 1620

Francis I, the King of France, was upset. "I would like to see the [part] in Adam's will which excludes France from the division of the world," he said. In the Bible, Adam is the first human being created by God. Francis I was saying that Spain and Portugal should not be the only nations allowed to claim the Americas. Francis I wanted the French to gain territory as well.

France was not the only power there to challenge the right of Spain and Portugal to dominate the Americas. Starting in the 1500s, other countries sent explorers and settlers by the thousands across the Atlantic. Competition for North American colonies was fierce and sometimes bloody. Also fierce and bloody were the conflicts that colonists had with the Native Americans who had lived on the land before the Europeans arrived.

European Countries Seek Colonies in North America

In the 1600s, France, England, and the Netherlands tried to join Spain and Portugal in establishing colonies in the Americas.

The Dutch Colonies The Dutch established colonies in the Caribbean to take advantage of the trade in sugar cane, a product highly valued in Europe. They also established a colony on the North American Continent, which they named New Netherland. However, the English seized this colony in 1664 and renamed it New York.

The French in Canada Soon after Columbus's discovery of a new land, the French began crossing the Atlantic to fish for cod off the Canadian coast. In 1608, Samuel de Champlain (SAM yoo ul duh sham PLAYN) established the first French settlement in Quebec. As they had in South America, Catholic priests and monks soon followed, converting Native Americans and making their way farther into the Canadian interior. Local Native Americans helped the French trade in furs. The fur trade led to exploration and to the claiming of land from the Great Lakes down the Mississippi to Louisiana.

The British in North America The British were successful colonists. The first British settle-ment, established in 1607, was in Jamestown, Virginia. Despite early perils of disease and starvation, the settlement finally flourished when the Native Americans taught settlers to grow tobacco.

In 1620, other English settlers—the Pilgrims—traveled to the northeastern coast and established the Plymouth colony. Unlike most colonists, these people came seeking religious freedom rather than profit. Because of the success of that small settlement, more and more British emigrated to northern America. To **emigrate** is to leave one's country to settle in another. The British eventually established a string of colonies along North America's East Coast.

✓ Reading Check   **Which five European countries established colonies in the Americas?**

The Mayflower Compact
By signing the Mayflower Compact, the Pilgrims pledged their obedience to the laws and government of their new colony. **Sequence** *When did the Pilgrims establish the Plymouth colony?*

The Effect of European Colonization on Native Americans

When Europeans arrived in North America, Native American groups lived throughout the land. For these people, the arrival of colonists brought great misfortune. European diseases hit these groups hard, just as they had the native people of South and Central America. Disease weakened or killed many native people. Those who survived faced the loss of their lands to the growing numbers of European colonists. Because the English colonies along the East Coast were growing the most rapidly, the Native Americans in this area faced the greatest problems.

In some cases, Native Americans tried to fight the colonists and slow the spread of their settlements. As colonists claimed more land, Native Americans resisted their advances. Bitter fighting resulted. Although they won some battles, Native Americans generally lost the wars. Year by year, group by group, they were steadily pushed westward as the British colonies expanded. This pattern of Native American defeat and removal would be repeated often as the British colonized and settled North America.

Target Skill

Identify Implied Main Ideas

In one sentence, state the main idea that this section details.

This reenactment of the first Thanksgiving in 1971 at Plymouth Plantation brought together descendants of Pilgrims and Native Americans who took part in the first Thanksgiving 350 years ago.

The French and Indian War As you have read, the English and the French were already rivals in India and Europe. They also regarded each other as rivals in the new lands. In 1754, they went to war in North America. This part of the conflict between the French and the English is known as the French and Indian War because the French were allies with several Native American groups. An **ally** is a person or group that joins with another to reach a common goal. The Native Americans had long served as guides for French fur traders and had become friendly with them. However, the French were defeated in the war and were eventually driven from most of North America.

Native American Legacy in America The Native American way of life contributed to the new culture that was developing in the new country. Native Americans helped both the Pilgrims and the settlers of Jamestown survive by teaching them how to grow crops. Native American trails formed the highways for westward movement. Hundreds of Native American names—of rivers, states, cities, and mountains—are preserved across the North American continent.

✓ **Reading Check** **Why did the Native Americans become allies of the French during the French and Indian War?**

Links to

Science

Herbal Medicine
European settlers brought their own plants to use as medicine to North America, but they also learned herbal remedies from Native Americans. For example, in the 1700s, the bark of a witch hazel plant was used by the Mohawks to treat bruised eyes. Other Native American groups used the boiled leaves of the witch hazel plant as a liniment for aching legs.

Section 3 Assessment

Key Terms
Review the key terms at the beginning of this section. Use each term in a sentence that explains its meaning.

Target Reading Skill
State the main ideas of this section.

Comprehension and Critical Thinking
1. (a) List What countries besides Spain and Portugal sought colonies in North America?
(b) Compare and Contrast How did the French and English colonies differ?

2. (a) Identify Name a place other than North America where England and France competed for influence and power.
(b) Draw Inferences What can you infer about the power of England and France in Europe, based on the outcome of their colonizing competition?
3. (a) Explain What was the general pattern of interaction between the English colonists and the Native Americans?
(b) Identify Point of View How do you think the English colonists viewed the misfortune suffered by the Native Americans in the years after colonization?

Writing Activity
You are an English settler on the East Coast of North America. Write a letter to relatives in England, describing your endeavor. Be sure to discuss the relationship of your colony with the Native Americans who live in the area.

For: An activity on Spanish conquests in the Americas
Visit: PHSchool.com
Web Code: mud-1730

Focus On
Plymouth Colony

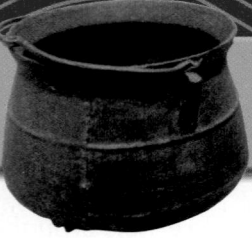

Think about what life would be like if you and your family had to grow your own food, sew your own clothes, and stay warm without power. The climate is frigidly cold in winter and hot and humid in summer. You have only simple tools with which to build your houses and grow your food. Life in Plymouth Colony in the early 1600s was hard work. Yet the men and women who lived there were able to create a thriving village. Historians have been able to learn much about what colonists' lives were like through the letters, official documents, and artifacts that have survived from that time.

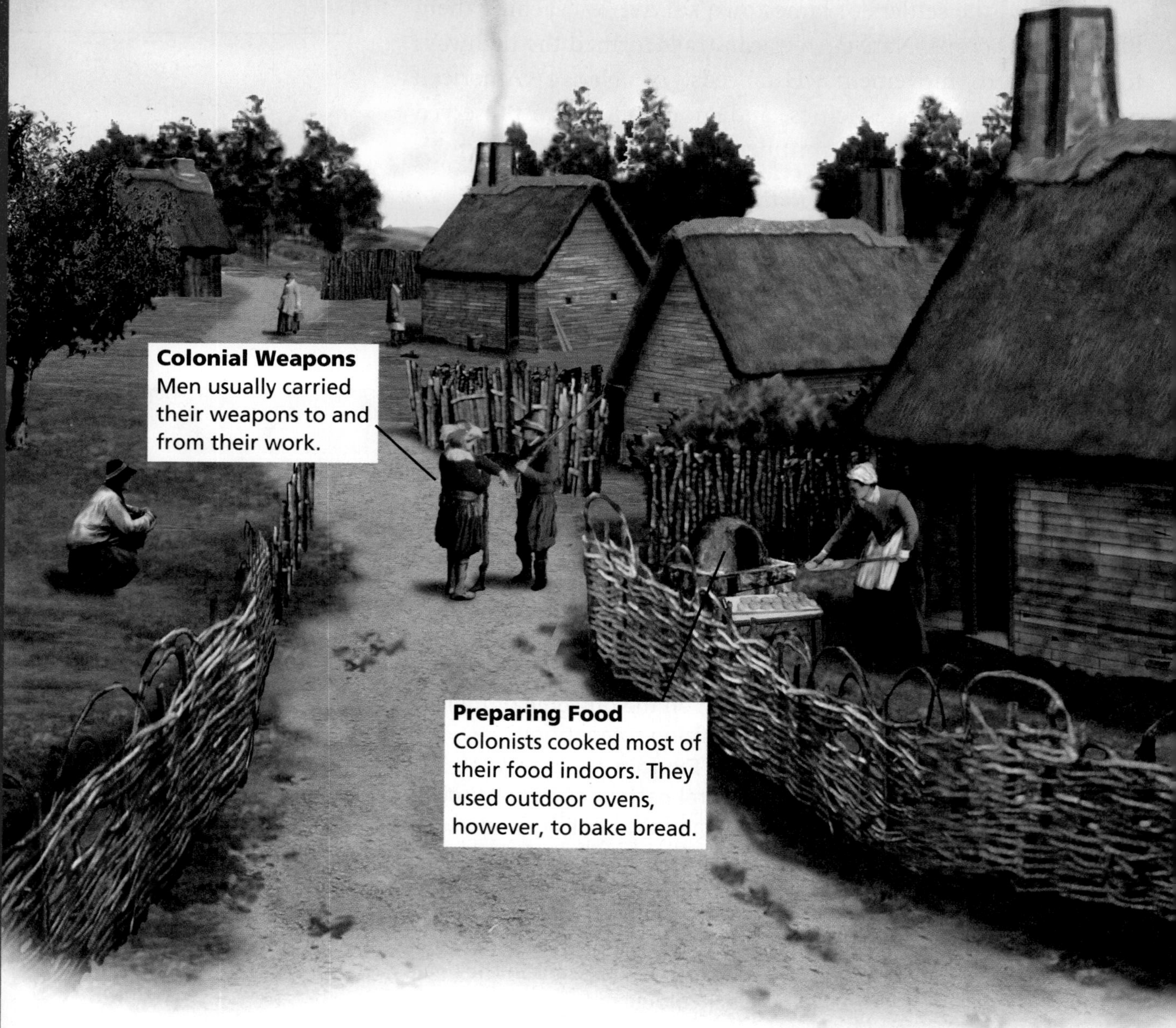

Colonial Weapons
Men usually carried their weapons to and from their work.
Preparing Food
Colonists cooked most of their food indoors. They used outdoor ovens, however, to bake bread.

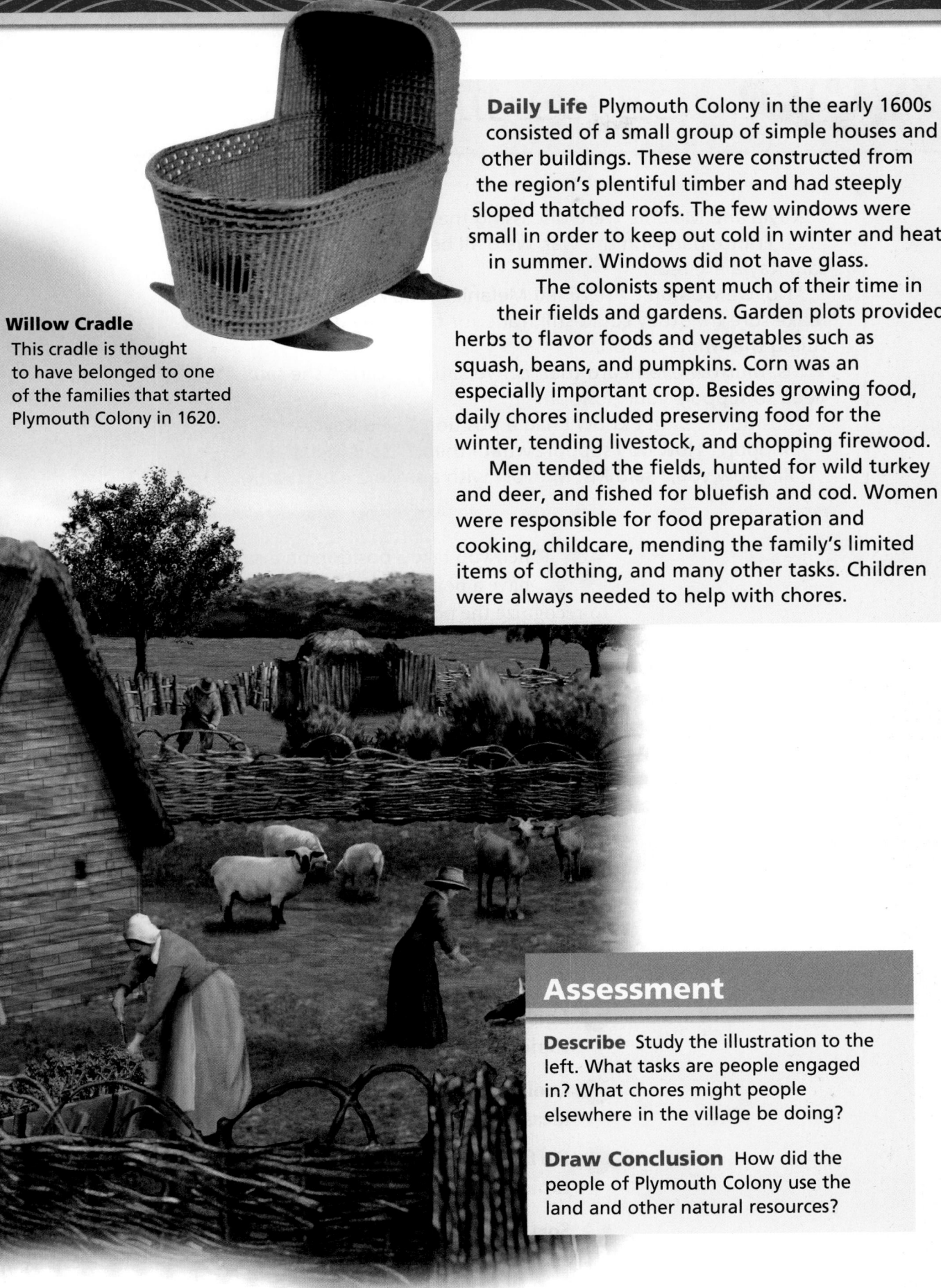

Willow Cradle
This cradle is thought to have belonged to one of the families that started Plymouth Colony in 1620.

Daily Life Plymouth Colony in the early 1600s consisted of a small group of simple houses and other buildings. These were constructed from the region's plentiful timber and had steeply sloped thatched roofs. The few windows were small in order to keep out cold in winter and heat in summer. Windows did not have glass.

The colonists spent much of their time in their fields and gardens. Garden plots provided herbs to flavor foods and vegetables such as squash, beans, and pumpkins. Corn was an especially important crop. Besides growing food, daily chores included preserving food for the winter, tending livestock, and chopping firewood.

Men tended the fields, hunted for wild turkey and deer, and fished for bluefish and cod. Women were responsible for food preparation and cooking, childcare, mending the family's limited items of clothing, and many other tasks. Children were always needed to help with chores.

Assessment

Describe Study the illustration to the left. What tasks are people engaged in? What chores might people elsewhere in the village be doing?

Draw Conclusion How did the people of Plymouth Colony use the land and other natural resources?

Kayla and Melanie were discussing the French and Indian War. "If France had won the war, we'd all be speaking French today," said Kayla excitedly.

"No, we wouldn't," rejoined Melanie. "The French just wanted to make sure that they could still trade for furs. They didn't care about ruling the whole nation."

Ms. Murrow overheard their conversation. "Girls," she said, "You need to support your position."

"Position? I didn't know I had a position," said Kayla.

"Support? How do I support what I think?" said Melanie.

"I'll show you," said Ms. Murrow with a smile.

When you take a position on a subject or a question, you have a point of view or attitude about it. It is important to recognize the positions you have on various topics. It is just as important to be able to support, or back up, your position with solid arguments, information, and authoritative sources.

©Smithsonian American Art Museum, Washington, DC/Art Resource, NY

Learn the Skill

Use these steps to learn how to support your position.

1. **Look at the information you already know about your topic.** Write your ideas on a sheet of paper.

2. **Look at arguments that oppose your position.** Write these ideas next to those you've already written.

3. **Do further research on the subject. Learn more about the topic.** Take notes on the subject.

4. **Sort facts from opinions.** Facts can be proven true, whereas opinions cannot be proven true.

If the Inca hadn't just had a civil war, the Spanish invasion could not have happened. The Inca were an old, proud civilization. They were wonderful architects and astronomers. Indeed, historian Frank Wright says of them, "The Inca were ahead of their counterparts in Europe in their scientific knowledge." The Spanish invaders, by contrast, were just adventurers, out to become rich. The Spanish didn't have superior technology. I think that their behavior toward the Inca was deplorable, and they didn't deserve to rule the country. The civil war drew the Inca's attention away from the threat of invasion. The Spanish used trickery to capture the Incan king. If he had not been captured, the Inca would never have been overrun.

Practice the Skill

Read the above paragraph. Identify the position taken in the paragraph. Then reread the paragraph, taking note of the following:

1. What do you already know about this topic that would help you agree or disagree with the author's premise?

2. Identify the counterarguments to the claims made in the article. For example, what is the counterargument to the statement, "The Spanish didn't have superior technology?"

3. Point to a sentence that shows that the author did some additional research on the subject.

4. Identify two words that indicate that the author's opinion on the subject, rather than factual information, is being offered. Name one example of factual information, something that can be verified.

Apply the Skill

Choose another student as a partner. One partner should prepare arguments for the following statement; the other partner should prepare arguments against the statement. "The *encomienda* system was an important way of developing the economic growth of the Spanish colonies." Take turns presenting your arguments in class.

Africa and the Atlantic Slave Trade

Prepare to Read

Objectives

In this section you will

1. Understand that the slave trade that began with the exploration of Africa and the colonization of South America and Central America also spread to North America.
2. Discover what the triangular trade was and how it expanded with the growth of the European colonization of North America.

Taking Notes

As you read this section, look for information about the growth of slavery in the Americas. Copy the graphic organizer below, and record your findings in it.

Target Reading Skill

Identify Main Ideas To remember information, good readers identify main ideas as they read. The most important point in a paragraph or section is the main idea. As you read, identify the main idea stated in each section.

Key Terms

- **enslaved** (en SLAYVD), *v.* made into a slave and treated as property
- **import** (im PAWRT), *v.* to bring in goods from a foreign country

Slavery in the Americas	
South America	**North America**
• Developed when population of Native Americans declined •	• •

Leg shackles worn by enslaved Africans

The journey of the enslaved African was a living nightmare. One day he or she was living as a free person in an African village. The next, he or she was captured by slave traders, placed in chains, and forced to march for days. At the end of the march was the slave trading fort and a dungeon where captured Africans might sit for weeks or months. Eventually, people would be brought from the dungeon and then loaded onto a ship. A couple of months later, those who survived the voyage would arrive in the Americas. This destination was the end of the journey—but the beginning of a lifetime of slavery.

This bitter story is one that could have been told by millions of Africans from the 1500s to the 1800s. During those centuries, trade in human beings from Africa thrived. This trade helped enrich traders in Europe, Africa, and the Americas. It provided much of the labor that built European colonies in the Americas. It also changed the cultures of the Americas, as Africans brought with them their traditions and values, which helped them endure enslavement.

Slavery in the Americas

In Chapter 16, you read about the Portuguese explorations under the leadership of Prince Henry the Navigator. In the 1400s, Portugal had explored the western coast of Africa. During that time, Portugal began capturing and trading enslaved human beings in Africa. **Enslaved** means held as the property of another person and to have no individual rights.

You have also read how the Spanish used enslaved Africans in their American colonies. The Spanish turned to this source of labor as vast numbers of Native Americans died from European diseases for which they had no immunity. The Portuguese also imported large numbers of enslaved Africans to Brazil. To **import** means to bring in products—in this case, people—from a foreign country.

The growing English colonies in North America also relied on enslaved Africans. This dependence on slaves was especially true in the southern regions, where climate and soil conditions favored crops such as tobacco and sugar. The raising of these crops required cheap labor if profits were to be made.

European colonists preferred enslaved Africans to other sources of labor. Africans came from very different cultures and were usually not Christian. This may have made it easier for the colonists to excuse their enslavement of human beings.

✓ **Reading Check** **Which European country began the European trade in African slaves?**

Learn what the African slave trade was like.

Identify Main Ideas Look at the third paragraph on this page. Which sentence represents the main idea of this paragraph?

Slavery
This drawing of a tobacco plantation was made by a European who lived at the time of slavery. **Analyze Images** *What attitude do you think the artist had about slavery?*

A TOBACCO PLANTATION

The Triangular Trade

Go Online
PHSchool.com Use Web Code
mup-0842 for an interactivity
on the triangular trade.

The trade in enslaved Africans was part of a larger trade pattern called the triangular trade, so called because it had three "sides." The first corner of the triangle was in Europe, where ships were loaded with manufactured goods. These goods were shipped to Africa, the second point on the triangle. Here Europeans traded the manufactured goods for enslaved Africans. Slave traders then sent the slaves to the Americas, the third point of the triangle. In the Americas, enslaved Africans were traded for raw materials, which were then shipped back to Europe for manufacturing, completing the triangle.

The journey of enslaved Africans across the Atlantic Ocean was known as the Middle Passage. Wrote one British critic, "Never can so much misery be found condensed in so small a place as in a slave ship during the Middle Passage." The ships were extremely crowded. Death rates on the voyage may have averaged as much as 20 percent.

Slavery became critical to the economic stability of several American colonies. In the 1600s and 1700s, it formed an important part of trade between Europe and the American colonies.

The door in the center of this Gorée Island "slave house" was sometimes called "the door of no return" because slaves had to pass through it to go to the slave ships.

✓ Reading Check   **What was the triangular trade?**

Section 4 Assessment

Key Terms

Review the key terms at the beginning of this section. Use each term in a sentence that explains its meaning.

 Target Reading Skill

Identify the main idea of the paragraphs under each heading in this section.

Comprehension and Critical Thinking

1. (a) Identify In which century did Europeans begin trading in African slaves?

(b) Identify Cause and Effect What event helped lead the Spanish turn to enslaved labor in their American colonies?

2. (a) Identify In what part of the English colonies was slavery most common?

(b) Draw Inferences Why do you think slavery was less common in the other colonies?

3. (a) Define What was the Middle Passage?

(b) Summarize Why did the Spanish turn to enslaved Africans as a source of labor for their American colonies?

Writing Activity

You are an enslaved African, waiting for shipment to the Americas from the dungeon of a coastal African trading fort. Write a journal entry about your feelings. Be sure to discuss what has happened to you and your thoughts about what the future may hold.

For: An activity on Spanish conquests in the Americas
Visit: PHSchool.com
Web Code: mud-1740

17 Review and Assessment

◆ Chapter Summary

Section 1: Conquest in the Americas

Aztec warriors

- The Spanish conquered large areas in the Americas because the Native Americans had inferior weapons and many died from diseases carried by the Spanish.
- Hernán Cortés led his Spanish soldiers and some Native Americans in the conquest of the Aztec empire in present-day Mexico.
- Francisco Pizarro led the Spanish conquest of the Incan Empire in present-day Peru.

Section 2: Colonies in Middle and South America

Spanish plantation

- The Spanish and the Portuguese colonized South America and southern portions of North America.
- Spanish colonies relied on the labor of Native Americans and some enslaved Africans.
- The Catholic Church played a role in governing the colonies.

Section 3: Colonies in North America

Pilgrim hat

- European powers such as England, France, and the Netherlands sought colonies in North America.
- The rivalry between the French and the English resulted in the French and Indian War, which the English won.
- Native American groups were forced from their land by the advance of colonies in North America.

Section 4: Africa and the Atlantic Slave Trade

Tobacco plantation

- Huge numbers of Africans were shipped to English, Spanish, and Portuguese colonies in the Americas.
- The triangular trade in slaves was a central part of colonial and European trade.
- Africans suffered unspeakable horrors in their journey from their homes to lives of slavery in the Americas.

◆ Key Terms

Select the proper term to complete the sentence.

1. Africans were captured in their villages and _____.
2. The _____ ruled in the name of the Spanish king or queen.
3. The deaths of large numbers of Native Americans led the Spanish to _____ enslaved Africans.
4. Cortés finally conquered Tenochtitlán after a long _____.
5. A Spanish _____ wanted to earn glory for himself, his country, and his god.
6. In their war with the British, the French had an _____ in friendly Native American groups.
7. Operating a _____ required large numbers of workers.

A conquistador
B siege
C viceroy
D plantation
E ally
F enslaved
G import

◆ Comprehension and Critical Thinking

8. (a) Explain Why were many Native Americans vulnerable to European diseases?
(b) Cause and Effect What effect did disease have on many Native American groups after the arrival of the Spanish?

9. (a) Identify What important event had occurred in the Inca empire around the time of Pizarro's arrival?
(b) Cause and Effect Why might this event have made it easier for Pizarro to conquer the Inca?

10. (a) Identify What factors helped bring an end to the encomienda system?
(b) Identify Point of View Why did the Catholic missionaries resist the encomienda system?
(c) Draw Conclusions How did the end of the encomienda system lead to the use of slavery in the Spanish colonies?

11. (a) Recall In what part of North America did the English have their colonies?
(b) Cause and Effect Name two consequences of the European invasion for the Native Americans.

12. (a) Identify What were the three legs of the triangular trade?

13. (b) Analyze Information What role did the slave trade play in the colonial trading system?

14. (a) Explain What was the main use of enslaved Africans in the English colonies?
(b) Draw Conclusions Why do you think enslaved Africans were packed so tightly into ships on the Middle Passage?

◆ Skills Practice

Supporting a Position In the Skills Activity, you learned how to support your position. Review the steps you followed to learn this skill. Then reread the part of Section 3 called The Effect of European Colonization on Native Americans. Identify and support your position on Native Americans and colonization.

◆ Writing Activity: Geography

Using the library or the Internet, research the term Columbian Exchange. Write a brief report on how the European arrival in the Americas not only changed life for Native Americans but also for Europeans. Include specific examples of items that were "exchanged" as a part of the Columbian Exchange.

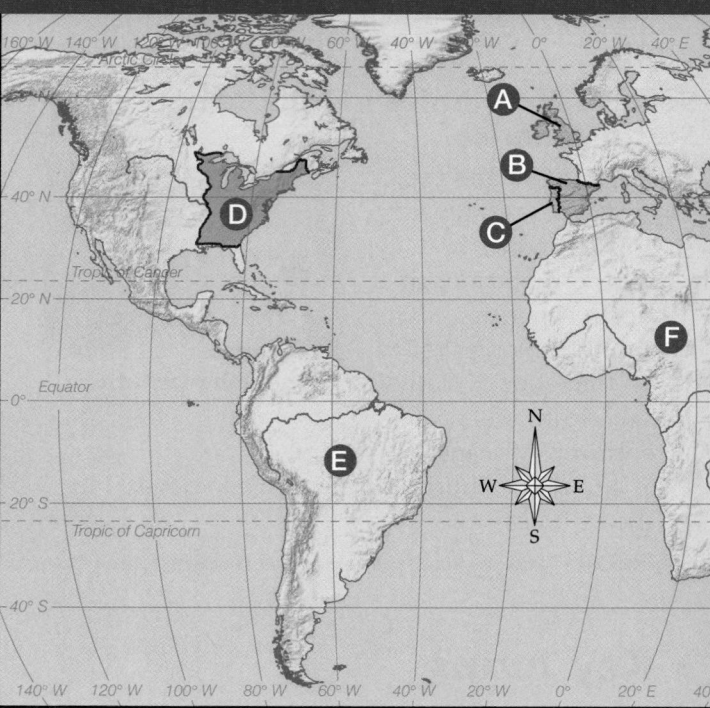

MAP★MASTER™
Skills Activity

Europe, Africa, and the Americas About 1800

Place Location For each place listed below, write the letter from the map that shows its location.

1. South America
2. Africa
3. Britain
4. Spain
5. Portugal
6. United States

Go Online
PHSchool.com Use Web Code **mup-1702** for step-by-step **map skills practice**.

Standardized Test Prep

Test-Taking Tips

Some questions on standardized tests ask you to find main ideas. Read the paragraph below. Then follow the tips to answer the sample question.

> Jean-Baptiste Point du Sable, the founder of Chicago, was born in the French colony of Haiti. His mother was black, and his father was a white Frenchman. Around 1779, he settled at the future site of Chicago with his Native American wife, Kittihawa. Point du Sable's life shows that the colonial Americas were a meeting place of different ethnic groups.

TIP As you read the paragraph, try to identify its main ideas, or most important points.

Pick the letter that best answers the question.
This paragraph shows that—

A colonial Americans moved frequently.

B ethnic groups have different customs.

C the colonial Americas were ethnically mixed.

D Chicago was a Haitian colony.

TIP Look for a key word that connects to the paragraph. In this case, the key word is *ethnic.*

Think It Through Start with the main idea, that Point du Sable's life shows how different ethnic groups mixed in the colonial Americas. Link this idea to the key word: ethnic, referring to groups with different customs. You can rule out A and D, which do not have to do with ethnic difference. B is a statement about ethnic groups, but the statement is not linked to the paragraph. The answer is C.

Practice Questions

Use the tips above and other tips in this book to help you answer the following question:

1. Portugal's colony in the Americas was located in
   A Peru.
   B the Caribbean.
   C Brazil.
   D Mexico.

Use the graph below to answer questions 2 and 3.

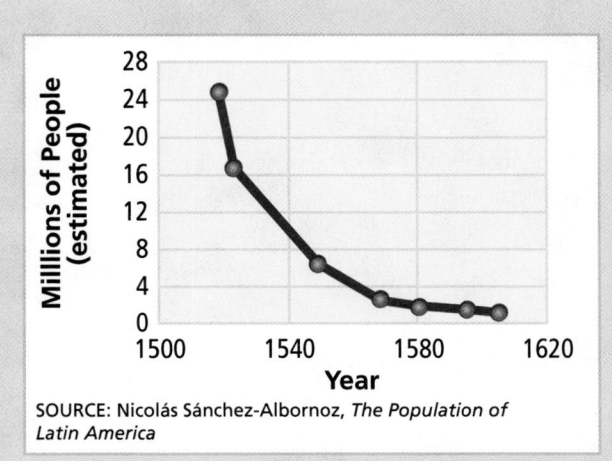

SOURCE: Nicolás Sánchez-Albornoz, *The Population of Latin America*

2. This graph most likely shows which of the following:
   A the change in the population of enslaved Africans in the Americas.
   B the change in the population of Native Americans in Mexico following the Spanish conquest.
   C the change in the numbers of British colonists following the French and Indian War.
   D the change in the number of Portuguese colonists after the establishment of Brazil.

3. Between which years was there the greatest decline in population?
   A between 1520 and 1540
   B between 1540 and 1580
   C between 1580 and 1610
   D decline was consistent for all years

Use Web Code **mua-1700** for **Chapter 17 self-test.**

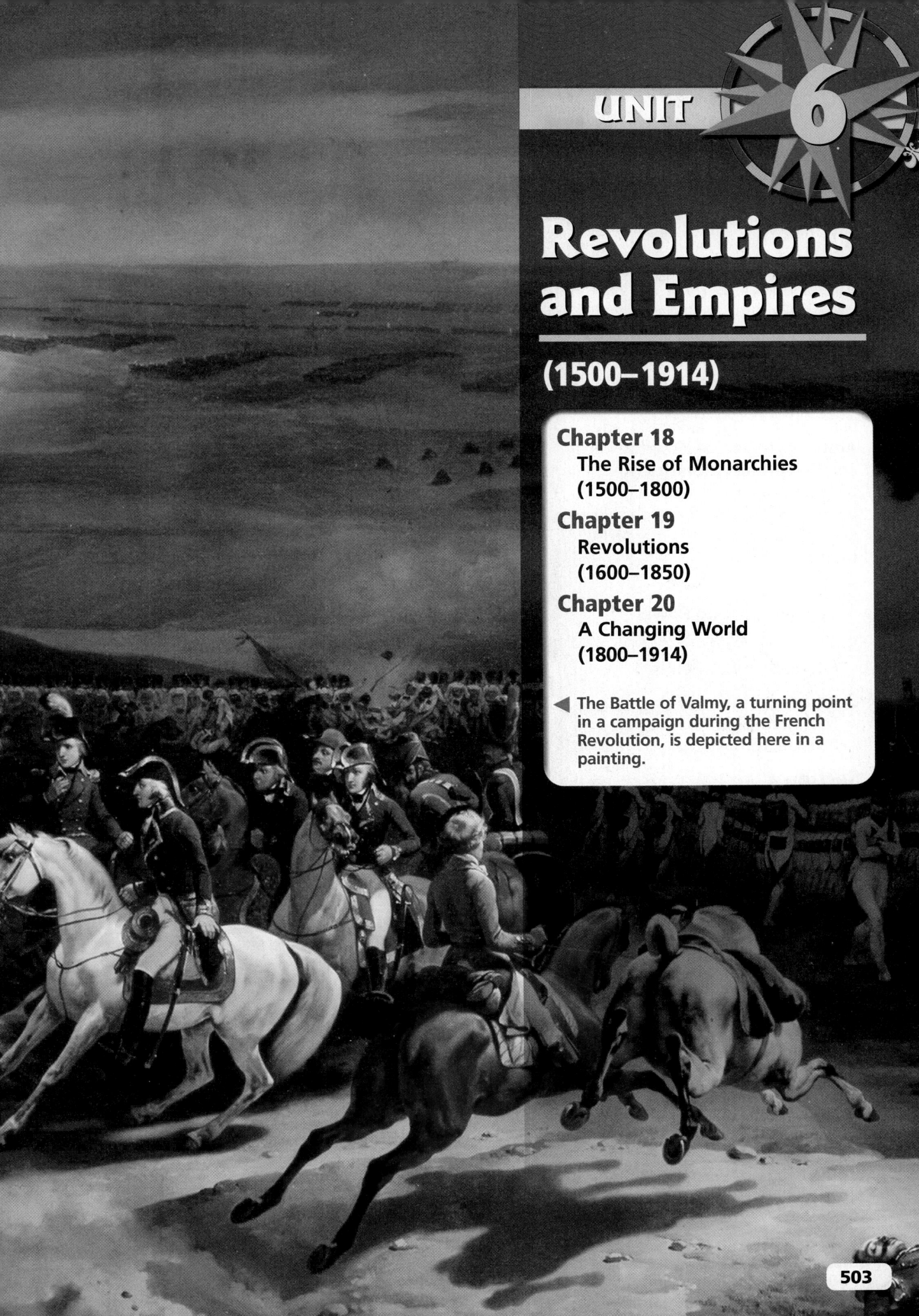

UNIT 6

Revolutions and Empires

(1500–1914)

Chapter 18
The Rise of Monarchies
(1500–1800)

Chapter 19
Revolutions
(1600–1850)

Chapter 20
A Changing World
(1800–1914)

◀ The Battle of Valmy, a turning point in a campaign during the French Revolution, is depicted here in a painting.

18 The Rise of Monarchies

Chapter Preview

In this chapter you will learn about the rise of strong monarchies in different parts of Europe. You will discover how rulers in Spain, France, Russia, Prussia, and Austria increased their own power and that of their countries. You will also examine how conflict between rulers and Parliament in England further limited monarchy there.

Section 1
Spain's Growing Power

Section 2
France's Power Peaks

Section 3
Monarchies in Russia, Prussia, and Austria

Section 4
Limited Monarchy in England

Target Reading Skill

Reading Process In this chapter you will focus on the reading process. The first step in this process is previewing. Previewing helps you set a purpose for reading, make predictions, ask questions, and use prior knowledge to better understand what you read.

▶ The Palace of Versailles was the official home of several French monarchs during the 1600s and 1700s.

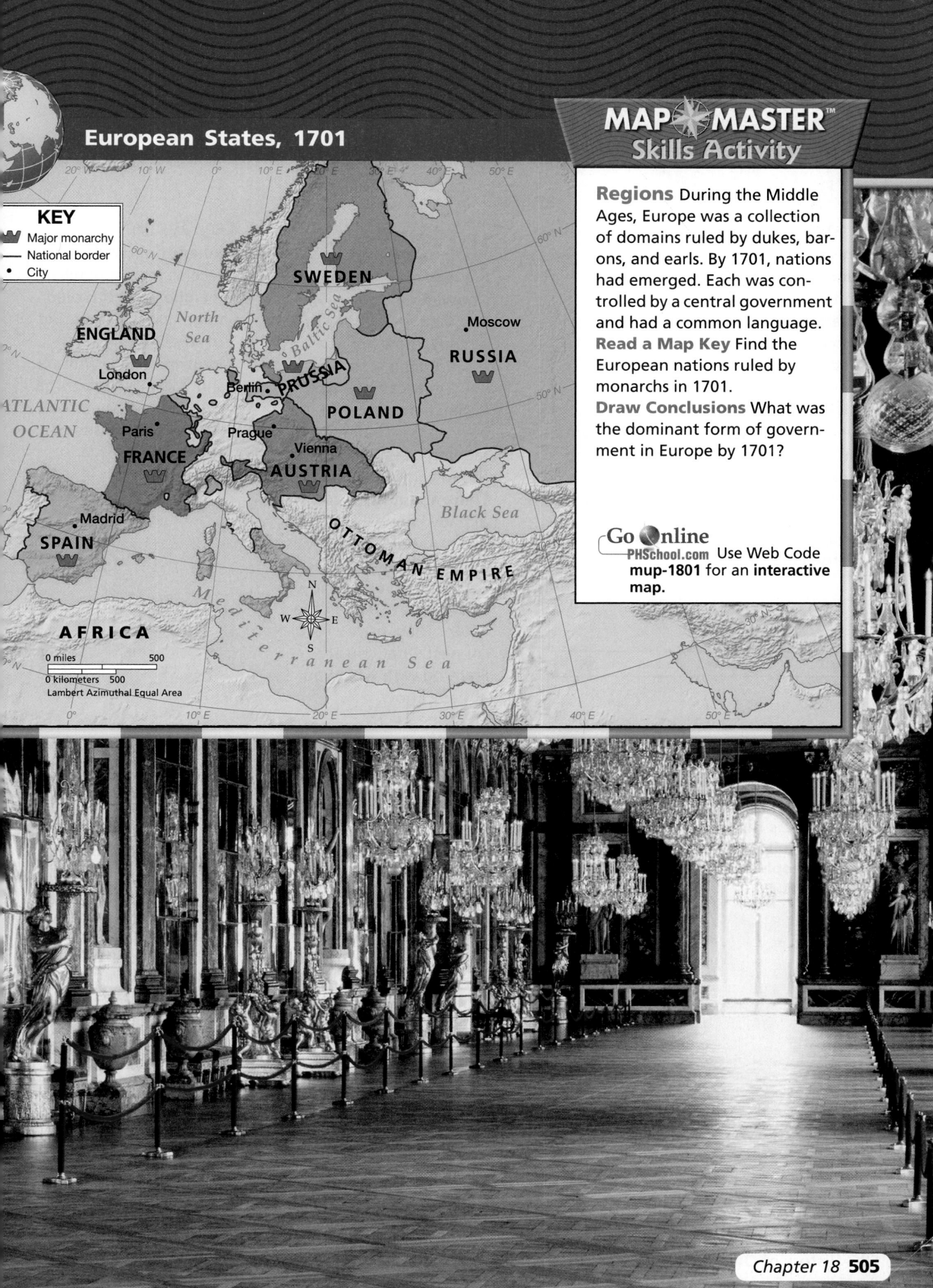

KEY
- Major monarchy
- National border
- City

SWEDEN

ENGLAND

North Sea

Baltic Sea

London

Moscow

RUSSIA

Berlin
PRUSSIA

POLAND

ATLANTIC OCEAN

Paris

Prague

Vienna

FRANCE

AUSTRIA

Black Sea

Madrid

SPAIN

OTTOMAN EMPIRE

AFRICA

Mediterranean Sea

0 miles 500
0 kilometers 500
Lambert Azimuthal Equal Area

Regions During the Middle Ages, Europe was a collection of domains ruled by dukes, barons, and earls. By 1701, nations had emerged. Each was controlled by a central government and had a common language.
Read a Map Key Find the European nations ruled by monarchs in 1701.
Draw Conclusions What was the dominant form of government in Europe by 1701?

Go Online
PHSchool.com Use Web Code
mup-1801 for an **interactive map.**

Spain's Growing Power

Prepare to Read

Objectives

In this section you will

1. Understand why the Spanish empire grew in the 1500s.
2. Learn about the reign of King Philip II.
3. Discover why Spain's power began to decline in the late 1500s.

Taking Notes

As you read this section, look for information about the growth of Spain's power under Charles I and Philip II. Copy the graphic organizer below and record your findings in it.

```
┌─────────────────────────────────────────┐
│ 1500s: Under Charles I, Spain controls   │
│ a large Empire                           │
└─────────────────────────────────────────┘
      ↓              ↓              ↓
┌─────────────────────────────────────────┐
│                                          │
│                                          │
└─────────────────────────────────────────┘
      ↓              ↓              ↓
┌─────────────────────────────────────────┐
│                                          │
│                                          │
└─────────────────────────────────────────┘
```

🎯 Target Reading Skill

Preview and Use Prior Knowledge Prior knowledge is what you already know about a topic. Building on what you know can help you understand new information. Before reading a section, look at the headings and images. Think about what you already know about the topic. As you preview this section, for example, write down what you already know about Spain in the 1500s. Then, as you read, connect what you are learning with what you already know.

Key Terms

- **inherit** (in HAYR it) *v.* to receive from a family member who has died
- **reign** (RAYN) *n.* a period of rule
- **Inquisition** (in kwuh ZIH shun) *n.* a Catholic organization that held trials for people accused of false beliefs

The Inquisition became well known for its harsh punishments. Here, officials carry out the orders of the Catholic Church to publicly execute people accused of having false beliefs.

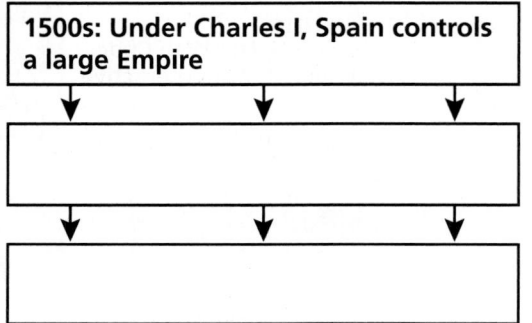

The man had been found guilty of having false religious beliefs. In Spain in the mid-1500s, the punishment for such a crime was severe. First, the man would be tied to a stake. Then, wood placed at his feet would be set on fire. In this way, he would be burned to death.

Philip II of Spain did not invent this punishment. Under his rule, however, Spanish officials made use of it. Philip II once told a person who had been sentenced to burn at the stake, "If my own son were guilty like you, I should lead him with my own hands to the stake."

In Spain of the mid-1500s, Philip II ruled over a vast empire with a firm hand. His style of leadership made him one of the most powerful rulers of one of the world's most powerful empires. Yet Philip's uncompromising ways also led to problems for Spain. In time, Spain would lose its place among the world's great empires.

The Spanish Empire Grows

The late 1400s began a golden era of great power in Spain. As you have read, Isabella and Ferdinand defeated the Moors in 1492. Spanish explorers claimed territory for Spain around the world. Spanish ships carried home tons of treasure from conquests in the Americas. Spain's power continued to grow under the leadership of Charles I.

King Charles I In 1517, Charles I became king of Spain. Charles also inherited a European empire. To **inherit** means to receive from a family member who has died. This empire included the Netherlands and parts of Italy. In 1519, Charles I of Spain became Charles V, emperor of the Holy Roman Empire. He now ruled over a huge area of Europe. As you have learned, Spain had also made conquests in the Americas and the Philippines. It was said that the sun never set on the lands Charles ruled.

A Difficult Reign Spain prospered under Charles I. Yet his **reign**, or period of rule, was full of challenges. A strong Catholic, Charles fought (and failed) to put down Martin Luther and his followers in the Holy Roman Empire. Charles also helped lead the Catholic Reformation, which you read about in Chapter 15. Spain faced a long series of military conflicts with France while Charles was in power. He also overcame military threats from the Ottomans (AHT uh munz), who ruled a powerful empire based in what is Turkey today.

✓ **Reading Check** By what two names was Charles known?

Links Across
The World

The Ottomans Suleyman (soo lay MAHN) the Magnificent was leader of the Ottoman Empire in the 1500s. The Ottomans were Muslims who controlled a large area of Europe, Asia, and North Africa. The capital of their empire was Istanbul. This city had once been the Byzantine capital of Constantinople. In the 1500s the Ottoman Empire was one of the world's great centers of learning, culture, and military strength. The Ottomans helped introduce Islam to eastern Europe, where it still exists today.

The Imperial Crown of the Holy Roman Empire

The Reign of Philip II

In the 1550s, an exhausted Charles gave up his thrones. His brother, Ferdinand, took charge of the Holy Roman Empire. Charles's son, Philip II, became king of Spain. Spain under Philip II was perhaps the most powerful and wealthy country on earth. Philip himself soon emerged as a strong ruler.

Philip and Religion Philip was a firm believer in the Catholic Church. He also believed in absolute rule. He held all authority, or power, over the government and lives of the people. He used various means to rid his lands of people who were not Catholic. One way he did this was through the Inquisition. The **Inquisition** was a Catholic organization that held trials for people accused of false beliefs. In some cases, people who refused to accept Catholic teachings were burned alive at the stake. Through the Inquisition, Philip was successful in driving Protestants, Jews, and Muslims out of Spain.

Philip Battles the Turks Philip II also faced continuing conflict with the Ottomans, who remained a threatening force to the east. In 1571, he organized a fleet that battled the Ottomans in the Mediterranean Sea. The Ottoman fleet was badly defeated in the Battle of Lepanto (BAT ul uv lih PAN toh).

Philip later turned to another enemy: England. In the late 1500s, England was ruled by the Protestant queen Elizabeth I. Philip had tried at one time to arrange a marriage to Elizabeth as a way of spreading the Catholic faith to England. When that plan failed, Philip II looked to conquer England.

√ Reading Check **What threat did Philip II face to the east?**

Preview and Use Prior Knowledge
What do you know about the Reformation that helps you understand Philip's actions against people who were not Catholic?

Trials of the Inquisition
This painting shows a trial held during the Inquisition. The Inquisition provided Philip with a way to drive out groups that did not want to unite under his absolute rule. **Draw Conclusions** *How did the Inquisition help Philip work toward his goal of absolute rule?*

Spain's Power in Decline

Spain in 1588 was considered a great naval power. To defeat England, Philip II put together a huge fleet of warships. The fleet was called the Spanish Armada (SPAN ish ahr MAH duh). Spain believed the Armada was unbeatable. It was not, however. A combination of English warships and bad weather nearly destroyed the Armada.

The defeat of the Armada weakened Spain. It was only one factor in Spain's decline, however. Even before the Armada, Spain had suffered losses fighting Protestantism in the Netherlands. These lands had been part of Spain, and the people there had resisted Philip's efforts to stamp out Protestantism. In 1581 parts of the Netherlands declared independence from Spain.

Spain was also spending large amounts of money to run its far-flung empire. The Jewish and Muslim populations had filled important roles in the Spanish economy. Now they were gone. This contributed to wider economic problems in Spain.

These and other problems contributed to the decline of Spain. Philip died in 1598. His successors were not effective leaders. Soon, new countries would replace Spain as the major power of Europe.

✓ **Reading Check** **What happened to the Spanish Armada?**

Citizen Heroes

Writer of the Times

Miguel de Cervantes (mee GEL du sur VAN tee) was a Spanish writer who lived during the reign of Philip II. He was wounded in the Battle of Lepanto. In the late 1500s, he began writing what would be his most famous work, the novel *Don Quixote* (dahn kee HO tee). One of the great novels of all time, *Don Quixote* is a humorous story that makes fun of Spain's medieval past.

Section 1 Assessment

Key Terms

Review the key terms listed at the beginning of this section. Use each term in a sentence that explains its meaning.

Target Reading Skill

Tell how something you already knew about Spain in the 1500s helped you understand something new.

Comprehension and Critical Thinking

1. (a) Identify Who became king of Spain in 1517?

(b) Identify Cause and Effect How did this ruler help the Spanish empire grow in the 1500s?

2. (a) Recall Who became king of Spain in the 1550s?

(b) Summarize What part did religion play in this ruler's reign?

3. (a) Define What was the Spanish Armada?

(b) Identify Cause and Effect What factors caused Spain's power to decline in the late 1500s?

Writing Activity

You are a Spanish official in the mid-1500s. Philip II has just been named king, and many people are interested in what kind of person he is. Write a brief profile of King Philip II that describes his beliefs and style of leadership.

For: An activity on the Spanish monarchs of the 1500s
Visit: PHSchool.com
Web Code: mud-1810

What kinds of ships were used during the late 1500s and the early1600s? What were they like inside? How did people live and work on these ships? The more you read about people in other places and times, the more questions you may have.

You can read to get information to answer your questions. You can also study diagrams and illustrations to learn more about people, places, and all kinds of things in the past. A cross-section diagram, for example, can give you a look inside a ship, such as the Mayflower. A cross-section is a drawing or image of something with a section cut away. Shortly after the English warships defeated the Spanish Armada, the Pilgrims sailed to the New World on the Mayflower, which you may recall from your reading in Chapter 17.

Learn the Skill

Use these steps to interpret a diagram or illustration.

1. **Read the title or caption.** A title will tell you what is shown. A caption often gives more details.

2. **Look at the diagram or illustration to get a general idea of what it shows.** Figure out what part of the object has been cut away in a cross-section diagram. Look beyond the parts of an illustration to get the whole picture.

3. **Use the labels or key to interpret the diagram or illustration.** A diagram or illustration may have labels that identify the parts of what is shown. If numbers or letters are used for the parts, a key explains what part is marked by each number or letter.

4. **Draw conclusions based on the diagram or illustration.** Information that you gather when you interpret a diagram or illustration can help you draw conclusions about people, places, and things. You might draw conclusions about how people lived or how something worked, for example.

Practice the Skill

Use a cross-section diagram to learn more about the Mayflower.

1 Make sure you understand what you are looking at. What part of the ship is cut away?

2 Use the labels to identify the parts of the ship. Match parts with labels, and labels with parts. What parts of the ship especially interest you?

3 Use the diagram to draw conclusions about the past. What do you think it was like to sail on the Mayflower?

Cross-Section of the Mayflower

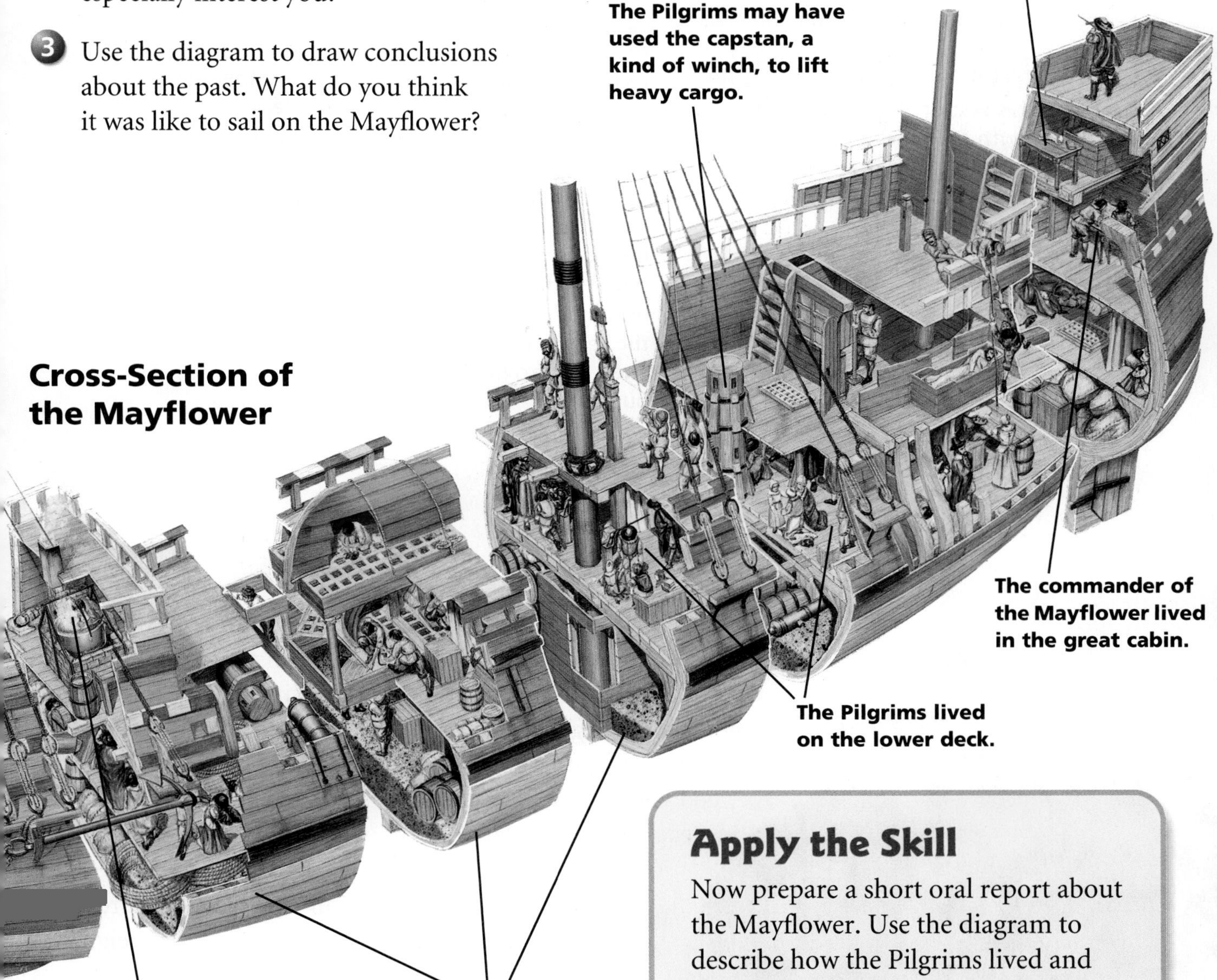

The Pilgrims may have used this room, called the round house, to plan their voyage to the New World.

The Pilgrims may have used the capstan, a kind of winch, to lift heavy cargo.

The commander of the Mayflower lived in the great cabin.

The Pilgrims lived on the lower deck.

The cook may have used the forcastle to prepare the pilgrims' meals.

The Pilgrims stored cargo in the hold.

Apply the Skill

Now prepare a short oral report about the Mayflower. Use the diagram to describe how the Pilgrims lived and worked on board such a ship. Explain what parts of the Mayflower were used for living purposes and what parts were used for working purposes.

Prepare to Read

Objectives

In this section you will

1. Understand developments in the 1500s and 1600s that led to the rise of a strong French monarchy.
2. Learn about France under King Louis XIV.

Taking Notes

As you read this section, look for information about the growth of France's power in the 1500s and 1600s. Copy the graphic organizer below, and record your findings in it.

The Rise of French Power

Target Reading Skill

Preview and Set a Purpose
When you set a purpose for reading, you give yourself a focus. Before reading a section, look at its headings and images to get an idea of what the section is about. Then set a purpose for reading the section. In this section, for example, your purpose might be to find out about developments in France before, during, and after the reign of Louis XIV. Then read to meet your purpose.

Key Terms

- **administration** (ad min is TRAY shun) *n.* a group of people who work with and for a leader
- **divine right of kings** (duh VYN ryt uv kingz) *n.* the theory that God decides who shall be king

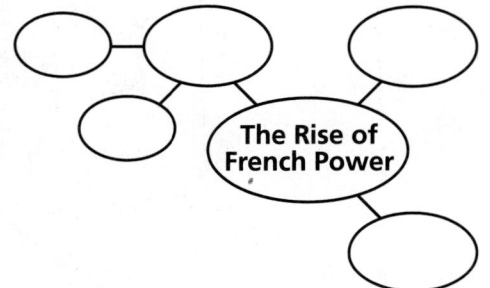

Louis XIV and his court gather in the gardens at the Palace of Versailles.

An observer once said of France's King Louis XIV, "With a [calendar] and a watch, even at a [great] distance . . . you could say precisely what he was doing." The king's daily routine was legendary. It began at 8:30 with an elaborate ceremony in which 100 people helped him rise and get ready for the day. It continued with a carefully scheduled series of events that organized each and every day.

Control and order were important to Louis XIV. Like Spain's Philip II, he was an absolute monarch. He controlled all features of life in France. His reign was also long. He held power in France for over half a century. During this time, Louis XIV helped France secure its place as one of the great powers of Europe. Louis XIV also became the model of the all-powerful monarch.

A Strong French Monarchy

France had suffered greatly during the troubled days of the Reformation. Violence was common between Catholics and Protestants, or Huguenots (HYOO guh nahtz) as they were known in France. The worst example was the 1572 St. Bartholomew's Day Massacre, in which Catholics murdered thousands of Huguenots in Paris and other French cities.

Henry IV Henry was a Huguenot who became king of France in 1589. However, he chose to become a member of the Catholic Church in order to win the support of important parties in France. At the same time, he put in place important protections for Huguenots. Under Henry IV, France enjoyed a period of religious peace. Henry IV also expanded the use of royal power in many areas of French life. His policies helped the French economy thrive.

Louis XIII and Cardinal Richelieu Henry IV died in 1610. He was followed by Louis XIII, who was only a young boy when he took the throne. A key figure in Louis XIII's administration was Cardinal Armand Richelieu (KAHRD un ul AHR mund RISH loo). **Administration** is a term used to describe the group of people who work with and for a leader. Richelieu shaped many government policies during the reign of Louis XIII. He sought to build relations with Protestant governments. At the same time, he greatly limited the growing power of Huguenots in France. The effect of his work was to strengthen the power of the French monarchy.

✓ **Reading Check** Under which king did Cardinal Richelieu serve?

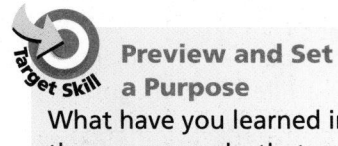

Preview and Set a Purpose
What have you learned in these paragraphs that meets your purpose of finding out about events in France before the reign of Louis XIV?

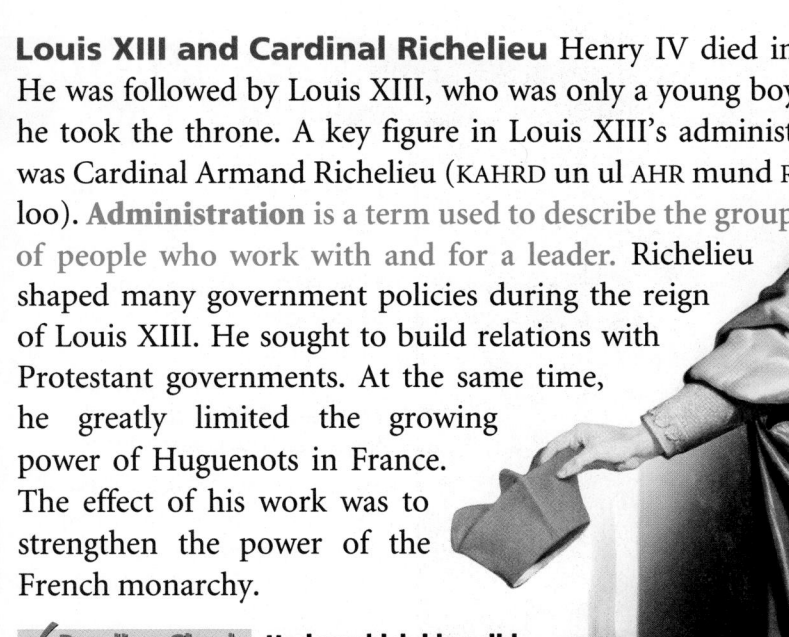

The Iron Cardinal
Cardinal Richelieu was granted a great deal of authority by Louis XIII. He became known as a forceful ruler, who was sometimes referred to as the "Iron Cardinal." **Analyze Images** *In this picture, what aspects of Richelieu's appearance help identify him as a person of great power?*

France Under Louis XIV

Louis XIV became king in 1643 when he was still a young boy. For this reason, he did not rule France directly until 1661. Between those years, France experienced a revolt known as the Fronde (frohnd). This uprising created great disorder in France and threatened the power of the king. Louis XIV decided that this should never happen again. At age 22, he finally took direct control of France. When he did so, he sought to rule as an absolute monarch.

The Sun King Louis XIV is famous for the remark, "I am the state." This statement reflected the idea that all government power flowed through him. Under Louis XIV, local officials, nobles, and others in France saw their power stripped away. Louis XIV, with the help of his advisors, ruled on all matters of French life. Indeed, he chose the sun—the center of the universe—as his symbol. Louis XIV is known as the Sun King.

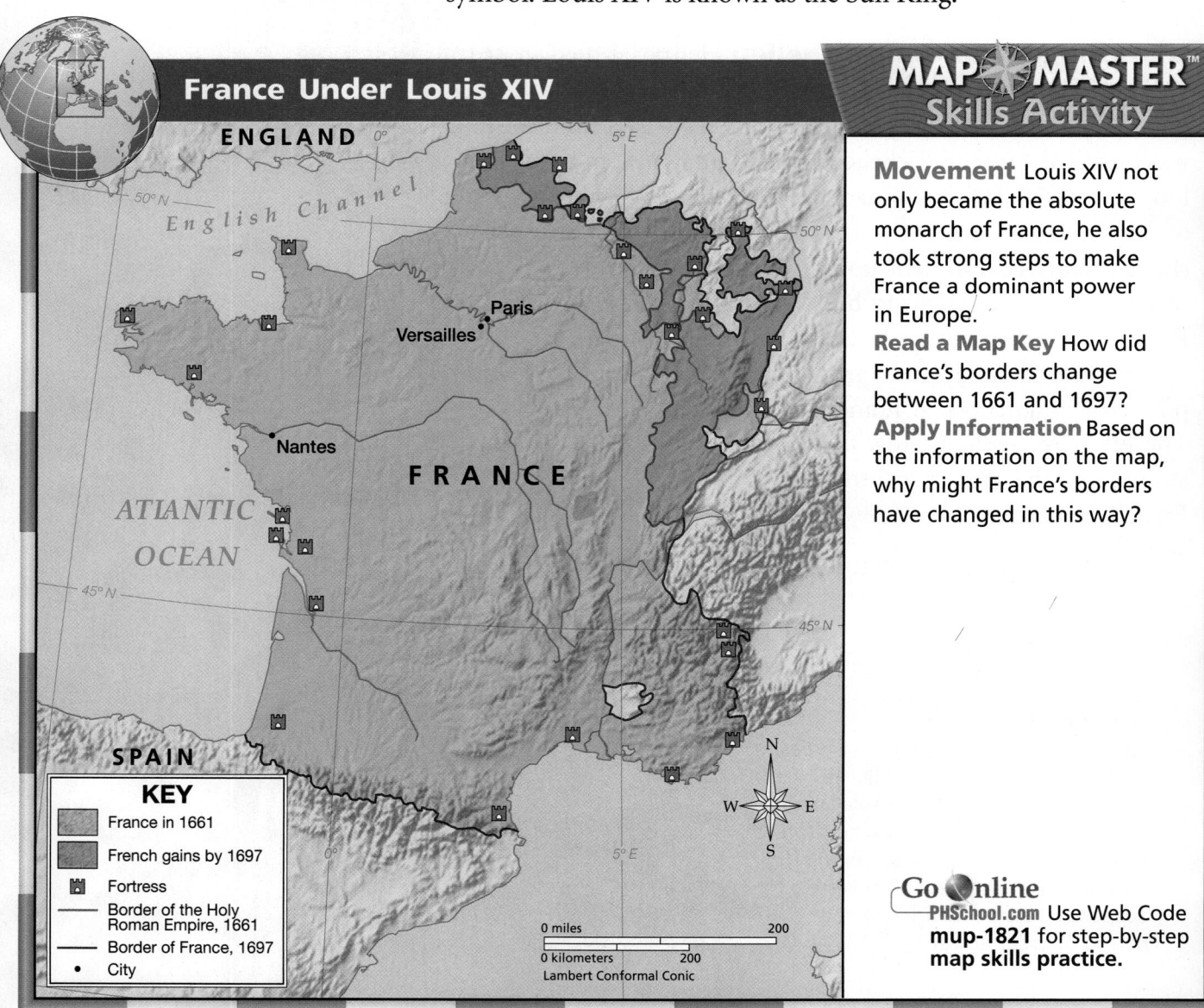

France Under Louis XIV

MAP MASTER™
Skills Activity

Movement Louis XIV not only became the absolute monarch of France, he also took strong steps to make France a dominant power in Europe.
Read a Map Key How did France's borders change between 1661 and 1697?
Apply Information Based on the information on the map, why might France's borders have changed in this way?

KEY
France in 1661
French gains by 1697
⌂ Fortress
— Border of the Holy Roman Empire, 1661
— Border of France, 1697
• City

0 miles 200
0 kilometers 200
Lambert Conformal Conic

Go Online
PHSchool.com Use Web Code **mup-1821** for step-by-step **map skills practice.**

Divine Rule Louis XIV also believed in the theory of the **divine right of kings.** This theory holds that God decides who shall be king. It meant that to rebel against the king was the same as rebelling against God.

Huguenots suffered terribly under Louis XIV, who was Catholic. Many fled France including leading merchants and artisans. The loss of these skilled people hurt the French economy.

Military Affairs Louis XIV was quite willing to use French military power. During his reign, France endured several wars. These included conflicts with the Dutch and the Spanish over control of the Netherlands. France's frequent warfare placed a great strain on the country. Most disastrous was the War of the Spanish Succession in the early 1700s. This conflict developed from a dispute over whether Louis XIV's grandson should become king of Spain. The war left France weak and in debt.

French Power Declines France was still a major force in Europe when Louis XIV died in 1715. Its peak of power, however, had passed. As you have read, it would soon lose its colonies in North America. England, the great sea power, was rising to the rank of Europe's leading power.

✓ **Reading Check** What was Louis XIV's religion, and how did that affect France?

French soldiers wore helmets such as these to protect their head, face, and neck during battle. The engravings on this helmet depict knights, horses, and scenes of battle.

Section 2 Assessment

Key Terms

Review the key terms listed at the beginning of this section. Use each term in a sentence that explains its meaning.

Target Reading Skill

What was your purpose for reading? Did you meet it? If not, what might have been a better purpose?

Comprehension and Critical Thinking

1. (a) **Identify** What was the St. Bartholomew's Day Massacre?

(b) **Evaluate** Why was the St. Bartholomew's Day Massacre significant?

2. (a) **Explain** Why did Louis XIV not hold power directly during the first years of his reign?

(b) **Identify Cause and Effect** How did the *Fronde* help shape Louis XIV's attitudes about government?

3. (a) **Recall** What was Louis XIV's policy toward Huguenots?

(b) **Draw Conclusions** How did French wars and the treatment of Huguenots combine to hurt France's economy?

Writing Activity

Suppose that you are a speech-writer for Louis XIV. Write a speech in which you explain your beliefs about the role of the king in French life. Be sure that your speech accurately reflects Louis XIV's ideas and attitudes.

For: An activity on France under Louis XIV
Visit: PHSchool.com
Web Code: mud-1820

The palace of Versailles is one of the most elaborate structures in the world. Picture gold, mirrors, tapestries, and magnificent furniture and works of art, and you will have some idea of what its rooms look like. Construction took more than 50 years and involved more than 36,000 workers. Officially opened in 1682, it served as France's royal palace until 1793. Today it is restored, and parts are open to tourists.

The gardens of Versailles are as magnificent as the palace. Talented French designers created perfect formal French gardens there. Both the palace and the gardens, as well as the people who strolled there, reflected the wealth and luxury of the reign of Louis XIV.

The Fountain of Apollo

Among the many fountains and waterworks at Versailles, the Fountain of Apollo is one of the most magnificent.

Designer of the King's Gardens
André le Notre was the architect and designer of the gardens at Versailles and one of the greatest garden and landscape designers in the world.

A Walk in the Gardens The Versailles gardens are vast. Close to the palace are flowerbeds that can be enjoyed from the upper floors. Beyond the palace, plantings are arranged in geometric patterns around fountains, pools, and statues. Every flowerbed, patch of grass, and path is precisely laid out. Trees and shrubs are trained and pruned into unusual shapes. Water pours, gushes, or bubbles from more than a thousand fountains. New, unexpected sights appear at every turn in the path.

The illustration to the left shows two members of Louis XIV's court strolling in the gardens. Their dress and even the way they stand and move mirrors the formality of the gardens. During the reign of Louis XIV, both men and women wore elaborate clothing decorated with tassels, lace, and embroidery. The clothing shown here was worn by the nobility around 1693. Notice that the man is carrying his hat. Even though his wig is too large to allow him to wear it, he carries his hat along as an important part of his costume. As he walks, his movements are like those used in ballet or fencing. They are graceful, precise, and formal.

Assessment

Describe Look closely at the illustration to the left. What details in the gardens and the people's dress do you notice?

Draw Conclusions How does the scene illustrate the wealth and the power of the king?

Prepare to Read

Objectives

In this section you will

1. Learn about the rise of the Russian monarchy.
2. Discover why strong monarchs came to power in other parts of Europe.

Taking Notes

As you read this section, look for information about how strong monarchies developed in the European nations of Russia, Prussia, and Austria. Copy the graphic organizer below, and record your findings in it.

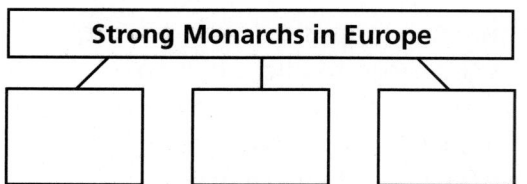

Target Reading Skill

Preview and Predict Making predictions helps you set a purpose for reading. Before reading a section, look at its headings, images, and anything else that stands out. Then predict what the section might discuss. As you read, compare what you read with your prediction. If what you learn doesn't support your prediction, revise the prediction.

Go Online
PHSchool.com Use Web Code **mup-0843** for an interactivity on the expansion of Russia.

Key Terms

- **czar** (zahr) *n.* the title given to the Russian monarch
- **heir** (ehr) *n.* a person who receives something from someone who has died

Peter I was the czar of Russia from 1689 to 1725. **Czar** was the title given to the Russian monarch. However, Peter I had a great love for the customs and manners of western Europe. In fact, he decided that the people of his native Russia should look and act like the people of western Europe. He ordered Russian men to shave off their beards. Those who did not would have to pay a tax—a beard tax! This was just one of the steps that Peter took to change the way Russians looked and acted.

You have read about the strong, all-powerful monarchies that developed in Spain and France around this time. Peter I—or Peter the Great as he became known—was a Russian example of a strong monarch. The trend toward a strong monarchy was taking place in many European nations, as you will learn.

This cartoon shows Peter I cutting the beard of a Russian boyar. Boyar was a title passed down among individuals from prominent families. These individuals formed a high-ranking class that helped govern Russia.

The Rise of the Russian Monarchy

Peter the Great did more than just change the way Russians looked and acted. He helped build Russia into one of the leading powers of Europe. Peter I built a great army. With this force he waged war on Sweden. His goal was to enlarge Russia and give it territory along the Baltic Sea. It was on this newly won territory that Peter built the city of St. Petersburg. It served as the capital of his all-powerful government.

The next great Russian leader was Catherine the Great. She led Russia from 1762 to 1796. She continued to expand Russia's territory. She also made major changes in the Russian economy and encouraged education. Her goal was to modernize farming and industry. She helped Russia keep and even expand its place among the great nations of Europe.

✔ **Reading Check** **Which two monarchs helped lead Russia to the front of European power?**

Target Skill **Preview and Predict** Is your prediction on target, according to what you've read so far? If not, revise or change it now.

Discovery CHANNEL **SCHOOL** **Video**
Learn how Peter the Great built Saint Petersburg.

MAP MASTER™ Skills Activity

Expansion of Russia, 1689–1796

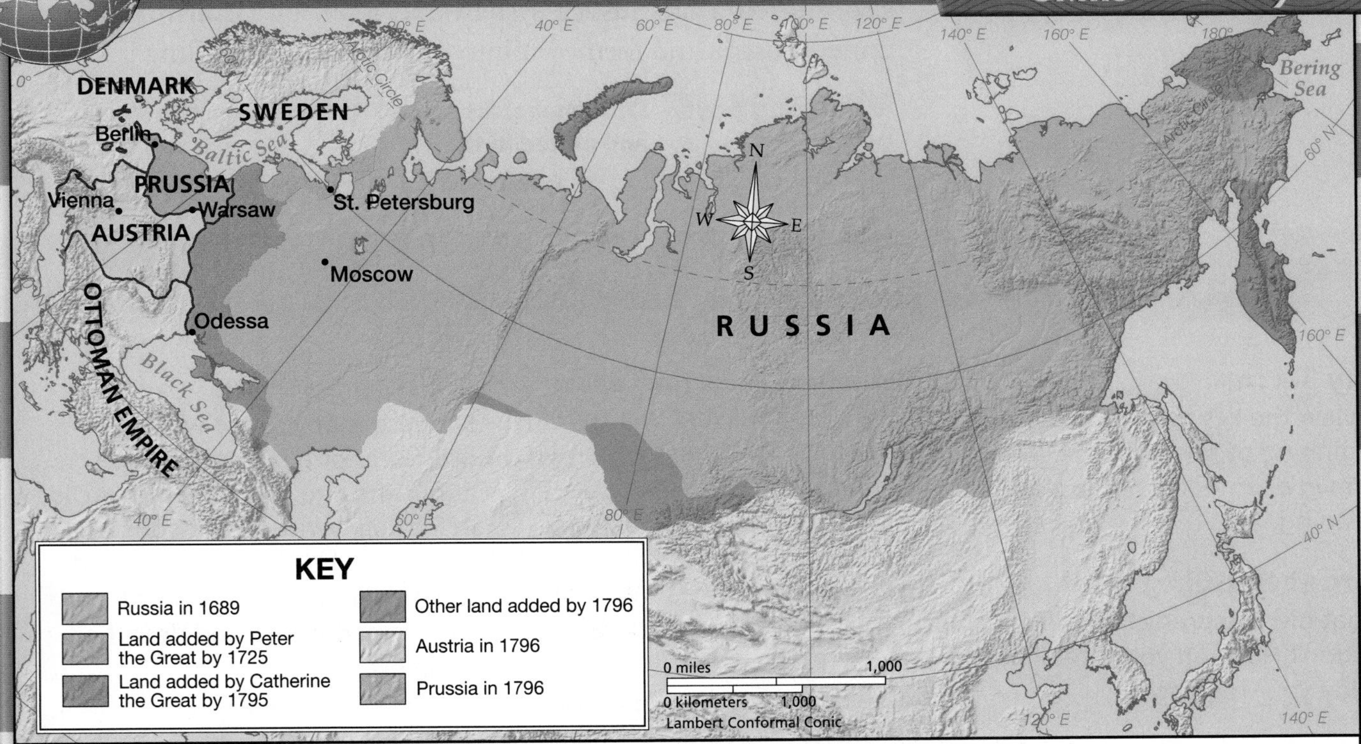

KEY

- Russia in 1689
- Land added by Peter the Great by 1725
- Land added by Catherine the Great by 1795
- Other land added by 1796
- Austria in 1796
- Prussia in 1796

0 miles 1,000
0 kilometers 1,000
Lambert Conformal Conic

DENMARK
SWEDEN
Berlin
PRUSSIA
Vienna
Warsaw
AUSTRIA
St. Petersburg
Moscow
Odessa
OTTOMAN EMPIRE
Black Sea
Baltic Sea
RUSSIA
Bering Sea
Arctic Circle

Place Russian territory expanded in the 1700s. Key gains included a warm-water port on the Black Sea.
Identify To which seas did the Russians gain access under the leadership of Peter the Great and Catherine the Great?
Analyze Information Why might access to European seas help Russia gain power?

Go Online
PHSchool.com Use Web code **mup-1831** for step-by-step map skills practice.

Frederick II of Prussia (top) and Maria Theresa of Austria

Other Strong European Monarchs

As you have read, monarchs in many European countries were exercising absolute rule in the 1600s and 1700s. This trend was also evident in the countries of Prussia and Austria.

Prussia Prussia rose to power in the late 1600s. Prussia's first ruler, Frederick William I, began building a powerful army that became the most important institution in Prussian life.

In 1740, Frederick II became king of Prussia. He used the army to expand Prussia. He also reformed Prussian education and the economy. For his role in building a strong and united Prussia, he is remembered as Frederick the Great.

Austria Maria Theresa's neighbors, including Frederick, declared war when she came to power in Austria in 1740. As a woman, she had not been raised to rule Austria. She came to the throne when her father died without a male heir. An **heir** is a person who receives something from someone who has died.

Maria Theresa ruled with great authority. She built a strong army that fought effectively against Frederick the Great's army. She also created a fair justice system and a strong government. She united Austria and formed it into one of Europe's leading powers.

✓ **Reading Check** What monarchs made Prussia and Austria strong and united in the 1700s?

Section 3 Assessment

Key Terms
Review the key terms listed at the beginning of this section. Use each term in a sentence that explains its meaning.

Target Reading Skill
What did you predict about this section? How did your prediction guide your reading?

Comprehension and Critical Thinking
1. (a) Identify What city did Peter the Great build?

(b) Analyze Aside from being Russia's capital, what was the significance of St. Petersburg and its location?
2. (a) Recall How did Frederick the Great expand Prussia?
(b) Draw Inferences What other changes did Frederick the Great make in Prussia?
3. (a) Explain Why was Maria Theresa not raised to rule her country?
(b) Draw Inferences What were Maria Theresa's main accomplishments?

Writing Activity
Suppose that you are writing a brochure for a museum exhibit about the age of strong monarchs in Europe. Write an introductory paragraph for the brochure. In it, summarize the trend toward strong monarchies and describe some examples.

For: An activity on the rise of strong monarchs in Russia, Prussia, and Austria
Visit: PHSchool.com
Web Code: mud-1830

Section 4 · Limited Monarchy in England

Prepare to Read

Objectives

In this section you will
1. Learn about England's strong monarchs in the 1600s and their conflicts with Parliament.
2. Understand the events and outcome of the English Civil War.
3. Explore the significance of the Restoration and the Glorious Revolution.

Taking Notes

As you read this section, look for information about how the long conflict between the king and Parliament in England led to the development of a limited monarchy. Copy the graphic organizer below, and record your findings in it.

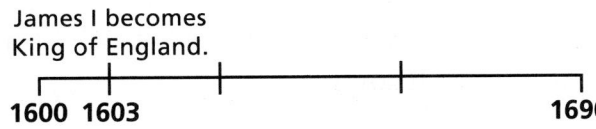

James I becomes King of England.

```
1600  1603            1690
```

Target Reading Skill

Preview and Ask Questions Asking questions before you read is another way to set a purpose for reading. Before you read a section, preview its headings and images to discover what it is about. Write down any questions you have. Then read to find answers to your questions.

Key Terms

- **civil war** (SIV ul wawr) *n.* a war among different parts of the same group or country
- **treason** (TREE zun) *n.* a betrayal of one's country

Charles I, the king of England, dressed with care. He wanted to be sure he was warm enough to avoid shivering. He did not want to appear frightened as he stood before his subjects, awaiting his execution.

In fact, Charles I did not appear frightened. He faced the crowd with dignity later that day. Although equipment was on hand to force him into place if he resisted, Charles did not put up a fight! He even instructed the executioner to wait for his signal to act. Then, he placed his head on the chopping block. A few moments later, he gave the agreed-upon signal with his hand. Seconds later, the deed was done. The people of England had executed their own king.

The execution of Charles I showed that absolute monarchs did not rule in all of Europe. England continued its long tradition of limiting the power of its monarchy.

Charles I being led to his execution

When Charles I tried to force the Protestant Scots to make changes in their religious practices, they rebelled. This rebellion forced Charles I to turn to Parliament for help. He called Parliament together in 1640.

England's Monarchs in the Early 1600s

You have read about the Magna Carta. That important document helped establish the ideas that English people had certain rights and that their monarch must obey the laws. These ideas became a strong tradition in English life. England's Parliament played a major role in helping the monarch govern.

The Reign of James I In 1603, Elizabeth I died without an heir. James I became king of England. He had already ruled as king of Scotland for 36 years. Now he saw himself as king of the area that would later be known as Great Britain.

James I described himself to the English Parliament as "an old and experienced king." He had some different ideas about leading England. He believed in the divine right of kings. He often acted as though he wanted to rule England by himself, without Parliament's input. These actions angered Parliament.

Charles I Follows Charles I followed his father James I to the throne in 1625. The new king was even more hostile toward Parliament than James I had been. In 1628, Charles I actually ordered an end to the meeting of Parliament. He did not allow another meeting until 1640.

Relations between Charles I and Parliament grew worse in the 1640s. Eventually, the king's enemies in Parliament formed an army. This army went to battle against forces loyal to the king. Civil war broke out in England. A **civil war** is a war among different parts of the same group or country.

✓ **Reading Check** How did James I and Charles I view Parliament?

English Civil War

The parliamentary force opposed to the king was known as the Roundheads. This term referred to its members' habit of wearing short hair. Their first major battle with the king's forces took place at Edgehill in 1642. The king's troops fought to save the monarchy. Charles I encouraged them during the battle with these words:

> **"Your king is both your cause, your quarrel, and your captain."**

The battle was a draw. In the years ahead, however, the Roundheads and their allies took control. By 1646 the king's armies had been defeated, and Charles I found himself a captive.

Charles I Executed The king's enemies were hardly a united force. They were soon fighting among themselves. A group led by Oliver Cromwell (AHL uh vur KRAHM wel) won this struggle. This group wanted to uphold people's rights against the absolute power of the king. Under Cromwell's leadership, Parliament put Charles I on trial. He was found guilty of **treason**, which is a betrayal of one's country. Charles was sentenced to death. This sentence was carried out in 1649.

Cromwell In Charge Without a king, England was now led by Oliver Cromwell and Parliament. However, Cromwell quickly discovered the difficulty in working with Parliament. By 1653 he had had enough. "I say you are no Parliament," he declared. "I will put an end to your sitting." Parliament was closed. Cromwell was now absolute ruler of England. He ruled not as king, but as lord protector.

✓ **Reading Check** **Of what crime was Charles I found guilty?**

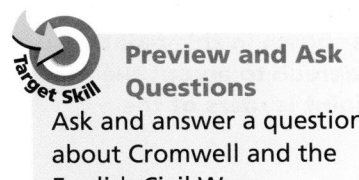

Preview and Ask Questions
Ask and answer a question about Cromwell and the English Civil War.

Siege at Basing House
During the English Civil War, Oliver Cromwell joined a lengthy siege on Basing House, the residence of a wealthy English citizen who remained loyal to Charles I.
Analyze Images *Based on this picture, why would Basing House have proven difficult to capture?*

The Restoration and Glorious Revolution

During Cromwell's rule, many people wanted a return of the monarchy. They even asked Cromwell to become king, but he refused. In 1658 Cromwell died. His son, Richard, took power.

The crowning of William III and Mary II as king and queen of England is shown in this painting. They agreed to accept the crown as joint leaders of the country.

Restoring the Monarchy In 1660, Charles I's son arrived in England with a small army. Charles II had escaped to France when his father was executed. The English people quickly supported him. Richard Cromwell was forced from power. Charles II became king of England, restoring the monarchy. Yet arguments with Parliament continued. Charles asked for money and troops from King Louis XIV of France to rule without Parliament.

Power Changes Hands When Charles' brother, James II, took power, conflict with Parliament grew. In 1688 Parliament asked Holland's ruler, William of Orange, to take power in England. James fled England. In 1689 William III and Mary II became England's king and queen. This change of power, called the Glorious Revolution, came about peacefully. The new monarchs agreed to a document known as the English Bill of Rights that made Parliament more powerful than the monarchy and protected English citizens.

✓ **Reading Check** Who followed James II as rulers of England?

 **Section 4 Assessment**

Key Terms

Review the key terms listed at the beginning of this section. Use each term in a sentence that explains its meaning.

Target Reading Skill

What questions did you ask that helped you learn something from this section?

Comprehension and Critical Thinking

1. (a) Identify Who was king when the English Civil War started?

(b) Drawing Conclusions What can you conclude from the fact that Charles I turned to Parliament for help in 1640?

2. (a) Identify Who led the Roundheads during the English Civil War?

(b) Draw Inferences Why might people of England have asked Cromwell to be king?

3. (a) Explain What was the English Bill of Rights?

(b) Predict How would limiting the power of the monarchy change relations between the monarch and Parliament in the future?

Writing Activity

The year is 1689. You are a newspaper reporter in England. Write a "news brief" summary of the major events involving Parliament and the monarchy in the past century.

For: An activity on English rulers and their conflict with Parliament in the 1600s
Visit: PHSchool.com
Web Code: mud-1840

Review and Assessment

◆ Chapter Summary

Section 1: Spain's Growing Power

- Spain emerged as an important power in Europe in the 1500s.
- King Philip II sought to rule Spain as an absolute ruler.
- Spain's power began to decline in the late 1500s.

The Imperial Crown of the Holy Roman Empire

Section 2: France's Power Peaks

- French kings sought to build a more powerful monarchy in the late 1500s and early 1600s.
- King Louis XIV became the model for the all-powerful European monarch.
- French power began to decline in the 1700s as a result of its various wars.

Louis XIV

Section 3: Monarchies in Russia, Prussia, and Austria

- Peter the Great and Catherine the Great were strong monarchs who helped make Russia a major European power.
- Frederick the Great helped build Prussia into a strong European power in the 1700s.
- Austria became another leading European power under Maria Theresa.

Section 4: Limited Monarchy in England

- Conflict between the monarchy and Parliament led to the English Civil War in the 1640s.
- England welcomed back the monarchy in 1660.
- Continuing conflict between Parliament and the monarchy led to the Glorious Revolution and the English Bill of Rights.

Charles I

◆ Key Terms

Each of the statements below contains a key term from the chapter. If the statement is true, write *true*. If it is false, rewrite the statement to make it true.

1. In Europe, to become the monarch a person usually had to inherit the throne.

2. A monarch's reign is the period in his or her life before he or she takes power.

3. A monarch's administration is made up of people who help him or her run the government.

4. The divine right of kings is the idea that kings should answer directly to their subjects.

5. The Russian monarch received advice from an official known as the czar.

6. Civil war is an armed conflict between two countries over territory.

◆ Comprehension and Critical Thinking

7. (a) **Recall** What was the Inquisition?
   (b) **Identify Cause and Effect** How did the Inquisition affect people who were not Catholic?
   (c) **Analyze Information** How did the Inquisition hurt Spain in the 1600s?

8. (a) **Define** What is absolute rule?
   (b) **Analyze** What made Louis XIV the model of an absolute ruler?
   (c) **Draw Inferences** Why did Louis XIV believe that the sun was a fitting image for his reign?

9. (a) **Recall** What was Peter the Great's attitude toward European culture?
   (b) **Synthesize Information** Explain how Peter the Great's military activities supported his interest in European life and culture.

10. (a) **Identify** Which English king was executed in the 1640s?
    (b) **Identify Point of View** Why do you think this ruler was tried for the crime of treason?

11. (a) **Define** What term is used to describe the event that brought about the reign of William III and Mary II?
    (b) **Draw Inferences** What can you infer from the fact that William III and Mary II agreed to the English Bill of Rights?

◆ Skills Practice

Interpreting Diagrams and Illustrations In the skills activity in this chapter, you learned how to interpret diagrams, such as a cross-section.

Review the steps you followed to learn this skill. Then use the diagram and illustration on pages 510–511 to answer the following questions.

1. In what part of the Mayflower did the commander live?
2. What was the capstan used for?

◆ Writing Activity: Science

Philip II hoped to conquer England with the help of the Spanish Armada. This huge fleet of warships was thought to be unbeatable. Do some research to discover how design and construction made the ships in the Spanish Armada strong. Write a brief report about your findings.

MAP MASTER™
Skills Activity

European States, 1700

Place Location For each place listed below, write the letter from the map that shows its location.

1. Austria
2. France
3. Prussia
4. Russia
5. Paris
6. Vienna

Go Online
PHSchool.com Use Web Code **mup-1802** for an interactive map.

Standardized Test Prep

Test-Taking Tips

Some questions on standardized tests ask you to analyze a graphic organizer. Study the concept web below. Then follow the tips to answer the sample question.

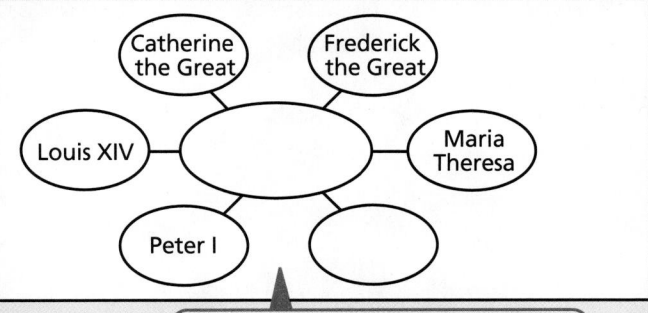

TIP As you review a chart or concept web, notice the kind of information included in each part.

Pick the letter that best answers the question.

Which title should go in the center of the web?
- **A** Spanish Kings
- **B** European Monarchs
- **C** James II
- **D** Britain's Parliament

TIP Try to find the BEST answer, because more than one answer choice sometimes seems possible.

Think it Through The question asks you to choose a title for the center of the web; in other words, an idea that covers the information in all of the outer circles. You can rule out A and D because none of the people on the web were Spanish or British. That leaves B or C. Since C is too specific, the answer must be B; they were all European monarchs.

Practice Questions

Use the graphic organizer above to answer Question 1. Choose the letter of the best answer to the question.

1. Which of the following would best fit the blank circle on the outside of the concept web?
   - **A** European monarchs
   - **B** Louis XIV
   - **C** Philip II
   - **D** Oliver Cromwell

Use the tips above and other tips in this book to help you answer the following questions.

2. Which of the following bests summarizes the significance of the Spanish Armada?
   - **A** It was a great victory at the peak of the French power.
   - **B** Its defeat led to the decline of Spanish power.
   - **C** It improved Russian access to the Baltic Sea.
   - **D** It helped make England a Catholic state.

3. Louis XIV is known for which of the following?
   - **A** the palace of Versailles
   - **B** the Inquisition
   - **C** the English Bill of Rights
   - **D** the founding of St. Petersburg

4. Which of the following figures are connected with the English Civil War?
   - **A** William III and Mary II
   - **B** James I
   - **C** Oliver Cromwell
   - **D** Cardinal Armand Richelieu

Go Online
PHSchool.com

Use Web Code mua–1805 for **Chapter 18** self-test.

19 Revolutions

Chapter Preview

This chapter will introduce you to a series of revolutions in Europe and North America. These revolutions brought dramatic changes in the sciences, government, and how people worked and produced goods.

Section 1
The Enlightenment

Section 2
Political Revolutions

Section 3
The Age of Napoleon

Section 4
The Early Industrial Age

**Target
Reading Skill**

Using Context In this chapter, you will focus on using context to help you understand unfamiliar words. Context refers to the words and sentences that surround unfamiliar words.

▶ During the War of Independence, General George Washington and his troops spent a miserable winter at their camp at Valley Forge, Pennsylvania.

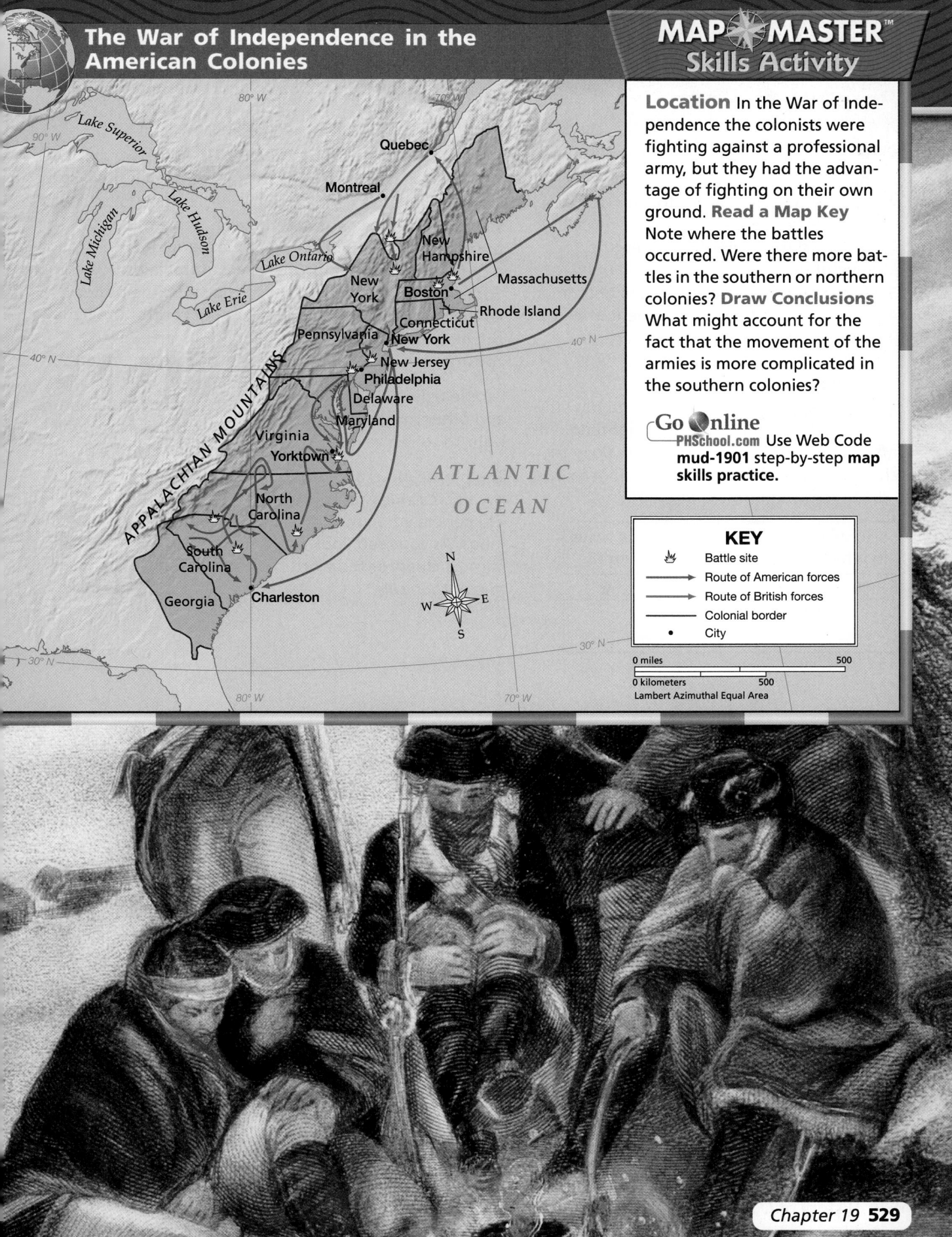

The War of Independence in the American Colonies

MAP★MASTER™ Skills Activity

Location In the War of Independence the colonists were fighting against a professional army, but they had the advantage of fighting on their own ground. **Read a Map Key** Note where the battles occurred. Were there more battles in the southern or northern colonies? **Draw Conclusions** What might account for the fact that the movement of the armies is more complicated in the southern colonies?

Go Online
PHSchool.com Use Web Code **mud-1901** step-by-step **map skills practice.**

KEY

♨	Battle site
→	Route of American forces
→	Route of British forces
—	Colonial border
•	City

0 miles 500
0 kilometers 500
Lambert Azimuthal Equal Area

Map labels: Lake Superior, Lake Michigan, Lake Huron, Lake Ontario, Lake Erie, Quebec, Montreal, New Hampshire, New York, Boston, Massachusetts, Rhode Island, Connecticut, New York, Pennsylvania, New Jersey, Philadelphia, Delaware, Maryland, Virginia, Yorktown, APPALACHIAN MOUNTAINS, North Carolina, South Carolina, Georgia, Charleston, ATLANTIC OCEAN, 90° W, 80° W, 70° W, 40° N, 30° N

The Enlightenment

Prepare to Read

Objectives

In this section you will
1. Learn about approaches to science that began in the 1500s.
2. Identify discoveries of the Scientific Revolution.
3. Understand the ideas of the Enlightenment.
4. Find out how the Enlightenment affected governments.

Taking Notes

As you read this section, summarize how the Scientific Revolution and the Enlightenment affected governments at the time. Copy the chart below, and record your findings in it.

Scientists apply new ideas to the ways in which they understand the world.

Target Reading Skill

Use Context Clues You can sometimes figure out the meaning of an unfamiliar word from clues in context. For example, you can use a context clue to figure out the meaning of the word *royalty*:

People believed that kings and other royalty had the right to collect taxes.

The phrase *kings and other royalty* is a clue that royalty are people who are like kings. As you read, look for context clues for the word *microorganisms*.

Key Terms

- **scientific method** (sy un TIF ik METH ud) *n.* a way of performing experiments
- **natural laws** (NACH ur ul lawz) *n.* the patterns that control the behavior of the universe
- **Enlightenment** (en LYT un munt) *n.* the belief that science and natural laws bring individuals and society to a more enlightened state
- **natural rights** (NACH ur ul rytz) *n.* the rights to life, liberty, and property

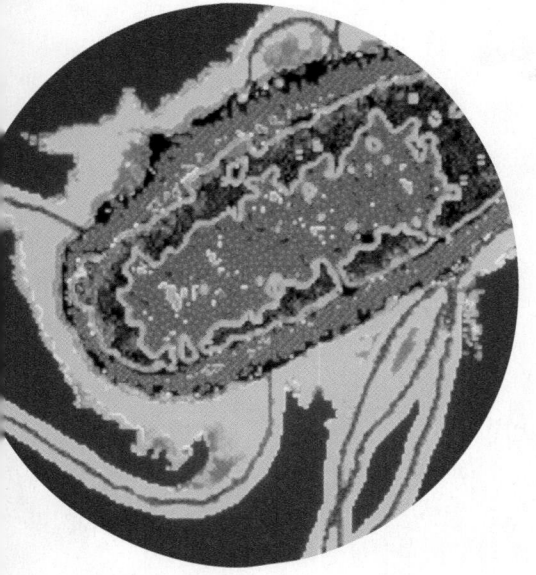

Leeuwenhoek was the first person to study bacteria.

In Medieval times, scientists thought that living things, such as maggots, developed from nonliving things, such as rotten meat. The belief was called the theory of spontaneous generation.

In the 1600s, a Dutch merchant named Antoni van Leeuwenhoek (ahn TOH nee van LAY vun hook) constructed microscopes to examine the quality of his cloth. His microscope was more powerful than any previously used. Through his microscope, he saw what looked like tiny moving objects. In 1674, he concluded that these must be tiny animals. Leeuwenhoek's discovery showed that the small insects that ate spoiled grain and meat had hatched from tiny eggs laid by adult insects.

Leeuwenhoek's theories eventually led to our understanding of microorganisms such as germs and bacteria. Leeuwenhoek's work, like that of others during the Enlightenment, helped people see science as a way to improve the world.

Scientific Discoveries Encourage New Attitudes

As new ideas inspired by humanism and the Reformation spread across Europe in the 1500s and 1600s, scientists had begun applying new ideas to the ways in which they understood the world. They began to rely more on reason and logic than on superstition or old theories to explain the world.

One example of the use of reason was the development of the **scientific method**, a step-by-step way of performing experiments. Using the scientific method, a scientist conducts an experiment in steps, changing a single process or ingredient in each step. The scientist carefully observes and records what happens, and then uses these observations to explain the results. Experiments performed using the scientific method can be repeated by others. Discoveries made by the scientists of this period not only increased knowledge about the world but also changed the way that people lived.

Sometimes these experiments gave results that contradicted the teachings of the Roman Catholic Church in Europe. In the early 1600s, Galileo Gallilei (gal uh LAY oh gal uh LAY) used his observations to prove that the sun was the center of the universe and that the planets revolved around the sun. However, the official Catholic Church teaching at that time was that Earth was at the center of the universe and that the sun and planets revolved around Earth.

After Galileo published the results of his research in 1632, he was brought to Rome, where a court found him guilty of violating Catholic Church teachings. He was sentenced to life imprisonment, a sentence he served by remaining confined in his house in Florence for the rest of his life. Other scientists and writers were jailed for opposing the Catholic Church, and their writings were banned.

Despite these challenges, new ideas and methods continued to spread throughout Europe. These ideas and methods would change not only how Europeans thought about science, but also how they thought about religion, politics, and many other aspects of human nature and society.

✓ **Reading Check** **How did the Catholic Church react when scientific theories differed from Church teachings?**

Go Online
PHSchool.com Use Web Code **mup-0844** for an interactivity on the scientific method.

Galileo and the Telescope
Galileo was the first person to use a telescope to study the stars and planets. **Infer** *How might a telescope have helped Galileo to make new discoveries?*

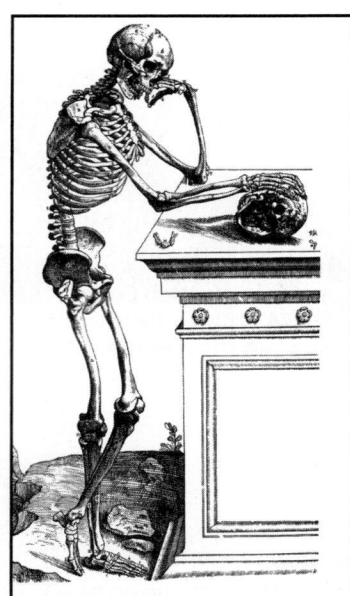

Revolutionizing Medicine
Vesalius demonstrated that accepted theories on the structure of the human body were not based on the study of human anatomy. He realized that previous physicians had merely applied information gathered from the structures of animals to that of the human body. **Infer** *What does the title page to Vesalius's book (above) suggest about how he learned about the human body?*

The Scientific Revolution

Galileo's work came during a period that historians now call the Scientific Revolution. From the mid-1500s through the mid-1700s, scientists made many significant discoveries in several different sciences. In 1543, Andreas Vesalius (AN dree us vih SAY lee us), a Flemish doctor, produced the first manual that used detailed pictures to show the structure of the human body. William Harvey, an English doctor, discovered that the human heart works like a pump and that blood is returned to the heart after it circulates through the body.

Beginning in 1637, the French philosopher René Descartes (ruh NAY day KAHRT) began to publish books proposing a system for geometry. He also used letters of the alphabet in math equations and analyzed how light was reflected from a mirror. His studies led to the development of analytic geometry. Descartes also proposed the idea that mathematics was the perfect model for reasoning in all of the sciences.

Robert Boyle, an Irish chemist, disproved the centuries-old idea that all matter was made of a combination of four things: air, water, earth, and fire. Boyle argued in the late 1600s that matter was made up of a more complex combination of chemicals. Boyle's work became the foundation of modern chemistry.

In the mid-1700s, the British scientist Sir Isaac Newton studied the motion of the planets and objects on the earth. His theories about **natural laws,** or the patterns that control the behavior of the universe, included the laws of motion and gravity. These laws explain everything from why a rock rolls down a hill to the way the Earth revolves around the sun. His studies helped explain some problems with the theories that Galileo had proposed a century earlier, but still upheld their basic principles.

These scientific discoveries and many others changed the way that people understood the world around them. People began to believe that science and reason could improve their lives. Although some of the explanations were later proven wrong, the dedication of these scientists to the scientific method and their belief in the use of reason continue to be the basis for science today.

An 1883 reproduction of the pendulum clock designed by Galileo

✓ Reading Check **How did William Harvey help increase scientific knowledge?**

New Ways of Thinking

In 1687, Newton published his ideas in a book called *Mathematical Principles of Natural Philosophy*. As scientists and thinkers across Europe understood Newton's work, they believed his approach could discover other natural laws. Their belief in the power of science and reason inspired them. They began to search for natural laws in human behavior as well.

To help them keep up with the pace of new discoveries, scientists began forming organizations through which they could share new knowledge and exchange ideas. The first of these organizations was created in Italy in the early 1600s. Two of the most important were formed in the mid-1660s: the Royal Society of London for the Promotion of Natural Knowledge and the Académie des Sciences (a ka day MEE day see AHNS) of Paris. These societies published papers explaining new discoveries in a way that could be understood by all scientists. Through these and other organizations like them, scientific knowledge spread rapidly throughout Germany, England, Italy, Russia, the Netherlands, and the American colonies.

This movement across Europe became known as the **Enlightenment** because of the belief that science and natural laws of behavior would bring individuals and society to a better, or more enlightened, state. It is sometimes called the Age of Reason because people believed they could understand the world with their intelligence. This way of thinking affected politics, art, literature, science, and religion.

Newton concluded that a prism separates light into the colors of the spectrum because each color refracts, or bends, by a different amount.

✔ **Reading Check** How were Enlightenment ideas communicated throughout Europe?

The Enlightenment Affects Government

As Enlightenment ideas about science and reason spread, new theories about politics and government were developed. These new theories emphasized the rights of individuals and new ways that society could be organized.

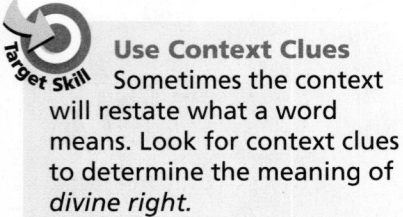

Use Context Clues Sometimes the context will restate what a word means. Look for context clues to determine the meaning of *divine right*.

The Conflict Over Divine Right to Rule In Chapter 18, you learned that the monarchs who ruled in Europe were believed to have divine right. According to this theory, the right to rule had been decided by God, and rulers had to answer to God only. The people they ruled had no say in the government and no right to speak out against it. In 1651, the English writer Thomas Hobbes published a book that strongly supported the power of royalty and the divine right to rule. He believed that without a strong government to control them, people would behave badly and their lives would be "solitary, poor, nasty, brutish, and short." He thought that people were naturally greedy and selfish and that they needed a king who could rule without any limits to preserve order.

Many Enlightenment thinkers disagreed with Hobbes' view of human nature. According to the French philosopher Descartes, "the power of forming a good judgment and of distinguishing the true from the false, which is properly speaking what is called good sense or reason, is by nature equal in all men." Descartes believed that any person who had a good education had the power to reason and make good decisions.

John Locke, an English writer, also opposed the theory of the divine right of kings. In his 1690 book, *Two Treatises of Government*, Locke applied Enlightenment ideas to government and challenged the divine right of kings. He argued that all people possessed certain **natural rights** when they were born, including the rights to life, liberty, and property. He also argued that the people should hold the power of government. According to his theory, a government should rule only if it followed natural laws and protected people's natural rights. Locke argued that the people should overthrow a government that does not do these things.

René Descartes

Enlightened Rulers Among the upper classes in Europe, the ideas of the Enlightenment became very popular. Even kings and queens became familiar with them.

Frederick the Great of Prussia ruled over much of what is now Germany and Poland from 1740 to 1786. He made changes within his country that reflected Enlightenment ideas. He retained absolute power, but he believed he should work for the common good. He helped peasant farmers and made laws so that they were fairer to all classes of people.

Catherine the Great of Russia (1762–1796) expanded the Russian educational and public health system. However, even as she made these changes, she also expanded landowners' authority over peasants.

Even though some monarchs started reforms during the Enlightenment, serfdom continued in Europe until the 1800s.

Joseph II of Austria (1765–1790) allowed religious tolerance and limited the power of the Catholic Church to take action in his kingdom. He reformed laws, established independent judges, freed the serfs, and allowed the publication of ideas that were opposed to his or to those of the church. However, many people in the upper class in his country opposed such big changes.

 **Reading Check** How did Enlightenment thinking affect some of the rulers in Europe?

Section 1 Assessment

Key Terms
Review the Key Terms at the beginning of this section. Use each term in a sentence that explains its meaning.

Target Reading Skill
Find the word *promotion* on page 533. What do you think *promotion* means? What clues help you arrive at this meaning?

Comprehension and Critical Thinking
1. (a) Define What is the scientific method?
(b) Identify Cause and Effect How did the scientific method change the practice of science?

2. (a) List List three areas of science affected by the Scientific Revolution.
(b) Summarize How did the Scientific Revolution affect thinkers across Europe?
3. (a) Identify What was the Enlightenment?
(b) Identify Cause and Effect How did Enlightenment ideas spread?
4. (a) Explain Explain how Enlightenment ideas helped some peasants and serfs in Europe.
(b) Compare and Contrast Contrast the ideas of Hobbes and Locke on what rights people and governments should have.

Writing Activity
Write a journal entry that lists some scientific discoveries in medicine or other areas that have been made during your life or during the last 50 years. Describe how they have changed your life or other people's lives.

For: An activity on the Scientific Revolution
Visit: PHSchool.com
Web Code: mud-1910

Prepare to Read

Objectives

In this section you will

1. Learn why Great Britain established colonies in North America.
2. Understand the American Revolution.
3. Identify reasons for the French Revolution.
4. Explore the effects of the French Revolution.

Taking Notes

As you read, identify ways that the American and French Revolutions were alike and different. Copy the chart below. Record your findings in it.

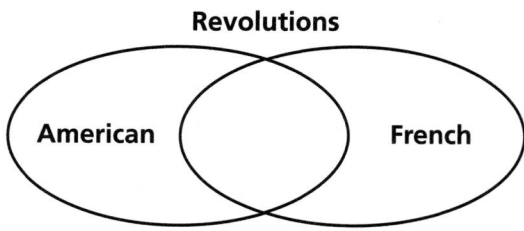

Revolutions

American · French

Target Reading Skill

Recognize Nonliteral Meanings Sometimes figurative language is used to convey meaning. As you read, look for words that have figurative meanings and substitute a word that gives a more literal meaning. Look at the word *spark* on this page. What is a word that you can use to replace *spark?*

Key Terms

- **colony** (KAHL uh nee) *n.* a territory that is ruled by another country and is usually very far from the ruling country
- **constitution** (kahn stuh TOO shun) *n.* a set of rules explaining the structure and powers of the government
- **democracy** (dih MAHK ruh see) *n.* a political system in which people freely elect government leaders

Founded in May 1607, Jamestown, Virginia, became Britain's first permanent settlement in North America.

Even as Enlightenment ideas were spreading throughout Europe, a radical new experiment was taking shape elsewhere. In a distant corner of the British Empire, settlers who had come to North America throughout the 1600s and 1700s began planning a new form of government.

By 1607, 105 settlers had established their first permanent North American homes in Virginia. By 1760, almost 1,700,000 Europeans lived in British North America. They built towns and shipped goods from coastal trading ports. Living outside of Europe, though, also had given them a new way of seeing things.

"We see with other eyes; we hear with other ears; and think with other thoughts, than those formerly used," wrote one of these leaders, Thomas Paine. Their new beliefs would spark a revolution in North America. The changes in this tiny imperial outpost would be felt throughout Europe and beyond in the next century.

Britain Establishes Colonies in North America

After Christopher Columbus had returned from the Caribbean, European nations sought ways to control new lands. They sent ships to claim lands and take advantage of the many resources they found. They also established permanent settlements to enforce their claims and to grow cash crops. Disputes and wars over the new settlements were common. In some cases, native populations resisted the settlers. Europeans from different areas also fought with one another for control. By the end of the Seven Years' War in 1763, Great Britain had won from the French most of what is now the United States east of the Mississippi River and much of Canada.

The new settlements in North America were called colonies. A **colony** is a territory that is ruled by another country and is usually very far from the ruling country. Great Britain used the North American colonies as a source of income. Private companies that had received charters, or special permission from the government to settle and govern the territory, had established some settlements. These companies invested in the settlements with the hope that they could eventually make a profit.

By the mid-1700s, the British government had brought most of the colonies under more direct authority. Governors ruled many of the colonies, and laws required that all goods shipped from the colonies had to be transported on British ships. The British government also provided protection from Native Americans and from other countries while regulating many aspects of life in the colonies.

Jamestown Colony
Today, parts of Jamestown have been reconstructed to show how the colony may have looked about 400 years ago.
Summarize *What is a colony?*

✓ **Reading Check** **Why did private companies help establish colonies in North America?**

and enslaved Africans, the founding principles of the United States were the clearest statements of freedom and equality by any government at that point in history.

on spreading the word of revolution.

✓ **Reading Check** **How were the Articles of Confederation and the Constitution different?**

Target Skill

Recognize Nonliteral Meanings
The word *raged* is used figuratively in the first sentence on this page. What is another word you could substitute for *raged*?

The American Revolution

As the Seven Years' War raged in Europe, British and French forces also fought each other in their North American colonies. Although the British drove the French out of much of North America, their battles against the French had been very costly. The British government had large debts to pay when the war

Effects of the French Revolution

The growing disorder in France and the fear of invasion led to a period of violence that lasted until 1794. During this period, called the Reign of Terror (rayn uv TEHR ur), bloody attacks and executions became common as leaders struggled to gain power.

Robespierre's arrest

They also sought to protect France from other kingdoms that felt threatened by the spread of democratic ideals.

As the National Assembly continued to meet, distinct political groups emerged. The most radical of them, called the Jacobins (JAK uh binz), were led by Maximilien Robespierre (mahk see mee LYAHN ROHBZ pyehr). The Jacobins declared a "policy of terror" against all opponents, including supporters of the king and nearly anyone else who disagreed with their policies.

Between September 1793 and 1794 more than 300,000 people were arrested. Approximately 17,000 of them were condemned to death and executed. Many more died in prisons or while awaiting trial. At the same time, the revolutionary government raised an army of more than one million men. Instead of a new representative government, Robespierre and the Jacobins had taken power and ruled as dictators.

Even as the Jacobins ruled through fear and terror, they instituted a number of democratic reforms through the National Assembly. They authorized free schooling for all children regardless of class and created a tax system based on a person's income. They tried to end slavery in France's colonies and created laws to protect people from high prices. The Jacobins also raised a large "citizen's army" that fought against European powers that opposed the changes in France. During the period of Jacobin rule, French armies pushed back invaders and went on the offensive. These wars are known as the French Revolutionary Wars.

Many of these reforms were not fully carried out. On July 27, 1794, leaders who opposed Robespierre had him arrested and accused him of being a tyrant. His execution the next day ended the Reign of Terror. It also opened the door for new competition between political groups.

Links to Art

The Death of Marat Jacobin leader Jean-Paul Marat (zhahn pawl mah rah) was assassinated by Charlotte Corday (shahr lut kawr day), a young Jacobin opponent who stabbed him as he bathed. Shortly after the assassination, Marat's death was depicted in an oil painting by Jacques-Louis David (zhahk loo ee dah veed), a leading artist who supported the Jacobins. His painting, "The Death of Marat," depicts Marat as a martyr, a person who gives his or her life for a noble cause. This and similar paintings by David of slain Jacobin leaders helped shape national opinion about the Jacobins.

After Robespierre's death, a new government called the Directory formed and abolished many of the Jacobin reforms. The Directory limited voting rights only to people who paid a certain amount of taxes. However, the Directory was severely weakened by conflicts with people who favored the old monarchy and those who wanted to return to Jacobin rule. Wars continued between France and European powers, making the disagreements within France stronger.

By the late 1790s, the French Revolutionary Wars had shifted from defending the French Revolution to conquering neighboring countries. French people were deeply divided about how best to rule their country, and many were simply tired of the violence, chaos, and rapid changes that had prevailed in France for a decade. In October 1799, some leaders opposed to the Directory looked to the French military for support. A young general named Napoleon Bonaparte (nuh POH lee un BOH nuh pahrt) had become a national hero after his victories in Italy. He returned to France and seized power, ending the revolution in France.

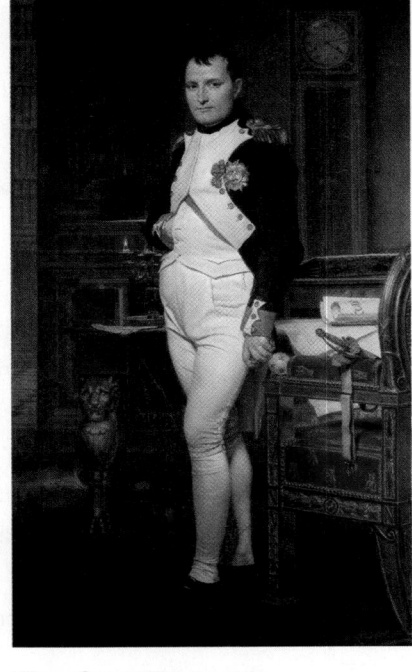

Napoleon Bonaparte

 **Reading Check** **What changes did the Directory propose after Robespierre's death?**

Section 2 Assessment

Key Terms
Review the Key Terms at the beginning of this section. Use each term in a sentence that explains its meaning.

Target Reading Skill
Find the phrase "opened the door" on page 542. Use the context of the sentence to determine what the phrase means. Then substitute a word or phrase for "opened the door" that gives its literal meaning.

Comprehension and Critical Thinking

1. (a) Define What is a colony?
(b) Explain How were British colonies governed?

2. (a) Identify Identify several complaints the American colonists had about British rule.
3. (a) Apply Information How did Americans change their form of government after they won the Revolutionary War?
4. (a) List List the three classes that existed in French society before the French Revolution.
(b) Explain How did members of France's third estate want to change the system of voting?
(c) Compare and Contrast How were the American and French Revolutions similar? How were they different?
5. (a) Identify What political group ruled during the Reign of Terror?

(b) Draw Conclusions In what ways did rulers during the Reign of Terror reflect or not reflect the ideals of the Enlightenment?

Writing Activity
You are a commoner or peasant during the French Revolution. Write a journal entry that describes why you are angry and what fears you have.

For: An activity on revolutions in France and America
Visit: PHSchool.com
Web Code: mud-1920

Problem Solving

> **Jack:** What's wrong, Maurice?
>
> **Maurice:** Oh, nothing. It's just that my life has been getting really busy lately, and I'm having trouble keeping track of everything. I have homework and rehearsals for the school play, not to mention practice for the team. I never know where I'm supposed to be.
>
> **Jack:** Sounds like you have a problem organizing your time. Or maybe you just have too many things to do.
>
> **Maurice:** I know. I'd better figure out some kind of solution before this situation gets out of hand.

Maurice has a problem to solve. Solving problems is an important skill that allows you to analyze a situation and make the best possible decision about it. When you study, analyzing how people in history tried to solve problems can help you better understand the choices they made and the effects of those choices.

Learn the Skill

Use these steps to solve problems.

1 **Identify the problem.** State the problem in your own words, and explain the effect of the problem.

2 **Gather information about the problem.** Use a graphic organizer to identify causes of the problem.

3 **List possible solutions for the problem.** Include several solutions, even though some may seem unrealistic to you at first. When you examine them, you may find that they have unexpected benefits.

4 **List advantages and disadvantages of each possible solution.** Your list should include at least one advantage and one disadvantage of each possible solution.

5 **Choose the best solution.** Once you have put the solution into practice for awhile, evaluate how effective it has been.

Practice the Skill

Read the passage below. Then follow the steps below to identify the best solution to the problem.

"During the 1700s, many businesses in the United Kingdom began to hire children. Children worked for lower wages than adults, and were not as likely as adults to cause labor troubles. Factory owners wanted to use the children's small, nimble fingers for tending machines. Children worked for low pay in dirty, poorly lighted factories, mills, and mines. They often performed jobs that really required adult strength. Many children worked to help support their unemployed parents. Orphans were often forced into labor. Similar conditions became common in the United States during the late 1700s.

Child workers were often deprived of the chance to attend school. Uneducated, the only work they were capable of doing was unskilled labor. Thus, they had little chance to better themselves."

1 Read the passage, and identify a problem that needs to be solved.

2 Use a graphic organizer to identify causes of the problem.

3 List possible solutions for the problem you have identified.

4 Evaluate the possible solutions by listing at least one advantage and one disadvantage for each.

5 Select the best possible solution.

Apply the Skill

Read about industrial cities on page 556, and use the problem-solving steps to identify possible solutions for poor living conditions for workers in cities. Select the best possible solution and explain your choice.

Prepare to Read

Objectives

In this section you will

1. Learn how Napoleon rose to power in France and began a large empire.
2. Understand some reforms that Napoleon made and why he finally lost power.

Taking Notes

As you read this section, notice how Napoleon affected Europe as a military leader and as a government leader. Copy the chart below and record your findings in it.

Napoleon's Influence on Europe	
Military Actions	**Government Actions**
• Wins early victories for France •	• Takes control of France •

Target Reading Skill

Use Context Clues
Sometimes the context gives a direct description of a word. The following sentence gives a direct description of the word *alliance*.

At one time, France and Spain formed an *alliance* to fight together against the British.

What does the word *alliance* mean?

Key Terms

- **Napoleonic Code** (nuh poh lee AHN ik kohd) *n.* a set of laws that protect individual liberty, the right to work, and the right to one's own opinions
- **blockade** (blah KAYD) *n.* the banning of trade
- **exile** (EK syl) *v.* to send away

Napoleon's Grand Army destroyed towns such as Kovno as it advanced towards Moscow.

In June 1812, Napoleon Bonaparte, French emperor and ruler of a large part of western Europe, attacked Russia. He hoped to defeat Russia and weaken Great Britain by cutting off trade. His Grand Army numbered 600,000, and had a history of spectacular success in war.

But the Russians fought well. When Napoleon's army reached Moscow, the city had been burned. Napoleon retreated in October as the winter began. The temperature sank as low as −40° F (−71° C). Many soldiers starved or froze to death.

The Berezina River (buh REZ ih nuh RIV ur) in Poland was choked with ice when the Grand Army tried to cross on a makeshift bridge. The Russian Army attacked from behind.

Half a million of his soldiers died, deserted, or were taken captive during the disastrous invasion of Russia. Napoleon's defeat led to his downfall. The Age of Napoleon did not last much longer, but its effects shaped the history of Europe throughout the nineteenth century.

Napoleon Takes Power and Builds an Empire

As French armies made gains against European empires in 1799, the power of the Directory was challenged. A young military officer, Napoleon Bonaparte, had achieved great fame fighting against the Austrian Empire in Italy. His victory had forced the Austrians to turn the lands over to France that today are Belgium and Luxembourg.

In 1799, Napoleon learned that Austria, Great Britain, Turkey and Russia had formed a new partnership to defeat France. Napoleon returned to Paris to save his country. He took advantage of political divisions in the Directory to seize power in November 1799. After ten years of revolution, many French people wanted a strong leader. In 1802, the people of France made Napoleon leader for life. In 1804, he took the title emperor, placing a crown on his own head during a ceremony in December of that year.

Napoleon continued his wars against the other European kingdoms, hoping to build the greatest empire in history. At the same time, he put some of the ideas of the French Revolution into practice in government.

He was successful in battle after battle. By 1812 he controlled most of Europe, including the countries that would later be Spain, Italy, Germany, the Netherlands, Switzerland, and Belgium. Napoleon also made alliances with other countries to extend his control of those countries. Often, he put friends and relatives in power in countries he had conquered to guarantee the friendship and support of those countries. His success at building an empire made him respected and feared across Europe and around the world. Only Great Britain remained a strong country and an enemy outside of his influence.

Napoleon's Empire
As emperor, Napoleon restored practices similar to those of the past monarchy. He asked the pope to bless his coronation. He also revived the titles and symbols of the nobility. **Analyze Images** *How does the painting of Napoleon's coronation suggest France's past monarchy?*

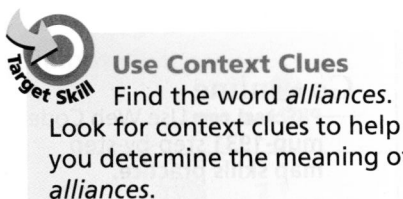

Use Context Clues
Target Skill Find the word *alliances*. Look for context clues to help you determine the meaning of *alliances*.

✓ **Reading Check** **How did Napoleon first become popular with the French people?**

Effects of Industrialization

Countries that industrialized were greatly affected by it. The Industrial Revolution changed city life, changed working conditions, and increased wealth.

Workers in a steel forge

Growth of Industrial Cities New factories of the Industrial Revolution drew large numbers of workers to fill the jobs. Cities grew rapidly, and workers often lived in slums. Sanitation, pollution, and disease became big problems in cities.

Harsh Working Conditions Factory workers often worked long hours under harsh conditions. Women and young children often performed the worst jobs. Many of the new machines were not safe and were often very loud. The air in textile mills was filled with dust from the cloth.

Growing Wealth Despite these problems, the standard of living for the working class in industrialized countries improved. The general prosperity led to rising populations, and cities assumed a new importance in industrialized countries.

✓ Reading Check **Why did new cities grow so quickly during the Industrial Revolution?**

 Section **4** Assessment

Key Terms
Review the Key Terms at the beginning of this section. Use each term in a sentence that explains its meaning.

Target Reading Skill
Find the phrase *gave birth* on page 555. Use context clues to figure out its meaning.

Comprehension and Critical Thinking
1. (a) Explain How did changes in farming methods affect population?

2. (a) List List two advantages Great Britain had that helped it lead the Industrial Revolution.
(b) Draw Conclusions How did James Watt's steam engine help the Industrial Revolution?
3. (a) Explain How did Great Britain lay the groundwork for industrialism in the United States?
(b) Compare and Contrast What features did the United States share with Great Britain that allowed industrialism to develop rapidly?
4. (a) Make Generalizations What were working conditions like for many factory workers?

Writing Activity
You are a child who has moved from a small village in Great Britain to a new city. Your whole family now lives in a small room and works in a textile mill. Write a journal entry that describes some of your feelings about the changes in your family's life.

For: An activity on the Industrial Revolution
Visit: PHSchool.com
Web Code: mud-1940

Review and Assessment

◆ Chapter Summary

Section 1: The Enlightenment

- Scientific discoveries in the 1500s and 1600s led people to believe that science could improve their lives.
- Enlightenment thinking spread across Europe and encouraged people to look for natural laws in the world around them and in how people were governed.
- Some people began to think that kings did not have a divine right to rule and a few rulers made changes that gave serfs and peasants more freedom.

Section 2: Political Revolutions

- The American colonies fought a war against Great Britain so that they could have a more representative government.
- The French people revolted against their king in hopes that they could have more influence in their government and be treated more fairly. However, the French Revolution resulted in the execution of thousands of people and did not create a strong government.

Section 3: The Age of Napoleon

- Napoleon took control of the government when it was weak.
- Napoleon fought wars throughout Europe and built a huge empire by conquering other countries.
- Napoleon reformed many laws and government systems in France and Europe.
- Most countries in Europe fought along-side Great Britain to defeat Napoleon.

Section 4: The Early Industrial Age

- Farming improvements led to a population increase in Great Britain and Europe and increased demand for consumer goods.
- Great Britain led the world in the Industrial Revolution.
- The United States quickly used British industrial methods and made improvements to become the leading industrial nation by 1850.
- Factories were often dangerous and many of the new cities around the factories were unhealthy places to live.

◆ Key Terms

Match the key terms below with the sentences that follow.

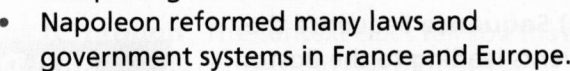

    a. **scientific method**

    b. **natural laws**

    c. **democracy**

    d. **blockade**

    e. **exiled**

1. One way to influence a country during a war is to use a _____.

2. A person who is _____ has been forced to leave his or her home country forever or for a specific period of time.

3. In a _____, people vote for their representatives.

4. To discover how high different types of balls bounce, you might use the _____.

5. To explain why balls bounce, your explanation might include _____.

Chapter 20 A Changing World

Chapter Preview

In this chapter you will examine reasons why Europeans changed their thinking about government. You will explore the changes revolutions brought to European nations. You will also learn how Europeans expanded their influence in the world through imperialism and colonization.

Section 1
Nationalism and Expansion in Europe

Section 2
Imperialism in Africa and the Middle East

Section 3
Imperialism in Asia and Latin America

Target Reading Skill

Main Idea In this chapter, you will focus on identifying details that give further information about the main idea of a paragraph or section.

▶ **Parliament Building in Vienna, Austria**

Europe in 1815

MAP MASTER™ Skills Activity

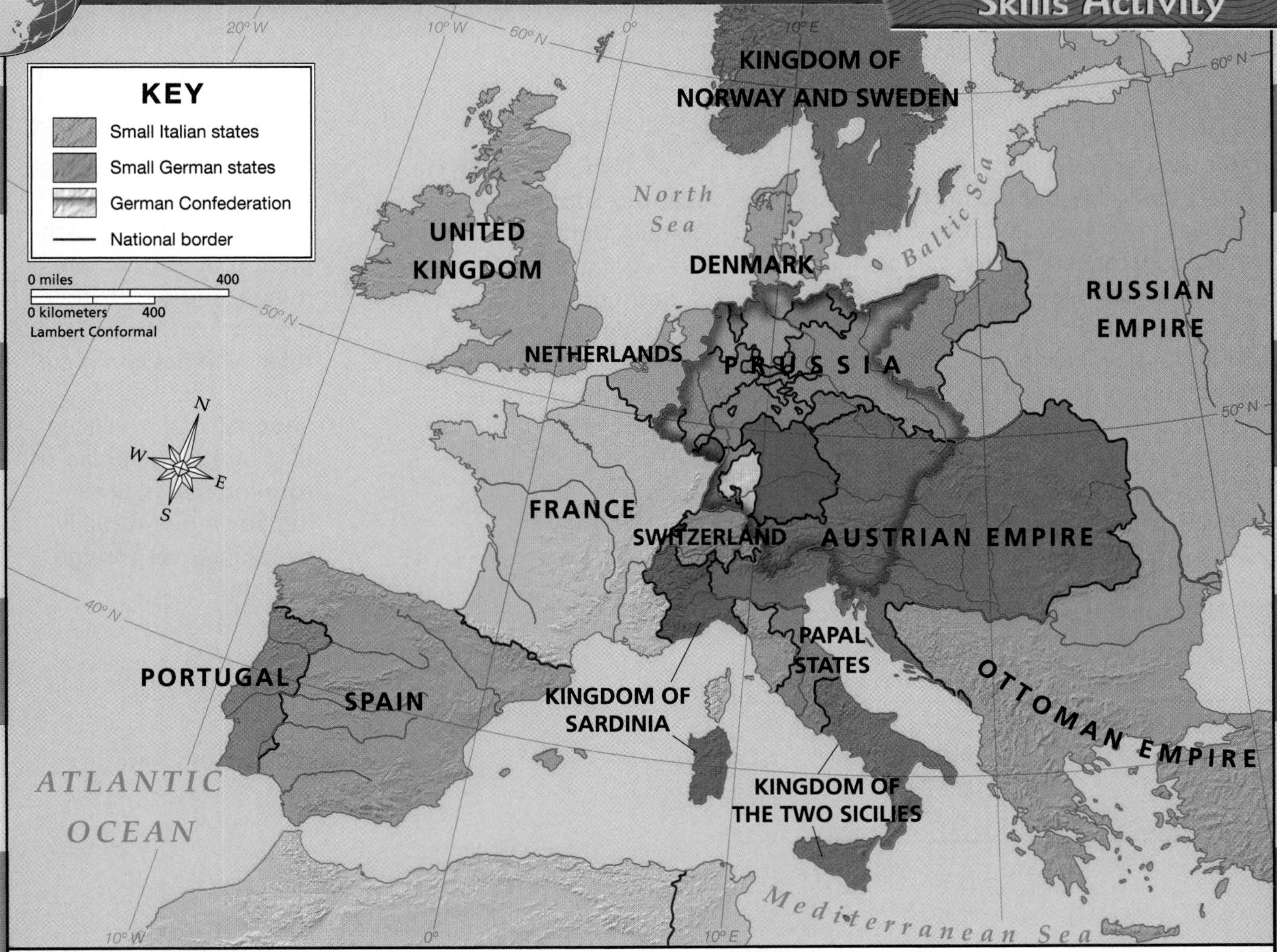
KEY
Small Italian states
Small German states
German Confederation
National border
0 miles 400
0 kilometers 400
Lambert Conformal
N
S
E
W
20° W
10° W
0°
10° E
60° N
50° N
40° N
KINGDOM OF NORWAY AND SWEDEN
North Sea
Baltic Sea
UNITED KINGDOM
DENMARK
RUSSIAN EMPIRE
NETHERLANDS
PRUSSIA
FRANCE
SWITZERLAND
AUSTRIAN EMPIRE
PAPAL STATES
PORTUGAL
SPAIN
KINGDOM OF SARDINIA
OTTOMAN EMPIRE
KINGDOM OF THE TWO SICILIES
ATLANTIC OCEAN
Mediterranean Sea

Regions After the defeat of Napoleon, European rulers negotiated new boundaries for many areas of the continent. These new boundaries were influenced by the power and ambition of the rulers involved. **Note** Which names on the map do you recognize as those of countries that exist today? Notice the names of those that no longer exist. What do many of them have in common? **Compare** Look at the map on page 548. Which countries gained territory at the expense of France or French-influenced states after Napoleon was defeated?

Go Online PHSchool.com Use Web Code **mup-2001** for step-by-step **map skills practice.**

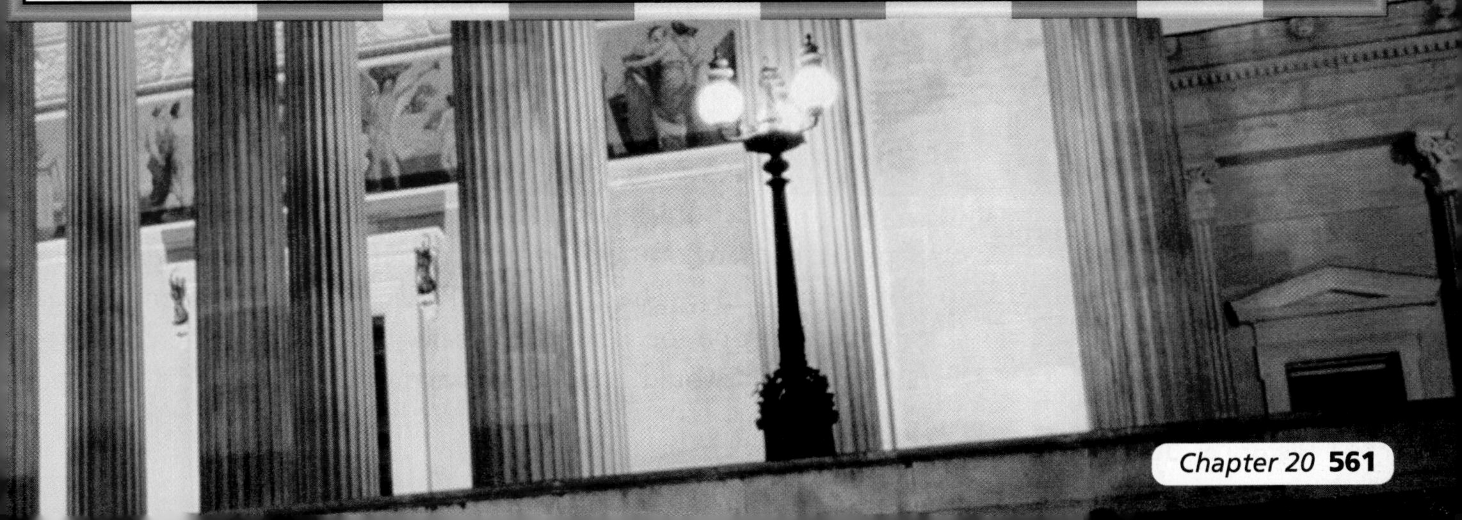

Nationalism and Expansion in Europe

Prepare to Read

Objectives

In this section you will

1. Learn how changes in Europe in the early 1800s led to a rise in nationalism.
2. Describe France after the fall of Napoleon.
3. Identify why revolutions swept across Europe in 1848.
4. Find out how European countries expanded their control to other parts of the world.

Taking Notes

As you read this section, add details that help explain the main idea of the section. Copy the chart below, and record your findings in it.

Nationalism and Expansion in Europe	
Moving Toward Nationalism	**Revolutions in France**
• People didn't think of themselves as part of a nation •	• Overthrow of the king in the July Revolution •

Target Reading Skill

Identify Supporting Details Details are smaller pieces of information that support or help explain the main idea. As you read, look for details that help explain the main idea.

Key Terms

- **nationalism** (NASH uh nul iz um) *n.* a feeling of strong loyalty or attachment to a culture, language, and/or territory
- **dictator** (DIK tay tur) *n.* a ruler who has complete power
- **imperialism** (im PIHR ee ul iz um) *n.* the policy of forming and maintaining an empire, usually by taking over foreign colonies

The Congress of Vienna, 1814

When Napoleon was defeated in 1814, governments from all over Europe met in Vienna, Austria, to discuss how Napoleon's empire would be divided. For nine months there were meetings during the day and extravagant parties, dances, and other events at night. Great Britain, Austria, Prussia, and Russia were the most powerful countries at the meetings. Each of these nations had secret plans for how the map of Europe was to be redrawn and how political order was to be reestablished. It was not long before these powerful nations grew to distrust one another.

In the end, kings and queens were put back into power in many of the countries and replaced the elected government of France. The Congress of Vienna helped prevent a large war in Europe for a hundred years. But many of the countries they created would not last. Too many people wanted an elected government.

The Rise of Nationalism

For centuries the empires of Europe were built through military victories and marriages between ruling families. Rulers fought wars to make their empires larger, or married their sons and daughters into other royal families to extend their control. Educated Europeans spoke and wrote in the same language—Latin and later French—and they shared the same religion, Christianity.

When common people in Europe thought about who they were, most would have identified themselves as the subject of a particular ruler, a native of a certain village, or a member of a particular religion. At the end of the 1700s, common people began to think of themselves as citizens of a nation united by shared interests, such as religion, language, and culture. Inspired by John Locke's Enlightenment ideas about the natural rights of individuals and the rise of the merchant middle class, Europeans of the late eighteenth and early nineteenth centuries became more interested in the governments who ruled them. The American and French Revolutions also brought great attention to these new ideas.

The belief in a separate nation was particularly strong in France after the French Revolution and under Napoleon. In an effort to unite French people under his rule, Napoleon encouraged national songs, holidays, flags, and other symbols to promote patriotic feelings for a specifically French nation. Napoleon's conquests in Europe helped spread these ideas about national pride throughout Europe. Some of the conquered groups of people believed that they had natural rights as well. They acknowledged or recognized that people in their own area had similar beliefs and wanted to create and vote for their own governments.

The rulers at the 1814–1815 Congress of Vienna tried to overcome this thinking by putting kings and queens from the old ruling families back into power, and by supporting the old idea of divine rights. But the move toward **nationalism,** or a feeling of strong loyalty or attachment to a culture, language, or territory, was too strong. People across Europe revolted against the royal families during the next 35 years because they wanted to create and govern their own countries.

✓ Reading Check   **Why was nationalism especially strong in France?**

Patriotic Symbols
The day after Napoleon's coronation, he ordered the eagle—a symbol of military victory—be placed on top of every flag in his army. **Identify** Name a symbol of government and explain what it represents.

France After the Fall of Napoleon

After Napoleon's defeat, the Congress of Vienna put Louis XVIII back into power in France. He allowed voters to elect representatives to parliament. These officials were given limited powers, but the most important powers remained with the king.

The July Revolution After Louis's death in 1824, his younger brother, Charles X, took the throne. Charles disagreed with Enlightenment ideas, such as the right of the people to vote and to publish their opinions in newspapers. When he tried to reject the French constitution and make these changes in the summer of 1830, the people of France revolted. The revolutionaries put into power a new king, Louis-Philippe, and wrote a new constitution that limited the power of the king and gave French citizens many more rights.

The Citizen King The parliament that named Louis-Philippe king stressed the importance of ruling with the consent of the people. Louis-Philippe soon came to be called the "citizen king." However, as his rule continued, there were many conflicts over the role of the king in government. Some wanted to strengthen the role of the king, but others thought his power should be reduced even more. Louis-Philippe survived many assassination attempts. In 1836 and again in 1840, Napoleon III, the nephew of the former emperor, tried to seize control of the French government.

The July Revolution, 1830
French men and women took over the streets of Paris in the summer of 1830, and forced Charles X to give up his throne in a revolt called the July Revolution. **Identify Causes** *What actions on the part of Charles X led to the July Revolution?*

✓ Reading Check **Why was Louis-Philippe known as the citizen king?**

Revolutions Across Europe

News of the changes in France inspired nationalists in other countries to fight against the kings restored to power by the Congress of Vienna. However, not all of the revolutions were successful for the nationalists. Revolts in Austria and Prussia were defeated with military force, but local revolts by nationalists in Italy and Switzerland had some success in changing their governments. Civil wars broke out in Spain and Portugal and involved troops from Britain and France. In Spain, these wars lasted until 1840.

The Polish Revolt The lands of present-day Poland had been divided up and ruled by other countries for many years. The Congress of Vienna put most of Poland under Russian control. Nationalists wanted to make Poland a single nation ruled by the Polish people. In 1830, they began a small revolt against the Russians, and for a short time, controlled the country. But the Russian army crushed the revolt the following year, and many of the rights the Polish people previously had were taken away.

Belgium's Quest for Independence A revolt in Belgium was the only one that succeeded in creating an independent country that year. The Vienna Congress had joined Belgium, Holland, and Luxembourg to form the Kingdom of the Netherlands. A Dutch king was given control of the joined nations in order to limit the power of the defeated France. People in these areas spoke different languages and had different religions and economic interests. They did not want to unify to form one new nation. When the revolt began, the Dutch king asked other European rulers for help. Some were too busy with revolts of their own, but Britain and France thought that it was in their best interest for Belgium to remain as an independent country. Belgium declared its independence on October 4, 1830.

Art and Revolution Although most of the revolts of 1830 were not immediately successful, nationalism continued to spread throughout Europe. A literary and arts movement in Europe called Romanticism celebrated the French revolutions and spread the idea that people had a natural right to rule themselves. In the following years, these ideas helped spark more revolts against the ruling empires.

✓ **Reading Check** **What was the effect of the uprising in Poland?**

The Triumphal Arches were built as a monument to celebrate the 50th anniversary of Belgium's independence.

Revolutions of 1848

Nationalist feelings, economic changes brought by the Industrial Revolution, and new theories about government continued to change the attitudes of people throughout Europe. Escalating frustrations with the old empires and rulers erupted throughout Europe in 1848, a year of revolutions.

France The French were happy at first with their elected king, Louis-Philippe. This changed when Louis-Philippe began to act more like a royal king from the past. He returned to the practice of arranged marriages and arranged a marriage for his daughter to the king of Belgium. The Industrial Revolution also brought changes that worked against Louis-Philippe. The Industrial Revolution created unhealthy cities filled with poorly paid workers. Philippe's government did little to clean up the cities and solve labor problems. Angered, the French protested and overthrew the king in 1848.

For the first time, the French held an election in which all citizens were allowed to vote. The voters elected Napoleon III for a four-year term as president. In 1852, he abolished the republic and declared himself emperor of France. He ruled as a **dictator,** a ruler who has complete power, until he was overthrown in 1870 following France's defeat in a war with Prussia.

The Austrian Empire The Congress of Vienna joined the present-day countries of Austria, Hungary, the Czech Republic, and much of Italy to form the Austrian empire. However, many of the citzens of this newly formed empire were unhappy about the merge. The 1848 revolution in France inspired students and workers in Vienna, Austria's capital, to revolt against the Austrian empire. They demanded that Prince Metternich resign and a constitutional government be created. In Hungary, nationalists demanded a constitution that protected basic rights and freedom for the serfs. The Czechs also revolted and issued the same demands. Although Metternich was forced to resign, Austrian troops were quick to put down the nationalist movements.

The Austrian empire was overwhelmed by this opposition at first and agreed to make most of the changes that the rebels wanted. But soon, they used their army to regain control in Austria and the Czech Republic. The Russian army helped them smash the revolution in Hungary. The royal empire was once again in control.

From President to Emperor
The nephew of Napoleon, Napoleon III was elected in 1848 to a single term as president. Knowing he could not run for a second term, he led a military coup, dissolved the Legislative Assembly, and declared a new constitution. He was crowned emperor in 1852. **Sequence** *When did Napoleon III's rule end?*

The revolts in Italy followed some of the same patterns. Nationalists and workers took control of many of the small states that made up Italy at the time, and established new elected governments. But the Austrian army again took control in northern Italy, and a French army took over in the south.

Germany The Congress of Vienna left the Prussian and Austrian empires as rivals for power over the land that is today Germany. A loose union of 39 independent states called the German Confederation was also established. The German population experienced rapid population growth in the early 1800s, but many of its people remained poor. At the same time, the more prosperous middle class wanted a greater say in government. German nationalists worked to establish a strong German state.

Motivated by events in France and Austria in 1848, Germans in Berlin rebelled against Prussia and demanded a new constitution. Germans in other cities organized similar uprisings. Germans met in Frankfurt to write a new constitution to unify the German states. When they failed to agree, Prussian forces again took control.

Although the revolutions of 1848 did not cause great change, their ideas remained popular, and the nationalist movement continued. Instead of armed revolts, nationalists later used elections to gain power. Italy became an independent country in 1861, as did Germany in 1871. In the last part of the 1800s, Europeans were interested in expanding their control to other parts of the world.

✔ **Reading Check** Why did the Austrian empire face many different nationalist revolts?

Identify Supporting Details
What details in the paragraph explain how the revolts in Italy were similar to other revolts in 1848?

The Austrian army is shown below, with an enlarged view of the crest found on the flags of the Austrian infantry.

European Expansion and Imperialism

The opposition to the ruling empires did not succeed in making independent nations across Europe in 1848, and armed revolutions there were rare in the following years. In many cases, elected groups helped govern alongside a king or queen. But even as the empires of Europe fought to maintain their control at home, they began expanding their power in Asia and Africa.

Imperialism The French and the British were the leaders in the move to expand their empires in the early 1800s. These two countries had fought for control of colonies in North America in the 1700s. Great Britain had driven the French out of most of North America in 1763, only to lose the American colonies during the American Revolution. In the 1800s, both countries would focus their energy on gaining new colonies in Africa and Asia. As the century continued, other powerful European countries also pushed to take control of new lands. They looked to expand their control through a new era of **imperialism,** forming and maintaining an empire by taking over foreign colonies.

Expanding European Empires European countries had established trading posts and ports around the world for centuries. Sometimes they took control of key harbors and islands so that they could support their ships. This led to a growing interest in the establishment of colonies.

An African ruler and her officer receive European naval officers, who are seated under an umbrella.

Europeans saw many benefits to possessing colonies. Colonies would give Europeans a stable supply of raw materials. Colonies would also provide new markets for goods produced in their home countries. In countries where overcrowding was a problem, the colonies promised new lands for settlement. European nations also believed that establishing colonies would prevent their rivals from becoming too powerful.

European countries developed industry before African and Asian countries. This gave the European countries greater wealth and more powerful weapons. These advantages allowed Europeans to conquer parts of Asia and Africa. Many Europeans wanted to improve the lives of Asian and African people. They thought that sharing European culture and religion with others would help them become more "civilized." Some others thought that the darker-skinned peoples of Asia and Africa were not equal to the lighter-skinned peoples of Europe. They thought it was natural that stronger peoples should destroy or conquer weaker peoples and rule the world.

An African carving showing a European Christian missionary

✓ **Reading Check** In which areas of the world did the Europeans look to expand their control?

Section 1 Assessment

Key Terms
Review the Key Terms at the beginning of this section. Use each term in a sentence that explains its meaning.

Target Reading Skill
State the details that support the main idea under the heading "Revolutions of 1848" on page 566.

Comprehension and Critical Thinking
1. (a) List List three ways that Napoleon helped promote the idea of a strong French nation.
(b) Make Generalizations How did Locke's ideas about natural rights affect the French people and other European nationalists?

2. (a) Identify Identify the "citizen king," and explain why he was called that.
(b) Analyze Cause and Effect How did the overthrow of Charles X change the rights of French citizens?
3. (a) Summarize Summarize the reasons for the 1848 revolts against the Austrian empire.
(b) Describe the effects of the 1848 revolutions.
4. (a) Identify the Main Idea Why did European countries seek colonies in Africa and Asia?
(b) Analyze Cause and Effect How did European attitudes about people in other parts of the world influence the spread of imperialist ideas?

Writing Activity
Think about the revolutions of 1830 and 1848 in Europe. Write a brief paragraph discussing lessons that we can draw today from those revolutions.

For: For an activity on changes in Europe in the 1800s
Visit: PHSchool.com
Web Code: mud-2011

Imperialism in Africa and the Middle East

Prepare to Read

Objectives

In this section you will

1. Identify the reasons for European colonization in Africa.
2. Examine how European powers made claims on the right to rule Africa.
3. Learn how Africans resisted European colonization.
4. Understand the causes of the Boer War.
5. Understand how Britain gained control of lands in the Middle East.

Taking Notes

As you read this section, consider how European trade with Africa changed with colonization. Identify similarities and differences between these two eras. Copy the chart below, and record your findings in it.

African-European Trade

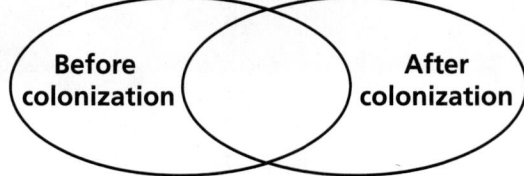

Before colonization   After colonization

Target Reading Skill

Identify Main Ideas
The main idea is the most important idea of a paragraph. Sometimes paragraphs have sentences that summarize or state the main idea. In other reading selections, the main idea may not be directly stated. When the main idea is implied, you must determine the main idea from key facts or ideas contained in the selection. As you read, consider what the sentences in the paragraph describe. Then connect these details to find the main idea.

Key Terms

- **monopoly** (muh NAHP uh lee) *n.* the areas in which only one government or company has the right to trade
- **partition** (pahr TISH un) *n.* a division
- **missionary** (MISH un her ee) *n.* the people who traveled to other places to convert others to their religions
- **campaigns** (kam PAYNZ) *n.* a series of military operations in a war

During the winter of 1884–1885, representatives from Europe's leading countries gathered in Berlin to settle disputes over the right to govern and trade in Africa. Belgium's King Leopold II sent Henry Morton Stanley to the Berlin Conference. An explorer, Stanley had previously gone to Africa in search of the missing British missionary and explorer David Livingstone. As one of the few at the conference who had actually traveled to Africa, Stanley used his reputation to successfully defend Leopold's claim to the Congo at the gathering.

This competition for African lands became known as the Scramble for Africa. It was just one step in a process by which European countries expanded their power through colonization.

Robert Fulton's *Clermont* was the first steamboat to demonstrate its efficiency in transporting passengers and freight.

European Interest in Africa Grows

At the beginning of the 1800s, European nations traded extensively with African kingdoms, particularly the kingdoms of Tripoli (TRIP uh lee), Tunis (TOO nis), Algiers (al JEERZ), and Morocco (muh RAH koh) on the northern coast. Farther south along the West African coast, European ships sailed the coastlines motivated by the fortunes to be made from the slave trade there.

Rarely did Europeans travel inland for trade. The major river along the western coast, the Congo, had a series of waterfalls and other barriers that made it impossible for their ships to sail upstream. Those who tried crossing by land fell victim to diseases from which they had no natural immunity. As the 1800s began, Africans and Arabs who traded from northern Africa and across the Red Sea controlled trade routes in the interior.

In the mid to late 1800s, European governments, companies, and churches began sending people to explore the continent's interior. These individuals established trade routes and started taking control of African lands. By the 1870s, Great Britain and France were in strong competition for trade routes along the Niger River (NY jur RIV ur) in western Africa. In the 1880s, King Leopold II of Belgium and Otto von Bismarck of Germany began making competing claims on other African territories.

✓ **Reading Check** **Describe trade between Europeans and Africans before the 1800s.**

Links to
Science

Steamship The development of the steamship in the early 1800s gave Europeans an important new tool for navigating upstream on Africa's rivers. Robert Fulton's 1807 steamboat trip from New York City to Albany demonstrated the invention's practical use. In 1819, the American steamship *Savannah* crossed the Atlantic Ocean. By the end of the 1800s, steamboats had become a common means of transportation on African rivers such as the Congo.

The Scramble for Africa

To avoid European wars over African lands, European leaders gathered in Berlin in 1884 to make rules about how they could claim land in Africa and establish trading monopolies. **Monopolies** are areas in which only one government or company has the right to trade. No African leaders were represented at the conference. New treaties among the Europeans stated that a country had to have authority over an area before it could claim that region. They also stated that a country had to notify the other countries of any new land claims.

Partition of Africa The arrangement made at the Berlin conference established **partitions,** or divisions, of African lands into separate areas with new borders. Although Britain lost some of its land claims, it still controlled a great deal of land in Africa. This arrangement made it possible for other countries to explore lands and make new claims over them. Seven countries—Spain, Belgium, Portugal, France, Great Britain, Italy, and Germany—established areas of control over the next two decades.

Chart Skills

In 1879 Africans had ruled more than 90 percent of the continent. By 1914, almost all Africans were under European rule. **Identify** Which European countries controlled the largest number of colonies in Africa? **Infer** How might the size or number of a country's colonial possessions reflect its military power?

European Land Claims in Africa

Country	Land Claims
Britain	Egypt, Sudan, part of Somalia, Gambia, Sierra Leone, Gold Coast (now Ghana), Nigeria, Uganda, Kenya, Zanzibar (now in Tanzania), Nyasaland (now Malawi), Rhodesia (now Zambia and Zimbabwe), Bechuanaland (now Botswana), Swaziland, Lesotho, South Africa
Belgium	The Congo (now Democratic Republic of the Congo)
France	Tunisia, Algeria, most of Morocco, Djibouti, Mauritania, Mali, Niger, Chad, Senegal, Guinea, Ivory Coast, Dahomey (now Benin), Ubangi-Shari (now Central African Republic), Gabon, Congo (now Republic of Congo), Comoros, Madagascar
Italy	Libya, Eritrea, most of Somalia
Germany	Togo, Cameroon, Tanganyika (now in Tanzania), Rwanda, Burundi, South West Africa (now Namibia)
Portugal	Cape Verde, Portuguese Guinea (now Guinea Bissau), São Tomé and Príncipe, Angola, Mozambique
Spain	part of Morocco, Western Sahara, Spanish Guinea (now Equatorial Guinea)

Colonial Rule European countries made claims in Africa because they wanted access to the continent's large supply of natural resources—and at cheap prices. Gold, diamonds, ivory, rubber, coffee, cotton, and cocoa were found in abundance. Once land claims were made, Europeans established colonial governments. Europeans quickly built roads and railways. Some governments turned this work over to private companies. In return, a company was granted the rights to a certain amount of land for every mile of road or railroad it built.

This arrangement sometimes led to extreme abuses of human rights. In the Congo, for example, Africans were often forced into slave labor on rubber plantations. This led to the deaths of between five and eight million Africans by the beginning of the 1900s.

Germany's population was growing at the end of the 1800s. Germans saw colonization in Africa as a way to reduce its population. The German government set aside land along railway lines for citizens to settle on, start trading companies and farms, and establish control over German colonies.

Christian Missionaries European governments generally left the education and health care of their colonial subjects in the hands of private groups. Christian **missionaries**, people who traveled to other places to convert others to their religions, opened schools and hospitals in many places, throughout the continent.

Students who learned European languages had an advantage over other Africans in finding jobs in the colonial governments and European companies. As a result, missionary schools were seen by some Africans as a way to escape a life of poverty and manual labor.

☑ **Reading Check** **Why did Europeans establish colonies in Africa?**

Gold in Ghana
The British gained control of the Gold Coast, now the nation of Ghana, in the late 1800s and made it a British colony in 1874. Gold mining was a key focus of the colony's economy. Ghana remained under British control until it became independent in 1957.
Summarize *Name some of the other natural resources in Africa that attracted European countries.*

Go Online
PHSchool.com Use Web Code
mup-0846 for an interactivity
on imperialism in Africa.

African Resistance to Colonization

Although Europeans were successful in taking over nearly all of Africa by 1914, they had to fight Africans for control of many places. When Europeans colonized an area, they brought their cultures and customs with them. Often Europeans expected people living in the colony to start doing things their way. They also took power away from people who lived in the colonies. People from colonized areas became tired of this treatment and wanted to end European rule. Larger African kingdoms were able to raise large armies to resist occupying forces. However, their musket guns gained through earlier trade were no match for new European fighting weapons, such as machine guns.

In southern Africa during the 1830s and 1840s, the Zulu (ZOO loo), led by their king, Dingane (ding GAHN), unsuccessfully fought Dutch settlers who attempted to settle the Natal region. As the scramble for Africa progressed, battles with the occupying armies became increasingly bloody. In separate **campaigns**, or series of military operations in a war, France achieved control of Madagascar (mad uh GAS kur) and Morocco, and Britain seized the Sudan.

A present-day Zulu village in South Africa

Ethiopia The Italians, who had made a claim on Ethiopia at the 1884 Berlin Conference, attempted to take control of Ethiopia in the early 1890s. The Ethiopian emperor, Menelik, resisted the Italians. In 1896, the disagreement led to a war in which the Ethiopians defeated the Italian army. After the war, Menelik extended his empire by conquering lands to the south and southwest as far as the ancient kingdom of Kaffa near Lake Turkana.

Liberia Liberia, located on the west coast of Africa, was a recognized independent country at the time of the scramble for Africa. It had been established as a republic in 1847 after being settled by freed slaves who had left the United States. During the colonial period, Britain and France forced Liberia to give up some of its land, but it maintained its political independence.

African Nationalists Even as the system of missionary schools in Africa was opening up the outside world to African students, Africans were also spreading new ideas about how they could take control of their own lives. Some members of wealthy merchant families began publishing newspapers critical of colonial rule. Some African bishops who had gained positions in European churches also made criticisms. The growing unrest led to independence movements in the twentieth century by these western-educated Africans. Some middle class Africans valued their African traditions and condemned western societies that upheld liberty and equality for whites only. By the early 1900s, African leaders pushed nationalist movements hoping to gain independence. They were called nationalists because they believed in independence and the right to rule their own nations.

Joseph Jenkins Roberts was the president of Liberia from 1845–1856 and 1872–1876. He lived in the mansion shown above.

✔ Reading Check **What two African countries were never colonized by Europeans?**

The Boer War

The Berlin Conference was not completely successful in preventing wars between Europeans in Africa. In southern Africa in the late 1800s and early 1900s, tensions increased between the British colonial government and Dutch settlers, eventually erupting into war.

The roots of the conflict were deep. After Britain seized control of the Cape Colony in southern Africa in 1806, many Dutch settlers, called Boers (bohrz), left the colony and founded two new republics, Transvaal (trans VAHL) and the Orange Free State. Meanwhile, the British had established a second colony, Natal (nuh TAHL), to the east of the Boer republics.

Strong cultural differences existed between the Cape Colony and the Boer republics. For example, in Cape Colony all men who had a certain level of wealth, regardless of race, were allowed to vote for representatives to the colony's parliament. In the Boer republics, only white people were recognized as citizens, and only white men could vote.

The discovery of diamonds in 1868 and gold in 1886 in the Boer republics renewed British interest in taking control of these lands. They made a claim on these lands at the Berlin Conference in 1884 and began working to establish authority over the Boers. During a bitter, two-year war that began in 1899, the British army defeated the Boer settlers and created a new country, South Africa, which would remain under white rule until 1994.

Reading Check How did the discovery of diamonds and gold in the Boer republics contribute to the Boer War?

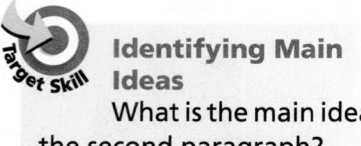

Identifying Main Ideas
What is the main idea of the second paragraph?

A Scene from the Boer War
With well-trained British troops numbering nearly 500,000 many expected the Boer forces to easily be shut down. However, the almost 88,000 Boer soldiers, mostly ordinary farmers, held off British troops for almost two years. **Describe** *Describe the action in this drawing of British soldiers under attack during a battle in the Boer War.*

Britain Seeks Control in the Middle East

The Ottoman Empire once ruled a large part of the Middle East. In 1798, Napoleon's armies invaded Egypt, an important Ottoman province. Although the Ottomans succeeded in driving out the French, an Egyptian officer in the Ottoman army, Muhammad Ali, established himself as ruler. Egypt remained part of the Ottoman Empire in name, but in practice it was an independent country.

After Ali's death in 1849, a series of weaker rulers controlled Egypt with British support. One ruler, Ali's son, Said Pasha (sah EED PAH shah), granted a French company the right to build a canal at Suez (SOO ez). This canal was seen as a way to link the Mediterranean and Red seas. It was not long before fighting broke out again. In response to a series of political revolts in the early 1880s, the British government sent troops to Egypt in 1882. British troops hoped to restore order and return Tawfiq (tow FEEK), who had been removed from the throne of Egypt. Through Tawfiq and his successors, Britain was able to maintain control of the country.

The Suez Canal
When the Suez Canal opened in 1869, ships traveling from Europe no longer had to sail around the southern tip of Africa to reach Asia. **Apply Information** *Which two seas were linked by the Suez Canal?*

✓ **Reading Check** **Why was the Suez Canal important?**

Section 2 Assessment

Key Terms
Review the Key Terms at the beginning of this section. Use each term in a sentence that explains its meaning.

Target Reading Skill
State the main idea under African Resistance to Colonization on page 574.

Comprehension and Critical Thinking
1. (a) Identify Why did European traders stay close to the African coast in the early 1800s?
(b) Apply Information How did expeditions into the African interior increase interest in establishing colonies in Africa?

2. (a) List List the nations involved in the scramble for Africa.
(b) Identify Effects Describe the effects of the Berlin Conference.
3. (a) Recall Why did most armed resistance by Africans fail?
(b) How did Western-style education lay the groundwork for African nationalism?
4. (a) Recall What discoveries increased British interest in the Boer republics?
(b) Compare and Contrast How were the Boer republics different from the British colonies?
5. (a) Summarize How did Great Britain gain control of Egypt?

(b) Analyze Causes Why did Great Britain restore Tawfiq to the Egyptian throne?

Writing Activity
Suppose that you are a reporter sent to cover the Berlin Conference. Write a news article describing the conference. Be sure to include all of the basic facts: what, why, where, and when.

For: An activity on African colonization
Visit: PHSchool.com
Web Code: mud-2021

Megan: Hi, Paul. How was your weekend? Did you do anything fun?
Paul: I didn't do anything too exciting on Saturday afternoon, but Sunday I finished a great book, *Taking It to the Hoop*.
Megan: I haven't heard of it. What's it about?
Paul: In a nutshell, the story is about two best friends who play basketball at a small-town high school. A coach from a big-time school comes to recruit one of them. The other one stays behind after high school to play at a small, local college. Still, they still manage to stay best friends and learn a lot from each other.

A summary is a brief statement that takes a larger selection and reduces it to its key points or main ideas. Paul's description of *Taking It to the Hoop* is an example of a summary. When telling Megan about the book, Paul selects key characters and plot developments. He leaves out many minor details. When you study, summarizing what you read can help you better understand and remember key information.

Learn the Skill

Use these steps to write a summary.

1 **Read the information carefully, and identify key ideas.** Record these key ideas in your notes.

2 **Review the key ideas, and consider how they are related.** Use a graphic organizer such as a web diagram or a flowchart to help you connect ideas.

3 **Write one or more sentences that summarize the main ideas and the connections between them.** Be brief and use your own words. Using your own words will help you understand and remember the information better.

4 **Review your summary and the source text to make sure that it is accurate and complete.** Your sentences should summarize the most important ideas.

Practice the Skill

The passage on the right is a statement given by a woman named Ilanga who lived in the Congo during the rule of King Leopold II. Her statement was reported by an American named Edgar Canisius. In 1903, Canisius published Ilanga's statement in a book opposing Leopold's Congo policies. Follow the steps below to write a summary of Ilanga's statement.

Soon after the sun rose over the hill, a large band of soldiers came into the village, and we all went into the houses and sat down. We were not long seated when the soldiers came rushing in shouting, and threatening Niendo [the village chief] with their guns. They rushed into the houses and dragged the people out. Three or four came to our house and caught hold of me, also my husband Oleka and my sister Katinga. We were dragged into the road, and were tied with cords about our necks, so that we could not escape. We were all crying, for now we knew that we were to be taken away as slaves. The soldiers . . . compelled us to march to the camp of Kibalanga [a Belgian military officer], who ordered the women to be tied up separately, ten to each cord, and the men in the same way. When we were all collected —and there were many from other villages whom we now saw, and many from Waniendo [Ilanga's village]—the soldiers brought baskets of food for us to carry.

1 Read the passage, and identify key phrases and actions. What event does the passage describe?

2 Make a flowchart to show the connections between the events Ilanga describes.

3 Write a two-sentence summary of Ilanga's statement in your own words.

4 Review the reading passage and your summary. Ask yourself whether your summary presents accurate and complete information about Ilanga's statement.

Apply the Skill

Review the information called The Scramble for Africa on pages 572–573, and write a one-paragraph summary of it. Be sure to highlight the most important information.

Imperialism in Asia and Latin America

Prepare to Read

Objectives

In this section you will
1. Understand how Britain gained influence in China and ruled India.
2. Find out how Japan successfully resisted Western colonial powers.
3. Learn the effects of revolutions that brought independence to Latin American countries.

Taking Notes

As you read this section, concentrate on how different areas were affected by foreign pressures. Copy the chart below and record your findings in it.

Imperialism in Asia and Latin America	
India	• British East India Company gains control
Japan	• U.S. forces trade with Japan •
Latin America	• Spain loses power in Europe

Target Reading Skill

Identify Implied Main Ideas Sometimes the main idea of a paragraph or section is implied rather than directly stated. For example, the implied main idea of the second paragraph on page 581 could be stated this way:

The weakness of the Chinese government allowed foreign powers to take control more easily.

As you read, note the main ideas that paragraphs and sections imply.

Key Terms

- **direct rule** (duh REKT rool) *n.* the use of colonial officials to control a colony
- **indirect rule** (in duh REKT rool) *n.* the use of local rulers to control a colony
- **extraterritorial rights** (eks truh tehr uh TAWR ee ul rytz) *n.* the rights of foreigners to be protected by the laws of their own nation
- **indigenous** (in DIJ uh nus) *adj.* the original inhabitants of a region
- **economic imperialism** (ek uh NAHM ik im PIHR ee ul iz um) *n.* the control of one country over another country through economic policies rather than military force

The British, under Captain Elliott, blast Canton in 1841.

In 1839, Lin Zexu (lin DZUH shoo) was sent to Canton, China, to help the government solve problems with British traders. Britain had been sending opium to China to exchange for tea. China's government realized that opium, a drug, harmed its people.

Lin shut down the opium trade in China. He even dumped about 20,000 chests of opium into the water. This marked the start of the Opium War.

The British sent ships to blockade Canton. The British were much better armed than the Chinese and defeated them by 1842. Instead of eliminating opium sales, the opium kept flowing and even more ports were opened to British traders.

Imperialism in Asia

In the early 1800s, China exported a variety of products, but it imported very few products. After the Opium War, the Chinese were forced to allow trade in more cities. Gradually, other countries began to influence how Chinese people lived.

The Taiping Weaken China By 1850, China's Qing (ching) dynasty could no longer manage the country's problems. A group called the Taiping (TY ping) led a 14-year battle against the government. During the war, foreign nations pressured China to sign treaties that would open additional ports to trade and grant western missionaries more freedom in the country.

Although some people in China worked to improve society using western ideas, others wanted to limit foreign power. When nationalists attacked foreigners in many Chinese cities in 1900, troops from Japan and Europe defeated them and forced China's government to allow more foreign influence.

British Expansion in India In 1600, Britain granted the East India Company a monopoly on trade with India. Over the next two centuries, the company bought spices, cotton, tea, and other products in exchange for silver. During this period, the French and Dutch also traded in India. However, a series of battles in Europe and India in the late 1600s and 1700s strengthened British control of European trade in India.

By the mid-1700s, India's Mughal Empire was weakened by internal revolts, and most of India fell under the control of weaker local princes. Over the next century, the East India Company gradually gained control of large parts of India.

Porcelain figures from the time of China's Qing dynasty

Opposition to British Rule Indian resentment against British policies spread across northern and central India. In 1857 and 1858, Indian soldiers under British command staged an unsuccessful revolt against British rule. Britain responded by ending the control of the East India Company and establishing **direct rule,** or the sending of colonial officials to control a colony, over areas formerly controlled by the company. They used a system called **indirect rule,** or the use of local rulers to control a colony, to control other parts of India.

During the last half of the 1800s, the British improved education and transportation in India. However, they also limited Indians' opportunities to become high government officials or army officers. In 1885, a group called the Indian National Congress formed to bring about changes to British rule.

Japan Opens to Trade In the early 1800s, Japan traded only with the Netherlands and China. Each country had permission to trade in only one port. In 1853, Matthew Perry of the United States Navy was sent to ask that Japan open all of its ports to trade. Although Japanese officials did not open all ports as Perry requested, they did open two ports to international trade. The Japanese government also granted extraterritorial rights. **Extraterritorial rights** meant that foreigners were subject to their own laws, rather than the laws of the host nation. Japan later made similar agreements with other nations.

Seizing Power In 1868, a small group of Japanese military commanders and aristocrats seized power from the Tokugawa (toh koo GAH wah) shoguns. The overthrow of the shoguns became known as the Meiji (MAY jee) Restoration. During the Meiji era, Japan's government invested in shipbuilding, railways, communications, coal mines, and machinery. The nation's educational system was reformed and its military modernized.

Japanese Imperialism Such changes made Japan one of Asia's most powerful countries. Japan began its own age of imperialism. During the late 1800s and early 1900s, Japan took control of areas such as Taiwan and the Korean peninsula. Japan also tried to take Manchuria, but Britain and the United States stopped Japan from claiming outright control.

√ **Reading Check** **Why did Matthew Perry visit Japan?**

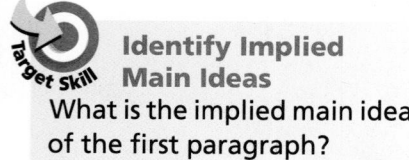

Identify Implied Main Ideas
What is the implied main idea of the first paragraph?

Meeting to Open Trade
In this scene, Matthew Perry is arriving for a meeting with the Japanese royal commissioner. **Infer** *How might the armed U.S. naval vessels and sailors who accompanied Perry have influenced the Japanese response to Perry's request?*

Independent Nations in Latin America

European powers had established colonies throughout North and South America during the 1600s. The British and French were strongest in North America, and Spain and Portugal held most of Central and South America. Much like other imperialists, they controlled the colonies' governments and took natural resources they needed. They also changed the schools, customs, and religious beliefs of the native people. As a result, nationalists in these colonies fought for independence, but struggled to establish stable governments and strong economies.

Present-day Rio de Janeiro

Nationalists Defeat Spain Spain controlled Mexico, most of Central America, and western South America. However, the spread of Enlightenment ideals, as well as Napoleon's invasion of Spain and Portugal, strengthened the colonies' desire for independence.

Between 1810 and 1824, a series of revolts ended Spanish rule in Latin America. José de San Martín led revolts in 1817 in Chile and in 1821 in Argentina. In northern South America, Simón Bolívar led forces that freed Venezuela, Panama, Colombia, Ecuador, Peru, and Bolivia between 1819 and 1825. Mexico gained its independence in 1821 after a failed rebellion in 1810–1815.

Guatemala, which then included most of Central America, declared independence from Spain in 1821. It then briefly formed a partnership with Mexico. By the 1830s, internal differences within the country caused it to split into the independent nations of Guatemala, Honduras, El Salvador, Nicaragua, and Costa Rica.

Brazil Gains Independence from Portugal In 1808, during Napoleon's invasion, Prince John, the ruling prince of Portugal, fled to Rio de Janeiro, the capital of Brazil. He then declared the city the capital of the Portuguese empire. Upon returning to Portugal in 1821, he named his son, Dom Pedro, ruler of Brazil. Pedro declared Brazil's independence in 1822 and adopted a new constitution in 1824. His son, Pedro II, succeeded him and undertook many projects to modernize Brazil, such as building railroads, telegraph systems, and schools.

Go Online
PHSchool.com Use Web Code **mup-0847** for an interactivity on independence in Latin America.

José de San Martín

In 1868, a group of samurai launched a political revolution under the slogan "A rich country, strong military." Their goal was to create a Japan strong enough to stand up to Western powers. The samurai led a revolt that unseated the Tokugawa shogunate and returned, or "restored," power to a 15-year-old emperor named Meiji. The Meiji Restoration lasted from 1868 to 1912 and was a major turning point in Japanese history. Under Meiji rule, Japan modernized with amazing speed and emerged as a growing economic and military power.

Emperor Meiji
Emperor Meiji ruled Japan from 1868 until his death in 1912. Meiji means "enlightened rule."

Becoming a Modern Country During the Meiji Restoration, Japan's leaders made great strides in modernizing the country and improving the economy. The government established a banking system, built railroads and factories, and organized a telegraph and postal system. Japanese leaders traveled to Western nations to learn about their technology, education, and customs. They brought back new ways of living and adapted them to Japanese needs. In the old Japan, the samurai alone were warriors. In 1871, Japan set up a national army in which all Japanese men were required to serve.

Works of art made during the Meiji Restoration documented the changes in Japan. The illustration to the left is a woodblock print published in 1888. Artists created hundreds of these prints during the Meiji era. Some prints showed achievements in transportation, such as the opening of Japan's first railway line and steam locomotive. Others showed new architecture, cars, modern bridges, and people wearing Western-style clothing and military uniforms. Such works of art reflected Japan's pride in becoming a modern nation.

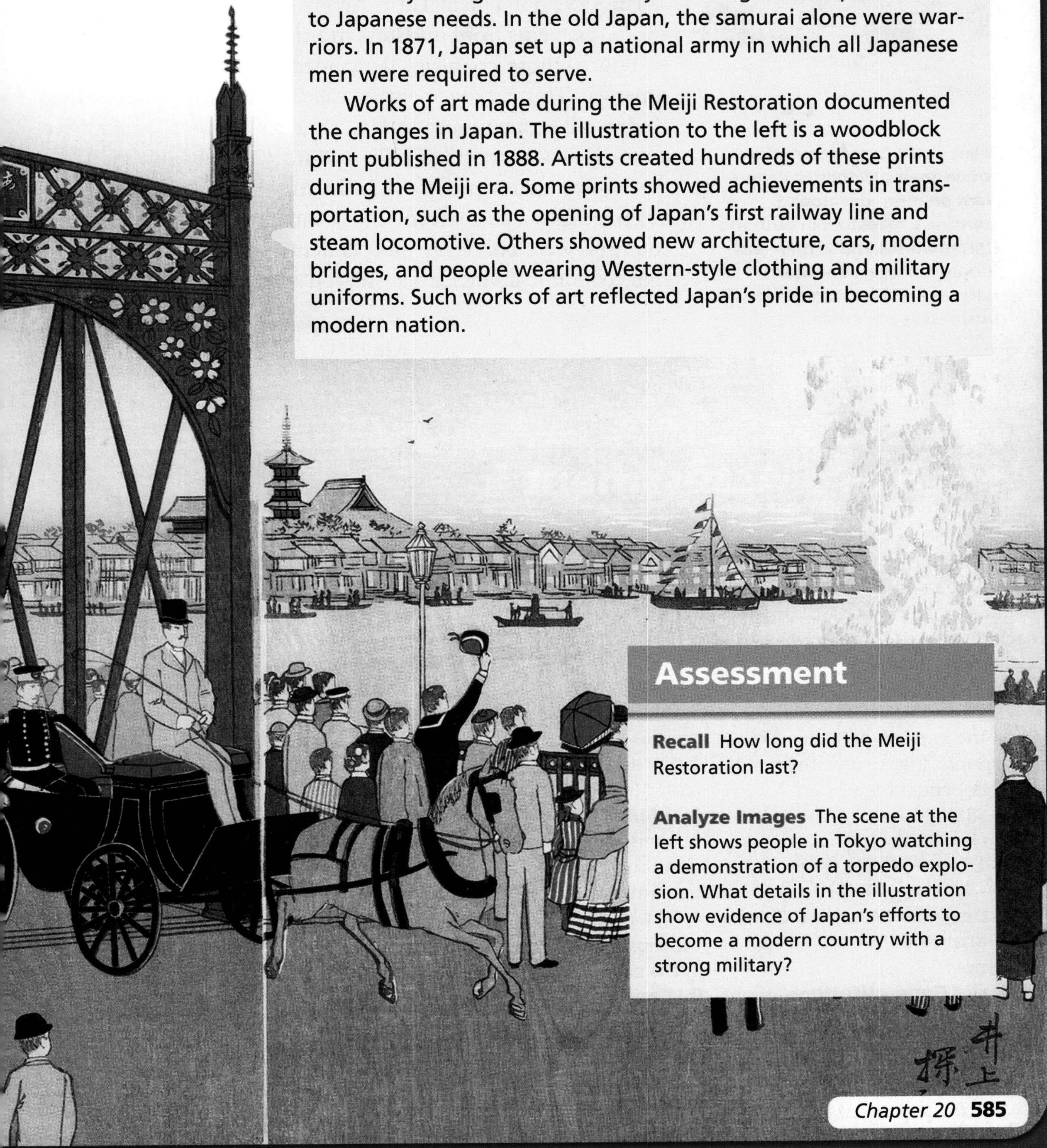

Assessment

Recall How long did the Meiji Restoration last?

Analyze Images The scene at the left shows people in Tokyo watching a demonstration of a torpedo explosion. What details in the illustration show evidence of Japan's efforts to become a modern country with a strong military?

Many Latin American nations found their economies dependent on more developed countries. Investors in both the United States and Britain lent money to Latin American nations and invested in local businesses and trade.

Independent States Most of the newly independent states in Latin America wrote constitutions that established federal republics, or nations with both a federal government and state or provincial governments. However, many of the new rulers ignored the constitutions and ruled as dictators. The descendants of European settlers did not share political power with **indigenous**, or original inhabitants. Large landowners and industrialists who relied on international trade gained increasing power and wealth while many other people remained poor.

The development of Latin American nations required loans and investments from investors in Britain and the United States. In return, those countries demanded much influence in Latin America. This arrangement is called **economic imperialism**. Under this system, one country controls another through economic policy rather than military force. Throughout the 1800s, the United States protected Latin American countries and its investments in them from European powers. Although these countries were politically independent, nationalists felt that foreign economic influence was still too strong.

 **Reading Check** What caused the power of Spain in Central America to weaken in 1821?

Section 3 Assessment

Key Terms
Review the Key Terms at the beginning of this section. Use each term in a sentence which explains its meaning.

Target Reading Skill
State the implied main idea of the paragraphs that follow the heading Independent States on page 586.

Comprehension and Critical Thinking
1. (a) Describe What was China's general attitude toward foreign influences?
(b) Make Generalizations How did Britain and other countries gain influence in China?

2. (a) Define Define direct rule and indirect rule.
(b) Draw Conclusions Why did the British government take control of India from the East India Company?
3. (a) Compare How were the policies of the governments of Japan and China similar in the early 1800s?
(b) Identify Effects What reforms during the Meiji Restoration contributed to Japan's development as an imperial power?
4. (a) Recall Which countries had the most control in Latin America in the early 1800s?
(b) Cause and Effect How did events in Europe affect colonies in Latin America?

Writing Activity
Suppose that you lived in a Latin American country during the 1800s. How would you feel about Spanish colonial rule and the struggle for independence? How would you feel about the later influence of British and American investors? Write a few sentences stating your opinions.

For: An activity on imperialism in Asia
Visit: PHSchool.com
Web Code: mud-2031

Review and Assessment

◆ Chapter Summary

Napoleon III

Section 1: Nationalism and Expansion

- The Congress of Vienna tried to put old rulers back into power and continue the large empires of Europe.
- Nationalists in France revolted against their kings in 1830 and 1848, and helped make changes in the government.
- Other revolutions across Europe were inspired by those in France, but were not immediately successful in creating independent nations.
- European countries in the last half of the 1800s used military and economic power to gain control in other areas of the world.

Section 2: Imperialism in Africa and the Middle East

- European countries took control of nearly all of Africa by 1914 and used the colonies for natural resources.
- Africans resisted colonization, but only Ethiopia and Liberia remained independent nations.
- Britain gained control of Egypt and the Suez Canal.

The Boer War

Section 3: Imperialism in Asia and Latin America

- China's government became weak late in the 1800s, and it was forced to allow foreign trade and influence in its culture.
- Great Britain's colony in India helped the British economy and influenced the way Indians lived.
- Japan adopted western ways of government and economy and became a strong country.
- Latin American countries achieved independence by the 1840s but fell under British and American economic influence.

San Martín

◆ Key Terms

Classify each of the following as an economics (E), government (G), or religion (R) term. Give reasons to explain your choices.

1. dictator
2. nationalism
3. monopoly
4. missionary
5. imperialism
6. direct rule
7. economic imperialism

◆ Comprehension and Critical Thinking

8. (a) Explain How did the European empires react to revolts in 1830 and 1848 in areas such as Austria, Poland, and Hungary?
(b) Infer How did the revolts of 1830 and 1848 help create the independent nations of Italy and Germany after 1850?

9. (a) List List some reasons for European imperialism in the 1800s.
(b) Analyze How successful was European imperialism in economic and political ways?

10. (a) Identify Which countries gained the greatest areas of control in Africa before 1914?
(b) Synthesize Why did these countries seek African colonies during this period?

11. (a) Identify Which African country was able to stop an invasion from Europe?
(b) Infer Why might it have been more successful in resisting European control?

12. (a) Explain How did the British help India during the late 1800s?
(b) Cause and Effect What were some ways that the economic changes in India created by British rule harmed the Indian people?

13. (a) Explain How did Japan learn about Western cultures after it opened its ports to foreign trade?
(b) Apply Information How were Britain and the United States able to gain so much influence in Latin America in the 1800s?

◆ Writing Activity: Language Arts

Choose one of the countries in Latin America that had become independent by the 1830s. Research the early years in this country's independence, and write a brief description of its attempts to set up a government that was not controlled by another country during the 50 years after their independence.

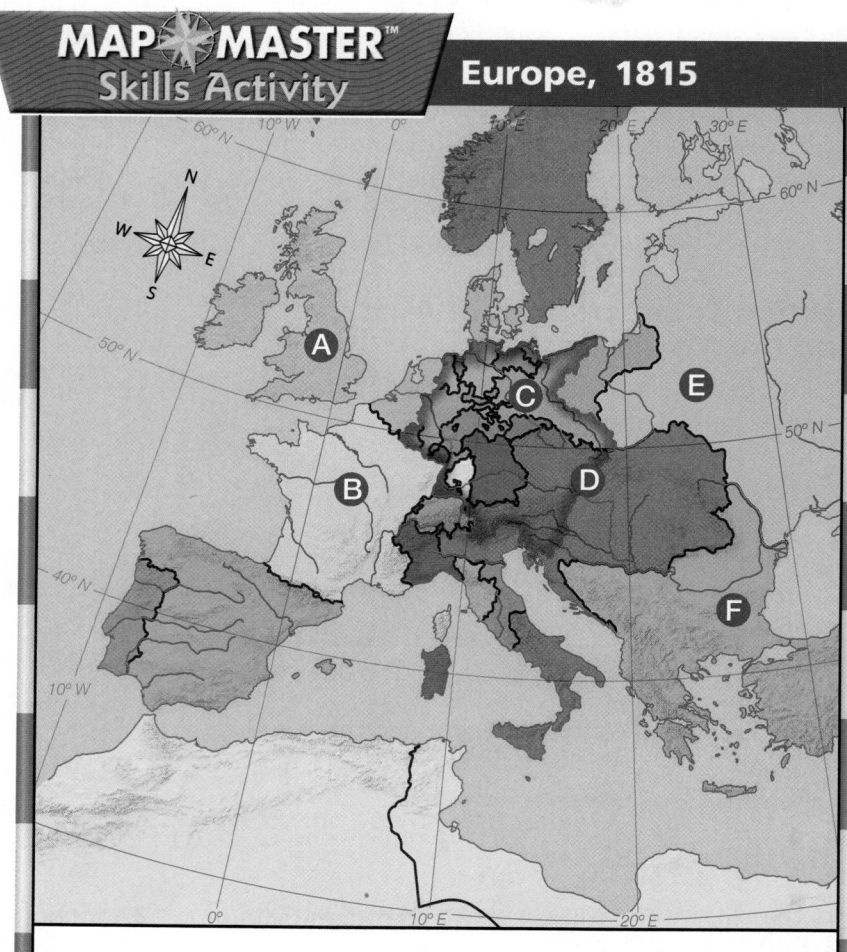

MAP MASTER™ Skills Activity

Europe, 1815

Place Location For each place listed below, write the letter from the map that shows its location.
1. Austrian Empire **3.** Ottoman Empire **5.** Prussia
2. France **4.** United Kingdom **6.** Russian Empire

Go Online
PHSchool.com Use Web code **mup-2003** for an **interactive map.**

Standardized Test Prep

Test-Taking Tips

Some questions on standardized tests ask you to analyze a reading selection. Study the passage below. Then follow the tips to help you answer the sample question.

> When Napoleon's army invaded Egypt in 1798, it brought with it a number of scientists and historians to study Egyptian culture. They made one of their most important discoveries outside the important coastal city of Alexandria. At the city of Rosetta, a soldier found a stone on which the same message was inscribed in several languages, including Greek and ancient Egyptian hieroglyphs, a form of picture writing. By comparing the messages on the Rosetta Stone, scholars were able to decipher hieroglyphs for the first time and learn a great deal about ancient Egyptian culture.

TIP Look for words that signal why certain ideas are important.

Pick the letter that best completes the statement. The message on the Rosetta Stone was written in both ancient Egyptian hieroglyphs and

TIP Look for these keywords in the passage to determine which is the correct answer.

A French

B Greek

C Alexandrian

D Egyptian hieroglyphs

Think It Through Answer C is not a language. Answer A is a language but is not mentioned in the passage. Both B and D are mentioned in the passage, but D is one of the languages identified in the question. Greek is the second language identified, so B is the correct answer.

Practice Questions

Use the tips above and other tips to help you answer the following questions.

1. What was one result of the Meiji Restoration in Japan?

   A Japan's military power grew.

   B Japan became a colony of Great Britain.

   C Japan's influence in Korea declined.

   D Japanese ships were barred from Chinese ports.

2. Which of the following countries did not participate in the scramble for Africa?

   A France

   B Portugal

   C Poland

   D Germany

3. What is one result of Napoleon's invasion of Spain and Portugal in 1808?

   A Napoleon became emperor of Brazil.

   B Control of Guatemala shifted from Portugal to Spain.

   C French became the official language in the Latin American colonies.

   D Colonies in Latin America began a series of rebellions against Spanish and Portuguese colonial rule.

4. Louis-Philippe of France was called the

   A false king

   B people's king

   C citizen king

   D constitutional king

Go Online
PHSchool.com

Use Web Code **mua-2004**
for **Chapter 20 self-test**

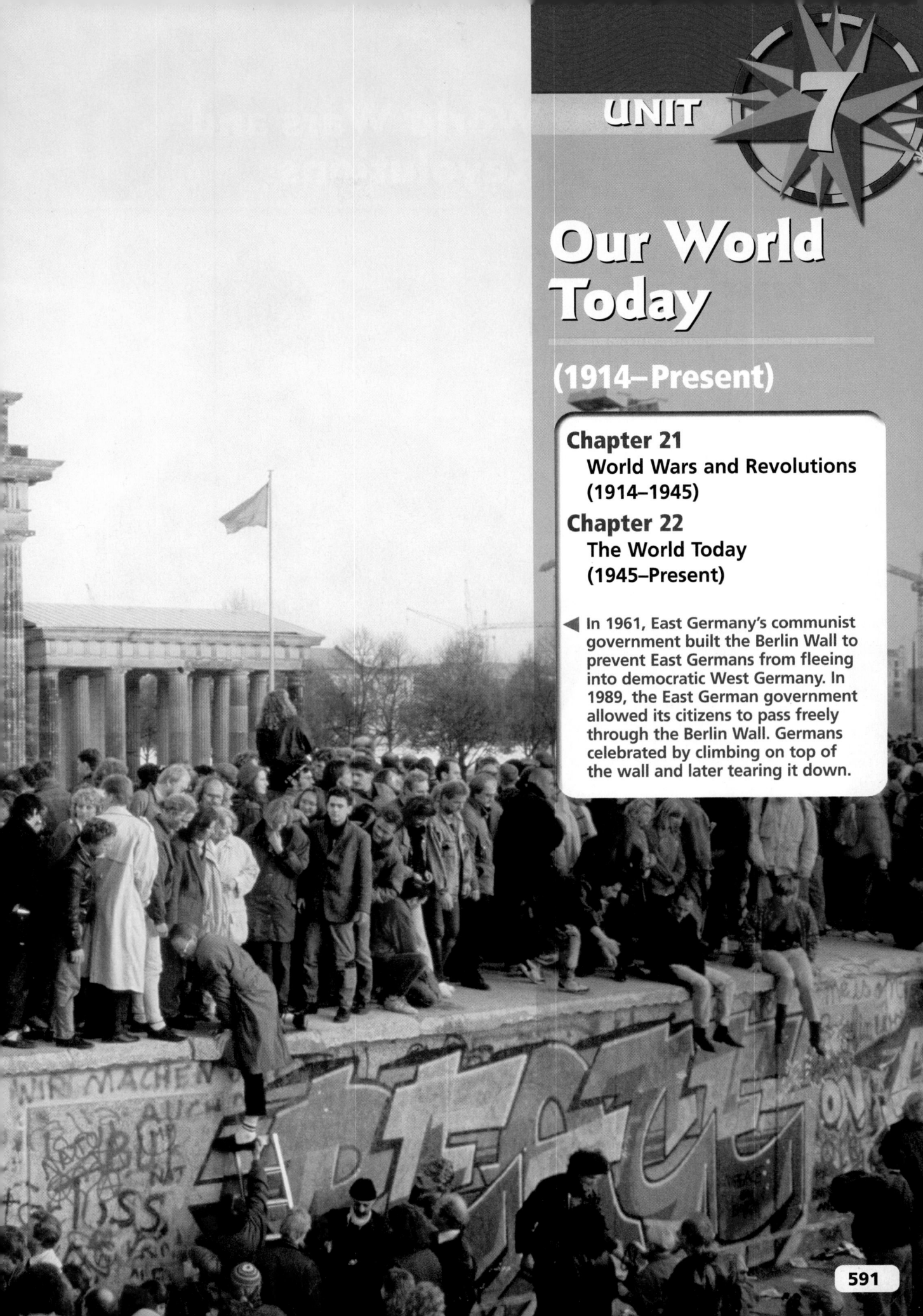

Our World Today

(1914–Present)

Chapter 21
World Wars and Revolutions
(1914–1945)

Chapter 22
The World Today
(1945–Present)

◀ In 1961, East Germany's communist government built the Berlin Wall to prevent East Germans from fleeing into democratic West Germany. In 1989, the East German government allowed its citizens to pass freely through the Berlin Wall. Germans celebrated by climbing on top of the wall and later tearing it down.

Chapter

21 World Wars and Revolutions

Chapter Preview

This chapter will introduce a major revolution and the two world wars that shaped the first half of the 1900s.

Section 1
World War I

Section 2
The Russian Revolution

Section 3
Crises Around the World

Section 4
World War II

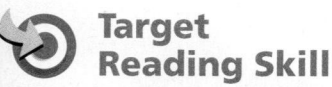

Target Reading Skill

Cause and Effect In this chapter you will learn to identify and see the relationship between the causes and the effects of historical events.

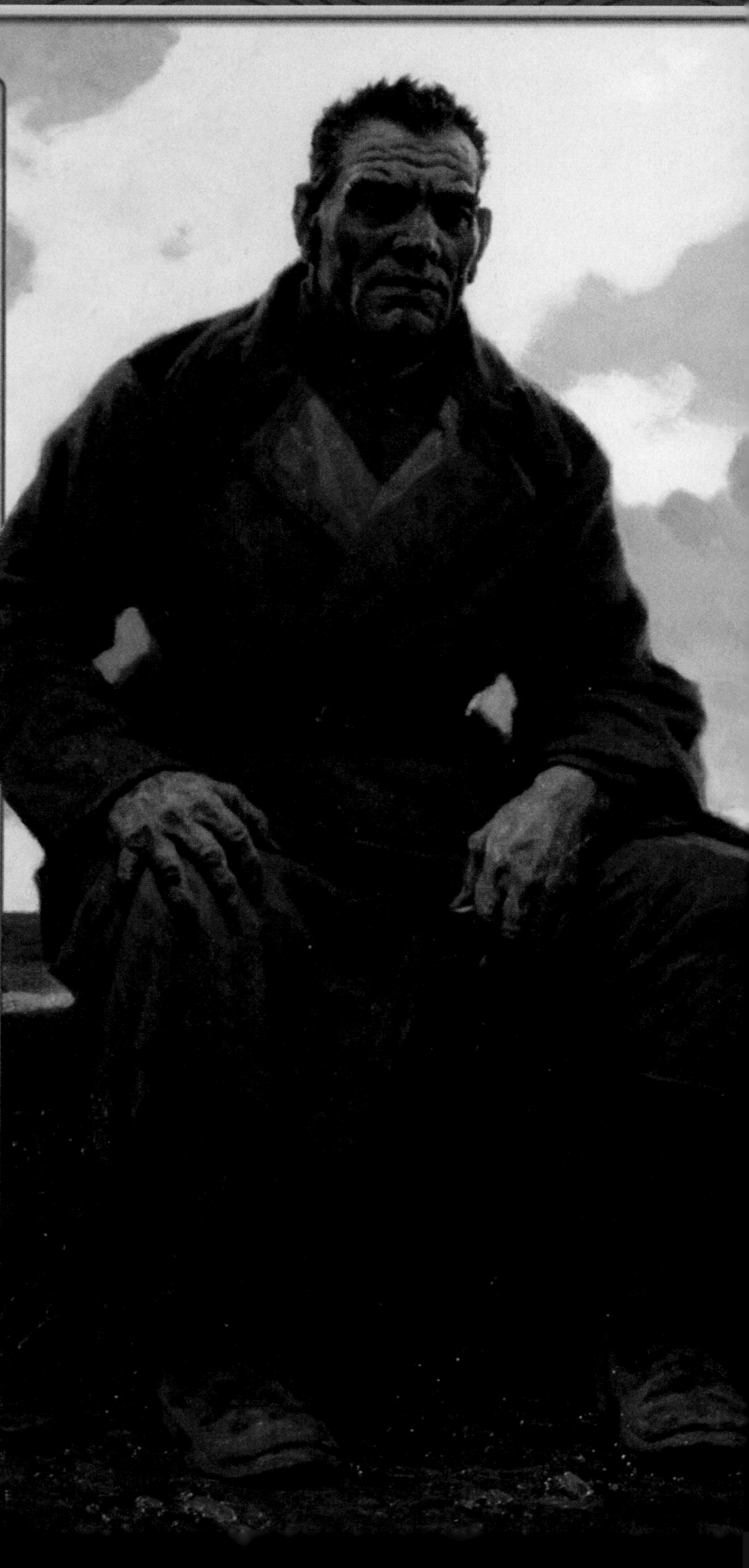

▶ Painting by B.V. Cerbakov called *The Invincible Soldier*

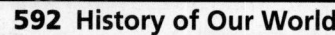

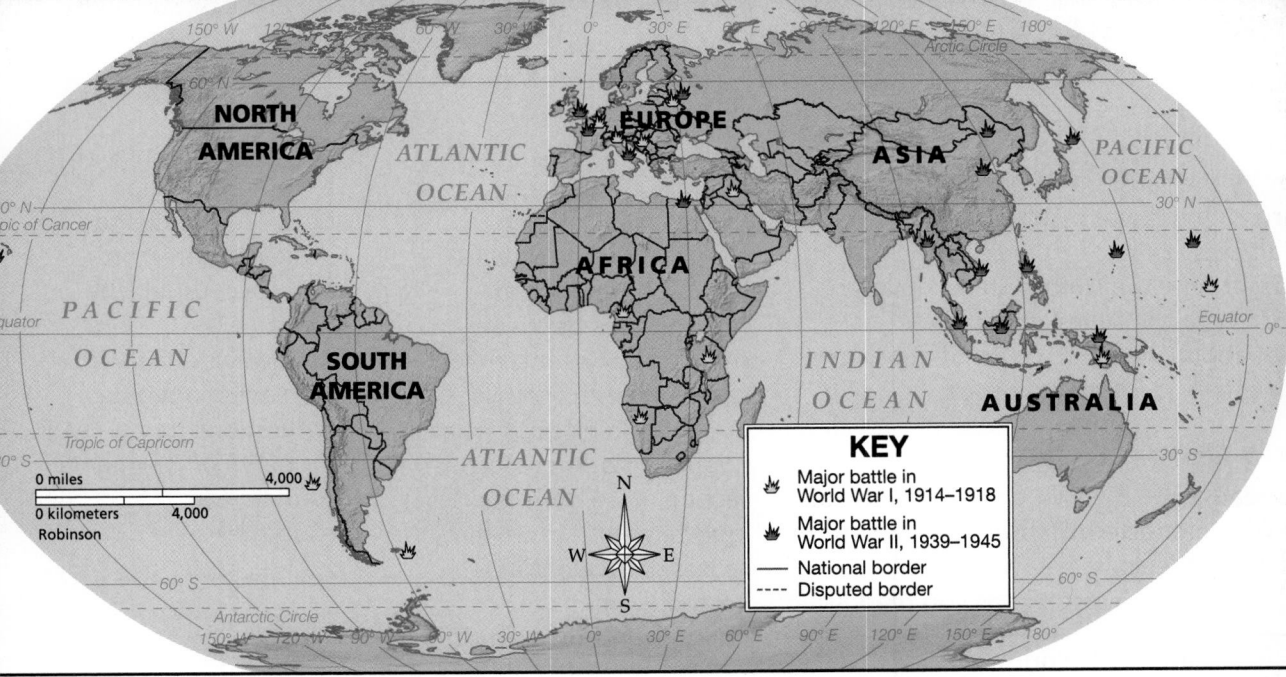

KEY

🔥 Major battle in World War I, 1914–1918

🔥 Major battle in World War II, 1939–1945

—— National border

---- Disputed border

Location The World Wars in the twentieth century affected the whole world, and that is the reason for their names. However, the fighting took place only in certain parts of the world. **Read a Map** Key Find the parts of the world where the battles of the World Wars were fought.

Analyze Information Which areas saw no battles in either war? Which areas were battlegrounds in only one of the wars? Which suffered during both wars?

Go Online
PHSchool.com Use Web Code **mup-2201** for step-by-step **map skills practice.**

World War I

Prepare to Read

Objectives

In this section you will
1. Identify the causes of World War I.
2. Learn why the war resulted in battlefield stalemates.
3. Find out how the United States' involvement led to the Allies' victory.
4. Learn about the harsh terms of peace and their effect on postwar Europe.

Taking Notes

As you read, note the two types of causes of World War I: long-term causes and short-term causes. Copy the chart below. Then fill it in with the causes you discover as you read.

Causes of World War I	
Long-Term Causes	**Short-Term Causes**
•	•
•	•
•	•

Target Reading Skill

Identify Causes and Effects Determining causes and effects will help you understand relationships between situations or events. A cause makes something happen. An effect is what happens. As you read this section, note both the long-term and short-term causes of World War I. Record them in your Taking Notes diagram.

Key Terms

- **alliance** (uh LY uns) *n.* a close association between nations to achieve a common objective, usually by treaty
- **neutral** (NOO trul) *adj.* not taking any side
- **reparations** (rep uh RAY shunz) *n. pl.* payments for harm done to other countries

Ignoring warnings of anti-Austrian unrest, the Archduke Francis Ferdinand and his wife Sophie set out on a tour of Sarajevo (sa ruh YAY voh). News of the visit angered Serbians who saw the Austrians as tyrants.

On June 28, 1914, the archduke and his wife rode through Sarajevo in an open car. During their drive, a bomb was hurled at the car. The bomb missed the archduke but injured an officer in another car. Later that day, the archduke asked to visit the wounded officer. As the car set out, a hidden gunman sprang forward and fired twice into the back seat. Moments later, the archduke and his wife were dead. This assassin's bullets set off the "gunpowder" that ignited a war that engulfed much of the world for four bloody years.

The assassination of Austria's archduke Ferdinand and his wife Sophie made headlines around the world.

British Troops in World War I
These soldiers are members of the British cavalry, or troops that serve on horseback. **Summarize** *What were the long-term causes of World War I?*

The Causes of World War I

Historians disagree about what caused World War I. Long-term causes such as *nationalism, imperialism,* and the *system of alliances* created by the great powers originated in the 1800s. The assassination of the Archduke Ferdinand, a short-term cause, also contributed to the war.

Nationalism Nationalism is a feeling of loyalty or attachment to a culture, language, or territory. Prior to World War I, nationalism in the Balkans (BAWL kunz), a region of southeastern Europe, had been strong. Greece, Montenegro (mahnt uh NEE groh), Serbia (SUR bee uh), Romania (roh MAY nee uh), Bulgaria (bul GEHR ee uh), and Albania (al BAY nee uh), had gained independence by 1914. But other nationalities, such as the Yugoslavs (yoo goh SLAHVZ), Czechs (cheks), Slovaks (SLOH vahks), and Poles, remained subject to foreign powers.

Serbia's effort to unite the region's Slavic peoples worried Austria-Hungary (AWS tree uh HUNG guh ree). One concern was Bosnia (BAHZ nee uh), which was pressing to break away from Austria-Hungary and combine with Serbia.

Nationalist feelings were also strong in western Europe. France wanted to recover Alsace-Lorraine (al SAYS law RAYN), which it lost to Germany in the Franco-Prussian (FRANG koh PRUSH un) War. Germany sought to increase its influence at France's expense. Germany also challenged Britain's control of the seas.

Imperialism Imperialism is the policy of building an empire, usually by taking over foreign colonies. Imperialist rivalries also led to World War I. France and Germany fought for control of Morocco (muh RAH koh). Britain and Germany each wanted maximum advantage in Africa and the Middle East. Russia and Austria-Hungary competed for influence in the Balkans.

Go Online
PHSchool.com Use Web Code
mup-0848 for an interactivity
on World War I's battle fronts.

Identify Causes and Effects

What was the effect of the system of alliances?

Alliances In 1914, the major powers of Europe were grouped together into two main **alliances,** or associations between nations to achieve a common goal. The goal of the European alliances was to protect members against attack by a nation outside the alliance. The two major European alliances in 1914 were the Triple Entente (ahn TAHNT), made up of France, Russia, and Britain, and the Triple Alliance, made up of Germany, Austria-Hungary, and Italy. In addition, smaller countries counted on major powers to defend them. For example, Serbia looked to Russia for support, while Belgium had an alliance with Britain. When one country moved toward war, the alliance system meant that several others became involved as well. In this way, a regional conflict could turn into a world war.

World War I, 1914–1918

MAP MASTER™ Skills Activity

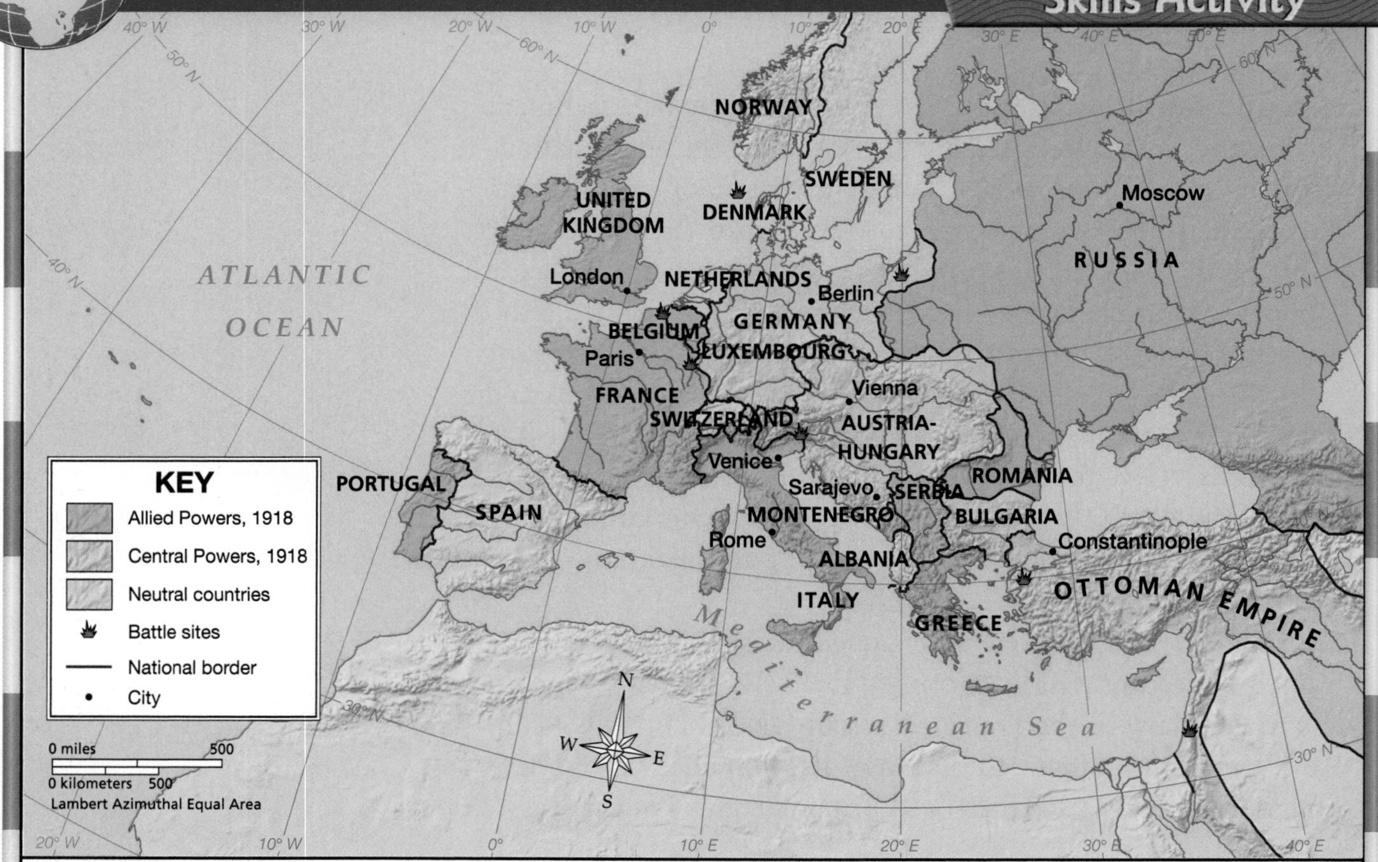

KEY
- Allied Powers, 1918
- Central Powers, 1918
- Neutral countries
- Battle sites
- National border
- City

0 miles 500
0 kilometers 500
Lambert Azimuthal Equal Area

Map labels: NORWAY, SWEDEN, Moscow, UNITED KINGDOM, DENMARK, RUSSIA, London, NETHERLANDS, Berlin, ATLANTIC OCEAN, BELGIUM, GERMANY, Paris, LUXEMBOURG, Vienna, FRANCE, SWITZERLAND, AUSTRIA-HUNGARY, Venice, ROMANIA, PORTUGAL, Sarajevo, SERBIA, SPAIN, MONTENEGRO, BULGARIA, Rome, Constantinople, ALBANIA, OTTOMAN EMPIRE, ITALY, GREECE, Mediterranean Sea

Regions World War I forced many European nations to take a position because of alliances they had made before the war. **Read a Map Key** Which countries were successful in staying out of the war? Note where the Allied Powers are. **Draw Conclusions** A front is a line of separation between warring sides. Which side had a disadvantage because they had to defend more than one front? Which side could more easily carry on trade and obtain supplies?

Go Online
PHSchool.com Use Web Code
mup-2111 for step-by-step map skills practice.

Declarations of War The spark that brought European alliances to war was the murder of Archduke Francis Ferdinand. The leaders of Austria-Hungary declared war on Serbia. They suspected the Serbians of organizing the killing of the archduke. Russia, alarmed by this attack on Serbia by its chief rival, announced that it was preparing its army.

Europe's alliance system drew more countries into the conflict. Germany moved to protect its ally, Austria-Hungary, by declaring war on Russia on August 1, 1914. Two days later, Germany declared war on Russia's ally, France. When Germany invaded Belgium to attack France, Britain responded. Belgium was a **neutral** country; that is, it had not taken any sides. On August 4, Britain declared war on Germany. Only a few weeks after the gunshots in Sarajevo, the entire European continent was at war.

✓ Reading Check   **What causes led to World War I?**

Battlefield Stalemate, 1914–1917

Germany had hoped to swiftly conquer France so that it could turn its attention to Russia. Although the Germans quickly came within miles of Paris, they met fierce resistance from French and British troops along the Marne River (mahrn RIV ur).

By the winter of 1915, the Allies (Great Britain, France, and Russia) and the Central Powers (Germany, Turkey, and Austria-Hungary) were stalled on both the western and eastern fronts. The vast armies began three long years of deadly trench warfare.

Most of the burden of battle fell on foot soldiers. The traditional horse-borne cavalry was of no use against the spray of bullets from modern machine guns. Air warfare was just beginning, and tanks were not invented until late in the war. Foot soldiers formed charges against enemy lines. They were cut down by artillery or poison gas from enemy troops who were protected by a network of trenches. By 1917 the French had 3.3 million persons dead and wounded, the British more than 1 million, and the Germans more than 2.5 million.

✓ Reading Check   **What dangers did foot soldiers face in battle?**

Advances in Military Technology
World War I was the first modern, fully industrialized war. Some weapons, such as the U-boat and the aircraft, changed the nature of fighting. The gas mask helped protect soldiers from gases that could cause rashes, blindness, and even death. **Predict** *Which invention do you think has done the most to change how wars are fought? Explain your answer.*

The British ocean liner *Lusitania* is pictured sinking after being attacked by a German submarine on May 7, 1915.

THE CALL TO DUTY

JOIN THE ARMY

FOR HOME AND COUNTRY

ADAPTED FROM THE SCULPTURE BY EDOARDO CAMMILLI

PUBLISHED BY RECRUITING COMMITTEE OF THE MAYORS COMMITTEE ON NATIONAL DEFENCE

World War I recruitment poster

US Involvement and Allied Victory

Germany started submarine warfare at the outset of war but had backed down due to U.S. pressure early in the war. By 1917 the Germans resumed using submarine warfare. After German submarines sank several American merchant ships, the United States declared war on Germany on April 6, 1917.

It was a timely decision that helped the Allies. After the Bolshevik Revolution of November 1917, which you will read about in the next section, Russia withdrew from combat. Russia's absence allowed the Germans to add more troops to the Western front. However, the arrival of American soldiers by the summer of 1918 was too much for the Germans, who finally signed an armistice, or cease-fire agreement, on November 11, 1918.

✓ Reading Check **Which event allowed the Germans to add more troops to the Western front?**

A Hard and Bitter Peace

The Treaty of Versailles (TREE tee uv vur SY) was signed in 1919 and was named after the French town in which it was signed. This treaty brought peace to a Europe exhausted by years of war.

The Treaty of Versailles The Treaty of Versailles forced Germany to formally accept responsibility for the war, to turn over territory to the Allied powers, and to give up its foreign colonies. It also limited Germany's armed forces to 100,000 volunteers and required Germany to pay **reparations**, payments for harm done to other countries, to the Allied powers. Many historians believe that the harshness of the treaty caused resentment among the Germans and became a cause of World War II.

The League of Nations A major feature of the Treaty of Versailles was the creation of the League of Nations. This international organization was one of the Fourteen Points that U.S. President Woodrow Wilson proposed to encourage democracy and prevent future wars.

The League, however, turned out to be mostly ineffective in a tense postwar world. Europe still had much to overcome from the war. Some 10 million men died during the war, and 20 million were wounded. Starvation was widespread throughout Europe. In 1919 European industrial production was one quarter of what it had been in 1914, and millions of people were out of work. This poverty and despair contributed to still another world war, only twenty years later.

President Woodrow Wilson addresses Congress.

 **Reading Check** What steps were taken to restore peace, encourage democracy, and prevent future wars?

Section 1 Assessment

Key Terms

Review the Key Terms at the beginning of this section. Use each term in a sentence that explains its meaning.

Target Reading Skill

What effect did modern weapons have on the war?

Comprehension and Critical Thinking

1. (a) Identify Cause and Effect Identify the main long-term and short-term causes of World War I.
(b) Explain How did the system of alliances in Europe lead to war?

2. (a) Identify Where did the German's westward drive stall?
(b) Explain Why did the foot soldiers bear most of the burden of battle in World War I?

3. (a) Recall What was the main reason for U.S. entry into World War I?
(b) Explain What was the most important effect of the U.S. entry into the war?

4. (a) Identify Cause and Effect Identify three key effects that the Treaty of Versailles had on Germany.
(b) Draw Conclusions Explain why the Treaty of Versailles is often considered a cause of World War II.

Writing Activity

Suppose that you were a government official in Europe just before the start of World War I. What kind of plan or treaty might you have suggested in order to prevent the outbreak of war? Be specific in your answer, drawing on what you have read about the political situation in 1914.

For: an activity on World War I
Visit: PHSchool.com
Web Code: mud-2110

Prepare to Read

Objectives

In this section you will

1. Understand why the Russian people revolted against the czar.
2. Learn about the revolutions in 1917.
3. Identify the main features of the new revolutionary government in Russia.
4. Understand why the Russian Revolution led to civil war and dictatorship.

Taking Notes

As you read this section, note at least three causes of the Russian Revolution. Copy the chart below and use it to record your findings.

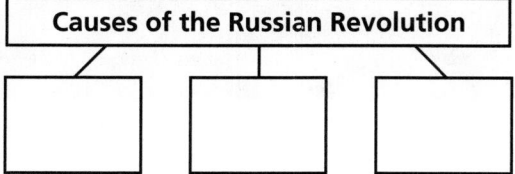

Causes of the Russian Revolution

Target Reading Skill

Recognize Multiple Causes Sometimes an effect can have more than one cause. For example, the Russian Revolution of October 1917 had many causes. As you read this section, identify at least three causes of the Russian Revolution. Record the information in your Taking Notes chart.

Key Terms

- **revolution** (rev uh LOO shun) *n.* a change or overthrow of a government or social system
- **socialism** (SOH shul iz um) *n.* a social system that seeks to abolish all forms of social classes and create a society of complete equality
- **capitalist** (KAP ut ul ist) *n.* a person who provides ideas and money for investing in businesses; a wealthy person
- **soviet** (SOH vee ut) *n.* an elected workers' council or committee set up by Russian laborers

Russian soldiers marching through the streets of Moscow

The modern world has been shaped by three major revolutions: the American Revolution of 1776, the French Revolution of 1789, and the Russian Revolution of 1917. A **revolution** is a change or overthrow of a government or social system.

The American Revolution was the most successful and lasting of the three. The French Revolution had a promising start, but ultimately ended in disorder and terror. The Russian Revolution, the boldest change, was the most miserable failure.

The people who led the Russian Revolution were the first to try to put the theories of socialism into practice. **Socialism** is a social system that seeks to abolish all forms of social classes and create a society of complete equality, with no private property or bosses. Far from fulfilling its promises to individuals of more control over their own lives, this revolution led to one of the harshest dictatorships in history.

Czar Nicholas II and his wife Alexandra surrounded by their children: Olga, Marie, Anastasia, Alexis, and Tatiana. Revolutionaries executed the royal family in 1918.

The Revolt against the Czar

A series of czars (zahrz) had ruled Russia for 400 years. The Russian czar had all the power of a king and ruled with the support of wealthy nobles and landowners. But many Russians had become upset with the way the Czar ruled. They demanded change.

The Czarist Regime In 1900 Russia was less democratically and economically developed than other European countries. Peasants who worked for nobles and had no say in the government made up the majority of the population. These peasants were very poor and had almost none of the freedoms that citizens of Western European countries enjoyed. Russia was also far behind economically because it relied mostly on farming long after the Industrial Revolution had taken hold in Western Europe and the United States.

Russia's Economy Starts to Catch Up By 1905, however, Russia began to develop. Although Russia lagged behind Western Europe, a small but important class of capitalists, people who provide ideas and money for investing in businesses, began to emerge in Russia. These capitalists financed and managed the building of factories and railroads.

This industrial growth created a class of industrial workers in Russia. Industrial workers were poor and often worked long hours in awful conditions. They were far smaller in number than the peasants. The workers only made up about 10 percent of Russia's population by 1917, but they were crucial to the workings of Russia's young manufacturing economy.

The Revolution of 1905 With these economic changes came political changes. Capitalists and professionals sought greater economic freedom and political power as part of the Constitutional Democratic Party. Meanwhile, urban workers supported the socialism of the Social Democratic Labor Party. This party soon split into two groups. The Mensheviks (MEN shuh viks) sought change through democratic means. The Bolsheviks (BOHL shuh viks) sought to overthrow the government through a revolution and to replace the government with dictatorial rule by the party. This philosophy is known as communism. The Bolsheviks, led by Vladimir Lenin (VLAD uh mihr LEN in), were later called the Communist Party.

The Mensheviks and Bolsheviks joined together in a large demonstration for reform in St. Petersburg, the Russian capital, on January 22, 1905. The czar's police fired guns into the crowd of peaceful marchers in an attack that later became known as "Bloody Sunday." The attack began a series of strikes and riots throughout Russia. Czar Nicholas II put down the protests with force, but he also introduced a series of small reforms. The reforms included limited freedom of speech, press, and assembly and the creation of Russia's first elected legislative body, the Duma (DOO mah). But the Duma had very little power.

✓ Reading Check **What was the largest social class in Russia in 1900?**

Bloody Sunday, 1905
The Revolution of 1905 began in St. Petersburg when troops opened fire on a defenseless crowd of workers marching to the czar's palace to ask for reforms. The attack became known as "Bloody Sunday."
Identify Effects *What events took place after Bloody Sunday?*

The Year of Revolution

The Czar's reforms of 1905 did not quiet Russia's growing revolutionary spirit. Russia's participation in World War I was a military, economic, and political disaster. The stage was set for revolution.

February to July 1917 Russia's horrible wartime conditions led to a series of massive strikes and demonstrations in the nation's capital, Petrograd (PEH truh grad), now called St. Petersburg. The Czar's troops, most of them from the peasant class, joined the protesters they were supposed to be battling. With no army to enforce his orders, Czar Nicholas II was forced to give up power. Later, he and his family were executed. Control passed to a temporary democratic government based on the Duma. The peasant-based Socialist Revolutionaries and the moderate Menshevik socialists controlled this government.

Revolutionary Rumblings While the Czar gave control to the Duma, the Petrograd workers formed their own elected body, the Soviet of Workers' and Soldiers' Deputies. This group was one of many **soviets,** or elected workers' councils set up by laborers. It challenged the Duma for control of Russia.

Lenin and other Bolshevik leaders had been banned from Russia since 1907. In April 1917, the German government allowed them to return to Russia, hoping that their revolutionary activities would undermine the Russian war effort. Back in Russia, Lenin and the Bolsheviks demanded "land, bread, and peace." Land would be for poor peasants, who had already begun seizing land and forming their own soviets. Bread was for hungry workers. Peace meant an end to Russia's participation in World War I. Most importantly, the Bolsheviks also demanded a government by and for the workers and peasants.

Bolshevik-led workers revolted in Petrograd in July 1917. The provisional, or temporary, government put down the July uprising, and Lenin escaped to Finland. Late in July 1917, Alexander F. Kerensky (al ig ZAN dur (F.) kuh REN skee) took control of the provisional government. He wanted a peaceful, gradual change and opposed the Bolsheviks' revolutionary approach.

October 1917 By the fall of 1917, some members of the provisional government had become more concerned about the soviets' growing power. One such person was General Kornilov (JEN ur ul kur NYEE luf), Kerensky's military chief. In late August 1917, Kornilov ordered troops to stop the soviets by moving on Petrograd. This action caught the attention of the opposition of both the Bolsheviks and Kerensky. Together, they defeated Kornilov's attempt to take over the government. Afterward, the workers became more extreme. In September 1917, the Bolsheviks won a majority in a number of key soviets including Petrograd, Moscow (MAHS kow), and several other cities.

The revolution grew daily. In October 1917, Lenin returned from Finland and urged the Bolsheviks to begin planning to take power. On October 25, 1917, armed Bolshevik workers entered the main government buildings in Petrograd and arrested the cabinet members. A week later the Bolshevik workers controlled Moscow. Kerensky was forced to leave. The Bolsheviks had led the world's first socialist revolution, but the hardest days for Lenin and the Russian Revolution still lay ahead.

Vladimir Lenin
Bolshevik leader Vladimir Lenin was one of the major forces of the Russian Revolution. In 1917, he led the Bolsheviks as they took over Russia's government and set up the world's first Communist state.
Identify Effects *How did the Bolshevik takeover affect private ownership of land in Russia?*

✓ **Reading Check** **Who ordered the takeover of the Russian government in August, 1917?**

A New Government

Changes spread quickly in the first months of the revolution, as the Bolsheviks seized power in other Russian cities. Lenin declared the formation of the world's first Communist state. Its capital was the city of Moscow. The Bolsheviks ended private ownership of land and distributed land to the peasants. All land was declared to belong to the people, and some 500 million acres were turned over to peasants. Workers were given control of factories, mines, and industries. The Bolshevik government took control of banks. Trade was outlawed, as was the ownership of most private property. The government formed a secret police unit, the Cheka (CHEK uh), to keep track of opponents of the new government.

✓ **Reading Check** **Name one feature of the new Russian government.**

Post-Revolutionary Russia

The new government quickly fulfilled its promise to withdraw from the war. In March 1918, the government signed the Treaty of Brest-Litovsk (TREE tee uv brest lih TAWFSK). The treaty forced Russia to give up large amounts of territory to Germany.

Civil War This treaty and other Bolshevik policies angered many Russians. The nobles wanted their land back, and capitalists wanted their factories back. Some workers and peasants thought the government was not equal enough. In 1918 many of these forces banded together in an armed revolt against the government. The anti-government forces, called the Whites, received aid from several foreign countries, including Britain, France, and the United States. These nations were concerned that if socialist revolution were to succeed in Russia, it might spread beyond Russia's borders.

After two years of civil war, the Bolshevik army, called the Reds, headed by Lenin's deputy Leon Trotsky (LEE ahn TRAHT skee), defeated the Whites in 1920. But the struggle took its toll on the Russian people. Under the Bolsheviks, the death penalty was restored, all opposition parties were outlawed, and freedom of the press was limited.

Recognize Multiple Causes
What multiple causes led to the armed revolt by the Whites against the government?

Leon Trotsky (inset) headed the Bolshevik Army.

קום צו אונדז אין קאלווירדט!

A communist poster calling for female workers

Dictatorship By the mid-1920s these emergency measures had become permanent. The Bolsheviks, now called the Communist Party, tried to revive the war-shattered economy in 1921 with their New Economic Policy, which allowed some economic freedom. In 1922, the Communists created the Soviet Union, which united the lands of the former Russian Empire. After Lenin's death in 1924, the Communist Party leader Joseph Stalin (JOH zuf STAH lin) took power and pushed for stricter government control, reversing the reforms of the New Economic Policy. Trotsky, Lenin's chosen successor, was forced out of the party in 1927 and was forced to leave the country in 1929. By the 1930s all power was held by Stalin, the new Soviet dictator.

✔ **Reading Check** **Who took power after Lenin died?**

Section 2 Assessment

Key Terms
Review the Key Terms at the beginning of this section. Use each term in a sentence that explains its meaning.

Target Reading Skill
Name three causes of the Russian Revolution in 1917.

Comprehension and Critical Thinking
1. (a) Identify Which two new social classes sprang up in Russia as it began to build factories?
(b) Identify Cause and Effect Which event caused the Czar to create the first Russian Duma?

2. (a) Draw Conclusions Why did the Germans decide to let Lenin back into Russia in April 1917?
(b) Draw Inferences Why do you think Bolsheviks and Mensheviks combined forces to put down the Kornilov coup attempt?
3. (a) Explain How did the new Bolshevik government address the needs of the peasants?
(b) Draw Inferences Why did foreign countries such as Britain, France, and the United States support the Whites?
4. (a) Identify Cause and Effect Name one important result of the Treaty of Brest-Litovsk.
(b) Explain Why were the capitalists and nobles opposed to the Bolshevik regime?

Writing Activity
Suppose that you are a news writer in 1918. Write an article that includes three or four key events of the Russian Revolution in the order in which they happened.

For: An activity on the Russian Revolution
Visit: PHSchool.com
Web Code: mud-2120

Crises Around the World

Prepare to Read

Objectives

In this section you will

1. Discover why people in the United States and Europe were hopeful at the start of the 1920s.
2. Understand the causes of the 1929 crash on Wall Street and the Great Depression.
3. Explore the two major responses to the Great Depression.
4. Learn about the growth of Japan as a major power.

Taking Notes

As you read this section, looks for the effects of the Great Depression on the world. Copy the chart below, and record three such effects.

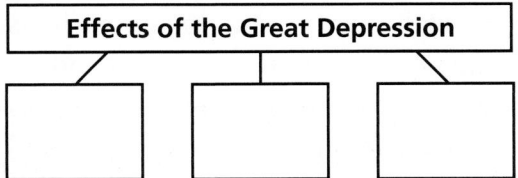

Effects of the Great Depression

Target Reading Skill

Understand Effects
Sometimes one cause may produce several effects. For example, the worldwide Great Depression of the 1930s had many different effects on countries around the world. As you read, note three effects of the Great Depression. Write them in your Taking Notes chart.

Key Terms

- **inflation** (in FLAY shun) *n.* an increase in both prices and the amount of money in circulation
- **depression** (dee PRESH un) *n.* a sharp and prolonged downturn in the economy
- **fascism** (FASH iz um) *n.* a nationalistic and anti-communist political movement that openly supports violence and dictatorship to achieve its aims
- **scapegoat** (SKAYP goht) *n.* a person or group that bears the blame for the mistakes of others

U.S. President Woodrow Wilson shared the popular belief that World War I had been "the war to end all wars." In his Fourteen Points, he outlined a plan for greater cooperation among the major powers. The centerpiece of his plan was the creation of the League of Nations, an international organization in which countries could settle their disputes through conversation and compromise rather than through war.

For a few years after the war, it appeared that Wilson's dream might come true. Prosperity slowly returned to Europe. Democracy was established in Germany, and international trade and cooperation were increasing. But, by the late 1920s, the world economy slowed down. Wilson's vision of a peaceful postwar world turned out to be an impossible dream. Tragically, "the war to end all wars" would be followed by an even bigger world war.

Pictured left to right, British Prime Minister David Lloyd George, American President Woodrow Wilson, and French Prime Minister Georges Clemenceau at the Versailles Peace Conference after World War I.

Go Online
PHSchool.com Use Web Code
mup-0849 for an interactivity
on the Jazz Age.

Inflation in Germany
Inflation caused the mark, Germany's currency, to lose most of its value in 1923. As a result, the German mark became almost worthless. Here, a man uses German mark notes to decorate an office. **Summarize** *Define inflation in your own words.*

A Time of Hope

The European powers entered the 1920s thinking that they had fought to make the world safe for democracy. In Great Britain, all male citizens finally achieved the right to vote in 1918, as did women in 1928. Women also won the right to vote in the United States in 1920, in Russia in 1917, and in Germany and most of Europe during the 1920s.

Concerned about the threat of communism, many European countries improved their treatment of workers. In the 1920s, most countries made the eight-hour working day standard for the first time. Other countries launched or expanded programs to guarantee public medical, accident, and old-age insurance to their citizens.

The economies of the Western countries were slow to recover from the war, mostly because of the drop in orders from war industries. Peacetime industries gradually increased their productivity, and so did the economies of the West. Europe and the United States underwent a major economic recovery between 1924 and 1929. The rise of the automobile created a demand for related industries, such as steel, rubber, oil, electrical equipment, and road building. New entertainment technologies such as radio and movies became thriving new industries. World trade reached all-time highs, and in 1929 European trade climbed to a level it would not equal again until 1954.

During this time the German economy suffered briefly. In 1923 it was hit by **inflation**, an increase in both prices and the amount of money in circulation. By the end of that year, one American dollar equaled 4 trillion German marks!

Thanks largely to aid and investment from the United States, Germany quickly recovered and enjoyed five years of prosperity under its new democratic government. During those years the German Weimar Republic (JUR mun VY mahr rih PUB lik), named after the city where its constitution was adopted, became a thriving center of international commerce and culture.

✓ **Reading Check** **What problem jolted the German economy in 1923?**

Unemployed men in a New York City bread line during the Great Depression

Worldwide Economic Depression

Unemployed men in a New York City bread line during the Great Depression

By the late 1920s, the economies of the United States and Europe slowed down. A series of causes led to a devastating worldwide economic crash.

Economic Instability Several factors contributed to the world's economic struggles. The wages of working people had not risen nearly as fast as profits. Production expanded faster than people's ability to buy goods, so sales began to drop. Similarly, the world market for farm goods remained slow throughout the 1920s.

The key cause of the economic slump, however, was Europe's heavy debt to the United States. By 1929, Europe had borrowed $2.9 billion from the United States. These loans were added to the debt still unpaid from the war. Britain and France financed these debts by demanding that Germany make its reparation payments. But Germany could pay reparations only by borrowing from the United States, so the solution became a part of the problem.

In 1928, Americans began to ask that their loans to Europeans be repaid. When the Europeans had trouble paying, U.S. banks had big problems.

This man sits by a shack in a "Hooverville" built to house Seattle's unemployed.

The Crash On October 24, 1929, the American stock market crashed. Within a month, American stock values dropped some 40 percent. Within three years, the average value of fifty major industrial stocks had collapsed from 252 to 61. In that time 5,000 American banks closed.

A newspaper headline announces a panic on Wall Street.

Reasons for the Crash Why the sudden collapse? When the banks tried to collect on their European loans, the funds were not available to repay them. The unpaid loans left the banks with no money. When people tried to withdraw their money from banks, the banks went out of business. In addition, when people lost their money in the stock market, they could not buy goods and soon factories began to close. People lost their jobs and could not find new ones.

The global economy also slowed down considerably. Between 1929 and 1932, world economic output dropped by 38 percent, and international trade fell by two thirds. In the United States, at that point the world's leading economy, national income shrank by more than half. The world was in a full-scale **depression**, a sharp and prolonged downturn in the economy.

As banks and businesses closed, the ranks of the unemployed swelled. By 1932, there were more than 40 million people out of work world-wide. Productive wage earners were reduced to accepting charity or relief from the state. This crisis became known as the Great Depression.

✓ **Reading Check** **Why did the banks run out of money?**

■ Graph Skills

The Great Depression
As banks and businesses failed, millions of workers around the world were without jobs. In once-prosperous western cities, people slept on park benches and lined up to eat in charity soup kitchens. Among the hardest hit were the powerhouses of the Industrial Revolution—Britain, Germany, and the United States. **Identify** What percentage of Britain's work force was unemployed in 1928? During what year did unemployment in Germany reach its highest point? **Draw Conclusions** What may have caused Germany's unemployment rate to decrease?

Unemployment in the U.S. and Europe, 1928–1938

- Hitler begins to re–arm Germany
- Roosevelt introduces New Deal
- Depression ends in Germany
- Great Depression begins

SOURCES: Historical Statistics of the United States: Colonial Times to 1970
International Historical Statistics Europe 1750–1988

- Germany
- Great Britain
- United States

Responses to the Great Depression

During the Great Depression, people demanded solutions. In the United States, France, and Britain, governments were able to make reforms within democratic systems of government. In Italy and Germany, however, the Great Depression resulted in **fascism**, a nationalist and anti-communist system of government that openly supports violence and dictatorship to achieve its aims.

Construction of the Ft. Loudoun Dam in Tennessee was a New Deal public works project.

The New Deal in the United States Franklin Delano Roosevelt (FRANGK lin DEL uh noh ROH zuh velt) became the President of the United States in 1933, at the low point of the Great Depression. Roosevelt's program of social reform and economic recovery, the New Deal, included huge public works projects. These projects created new jobs, unemployment insurance, and social security. These projects also expanded organizing rights for labor unions, reformed the banking system, and began price supports for farmers.

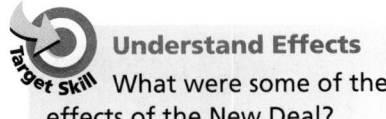

Understand Effects What were some of the effects of the New Deal?

The Rise of Fascism in Italy Italians were on the winning side in World War I, but the war left Italy with a poor economy and widespread unemployment. In the 1921 elections, the Socialists and Communists won a large majority in the parliament.

Italian army and business leaders, however, feared a communist takeover. They turned to Benito Mussolini (beh NEE toh moo suh LEE nee), a former socialist who had founded a fascist movement in 1919.

Although they held only a handful of seats in the Parliament, in 1922 Mussolini and his followers met no resistance. The fascists replaced Italy's democracy by force, outlawing other political parties, ending freedom of the press, and breaking up the labor unions.

The Rise of Hitler and Nazism in Germany

Adolf Hitler (AD awlf HIT lur) emerged from World War I as an honored soldier and a nationalist. He was determined to overcome what he saw as Germany's disgrace in World War I. In 1923, while in prison for leading an unsuccessful revolt, Hitler recorded his philosophy in the book *Mein Kampf* (myn kahmpf), which means "my struggle."

Nazi party officials salute Adolf Hitler at a meeting of the German parliament.

Between 1924 and 1929, Germany seemed to be on a path to democracy. With the beginning of the Depression, however, Hitler and his ideas gained a wider audience. At the time, Hitler was the leader of the National Socialist German Workers' Party, called "Nazis" (NAHT seez) for short. The party called for German-speaking peoples to unite in a crusade against communists and Jews. The Jews were blamed for Germany's defeat in the war. As a result, they became a **scapegoat,** or a person or group that bears the blame for the mistakes of others.

Hitler's message appealed to Germans who wished for stronger leadership. In the July 1932 elections, the Nazis became the largest party in the German parliament. In January 1933, German president Paul von Hindenburg (pawl vawn HIN dun burg) appointed Hitler chancellor, or leader, of Germany.

Hitler soon broke his pledge to preserve democratic rights. He outlawed opposition political parties and broke up the trade unions. Jews endured the worst treatment. The Nazis passed a series of laws robbing Jews of their property and their civil rights. Synagogues were destroyed or vandalized with the approval of the government. The Nazis sent Jews, as well as Gypsies, Slavs, communists, and other persecuted minorities that the Nazis considered inferior, to concentration camps, where more than 6 million Jews were murdered.

With a vast public works program, Hitler eliminated much of Germany's unemployment and brought some prosperity. But he also abolished free speech, free elections, and racial and religious harmony. On these foundations of violence and hate, Hitler set his nation on the march to yet another war.

Find out about the Holocaust.

All Jews in Nazi-occupied Europe were ordered to wear a yellow Star of David.

✓ Reading Check   What were members of the National Socialist German Workers' Party called?

Practice the Skill

Reread Chapter 21, Section 3, Crises Around the World. Then use the steps on the opposite page to draw inferences and a conclusion about the causes of revolutions.

1 Answer these questions in order to help you find facts. What problems did U.S. bankers have in collecting on European loans? What role did the Germans have in the loan repayment cycle?

2 Use the facts to create at least two inferences, or educated guesses. State your inferences as "if … then" sentences. For example: If countries are borrowing money to pay off loans, then they are more likely to encounter large-scale economic problems.

3 Using the inference you have written, what conclusion can you draw about why the Great Depression occurred?

Apply the Skill

Turn to Section 3 of Chapter 21 and reread the paragraphs under the heading The Rise of Hitler and Nazism in Germany. Use the steps on the opposite page to draw inferences about why Hitler was able to turn Germany into a fascist state.

World War II

Prepare to Read

Objectives

In this section you will
1. Explore the causes of World War II.
2. Learn about Germany's early successes in the war.
3. Discover how 1941 was a turning point in the war.
4. Understand why the Allies achieved success in the years 1942–1945.

Taking Notes

As you read this section, note the key words that signal the sequence of causes and effects in World War II. Use the chart below to note at least three such words and the cause or effect that each signals.

Signal Word	Cause or Event Signaled
•	•
•	•
•	•

🎯 Target Reading Skill

Recognize Cause-and-Effect Signal Words
Causes and effects follow each other in a certain sequence, or time order. This section contains information about many of the important events of World War II. To help keep the order of events clear, look for words such as *before, after, meanwhile, then,* and *next* that signal the order in which events took place. Use your Taking Notes chart as a guide.

Key Terms

- **Holocaust** (HAHL uh kawst) *n.,* the term used to refer to the Nazis' murder of 6 million Jews during World War II
- **appeasement** (uh PEEZ munt) *n.,* the giving in to the demands of an aggressor in order to keep the peace
- **atomic bomb** (uh TAHM ik BAHM) *n.,* an extremely destructive bomb whose power results from the chain reaction of nuclear fission

What does evil look like? For many people, the Holocaust is the most evil event of the modern era. The word **Holocaust** means "sacrifice or destruction through fire" and is used to refer to the Nazis' murder of 6 million Jews during World War II.

Adolf Hitler and his supporters had devised plans for what he considered the "Jewish problem." The scale and savagery of the Holocaust has been unequaled in history. The record of the Nazi's slaughter is a vivid reminder of the monstrous results of racism and intolerance.

A soldier stands guard as a train full of prisoners enters a Nazi concentration camp.

Causes of World War II

In many ways World War II resulted from the unfinished business of World War I. The nationalism that arose in 1914 did not disappear in 1918. Instead, it drew new strength from those who were defeated in World War I, especially the Germans.

Resentment Over the Treaty of Versailles Many Germans felt humiliated by the terms of the Treaty of Versailles. The German Nazi leader, Adolf Hitler, wanted to overcome this humiliation. Germany stopped paying the required reparations. After he became chancellor, Hitler withdrew Germany from the League of Nations and ignored the treaty's other provisions. He began to build up Germany's army. He reintroduced the draft and sent soldiers into the Rhineland (RYN land), a German territory placed off-limits to military activity by the treaty. Meanwhile, Fascist Italy had conquered the African nation of Ethiopia. In October 1936, Germany and Italy signed a treaty creating the Rome-Berlin Axis.

Appeasement In March 1938, Hitler announced the unification of Germany and Austria. In September 1938 he announced his desire to take over the Sudeten (soo DAYT un) area of Czechoslovakia (chek uh sloh VAH kee uh). France and Britain still followed a policy of **appeasement**, or the giving in to the demands of an aggressor in order to keep the peace. By signing the Munich Pact (MYOO nik pakt) on September 29, 1938, France and Great Britain recognized Hitler's takeover of the Sudeten area.

The Final Steps to War Hitler continued to extend his empire. In March 1939, he ignored the Munich Pact by occupying the rest of Czechoslovakia. Italy also extended its boundaries. In April Italy invaded Albania (al BAY nee uh). Great Britain and France began to prepare their own militaries. They formed alliances with Turkey, Greece, Romania, and Poland.

Meanwhile, Germany and the Soviet Union promised not to attack each other. Certain that he would not have to fight Russia, Hitler invaded Poland on September 1, 1939. Britain and France declared war on Germany on September 3. World War II had begun.

Hitler's Road to War
Above, Adolph Hitler is pictured on German postage stamps as leader of Germany. Below, German soldiers march through a street in Poland after Germany's 1939 invasion of Poland. **Identify Effects** *How did Britain and France respond after Germany invaded Poland?*

✓ **Reading Check** **How was the Munich Pact an example of appeasement?**

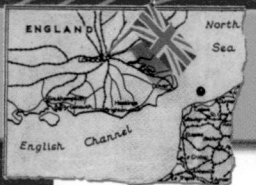

In May 1940, Great Britain's Prime Minister Winston Churchill entered one of the basement rooms beneath a government building in London and said, "This is the room from which I'll direct the war." The room Churchill spoke of was part of the Cabinet War Rooms, a secret complex of specially equipped and protected underground rooms. During World War II, London suffered heavy bombing by German aircraft and threats of invasion. At such times, Churchill and his advisors met in the Cabinet War Rooms to discuss the war and to plan for their country's defense. Concrete, steel beams, heavy timber, and a special ventilation system protected the rooms from attack.

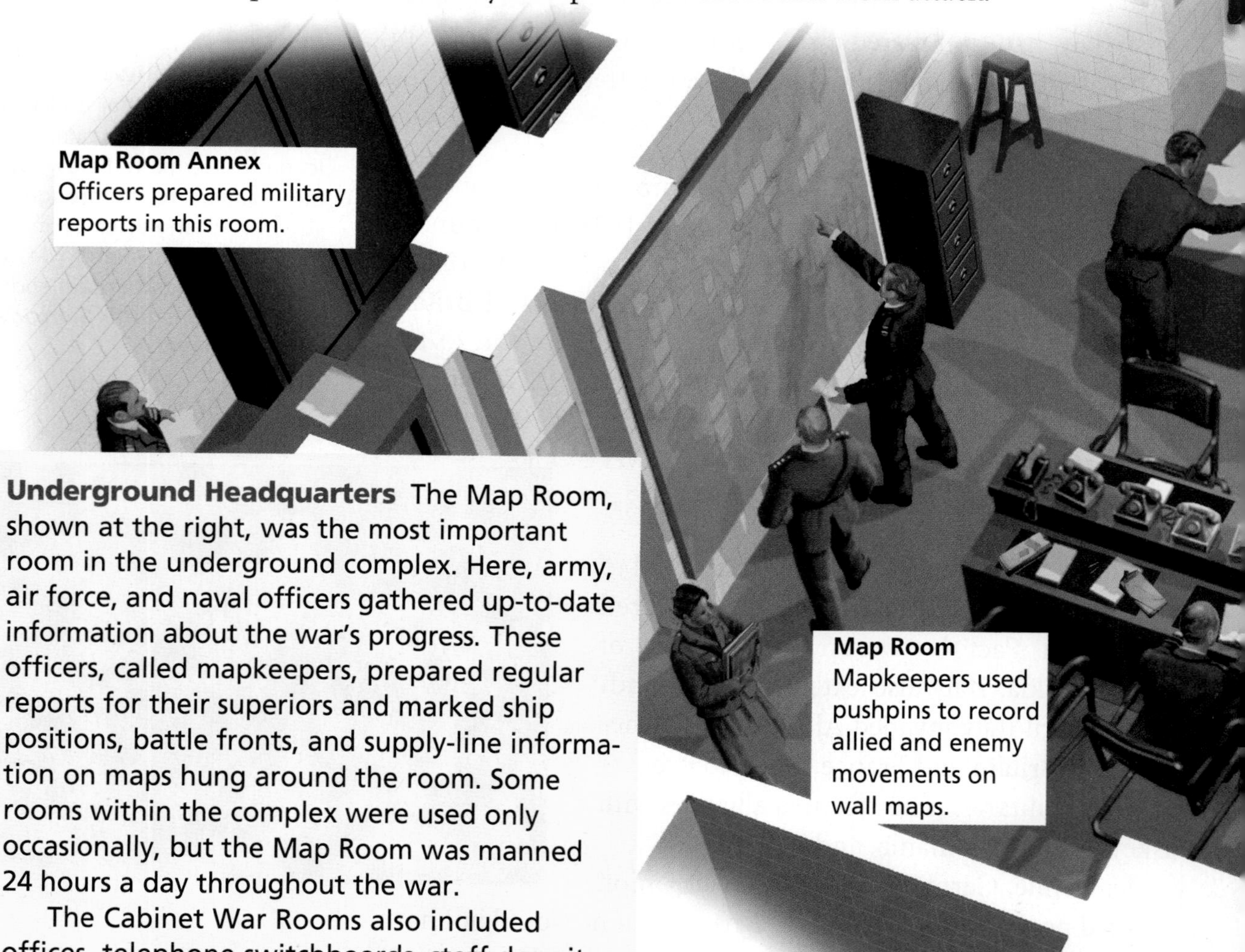

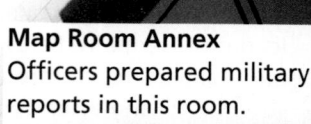

Map Room Annex
Officers prepared military reports in this room.

Underground Headquarters The Map Room, shown at the right, was the most important room in the underground complex. Here, army, air force, and naval officers gathered up-to-date information about the war's progress. These officers, called mapkeepers, prepared regular reports for their superiors and marked ship positions, battle fronts, and supply-line information on maps hung around the room. Some rooms within the complex were used only occasionally, but the Map Room was manned 24 hours a day throughout the war.

The Cabinet War Rooms also included offices, telephone switchboards, staff dormitories, a mess room where snacks were served, and a transatlantic telephone room—disguised as a bathroom—where Churchill had a direct phone line to the President of the United States.

Map Room
Mapkeepers used pushpins to record allied and enemy movements on wall maps.

Winston Churchill inspects a bomb crater in London, 1940.

Map Room Exhibit
This is how the Map Room looked while it was in use. Today, the Cabinet War Rooms are a museum.

Telephone switchboard operators in the Cabinet War Rooms, 1945

Prime Minister's Room
This was Winston Churchill's office, from which he made some of his wartime radio broadcasts. Occasionally, he slept here.

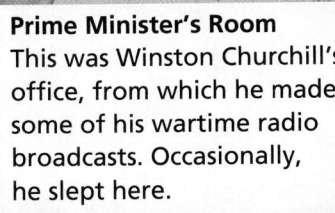

Assessment

Describe What were the Cabinet War Rooms?

Infer Why was it important for Churchill and his war advisors to remain safe from enemy attacks?

Early German Successes and the Battle of Britain

In April 1940, the German army conquered Denmark and by June had conquered Norway. In May the Germans invaded Luxembourg, Belgium, and the Netherlands on their way to France.

The Fall of France On May 13, German forces reached the Maginot Line (MAZH uh noh lyn), the fortified line of defense the French had built to protect against a German attack. But the Maginot Line failed to stop the powerful German forces. France fell by late June 1940, and the Germans set up a puppet government in France under Marshal Pétain (MAHR shul pay TAN). Germany now controlled all of Western Europe except Britain and neutral countries such as Switzerland, Sweden, and Spain.

The Battle of Britain British forces at Dunkirk in France managed to escape from the Germans and returned to Britain. As the only major European democracy not in Hitler's hands, Britain fought ferociously. Under the leadership of their prime minister, Winston Churchill, British pilots held off the Nazi air force in a series of fights known as "the   Battle of Britain."

✓ Reading Check **What was the Maginot Line?**

Below: Allied troops on the dunes at Dunkirk lined up to board ships bound for England. Inset: Soldiers waiting for their ship to depart for England.

herman Tank

st used in World War I, tanks are combat
hicles that are covered with armor and equipped
th machine guns and artillery capabilities. Steel
cks wrapped around wheels move the tank.
uring World War II, Germany developed new
nks. In response, the United States built the M-4,
own as the Sherman tank after a famous Civil
ar general. The Sherman tank became the most
mmon tank among the Allied forces.

Sherman Tank in France, 1944
The United States built more than
80,000 tanks during World War II,
including more than 50,000 Shermans.

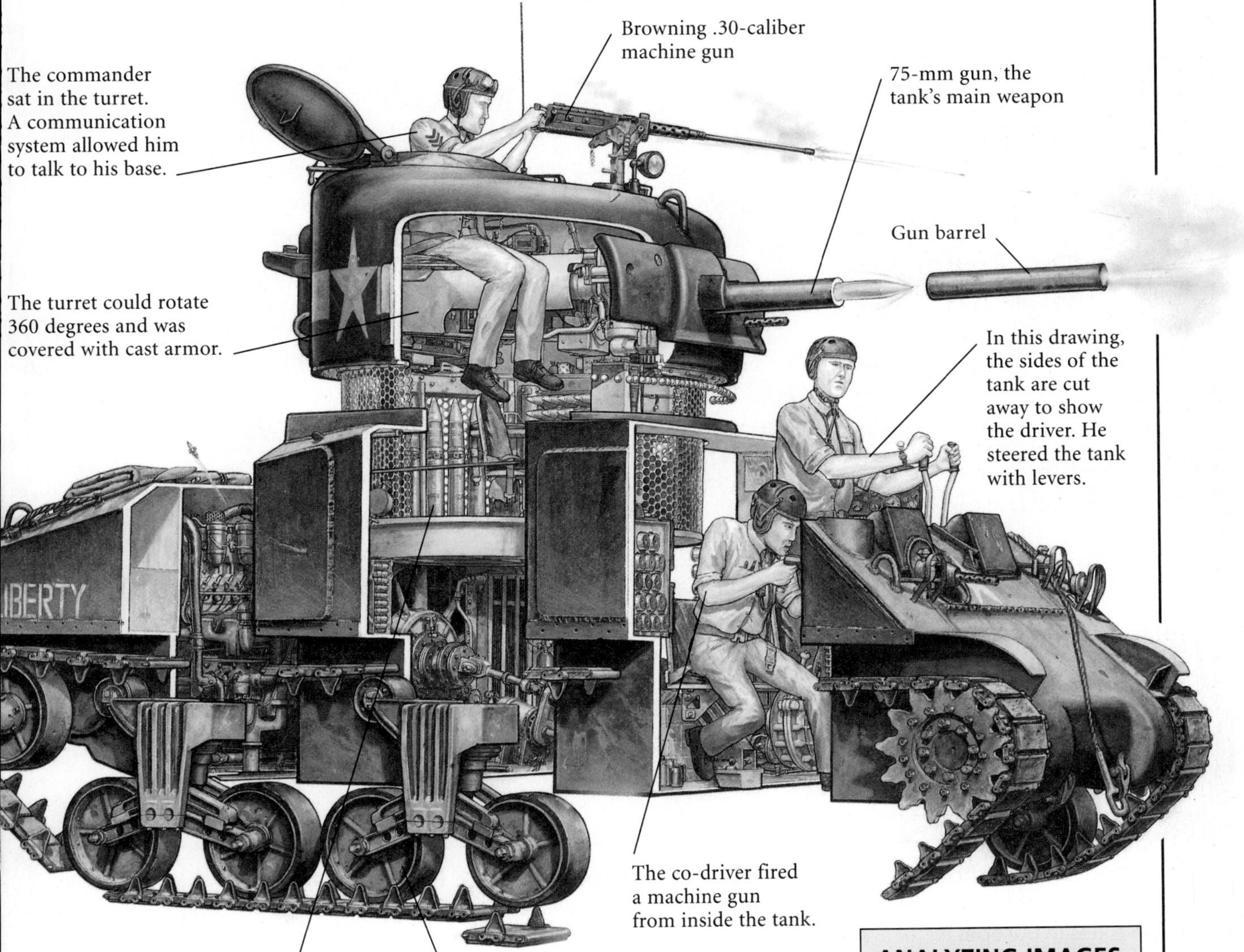

Browning .30-caliber
machine gun

75-mm gun, the
tank's main weapon

The commander
sat in the turret.
A communication
system allowed him
to talk to his base.

Gun barrel

The turret could rotate
360 degrees and was
covered with cast armor.

In this drawing,
the sides of the
tank are cut
away to show
the driver. He
steered the tank
with levers.

IBERTY

The co-driver fired
a machine gun
from inside the tank.

The Sherman fired artillery
shells that could pierce
the armor of enemy tanks.

A system of wheels inside a
steel track allowed the tank to
roll easily over uneven ground.

ANALYZING IMAGES
Why might a rotating
turret on a tank
be needed?

1941: Turning Points in the War

Hitler's army had quickly captured most of Western Europe. Things changed, however, when German forces faced the harsh Russian winter and the entry of the United States into the war.

World War II in Europe and North Africa

MAP★MASTER™
Skills Activity

KEY

- Axis Powers, 1942
- Under Axis control by 1942
- Areas occupied by Germany by 1942
- Allied territory, 1942
- Axis satellites
- Neutral nations
- City severely bombed by the Allies
- City severely bombed by the Germans
- Ⓥ Allied victory
- National border
- • City

0 miles 500
0 kilometers 500
Lambert Azimuthal Equal Area

Regions The map shows the extent of Axis and Allied powers in 1942. For the first few years of World War II, the Axis powers seemed to have the advantage of the Allies in Europe. **Read a Map Key** Identify those areas under the control of Germany and the Axis Powers. Note the additional countries that were neutral. **Draw Conclusions** Why was geography on the side of the Axis Powers at this point in the war?

Go Online
PHSchool.com Use Web Code mup-2141 for step-by-step map skills practice.

Germany Invades the Soviet Union In the spring of 1941, after adding Yugoslavia and Greece to his conquests, Hitler proceeded to attack the Soviet Union. Ignoring his treaty with the Soviets, Hitler ordered his troops into Russia on June 22, 1941. At first, German troops easily advanced through the Ukraine (yoo KRAYN) and came within sight of Moscow. Then the harsh Russian winter set in. A Russian attack near Moscow pushed back Germans troops who were ill-prepared for the freezing temperatures.

The United States Enters the War Although formally neutral, the United States had been doing its best to help Britain and the other Allies with aid under the Lend-Lease program. Japan, meanwhile, was expanding and challenged American interests in Asia. This changed when Japanese planes attacked the U.S. naval base at Pearl Harbor, Hawaii, on December 7, 1941. They damaged or destroyed 19 ships, smashed American planes on the ground, and killed more than 2,200 people. This disaster caused the American public to support an immediate American entry into the war. Upon its declaration of war the following day, the United States faced the challenge of facing Japan in the Pacific while fighting against Germany in Europe.

The Battle of Stalingrad One of Germany's failures came on the snowy, frozen battlefields of Russia during the winter of 1942. In September of that year, more than 500,000 German troops attacked the city of Stalingrad (stah lin GRAHT). The remaining Russian forces, resolving not to let the city fall, disrupted the German supply lines in November. The starving, frozen German army was stunned by the Soviet resistance. At the end of January 1943, 91,000 German troops surrendered. After this first major defeat for Germany, the Soviet forces began pushing westward.

Victory in Europe Following campaigns in North Africa and Italy, the Allies opened a western front against the weakened Germans. On June 6, 1944, Allied warships carrying 156,000 troops landed at Normandy (NAWR mun dee), on the northern coast of France. Known as D-Day, the Normandy landing was the start of a massive Allied campaign eastward. Within six months, the Allied armies had reached Germany. After one last attempt for success in December 1944, known as the Battle of the Bulge, the German army collapsed. The Allies declared victory in Europe on May 8, 1945.

Go Online
PHSchool.com Use Web Code **mup-0850** for an interactivity on World War II.

Target Skill **Recognize Cause-and-Effect Signal Words**
Identify signal words in the paragraph titled Germany Invades the Soviet Union.

Links to Science

The Manhattan Project By the 1930s, scientists knew that if they could split the atom, they could make a bomb that would release unheard-of amounts of energy. The United States had a secret program, the Manhattan Project, that was trying to create such a bomb. The project scientists exploded the world's first atomic blast in New Mexico in July 1945. A month later, an atomic bomb was used against Japan.

Victorious Allied troops return home.

Victory in the Pacific Although Japanese forces triumphed early in the war, 1942 saw Allied victories at the Battle of the Coral Sea, the Battle of Midway, and the Battle of Guadalcanal (gwahd ul kuh NAL). The first U.S. bombs fell on Tokyo in April 1942. Although the bombs did little real damage, the event did much to raise American morale. It also caused the Japanese to move resources to air defense.

By September 1944, the Allies were advancing on the Philippines. The Battle of Leyte (LAYT ee) Gulf in October 1944 hurt the Japanese navy. In the spring of 1945, U.S. forces captured the Japanese islands of Iwo Jima (EE woh JEE muh) and Okinawa (oh kuh NAH wuh), and then began pounding Japan from the air. The U.S. air campaign ended with the dropping of an **atomic bomb, an extremely destructive bomb whose power results from the chain reaction of nuclear fission,** on the cities of Hiroshima (HIHR uh SHEE muh), and Nagasaki (nah guh SAH kee). Both cities were completely destroyed. Japan surrendered only five days later and signed a peace agreement on September 2, 1945. With the Japanese surrender, World War II came to an end.

✓ **Reading Check** What events signaled a turning point in the war?

Section 4 Assessment

Key Terms
Review the Key Terms at the beginning of this section. Use each term in a sentence that explains its meaning.

 **Target Reading Skill**
Review the section Germany Invades the Soviet Union. Find the words that signal the sequence that leads up to and includes Germany's advance on Moscow.

Comprehension and Critical Thinking
1. (a) Recall Which area was turned over to Germany as a result of the Munich Pact?

(b) Explain Why did France, Great Britain, and the United States do nothing, at first, to oppose Hitler's aggressive policies?
2. (a) Recall What effect did the Maginot Line have on German soldiers?
(b) Summarize How did things go for Germany during the first year of the war?
3. (a) Identify Cause and Effect How did the attack on Pearl Harbor affect American public opinion?
(b) Explain How did Hitler betray the Soviet Union during the war?
4. (a) Identify What was the first major defeat for Germany during World War II?

(b) Draw Inferences What effect did the dropping of the atomic bomb have on World War II?

Writing Activity
Write a summary of the causes of World War II. Be sure to include the key events that led up to war.

For: An activity on World War II
Visit: PHSchool.com
Web Code: mud-2140

21 Review and Assessment

◆ Chapter Summary

World War I gas mask

Section 1: World War I

- Nationalism, imperialism, and the system of alliances put the world on the brink of a world war at the start of the 1900s.
- An assassination in Eastern Europe was the spark that set off World War I.
- Battlefield stalemates and new automatic weapons caused fearful death tolls throughout Europe.
- The United States entered the war and turned the tide in favor of the Allies.
- The Treaty of Versailles ended the war but created resentment in Germany that would lead to another war two decades later.

Section 2: The Russian Revolution

- The Russian people revolted against the czar in the hope of overcoming poverty and gaining greater control over their own lives.
- In 1917 the Bolsheviks led the Russian people in the world's first socialist revolution.
- The first year of the revolution offered both the promise of radical reform and the threat of dictatorship.
- Opposition to the revolution inside and outside of Russia caused a tough two-year civil war that undermined the original goals and ideals of the revolution and led to Stalin's dictatorship.

Section 3: Crises Around the World

- Europe emerged from the war with new hopes for democracy and prosperity in the 1920s.
- The late 1920s were darkened by a worldwide depression that put tens of millions of people out of work.
- The desperate conditions in Italy and Germany led to the rise of fascist dictatorships.
- Japan emerged as a major world power and posed a threat to the security of China and the United States.

Section 4: World War II

- Nazi aggression in Europe set off World War II.
- Germany achieved quick successes early in the war.
- The entry of the United States into the war and German setbacks in Russia marked a turning point in the war.
- From 1942 to 1945, Germany and Japan suffered a series of reverses that turned the tide of the war and sent them to eventual defeat.

Germany invades Poland, 1939

◆ Key Terms

Each of the statements below contains a key term from the chapter. If the statement is true, write *true*. If it is false, rewrite the statement to make it true.

1. An **alliance** is the division of land after a war.

2. **Reparations** are the rebuilding activities that go on after a war in areas that have been destroyed or damaged by large battles.

3. **Socialism** is a social system that seeks to abolish all forms of social classes and create a society of complete equality.

4. A **soviet** is someone who comes from Russia.

5. A **depression** is a sharp and prolonged downturn in the economy.

6. **Inflation** is an increase in prices and the amount of money in circulation.

7. **Appeasement** is the act of invading another country.

8. **Fascism** is a strongly nationalistic, anticommunist, and violent political outlook.

◆ Comprehension and Critical Thinking

9. (a) **Identify** What event was considered a short-term cause of World War I?
   (b) **Draw Inferences** In what way was imperialism an outgrowth of nationalism in the years before World War I?

10. (a) **Summarize** What were some of the key points of the Treaty of Versailles?
    (b) **Evaluate Information** In your view, what was the fairest feature of the Treaty of Versailles? The least fair?

11. (a) **Recall** What democratic features of the Russian Revolution did not survive the civil war of 1918–1920?
    (b) **Explain** How did the Communist party change after Lenin's death?

12. (a) **Identify** Which two European countries had fascist governments by the 1930s?
    (b) **Explain** Which social problem was most responsible for promoting the growth of fascism in Europe in the 1920s?

13. (a) **Recall** What policy did the Allies pursue toward Hitler before 1938?
    (b) **Evaluate Information** Do you think World War II could have been prevented if the Allies had stood up to Hitler sooner? Why or why not?

14. (a) **Identify** What were the key factors in the German defeat in Russia in 1943?
    (b) **Draw Inferences** What was the single most important factor in ending World War II?

◆ Skills Practice

Making Inferences In the skills activity in this chapter you learned how to draw inferences. You also learned how to draw a conclusion from two or more inferences. Review the steps for this skill. Then reread Responses to the Great Depression. List several inferences you can draw about the events described there. Finally, use your inferences to draw a conclusion about those events.

◆ Writing Activity: Language Arts

Suppose you are a newspaper writer in Russia during the winter of 1942. Your assignment is to write a brief news report on the Battle of Stalingrad. Your report should describe the conditions and outcomes of this battle.

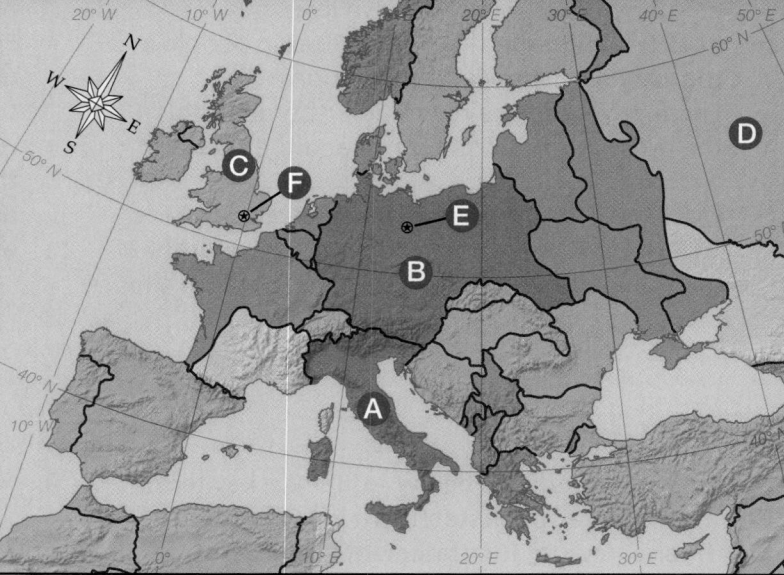

Place Location For each place listed below, write the letter from the map that shows its location.

1. Berlin   3. Germany   5. Soviet Union
2. London   4. United Kingdom   6. Italy

Go **Online**
PHSchool.com Use Web Code **mup-2102** for an **interactive map**.

Standardized Test Prep

◆ Test-Taking Tips

Some questions on standardized tests ask you to analyze point of view. Read the passage below. Then follow the tips to answer the sample question.

In 1917, Vladimir Lenin took control of Russia. Upon hearing about the overthrow of Russia's government, someone remarked: It is very good news indeed! Soon, the Russians will leave the world war. That will hurt the Allies and help us.

TIP Make sure you understand what the question is asking: Who made the comments that begin with the words "It is very good news indeed!"

Pick the letter that best answers the question.

Who might have made this statement?

A a French soldier fighting in the trenches

B a Russian nobleman friendly to Czar Nicholas

C a German general fighting in France

D an American soldier in Pearl Harbor after it was bombed

TIP Use logic, or good reasoning, to be sure you choose an answer that makes sense.

Think It Through You can eliminate D right away: Pearl Harbor was not bombed until World War II. Next think about the significance of Lenin coming to power: Czar Nicholas lost his throne. So you can rule out B. Then think about which side benefited from Lenin taking Russia out of the war. Russia was an ally of France and Britain, so you can rule out A: French soldiers would not consider this good news. The answer is C.

Practice Questions

Use the tips above and other tips in this book to help you answer the following questions.

1. A person from which country would be more likely to feel that the Treaty of Versailles was unfair?
   A France
   B Germany
   C Great Britain
   D Luxembourg

2. Who would be most likely to support socialism?
   A a capitalist
   B a dictator
   C a worker
   D a noble

Use the quotation below to answer the question that follows.

"I've lost everything. Since the stock market crashed, my stocks are worthless and I can't find a job. Our economy is in shambles."

3. The person responsible for the quote above was probably talking about which event?
   A The Great Depression
   B The Russian Revolution
   C The New Deal
   D The Treaty of Versailles

Go Online
PHSchool.com
Use Web Code **mua-2101**
for **Chapter 21 self-test.**

Chapter

22 The World Today

Chapter Preview

This chapter will introduce you to the events and forces that have shaped the world since the end of World War II.

Section 1
Europe and North America

Section 2
Latin America

Section 3
Asia

Section 4
Africa and the Middle East

Section 5
The World in a New Century

Target Reading Skill

Clarifying Meaning In this chapter you will focus on several techniques for clarifying meaning as you read: rereading or reading ahead, paraphrasing, and summarizing.

▶ Billowing in the background are the flags from 103 countries that participated in the 1992 World's Fair. Its theme was "The Age of Discovery."

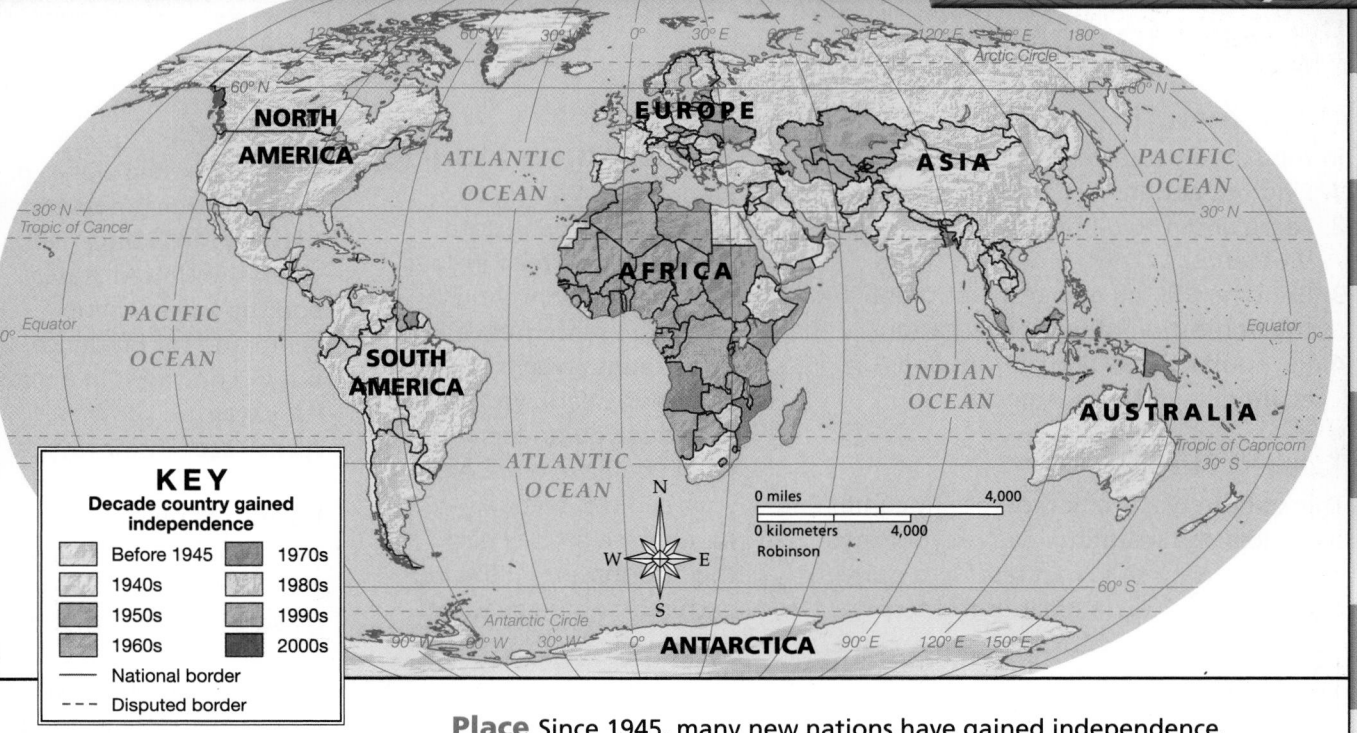

MAP MASTER™
Skills Activity

KEY
Decade country gained independence

- Before 1945
- 1940s
- 1950s
- 1960s
- 1970s
- 1980s
- 1990s
- 2000s
- —— National border
- - - - Disputed border

Go Online
PHSchool.com Use Web Code
mup-2200 for step-by-step
map skills practice.

Place Since 1945, many new nations have gained independence.
Identify On which two continents are most of the new nations located?
Draw Conclusions What does this map suggest about the European colonial empires that were built during the 1800s?

Prepare to Read

Objectives

In this section you will
1. Find out about the Cold War.
2. Learn about two hot wars: Korea and Vietnam.
3. Examine the fall of the Soviet Union and the unification of European nations.
4. Recognize the strong nations and economies in North America.

Taking Notes

Think about ways to paraphrase by combining sentences and restating ideas in your own words. Refer to this chart later as a guide to restating other main ideas in this section.

The division of control over Axis countries broke wartime alliances.

↓↓↓

Distrust developed between the United States and the Soviet Union.

↓↓↓

🎯 Target Reading Skill

Paraphrase When you paraphrase, you restate what you have read in your own words. By "saying back" the sentences or paragraphs (even if it is in your own head), you make sure that you understand what you have read. As you read this section, paraphrase or "say back" the information following each red or blue heading.

Key Terms

- **Cold War** (kohld wawr) *n.* the name for the period between 1945 and 1989, when the United States and the Soviet Union competed for influence but did not fight in a military war
- **Arms Race** (ahrmz rays) *n.* during the Cold War, the buildup of military forces by the United States and the Soviet Union
- **glasnost** (GLAHS nawst) *n.* openness
- **perestroika** (pehr uh STROI kuh) *n.* the restructuring of the Soviet government and economy

Two people looking over the top of the Berlin Wall, 1962

Berlin was a focus of Cold War tensions after World War II. After the war, East Berlin became part of Soviet-occupied communist East Germany, while West Berlin had a democratic government. In the 1950s, thousands of East Germans fled into West Berlin. To stop the loss of workers, East Germany built a wall in 1961 between East and West Berlin. The communists shot people trying to cross into West Berlin.

After a series of protests against East Germany's communist government, an East German leader said on November 9, 1989, that people would be allowed to cross the Berlin Wall. He meant that East Germans could apply for permits to cross the wall, but thousands of East Germans gathered at the wall and demanded to be let through. The wall was opened and later destroyed. Its destruction signaled the end of Soviet-style communism.

The Cold War

During World War II, the Soviet Union and the nations of the West worked together to defeat Nazi Germany. After the war, the Allies had to decide how to divide control over Europe. Much of Eastern Europe was controlled by the Soviet Union, which put Communist governments in place. Democratic governments were established in Western Europe. During these years, a great distrust developed between the Soviet Union and democratic nations in the West, led by the United States.

Within a few years, the communist countries in Eastern Europe had built strong defenses and tried to isolate their citizens from the West by preventing travel and controlling the spread of information and ideas. Winston Churchill, who led Great Britain during World War II, said that the Soviets had built an "iron curtain" between the communist countries and the West.

This mistrust between the United States and other Western democracies and the Communist dictatorships grew into a conflict called the **Cold War**. This was a conflict between 1945 and 1989 in which Western democracies and Eastern communist countries competed for power without using their armies directly against one another. Although they did not fight each other directly, the United States and Soviet Union built up their armies and weapons to discourage the other side from attacking. This buildup, called the **Arms Race,** included new missiles that could fly to targets hundreds of miles away and attack with nuclear bombs. It also led to new advancements in airplanes and jets, tanks, and many other weapons systems.

During the Cold War, the Soviet Union and China supported groups that wanted to establish communist governments in their own countries. The Soviet Union and China sent money, supplies, and even their own advisers and soldiers to many countries throughout the world to spread communist ideas. The United States and other Western countries decided to fight the spread of communism by supporting governments and political groups that opposed communism. The tensions between the Western democracies and the communist powers set the stage for two key battlegrounds: Korea and Vietnam.

✓ **Reading Check** What was the Cold War?

Walk in Space
Astronaut Edward White was the first person from the United States to walk in space. This walk took place on June 3, 1965. In 1969, the United States landed the first man on the moon. **Analyze** *Why do you think space exploration was important to the United States in the 1960s?*

Target Skill
Paraphrase
Paraphrase or restate the information in the section titled The Cold War.

Go Online
PHSchool.com Use Web Code **mup-0851** for an interactivity on the Cold War world.

Two Hot Wars: Korea and Vietnam

The wars in Korea and Vietnam played a large part in the Cold War tensions between the United States and Soviet Union. Korea and Vietnam were countries where the Cold War escalated into hot wars—or actual military confrontations—between Communist and U.S.-backed forces.

Vietnam War Protest
The Vietnam War created deep divisions among Americans. Some people supported U.S. involvement in Vietnam. Others called for the withdrawal of U.S. troops. Here, college students protest against the Vietnam War. **Sequence** *When did the United States become involved in Vietnam?*

Korea After World War II, Korea was divided at the 38th parallel of latitude. North Korea became a communist ally of the Soviet Union, and the United States supported the noncommunist government in South Korea. Tension developed as governments in both the north and the south claimed the right to rule Korea.

In 1950, the communists attacked to try to bring all of Korea under communist control. U.S. forces, under the command of General Douglas MacArthur, were sent to push the invaders out of South Korea. U.S. forces were backed by the United Nations, an organization created after World War II to maintain international peace. MacArthur drove the invaders across the 38th parallel. In response, China sent troops to help the North Koreans.

Fighting continued until an armistice was signed in 1953. The two sides agreed to stop fighting and to keep the country divided as it had been before the war.

Vietnam By the early 1960s, the United States became involved in Vietnam. Like Korea, this Southeast Asian nation was divided into a communist northern state and a noncommunist southern state. Similarly, rebels in the south (known as the Viet Cong) also wanted to unite the country under communist rule and tried to overthrow the government in South Vietnam. To prevent these rebels from winning power, the U.S. sent economic and military aid, in addition to United States troops, to South Vietnam.

Even with massive help from the United States, South Vietnam could not defeat the Viet Cong and their North Vietnamese allies. After years of fighting and thousands of U.S. and Vietnamese deaths, the United States withdrew its troops from South Vietnam in 1973. Communist forces overran South Vietnam and united Vietnam under communist rule in 1975.

✓ Reading Check **Why did the United States enter the wars in Korea and Vietnam?**

The Soviet Union Falls and Europe Unites

In 1985, Mikhail Gorbachev (mee kah EEL GAWR buh chawf) came to power in the Soviet Union. Gorbachev hoped to bring change and reform to the Soviet Union. Meanwhile, economic cooperation helped Western European countries join together to compete with the world's economic superpowers.

The End of the Soviet Union Gorbachev sought an end to costly Cold War tensions and began to change the economy to one more like those in democracies. He launched a two-pronged effort at reform. First, he called for **glasnost** (GLAHS nawst), or openness. He ended censorship and encouraged people to openly discuss the country's problems. Second, he urged **perestroika** (pehr uh STROI kuh), which meant the restructuring of the government and economy.

When the changes did not work at first, some people tried to overthrow him and bring back the old-style communism. Their attempted overthrow failed, but it further weakened the Soviet Union. In 1991, Gorbachev resigned as president. After 74 years the old Soviet Union came to an end in 1991.

The republics that had been put together in 1922 to form the Soviet Union now became independent again. The Russian Federation, or Russia, remains by far the largest and most powerful. Several former Soviet republics have formed economic alliances with Russia. Others have joined the European Union.

Citizen Heroes

Mikhail Gorbachev

As the general secretary of the Communist Party of the Soviet Union (CPSU), and then as the president of the Soviet Union, Mikhail Gorbachev worked to bring democracy to his country. In addition to democracy, Gorbachev was also interested in improving his country's slow-growing economy. During his term as president, Gorbachev improved the Soviet Union's relationship with Western and Eastern countries. These reforms changed the political nature of Europe. For his part in bringing an end to communism in the Soviet Union and encouraging the end of communism in other European nations, Gorbachev was awarded the Nobel Peace Prize in 1990.

Russian president Boris Yeltsin (holding a sheet of paper) stands on top of a tank and condemns the attempted coup by Communist hard-liners before a crowd of people in Moscow.

European Union Members in 2003

EU Members	Joined
Founding members: Belgium, France, Germany, Italy, Luxembourg, the Netherlands	1958
Denmark, Ireland, United Kingdom	1973
Greece	1981
Portugal, Spain	1986
Austria, Finland, Sweden	1995
Cyprus, Czech Republic, Estonia, Hungary, Latvia, Lithuania, Malta, Poland, Slovakia, Slovenia	2004

Toward European Unity Economic cooperation helped Western Europe recover from World War II. In 1952 France, West Germany, Belgium, Italy, the Netherlands, and Luxembourg (LUK sum burg) set up the European Coal and Steel Community. This agency set prices, regulated coal and steel industries, and increased economic growth in Western Europe.

These same nations also signed a treaty to form the European Community or Common Market. The Common Market expanded free trade, ended tariffs on goods, and allowed workers and capital to move freely across national borders. It set up the European Parliament. Citizens of Common Market Countries elected this multinational body. Its powers were limited, however, because member states remained independent.

European Union In the 1980s and 1990s, the Common Market expanded further and took the name European Union (EU). The EU pushed for complete economic unity and greater political unity. It eliminated national passports, which gave citizens from member states greater mobility, or freedom to move around. It also ended most tariffs. In 1999, the EU began launching the euro, a single currency to be used by EU members. The EU was a powerful force and helped Europe compete with economic superpowers like the United States and Japan.

✓ **Reading Check** **How did Europeans benefit from the formation of the European Union?**

■ Chart Skills

The European Union
In 2003, the EU was made up of 15 member nations. Ten additional nations joined the EU in 2004, increasing the size of both the EU's population and land area.
Identify In what year did the most EU members join?
Predict Will the number of EU members shrink or grow over time? Why?

The euro, official currency of the European Union

Strong Nations and Economies in North America

When the communist government collapsed in the Soviet Union in 1991, the United States stood alone as the world's only superpower. Militarily, the United States is the strongest country in the world and spends more on defense than all the other countries of the world combined. The United States has remained a rich nation and is a magnet for immigrants.

Like the United States, Canada is also a nation shaped by immigrants. Canada, too, ranks among the major democratic, industrial powers. Through quiet diplomacy, Canada is a strong member of NATO, and its troops serve in UN peacekeeping missions around the world.

Economic competition led to disputes over trade and tariffs between the United States and Canada. A key step to solving these issues was the creation of a free-trade zone between the two nations. NAFTA later extended this zone to Mexico.

The Pentagon, called such because of its five-sided shape, is the headquarters of the United States Department of Defense.

✓ **Reading Check** **What makes the United States the world's only superpower?**

Section 1 Assessment

Key Terms
Review the Key Terms at the beginning of this section. Use each term in a sentence that explains its meaning.

Target Reading Skill
Paraphrase the paragraph under the heading Vietnam on page 632.

Comprehension and Critical Thinking
1. (a) Identify Identify the two main kinds of government in Eastern and Western Europe.
(b) Analyze Information What was the connection between the Cold War and the Arms Race?
2. (a) Recall How were Korea and Vietnam divided?

(b) Explain What role did the Cold War play in the Korean and Vietnam Wars?
3. (a) List List examples of the changes and reforms Gorbachev brought to the Soviet Union.
(b) Identify Cause and Effect What was the main effect of the fall of the Soviet Union?
4. (a) Identify What was the main reason for the formation of the Common Market?
(b) Draw Inferences How does being in the European Union make the individual countries stronger?
5. (a) Draw Conclusions What was the world's other superpower before 1991?
(b) Summarize What are the two main sources of U.S. strength?

Writing Activity
Suppose that you were an East German who was able to peacefully walk through the Berlin Wall after it was opened in 1989. Write a journal entry describing some of your thoughts about the Wall before it was opened, and discuss some of your hopes now that it is open.

For: An activity on the Cold War
Visit: PHSchool.com
Web Code: mud-2211

Prepare to Read

Objectives

In this section you will

1. Understand why Mexico has experienced reform, but little economic growth in recent years.
2. Learn about revolutions and wars in Central America.
3. Find out about unstable governments and economies in South America.
4. Learn about the Cuban Revolution.

Taking Notes

As you read this section, summarize events and ideas related to the changes in Latin America since World War II. Organize your findings into a table like the one below.

Changes in Latin America Since World War II	
Mexico	Joins the U.S. and Canada under NAFTA; PRI loses

Target Reading Skill

Reread or Read Ahead Rereading and reading ahead are strategies that can help you understand words and ideas in the text. If you do not understand a certain passage, reread it to look for connections among the words and sentences. It might also help to read ahead, because a word or idea may be clarified further on.

Key Terms

- **NAFTA (North American Free Trade Agreement)** (NAF tuh) *n.* a trade agreement that lowered tariffs and trade barriers among the U.S., Canada, and Mexico
- **guerrilla** (guh RIL uh) *n.* a member of a small defensive force of soldiers that makes surprise raids
- **Sandinista** (san duh NEES tuh) *n.* a member of a political movement that overthrew the Somoza regime in Nicaragua

Department of Defense photograph showing Soviet ships being loaded in Cuba

In October of 1962, the world watched as the United States and the Soviet Union were on the edge of a global nuclear war. The Soviets sent missiles to Cuba. Located 90 miles away from the U.S. coast, any missiles they launched were capable of hitting targets throughout the United States, including Los Angeles, Chicago, and the eastern U.S. When U.S. spy planes discovered the missles, the U.S. government and President John F. Kennedy ordered a blockade by the navy to prevent further shipments of missiles. U.S. armed forces were ready for an attack. The Soviets were also prepared to use nuclear weapons should the United States invade Cuba.

After thirteen days, Kennedy and Soviet Premier Khrushchev (KROOSH chawf) reached a compromise. Their secret negotiations resulted in an agreement by the Soviets to remove nuclear weapons from Cuba and by the U.S. to remove nuclear weapons in Turkey. This ended the Cuban Missile Crisis.

NAFTA Border Inspection
NAFTA links the markets of Mexico, the United States, and Canada. Trucks containing goods from Mexico are inspected at the California border.
Draw Inferences *What kinds of goods do you think are being transported in the picture?*

Mexico: Reform but Little Growth

Since World War II, Mexico's attempts at economic growth have had mixed results. A major oil producer, Mexico has struggled to pay a heavy foreign debt. This debt has prevented the economy from growing and has kept much of the population in poverty. For example, the average yearly income per person in Mexico was only $5,910 in 2002. Hopes for growth rose in 1994, when Mexico joined Canada and the United States in the **North American Free Trade Agreement (NAFTA)**. This trade agreement sharply lowered tariffs and investment barriers among the three countries. NAFTA has brought some new business and investment opportunities to Mexico. At the same time, however, it hurt Mexican manufacturers who could not compete with the amount of goods brought in from the United States.

In addition to trade, the Mexican people have also looked to reform their government. The Institutional Revolutionary Party, or PRI, had been in control of Mexican government since 1929. When the PRI finally lost power to Vicente Fox after the 2000 presidential election, many expected the economy to grow and the rights of Mexican workers to be better protected. However, many Mexicans remain unhappy with the lack of economic progress under Fox's administration. Critics of NAFTA fault Fox for allowing investments by foreign countries without adequate protection for workers and the environment.

✓ **Reading Check** What is NAFTA?

Revolutions and Wars in Central America

In the past thirty years Central America has been a troubled region in the Americas. The three major countries there, Guatemala (gwaht uh MAH luh), El Salvador (el SAL vuh dawr), and Nicaragua (nik uh RAH gwuh), have suffered from bloody civil wars.

Reread or Read Ahead Reread the section on El Salvador to help you better understand the meaning of *guerrilla,* which is also used in the paragraph that follows.

Guatemala Through the first half of the twentieth century, dictators and military strongmen ruled Guatemala. Most of these leaders were supported with aid from the United States. In 1944, liberal governments began reforms until they were overthrown in 1954. Harsh military governments followed and the country was soon in a civil war. Since 1996, a democratic government has been in control, but the military remains a powerful force.

Contra rebels in Nicaragua

El Salvador Civil war broke out in 1979 between a right-wing government and left wing **guerrillas**, members of a small defensive force of soldiers that make surprise raids. Although the United States pressed the government to make some reforms, they also gave military and financial aid to the Salvadoran (sal vuh DAWR un) government. The twelve-year war ended in 1992.

Nicaragua The Somoza (soh MOH zah) family ruled Nicaragua from 1936 to 1979. In July 1979 left-wing guerrillas known as the **Sandinistas** drove the Somoza family from power. The Sandinistas threatened U.S. interests. To stop them, the United States supported the contras, or guerrillas who fought against the Sandanistas in the 1980s. The contras increased their attacks until the 1984 presidential election. A peace treaty was finally signed in 1987. Moderate governments have been in power since then.

✓ Reading Check **How did the United States help the Salvadoran government?**

Unstable Governments and Economies in South America

Go Online
PHSchool.com Use Web Code
mup-0852 for an interactivity
on Latin America's economy.

For both Argentina and Brazil, economic swings have contributed to political and social unrest. In both nations, periods of dictatorship and military rule have limited the growth of democracy.

Brazil In 1964, the military established a dictatorship that lasted nearly twenty years. Although the economy boomed during these years, the people longed for democracy, which the military granted in stages until a full presidential election was held in 1989. This signaled a full return to democracy. Despite some economic progress, Brazil's poverty and inequality eventually led to the election of a socialist president.

Argentina Argentina emerged from World War II firmly in the control of a former army colonel, Juan Perón (hwahn pay RAWN), and his wife, Eva. After having won two consecutive presidential elections, Perón was ousted in 1955 by the military. Civilian and military governments came and went for the next two decades until Perón was reelected in the 1973 elections. After his death in 1974, his wife ruled for two years until she was overthrown by the military. This began a period of ruthless dictatorship. During the 1980s, the military waged a "dirty war" against leftist opponents of the regime until a civilian government was restored in 1983. In 2001, Argentina was shaken by an economic crisis that led to strikes, demonstrations, and a change of government.

✓ **Reading Check** **Who was the target of the "dirty war?"**

Links to Art

Evita The English composer Andrew Lloyd Webber transformed the life of Eva Perón into a theatrical extravaganza in his musical *Evita*. Webber's musical dramatically portrayed the relationship of Maria Eva Duarte de Perón (muh REE uh EE vuh DWAHRT ee day pay RAWN) and her beloved country, Argentina. Webber's musical premiered in London in 1978 and opened on Broadway in 1979. His musical received some of the entertainment world's top honors. *Evita* won seven Tony awards, and its original cast won a Grammy for their soundtrack album.

The wife of Juan Perón, Eva, became an important political figure and was thought of as a champion of the poor.

The Cuban Revolution

Cuban leader Fidel Castro in 1984

Fulgencio Batista (fool HEN see oh bah TEE stah) ruled the island nation of Cuba throughout the 1950s. In 1959, a revolutionary movement of workers and peasants led by Fidel Castro overthrew Batista's right-wing dictatorship. Castro began to seize the assets of U.S.-owned companies and turned more and more to the Soviet Union for support. In 1961, a U.S.-backed invasion at the Bay of Pigs failed to remove Castro from power. The next year, the United States discovered Soviet missiles in Cuba. The world went to the brink of nuclear war before the Soviets agreed to withdraw their missiles. Castro has remained in power since then and has enforced a strict communist rule. Although Castro has helped bring advances in health care and education, he also has one of the worst human-rights records in the region.

 **Reading Check** **In what year did Fidel Castro come to power in Cuba?**

Section 2 Assessment

Key Terms
Review the Key Terms at the beginning of this section. Use each term in a sentence that explains its meaning.

Target Reading Skill
What word or idea were you able to clarify by rereading or reading ahead?

Comprehension and Critical Thinking
1. (a) Explain Why was Nafta a sign of hope for Mexico?
(b) Summarize Summarize the reason that NAFTA did not help Mexico's employment situation as much as some had hoped.

2. (a) Recall How has government in Guatemala changed in the twentieth century?
(b) Summarize Why did the United States support the contras in Nicaragua?
3. (a) Explain What factors led to the election of Brazil's first socialist president?
(b) Predict Do you think that it is likely that Argentina will have another military takeover in the future? Why or why not?
4. (a) Identify Which military action against Cuba had the backing of the United States?
(b) Explain Why did the world nearly have a nuclear war over Cuba?

Writing Activity
Suppose that you lived on the coast of Florida and saw people floating on rafts, trying to escape from Castro's dictatorship in Cuba and reach the United States. Describe what you saw and what you think about the fact that people are willing to risk their lives to get to the United States.

Go Online PHSchool.com

For: An activity on revolutions and wars in Central America
Visit: PHSchool.com
Web Code: mud-2221

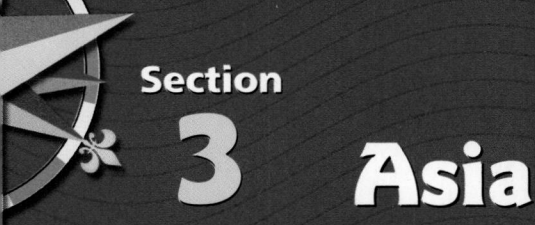

Section 3

Asia

Prepare to Read

Objectives

In this section you will
1. Learn about Japan's recovery from World War II, and its strong postwar economy.
2. Understand the long-standing tensions between India and Pakistan.
3. Find out about China's move toward a more open economy.

Taking Notes

As you read this section, paraphrase the main ideas of each major topic in your own words to make sure that you have understood it. Devote at least one sentence to each main idea. Use a chart like the one below to help you paraphrase.

Asia	
Japan's Recovery and Strong Economy	
India and Pakistan: Still Enemies	

Target Reading Skill

Paraphrase Paraphrasing can help you understand what you read. When you paraphrase, you restate what you have read in your own words. As you read this section, paraphrase or "say back" the information following each red or blue heading.

Key Terms

- **Kashmir** (KASH mihr) *n.* a mostly Muslim area in the northern part of the Indian subcontinent that is claimed by both India and Pakistan

Wartime destruction left cities crumbling throughout Japan. More than half of the homes in Tokyo had been destroyed. Agricultural production also suffered, as bad weather left rice harvests at only two thirds of the prewar level.

With the end of the war came the need to rebuild. In 1945, for the first time in history, Japan had to accept foreign occupation. They selectively borrowed western ideas and technology and put them to their own use. In time, Japan emerged as an economic superpower.

Tokyo skyline

Japan's Recovery and Strong Economy

With many cities and factories destroyed in Japan during World War II, the Japanese economy struggled and inflation was high. Rebuilding was necessary if the economy was to recover and grow.

With help from the United States, Japan rebounded quickly and its economy became one of the fastest-growing after the war. True growth and changes began in 1949 and Japan became a powerhouse in manufacturing, trade, and modern transportation. By the 1970s, Japan was a leader in the manufacture of electronics and its brands dominated the market for TVs and stereos. Later Japan improved the technology in this market and led the world in making VCRs, DVD players, and computer components. By the 1970s, Japan's auto industry was producing cars of such good quality and reliability that it began to overtake the automakers in the United States. Today, one of Japan's auto companies is the largest-selling car brand in the United States.

Since 1990, however, the Japanese economy has slowed considerably. Corporations are not investing as much, and prices keep falling. Major public-works projects have failed to bring Japan out of its economic slump.

✓ Reading Check **What items does Japan manufacture?**

Japan's Automobile Industry
Japan's success was built on producing goods for exports. Here automobile workers install seats in cars. **Identify** *What other goods does Japan export?*

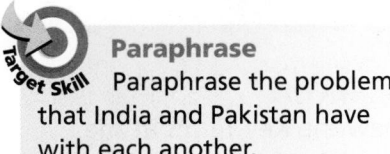

Tension Between India and Pakistan

After a long struggle led by Mohandas Gandhi, Jawaharlal Nehru, and Mohammed Ali Jinnah, British India won its independence in 1947. It was divided into two nations: the mainly Hindu India and the mainly Muslim Pakistan. India adopted a democratic form of government that has lasted to the present. Pakistan, on the other hand, has gone through periods of both democracy and military dictatorship.

Relations between these two rivals have always been tense. India and Pakistan have fought three major wars—in 1947, 1965, and 1971—and have often been on the verge of another through much of the past 35 years. These conflicts centered on **Kashmir,** a mostly Muslim area in the northern Indian subcontinent that is claimed by both India and Pakistan. The United Nations sponsored a peace plan in 1949 that divided Kashmir pending a vote by its inhabitants. However, the vote never occurred, and fighting over Kashmir broke out again in later years.

The prospect of war between these two longtime rival countries grew more dangerous when both successfully tested nuclear bombs in 1998. Although the countries avoided serious conflicts during the early 2000s, tensions remained.

✓ Reading Check   **Which territory has remained a source of conflict between India and Pakistan?**

Monastery in Kashmir
While most people in Kashmir are Muslims, this Buddhist monastery shows the presence of religious minorities. Hindus are another important minority in Kashmir. **Infer** *How might religious differences contribute to the conflict over Kashmir?*

Paraphrase
Paraphrase the problem that India and Pakistan have with each another.

Nixon's visit to China in 1972 was the first by a U.S. President while in office and helped to improve the strained U.S.-China relationship.

China's Move Toward an Open Economy

After the Communist takeover of China in 1949, the country became a one-party dictatorship on the model of the Soviet Union, with complete government control of the economy. Like the Soviets, the Chinese Communists built up a strong base of heavy industry and military power—China successfully tested its first atomic bomb in 1967. But there were fewer choices of consumer goods, and these were of poor quality.

By the 1970s, China's economy was stalled. The communist government sought to make contact with its long-time enemy, the United States. In 1979, the two countries established formal diplomatic relations. In these years China began to open up its economy to greater outside investment from private corporations. That process sped up China's development so much that it has been one of the world's fastest-growing economies since 1979.

 **Reading Check** **When did China and the United States establish formal diplomatic relations?**

Section 3 Assessment

Key Terms
Review the Key Terms at the beginning of this section. Use each term in a sentence that explains its meaning.

Target Reading Skill
Paraphrasing In a brief paragraph, paraphrase the information under the section on Japan.

Comprehension and Critical Thinking
1. (a) Identify Which two industries fueled the Japanese economy after the war?

(b) Explain Why has the Japanese economy slowed down in recent years?

2. (a) Recall What is the dominant religion in India?

(b) Infer How have different religions affected the relationship between India and Pakistan?

3. (a) Synthesize Information What were the strengths and weaknesses of China's communist economy?

(b) Identify Cause and Effect What is a major cause of the rapid growth of the Chinese economy in recent years?

Writing Activity
Write a brief paragraph that paraphrases the information on this page about China's government and economy.

For: An activity on postwar Asia
Visit: PHSchool.com
Web Code: mud-2231

Africa and the Middle East

Prepare to Read

Objectives

In this section you will
1. Learn about the new countries in Africa and some of the challenges facing African nations today.
2. Learn about the Arab-Israeli conflict.
3. Understand the importance of oil in the Middle East and the Persian Gulf.

Taking Notes

As you read this section, summarize the events and ideas related to the changes in Africa and the Middle East since World War II. Use an outline format like the one that is partially filled in below, and record your findings in it.

I. Challenges for Africa Today
  A. Economic problems
  B.
  C.
II. Middle East
  A.
  B.
  C.

Target Reading Skill

Summarize You can better understand a text if you pause occasionally to summarize—to review what you have read so far. Summarize using the following steps:

1. Identify main ideas.
2. State them in the order in which they appear.
3. Note when one event causes another event.

Key Terms

- **apartheid** (uh PAHR tayt) *n.* a system of strict racial separation
- **AIDS** (aydz) *n.* a disease that is caused by the virus HIV and that leads to the gradual collapse of the immune system and is fatal

Kwame Nkrumah speaks to a crowd in Ghana.

It was a great day in world history. A new country was about to be born. More than seventy other countries sent representatives to witness the event.

For many years, the West African region known as the Gold Coast had been a British colony. On this day in 1957, it was breaking its colonial links. The Gold Coast had been ruled by the Portuguese, the Dutch, and then the British. Finally Africans would govern it. It would also leave its European name behind and take one that had belonged to an ancient African kingdom—Ghana (GAH nuh).

"We must set an example to all of Africa," Ghana's new leader Kwame Nkrumah (KWAH mee un KROO muh) said that day. He was right. After Ghana showed the way, the rest of Africa gradually won its independence from the colonial powers.

Learn more about the history of apartheid.

New Nations in Africa and Internal Struggles

For Africa, the years after World War II were a time of hope. It was a time of liberation from colonial masters. In 1957, Ghana became the first nation to achieve independence in Sub-Saharan Africa—the part of Africa south of the Sahara. Within about twenty years, more than forty African nations had achieved independence. By 1990, all of the other colonies had declared their independence.

Ethnic Conflict and Dictatorship The independent nations that emerged in Africa after World War II contained hundreds of ethnic groups. Many one-party states sprang up and allowed dictators to take control of weak governments. These military dictatorships tried to force differing ethnic groups to live in peace. Throughout the 1990s, however, most African countries had some kind of elected government in place.

Apartheid All-white governments governed South Africa until 1994, even though the great majority of the population is black. These governments enforced the policy of **apartheid**, a system of strict of racial separation, which required that whites, blacks, Asians, and people of mixed ancestry live in separate areas and have their own governing bodies. Under apartheid, only whites could vote. In 1993, a new constitution was adopted that did away with apartheid.

AIDS Crisis Beginning in the 1980s, a global health crisis developed with the spread of **AIDS**, a condition caused by the HIV virus that leads to the gradual collapse of the immune system and is fatal. This modern plague has hit harder in Africa than anywhere else. In several African countries, more than a quarter of the adult population is infected.

Poverty Overall, Africa is rich in natural resources such as oil and diamonds, yet Africa remains the poorest continent in the world. The reasons for this poverty include trade practices that are unfair to Africans and poor farming conditions. Africans are working hard to improve their nations.

✓ Reading Check What are the struggles that Africa faces?

Citizen Heroes

Nelson Mandela
1918–

Nelson Mandela (NEL sun man DEL uh) fought against racial inequality in South Africa. Mandela became the leader of the African National Congress militant wing. The government jailed Mandela in 1964, accusing him of conspiring to overthrow the government. He remained in prison for more than a quarter of a century. He was released in 1990 and was named head of the ANC. In 1993 he was awarded the Nobel Peace Prize. In the first election in which all could vote, Mandela was elected president of South Africa.

Nelson Mandela casting his vote in the first all-race election in South Africa

MAP★MASTER™
Skills Activity

Movement The areas under Israeli control have shifted since Israel's borders were drawn in 1949.

Read a Map Key Find areas taken over by Israel after its establishment as an independent state.

Analyze Images How did the amount of land controlled by Israel change after 1949?

KEY

- ▓ Israel in 1949
- ░ Occupied by Israel after 1967 war
- ▒ Occupied by Israel in 1967 but returned to Egypt in 1982
- ▓ Arab Countries
- ⊛ National capital
- — National border

0 miles 100
0 kms 100
Lambert Conformal Conic

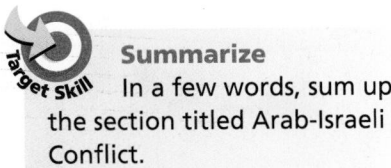

Go **O**nline
PHSchool.com Use Web Code **mup-2241** for step-by-step **map skills practice.**

Arab-Israeli Conflict

After the Holocaust, many Jews wished for a land they could call their own. That wish became a reality in 1948 with the founding of the State of Israel in the region formerly called Palestine or Judaea.

Before large-scale Jewish immigration in the 1900s, however, the region had a mainly Muslim Arab population. Many Arabs resented and rejected Israel's control of this land.

Neighboring Arab countries attacked Israel in 1948, but Israel fought off these attacks. Thousands of Palestinian Arabs fled to the Arab-controlled West Bank and Gaza Strip. When Israel was again attacked by Arab forces in 1967, Israel took control of the West Bank, the Gaza Strip, and parts of Syria and Egypt.

Since 1967, Israel and the Palestinian Arabs have faced a difficult conflict. Many Palestinian Arabs seek a state of their own in the West Bank and Gaza. However, Israeli settlements in the West Bank, Palestinian attacks against Israeli civilians, and Israeli retaliations against Palestinians have fueled mistrust. While many Israelis and Arabs want peace, it has been difficult to achieve.

Summarize In a few words, sum up the section titled Arab-Israeli Conflict.

✓ **Reading Check** How did Israel's Arab neighbors respond to its founding?

Chapter 22 Section 4 **647**

Go Online
PHSchool.com Use Web Code
mup-0853 for an interactivity on oil resources and consumption.

The Importance of Oil in the Middle East and the Persian Gulf

Oil is a source of power for most of the world's factories, electrical systems, cars, and airplanes. Without oil, industrial economies could not function. But the most advanced countries, the ones that depend on oil, do not contain most of the oil on their land. So those industrial powerhouses—the United States, Europe, and Japan—must find oil elsewhere.

Interest in Middle East's Oil In 1960, the Middle Eastern oil powers led the way in forming the Organization of Petroleum Exporting Countries (OPEC). OPEC sought to give exporters more control over the world price of oil.

The United States is the world's largest user of oil. Japan is the world's second-biggest consumer of oil. Much of the oil consumed by these nations is imported from the Middle East and the Persian Gulf. This is because the Middle East contains 65 percent of the world's known reserves of oil. It is not surprising, then, that several countries have taken a keen interest in events in the Middle East and the Persian Gulf.

■ Chart Skills

The Power of Oil
Industrialized nations depend on imported oil to produce electricity, run factories, and fuel vehicles.
Infer How might oil-rich countries influence oil prices?

Worldwide Crude Oil Production

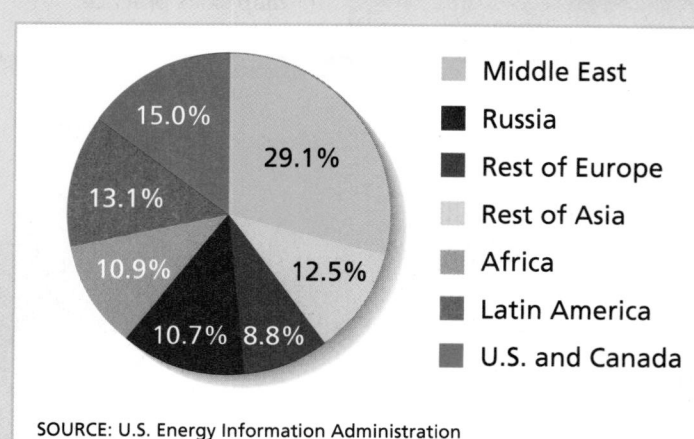

15.0%
29.1%
13.1%
10.9%
12.5%
10.7% 8.8%

- Middle East
- Russia
- Rest of Europe
- Rest of Asia
- Africa
- Latin America
- U.S. and Canada

SOURCE: U.S. Energy Information Administration

Expanding U.S. Role in the Middle East and Persian Gulf The three countries with the largest reserves of oil in the world are Saudi Arabia, Iraq, and Iran, in that order. To promote stability in Saudi Arabia, the United States has supported a conservative monarchy there. The country has no constitution and is run according to strict Muslim religious law. The United States has also been heavily involved in Iran, an oil-rich nation in the Persian Gulf region.

Iraq was ruled by the socialist Ba'ath Party (BAH ahth) from 1968 until 2003. After Iraq invaded the oil-rich kingdom of Kuwait (koo WAYT) in 1990, the United States led an international military coalition to drive Iraq's troops out of Kuwait. But Iraq's brutal dictator, Saddam Hussein (suh DAHM hoo SAYN), was left in power. More than ten years of peaceful international pressure against the policies of Hussein's dictatorship brought no changes, so the United States again went to war against Iraq in March 2003 with a much smaller coalition than in 1990. This time the United States overthrew Hussein's government.

Even after the United States declared victory in 1991, Kuwait City was still a dangerous place.

✓ **Reading Check** **Why do many countries have an interest in what happens in the Middle East and the Persian Gulf?**

Section 4 Assessment

Key Terms

Review the Key Terms at the beginning of this section. Use each term in a sentence that explains its meaning.

Target Reading Skill

Write an outline summary of the key challenges facing African nations today.

Comprehension and Critical Thinking

1. (a) Explain What is apartheid?
(b) Draw Inferences Why do you think Africa has been hit so much harder by AIDS than other parts of the world have?

2. (a) Recall Which historical event led many Jews to wish for a homeland of their own?
(b) Predict Do you think the conflict between Israel and the Palestinians will ever be resolved? If so, how?
3. (a) Identify Which two countries are the world's largest consumers of oil?
(b) Draw Inferences Why do you think it is important for the United States to have a good relationship with oil-rich nations in the Middle East?

Writing Activity

You are a citizen of South Africa in 1994, and you saw the newly elected president, Nelson Mandela, join hands with members of the white government that had ruled the country for years. Describe your hopes and fears for the future of your country at that moment.

For: An activity on Africa and the Middle East
Visit: PHSchool.com
Web Code: mud-2241

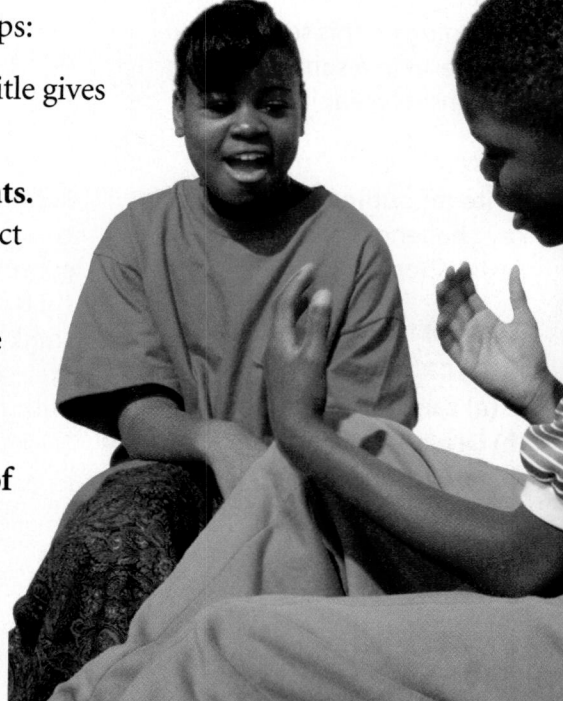

Skills for Life
Making Predictions

> Chris and Fran were waiting for the bus after school. "I am so hungry!" Chris cried.
>
> "Me, too," said his sister. "I bet we have pizza for dinner."
>
> "No way! I bet Mom is making my favorite—roast beef!"
>
> "Chris," Fran answered, "You know that this is Mom's night to volunteer at the hospital. There's no way she's making a big roast beef dinner just for you."
>
> "Well, I remember that this night last week we did have roast beef."
>
> "That's because Mom didn't go to the hospital that night. You're having pizza tonight!"
>
> When they got home, they rushed in to see who had made the right prediction.
>
> Their father popped his head through the kitchen door. "Mom is working late at the hospital tonight. Get washed up for dinner—I just ordered in Chinese food."

We make predictions all the time: what we might have for dinner, who will win the big game, how you will do on a big test. Predicting can help you become a better, more thoughtful reader. When you look over a book or chapter before you read it, you will know what to expect and will get more from your reading.

Learn the Skill

To predict before reading, use the following steps:

1. **Read the title of the book or chapter.** The title gives you clues as to what you are about to read.

2. **In a book, read through the table of contents.** The table of contents breaks down the subject matter in more detail.

3. **For an article or textbook chapter, read the headings.** The headings tell you what each section is about.

4. **Read the questions that appear at the end of a section or chapter.** Reading the questions in advance provides a focus and alerts you to key facts or issues.

Practice the Skill

Look at the table of contents in one of your other textbooks. Read the headings of two chapters that you have not read yet. From those headings, predict what kinds of facts or issues the chapter will cover.

1 First Chapter—Heading: _____

Prediction about what the chapter will cover:

_____

_____

_____

_____

2 Second Chapter—Heading: _____

Prediction about what the chapter will cover:

_____

_____

_____

Apply the Skill

Given their titles, make a prediction about the subject and the likely point of view of each of the following articles:

1. "Oil vs. Solar Energy: Powering the Future"
2. "Japanese Cars: Profiting from Quality"
3. "Internet Research: A Guide Through the Jungle"

The World in a New Century

Prepare to Read

Objectives

In this section you will
1. Explain the impact of TV and computers.
2. Learn about the global economy.
3. Find out about growing threats to the world's security.
4. Explore the major concerns about the world's environment.

Taking Notes

For each of the major headings, summarize the key points in a bulleted list like the one below.

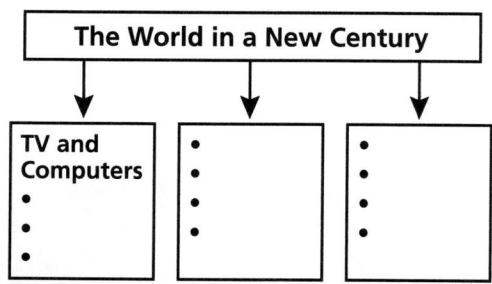

The World in a New Century

TV and Computers
-
-
-
-

-
-
-
-

-
-
-
-

Target Reading Skill

Summarizing You can better understand a text if you pause occasionally to summarize, or to restate the key points briefly in your own words. A good summary

- includes all of the important events and details.

- makes clear the order in which important events occurred.

- indicates connections among events or details.

Key Terms

- **United Nations** (yoo NYT id NAY shunz) *n. pl.* an international organization founded in 1946 in which nations can discuss and act on world issues
- **terrorism** (TEHR ur iz um) *n.* the deliberate use of violence to achieve political goals
- **environment** (en VY run munt) *n.* the elements that surround all living things and make life possible

In the 1600s, scientists in Europe built machines that used gears and levers to automatically add, subtract, and multiply. More than 300 years later, electronics were first used in making calculations. This led to the development of the first computers.

The first computers were enormous. One of the first large computers was called ENIAC (Electronic Numerical Integrator and Computer). Built in Pennsylvania in the 1940s, ENIAC weighed about 30 tons and fit inside the basement of the University of Pennsylvania. ENIAC could solve in about twenty seconds problems that would otherwise take one or two days by hand.

In the 1950s, the UNIVAC (Universal Automatic Computer) became the first computer to be sold widely to corporations. Although much smaller than ENIAC, UNIVAC still weighed 8 tons! Now, computers 10,000 times faster than ENIAC weigh less than five pounds and can be carried easily.

A UNIVAC comput processing U.S. Census data

The World Wide Web
The World Wide Web refers to all the publicly accessible Web sites in the world. These Web sites are accessed on the Internet, a worldwide network of interconnected computers. **Summarize** *How has the Internet changed the way people communicate?*

TV and Computers

After World War II, the U.S. economy did well. People could now afford products that made life easier. Out of this environment came many of the technologies we take for granted today.

Television After World War II, television became popular in the United States. In 1950, about 9 percent of American households owned a television. Twelve years later, 90 percent of America's households owned TVs. Today, that figure is close to 100 percent.

The major networks began nightly broadcasts in 1948. At first, Americans relied on TV mostly for entertainment. However, with several major stories of the 1960s—the assassination of President Kennedy, the Vietnam War, and the moon landing—Americans turned to the television as a major news source. With the popularity of cable TV in the 1970s, American's choices expanded from three networks to dozens of networks. Today, viewers can choose from a wide variety of networks.

Computers and the Internet The first home computers became available in 1975. Americans started using computers much more slowly than they had televisions. By 1990, only 15 percent of American households owned computers. That number grew during the 1990s. By 1997, 35 percent of American households owned at least one computer, and by 2004, the figure had risen to 79 percent.

One major force behind the growing number of home computer users is the Internet (IN tur net). The Internet has revolutionized the way people communicate. With e-mail, instant messaging, chat rooms, and newsgroups, people can communicate with others all over the world in a matter of seconds. In addition, the World Wide Web has proven to be a source for both information and entertainment.

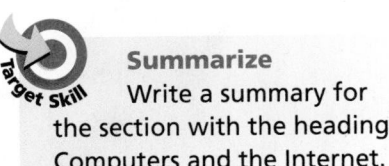

Summarize
Write a summary for the section with the heading Computers and the Internet.

√ Reading Check **How has the Internet affected communication?**

Focus On
1950s Living Room

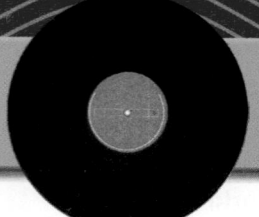

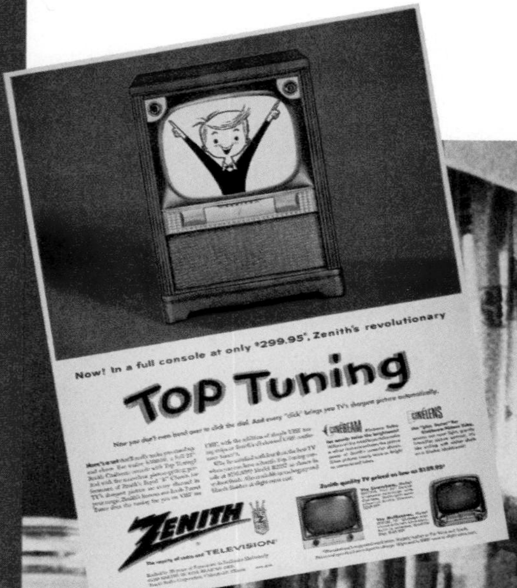

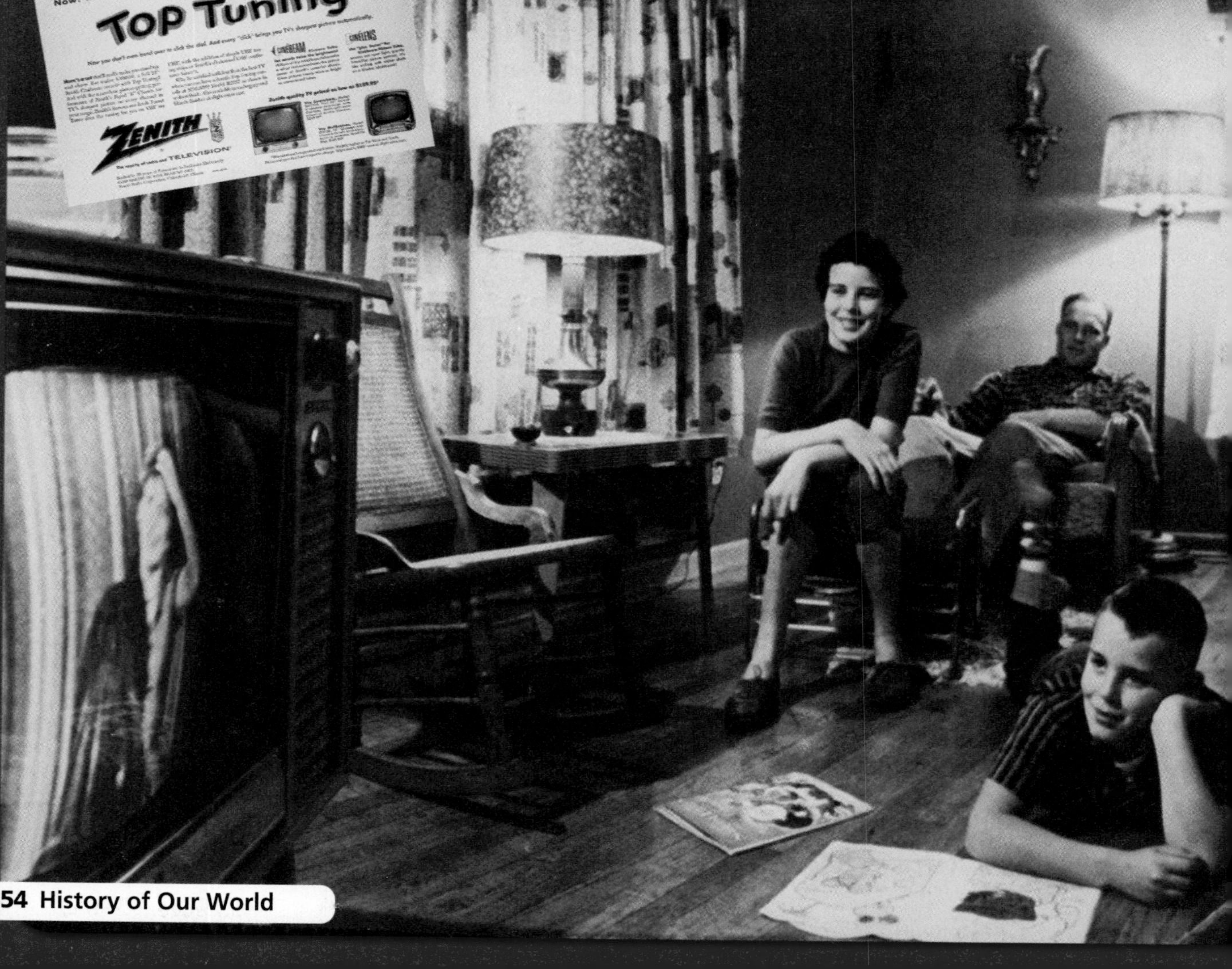

1950s Television Ad
Like many TV models of the 1950s, this television set is encased in wood. Until remote control TVs were introduced in 1956, Americans got up to change the channel.

Now! In a full console at only $299.95*, Zenith's revolutionary
Top Tuning
ZENITH
TELEVISION

In the 1950s, American life was transformed by television. In 1950s, about 9 percent of households in the United States owned a TV. By 1960, that figure had increased to 87 percent. During the 1950s, the question of where to put the TV was often answered by putting this relatively new device in the living room. There, it often became the central feature in the room, around which every member of the family would gather to watch such top-rated programs as *I Love Lucy*, *Walt Disney*, and *The Ed Sullivan Show*.

The Set of *I Love Lucy*
During the 1950s, millions of families tuned in each week to watch *I Love Lucy,* one of the most successful television shows in history.

Television in the 1950s Living Room

Television transformed the American living room as well as American life. Before television, living room furniture was typically grouped around the fireplace. By the early 1950s, however, decorating magazines and home designers were advising Americans to make the television set the central focus of the living room. As shown in the large picture, many living rooms were organized so that all seating faced the television set.

During the 1950s, television broadcasting was mostly aimed at the entire family. The living room became the place where the family would gather around the television to watch the same programs. The mid-1950s family in the picture—grandparents included—is watching *The Ed Sullivan Show* in their living room. Broadcast from 1948 to 1971, *The Ed Sullivan Show* featured a variety of musical and comedy performers every Sunday night.

Assessment

Recall How did television set ownership change between 1950 and 1960?

Contrast Most American households during the 1950s owned just one television set. TV programs were broadcast on black and white sets. How has television changed since the 1950s?

A Global Economy

The last half of the twentieth century was a time of increased globalization (gloh bul ih ZAY shun), or cooperation and contact among nations through culture, politics, and trade. The postwar trend toward political globalization began with the founding of the United Nations (UN) in 1946. The **United Nations (UN)** serves as a place where nations can discuss and act on the world's political disputes and problems like poverty and disease.

International trade is another important part of globalization. Several trade agreements and organizations created during the 1990s increased global trade. In section 2 of this chapter, you learned about the North American Free Trade Agreement (NAFTA), which was signed in 1992 and lowered tariffs between the United States, Canada, and Mexico. The World Trade Organization (WTO), created in 1995, also helps increase trade by setting rules for international trade and resolving international trade disputes.

√ Reading Check   **What is the purpose of the UN?**

The United Nations
The United Nations meets in this building in New York City.
Predict *How might the world's political disputes be handled if the United Nations had not been formed?*

Threats to the World's Security

In the early 2000s, threats to the world's security raised growing concerns. One serious threat was **terrorism,** or the deliberate use of violence to spread fear and to achieve political goals.

On September 11, 2001, two hijacked jetliners destroyed the World Trade Center in New York City. Another plane crashed into the Pentagon in Virginia. A fourth hijacked plane crashed into a field in Pennsylvania after passengers overtook the hijackers.

Thousands were injured or killed in these attacks. Thousands were injured or killed in later attacks in other countries, including Britain, Spain, Egypt, and Indonesia.

These attacks were carried out by a radical Muslim terrorist group called al Qaeda (ahl KY duh) and by related Muslim groups. Most Muslims around the world condemned these attacks. At the time of the 2001 attacks, al Qaeda was based in Afghanistan, in central Asia. Al Qaeda was supported by the Taliban, a radical Muslim group that held power there. The United States organized a military coalition that removed the Taliban from power in Afghanistan and destroyed al Qaeda's base.

Aggressive military dictators posed another threat to the world's security. The United States saw Saddam Hussein, the brutal dictator of Iraq, as a continuing threat to regional and global security. The United States led a coalition of forces that removed him from power in 2003. These forces remained in Iraq in an effort to restore a stable government.

A third threat to the world's security was the spread of nuclear weapons. For years, international negotiators tried to stop North Korea from building nuclear weapons. In 2005, however, North Korea announced that it had such weapons. In the early 2000s, the United States worked with other nations in an effort to keep Iran from developing nuclear weapons technology. Iran's location next to Iraq in the oil-rich Middle East made its nuclear efforts a cause for special concern.

✔ Reading Check **What terrorist group carried out the September 11 attacks?**

Citizen Heroes

Americans Respond to September 11, 2001

Americans were quick to respond to the September 11 attacks. Millions volunteered, gave blood, or made donations to help the victims or the rescuers. Across the nation, people displayed flags and held candlelight vigils (such as the one shown in the photograph above) to show their unity and to mourn for those who died in the attacks. The spirit of unity extended overseas. The headline of one French newspaper captured the feeling of many in the world: "WE ARE ALL AMERICANS."

Environmental Issues

The past thirty years have been a time of growing interest in the **environment**, or the elements that surround all living things and that make life possible. Concern about environmental pollution led to the first Earth Day in 1970, the same year in which President Nixon established the Environmental Protection Agency (EPA). Some three decades later, however, pollution still threatens the world environment. Acid rain and global warming also put our environment at risk.

Acid rain is caused when sulfuric acid (sul FYOOR ik AS id) is released into the air from industrial and power plants. Acid rain can harm lakes, trees, and crops. Scientists believe that global warming is caused by "greenhouse gases" from cars and factories, which trap the sun's warmth in the atmosphere. The EPA reports that even though people in the United States consume more energy now than they did in 1970, the air is now cleaner than it was then.

An Earth Day Celebration

 **Reading Check** **Why did President Nixon establish the EPA?**

Section 5 Assessment

Key Terms
Review the Key Terms at the beginning of this section. Use each term in a sentence that explains its meaning.

Target Reading Skill
Write a brief paragraph in which you summarize the United States' response to the September 11 attacks.

Comprehension and Critical Thinking
1. (a) Recall When did television start to become popular in the United States?

(b) Find Main Idea and Details When did television become a major source for news?

2. (a) Explain How does NAFTA help increase trade?
(b) Summarize What is the purpose of the WTO?

3. (a) Recall Along what three fronts did President Bush launch his campaign against terrorism?
(b) Summarize What domestic steps did the United States take to address the problems of terrorism?

4. (a) Recall How long has the environment been a major issue in the United States?
(b) Predict What do you think will happen if nothing is done about global warming?

Writing Activity
Write a letter to your congressperson in which you express concern about a threat to the environment in or near your local community.

For: An activity on the world in the twenty-first century
Visit: PHSchool.com
Web Code: mud-2251

Review and Assessment

◆ Chapter Summary

Nelson Mandela

Section 1: Europe and North America

- Tension between the United States and the Soviet Union led to the Cold War.
- Cold War tensions erupted into two hot wars in Korea and in Vietnam.
- An ailing Communist system finally collapsed in the Soviet Union and Eastern Europe.
- European nations joined the European Union, which created economic unity and increased political unity between its member nations.
- The United States emerged as the world's only superpower and formed new trade agreements with its North American neighbors.

Section 2: Latin America

- Despite reforms, the Mexican economy continues to struggle.
- Civil wars plagued Central American countries in the 1970s and 1980s.
- South American governments and economies have worked to overcome instability.
- The Cuban Revolution posed a challenge to democracy in the Americas.

Section 3: Asia

- Japan made a dramatic economic recovery from the destruction of World War II.
- India and Pakistan remained enemies over disputed territory.
- In the 1980s, China began to move toward a more open economy.

Section 4: Africa and the Middle East

- Newly independent African nations faced internal struggles.
- African nations face struggle with health issues and poverty.
- Israel faced continuing challenges from neighboring Arab nations and the Palestinians.
- Tensions over oil threatened the peace of the Middle East.

Section 5: The World in a New Century

- TV, computers, and the Internet changed society.
- The global economy has increased international trade and communication.
- Terrorism brings peril to the nations of the world.
- The environment faces a series of serious challenges, old and new.

September 11, 2001, memorial service

◆ Key Terms

Match the definition in column 1 to the correct key term in column 2.

1. Openness
2. The buildup of military forces during the Cold War
3. A trade agreement between the U.S., Canada, and Mexico
4. Muslim area claimed by India and Pakistan
5. A system of racial separation

A. NAFTA
B. Kashmir
C. apartheid
D. glasnost
E. Arms Race

◆ Comprehension and Critical Thinking

6. (a) Recall Which two major powers squared off against each other during the Cold War?
(b) Draw Inferences Why might people have tried to overthrow Mikhail Gorbachev?

7. (a) Explain What was the Cuban Missile Crisis, and how did the United States respond to it?
(b) Draw Conclusions Why do you think Mexico signed the NAFTA treaty?

8. (a) Recall How did Communist control affect China's economy?
(b) Predict What do you think will be the outcome of China's new open economic policies?

9. (a) Recall How did the governments of African colonies change in the years after World War II, and how did they change in the decades that followed?
(b) Synthesize Why have many nations taken an interest in events in the Middle East?

10. (a) Identify Who was responsible for the terrorist attacks of September 11, 2001, and how did the United States respond to those attacks?

(b) Predict Which do you think is a greater threat to the future of humanity—terrorism or global warming? Why?

◆ Skills Practice

Predicting In the Skills Activity in this chapter, you learned about predicting content as a way of getting more out of your reading.

Review the steps you followed to learn this skill. Then make a prediction about the future role of the Internet in society. Be careful to base your predictions on what you have already learned about the impact of the Internet on society.

◆ Writing Activity

In this chapter, you learned about the advances in technology that occurred after World War II. Do research on the following topic: How has technology changed entertainment? Focus your research on one aspect of entertainment such as television, music/radio, or computers and show how this has changed from World War II to the present. Write a paper based on your research. Share your report with the class.

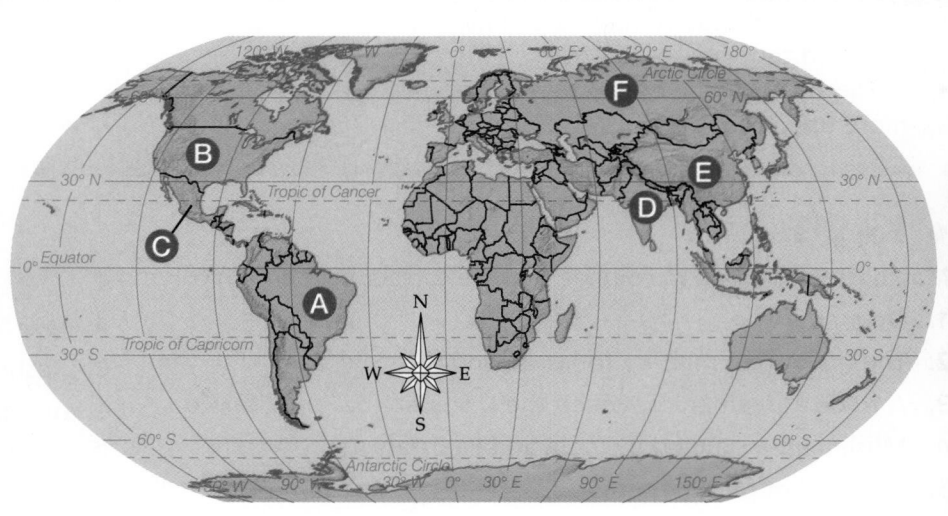

MAP MASTER™ Skills Activity

The World Today

Place Location For each place listed below, write letter from the map that shows its location.
1. Brazil
2. China
3. India
4. United States
5. Mexico
6. Russia

Go Online
PHSchool.com Use Web Code **mup-2202** for an **interactive map.**

Standardized Test Prep

Test-Taking Tips

Some questions on standardized tests ask you to analyze a reading selection. Read the paragraph below. Then follow the tips to answer the sample question.

> Vicente Fox, who was elected Mexico's president in 2000, was born in 1942. Fox brought a business background to government, studying in both Mexico and the United States. He worked for Coca-Cola for many years before turning to politics. Concerned about Mexico's economy, he first ran for office in 1987. Fox became President in 2000, ending 71 years of rule for Mexico's International Revolutionary Party.

TIP When you are reading a paragraph, pay attention to the structure. Did the author use cause-effect, topics, or chronological order (as in this paragraph)?

Pick the letter that best answers the question.

What information would you expect to find in the next paragraph of an article about Vicente Fox?

TIP Use what you already know about history, geography, or government to help you answer social studies questions.

- **A** what Fox's childhood was like
- **B** when Fox first ran for office
- **C** how Fox's presidency affected Mexico
- **D** what Fox did while working for Coca-Cola

Think It Through Start with the structure of the paragraph. The events go from earliest to latest. You can rule out A—something that happened in Fox's early years. You can also rule out D, which also happened before Fox entered politics. That leaves B and C. The paragraph ends by talking about Fox's presidency. Because B talks about Fox's first political office, you can rule this choice out. You would expect the next paragraph to tell you more about Fox's presidency. The answer is C.

Practice Questions

Use the tips above and other tips in this book to help you answer the following questions.

1. In which year did the Soviet Union fall?
- **A** 1945
- **B** 1985
- **C** 1991
- **D** 2001

2. India and Pakistan have fought for years over which territory?
- **A** Gaza Strip
- **B** West Bank
- **C** Iraq
- **D** Kashmir

Read the paragraph below to help you answer the following question.

> The war in Korea ended in 1954 with a stalemate. The front lines of battle eventually became the boundary between North Korea and South Korea.

3. What information would you expect to find in the previous paragraph of an article about the Korean War?
- **A** life in North Korea today
- **B** the causes of the Korean War
- **C** how the Korean War ended
- **D** the start of the Vietnam War

Go Online
PHSchool.com
Use Web Code **mua-2206**
for **Chapter 22 self-test.**

Projects

Create your own projects to learn more about world history. At the beginning of this book, you were introduced to these **Guiding Questions** for studying the chapters and special features. But you can also find answers to these questions by doing projects on your own or with a group.

1. **Geography** How did physical geography affect the development and growth of societies around the world?

2. **History** How did each society's belief system affect its historical accomplishments?

3. **Culture** What were the beliefs and values of people in these societies?

4. **Government** What types of governments were formed in these societies and how did they develop?

5. **Economics** How did each society develop and organize its economic activities?

Project

STAGE A DEBATE

Researching Modern Societies
Which of the modern societies in this book made the greatest contributions to the world? Stage a debate with representatives from each society. To support your argument, research your society's form of government, art, inventions, language, science, and literature. Visual aids such as pictures and posters could make your arguments more convincing.

Colossal statue of a seated Buddha at Kyaikpun Pagoda, Burma (Myanmar)

Project

CREATE A TRAVEL GUIDE

Travel the Ancient World
As you study each civilization in this book, write a chapter for a travel guide to the world of ancient times. Create a map for each place, and write about its geography and history. Include a picture of a special place or an interesting feature of each civilization that is a "must see" for travelers. When you have finished all of the chapters, combine them to make a travel guidebook.

Reference

Table of Contents

Ancestors: In Search of Human Origins

by Donald Johanson, Lenora Johanson, and Blake Edgar

Prepare to Read

Objectives

In this selection you will

1. Learn about the work of archaeologists studying early humans.

2. Learn how to frame questions that can be answered through research.

Background

One of the great questions in archaeology is how did the first tool-using humans make a living. At present, not enough is known about early humans to be sure. However, this big question has led to smaller questions that can be answered by study and research. In this excerpt, archaeologist Donald Johanson describes such research. It was carried out at a game ranch in South Africa.

Vocabulary *Builder*

carcass (KAR kuhs) *n.* dead body

blind (blīnd) *n.* hiding place for hunters

hominid (HAHM uh nihd) *n.* a modern human or a member of an earlier group that may have included ancestors or relatives of modern humans

viscera (VIH suh ruh) *n.* internal organs

connoisseur (kon uh SIHR) *n.* expert

One night Herb Friedl, our hunter guide, took an impala [antelope] carcass and tied it to a bush not far from our camp. Then he turned on a tape of wild-animal sounds to lure hyenas. . . .

Right on schedule, five hyenas appeared out of nowhere. We watched them tear through the carcass. . . . After we filmed the hyenas feeding, we frightened them away and retrieved the carcass.

The next morning, on the edge of a plain as large as a football field, Rob [Blumenschine] and I sat in a blind watching the same impala

Impalas drinking at a watering hole.

carcass. . . . After three hours of watching and waiting, we saw a black-and-chestnut-colored bateleur eagle descend upon the remains. The eagle clasped the impala with its talons and began tearing flesh off the carcass with its down-curved beak.

Suddenly, a group of white-headed vultures appeared. The eagle flew off and the vultures covered the carcass, squabbling and jostling for space. Within ten minutes the vultures stripped off all the remaining flesh. . . .

Rising out of our blind, Rob and I approached the carcass. Had we been hominids searching for food, the sight of vultures circling and descending would have lured us here. The birds flew off noisily as soon as they sensed us coming. That meant our ancestors probably had little trouble chasing this carnivore, at least, from a kill. We found a devastated carcass. Skin sagged over empty space that had once held flesh. . . .

I looked at it dubiously. "What's left on this thing to eat?"

"There's a great meal here for the taking if you know what to do," Rob cried with enthusiasm I could not share. "But you can't process a carcass of this size or larger with your hands. You'll need stone tools to get to the nutrients."

Rob grabbed one of the bloody limb bones and laid it on a flat rock. . . . He took a battered piece of quartz out of his backpack to use as his hammerstone. The hammerstone is a bone breaker, one of the essential elements of the earliest tool kit. . . .

Rob delivered a sharp blow to each end of the impala leg bone and then twisted it with his hands. The bone splintered into jagged, spiral fragments and an eight-inch rod of pink marrow slid out. "Not counting the <u>viscera</u>, the marrow bones are the major source of fat in a healthy animal," he said. "Lion and leopard kills usually have plenty of marrow left on them."

"How nutritious a meal does marrow make?" I asked.

Rob has calculated that a healthy, well-fed adult impala would yield 1,500 calories worth of marrow from the twelve major limb bones. . . .

A hyena and vultures surround a carcass

"It's a full meal, all right," he said . . . "and it only takes about ten minutes to process."

"The first fast food?"

"A great food source, isn't it?" Rob said with a <u>connoisseur's</u> relish. "There's no other way you could get so many calories so fast out here."

I was powerfully struck by just how much marrow there was and how many nutrients it provided. These limb bones were the power bars of the past.

Source: *Ancestors: In Search of Human Origins*, Donald Johanson, Lenora Johanson, and Blake Edgar

Analyze Primary Sources: *Frame Questions*

1. Good historical questions inspire interesting research. Read the questions below. Which one do you think led to Donald Johanson's experiment with Rob Blumenschine?
   A How many calories are in the bone marrow of an antelope?
   B Was it possible for early humans to live by scavenging food?
   C What kinds of stone tools did early humans have in their tool kits?
   D Did early humans prefer eating bone marrow to fresh meat?

2. Not all historical questions can be answered by study and research. Reread the questions at left. Which one do you think may never be answered? Explain your choice.

3. Think of a good question that you think Johanson and Blumenschine could answer about scavenging if they did more research.

A Student's Life in Sumer

Prepare to Read

Objectives

In this selection you will

1. Learn about the life of a student in ancient Sumer.

2. Distinguish between information that is relevant to a researcher and irrelevant to a researcher.

Background

Archaeologists excavated documents in the form of essays written by a schoolteacher about 2000 B.C. The essays describe the life of a student in ancient Sumer. These documents are important because they are written history. Primary documents—such as essays, diaries, and journals—give historians important information about the past.

As you read excerpts from the essay "School Days," think about the information that you can gather about school life in ancient Sumer.

Vocabulary Builder

punctuality (puhnk choo AL ih tee) *n.* being on time; promptness

curtsy (KERT see) *n.* a bow of respect

loiter (LOI ter) *v.* stop and play along the way

I recited my tablet, ate my lunch, prepared my (new) tablet, wrote it, finished it; then my model tablets were brought to me; and in the afternoon my exercise tablets were brought to me. When school was dismissed, I went home, entered the house, and found my father sitting there. I explained . . . my exercise tablets to my father, . . . recited my tablet to him, and he was delighted. . . .

[The schoolboy then gives the servants the following orders.] I am thirsty, give me water to drink; I am hungry, give me bread to eat; wash my feet, set up (my) bed, I want to go to sleep. Wake me early in the morning, I must not be late. . . .

When I arose early in the morning, I faced my mother and said to her: "Give me my lunch, I want to go to school!" My mother gave me two rolls, and I set out. . . .

In school the fellow in charge of <u>punctuality</u> said: "Why are you late?" Afraid and with a pounding heart, I entered before my teacher and made a respectful <u>curtsy</u>.

My headmaster read my tablet, said: "There is something missing,". . . The fellow in charge of neatness said: "You <u>loitered</u> in the street and did not straighten up your clothes," The fellow in charge of silence said: "Why did you talk without permission?". . .The fellow in charge of good behavior said: "Why did you rise without permission?". . .The fellow in charge of Sumerian said: "Why didn't you speak Sumerian?. . ."

[The teacher speaks to the schoolboy.] Young fellow, (because) you hated not my words, neglected them not, (may you) complete the scribal [writer's] art from beginning to end. Because you . . . paid me a salary larger than my efforts (deserve), (and) have honored me, . . . may your exercises contain no faults. Of your brothers, may you be their leader; of your friends may you be their chief; may you rank the highest among the schoolboys. . . . You have carried out well the school's activities, you are a man of learning.

Source: "School Days,"
Anonymous Author

Ancient scribes

Analyze Primary Sources: *Distinguish Relevant Information*

1. Which parts of the essay about a student's life in ancient Sumer could a historian verify?

2. Which statements in this essay would not be useful to a historian who wants to write an article about education in ancient Sumer?

3. What information in this essay would be essential for someone who is studying ancient teaching methods?

4. Historians learn about the past by studying written documents. By studying the written language, historians learn about ideas that are important to a society. Think of a question that a historian might ask about Sumerian society from reading the essay.

Psalm 23
Selections from the Book of Proverbs

Prepare to Read

Objectives

In this selection you will

1. Learn about some of the teachings of the Hebrew Bible.

2. Distinguish between information that is relevant to a researcher and irrelevant to a researcher.

Background

The book of Psalms and the Book of Proverbs are both part of the Hebrew Bible. According to Hebrew tradition, David is given credit for many of the songs in the Book of Psalms. In Psalm 23, David compares the God of Israel to a shepherd watching over his sheep.

Solomon, the son of David, is given credit for many of the poems and sayings in the Book of Proverbs. The collection touches on how to live an honest, responsible life. Following Psalm 23 are some of selections from the Book of Proverbs.

Vocabulary *Builder*

anoint (uh NOINT) *v.* to put oil on someone's head or body

boast (bohst) *v.* to speak highly of oneself or what one owns

entice (ihn TICE) *v.* to persuade someone to do something by offering them something nice

23 A psalm of David.

The LORD is my shepherd;
    I lack nothing.
He makes me lie down in green pastures;
    He leads me to water in places of repose;
    He renews my life;
    He guides me in right paths
    as befits His name.

Though I walk through a valley of deepest darkness,
    I fear no harm, for You are with me;
    Your rod and Your staff—they comfort me.

You spread a table for me in full view of my enemies;
    You <u>anoint</u> my head with oil;
    my drink is abundant.
Only goodness and steadfast love shall pursue me
    all the days of my life,
    and I shall dwell in the house of the LORD
    for many long years.

Source: TANAKH The Holy Scriptures
(translation according to the traditional Hebrew text)

Selections From the Book of Proverbs

Do not <u>boast</u> of tomorrow,
For you do not know what the day will bring.

My son if sinners <u>entice</u> you, do not yield.

Let the mouth of another praise you, not yours,
The lips of a stranger, not your own.

Repute is preferable to great wealth,
Grace is better than silver and gold.

Rich man and poor man meet;
The Lord made them both.

My son, do not forget my teaching,
But let your mind retain my commandments

Train a lad in the way he ought to go;
He will not swerve from it even in old age.

Source: TANAKH The Holy Scriptures
(translation according to the traditional Hebrew text)

A shepherd watches over his sheep.

Analyze Primary Sources: *Distinguish Relevant Information*

1. Which lines in the psalm would be useful to a historian who is studying the way sheep were tended in ancient Israel?

2. The word translated "LORD" in the first verse is a name that is used only for the God of Israel. What might that indicate about the author of this psalm?

3. Which lines in the psalm remind you that the "sheep" in the psalm is a person and not an actual sheep?

4. How might a historian verify whether the shepherding practices mentioned in the psalm were common in Israel during the time of David?

5. Why might a historian credit Solomon with gathering parts of the collection of the Book of Proverbs?

6. What important values were taught to children during this time?

7. Why might this information be important to historians?

Mauryan Empire: Asoka's Political and Moral Achievements

Prepare to Read

Objectives

In this selection you will

1. Learn about the influence of Buddhism on the Mauryan king Asoka.

2. Distinguish between information that is relevant to a researcher and irrelevant to a researcher.

Background

Asoka became the third king of the Mauryan Empire about 269 B.C. As a young man, he had the reputation of being fierce, cruel, and aggressive. Today, he is known as one of the world's greatest rulers.

Asoka began studying the teachings of Buddhism before he became emperor; however, he did not take the religion's teachings of peace and harmony seriously until he had fought in the battle of Kalinga. This excerpt describes how that battle changed Asoka's life.

Vocabulary *Builder*

<u>hilarious</u> (hih LAIR ee uhs) *adj.* noisy and cheerful

<u>pomp</u> (pahmp) *n.* all the impressive clothes, decorations, music, etc. that are traditional for an important public ceremony

<u>turmoil</u> (TER moil) *n.* a state of confusion and trouble

<u>annex</u> (uh NEHKS) *v.* to add

<u>humanity</u> (hyoo MAN ih tee) *n.* people

<u>jubilation</u> (jyoo bih LAY shuhn) *n.* happy celebration; rejoicing

<u>illuminate</u> (ih LOO mih nayt) *v.* to light up; make bright

---

It happened in about 261 B.C. . . . Since early morning, men, women, and children had been gathering in large numbers. . . . They were in a <u>hilarious</u> mood as this was their first opportunity to welcome Emperor Asoka after his victory in the Kalinga war. The city of Pataliputra wore a festive look with national flags fluttering high in the sky all along the main highway leading to the place of the public meeting.

There seemed nothing surprising in this exhibition of <u>pomp</u> and show by the . . . citizens of the Mauryan Empire. The victory in the Kalinga war was an achievement of which they could be justly proud. As a result of their ultimate victory, the people of Magadha had almost forgotten the troubles and <u>turmoils</u> through which they had to pass when the war was on. The Jawans, who had accomplished heroic deeds and were instrumental in <u>annexing</u> Kalinga, were expecting high awards . . . for their . . . bravery. . . .

At last, Asoka accompanied by the Buddhist Sage, Moggaliputta Tissa arrived on the scene and the vast mass of <u>humanity</u> burst into cries of joy. When the King . . . ascended the rostrum especially erected for the purpose, the public <u>jubilation</u> cooled down. And when Asoka arose to deliver his address, all eyes turned toward him; there was pin-drop silence. The people thought that they were now going to get a pat from the royalty for their deeds of gallantry and supreme sacrifices.

But they were disillusioned when the king started speaking in an entirely different tone. He said, "Brothers and Sisters, after the victory

in the Kalinga war we have assembled here today for the first time. Perhaps you have come here to celebrate the victory with high expectations. But . . . I am unable to celebrate this occasion in the way you might have liked. I am fully conscious of the hardships faced and the sacrifices made by all of you in turning the scales in our favor in the Kalinga war. I am indeed thankful to you all for the help and cooperation you gave to government in the shape of men and material. I am, however, ashamed of the large-scale destruction brought about by the Kalinga war. . . . Moggaliputta Tissa has removed darkness from my eyes and <u>illuminated</u> my mind. I have now fully realized that for the sake of self-glory, for the sake of territorial expansion and for the sake of humiliating others, it is a crime . . . to massacre thousands . . . to destroy . . . the property of others . . . and to uproot a large number of people from their . . . homes. It is such a crime which can never be pardoned . . . The horrible results of this mass destruction and untold misery have served as an eye-opener to me. I am grateful . . . to Moggaliputta Tissa due to whose kind guidance I have found solace [comfort] in the Teachings of the Compassionate Buddha."

"Since the message of . . . the Buddha stands for peace and universal brotherhood," Asoka declared . . . "from today onward . . . I shall endeavor to win the hearts . . . of my empire, by persuasion and love instead of by the use of force and sword."

Source: *Asoka the Great,*
D. C. Ahir

Asoka

Analyze Primary Sources: *Distinguish Relevant Information*

1. Which statements in Asoka's speech can help you to understand his point of view on the Kalinga war?
2. Which statements in this excerpt would be relevant to a historian studying the results of the battle of Kalinga?
3. Which statements in this excerpt would not be useful in determining the people's reaction to Asoka's speech?
4. How did Asoka's study of Buddhism affect the people of the Mauryan Empire?

Chinese Politics: Confucius and Good Government

Prepare to Read

Objectives

In this selection you will

1. Learn about Confucian ideas about good government.

2. Determine Confucius's point of view on how a person in authority should act.

Background

Born in China in 551 B.C., Confucius became a Chinese philosopher and teacher. His ideas on education and government had a profound impact on Chinese society for many centuries.

In this selection from *The Analects,* Confucius discusses his philosophy of good government.

Vocabulary *Builder*

beneficent (buh NEHF uh suhnt) *adj.* doing things to help people; generous

expenditure (ehk SPEHN dih chur) *n.* the amount of money that a person or government spends

covetous (KUHV ih tuhs) *adj.* having a very strong desire to have something that someone else has

benevolent (buh NEHV uh luhnt) *adj.* kindly

awe (aw) *n.* a feeling of great respect and admiration for someone or something

propriety (proh PRĪ ih tee) *n.* proper behavior

Tzu-chang asked Confucius, saying, "In what way should a person in authority act in order that he may conduct government properly?" The Master replied, "Let him honor the five excellent, and banish away the four bad, things; then may he conduct government properly." Tzu-chang said, "What are meant by the five excellent things?" The Master said, "When the person in authority is <u>beneficent</u> without great <u>expenditure</u>; when he gives tasks [to] the people without their complaining; when he [tries to get] what he desires without being <u>covetous</u>; when he maintains a dignified ease without being proud; when he is majestic without being fierce."

Tzu-chang said, "What is meant by being beneficent without great expenditure?" The Master replied, "When the person in authority makes more beneficial to the people the things from which they naturally derive benefit; is not this being beneficent without great expenditure? When he chooses the labors which are proper, and makes them labor on them, who will [complain]? When his desires are set on <u>benevolent</u> government, and he secures it, who will accuse him of covetousness? Whether he has to do with many people or few, or with things great or small, he does not dare to indicate any disrespect; is not this to maintain a dignified ease without any pride? He adjusts his clothes and cap, and throws a dignity into his looks, so that, thus dignified, he is looked at with <u>awe</u>; is not this to be majestic without being fierce?"

Tzu-chang then asked, "What are meant by the four bad things?" The Master said, "To put the people to death without having instructed them; this is called cruelty. To require from them, suddenly, the full [sum] of work, without having given them warning; this is called oppression. To issue orders as if without urgency, at first, and when the time comes, to insist on them with severity; this is called injury. And, generally, in the giving pay or rewards to men, to do it in a stingy way; this is called acting the part of a mere official."

The Master said, "Without recognizing the laws of Heaven, it is impossible to be a superior man."

"Without an acquaintance with the rules of <u>propriety</u>, it is impossible for the character to be established."

"Without knowing the force of words, it is impossible to know men."

Source: *The Analects,* Confucius

Confucius

Analyze Primary Sources: *Detect Point of View*

1. The question Confucius tries to answer in this excerpt concerns

   A a leader's ability to persuade others.

   B a leader's decision to govern fairly.

   C the qualities that a good leader needs.

   D the importance of being a proud leader.

2. What is Confucius's viewpoint on how to govern?

   A The best leaders work to meet their own desires.

   B It is important to be proud and fierce.

   C The best leaders understand human nature.

   D The best leaders know that people should work hard.

3. Who was Confucius trying to persuade with his argument? Do you think he succeeded? Explain.

Qin Dynasty: The Achievements of Shi Huangdi

Prepare to Read

Objectives

In this selection you will

1. Read a historical account of the rule of a Chinese emperor.

2. Assess whether the information in the account is reliable as historical evidence.

Background

Shi Huangdi ruled as emperor of China during the Qin Dynasty from 221–210 B.C. He is best known as the first emperor to unify China.

Sima Qian, the grand historian of the Han Dynasty, collected many sources from the Qin Dynasty that he included in his book *The Records of the Grand Historian*. In the excerpt, Sima Qian quotes an inscription found on a memorial that Shi Huangdi built.

Vocabulary *Builder*

<u>inaugurate</u> (in AW gyoo rayt) *v.* to install in office with a ceremony

<u>pacify</u> (PAS ih fy) *v.* make calm; quiet down

<u>diligently</u> (DIHL uh jehnt lee) *adv.* with a lot of care and effort

<u>uniform</u> (YOO nuh form) *adj.* always the same

A new age is <u>inaugurated</u> by the Emperor;
Rules and measures are rectified, . . .
Human affairs are made clear
And there is harmony between fathers and
    sons.
The Emperor in his [wise ways] [kindness]
    and justice
Has made all laws and principles
    [understandable].

He set forth to <u>pacify</u> the east,
To inspect officers and men;
This great task accomplished
He visited the coast.
Great are the Emperor's achievements,
Men attend <u>diligently</u> to basic tasks,
Farming is encouraged, . . .

All the common people prosper;
All men under the sky
Toil with a single purpose;
Tools and measures are made <u>uniform</u>,
The written script is standardized;
Wherever the sun and moon shine,

Wherever one can go by boat or by carriage,
Men carry out their orders
And satisfy their desires;
For our Emperor in [keeping] with the time
Has regulated local customs,
Made waterways and divided up the land.
Caring for the common people,
He works day and night without rest;
He defines the laws, leaving nothing in
    doubt,

Making known what is forbidden.
The local officials have their duties,
Administration is smoothly carried out,
All is done correctly, all according to plan.
The Emperor in his wisdom
Inspects all four quarters of his
    [kingdom]. . . .

Source: *The Records of the Grand Historian,*
Sima Qian

Shi Huangdi

Analyze Primary Sources: *Draw Conclusions*

1. According to Huangdi's memorial, during his reign

   A citizens no longer paid taxes.

   B many new lands were conquered.

   C ordinary citizens lived well.

   D cruel governors ruled the land.

2. How might historians describe the time of Huangdi's rule?

   A a time of great economic growth

   B a time when decisions favored the wealthy

   C a time of social unrest

   D a time of warring states

3. Should historians trust the list of accomplishments written on the memorial when they write about Shi Huangdi? Why or why not?

4. What questions might historians want to ask about the source before accepting the inscription as an accurate description of Shi Huangdi's accomplishments?

The Peloponnesian War: The Plague in Athens

Prepare to Read

Objectives

In this selection you will

1. Read a historian's account of a plague in ancient Athens, Greece.

2. Examine the historian's sources and draw conclusions about the impact of the event on Athens.

Background

The Peloponnesian War, fought between Athens and Sparta, broke out in 431 B.C. Thucydides wrote the *History of the Peloponnesian War,* which includes eyewitness accounts of the war and a description of the plague of Athens. Thucydides contracted the plague, but he recovered to write a detailed account of the tragedy.

Vocabulary *Builder*

devastation (dehv uh STAY shuhn) *n.* very bad damage or complete destruction

virulent (VIR uh lehnt) *adj.* poisonous; deadly

unprecedented (uhn PREHS uh dehnt ehd) *adj.* never having happened before

calamity (kuh LAM ih tee) *n.* a great misfortune such as a flood or fire

At the beginning of the following summer the Peloponnesians and their allies . . . invaded Attica, again under the command of the Spartan King Archidamus. . . . Taking up their positions, they set about the <u>devastation</u> of the country.

They had not been many days in Attica before the plague first broke out among the Athenians. Previously attacks of the plague had been reported from many other places in the neighborhood of Lemnos and elsewhere, but there was no record of the disease being so <u>virulent</u> anywhere else or causing so many deaths as it did in Athens. . . .

The plague originated, so they say, in Ethiopia in upper Egypt, and spread from there into Egypt itself and Libya and much of the territory of the King of Persia. In the city of Athens it appeared suddenly, and the first cases were among the population of Piraeus, where there were no wells at that time, so that

it was supposed by them that the Peloponnesians had poisoned the reservoirs. Later, however, it appeared also in the upper city, and by this time the deaths were greatly increasing in number. . . .

Words indeed fail one when one tries to give a general picture of this disease; and as for the sufferings of individuals, they seemed almost beyond the capacity of human nature to endure. Here in particular is a point where this plague showed itself to be something quite different from ordinary diseases: though there were many dead bodies lying about unburied, the birds and animals that eat human flesh either did not come near them or, if they did taste the flesh, died of it afterwards. . . .

A factor which made matters much worse than they were already was the removal of people from the country into the city, and this particularly affected the incomers. There were no houses for them, and, living as they did during the hot season in badly ventilated huts, they died like flies. . . . For the catastrophe was so overwhelming that men, not knowing what would happen next to them, became indifferent to every rule of religion or of law. . . .

[Also] Athens owed to the plague the beginnings of a state of <u>unprecedented</u> lawlessness. Seeing how quick and abrupt were the changes of fortune which came to the rich who suddenly died and to those who had previously been penniless but now inherited their wealth, people now began openly to venture [take a chance] on acts of self-indulgence which before then they used to keep dark. . . . No fear of god or law of man had a restraining influence.

This, then, was the <u>calamity</u> which fell upon Athens. . . . At this time of distress people naturally recalled old oracles, and among them was a verse which the old men claimed had been delivered in the past and which said:

War with the Dorians comes, and a death will come at the same time.

. . . What was actually happening seemed to fit in well with the words of this oracle . . . the plague broke out directly after the Peloponnesian invasion, and never affected the Peloponnese at all, or not seriously; its full force was felt at Athens. . . ."

Source: *History of the Peloponnesian War,*
Thucydides

Soldiers preparing for battle

Analyze Primary Sources: *Draw Conclusions*

1. What question was Thucydides trying to answer in this excerpt?

2. What does Thucydides tell the reader about his sources?

3. What is Thucydides' point of view on the events described in this excerpt?

4. What conclusions can you draw regarding the impact of the plague on Athenian society?

Republic to Empire: Julius Caesar

Prepare to Read

Objectives
In this selection you will

1. Read a historian's account of Julius Caesar.

2. Examine the historian's opinion of Julius Caesar as a leader.

Background
Julius Caesar remains a colorful and controversial historical figure. His achievements are many. Caesar served the Roman Republic as an accomplished orator, politician, general, and statesman.

In *Lives of the Caesars*, Roman historian Suetonius writes about Julius Caesar's life and character.

Vocabulary *Builder*
desist (dih SIST) *v.* to stop doing something
perpetuity (pehr peh TOO ih tee) *n.* for all future time
arrogance (AIR oh gans) *n.* too much pride
insolence (IHN suh lehns) *n.* insulting behavior

When people spoke of him critically, he was content to urge in public that they should desist. He was able to carry with good grace the harm to his reputation caused by the most [unflattering or unkind] book written by Aulus and Caecina and the highly abusive poems of Pitholaus.

However, other things he did and said outweighed these, so that it is thought he abused his power and was justly killed. Not only did he accept excessive honors—one consulship after another, the dictatorship in perpetuity, responsibility for morals, as well as the . . . title "Father of his Fatherland," a statue displayed with those of the kings, and a raised seat at the theater—he even allowed privileges to be given to him which were greater than is right for mortals: a golden seat in the senate house and in front of the speaker's platform, a chariot . . . in the procession for the circus games, temples, altars, statues placed beside those of the gods . . . and a month of the year named after him. Indeed there were no honors which he did not either give to someone or receive as he willed.

His public sayings, as recorded by Titus Ampius, were characterized by equal arrogance: "The republic is nothing—just a name, without substance or form. . . ." "Men should now have more consideration in speaking with me and regard what I say as law." Such was the level of insolence he reached. . . .

. . . At the time of the Latin Festival he was returning to the city, among . . . demonstrations by the people, one member of the crowd had placed a laurel crown, bound with a white ribbon, on his statue and the tribunes . . . had given orders that the ribbon should be removed from the crown and that the man should be thrown into chains. Caesar, regretting, perhaps, that the reference to kingship had met with such a poor reception, or else, as he claimed, that he had been robbed of the glory to be had from refusing the honor, took the tribunes severely to task and deprived them of their authority. And after that time he was never able to shake off the rumor that his ambition was to take the title of king, even though, when the common people greeted him as king, he replied that he was not King but Caesar. . . .

Source: *Lives of the Caesars*, Suetonius

Caesar crosses the Rubicon.

Analyze Primary Sources: *Distinguish Facts From Opinions*

1. Which statements in this excerpt about Julius Caesar are facts?

2. Read the following passage. Which statements are facts and which are opinions?

   His public sayings, as recorded by Titus Ampius, were characterized by equal arrogance [self-importance]: "The republic is nothing—just a name, without substance or form. . . ." "Men should now have more consideration in speaking with me and regard what I say as law."

3. What opinion do you think Suetonius had of Julius Caesar?

4. What can historians learn from this historical narrative?

The Government of the Roman Empire: The Persecution of Christians

Prepare to Read

Objectives

In this selection you will

1. Read two letters from Ancient Rome regarding the persecution of Christians.

2. Determine the purpose of the letters and describe the emperor's point of view on how people accused of being Christians should be tried.

Background

The Romans were tolerant of different religions. However, all Roman citizens had to honor the Roman gods and pay homage to the emperor. Christians, who worshiped only one god, often faced persecution. In the following letters, Pliny, a Roman governor, asks the emperor Trajan for advice about how to deal with the Christians.

Vocabulary *Builder*

<u>repentance</u> (rih PEHN tens) *n.* sorrow for doing wrong

<u>denounce</u> (dih NOWNCE) *v.* accuse; give information against

<u>folly</u> (FAHL lee) *n.* being foolish; unwise behavior

<u>edict</u> (EE dihkt) *n.* a decree or order proclaimed by an authority that has the force of law

<u>warrant</u> (WOR ihnt) *v.* to be a good enough reason for something

Pliny to Emperor Trajan

. . . I have never participated in trials of Christians. I therefore do not know what offenses it is the practice to punish or investigate, and to what extent. And I have been not a little hesitant as to whether there should be any distinction on account of age or no difference between the very young and the more mature; whether pardon is to be granted for <u>repentance</u> or, if a man has once been a Christian, it does him no good to have ceased to be one; whether the name itself, even without offenses, or only the offenses associated with the name are to be punished.

Meanwhile, in the case of those who were <u>denounced</u> to me as Christians, I have observed the following procedure: I [questioned] these as to whether they were Christians; those who confessed I interrogated a second and a third time, threatening them with punishment; those who persisted I ordered executed. For I had no doubt that, whatever the nature of their beliefs, . . . [they] surely deserved to be punished. There were others possessed of the same <u>folly</u>; but because they were Roman citizens, I signed an order for them to be transferred to Rome.

Soon accusations spread, as usually happens, because of the proceedings going on, and several incidents occurred. An anonymous [written by an unknown person] document was published containing the names of many persons. Those who denied that they were or had been Christians, when they prayed to the gods in words dictated by me, offered prayer . . . to your image, which I had ordered to be brought for this purpose together with statues of the gods, and moreover . . . none of . . .

those who are really Christians, it is said, can be forced to do—these I thought should be discharged. Others named by the informer declared that they were Christians, but then denied it, asserting that they had been but had ceased to be, some three years before, others many years, some as much as twenty-five years. They all worshiped your image and the statues of the gods, and cursed Christ.

They asserted, however . . . their fault . . . had been that they were accustomed to meet on a fixed day before dawn and sing . . . a hymn to Christ as to a god, and to bind themselves by oath. . . . When this was over, it was their custom to depart and to assemble again to partake of food. . . . Even this, they agreed to, they had ceased to do after my <u>edict</u> by which, in agreement with your instructions, I had forbidden political associations. . . . I discovered nothing but . . . excessive superstition.

I therefore postponed the investigation and hastened to consult you. For the matter seemed to me to <u>warrant</u> consulting you, especially because of the number involved. For many persons of every age, every rank, and also of both sexes are and will be endangered. For . . . this superstition has spread not only to the cities but also to the villages and farms. But it seems possible to check and cure it. It is certainly quite clear that . . . the established religious rites, long neglected, are being resumed. . . . Hence it is easy to imagine what a great number of people can be reformed if an opportunity for repentance is given.

Pliny

Emperor Trajan

Trajan to Pliny

You observed proper procedure, my dear Pliny, in sifting the cases of those who had been denounced [formally accused] to you as Christians. For it is not possible to lay down any general rule to serve as a kind of fixed standard. They are not to be sought [gone after] out; if they are denounced and proved guilty, they are to be punished, with this reservation, that whoever denies that he is a Christian and really proves it—that is, by worshiping our gods—even though he was under suspicion in the past, shall obtain pardon through repentance. But anonymously posted accusations ought to have no place in any prosecution. For this is . . . out of keeping with the spirit of our age.

Source: *Ancestors: Medieval Sourcebook: Pliny on the Christians*

Analyze Primary Sources: *Detect Point of View*

1. What problem was Pliny trying to solve in this excerpt?
2. What is Trajan's point of view on the prosecution of the Christians?

3. What information does Pliny give about his sources in the letter?
4. How might historians use these letters?

Roman Engineering

Prepare to Read

Objectives

In this selection you will

1. Read first-person accounts of some of the Romans' engineering accomplishments.

2. Determine which statements in the accounts are fact and which are opinion.

Background

The Romans were well known for their achievements in engineering, especially for their roads and aqueducts. Roads connected distant parts of their empire and helped in spreading Roman culture. Aqueducts carried fresh water to cities for drinking and bathing. The roads and aqueducts were so well built that many are still in use today. Following are some eyewitness accounts of the building of Roman roads and aqueducts. As you read, try to distinguish the facts from the opinions.

Vocabulary *Builder*

intensify (ihn TEHN suh fī) *v.* to increase in size or strength

eddy (EHD ee) *v.* to circle

ventilation (vehnt uhl AY shuhn) *n.* fresh air

treacherous (TREHCH uhr uhs) *adj.* dangerous

divert (duh VERT) *v.* to change direction

despondent (dih SPAHN duhnt) *adj.* hopeless

attribute (uh TRIHB yoot) *v.* to assign responsibility for

blunder (BLUHN duhr) *n.* mistake

diverge (dī VERJ) *v.* to go in different directions

> The network of roads near Naples included a 2,300-foot-long tunnel. The Roman philosopher and playwright Seneca described his passage through this tunnel.

[After enduring a mud-soaked overland walk] we then faced a sand-dusting in the Naples tunnel. Nothing is longer than that prison, nothing more gloomy than the torches [sold to travelers at the entrance] there, which <u>intensify</u> the darkness rather than enabling us to see through it. In any case, even if the place had any light, the dust would conceal it. Dust is a serious nuisance even in the open. You can imagine what it's like in that place, where it just <u>eddies</u> around, and since there's no <u>ventilation</u>, it settles on those who have stirred it up.

> Statius, a Roman poet, wrote this account of workers building part of the Via Appia, the road from Rome to southern Italy.

Here the first task is to start with [a long trench], cut back the edges and hollow out the earth far down with deep excavation; next, to refill the scooped out trenches with other material and prepare a bed . . . so that the earth shall not wobble nor the spiteful ground provide a <u>treacherous</u> bed for the weight of [the paving] slabs; then to bind the road with blocks rammed in on both sides and numerous pegs. How many hands labor together! Some cut down [trees] and strip mountains, some smooth stakes and beams with iron; others bind together the slabs . . . [while] some dry up thirsty pools by hand and <u>divert</u> lesser streams far away.

I found everybody sad and <u>despondent</u>. They had given up all hopes that the opposite sections of the tunnel would meet, because each section had already been excavated beyond the middle of the mountain. As always happens in these cases, the fault was <u>attributed</u> to me, the engineer, as though I had not taken all precautions to ensure the success of the work. What could I have done better? For I began by surveying and taking the levels of the mountain, I drew plans and sections of the whole work. . . . And to take extra precaution, I summoned the contractor and his workmen and began the excavation in their presence with the help of two gangs of experienced veterans. . . . What more could I have done? After four years' absence, expecting every day to hear the good tidings of the water at Saldae, I arrived. The contractor and his assistants had made <u>blunder</u> upon blunder. In each section of the tunnel they had <u>diverged</u> from the [straight] line, each towards the right, and had I waited a little longer before coming, Saldae would have possessed two tunnels instead of one!

—Source: *Roman Roads and Aqueducts,* Don Nardo

> The Roman engineer Nonius Datus designed an aqueduct near Saldae, in North Africa. Returning to the construction site after some time away, he described mistakes by workers digging a tunnel for the aqueduct.

Roman aqueduct

Analyze Primary Sources: *Distinguish Facts From Opinions*

1. Read the following statement: "Nothing is longer than that prison, nothing more gloomy than the torches [sold to travelers at the entrance] there, which intensify the darkness rather than enabling us to see through it." Is this a fact or an opinion? Explain your answer.

2. Which statements in Statius' account of building the Via Appia are facts? Which are opinions?

3. Which statements in Nonius Datus' excerpt are facts? Which are opinions?

Travels of Ibn Battuta

Prepare to Read

Objectives

In this selection you will

1. Read descriptions of various cities within the Muslim world during the 1300s.

2. Assess the credibility and accuracy of the descriptions and draw conclusions about life in the Muslim world during the 1300s.

Background

Ibn Battuta was born in Tangiers, Morocco, in 1304. He set out in 1325 with the idea of taking a hajj to the Muslim holy city of Mecca. He had no idea that he would spend the next 30 years of his life traveling. At the end of his life, Battuta wrote a book about his experiences. As you read this excerpt, think about what life was like in the Muslim Empire during the Middle Ages.

Vocabulary *Builder*

decree (dee KREE) *v.* to order; to decide

sanctity (SANGK tuh tee) *n.* sacred; holy

chamber (CHAYM buhr) *n.* room

veneration (vehn uh RAY shuhn) *n.* deep respect

vie (vī) *v.* to struggle or compete

I left Tangiers, my birthplace, on . . . [June 14, 1325] . . . with the intention of making the Pilgrimage to the Holy House [at Mecca] and the Tomb of the Prophet [at Medina]. . . .

On reaching the city of Tilimsan . . . I found there two ambassadors of the Sultan of Tunis, who left the city on the same day that I arrived. . . . [A]fter a stay of three days in the city . . . I rode after them with all speed. I overtook them at the town of Miliana, where we stayed ten days, as both ambassadors fell sick on account of the summer heats. . . . I left their party there and pursued my journey, with a company of merchants from Tunis.

On reaching . . . [Algiers] we halted outside the town for a few days, until the former party rejoined us, when we went on together . . . and so reached Bijaya. . . .

At Bijaya I fell ill of a fever, and one of my friends advised me to stay there till I recovered. But I refused, saying, "If God decrees my death,

it shall be on the road with my face set toward Mecca." "If that is your resolve," he replied, "sell your . . . heavy baggage, and I shall lend you what you require. In this way you will travel light. . . ." I followed his advice and he did as he had promised—may God reward him!

On reaching . . . [Constantine] we camped outside the town, but a heavy rain forced us to leave our tents during the night and take refuge in some houses there. Next day the governor of the city came to meet us. Seeing my clothes all soiled by the rain he gave orders that they should be washed at his house, and in place of my old worn headcloth sent me a headcloth of fine Syrian cloth, in one of the ends of which he had tied two gold . . . [coins]. This was the first alms I received on my journey. . . .

At length on April 5 [1326] we reached Alexandria. It is a beautiful city, well-built and fortified with four gates and a magnificent port. . . .

One of the learned men of Alexandria was . . . Burhan ad-Din, whom I met during my stay and whose hospitality I enjoyed for three days. One day as I entered his room he said to me, "I see that you are fond of traveling through foreign lands." I replied, "Yes, I am" (though I had as yet no thought of going to such distant lands as India or China). Then he said "You must certainly visit my brother Farid ad-Din in India, and my brother Rukin ad-Din in Sind, and my brother Burhan ad-Din in China. . . ." I was amazed at his prediction and the idea of going to these countries having been cast into my mind, my journeys never ceased until I had met these three that he named and conveyed his greeting to them. . . .

At Cairo too is the great cemetery of al-Qarafa, which is a place of peculiar <u>sanctity</u> and contains the graves of innumerable scholars and pious believers. In the Qarafa the people build beautiful pavilions surrounded by walls, so that they look like houses. They also build <u>chambers</u> and hire Koran-readers who recite night and day in agreeable voices. . . .

From Cairo I traveled into Upper Egypt. . . . [From here] my way lay through a number of towns and villages to . . . [Minia], a large town which is built on the bank of the Nile, and most emphatically excels all the other towns of Upper Egypt. . . .

On the way from Hebron to Jerusalem, I visited Bethlehem, the birthplace of Jesus. The site is covered by a large building; the Christians regard it with intense <u>veneration</u> and hospitably entertain all who alight at it.

Mosque in Damascus

We then reached Jerusalem . . . third in excellence after the two holy shrines of Mecca and Medina and the place whence the Prophet was caught up into heaven. . . . The sacred mosque is the most beautiful building, and is said to be the largest mosque in the world. . . .

I entered Damascus on . . . [August 9, 1326]. . . . Damascus surpasses all other cities in beauty, and no description, however full, can do justice to its charms.

The people of Damascus <u>vie</u> with one another in building mosques, religious houses, colleges. . . . All strangers . . . are handsomely treated and care is taken that they are not forced to any action that might injure their self-respect.

—Source: *Travels in Asia and Africa 1325–1354*, Ibn Battuta

Analyze Primary Sources: *Draw Conclusions*

1. Should historians trust Ibn Battuta's account? Why or why not?

2. What questions might historians ask before accepting this description as accurate?

3. What can you conclude from this excerpt about life in the Muslim Empire during the Middle Ages?

West African Folk Tale

Prepare to Read

Objectives

In this selection you will

1. Read a traditional folk tale from West Africa that pokes fun at human nature.

2. Draw conclusions about West African culture based on evidence and details in the selection.

Background

Folk tales are an important part of West African culture. West Africans use folk tales to pass on beliefs and values from one generation to the next. Meant to entertain as well as to teach lessons, these stories are often humorous or far-fetched. As you read this folk tale, ask yourself what point the story is making about human nature.

Vocabulary *Builder*

<u>ford</u> (ford) *n.* shallow place where a river can be crossed
<u>refrain</u> (rih FRAYN) *v.* to hold back from doing something
<u>scowl</u> (scowl) *v.* to frown

O nce, . . . a country man went out to his garden to dig up some yams to take to market. While he was digging, one of the yams said to him, "Well, at last you're here. You never weeded me, but now you come around with your digging stick. Go away and leave me alone!"

The farmer turned around and looked at his cow in amazement. . . .

"Did you say something?" he asked.

The cow . . . said nothing, but the man's dog spoke up. "It wasn't the cow who spoke to you," the dog said. "It was the yam. The yam says leave him alone."

The man became angry, because his dog had never talked before, and he didn't like his tone besides. So he took his knife and cut a branch from a palm tree to whip his dog. Just then the palm tree said, "Put that branch down!"

The man was getting very upset about the way things were going, and he started to throw the palm branch away, but the palm branch said, "Man, put me down softly!"

He put the branch down gently on a stone, and the stone said, "Hey, take that thing off me!"

That was enough, and the frightened farmer started to run for his village. On the way he met a fisherman going the other way with a fish trap on his head.

"What's the hurry?" the fisherman asked.

"My yam said, 'Leave me alone!' Then the dog said, 'Listen to what the yam says!' When I went to whip the dog with a palm branch the tree said, 'Put that branch down!' Then the palm branch said, 'Do it softly!' Then the stone said, 'Take that thing off me!'"

"Is that all?" the man with the fish trap asked. "Is that so frightening?"

"Well," the man's fish trap said, "did he take it off the stone?"

"Wah!" the fisherman shouted. He threw the fish trap on the ground and began to run with the farmer, and on the trail they met a weaver with a bundle of cloth on his head.

"Where are you going in such a rush?" he asked them.

"My yam said, 'Leave me alone!'" the farmer said. "The dog said, 'Listen to what the yam says!' The tree said, 'Put that branch down!' The branch said, 'Do it softly!' And the stone said, 'Take that thing off me!'"

"And then," the fisherman continued, "the fish trap said, 'Did he take it off?'"

"That's nothing to get excited about," the weaver said. "No reason at all."

"Oh, yes it is," his bundle of cloth said. "If it happened to you you'd run too!"

"Wah!" the weaver shouted. He threw his bundle on the trail and started running with the other men.

They came panting to the <u>ford</u> in the river and found a man bathing. "Are you chasing a gazelle?" he asked them.

The first man said breathlessly, "My yam talked at me, and it said, 'Leave me alone!' And my dog said, 'Listen to your yam!' And when I cut myself a branch, the tree said, 'Put that branch down!' And the branch said, 'Do it softly!' And the stone said, 'Take that thing off me!'"

The fisherman panted. "And my trap said, 'Did he?'"

The weaver wheezed. "And my bundle of cloth said, 'You'd run too!'"

"Is that why you're running?" the man in the river asked.

"Well, wouldn't you run if you were in their position?" the river said.

The man jumped out of the water and began to run with the others. They ran down the main street of the village to the house of the chief. The chief's servant brought his stool out, and he came and sat on it to listen to their complaints. The men began to recite their troubles.

"I went out to my garden to dig yams," the farmer said, waving his arms. "Then everything began to talk! My yam said, 'Leave me alone!' My dog said, 'Pay attention to your yam!' The tree said, 'Put that branch down!' The branch said, 'Do it softly!' And the stone said, 'Take it off me!'"

"And my fish trap said, 'Well, did he take it off?'" the fisherman said.

"And my cloth said, 'You'd run too!'" the weaver said.

"And the river said the same," the bather said hoarsely, his eyes bulging.

The chief listened to them patiently, but he couldn't <u>refrain</u> from <u>scowling</u>. "Now this is really a wild story," he said at last. "You'd better all go back to your work before I punish you for disturbing the peace."

So the men went away, and the chief shook his head and mumbled to himself. "Nonsense like that upsets the community."

"Fantastic, isn't it?" his stool said. "Imagine a talking yam!"

—Source: *The Cow-Tail Switch and Other West African Stories*, Harold Courlander and George Herzog

Analyze Primary Sources: *Draw Conclusions*

1. How does the story poke fun at human nature?

2. Which details in the story reflect the way of life of the people of West Africa?

3. What conclusions about West African culture can you draw from this folk tale?

Inca Creation Myth

Objectives

In this selection you will

1. Read a myth describing the origins and development of the Inca people of South America.

2. Identify which parts of the story historians might be able to verify as fact.

Background

The Incas built one of the largest and wealthiest empires in South America in the 1400s. They called their empire Tahuantinsuyu, the four united quarters. The Incas had a complex political and religious system. They worshiped many gods, and their religious ceremonies centered on the rain and the sun. They believed that Viracocha, their most important god, created nature. Special teachers, called *amautas,* recited Inca history in the form of legends and myths like this one.

Vocabulary *Builder*

tongue (tuhng) *n.* language

hoard (hord) *n.* supply that is stored up and hidden

acquisitive (uh KWIHZ uh tihv) *adj.* greedy

fastness (FAST nihs) *n.* secure, fortified place

parched (pahrcht) *adj.* dry

multitude (MUHL tuh tood) *n.* very large number of people

The Sun rises and sets, the world spins, people live and die. Such are the cycles of time, which have endured through all the ages. Those who speak the Quechua <u>tongue</u> call this Pachacuti.

The age of the first Sun was born in the darkness of the beginning. The people then were primitive creatures, cousins to the *wari,* a beast which is part-llama, part-alpaca. Some of these people . . . worshipped Viracocha, saying that he had made them; others said Pachacamac. Knowing no better, they clothed themselves in leaves.

The age of the second Sun belonged to the Wari Runa, the *wari* people, a race with a little more learning. Dressed in animal skins, they tended the soil and grew a few simple crops.

Their god was Viracocha. A great flood ended their peaceful lives.

The age of the third Sun was a good time and a bad time. It belonged to the Purun Runa, the wild people. Their god was Pachacamac and they enjoyed the bounty he had provided. They spun wool into yarn and wove and colored the yarn to make cloth for clothing. They planted and harvested their own crops. They mined the Earth for her <u>hoard</u> of gold, silver and precious stones, which they turned into jewelry and other fine ornaments. With good food in their bellies and warm clothes on their backs, they were healthy and strong and increased in number. Soon there was not enough space for them in their highland home and they spread out into the lowlands. But now, instead of sharing what they had, the people became afraid of losing it. Possessive, <u>acquisitive</u> and defensive—of territory, of possessions—they banded together in towns, each under the rulership of a different king. For the first time, the people went to war with each other.

The age of the fourth Sun continued the mood of the third. This was the time of the Auca Runa, the warlike people. From their stone houses and <u>fastnesses</u> on the tops of mountains, they kept a lookout and guarded themselves against attack. Conflict and divisions marked this age. The people were divided into *ayllus*, kinship groups, according to their blood. The land, too, was divided; it became Tahuantinsuyu, the land of the four united quarters.

The age of the fifth Sun was the age of the glorious Inca empire, which stretched north, south, east and west across Tahuantinsuyu, over coastal desert, frozen mountain and fertile valley, and dazzled with its imperial wonders: its network of roads, which allowed for good communications and the rapid movement of troops; its irrigation systems, which brought water to a <u>parched</u> earth; its agricultural terraces, climbing up the hillsides like stairways for giants, which produced not only enough food for the <u>multitude</u>, but a surplus; its monumental buildings, erected without the

benefit of iron tools or the wheel, and constructed of stones which interlock with such fine precision that barely a whisper can pass between them; its handicrafts in weaving and ceramics and jewelry and gold; and, presiding above it all, the High King himself, the Inca.

—Source: *Tales of the Plumed Serpent,*
Diana Ferguson

Inca religious ceremony

Analyze Primary Sources: *Distinguish Relevant Information*

1. Which statements in this myth are relevant to understanding its purpose?

2. Which parts of this myth might a historian be able to verify? How might a historian verify the names of people?

3. What information about Inca culture in this myth might a historian not be able to verify?

Trade in Ming China

Prepare to Read

Objectives
In this selection you will

1. Read a government official's account of trade in various regions of China during the early 1500s.

2. Distinguish between facts and opinions in the selection.

Background
During the time of Mongol rule, overland trade flourished between China, Central Asia, and Europe. Caravans carrying silk and spices traveled the Silk Road and other routes. Chinese merchants also sailed to ports in Southeast Asia and India. In the mid-1400s, however, the Ming Dynasty ended overseas expeditions. A Ming government official wrote this essay about merchants and trade in the early 1500s.

Vocabulary *Builder*

boast (bohst) *v.* to brag
transformation (trans for MAY shuhn) *n.* complete change
prohibit (proh HIHB iht) *v.* to forbid or not allow something
rigid (RIHJ ihd) *adj.* strict
recalcitrant (rih KAL sih truhnt) *adj.* refusing to obey
refrain (rih FRAYN) *v.* to stop from doing something

Merchants <u>boast</u> that their wisdom and ability are such as to give them a free hand in affairs. They believe that they know all the possible <u>transformations</u> in the universe and therefore can calculate all the changes in the human world, and that the rise and fall of prices are under their command. They are confident that they will not make one mistake in a hundred in their calculations. These merchants do not know how insignificant their wisdom and ability really are. . . .

Because I have traveled to many places during my career as an official, I am familiar with commercial activities and business conditions in various places. The capital is located in an area with mountains at its back and a great plain stretching in front. The region is rich in millet, grain, donkeys, horses, fruit, and vegetables, and has become a center where goods from distant places are brought. Those who engage in commerce, including the foot peddler, the cart peddler, and the shopkeeper, display not only clothing and fresh foods from the fields but also numerous luxury items such as priceless jade from K'un-lun, . . . gold from Yunnan, and coral from Vietnam. These precious items, coming from the mountains or the sea, are not found in central China. But people in remote areas and in other countries, unafraid of the dangers and difficulties of travel, transport these items step by step to the capital, making it the most prosperous place in the empire. . . .

The profits from the tea and salt trades are especially great but only large-scale merchants can undertake these businesses. Furthermore, there are government regulations on their distribution, which prohibit the sale of tea in the Northwest and salt in the Southeast. Since tea is produced primarily in the Southeast, <u>prohibiting</u> its sale to the non-Chinese on the northern border is wise and can be enforced.

Chinese ship

Selling privately produced salt where it is manufactured is also prohibited. This law is rigidly applied to all areas where salt was produced during the Ming dynasty. Yet there are so many private salt producers there now that the regulation seems too <u>rigid</u> and is hard to enforce. . . .

Foreigners [in the Northwest] are <u>recalcitrant</u> and their greed knows no bounds. At the present time our nation spends over one million cash yearly from our treasury on these foreigners, still we cannot rid ourselves of their demands. What is more, the greedy heart is unpredictable. If one day they break the treaties and invade our frontiers, who will be able to defend us against them? I do not think our present trade with them will ensure us a century of peace.

As to the foreigners in the Southeast, their goods are useful to us just as ours are to them. . . . Moreover, the Southeast sea foreigners are more concerned with trading with China than with gaining gifts from China. Even if they send a large tribute offering only to receive small gifts in return, they will still be content. In addition, trading with them can enrich our people. So why do we <u>refrain</u> from the trade?

Some people may say that the Southeast sea foreigners have invaded us several times so they are not the kind of people with whom we should trade. But they should realize that the Southeast sea foreigners need Chinese goods and the Chinese need their goods. If we prohibit the natural flow of this merchandise, how can we prevent them from invading us? I believe that if the sea trade were opened, the trouble with foreign pirates would cease. These Southeast sea foreigners are simple people, not to be compared to the unpredictable Northeast sea foreigners. Moreover, China's exports in the Northwest trade come from the national treasury. Whereas the Northwest foreign trade ensures only harm, the sea trade provides us with only gain. . . .

—Source: *World History in Documents: A Comparative Reader,*
edited by Peter N. Stearns

Analyze Primary Sources: *Distinguish Facts From Opinions*

1. Read the first paragraph. Does it contain a factual discussion about merchants or the author's opinion? Explain your answer.

2. Which statements in the second paragraph are facts?

3. Which statements in the description of foreigners are opinions?

Magna Carta

Objectives

In this selection you will

1. Describe some of the early rights that nobles demanded from the king of England in 1215.

2. Determine the purpose of the document.

Background

When King John came to the English throne in 1199, he made great demands on his subjects. For example, he increased the nobles' taxes and length of military service. People who lost court cases had to pay enormous penalties. King John also fought with church leaders. The nobles and church leaders demanded that the king recognize their rights. In 1215, they forced King John to approve the Magna Carta, or Great Charter. In this excerpt, the pronouns *we* and *our* refer to King John.

Vocabulary *Builder*

inviolate (ihn VĪ uh liht) *adj.* unbroken

scutage (SKYOOT ihj) *n.* tax

levy (LEHV ee) *v.* to make someone pay a tax

remit (rih MIHT) *v.* to excuse or cancel

allay (a LAY) *v.* to calm or quiet

concession (kuhn SEHSH uhn) *n.* something given in order to end an argument

transgression (trans GREHSH uhn) *n.* something that is against the rules

redress (rih DREHS) *v.* to correct something that is wrong

---

1. . . . the English Church shall be free, and shall have her rights entire, and her liberties <u>inviolate</u>; and we will that it be thus observed. . . . We also have granted to all freemen of our kingdom, for us and our heirs forever, all the underwritten liberties, to be had and held by them and their heirs, of us and our heirs forever.

12. No <u>scutage</u> or aid shall be imposed on our kingdom, unless by common counsel of our kingdom, except for ransoming our person, for making our eldest son a knight, and for marrying our eldest daughter once; and for them there shall be <u>levied</u> no more than a reasonable aid. . . .

13. And the city of London shall have all its ancient liberties and free customs, by land as well as by water; furthermore, we decree and grant that all other cities, boroughs, towns, and ports shall have all their liberties and free customs.

28. No constable or other bailiff of ours shall take corn or other provisions from anyone without immediately [offering] money . . . unless he can have postponement . . . by permission of the seller.

29. No constable shall [force] any knight to give money instead of castle guard, when he is willing to perform it in his own person, or (if he himself cannot do it from any reasonable cause) then by another reliable man; and if we have led him or sent him upon military service, he shall be quit of guard, in proportion to the time during which he has been on service because of us.

30. No sheriff or bailiff of ours, or other person, shall take the horses or carts of

any freeman for transport duty, against the will of the freeman.

38. No bailiff for the future shall, upon his unsupported complaint, put anyone to his "law," without credible witnesses brought for this purpose.

39. No freeman shall be taken or imprisoned . . . or exiled or in any way destroyed . . . except by the lawful judgment of his peers or by the law of the land.

40. To no one will we sell, to no one will we refuse or delay, right or justice.

42. It shall be lawful in future for anyone (excepting always those imprisoned or outlawed in accordance with the law of the kingdom, and natives of any country at war with us, and merchants, who shall be treated as if above provided) to leave our kingdom and to return, safe and secure by land and water, except for a short period in time of war, on grounds of public policy—reserving always the allegiance due to us.

45. We will appoint as justices, constables, sheriffs, or bailiffs only such as know the law of the realm and mean to observe it well.

55. All fines made by us unjustly and against the law of the land, shall be entirely remitted. . . .

61. Since, moreover, for God and the amendment of our kingdom and for the better allaying of our quarrel that has arisen between us and our barons, we have granted all these concessions . . . we

King John signing the Magna Carta

give and grant to them the underwritten security, namely, that the barons choose five-and-twenty barons of the kingdom . . . who shall be obliged to observe and hold . . . the peace and liberties which we have granted and confirmed to them by this present Charter, so that if we . . . or any one of our officers, shall in anything be at fault towards anyone, or shall have broken any one of the articles . . . and the offence be notified to four barons of the . . . five-and-twenty, the said four barons shall come to us and, laying the transgression before us, petition to have that transgression redressed without delay. And if we shall not have corrected the transgression . . . within forty days . . . the four barons aforesaid shall refer the matter to the rest of the . . . barons, and those . . . barons shall . . . distress us in all possible ways, namely, by seizing our castles, lands, possessions, and in any other way they can, until redress has been obtained as they deem fit. . . .

—Source: Magna Carta, 1215

Analyze Primary Sources: *Draw Conclusions*

1. What was the purpose for writing the Magna Carta?

2. What issues was the Magna Carta trying to resolve?

3. What is the Magna Carta's point of view on individual rights?

The Bubonic Plague

Prepare to Read

Objectives

In this selection you will

1. Read an account of the bubonic plague in Florence during the 1300s.

2. Draw conclusions about the impact of the plague on society and culture.

Background

From 1347 to 1352, the bubonic plague, or Black Death, devastated Europe. Giovanni Boccaccio described what he saw when the plague struck Florence. As you read his account, think about how the disease changed the lives of the people of Florence.

Vocabulary *Builder*

pestilence (PEHS tuh luhns) *n.* deadly disease

infirmity (ihn FER muh tee) *n.* sickness

affirm (uh FERM) *v.* to say that something is true

affliction (uh FLIHK shuhn) *n.* something that causes pain or suffering

ferocity (fuh RAHS uh tee) *n.* fierceness

There came into the noble city of Florence, the most beautiful of all Italian cities, a deadly <u>pestilence</u>, which . . . had originated in . . . [China], where it destroyed countless lives, scarcely resting in one place before it moved to the next, and turning westward its strength grew monstrously. . . .

To cure these <u>infirmities</u> neither the advice of physicians nor the power of medicine appeared to have any value or profit; . . . as a consequence, very few were ever cured; all died three days after the appearance of the first outward signs. . . . But what gave this pestilence particularly severe force was that whenever the diseased mixed with healthy people, like a fire through dry grass or oil it would rush upon the healthy. And this wasn't the worst of the evil: for not only did it infect healthy persons who [talked] or mixed with the sick, but also touching bread or any other object which had been handled or worn by the sick would transport the sickness from the victim to the one touching the object. . . .

Because of all these things . . . fears and imaginings were born in those left alive, and all of them took . . . the most cruel precaution: to avoid and run away from the sick and their things; by doing this, each person believed they could preserve their health. Others were of the opinion that they should live moderately and guard against all excess. . . . Others, who disagreed with this, <u>affirmed</u> that . . . enjoying oneself . . . was the best medicine. . . . With so much <u>affliction</u> and misery, all reverence for the laws, both of God and of man, fell apart and dissolved, because the ministers . . . of the laws were either dead or ill like everyone else, or were left with so few officials that they were unable to do their duties; as a result, everyone was free to do whatever they pleased. Many other people steered a middle course between these two extremes, neither restricting their diet like the first group, nor indulging so liberally . . . like the second group . . . and, instead of locking themselves away, these people walked about freely, holding in their hands a posy of flowers, or fragrant herbs . . . which sometimes they pressed to their nostrils, believing it would comfort the brain with smells of that sort because of the stink of the corpses, sick bodies, and medicines polluted the air all about the city. Others held a more cruel opinion, one that in the end probably guaranteed their safety, saying that there was no better or more effective medicine against the disease than to run away from it. . . .

One citizen avoided another, everybody neglected their neighbors and rarely or never visited their parents and relatives unless from a distance; the ordeal had so withered the hearts of men and women that brother abandoned brother, and the uncle abandoned his nephew and the sister her brother and many times, wives abandoned their husbands, and, what is even more incredible and cruel, mothers and fathers abandoned their children and would refuse to visit them. . . .

How much more can be said of the cruelty of heaven, and possibly, in part, that of humanity, which between March and July of that year, because of the <u>ferocity</u> of the pestilence and the fact that many of the sick were poorly cared for or abandoned in their hour of need by people frightened for their health, killed off one hundred thousand human creatures for certain within the walls of the city of Florence.

—Source: *The Decameron*, Giovanni Boccaccio

Painting of the Black Death

Analyze Primary Sources: *Draw Conclusions*

1. Is this description of the plague believable or exaggerated? Explain.

2. What questions might historians want to ask before accepting this as an accurate description of what happened in Florence?

3. What can you conclude from this description about how life changed in Florence as a result of the plague?

The New Education

Objectives

In this selection you will

1. Consider one writer's views on the importance of education during the Renaissance.

2. List the arguments the writer makes in favor of the study of literature.

Background

During the Renaissance, humanists looked to nature and science to explain the world around them. The invention of the printing press made books more widely available and sparked a revival in learning. Education also changed. An Italian teacher named Petrus Paulus Vergerius wrote this essay on "The New Education" for Ubertino, the son of the lord of Padua, around 1400.

Vocabulary *Builder*

irksome (ERK suhm) *adj.* annoying

proficient (proh FIHSH uhnt) *adj.* able to do something very well

tenacious (tuh NAY shuhs) *adj.* firmly held

accord (uh KORD) *v.* to give

precept (PREE sehpt) *n.* rule

supplement (SUHP luh mehnt) *v.* to add

rudiment (ROO duh mehnt) *n.* basic part

We call those studies liberal which are worthy of a free man; those studies by which we attain and practice virtue and wisdom; that education which calls forth, trains and develops those highest gifts of body and of mind . . . which are rightly judged to rank next in dignity to virtue only. . . . It is, then, of the highest importance that even from infancy this aim, this effort, should constantly be kept alive in growing minds. . . .

Our youth of today, it is to be feared, is backward to learn; studies are accounted <u>irksome</u>. Boys hardly weaned begin to claim their own way, at a time when every art should be employed to bring them under control and attract them to [serious] studies. . . .

In your own case, Ubertinus, you had before you the choice of training in Arms or in Letters. Either holds a place of distinction amongst the pursuits which appeal to men of noble spirit; either leads to fame and honor in the world. It would have been natural that you, the [heir] of a House ennobled by its [skill] in arms, should have been content to . . . devote yourself wholly to that discipline. But to your credit you elected to become <u>proficient</u> in both alike: to add to the career of arms traditional in your family, an equal success in that other great discipline of mind and character, the study of Literature. . . .

Indeed the power which good books have of diverting our thoughts from unworthy or distressing themes is another support to my argument for the study of letters. . . . In them we see unfolded before us vast stores of knowledge, for our delight, it may be, or for our inspiration. In them are contained the records of the great achievements of men; the wonders of Nature. . . . And, most important of all, this Knowledge is not liable to decay. . . .

Literature indeed exhibits not facts alone, but thoughts, and their expression. . . . Books

Renaissance painting of a gathering of scholars

indeed are a higher—a wider, more <u>tenacious</u>—memory, a store-house which is the common property of us all. . . .

We come now to the consideration of the various subjects which may rightly be included under the name of "Liberal Studies." Amongst these I <u>accord</u> the first place to History, on grounds both of its attractiveness and of its [usefulness], qualities which appeal equally to the scholar and to the statesman. Next in importance ranks Moral Philosophy, which indeed is, in a peculiar sense, a "Liberal Art," in that its purpose is to teach men the secret of true freedom. History, then, gives us the concrete examples of the <u>precepts</u> [taught] by philosophy. The one shows what men should do, the other what men have said and done in the past, and what practical lessons we may draw therefrom for the present day. I would indicate as the third main branch of study, Eloquence [expression], which indeed holds a place of distinction amongst the refined Arts. By philosophy we learn the essential truth of things. . . .

And history provides the light of experienced . . . wisdom fit to <u>supplement</u> the force of reason and the persuasion of eloquence. For we allow that soundness of judgment, wisdom of speech, integrity of conduct are the marks of a true liberal . . . [mind].

The Art of Letters, however, rests upon a different footing. It is a study adapted to all times and to all circumstances, to the investigation of fresh knowledge or to the recasting and application of old. Hence the importance of grammar and of the rules of composition must be recognized at the outset, as the foundation on which the whole study of Literature must rest: and closely associated with these <u>rudiments</u>, the art of . . . Logical argument. . . .

The principal "Disciplines" have now been reviewed. It must not be supposed that a liberal education requires acquaintance with them all: for a thorough mastery of even one of them might fairly be the achievement of a lifetime. . . .

Source: "The New Education,"
Petrus Paulus Vergerius

Analyze Primary Sources: *Detect Point of View*

1. What argument is Vergerius trying to resolve in this excerpt?

2. How does Vergerius view the "youth of today"?

3. What is his perspective on education?

Primary Source

The Conquest of Mexico

Prepare to Read

Objectives

In this selection you will

1. Read an Aztec account of the arrival of the Spanish in Mexico.

2. Draw conclusions about the Aztecs' reaction to the arrival of the Spanish.

Background

The Aztecs built a great empire in Mexico. By 1519, Tenochtitlán, the Aztec capital, had a population of more than 200,000. In 1519, Hernan Cortés and his troops landed on the east coast of Mexico and marched into the Aztec capital. The following is an Aztec account of the arrival of the Spanish.

Vocabulary *Builder*

<u>resound</u> (rih ZOWND) *v.* to echo

<u>entrails</u> (EHN traylz) *n.* internal organs

<u>pestilent</u> (PEHS tuh luhnt) *adj.* deadly

<u>distraught</u> (dih STRAWT) *adj.* worried

A few days later a . . . [common man] came to the city from Mictlancuauhtla. No one had sent him, none of the officials; he came of his own accord. He went directly to the palace of Motecuhzoma and said to him: "Our lord and king, forgive my boldness. I am from Mictlancuauhtla. When I went to the shores of the great sea, there was a mountain range or small mountain floating in the midst of the water, and moving here and there without touching the shore. My lord, we have never seen the like of this, although we guard the coast and are always on watch. . . ."

"Our lord and king, it is true that strange people have come to the shores of the great sea. They were fishing from a small boat, some with rods and others with a net. . . . On their heads they wore red kerchiefs, or bonnets of a fine scarlet color, and some wore large round hats . . . which must have been sunshades. They have very light skin, much lighter than ours. They all have long beards, and their hair comes only to their ears. . . ."

Motecuhzoma was astonished and terrified by their report. . . .

He was also terrified to learn how the cannon roared, how its noise <u>resounded</u>, how it caused one to faint and grow deaf. The messengers told him: "A thing like a ball of stone comes out of its <u>entrails</u>: it comes out shooting sparks and raining fire. The smoke that comes out with it has a <u>pestilent</u> odor, like that of rotten mud. This odor penetrates even to the brain and causes the greatest discomfort. . . ."

The messenger also said: "Their trappings and arms are all made of iron. They dress in iron and wear iron . . . on their heads. Their swords are iron; their bows are iron; their shields are iron; their spears are iron. Their deer carry them on their backs wherever they wish to go. These deer, our lord, are as tall as the roof of a house. . . ."

Motecuhzoma was <u>distraught</u> and bewildered; he was filled with terror, not knowing what would happen to the city. The people were also terrified, debating the news among themselves. There were meetings and arguments and gossip in the street; there was weeping. . . . The people were downcast: they went about with their heads bowed down and greeted each other with tears. . . .

Then the Spaniards fired one of their cannons, and this caused great confusion in the city. The people scattered in every direction; they fled without rhyme or reason; they ran off as if they were being pursued. . . . They were all overcome by terror, as if their hearts had fainted. And when night fell, the panic spread through the city and their fears would not let them sleep. . . .

While the Spaniards were in Tlaxcala, a great plague broke out here in Tenochtitlán. It began to spread during the thirteenth month and lasted for seventy days, striking everywhere in the city and killing a vast number of our people. Sores erupted on our faces, our breasts, our bellies; we were covered with agonizing sores from head to foot. . . .

A great many died from this plague, and many others died of hunger. They could not get up to search for food, and everyone else was too sick to care for them, so they starved to death in their beds. . . .

And now the Spaniards came back again. . . .

The Spaniards wasted no time as they loaded and fired the cannons. The smoke

Battle between Spanish and Aztecs

belched out in black clouds that darkened the sky, as if night were falling. . . . When the smoke cleared away, the Spaniards could not see a single Aztec. . . .

The Spanish blockade caused great anguish in the city. The people were tormented by hunger, and many starved to death. There was no fresh water to drink. . . .

The only food was lizards, swallows, corncobs, and the salt grasses of the lake. The people also ate water lilies . . . and chewed on deerhides and pieces of leather. They roasted and seared and scorched whatever they could find and then ate it. They ate the bitterest weeds and even dirt.

Nothing can compare with the horrors of that siege and the agonies of the starving. We were so weakened by hunger that, little by little, the enemy forced us to retreat. Little by little they forced us to the wall. . . .

—Source: *The Broken Spears:*
The Aztec Account of the Conquest of Mexico,
edited by Miguel Leon-Portilla

Analyze Primary Sources: *Draw Conclusions*

1. Is this a reliable description of the arrival of the Spanish? Why or why not?

2. What questions might historians ask about this source before accepting it as accurate?

3. What can you conclude from this description about how the Aztecs reacted to the arrival of the Spanish?

Declaration of the Rights of Man and the Citizen

Prepare to Read

Objectives
In this selection you will

1. Analyze the document in which the French declared their rights during the French Revolution.

2. Compare this document to the American Declaration of Independence, which was written thirteen years before this document.

Background
The French National Assembly issued this document in 1789 after having overthrown the government in the early stages of the French Revolution. The document lists what the writers believed to be the natural rights of French citizens and establishes the equality of all citizens before the law.

Vocabulary *Builder*

auspices (AWS puh siz) *n.* approval and support

imprescriptible (im prih SKRIP tuh buhl) *adj.* that cannot rightfully be taken away

indispensable (in dih SPEN suh buhl) *adj.* absolutely necessary

---

Therefore the National Assembly recognizes and proclaims, in the presence and under the <u>auspices</u> of the Supreme Being, the following rights of man and of the citizen:

1. Men are born and remain free and equal in rights. Social distinctions may be founded only upon the general good.

2. The aim of all political association is the preservation of the natural and <u>imprescriptible</u> rights of man. These rights are liberty, property, security, and resistance to oppression. . . .

4. Liberty consists in the freedom to do everything which injures no one else. . . .

5. Law can only prohibit such actions as are hurtful to society. . . .

6. Law is the expression of the general will. Every citizen has a right to participate personally, or through his representative, in its formation. It must be the same for all, whether it protects or punishes. All

A revolutionary in France, 1792

Women marching to the royal palace of Versailles during the French Revolution

citizens, being equal in the eyes of the law, are equally eligible to all dignities and to all public positions and occupations, according to their abilities, and without distinction except that of their virtues and talents.

7. No person shall be accused, arrested, or imprisoned except in the cases and according to the forms prescribed by law. . . .

9. As all persons are held innocent until they shall have been declared guilty, if arrest shall be deemed <u>indispensable</u>, all harshness not essential to the securing of

the prisoner's person shall be severely repressed by law. . . .

11. The free communication of ideas and opinions is one of the most precious of the rights of man. Every citizen may, accordingly, speak, write, and print with freedom. . . .

13. A common contribution is essential for the maintenance of the public [military] forces and for the cost of administration. This should be equitably distributed among all the citizens in proportion to their means.

Analyze Primary Sources: *Make Comparisons*

1. This document was modeled in part on the English Bill of Rights and the American Declaration of Independence. Locate a copy of the American Declaration and identify three statements that are similar in both documents.

2. Which article above specifically protects citizens from police brutality and torture?

3. Give one real-life example of each of the four natural rights listed under article 2.

Hard Times by Charles Dickens

Prepare to Read

Objectives

In this selection you will

1. Read a fictional description of work in a factory during the early Industrial Revolution.

2. Make inferences about the ideas that the author is trying to convey through his writing.

Background

In his novel *Hard Times*, British writer Charles Dickens protests the dehumanizing conditions of factory life in England during the early years of the Industrial Revolution. In this excerpt, Dickens describes a morning in a fictional factory town named Coketown. (Coke is a form of coal.)

Vocabulary *Builder*

clog (klahg) *n.* a shoe with a wooden sole

melancholy (MEL uhn kahl ee) *adj.* sad

monotony (muh NAHT uhn ee) *n.* tedious sameness, repetition

consign (kuhn SYN) *v.* to give over to another's care

decomposition (dee kahm puh ZISH uhn) *n.* break up

unfathomable (un FATH uhm uh buhl) *adj.* not capable of being understood

meanest (MEEN ist) *adj.* most humble, lowest status

shrouded (SHROWD id) *v.* covered

The Fairy palaces burst into illumination, before pale morning showed the monstrous serpents of smoke trailing themselves over Coketown. A clattering of <u>clogs</u> upon the pavement; a rapid ringing of bells; and all the <u>melancholy</u> mad elephants, polished and oiled up for the day's <u>monotony</u>, were at their heavy exercise again.

Stephen bent over his loom, quiet, watchful, and steady. A special contrast, as every man was in the forest of looms where Stephen worked, to the crashing, smashing, tearing piece of mechanism at which he laboured. Never fear, good people of an anxious turn of mind, that Art will <u>consign</u> Nature to Oblivion. Set anywhere, side by side, the work of God and the work of man; and the former, even though it be a troop of Hands of

Young girl in a cotton mill, 1908

Industrial factories in London, England

very small account, will gain in dignity from the comparison.

So many hundred Hands in this Mill; so many hundred horse Steam Power. It is known, to the force of a single pound weight, what the engine will do; but, not all the calculators of the National Debt can tell me the capacity for good or evil, for love or hatred, for patriotism or discontent, for the <u>decomposition</u> of virtue into vice, or the reverse, at any single moment in the soul of one of these its quiet servants, with the composed faces and the regulated actions. There is no mystery in it; there is an <u>unfathomable</u> mystery in the <u>meanest</u> of them, for ever. . . .

The day grew strong, and showed itself outside, even against the flaming lights within. The lights were turned out, and the work went on. The rain fell, and the Smoke-serpents, submissive to the curse of all that tribe, trailed themselves upon the earth. In the waste-yard outside, the steam from the escape pipe, the litter of barrels and old iron, the shining heaps of coals, the ashes everywhere, were <u>shrouded</u> in a veil of mist and rain.

The work went on, until the noon-bell rang. More clattering upon the pavements. The looms, and wheels, and Hands all out of gear for an hour.

Analyze Primary Sources: *Making Inferences*

1. (a) Why does Dickens refer to the factory workers as "Hands"? (b) What seems to be his attitude toward the workers?

2. What descriptive words does Dickens use to set the scene for this factory town? What does this description imply about his attitude toward the Industrial Revolution?

3. What objects do you think Dickens is describing as "melancholy mad elephants"?

Churchill Rallies the British

Objectives

In this selection you will

1. Read excerpts from two speeches given by British Prime Minister Winston Churchill during World War II.

2. Determine the purpose of Churchill's speeches.

Background

Winston Churchill delivered the two speeches excerpted below to British Parliament in June 1940. At the time, Germany's Adolf Hitler had conquered nearly all of mainland Europe and was preparing to attack the British Isles. In the first excerpt, Churchill describes the "Miracle of Dunkirk" during which British ships rescued more than 300,000 British and French troops trapped by the German army on the northern coast of France on the beaches of Dunkirk.

Vocabulary *Builder*

embark (em BAHRK) *v.* to put aboard a vehicle for transportation

menace (MEN uhs) *n.* threat

flag (flag) *v.* to become unsteady or spiritless

continuity (kahn tuh NOO uh tee) *n.* uninterrupted duration

abyss (uh BIS) *n.* bottomless pit

protract (proh TRAKT) *v.* continue or extend outward

June 4, 1940

The enemy attacked on all sides with great strength and fierceness, and their main power, the power of their far more numerous Air Force, was thrown into the battle or else concentrated upon Dunkirk and the beaches. Pressing in upon the narrow exit, both from the east and from the west, the enemy began to fire with cannon upon the beaches by which alone the shipping could approach or depart. . . . .

Meanwhile, the Royal Navy, with the willing help of countless merchant seamen, strained every nerve to <u>embark</u> the British and Allied troops; 220 light warships and 650 other vessels were engaged. They had to operate upon the difficult coast, often in adverse weather, under an almost ceaseless hail of bombs and an increasing concentration of artillery fire. Nor were the seas, as I have said, themselves free from mines and torpedoes. It was in conditions such as these that our men carried on, with little or no rest, for days and nights on end, making trip after trip across the dangerous waters, bringing with them always men whom they had rescued. The numbers they have brought back are the measure of their devotion and their courage. . . . .

I have, myself, full confidence that if all do their duty, if nothing is neglected, and if the best arrangements are made, as they are being made, we shall prove ourselves once again able to defend our Island home, to ride out the storm of war, and to outlive the <u>menace</u> of tyranny, if necessary for years, if necessary alone. . . . Even though large tracts of Europe and many old and famous States have fallen or may fall into the grip of the Gestapo and all the odious apparatus of Nazi rule, we shall not <u>flag</u> or fail. We shall go on to the end, we shall fight in France, we shall fight on the seas and oceans, we shall fight with growing confidence and growing strength in the air, we shall defend our Island, whatever the cost may be, we shall fight on the beaches, we shall fight on the landing grounds, we shall fight in the fields and in the streets, we shall fight in the hills; we shall never surrender, and even if, which I do not for a moment believe, this Island or a large part of it were subjugated and starving, then our Empire beyond the seas, armed and guarded by the British Fleet, would carry on the struggle, until, in God's good time, the New World, with all its power and might, steps forth to the rescue and the liberation of the old.

Winston Churchill

June 18, 1940

What General Weygand called the Battle of France is over. I expect that the Battle of Britain is about to begin. Upon this battle depends the survival of Christian civilization. Upon it depends our own British life, and the long <u>continuity</u> of our institutions and our Empire. The whole fury and might of the enemy must very soon be turned on us. Hitler knows that he will have to break us in this Island or lose the war. If we can stand up to him, all Europe may be free and the life of the world may move forward into broad, sunlit uplands. But if we fail, then the whole world, including the United States, including all that we have known and cared for, will sink into the <u>abyss</u> of a new Dark Age made more sinister, and perhaps more <u>protracted</u>, by the lights of perverted science. Let us therefore brace ourselves to our duties, and so bear ourselves that, if the British Empire and its Commonwealth last for a thousand years, men will still say, "This was their finest hour."

Analyze Primary Sources: *Determine the Author's Purpose*

1. What do you think was the purpose of these speeches by Churchill?

2. Who is Churchill referring to when he says "the New World"?

3. What does Churchill mean when he says "the Battle of Britain is about to begin"?

The World: Political

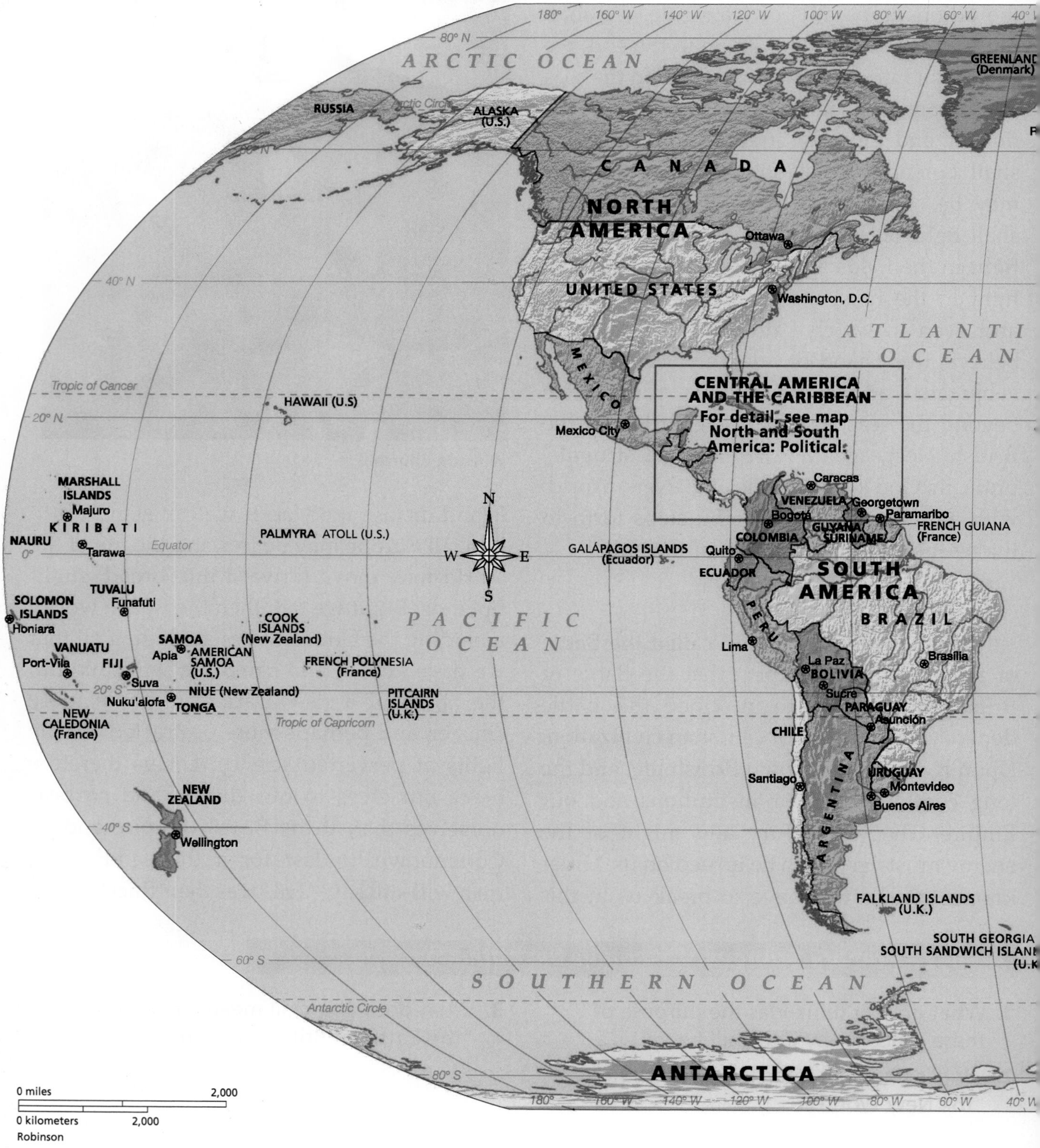

ARCTIC OCEAN

GREENLAND (Denmark)

RUSSIA

ALASKA (U.S.)

CANADA

NORTH AMERICA

Ottawa

UNITED STATES

Washington, D.C.

ATLANTIC OCEAN

MEXICO

Tropic of Cancer

HAWAII (U.S)

Mexico City

CENTRAL AMERICA AND THE CARIBBEAN
For detail, see map North and South America: Political.

Caracas

MARSHALL ISLANDS
Majuro

KIRIBATI

VENEZUELA Georgetown
Bogotá Paramaribo
COLOMBIA GUYANA FRENCH GUIANA (France)
SURINAME

NAURU
Tarawa

PALMYRA ATOLL (U.S.)

Equator

GALÁPAGOS ISLANDS (Ecuador)
Quito
ECUADOR

SOUTH AMERICA

BRAZIL

SOLOMON ISLANDS
Honiara

TUVALU
Funafuti

COOK ISLANDS (New Zealand)

PERU

Lima

La Paz
BOLIVIA
Sucre

Brasília

VANUATU
Port-Vila

SAMOA
Apia AMERICAN SAMOA (U.S.)

FIJI
Suva

Nuku'alofa TONGA

FRENCH POLYNESIA (France)

NIUE (New Zealand)

PITCAIRN ISLANDS (U.K.)

PARAGUAY
Asunción

NEW CALEDONIA (France)

Tropic of Capricorn

CHILE

URUGUAY
Montevideo

NEW ZEALAND

Santiago

ARGENTINA

Buenos Aires

Wellington

PACIFIC OCEAN

FALKLAND ISLANDS (U.K.)

SOUTH GEORGIA SOUTH SANDWICH ISLAND (U.K.)

SOUTHERN OCEAN

Antarctic Circle

ANTARCTICA

0 miles 2,000
0 kilometers 2,000
Robinson

SVALBARD
(Norway)

EUROPE AND SOUTHWEST ASIA
For detail, see maps Europe: Political
and Asia: Political.

RUSSIA

Arctic Circle

ASIA

Moscow

EUROPE

KAZAKHSTAN
UZBEKISTAN
Astana
Tashkent   Bishkek

MONGOLIA

Ulaanbaatar

Beijing   NORTH
KOREA   P'yŏngyang   JAPAN
Tokyo

40° N

Algiers   Tunis
TUNISIA
Rabat   Tripoli
MOROCCO

TURKMENISTAN
Ashgabat
Tehran
IRAN   Kabul
AFGHANISTAN
Islamabad

KYRGYZSTAN
Dushanbe
TAJIKISTAN

CHINA

Seoul
SOUTH
KOREA

Cairo

Kuwait
KUWAIT
Manama   BAHRAIN
QATAR
Riyadh   Doha   U.A.E.
Abu Dhabi   Muscat

Thimphu

Taipei
TAIWAN

PACIFIC
OCEAN

Tropic of Cancer

ALGERIA   LIBYA   EGYPT

NEPAL

PAKISTAN

New Delhi

BHUTAN

Kathmandu
BANGLADESH

AFRICA

NIGER

SAUDI
ARABIA   YEMEN

OMAN

INDIA

Dhaka

MYANMAR   Hanoi

20° N

ST AFRICA
tail, see map
a: Political.

CHAD

Khartoum

ERITREA

Sanaa

SOCOTRA
(Yemen)

Yangon   Vientiane   VIETNAM
THAILAND   CAMBODIA
Bangkok
Phnom Penh

LAOS

PHILIPPINES
Manila

NORTHERN
MARIANA
ISLANDS
(U.S.)

N'Djamena   SUDAN   Asmara   DJIBOUTI

NIGERIA   Abuja
CAMEROON
Yaoundé

CENTRAL
AFRICAN
REPUBLIC

Djibouti

Addis Ababa
ETHIOPIA

ANDAMAN
& NICOBAR
ISLANDS
(India)

PALAU

GUAM
(U.S.)
Koror

Palikir

Bangui   UGANDA

Colombo   SRI LANKA

BRUNEI   Bandar Seri Begawan

FEDERATED STATES
OF MICRONESIA

Malabo

DEMOCRATIC
REPUBLIC
OF THE
CONGO

Male
MALDIVES

Kuala Lumpur
MALAYSIA
Singapore   SINGAPORE

Equator

0°

TORIAL GUINEA
São Tomé

GABON
Libreville
CONGO
Brazzaville

Kampala
Kigali   KENYA   Nairobi
RWANDA
BURUNDI
Bujumbura

Mogadishu

INDONESIA

PAPUA
NEW
GUINEA

MÉ & PRÍNCIPE

SOMALIA

TANZANIA

Dodoma

Victoria
SEYCHELLES

Jakarta

Dili

Port Moresby

CABINDA
(Angola)

Kinshasa

Dar es Salaam

EAST TIMOR

Luanda   Lilongwe
ANGOLA   MALAWI
ZAMBIA
Lusaka

COMOROS
Moroni

AUSTRALIA

MOZAMBIQUE

MADAGASCAR

Harare

Antananarivo
MAURITIUS
Port Louis

AUSTRALIA

NAMIBIA   ZIMBABWE
Windhoek   BOTSWANA
Gaborone
Pretoria   Maputo
Bloemfontein   Mbabane
Maseru   SWAZILAND
SOUTH   LESOTHO
Cape Town   AFRICA

RÉUNION
(France)

Tropic of Capricorn

20° S

LANTIC
CEAN

INDIAN
OCEAN

Canberra

40° S

SOUTHERN   OCEAN

Antarctic Circle

ANTARCTICA

80° S

0°   20° E   40° E   60° E   80° E   100° E   120° E   140° E

KEY

———   National border

- - -   Disputed border

⊛   National capital

The World: Physical

0 miles 2,000
0 kilometers 2,000
Robinson

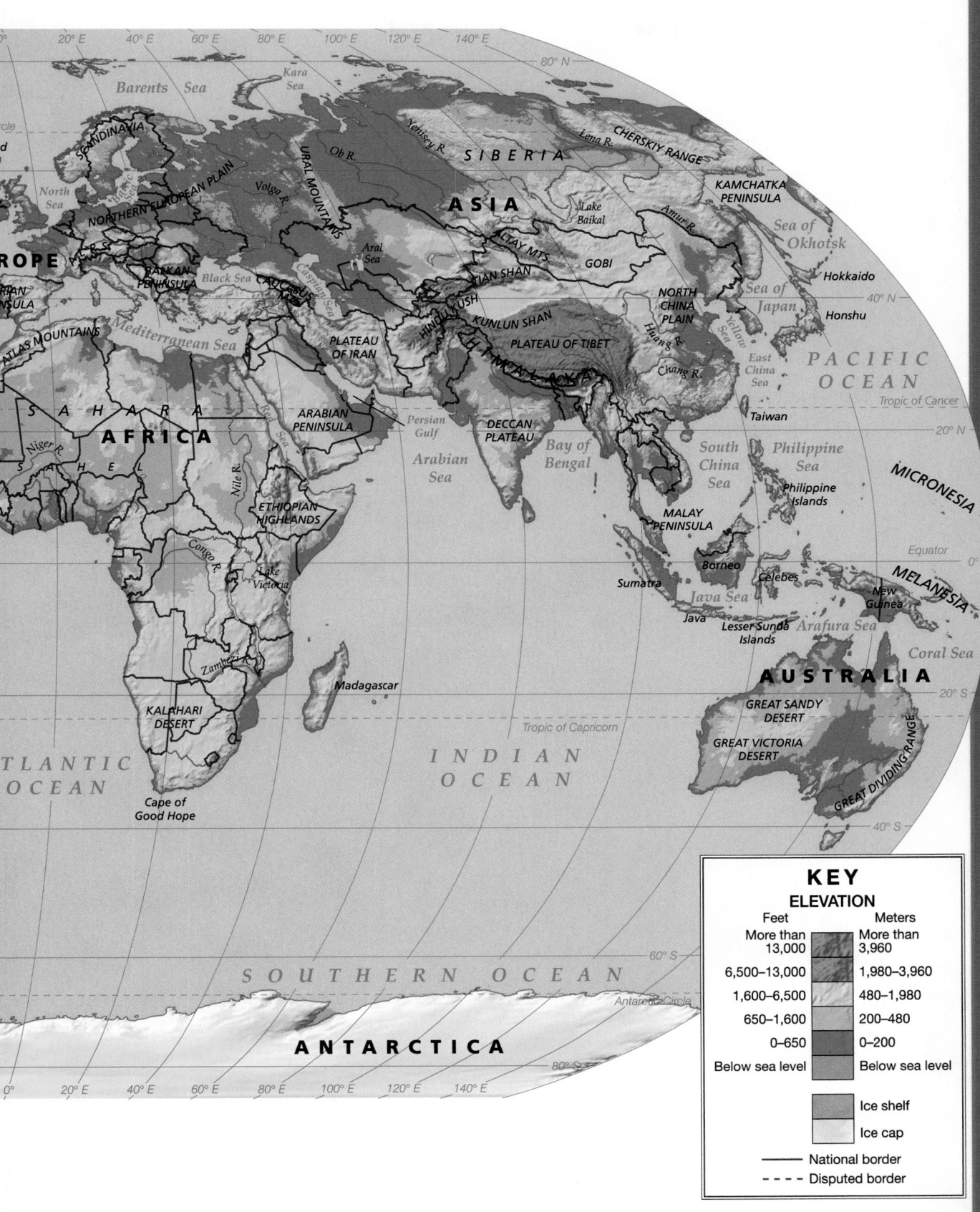

KEY

ELEVATION

Feet		Meters
More than 13,000		More than 3,960
6,500–13,000		1,980–3,960
1,600–6,500		480–1,980
650–1,600		200–480
0–650		0–200
Below sea level		Below sea level

Ice shelf

Ice cap

————— National border

– – – – – Disputed border

North and South America: Political

ASIA

Bering Strait

ARCTIC OCEAN

180°
160° W
140° W

Beaufort Sea

Bering Sea

ALASKA (U.S.)

GREENLAND (Denmark)

40° W

EUROPE

Baffin Bay

Great Bear Lake

Great Slave Lake

Labrador Sea

80° N

Hudson Bay

60° N

C A N A D A

40° N

Lake Winnipeg

Great Lakes

Ottawa

U N I T E D S T A T E S

New York City

Ohio R.

Washington, D.C.

ATLANTIC OCEAN

Los Angeles

Rio Grande

Mississippi R.

20° N

DOMINICAN REPUBLIC

VIRGIN ISLANDS (U.S.)

ST. KITTS & NEVIS

ANTIGUA & BARBUDA

Tropic of Cancer

BAHAMAS

PUERTO RICO (U.S.)

GUADELOUPE (France)

MEXICO

Havana   Nassau

DOMINICA

Gulf of Mexico

CUBA

MARTINIQUE (France)

ST. LUCIA

Mexico City

JAMAICA

HAITI

BARBADOS

PACIFIC OCEAN

Belmopan

BELIZE

Kingston

Santo Domingo

ST. VINCENT & THE GRENADINES

GUATEMALA

HONDURAS

Port-au-Prince

GRENADA

Guatemala

Tegucigalpa

Caribbean Sea

TRINIDAD & TOBAGO

San Salvador

NICARAGUA

Caracas   Georgetown

EL SALVADOR

Managua

VENEZUELA

Paramaribo

San José

Panama

GUYANA

Cayenne

COSTA RICA

Bogotá

SURINAME

FRENCH GUIANA (France)

PANAMA

COLOMBIA

0°

Equator

GALÁPAGOS ISLANDS (Ecuador)

Quito

Amazon R.

ECUADOR

PERU

B R A Z I L

São Francisco R.

N

W   E

S

Lima

Brasília

20° S

Lake Titicaca

La Paz

BOLIVIA

Rio de Janeiro

Sucre

PARAGUAY

Paraná R.

São Paulo

Tropic of Capricorn

CHILE

Asunción

URUGUAY

Santiago

Buenos Aires

Montevideo

ARGENTINA

Río de la Plata

40° S

ATLANTIC OCEAN

FALKLAND ISLANDS (U.K.)

Tierra del Fuego

Cape Horn

KEY

⎯ National border

⊛ National capital

• Other city

0 miles   2,000

0 kilometers   2,000

Lambert Azimuthal Equal Area

160° W   140° W   120° W   100° W   80° W   60° W   40° W   20° W

North and South America: Physical

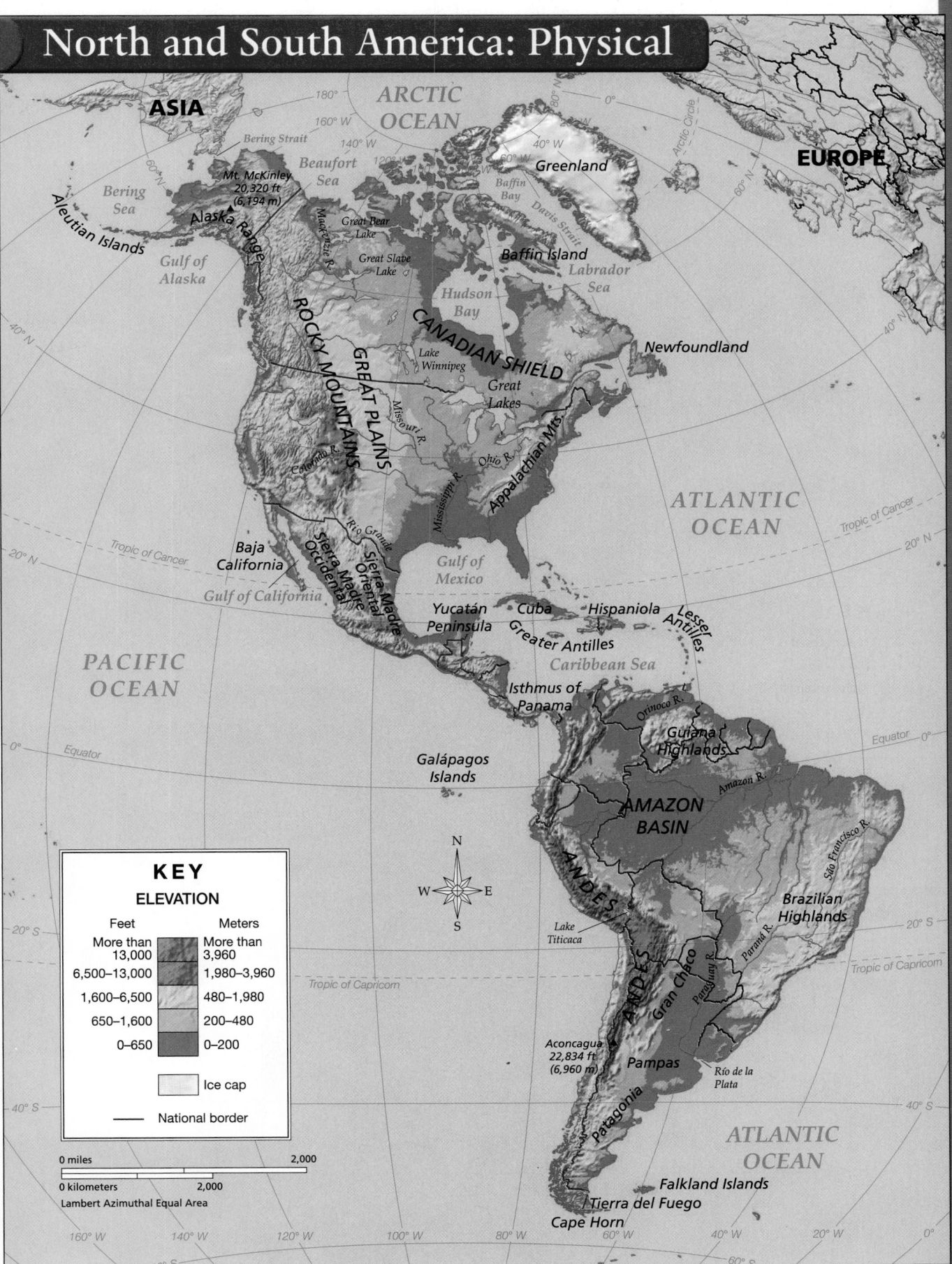

ASIA

ARCTIC OCEAN

EUROPE

Bering Strait

Beaufort Sea

Greenland

Bering Sea

Mt. McKinley 20,320 ft (6,194 m)

Alaska Range

Great Bear Lake

Baffin Bay

Davis Strait

Aleutian Islands

Gulf of Alaska

Mackenzie R.

Great Slave Lake

Baffin Island

Labrador Sea

CANADIAN SHIELD

Hudson Bay

Newfoundland

ROCKY MOUNTAINS

Lake Winnipeg

GREAT PLAINS

Missouri R.

Great Lakes

Colorado R.

Ohio R.

Appalachian Mts.

ATLANTIC OCEAN

Tropic of Cancer

Río Grande

Mississippi R.

Baja California

Sierra Madre Oriental

Sierra Madre Occidental

Gulf of California

Gulf of Mexico

Tropic of Cancer

Yucatán Peninsula

Cuba

Hispaniola

Lesser Antilles

Greater Antilles

PACIFIC OCEAN

Caribbean Sea

Isthmus of Panama

Orinoco R.

Guiana Highlands

Galápagos Islands

Equator

Equator

AMAZON BASIN

Amazon R.

ANDES

São Francisco R.

Lake Titicaca

Brazilian Highlands

KEY

ELEVATION

Feet	Meters
More than 13,000	More than 3,960
6,500–13,000	1,980–3,960
1,600–6,500	480–1,980
650–1,600	200–480
0–650	0–200

Ice cap

National border

Tropic of Capricorn

Gran Chaco

Paraguay R.

Paraná R.

Tropic of Capricorn

Aconcagua 22,834 ft (6,960 m)

Pampas

Río de la Plata

Patagonia

ATLANTIC OCEAN

0 miles 2,000

0 kilometers 2,000

Lambert Azimuthal Equal Area

Falkland Islands

Tierra del Fuego

Cape Horn

N W E S

United States: Political

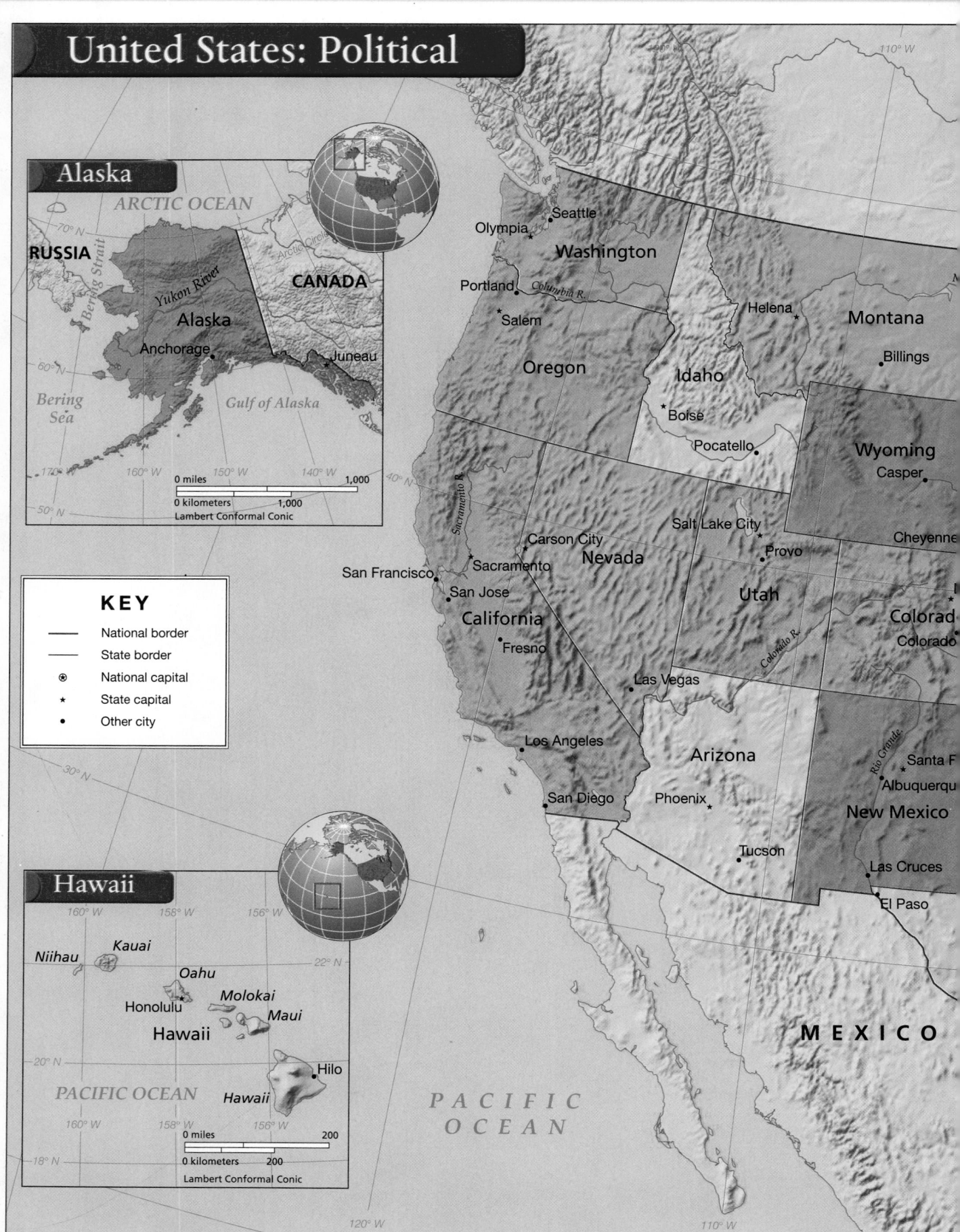

Alaska

ARCTIC OCEAN

RUSSIA

CANADA

Yukon River

Bering Strait

Arctic Circle

70° N

Alaska

Anchorage

Juneau

60° N

Bering Sea

Gulf of Alaska

170° W   160° W   150° W   140° W

50° N

0 miles   1,000
0 kilometers   1,000
Lambert Conformal Conic

KEY

— National border

— State border

⊛ National capital

★ State capital

• Other city

Hawaii

160° W   158° W   156° W

Niihau   Kauai

Oahu   22° N

Honolulu   Molokai

Maui

Hawaii

20° N

Hilo

PACIFIC OCEAN   Hawaii   18° N

160° W   158° W   156° W

0 miles   200
0 kilometers   200
Lambert Conformal Conic

Seattle
Olympia
Washington
Portland   Columbia R.
Salem   Helena   Montana
Oregon   Idaho   Billings
Boise
Pocatello   Wyoming
Casper
Salt Lake City   Cheyenne
Carson City   Provo
San Francisco   Sacramento   Nevada
San Jose   Utah   Colorad
California   Colorado R.   Colorado
Fresno
Las Vegas
Los Angeles   Arizona   Rio Grande   Santa F
San Diego   Phoenix   Albuquerqu
Tucson   New Mexico
Las Cruces
El Paso

MEXICO

PACIFIC OCEAN

110° W   40° N   30° N   120° W   110° W

CANADA

North Dakota
· Bismarck
· Fargo

South Dakota
· Pierre
· Sioux Falls

Minnesota
Minneapolis ·
· St. Paul

Wisconsin
Milwaukee ·
Madison ·

Lake Superior

Michigan
Grand Rapids ·
Lansing ·
Lake Huron

Lake Michigan

Nebraska
· Omaha
· Lincoln
Missouri R.

Iowa
Des Moines ·
Cedar Rapids ·

Illinois
· Chicago

Fort Wayne ·

Indiana
· Indianapolis
Springfield ·

Detroit ·
Lake Erie

Ohio
Cleveland ·
Pittsburgh ·
Columbus ·

Cincinnati ·
Ohio R.

Lake Ontario

New York
· Buffalo

Albany ·

Pennsylvania
Harrisburg ·

Vermont
Montpelier ·

Maine
· Augusta
Portland

New Hampshire
· Concord

Boston
Massachusetts
Providence ·
Hartford ·
Connecticut
Rhode Island

New York City ·

New Jersey
· Trenton
Philadelphia ·

Kansas
· Topeka
· Wichita
Arkansas R.

Kansas City ·
Jefferson City ·
St. Louis ·

Missouri

Louisville ·

Frankfort ·

Kentucky

West
Virginia
Charleston ·

Baltimore ·
Washington, D.C.
Richmond ·

Dover ·
Delaware
Annapolis ·
Maryland
District of Columbia
Norfolk ·

Virginia

Oklahoma
· Tulsa
Oklahoma City ·

Arkansas
Fort Smith ·
Little Rock ·
Mississippi R.
Memphis ·

Nashville ·
Tennessee

Knoxville ·

Tennessee R.

North Carolina
· Raleigh
· Charlotte

South Carolina
· Columbia
Charleston ·

ATLANTIC
OCEAN

Texas
· Dallas
Fort Worth ·

Red R.

Shreveport ·
Louisiana

Mississippi
Jackson ·

Birmingham ·

Alabama
Montgomery ·

Atlanta ·

Columbus ·
Georgia

Savannah ·

· Austin
· San Antonio
Houston ·

Baton Rouge ·
Gulfport ·
New Orleans

Mobile ·

Tallahassee ·

Jacksonville ·

Florida
Orlando ·
Tampa ·

Gulf of Mexico

N
W · E
S

Miami ·

0 miles   250
0 kilometers   250
Lambert Azimuthal Equal Area

50° N
40° N
30° N
100° W   90° W   80° W   70° W

Africa: Political

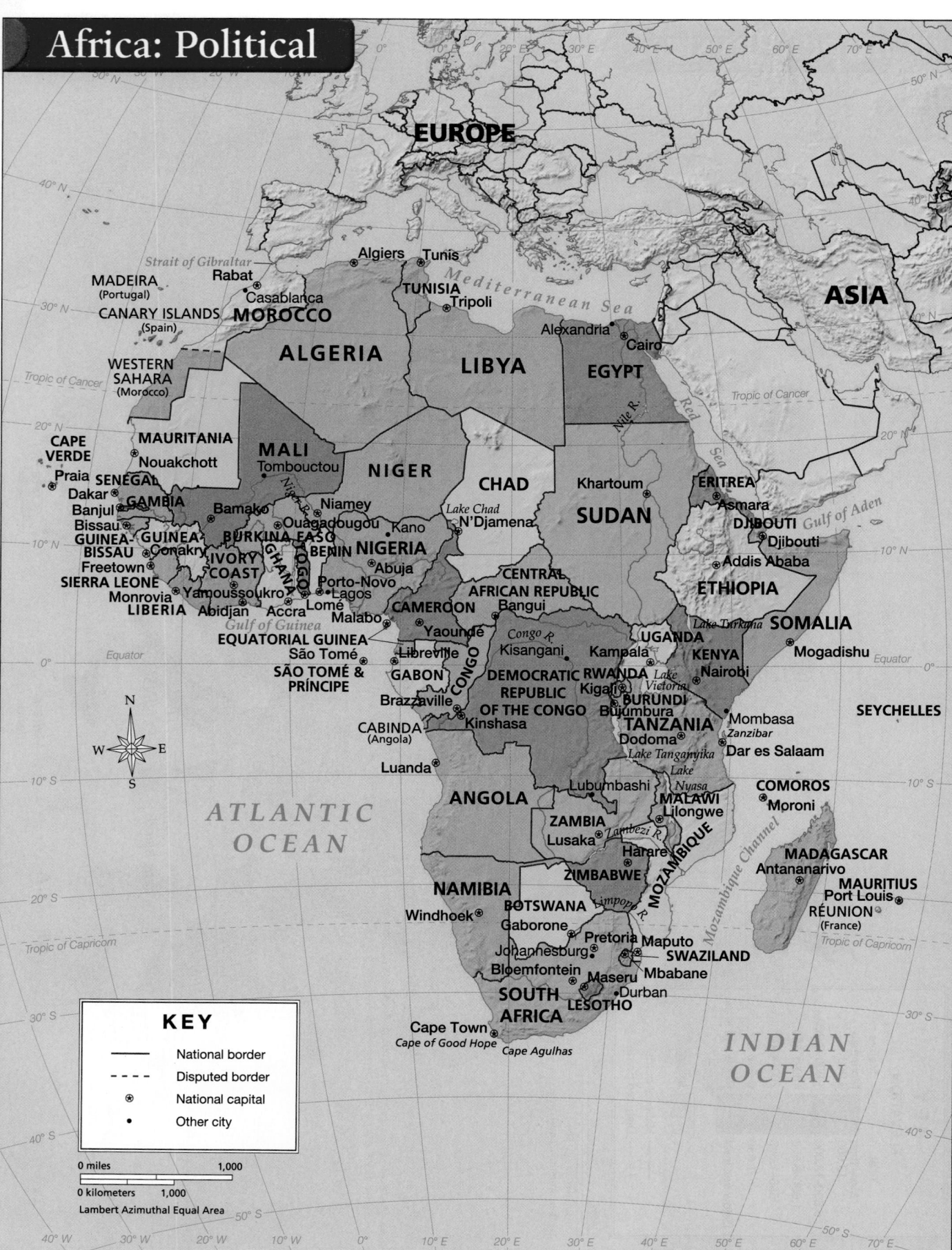

EUROPE

ASIA

Strait of Gibraltar

MADEIRA (Portugal)

CANARY ISLANDS (Spain)

Algiers • Tunis

Rabat •

Mediterranean Sea

Casablanca •

TUNISIA

MOROCCO

• Tripoli

Alexandria ⊗

• Cairo

WESTERN SAHARA (Morocco)

ALGERIA

LIBYA

EGYPT

Tropic of Cancer

Nile R.

Red Sea

Tropic of Cancer

CAPE VERDE

MAURITANIA

Nouakchott ⊗

MALI

Tombouctou •

NIGER

CHAD

Khartoum ⊗

ERITREA

Asmara ⊗

Praia ⊗

SENEGAL

Dakar ⊗

GAMBIA

Bamako ⊗

Niamey ⊗

Lake Chad

N'Djamena •

SUDAN

DJIBOUTI

Gulf of Aden

Banjul ⊗

Niger R.

Ouagadougou ⊗

Kano •

• Djibouti

Bissau ⊗

GUINEA-

Conakry ⊗

BURKINA FASO

NIGERIA

Addis Ababa •

BISSAU

GUINEA

IVORY COAST

GHANA

BENIN

Abuja ⊗

CENTRAL AFRICAN REPUBLIC

ETHIOPIA

Freetown ⊗

SIERRA LEONE

Yamoussoukro ⊗

Porto-Novo ⊗

Bangui ⊗

SOMALIA

Monrovia ⊗

LIBERIA

Abidjan •

Accra ⊗

Lomé ⊗

Lagos •

CAMEROON

Lake Turkana

Mogadishu ⊗

Equator

Gulf of Guinea

Malabo ⊗

Yaoundé ⊗

Congo R.

UGANDA

Equator

EQUATORIAL GUINEA

Libreville ⊗

Kisangani •

Kampala ⊗

KENYA

SÃO TOMÉ & PRÍNCIPE

São Tomé ⊗

GABON

CONGO

DEMOCRATIC REPUBLIC OF THE CONGO

RWANDA

Kigali ⊗

Lake Victoria

Nairobi ⊗

Brazzaville ⊗

BURUNDI

Bujumbura ⊗

Mombasa •

SEYCHELLES

CABINDA (Angola)

Kinshasa ⊗

TANZANIA

Dodoma ⊗

Zanzibar

Dar es Salaam •

Luanda ⊗

Lake Tanganyika

10° S

ANGOLA

Lubumbashi •

Lake Nyasa

MALAWI

Lilongwe ⊗

COMOROS

Moroni ⊗

10° S

ZAMBIA

Lusaka ⊗

Zambezi R.

ATLANTIC OCEAN

Harare ⊗

MOZAMBIQUE

Mozambique Channel

MADAGASCAR

Antananarivo ⊗

NAMIBIA

BOTSWANA

ZIMBABWE

MAURITIUS

Port Louis ⊗

RÉUNION (France)

Windhoek ⊗

Gaborone ⊗

Limpopo R.

Tropic of Capricorn

Tropic of Capricorn

Pretoria ⊗

Maputo ⊗

SWAZILAND

Johannesburg •

Mbabane ⊗

Bloemfontein ⊗

Maseru ⊗

INDIAN OCEAN

SOUTH AFRICA

LESOTHO

• Durban

Cape Town ⊗

Cape of Good Hope

Cape Agulhas

KEY

—— National border

- - - Disputed border

⊗ National capital

• Other city

0 miles   1,000

0 kilometers 1,000

Lambert Azimuthal Equal Area

Africa: Physical

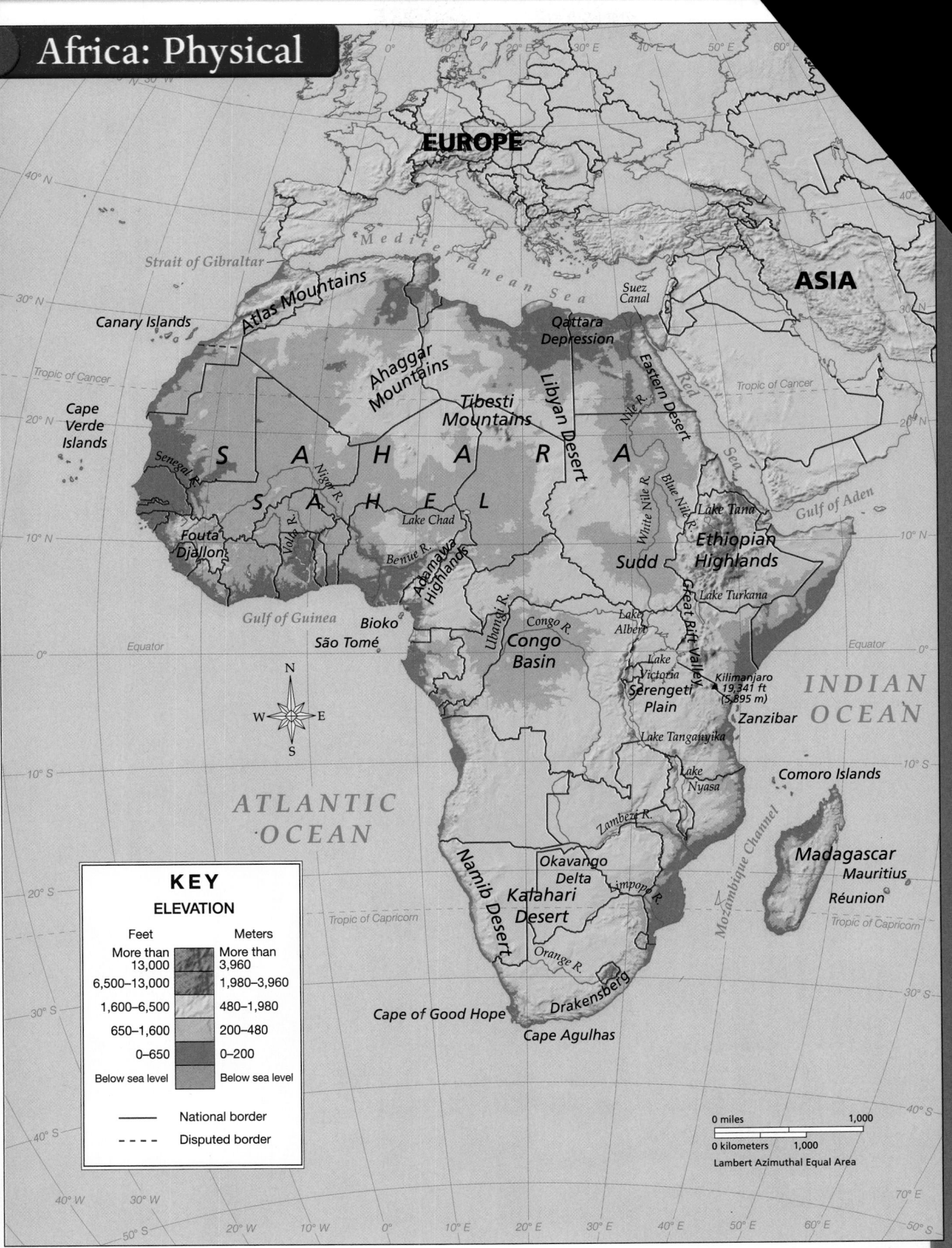

EUROPE

ASIA

Strait of Gibraltar

Canary Islands

Atlas Mountains

Tropic of Cancer

Cape Verde Islands

Ahaggar Mountains

Tibesti Mountains

Libyan Desert

Qattara Depression

Eastern Desert

Suez Canal

Nile R.

Red Sea

Tropic of Cancer

S A H A R A

Senegal R.

Niger R.

Volta R.

Lake Chad

Benue R.

Adamawa Highlands

S A H E L

White Nile R.

Blue Nile R.

Lake Tana

Gulf of Aden

Fouta Djallon

Sudd

Ethiopian Highlands

Gulf of Guinea

Bioko

São Tomé

Ubangi R.

Congo R.

Congo Basin

Lake Albert

Lake Turkana

Great Rift Valley

Equator

Lake Victoria

Serengeti Plain

Kilimanjaro 19,341 ft (5,895 m)

Zanzibar

INDIAN OCEAN

Equator

Lake Tanganyika

ATLANTIC OCEAN

Lake Nyasa

Comoro Islands

Zambezi R.

Mozambique Channel

Madagascar

Mauritius

Réunion

Namib Desert

Okavango Delta

Kalahari Desert

Limpopo R.

Tropic of Capricorn

Orange R.

Drakensberg

Tropic of Capricorn

Cape of Good Hope

Cape Agulhas

KEY

ELEVATION

Feet		Meters
More than 13,000		More than 3,960
6,500–13,000		1,980–3,960
1,600–6,500		480–1,980
650–1,600		200–480
0–650		0–200
Below sea level		Below sea level

———— National border

– – – – Disputed border

N
W E
S

0 miles 1,000

0 kilometers 1,000

Lambert Azimuthal Equal Area

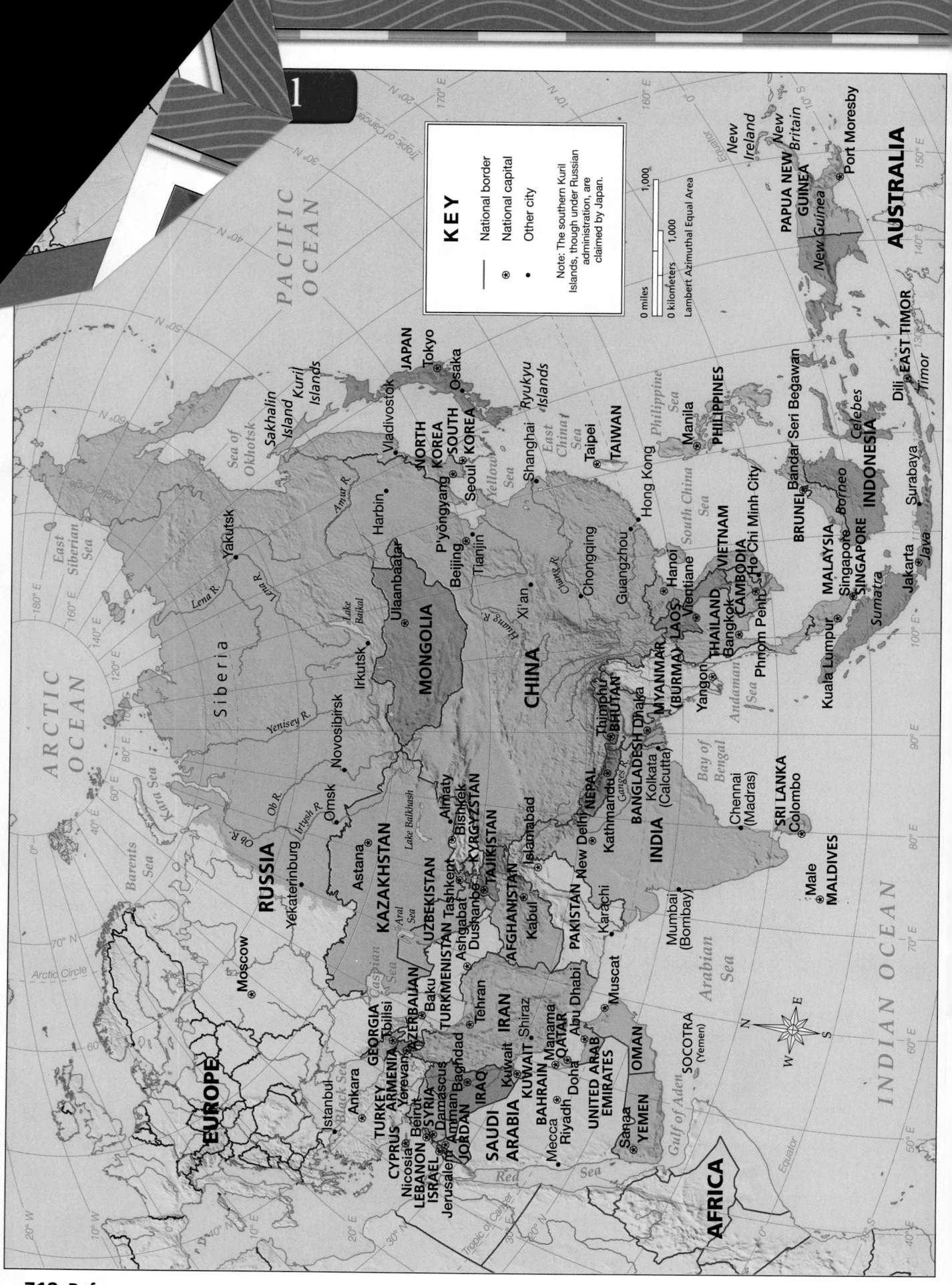

KEY

National border
⊛ National capital
• Other city

Note: The southern Kuril
Islands, though under Russian
administration, are
claimed by Japan.

0 miles   1,000
0 kilometers   1,000
Lambert Azimuthal Equal Area

Asia: Physical

KEY

ELEVATION

Feet	Meters
More than 13,000	More than 3,960
6,500–13,000	1,980–3,960
1,600–6,500	480–1,980
650–1,600	200–480
0–650	0–200
Below sea level	Below sea level

—— National border

PACIFIC OCEAN

ARCTIC OCEAN

INDIAN OCEAN

EUROPE

AFRICA

New Ireland
New Britain
New Guinea
Moluccas
Celebes
Lesser Sunda Islands
Timor
Borneo
Java
Sumatra
Malay Peninsula
Mindanao
Luzon
Philippine Sea
Taiwan
Hainan
South China Sea
East China Sea
Yellow Sea
Korean Peninsula
North China Plain
Sea of Japan
Honshū
Shikoku
Kyūshū
Ryukyu Islands
Hokkaidō
Kuril Islands
Sakhalin Island
Kamchatka Peninsula
Sea of Okhotsk
Kolyma Mts.
Cherskiy Range
Stanovoy Range
Amur R.
Lena R.
Lake Baikal
Mongolian Plateau
GOBI
Altay Mts.
North Siberian Lowland
Central Siberian Plateau
Yenisey R.
Ob R.
Irtysh R.
Lake Balkhash
Aral Sea
Kara-Kum Desert
Tian Shan
Taklimakan Desert
Kunlun Shan
Tibetan Plateau
Mt. Everest 29,035 ft (8,850 m)
HIMALAYA
Hindu Kush
Thar Desert
Ganges R.
Indus R.
INDIAN PENINSULA
Deccan Plateau
Western Ghats
Eastern Ghats
Sri Lanka
Bay of Bengal
Andaman Islands
Andaman Sea
Strait of Malacca
Irrawaddy R.
Indochina Peninsula
Mekong R.
Chang R.
Huang R.
URAL MOUNTAINS
Ob R.
Kara Sea
Barents Sea
Arctic Circle
CAUCASUS MTS.
Black Sea
Plateau of Anatolia
Cyprus
Mediterranean Sea
Tigris R.
Euphrates R.
Caspian Sea
Plateau of Iran
Persian Gulf
ARABIAN PENINSULA
Rub' al-Khali Desert
Arabian Sea
Gulf of Aden
Socotra
Red Sea
East Siberian Sea

Tropic of Cancer
Tropic of Cancer
Equator
Arctic Circle

1,000
1,000
0 miles
0 kilometers
Lambert Azimuthal Equal Area

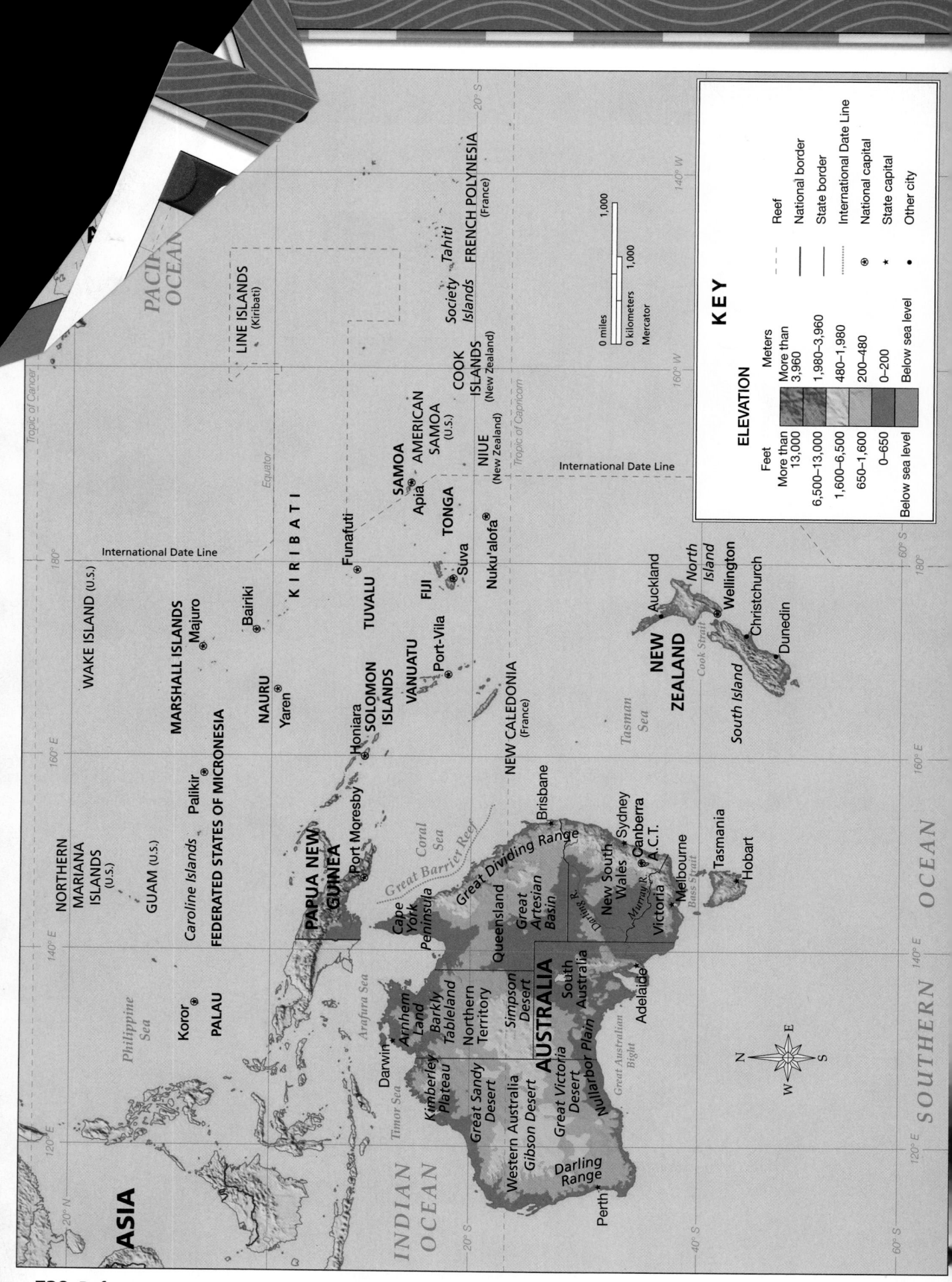

ASIA

INDIAN
OCEAN

PACIFIC
OCEAN

Tropic of Cancer

20° N

*Philippine
Sea*

NORTHERN
MARIANA
ISLANDS
(U.S.)

GUAM (U.S.)

Koror ⊛
PALAU

Equator

*Timor
Sea*

Arafura Sea

Caroline Islands   Palikir ⊛
FEDERATED STATES OF MICRONESIA

WAKE ISLAND (U.S.)

180°
International Date Line

MARSHALL
ISLANDS
Majuro
⊛

Bairiki
⊛

K I R I B A T I

LINE ISLANDS
(Kiribati)

FRENCH POLYNESIA
(France)

Tahiti

*Society
Islands*

COOK
ISLANDS
(New Zealand)

NIUE
(New Zealand)

SAMOA
Apia ⊛
AMERICAN
SAMOA
(U.S.)

TONGA
Nuku'alofa ⊛

Funafuti ⊛
TUVALU

NAURU
Yaren ⊛

SOLOMON
ISLANDS
Honiara ⊛

VANUATU
Port-Vila ⊛

FIJI
Suva ⊛

PAPUA NEW
GUINEA
Port Moresby ⊛

*Great Coral
Sea*

Great Barrier Reef

Cape
York
Peninsula

Darwin ★
Arnhem
Land

Kimberley
Plateau

Barkly
Tableland

Northern
Territory

Queensland

Great
Artesian
Basin

Brisbane

Great Dividing Range

Sydney
Canberra
A.C.T.
New South
Wales
Melbourne
Victoria ★
Murray R.
Darling R.

NEW CALEDONIA
(France)

*Tasman
Sea*

NEW
ZEALAND

*North
Island*

Auckland
Wellington
Christchurch
Cook Strait
South Island
Dunedin

Tasmania
Hobart
Bass Strait

Western Australia
Gibson Desert

Great Sandy
Desert

Simpson
Desert

South
Australia

AUSTRALIA

Great Victoria
Desert

Nullarbor Plain
*Great Australian
Bight*

Adelaide ★

Darling
Range

Perth ★

N
W   E
S

SOUTHERN   OCEAN

Tropic of Capricorn

International Date Line

20° S

40° S

60° S

120° E

140° E

160° E

180°

160° W

140° W

20° S

40° S

120° E   140° E   160° E

KEY

ELEVATION

Feet	Meters
More than 13,000	More than 3,960
6,500–13,000	1,980–3,960
1,600–6,500	480–1,980
650–1,600	200–480
0–650	0–200
Below sea level	Below sea level

– – – Reef
—— National border
—— State border
······ International Date Line
⊛ National capital
★ State capital
• Other city

0 miles   1,000
0 kilometers   1,000
Mercator

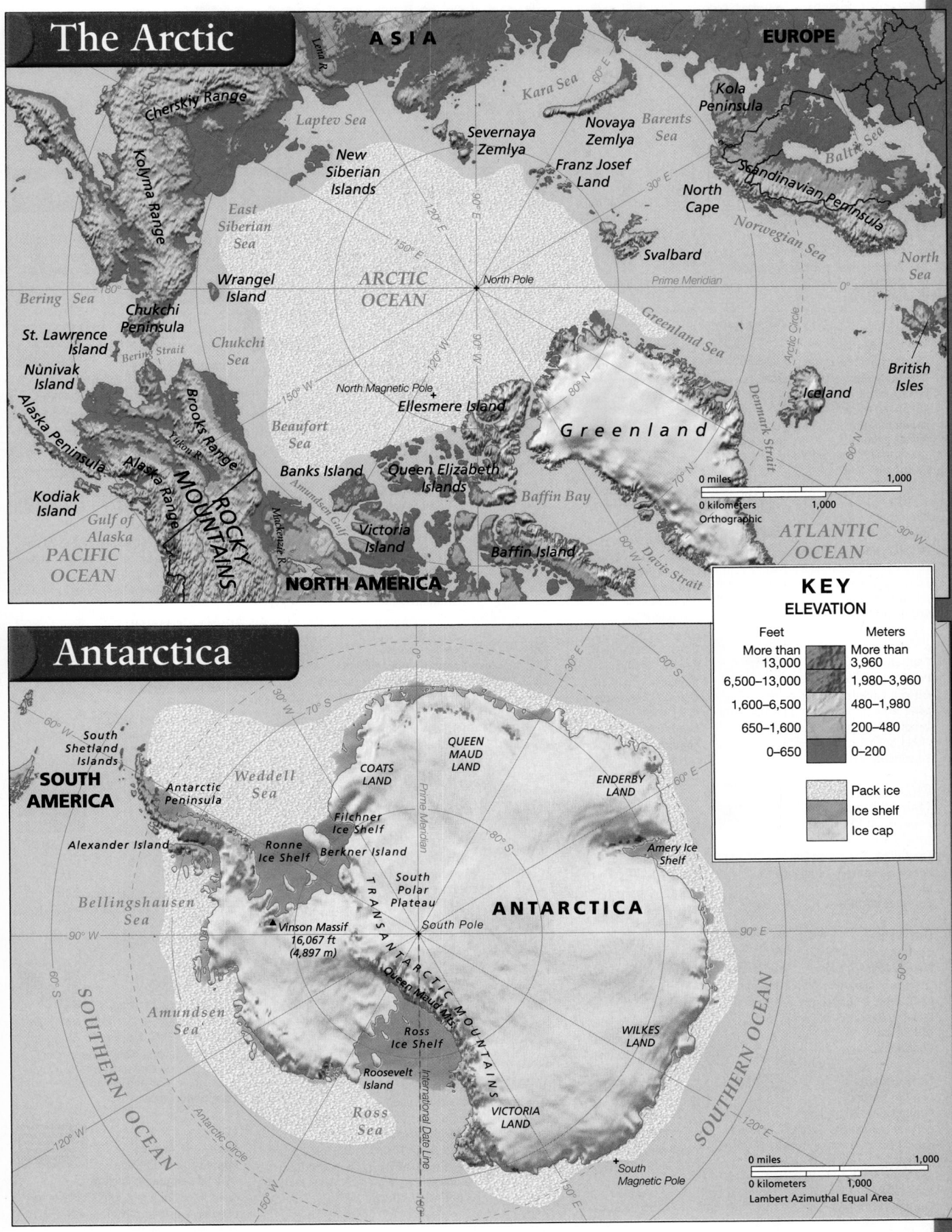

The Arctic

ASIA
EUROPE

Lena R.
Cherskiy Range
Laptev Sea
Kara Sea
Severnaya Zemlya
Novaya Zemlya
Barents Sea
Kola Peninsula
Baltic Sea
New Siberian Islands
Franz Josef Land
North Cape
Scandinavian Peninsula
Kolyma Range
East Siberian Sea
ARCTIC OCEAN
North Pole
Svalbard
Norwegian Sea
Prime Meridian
North Sea
Wrangel Island
Greenland Sea
Bering Sea
Chukchi Peninsula
Chukchi Sea
Arctic Circle
Iceland
British Isles
St. Lawrence Island
North Magnetic Pole
Ellesmere Island
Denmark Strait
Nunivak Island
Beaufort Sea
Greenland
Brooks Range
Yukon R.
Alaska Peninsula
Alaska Range
ROCKY MOUNTAINS
Banks Island
Queen Elizabeth Islands
Baffin Bay
0 miles 1,000
0 kilometers 1,000
Orthographic
ATLANTIC OCEAN
Kodiak Island
Gulf of Alaska
Mackenzie R.
Amundsen Gulf
Victoria Island
Baffin Island
Davis Strait
PACIFIC OCEAN
NORTH AMERICA
Bering Strait

Antarctica

KEY
ELEVATION

Feet		Meters
More than 13,000		More than 3,960
6,500–13,000		1,980–3,960
1,600–6,500		480–1,980
650–1,600		200–480
0–650		0–200

Pack ice
Ice shelf
Ice cap

South Shetland Islands
SOUTH AMERICA
Antarctic Peninsula
Weddell Sea
COATS LAND
QUEEN MAUD LAND
ENDERBY LAND
Filchner Ice Shelf
Prime Meridian
Alexander Island
Ronne Ice Shelf
Berkner Island
Amery Ice Shelf
Bellingshausen Sea
South Polar Plateau
ANTARCTICA
▲ Vinson Massif 16,067 ft (4,897 m)
South Pole
TRANSANTARCTIC MOUNTAINS
SOUTHERN OCEAN
Amundsen Sea
Queen Maud Mts.
WILKES LAND
Ross Ice Shelf
Roosevelt Island
International Date Line
VICTORIA LAND
Ross Sea
Antarctic Circle
South Magnetic Pole
SOUTHERN OCEAN
0 miles 1,000
0 kilometers 1,000
Lambert Azimuthal Equal Area

Country Databank

Africa

Algeria
Capital: Algiers
Population: 32.3 million
Official Languages: Arabic and Tamazight
Land Area: 2,381,740 sq km; 919,590 sq mi
Leading Exports: petroleum, natural gas, petroleum products
Continent: Africa

Angola
Capital: Luanda
Population: 10.6 million
Official Language: Portuguese
Land Area: 1,246,700 sq km; 481,551 sq mi
Leading Exports: crude oil, diamonds, refined petroleum products, gas, coffee, sisal, fish and fish products, timber, cotton
Continent: Africa

Benin
Capital: Porto-Novo
Population: 6.9 million
Official Language: French
Land Area: 110,620 sq km; 42,710 sq mi
Leading Exports: cotton, crude oil, palm products, cocoa
Continent: Africa

Botswana
Capital: Gaborone
Population: 1.6 million
Official Language: English
Land Area: 585,370 sq km; 226,011 sq mi
Leading Exports: diamonds, copper, nickel, soda ash, meat, textiles
Continent: Africa

Burkina Faso
Capital: Ouagadougou
Population: 12.6 million
Official Language: French
Land Area: 273,800 sq km; 105,714 sq mi
Leading Exports: cotton, animal products, gold
Continent: Africa

Burundi
Capital: Bujumbura
Population: 6.4 million
Official Languages: Kirundi and French
Land Area: 25,650 sq km; 9,903 sq mi
Leading Exports: coffee, tea, sugar, cotton, hides
Continent: Africa

Cameroon
Capital: Yaoundé
Population: 16.1 million
Official Languages: English and French
Land Area: 469,440 sq km; 181,251 sqmi
Leading Exports: crude oil and petroleum products, lumber, cocoa, aluminum, coffee, cotton
Continent: Africa

Cape Verde
Capital: Praia
Population: 408,760
Official Language: Portuguese
Land Area: 4,033 sq km; 1,557 sq mi
Leading Exports: fuel, shoes, garments, fish, hides
Location: Atlantic Ocean

Central African Republic
Capital: Bangui
Population: 3.6 million
Official Language: French
Land Area: 622,984 sq km; 240,534 sq mi
Leading Exports: diamonds, timber, cotton, coffee, tobacco
Continent: Africa

Chad
Capital: N'Djamena
Population: 9 million
Official Languages: Arabic and French
Land Area: 1,259,200 sq km; 486,177 sq mi
Leading Exports: cotton, cattle, gum arabic
Continent: Africa

Comoros
Capital: Moroni
Population: 614,382
Official Languages: Arabic, Comoran, and French
Land Area: 2,170 sq km; 838 sq mi
Leading Exports: vanilla, ylang-ylang, cloves, perfume oil, copra
Location: Indian Ocean

Congo, Democratic Republic of the
Capital: Kinshasa
Population: 55.2 million
Official Language: French
Land Area: 2,267,600 sq km; 875,520 sq mi
Leading Exports: diamonds, copper, coffee, cobalt, crude oil
Continent: Africa

Congo, Republic of the
Capital: Brazzaville
Population: 3.3 million
Official Language: French
Land Area: 341,500 sq km; 131,853 sq mi
Leading Exports: petroleum, lumber, sugar, cocoa, coffee, diamonds
Continent: Africa

Djibouti
Capital: Djibouti
Population: 472,810
Official Languages: Arabic and French
Land Area: 22,980 sq km; 8,873 sq mi
Leading Exports: reexports, hides and skins, coffee (in transit)
Continent: Africa

Egypt
Capital: Cairo
Population: 70.7 million
Official Language: Arabic
Land Area: 995,450 sq km; 384,343 sq mi
Leading Exports: crude oil and petroleum products, cotton, textiles, metal products, chemicals
Continent: Africa

Equatorial Guinea
Capital: Malabo
Population: 498,144
Official Languages: Spanish and French
Land Area: 28,050 sq km; 10,830 sq mi
Leading Exports: petroleum, timber, cocoa
Continent: Africa

Eritrea
Capital: Asmara
Population: 4.5 million
Official Language: Tigrinya
Land Area: 121,320 sq km; 46,842 sq mi
Leading Exports: livestock, sorghum, textiles, food, small manufactured goods
Continent: Africa

Ethiopia
Capital: Addis Ababa
Population: 67.7 million
Official Language: Amharic
Land Area: 1,119,683 sq km; 432,310 sq mi
Leading Exports: coffee, qat, gold, leather products, oilseeds
Continent: Africa

Gabon
Capital: Libreville
Population: 1.2 million
Official Language: French
Land Area: 257,667 sq km; 99,489 sq mi
Leading Exports: crude oil, timber, manganese, uranium
Continent: Africa

Gambia
Capital: Banjul
Population: 1.5 million
Official Language: English
Land Area: 10,000 sq km; 3,861 sq mi
Leading Exports: peanuts and peanut products, fish, cotton lint, palm kernels
Continent: Africa

Ghana
Capital: Accra
Population: 20.2 million
Official Language: English
Land Area: 230,940 sq km; 89,166 sq mi
Leading Exports: gold, cocoa, timber, tuna, bauxite, aluminum, manganese ore, diamonds
Continent: Africa

Guinea
Capital: Conakry
Population: 7.8 million
Official Language: French
Land Area: 245,857 sq km; 94,925 sq mi
Leading Exports: bauxite, alumina, gold, diamonds, coffee, fish, agricultural products
Continent: Africa

Guinea-Bissau
Capital: Bissau
Population: 1.4 million
Official Language: Portuguese
Land Area: 28,000 sq km; 10,811 sq mi
Leading Exports: cashew nuts, shrimp, peanuts, palm kernels, lumber
Continent: Africa

Ivory Coast
Capital: Yamoussoukro
Population: 16.8 million
Official Language: French
Land Area: 318,000 sq km; 122,780 sq mi
Leading Exports: cocoa, coffee, timber, petroleum, cotton, bananas, pineapples, palm oil, cotton, fish
Continent: Africa

Kenya
Capital: Nairobi
Population: 31.3 million
Official Languages: Swahili and English
Land Area: 569,250 sq km; 219,787 sq mi
Leading Exports: tea, horticultural products, coffee, petroleum products, fish, cement
Continent: Africa

Lesotho
Capital: Maseru
Population: 2.2 million
Official Languages: Sesotho and English
Land Area: 30,355 sq km; 11,720 sq mi
Leading Exports: manufactured goods (clothing, footwear, road vehicles), wool and mohair, food and live animals
Continent: Africa

Liberia
Capital: Monrovia
Population: 3.3 million
Official Language: English
Land Area: 96,320 sq km; 37,189 sq mi
Leading Exports: rubber, timber, iron, diamonds, cocoa, coffee
Continent: Africa

Libya
Capital: Tripoli
Population: 5.4 million
Official Language: Arabic
Land Area: 1,759,540 sq km; 679,358 sq mi
Leading Exports: crude oil, refined petroleum products
Location: Indian

Madagascar
Capital: Antananarivo
Population: 16.5 million
Official Languages: French and Malagasy
Land Area: 581,540 sq km; 224,533 sq mi
Leading Exports: coffee, vanilla, shellfish, sugar, cotton cloth, chromite, petroleum products
Location: Indian Ocean

Malawi
Capital: Lilongwe
Population: 10.7 million
Official Languages: English and Chichewa
Land Area: 94,080 sq km; 36,324 sq mi
Leading Exports: tobacco, tea, sugar, cotton, coffee, peanuts, wood products, apparel
Continent: Africa

Mali
Capital: Bamako
Population: 11.3 million
Official Language: French
Land Area: 1,220,000 sq km; 471,042 sq mi
Leading Exports: cotton, gold, livestock
Continent: Africa

Mauritania
Capital: Nouakchott
Population: 2.8 million
Official Language: Arabic
Land Area: 1,030,400 sq km; 397,837 sq mi
Leading Exports: iron ore, fish and fish products, gold
Continent: Africa

Mauritius
Capital: Port Louis
Population: 1.2 million
Official Language: English
Land Area: 2,030 sq km; 784 sq mi
Leading Exports: clothing and textiles, sugar, cut flowers, molasses
Location: Indian Ocean

Morocco
Capital: Rabat
Population: 31.2 million
Official Language: Arabic
Land Area: 446,300 sq km; 172,316 sq mi
Leading Exports: phosphates and fertilizers, food and beverages, minerals
Continent: Africa

Mozambique
Capital: Maputo
Population: 19.6 million
Official Language: Portuguese
Land Area: 784,090 sq km; 302,737 sq mi
Leading Exports: prawns, cashews, cotton, sugar, citrus, timber, bulk electricity
Continent: Africa

Namibia
Capital: Windhoek
Population: 1.8 million
Official Language: English
Land Area: 825,418 sq km; 318,694 sq mi
Leading Exports: diamonds, copper, gold, zinc, lead, uranium, cattle, processed fish, karakul skins
Continent: Africa

Niger
Capital: Niamey
Population: 11.3 million
Official Language: French
Land Area: 1,226,700 sq km; 489,073 sq mi
Leading Exports: uranium ore, livestock products, cowpeas, onions
Continent: Africa

Nigeria
Capital: Abuja
Population: 129.9 million
Official Language: English
Land Area: 910,768 sq km; 351,648 sq mi
Leading Exports: petroleum and petroleum products, cocoa, rubber
Continent: Africa

Rwanda
Capital: Kigali
Population: 7.4 million
Official Languages: Kinyarwanda, French, and English
Land Area: 24,948 sq km; 9,632 sq mi
Leading Exports: coffee, tea, hides, tin ore
Continent: Africa

São Tomé and Príncipe
Capital: São Tomé
Population: 170,372
Official Language: Portuguese
Land Area: 1,001 sq km; 386 sq mi
Leading Exports: cocoa, copra, coffee, palm oil
Location: Atlantic Ocean

Senegal
Capital: Dakar
Population: 10.6 million
Official Language: French
Land Area: 192,000 sq km; 74,131 sq mi
Leading Exports: fish, groundnuts (peanuts), petroleum products, phosphates, cotton
Continent: Africa

Seychelles
Capital: Victoria
Population: 80,098
Official Languages: English and French
Land Area: 455 sq km; 176 sq mi
Leading Exports: canned tuna, cinnamon bark, copra, petroleum products (reexports)
Location: Indian Ocean

Sierra Leone
Capital: Freetown
Population: 5.6 million
Official Language: English
Land Area: 71,620 sq km; 27,652 sq mi
Leading Exports: diamonds, rutile, cocoa, coffee, fish
Continent: Africa

Somalia
Capital: Mogadishu
Population: 7.8 million
Official Languages: Somali and Arabic
Land Area: 627,337 sq km; 242,215 sq mi
Leading Exports: livestock, bananas, hides, fish, charcoal, scrap metal
Continent: Africa

South Africa
Capital: Cape Town, Pretoria, and Bloemfontein
Population: 43.6 million
Official Languages: Eleven official languages: Afrikaans, English, Ndebele, Pedi, Sotho, Swazi, Tsonga, Tswana, Venda, Xhosa, and Zulu
Land Area: 1,219,912 sq km; 471,008 sq mi
Leading Exports: gold, diamonds, platinum, other metals and minerals, machinery and equipment
Continent: Africa

Sudan
Capital: Khartoum
Population: 37.1 million
Official Language: Arabic
Land Area: 2,376,000 sq km; 917,374 sq mi
Leading Exports: oil and petroleum products, cotton, sesame, livestock, groundnuts, gum arabic, sugar
Continent: Africa

Swaziland
Capital: Mbabane
Population: 1.1 million
Official Languages: English and siSwati
Land Area: 17,20 sq km; 6,642 sq mi
Leading Exports: soft drink concentrates, sugar, wood pulp, cotton yarn, refrigerators, citrus and canned fruit
Continent: Africa

Tanzania
Capital: Dar es Salaam and Dodoma
Population: 37.2 million
Official Languages: Swahili and English
Land Area: 886,037 sq km; 342,099 sq mi
Leading Exports: gold, coffee, cashew nuts, manufactured goods, cotton
Continent: Africa

Togo
Capital: Lomé
Population: 5.2 million
Official Language: French
Land Area: 54,385 sq km; 20,998 sq mi
Leading Exports: cotton, phosphates, coffee, cocoa
Continent: Africa

Tunisia

Capital: Tunis
Population: 9.8 million
Official Language: Arabic
Land Area: 155,360 sq km; 59,984 sq mi
Leading Exports: textiles, mechanical goods, phosphates and chemicals, agricultural products, hydrocarbons
Continent: Africa

Uganda
Capital: Kampala
Population: 24.7 million
Official Language: English
Land Area: 199,710 sq km; 77,108 sq mi
Leading Exports: coffee, fish and fish products, tea, gold, cotton, flowers, horticultural products
Continent: Africa

Zambia
Capital: Lusaka
Population: 10.1 million
Official Language: English
Land Area: 740,724 sq km; 285,994 sq mi
Leading Exports: copper, cobalt, electricity, tobacco, flowers, cotton
Continent: Africa

Zimbabwe
Capital: Harare
Population: 11.3 million
Official Language: English
Land Area: 386,670 sq km; 149,293 sq mi
Leading Exports: tobacco, gold, iron alloys, textiles and clothing
Continent: Africa

Asia and the Pacific

Afghanistan
Capital: Kabul
Population: 27.8 million
Official Languages: Pashtu and Dari
Land Area: 647,500 sq km; 250,000 sq mi
Leading Exports: agricultural products, hand-woven carpets, wool, cotton, hides and pelts, precious and semiprecious gems
Continent: Asia

Armenia
Capital: Yerevan
Population: 3.3 million
Official Language: Armenian
Land Area: 29,400 sq km; 10,965 sq mi
Leading Exports: diamonds, scrap metal, machinery and equipment, brandy, copper ore
Continent: Asia

Australia
Capital: Canberra
Population: 19.6 million
Official Language: English
Land Area: 7,617,930 sq km; 2,941,283 sq mi
Leading Exports: coal, gold, meat, wool, alumina, iron ore, wheat, machinery and transport equipment
Continent: Australia

Azerbaijan
Capital: Baku
Population: 7.8 million
Official Language: Azerbaijani
Land Area: 86,100 sq km; 33,243 sq mi
Leading Exports: oil and gas, machinery, cotton, foodstuffs
Continent: Asia

Bahrain
Capital: Manama
Population: 656,397
Official Language: Arabic
Land Area: 665 sq km; 257 sq mi
Leading Exports: petroleum and petroleum products, aluminum, textiles
Continent: Asia

Bangladesh
Capital: Dhaka
Population: 133.4 million
Official Language: Bengali
Land Area: 133,910 sq km; 51,705 sq mi
Leading Exports: garments, jute and jute goods, leather, frozen fish and seafood
Continent: Asia

Bhutan
Capital: Thimphu
Population: 2.1 million
Official Language: Dzongkha
Land Area: 47,000 sq km; 18,147 sq mi
Leading Exports: electricity, cardamom, gypsum, timber, handicrafts, cement, fruit, precious stones, spices
Continent: Asia

Brunei
Capital: Bandar Seri Begawan
Population: 350,898
Official Language: Malay
Land Area: 5,270 sq km; 2,035 sq mi
Leading Exports: crude oil, natural gas, refined products
Continent: Asia

Cambodia
Capital: Phnom Penh
Population: 12.8 million
Official Language: Khmer
Land Area: 176,520 sq km; 68,154 sq mi
Leading Exports: timber, garments, rubber, rice, fish
Continent: Asia

China
Capital: Beijing
Population: 1.29 billion
Official Languages: Mandarin and Chinese
Land Area: 9,326,410 sq km; 3,600,927 sq mi
Leading Exports: machinery and equipment, textiles and clothing, footwear, toys and sports goods, mineral fuels
Continent: Asia

Cyprus
Capital: Nicosia
Population: 767,314
Official Languages: Greek and Turkish
Land Area: 9,240 sq km; 3,568 sq mi
Leading Exports: citrus, potatoes, grapes, wine, cement, clothing and shoes
Location: Mediterranean Sea

East Timor
Capital: Dili
Population: 952,618
Official Languages: Tetum and Portuguese
Land Area: 15,007 sq km; 5,794 sq mi
Leading Exports: coffee, sandalwood, marble
Continent: Asia

Fiji
Capital: Suva
Population: 856,346
Official Language: English
Land Area: 18,270 sq km; 7,054 sq mi
Leading Exports: sugar, garments, gold, timber, fish, molasses, coconut oil
Location: Pacific Ocean

Georgia
Capital: Tbilisi
Population: 5 million
Official Languages: Georgian and Abkhazian
Land Area: 69,700 sq km; 26,911 sq mi
Leading Exports: scrap metal, machinery, chemicals, fuel reexports, citrus fruits, tea, wine, other agricultural products
Continent: Asia

India
Capital: New Delhi
Population: 1.05 billion
Official Languages: Hindi and English
Land Area: 2,973,190 sq km; 1,147,949 sq mi
Leading Exports: textile goods, gems and jewelry, engineering goods, chemicals, leather manufactured goods
Continent: Asia

Indonesia
Capital: Jakarta
Population: 231.3 million
Official Language: Bahasa Indonesia
Land Area: 1,826,440 sq km; 705,188 sq mi
Leading Exports: oil and gas, electrical appliances, plywood, textiles, rubber
Continent: Asia

Iran
Capital: Tehran
Population: 66.6 million
Official Language: Farsi
Land Area: 1,636,000 sq km; 631,660 sq mi
Leading Exports: petroleum, carpets, fruits and nuts, iron and steel, chemicals
Continent: Asia

Iraq
Capital: Baghdad
Population: 24.7 million
Official Language: Arabic
Land Area: 432,162 sq km; 166,858 sq mi
Leading Exports: crude oil
Continent: Asia

Israel
Capital: Jerusalem
Population: 6.0 million
Official Languages: Hebrew, Arabic
Land Area: 20,330 sq km; 7,849 sq mi
Leading Exports: machinery and equipment, software, cut diamonds, agricultural products, chemicals, textiles and apparel
Continent: Asia

Japan
Capital: Tokyo
Population: 127 million
Official Language: Japanese
Land Area: 374,744 sq km; 144,689 sq mi
Leading Exports: motor vehicles, semiconductors, office machinery, chemicals
Continent: Asia

Jordan
Capital: Amman
Population: 5.3 million
Official Language: Arabic
Land Area: 91,971 sq km; 35,510 sq mi
Leading Exports: phosphates, fertilizers, potash, agricultural products, manufactured goods, pharmaceuticals
Continent: Asia

Kazakhstan
Capital: Astana
Population: 16.7 million
Official Language: Kazakh
Land Area: 2,669,800 sq km; 1,030,810 sq mi
Leading Exports: oil and oil products, ferrous metals, machinery, chemicals, grain, wool, meat, coal
Continent: Asia

Kiribati
Capital: Bairiki (Tarawa Atoll)
Population: 96,335
Official Language: English
Land Area: 811 sq km; 313 sq mi
Leading Exports: copra, coconuts, seaweed, fish
Location: Pacific Ocean

Korea, North
Capital: Pyongyang
Population: 22.3 million
Official Language: Korean
Land Area: 120,410 sq km; 46,490 sq mi
Leading Exports: minerals, metallurgical products, manufactured goods (including armaments), agricultural and fishery products
Continent: Asia

Korea, South
Capital: Seoul
Population: 48.3 million
Official Language: Korean
Land Area: 98,190 sq km; 37,911 sq mi
Leading Exports: electronic products, machinery and equipment, motor vehicles, steel, ships, textiles, clothing, footwear, fish
Continent: Asia

Kuwait
Capital: Kuwait City
Population: 2.1 million
Official Language: Arabic
Land Area: 17,820 sq km; 6,880 sq mi
Leading Exports: oil and refined products, fertilizers
Continent: Asia

Kyrgyzstan
Capital: Bishkek
Population: 4.8 million
Official Languages: Kyrgyz and Russian
Land Area: 191,300 sq km; 73,861 sq mi
Leading Exports: cotton, wool, meat, tobacco, gold, mercury, uranium, hydropower, machinery, shoes
Continent: Asia

Laos
Capital: Vientiane
Population: 5.8 million
Official Language: Lao
Land Area: 230,800 sq km; 89,112 sq mi
Leading Exports: wood products, garments, electricity, coffee, tin
Continent: Asia

Lebanon

Capital: Beirut
Population: 3.7 million
Official Language: Arabic
Land Area: 10,230 sq km; 3,950 sq mi
Leading Exports: foodstuffs and tobacco, textile, chemicals, precious stones, metal and metal products, electrical equipment and products, jewelry, paper and paper products
Continent: Asia

Malaysia

Capital: Kuala Lumpur and Putrajaya
Population: 22.7 million
Official Language: Bahasa Malaysia
Land Area: 328,550 sq km; 126,853 sq mi
Leading Exports: electronic equipment, petroleum and liquefied natural gas, wood and wood products, palm oil, rubber, textiles, chemicals
Continent: Asia

Maldives

Capital: Malé
Population: 320,165
Official Language: Dhivehi (Maldivian)
Land Area: 300 sq km; 116 sq mi
Leading Exports: fish, clothing
Location: Indian Ocean

Marshall Islands

Capital: Majuro
Population: 73,360
Official Languages: Marshallese and English
Land Area: 181.3 sq km; 70 sq mi
Leading Exports: copra cake, coconut oil, handicrafts
Location: Pacific Ocean

Micronesia, Federated States of

Capital: Palikir (Pohnpei Island)
Population: 135,869
Official Language: English
Land Area: 702 sq km; 271 sq mi
Leading Exports: fish, garments, bananas, black pepper
Location: Pacific Ocean

Mongolia

Capital: Ulaanbaatar
Population: 2.6 million
Official Language: Khalkha Mongolian
Land Area: 1,555,400 sq km; 600,540 sq mi
Leading Exports: copper, livestock, animal products, cashmere, wool, hides, fluorspar, other nonferrous metals
Continent: Asia

Myanmar (Burma)

Capital: Rangoon (Yangon)
Population: 42.2 million
Official Language: Burmese (Myanmar)
Land Area: 657,740 sq km; 253,953 sq mi
Leading Exports: apparel, foodstuffs, wood products, precious stones
Continent: Asia

Nauru

Capital: Yaren District
Population: 12,329
Official Language: Nauruan
Land Area: 21 sq km; 8 sq mi
Leading Exports: phosphates
Location: Pacific Ocean

Nepal

Capital: Kathmandu
Population: 25.9 million
Official Language: Nepali
Land Area: 136,800 sq km; 52,818 sq mi
Leading Exports: carpets, clothing, leather goods, jute goods, grain
Continent: Asia

New Zealand

Capital: Wellington
Population: 3.8 million
Official Languages: English and Maori
Land Area: 268,680 sq km; 103,737 sq mi
Leading Exports: dairy products, meat, wood and wood products, fish, machinery
Location: Pacific Ocean

Oman

Capital: Muscat
Population: 2.7 million
Official Language: Arabic
Land Area: 212,460 sq km; 82,030 sq mi
Leading Exports: petroleum, reexports, fish, metals, textiles
Continent: Asia

Pakistan

Capital: Islamabad
Population: 147.7 million
Official Languages: Urdu and English
Land Area: 778,720 sq km; 300,664 sq mi
Leading Exports: textiles (garments, cotton cloth, and yarn), rice, other agricultural products
Continent: Asia

Palau

Capital: Koror
Population: 19,409
Official Languages: English and Palauan
Land Area: 458 sq km; 177 sq mi
Leading Exports: shellfish, tuna, copra, garments
Location: Pacific Ocean

Papua New Guinea

Capital: Port Moresby
Population: 5.2 million
Official Language: English
Land Area: 452,860 sq km; 174,849 sq mi
Leading Exports: oil, gold, copper ore, logs, palm oil, coffee, cocoa, crayfish, prawns
Location: Pacific Ocean

Philippines

Capital: Manila
Population: 84.5 million
Official Languages: Filipino and English
Land Area: 298,170 sq km; 115,123 sq mi
Leading Exports: electronic equipment, machinery and transport equipment, garments, coconut products
Continent: Asia

Qatar

Capital: Doha
Population: 793,341
Official Language: Arabic
Land Area: 11,437 sq km; 4,416 sq mi
Leading Exports: petroleum products, fertilizers, steel
Continent: Asia

Samoa

Capital: Apia
Population: 178,631
Official Languages: Samoan and English
Land Area: 2,934 sq km; 1,133 sq mi
Leading Exports: fish, coconut oil cream, copra, taro, garments, beer
Location: Pacific Ocean

Saudi Arabia

Capital: Riyadh and Jiddah
Population: 23.5 million
Official Language: Arabic
Land Area: 1,960,582 sq km; 756,981 sq mi
Leading Exports: petroleum and petroleum products
Continent: Asia

Singapore

Capital: Singapore
Population: 4.5 million
Official Languages: Malay, English, Mandarin, Chinese, and Tamil
Land Area: 683 sq km; 264 sq mi
Leading Exports: machinery and equipment (including electronics), consumer goods, chemicals, mineral fuels
Continent: Asia

Solomon Islands

Capital: Honiara
Population: 494,786
Official Language: English
Land Area: 27,540 sq km; 10,633 sq mi
Leading Exports: timber, fish, copra, palm oil, cocoa
Location: Pacific Ocean

Sri Lanka

Capital: Colombo
Population: 19.6 million
Official Language: Sinhala, Tamil, and English
Land Area: 64,740 sq km; 24,996 sq mi
Leading Exports: textiles and apparel, tea, diamonds, coconut products, petroleum products
Continent: Asia

Syria

Capital: Damascus
Population: 17.2 million
Official Language: Arabic
Land Area: 184,050 sq km; 71,062 sq mi
Leading Exports: crude oil, textiles, fruits and vegetables, raw cotton
Continent: Asia

Taiwan

Capital: Taipei
Population: 22.5 million
Official Language: Mandarin Chinese
Land Area: 32,260 sq km; 12,456 sq mi
Leading Exports: machinery and electrical equipment, metals, textiles, plastics, chemicals
Continent: Asia

Tajikistan

Capital: Dushanbe
Population: 6.7 million
Official Language: Tajik
Land Area: 142,700 sq km; 55,096 sq mi
Leading Exports: aluminum, electricity, cotton, fruits, vegetables, oil, textiles
Continent: Asia

Thailand

Capital: Bangkok
Population: 62.5 million
Official Language: Thai
Land Area: 511,770 sq km; 197,564 sq mi
Leading Exports: computers, transistors, seafood, clothing, rice
Continent: Asia

Tonga

Capital: Nuku'alofa
Population: 106,137
Official Languages: Tongan and English
Land Area: 718 sq km; 277 sq mi
Leading Exports: squash, fish, vanilla beans, root crops
Location: Pacific Ocean

Turkey

Capital: Ankara
Population: 67.3 million
Official Language: Turkish
Land Area: 770,760 sq km; 297,590 sq mi
Leading Exports: apparel, foodstuffs, textiles, metal manufactured goods, transport equipment
Continent: Asia

Turkmenistan

Capital: Ashgabat
Population: 4.7 million
Official Language: Turkmen
Land Area: 488,100 sq km; 188,455 sq mi
Leading Exports: gas, oil, cotton fiber, textiles
Continent: Asia

Asia and the Pacific (continued)

Tuvalu

Capital: Fongafale
Population: 10,800
Official Language: English
Land Area: 26 sq km; 10 sq mi
Leading Exports: copra, fish
Location: Pacific Ocean

United Arab Emirates
Capital: Abu Dhabi
Population: 2.4 million
Official Language: Arabic
Land Area: 82,880 sq km; 32,000 sq mi
Leading Exports: crude oil, natural gas, reexports, dried fish, dates
Continent: Asia

Uzbekistan
Capital: Tashkent
Population: 25.5 million
Official Language: Uzbek
Land Area: 425,400 sq km; 164,247 sq mi
Leading Exports: cotton, gold, energy products, mineral fertilizers, ferrous metals, textiles, food products, automobiles
Continent: Asia

Vanuatu
Capital: Port-Vila
Population: 196,178
Official Languages: English, French, and Bislama
Land Area: 12,200 sq km; 4,710 sq mi
Leading Exports: copra, kava, beef, cocoa, timber, coffee
Location: Pacific Ocean

Vietnam
Capital: Hanoi
Population: 81.1 million
Official Language: Vietnamese
Land Area: 325,320 sq km; 125,621 sq mi
Leading Exports: crude oil, marine products, rice, coffee, rubber, tea, garments, shoes
Continent: Asia

Yemen
Capital: Sanaa
Population: 18.7 million
Official Language: Arabic
Land Area: 527,970 sq km; 203,849 sq mi
Leading Exports: crude oil, coffee, dried and salted fish
Continent: Asia

Europe and Russia

Albania
Capital: Tiranë
Population: 3.5 million
Official Language: Albanian
Land Area: 27,398 sq km; 10,578 sq mi
Leading Exports: textiles and footwear, asphalt, metals and metallic ores, crude oil, vegetables, fruits, tobacco
Continent: Europe

Andorra
Capital: Andorra la Vella
Population: 68,403
Official Language: Catalan
Land Area: 468 sq km; 181 sq mi
Leading Exports: tobacco products, furniture
Continent: Europe

Austria
Capital: Vienna
Population: 8.2 million
Official Language: German
Land Area: 82,738 sq km; 31,945 sq mi
Leading Exports: machinery and equipment, motor vehicles and parts, paper and paperboard, metal goods, chemicals, iron and steel, textiles, foodstuffs
Continent: Europe

Belarus
Capital: Minsk
Population: 10.3 million
Official Languages: Belarussian and Russian
Land Area: 207,600 sq km; 80,154 sq mi
Leading Exports: machinery and equipment, mineral products, chemicals, textiles, food stuffs, metals
Continent: Europe

Belgium
Capital: Brussels
Population: 10.3 million
Official Languages: Dutch and French
Land Area: 30,230 sq km; 11,172 sq mi
Leading Exports: machinery and equipment, chemicals, metals and metal products
Continent: Europe

Bosnia and Herzegovina
Capital: Sarajevo
Population: 4.0 million
Official Language: Serbo-Croat
Land Area: 51,129 sq km; 19,741 sq mi
Leading Exports: miscellaneous manufactured goods, crude materials
Continent: Europe

Bulgaria
Capital: Sofía
Population: 7.6 million
Official Language: Bulgarian
Land Area: 110,550 sq km; 42,683 sq mi
Leading Exports: clothing, footwear, iron and steel, machinery and equipment, fuels
Continent: Europe

Croatia
Capital: Zagreb
Population: 4.4 million
Official Language: Croatian
Land Area: 56,414 km; 21,781 sq mi
Leading Exports: transport equipment, textiles, chemicals, foodstuffs, fuels
Continent: Europe

Czech Republic
Capital: Prague
Population: 10.3 million
Official Language: Czech
Land Area: 78,276 sq km; 29,836 sq mi
Leading Exports: machinery and transport equipment, intermediate manufactured goods, chemicals, raw materials and fuel
Continent: Europe

Denmark
Capital: Copenhagen
Population: 5.4 million
Official Language: Danish
Land Area: 42,394 sq km; 16,368 sq mi
Leading Exports: machinery and instruments, meat and meat products, dairy products, fish, chemicals, furniture, ships, windmills
Continent: Europe

Estonia
Capital: Tallinn
Population: 1.4 million
Official Language: Estonian
Land Area: 43,211 sq km; 16,684 sq mi
Leading Exports: machinery and equipment, wood products, textiles, food products, metals, chemical products
Continent: Europe

Finland
Capital: Helsinki
Population: 5.2 million
Official Languages: Finnish and Swedish
Land Area: 305,470 sq km; 117,942 sq mi
Leading Exports: machinery and equipment, chemicals, metals, timber, paper, pulp
Continent: Europe

France
Capital: Paris
Population: 59.8 million
Official Language: French
Land Area: 545,630 sq km; 310,668 sq mi
Leading Exports: machinery and transportation equipment, aircraft, plastics, chemicals, pharmaceutical products, iron and steel, beverages
Continent: Europe

Germany
Capital: Berlin
Population: 83 million
Official Language: German
Land Area: 349,223 sq km; 134,835 sq mi
Leading Exports: machinery, vehicles, chemicals, metals and manufactured goods, foodstuffs, textiles
Continent: Europe

Greece
Capital: Athens
Population: 10.6 million
Official Language: Greek
Land Area: 130,800 sq km; 50,502 sq mi
Leading Exports: food and beverages, manufactured goods, petroleum products, chemicals, textiles
Continent: Europe

Holy See
(Vatican City)
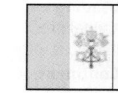
Capital: Vatican City
Population: 900
Official Languages: Latin and Italian
Land Area: 0.44 sq km; 0.17 sq mi
Leading Exports: no information available
Continent: Europe

Hungary
Capital: Budapest
Population: 10.1 million
Official Language: Hungarian
Land Area: 92,340 sq km; 35,652 sq mi
Leading Exports: machinery and equipment, other manufactured goods, food products, raw materials, fuels and electricity
Continent: Europe

Iceland
Capital: Reykjavík
Population: 279,384
Official Language: Icelandic
Land Area: 100,250 sq km; 38,707 sq mi
Leading Exports: fish and fish products, animal products, aluminum, diatomite, ferrosilicon
Location: Atlantic Ocean

Ireland
Capital: Dublin
Population: 3.9 million
Official Languages: Irish Gaelic and English
Land Area: 68,890 sq km; 26,598 sq mi
Leading Exports: machinery and equipment, computers, chemicals, pharmaceuticals, live animals, animal products
Continent: Europe

Italy
Capital: Rome
Population: 57.7 million
Official Language: Italian
Land Area: 294,020 sq km; 113,521 sq mi
Leading Exports: fruits, vegetables, grapes, potatoes, sugar beets, soybeans, grain, olives, beef, diary products, fish
Continent: Europe

Latvia
Capital: Riga
Population: 2.4 million
Official Language: Latvian
Land Area: 63,589 sq km; 24,552 sq mi
Leading Exports: wood and wood products, machinery and equipment, metals, textiles, foodstuffs
Continent: Europe

Liechtenstein
Capital: Vaduz
Population: 32,842
Official Language: German
Land Area: 160 sq km; 62 sq mi
Leading Exports: small specialty machinery, dental products, stamps, hardware, pottery
Continent: Europe

Lithuania
Capital: Vilnius
Population: 3.6 million
Official Language: Lithuanian
Land Area: 65,200 sq km; 25,174 sq mi
Leading Exports: mineral products, textiles and clothing, machinery and equipment, chemicals, wood and wood products, foodstuffs
Continent: Europe

Luxembourg
Capital: Luxembourg
Population: 448,569
Official Languages: Luxembourgish, French, and German
Land Area: 2,586 sq km; 998 sq mi
Leading Exports: machinery and equipment, steel products, chemicals, rubber products, glass
Continent: Europe

Macedonia, The Former Yugoslav Republic of
Capital: Skopje
Population: 2.1 million
Official Languages: Macedonian and Albanian
Land Area: 24,856 sq km; 9,597 sq mi
Leading Exports: food, beverages, tobacco, miscellaneous manufactured goods, iron and steel
Continent: Europe

Malta
Capital: Valletta
Population: 397,499
Official Languages: Maltese and English
Land Area: 316 sq km; 122 sq mi
Leading Exports: machinery and transport equipment, manufactured goods
Location: Mediterranean Sea

Moldova
Capital: Chişinău
Population: 4.4 million
Official Language: Moldovan
Land Area: 33,371 sq km; 12,885 sq mi
Leading Exports: foodstuffs, textiles and footwear, machinery
Continent: Europe

Monaco
Capital: Monaco
Population: 31,987
Official Language: French
Land Area: 1.95 sq km; 0.75 sq mi
Leading Exports: no information available
Continent: Europe

Montenegro
Capital: Podgorica
Population: 620,145
Official Language: Serbian
Land Area: 13,812 sq km; 5,333 sq mi
Leading Exports: food products
Continent: Europe

Netherlands
Capital: Amsterdam and The Hague
Population: 16.1 million
Official Language: Dutch
Land Area: 33,883 sq km; 13,082 sq mi
Leading Exports: machinery and equipment, chemicals, fuels, foodstuffs
Continent: Europe

Norway
Capital: Oslo
Population: 4.5 million
Official Language: Norwegian
Land Area: 307,860 sq km; 118,865 sq mi
Leading Exports: petroleum and petroleum products, machinery and equipment, metals, chemicals, ships, fish
Continent: Europe

Poland
Capital: Warsaw
Population: 38.6 million
Official Language: Polish
Land Area: 304,465 sq km; 117,554 sq mi
Leading Exports: machinery and transport equipment, intermediate manufactured goods, miscellaneous manufactured goods, food and live animals
Continent: Europe

Portugal
Capital: Lisbon
Population: 10.1 million
Official Language: Portuguese
Land Area: 91,951 sq km; 35,502 sq mi
Leading Exports: clothing and footwear, machinery, chemicals, cork and paper products, hides
Continent: Europe

Romania
Capital: Bucharest
Population: 22.3 million
Official Language: Romanian
Land Area: 230,340 sq km; 88,934 sq mi
Leading Exports: textiles and footwear, metals and metal products, machinery and equipment, minerals and fuels
Continent: Europe

Russia
Capital: Moscow
Population: 145 million
Official Language: Russian
Land Area: 16,995,800 sq km; 6,592,100 sq mi
Leading Exports: petroleum and petroleum products, natural gas, wood and wood products, metals, chemicals, and a wide variety of civilian and military manufactured goods
Continents: Europe and Asia

San Marino
Capital: San Marino
Population: 27,730
Official Language: Italian
Land Area: 61 sq km; 24 sq mi
Leading Exports: building stone, lime, wood, chestnuts, wheat, wine, baked goods, hides, ceramics
Continent: Europe

Serbia
Capital: Belgrade
Population: 9.4 million
Official Language: Serbian
Land Area: 88,361 sq km; 34,116 sq mi
Leading Exports: food and live animals, manufactured goods, raw materials
Continent: Europe

Slovakia
Capital: Bratislava
Population: 5.4 million
Official Language: Slovak
Land Area: 48,800 sq km; 18,842 sq mi
Leading Exports: machinery and transport equipment, intermediate manufactured goods, miscellaneous manufactured goods, chemicals
Continent: Europe

Slovenia
Capital: Ljubljana
Population: 1.9 million
Official Language: Slovene
Land Area: 20,151 sq km; 7,780 sq mi
Leading Exports: manufactured goods, machinery and transport equipment, chemicals, food
Continent: Europe

Spain
Capital: Madrid
Population: 40.1 million
Official Languages: Spanish, Galician, Basque, and Catalan
Land Area: 499,542 sq km; 192,873 sq mi
Leading Exports: machinery, motor vehicles, foodstuffs, other consumer goods
Continent: Europe

Europe and Russia (continued)

Sweden
Capital: Stockholm
Population: 8.9 million
Official Language: Swedish
Land Area: 410,934 sq km; 158,662 sq mi
Leading Exports: machinery, motor vehicles, paper products, pulp and wood, iron and steel products, chemicals
Continent: Europe

Switzerland
Capital: Bern
Population: 7.3 million
Official Languages: German, French, and Italian
Land Area: 39,770 sq km; 15,355 sq mi
Leading Exports: machinery, chemicals, metals, watches, agricultural products
Continent: Europe

Ukraine
Capital: Kiev
Population: 48.4 million
Official Language: Ukrainian
Land Area: 603,700 sq km; 233,090 sq mi
Leading Exports: ferrous and nonferrous metals, fuel and petroleum products, machinery and transport equipment, food products
Continent: Europe

United Kingdom
Capital: London
Population: 59.8 million
Official Languages: English and Welsh
Land Area: 241,590 sq km; 93,278 sq mi
Leading Exports: manufactured goods, fuels, chemicals, food, beverages, tobacco
Continent: Europe

Latin America

Antigua and Barbuda
Capital: Saint John's
Population: 67,448
Official Language: English
Land Area: 442 sq km; 171 sq mi
Leading Exports: petroleum products, manufactured goods, machinery and transport equipment, food and live animals
Location: Caribbean Sea

Argentina
Capital: Buenos Aires
Population: 37.8 million
Official Language: Spanish
Land Area: 2,736,690 sq km; 1,056,636 sq mi
Leading Exports: edible oils, fuels and energy, cereals, feed, motor vehicles
Continent: South America

Bahamas
Capital: Nassau
Population: 300,529
Official Language: English
Land Area: 10,070 sq km; 3,888 sq mi
Leading Exports: fish and crawfish, rum, salt, chemicals, fruit and vegetables
Location: Caribbean Sea

Barbados
Capital: Bridgetown
Population: 276,607
Official Language: English
Land Area: 431 sq km; 166 sq mi
Leading Exports: sugar and molasses, rum, other foods and beverages, chemicals, electrical components, clothing
Location: Caribbean Sea

Belize
Capital: Belmopan
Population: 262,999
Official Language: English
Land Area: 22,806 sq km; 8,805 sq mi
Leading Exports: sugar, bananas, citrus, clothing, fish products, molasses, wood
Continent: North America

Bolivia
Capital: La Paz and Sucre
Population: 8.5 million
Official Language: Spanish, Quechua, and Aymara
Land Area: 1,084,390 sq km; 418,683 sq mi
Leading Exports: soybeans, natural gas, zinc, gold, wood
Continent: South America

Brazil
Capital: Brasília
Population: 176 million
Official Language: Portuguese
Land Area: 8,456,510 sq km; 3,265,059 sq mi
Leading Exports: manufactured goods, iron ore, soybeans, footwear, coffee, autos
Continent: South America

Chile
Capital: Santiago
Population: 15.5 million
Official Language: Spanish
Land Area: 748,800 sq km; 289,112 sq mi
Leading Exports: copper, fish, fruits, paper and pulp, chemicals
Continent: South America

Colombia
Capital: Bogotá
Population: 41 million
Official Language: Spanish
Land Area: 1,038,700 sq km; 401,042 sq mi
Leading Exports: petroleum, coffee, coal, apparel, bananas, cut flowers
Continent: South America

Costa Rica
Capital: San José
Population: 3.8 million
Official Language: Spanish
Land Area: 51,660 sq km; 19,560 sq mi
Leading Exports: coffee, bananas, sugar, pineapples, textiles, electronic components, medical equipment
Continent: North America

Cuba
Capital: Havana
Population: 11.2 million
Official Language: Spanish
Land Area: 110,860 sq km; 42,803 sq mi
Leading Exports: sugar, nickel, tobacco, fish, medical products, citrus, coffee
Location: Caribbean Sea

Dominica
Capital: Roseau
Population: 73,000
Official Language: English
Land Area: 754 sq km; 291 sq mi
Leading Exports: bananas, soap, bay oil, vegetables, grapefruit, oranges
Location: Caribbean Sea

Dominican Republic
Capital: Santo Domingo
Population: 8.7 million
Official Language: Spanish
Land Area: 48,380 sq km; 18,679 sq mi
Leading Exports: ferronickel, sugar, gold, silver, coffee, cocoa, tobacco, meats, consumer goods
Location: Caribbean Sea

Ecuador
Capital: Quito
Population: 13.5 million
Official Language: Spanish
Land Area: 276,840 sq km; 106,888 sq mi
Leading Exports: petroleum, bananas, shrimp, coffee, cocoa, cut flowers, fish
Continent: South America

El Salvador
Capital: San Salvador
Population: 6.4 million
Official Language: Spanish
Land Area: 20,720 sq km; 8,000 sq mi
Leading Exports: offshore assembly exports, coffee, sugar, shrimp, textiles, chemicals, electricity
Continent: North America

Grenada
Capital: Saint George's
Population: 89,211
Official Language: English
Land Area: 344 sq km; 133 sq mi
Leading Exports: bananas, cocoa, nutmeg, fruit and vegetables, clothing, mace
Location: Caribbean Sea

Guatemala
Capital: Guatemala City
Population: 13.3 million
Official Language: Spanish
Land Area: 108,430 sq km; 41,865 sq mi
Leading Exports: coffee, sugar, bananas, fruits and vegetables, cardamom, meat, apparel, petroleum, electricity
Continent: North America

Guyana
Capital: Georgetown
Population: 698,209
Official Language: English
Land Area: 196,850 sq km; 76,004 sq mi
Leading Exports: sugar, gold, bauxite/alumina, rice, shrimp, molasses, rum, timber
Continent: South America

Haiti
Capital: Port-au-Prince
Population: 7.1 million
Official Language: French and French Creole
Land Area: 27,560 sq km; 10,641 sq mi
Leading Exports: manufactured goods, coffee, oils, cocoa
Location: Caribbean Sea

Honduras
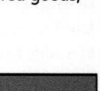
Capital: Tegucigalpa
Population: 6.6 million
Official Language: Spanish
Land Area: 111,890 sq km; 43,201 sq mi
Leading Exports: coffee, bananas, shrimp, lobster, meat, zinc, lumber
Continent: North America

Jamaica
Capital: Kingston
Population: 2.7 million
Official Language: English
Land Area: 10,831 sq km; 4,182 sq mi
Leading Exports: alumina, bauxite, sugar, bananas, rum
Location: Caribbean Sea

Mexico
Capital: Mexico City
Population: 103.4 million
Official Language: Spanish
Land Area: 1,923,040 sq km; 742,486 sq mi
Leading Exports: manufactured goods, oil and oil products, silver, fruits, vegetables, coffee, cotton
Continent: North America

Nicaragua
Capital: Managua
Population: 5 million
Official Language: Spanish
Land Area: 120,254 sq km; 46,430 sq mi
Leading Exports: coffee, shrimp and lobster, cotton, tobacco, beef, sugar, bananas, gold
Continent: North America

Panama
Capital: Panama City
Population: 2.9 million
Official Language: Spanish
Land Area: 75,990 sq km; 29,340 sq mi
Leading Exports: bananas, shrimp, sugar, coffee, clothing
Continent: North America

Paraguay
Capital: Asunción
Population: 5.9 million
Official Language: Spanish
Land Area: 397,300 sq km; 153,398 sq mi
Leading Exports: electricity, soybeans, feed, cotton, meat, edible oils
Continent: South America

Peru
Capital: Lima
Population: 28 million
Official Languages: Spanish and Quechua
Land Area: 1,280,000 sq km; 494,208 sq mi
Leading Exports: fish and fish products, gold, copper, zinc, crude petroleum and byproducts, lead, coffee, sugar, cotton
Continent: South America

Saint Kitts and Nevis
Capital: Basseterre
Population: 38,736
Official Language: English
Land Area: 261 sq km; 101 sq mi
Leading Exports: machinery, food, electronics, beverages, tobacco
Location: Caribbean Sea

Saint Lucia
Capital: Castries
Population: 160,145
Official Language: English
Land Area: 606 sq km; 234 sq mi
Leading Exports: bananas, clothing, cocoa, vegetables, fruits, coconut oil
Location: Caribbean Sea

Saint Vincent and the Grenadines
Capital: Kingstown
Population: 116,394
Official Language: English
Land Area: 389 sq km; 150 sq mi
Leading Exports: bananas, eddoes and dasheen, arrowroot starch, tennis racquets
Location: Caribbean Sea

Suriname
Capital: Paramaribo
Population: 436,494
Official Language: Dutch
Land Area: 161,470 sq km; 62,344 sq mi
Leading Exports: alumina, crude oil, lumber, shrimp and fish, rice, bananas
Continent: South America

Trinidad and Tobago
Capital: Port-of-Spain
Population: 1.2 million
Official Language: English
Land Area: 5,128 sq km; 1,980 sq mi
Leading Exports: petroleum and petroleum products, chemicals, steel products, fertilizer, sugar, cocoa, coffee, citrus, flowers
Location: Caribbean Sea

Uruguay
Capital: Montevideo
Population: 3.4 million
Official Language: Spanish
Land Area: 173,620 sq km; 67,100 sq mi
Leading Exports: meat, rice, leather products, wool, vehicles, dairy products
Continent: South America

Venezuela
Capital: Caracas
Population: 24.3 million
Official Language: Spanish
Land Area: 882,050 sq km; 340,560 sq mi
Leading Exports: petroleum, bauxite and aluminum, steel, chemicals, agricultural products, basic manufactured goods
Continent: South America

United States and Canada

Canada
Capital: Ottawa
Population: 31.9 million
Official Languages: English and French
Land Area: 9,220,970 sq km; 3,560,217 sq mi
Leading Exports: motor vehicles and parts, industrial machinery, aircraft, telecommunications equipment, chemicals, plastics, fertilizers, wood pulp, timber, crude petroleum, natural gas, electricity, aluminum
Continent: North America

United States
Capital: Washington, D.C.
Population: 281.4 million
Official Language: English
Land Area: 9,158,960 sq km; 3,536,274 sq mi
Leading Exports: capital goods, automobiles, industrial supplies and raw materials, consumer goods, agricultural products
Continent: North America

SOURCE: CIA World Factbook Online, 2002

Glossary of Geographic Terms

basin
an area that is lower than surrounding land areas; some basins are filled with water

bay
a body of water that is partly surrounded by land and that is connected to a larger body of water

butte
a small, high, flat-topped landform with cliff-like sides

 butte

canyon
a deep, narrow valley with steep sides; often with a stream flowing through it

cataract
a large waterfall or steep rapids

◀ **cataract**

delta
a plain at the mouth of a river, often triangular in shape, formed where sediment is deposited by flowing water

flood plain
a broad plain on either side of a river, formed whe sediment settles during floods

glacier
a huge, slow-moving mass of snow and ice

hill
an area that rises above surrounding land and has rounded top; lower and usually less steep than a mountain

island
an area of land completely surrounded by water

isthmus
a narrow strip of land that connects two larger areas of land

mesa
a high, flat-topped landform with cliff-like sides; larger than a butte

mountain
a landform that rises steeply at least 2,000 feet (610 meters) above surrounding land; usually wide at the bottom and rising to a narrow peak or ridge

▶ **glacier**

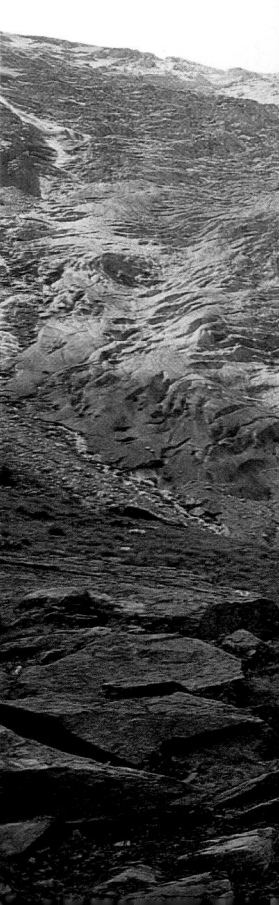

◄ delta

ountain pass
ap between mountains

ninsula
area of land almost completely surrounded by
er but connected to the mainland

ain
rge area of flat or gently rolling land

teau
rge, flat area that rises above the surrounding
d; at least one side has a steep slope

er mouth
point where a river enters a lake or sea

strait
a narrow stretch of water that connects two larger
bodies of water

tributary
a river or stream that flows into a larger river

valley
a low stretch of land between mountains or hills;
land that is drained by a river

volcano
an opening in Earth's surface through which
molten rock, ashes, and gases escape from
the interior

► **volcano**

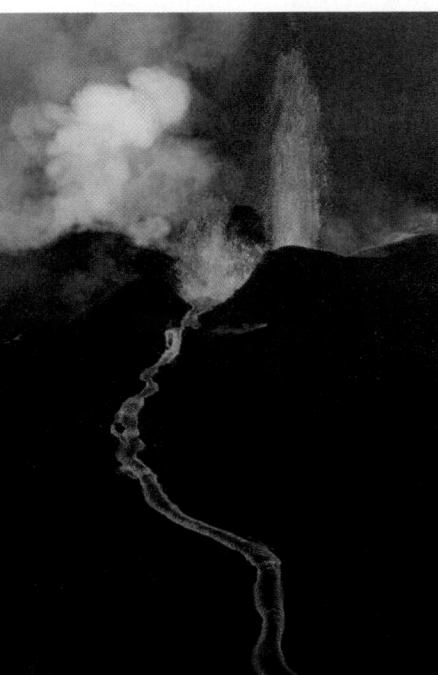

Gazetteer

A

Acropolis (37°58' N, 23°43' E) a hill in Athens, Greece, on which many temples and archaeological sites are located, p. 186

Aegean Sea (39° N, 25° E) the sea that separates Greece and Turkey and contains many small islands, p. 170

Africa (10° N, 22° E) the world's second-largest continent, surrounded by the Mediterranean Sea, the Atlantic Ocean, and the Red Sea, p. 7

Aksum (14°8' N, 38°43' E) an ancient town in northern Ethiopia; a powerful kingdom and trade center about A.D. 200–600, p. 327

Albania (41° N, 20° E) a European country located in the Balkans, p. 595

Alexandria (31°12' N, 29° 54' E) an ancient Hellenistic city in Egypt, p. 221

Alsace-Lorraine a region in northeastern France, near the German border, p. 595

Andes (20° S, 67° W) a mountain system extending along the western coast of South America, p. 14

Anyang (36°6' N, 114°21' E) capital of the Shang dynasty in ancient China, p. 22

Arabian Peninsula (25° N, 45° E) a peninsula in Southwest Asia on which the present-day nations of Saudi Arabia, Yemen, Oman, the United Arab Emirates, Qatar, Bahrain, and Kuwait are located, p. 100

Arctic Circle a line of latitude around Earth near the North Pole, p. 14

Argentina (34° S, 64° W) a country in South America, p. 336

Asia (50° N, 100° E) the world's largest continent, surrounded by the Arctic Ocean, the Pacific Ocean, the Indian Ocean, and Europe, p. 7

Asia Minor (39° N, 32° E) a peninsula in western Asia between the Black Sea and the Mediterranean Sea; within the site of present-day eastern Turkey, p. 40

Assyria (36° N, 43° E) a historical kingdom in northern Mesopotamia around present-day Iraq and Turkey, p. 38

Athens (37°58' N, 23°43' E) a city-state in ancient Greece; the capital city of present-day Greece, p. 175

Atlantic Ocean (5° S, 25° W) the second-largest of the world's oceans; extends from western Europe and Africa to eastern North and South America, p. 49

Austria (47° N, 13° E) a country in Central Europe, p. 520

B

Babylonia (32° N, 44° E) an ancient region around southeastern Mesopotamia and between the Tigris and Euphrates Rivers; present-day Iraq, p. 35

Baghdad (33°30' N, 44°30' E) capital city of present-day Iraq; capital of the Muslim empire during Islam's golden age, p. 302

Bangladesh (24° N, 90° E) a coastal country in South Asia, officially the People's Republic of Bangladesh, p. 107

Belgium (51° N, 4° E) a country in western Europe, p. 437

Benin (6°19' N, 5°41' E) a kingdom in the West African rain forest; major cultural and trading center; may have borrowed traditions from Ile-Ife; located in present-day Nigeria, p. 322

Berlin (52°31' N, 13°24' E) the capital of Germany, p. 630

Bethlehem (31°43' N, 35°12' E) the Judaean town where Jesus was said to have been born, p. 260

Bolivia (17° S, 65° W) a country in South America, p. 336

Bosporus (41°6' N, 29°4' E) a narrow strait that separates Europe and Asia and connects the Black Sea with the Sea of Marmara, p. 286

Brazil (10° S, 55° W) the largest country in South America, p. 467

Bulgaria (43° N, 25° E) a European country located in the Balkans, p. 595

Byzantium (41°1' N, 28°58' E) a city in the Roman Empire; the site of present-day Istanbul, Turkey, p. 275

C

Cahokia (38°34' N, 90°11' W) a village in what is now the state of Illinois; formerly a large, prehistoric city known for its Native American mounds, p. 355

Cairo (30°3' N, 31°15' E) the capital and largest city in Egypt, located on the Nile River, p. 75

Calicut (11°15' N, 75°46' E) a city in India that was once a European trading center, p. 457

Cameroon (6° N, 12° E) a country in eastern Africa, p. 572

Canaan (32° N, 35° E) a region occupied by the ancient Israelites, later known as Palestine, located between the Syrian Desert and the Mediterranean Sea; on a site including present-day Israel and part of Jordan, p. 52

Cape of Good Hope (34°24' S, 18°30' E) the southern-most tip of Africa; named in 1488 by Bartholomeu Dias, a Portuguese sailor, p. 457

Caribbean Islands islands that lie off the southwest coast of North America, p. 480

Carthage (36°52' N, 10°20' E) an ancient city on the northern coast of Africa that controlled much of the North African coast and other Mediterranean territories; now a suburb of the city of Tunis, p. 233

Ceuta (35°53' N, 5°19' W) a city in North Africa that is controlled by the Spanish, p. 456

Chang River (31°48' N, 121°10' E) the longest river in China and Asia and the third-longest river in the world (also called the Yangzi River), p. 137

Chang'an (34°15' N, 108°52' E) a city in northern China; in ancient times the eastern end of the Silk Road; also called Xi'an, p. 365

Chile (30° S, 71° W) a country on the west coast of South America, p. 14

China (35° N, 105° E) a country occupying most of the mainland of East Asia, p. 22

Colosseum (41°54' N, 12°29' E) a large arena built in Rome around A.D. 70; site of contests and combats between people and animals, p. 244

Congo River (6° S, 12° E) a river in west-central Africa; the second largest river in Africa, p. 571

Constantinople (41°1' N, 28°58' E) formerly the ancient city of Byzantium, renamed in A.D. 330 after the Roman emperor, Constantine, who made it the new capital of the Eastern Roman, or Byzantine, Empire; now Istanbul, Turkey, p. 275

Costa Rica (10° N, 84° W) a country in Central America, p. 583

Crete (35°15' N, 25° E) an island of Greece, southeast of the mainland, home to the ancient Minoan civilization, p. 170

Cuba (21°30' N, 80° W) an island country located in the West Indies, p. 636

Cuzco (13°31' S, 71°59' W) a city in Peru; the capital city of the ancient Incan empire, p. 338

Czech Republic (50° N, 15° E) a country in eastern Europe, p. 566

D

Damascus (33°30' N, 36°18' E) the capital of and largest city in Syria, p. 262

Delhi (28°40' N, 77°13' E) the third-largest city in India, popularly known as Old Delhi, p. 382

Delphi (38°30' N, 22°29' E) an ancient town in central Greece, site of the oracle of Apollo, p. 183

Denmark (56° N, 10° E) a country in northern Europe; considered part of Scandinavia, p. 396

Djenné (13°54' N, 4°33' W) a city in Mali, Africa; was an important center of Muslim learning in the Kingdom of Mali in the 1300s, p. 320

E

East Africa an eastern region of the continent of Africa that is made up of the countries of Burundi, Kenya, Rwanda, Tanzania, Uganda, and Somalia, p. 12

Ecuador (2° S, 78° W) a country in northwest South America, p. 336

Egypt (27° N, 30° E) a country in North Africa, p. 9

El Salvador (14° N, 89° W) a country in Central America, p. 583

England (53° N, 2° W) an island country in western Europe, p. 412

Ethiopia (9° N, 39° E) a country in East Africa, officially the People's Republic of Ethiopia, p. 69

Euphrates River (31° N, 47°25' E) a river that flows south from Turkey through Syria and Iraq, p. 22

Europe (50° N, 28° E) the world's second-smallest continent; a peninsula of the Eurasian landmass bounded by the Arctic Ocean, the Atlantic Ocean, the Mediterranean Sea, and Asia, p. 6

F

Fertile Crescent a region in Southwest Asia; site of the world's first civilizations, p. 32

Florence (43°46' N, 11°15' E) a city in the Tuscany region of central Italy, p. 433

France (46° N, 2° E) a country in western Europe, p. 233

G

Gambia (13° N, 15° W) a country in western Africa, p. 572

Ganges River (23°22' N, 90°32' E) a river in northern India and Bangladesh that flows from the Himalayas to the Bay of Bengal, p. 108

Gaul (46° N, 2° E) a region inhabited by the ancient Gauls, including present-day France and parts of Belgium, Germany, and Italy, p. 233

Germany (51° N, 10° E) a country in central Europe, p. 416

Ghana (8° N, 1° W) a country in West Africa; officially known as the Republic of Ghana, p. 319

Giza (30°1' N, 31°13' E) an ancient city of Upper Egypt; site of the Sphinx and the Great Pyramid, p. 84

Gobi Desert (43° N, 105° E) a desert in Mongolia and northern China, p. 364

Grand Canal (32°12' N, 119°31' E) the 1,085-mile (1,747 km) channel connecting the Huang and Chang rivers in China; the longest artificially made waterway in the world, p. 366

Great Plains (42° N, 100° W) a mostly flat and grassy region in western North America; home to the Plains Indians, p. 357

Great Wall of China (41° N, 117° E) a wall that extends about 1,400 miles across northern China; built in the third century B.C., p. 150

Great Zimbabwe (20°17' S, 30° 57' E) a former kingdom in the highlands of Southern Africa, founded in A.D. 1100, p. 329

Greece (39° N, 22° E) a country in southeastern Europe; site of a great ancient civilization, p. 127

Greenland (70° N, 40° W) a large, self-governing island in the northern Atlantic Ocean; part of Denmark, p. 397

Guatemala (15° N, 90° W) a country in Central America, p. 583

Gulf of Mexico (25° N, 90° W) an arm of the Atlantic Ocean in southeastern North America, bordering on eastern Mexico, the southeastern United States, and Cuba, p. 347

Gupta Empire an empire that ruled northern India in the 300s and 400s A.D., p. 130

H

Harappa (30°38' N, 72°52' E) an ancient city of the Indus civilization; a village in present-day Pakistan, p. 108

Himalayas (the) (28° N, 84° E) a mountain system in south central Asia that extends along the border between India and Tibet and through Pakistan, Nepal, and Bhutan, p. 106

Hindu Kush (36° N, 72° E) a mountain range in central Asia, p. 107

Hiroshima (34°24' N, 132°27' E) Japanese city located on Honshu Island, site of atomic bomb detonation, p. 624

Holy Land (32° N, 35° E) a small region at the eastern edge of the Mediterranean Sea that includes modern Israel; considered holy by Jews, Christians, and Muslims, p. 409

Huang River (37°32' N, 118°19' E) the second-longest river in China, beginning in Tibet and emptying into the Yellow Sea, p. 22

Hungary (47° N, 20° E) a country in eastern Europe, p. 566

I

Iberian Peninsula (40° N, 5° W) the peninsula in Europe on which Spain and Portugal are located, p. 455

Ile-Ife (7°30' N, 4°30' E) the capital of a kingdom in present-day Nigeria; major cultural and trading center, p. 322

Incan Empire an empire ruled by the Incas between the 1300s and the 1500s that stretched along the Andes through present-day Ecuador, Peru, Bolivia, Chile, and Argentina, p. 336

India (20° N, 77° E) a large country in South Asia, p. 17

Indian Ocean (10° S, 70° E) the world's third-largest ocean, lying between Africa, Asia, and Australia, p. 107

Indus River (24°20' N, 67°47' E) a river that rises in Tibet, crosses the Himalaya Mountains, and flows through India and Pakistan into the Arabian Sea; its valley was the home of India's earliest communities, p. 22

Iran (32° N, 53° E) a country in Southwest Asia, p. 42

Iraq (33° N, 44° E) a country in Southwest Asia, p. 15

Isthmus of Panama (9° N, 80° W) a strip of land that connects the continents of North America and South America, p. 460

Israel (32° N, 35° E) an ancient kingdom of the Hebrews; a present-day country in Southwest Asia, p. 53

Italy (43° N, 13° E) a boot-shaped country in southern Europe, including the islands of Sicily and Sardinia, p. 229

J

Japan (36° N, 138° E) an island country in the Pacific Ocean off the east coast of Asia, p. 123

Jerusalem (31°46' N, 35°14' E) the capital city of modern Israel; a holy city for Jews, Christians, and Muslims, p. 53

Judah the name of the southern half of the Kingdom of the Israelites (the northern half retaining the name Israel), with Jerusalem as its capital; later called Judaea, p. 53

Judaea (31°35' N, 35° E) a Roman province centered on the ancient region of Judah, Roman Judaea including present-day Israel, Gaza, and the West Bank, p. 260

K

Kemet the term used by ancient Egyptians to describe their land, meaning "the black land," a reference to the dark soil left by the Nile River, p. 71

Kilwa (9°18' S, 28°25' E) a medieval Islamic city-state on an island near present-day Tanzania, p. 326

Knossos (35°20' N, 25°10' E) an ancient city on the island of Crete, occupied by the Minoans, a Bronze-Age civilization, p. 170

Koreas the nations of the Democratic People's Republic of Korea (North Korea) (40° N, 127° E) and the Republic of Korea (South Korea) (37° N, 128° E), which occupy the Korean peninsula in East Asia, p. 123

Kuwait (29° N, 48° E) a country on the Arabian Peninsula, in southwest Asia, p. 649

Kyoto (35°5' N, 135°45' E) a city in west central Japan; was Japan's capital until the late 1800s, p. 376

L

Lake Nasser (22°40' N, 32° E) a lake located in southeast Egypt and northern Sudan, formed by the construction of the Aswan Dam on the Nile River, p. 72

Lake Texcoco (19°30' N, 99° W) a lake, now drained, in central Mexico, where Mexico City now stands; formerly the site of the ancient Aztec capital of Tenochtitlán, p. 344

Liberia (6° N, 9° W) a country in western Africa, p. 575

Libya (27° N, 17° E) a country in North Africa, p. 572

Lower Egypt (31° N, 31° E) an area in ancient and present-day Egypt, in the northern Nile River region, p. 70

Lower Nubia an ancient region in northern Africa extending from the Nile Valley in Egypt to present-day Sudan; specifically, between the first and second Nile cataracts, p. 69

M

Macedonia (41° N, 23° E) an ancient kingdom on the Balkan Peninsula in southeastern Europe, the site of the present-day nation of Macedonia, northern Greece, and southwest Bulgaria, p. 79

Machu Picchu (13°7' S, 72°34' W) an ancient city in the Andes Mountains built during the Incan Empire; located near the present-day city of Cuzco in Peru, p. 336

Madagascar (19° S, 46° E) an island country off the coast of southeastern Africa, p. 574

Maginot Line a fortified line of defense built by the French to protect against a German attack prior to World War II, p. 620

Mali (17° N, 4° W) a country in West Africa, officially the Republic of Mali; powerful West African trading kingdom from about 1240 to 1500, p. 318

Manchuria (47° N, 125° E) a historical province located in northeastern China; invaded by the Japanese prior to World War II, p. 613

Marathon (38°10' N, 23°58' E) a village in ancient Greece, northeast of Athens, where the ancient Greeks defeated the Persians in 490 B.C., p. 210

Marne River (48°49' N, 2°24' E) a river in northeastern France; site of two major World War I battles, p. 597

Mauritania (20° N, 12° W) a country in northwestern Africa, p. 572

Maurya Empire the Indian empire founded by Chandragupta; empire that began with his kingdom in northeastern India and spread to most of northern and central India, p. 126

Mecca (21°27' N, 39°49' E) a city in western Saudi Arabia; birthplace of the prophet Muhammad; the holiest Muslim city, p. 294

Medina (41°8' N, 81°52' W) a city in western Saudi Arabia; one of the two holiest cities of Islam (the other being Mecca), p. 295

Mediterranean Sea (35° N, 20° E) the large sea that separates Europe and Africa, p. 32

Memphis (29°51' N, 31°15' E) an ancient city in Lower Egypt; capital of many ancient Egyptian dynasties, p. 75

Meroë (16°56' N, 33°43' E) a city in ancient Nubia; in present-day Sudan, p. 97

Mesopotamia (34° N, 44° E) an ancient region between the Tigris and Euphrates Rivers in Southwest Asia, p. 31

Mexico (23° N, 102° W) a country in North America, p. 344

Mohenjo-Daro (27°18' N, 68°15' E) an ancient city on the Indus River in Pakistan, p. 108

Moluccas (2° S, 128° E) islands currently part of Indonesia; once known as the Spice Islands, were prized by Europeans for spices, p. 466

Montenegro (42°30' N, 19°18' E) a Balkan republic; formerly part of Yugoslavia, p. 595

Morocco (32° N, 5° W) a country in North Africa, p. 571

Moscow (55°45' N, 37°35' E) the capital of Russia, p. 604

Mount Olympus (40°5' N, 22°21' E) Greece's highest mountain, site where ancient Greeks believed their gods dwelled, p. 182

Mycenae (37°44' N, 22°45' E) an ancient city on the mainland of Greece, home to one of Greece's earliest civilizations, p. 171

N

Nagasaki (32°48' N, 129°55' E) a city on the island of Kyushu, Japan, p. 474

Namibia (22° S, 17° E) a country in southwestern Africa, p. 572

Napata one of the three most powerful Nubian kingdoms, located in Upper Nubia, p. 97

Netherlands (52° N, 6° E) a country in northwestern Europe; also known as Holland, p. 437

New Babylonian Empire a revival of the old Babylonian empire stretching from the Persian Gulf to the Mediterranean Sea, p. 41

Nicaragua (13° N, 85° W) a country in Central America, p. 583

Niger (16° N, 8° E) a country in western Africa, p. 572

Nigeria a country in western Africa, p. 572

Nile River (30°10' N, 31°6' E) the longest river in the world, flowing through northeastern Africa into the Mediterranean Sea, p. 9

Normandy a region in northwestern France where the D-Day invasion by the Allies took place during World War II, p. 623

North China Plain a large plain in East Asia, built up by soil deposits of the Huang River, p. 137

Norway (62° N, 10° E) a country in northwestern Europe, occupying the western part of the Scandinavian peninsula, p. 396

Nubia (21° N, 33° E) a desert region and ancient kingdom in the Nile River Valley, in present-day southern Egypt and northern Sudan, p. 69

O

Orléans (47°55' N, 1°54' E) a city in north-central France; a battle site during the Hundred Years' War where the French under the leadership of Joan of Arc defeated the English, p. 419

Ottoman Empire an empire centered in present-day Turkey that ruled parts of Southeastern Europe, North Africa, and Southwest Asia between the 1400s and 1918, p. 304

P

Pacific Ocean (10° S, 150° W) the largest of the world's oceans; extends from the western Americas to eastern Asia and Australia, p. 347

Pakistan (30° N, 70° E) a country in South Asia between India and Afghanistan; officially, the Islamic Republic of Pakistan, p. 22

Paris (48°52' N, 2° 20' E) the capital of France, p. 407

Parthenon (37°58' N, 23°43' E) the chief temple of the Greek goddess Athena, on the hill of the Acropolis in Athens, Greece, p. 181

Pearl Harbor (21°21' N, 157°57' W) a U.S. naval base located in Hawaii that was bombed by the Japanese in World War II, p. 623

Peloponnesus (37°30' N, 22° E) a large peninsula in southern Greece, p. 212

Persia (32° N, 53° E) the historical name for a region in present-day Iran, p. 157

Persian Empire *n.* an ancient empire centered in modern Iran that covered the Fertile Crescent, Egypt, Asia Minor, and parts of Central Asia and India, p. 42

Persian Gulf (27° N, 51° E) an arm of the Arabian Sea, located between the Arabian Peninsula and southwest Iran, p. 32

Peru (10° S, 76° W) a country in northwestern South America, p. 336

Phoenicia (34° N, 36° E) an ancient region in present-day Lebanon, p. 49

Poland (52° N, 19° E) a country in eastern Europe, p. 565

Portugal (40° N, 8° W) a country in western Europe; occupies the Iberian Peninsula with Spain, p. 329

Prussia a kingdom in central and eastern Europe that included parts of what are now Russia, Poland, and Germany, p. 520

R

Red Sea (20° N, 38° E) a narrow sea located between northeast Africa and the Arabian Peninsula; connected to the Arabian Sea in the south, p. 71

Rio de Janeiro (22°54' S, 43°14' W) a city in Brazil, p. 583

Romania (46° N, 26° E) a European country located in the Balkans, p. 595

Rome (41°54' N, 12°29' E) the capital city of Italy; the capital of the ancient Roman Empire, p. 100

Runnymede (51°26' N, 0°34' W) a meadow along the Thames River in England, p. 418

Russia (40° N, 84° W) a country in northern Eurasia, p. 284

S

Sahara (26° N, 13° E) the largest tropical desert in the world, covering almost all of North Africa, p. 71

Sarajevo (43°52' N, 18°25' E) capital city of Bosnia and Herzegovina, p. 594

Senegal (14° N, 14° W) a country in western Africa, p. 572

Serbia (44° N, 21° E) a Balkan republic; formerly part of Yugoslavia, p. 595

Sierra Leone (9° N, 12° W) a country in western Africa, p. 572

Silk Road an ancient trade route between China and Europe, p. 156

Sinai Peninsula (29°30' N, 34° E) a peninsula in Egypt at the northern end of the Red Sea that links southwest Asia with northeast Africa, p. 52

Songhai (16°N, 0°) an ancient empire and trading state in West Africa that reached its peak in the 1400s, p. 321

South Africa (30° S, 26° E) the southernmost country in Africa, officially known as the Republic of South Africa, p. 310

Spain (40° N, 4° W) a country in western Europe; with Portugal, occupies the Iberian Peninsula, p. 233

Sparta (37°5' N, 22°27' E) an ancient city-state in Greece, p. 180

Stalingrad historic name for Volgograd, a city in southwestern Russia, p. 623

Sudan (15° N, 30° E) a country in northeastern Africa, p. 572

Suez Canal (29°55' N, 32°33' E) a canal that links the Mediterranean and Red Seas, p. 577

Sumer (31° N, 46° E) the site of the earliest-known civilization, located in Mesopotamia, in present-day southern Iraq; later became part of Babylonia, p. 30

Sweden (62° N, 15° E) a country in northern Europe, occupying the eastern half of the Scandinavian Peninsula, p. 396

Syria (35° N, 38° E) a country in Southwest Asia, p. 15

T

Taj Mahal (27°10' N, 78°3' E) a spectacular tomb near Agra, India, built by the Mughal emperor Shah Jahan in memory of his wife, Mumtaz Mahal, p. 386

Tanzania (6° S, 35° E) a coastal country in south-eastern Africa, p. 12

Tenochtitlán (19°29' N, 99°9' W) the capital city of the Aztec empire, located on islands in Lake Texcoco, now the site of Mexico City, p. 344

Thames River (51°28' N, 0.43' E) a river in southern England that flows to the North Sea, p. 418

Tiber River (41°44' N, 12°14' E) a major river in Italy that rises in the mountains of central Italy and empties into the Tyrrhenian Sea; flows through Rome, p. 228

Tibet (32° N, 88° E) a historical region in central Asia north of the Himalayas; currently under Chinese control, p. 123

Tigris River (31° N, 47°25' E) a river in Iraq and Turkey, p. 22

Tombouctou (16°46' N, 3°1' W) a city in Mali near the Niger River; in the past an important center of Islamic education and a trans-Saharan caravan stop (also spelled Timbuktu), p. 321

Troy (39°57' N, 26°15' E) an ancient city in north-western Anatolia, the Asian part of Turkey; the site of the mythical Trojan War, p. 171

Turkey (39° N, 35° E) a country located in South-west Asia, p. 40

Tyre (33°16' N, 35°11' E) a rich trade port and the major city of Phoenicia, located on the eastern Mediterranean Sea in present-day southern Lebanon, p. 48

U

Ukraine (49° N, 32° E) a country in eastern Europe, p. 623

Upper Egypt (26° N, 32° E) an area in ancient and present-day Egypt in the Nile Valley, south of the river's delta and the 30th northern parallel, p. 70

Upper Nubia an ancient region in northeastern Africa that extended from the Nile Valley in Egypt to present-day Sudan; specifically, between the second and sixth cataracts, p. 69

Ur (30°57' N, 46°9' E) a city in ancient Sumer in southern Mesopotamia, located in present-day southeast Iraq, p. 22

V

Venice (45°27' N, 12°21' E) a city and major seaport in northern Italy known for its canals, p. 288

Versailles (48°48' N, 2°1' E) a town in France, where the Treaty of Versailles that ended World War I was signed, p. 598

Vienna (48°13' N, 16°2' E) the capital city of Austria, p. 562

Vietnam (16° N, 108° E) a country located in Southeast Asia, p. 123

W

West Africa the countries in the western region of Africa, p. 310

Wittenberg (51°52' N, 12°39' E) the city in Germany where Martin Luther posted his 95 Theses, p. 442

Z

Zimbabwe (20° S, 30° E) a country in Southern Africa, p. 330

Biographical Dictionary

A

Abraham (AY bruh ham) the first leader of the Israelites, who, according to the Torah, led his family to Canaan, p. 51

Akbar (AK bahr) (1542–1605) the greatest of the Mughal emperors and reformers of India, p. 384

Akhenaton (ah keh NAH tun) (died *c.* 1354 B.C.) a king of ancient Egypt (*c.* 1372–1354 B.C.) who introduced monotheism, p. 82

Alexander the Great (al ig ZAN dur thuh grayt) the king of Macedonia from 356 to 323 B.C.; conquerer of Persia and Egypt and invader of India, p. 79

Archimedes (ahr kuh MEE deez) (born 290 B.C.) a Greek inventor and mathematician; calculated the surface area and volume of a sphere, p. 222

Aristarchus (AIR uh STAHR kus) (lived *c.* 310–230 B.C.) a Greek astronomer who was the first to hold the theory that Earth moves around the sun, p. 222

Aristotle (AIR uh STAHT ul) (384–322 B.C.) a Greek philosopher who was a student of Plato and became a famous teacher; wrote about and taught logic, politics, science, and poetry, p. 216

Asoka (uh SOH kuh) (died *c.* 238 B.C.) Chandragupta's grandson and last major emperor of India's Maurya empire; credited with having built the greatest empire in India's history; helped spread Buddhism, p. 128

Atahualpa (ah tuh WAHL puh) (1502–1533) the last king of the Incas; captured, held for ransom, and murdered by Spanish conquerors after the ransom was delivered, p. 483

Augustus (aw GUS tus) (63 B.C.–A.D. 14) the first Roman emperor; ruled after Julius Caesar's death in 44 B.C. until his own death; named Octavian, he was awarded the title of Augustus in 27 B.C., p. 235

B

Babur (BAH bur) (1483–1530) a descendant of Genghis Khan and Timur; founder of the Mughal dynasty and emperor from 1526 to 1530, p. 384

Balboa, Vasco Núñez de (VAHS koh NOO nyeth theh bal BOH uh) (1475–1519) a Spanish explorer who discovered the Isthmus of Panama; also led an expedition that reached the Pacific Ocean, p. 460

Batista, Fulgencio (fool HEN see oh bah TEE stah) (1901–1973) ruler of Cuba from 1933 to 1944 and from 1952 to 1959, p. 640

Bismarck, Otto von (1815–1898) German chancellor who made competing claims with Leopold II of Belgium for African territory, p. 571

Bolívar, Simón (1783–1830) South American revolutionary who helped liberate Ecuador, Peru, and Bolivia, p. 583

Bonaparte, Napoleon (nuh POH lee un BOH nuh pahrt) (1769–1821) French emperor from 1799 to 1814; exiled to Elba in 1814, but returned in 1815 and resumed power until Battle of Waterloo in the same year, p. 543

Boyle, Robert (1627–1691) Irish chemist whose work laid the foundation for modern chemistry, p. 532

C

Cabral, Pedro Alvarez (PAY droh AL vuh rez kuh BRAHL) (*c.* 1467–1520) Portuguese explorer; claimed Brazil for Portugal; later sailed to India, p. 467

Caligula (kuh LIG yuh luh) (A.D. 12–41) a Roman emperor (A.D. 37–41) believed to be insane for much of his rule; responsible for many disturbances during his reign, p. 242

Calvin, John (jahn KAL vin) (1509–1564) the founder of the Calvinist church; preached idea of predestination, p. 447

Castro, Fidel (born 1926) Communist leader of Cuba who overthrew Batista in 1959, p. 640

Catherine the Great (1729–1796) czarina of Russia from 1762 to 1796, expanded Russian territory and modernized farming and industry, p. 519

Cervantes, Miguel de (mee GEL du sur VAN tee) (1547–1616) Spanish novelist who wrote *Don Quixote*, p. 509

Champollion, Jean François (zhahn frahn SWAH shahm poh LY OHN) (A.D. 1790–1832) a French scholar; first to decode Egyptian hieroglyphics, p. 92

Chandragupta (chun druh GOOP tuh) (died 297 B.C.) founded India's Maurya empire in 321 B.C.; unified most of India under one ruler, p. 126

Charlemagne (SHAHR luh mayn) (742–814) king of the Franks who conquered much of Western Europe; patron of literature and learning, p. 396

Charles I (1500–1558) king of Spain who later became Charles V, emperor of the Holy Roman Empire; ruled from 1519 to 1558, p. 507

Charles I (1600–1649) king of England from 1625 to 1649; fight with Parliament resulted in civil war, p. 521

Churchill, Winston (WIN stun CHUR chil) (1874–1965) British prime minister who led Great Britain during World War II, p. 620

Cicero (SIS uh roh) (106–43 B.C.) the greatest and best-known Roman orator and the author of many famous speeches; also famous as a philosopher and politician, p. 246

Columbus, Christopher (KRIS tuh fur kuh LUM bus) (1451–1506) an Italian navigator who discovered the Americas while looking for a sea route from Europe to Asia, p. 458

Commodus (KAHM uh dus) (A.D. 161–192) a Roman emperor who succeeded his father, Marcus Aurelius; a poor ruler who was assassinated and whose reign marked the beginning of the decline of the Roman Empire, p. 242

Confucius (kun FYOO shus) (551–479 B.C.) a Chinese philosopher and teacher; originator of Confucianism; greatly influenced Chinese life, p. 141

Constantine (KAHN stun teen) (c. A.D. 278–337) the emperor of Rome from A.D. 312 to 337; encouraged the spread of Christianity, p. 270

Cortés, Hernán (hur NAHN kohr TEZ) (1485–1547) a Spanish explorer who reached Mexico in 1519, conquered the Aztecs, and won Mexico for Spain, p. 482

Cromwell, Oliver (AHL uh vur KRAHM well) (1599–1658) lord protector of England after English Civil War, p. 523

Cyrus the Great (SY rus thuh grayt) (c. 590–529 B.C.) the founder of the Persian Empire in the mid-500s B.C., p. 41

D

da Gama, Vasco (VAHS koh duh GAM uh) (c. 1469–1524) a Portuguese navigator who was the first European to sail to India; his voyage opened the way for the expansion of the Portuguese empire, p. 457

da Vinci, Leonardo (lee uh NAHR doh duh VIN chee) (1452–1519) an Italian artist, scientist, inventor; many of his works, including the Mona Lisa, were not finished, p. 430

David (DAY vid) (died c. 972 B.C.) the king of the Israelites from about 1012 to 972 B.C.; unified the Jews into a settled nation and established a capital at the city of Jerusalem, p. 53

David, Jacques-Louis (zhahk loo EE dah VEED) (1748–1825) French painter and Jacobin supporter, p. 542

Deborah (DEB uh ruh) (c. 1100s B.C.) a judge and prophet in the Jewish Bible, p. 58

Democritus (dih MAHK ruh tus) (c. 460–c. 370 B.C.) a Greek philosopher who proposed that the universe is made up of atoms, p. 184

Demosthenes (dih MAHS thuh neez) (384–322 B.C.) a Greek orator who issued powerful speeches against King Philip of Macedonia; the speeches became known as *Philippics*, p. 217

Descartes, René (ruh NAY day KAHRT) (1596–1650) French philosopher whose ideas led to the development of analytic geometry, p. 532

Dingane (ding GAHN) (*c.* 1795–1840) king of Zulu people; unsuccessfully challenged Dutch settlers in the Natal region, p. 574

Diocletian (dy uh KLEE shuhn) (A.D. 245–316) the emperor of Rome from A.D. 284 to 305; reorganized the Roman government, p. 265

Dias, Bartolomeu (bahr too loo MEE oo DEE us) (*c.* 1450–1500) a Portuguese explorer, first to sail around southern tip of Africa, p. 457

Donatello (doh nuh TEL oh) (*c.* 1386–1466) a Renaissance sculptor, p. 433

Durer, Albrecht (ahl brekt DYOOR ur) (1471–1528) German painter; master of woodcuts and engravings; Italian style reflected in his work, p. 437

E

Erasmus, Desiderius (des uh DIHR ee us ih RAZ mus) (1466–1536) a Roman Catholic priest; leading figure of Christian Humanism; mocked certain Church practices, p. 435

Eratosthenes (ehr uh TAHS thuh neez) (*c.* 275– *c.* 195 B.C.) a Greek scholar who headed the library at Alexandria; a noted astronomer who wrote about many subjects, p. 222

Euclid (YOO klid) (*c.* 300 B.C.) a Greco-Roman mathematician; known for the Elements, a book on geometry, p. 222

F

Ferdinand, Francis (1863–1914) Archduke of Austria; his and his wife's assassination by a Balkan revolutionary led to the start of World War I, p. 594

Fox, Vicente (born 1942) Mexican president; his election ended 71 years of government control by the PRI, p. 637

Frederick William I (1688–1740) king of Prussia from 1713 to 1740; known as Frederick the Great, p. 520

G

Gallilei, Galileo (gal uh LEE oh gal uh LAY) (1564–1642) Italian astronomer; proved that the planets in our solar system revolve around the sun, p. 531

Gautama, Siddhartha (sih DAHR tuh gow tuh muh) (born after 500 B.C. and died before 350 B.C.) the founder of Buddhism; a prince who left his family and gave up his wealth to try to find the cause of human suffering; also known as the Buddha, p. 119

Gorbachev, Mikhail (mee kah EEL GAWR buh chawf) (born 1931) Soviet leader; led reforms in the U.S.S.R., including glasnost and perestroika, p. 633

Gregory VII (GREG uh ree thuh SEV unth) (*c.* A.D. 1020–1085) a pope who reigned from A.D. 1073 to 1085; considered one of the great papal reformers of the Middle Ages, p. 416

Gutenberg, Johannes (yoh HAHN us GOOT un burg) (died 1468) a German printer who invented movable type, p. 434

H

Hadrian (HAY dree un) (76–138) emperor of Rome from 117 to 138; one of Rome's greatest emperors; worked to unify the empire, p. 242

Hammurabi (hah muh RAH bee) (died 1750 B.C.) the king of Babylon from about 1792 to 1750 B.C.; creator of the Babylonian empire; established one of the oldest codes of law, p. 39

Hatshepsut (haht SHEP soot) (died *c.* 1458 B.C.) the stepmother of Thutmose III; ruled Egypt as regent and then as pharaoh; achieved economic success, especially in trade, p. 74

Henry (HEN ree) (1394–1460) a prince of Portugal; advanced Portuguese navigation and trade, p. 456

Henry IV (HEN ree thuh fawrth) (1050–1106) a king of Germany and the Holy Roman Empire; argued with Pope Gregory VII and was banned from the Church, p. 416

Henry IV (HEN ree thuh fawrth) (1553–1610) king of France from 1589 to 1610; a Huguenot who converted to the Roman Catholic Church, p. 513

Henry VIII (HEN ree thuh ayth) (1491–1547) the king of England from 1509 to 1547; had six wives; separated the English Church from Catholicism to begin the English Reformation, p. 446

Herodotus (huh RAHD uh tus) (c. 484–420 B.C.) a Greek author who traveled throughout the known world; wrote about the wars between Greece and Persia in the *History*, the first major historical work of ancient times, p. 68

Hitler, Adolf (AD awlf HIT lur) (1889–1945) brutal German dictator who led Nazi Germany during World War II, p. 612

Hobbes, Thomas (1588–1679) English writer; author of *Leviathan*, a book that strongly supported the power of royalty and the divine right of kings, p. 534

Homer (HOH mur) (c. 800 B.C.) a Greek poet; credited with composing the epics the *Iliad* and the *Odyssey*, p. 171

Hussein, Saddam (suh DAHM hoo SAYN) (born 1937) Iraqi dictator from 1979 to 2003, p. 649

I

Ibn Battuta (IB un bah TOO tuh) (1304–1369) a North African traveler who wrote about his travels across Africa and Asia, p. 317

Ieyasu, Tokugawa (toh koo GAH wah, ee yay AH soo) (1543–1616) the founder of the last shogunate in Japan; closed his country off from the rest of the world, p. 378

J

Jahan, Shah (shah juh HAHN) (1592–1666) a Mughal emperor of India and builder of the Taj Mahal, p. 386

Jesus (JEE zus) (c. 6-4 B.C.–c. A.D. 30) the founder of Christianity; believed by Christians to be the Messiah; executed by the Roman government; believed to have appeared to his followers after his death and to have risen bodily to heaven, p. 259

Joan of Arc (john uv ahrk) (c. 1412–1431) a peasant girl who led the French army to victory over the English in the Hundred Years' War, p. 419

John I (jahn thuh furst) (1167–1216) the king of England who was forced to sign the Magna Carta in 1215 under threat of civil war, p. 418

Joseph II (1741–1790) Holy Roman emperor from 1765 to 1790; made reforms based on Enlightenment ideas, p. 535

Julius Caesar (JOOL yus SEE zur) (c. 100–44 B.C.) a Roman political and military leader; became dictator for life and was assassinated by Roman senators in the same year; greatly improved the Roman government, p. 234

Justinian (juh STIN ee un) (A.D. 483–565) a Byzantine emperor, responsible for codifying Roman law; his code influenced all later laws, p. 246

K

Kennedy, John F. (1917–1963) U.S. president from 1961 to 1963, p. 636

Kerensky, Alexander F. (al ig ZAN dur (F.) kuh REN skee) (1881–1970) Soviet revolutionary who led the Soviet revolutionary government from July 1917 to October 1917, p. 603

Khrushchev, Nikita (nih KEE tah KROO shawf) (1894–1971) Soviet Premier from 1958 to 1964, p. 636

Kublai Khan (KOO bly kahn) (A.D. 1215–1294) a Mongol emperor of China, p. 37

L

Laozi (LOW dzih) (c. 500s B.C.) a Chinese philosopher and the founder of Taoism, p. 147

Leeuwenhoek, Antoni van (ahn TOH nee van LAY vun hook) (1632–1723) Dutch merchant who discovered microorganisms, p. 530

Lenin, Vladimir (vlad uh MIHR LEN in) (1870–1924) Russian leader of the Bolshevik party that overthrew Czar Nicholas II, p. 602

Leopold II (1835–1909) Belgian king from 1865 to 1909; asserted claim of the Congo, p. 570

Licinius (ly SIN ee us) (died A.D. 325) took control of the eastern part of the Roman Empire in 313; co-emperor with Constantine; continued to allow religious persecution in the east; was defeated in 324 by Constantine, p. 274

Lin Zexu (lin DZUH shoo) (1785–1850) Chinese scholar who shut down British opium trade, leading to Opium Wars, p. 580

Liu Bang (LYOH bahng) (256–195 B.C.) the founder of the Han dynasty of China in 202 B.C.; born a peasant; stabilized the government and promoted education, p. 152

Locke, John (1632–1704) English author who opposed the theory of the divine right of kings; wrote *Two Treatises of Government*, p. 534

Louis XIV (1638–1715) king of France from 1643 to 1715, known as the Sun King, p. 512

Louis-Philippe (1773–1850) king of France from 1830 to 1848; known as the "citizen king," p. 564

Loyola, Ignatius (ig NAY shus loy OH luh) (c. 1491–1556) founded the Society of Jesus; Jesuits worked to educate people and spread Catholicism, p. 448

Luther, Martin (MAHRT un LOO thur) (1483–1546) a German teacher who founded the Protestant Reformation of the 1500s in revolt against the Roman Catholic Church, p. 440

M

MacArthur, Douglas (1880–1964) American General who led U.S. troops in the Pacific Theatre during World War II and in Korea during the Korean War, p. 632

Magellan, Ferdinand (FUR duh nand muh JEL un) (c. 1480–1521) a Portuguese explorer whose crew was the first to sail around the world; he was killed during the voyage, p. 461

Mandela, Nelson (NEL sun man DEL us) (born 1918) African National Congress leader who fought against apartheid; jailed for 27 years before being released in 1990; later became president of South Africa, p. 646

Mansa Musa (MAHN sah moo SAH) (died c. 1332) a Muslim emperor of Mali known for his pilgrimage to Mecca in 1324; encouraged the arts and learning, p. 318

Marat, Jean-Paul (zhahn pawl mah RAH) (1743–1793) French revolutionary Jacobin leader assassinated by Charlotte Corday, p. 542

Marcus Aurelius (MAHR kus aw REE lee uhs) (A.D. 121–180) a Roman emperor; generally tolerant and promoter of humanitarian causes, p. 242

Martial (MAHR shul) (c. A.D. 40–104) a Roman poet; wrote poems about the early Roman Empire, p. 252

Mary II (1662–1694) queen of England from 1689 to 1694; married to William III of the Netherlands; both came to power in England with the Glorious Revolution, p. 524

Menelik (1844–1913) Ethiopian emperor whose forces defeated the Italian army in 1896, p. 575

Menes (MEE neez) (c. 2900s B.C.) the legendary founder of the first Egyptian dynasty; according to tradition, unified Upper and Lower Egypt around 3100 B.C. or earlier and founded the capital of Memphis; possibly King Narmer of the carving known as the Narmer Palette, p. 75

Michelangelo (my kul AN jul loh) (1475–1564) an Italian Renaissance artist; famous for painting the ceiling of the Sistine Chapel, p. 433

More, Sir Thomas (sur TAHM us mawr) (1477–1535) an English writer, author of *Utopia*, a novel that pointed out problems in society, p. 435

Moses (MOH zuz) (*c.* 1200s B.C.) the Israelite leader who, according to the Torah, led the Israelites from Egypt to Canaan; said to have received the Ten Commandments from God, p. 52

Muhammad (muh HAM ud) (*c.* A.D. 570–632) the prophet of Islam who Muslims believe proclaimed the message of God; considered by Muslims to be the last of the prophets, p. 292

Mussolini, Benito (beh NEE toh moo suh LEE nee) (1883–1945) Italian dictator who founded the fascist moverment, p. 611

Napoleon III (nuh POH lee un thuh thurd) (1808–1873) elected president of France in 1848; abolished French republic in 1852 and declared himself emperor; overthrown in 1870, p. 566

Nebuchadnezzar II (nehb uh kuhd NEHZ uhr thuh SEK und) (*c.* 630–561 B.C.) the king of the New Babylonian empire from about 605 to 561 B.C., p. 41

Nero (NEE roh) (*c.* A.D. 37–68) the Roman emperor from A.D. 54 to 68; known for his cruel treatment of the Christians, p. 242

Newton, Sir Isaac (1642–1727) British physicist who developed theories about natural laws, such as the laws of motion and gravity, p. 532

Nicholas II (1868–1918) Russian czar who ruled from 1894 to 1917, p. 602

Nkrumah, Kwame (KWAH mee un KROO muh) (1909–1972) first president of Ghana, p. 645

Octavian (AHK tay vee un) (63 B.C.–A.D. 14) Rome's first emperor; strong leader whose rule led to peace and wealth; also known as Augustus, p. 235

Omar Khayyam (oh mayr ky AHM) (1048–1131) Persian poet, mathematician, and astronomer, p. 300

P

Paul (PAWL) (died *c.* A.D. 64) a disciple of Jesus; spent his later life spreading Jesus' teachings; helped turn Christianity into an organized religion, p. 262

Peter the Hermit (PEET ur thuh HUR mit) (*c.* 1050–1115) a French religious leader who led one of the bands of the First Crusade, p. 412

Petrarch, Francesco (frahn CHES koh PEA trahrk) (1304–1374) an Italian poet; first great humanist; loved the works of Cicero and other Latin writers; studied the ancient Romans, p. 432

Pericles (PEHR uh kleez) (*c.* 495–429 B.C.) an Athenian leader; played a major role in the development of democracy and the Athenian empire, p. 180

Perón, Juan (hwahn pay RAWN) (1895–1974) Argentinean president from 1946 to 1955 and from 1973 to 1974, p. 639

Perry, Matthew (1794–1858) American naval commander who tried to establish increased trade with Japan, p. 582

Peter I (1672–1725) czar of Russia from 1689 to 1725; known as Peter the Great; greatly expanded Russian territory, p. 518

Philip (FIL ip) (382–336 B.C.) a king of Macedonia; seized power in 359 B.C.; conquered the Greek city-states; father of Alexander the Great, p. 216

Philip II (FIL ip thuh SEK und) (1527–1598) Spanish king from 1556 to 1598; responsible for the Inquisition and the Spanish Armada, p. 508

Pizarro, Francisco (frahn SEES koh pea SAHR oh) (*c.* 1475–1541) Spanish explorer who conquered the Incan empire and claimed Peru for Spain, p. 341

Plato (PLAYT oh) (*c.* 427-347 B.C.) a Greek philosopher and student of Socrates; founded the Academy of Athens and wrote *The Republic,* p. 185

Polo, Marco (MAHR koh POH loh) (1254–1324) employed by Kublai Khan for 17 years; wrote about his travels after returning to Europe; sparked increased trade between Europe and China, p. 371

Ptolemy V (TAHL uh mee thuh fifth) (died 180 B.C.) the king of ancient Egypt from 205 to 180 B.C., married to Cleopatra; his ascension to the throne is recorded on the Rosetta Stone, p. 92

R

Rabelais, François (frahn SWAH rab uh LAY) (*c.* 1483–1553) a French Renaissance writer; author of Gargantua and Pantagruel, a tale that attacks critics of humanist learning, p. 436

Richelieu, Cardinal Armand (KAHRD un ul ahr mund RISH loo) (1585–1642) French cardinal; served in the administration of King Louis XIII, p. 513

Robespierre, Maximilien (mahk see mee LAYHN ROHBZ pyehr) (1758–1794) Jacobin leader during French Reign of Terror, p. 542

Romulus Augustulus (RAHM yuh lus oh GUS chuh lus) (died *c.* A.D. 476) the last Roman emperor; ruled from A.D. 475 to 476, p. 276

Roosevelt, Franklin Delano (FRANGK lin DEL uh noh ROH zuh velt) (1882–1945) U.S. president from 1933 to 1945; created the New Deal to help America recover from the Great Depression, p. 611

S

Saladin (SAL uh din) (*c.* 1137–1193) a Muslim leader who became sultan of Egypt and ultimately defeated the Crusades; was also a man of learning and a patron of the arts, p. 412

San Martín, José de (1778–1850) South American revolutionary who helped liberate Chile, Argentina, and Peru, p. 583

Sargon II (SAHR gahn thuh sek und) (died 705 B.C.) Assyrian king (722–705 B.C.); conquered Babylonia; founded the last great Assyrian dynasty, p. 38

Saul (sawl) (*c.* 1000s B.C.) the first king of the Israelites, p. 53

Seneca (SEN ih kuh) (*c.* 4 B.C.–A.D. 65) a writer, philosopher, and statesman of ancient Rome, p. 255

Shakespeare, William (WIL yum SHAYK spihr) (1564–1616) wrote at least 37 verse plays based on plots borrowed from ancient works; interested in the human character, p. 436

Shi Huangdi (shur hwahng DEE) (*c.* 259–210 B.C.) the founder of the Qin dynasty and China's first emperor; ruled from about 221 to 210 B.C., p. 149

Sima Qian (sih MAH chen) (*c.* 135–87 B.C.) a Chinese scholar, astronomer, and historian; wrote the most important history of ancient China, Historical Records, p. 159

Socrates (SAHK ruh teez) (*c.* 470–399 B.C.) an Athenian philosopher of the late 400s B.C.; taught by using a method of questioning; helped form many values of Western culture; put to death for challenging Athenian values, p. 184

Solomon (SAHL uh mun) (died *c.* 932 B.C.) the king of the Israelites from about 972 to 932 B.C., after his father King David; built cities, a temple, and established foreign trade and alliances, p. 53

Solon (SOH lun) (*c.* 630–560 B.C.) an Athenian statesman; made Athens more democratic, p. 175

Stalin, Joseph (JOH zuf STAH lin) (1879–1953) brutal Russian dictator who took power in 1924, following the Russian Revolution, p. 606

Suleyman the Magnificent (soo lay MAHN) (1494–1566) leader of the Ottoman Empire from 1520 to 1566, p. 507

Sundiata (sun JAH taah) (died 1255) West African king; founded the Kingdom of Mali, p. 320

T

Taharka (tuh HAHR kuh) a prince of Nubia; became king of Nubia and Egypt in 690 B.C., p. 96

Tang Taizong (tahng ty ZAWNG) (A.D. 600–649) second emperor of the Tang dynasty, p. 366

Thales (THAY leez) (*c.* 636–546 B.C.) Greek philosopher; the first recorded Western philosopher; looked for ways to explain the physical world other than with mythological explanations, p. 184

Theresa, Maria (1717–1780) monarch who ruled Austria from 1740 to 1780, p. 520

Thutmose III (thoot MOH suh thuh thurd) (died 1426 B.C.) the stepson of Hatshepsut; considered the greatest pharaoh of Egypt's New Kingdom; expanded the empire to include Syria and Nubia; reigned from about 1479 to 1425 B.C., p. 78

Timur (tee MOOR) (1336–1405) a Turkish conqueror active in India, Russia, and the Mediterranean, known for his brutality, p. 382

Trajan (TRAY jun) (A.D. 53–117) Roman emperor who ruled at the empire's height, A.D. 98–117, p. 520

Trotsky, Leon (LEE ahn TRAHK skee) (1879–1940) Bolshevik leader who led the Reds to defeat the Whites in 1920, p. 605

Tutankhamen (toot ahng KAH mun) a king of ancient Egypt from about 1333 to 1323 B.C.; well-known because the excavation of his tomb in 1922 provided new knowledge about Egyptian art and history, p. 77

U

Urban II (UR bun thuh SEK und) (*c.* A.D. 1035–1099) a pope who developed reforms begun by Pope Gregory VII, began the Crusades, and built political power for the papacy, p. 409

V

van Eyck, Jan (yahn van yk) (*c.* 1390–1441) a Flemish Renaissance painter; master of realistic portraits, p. 437

Vesalius, Andreas (AN dree us vih SAY lee us) (1514–1564) produced the first manual with pictures that showed the structure of the human body, p. 532

Virgil (VUR jul) (70–19 B.C.) a Roman poet and the author of the *Aeneid,* an epic that glorifies Roman ideals in the age of Augustus, p. 240

W

Washington, George (1732–1799) Revolutionary War leader and first U. S. president, p. 528

Watt, James (1736–1819) Scottish inventor who adapted the steam engine for uses other than pumping water from mines, p. 554

Whitney, Eli (1765–1825) American inventor who first developed interchangeable parts, p. 555

William III (1650–1702) king of England from 1689 to 1702; married to Mary II; came to power with the Glorious Revolution, p. 524

Wilson, Woodrow (1856–1924) U.S. president from 1913 to 1921; his Fourteen Points led to the League of Nations, the precursor to the United Nations, p. 599

Wudi (WOO dee) (*c.* 156–86 B.C.) the Chinese emperor from 140 to 86 B.C.; expanded the Chinese empire under the Han dynasty; made Confucianism the state religion, p. 152

Y

Yoritomo, Minamoto (mee nah moh toh yoh ree TOH moh) (1147–1199) the founder of the shogunate, a Japanese feudal system that lasted for 700 years, p. 378

Z

Zwingli, Ulrich (ool rik zwing lee) (1484–1531) a religious reformer who believed that the Bible alone contained all religious truth, p. 447

Glossary

A

absolute power (AB suh loot POW ur) *n.* complete control over someone or something, p. 75

acropolis (uh KRAH puh lis) *n.* the fortified hill of an ancient Greek city; the acropolis of Athens when spelled with a capital *A*, p. 172

administration (ad min is TRAY shun) *n.* a group of people who work with and for a leader, p. 513

afterlife (AF tur lyf) *n.* a life after death, p. 80

agora (AG uh ruh) *n.* a public market and meeting place in an ancient Greek city; the agora of Athens when spelled with a capital *A*, p. 199

ahimsa (uh HIM sah) *n.* the Hindu idea of nonviolence, p. 117

AIDS (aydz) n. a condition caused by the HIV virus that leads to the gradual collapse of the immune system and is fatal, p. 646

Aksum (AHK soom) *n.* an important East African center of trade, p. 327

alliance (uh LY uns) *n.* a close association between nations to achieve a common objective, p. 596

ally (AL eye) *n.* a country or group that is united with another for a common purpose, p. 491

alphabet (AL fuh bet) *n.* a set of symbols that represent the sounds of a language, p. 50

Ancestral Puebloans (an SES trul PWEB loh unz) *n.* one of the ancient Native American peoples of the Southwest, p. 355

Andes (AN dees) *n.* a mountain chain in western South America, p. 14

apartheid (uh PAHR tayt) *n.* a system of strict racial separation, p. 646

appeasement (uh PEEZ munt) *n.* the giving in to an aggressor in order to keep the peace, p. 617

apprentice (uh PREN tis) *n.* an unpaid person training in a craft or trade, p. 407

aqueduct (AK wuh dukt) *n.* a structure that carries water over long distances, p. 244

arch (ahrch) *n.* a curved structure used as a support over an open space, as in a doorway, p. 244

archaeologist (ahr kee AWL uh jist) *n.* a scientist who examines objects such as bones and tools to learn about past peoples and cultures, p. 7

archipelago (ahr kuh PEL uh goh) *n.* a group or chain of many islands, p. 375

Arms Race (ahrmz rays) *n.* the buildup of military forces during the Cold War by the United States and Soviet Union, p. 631

aristocrat (uh RIS tuh krat) *n.* a member of a rich and powerful family, p. 174

artisan (AHR tuh zun) *n.* a skilled worker who practices a trade, such as jewelry making, ceramics, or sculpture, p. 21

assassinate (uh SAS uh nayt) *v.* to commit murder for political reasons, p. 218

astronomer (uh STRAHN uh mur) *n.* a scientist who studies the stars and other objects in the sky, p. 92

Athens (ATH unz) *n.* a city-state in ancient Greece; the capital of modern-day Greece, p. 198

atomic bomb (uh TAHM ik BAHM) *n.* an extremely destructive bomb whose power results from the chain reaction of nuclear fission, p. 624

avatar (AV uh tahr) *n.* a representation of a Hindu god or goddess in human or animal form, p. 115

Aztecs (AZ teks) *n.* a people who lived in the Valley of Mexico, p. 344

B

Babylon (BAB uh lun) *n.* the capital of Babylonia; a city of great wealth and luxury, p. 39

Bantu (BAN too) *n.* a large group of central and southern Africans who speak related languages, p. 310

barbarian (bahr BEHR ee un) *n.* a wild and uncivilized person, p. 216

battering ram (BAT ur ing ram) *n.* a powerful weapon having a wooden beam mounted on wheels; used to knock down walls or buildings, p. 41

bazaar (buh ZAHR) *n.* a market selling different kinds of goods, p. 39

Benin (beh NEEN) *n.* a kingdom in the West African rain forest, p. 322

blockade (blah KAYD) *n.* an action taken to isolate an enemy and cut off its supplies, p. 213

brahman (BRAH mun) *n.* a single spiritual power that Hindus believe lives in everything, p. 115

C

caliph (KAY lif) *n.* a Muslim ruler, p. 302

campaigns (kam PAYNZ) *n.* a series of military operations, p. 574

capitalist (KAP ut ul ist) *n.* someone who provides ideas and money for investing in businesses, p. 601

caravan (KA ruh van) *n.* a group of traders traveling together, p. 39

caste (kast) *n.* a social class of people, p. 111

caste system (kast SIS tum) *n.* a Hindu social class system that controlled every aspect of daily life, p. 111

cataract (KAT uh rakt) *n.* a large waterfall or steep rapids, p. 69

census (SEN sus) *n.* an official count of people living in a place, p. 253

chivalry (SHIV ul ree) *n.* the code of honorable conduct for knights, p. 408

circumnavigation (sir kum nav ih GAY shun) *n.* going completely around the Earth, especially by water, p. 461

circus (SUR kus) *n.* an arena in ancient Rome; also the show held there, p. 255

citadel (SIT uh del) *n.* a fortress in a city, p. 108

city-state (SIH tee stayt) *n.* a city that has its own independent government and often controls much of the surrounding land, p. 33

civil service (SIV ul SUR vis) *n.* the group of people whose job it is to carry out the work of the government, p. 148

civil war (SIV ul wawr) *n.* a war between different regions of one country, p. 483

civilization (sih vuh luh ZAY shun) *n.* a society with cities, a central government run by official leaders, and workers who specialize in certain jobs, leading to social classes; characterized by writing, art, and architecture, p. 23

clan (klan) *n.* a group of families that trace their roots to the same ancestor, p. 314

clergy (KLUR jee) *n.* persons with authority to perform religious services, p. 403

code (kohd) *n.* an organized list of laws or rules, p. 44

Cold War (kohld wawr) *n.* the name for the period between 1945 and 1989, when the U.S. and USSR competed for influence but did not fight in a military war, p. 631

colony (KAHL uh nee) *n.* a territory ruled over by a distant state, p. 470

Colosseum (kahl uh SEE um) *n.* a large arena built in Rome around A.D. 70; site of contests and combats between people and animals, p. 244

Columbian Exchange (kuh LUM bee un eks CHAYNJ) *n.* the movement of plants and animals between the Western and Eastern Hemispheres after the voyages of Columbus, p. 487

conquistador (kahn KEES tuh dawr) *n.* a Spanish conqueror of the Americas in the sixteenth century, p. 341

Constantinople (kahn stan tun NOH pul) *n.* the capital of the eastern Roman Empire and later of the Byzantine Empire, p. 275

constitution (kahn stuh TOO shun) *n.* a set of rules defining the structure and powers of a government, p. 539

consul (KAHN sul) *n.* one of two officials who led the ancient Roman Republic, p. 232

convert (kun VURT) *v.* to change one's beliefs; in particular, to change one's religion, p. 128

covenant (KUV uh nunt) *n.* a promise made by God; a binding agreement, p. 57

Crusades (kroo SAYDZ) *n.* a series of military expeditions launched by Christian Europeans to win the Holy Land back from Muslim control, p. 410

cuneiform (kyoo NEE uh fawrm) *n.* a form of writing that uses groups of wedges and lines; used to write several languages of the Fertile Crescent, p. 46

currency (KUR un see) *n.* the kind of money used by a group or a nation, p. 151

Cuzco (KOOZ koh) *n.* the capital city of the Incan Empire, located in present-day Peru, p. 338

czar (zahr) *n.* the Russian monarch, p. 518

D

delta (DEL tuh) *n.* a triangular plain at the mouth of a river, formed when sediment is deposited by flowing water, p. 70

democracy (dih MAHK ruh see) *n.* a form of government in which citizens govern themselves, p. 175

depression (dee PRESH un) *n.* a sharp and prolonged downturn in the economy, p. 610

dharma (DAHR muh) *n.* the religious and moral duties of Hindus, p. 117

diaspora (dy AS pur uh) *n.* the scattering of people who have a common background or beliefs, p. 60

dictator (DIK tay tur) *n.* a ruler who has total control of the government, p. 232

dike (dyk) *n.* a protective wall that controls or holds back water, p. 138

direct rule (duh REKT rool) *n.* the sending of colonial officials to control a colony, p. 581

disciple (dih SY pul) *n.* a follower of a person or belief, p. 260

divine right of kings (duh VYN ryt uv kingz) *n.* the idea that God decides who shall be king, p. 515

domesticate (duh MES tih kayt) *v.* to adapt wild plants for human use; to tame wild animals and breed them for human use, p. 16

dynasty (DY nus tee) *n.* a series of rulers from the same family, p. 75

E

economic imperialism (ek uh NAHM ik im PIHR ee ul iz um) *n.* one country's control over another country through economic policies rather than military force, p. 586

emigrate (em ih grayt) *v.* to leave one country or region to settle in another, p. 489

empire (EM pyr) *n.* many territories and people controlled by one government, p. 39

encomienda (en koh mee EN dah) *n.* the right granted by the king to certain Spanish colonists to force the Native Americans to work for them, p. 487

Enlightenment (en LYT un munt) *n.* the belief that science and natural laws bring individuals and society to a more enlightened state, p. 533

enslaved (en SLAYVD) *v.* made into a slave and treated as property, p. 497

environment (en VY run munt) *n.* the elements that surround all living things and make life possible, p. 658

epic (EP ik) *n.* a long poem that tells a story, p. 171

epistle (ee PIS ul) *n.* a letter; in the Christian Bible, any of the letters written by disciples to Christian groups, p. 262

excommunication (eks kuh myoo nih KAY shun) *n.* expelling someone from the Church, p. 403

exile (EK syl) *v.* to force someone to live in another place or country, p. 53

extended family (ek STEN did FAM uh lee) *n.* closely related people of several generations, p. 140

extraterritorial rights (eks truh tehr uh TAWR ee ul rytz) *n.* the rights of foreigners to be protected by the laws of their own nation, p. 582

F

factories (FAK tuh reez) *n.* large buildings in which workers produce goods, p. 551

famine (FAM in) *n.* a time when there is so little food that many people starve, p. 52

fascism (FASH iz um) *n.* a nationalistic system of government that endorses violence and dictatorship to achieve its aims, p. 611

Fertile Crescent (FUR tul KRES unt) *n.* a region in Southwest Asia; site of the world's first civilizations, p. 32

feudalism (FYOOD ul iz um) *n.* in Europe, a system in which land was owned by kings or lords but held by vassals in return for their loyalty; in Japan, a system in which poor people are legally bound to work for wealthy landowners, p. 377

G

geography (jee AHG ruh fee) *n.* the study of Earth's surface and the processes that shape it, p. 9

Ghana (GAH nah) *n.* the first West African kingdom based on the gold and salt trades, p. 319

Giza (GEE zuh) *n.* an ancient Egyptian city; site of the Great Pyramid, p. 84

gladiator (GLAD ee ayt ur) *n.* in ancient Rome, a person who fought to the death in an arena for the entertainment of the public; usually a slave, p. 255

glasnost (GLAHS nawst) *n.* openness, p. 633

Great Plains (grayt playnz) *n.* a mostly flat and grassy region of western North America, p. 357

Great Zimbabwe (grayt zim BAHB way) *n.* a powerful East African kingdom, p. 329

guerrilla (guh RIL uh) *n.* a member of a small defensive force of soldiers that makes surprise raids, p. 638

guild (gild) *n.* a medieval organization of crafts workers or tradespeople, p. 407

H

Hellenistic (hel uh NIS tik) *adj.* a term that describes Greek history or culture after the death of Alexander the Great, including the three main kingdoms formed by the breakup of Alexander's empire, p. 220

helot (HEL ut) *n.* a member of a certain class of servants in ancient Sparta, p. 207

heir (ehr) *n.* a person who inherits something from someone who has died, p. 520

hieroglyphs (HY ur oh glifs) *n.* a kind of picture writing in which some pictures stand for ideas or things and others stand for sounds; the written signs and symbols used by the Egyptians, the Mayan people, and other groups, p. 91

history (HIS tuh ree) *n.* the written and other recorded events of people, p. 7

Holocaust (HAHL uh kawst) *n.* the term used to refer to the Nazis' murder of six million Jews during World War II, p. 616

Holy Land (HOH lee land) *n.* Jerusalem and parts of the surrounding area where Jesus lived and taught, p. 409

hominid (HAHM uh nid) *n.* a modern human or a member of an earlier group that may have included ancestors or relatives of modern humans, p. 12.

humanism (HYOO muh niz um) *n.* an interest in the classics, p. 432

Hundred Years' War (HUN drud yeerz wawr) *n.* a series of conflicts between England and France, 1337–1453, p. 419

I

Ile-Ife (EE lay EE fay) *n.* the capital of a kingdom of the West African rain forest, p. 322

immortal (ih MAWR tul) *n.* someone or something that lives forever, p. 182

imperialism (im PIHR ee ul iz um) *n.* the policy of forming and maintaining an empire, usually by taking over foreign colonies, p. 568

import (im PAWRT) *v.* to bring in goods from a foreign country, p. 497

Incas (ING kuhz) *n.* the people of a powerful South American empire during the 1400s and 1500s, p. 336

indigenous (in DIJ uh nus) *adj.* refers to the original inhabitants of a region, p. 586

indirect rule (in duh REKT rool) *n.* the use of local rulers to control a colony, p. 581

indulgence (in DUL juns) *n.* an official pardon given by the pope in return for money in the Middle Ages; people could pay the Catholic Church to be forgiven for their sins, a practice opposed by Martin Luther, p. 440

Industrial Revolution (in DUS tree ul rev uh LOO shun) *n.* the development of new machines and the creation of factories, p. 551

inflation (in FLAY shun) *n.* an economic situation in which there is more money with less value, p. 273

inherit (in HAYR it) *v.* to receive from a family member who has died, p. 507

Inquisition (in kwuh ZIH shun) *n.* a Catholic organization that held trials for people accused of false beliefs, p. 508

interchangeble parts (in tur CHAYNJ uh bil partz) *n.* parts that are identical in size, shape, and quality and that allow products to be assembled quickly and efficiently, p. 555

irrigation (ih ruh GAY shun) *n.* a method of supplying land with water through a network of canals, p. 20

isthmus (IS mis) *n.* a narrow strip of land connecting two larger areas of land, p. 460

J

Jerusalem (juh ROOZ uh lum) *n.* a city in the Holy Land, regarded as sacred by Christians, Muslims, and Jews, p. 53

Justinian's Code (jus TIN ee unz kohd) *n.* an organized collection and explanation of Roman laws for use in the Byzantine Empire, p. 287

K

Kashmir (KASH mihr) *n.* a mostly Muslim area in the northern part of the Indian subcontinent that is claimed by both India and Pakistan, p. 643

Kilwa (KEEL wah) *n.* one of the many trading cities on the East African coast, p. 326

kiva (KEE vah) *n.* a round room used by the Pueblo people for religious ceremonies, p. 356

knight (nyt) *n.* a man who received honor and land in exchange for serving a lord as a soldier, p. 394

Kyoto (kee OH toh) *n.* the capital city of medieval Japan, p. 376

L

loess (LOH es) *n.* a yellow-brown soil, p. 138

Lower Nubia (LOH ur NOO bee uh) *n.* an ancient region in northern Africa extending from the Nile Valley in Egypt to present-day Sudan; specifically, between the first and second Nile cataracts, p. 97

M

Magna Carta (MAG nuh KAHR tuh) *n.* the "Great Charter," in which the king's power over his nobles was limited, agreed to by King John of England in 1215, p. 418

maize (mayz) *n.* corn, p. 345

Mali (MAH lee) *n.* a rich kingdom of the West African savanna, p. 318

manor (MAN ur) *n.* a large estate, often including farms and a village, ruled by a lord, p. 397

martyr (MAHR tur) *n.* a person who dies for a cause in which he or she believes, p. 265

Maurya Empire (MOWR yuh EM pyr) *n.* the Indian empire founded by Chandragupta, beginning with his kingdom in northeastern India and spreading to most of northern and central India, p. 126

Mayas (MAH yuhz) *n.* a people who established a great civilization in Middle America, p. 345

Mecca (MEK uh) *n.* an Arabian trading center and Muhammad's birthplace, p. 294

medieval (mee dee EE vul) *adj.* referring to the Middle Ages, p. 286

meditate (MED uh tayt) *v.* to focus the mind inward in order to find spiritual awareness or relaxation, p. 120

mercenary (MUR suh neh ree) *n.* a soldier who serves for pay in a foreign army, p. 272

merit system (MEHR it SIS tum) *n.* a system of hiring people on the basis of their abilities, p. 367

messiah (muh SY uh) *n.* a savior in Judaism and Christianity, p. 260

Middle Ages (MID ul AY juz) *n.* the years between ancient and modern times, p. 286

migrate (MY grayt) *v.* to move from one place to settle in another area, p. 110

migration (my GRAY shun) *n.* the movement from one country or region to settle in another, p. 310

missionary (MISH un ehr ee) *n.* a person who spreads his or her religious beliefs to others, p. 121

Model Parliament (MAHD ul PAR luh munt) *n.* a council of lords, clergy, and common people that advised the English king on government matters, p. 418

monopoly (muh NAHP uh lee) *n.* the exclusive control of goods or services in a market, p. 469

monotheism (MAHN oh thee iz um) *n.* the belief in one god, p. 51

monsoon (mahn SOON) *n.* a strong, seasonal wind that blows across East Asia, p. 107

mosque (mahsk) *n.* a Muslim house of worship, p. 295

Mound Builders (mownd BIL durz) *n.* Native American groups who built earthen mounds, p. 352

movable type (MOO vuh bul typ) *n.* individual letters and marks that can be arranged and rearranged quickly, p. 434

Mughal Empire (MOO gul EM pyr) *n.* a Muslim state that ruled India from the 1500s to the 1700s, p. 384

mummy (MUM ee) *n.* a dead body preserved in lifelike condition, p. 82

Muslim (MUZ lum) *n.* a follower of Islam, p. 294

myth (mith) *n.* a traditional story; in some cultures, a legend that explains people's beliefs, p. 34

N

NAFTA (North American Free Trade Agreement) (NAF tuh) *n.* a trade agreement that lowered tariffs and trade barriers among the U.S., Canada, and Mexico, p. 637

Napoleonic code (nuh poh lee AHN ik kohd) *n.* a set of laws that protect individual liberty, the right to work, and the right to one's own opinions, p. 548

nation (NAY shun) *n.* a community of people that shares territory and a government, p. 417

nationalism (NASH uh nul iz um) *n.* a feeling of strong loyalty or attachment to a culture, language, and/or territory, p. 563

natural laws (NACH ur ul laws) *n.* the patterns that control the behavior of the universe, p. 532

natural rights (NACH ur ul rytz) *n.* the rights to life, liberty, and property, p. 534

neutral (NOO trul) *adj.* not taking any sides, p. 597

nirvana (nur VAH nuh) *n.* the lasting peace that Buddhists seek by giving up selfish desires, p. 121

nomad (NOH mad) *n.* a person with no permanent home who moves from place to place in search of food, water, or pasture, p. 14

Nubia (NOO bee uh) *n.* a desert region and ancient kingdom in the Nile River Valley, in present-day southern Egypt and northern Sudan, p. 69

O

oasis (oh AY sis) *n.* an area of vegetation within a desert, fed by springs and underground water, p. 293

oracle (AWR uh kul) *n.* in ancient Greece, a sacred site where a god or goddess was consulted; any priest or priestess who spoke for the gods, p. 183

oral history (AWR ul HIS tuh ree) *n.* accounts of the past that people pass down by word of mouth, p. 314

oral traditions (AWR ul truh DISH unz) *n.* stories passed down through generations by word of mouth, p. 8

ore (awr) *n.* a mineral or a combination of minerals mined for the production of metals, p. 97

P

papyrus (puh PY rus) *n.* an early form of paper made from a reedlike plant found in the marshy areas of the Nile delta, p. 91

partition (pahr TISH un) *n.* a division, p. 572

patrician (puh TRISH un) *n.* a member of a wealthy, upper-class family in the Roman Republic, p. 231

Peloponnesian War (pel uh puh NEE shun wawr) *n.* (431–404 B.C.) a war fought for 27 years between Athens and Sparta in ancient Greece, p. 212

perestroika (pehr uh STROI kuh) *v.* the restructuring of the Soviet government and economy, p. 633

persecution (pur sih KYOO shun) *n.* causing injury or distress to others because of their religion, race, or political beliefs, p. 474

pharaoh (FAIR oh) *n.* a king of ancient Egypt, p. 74

philosopher (fih LAHS uh fur) *n.* someone who uses reason to understand the world; in Greece, the earliest philosophers used reason to explain natural events, p. 184

philosophy (fih LAHS uh fee) *n.* a system of beliefs and values, p. 146

pilgrim (PIL grum) *n.* a person who journeys to a sacred place, p. 410

plague (playg) *n.* a widespread disease, p. 213

plantation (plan TAY shun) *n.* a large estate or farm, p. 487

plebeian (plih BEE un) *n.* an ordinary citizen in the ancient Roman Republic, p. 231

polytheism (PAHL ih thee iz um) *n.* the belief in many gods, p. 34

prehistory (pree HIS tuh ree) *n.* before history; the events in the period of time before writing was invented, p. 7

prophet (PRAHF it) *n.* a religious teacher who is regarded as speaking for God or a god, p. 59

Protestants (PRAHT us tunts) *n.* Christians who are not members of the Catholic or Orthodox churches; in this text, the Christians who broke away from the Roman Catholic Church, p. 447

province (PRAH vins) *n.* a unit of an empire; in the Roman Empire, each one having a governor supported by an army, p. 241

pueblo (PWEB loh) *n.* a cluster of Native American stone or adobe dwellings, p. 356

pyramid (PIH ruh mid) *n.* a huge building with four sloping triangle-shaped sides; built as a royal tomb in Egypt, p. 84

Q

quipu (KEE poo) *n.* a group of knotted strings used by the Mayas to record information, p. 339

Quran (koo RAHN) *n.* the holy book of Islam, p. 296

R

Reformation (ref ur MAY shun) *n.* the term used to describe Luther's break with the Church and the movement it inspired, p. 443

regent (REE junt) *n.* someone who rules for a child until the child is old enough to rule, p. 78

reign (RAYN) *n.* a period of rule, p. 507

reincarnation (ree in kahr NAY shun) *n.* the rebirth of the soul in the body of another living being, p. 117

Renaissance (REN uh sahns) *n.* a widespread change in culture that took place in Europe beginning in the 1300s, p. 430

reparations (rep uh RAY shunz) *n. pl.* payments for harm done to other countries, p. 598

republic (rih PUB lik) *n.* a type of government in which citizens who have the right to vote select their leaders, p. 231

revolution (rev uh LOO shun) *n.* a change or overthrow of a government or social system, p. 600

S

Sahara (suh HAR uh) *n.* a huge desert stretching across most of North Africa, p. 71

salvation (sal VAY shun) *n.* access to heaven, in religious terms, p. 442

samurai (SAM uh ry) *n.* the warriors in Japan who swore to serve their leaders and obeyed a strict code of rules without question, p. 377

Sandinista (san duh NEES tuh) *n.* a member of a political movement that overthrew the Somoza regime in Nicaragua, p. 638

savanna (suh VAN uh) *n.* an area of grassland with scattered trees and bushes, p. 311

scapegoat (SKAYP goht) *n.* a person or group that bears the blame for the mistakes of others, p. 612

schism (SIZ um) *n.* a split, particularly in a church or religion, p. 288

scientific method (sy un TIF ik METH ud) *n.* a way of performing experiments, p. 531

scribe (skryb) *n.* in ancient civilizations, a specially trained person who knew how to read, write and keep records, p. 30

serf (surf) *n.* a farm worker considered part of the manor on which he or she worked, p. 399

shogun (SHOH gun) *n.* the supreme military commander of Japan, p. 378

siege (seej) *n.* the surrounding and blockading of a town by an army intent on capturing it, p. 482

silk (silk) *n.* a valuable cloth originally made only in China from threads spun by caterpillars called silkworms, p. 158

Silk Road (silk rohd) *n.* a chain of trade routes stretching from China to the Mediterranean Sea, p. 156

silt (silt) *n.* a fine soil found on river bottoms, p. 70

slash-and-burn agriculture (slash-and-burn AG rih kul chur) *n.* a farming technique in which trees are cut down and burned to clear and fertilize the land, p. 345

slavery (SLAY vur ee) *n.* the condition of being owned by and forced to work for someone else, p. 202

social class (SOH shul klas) *n.* a group, or class, that is made up of people with similar backgrounds, income, and ways of living, p. 24

socialism (SOH shul iz um) *n.* a social system that seeks to abolish all forms of social classes and create a society of complete equality, p. 600

Song (sawng) *n.* a dynasty that ruled China after the Tang, p. 367

Songhai (SAWNG hy) *n.* a powerful kingdom of the West African savanna, p. 321

soviet (SOH vee ut) *n.* an elected workers' council or committee, p. 603

Sparta (SPAHR tuh) *n.* a city-state in the southern part of ancient Greece, p. 206

Stone Age (stohn ayj) *n.* a period of time during which people made lasting tools and weapons mainly from stone; the earliest-known period of human culture, p. 13

subcontinent (SUB kahn tih nunt) *n.* a large landmass that juts out from a continent; India is considered a subcontinent, p. 107

Sufis (SOO feez) *n.* a Muslim group that believed they could draw closer to God through prayer, fasting, and a simple life, p. 303

sultan (SUL tun) *n.* a Muslim ruler, p. 304

surplus (SUR plus) *n.* more of a thing or product than is needed, p. 21

Swahili (swah HEE lee) *n.* a Bantu language with Arabic words, spoken along the East African coast, p. 329

T

Taj Mahal (tahzh muh HAHL) *n.* a tomb built by Shah Jahan of India for his wife, p. 386

Tang (tahng) *n.* a dynasty that ruled China for almost 300 years, p. 365

Tenochtitlán (teh nawch tee TLAHN) *n.* the capital city of the Aztecs, p. 344

terraces (TEHR us iz) *n.* steplike ledges cut into mountains to make land suitable for farming, p. 340

terrorism (TEHR ur iz um) *n.* the deliberate use of violence to achieve political goals, p. 657

textiles (TEKS tylz) *n.* woven or knitted cloths, p. 551

tolerance (TAHL ur uns) *n.* the acceptance of differences, p. 129

Torah (TOR uh) *n.* the first five books of the Jewish Bible that record events and laws important to the Israelites, p. 56

tragedy (TRAJ uh dee) *n.* a type of serious drama that ends in disaster for the main character, p. 187

treason (TREE zun) *n.* the betrayal of one's country, p. 523

tribute (TRIB yoot) *n.* a regular payment made to a powerful state or nation by a weaker one, p. 181

troubadour (TROO buh dawr) *n.* a traveling poet and musician of the Middle Ages, p. 408

tyrant (TY runt) *n.* a ruler in ancient Greece who took power by force, with the support of the middle and working classes, p. 174

U

United Nations (yoo NYT id NAY shunz) *n. pl.* an international organization founded in 1946 in which nations can discuss and act on world issues, p. 656

Upper Nubia (UP ur NOO bee uh) *n.* an ancient region in northeastern Africa that extended from the Nile Valley in Egypt to present-day Sudan; specifically, between the second and sixth cataracts, p. 97

or (VEN dur) *n.* a seller of goods, p. 199

(VEE toh) *n.* the rejection of any planned
or rule by a person in power; the Latin word
orbid," p. 232

by (VYS roy) *n.* a governor of a country or
who rules as the representative of a king
en, p. 486

VIL uh) *n.* a country estate usually owned by
thy family; an important source of food and
for ancient Rome, p. 254

rd (WAWR lawrd) *n.* a local leader of an armed
p. 153

rat (ZIG oo rat) *n.* in ancient Sumeria, the
the temple to the main god or goddess
ty, p. 34

strianism (zoh roh AS tree un iz um) *n.* a
n that developed in ancient Persia, p. 42

Index

The m, g, q, or p following the number refers to maps (m), charts, tables or graphs (g), quotes (q), or pictures (p).

Maurya Empire, 126–129, 127p, 131, 133, 670

Mayan civilization, M14p, 345, 485

Mecca, 294, 295

Medes, 40

Medici, Cosimo de, 433, 433p

medicine
in American colonies, 491
in ancient China, 159g
in ancient Egypt, 87, 87p, 93
in China, 369
Muslim advances in, 303, 303p
Scientific Revolution and, 532, 532p

medieval period, 286, 395–399, 402–408, 435

Medina, 295

meditation, 120

Mediterranean Sea, 69, 71, 229, 241, 431

Meiji, emperor of Japan, 582, 584, 584p

Meiji Restoration, 582, 584–585, 584p–585p

Mein Kampf **(Hitler),** 612

men
of Athens, 199, 223
role in prehistoric times, 15
role of in Aztec society, 348
of Rome, 253, 277
of Sparta, 208, 208p, 223

Menelik, 575

Menes, 75

Mensheviks, 602, 603

mercantilism, 489

Mercator projection, M6, M6p

mercenaries, 272

meridians of longitude, M5, M5p

merit system. See civil service

Meroë culture, 99–100

Mesopotamia, 31m
agriculture in, 36p, 36–37, 37p
animal hitching post from, 10p
Assyrian civilization, 38–39, 40–41, 41p
Babylonian civilization, 39–40, 42, 44–45
development of writing in, 45–47, 46p
invasions of, 71
legacy of, 43–47
Sumerian civilization, 30–35

Mesopotamian tablet, 46q

messiah, 260, 261

Metternich, prince of Austria, 566

Mexico, 472, 478p–479p, 659, 661, 729
Aztec civilization, 344p, 347–349
independence for, 583
Mayan civilization, 345–346
NAFTA and, 637, 637p
Spanish conquest, 482, 698–699

Michelangelo, 433

Micronesia, Federated States of, 725

microorganisms, 530p

Middle Ages, 286, 421
banking in, 413p
Christianity during, 402p, 402–405
Crusades during, 409–413, 411m
feudalism and manorialism, 395–399, 400p, 400–401, 401p
power of the kings during, 416–420

Middle America, 359, 500m.
See also Latin America
agriculture in, 16
Aztec Empire, 344, 347–349
civilizations of, 335m
civil wars, 659
colonies in, 569
countries of, 712m, 730
independent nations in, 583, 586, 587
land use in, M16m
Mayan civilization, 345–347
migration to, M14m
physical geography of, 337m, 669m
pyramids of, M14p
revolutions in, 638, 638p
Spanish and Portuguese claims in, 482, 485m, 485–493, 499

middle class, 407, 421

Middle East, 304, 659
Arab-Israeli conflict, 647, 647m
British imperialism and, 577, 577p
oil production, 648 , 648p, 648g

Middle Way, 120–121

Midway, Battle of, 624

migration
in Africa, 310, 312, 313m, 314–315
to Americas, M14, M14m, M14, M14m
of early man, 14
into India, 110
of Israelites, 51–53
maps of, M14m–M15m
of modern humans, 5m
push/pull factors, M15

Minamoto Yoritomo, 378

Minoan civilization, 170, 170p, 189

missionaries
in Africa, 573
of Buddhism, 121, 123, 129, 133, 158
of Christianity, 474, 573

Mississippian culture, 355

Mississippi River, 337, 337m, 354

Moctezuma, 349, 481p, 482

Model Parliament, 418, 420

Mohenjo-Daro, Pakistan, 108–109, 109p, 112p, 112–113, 113p, 131

Moldova, 727

Moluccas. See Spice Islands

Mombasa Harbor, Kenya, 329p

Monaco, 727

Mona Lisa, 430, 430p, 433

monarchies, 506–509, 512–515, 518–520, 521–524

monasticism, 405

money. See currency

Mongolia, 725

Mongols, 370p
attack on Japan, 378, 378p
conquest of China, 370, 387
invasion of India, 382, 387
rule of India, 384–386

monopoly, 469, 572

monotheism, 51, 56, 57–60, 82

monsoons, 107m, 107–108, 137

Montenegro, 729

Monument of Discovery, 452p–453p

monuments, 72

Moors, 455, 458, 481

More, Sir Thomas, 435

Morocco, 321, 571, 574, 723

Morse, Samuel, 555

Moses, 52, 57–58

mosque, 295, 320p

Mound Builders, 337, 352–355, 354m

Moundville, 355

mountain pass, 383p

movable type, 369, 369p, 434, 434p

O

oasis, 293–294, 311p

obas, 323

Oceania, 720m

Octavian. *See* Augustus

Odyssey (Homer), 171, 192–195

Ohio River, 354

oil production, 648, 648g, 659

Olmec, 345, 345p

Olympic Games, 182, 188

Oman, 725

onis, 322

OPEC. *See* Organization of Petroleum Exporting Countries (OPEC)

Opium Wars, 580, 580p

oracles, 183

oral traditions, 8, 8p, 172, 260, 314

Orange Free State, 576

orbit, M2, M2p–M3p

ore, 97

Organization of Petroleum Exporting Countries (OPEC), 648p

Orléans, Battle of, 419

Osiris, 81, 81p

Ottoman Empire
control in Middle East, 577
expansion, 304
Spain and, 507, 508

P

Pacific
countries of, 724–726

Pacific Ocean, 460

pagan, 263

Paine, Thomas, 536

Pakistan, 22, 107, 643, 659, 725

Palace of Versailles, 504p–505p, 512p, 516–517, 516p–517p

Palau, 725

Palestinians, 647

Panama, 583, 729

Pangaea, 107

paper, 91, 159, 160

Papua New Guinea, 725

papyrus, 91

Paraguay, 729

parallels of latitude, M4, M4p

Paris, 407, 407p

Parliament, 522–524, 525, 538

Parthenon, 181, 186, 187p, 212

partition, 572

Passover, 60

paterfamilias, 256

patricians, 231, 233, 234

Paul (disciple of Jesus), 262, 262p

Paul III, pope, 448

Peace of Augsburg, 443

Pearl Harbor attack, 623

peasants, 380, 398–399, 399p, 400, 421

Pedro II, ruler of Brazil, 583

Peloponnesian League, 212–213

Peloponnesian War, 212–213, 676–677

peninsula, 169

Pentagon, 635p

perestroika, 633

Pericles, 180, 180p, 181, 186, 201q, 213

Perón, Eva, 639, 639p

Perón, Juan, 639, 639p

Perry, Matthew, 582

persecution of Christians, 264–265, 274, 474, 680–681

Persia, 301

Persian Empire, 42, 210–211, 212m, 218, 288

Persian Gulf, 648p, 648–649

Persian Wars, 210–211, 223

Peru, 336, 483, 583, 729

Pétain, Marshal, 620

Peter the Great, czar of Russia, 518p, 518–519, 525

Peter the Hermit, 412

Petra, 33

Petrarch, Francesco, 432

pharaoh, 74–76

Philip, king of Macedonia, 216p, 216–218, 217p, 223

Philippics, 217

Philip II, king of Spain, 506, 508, 525

Philippines, 472, 725

philosophers/philosophy, 199p
of Confucius, 146
of Greece, 184–185, 189, 216
of Renaissance, 435
of Rome, 243
of Taoism, 147

Phoenicians, 48p, 48–50, 49m, 50, 50p

physical geography
of Africa, 311, 331
of Americas, 337, 337m
of ancient Greece, 169, 169p
of China, 136–138, 161
effect on civilization, 9, 22
of India, 106–107, 131
of Japan, 375 , 375m
of Mesopotamia, 31–32
of Nile River, 68–71, 101
of Rome, 229, 247

physical maps, M11m, 710m, 713m, 717m, 719m, 721m, 723m

pilgrims, 410–411, 412, 489

Pizarro, Francisco, 341, 483, 499

plague, 213, 407, 415, 415p

plantations, 487

Plateau of Tibet, 365

Plato, 185, 435

plebeians, 231, 233, 234

Pleiade, 436

Pliny, 680–681

Plymouth colony, 489, 490p, 492–493, 492p–493p

pok-ta-tok, 346

Poland, 565, 617, 727

political maps, M10m, 708m, 712m, 714m, 716m, 718m, 720m, 722m

pollution, 658

Polo, Marco, 371, 371p

polytheism, 63
in Africa, 322
of ancient Greece, 182–183, 183g
of ancient Rome, 229, 230, 243
of Aztecs, 348
of Egyptians, 80–85
of Greece, 168, 168p, 173–174
Hinduism, 114–118, 116p, 118p, 122, 131, 383–384
of Mayans, 345
of Sumerians, 34–35

X

Y

Z

Acknowledgments

Cover Design
Pronk&Associates

Staff Credits
The people who made up *Prentice Hall History of Our World* team— representing design services, editorial, editorial services, educational technology, marketing, market research, photo research and art development, production services, project office, publishing processes, and rights & permissions—are listed below. Bold type denotes core team members.

Penny Baker, **Joyce Barisano**, Peter Brooks, Kerry Lyn Buckley, John Carle, Marianne Frasco, Kerri Hoar, Jen Paley, Deborah Levheim, Raymond Parenteau, **Kirsten Richert, Nancy Rogier**, Robin Samper, Mildred Schulte, Sarah Yezzi

Additional Credits
William Bingham, Jason Cuoco, Ella Hanna, Jeffrey LaFountain, William McAllister, John McClure, Michael McLaughlin, Leslie Pierson, Enrique Sevilla, Michele Stevens, Debra Taffet, The Mazer Corporation, Jeff Zoda

The DK Designs team who contributed to *Prentice Hall History of Our World* were as follows: Damien Demaj, Nigel Duffield, Leyla Ostovar, David Roberts, Pamela Shiels, Rob Stokes, Gail Townsley, Iorwerth Watkins

Maps
Maps and globes were created by **DK Cartography**. The team consisted of: Tony Chambers, Damien Demaj, Julia Lunn, Ed Merritt, David Roberts, Ann Stephenson, Gail Townsley, Iorwerth Watkins

Illustrations
Kenneth Batelman: 78, 285; KJA-artists.com: 18, 18–19, 36, 36–37, 86, 86–87, 112, 112–113, 154, 154–155, 155, 176, 176-177, 186, 186–187, 204, 204–205, 222, 266, 266–267, 298, 298–299, 324, 324–325, 351, 351–352, 380, 380–381, 400, 400–401, 401, 462, 462–463, 492, 492–493, 516, 552, 552–553, 618, 618–619; Jill Ort: 232, 271, 279, 291, 292, 300, 364, 374, 382; Jen Paley: 06, 11, 12, 20, 21, 22, 30, 38, 43, 45, 47, 48, 50, 56, 68, 74, 76, 80, 88, 91, 96, 106, 114,119, 120, 125, 126, 136, 144, 149, 151, 156, 159, 163, 168, 172, 180, 183, 191, 198, 206, 210, 216, 225, 228, 239, 240, 252, 259, 269, 270, 291, 295, 310, 318, 321, 326, 336, 342, 344, 352, 361, 369, 372, 373, 394, 402, 409, 416, 423; Lisa Smith-Ruvalcaba: 146

Photos
Cover Photos
Lee Snider/Corbis Magma; The British Museum/Topham0HIP/The Image Works.

Title Page
Lee Snider/Corbis Magma; The British Museum/Topham0HIP/The Image Works.

Table of Contents
iv–v, Vanni Archive/Corbis; **v t,** George Holton/Photo Researchers, Inc.; **vi,** Woodfin Camp & Associates; **vii,** Réunion des Musées Nationaux/Art Resource, NY; **x,** University of Witwatersrand, Johannesburg, South Africa/Bridgeman Art Library; **viii–ix,** Ric Ergenbright/Corbis

Learning With Technology
xiii tr, bc, Discovery School Channel

Reading and Writing Handbook
Michael Newman/PhotoEdit; **RW1,** Walter Hodges/Getty Images, Inc.; **RW2,** Digital Vision/Getty Images, Inc.; **RW3,** Will Hart/PhotoEdit; **RW5,** Jose Luis Pelaez, Inc./Corbis

MapMaster
James Hall/Dorling Kindersley; **M1,** Mertin Harvey/Gallo Images/Corbis; **M2–3 m,** NASA; **M2–3,** (globes) Planetary Visions; **M5 br,** Barnabas Kindersley/Dorling Kindersley; **M6 tr,** Mike Dunning/Dorling Kindersley; **M10 b,** Bernard and Catherine Desjeux/Corbis; **M11,** Hutchison Library; **M12 b,** Pa Photos; **M13 r,** Panos Pictures; **M14 t,** MSCF/NASA; **M14 l,** Macduff Everton/Corbis; **M15 b,** Ariadne Van Zandbergen/Lonely Planet Images; **M16 l,** Bill Stormont/Corbis; **M16 b,** Pablo Corral/Corbis; **M17 t,** Les Stone/Sygma/Corbis; **M17 b,** W. Perry Conway/Corbis

Guiding Questions
1tl, Bettmann/Corbis; **1br,** Richard Haynes

Unit 1
2–3, American Museum of Natural History

Chapter One
4–5, Philip & Karen Smith/Getty Images, Inc.; **6,** Sygma/Corbis; **7 c,** National Geographic Image Collection; **7 cr,** South Tyrol Archaeology Museum; **7 bl,** South Tyrol Archaeology Museum; **8 tl,** George Holton/Photo Researchers, Inc.; **8 b,** M.&E. Bernheim/Woodfin Camp & Associates; **9,** James Strachan/Getty Images, Inc.; **10 t,** Wolfgang Kaehler/Corbis; **10 b,** Dorling Kindersley/The British Museum; **11 cl,** The Granger Collection, New York; **11 br,** Richard T. Nowitz/Corbis; **11 cl,** The Granger Collection, New York; **12,** John Reader/Science Photo Library/Photo Researchers, Inc.; **13 cr,** Dorling Kindersley/The Museum of London; **13 b,** Peter Johnson/Corbis; **14 cl,** Discovery Channel School; **14 b,** Lauren Goodsmith/The Image Works; **16 t,** Peter Adams/Index Stock Imagery, Inc.; **16 cl,** Robert S. Peabody Museum of Archaeology, Phillips Academy, Andover, Massachusetts All Rights Reserved/Robert S. Peabody Museum of Archaeology; **17,** J. C. Stevenson/Animals Animals/Earth Scenes; **18 bc,** Musee des Antiquites Nationales, St-Germain-en-Laye, France/ Bridgeman Art Library; **18 br,** #55014847/Lynton Gardiner /American Museum of Natural History; **18–19,** The Granger Collection, New York; **19 br,** Ashmolean Museum, Oxford, UK/Bridgeman Art Library; **19 tc,** Peter H. Buckley/Pearson Education/PH College; **19 tr,** #4938(9)/D. Finnin/C. Chesek/ American Museum of Natural History; **20,** James R. Holland/Stock Boston/ PictureQuest; **21,** Pictures of Record, Inc.; **22,** SuperStock, Inc.; **23 cr,** University Museum of Archaeology and Anthropology, Cambridge/Dorling Kindersley; **23 bc,** Dorling Kindersley/ University Museum of Archaeology and Anthropology, Cambridge; **24,** Erich Lessing/Art Resource, NY; **25 tr,** SuperStock, Inc.; **25 bc,** J. C. Stevenson/Animals Animals/Earth Scenes

Chapter Two
28–29, Ed Kashi Photography/IPN; **30,** Dorling Kindersley/The British Museum; **31,** Nik Wheeler/Corbis; **32–33,** The British Museum, London, UK/Bridgeman Art Library; **33 tr,** Discovery Channel School; **34 tl,** Victor J. Boswell/Oriental Institute Museum/University of Chicago; **34b,** Hirmer Fotoarchiv; **35,** British Museum, London UK/Bridgeman Art Library; **37 tl,** The Art Archive/Egyptian Museum Turin/Dagli Orti; **37 cr,** Erich Lessing/Art Resource, NY; **37 br,** Ashmolean Museum, University of Oxford, UK/Bridgeman Art Library; **38,** Musee du Louvre, Paris/SuperStock, Inc.; **39,** Erich Lessing/Art Resource, NY; **40–41,** Dorling Kindersley /The British Museum; **42,** The Art Archive, Musée du Louvre Paris/Dagli Orti; **43,** Musee du Louvre/Art Resource, NY; **44,** Scala/Art Resource, NY; **46 t,** The Granger Collection, New York; **48 cl, bc,** Courtesy of P'til Tekhelet,The Association for the Promotion and Distribution of Tekhelet Jerusalem, Israel; **48 br,** Dr. Davis S. Reese; **46 b,** Steve Gorton/Dorling Kindersley; **49,** Chris Howson/Dorling Kindersley; **50,** Michael Holford Photographs; **52,** Ziv Koren/Polaris Images; **53,** Hulton/ Getty Images, Inc.; **54 tr,** Eyewire Collection/Getty Images, Inc.; **54 cl,** Bob Daemmrich/The Image Works; **55,** Giraudon/Art Resource, NY; **56,** PhotoEdit; **57 t,** The Granger Collection, New York; **57 c,** Dorling Kindersley /The British Museum; **58,** www.asap.co.il; **60,** Erich Lessing/Art Resource, NY; **61 t,** Dorling Kindersley /The British Museum; **61 cr,** Scala/Art Resource, NY

Unit 2
64–65, Bettmann/Corbis

Chapter Three
66–67, Erich Lessing/Art Resource, NY; **68,** Werner Forman/Art Resource, NY; **69 t,** Bettmann/Corbis; **69 cr,** Discovery Channel School; **70–71,** Wolfgang Kaehler Photography; **71 cr,** John Elk III/Lonely Planet Images; **72,** Richard Nowitz Photography; **73,** Museum of Fine Arts, Boston: Harvard University—Museum of Fine Arts Expedition 21.318; **74,** Araldo de Luca/Corbis; **75,** The Art Archive/Egyptian Museum, Cairo/Dagli Orti; **77,** The Art Archive/Egyptian Museum, Cairo/Dagli Orti; **78,** Miles Ertman/Masterfile Corporation; **79,** Erich Lessing/Art Resource, NY; **80,** Erich Lessing/Art Resource, NY; **81 bc,** Dorling Kindersley/The British Museum, London, UK; **81 bl,** Réunion des Musées Nationaux/Art Resource, NY; **81 br,** Scala/Art Resource, NY; **82 cl,** Dorling Kindersley/Manchester Museum; **82 cr,** Sandro Vannini/Corbis; **83 tl,** L. Mayer/Mary Evans Picture Library; **83 tr,** Dorling Kindersley; **83 b,** Dorling Kindersley; **84,** Paul Solomon/Woodfin Camp & Associates; **85,** Erich Lessing/Art Resource, NY; **86,** Kenneth Garrett/National Geographic Image

tion; **87,** Dorling Kindersley/The British Museum; **88,** National Geographic Collection; **89,** Erich Lessing/Art Resource, NY; **90 cl,** Gianni Dagli orbis; **90 br,** Robert Frerck/Odyssey/Chicago.; **91,** Scala/Art Resource, NY; Dorling Kindersley/The British Museum; **92 c,** Louvre, Paris, /Lauros/Giraudon /Bridgeman Art Library; **92 cl,** The Granger Collection, York; 093, The Art Archive/Musée du Louvre Paris/Dagli Orti; **94 b,** m/The Image Works; **94 t,** Scala/Art Resource, NY; **96,** The Granger tion, New York; **97,** Archivo Iconografico, S.A./Corbis; **98,** Museum of Fine oston: Harvard University - Museum of Fine Arts Expedition 13.4081 and 69; **99 cr,** Topham/ The Image Works; **99 br,** Tim Kendall; **100,** from K. s, Denkmaeler aus Aegypten and Aethiopien...(Berlin:Nicolaische handlung, 1842-45), Abt. 5, pl. 56.; **101 t,** Werner Forman/Art Resource, NY; , The Granger Collection, New York

ter Four
05, Dinodia; **106–107,** Zane Williams/Panoramic Images; **108 cl,** National m of Karachi, Karchi, Pakistan/Bridgeman Art Library; **108 b,** Jehangir r/Woodfin Camp & Associates; **109b,** Woodfin Camp & Associates; **109 tr,** s & Josette Lenars/Corbis, **110,** Chris Lisle/Corbis; **111,** Victoria & Albert m, London/Art Resource, NY; **113,** National Museum of Karachi, Karachi, an/Bridgeman Art Library; **114,** Corbis Digital Stock; **115,** Jacob ka/ Index Stock Imagery, Inc.; **116,** Woodfin Camp & Associates; **117,** The Museum/Bridgeman Art Library; **118,** Eve Arnold/Magnum Photos; **119,** oltin/Boltin Picture Library; **120–121,** John W. Banagan/Getty Images, Inc.; orling Kindersley/The Ashmolean Museum; **123,** Hugh Sitton/Getty Images, 24, AP/Wide World Photos; **125,** Russ Lappa; **126,** Musee Guimet, Paris, e/ Flammarion/Bridgeman Art Library; **127,** Burstein Collection/Corbis; **129** covery Channel School; **129 b,** Chris Lisle/Corbis; **130,** R. Ashworth/Ancient Architecture Collection Ltd.; **131 t,** Jehangir Gazdar/Woodfin Camp & ates; **131 cl,** The British Museum/Bridgeman Art Library; **131 cr,** Burstein tion/Corbis

ter Five
135, David Allan Brandt/Getty Images, Inc.; **136,** Wolfgang Kaehler graphy; **137 tr,** The Granger Collection, New York; **137 b,** AP/Wide World s; **138 tr,** Chris Stowers/Panos Pictures; **138 b,** Gina Corrigan/Robert Harding l Imagery; **139,** Art Directors/Helene Rogers/Trip Photographic; **140 tl,** The ger Collection, New York; **140 br,** The Great Bronze Age of China/ politan Museum; **141,** Réunion des Musées Nationaux/Art Resource, NY; Michael Newman/PhotoEdit; **143 tr,** Michael Newman/PhotoEdit;**143 b,** Julia low; Eye Ubiquitous/Corbis; **144,** Victoria Vebell Bruck; **145,** The Granger ction, New York; **146 tl,** The Granger Collection, New York; **146 tc,** Reed ner/Corbis; **146 tr,** Carlos Spaventa/Getty Images, Inc.; **146 cr,** The British um/The Art Archive; **146 bl,** Bettmann/Corbis; **147 tl,** Bonnie n/ PhotoEdit; **147 br,** Bibliotheque Nationale, Paris, France/Archives met/ Bridgeman Art Library; **148,** Bibliotheque Nationale, Paris, e/Bridgeman Art Library; **149,** Keren Su/China Span; **150 tl,** Alvis s/SuperStock, Inc.; **150 bl,** Discovery Channel School; **151 tr,** Giraudon/Art rce, NY; **151 bc,** Réunion des Musées Nationaux/Art Resource, NY; **152,** The h Museum/Bridgeman Art Library; **153,** People's Republic of China/ udon/Bridgeman Art Library; **155,** The Art Archive/Musée Cernuschi /Dagli Orti; **156,** Keren Su/China Span, **157,** Réunion des Musées/Art rce, NY; **158 cr,** Cary Wolinsky/Aurora & Quanta Productions Inc.; **158 tl,** Granger Collection, New York; **159 tr,** Dorling Kindersley/The British um; **159 cr,** Alan Hills and Geoff Brightling/Dorling Kindersley; **159 br,** Geoff tling/Dorling Kindersley; **160,** The Metropolitan Museum of Art, Purchase, Dillon Fund, 1977. (1977.78) Photograph by Malcom Varon. Photograph 0 The Metropolitan Museum of Art; **161 tr,** Keren Su/China Span; **161 cl,** The ger Collection, New York

3
-165, Zephyr Picture/Index Stock Imagery

pter Six
-167, Picture Finders, Ltd./Leo De Wys Stock Photo Agency/eStock ography; **167,** James Hall/Dorling Kindersley; **168,** Erich Lessing/Art rce, NY; **169,** Colin Paterson/SuperStock, Inc.; **170 b,** Gianni Dagli /Corbis; **170 t,** Gianni Dagli Orti/Corbis; **171 t,** Discovery Channel School; b, Ulf Sjostedt/Getty Images, Inc.; **172,** Dorling Kindersley/The British um; **173 tr,** Archivo Inconografico, S.A./Corbis; **173 c,** Richard Bonson/ ing Kindersley; **174,** Réunion des Musées Nationaux/Art Resource, NY;

175 t, b, The Art Archive/ Agora Museum Athens/Dagli Orti; **177 tr,** Donald Cooper/Photostage, Ltd.; **177 b,** Scala/Art Resource, NY; **178 tl,** The Art Archive/The British Museum/Eileen Tweedy; **178 bl,** David Young-Wolff/PhotoEdit; **179,** Bettmann/Corbis; **180,** The Granger Collection, New York; **181 tr,** Dorling Kindersley/The British Museum; **181 b,** The Art Archive/ Archaeological Museum Spina Ferrara/Dagli Orti; **182,** David Lees/Corbis; **183 tl,** Steve Vidler/SuperStock, Inc.; **183 tr,** Staatliche Museen, Berlin, Germany/ Bridgeman Art Library; **184–185,** Alinari/Art Resource, NY; **186–187,** Vanni Archive/Corbis; **187 tc,** The Art Archive/Dagli Orti; **187 tr,** The Art Archive/ Archaeological Museum Piraeus/Dagli Orti; **188 tl,** Hulton Archive/Getty Images; **188 c,** Gianni Dagli Orti/Corbis; **189 tr,** Gianni Dagli Orti/Corbis; **189 cl,** David Lees/Corbis

Literature
192, Alinari/Regione Umbria/Art Resource, NY; **193,** Dorling Kindersley/The British Museum; **194,** Erich Lessing/Art Resource, NY; **195 tl,** Joe Malone Agency/Jon Arnold Images/Alamy Images; **195 cr,** Gustavo Tomsich/Corbis

Chapter Seven
196–197, Bernard Van Berg/Image Bank/Getty Images, Inc; **198,** Scala/Art Resource, NY; **199 t,** Richard T. Norwitz/Corbis; **199 b,** The Art Archive / Musée du Louvre Paris / Dagli Orti; **200 tl,** Dorling Kindersley/British Museum; **200–201,** Erich Lessing/Art Resource, NY; **201 tr,** Réunion des Musées Nationaux/Art Resource, NY; **202,** Dorling Kindersley/The British Museum **203,** The Art Archive/Agora Museum Athens/Dagli Orti; **205,** Erich Lessing/Art Resource, NY; **206,** Gian Berto Vanni/Art Resource, NY; **207,** The Art Archive/Dagli Orti; **208 t,** Dorling Kindersley /The British Museum; **208–209,** Jose Miralles/S.I. International; **211,** Erich Lessing/Art Resource. NY; **212c,** Dorling Kindersley/The British Museum; **212 b,** Discovery Channel School **213,** Erich Lessing/Art Resource, NY; **214 tr,** Dorling Kindersley/TheBritish Museum; **214 bl,** Wolfgang Kaehler/Corbis; **216,** Gianni Dagli Orti/Corbis; **217 cr,** Réunion des Musées Nationaux/Art Resource, NY; **217 b,** Bettmann/Corbis; **218 cl,** The Granger Collection, New York; **218 b,** David Lees/Corbis; **220 c,** Bettmann/Corbis; **220 tr,** Alistair Duncan/Dorling Kindersley; **221,** Art Resource, NY; **222,** Pearson Learning Group; **223,** Erich Lessing/Art Resource, NY; **224 c,** Jose Miralles/S.I. International; **224 b,** The Granger Collection, New York

Chapter Eight
226–227; David McLain/Aurora Photos; **228,** Enzo & Paolo Ragazzini/Corbis; **229,** Tim Thompson/Corbis; **230,** The Granger Collection, New York; **231,** Scala/Art Resource, NY; **233,** The Metropolitan Museum of Art, Rogers Fund, 1965 (65.183.2) Photograph ©1984 The Metropolitan Museum of Art; **234,** Bettmann/Corbis; **235,** Raymond V. Schoder/Pearson Education U.S. ELT/Scott Foresman; **236 t,** The Art Archive/Jan Vinchon Numismatist Paris/Dagli Orti; **236–237,** Scala/Art Resource, NY; **237 t,** Araldo de Luca/Corbis; **237 b,** Tom Carter/PhotoEdit; **238,** Michael S. Yamshita/Corbis; **239 br,** Dorling Kindersley/ The British Museum; **240,** Richard T. Nowitz/Corbis; **241 cr,** Stock Montage; **241 b,** Dorling Kindersley/The British Museum; **242,** Nimatallah/Art Resource, NY; **243 cr,** Alinari/Art Resource, NY; **243 bc,** Vanni Archive/Corbis; **244 bl,** Discovery Channel School; **244 cl,** Dallas and John Heaton/Corbis; **245 t,** Max Alexander/Dorling Kindersley; **245 b,** Dorling Kindersley; **247 tr,** The Granger Collection, New York; **247 cr,** Richard T. Nowitz/Corbis

Chapter Nine
250–251, Richard Glover/Corbis; **252,** The Metropolitan Museum of Art; **253,** Dorling Kindersley /The British Museum; **254 tl,** Dorling Kindersley/The British Museum; **254 b,** Pearson; **255,** Réunion des Musées Nationaux/Art Resource, NY; **256,** Erich Lessing/Art Resource, NY; **257 bl, br,** Dorling Kindersley; **258 t,** Dorling Kindersley/The British Museum; **258 bc,** Discovery School Channel; **259,** Erich Lessing/Art Resource, NY; **260 tl,** Scala/Art Resource, NY; **260–261,** Scala/Art Resource, NY; **262,** Arte & Immagini srl/Corbis; **263,** Scala/Art Resource, NY; **264,** Hubert Robert (1733–1808). *The Burning of Rome.* 0.76 x 0.93 m. Oil on canvas. Musee des Beaux-Arts Andre Malraux, Le Havre, France. Giraudon/Art Resource, NY; **265,** The Art Archive/Palazzo Barberini Rome/Dagli Orti; **266 cl,** Erich Lessing/Art Resource, NY; **266 b,** Erich Lessing/Art Resource, NY; **267 bl,** The Art Archive/Museo Civico Riva del Garda/Dagli Orti; **268,** Spencer Grant/PhotoEdit; **269 t,** The Art Archive/Dagli Orti; **269 b,** Panorama Images/The Image Works; **270,** Robert Frerck/Odyssey/Chicago.; **271 cl,** The Granger Collection, New York; **271 tr,** Dorling Kindersley/The British Museum; **271 cr,** Private Collection/ Bridgeman Art Library; **272,** Reunion des Musees Nationaux/Art Resource, NY; **273,** Archivo

ter Sixteen

453, Robert Everts/Getty Images Inc./Stone/Allstock; **454 t,** Royal Geographic ty; **454 b,** Science Museum/Science & Society Picture Library; **r,** Michelle Garrett/Corbis; **455 b,** Private Collection/Phillips, The International Art Auctioneers/The Bridgeman Art Library; **456,** Granger Collection, New York; **r,** The Granger Collection, New York; **457 bl,** Corbis; **457 br,** University of atersrand, Johannesburg, South Africa/Bridgeman Art Library; **459 t,** ann/Corbis; **459 c,** Peter Dennis/Dorling Kindersley; **459 b,** Corbis; **461,** The Archive/Marine Museum Lisbon/Dagli Orti/The Picture Desk; **462,** David Corbis; **463,** David Lees/Corbis; **464,** Private Collection/Bridgeman Art Library; **t,** Colin Prior/Stone Allstock/Getty Images, Inc.; **465 b,** Victoria & Albert um, London, UK/Bridgeman Art Library; **466 c,** Archivo Iconografico, S.A./ s; **466 b,** Archivo Iconografico,S.A./Corbis; **467,** Hulton Archive/Getty Images; **469,** The Art Archive/Museo de la Torre del Oro Seville/Dagli Orti/The Picture ; **470,** Hulton Archive/Getty Images; **471,** Judith Miller/Dorling Kindersley/ 's; **472 cl,** Judith Miller/Dorling Kindersley/Sloan's; **472 bc,** Dorling Kindersley/ British Museum; **472–473,** Historical Picture Archive/Corbis; **473 cr,** Judith r/Dorling Kindersley/Sloan's; **473 b,** Discovery Channel School **474,** Private ction/The Stapleton Collection/Bridgeman Art Library; **475 t,** Science um/ Science & Society Picture Library; **475 c,** Hulton Archive/Getty Images; **,** Judith Miller/Dorling Kindersley/Sloan's

ter Seventeen

479, Randy Faris/Corbis; **480,** Steve Dunwell Photography/Getty Images, Inc.; **t,** Biblioteca Nacional, Madrid, Spain/Bridgeman Art Library; **481 cr,** nann/Corbis; **482,** Charles & Josette Lenars/Bettmann/Corbis; **483,** Dorling ersley/The British Museum; **484,** The Granger Collection; **486,** Snark/Art rce, NY; **488,** Courtesy of the Pilgrim Society, Plymouth, Massachusetts; **489,** Morgan/Courtesy of the Pilgrim Society, Plymouth, Massachusetts; **490,** nann/Corbis; **492,** Courtesy of Pilgrim Hall Museum, Plymouth, Massachusetts; Courtesy of Pilgrim Hall Museum, Plymouth, Massachusetts; **494,** Smithsonian ican Art Museum, Washington, DC/Art Resource, NY; **495 bc, b,** Archivo ografico, S.A./Corbis; **495 t,** Werner Forman/Art Resource; **496,** Tom rlitz/ Stone-Allstock/Getty Images, Inc.; **497 b,** The Granger Collection; **497 t,** overy Channel School; **498,** Wolfgang Kaehler/Corbis; **499 tl,** Biblioteca onal, Madrid, Spain/Bridgeman Art Library; **499 tr,** Courtesy of the Pilgrim ty, Plymouth, Massachusetts; **499 bl,** Snark/Art Resource, NY; **499 br,** The ger Collection

6

503, Giraudon/Art Resource, NY

ter Eighteen

505, Archivo Iconografico, S.A./Corbis; **506,** Bettmann/Corbis; **507,** Austrian ives/Corbis; **508,** Archivo Iconografico, S.A./Corbis; **510–511,** Jonathan r/Dorling Kindersley; **512,** Chateau de Versailles, France/Giraudon/Bridgeman Library; **513,** National Gallery Collection; By kind permission of the Trustees e National Gallery, London/Corbis; **515,** Dorling Kindersley/By kind permission e Trustees of the Wallace Collection; **516 bl,** Bill Ross/Corbis; **516–517,** Archivo ografico; **517 tl,** Gerard Blot/Réunion des Musées Nationaux/Art Resource, NY Corbis; **518,** Arch fur Kunst und Geschichte, Berlin; **519,** Discovery Channel ol; **520 c,** Archivo Iconografico, S.A./Corbis; **520 t,** Bettmann/Corbis; **521,** Private ction/Ken Welsh/Bridgeman Art Library; **522,** Boston Public Library, Boston, sachusetts, USA/Bridgeman Art Library; **523,** Ernest Crofts/Bridgeman Art ry; **524,** FPG/Taxi/Getty Images, Inc.; **525,** Private Collection/Ken h/ Bridgeman Art Library; **525 bl,** Chateau de Versailles, France/Giraudon/ geman Art Library; **525 tl,** Austrian Archives/Corbis; **525 tr,** Archivo ografico, S.A./Corbis

ter Nineteen

-529, Bettmann/Corbis; **530,** Dr. Linda Stannard, UCT/ Science Photo Library; Bettmann/Corbis; **532,** Bettmann/Corbis; **532–533,** Dorling Kindersley/Science eum/Science & Society Picture Library; **533,** Loudan/The Granger Collection; Bettman/Corbis; **535,** Dorling Kinderlsey/The British Library; **536,** nann/ Corbis; **537,** Richard T. Nowitz/Corbis; **538,** Bettmann/Corbis; **539,** nann/ Corbis; **541,** Gianni Dagli Orti/Corbis; **542,** Archivo Iconografico, /Corbis; **543,** Jacques-Louis David (French, 1748–1825) "Napoleon in His Study" , oil on canvas, 2.039 x 1.251 (80 1/4 x 49 1/4); framed: 2.439 x 1.651 x .152 (96 x 6). National Gallery of Art, Washington. Samuel H. Kress Collection. (c)Board

of Trustees, National Gallery of Art, Washington. Photo by: Lyle Peterzell.; **544,** David Young-Wolff/Photo Edit; **545 t,** Photo Researchers, Inc.; **545 b,** Phil Borden/ PhotoEdit; **546,** Erich Lessing/Art Resource, NY; **547,** Giraudon/Art Resource, NY; **549,** SuperStock; **550,** Bettmann/Corbis; **551,** Joe Cornish/Dorling Kindersley; **553 t,** Bettmann/Corbis; **554 b,** Bettmann/Corbis; **554 t,** Judith Miller/Dorling Kindersley/Sloan's; **555 cr,** Dorling Kindersley; **555 b,** Tima Chambers/Dorling Kinderlsey/National Maritime Museum; **556,** Peter Severin Kroyer (1851–1909), The Biermeister & Main Steel Forge. Statens Museum for Kunstm, Copenhagen, Denmark/ Bridgeman Art Library, London/SuperStock, Inc.; **557 tl,** Science Museum/Science & Society Picture Library/Dorling Kindersley; **557 bl,** Bettmann/Corbis; **557 tr,** Giraudon/Art Resource, NY; **557 br,** Bettmann/Corbis

Chapter Twenty

560–561, Jon Arnold/Getty Images, Inc.; **562,** Scala/Art Resource, NY; **563,** Dorling Kindersley; **564,** Erich Lessing/Art Resource, NY; **565,** Bryan Pickering; Eye Ubiquitous/Corbis; **566,** Reunion des Musees Nationaux/Art Resource, NY; **567 cr, b,** Erich Lessing/Art Resource, NY; **568,** Bettmann/Corbis; **569,** Werner Forman/Art Resource, NY; **571,** Bettmann/Corbis; **572–573,** Mandy Groszko; **573 tr,** Harry Taylor/Dorling Kindersley/Natural History Museum; **574,** Collart Herve/Corbis Sygma; **575 t, c,** Corbis; **576,** Bettmann/Corbis; **577,** popperfoto.com; **578,** David Madison/Getty Images, Inc.; **579 t,** Robert J. Ross/Peter Arnold, Inc.; **579 b,** Judith Miller/Dorling Kindersley/Sloan's; **580,** Bettmann/ Corbis; **581,** Judith Miller/Dorling Kindersley/Sloan's; **582,** Bettmann/Corbis; **583 t,** Manfred Gottschalk/AGE Fotostock America, Inc.; **583 b,** Robert Frerck/ Odyssey/Chicago; **584 t,** Museum of Fine Art, Boston; **584 cr,** Mary Evans Picture Library; **584–585,** Museum of Fine Art, Boston; **586 t,** Royalty-Free/Corbis; **586 b,** AP/Wide World Photos; **587 tl,** Reunion des Musees Nationaux/Art Resource, NY **587 bl,** Bettmann/Corbis; **587 br,** Robert Frerck/Odyssey/Chicago

Unit 7

590–591, Anthony Suau/Getty Images, Inc.

Chapter Twenty One

592–593, Scala/Art Resource, NY; **594 bl, b,** Bettmann/Corbis; **595,** Corbis; **597 t,** Hulton-Deutsch Collection/Corbis; **597 cr,** Archive Holdings Inc./Getty Images, Inc.; **597 b,** Hulton Archive/Getty Images, Inc.; **598 t,** Hulton Archive/Getty Images, Inc.; **598 cl,** Swim Ink/Corbis; **599,** Bettmann/Corbis; **600,** Scala/Art Resource, NY, **601,** Bettmann/Corbis; **602,** Hulton Archive/Getty Images, Inc.; **603,** Hulton-Deutsch Collection/Corbis; **604,** Brown Brothers; **605 cr,** Brown Brothers **605 b,** Corbis; **606,** Swim Ink/Corbis; **607,** Hulton Archive/Getty Images, Inc.; **608 cl,** Archivo Iconografico, S.A./Corbis; **608 b,** Bettmann/Corbis;. **609 b,** Museum of History & Industry/Corbis; **609 t,** Bettmann/Corbis; **610,** Taxi/Getty Images, Inc.; **611,** Corbis; **612 t,** Corbis; **612 c,** Discovery School Channel; **612 b,** Dorling Kindersley/with permission from the Trustees of the Imperial War Museum; **613,** Hulton Archive/Getty Images, Inc.; **614,** Richard Hutchings/Corbis; **615,** Bettmann/Corbis; **616,** Hulton Archive/Getty Images, Inc.; **617 b,** Corbis; **617 t,** Corbis; **619 tl, tc, tr,** Imperial War Museum; **620 cl,** Hulton Archive/Getty Images, Inc.; **620 b,** Hulton-Deutsch Collection/Corbis; **621 t,** Tony Vaccaro/Sygme/Corbis; **621 c,** Richard Chasemore/ Dorling Kindersley; **623,** Archive Holdings, Inc./Getty Images, Inc.; **624,** AP/Wide World Photo; **625 tl,** Archive Holdings, Inc./Getty Images, Inc.; **625 br,** Corbis

Chapter Twenty Two

628–629, Julio Donoso/Corbis; **630,** Bettmann/Corbis; **631,** Hulton Archive/Getty Images, Inc.; **632,** Courtesy Indiana University Archives & Photographic Services; **633,** AP/Wide World Photos; **634 bc,** Matthias Kulka/Corbis; **634 br,** Andrew Brookes/Corbis; **635,** Peter Gridley/Getty Images, Inc.; **636,** Bettmann/Corbis; **637,** Steve Starr/Corbis; **638,** Bill Gentile/Corbis; **639,** Bettmann/Corbis; **640,** Jaques M. Chenet/Corbis; **641,** Jose Fuste Raga/Corbis; **642,** Tom Wagner/Corbis Saba; **643,** Chris Lisle/Corbis; **644,** Corbis; **645,** Bettmann/Corbis; **646,** AP/Wide World Photos; **648,** Kevin McKiernan/Sipa Press; **649,** Bettmann/Corbis; **650,** Myrleen Ferguson Cate/PhotoEdit; **651,** ISSEI KATO/Reuters Newmedia Inc/Corbis; **652 t,** Clive Streeter/Dorling Kindersley; **652 cl,** The Granger Collection, New York; **652–653,** A Y Owen/Getty Images, Inc.; **653 tl,** Bettmann/Corbis; **654,** Mark Mangold/U.S. Bureau of the Census; **655,** UIUC/National Center for Supercomputing Applications; **656,** Alan Schein Photography/Corbis; **657,** Reuters/Corbis; **658,** Todd A. Gipstein/Corbis; **659 tr,** AP/Wide World Photos; **659 br,** Reuters/Corbis

Text

Grateful acknowledgment is made to the following for copyrighted material: